Understanding the Theory and Design of Organizations

11e

Richard L. Daft
VANDERBILT UNIVERSITY

SOUTH-WESTERN
CENGAGE Learning

Australia • Brazil • Japan • Korea • Mexico • Singapore • Spain • United Kingdom • United States

Understanding the Theory & Design of Organizations
Eleventh International Edition
Richard L. Daft

With the Assistance of Patricia G. Lane

Vice President of Editorial, Business: Jack W. Calhoun

Publisher: Erin Joyner

Executive Editor: Scott Person

Developmental Editor: Erin Guendelsberger

Sr. Editorial Assistant: Ruth Belanger

Marketing Manager: Jonathan Monahan

Media Editor: Rob Ellington

Manufacturing Planner: Ron Montgomery

Sr. Marketing Communications Manager: Jim Overly

Art and Cover Direction, Production Management, and Composition: PreMediaGlobal

Cover Designer: Patti Hudepohl

Cover Photo Credits:

B/W Image: iStockphoto

Color Image: Shutterstock Images/Yuri Arcurs

Rights Acquisitions Specialist: Amber Hosea

Library of Congress Control Number: 2012931503

International Edition:

ISBN-13: 978-1-111-82662-8

ISBN-10: 1-111-82662-5

Cengage Learning International Offices

Asia
www.cengageasia.com
tel: (65) 6410 1200

Australia/New Zealand
www.cengage.com.au
tel: (61) 3 9685 4111

Brazil
www.cengage.com.br
tel: (55) 11 3665 9900

India
www.cengage.co.in
tel: (91) 11 4364 1111

Latin America
www.cengage.com.mx
tel: (52) 55 1500 6000

UK/Europe/Middle East/Africa
www.cengage.co.uk
tel: (44) 0 1264 332 424

Represented in Canada by
Nelson Education, Ltd.
www.nelson.com
tel: (416) 752 9100 / (800) 668 0671

Cengage Learning is a leading provider of customized learning solutions with office locations around the globe, including Singapore, the United Kingdom, Australia, Mexico, Brazil, and Japan. Locate your local office at: **www.cengage.com/global**

For product information: **www.cengage.com/international**
Visit your local office: **www.cengage.com/global**
Visit our corporate website: **www.cengage.com**

Printed in Canada
1 2 3 4 5 6 7 16 15 14 13 12

About the Author

Richard L. Daft, Ph.D., is the Brownlee O. Currey, Jr., Professor of Management in the Owen Graduate School of Management at Vanderbilt University. Professor Daft specializes in the study of organization theory and leadership. Professor Daft is a Fellow of the Academy of Management and has served on the editorial boards of *Academy of Management Journal, Administrative Science Quarterly,* and *Journal of Management Education.* He was the Associate Editor-in-Chief of *Organization Science* and served for three years as associate editor of *Administrative Science Quarterly.*

Professor Daft has authored or co-authored 13 books, including *The Executive and the Elephant: A Leader's Guide to Building Inner Excellence* (Jossey-Bass 2010), *Management* (Cengage/South-Western, 2012), *The Leadership Experience* (Cengage/South-Western, 2011), and *What to Study: Generating and Developing Research Questions* (Sage, 1982). He also published *Fusion Leadership: Unlocking the Subtle Forces That Change People and Organizations* (Berrett-Koehler, 2000) with Robert Lengel. He has authored dozens of scholarly articles, papers, and chapters. His work has been published in *Administrative Science Quarterly, Academy of Management Journal, Academy of Management Review, Organizational Dynamics, Strategic Management Journal, Journal of Management, Accounting Organizations and Society, Management Science, MIS Quarterly, California Management Review,* and *Organizational Behavior Teaching Review.* Professor Daft has been awarded several government research grants to pursue studies of organization design, organizational innovation and change, strategy implementation, and organizational information processing.

Professor Daft is also an active teacher and consultant. He has taught management, leadership, organizational change, organizational theory, and organizational behavior. He has been involved in management development and consulting for many companies and government organizations, including Allstate Insurance, American Banking Association, Bell Canada, Bridgestone, National Transportation Research Board, NL Baroid, Nortel, TVA, Pratt & Whitney, State Farm Insurance, Tenneco, Tennessee Emergency Pediatric Services, the United States Air Force, the United States Army, J. C. Bradford & Co., Central Parking System, USAA, United Methodist Church, Entergy Sales and Service, Bristol-Myers Squibb, First American National Bank, and the Vanderbilt University Medical Center.

Brief Contents

Contents

Preface

My vision for the Eleventh Edition of *Understanding the Theory & Design of Organizations* is to integrate current organization design problems with significant ideas and theories in a way that is engaging and enjoyable for students. There is an average of 39 new citations per chapter for new findings and examples that make the Eleventh Edition current and applicable for students. In addition, significant elements of this edition include "Managing by Design Questions" and "How Do You Fit the Design?" boxes, along with updates to every chapter that incorporate the most recent ideas, new case examples, new book reviews, and new end-of-part integrative cases. The research and theories in the field of organization studies are rich and insightful and will help students and managers understand their organizational world and solve real-life problems. My mission is to combine the concepts and models from organizational theory with changing events in the real world to provide the most up-to-date view of organization design available.

Distinguishing Features of the Eleventh Edition

Many students in a typical organization theory course do not have extensive work experience, especially at the middle and upper levels, where organization theory is most applicable. Moreover, word from the field is that many students today often do not read the chapter opening examples or boxed examples, preferring instead to focus on chapter content. To engage students in the world of organizations, the Eleventh Edition uses "Managing by Design Questions" at the start of each chapter. These questions immediately engage students in thinking and expressing their beliefs and opinions about organization design concepts. Another in-chapter feature, "How Do You Fit the Design?" engages students in how their personal style and approach will fit into an organization. Other student experiential activities that engage students in applying chapter concepts include new "Book Marks," new "In Practice" examples, and new integrative cases for student analysis. The total set of features substantially expands and improves the book's content and accessibility. These multiple pedagogical devices are used to enhance student involvement in text materials.

How Do You Fit the Design? The "How Do You Fit the Design?" feature presents a short questionnaire in each chapter about the student's own style and preferences to quickly provide feedback about how they fit particular organizations or situations. For example, questionnaire topics include "Your Strategy Strength," "Are You Ready to Fill an International Role?" "Corporate Culture Preference," "Is Goal-Setting Your Style?" "Making Important Decisions," and "Personal Networking." These short feedback questionnaires connect the student's personal preferences to chapter material to heighten interest and show the relevance of the concepts.

Managing by Design Questions Each chapter opens with three short opinion questions that engage students in clarifying their thoughts about upcoming material and concepts. These questions are based on the idea that when students express their opinions first, they are more open to and interested in receiving material that is relevant to the questions. Example questions, which ask students to agree or disagree, include:

The best measures of business performance are financial.
Managers in business organizations should not get involved in political activities.
A CEO's top priority is to make sure the organization is designed correctly.
A manager should emphasize shared values, trust, and commitment to the organization's mission as the primary means of controlling employee behavior.

As a follow-up to the three "Managing by Design" questions, each chapter contains three "Assess Your Answer" inserts that allow students to compare their original opinions with the "correct" or most appropriate answers based on chapter concepts. Students learn whether their mental models and beliefs about organizations align with the world of organizations.

Book Marks "Book Marks," a unique feature of this text, represent book reviews that reflect current issues of concern for managers working in real-life organizations. These reviews describe the varied ways companies are dealing with the challenges of today's changing environment. New "Book Marks" in the Eleventh Edition include *Good Strategy, Bad Strategy: The Difference and Why It Matters; The Checklist Manifesto: How to Get Things Right*; *Delivering Happiness: A Path to Profits, Passion, and Purpose*; and *Little Bets: How Breakthrough Ideas Emerge from Small Discoveries.*

In Practice This edition contains many new "In Practice" examples that illustrate theoretical concepts in organizational settings. Many examples are international, and all are based on real organizations. New "In Practice" cases used within chapters include Deutsche Lufthansa, Acer, Inc., Netflix, Huawei Technologies, Disney/Pixar, Anheuser-Busch InBev, Sealy, Shizugawa Evacuation Center, Mimeo, Seattle Children's Hospital, SAS, Meliá Hotels International (Sol Meliá), Cognizant, Menlo Innovations, Facebook, CitiMortgage, *The Atlantic*, Cisco Systems, Every Child Succeeds, Fukushima Daiichi (Toyko Power Company), KFC (Yum Brands), Southwest Airlines, Corning Inc., Sandberg Furniture, GlaxoSmithKline, Washington, D.C. Metropolitan Police, Volvo, Barnes & Noble, Johns Hopkins Medicine, Nokia, W. L. Gore, Sony, *The New York Times*, Smart Balance, Service Employees International Union, BP/Transocean, Kaplan/*The Washington Post*, Toyota Motor, Borders Group, and Google.

Manager's Briefcase Located in the chapter margins, this feature tells students how to use concepts to analyze cases and manage organizations.

Text Exhibits Frequent exhibits are used to help students visualize organizational relationships, and the artwork has been redone to communicate concepts more clearly.

Design Essentials This summary and interpretation section tells students how the essential chapter points are important in the broader context of organization theory.

Case for Analysis These cases are tailored to chapter concepts and provide a vehicle for student analysis and discussion. New cases for analysis include "Covington Corrugated Parts & Services," "Why Is Cooperation So Hard?" "Is Anybody Listening?" and "The New Haven Institute."

Integrative Cases The integrative cases at the end of each part have been significantly expanded and positioned to encourage student discussion and involvement. The new cases include Developing Global Teams to Meet Twenty-First Century Challenges at W. L. Gore & Associates; IKEA: Scandinavian Style; Perdue Farms; Lean Initiatives and Growth at Orlando Metering Company; Cisco Systems: Evolution of Structure; First Union: An Office Without Walls; and Costco: Join the Club. Previous cases that have been retained include The Donor Services Department; Royce Consulting; The Plaza Inn; Custom Chip, Inc.; and Hartland Memorial Hospital.

New Concepts

Many concepts have been added or expanded in this edition. New material has been added on organic and mechanistic designs; the role of contingency factors; open systems; sustainability; organizational effectiveness as a social construct; the strategic constituents approach to assessing effectiveness; the competing values model; relational coordination; the BRIC countries, particularly China, as a growing aspect of the international environment; reverse (trickle-up) innovation; manufacturing processes management (MPM); the trend toward lean services; shifting approaches to e-business design; social networking and other social media tools; downsizing alternatives; the shared value model; differences among episodic change, continuous change, and disruptive change; bottom-up techniques for encouraging technology change; management innovation and the dual-core approach; the change curve; using soft power and political tactics; and reciprocity as an influence tactic. In addition, coping with the complexity of today's global environment is explored thoroughly in Chapter 5.

Chapter Organization

Each chapter is highly focused and is organized into a logical framework. Many organization theory textbooks treat material in sequential fashion, such as "Here's View A, Here's View B, Here's View C," and so on. *Understanding the Theory & Design of Organizations* shows how they apply in organizations. Moreover, each chapter sticks to the essential point. Students are not introduced to extraneous material or confusing methodological squabbles that occur among organizational researchers. The body of research in most areas points to a major trend, which is reported here. Several chapters develop a framework that organizes major ideas into an overall scheme.

This book has been extensively tested on students. Feedback from students and faculty members has been used in the revision. The combination of organization theory concepts, book reviews, examples of leading organizations, self-insight questionnaires, case illustrations, experiential exercises, and other teaching devices is designed to meet student learning needs, and students have responded favorably.

Supplements

Instructor's Manual Available on the website, the Instructor's Manual contains chapter overviews, chapter outlines, lecture enhancements, discussion questions, discussion of workbook activities, discussion of chapter cases, and case notes for integrative cases.

Test Bank Available on the website, the Test Bank consists of multiple choice, true/false, and essay questions tagged to AACSB guidelines.

ExamView A computerized version of the Test Bank is available on the website. ExamView contains all of the questions in the test bank. This program is easy-to-use test creation software. Instructors can add or edit questions, instructions, and answers and can select questions (randomly or numerically) by previewing them on the screen. Instructors can also create and administer quizzes online, whether over the Internet, a local area network (LAN), or a wide area network (WAN).

PowerPoint Lecture Presentation Available on the website, the PowerPoint Lecture Presentation enables instructors to customize their own multimedia classroom presentations. Prepared in conjunction with the text and instructor's resource guide, the package contains approximately 150 slides. It includes exhibits from the text as well as outside materials to supplement chapter concepts. Material is organized by chapter and can be modified or expanded for individual classroom use.

Video/DVD (ISBN: 978-1-111-82585-0) This DVD includes video segments related to organization design concepts. They are designed to visually reinforce key concepts.

MANAGEMENT CourseMate Engaging, trackable, and affordable, the new MANAGEMENT CourseMate website offers a dynamic way to bring course concepts to life with interactive learning, study, and exam preparation tools that support this printed edition of the text. Watch student comprehension soar with all-new flashcards and engaging games. A complete e-book provides the choice of an entire online learning experience. MANAGEMENT CourseMate goes beyond the book to deliver what students need!

Text Companion Website Access important teaching resources on this companion website. For your convenience, you can download electronic versions of the instructor supplements at the password-protected section of the site, including the Instructor's Manual, Test Bank, ExamView, and PowerPoint® presentations.

To access these additional course materials and companion resources, please visit www.cengagebrain.com. At the CengageBrain.com home page, search for the ISBN of your title (from the back cover of your book) using the search box at the top of the page. This will take you to the product page where free companion resources can be found.

Acknowledgments

Textbook writing is a team enterprise. The Eleventh Edition has integrated ideas and hard work from many people to whom I am grateful. Reviewers and focus group participants made an especially important contribution. They praised many features, were critical of things that didn't work well, and offered valuable suggestions.

David Ackerman
University of Alaska, Southeast

Kristin Backhaus
SUNY New Paltz

Michael Bourke
Houston Baptist University

Suzanne Clinton
Cameron University

Pat Driscoll
Texas Woman's University

Jo Anne Duffy
Sam Houston State University

Cheryl Duvall
Mercer University

Allen D. Engle, Sr.
Eastern Kentucky University

Patricia Feltes
Missouri State University

Robert Girling
Sonoma State University

Yezdi H. Godiwalla
University of Wisconsin-Whitewater

John A. Gould
University of Maryland

George Griffin
Spring Arbor University

Leda McIntyre Hall
Indiana University, South Bend

Ralph Hanke
Pennsylvania State University

Bruce J. Hanson
Pepperdine University

Patricia Holahan
Stevens Institute of Technology

Jon Kalinowski
Minnesota State University, Mankato

Guiseppe Labianca
Tulane University

Jane Lemaster
University of Texas–Pan American

Kim Lukaszewski
SUNY New Paltz

Steven Maranville
University of Saint Thomas

Rick Martinez
Baylor University

Ann Marie Nagye
Mountain State University

Janet Near
Indiana University

Julie Newcomer
Texas Woman's University

Asbjorn Osland
George Fox University

Laynie Pizzolatto
Nicholls State University

Samantha Rice
Abilene Christian University

Richard Saaverda
University of Michigan

W. Robert Sampson
University of Wisconsin, Eau Claire

Amy Sevier
University of Southern Mississippi

W. Scott Sherman
Pepperdine University

Marjorie Smith
Mountain State University

R. Stephen Smith
Virginia Commonwealth University

Thomas Terrell
Coppin State College

Jack Tucci
Southeastern Louisiana University

Isaiah Ugboro
North Carolina A&T State University

Richard Weiss
University of Delaware

Judith White
Santa Clara University

Jan Zahrly
University of North Dakota

Among my professional colleagues, I am grateful to my friends and colleagues at Vanderbilt's Owen School—Bruce Barry, Neta Moye, Rich Oliver, David Owens, Ranga Ramanujam, and Bart Victor—for their intellectual stimulation and feedback. I also owe a special debt to Dean Jim Bradford and Associate Dean Ray Friedman for providing the time and resources for me to stay current on the organization design literature and develop the revisions for the text.

I want to extend special thanks to my editorial associate, Pat Lane. She skillfully wrote materials on a variety of topics and special features, found resources, and did an outstanding job with the copyedited manuscript and page proofs. Pat's personal enthusiasm and care for the content of this text enabled the Eleventh Edition to continue its high level of excellence. I also thank DeeGee Lester for her work drafting new end-of-chapter cases and end-of-part integrative cases for this edition. DeeGee's creative writing skills brought to life key organizational issues that students will enjoy discussing and solving.

The team at South-Western also deserves special mention. Scott Person did a great job of designing the project and offering ideas for improvement. Erin Guendelsberger was superb to work with as Developmental Editor, keeping the people and project on schedule while solving problems creatively and quickly. Pooja Khurana, Project Manager, provided superb project coordination and used her creativity and management skills to facilitate the book's on-time completion. Jon Monahan, Marketing Manager, provided additional support, creativity, and valuable market expertise.

Finally, I want to acknowledge the love and contributions of my wife, Dorothy Marcic. Dorothy has been very supportive of my textbook projects and has created an environment in which we can grow together. She helped the book take a giant step forward with her creation of the Workbook and Workshop student exercises. I also want to acknowledge the love and support of my daughters, Danielle, Amy, Roxanne, Solange, and Elizabeth, who make my life special during our precious time together.

Richard L. Daft
Nashville, Tennessee
January 2012

Part One

Introduction to Organization Theory and Design

Chapter 1

Introduction to Organizations

©Marilyn Nieves, iStock

Learning Objectives

After reading this chapter you should be able to:

1. Define an organization and the importance of organizations in society.
2. Identify current challenges facing organizations.
3. Understand how organization design concepts apply to a major company like Xerox.
4. Recognize the structural dimensions of organizations and the contingencies that influence structure.
5. Understand efficiency and effectiveness, and the stakeholder approach to measuring effectiveness.
6. Explain historical perspectives on organizations.
7. Describe Mintzberg's five basic parts of an organization.
8. Explain the differences in organic and mechanistic organization designs and the contingency factors typically associated with each.

Before reading this chapter, please check whether you agree or disagree with each of the following statements:

1 **An organization can be understood primarily by understanding the people who make it up.**

I AGREE ______ I DISAGREE ______

2 **The primary role of managers in business organizations is to achieve maximum efficiency.**

I AGREE ______ I DISAGREE ______

3 **A CEO's top priority is to make sure the organization is designed correctly.**

I AGREE ______ I DISAGREE ______

A LOOK INSIDE | XEROX CORPORATION

On the eve of the twenty-first century, Xerox Corporation seemed on top of the world, with fast-rising earnings, a soaring stock price, and a new line of computerized copier-printers that were technologically superior to rival products. Less than two years later, however, many considered Xerox a has-been, destined to fade into history. Consider the following events:

- Sales and earnings plummeted as rivals caught up with Xerox's high-end digital machines, offering comparable products at lower prices.
- Xerox's losses for the opening year of the twenty-first century totaled $384 million, and the company continued to bleed red ink. Debt mounted to $18 billion.
- The company's stock fell from a high of $64 to less than $4, amid fears that Xerox would file for federal bankruptcy protection. Over an 18-month period, Xerox lost $38 billion in shareholder wealth.
- Twenty-two thousand Xerox workers lost their jobs, further weakening the morale and loyalty of remaining employees. Major customers were alienated, too, by a restructuring that threw salespeople into unfamiliar territories and tied billing up in knots, leading to mass confusion and billing errors.
- The company was fined a whopping $10 million by the Securities and Exchange Commission (SEC) for accounting irregularities and alleged accounting fraud.

What went wrong at Xerox? The company's deterioration is a classic story of organizational decline. Although Xerox appeared to fall almost overnight, the organization's problems were connected to a series of organizational blunders over a period of many years.

"BUROX" TAKES HOLD

Xerox was founded in 1906 as the Haloid Company, a photographic supply house that developed the world's first xerographic copier, introduced in 1959. Without a doubt, the 914 copier was a money-making machine. By the time it was retired in the early 1970s, the 914 was the best-selling industrial product of all time, and the new name of the company, Xerox, was listed in the dictionary as a synonym for photocopying. Yet, like many profitable organizations, Xerox became a victim of its own success. Leaders no doubt knew that the company needed to move beyond copiers to sustain its growth, but they found it difficult to look beyond the 70 percent gross profit margins of the 914 copier.

Xerox's Palo Alto Research Center (PARC), established in 1970, became known around the world for innovation—many of the most revolutionary technologies in the computer industry, including the personal computer, graphical user interface, Ethernet, and laser printer, were invented at PARC. But the copier bureaucracy, or *Burox* as it came to be known, blinded Xerox leaders to the enormous potential of these innovations. While Xerox was plodding along selling copy machines, younger, smaller, and hungrier companies were developing PARC technologies into tremendous money-making products and services.

The dangers of Burox became dramatically clear when the company's xerography patents began expiring. Suddenly, Japanese rivals such as Canon and Ricoh were selling copiers at the cost it took Xerox to make them. Market share declined from 95 percent to 13 percent by 1982. And with no new products to make up the difference, the company had to fight hard to cut costs and reclaim market share by committing to Japanese-style techniques and total quality management. Through the strength of his leadership, CEO David Kearns was able to rally the troops and rejuvenate the company by 1990. However, he also set Xerox on a path to future disaster. Seeing a need to diversify, Kearns moved the company into insurance and financial services on a large scale. When he turned leadership over to Paul Allaire in 1990, Xerox's balance sheet was crippled by billions of dollars in insurance liabilities.

ENTERING THE DIGITAL AGE

Allaire wisely began a methodical, step-by-step plan for extricating Xerox from the insurance and financial services business. At the same time, he initiated a mixed strategy of cost cutting and new-product introductions to get the stodgy company moving again. Xerox had success with a line of digital presses and new high-speed digital copiers, but it fumbled again by underestimating the threat of the desktop printer. By the time Xerox introduced its own line of inkjet printers, the game was already over.

Desktop printing, combined with the increasing use of the Internet and e-mail, cut heavily into Xerox's sales of copiers. People didn't need to make as many photocopies, but they still needed effective ways to create and share documents. Rebranding Xerox as "The Document Company," Allaire pushed into the digital era, hoping to remake Xerox in the image of the rejuvenated IBM, offering not just "boxes (machines)" but complete document management solutions.

As part of that strategy, Allaire picked Richard Thoman, who was then serving as Louis Gerstner's right-hand man at IBM, as his successor.

Thoman came to Xerox as president, chief operating officer, and eventually CEO, amid high hopes that the company could regain the stature of its glory years. Only 13 months later, as revenues and the stock price continued to slide, he was fired by Allaire, who had remained as Xerox's chairman.

A DYSFUNCTIONAL CULTURE

Allaire and Thoman blamed each other for the failure to successfully implement the digital strategy. Outsiders, however, believe the failure had much more to do with Xerox's dysfunctional culture. The culture was already slow to adapt, and some say that under Allaire it became almost totally paralyzed by politics. Thoman was brought in to shake things up, but when he tried, the old guard rebelled. A management struggle developed, with the outsider Thoman and a few allies on one side lined up against Allaire and his group of insiders who were accustomed to doing things the Xeroid way. Recognized for his knowledge, business experience, and intensity, Thoman was also considered to be somewhat haughty and unapproachable. He was never able to exert substantial influence with key managers and employees or to gain the support of board members, who continued to rally behind Allaire.

The failed CEO succession illustrates the massive challenge of reinventing a century-old company. By the time Thoman arrived, Xerox had been going through various rounds of restructuring, cost cutting, rejuvenating, and reinventing for nearly two decades, but little had really changed. Some observers doubted that anyone could fix Xerox because the culture had become too dysfunctional and politicized. "There was always an in-crowd and an out-crowd," says one former executive. "They change the branches, but when you look closely, the same old monkeys are sitting in the trees."

AN INSIDER SHAKES THINGS UP

In August 2001, Allaire turned over the CEO reins to Anne Mulcahy, a popular 24-year veteran, who had started at Xerox as a copier saleswoman and worked her way up the hierarchy. Despite her insider status, Mulcahy proved that she was more than willing to challenge the status quo. She surprised skeptical analysts, stockholders, and employees by engineering one of the most extraordinary business turnarounds in recent history.

How did she do it? Few people thought Mulcahy would take the tough actions Xerox needed to survive, but she turned out to be a strong decision maker. She quickly launched a turnaround plan that included massive cost cutting and the closing of several money-losing operations, including the division she had previously headed. She was brutally honest about "the good, the bad, and the ugly" of the company's situation, as one employee put it, but she also showed that she cared about what happened to employees and she gave them hope for a better future. People knew she was working hard to save the company. After major layoffs, Mulcahy walked the halls to tell people she was sorry and let them vent their anger. She personally negotiated the settlement of a long investigation into fraudulent accounting practices, insisting that her personal involvement was necessary to signal a new commitment to ethical business practices. She appealed directly to creditors, begging them not to pull the plug until a new management team could make needed changes.

Mulcahy transferred much of production to outside contractors and refocused Xerox on innovation and service. In addition to introducing new products, Xerox moved into high-growth areas such as document management services, IT consulting, and digital press technology. A series of small acquisitions enabled the company to enter new markets and expand its base of small and medium-sized business customers.

A NEW ERA AT XEROX

Mulcahy also thought carefully about succession plans, and in 2009 she handed the top job to her second-in-command, Ursula Burns, who became the first African-American woman to head a *Fortune* 500 company. Burns, like Mulcahy, spent decades climbing the ranks at Xerox, actually starting her career there as an intern before earning a master's degree in engineering from Columbia University. Within days of being named CEO, Burns was on a plane, taking a 30-day tour to meet with staff and discuss ways to increase sales. Just weeks after she took over, she announced the biggest acquisition in the company's history—the buyout of outsourcing firm Affiliated Computer Services. As a result of the acquisition, Xerox boosted its services revenue from 23 percent to 50 percent within a year. This signaled the beginning of Burns's new course focused on becoming a state-of-the-art technology resource that other businesses rely on to operate more efficiently. In addition to offering hardware, Xerox now provides everything from mobile printing to cloud services to business process outsourcing. Burns is emphasizing collaboration with other organizations, such as Cisco Systems, which partners with the company to provide managed print tools, mobile printing, and cloud IT outsourcing services. She has also formed numerous partnerships with smaller organizations, in the United States and abroad, to offer both products and services.

Xerox has won accolades for its leaders' commitment to ethical and socially responsible behavior. It has been recognized as one of the World's Most Ethical Companies by the Ethisphere Institute; voted the World's Most Admired Company in the computer industry in *Fortune* magazine's survey; named one of the 100 Best Corporate Citizens by *Corporate Responsibility Officer* magazine; and ranked Number 1 in the Green Outsourcing Survey list. In addition, Xerox is recognized for its commitment to diversity and is considered one of the best places to work for women and minorities.

A decade or so after this American icon almost crashed, Xerox is once again admired in the corporate world. Has the "perfect storm" of troubles been replaced with a "perfect dawn?" Burns and her top management team believe Xerox is positioned to be resilient in the face of the current economic slowdown, but in the rapidly changing world of organizations, nothing is ever certain.[1]

Welcome to the real world of organization theory and design. The shifting fortunes of Xerox illustrate organization theory in action. Xerox managers were deeply involved in organization theory and design each day of their working lives—but many never realized it. Company managers didn't fully understand how the organization related to the environment or how it should function internally. Organization theory concepts have enabled Anne Mulcahy and Ursula Burns to analyze and diagnose what is happening and the changes needed to help Xerox keep pace with a fast-changing world. Organization theory gives us the tools to explain the decline of Xerox, understand Mulcahy's turnaround, and recognize some steps Burns can take to keep Xerox competitive.

Similar problems have challenged numerous organizations. American Airlines, for example, was once the largest airline in the United States, but managers have been struggling for the past decade to find the right formula to keep the once-proud company competitive. American's parent company, AMR Corporation, accumulated \$11.6 billion in losses from 2001 to 2011 and hasn't had a profitable year since 2007.[2] Or consider the dramatic organizational missteps illustrated by the 2008 crises in the mortgage industry and finance sector in the United States. Bear Stearns disappeared and Lehman Brothers filed for bankruptcy. American International Group (AIG) sought a bailout from the U.S. government. Another icon, Merrill Lynch, was saved by becoming part of Bank of America, which had already snapped up struggling mortgage lender Countrywide Financial Corporation.[3] The 2008 crisis in the U.S. financial sector represented change and uncertainty on an unprecedented scale, and it would, to some extent, affect managers in all types of organizations and industries around the world for years to come.

Organization Theory in Action

Organization theory and design gives us the tools to evaluate and understand how a huge, powerful firm like Lehman Brothers can die and a company like Bank of America can emerge almost overnight as a giant in the industry. It enables us to comprehend how a band like the Rolling Stones, which operates like a highly sophisticated global business organization, can enjoy phenomenal success for nearly half a century, while some musical groups with equal or superior talent don't survive past a couple of hit songs. Organization theory helps us explain what happened in the past, as well as what may happen in the future, so that we can manage organizations more effectively.

Topics

Each of the topics to be covered in this book is illustrated in the Xerox case. Indeed, managers at organizations such as Xerox, Lehman Brothers, American Airlines, and even the Rolling Stones are continually faced with a number of challenges. For example:

- How can the organization adapt to or control such external elements as competitors, customers, government, and creditors in a fast-paced environment?
- What strategic and structural changes are needed to help the organization attain effectiveness?
- How can the organization avoid management ethical lapses that could threaten its viability?
- How can managers cope with the problems of large size and bureaucracy?
- What is the appropriate use of power and politics among managers?
- How should internal conflict and coordination between work units be managed?
- What kind of corporate culture is needed and how can managers shape that culture?
- How much and what type of innovation and change is needed?

These are the topics with which organization theory and design is concerned. Organization theory concepts apply to all types of organizations in all industries.

BRIEFCASE

As an organization manager, keep these guidelines in mind:

Do not ignore the external environment or protect the organization from it. Because the environment is unpredictable, do not expect to achieve complete order and rationality within the organization. Strive for a balance between order and flexibility.

Managers at Hyundai, for example, turned the Korean auto manufacturer once known for producing inexpensive no-frills cars with a poor reputation into the world's fifth largest automaker by relentlessly focusing on quality, cost-control, and customer satisfaction. Bob Iger and his top management team revitalized the Walt Disney Company by effectively managing internal conflicts and enhancing coordination both within the company and with outside partners. Managers at high-end cosmetics firm Estée Lauder undertook a major reorganization to improve sales in a weak economy.[4] All of these companies are using concepts based in organization theory and design. Organization theory also applies to nonprofit organizations such as the United Way, the American Humane Association, local arts organizations, colleges and universities, and the Make-A-Wish Foundation, which grants wishes to terminally ill children.

Organization theory and design draws lessons from organizations such as Xerox, Walt Disney Company, and United Way and makes those lessons available to students and managers. As our opening example of Xerox shows, even large, successful organizations are vulnerable, lessons are not learned automatically, and organizations are only as strong as their decision makers. Organizations are not static; they continuously adapt to shifts in the external environment. Today, many companies are facing the need to transform themselves into dramatically different organizations because of new challenges in the environment.

Current Challenges

Research into hundreds of organizations provides the knowledge base to make Xerox and other organizations more effective. Challenges facing organizations today are different from those of the past, and thus the concept of organizations and organization design is evolving. The world is changing more rapidly than ever before, and managers are responsible for positioning their organizations to adapt to new needs. Some specific challenges today's managers and organizations face are globalization, intense competition, rigorous ethical scrutiny, the need for rapid response, adapting to a digital world, and embracing diversity.

Globalization. The cliché that the world is getting smaller is dramatically true for today's organizations. With rapid advances in technology and communications, the time it takes to exert influence around the world from even the most remote locations has been reduced from years to only seconds. Markets, technologies, and organizations are becoming increasingly interconnected.[5] Today's successful organizations feel "at home" anywhere in the world. Companies can locate different parts of the organization wherever it makes the most business sense: top leadership in one country, technical brainpower and production in other locales.

Related trends are global *outsourcing*, or contracting out some functions to organizations in other countries, and *strategic partnering* with foreign firms to gain a global advantage. Cross-border acquisitions and the development of effective business relationships in other countries are vital to many organizations' success. Large multinational corporations are actively searching for managers with strong international experience and the ability to move easily between cultures. A poll by the Association of Executive Search Consultants found China, India, and Brazil to be the top three countries in which companies want star talent, reflecting these organizations' increasing investment in those regions.[6]

Intense Competition. This growing global interdependence creates new advantages, but it also means that the environment for companies has become extremely competitive. Only 24 percent of managers responding to Bain & Company's recent global Management Tools and Trends survey believe the market leaders of today will still be the market leaders five years from now.[7] Customers want low prices for quality goods and services, and the organizations that can meet that demand will win. Outsourcing firms in low-wage countries can often do work for 50 to 60 percent less than companies based in the United States, for instance, so U.S. firms that provide similar services have to search for new ways to compete or go into new lines of business.[8] One entrepreneur with a new type of battery for notebook computers is having the product manufactured by a factory in Shenzhen, China. She wanted to produce it in the United States, but U.S. contract manufacturers wanted millions of dollars up front, a demand not made by any of the manufacturers she met with in China.[9]

In today's weak economy, companies in all industries are feeling pressure to drive down costs and keep prices low, yet at the same time they are compelled to invest in research and development or get left behind in the global drive for innovation. Consider McDonald's. Even as managers were seeking ways to expand the menu and draw in new customers, McDonald's labs were testing how to cut the cost of making basic items on the Dollar Menu. With the price of ingredients such as cheese, beef, and buns going up, McDonald's had to cut internal costs or lose money on its dollar-menu products.[10] Auto insurers searched for new ways to compete as drivers faced with steep gas prices looked for ways to cut their transportation costs.[11] Casual restaurant chains battled to draw in customers as people cut back on eating out. Grocers, too, felt the sting. Faced with higher transportation costs, managers at Supervalu raised their prices, but sales and profits plunged. They adjusted their strategy to promote cheaper store brands, work with manufacturers to design innovative promotions and coupons, and introduce new lines of products at lower prices.[12]

Ethics and Sustainability. Today's managers face tremendous pressure from the government and the public to hold their organizations and employees to high ethical and professional standards. Following widespread moral lapses and corporate financial scandals, organizations are under scrutiny as never before. Every decade seems to experience its share of scoundrels, but the pervasiveness of ethical lapses during the first decade of this century has been astounding. A survey of 20,000 people in 19 countries, conducted by market research firm GfK for *The Wall Street Journal*, found that 55 percent of respondents believe cheating in business is more common today than it was 10 years ago.[13] Another survey by The Ethics Resource Center revealed that more than half of American employees have observed at least one type of ethical misconduct (e.g., theft, lying) per year in their organizations.[14]

In addition to calls for higher ethical standards, people are demanding a stronger commitment by organizations to social responsibility, particularly when it comes to protecting the natural environment. *Going green* has become a new business imperative, driven by shifting social attitudes, new government policies, climate changes, and the information technology that quickly spreads news of a corporation's negative impact on the environment. Many companies are embracing the philosophy of **sustainability**, which refers to economic development that generates wealth and meets the needs of the current generation while saving the environment so future generations can meet their needs as well.[15] Walmart has become a surprise darling of the sustainability movement with its implementation of an energy-efficient trucking fleet, its growing use of green materials in buildings, and its zero waste initiative that aims to eliminate all the company's landfill waste by 2025. In addition, Walmart is pushing these initiatives down to suppliers, which could have a tremendous impact.[16]

Speed and Responsiveness. A fourth significant challenge for organizations is to respond quickly and decisively to environmental changes, organizational crises, or shifting customer expectations. For much of the twentieth century, organizations operated in a relatively stable environment, so managers could focus on designing structures and systems that kept the organization running smoothly and efficiently. There was little need to search for new ways to cope with increased competition, volatile environmental shifts, or changing customer demands. Today, globalization and advancing technology have accelerated the pace at which organizations in all industries must roll out new products and services to stay competitive. Today's customers want products and services tailored to their exact needs, and they want them *now*. Manufacturing firms that relied on mass production and distribution techniques must be prepared with new computer-aided systems that can produce one-of-a-kind variations and streamlined distribution systems that deliver products directly from the manufacturer to the consumer. Service firms are also searching for new ways to provide value. Allstate Insurance, for example, enhanced responsiveness to customers with its Your Choice Auto program, which gives drivers the opportunity to choose the insurance perks they want. Allstate managers recognize that what appeals to drivers can change quickly as gasoline prices shift.[17]

Considering the turmoil and flux inherent in today's world, the mindset needed by organizational managers is to expect the unexpected and be prepared for rapid change and potential crises. Crisis management has moved to the forefront in light of devastating natural disasters and terrorist attacks all over the world; a weak global economy, sovereign debt crises, growing unemployment, and weakening consumer confidence; widespread ethical scandals; and, in general, an environment that may shift dramatically at a moment's notice.

The Digital World. Today's realm of the Internet, social networking, blogs, online collaboration, Web-based communities, podcasting, mobile devices, Twittering, Facebooking, You Tube-ing, and Skype-ing is radically different from the world many managers are familiar and comfortable with.[18] The digital revolution has changed everything—not just how we communicate with one another, find information, and share ideas, but also how organizations are designed and managed, how businesses operate, and how employees do their jobs.

New and emerging digital tools enable many employees to perform much of their work on computers, perhaps working in virtual teams and connected electronically to colleagues around the world. In addition, rather than competing as independent entities, organizations are breaking down boundaries and collaborating with other organizations and individuals to provide innovative products and services.[19] Procter & Gamble doubled the success rate of new product introductions by using an "open innovation" approach rather than inventing and producing everything in-house.[20] Even the Federal Bureau of Investigation is taking a more open, collaborative approach. In 2011, the FBI posted on its Web site two notes written in code that were found in the pocket of a murder victim in Missouri in 1999, asking for the public's help in cracking the code that investigators have so far been unable to decipher.[21] These advances mean that an organization's managers not only need to be technologically savvy but are also responsible for managing a web of relationships that reaches far beyond the boundaries of the physical organization, building flexible e-links between a company and its employees, suppliers, contract partners, and customers.[22]

Diversity. As organizations increasingly operate on a global playing field, the workforce—as well as the customer base—grows increasingly diverse. Many of today's leading organizations have an international face. Look at the makeup of consulting firm McKinsey & Company. In the 1970s most consultants were American, but by the turn of the century McKinsey's chief partner was a foreign national (Rajat Gupta from India), only 40 percent of consultants were American, and the firm's foreign-born consultants came from 40 different countries.[23] Pepsi Co is currently led by Indra Nooyi, an India-born woman, and Coca-Cola is headed by Turkish American Muhtar Kent.

In addition to coping with global diversity, managers in the United States realize the nation's domestic population is changing dramatically. About a third of current population growth in the United States is due to immigration, and immigration is expected to continue being a positive element in coming decades.[24] The number of Hispanics in the U.S. workforce is expected to increase by 7.3 million between 2008 and 2018, and Hispanics will make up 17.6 percent of the workforce by 2018.[25] In addition to greater racial and cultural diversity in the workplace, women became the majority of the workforce for the first time in U.S. history in 2010.[26] Ursula Burns, the CEO of Xerox, captures how times have changed since she graduated from college in 1980: "I assure you that no one at my commencement was pointing at me and predicting that I'd become a CEO. *Women* presidents of large global companies were non-existent. *Black* women presidents of large companies were unimaginable."[27] The growing diversity within organizations brings vitality and many benefits but also a variety of challenges, such as maintaining a strong corporate culture while supporting diversity, balancing work and family concerns, and coping with the conflict brought about by varying cultural styles.

Purpose of this Chapter

The purpose of this chapter is to explore the nature of organizations and organization theory today. Organization theory has developed from the systematic study of organizations by scholars. Concepts are obtained from living, ongoing organizations. Organization theory has a practical application, as illustrated by the Xerox case. It helps managers understand, diagnose, and respond to emerging organizational needs and problems.

The next section begins with a formal definition of organization and then explores introductory concepts for describing and analyzing organizations, including various structural dimensions and contingency factors. We introduce the concepts of effectiveness and efficiency and describe the stakeholder approach, which considers what different groups want from the organization. Succeeding sections examine the history of organization theory and design, a framework for understanding organizational configuration, the distinction between

mechanistic and organic designs, organizations as open systems, and how organization theory can help people manage complex organizations in a rapidly changing world. The chapter closes with a brief overview of the themes to be covered in this book.

What Is an Organization?

Organizations are hard to see. We see outcroppings, such as a tall building, a computer workstation, or a friendly employee, but the whole organization is vague and abstract and may be scattered among several locations, even around the world. We know organizations are there because they touch us every day. Indeed, they are so common that we take them for granted. We hardly notice that we are born in a hospital, have our birth records registered in a government agency, are educated in schools and universities, are raised on food produced on corporate farms, are treated by doctors engaged in a joint practice, buy a house built by a construction company and sold by a real estate agency, borrow money from a bank, turn to police and fire departments when trouble erupts, use moving companies to change residences, and receive an array of benefits from various government agencies.[28] Most of us spend many of our waking hours working in an organization of one type or another.

Definition

Organizations as diverse as a bank, a corporate farm, a government agency, and Xerox Corporation have characteristics in common. The definition used in this book to describe organizations is as follows: **organizations** are (1) social entities that (2) are goal-directed, (3) are designed as deliberately structured and coordinated activity systems, and (4) are linked to the external environment.

An organization is not a building or a set of policies and procedures; organizations are made up of people and their relationships with one another. An organization exists when people interact with one another to perform essential functions that help attain goals. An organization is a means to an end. We might think of an organization as a tool or instrument used by owners and managers to accomplish a specific purpose. The purpose will vary, but the central aspect of an organization is the coordination of people and resources to collectively accomplish desired ends.[29] Managers deliberately structure and coordinate organizational resources to achieve the organization's purpose. However, even though work may be structured into separate departments or sets of activities, most organizations today are striving for greater horizontal coordination of work activities, often using teams of employees from different functional areas to work together on projects. Boundaries between departments, as well as those between organizations, are becoming more flexible and diffuse as companies face the need to respond to changes in the external environment more rapidly. An organization cannot exist without interacting with customers, suppliers, competitors, and other elements of the external environment. Today, some companies are even cooperating with their competitors, sharing information and technology to their mutual advantage.

From Multinationals to Nonprofits

Some organizations are large, multinational corporations, others are small, family-owned businesses, and still others are nonprofit organizations or governmental agencies. Some manufacture products such as automobiles, flat-panel televisions, or light bulbs, whereas others provide services such as legal representation, Internet and telecommunications services, mental health resources, or car repair. Later in this text, Chapter 12 discusses size and life cycle and describes some differences between small and large organizations. Chapter 13 will look at the distinctions between manufacturing and service technologies.

Another important distinction is between for-profit businesses and *nonprofit organizations*. All of the topics in this text apply to nonprofit organizations such as the Salvation Army, the World Wildlife Fund, the Save the Children Foundation, and Chicago's La Rabida Hospital, which is dedicated to serving the poor, just as they do to businesses such as Xerox, GameSpot, Sirius XM Radio, and Dunkin' Donuts. However, there are some important distinctions to keep in mind. The primary difference is that managers in businesses direct their activities toward earning money for the company, whereas managers in nonprofits direct their efforts toward generating some kind of social impact. The unique characteristics and needs of nonprofit organizations present unique challenges for organizational leaders.[30]

Financial resources for nonprofits typically come from government appropriations, grants, and donations rather than from the sale of products or services to customers. In businesses, managers focus on improving the organization's products and services to increase sales revenues. In nonprofits, however, services are typically provided to nonpaying clients, and a major problem for many organizations is securing a steady stream of funds to continue operating. Nonprofit managers, committed to serving clients with limited funds, must focus on keeping organizational costs as low as possible and demonstrating a highly efficient use of resources. Moreover, for-profit firms often compete with nonprofits for limited donations through their own philanthropic fundraising efforts.[31] Another problem is that, since nonprofit organizations do not have a conventional "bottom line," managers often struggle with the question of what constitutes organizational effectiveness. It is easy to measure dollars and cents, but nonprofits have to measure intangible goals such as "improve public health," "make a difference in the lives of the disenfranchised," or "enhance appreciation of the arts."

Managers in nonprofit organizations also deal with many diverse stakeholders and must market their services to attract not only clients (customers) but also volunteers and donors. This can sometimes create conflict and power struggles among organizations, as illustrated by the Make-A-Wish Foundation, which has found itself at odds with small, local wish-granting groups as it expands to cities across the United States. The more kids a group can count as helping, the easier it is to raise funds. Local groups don't want Make-A-Wish invading their turf, particularly at a time when charitable donations in general have declined along with the declining economy. Small groups are charging that Make-A-Wish is abusing the power of its national presence to overwhelm or absorb the smaller organizations. "We should not have to compete for children and money," says the director of the Indiana Children's Wish Fund. "They [Make-A-Wish] use all their muscle and money to get what they want."[32]

Thus, the organization design concepts discussed throughout this book, such as dealing with issues of power and conflict, setting goals and measuring effectiveness,

BRIEFCASE

As an organization manager, keep this guideline in mind:

Consider the needs and interests of all stakeholders when setting goals and designing the organization to achieve effectiveness.

coping with environmental uncertainty, implementing effective control mechanisms, and satisfying multiple stakeholders, apply to nonprofit organizations such as the Indiana Children's Wish Fund just as they do to businesses such as Xerox. These concepts and theories are adapted and revised as needed to fit the unique needs and problems of various small, large, profit, or nonprofit organizations.

Importance of Organizations

It may seem hard to believe today, but organizations as we know them are relatively recent in the history of humankind. Even in the late nineteenth century there were few organizations of any size or importance—no labor unions, no trade associations, and few large businesses, nonprofit organizations, or governmental agencies. What a change has occurred since then! The development of large organizations transformed all of society, and, indeed, the modern corporation may be the most significant innovation of the past 100 years.[33] This chapter's Book Mark examines the rise of the corporation and its significance in our society.

Organizations are all around us and shape our lives in many ways. But what contributions do organizations make? Why are they important? Exhibit 1.1 indicates seven reasons organizations are important to you and to society. First, recall that an organization is a means to an end. Organizations bring together resources to

EXHIBIT 1.1
Importance of Organizations

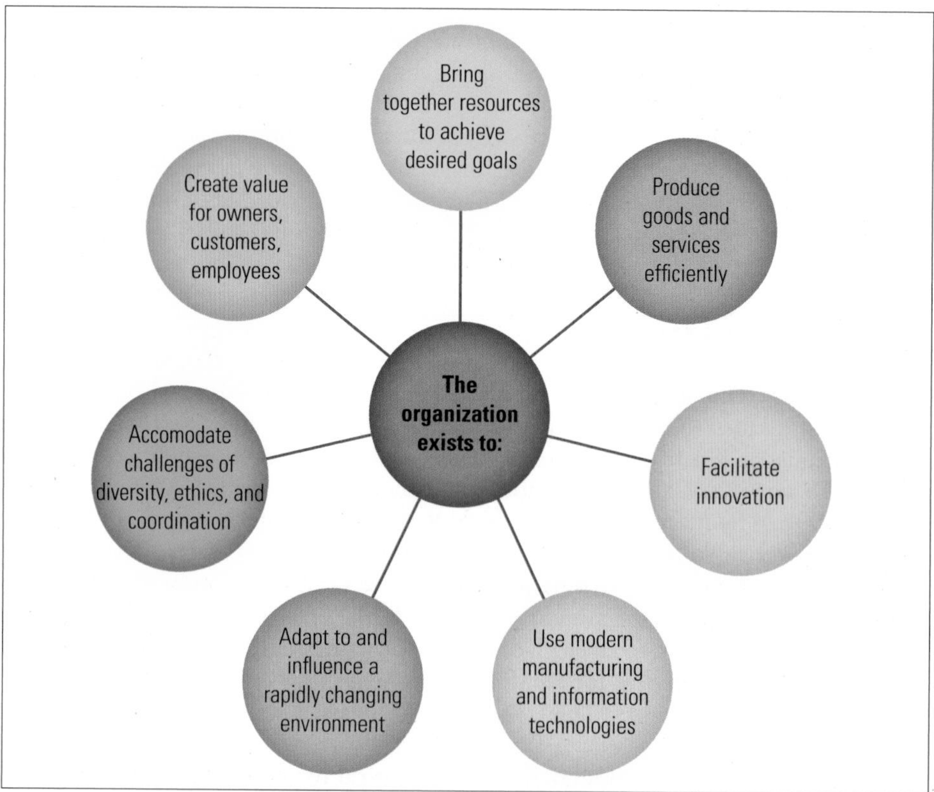

BOOKMARK

1.0 HAVE YOU READ THIS BOOK?

The Company: A Short History of a Revolutionary Idea

By John Micklethwait and Adrian Wooldridge

"The limited liability corporation is the greatest single discovery of modern times," is one conclusion of the concise and readable book *The Company: A Short History of a Revolutionary Idea* by John Micklethwait and Adrian Wooldridge. Companies are so ubiquitous today that we take them for granted, so it may come as a surprise that the company as we know it is a relatively recent innovation. Although people have joined together in groups for commercial purposes since ancient Greek and Roman times, the modern company has its roots in the late nineteenth century. The idea of a *limited liability company* that was legally an "artificial person" began with the Joint Stock Companies Act, enacted by the London Board of Trade in 1856. Today the company is seen as "the most important organization in the world." Here are a few reasons why:

- The corporation was the first autonomous legal and social institution that was within society yet independent of the central government.
- The concept of a limited liability company unleashed entrepreneurs to raise money because investors could lose only what they invested. Increasing the pool of entrepreneurial capital spurred innovation and generally enriched the societies in which companies operated.
- The company is the most efficient creator of goods and services that the world has ever known. Without a company to harness resources and organize activities, the cost to consumers for almost any product we know today would be impossible to afford.
- Historically, the corporation has been a force for civilized behavior and provided people with worthwhile activities, identity, and community, as well as a paycheck.
- The Virginia Company, a forerunner of the limited liability corporation, helped introduce the revolutionary concept of democracy to the American colonies.
- The modern multinational corporation began in Britain in the third quarter of the 1800s with the railroads, which built rail networks throughout Europe by shipping into each country the managers, materials, equipment, and labor needed.

During the past few years, it seems that large corporations have been increasingly in conflict with societies' interests. Yet large companies have been reviled throughout modern history—consider the robber barons at the beginning of the twentieth century—and the authors suggest that recent abuses are relatively mild compared to some incidents from history. Everyone knows that corporations can be scoundrels, but overall, Micklethwait and Wooldridge argue, their force has been overwhelmingly for the cumulative social and economic good.

The Company: A Short History of a Revolutionary Idea, by John Micklethwait and Adrian Wooldridge, is published by The Modern Library.

accomplish specific goals. A good example is Northrup Grumman Newport News (formerly Newport News Shipbuilding), which builds nuclear-powered, Nimitz-class aircraft carriers. Putting together an aircraft carrier is an incredibly complex job involving 47,000 tons of precision-welded steel, more than 1 million distinct parts, 900 miles of wire and cable, and more than seven years of hard work by 17,800 employees.[34] How could such a job be accomplished without an organization to acquire and coordinate these varied resources?

Organizations also produce goods and services that customers want at competitive prices. Companies look for innovative ways to produce and distribute desirable goods and services more efficiently. Two ways are through e-business and through the use of digital manufacturing technologies. For example, managers at Sandberg Furniture, based in Vernon, California, have been able to keep the 122-year-old family-owned company competitive against stiff foreign competition by using advanced technology.

Sandberg Furniture

IN PRACTICE

At one time, the Southern California furniture industry was a $1.3-billion-a-year business employing more than 60,000 workers. Today, though, inexpensive imported furniture from China has put many of the once-thriving companies out of business. How have managers kept Sandberg Furniture going? "We've had to be very efficient," says CEO John Sandberg, great-grandson of the founder. Managers embarked on some major changes after they discovered that retailers could import completed products for less than the cost of Sandberg's materials. "I knew we were in trouble," Sandberg says.

Today, Sandberg Furniture is a leader in the technology for making paper-laminate, moderately-priced laminated bedroom furniture. Two Schelling panel saws from Austria make software programmed cuts of the laminated wood and leave as little waste as possible. Another machine cuts, bends, and glues a single piece of laminate, which eliminates the need for more machines (and people) to put together four or five separate pieces. The company has also created a proprietary finishing technology that not only makes the furniture scratch-, dent-, and chemical-resistant but also creates a finish that makes a lightweight piece of laminated wood look like a heavy block of marble.

Sandberg can now do the same work that 450 people once did with about 150 employees because of the advanced technology and cross-training of workers.[35]

Faced with tough competition, strict environmental regulations in California, and other challenges, investing in advanced technology to increase efficiency was the only way Sandberg Furniture could survive. Redesigning organizational structures and management practices can also contribute to increased efficiency. Organizations create a drive for innovation rather than a reliance on standard products and outmoded approaches to management and organization design.

Organizations adapt to and influence a rapidly changing environment. Consider Facebook, which continues to adapt and evolve along with the evolving Internet and social media environment. In July 2011, the company introduced a free video-calling feature to its 750,000 worldwide members. Founder and CEO Mark Zuckerberg wants managers who aren't afraid to break things in order to make them better. Facebook's management team encourages a culture of fearlessness, helping the company win the top spot on *Fast Company*'s 2010 list of the world's 50 most innovative companies (it dropped to Number 3 in 2011, behind Apple and Twitter). Even during grim economic times, Facebook was increasing its engineering team, investing in new ideas, and pushing people to take risks for the future.[36] Many organizations have entire departments charged with monitoring the external environment and finding ways to adapt to or influence that environment.

Through all of these activities, organizations create value for their owners, customers, and employees. Managers analyze which parts of the operation create value and which parts do not; a company can be profitable only when the value it creates is greater than the cost of resources. For example, Vizio Inc., which seemed to come out of nowhere to become the Number 1 seller of flat-panel HDTVs in the United States, creates value by using existing LCD technology and developing an equity partnership with a contract manufacturer rather than producing televisions in-house. By keeping its costs low, the California-based company has been able to sell flat-panel HDTVs at about half the cost of those sold by major electronics manufacturers.[37]

Finally, organizations must cope with and accommodate today's challenges of workforce diversity and growing concerns over ethics and sustainability, as well as find effective ways to motivate employees to work together to accomplish organizational goals.

Dimensions of Organization Design

Organizations shape our lives, and well-informed managers can shape organizations. The first step for understanding organizations is to look at the features that describe specific organizational design traits. These features describe organizations in much the same way that personality and physical traits describe people.

Exhibit 1.2 illustrates two types of interacting features of organizations: structural dimensions and contingency factors. **Structural dimensions** provide labels to describe the internal characteristics of an organization. They create a basis for measuring and comparing organizations. **Contingency factors** encompass larger elements that influence structural dimensions, including the organization's size, technology, environment, culture, and goals. Contingency factors describe the organizational setting that influences and shapes the structural dimensions. Contingency factors can be confusing because they represent both the organization and the environment. These factors can be envisioned as a set of overlapping elements that shape an organization's structure and work processes, as illustrated in Exhibit 1.2. To understand and evaluate organizations, one must examine both structural dimensions and contingency factors.[38] These features of organization design interact with one another and can be adjusted to accomplish the purposes listed earlier in Exhibit 1.1.

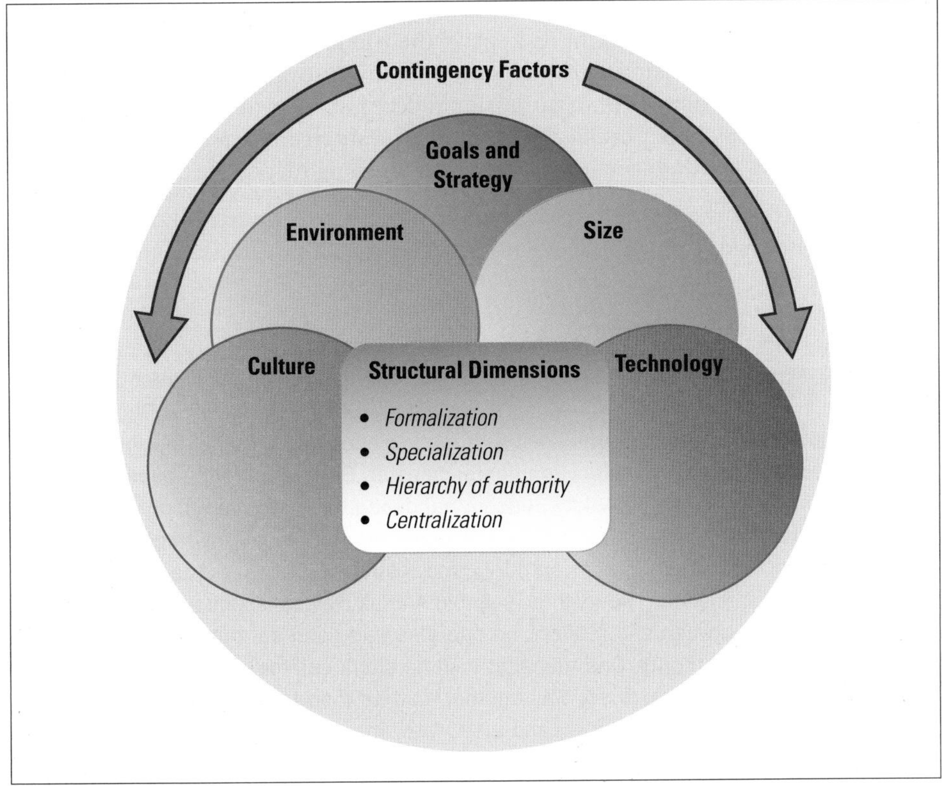

EXHIBIT 1.2
Interacting Structural Dimensions of Design and Contingency Factors

Structural Dimensions

Key structural dimensions of organizations include formalization, specialization, hierarchy of authority, and centralization.

1. *Formalization* pertains to the amount of written documentation in the organization. Documentation includes procedures, job descriptions, regulations, and policy manuals. These written documents describe behavior and activities. Formalization is often measured by simply counting the number of pages of documentation within the organization. Large universities, for example, tend to be high on formalization because they have several volumes of written rules for such things as registration, dropping and adding classes, student associations, dormitory governance, and financial assistance. A small, family-owned business, in contrast, may have almost no written rules and would be considered informal.
2. *Specialization* is the degree to which organizational tasks are subdivided into separate jobs. If specialization is extensive, each employee performs only a narrow range of tasks. If specialization is low, employees perform a wide range of tasks in their jobs. Specialization is sometimes referred to as the *division of labor.*
3. *Hierarchy of authority* describes who reports to whom and the span of control for each manager. The hierarchy is depicted by the vertical lines on an organization chart, as illustrated in Exhibit 1.3. The hierarchy is related to *span of control* (the number of employees reporting to a supervisor). When spans of control are narrow, the hierarchy tends to be tall. When spans of control are wide, the hierarchy of authority will be shorter.
4. *Centralization* refers to the hierarchical level that has authority to make decisions. When decision making is kept at the top level, the organization is centralized. When decisions are delegated to lower organizational levels, it is decentralized. Examples of organizational decisions that might be centralized or decentralized include purchasing equipment, establishing goals, choosing suppliers, setting prices, hiring employees, and deciding marketing territories.

To understand the importance of paying attention to structural dimensions of organization design, think about what happened at the BP-Transocean Deepwater Horizon oil rig.

BP Transocean Deepwater Horizon Oil Rig

IN PRACTICE

In the spring of 2010, a Transocean oil rig drilling a well for oil giant BP at Deepwater Horizon exploded in the Gulf of Mexico, killing 11 crew members and setting off an environmental disaster. Setting aside the question of what caused the explosion in the first place, once it happened the structure aboard the rig exacerbated the situation. Activities were so loosely organized that no one seemed to know who was in charge or what their level of authority and responsibility was. When the explosion occurred, confusion reigned. Twenty-three-year-old Andrea Fleytas issued a mayday (distress signal) over the radio when she realized no one else had done so, but she was chastised for overstepping her authority. One manager said he didn't call for help because he wasn't sure he had authorization to do so. Still another said he tried to call to shore but was told the order needed to come from someone else. Crew members knew the emergency shutdown needed to be triggered, but there was confusion over who had the authority to give the OK. As fire spread, several minutes passed before people received directions to evacuate.

EXHIBIT 1.3
Organization Chart Illustrating the Hierarchy of Authority for a Community Job Training Program

Board of Directors
Executive Committee
Advisory Committees

Level 1
Executive Director

Level 2
Assistant Executive Director for Community Services
Assistant Executive Director for Human Services

Level 3
Director Economic Dev.
Director Regional Planning
Director Housing
Director Criminal Justice
Director Finance
Assistant Director Finance
Director AAA
Director CETA

Level 4
Housing Coordinator
Alcoh. Coordinator
Public Information Coordinator
Accountant
Program Spec. AAA
Program Planner AAA
Contract Fiscal Mgr.
CETA Intake & Orient
Lead Couns.
CETA Couns. Devs. Title II ABC
CETA Couns. Devs. Youth IV
Lead Couns.
CETA Couns. Devs. Title II D & VI & VII
CETA Planner

Level 5
Secretary
Records Clerk
Secretary
Administrative Assistant
Payroll Clerk
Secretary
IT Specialist
Staff Clerk
Administrative Assistant

Again, an alarmed Fleytas turned on the public address system and announced that the crew was abandoning the rig. "The scene was very chaotic," said worker Carlos Ramos. "There was no chain of command. Nobody in charge."

In the aftermath of the explosion and oil spill, several federal agencies are also on the hot seat because of loose oversight and confusion over responsibility that led to delays and disagreements that prolonged the suffering of local communities. A federal law put in place after the 1989 Exxon Valdez oil spill requires national and regional plans laying out clear lines of authority and responsibility for everyone involved should such an event occur. However, the plans were confusing, faulty, or inadequate when it actually happened. For example, weeks after the rig sank, oil was seeping into the marshes around Grand Isle, Louisiana, but the boats supposed to be laying out boom to corral the oil were gathered on the wrong side of the bay. No one knew who had the authority to move them into the right area. At the Senate hearing seven weeks after the explosion that started the whole mess, Billy Nungesser, the president of Plaquemines Parish, Louisiana, said, "I still don't know who's in charge. Is it BP? Is it the Coast Guard?" Senator Bill Nelson of Florida captured the problem of poor structural design when he said, "The information is not flowing. The decisions are not timely. The resources are not produced. And as a result, you have a big mess."[39]

Contingency Factors

BRIEFCASE

As an organization manager, keep these guidelines in mind:

Think of the organization as a means to an end. It is a way to organize people and resources to accomplish a specific purpose. Describe the organization according to its degree of formalization, specialization, centralization, and hierarchy. Look at contingency factors of size, technology, the environment, goals and strategy, and the organizational culture.

Understanding structural dimensions alone does not help us understand or appropriately design organizations. It is also necessary to look at contingency factors, including size, organizational technology, the external environment, goals and strategy, and organizational culture.

1. *Size* can be measured for the organization as a whole or for specific components, such as a plant or division. Because organizations are social systems, size is typically measured by the number of employees. Other measures such as total sales or total assets also reflect magnitude, but they do not indicate the size of the human part of the system.
2. *Organizational technology* refers to the tools, techniques, and actions used to transform inputs into outputs. It concerns how the organization actually produces the products and services it provides for customers and includes such things as flexible manufacturing, advanced information systems, and the Internet. An automobile assembly line, a college classroom, and an overnight package delivery system are technologies, although they differ from one another.
3. The *environment* includes all elements outside the boundary of the organization. Key elements include the industry, government, customers, suppliers, and the financial community. The environmental elements that affect an organization the most are often other organizations.
4. The organization's *goals and strategy* define the purpose and competitive techniques that set it apart from other organizations. Goals are often written down as an enduring statement of company intent. A strategy is the plan of action that describes resource allocation and activities for dealing with the environment and for reaching the organization's goals. Goals and strategies define the scope of operations and the relationship with employees, customers, and competitors.
5. An organization's *culture* is the underlying set of key values, beliefs, understandings, and norms shared by employees. These underlying values and norms may

pertain to ethical behavior, commitment to employees, efficiency, or customer service, and they provide the glue to hold organization members together. An organization's culture is unwritten but can be observed in its stories, slogans, ceremonies, dress, and office layout.

The four structural dimensions and five contingency factors discussed here are interdependent. Certain contingency factors will influence the appropriate degree of specialization, formalization, and so forth for the organization. For example, large organization size, a routine technology, and a stable environment all tend to create an organization that has greater formalization, specialization, and centralization. More detailed relationships among contingency factors and structural dimensions are explored throughout this book.

1 **An organization can be understood primarily by understanding the people who make it up.**

ANSWER: *Disagree.* An organization has distinct characteristics that are independent of the nature of the people who make it up. All the people could be replaced over time while an organization's structural dimensions and contingency factors would remain similar.

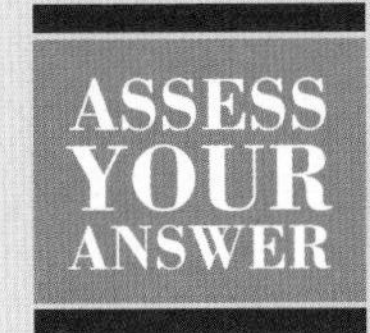

The organizational features illustrated in Exhibit 1.2 provide a basis for measuring and analyzing characteristics that cannot be seen by the casual observer, and they reveal significant information about an organization. Consider, for example, the dimensions of Ternary Software compared with those of Walmart and a governmental agency.

IN PRACTICE

Ternary Software Inc.

Brian Robertson is one of the founders of Ternary Software and holds the title of CEO. But as for having the power and authority typically granted to a top executive, forget about it. Consider a recent strategy meeting where a programmer criticized Robertson's plan to replace the company's profit-sharing program with an ad hoc bonus system based on performance. After much discussion, the CEO's plan was soundly rejected in favor of keeping the profit-sharing program and using monthly bonus incentives.

At Ternary, a company that writes software on contract for other organizations, everyone has a voice in making important decisions. A seven-member policy-setting team that includes two frontline workers elected by their peers consults with other teams throughout the company, ultimately giving every employee a chance to participate in decision making. Meetings are highly informal and people are invited to share feelings as well as business ideas. Any time a new item on the agenda is brought up for discussion, each person is asked for his or her gut reaction. Then, people get to state objections, offer alternative ideas, rework proposals, and perhaps throw out management's suggestions and plans.

Contrast Ternary's approach to that of Walmart, which achieves its competitive edge through internal cost efficiency. A standard formula is used to build each store, with uniform displays and merchandise. Walmart's administrative expenses are the lowest of any chain. The distribution system is a marvel of efficiency. Goods can be delivered to any store in less than two days after an order is placed. Stores are controlled from the top,

although store managers have some freedom to adapt to local conditions. Employees follow standard procedures set by management and have little say in decision making. However, performance is typically high, and most employees consider that the company treats them fairly.

An even greater contrast is seen in many government agencies or nonprofit organizations that rely heavily on public funding. Most state humanities and arts agencies, for example, are staffed by a small number of highly trained employees, but workers are overwhelmed with rules and regulations and swamped by paperwork. Employees who have to implement rule changes often don't have time to read the continuous stream of memos and still keep up with their daily work. Employees must require extensive reporting from their clients in order to make regular reports to a variety of state and federal funding sources.[40]

Exhibit 1.4 illustrates several structural dimensions and contingency factors of Ternary Software, Walmart, and the state arts agency. Ternary is a small organization that ranks very low with respect to formalization and centralization and has a medium degree of specialization. Horizontal collaboration to serve customers with innovative products is emphasized over the vertical hierarchy. Walmart is much more formalized, specialized, and centralized, with a strong vertical hierarchy. Efficiency is more important than new products and services, so most activities are guided by standard regulations. The arts agency, in contrast to the other organizations, reflects its status as a small part of a large government bureaucracy. The agency is overwhelmed with rules and standard procedures. Rules are dictated from the top and communication flows down a strong vertical chain of command.

Structural dimensions and contingency factors can thus tell a lot about an organization and about differences among organizations. These various organization design features are examined in more detail in later chapters to determine the appropriate level of each structural dimension needed to perform effectively based on various contingency factors.

EXHIBIT 1.4
Differing Characteristics of Three Organizations

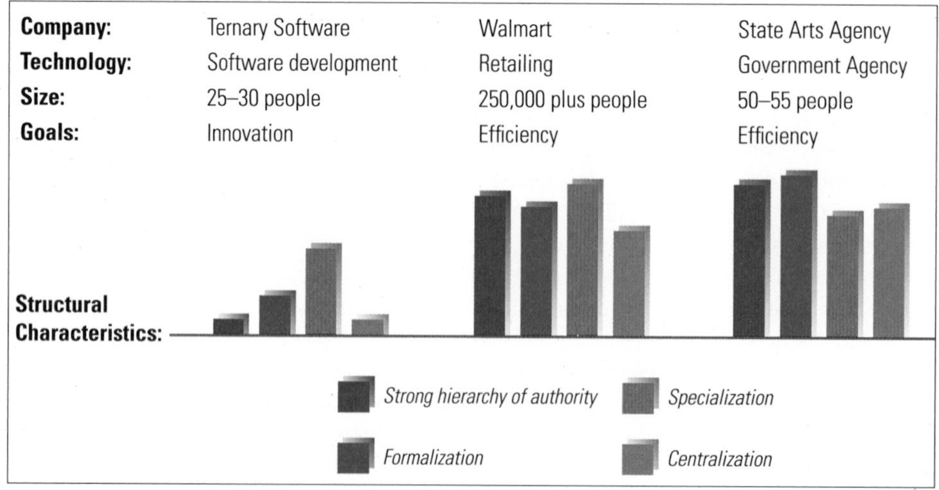

Performance and Effectiveness Outcomes

The whole point of understanding structural dimensions and contingency factors is to design the organization in such a way as to achieve high performance and effectiveness. Managers adjust various aspects of the organization to most efficiently and effectively transform inputs into outputs and provide value. **Efficiency** refers to the amount of resources used to achieve the organization's goals. It is based on the quantity of raw materials, money, and employees necessary to produce a given level of output. **Effectiveness** is a broader term, meaning the degree to which an organization achieves its goals.

To be effective, organizations need clear, focused goals and appropriate strategies for achieving them. The concept of effectiveness, including goals and strategies and various approaches to measuring effectiveness, will be discussed in detail in Chapter 3. Many organizations apply new technology to improve efficiency and effectiveness. To increase efficiency during the recent recession, Deloitte LLP cut travel budgets for consultants and began using Web and video conferencing for meetings that don't involve clients.[41] A physician's office in Philadelphia increased efficiency by using information technology to reduce paperwork and streamline procedures, enabling the practice to handle more patients with three fewer office employees. The new system improved effectiveness too. Staff can locate information more quickly and make fewer mistakes, leading to a higher quality of care and better customer service.[42]

Achieving effectiveness is not always a simple matter because different people want different things from the organization. For customers, the primary concern is high-quality products and services at a reasonable price, whereas employees are mostly concerned with adequate pay, good working conditions, and job satisfaction. Managers carefully balance the needs and interests of various *stakeholders* in setting goals and striving for effectiveness. This is referred to as the **stakeholder approach**, which integrates diverse organizational activities by looking at various organizational stakeholders and what they want from the organization. A **stakeholder** is any group within or outside of the organization that has a stake in the organization's performance. The satisfaction level of each group can be assessed as an indication of the organization's performance and effectiveness.[43]

2 The primary role of managers in business organizations is to achieve maximum efficiency.

ANSWER: *Disagree.* Efficiency is important, but organizations must respond to a variety of stakeholders, who may want different things from the organization. Managers strive for both efficiency and effectiveness in trying to meet the needs and interests of stakeholders. Effectiveness is often considered more important than efficiency.

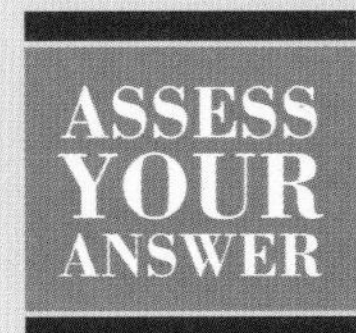

Exhibit 1.5 illustrates various stakeholders and what each group wants from the organization. Stakeholder interests sometimes conflict, and organizations often find it difficult to simultaneously satisfy the demands of all groups. A business might have high customer satisfaction, but the organization might have difficulties with creditors or supplier relationships might be poor. Consider Walmart. Customers

EXHIBIT 1.5
Major Stakeholder Groups and What They Expect

love its efficiency and low prices, but the low-cost emphasis has caused friction with suppliers. Some activist groups argue that Walmart's tactics are unethical because they force suppliers to lay off workers, close factories, and outsource to manufacturers from low-wage countries. One supplier said clothing is being sold at Walmart so cheaply that many U.S. companies couldn't compete even if they paid their workers nothing. The challenges of managing such a huge organization have also led to strains in relationships with employees and other stakeholder groups, as evidenced by recent gender discrimination suits and complaints about low wages and poor benefits.[44] The example of Walmart provides a glimpse of how difficult it can be for managers to satisfy multiple stakeholders. In all organizations, managers have to evaluate stakeholder concerns and establish goals that can achieve at least minimal satisfaction for major stakeholder groups.

The Evolution of Organization Theory and Design

Organization theory is not a collection of facts; it is a way of thinking about organizations and how people and resources are organized to collectively accomplish a specific purpose.[45] Organization theory is a way to see and analyze organizations more accurately and deeply than one otherwise could. The way to see and think about organizations is based on patterns and regularities in organizational design and behavior. Organization scholars search for these regularities, define them, measure them, and make them available to the rest of us. The facts from the research are not as important as the general patterns and insights into organizational functioning gained from a comparative study of organizations. Insights from organization design research can help managers improve organizational efficiency and effectiveness, as well as strengthen the quality of organizational life.[46] One area of insight is how organization design and management practices have varied over time in response to changes in the larger society.

Historical Perspectives

You may recall from an earlier management course that the modern era of management theory began with the classical management perspective in the late nineteenth and early twentieth century. The emergence of the factory system during the Industrial Revolution posed problems that earlier organizations had not encountered. As work was performed on a much larger scale by a larger number of workers, people began thinking about how to design and manage work in order to increase productivity and help organizations attain maximum efficiency. The classical perspective, which sought to make organizations run like efficient, well-oiled machines, is associated with the development of hierarchy and bureaucratic organizations and remains the basis of much of modern management theory and practice. In this section, we will examine the classical perspective, with its emphasis on efficiency and organization, as well as other perspectives that emerged to address new concerns, such as employee needs and the role of the environment. Elements of each perspective are still used in organization design, although they have been adapted and revised to meet changing needs. These different perspectives can also be associated with different ways in which managers think about and view the organization, called manager frame of reference. Complete the questionnaire in the "How Do You Fit the Design?" box on page 26 to understand your frame of reference.

Efficiency Is Everything. Pioneered by Frederick Winslow Taylor, **scientific management** emphasizes scientifically determined jobs and management practices as the way to improve efficiency and labor productivity. Taylor proposed that workers "could be retooled like machines, their physical and mental gears recalibrated for better productivity."[47] He insisted that management itself would have to change and emphasized that decisions based on rules of thumb and tradition should be replaced with precise procedures developed after careful study of individual situations.[48] To use this approach, managers develop precise, standard procedures for doing each job, select workers with appropriate abilities, train workers in the standard procedures, carefully plan work, and provide wage incentives to increase output.

Taylor's approach is illustrated by the unloading of iron from railcars and reloading finished steel for the Bethlehem Steel plant in 1898. Taylor calculated that with correct movements, tools, and sequencing, each man was capable of loading 47.5 tons per day instead of the typical 12.5 tons. He also worked out an incentive system that paid each man $1.85 per day for meeting the new standard, an increase from the previous rate of $1.15. Productivity at Bethlehem Steel shot up overnight. These insights helped to establish organizational assumptions that the role of management is to maintain stability and efficiency, with top managers doing the thinking and workers doing what they are told.

How Do You Fit the Design?

EVOLUTION OF STYLE

This questionnaire asks you to describe yourself. For each item, give the number "4" to the phrase that best describes you, "3" to the item that is next best, and on down to "1" for the item that is least like you.

1. My strongest skills are:
___ **a.** Analytical skills
___ **b.** Interpersonal skills
___ **c.** Political skills
___ **d.** Flair for drama

2. The best way to describe me is:
___ **a.** Technical expert
___ **b.** Good listener
___ **c.** Skilled negotiator
___ **d.** Inspirational leader

3. What has helped me the most to be successful is my ability to:
___ **a.** Make good decisions
___ **b.** Coach and develop people
___ **c.** Build strong alliances and a power base
___ **d.** Inspire and excite others

4. What people are most likely to notice about me is my:
___ **a.** Attention to detail
___ **b.** Concern for people
___ **c.** Ability to succeed in the face of conflict and opposition
___ **d.** Charisma

5. My most important leadership trait is:
___ **a.** Clear, logical thinking
___ **b.** Caring and support for others
___ **c.** Toughness and aggressiveness
___ **d.** Imagination and creativity

6. I am best described as:
___ **a.** An analyst
___ **b.** A humanist
___ **c.** A politician
___ **d.** A visionary

Scoring: Compute your scores according to the following rater. The higher score represents your way of viewing the organization and will influence your management style.

Structure = 1a + 2a + 3a + 4a + 5a + 6a = ________
Human Resource = 1b + 2b + 3b + 4b + 5b + 6b = ________
Political = 1c + 2c + 3c + 4c + 5c + 6c = ________
Symbolic = 1d + 2d + 3d + 4d + 5d + 6d = ________

Interpretation: Organization managers typically view their world through one or more mental frames of reference. (1) The *structural frame* of reference sees the organization as a machine that can be economically efficient with vertical hierarchy and routine tasks that give a manager the formal authority to achieve goals. This manager way of thinking became strong during the era of scientific management when efficiency was everything. (2) The *human resource frame* sees the organization as its people, with manager emphasis given to support, empowerment, and belonging. This manager way of thinking gained importance after the Hawthorne studies. (3) The *political frame* sees the organization as a competition for scarce resources to achieve goals, with manager emphasis on building agreement among diverse groups. This frame of reference reflects the need for organizations to share information, have a collaborative strategy, and to have all parts working together. (4) The *symbolic frame* sees the organization as theater, with manager emphasis on symbols, vision, culture, and inspiration. This manager frame of reference is important for managing an adaptive culture in a learning organization.

Which frame reflects your way of viewing the world? The first two frames of reference—structural and human resource—are important for newer managers at the lower and middle levels of an organization. These two frames usually are mastered first. As managers gain experience and move up the organization, they should acquire political and collaborative skills (Chapter 7) and also learn to use symbols to shape cultural values (Chapter 9). It is important for managers not to be stuck in one way of viewing the organization because their progress may be limited.

Source: Roy G. Williams and Terrence E. Deal, *When Opposites Dance: Balancing the Manager and Leader Within* (Palo Alto, CA: Davies-Black, 2003), pp. 24–28. Reprinted with permission.

The ideas of creating a system for maximum efficiency and organizing work for maximum productivity are deeply embedded in our organizations. A *Harvard Business Review* article discussing innovations that shaped modern management puts scientific management at the top of its list of 12 influential innovations.[49]

How to Get Organized. Another subfield of the classical perspective took a broader look at the organization. Whereas scientific management focused primarily on the technical core—on work performed on the shop floor—**administrative principles** looked at the design and functioning of the organization as a whole. For example, Henri Fayol proposed 14 principles of management, such as "each subordinate receives orders from only one superior" (unity of command) and "similar activities in an organization should be grouped together under one manager" (unity of direction). These principles formed the foundation for modern management practice and organization design.

The scientific management and administrative principles approaches were powerful and gave organizations fundamental new ideas for establishing high productivity and increasing prosperity. Administrative principles in particular contributed to the development of **bureaucratic organizations**, which emphasized designing and managing organizations on an impersonal, rational basis through such elements as clearly defined authority and responsibility, formal recordkeeping, and uniform application of standard rules. Although the term *bureaucracy* has taken on negative connotations in today's organizations, bureaucratic characteristics worked extremely well for the needs of the Industrial Age. One problem with the classical perspective, however, is that it failed to consider the social context and human needs.

What about People? Early work on industrial psychology and human relations received little attention because of the prominence of scientific management. However, a major breakthrough occurred with a series of experiments at a Chicago electric company, which came to be known as the **Hawthorne Studies**. Interpretations of these studies at the time concluded that positive treatment of employees improved their motivation and productivity. The publication of these findings led to a revolution in worker treatment and laid the groundwork for subsequent work examining treatment of workers, leadership, motivation, and human resource management. These human relations and behavioral approaches added new and important contributions to the study of management and organizations.

However, the hierarchical system and bureaucratic approaches that developed during the Industrial Revolution remained the primary approach to organization design and functioning well into the 1980s. In general, this approach worked well for most organizations until the past few decades. During the 1980s, though, it began to cause problems. Increased competition, especially on a global scale, changed the playing field.[50] North American companies had to find a better way.

Can Bureaucracies Be Flexible? The 1980s produced new corporate cultures that valued lean staff, flexibility and learning, rapid response to the customer, engaged employees, and quality products. Organizations began experimenting with teams, flattened hierarchies, and participative management approaches. For example, in 1983, a DuPont plant in Martinsville, Virginia, cut management layers from eight to four and began using teams of production employees to solve problems and take

BRIEFCASE

As an organization manager, keep these guidelines in mind:

Be cautious when applying something that works in one situation to another situation. All organizational systems are not the same. Use organization theory to identify the correct structure and management systems for each organization.

over routine management tasks. The new design led to improved quality, decreased costs, and enhanced innovation, helping the plant be more competitive in a changed environment.[51] Rather than relying on strict rules and hierarchy, managers began looking at the entire organizational system, including the external environment.

Since the 1980s, organizations have undergone even more profound and far-reaching changes. Flexible approaches to organization design have become prevalent. Recent influences on the shifting of organization design include the Internet and other advances in communications and information technology; globalization and the increasing interconnection of organizations; the rising educational level of employees and their growing quality-of-life expectations; and the growth of knowledge- and information-based work as primary organizational activities.[52]

It All Depends: Key Contingencies

Many problems occur when all organizations are treated as similar, which was the case with scientific management and administrative principles that attempted to design all organizations alike. The structures and systems that work in the retail division of a conglomerate will not be appropriate for the manufacturing division. The organization charts and financial procedures that are best for an entrepreneurial Internet firm like Twitter will not work for a large food processing plant at Kraft or a large nonprofit organization such as the United Way.

A basic premise of this text is that effective organization design means understanding various contingencies and how organizations can be designed to fit contingency factors. **Contingency** means that one thing depends on other things, and for organizations to be effective there must be a "goodness of fit" between their structure and various contingency factors.[53] What works in one setting may not work in another setting. There is no "one best way." Contingency theory means *it depends*. For example, a government agency may experience a certain environment, use a routine technology, and desire efficiency. In this situation, a management approach that uses bureaucratic control procedures, a hierarchical structure, and formalized communications would be appropriate. Likewise, a free-flowing design and management processes work best in a high-tech company that faces an uncertain environment with a non-routine technology. The correct approach is contingent on the organization's situation. Later in the chapter, we will examine two fundamental approaches to organization design, along with the typical contingency factors associated with each approach.

An Example of Organizational Configuration

An important insight from organization design researchers is how organizations are configured—that is, what parts make up an organization and how do the various parts fit together? An organization's design or configuration will reflect contingency factors along recognizable patterns. One framework proposed by Henry Mintzberg suggests that every organization has five parts.[54] These parts, illustrated in Exhibit 1.6, include the technical core, top management, middle management, technical support, and administrative support.

Technical Core. The technical core includes people who do the basic work of the organization. This part actually produces the product and service outputs of the

EXHIBIT 1.6
Five Basic Parts of an Organization

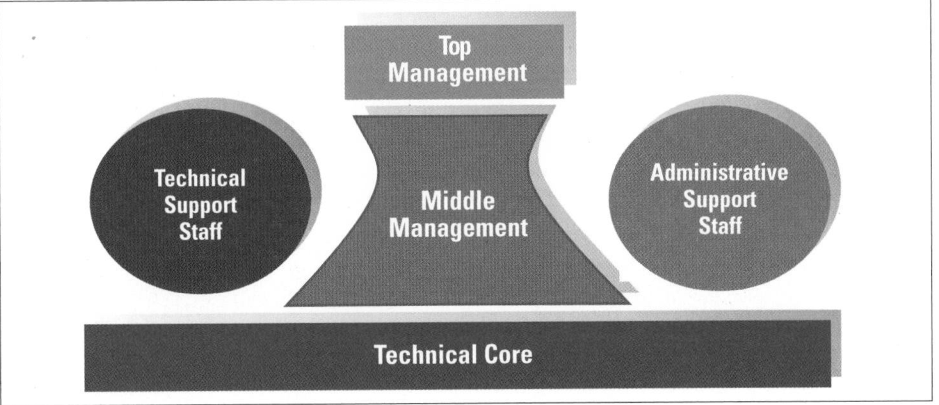

Source: Based on Henry Mintzberg, *The Structuring of Organizations* (Englewood Cliffs, N.J.: Prentice-Hall, 1979), 215–297; and Henry Mintzberg, "Organization Design: Fashion or Fit?" *Harvard Business Review* 59 (January-February 1981), 103–116.

organization. This is where the primary transformation from inputs to outputs takes place. The technical core is the production department in a manufacturing firm, the teachers and classes in a university, and the medical activities in a hospital.

Technical Support. The technical support function helps the organization adapt to the environment. Technical support employees such as engineers, researchers, and information technology professionals scan the environment for problems, opportunities, and technological developments. Technical support is responsible for creating innovations in the technical core, helping the organization change and adapt.

Administrative Support. The administrative support function is responsible for the smooth operation and upkeep of the organization, including its physical and human elements. This includes human resource activities such as recruiting and hiring, establishing compensation and benefits, and employee training and development, as well as maintenance activities such as cleaning of buildings and service and repair of machines.

Management. Management is a distinct function, responsible for directing and coordinating other parts of the organization. Top management provides direction, planning, strategy, goals, and policies for the entire organization or major divisions. Middle management is responsible for implementation and coordination at the departmental level. In traditional organizations, middle managers are responsible for mediating between top management and the technical core, such as implementing rules and passing information up and down the hierarchy.

BRIEFCASE

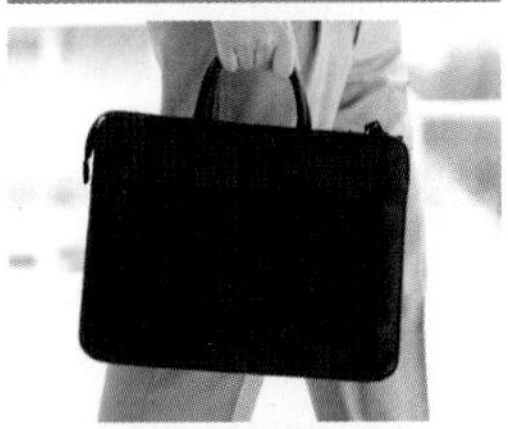

As an organization manager, keep these guidelines in mind:

When designing an organization, consider five basic parts—technical core, technical support, administrative support, top management, and middle management—and how they work together for maximum organizational effectiveness.

3 A CEO's top priority is to make sure the organization is designed correctly.

ANSWER: *Agree.* Top managers have many responsibilities, but one of the most important is making sure the organization is designed correctly. Organization design organizes and focuses people's work and shapes their response to customers and other stakeholders. Managers consider both structural dimensions and contingency factors as well as make sure the various parts of the organization work together to achieve important goals.

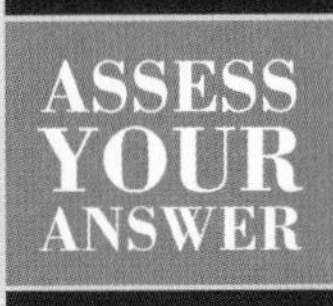

BRIEFCASE

As an organization manager, keep these guidelines in mind:

Think about whether the organization should have a mostly mechanistic design (associated with large size, efficiency strategy, a stable environment, a rigid culture, and a manufacturing technology) or a mostly organic design (associated with smaller size, innovation strategy, a changing environment, an adaptive culture, and a service technology).

The size and interaction of these five parts can vary widely among organizations. One organization might have a large technical support staff and minimal administrative support staff, whereas the reverse might be true for another company. In real-life organizations, the five parts are interrelated and often serve more than one function. For example, managers coordinate and direct parts of the organization, but they may also be involved in administrative and technical support. The point is that understanding these five parts provides a way to think about the various human components that make up an organization.

Organic and Mechanistic Designs

Organizations can also be categorized along a continuum ranging from a mechanistic design to an organic design. Tom Burns and G.M. Stalker first used the terms organic and mechanistic to describe two extremes of organization design after observing industrial firms in England.[55] In general, a **mechanistic** design means that the organization is characterized by machine-like standard rules, procedures, and a clear hierarchy of authority. Organizations are highly formalized and are also centralized, with most decisions made at the top. An **organic** design means that the organization is much looser, free-flowing, and adaptive. Rules and regulations often are not written down or, if written down, are flexibly applied. People may have to find their own way through the system to figure out what to do. The hierarchy of authority is looser and not clear-cut. Decision-making authority is decentralized.

Various contingency factors will influence whether an organization is more effective with a primarily mechanistic or a primarily organic design. Exhibit 1.7 summarizes the differences in organic and mechanistic designs based on five elements: structure, tasks, formalization, communication, and hierarchy. The exhibit also lists the typical contingency factors associated with each type of design.

- *Centralized Versus Decentralized Structure.* Centralization and decentralization pertain to the hierarchical level at which decisions are made. In a mechanistic design, the structure is centralized, whereas an organic design uses decentralized decision making. **Centralization** means that decision authority is located near the top of the organizational hierarchy. Knowledge and control of activities are centralized at the top of the organization, and employees are expected to do as they are told. With **decentralization**, decision making authority is pushed down to lower organizational levels. In a highly organic organization, knowledge and control of activities are located with employees rather than with supervisors or top executives. People are encouraged to take care of problems by working with one another and with customers, using their discretion to make decisions.
- *Specialized Tasks Versus Empowered Roles.* A **task** is a narrowly defined piece of work assigned to a person. With a mechanistic design, tasks are broken down into specialized, separate parts, as in a machine, with each employee performing activities according to a specific job description. A **role**, in contrast, is a part in a dynamic social system. A role has discretion and responsibility, allowing the person to use his or her discretion and ability to achieve an outcome or meet a goal. In an organization with an organic design, employees play a role in the team or department and roles may be continually redefined or adjusted.

EXHIBIT 1.7
Organic and Mechanistic Designs

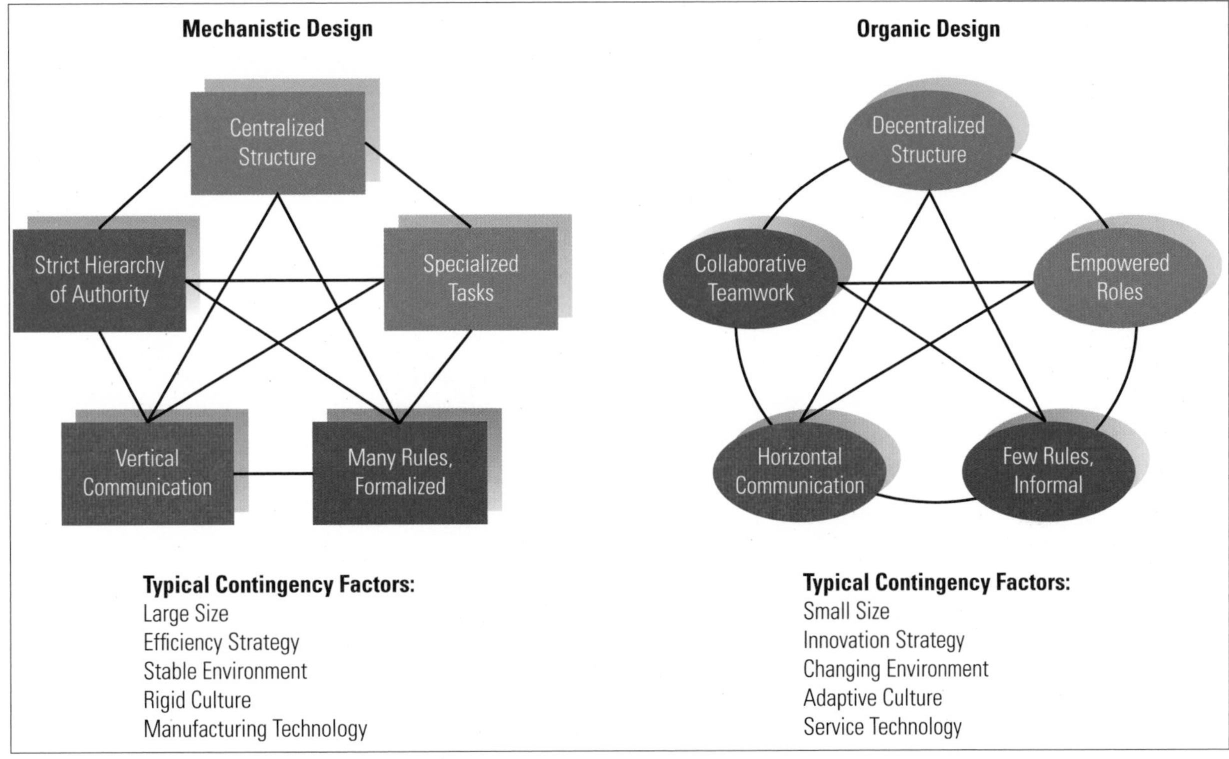

- *Formal Versus Informal Systems.* With a mechanistic design, there are numerous rules, regulations, and standard procedures. Formal systems are in place to manage information, guide communication, and detect deviations from established standards and goals. With an organic design, on the other hand, there are few rules or formal control systems. Communication and information sharing is informal.
- *Vertical Versus Horizontal Communication.* Mechanistic organizations emphasize vertical communication up and down the hierarchy. Top managers pass information downward to employees about goals and strategies, job instructions, procedures, and so forth, and in turn ask that employees provide information up the hierarchy concerning problems, performance reports, financial information, suggestions and ideas, and so forth. In an organic organization, there is greater emphasis on horizontal communication, with information flowing in all directions within and across departments and hierarchical levels. The widespread sharing of information enables all employees to have complete information about the company so they can act quickly. In addition, organic organizations maintain open lines of communication with customers, suppliers, and even competitors to enhance learning capability.
- *Hierarchy of Authority Versus Collaborative Teamwork.* In organizations with a mechanistic design, there is a close adherence to vertical hierarchy and the formal chain of command. Work activities are typically organized by common

function from the bottom to the top of the organization and there is little collaboration across functional departments. The entire organization is controlled through the vertical hierarchy. An organic design, on the other hand, emphasizes collaborative teamwork rather than hierarchy. Structure is created around horizontal workflows or processes rather than departmental functions, with people working across department and organizational boundaries to solve problems. The vertical hierarchy is dramatically flattened, with perhaps only a few senior executives in traditional support functions such as finance or human resources. Self-directed teams are the fundamental work unit in highly organic organizations.

Contemporary Design Ideas

To some extent, organizations are still imprinted with the hierarchical, formalized, mechanistic approach that arose in the nineteenth century with Frederick Taylor. Yet current challenges require greater flexibility for most organizations. Cisco Systems provides an example of an organization where managers shifted from a mechanistic to an organic design to meet new contingencies.

Cisco Systems

IN PRACTICE

Cisco Systems started out as a typical hierarchical organization with a command-and control mindset. Most decisions were made by top managers, and employees were expected to perform their jobs as directed, obey the rules, and follow formal procedures. That all changed after the dot-com bubble burst in the early 2000s and Cisco's stock dropped 86 percent virtually overnight.

CEO John Chambers believed the company needed a new approach to management and organization design if it was to survive. He knew collaborative teamwork would be required to get the company growing again. In addition, Chambers thought employees would be more creative, more productive, and more committed to rebuilding the organization if they had more autonomy and fewer limitations. So, he essentially threw out the old structures and controls. Now, rather than having proposals and suggestions sent to top executives for approval, a network of councils and boards that cross functional, departmental, and hierarchical lines are empowered to launch new businesses. One board made up of volunteer self-identified "sports freaks" built a product called StadiumVision, which allows venue owners to push video and digital content such as advertising to fans in the stadium. Now a multibillion-dollar business, StadiumVision came together in less than four months, without the CEO ever being involved in the decision.

Command and control is a thing of the past, Chambers asserts, with the future belonging to those companies that build leadership throughout the organization and take a more flexible and organic approach to design. The organic approach helped Cisco emerge from the dot-com crisis more profitable than ever and the company has since outperformed many technology rivals.[56]

However, not every organization performs better with a strong organic design. Sometimes standard procedures, formal rules, and a more mechanistic approach serve an important function. As an illustration, after the spring 2011 earthquake and tsunami devastated areas of Japan, formal rules, orderly systems, and bureaucratic procedures were critical to the smooth operation of evacuation centers. Not only did this mechanistic approach keep the centers running in an orderly fashion, but the rules, procedures, and top-down communication gave people a sense of normalcy and reassurance, helping to reduce psychological and physical stress.[57] Similarly, the organization aboard a nuclear aircraft carrier typically follows a mechanistic approach, with formal rules, a strict chain of command, and standard operating procedures. If people and activities are not well-ordered, too many things can quickly go awry when launching and landing planes from an oil-slicked deck in the middle of the ocean. Thus, mechanistic characteristics can be highly effective in the right situations. In general, however, most organizations are shifting toward more organic designs because of the turbulence of the external environment and the need for innovation, adaptability, and a fast response to customers or clients.[58] Organizations have to change as the environment changes because organizations are open systems.

Open Systems

The distinction between closed and open systems was a significant development in the study of organizations.[59] A **closed system** would not depend on or interact with the environment. It would be autonomous, closed off and sealed from the outside world. Although a true closed system cannot exist, early management and organization design concepts, such as scientific management, took a closed-systems approach by focusing on improving efficiency through modifications of internal systems. Yet to fully understand organizations requires viewing them as open systems. An **open system** must interact with the environment in order to survive. Open systems cannot seal themselves off and must continuously adapt to the environment.

To be successful, an organization must be managed as an open system. The organization has to find and obtain needed resources, interpret and act on environmental threats and opportunities, distribute products and services, and control and coordinate internal activities in the face of outside changes and uncertainty.

The term **system** means a set of interrelated parts that function as a whole to achieve a common purpose.[60] These interrelated parts of a system are called **subsystems**. Changes in one part of the system affect other parts, and managers need to understand the whole organization, rather than just the separate elements.[61] Subsystems in an organization perform specific functions required for organizational survival, such as production, boundary spanning, maintenance, adaptation, and management. Boundary systems, for example, are responsible for exchanges with the external environment. They include activities such as purchasing supplies, marketing products and services, and competitive intelligence. These various subsystem functions are carried out by the five basic organizational parts described earlier and illustrated in Exhibit 1.6.

BRIEFCASE

As an organization manager, keep these guidelines in mind:

Remember that organizations are open systems made up of various subsystems that perform functions such as production, boundary spanning, maintenance, adaptation, and management. Don't make changes in one subsystem of the organization without considering how the changes will affect other subsystems.

Chaos Theory

For most of the nineteenth and early twentieth centuries, mechanistic designs and closed-system thinking predominated. Newtonian science, which suggests that the world functions as a well-ordered machine, continued to guide managers' thinking about organizations.[62] The environment was perceived as orderly and predictable, and the role of managers was to maintain stability. Organizations became large and complex, and boundaries between functional departments and between organizations were distinct. Internal structures grew more complex, vertical, and

bureaucratic. Leadership was based on solid management principles and tended to be autocratic; communication was primarily through formal memos, letters, and reports. Managers did all the planning and "thought work," while employees did the manual labor in exchange for wages and other compensation. This mechanistic approach worked quite well for the Industrial Age.[63]

The environment for today's companies, however, is anything but stable. With the turbulence of recent years, managers can no longer maintain an illusion of order and predictability. The science of **chaos theory** suggests that relationships in complex, open systems—including organizations—are nonlinear and made up of numerous interconnections and divergent choices that create unintended effects and render the whole unpredictable.[64] The world is full of uncertainty, characterized by surprise, rapid change, and confusion. Managers can't measure, predict, or control in traditional ways the unfolding drama inside or outside the organization. However, chaos theory also recognizes that this randomness and disorder occurs within certain larger patterns of order. The ideas of chaos theory suggest that organizations should be viewed more as natural systems than as well-oiled, predictable machines, leading to an increase in the use of organic design approaches.

Framework for the Book

How does a course in organization theory differ from a course in management or organizational behavior? The answer is related to the concept called *level of analysis*.

Levels of Analysis

As just described, each organization is a system that is composed of various subsystems. Organization systems are nested within systems, and one **level of analysis** has to be chosen as the primary focus. Four levels of analysis normally characterize organizations, as illustrated in Exhibit 1.8. The individual human being is the basic building block of organizations. The human being is to the organization what a cell is to a biological system. The next higher system level is the group or department. These are collections of individuals who work together to perform group tasks.

EXHIBIT 1.8
Levels of Analysis in Organizations

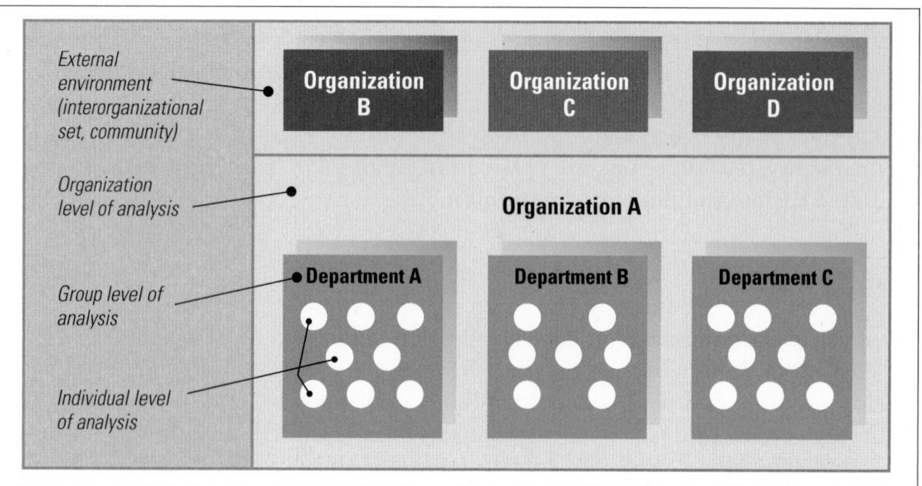

Source: Based on Andrew H. Van De Ven and Diane L. Ferry, *Measuring and Assessing Performance* (New York: Wiley, 1980), 8; and Richard L. Daft and Richard M. Steers, *Organizations: A Micro/Macro Approach* (Glenview, IL: Scott, Foresman, 1986), 8.

The next level of analysis is the organization itself. An organization is a collection of groups or departments that combine into the total organization.

Organizations themselves can be grouped together into the next higher level of analysis, which is the inter-organizational set and community. The inter-organizational set is the group of organizations with which a single organization interacts. Other organizations in the community make up an important part of an organization's environment.

Organization theory focuses on the organizational level of analysis, but with concern for groups and the environment. To explain the organization, one should look not only at its characteristics but also at the characteristics of the environment and of the departments and groups that make up the organization. The focus of this book is to help you understand organizations by examining their specific characteristics, the nature of and relationships among groups and departments that make up the organization, and the collection of organizations that make up the environment.

Are individuals included in organization theory? Organization theory does consider the behavior of individuals, but in the aggregate. People are important, but they are not the primary focus of analysis. Organization theory is distinct from organizational behavior.

Organizational behavior is the micro approach to organizations because it focuses on the individuals within organizations as the relevant units of analysis. Organizational behavior examines concepts such as motivation, leadership style, and personality and is concerned with cognitive and emotional differences among people within organizations.

Organization theory is a macro examination of organizations because it analyzes the whole organization as a unit. Organization theory is concerned with people aggregated into departments and organizations and with the differences in structure and behavior at the organization level of analysis. Organization theory might be considered the sociology of organizations, while organizational behavior is the psychology of organizations.

Organization theory is directly relevant to top- and middle-management concerns and partly relevant to lower management. Top managers are responsible for the entire organization and must set goals, develop strategy, interpret the external environment, and decide organization structure and design. Middle management is concerned with major departments, such as marketing or research, and must decide how the department relates to the rest of the organization. Middle managers must design their departments to fit work-unit technology and deal with issues of power and politics, intergroup conflict, and information and control systems, each of which is part of organization theory. Organization theory is only partly concerned with lower management because this level of supervision is concerned with employees who operate machines, create services, or sell goods. Organization theory is concerned with the big picture of the organization and its major departments.

BRIEFCASE

As an organization manager, keep this guideline in mind:

Make yourself a competent, influential manager by using the frameworks that organization theory provides to interpret and understand the organization around you.

Plan of the Book

The topics within the field of organization theory and design are interrelated. Chapters are presented so that major ideas unfold in logical sequence. The framework that guides the organization of the book is shown in Exhibit 1.9. Part 1

EXHIBIT 1.9
Framework for the Book

Part 1 Introduction to Organization Theory and Design

CHAPTER 1
Introduction to Organizations

Part 2 Organizational Strategy and Structure

CHAPTER 2
Structural Design for Organizations

CHAPTER 3
Strategy and Effectiveness

Part 3 External Factors and Design

CHAPTER 4
Relationships Between Organizations

CHAPTER 5
Global Organization Design

CHAPTER 6
The Impact of Environment

Part 4 Managing Organizational Processes

CHAPTER 7
Organizational Conflict and Politics

CHAPTER 8
Organizational Decision-Making

CHAPTER 9
Corporate Culture and Values

CHAPTER 10
Organizational Innovation

Part 5 Internal Factors and Design

CHAPTER 11
Information and Control Processes

CHAPTER 12
Organization Size and Life Cycle

CHAPTER 13
Workplace Technology and Design

introduces the basic idea of organizations as social systems and the essential concepts of organization theory and design. This discussion provides the groundwork for Part 2, which is about strategic management, goals and effectiveness, and the fundamentals of organization structure. This section examines how managers help the organization achieve its purpose, including the design of an appropriate structure, such as a functional, divisional, matrix, or horizontal structure. Part 3 looks at the various open system elements that influence organization structure and design, including the external environment, inter-organizational relationships, and the global environment.

Parts 4 and 5 look at processes inside the organization. Part 4 discusses dynamic processes that exist within and between major organizational departments and includes topics such as innovation and change, culture and ethical values, decision-making processes, managing intergroup conflict, and power and politics. Part 5 describes how organization design is related to the contingency factors of manufacturing and service technology, and organizational size and life cycle.

Plan of Each Chapter

Each chapter begins with opening questions to immediately engage the student in the chapter content. Theoretical concepts are introduced and explained in the body of the chapter. Several *In Practice* segments are included in each chapter to illustrate the concepts and show how they apply to real organizations. Each chapter also contains a *How Do You Fit the Design?* questionnaire that draws students more deeply into a particular topic and enables them to experience organization design issues in a personal way. A *Book Mark* is included in each chapter to present organizational issues that today's managers face in the real world. These short book reviews discuss current concepts and applications to deepen and enrich the student's understanding of organizations. The examples and book reviews illustrate the dramatic changes taking place in management thinking and practice. Key points for designing and managing organizations are highlighted in the *Briefcase* items throughout the chapter. Each chapter closes with a *Design Essentials* section that reviews and explains important theoretical concepts.

Design Essentials

- Organization theory provides tools to understand, design, and manage organizations more effectively, including issues such as how to adapt to a changing environment, cope with increasing size and complexity, manage internal conflict and coordination, and shape the right kind of culture to meet goals.
- Managers today face new challenges, including globalization, intense competition, rigorous ethical scrutiny and the demand for sustainability, a need for rapid response, adapting to the digital world, and increasing diversity.
- Organizations are highly important, and managers are responsible for shaping organizations to perform well and meet the needs of society. The structural dimensions of formalization, specialization, hierarchy of authority, and centralization and the contingency factors of size, organizational technology, environment, goals and strategy, and culture provide labels for measuring and analyzing organizations.

These characteristics vary widely from organization to organization. Subsequent chapters provide frameworks for analyzing organizations with these concepts.

- Many types of organizations exist. One important distinction is between for-profit businesses, in which managers direct their activities toward earning money for the company, and nonprofit organizations, in which managers direct their efforts toward generating some kind of social impact. Managers strive to design organizations to achieve both efficiency and effectiveness. Effectiveness is complex because different stakeholders have different interests and needs that they want satisfied by the organization.
- Organization design perspectives have varied over time. Managers can understand organizations better by gaining a historical perspective and by understanding the basics of organizational configuration. Five parts of the organization are the technical core, top management, middle management, technical support, and administrative support. Different configurations of these parts help organizations meet different needs.
- Organization designs fall on a scale ranging from mechanistic to organic. A mechanistic design is characterized by a centralized structure, specialized tasks, formal systems, vertical communication, and a strict hierarchy of authority. An organic design is characterized by a decentralized structure, empowered roles, informal systems, horizontal communication, and collaborative teamwork. Challenges in today's environment are causing many organizations to shift to more organic designs, although mechanistic characteristics are still valuable for some situations.
- Organizations are open systems that must interact with the environment. A system is a set of interrelated parts that function as a whole to achieve a common purpose. The interrelated parts of a system are called subsystems. Subsystems perform specific functions such as production, boundary spanning, maintenance, adaptation, and management.
- Most concepts in organization theory pertain to the top- and middle-management levels of the organization. This book is concerned more with the topics of those levels than with the operational-level topics of supervision and motivation of employees, which are discussed in courses on organizational behavior.

Key Concepts

administrative principles
bureaucratic organizations
centralization
chaos theory
closed system
contingency factors
contingency
decentralization
effectiveness
efficiency
Hawthorne Studies
level of analysis
mechanistic
open system
organic
organization theory
organizational behavior
organizations
role
scientific management
stakeholder
stakeholder approach
structural dimensions
subsystems
sustainability
system
task

Discussion Questions

1. What is the definition of *organization*? Briefly explain each part of the definition as you understand it.
2. Describe some ways in which the digital world has influenced or affected an organization with which you are familiar, such as your college or university, a local retailer or restaurant, a volunteer organization, a club to which you belong, or even your family. Can you identify both positive and negative aspects of this influence?
3. Explain how Mintzberg's five basic parts of the organization (Exhibit 1.6) fit together to perform needed functions. If an organization had to give up one of these five parts, such as during a severe downsizing, which one could it survive the longest without? Discuss.
4. A handful of companies on the *Fortune* 500 list are more than 100 years old, which is rare. What organizational characteristics do you think might explain 100-year longevity?
5. Can an organization be efficient without being effective? Can an inefficient organization still be an effective one? Explain your answers.
6. What is the difference between formalization and specialization? Do you think an organization high on one dimension would also be high on the other? Discuss.
7. What does *contingency* mean? What are the implications of contingency theory for managers?
8. What are the primary differences between an organic and a mechanistic organization design? Which type of organization do you think would be easier to manage? Discuss.
9. Explain the difference between an open system and a closed system. Can you give an example of a closed system? How is the stakeholder approach related to the concept of open and closed systems?
10. What are some differences one might expect among stakeholder expectations for a nonprofit organization versus a for-profit business? Do you think nonprofit managers have to pay more attention to stakeholders than do business managers? Discuss.
11. Early management theorists believed that organizations should strive to be logical and rational, with a place for everything and everything in its place. Discuss the pros and cons of this approach for today's organizations.

Chapter 1 Workbook Measuring Dimensions of Organizations[65]

Analyze two organizations along the following dimensions. Indicate where you think each organization would fall on each of the scales. Use an X to indicate the first organization and an * to show the second.

You may choose any two organizations you are familiar with, such as your place of work, the university, a student organization, your church or synagogue, or your family.

Formalization

Many written rules	1 2 3 4 5 6 7 8 9 10	Few rules

Specialization

Separate tasks and roles	1 2 3 4 5 6 7 8 9 10	Overlapping tasks

Hierarchy

Tall hierarchy of authority	1 2 3 4 5 6 7 8 9 10	Flat hierarchy of authority

Technology

Product	1 2 3 4 5 6 7 8 9 10	Service

External Environment

Stable	1 2 3 4 5 6 7 8 9 10	Unstable

	Culture	
Clear norms and values	1 2 3 4 5 6 7 8 9 10	Ambiguous norms and values
	Goals	
Well-defined goals	1 2 3 4 5 6 7 8 9 10	Goals not defined
	Size	
Small	1 2 3 4 5 6 7 8 9 10	Large
	Organizational Mindset	
Mechanistic system	1 2 3 4 5 6 7 8 9 10	Organic system

Questions

1. What are the main differences between the two organizations you evaluated?
2. Would you recommend that one or both of the organizations have different ratings on any of the scales? Why?

CASE FOR ANALYSIS Rondell Data Corporation[66]

"Damn it, he's done it again!" Frank Forbus threw the stack of prints and specifications down on his desk in disgust. The Model 802 wide-band modulator, released for production the previous Thursday, had just come back to Frank's Engineering Services Department with a caustic note that began, "This one can't be produced either . . . ." It was the fourth time production had kicked the design back.

Frank Forbus, director of engineering for Rondell Data Corporation, was normally a quiet man. But the Model 802 was stretching his patience; it was beginning to look just like other new products that had hit delays and problems in the transition from design to production during the eight months Frank had worked for Rondell. These problems were nothing new at the sprawling old Rondell factory; Frank's predecessor in the engineering job had run afoul of them, too, and had finally been fired for protesting too vehemently about the other departments. But the Model 802 should have been different. Frank had met two months before (July 3, 1998) with the firm's president, Bill Hunt, and with factory superintendent Dave Schwab to smooth the way for the new modulator design. He thought back to the meeting . . . .

"Now we all know there's a tight deadline on the 802," Bill Hunt said, "and Frank's done well to ask us to talk about its introduction. I'm counting on both of you to find any snags in the system and to work together to get that first production run out by October 2nd. Can you do it?"

"We can do it in production if we get a clean design two weeks from now, as scheduled," answered Dave Schwab, the grizzled factory superintendent. "Frank and I have already talked about that, of course. I'm setting aside time in the machine shop, and we'll be ready. If the design goes over schedule, though, I'll have to fill in with other runs, and it will cost us a bundle to break in for the 802. How does it look in engineering, Frank?"

"I've just reviewed the design for the second time," Frank replied. "If Ron Porter can keep the salesmen out of our hair and avoid any more last-minute changes, we've got a shot. I've pulled the draftsmen off three other overdue jobs to get this one out. But, Dave, that means we can't spring engineers loose to confer with your production people on manufacturing problems."

"Well, Frank, most of those problems are caused by the engineers, and we need them to resolve the difficulties. We've all agreed that production bugs come from both of us bowing to sales pressure, and putting equipment into production before the designs are really ready. That's just what we're trying to avoid on the 802. But I can't have 500 people sitting on their hands waiting for an answer from your people. We'll have to have some engineering support."

Bill Hunt broke in. "So long as you two can talk calmly about the problem I'm confident you can resolve it. What a relief it is, Frank, to hear the way you're approaching this. With Kilmann (the previous director of engineering) this conversation would have been a shouting match. Right, Dave?" Dave nodded and smiled.

"Now there's one other thing you should both be aware of," Hunt continued. "Doc Reeves and I talked last night about a new filtering technique, one that might improve the signal-to-noise ratio of the 802 by a factor of two. There's a chance Doc can come up with it before the 802 reaches production, and if it's possible, I'd like to use the new filters. That would give us a real jump on the competition."

Four days after that meeting, Frank found that two of his key people on the 802 design had been called to production for emergency consultation on a bug found in final assembly: two halves of a new data transmission interface wouldn't fit together because recent changes in the front end required a different chassis design for the back end.

Another week later, Doc Reeves walked into Frank's office, proud as a new parent, with the new filter design. "This won't affect the other modules of the 802 much," Doc had said. "Look, it takes a few connectors, some changes in the wiring harness, and some new shielding, and that's all."

Frank had tried to resist the last-minute design changes, but Bill Hunt had stood firm. With a lot of overtime by the engineers and draftsmen, engineering services should still be able to finish the prints in time.

Two engineers and three draftsmen went onto 12-hour days to get the 802 ready, but the prints were still five days late reaching Dave Schwab. Two days later, the prints came back to Frank, heavily annotated in red. Schwab had worked all day Saturday to review the job and had found more than a dozen discrepancies in the prints—most of them caused by the new filter design and insufficient checking time before release. Correction of those design faults had brought on a new generation of discrepancies; Schwab's cover note on the second return of the prints indicated he'd had to release the machine capacity he'd been holding for the 802. On the third iteration, Schwab committed his photo and plating capacity to another rush job. The 802 would be at least one month late getting into production. Ron Porter, vice president for sales, was furious. His customer needed 100 units NOW, he said. Rondell was the customer's only late supplier.

"Here we go again," thought Frank Forbus.

Company History

Rondell Data Corporation traced its lineage through several generations of electronics technology. Its original founder, Bob Rondell, had set the firm up in 1939 as "Rondell Equipment Company" to manufacture several electrical testing devices he had invented as an engineering faculty member at a large university. The firm branched into radio broadcasting equipment in 1947 and into data transmission equipment in the late 1960s. A well-established corps of direct salespeople, mostly engineers, called on industrial, scientific, and government accounts, but concentrated heavily on original equipment manufacturers. In this market, Rondell had a long-standing reputation as a source of high-quality, innovative designs. The firm's salespeople fed a continual stream of challenging problems into the Engineering Department, where the creative genius of Ed "Doc" Reeves and several dozen other engineers "converted problems to solutions" (as the sales brochure bragged). Product design formed the spearhead of Rondell's growth.

By 1998, Rondell offered a wide range of products in its two major lines. Broadcast and telecommunications equipment sales now accounted for more than half of company sales. In the field of data transmission, an increasing number of orders called for unique specifications, ranging from specialized display panels to entirely untried designs.

The company had grown from a few dozen employees in the early years to over 800 in 1998. (Exhibit 1.10 shows the 1998 organization chart of key employees.) Bill Hunt, who had been with the company since 1972, had presided over much of that growth, and he took great pride in preserving the "family spirit" of the old organization. Informal relationships between Rondell's veteran employees formed the backbone of the firm's day-to-day operations; all the managers relied on personal contact, and Hunt often insisted that the absence of bureaucratic red tape was a key factor in recruiting outstanding engineering talent. The personal management approach extended throughout the factory. All exempt employees were paid on a straight salary plus a share of the profits. Rondell boasted an extremely loyal group of senior employees and very low turnover in nearly all areas of the company.

The highest turnover job in the firm was Frank Forbus's. Frank had joined Rondell in January 1998, replacing Jim Kilmann, who had been director of engineering for only 10 months. Kilmann, in turn, had replaced Tom MacLeod, a talented engineer who had made a promising start but had taken to drink after a year in the job. MacLeod's predecessor had been a genial old-timer who retired at 70 after 30 years in charge of engineering. (Doc Reeves had refused the directorship in each of the recent changes, saying, "Hell, that's no promotion for a bench man like me. I'm no administrator.")

For several years, the firm had experienced a steadily increasing number of disputes between research, engineering, sales, and production people—disputes generally centered on the problem of new product introduction. Quarrels between departments became more numerous under MacLeod, Kilmann, and Forbus. Some managers associated those disputes with the company's recent decline

EXHIBIT 1.10
Rondell Data Corporation
1998 Organization Chart

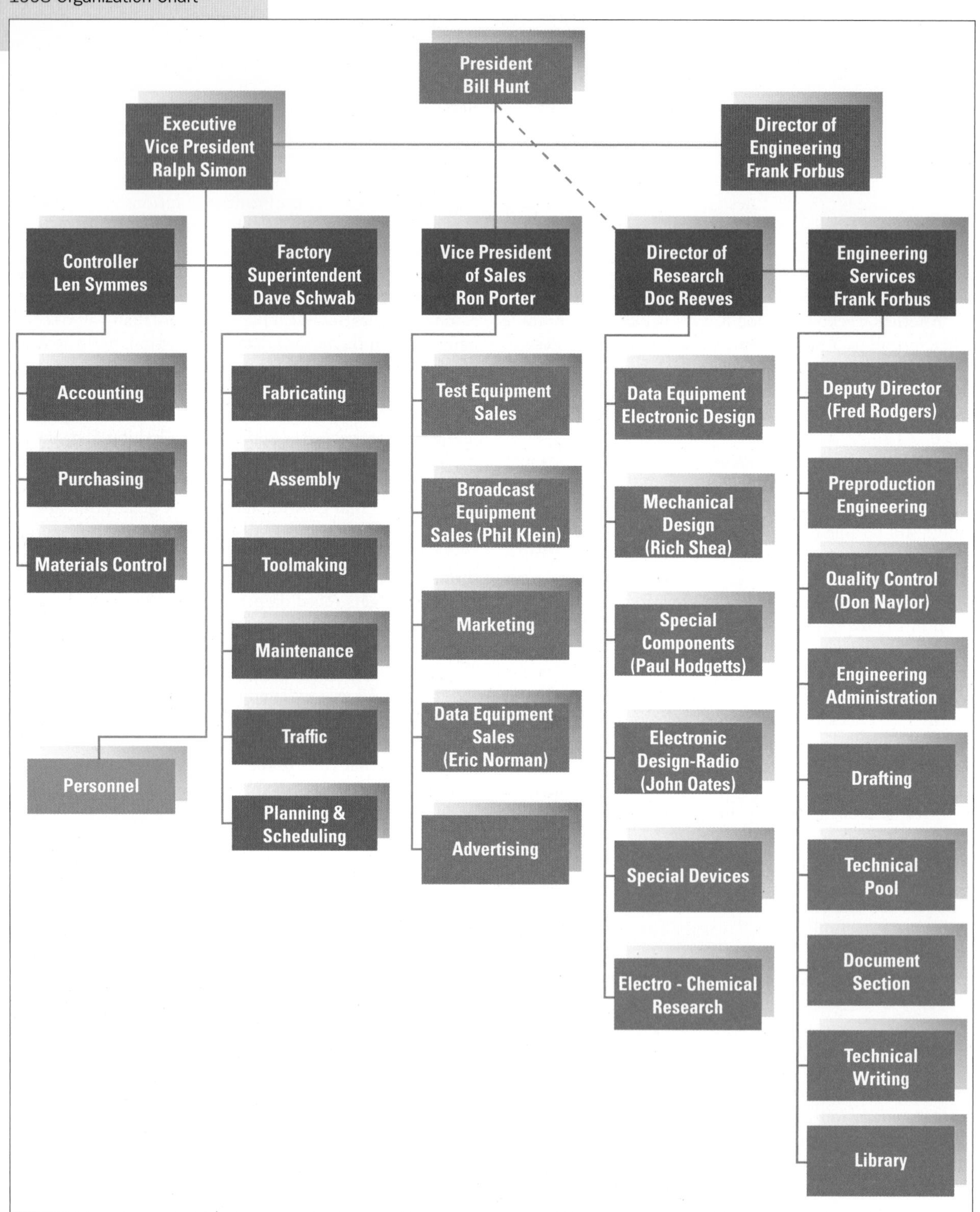

in profitability—a decline that, in spite of higher sales and gross revenues, was beginning to bother people in 1998. President Bill Hunt commented:

Better cooperation, I'm sure, could increase our output by 5–10 percent. I'd hoped Kilmann could solve the problems, but pretty obviously he was too young, too arrogant. People like him—conflict type of personality—bother me. I don't like strife, and with him it seemed I spent all my time smoothing out arguments. Kilmann tried to tell everyone else how to run their departments, without having his own house in order. That approach just wouldn't work here at Rondell. Frank Forbus, now, seems much more in tune with our style of organization. I'm really hopeful now.

Still, we have just as many problems now as we did last year. Maybe even more. I hope Frank can get a handle on engineering services soon . . . .

The Engineering Department: Research

According to the organization chart (see Exhibit 1), Frank Forbus was in charge of both research (really the product development function) and engineering services (which provided engineering support). To Forbus, however, the relationship with research was not so clear-cut:

Doc Reeves is one of the world's unique people, and none of us would have it any other way. He's a creative genius. Sure, the chart says he works for me, but we all know Doc does his own thing. He's not the least bit interested in management routines, and I can't count on him to take any responsibility in scheduling projects, or checking budgets, or what-have-you. But as long as Doc is director of research, you can bet this company will keep on leading the field. He has more ideas per hour than most people have per year, and he keeps the whole engineering staff fired up. Everybody loves Doc—and you can count me in on that, too. In a way, he works for me, sure. But that's not what's important.

Doc Reeves—unhurried, contemplative, casual, and candid—tipped his stool back against the wall of his research cubicle and talked about what was important:

Development engineering. That's where the company's future rests. Either we have it there, or we don't have it.

There's no kidding ourselves that we're anything but a bunch of Rube Goldbergs here. But that's where the biggest kicks come from—from solving development problems, and dreaming up new ways of doing things. That's why I so look forward to the special contracts we get involved in. We accept them not for the revenue they represent, but because they subsidize the basic development work which goes into all our basic products.

This is a fantastic place to work. I have a great crew and they can really deliver when the chips are down. Why, Bill Hunt and I (he gestured toward the neighboring cubicle, where the president's name hung over the door) are likely to find as many people here at work at 10:00 P.M. *as at 3:00 in the afternoon. The important thing here is the relationships between people; they're based on mutual respect, not on policies and procedures. Administrative red tape is a pain. It takes away from development time.*

Problems? Sure, there are problems now and then. There are power interests in production, where they sometimes resist change. But I'm not a fighting man, you know. I suppose if I were, I might go in there and push my weight around a little. But I'm an engineer and can do more for Rondell sitting right here or working with my own people. That's what brings results.

Other members of the Research Department echoed Doc's views and added some additional sources of satisfaction with their work. They were proud of the personal contacts they built up with customers' technical staffs—contacts that increasingly involved travel to the customers' sites to serve as expert advisers in the preparation of overall system design specifications. The engineers were also delighted with the department's encouragement of their personal development, continuing education, and independence on the job.

But there were problems, too. Rick Shea, of the mechanical design section, noted:

In the old days I really enjoyed the work—and the people I worked with. But now there's a lot of irritation. I don't like someone breathing down my neck. You can be hurried into jeopardizing the design.

John Oates, head of the electronic design section, was another designer with definite views:

Production engineering is almost nonexistent in this company. Very little is done by the preproduction section in engineering services. Frank Forbus has been trying to get preproduction into the picture, but he won't succeed because you can't start from such an ambiguous position. There have been three directors of engineering in three years. Frank can't hold his own against the others in the company, Kilmann was too aggressive. Perhaps no amount of tact would have succeeded.

Paul Hodgetts was head of special components in the research and development department. Like the rest of the department, he valued bench work. But he complained of engineering services:

The services don't do things we want them to do. Instead, they tell us what they're going to do. I should probably go to Frank, but I don't get any decisions there. I know I should go through Frank, but this holds things up, so I often go direct.

The Engineering Department: Engineering Services

The Engineering Services Department provided ancillary services to R & D and served as liaison between engineering and the other Rondell departments. Among its main functions were drafting; management of the central technicians' pool; scheduling and expediting engineering products; documentation and publication of parts lists and engineering orders; preproduction engineering (consisting of the final integration of individual design components into mechanically compatible packages); and quality control (which included inspection of incoming parts and materials, and final inspection of subassemblies and finished equipment). Top management's description of the department included the line, "ESD is responsible for maintaining cooperation with other departments, providing services to the development engineers, and freeing more valuable people in R & D from essential activities that are diversions from and beneath their main competence."

Many of Frank Forbus's 75 employees were located in other departments. Quality control people were scattered through the manufacturing and receiving areas, and technicians worked primarily in the research area or the prototype fabrication room. The remaining ESD personnel were assigned to leftover nooks and crannies near production or engineering sections.

Frank Forbus described his position:

My biggest problem is getting acceptance from the people I work with. I've moved slowly rather than risk antagonism. I saw what happened to Kilmann, and I want to avoid that. But although his precipitate action had won over a few of the younger R & D people, he certainly didn't have the department's backing. Of course, it was the resentment of other departments that eventually caused his discharge. People have been slow accepting me here. There's nothing really overt, but I get a negative reaction to my ideas.

My role in the company has never been well defined really. It's complicated by Doc's unique position, of course, and also by the fact that ESD sort of grew by itself over the years, as the design engineers concentrated more and more on the creative parts of product development. I wish I could be more involved in the technical side. That's been my training, and it's a lot of fun. But in our setup, the technical side is the least necessary for me to be involved in.

Schwab (production head) is hard to get along with. Before I came and after Kilmann left, there were six months intervening when no one was really doing any scheduling. No work loads were figured, and unrealistic promises were made about releases. This puts us in an awkward position. We've been scheduling way beyond our capacity to manufacture or engineer.

Certain people within R & D—for instance, John Oates, head of the electronic design section—understand scheduling well and meet project deadlines, but this is not generally true of the rest of the R & D department, especially the mechanical engineers who won't commit themselves. Most of the complaints come from sales and production department heads because items—like the 802—are going to production before they are fully developed, under pressure from sales to get out the unit, and this snags the whole process. Somehow, engineering services should be able to intervene and resolve these complaints, but I haven't made much headway so far. I should be able to go to Hunt for help, but he's too busy most of the time, and his major interest is the design side of engineering, where he got his own start. Sometimes he talks as though he's the engineering director as well as president. I have to put my foot down; there are problems here that the front office just doesn't understand.

Salespeople were often observed taking their problems directly to designers, while production frequently threw designs back at R & D, claiming they could not be produced and demanding the prompt attention of particular design engineers. The latter were frequently observed in conference with production supervisors on the assembly floor. Frank went on:

The designers seem to feel they're losing something when one of us tries to help. They feel it's a reflection on them to have someone take over what they've been doing. They seem to want to carry a project right through to the final stages, particularly the mechanical people. Consequently, engineering services people are used below their capacity to contribute and our department is denied functions it should be performing. There's not as much use made of engineering services as there should be.

Frank Forbus's technician supervisor added his comments:

Production picks out the engineer who'll be the "bum of the month." They pick on every little detail instead of using their heads and making the minor changes that have to be made. The 15-to-20-year people shouldn't have to prove their ability any more, but they spend four hours defending themselves and four hours getting the job done. I have no one to go to when I need help. Frank Forbus is afraid. I'm trying to help him but he can't help me at this time. I'm responsible for fifty people and I've got to support them.

Fred Rodgers, whom Frank had brought with him to the company as an assistant, gave another view of the situation:

I try to get our people in preproduction to take responsibility, but they're not used to it and people in other departments don't usually see them as best qualified to solve the problem. There's a real barrier for a newcomer here. Gaining people's confidence is hard. More and more, I'm wondering whether there really is a job for me here.

(Rodgers left Rondell a month later.) Another of Forbus's subordinates gave his view:

If Doc gets a new product idea, you can't argue. But he's too optimistic. He judges that others can do what he does—but there's only one Doc Reeves. We've had 900 production change orders this year—they changed 2,500 drawings. If I were in Frank's shoes I'd put my foot down on all this new development. I'd look at the reworking we're doing and get production set up the way I wanted it. Kilmann was fired when he was doing a good job. He was getting some system in the company's operations. Of course, it hurt some people. There is no denying that Doc is the most important person in the company. What gets overlooked is that Hunt is a close second, not just politically but in terms of what he contributes technically and in customer relations.

This subordinate explained that he sometimes went out into the production department but that Schwab, the production head, resented this. Personnel in production said that Kilmann had failed to show respect for old-timers and was always meddling in other departments' business. This was why he had been fired, they contended.

Don Taylor was in charge of quality control. He commented:

I am now much more concerned with administration and less with work. It is one of the evils you get into. There is tremendous detail in this job. I listen to everyone's opinion. Everybody is important. There shouldn't be distinctions—distinctions between people. I'm not sure whether Frank has to be a fireball like Kilmann. I think the real question is whether Frank is getting the job done. I know my job is essential. I want to supply service to the more talented people and give them information so they can do their jobs better.

The Sales Department

Ron Porter was angry. His job was supposed to be selling, he said, but instead it had turned into settling disputes inside the plant and making excuses to waiting customers. He jabbed a finger toward his desk:

You see that telephone? I'm actually afraid nowadays to hear it ring. Three times out of five, it will be a customer who's hurting because we've failed to deliver on schedule. The other two calls will be from production or ESD, telling me some schedule has slipped again.

The Model 802 is typical. Absolutely typical. We padded the delivery date by six weeks, to allow for contingencies. Within two months, the slack had evaporated. Now it looks like we'll be lucky to ship it before Christmas. (It was now November 28.) We're ruining our reputation in the market. Why, just last week one of our best customers—people we've worked with for 15 years—tried to hang a penalty clause on their latest order.

We shouldn't have to be after the engineers all the time. They should be able to see what problems they create without our telling them.

Phil Klein, head of broadcast sales under Porter, noted that many sales decisions were made by top management. Sales was understaffed, he thought, and had never really been able to get on top of the job.

We have grown further and further away from engineering. The director of engineering does not pass on the information that we give him. We need better relationships there. It is very difficult for us to talk to customers about development problems without technical help. We need each other. The whole of engineering is now too isolated from the outside world. The morale of ESD is very low. They're in a bad spot—they're not well organized.

People don't take much to outsiders here. Much of this is because the expectation is built up by top management that jobs will be filled from the bottom. So it's really tough when an outsider like Frank comes in.

Eric Norman, order and pricing coordinator for data equipment, talked about his own relationship with the Production Department:

Actually, I get along with them fairly well. Oh, things could be better of course, if they were more cooperative generally. They always seem to say, "It's my bat and ball, and we're playing by my rules." People are afraid to make production mad; there's a lot of power in there. But you've got to understand that production has its own set of problems. And nobody in Rondell is working any harder than Dave Schwab to try to straighten things out.

The Production Department

Dave Schwab had joined Rondell just after the Vietnam War, in which he had seen combat duty as well as intelligence duty. Both experiences had been useful in his first year of civilian employment at Rondell. The factory superintendent and several middle managers had been, apparently, indulging in highly questionable side deals with Rondell's suppliers. Dave Schwab had gathered evidence, revealed the situation to Bill Hunt, and stood by the president in the ensuing unsavory situation. Seven months after joining the company, Dave was named factory superintendent.

His first move had been to replace the fallen managers with a new team from outside. This group did not share the traditional Rondell emphasis on informality and friendly personal relationships and had worked long and hard to install systematic manufacturing methods and procedures. Before the reorganization, production had controlled purchasing, stock control, and final quality control (where final assembly of products in cabinets was accomplished). Because of the wartime events, management decided on a checks-and-balance system of organization and removed these three departments from production jurisdiction. The new production managers felt they had been unjustly penalized by this organization, particularly since they had uncovered the behavior that was detrimental to the company in the first place.

By 1998, the production department had grown to 500 employees, 60 percent of whom worked in the assembly area—an unusually pleasant environment that had been commended by *Factory* magazine for its colorful decoration, cleanliness, and low noise level. An additional 30 percent of the work force, mostly skilled machinists, staffed the finishing and fabrication department. About 60 others performed scheduling, supervisory, and maintenance duties. Production workers were nonunion, hourly-paid, and participated in both the liberal profit-sharing program and the stock purchase plan. Morale in production was traditionally high, and turnover was extremely low.

Dave Schwab commented:

To be efficient, production has to be a self-contained department. We have to control what comes into the department and what goes out. That's why purchasing, inventory control, and quality ought to run out of this office. We'd eliminate a lot of problems with better control there. Why, even Don Taylor in QC would rather work for me than for ESD; he's said so himself. We understand his problems better.

The other departments should be self-contained too. That's why I always avoid the underlings and go straight to the department heads with any questions. I always go down the line.

I have to protect my people from outside disturbances. Look what would happen if I let unfinished, half-baked designs in here—there'd be chaos. The bugs have to be found before the drawings go into the shop, and it seems I'm the one who has to find them. Look at the 802, for example. (Dave had spent most of Thanksgiving red-penciling the latest set of prints.) ESD should have found every one of those discrepancies. They just don't check drawings properly. They change most of the things I flag, but then they fail to trace through the impact of those changes on the rest of the design. I shouldn't have to do that. And those engineers are tolerance crazy. They want everything to a millionth of an inch. I'm the only one in the company who's had any experience with actually machining things to a millionth of an inch. We make sure that the things that engineers say on their drawings actually have to be that way and whether they're obtainable from the kind of raw material we buy.

That shouldn't be production's responsibility, but I have to do it. Accepting bad prints wouldn't let us ship the order any quicker. We'd only make a lot of junk that had to be reworked. And that would take even longer.

This way, I get to be known as the bad guy, but I guess that's just part of the job. (He paused with a wry smile.) Of course, what really gets them is that I don't even have a degree.

Dave had fewer bones to pick with the Sales Department because, he said, they trusted him.

When we give Ron Porter a shipping date, he knows the equipment will be shipped then.

You've got to recognize, though, that all of our new-product problems stem from sales making absurd commitments on equipment that hasn't been fully developed. That always means trouble. Unfortunately, Hunt always backs sales up, even when they're wrong. He always favors them over us.

Ralph Simon, age 65, executive vice president of the company, had direct responsibility for Rondell's production department. He said:

> *There shouldn't really be a dividing of departments among top management in the company. The president should be czar over all. The production people ask me to do something for them, and I really can't do it. It creates bad feelings between engineering and production, this special attention that they [R & D] get from Bill. But then Hunt likes to dabble in design. Schwab feels that production is treated like a poor relation.*

The Executive Committee

At the executive committee meeting on December 6, it was duly recorded that Dave Schwab had accepted the prints and specifications for the Model 802 modulator, and had set Friday, December 29, as the shipping date for the first 10 pieces. Bill Hunt, in the chairperson's role, shook his head and changed the subject quickly when Frank tried to open the agenda to a discussion of interdepartmental coordination.

The executive committee itself was a brainchild of Rondell's controller, Len Symmes, who was well aware of the disputes that plagued the company. Symmes had convinced Bill Hunt and Ralph Simon to meet every two weeks with their department heads, and the meetings were formalized with Hunt, Simon, Ron Porter, Dave Schwab, Frank Forbus, Doc Reeves, Symmes, and the personnel director attending. Symmes explained his intent and the results:

> *Doing things collectively and informally just doesn't work as well as it used to. Things have been gradually getting worse for at least two years now. We had to start thinking in terms of formal organization relationships. I did the first organization chart, and the executive committee was my idea too—but neither idea is contributing much help, I'm afraid. It takes top management to make an organization click. The rest of us can't act much differently until the top people see the need for us to change.*
>
> *I had hoped the committee especially would help get the department managers into a constructive planning process. It hasn't worked out that way because Mr. Hunt really doesn't see the need for it. He uses the meetings as a place to pass on routine information.*

Merry Christmas

"Frank, I didn't know whether to tell you now, or after the holiday." It was Friday, December 22, and Frank Forbus was standing awkwardly in front of Bill Hunt's desk.

"But, I figured you'd work right through Christmas Day if we didn't have this talk, and that just wouldn't have been fair to you. I can't understand why we have such poor luck in the engineering director's job lately. And I don't think it's entirely your fault. But . . . ."

Frank only heard half of Hunt's words, and said nothing in response. He'd be paid through February 28. . . . He should use the time for searching . . . .Hunt would help all he could . . . .Jim Kilmann was supposed to be doing well at his own new job, and might need more help . . . .

Frank cleaned out his desk and numbly started home. The electronic carillon near his house was playing a Christmas carol. Frank thought again of Hunt's rationale: Conflict still plagued Rondell—and Frank had not made it go away. Maybe somebody else could do it.

"And what did Santa Claus bring you, Frankie?" he asked himself.

"The sack. Only the empty sack."

Notes

1. This case is based on Anthony Bianco and Pamela L. Moore, "Downfall: The Inside Story of the Management Fiasco at Xerox," *BusinessWeek* (March 5, 2001), 82–92; Robert J. Grossman, "HR Woes at Xerox," *HR Magazine* (May 2001), 34–45; Jeremy Kahn, "The Paper Jam from Hell," *Fortune* (November 13, 2000), 141–146; Pamela L. Moore, "She's Here to Fix the Xerox," *BusinessWeek* (August 6, 2001), 47–48; Claudia H. Deutsch, "At Xerox, the Chief Earns (Grudging) Respect," *The New York Times* (June 2, 2002), section 3, 1, 12; Olga Kharif, "Anne Mulcahy Has Xerox by the Horns," *BusinessWeek Online* (May 29, 2003); Amy Yee, "Xerox Comeback Continues to Thrive," *Financial Times* January 26, 2005, 30; George Anders, "Corporate News; Business: At Xerox, Jettisoning Dividend Helped Company Out of a Crisis," *The Asian Wall Street Journal* (November 28, 2007), 6; Andrew Davidson, "Xerox Saviour in the Spotlight," *Sunday Times* (June 1, 2008), 6; Betsy Morris, "The Accidental CEO," *Fortune* (June 23, 2003), 58–67; Matt Hartley, "Copy That: Xerox Tries Again to Rebound," *The Globe and Mail* (January 7, 2008), B1; Nanette Byrnes and Roger O. Crockett, "An Historic Succession at Xerox," *BusinessWeek* (June 8, 2009), 18–22; William M. Bulkeley, "Xerox Names Burns Chief as Mulcahy Retires Early," *The Wall Street Journal* (May 22, 2009), B1; Geoff Colvin, "C-Suite Strategies: Ursula Burns Launches Xerox Into the Future," *Fortune* (April 22, 2010), http://money.cnn.com/2010/04/22/news/companies/xerox_ursula_burns.fortune/ (accessed July 1, 2011); Kelley Damore, "Burns: Blazing a New Trail,"

CRN (May 1, 2011), 48; Dana Mattioli, "Xerox Makes Push for Faster Services Growth," *The Wall Street Journal Online* (May 10, 2011), http://online.wsj.com/article/SB10001424052748703730804576315431127121172.html (accessed July 1, 2011); Scott Campbell, "Xerox: Channeling New Energy," *CRN* (May 1, 2011), 3; "Ethisphere Announces 2010 World's Most Ethical Companies," *Business Wire* (March 22, 2010); and "Xerox Recognized for Commitment to Citizenship: Awards Focus on Corporate Reputation, Ethics and Governance, Sustainability, Diversity, and a Commitment to Work-Life Balance," *Business Wire* (June 24, 2009).

2. Susan Carey and Timothy W. Martin, "American Air Strains for Lift," *The Wall Street Journal* (July 2, 2011), B1.
3. Matthew Karnitschnig, Carrick Mollenkamp, and Dan Fitzpatrick, "Bank of America Eyes Merrill," *The Wall Street Journal* (September 15, 2008), A1; Carrick Mollenkamp and Mark Whitehouse, "Old-School Banks Emerge Atop New World of Finance," *The Wall Street Journal* (September 16, 2008), A1, A10.
4. Mike Ramsey and Evan Ramstad, "Once a Global Also-Ran, Hyundai Zooms Forward," *The Wall Street Journal* (July 30, 2011), A1; Richard Siklos, "Bob Iger Rocks Disney," *Fortune* (January 19, 2009), 80–86; Ellen Byron, "Lauder Touts Beauty Bargains," *The Wall Street Journal* (May 5, 2009).
5. Harry G. Barkema, Joel A. C. Baum, and Elizabeth A. Mannix, "Management Challenges in a New Time," *Academy of Management Journal* 45, no. 5 (2002), 916–930.
6. Joann S. Lublin, "Hunt Is On for Fresh Executive Talent—Cultural Flexibility in Demand," *The Wall Street Journal* (April 11, 2011), B1.
7. Darrell Rigby and Barbara Bilodeau, "Management Tools and Trends 2009," Bain & Company (May 22, 2009), http://www.bain.com/publications/articles/management-tools-and-trends-2009.aspx (accessed July 5, 2011).
8. Keith H. Hammonds, "The New Face of Global Competition," *Fast Company* (February 2003), 90–97; and Pete Engardio, Aaron Bernstein, and Manjeet Kripalani, "Is Your Job Next?" *BusinessWeek* (February 3, 2003), 50–60.
9. Pete Engardio, "Can the U.S. Bring Jobs Back from China?" *BusinessWeek* (June 30, 2008), 38ff.
10. Janet Adamy, "McDonald's Tests Changes in $1 Burger As Costs Rise," *The Wall Street Journal* (August 4, 2008), B1.
11. Lavonne Kuykendall, "Auto Insurers Paying Up to Compete for Drivers," *The Wall Street Journal* (April 9, 2008), B5.
12. Chris Serres, "As Shoppers Cut Back, Grocers Feel the Squeeze," *Star Tribune* (July 23, 2008), D1.
13. Adam Cohen, "Who Cheats? Our Survey on Deceit," *The Wall Street Journal* (June 27, 2008).
14. Survey results reported in Don Hellriegel and John W. Slocum Jr., *Organizational Behavior,* 13th ed. (Cincinnati, OH: South-Western/Cengage Learning, 2011), 37.
15. This definition is based on Marc J. Epstein and Marie-Josée Roy, "Improving Sustainability Performance: Specifying, Implementing and Measuring Key Principles," *Journal of General Management* 29, no. 1 (Autumn 2003), 15–31; World Commission on Economic Development, *Our Common Future* (Oxford: Oxford University Press, 1987); and Marc Gunther, "Tree Huggers, Soy Lovers, and Profits," *Fortune* (June 23, 2003), 98–104.
16. Ann Zimmerman, "Retailer's Image Moves from Demon to Darling," *The Wall Street Journal Online* (July 16, 2009), http://online.wsj.com/article/SB124770244854748495.html?KEYWORDS=%22Retailer%E2%80%99s+Image+Moves+from+Demon+to+Darling%22 (accessed July 24, 2009); Samuel Fromartz, "The Mini-Cases: 5 Companies, 5 Strategies, 5 Transformations," *MIT Sloan Management Review* (Fall 2009), 41–45; and Ram Nidumolu, C. K. Prahalad, and M. R. Rangaswami, "Why Sustainability Is Now the Key Driver of Innovation," *Harvard Business Review* (September 2009), 57–64.
17. Kuykendall, "Auto Insurers Paying Up to Compete."
18. This section is based partly on Fahri Karakas, "Welcome to World 2.0: The New Digital Ecosystem," *Journal of Business Strategy* 30, no. 4 (2009), 23–30.
19. S. Nambisan and M. Sawhney, *The Global Brain: Your Roadmap for Innovating Faster and Smarter in a Networked World* (Philadelphia, PA: Wharton School Publishing, 2007); and Karakas, "Welcome to World 2.0."
20. Karakas, "Welcome to World 2.0."
21. "Help Solve an Open Murder Case," FBI website (March 29, 2011), http://www.fbi.gov/news/stories/2011/march/cryptanalysis_032911 (accessed July 7, 2011).
22. Andy Reinhardt, "From Gearhead to Grand High Pooh-Bah," *BusinessWeek* (August 28, 2000), 129–130.
23. G. Pascal Zachary, "Mighty Is the Mongrel," *Fast Company* (July 2000), 270–284.
24. Jennifer Cheeseman Day, "National Population Projections," Population Profile of the United States, U.S. Census Bureau, http://www.census.gov/population/www/pop-profile/natproj.html (accessed May 6, 2011); and Laura B. Shrestha and Elayne J. Heisler, "The Changing Demographic Profile of the United States," *Congressional Research Service* (March 31, 2011), http://www.fas.org/sgp/crs/misc/RL32701.pdf (accessed May 6, 2011).
25. "Employment Projections: 2008–2018 Summary," U.S. Department of Labor, Bureau of Labor Statistics (December 10, 2009), http://www.bls.gov/news.release/ecopro.nr0.htm (accessed September 21, 2010).
26. Hanna Rosin, "The End of Men," *The Atlantic Monthly* (July–August 2010), http://www.theatlantic.com/magazine/archive/2010/07/the-end-of-men/8135/ (accessed December 25, 2010).
27. Ursula M. Burns, "Lead with Values; Make the Worst the Best of Times," *Leadership Excellence* (February 2010), 7.
28. Howard Aldrich, *Organizations and Environments* (Englewood Cliffs, N.J.: Prentice-Hall, 1979), 3.
29. Royston Greenwood and Danny Miller, "Tackling Design Anew: Getting Back to the Heart of Organizational Theory," *Academy of Management Perspectives* (November 2010), 78–88.
30. This section is based on Peter F. Drucker, *Managing the Non-Profit Organization: Principles and Practices* (New York: HarperBusiness, 1992); Thomas Wolf, *Managing a Nonprofit Organization* (New York: Fireside/Simon & Schuster, 1990); and Jean Crawford, "Profiling the Non-Profit Leader of Tomorrow," *Ivey Business Journal* (May–June 2010).

31. Christine W. Letts, William P. Ryan, and Allen Grossman, *High Performance Nonprofit Organizations* (New York: John Wiley & Sons, Inc., 1999), 30–35; Crawford, "Profiling the Non-Profit Leader of Tomorrow."
32. Lisa Bannon, "Dream Works: As Make-a-Wish Expands Its Turf, Local Groups Fume," *The Wall Street Journal* (July 8, 2002), A1, A8.
33. Robert N. Stern and Stephen R. Barley, "Organizations and Social Systems: Organization Theory's Neglected Mandate," *Administrative Science Quarterly* 41 (1996), 146–162.
34. Philip Siekman, "Build to Order: One Aircraft Carrier," *Fortune* (July 22, 2002), 180[B]–180[J].
35. Ronald D. White, "Efficiency Helps Vernon Furniture Factory Keep Its Edge," *The Los Angeles Times* (May 1, 2011), http://articles.latimes.com/2011/may/01/business/la-fi-made-in-california-furniture-20110501 (accessed July 8, 2011).
36. Art Wittmann, "How Skype/Facebook Will Kill the Phone Network," *InformationWeek* (July 7, 2011), http://www.informationweek.com/news/telecom/unified_communications/231001171 (accessed July 8, 2011); Ellen McGirt, "1: Facebook," *Fast Company* (March 2010), 54–57, 110 (part of the section "The World's 50 Most Innovative Companies"); and "The World's Most Innovative Companies 2011," *Fast Company*, http://www.fastcompany.com/most-innovative-companies/2011/ (accessed September 29, 2011).
37. Christopher Lawton, Yukari Iwatani Kane, and Jason Dean, "Picture Shift: U.S. Upstart Takes on TV Giants in Price War," *The Wall Street Journal* (April 15, 2008), A1; and "Consumers Make Vizio the #1 LCD HDTV in North America," Vizio Website, http://www.vizio.com/news/ConsumersMakeVIZIOthe1FlatPanelHDTVinNorthAmerica/ (accessed July 6, 2011).
38. The discussion of structural dimensions and contingency factors was heavily influenced by Richard H. Hall, *Organizations: Structures, Processes, and Outcomes* (Englewood Cliffs, N.J.: Prentice-Hall, 1991); D. S. Pugh, "The Measurement of Organization Structures: Does Context Determine Form?" *Organizational Dynamics* 1 (Spring 1973), 19–34; and D. S. Pugh, D. J. Hickson, C. R. Hinings, and C. Turner, "Dimensions of Organization Structure," *Administrative Science Quarterly* 13 (1968), 65–91.
39. Ian Urbina, "In Gulf, It Was Unclear Who Was in Charge of Oil Rig," *The New York Times,* June 5, 2010; Douglas A. Blackmon, Vanessa O'Connell, Alexandra Berzon, and Ana Campoy, "There Was 'Nobody in Charge,'" *The Wall Street Journal,* May 27, 2010; Campbell Robertson, "Efforts to Repel Gulf Oil Spill Are Described as Chaotic," *The New York Times*, June 14, 2010.
40. Jaclyne Badal, "Can a Company Be Run As a Democracy? *The Wall Street Journal* (April 23, 2007), B1; "An Interview with Brian Robertson, President of Ternary Software, Inc.," http://integralesforum.org/fileadmin/user_upload/FACH-GRUPPEN/FG_imove/downloads/Interview_with_Brian_Robertson_2006-02-08_v2_01.pdf (accessed July 6, 2011); and John Huey, "Wal-Mart: Will It Take Over the World?" *Fortune* (January 30, 1989), 52–61.
41. Dana Mattioli, "CEOs Fight to Prevent Discretionary Spending from Creeping Back Up," *The Wall Street Journal* (July 12, 2010).
42. Steve Lohr, "Who Pays for Efficiency?" *The New York Times* (June 11, 2007), H1.
43. T. Donaldson and L. E. Preston, "The Stakeholder Theory of the Corporation: Concepts, Evidence, and Implications," *Academy of Management Review* 20 (1995), 65–91; Anne S. Tusi, "A Multiple-Constituency Model of Effectiveness: An Empirical Examination at the Human Resource Subunit Level," *Administrative Science Quarterly* 35 (1990), 458–483; Charles Fombrun and Mark Shanley, "What's in a Name? Reputation Building and Corporate Strategy," *Academy of Management Journal* 33 (1990), 233–258; and Terry Connolly, Edward J. Conlon, and Stuart Jay Deutsch, "Organizational Effectiveness: A Multiple-Constituency Approach," *Academy of Management Review* 5 (1980), 211–217.
44. Charles Fishman, "The Wal-Mart You Don't Know—Why Low Prices Have a High Cost," *Fast Company* (December 2003), 68–80.
45. Greenwood and Miller, "Tackling Design Anew."
46. Greenwood and Miller, "Tackling Design Anew;" and Roger L. M. Dunbar and William H. Starbuck, "Learning to Design Organizations and Learning from Designing Them," *Organization Science* 17, no. 2 (March–April 2006), 171–178.
47. Quoted in Cynthia Crossen, "Early Industry Expert Soon Realized a Staff Has Its Own Efficiency," *The Wall Street Journal* (November 6, 2006), B1.
48. Robert Kanigel, *The One Best Way: Frederick Winslow Taylor and the Enigma of Efficiency* (New York: Viking, 1997); Alan Farnham, "The Man Who Changed Work Forever," *Fortune* (July 21, 1997), 114; and Charles D. Wrege and Ann Marie Stoka, "Cooke Creates a Classic: The Story Behind F. W. Taylor's Principles of Scientific Management," *Academy of Management Review* (October 1978), 736–749. For a discussion of the impact of scientific management on American industry, government, and nonprofit organizations, also see Mauro F. Guillèn, "Scientific Management's Lost Aesthetic: Architecture, Organization, and the Taylorized Beauty of the Mechanical," *Administrative Science Quarterly* 42 (1997), 682–715.
49. Gary Hamel, "The Why, What, and How of Management Innovation," *Harvard Business Review* (February 2006), 72–84.
50. Amanda Bennett, *The Death of the Organization Man* (New York: William Morrow, 1990).
51. Ralph Sink, "My Unfashionable Legacy," *Strategy + Business* (Autumn 2007), http://www.strategy-business.com/press/enewsarticle/enews122007?pg=0 (accessed August 7, 2008).
52. Dunbar and Starbuck, "Learning to Design Organizations."
53. Johannes M. Pennings, "Structural Contingency Theory: A Reappraisal," *Research in Organizational Behavior* 14 (1992), 267–309.
54. Henry Mintzberg, *The Structuring of Organizations: The Synthesis of the Research* (Englewood Cliffs, N.J.: Prentice-Hall, 1979), 215–297; Henry Mintzberg, "Organization Design: Fashion or Fit?" *Harvard Business Review* 59 (January–February 1981), 103–116; and Henry Mintzberg, *Mintzberg on Management: Inside Our Strange World of Organizations* (New York: The Free Press,1989).
55. Tom Burns and G. M. Stalker, *The Management of Innovation* (London: Tavistock, 1961).

56. Jena McGregor, "'There Is No More Normal,'" *Business-Week* (March 23 & 30, 2009), 30–34; and Ellen McGirt, "Revolution in San Jose," *Fast Company* (January 2009), 88–94, 134–136.
57. Daisuke Wakabayashi and Toko Sekiguchi, "Disaster in Japan: Evacuees Set Rules to Create Sense of Normalcy," *The Wall Street Journal* (March 26, 2011), A1.
58. Niels Billou, Mary Crossan, and Gerard Seijts, "Coping with Complexity," *Ivey Business Journal* (May–June 2010), http://www.iveybusinessjournal.com/topics/leadership/coping-with-complexity (accessed May 10, 2010).
59. James D. Thompson, *Organizations in Action* (New York: McGraw-Hill, 1967), 4–13.
60. Ludwig von Bertalanffy, Carl G. Hempel, Robert E. Bass, and Hans Jonas, "General Systems Theory: A New Approach to Unity of Science," *Human Biology* 23 (December 1951), 302–361; and Kenneth E. Boulding, "General Systems Theory—The Skeleton of Science," *Management Science* 2 (April 1956), 197–208.
61. This discussion is based on Peter M. Senge, *The Fifth Discipline: The Art and Practice of the Learning Organization* (New York: Doubleday, 1990); John D. Sterman, "Systems Dynamics Modeling: Tools for Learning in a Complex World," *California Management Review* 43, no. 4 (Summer, 2001), 8–25; and Ron Zemke, "Systems Thinking," *Training* (February 2001), 40–46.
62. This discussion is based in part on Toby J. Tetenbaum, "Shifting Paradigms: From Newton to Chaos," *Organizational Dynamics* (Spring 1998), 21–32.
63. William Bergquist, *The Postmodern Organization* (San Francisco: Jossey-Bass, 1993).
64. Based on Tetenbaum, "Shifting Paradigms: From Newton to Chaos"; and Richard T. Pascale, "Surfing the Edge of Chaos," *Sloan Management Review* (Spring 1999), 83–94.
65. Copyright 1996 by Dorothy Marcic. All rights reserved.
66. John A. Seeger, Professor of Management, Bentley College. Reprinted with permission.

INTEGRATIVE CASE 1.0

1.0

Developing Global Teams to Meet 21st Century Challenges at W. L. Gore & Associates*

In 2008, W. L. Gore & Associates celebrated its 50th year in business. During the first four decades of its existence, Gore became famous for its products and for its use of business teams located in a single facility. To facilitate the development of teams, corporate facilities were kept to 200 associates or fewer. Due to the challenges of a global marketplace, business teams are no longer in a single facility. They are now often spread over three continents. Products are sold on six continents and used on all seven, as well as under the ocean and in space. The challenge of having a successful global presence requires virtual teams to enable a high degree of coordination in the development, production, and marketing of products to customers across the world. As previously, teams are defined primarily by product, but no longer by facility. Team members are now separated by thousands of miles, multiple time zones, and a variety of languages and cultures. Growth and globalization present significant challenges for W. L. Gore as it strives to maintain a family-like, entrepreneurial culture. According to Terri Kelly, the president of Gore and a 25-year associate:[1]

In the early days, our business was largely conducted at the local level. There were global operations, but most relationships were built regionally, and most decisions were made regionally. That picture has evolved dramatically over the last 20 years, as businesses can no longer be defined by brick and mortar. Today, most of our teams are spread across regions and continents. Therefore, the decision-making process is much more global and virtual in nature, and there's a growing need to build strong relationships across geographical boundaries. The globalization of our business has been one of the biggest changes I've seen in the last 25 years.

Elements of the culture at Gore are captured in Exhibit 1. The core belief in the need to take the long-term view in business situations, and to make and keep commitments, drives cooperation among individuals and small teams. This is supported by key practices that replace a traditional, hierarchical structure with flexible relationships and a sense that all workers are "in the same boat." The ultimate focus is on empowering talented associates to deliver highly innovative products.

Despite substantial growth, the core values have not changed at Gore. The objective of the company, "to make money and have fun," set forth by the founder Wilbert (Bill) Gore is still part of the Gore culture. Associates around the world are asked to follow the company's four guiding principles:

1. Try to be fair.
2. Encourage, help, and allow other associates to grow in knowledge, skill, and scope of activity and responsibility.
3. Make your own commitments, and keep them.
4. Consult with other associates before taking actions that may be "below the waterline."

The four principles are referred to as *fairness, freedom, commitment,* and *waterline.* The waterline principle is drawn from an analogy to ships. If someone pokes a hole in a boat above the waterline, the boat will be in relatively little real danger. If, however, someone pokes a hole below the waterline, the boat is in immediate danger of sinking. The expectation is that "waterline" issues will be discussed across teams, plants, and continents as appropriate before those decisions are made. This principle is still emphasized even though team members who need to share in the decision-making process are now spread across the globe.

Commitment is spoken of frequently at Gore. The commitment principle's primary emphasis is on the freedom associates have to make their own commitments rather than having others assign them to projects or tasks. But commitment may also be viewed as a mutual commitment between associates and the enterprise. Associates worldwide commit to making contributions to the company's success. In return, the company is committed to providing a challenging, opportunity-rich work environment that is responsive to associate needs and concerns.

Background

Gore was formed by Wilbert L. "Bill" Gore and his wife in 1958. The idea for the business sprang from Bill's personal,

*Developing Global Teams to Meet 21st Century Challenges at W. L. Gore & Associates," by Frank Shipper, Charles Manz, and Greg L. Stewart.

[1]This case was prepared by Frank Shipper, Professor of Management, Franklin P. Perdue School of Business; Charles C. Manz, Nirenberg Professor of Leadership, Isenberg School of Management, and Greg L. Stewart, Professor & Tippie Research Fellow, Tippie College of Business. Many sources were helpful in providing material for this case, most particularly associates at Gore who generously shared their time and viewpoints about the company to help ensure that the case accurately reflected the company's practices and culture. They provided many resources, including internal documents and stories of their personal experiences.

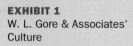

EXHIBIT 1
W. L. Gore & Associates' Culture

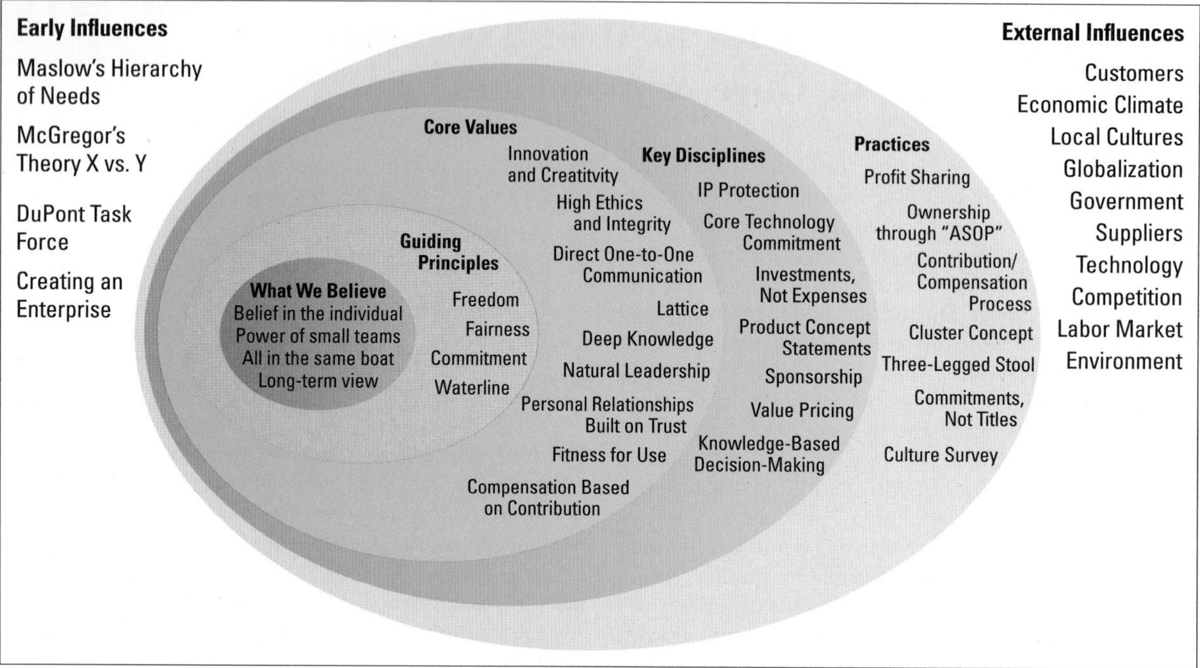

technical, and organizational experiences at E. I. du Pont de Nemours & Co. and, particularly, his involvement in the characterization of a chemical compound with unique properties. The compound, called polytetrafluorethylene (PTFE), is now marketed by DuPont under the Teflon brand name. Bill saw a wide variety of potential applications for this unique new material, and when DuPont showed little interest in pursuing most of them directly, he decided to form his own company and start pursuing the concepts himself. Thus, Gore became one of DuPont's first customers for this new material.

Since then, Gore has evolved into a global enterprise, with annual revenues of more than $2.5 billion, supported by more than 8,500 associates worldwide. This placed Gore at No. 180 on *Forbes* magazine's 2008 list of the 500 largest private companies in the United States. The enterprise's unique, and now famous, culture and leadership practices have helped make Gore one of only a select few companies to appear on all of the U.S. "100 Best Companies to Work For" rankings since they were introduced in 1984.

Bill Gore was born in Meridian, Idaho, in 1912. By age six, according to his own account, he was an avid hiker in Utah. Later, at a church camp in 1935, he met Genevieve (Vieve), his future wife. In their eyes, the marriage was a partnership. He would make breakfast and Vieve, as everyone called her, would make lunch. The partnership lasted a lifetime.

Bill Gore attended the University of Utah and earned a bachelor of science in chemical engineering in 1933, and a master of science in physical chemistry in 1935. He began his professional career at American Smelting and Refining in 1936, moved to Remington Arms, a DuPont subsidiary, in 1941, and then to DuPont's headquarters in 1945. He held positions as research supervisor and head of operations research. While at DuPont, he felt a sense of excited commitment, personal fulfillment, and self-direction while working with a task force to develop applications for PTFE.

Having followed the development of the electronics industry, he felt that PTFE had ideal insulating characteristics for use with such equipment. He tried many ways to make a PTFE-coated ribbon cable but with no success until a breakthrough in his home basement laboratory. One night, while Bill was explaining the problem to his 19-year-old son, Bob, the young Gore saw some PTFE sealant tape and asked his father, "Why don't you try this tape?" Bill explained that everyone knew that you could not bond PTFE to itself. After Bob went to bed, however, Bill remained in the basement lab and proceeded to try what conventional wisdom said could not be done. At about 5:00 AM Bill woke up Bob, waving a small piece of cable around and saying excitedly, "It works, it works." The following night father and son returned to the basement lab to make ribbon cable insulated with PTFE. Because the idea came from Bob, the patent for the cable was issued in his name.

After a while, Bill Gore came to realize that DuPont wanted to remain a supplier of raw materials for industrial buyers and not a manufacturer of high-tech products for end-use markets. Bill and Vieve began discussing the possibility of starting their own insulated wire and cable business. On January 1, 1958, their wedding anniversary, they founded Gore. The basement of their home served as their first facility. After finishing breakfast, Vieve turned to her husband of 23 years and said, "Well, let's clear up the dishes, go downstairs, and get to work."

When Bill Gore (a 45-year-old with five children to support) left DuPont, he put aside a career of 17 years and a good, secure salary. To finance the first two years of their new business, he and Vieve mortgaged their house and took $4,000 from savings. All their friends cautioned them against taking such a big financial risk.

The first few years were challenging. Some of the young company's associates accepted stock in the company in lieu of salary. Family members who came to help with the business lived in the home as well. At one point, 11 associates were living and working under one roof. One afternoon, while sifting PTFE powder, Vieve received a call from the City of Denver's water department. The caller wanted to ask some technical questions about the ribbon cable and asked for the product manager. Vieve explained that he was not in at the moment. (Bill and two other key associates were out of town.) The caller asked next for the sales manager and then for the president. Vieve explained that "they" were also not in. The caller finally shouted, "What kind of company is this anyway?" With a little diplomacy the Gores were eventually able to secure an order from Denver's water department for around $100,000. This order put the company over the start-up hump and onto a profitable footing. Sales began to take off.

During the decades that followed, Gore developed a number of new products derived from PTFE, the best-known of which is GORE-TEX® fabric. The development of GORE-TEX® fabric, one of hundreds of new products that followed a key discovery by Bob Gore, is an example of the power of innovation. In 1969, Gore's Wire and Cable Division was facing increased competition. Bill Gore began to look for a way to expand PTFE: "I figured out that if we could ever unfold those molecules, get them to stretch out straight, we'd have a tremendous new kind of material." The new PTFE material would have more volume per pound of raw material with no adverse effect on performance. Thus, fabricating costs would be reduced and profit margins increased. Bob Gore took on the project; he heated rods of PTFE to various temperatures and then slowly stretched them. Regardless of the temperature or how carefully he stretched them, the rods broke. Working alone late one night after countless failures, Bob in frustration stretched one of the rods violently. To his surprise, it did not break. He tried it again and again with the same results. The next morning, Bill Gore recalled, "Bob wanted to surprise me so he took a rod and stretched it slowly. Naturally, it broke. Then he pretended to get mad. He grabbed another rod and said, 'Oh, the hell with this,' and gave it a pull. It didn't break—he'd done it." The new arrangement of molecules not only changed the Wire and Cable Division, but led to the development of GORE-TEX® fabric and many other products.

In 1986, Bill Gore died while backpacking in the Wind River Mountains of Wyoming. Vieve Gore continued to be involved actively in the company and served on the board of directors until her death at 91 in 2005.

Gore has had only four presidents in its 50-year history. Bill Gore served as the president from the enterprise's founding in 1958 until 1976. At that point, his son Bob became president and CEO. Bob has been an active member of the firm from the time of its founding, most recently as chairman of the board of directors. He served as president until 2000, when Chuck Carroll was selected as the third president. In 2005, Terri Kelly succeeded him. As with all the presidents after Bill Gore, she is a long-time employee. She had been with Gore for 22 years before becoming president.

The Gore family established a unique culture that continues to be an inspiration for associates. For example, Dave Gioconda, a current product specialist, recounted meeting Bob Gore for the first time—an experience that reinforced Gore's egalitarian culture:

Two weeks after I joined Gore, I traveled to Phoenix for training . . . I told the guy next to me on the plane where I worked, and he said, "I work for Gore, too." "No kidding?" I asked. "Where do you work?" He said, "Oh, I work over at the Cherry Hill plant.". . .

I spent two and a half hours on this plane having a conversation with this gentleman who described himself as a technologist and shared some of his experiences. As I got out of the plane, I shook his hand and said, "I'm Dave Gioconda, nice to meet you." He replied, "Oh, I'm Bob Gore." That experience has had a profound influence on the decisions that I make.

Due to the leadership of Bill, Vieve, Bob, and many others, Gore was selected as one of the U.S. "100 Best Companies to Work For" in 2009 by *Fortune* magazine for the twelfth consecutive year. In addition, Gore was included in all three *100 Best Companies to Work For in America* books (1984, 1985, and 1993). It is one of only a select few companies to appear on all 15 lists. Gore has been selected also as one of the best companies to work for in France, Germany, Italy, Spain, Sweden, and the United Kingdom.

As a privately held company, Gore does not make its financial results public. However, it does share financial results with all associates on a monthly basis. In 2008, *Fortune* magazine reported that Gore's sales grew just over 7 percent in 2006, the latest year for which data were available.

Competitive Strategy at W. L. Gore

For product management, Gore is now divided into four divisions: Electronics, Fabrics, Industrial, and Medical. The Electronic Products Division (EPD) develops and manufactures high-performance cables and assemblies as well as specialty materials for electronic devices. The

EXHIBIT 2
Coordinating Technology, Manufacturing, and Sales at Gore

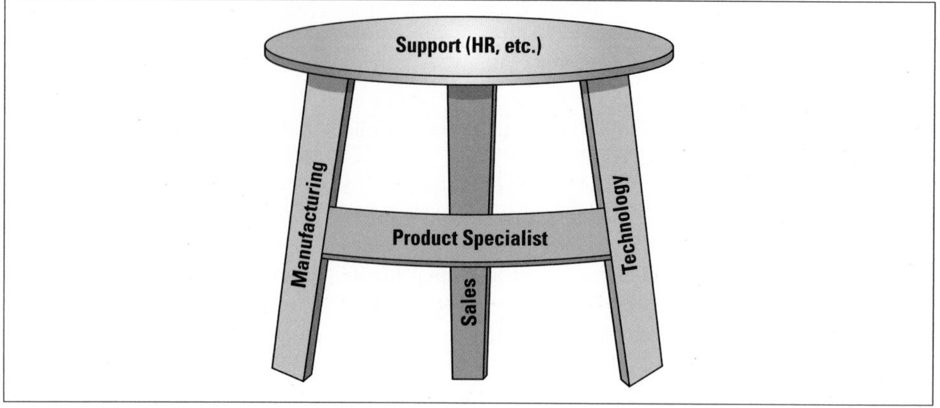

Fabrics Division develops and provides fabric to the outdoor clothing industry as well as the military, law enforcement, and fire protection industries. Gore fabrics marketed under the GORE-TEX®, WINDSTOPPER®, CROSSTECH®, and GORE® CHEMPAK® brands provide the wearer protection while remaining comfortable. The Industrial Products Division (IPD) makes filtration, sealant, and other products. These products meet diverse contamination and process challenges in many industries. The Gore Medical Products Division (MPD) provides products such as synthetic vascular grafts, interventional devices, endovascular stent-grafts, surgical patches for hernia repair, and sutures for use in vascular, cardiac, general surgery, and oral procedures. Although they are recognized as separate divisions, they frequently work together.

Since it has four divisions that serve different industries, Gore can be viewed as a diversified conglomerate. Bob Winterling, a financial associate, described how the four divisions work together financially as follows:

The thing I love about Gore is that we have four very diverse divisions. During my time here, I've noticed that when one or two divisions are down, you always have one, two, or three that are up. I call them cylinders. Sometimes all four cylinders are working really well; not all the time though. Normally it's two or three, but that's the luxury that we have. When one is down, it's good to know that another is up.

At the end of 2007, all four divisions were performing well. Having four diversified divisions not only protects against swings in any one industry, but it also provides multiple investment opportunities. Entering 2008, Gore was investing in a large number of areas, with the heaviest area of investment in the Medical Products Division. This was a conscious choice, as these opportunities were judged to be the largest intersection between Gore's unique capabilities and some very large, attractive market needs. As Brad Jones, an enterprise leader, said, "All opportunities aren't created equal, and there's an awful lot of opportunity that's screaming for resources in the medical environment." At the same time, the leadership at Gore scrutinizes large investments so those in what Brad Jones refers to as "big burn" projects are not made unless there is a reasonable expectation of a payoff.

Developing Quality Products by Creating and Protecting Core Technology

The competitive objective of Gore is to use core technology derived from PTFE and ePTFE to create highly differentiated and unique products. In every product line the goal is not to produce the lowest cost goods but rather to create the highest quality goods that meet and exceed the needs of customers. Of course, Gore works hard to maintain competitive pricing, but the source of competitive advantage is clearly quality and differentiation. Gore is a company built on technological innovations.

Leaders at Gore often refer to a three-legged stool to explain how they integrate operations. As shown in Exhibit 2, the three legs of the stool are technology, manufacturing, and sales. For each product, the legs of the stool are tied together by a product specialist. For instance, a product specialist might coordinate efforts to design, make, and sell a vascular graft. Another product specialist would coordinate efforts related to the creation and marketing of fabric for use in winter parkas. Support functions such as human resources, information technology, and finance also help tie together various aspects of technology, manufacturing, and sales.

Gore's Fabrics Division practices cooperative marketing with the users of its fabrics. In most cases, Gore does not make the finished goods from its fabrics; rather, it supplies the fabrics to manufacturers such as North Face, Marmot, L. L. Bean, Salomon, Adidas, and Puma. On each garment is a tag indicating that it is made using GORE-TEX® fabric. According to a former president of Cotton Inc., Gore is a leader in secondary branding. For example, a salesman in a golf pro shop related how he initially tried to explain that he had GORE-TEX® fabric rain suits made by various manufacturers. After realizing that his customers did not care who manufactured it, only that it was made from GORE-TEX® fabric, he gave up and just led the customers to the GORE-TEX® fabric rain suits.

Because of its commitment to producing superior goods, Gore emphasizes product integrity. For example, only certified and licensed manufacturers are supplied with Gore's fabrics. Gore maintains "rain-rooms" in which to test new garment designs. Shoes with GORE-TEX® fabric in them will be flexed in water approximately 300,000 times to ensure that they are waterproof.

After all the preventive measures, Gore stands behind its products regardless of who the manufacturer is and even if the defect is cosmetic in nature. Susan Bartley, a manufacturing associate, recounted a recent recall:

A cosmetic flaw, not a fitness-for-use flaw, was found in finished garments, so we (Gore) bought back the garments from the manufacturer, because we didn't want those garments out on the market.

Such recalls due to either cosmetic or fitness-for-use flaws happen infrequently. One associate estimated that the last one happened 10 years before the most recent one. Gore is, however, committed to the quality of its products and will stand behind them.

Gore's Fabrics sales and marketing associates believe positive buyer experiences with one GORE-TEX® product (for instance, a ski parka) carry over to purchases of other GORE-TEX® products (gloves, pants, rain suits, boots, and jackets). Also, they believe that positive experiences with their products will be shared among customers and potential customers, leading to more sales.

The sharing and enhancing of knowledge is seen as key to the development of current and future products. Great emphasis is placed on sharing knowledge. According to Terri Kelly,

There's a real willingness and openness to share knowledge. That's something I experienced 25 years ago, and it's not changed today. This is a healthy thing. We want to make sure folks understand the need to connect more dots in the lattice.

Associates make a conscious effort to share technical knowledge. For example, a core leadership team consisting of eight technical associates gets together every other month, reviews each other's plans, and looks for connections among the upcoming products. According to Jack Kramer, an enterprise leader, "We put a lot of effort into trying to make sure that we connect informally and formally across a lot of boundaries." One way in which associates connect formally to share knowledge is through monthly technical meetings. At the monthly meetings, scientists and engineers from different divisions present information to other associates and colleagues. Attended regularly by most technical associates in the area, these presentations are often described as "passionate" and "exciting."

Even though Gore shares knowledge within the organization, much of its highly technical know-how must be protected for competitive reasons. In a global environment, protection of specialized knowledge is a challenge. Some of the technology is protected by patents. In fact, some of the products are protected by an umbrella of patents. Normally, under U.S. law, patents expire 20 years from the earliest claimed filing date. Thus, the original patents have expired on GORE-TEX® fabric and some other products. Globally, patent procedures, protection, and enforcement vary. Both products and the processes are patentable. To protect its knowledge base, Gore has sought and been granted more than 2,000 patents worldwide in all areas in which it competes, including electronics, medical devices, and polymer processing. However, patents can sometimes be difficult or expensive to enforce, especially globally. Therefore, some of the technology is protected internally. Such knowledge is commonly referred to as *proprietary*.

Within Gore, proprietary knowledge is shared on a need-to-know basis. Associates are encouraged to closely guard such information. This principle can lead to some awkward moments. Terri Kelly was visiting Shenzhen, China and was curious about a new laminate that was being commercialized. The development engineer leader kept dodging her questions. Finally he smiled and said, "Now, Terri. Do you have a need to know?"

As Terri retold the incident, "He played back exactly what he was supposed to, which is don't share with someone, even if it's a CEO, something that they have no need to know." When this incident happened, she laughed and said, "You're right. I'm just being nosy."

Terri continued, "And everyone's—I could see the look in their eyes—thinking, 'Is he going to get fired?' He had taken a great personal risk, certainly for that local culture. We laughed, and we joked, and for the next week it became the running joke." Through stories like this the culture is shared with others in Gore.

The sharing and enhancing of its technology have brought recognition from many sources. From the United Kingdom, Gore received the Pollution Abatement Technology Award in 1989 and the Prince Philip Award for Polymers in the Service of Mankind in 1985. In addition, Gore received or shared in receiving the prestigious Plunkett Award from DuPont—for innovative uses of DuPont fluoropolymers—nine times between 1988 and 2006. Bill and Vieve Gore, as well as Bob Gore, received numerous honors for both their business and technical leadership.

Continuing Globalization and Deliberate Growth

Ever since the company was founded, Gore has recognized the need for globalization. Gore established its first international venture in 1964, only six years after its founding. By 2008, it had facilities in two dozen countries and manufacturing facilities in six countries distributed across four continents (See Exhibit 3). One example of Gore's global reach is the fact that it is the dominant supplier of artificial vascular grafts to the global medical community. Gore's Fabrics Division also generates most of its sales overseas.

In addition to globalization, Gore has a strategy of continued growth. Growth is expected to come from

EXHIBIT 3
Locations of Gore's Global Facilities

W. L. Gore & Associates — Worldwide Locations

two sources. One source will be from Gore associates contributing innovative ideas. The Gore culture is designed to foster such innovation and allow ideas to be energetically pursued, developed, and evaluated. These ideas will lead to new products and processes. Within Gore this form of growth is referred to as organic. Gore encourages both new products and extensions of existing products. To encourage innovation all associates are encouraged to ask for and receive raw material to try out their ideas. Through this process multiple products have come from unexpected areas. For example, the idea for dental floss came from the Industrial and not the Medical Division. Two associates who were fabricating space suits took to flossing their teeth with scraps. Thus, Gore's highly successful dental floss, GLIDE® floss, was born. GORE™ RIDE ON® bike cables came from a couple of passionate mountain bikers in the Medical Division. ELIXIR® guitar strings also came from the Medical Division from an associate who was also a musician. Due to Gore's track record of developing innovative products, *Fast Company* magazine called it "pound for pound, the most innovative company in America."

A second but much less significant source of growth can come from external acquisitions. Gore evaluates opportunities to acquire technologies and even companies based on whether they offer a unique capability that could complement an existing, successful business. The leadership at Gore considers this strategy a way to stack the probability deck in its favor by moving into market spaces its associates already know very well. To facilitate this growth strategy, Gore has a few associates who evaluate acquisition opportunities at the enterprise level. They do not do this in isolation, but in concert with leaders within each division.

By a multi-billion dollar corporate standard, the acquisitions made by Gore are small. To date, the largest company acquired employed approximately 100 people. Another attribute of these acquisitions is that no stock swap occurs. Since Gore is a privately held company, stock swaps are not an option. Acquisitions are made with cash.

A clear issue to any acquisition that Gore considers is cultural compatibility. Gore will consider the leadership style in an acquired company. According to Brad Jones, "If you're acquiring a couple patents and maybe an inventor, that's not a big issue, although if he's a prima donna inventor, it will be an issue." When acquiring a company, the culture that made it successful is closely examined. Issues regarding integrating the acquired company's culture with Gore's, and whether Gore's culture will add value to the acquired company, are just two of many cultural considerations. Gore wants to be able to expand when necessary by buying complementary organizations and their associated technologies, but not at the expense of its culture of 50 years.

Occasionally, Gore must divest itself of a product. One example is GLIDE® dental floss. The product, developed by Gore, was well received by consumers due to its smooth texture, shred resistance, and ability to slide easily between teeth. To meet demand when the product took off, leaders were processing credit cards; human resource people and accountants were out on the manufacturing floor packaging GLIDE® floss, and everybody else in the facility pitched in to make sure that the product got out the door. One associate observed that by rolling up their sleeves and pitching in, leaders built credibility with other associates.

Not long after its introduction, mint flavor GLIDE® floss became the biggest selling dental floss. That attracted the attention of the traditional dental floss manufacturers. Eventually, Procter & Gamble (P&G) and Gore reached an agreement whereby P&G bought the rights to market GLIDE® floss, while Gore continued to manufacture it.

Gore made this agreement with the understanding that no one would be laid off. The announcement of the agreement was made to all the GLIDE® floss team members on a Thursday. It did come as a shock to some. By Monday, however, the same team was working on a transition plan. Associates that were not needed in the manufacturing or selling of GLIDE® floss were absorbed into other fast-growing Gore businesses. In addition, everybody in the enterprise received a share of the profit from the P&G purchase.

Leadership at Gore

Competitive strategy at Gore is supported by a unique approach to leadership. Many people step forward and take on a variety of leadership roles, but these roles are not part of a hierarchical structure and traditional authority is not vested in the roles. Leadership is a dynamic and fluid process where leaders are defined by 'followership.' Future leaders emerge because they gain credibility with other associates. Gore refers to this process as "Natural Leadership." Credibility is gained by demonstrating special knowledge, skill, or experience that advances a business objective, a series of successes, and involving others in significant decisions.

Associates step forward to lead when they have the expertise to do so. Within Gore this practice is referred to as *knowledge-based decision-making*. Based on this practice, decisions are ". . . made by the most knowledgeable person, not the person in charge," according to Terri Kelly. This form of decision making flows naturally from the four guiding principles established by Bill Gore.

Leadership responsibilities can take many forms at Gore. In an internal memo Bill Gore described the following kinds of leaders and their roles:

1. *The Associate who is recognized by a team as having a special knowledge, or experience* (for example, this could be a chemist, computer expert, machine operator, salesman, engineer, lawyer). This kind of leader gives the team *guidance in a special area.*
2. *The Associate the team looks to for coordination of individual activities in order to achieve the agreed on objectives of the team.* The role of this leader is to persuade team members to *make the commitments* necessary for success (commitment seeker).
3. *The Associate who proposes necessary objectives and activities and seeks agreement and team consensus on objectives.* This leader is perceived by the team membership as having a good grasp of how the objectives of the team fit in with the broader objectives of the enterprise. This kind of leader is often also a "commitment seeking" leader.
4. *The leader who evaluates the relative contribution of team members (in consultation with other sponsors) and reports these contribution evaluations to a compensation committee.* This leader may also participate in the compensation committee on relative contribution and pay and *reports changes in compensation* to individual Associates. This leader is then also a compensation sponsor.
5. The leader who coordinates the research, manufacturing, and marketing of one product type within a business, interacting with team leaders and individual Associates who have commitments to the product type. These leaders are usually called *product specialists*. They are respected for their knowledge and dedication to their products.
6. *Plant leaders* who help coordinate activities of people within a plant.
7. *Business leaders* who help coordinate activities of people in a business.
8. *Functional leaders* who help coordinate activities of people in a functional area.
9. *Corporate leaders* who help coordinate activities of people in different businesses and functions and who try to promote communication and cooperation among all Associates.
10. *Intrapreneuring Associates who organize new teams* for new businesses, new products, new processes, new devices, new marketing efforts, or new or better methods of all kinds. These leaders invite other Associates to "sign up" for their project.

Developing a Unique and Flexible Leadership Structure

The leadership structure that works at Gore may have the world's shortest organizational pyramid for a company of its size. Gore is a company largely without titles, hierarchical

organization charts, or any other conventional structural arrangement typically employed by enterprises with billions of dollars in sales revenues and thousands of employees.

There are few positions at Gore with formal titles presented to the public. Due to laws of incorporation, the company has a president, Terri Kelly, who also functions as CEO. Terri is one of four members of the cross-functional Enterprise Leadership Team, the team responsible for the overall health and growth of the enterprise.

The real key to the egalitarian culture of Gore is the use of a unique lattice rather than a hierarchical structure (See Exhibit 4). The features of Gore's lattice structure include the following:

1. Direct lines of communication—person to person—with no intermediary.
2. No fixed or assigned authority.
3. Sponsors, not bosses.
4. Natural leadership as evidenced by the willingness of others to follow.
5. Objectives set by those who must "make them happen."
6. Tasks and functions organized through commitments.

The lattice structure, as described by the people at Gore, is complex and depends on interpersonal interactions, self-commitment to group-known responsibilities, natural leadership, and group-imposed discipline. According to Bill Gore, "Every successful organization has an underground lattice. It's where the news spreads like lightning, where people can go around the organization to get things done."

One potential disadvantage of such a lattice structure could be a lack of quick response times and decisive action. Gore associates say adamantly that this is not the case, and they distinguish between two types of decisions. First, for time-critical decisions, they maintain that the lattice structure is faster in response than traditional structures because interaction is not hampered by bureaucracy. The leader who has responsibility assembles a knowledge-based team to examine and resolve the issue. The team members can be recruited by the leader from any area of the company if their expertise is needed. Once the issue is resolved the team ceases to exist, and its members return to their respective areas. Associate Bob Winterling asserted, "We have no trouble making crisis decisions, and we do it very swiftly and very quickly."

The other response is for critical issues that will have a significant impact on the enterprise's long-term operations. Associates will admit that such decisions can sometimes take a little longer than they would like. Chrissy Lyness, another financial associate, stated,

> *We get the buy-in up front instead of creating and implementing the solution and putting something out there that doesn't work for everybody. That can be frustrating to new associates, because they're used to a few people putting their heads together, saying, "This is what we're going to do. This is a solution." That's not the way it works at Gore.*
>
> *Here, you spend a lot of time at the beginning of the decision-making process gaining feedback, so that when you come out of that process, you have something that's going to work, and the implementation is actually pretty easy.*

The associates at Gore believe that time spent in the beginning, tapping into the best ideas and gaining consensus, pays off in the implementation. They believe that authoritarian decision-making may save time initially, but the quality of the decision will not be as good as one made by consensus.

EXHIBIT 4
Gore's Lattice Structure

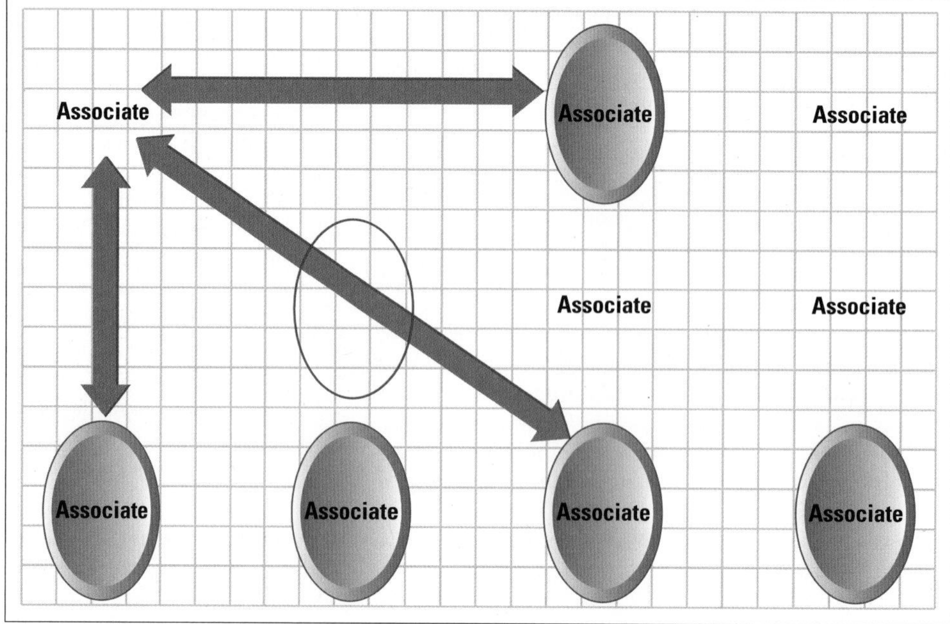

In addition, they believe that authoritarian decisions will take longer to implement than those made by consensus.

The egalitarian culture is also supported informally. For example, all associates are referred to and addressed by their first names. This is as true for the president as for any other associate.

Gore's leaders believe that its unique organization structure and culture have proven to be significant contributors to associate satisfaction and retention. *Fortune* magazine reports a turnover rate of 5 percent for Gore. In addition, it reports 19,108 applicants for 276 new jobs in 2008. In other words, it is harder to get a job at Gore than to get accepted at an elite university.

Global Human Resource Practices

The competitive strategy of using cutting-edge technology, empowered teams, and collaborative leadership to create high-quality goods is supported by a number of innovative human resources (HR) practices, globally. Many HR initiatives are designed to support the concept that all associates are stakeholders in the enterprise and have a shared responsibility for its success. Parking lots have no reserved parking spaces for leaders. Dining areas—only one in each plant—are set up as focal points for associate interaction. As an associate in Arizona explained, "The design is no accident. The lunchroom in Flagstaff has a fireplace in the middle. We want people to like to be here." The location of a plant is also no accident. Sites are selected on the basis of transportation access, nearby universities, beautiful surroundings, and climate appeal. To preserve the natural beauty of the site on which a production facility was built in 1982, Vieve Gore insisted that the large trees be preserved, much to the dismay of the construction crews. The Arizona associate explained the company's emphasis on selecting attractive plant sites, stating, "Expanding is not costly in the long run. Losses are what you make happen by stymieing people and putting them into a box." Such initiatives are practiced at Gore facilities worldwide.

Getting the Right People on Board

Gore receives numerous applicants for every position. Initially, job applicants at Gore are screened by personnel specialists. Then each candidate who passes the initial screening is interviewed by a group of associates from the team in which the person will work. Finally, personnel specialists contact multiple references before issuing a job offer. Recruitment is described by Donna Frey, leader of the global human resources function and one of four members of the Enterprise Leadership Team (ELT), as a two-way process. She explained:

Our recruiting process is very much about us getting to know the applicants and them getting to know us. We are very open and honest about who we are, the kind of organization we have, the kind of commitments we want and whether or not we think that the applicant's values are aligned with ours. Applicants talk to a number of people that they'll be working directly with if hired. We work very hard in the recruiting process to really build a relationship, get to know people and make sure that we're bringing people in who are going to fit this enterprise.

When someone is hired at Gore, an experienced associate makes a commitment to be the applicant's sponsor. The sponsor's role is to take a personal interest in the new associate's contributions, interests, and goals, acting as both a coach and an advocate. The sponsor tracks the new associate's progress, offers help and encouragement, points out weaknesses and suggests ways to correct them, and concentrates on how the associate can better make use of his or her strengths. Sponsoring is not a short-term commitment. When individuals are hired initially, they are likely to have a sponsor in their immediate work area. As associates' commitments change or grow, it is normal for them to change sponsors, or in some cases add a second sponsor. For instance, if they move to a new job in another area of the company, they may gain a sponsor and then decide whether to keep their former sponsor or not. Because sponsorship is built on the personal relationship between two people, the relationship most often continues even if the official sponsorship role does not.

New associates are expected to focus on building relationships during the first three to six months of their careers. Donna Frey described the first months for a new associate at Gore as follows:

When new associates join the enterprise, they participate in an orientation program. Then, each new associate works with a starting sponsor to get acclimated and begin building relationships within Gore. The starting sponsor provides the new hire with a list of key associates he/she should meet with during the next few months.

We encourage the new hire to meet with these associates one-on-one. It's not a phone conversation, but a chance to sit down with them face-to-face and get to know them.

This process helps demonstrate the importance of relationships. When you're hiring really good people, they want to have quick wins and make contributions, and building relationships without a clear goal can be difficult. Often, new associates will say, "I don't feel like I'm contributing. I've spent three months just getting to know people." However, after a year they begin to realize how important this process was.

To ensure that new associates are not overwhelmed by what is probably their first experience in a non-hierarchical organization, Gore has a two-day orientation program it calls Building on the Best. New associates are brought together with other new associates after two or three months to participate in the program, which addresses many of Gore's key concepts, who Gore is, and how the enterprise works. The program includes group activities and interactive presentations given by leaders and other longtime associates.

Helping Associates Build and Maintain Relationships

Gore recognizes the need to maintain initial relationships, continuously develop new ones, and cement ongoing relationships. One way this is fostered is through its digital voice exchange called Gorecom. According to Terri Kelly, "Gorecom is the preferred media if you want a quick response." An oral culture is fostered because it encourages direct communication.

To further foster the oral culture, team members and leaders are expected to meet face-to-face regularly. For team members and especially leaders, this can mean lots of travel. As one technical associate joked, "Probably, in the last 12 years, I spent three years traveling internationally, a couple weeks at a time."

Another way that Gore facilitates the development of teams and individuals is through training. An associate in Newark noted that Gore "works with associates who want to develop themselves and their talents." Associates are offered a variety of in-house training opportunities, not only in technical and engineering areas but also in leadership development. In addition, the company has established cooperative education programs with universities and other outside providers.

In many ways, Gore can feel like an extended family for its associates and the communities in which they live. Based on their own interests and initiatives, associates give back to their communities through schools, sports clubs, universities, and other local organizations. Recently, Gore has encouraged its U.S. associates' community outreach activities by providing up to eight hours of paid time off for such efforts. Through this program associates worked nearly 7,800 hours at non-profits in Gore's last fiscal year. In reality, Gore associates volunteer much more of their personal time. The associates individually or in teams decide on how to commit their time and to which organizations.

Rewarding Associates for Contributions

Compensation at Gore has both short-term and long-term equity-sharing components. Its compensation goal is to ensure internal fairness and external competitiveness. To ensure fairness, associates are asked to rank their team members each year in order of contribution to the enterprise. In addition, team members are asked to comment on their rationale behind the ranking, as well as on particular strengths or potential areas of improvement for the associates. To ensure competitiveness, each year Gore benchmarks the salary of its associates against a variety of functions and roles with their peers at other companies.

Gore also uses profit sharing as a form of short-term compensation. Profits remaining after business requirements are met are distributed among associates as profit sharing. Profit shares are distributed when established financial goals are reached. Every month the business results are reviewed with associates, and people know whether they are on track to meet forecasts. The first profit sharing occurred in 1960, only two years after the founding of the company.

Beyond short-term equity sharing, Gore has an associates' stock ownership program (ASOP). Each year Gore contributes up to 12 percent of pay to an account that purchases Gore stock for associates who have more than one year of service. Associates have ownership of the account after three years of service, when they become 100 percent vested. Gore also has a 401(K) Plan. It provides a contribution of up to 3 percent of pay to each associates' personal investment accounts. Associates are eligible after one month of service. Associates are 100 percent vested immediately.

A particular area where Gore's practices differ from traditional practices at other organizations is in how the majority of the sales force is compensated. They are paid not on commission, but with salary, stock through ASOP, and profit sharing with all the other associates.[2] When a sales associate was asked to explain this practice, he responded as follows:

The people who are just concerned with making their sales numbers in other companies usually struggle when they come to Gore. We encourage folks to help others. For example, when we hire new sales associates, we ask experienced sales associates to take some time to help get them acclimated to Gore and how we do things. In other companies where I've worked, that would have been seen as something that would detract from your potential to make your number, so you probably wouldn't be asked to do such a thing.

In other words, they see individual sales commissions as detracting from mentoring and sharing what is at the core of the Gore culture.

The entire package of compensation extends beyond direct monetary payments. As with most companies, associates receive a range of benefits, such as medical and dental insurance. Another benefit extended to associates is onsite child care. In addition, in *Fortune* magazine's 2008 story about Gore being one of the "100 Best Companies to Work For," onsite fitness centers are listed as benefits. Gore does have such benefits, but they are not driven from the top-down. Gore does support multiple wellness programs, but there is not one enterprise-wide program. In keeping with Gore's principles and philosophy, Gore looks for an associate or a group of associates to initiate a program. For example, in the Fabrics Division an associate who is a committed runner will champion a group at lunchtime. Gore will then support such activities with fitness centers, softball fields, volleyball courts, and running trails. Pockets of associates all over Gore pursue these and other wellness activities.

[2] Gore's ASOP is similar legally to an employee stock ownership plan (ESOP). Again, Gore simply has never allowed the word *employee* in any of its documentation.

GORE™ RIDE ON® Bike Cables: An Example of Strategy, Leadership, and HR in Action

A good example of strategy, leadership, and effective talent deployment is illustrated by the development of a product called GORE™ RIDE ON® bike cables. Initially, the cables were derailleur and brake cables for trail bikes. They were developed by some trail bike enthusiasts at the medical facilities in Flagstaff, Arizona in the 1990s. When the trail bike market declined, the product was withdrawn from the market. In 2006, a group of young engineers went to Jack Kramer, a technical leader at Gore, and said that they wanted to learn what it takes to develop a new product by reviving the cables. His response was, "You need someone who has some experience before you go off and try to do that."

One of the young engineers approached Lois Mabon, a product specialist who had about 16 years of experience at Gore and worked in the same facility, and asked her to be the group's coach. Lois went back to Jack and talked to him. He was still not sold on the idea, but he allowed Lois to find out what had happened to the bike cables and explore with the group what it would take to bring a new product to market. Within Gore, associates are encouraged to set aside some *dabble* time. Dabble time is when people have the freedom to develop new products and evaluate their viability. After some exploration of what happened to the cables, Lois led a group that made a presentation to Jack and some others in the company, and even though they still were not sure, they said, "All right, keep working on it."

After about 10 months of exploring the possibility, a team of excited and passionate associates developed a set of GORE™ RIDE ON® products. In their exploration, the team learned that the road bike market is larger than the trail bike market, and there might potentially be a product for the racing market.

A presentation, referred to within Gore as a "Real-Win-Worth" presentation, was prepared and presented to the Industrial Products Division (IPD) leadership team. Real-Win-Worth is a rigorous discipline that Gore uses to help hone in on the most promising new opportunities. The three issues that must be addressed in "Real-Win-Worth" are as follows: Is the idea real? Can Gore win in the market? And is it worth pursuing? After listening and questioning the presenters, the IPD leadership team responded, "You know what? You do have some really good ideas. Let's do a market study on it. Let's see if the market is interested."

Some samples of the new product were made and taken to 200 top bike stores across the United States. They were handed out to the store owners and, in turn, the store owners were asked to fill out a survey. The survey focused on three questions: Is this a product you would buy? Is it a product you would recommend to your customers? How would you compare this to the other products out in the industry?

An analysis of the surveys showed that 65 to 75 percent of all respondents would either definitely buy the product or were interested in it. Based on these results, the team concluded that people would really want to buy the product.

So with that data in hand, another presentation was made to the IPD leadership team in August 2006. The response was, "Okay, go launch it." The product team had 12 months to improve the mountain bike cables, develop the new road bike cables, redesign the packaging, redesign the logo, set up production, and do everything else that is associated with a new product introduction.

Every Gore division was involved in producing the cables. The product is overseen by a team in the Industrial Products Division. The GORE BIKE WEAR™ products team in the Fabrics Division serves as the sales team. The Medical Products Division makes a component that goes in it. And the Electronics Products Division coats the cables.

In September 2007 the product was officially launched at two bike shows. The first one was the Euro-Bike on Labor Day and the other was the Interbike show held in Las Vegas at the end of September. The top 100 GORE BIKE WEAR™ product customers and shops were invited to these shows.

In fewer than three months Gore had sold approximately 8,000 pairs of cables. In addition, Gore had teamed with one of the top shifter manufacturers to co-market their products. The shift manufacturer uses the Gore cables in its best-selling shifter line, introduced in November 2007.

Facing the Future Together

Associates at Gore believe that their unique organizational culture will allow the company to continue maximizing individual potential while cultivating an environment where creativity can flourish. The unique culture results from an unwavering commitment to the use of cutting-edge technology for developing high-quality products. This strategy is carried out through a unique approach to leadership and human resource management. The record of success is demonstrated not only by high financial profitability but also the creation of a highly desirable workplace. Nevertheless, success in the past cannot be seen as assurance of success in the future. As Brad Jones of the Enterprise Leadership Team said:

Twenty or thirty years ago, markets in different parts of the world were still somewhat distinct and isolated from one another. At that time, we could have pretty much the entire global business team for a particular market niche located in a building. Today, as our markets become more global in nature, we are increasingly seeing the need to support our customers with global virtual teams. How do our paradigms and practices have to change to accommodate those changing realities? Those are active discussions that apply across these many different businesses.

The answer of how Gore will evolve to meet these challenges is not something that will be decided by an isolated CEO or an elite group of executives. Critical decisions, those below the waterline, have never been made that way, and there is no expectation that this will change.

INTEGRATIVE CASE 2.0
The Donor Services Department*

Joanna Reed was walking home through fallen tree blossoms in Guatemala City. Today, however, her mind was more on her work than the natural beauty surrounding her. She unlocked the gate to her colonial home and sat down on the porch, surrounded by riotous toddlers, pets, and plants, to ponder the recommendations she would make to Sam Wilson. The key decisions she needed to make about his Donor Services Department concerned who should run the department and how the work should be structured.

Joanna had worked for a sponsorship agency engaged in international development work with poor people for six years. She and her husband moved from country to country setting up new agencies. In each country, they had to design how the work should be done, given the local labor market and work conditions.

After a year in Guatemala, Joanna, happily pregnant with her third child, had finished setting up the Donor Services Department for the agency and was working only part-time on a research project. A friend who ran a "competing" development agency approached her to do a consulting project for him. Sam Wilson, an American, was the national representative of a U.S.-based agency that had offices all over the world. Sam wanted Joanna to analyze his Donor Services Department, because he'd received complaints from headquarters about its efficiency. Since he'd been told that his office needed to double in size in the coming year, he wanted to get all the bugs worked out beforehand. Joanna agreed to spend a month gathering information and compiling a report on this department.

Sponsorship agencies, with multimillion-dollar budgets, are funded by individuals and groups in developed countries who contribute to development programs in less-developed countries (LDCs). Donors contribute approximately $20.00 per month plus optional special gifts. The agencies use this money to fund education, health, community development, and income-producing projects for poor people affiliated with their agency in various communities. In the eyes of most donors, the specific benefit provided by sponsorship agencies is the personal relationship between a donor and a child and his or her family in the LDC. The donors and children write back and forth, and the agency sends photos of the child and family to the donors. Some donors never write the family they sponsor; others write weekly and visit the family on their vacations. The efficiency of a Donor Services Department and the quality of their translations are key ingredients to keeping donors and attracting new ones. Good departments also never lose sight of the fact that sponsorship agencies serve a dual constituency—the local people they are trying to help develop and the sponsors who make that help possible through their donations.

What Is a Donor Services Department in a Sponsorship Agency Anyway?

The work of a Donor Services Department consists of more than translating letters, preparing annual progress reports on the families, and answering donor questions directed to the agency. It also handles the extensive, seemingly endless paperwork associated with enrolling new families and assigning them to donors, reassignments when either the donor or the family stops participating, and the special gifts of money sent (and thank you notes for them). Having accurate enrollment figures is crucial because the money the agency receives from headquarters is based upon these figures and affects planning.

The Department Head

Joanna tackled the challenge of analyzing the department by speaking first with the department head (see the organizational chart in Exhibit 1). José Barriga, a charismatic, dynamic man in his forties, was head of both Donor Services and Community Services. In reality, he spent virtually no time in the Donor Services Department and was not bilingual. "My biggest pleasure is working with the community leaders and coming up with programs that will be successful. I much prefer being in the field, driving from village to village talking with people, to supervising paperwork. I'm not sure exactly what goes on in Donor Services, but Elena, the supervisor, is very responsible. I make it a point to walk through the department once a week and say hello to everyone, and I check their daily production figures."

The Cast of Characters in the Department

Like José, Sam was also more interested in working with the communities on projects than in immersing himself in the details of the more administrative departments. In part, Sam had contracted Joanna because he rightfully worried that Donor Services did not receive the attention it deserved from José, who was very articulate and personable but seldom had time to look at anything beyond case histories. José never involved himself in the internal affairs of the department. Even though he was not considered

*Joyce S. Osland, San Jose State University.

much of a resource to them, he was well liked and respected by the staff of Donor Services, and they never complained about him.

The Supervisor

This was not the case with the supervisor José had promoted from within. Elena had the title of departmental supervisor, but she exercised very little authority. A slight, single woman in her thirties, Elena had worked for the organization since its establishment ten years earlier. She was organized, meticulous, dependable, and hard working. But she was a quiet, non-assertive, nervous woman who was anything but proactive. When asked what changes she would make if she were the head of the department, she sidestepped the question by responding, "It is difficult to have an opinion on this subject. I think that the boss can see the necessary changes with greater clarity."

Elena did not enjoy her role as supervisor, which was partly due to the opposition she encountered from a small clique of long-time translators. In the opinion of this subgroup, Elena had three strikes against her. One, unlike her subordinates, she was not bilingual. "How can she be the supervisor when she doesn't even know English well? One of us would make a better supervisor." Bilingual secretaries in status-conscious Guatemala see themselves as a cut above ordinary secretaries. This group looked down on Elena as being less skilled and educated than they were, even though she was an excellent employee. Second, Elena belonged to a different religion than the organization itself and almost all the other employees. This made no difference to Sam and José but seemed important to the clique who could be heard making occasional derogatory comments about Elena's religion.

The third strike against Elena was her lack of authority. No one had ever clarified how much authority she really possessed, and she herself made no effort to assume control of the department. "My instructions are to inform Don José Barriga of infractions in my daily production

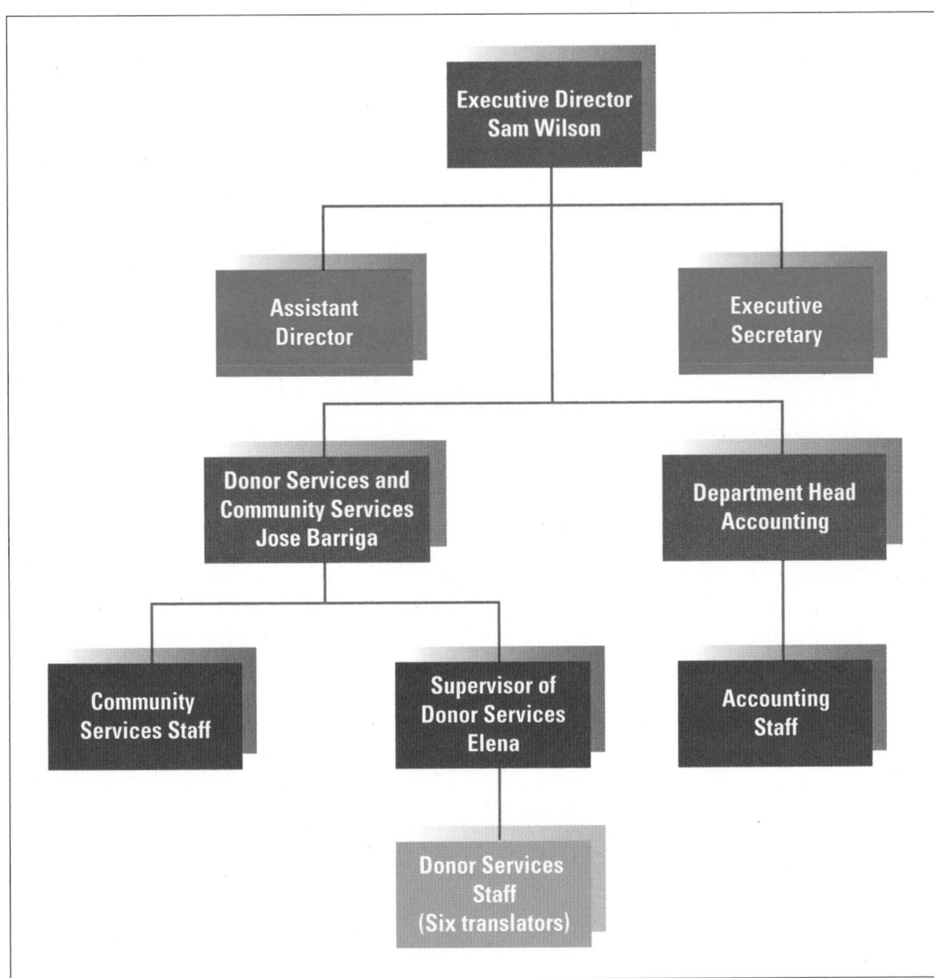

EXHIBIT 1
Organizational Chart—Donor Services Department

memo. I'm not supposed to confront people directly when infractions occur, although it might be easier to correct things if I did." ("Don" is a Latin American honorific used before the first name to denote respect.)

This subgroup showed their disdain and lack of respect for Elena by treating her with varying degrees of rudeness and ignoring her requests. They saw her as a watchdog, an attitude furthered by José who sometimes announced, "We (senior management) are not going to be here tomorrow, so be good because Elena will be watching you." When Sam and José left the office, the clique often stopped working to socialize. They'd watch Elena smolder out of the corner of their eyes, knowing she would not reprimand them. "I liked my job better before I became supervisor," said Elena. "Ever since, some of the girls have resented me, and I'm not comfortable trying to keep them in line. Why don't they just do their work without needing me to be the policeman? The only thing that keeps me from quitting is the loyalty I feel for the agency and Don José."

The Workers

In addition to the clique already mentioned, there were three other female translators in the department. All the translators but one had the same profile: in their twenties, of working-class backgrounds, and graduates of bilingual secretary schools, possessing average English skills. (As stated earlier, in Latin America, being a bilingual secretary is a fairly prestigious occupation for a woman.) The exception in this group was the best translator, Magdalena, a college-educated recent hire in her late thirties who came from an upper-class family. She worked, not because she needed the money, but because she believed in the mission of the agency. "This job lets me live out my religious beliefs and help people who have less advantages than I do." Magdalena was more professional and mature than the other translators. Although all the employees were proud of the agency and its religious mission, the clique members spent too much time socializing and skirmishing with other employees within and without the department.

The three translators who were not working at full capacity were very close friends. The leader of this group, Juana, was a spunky, bright woman with good oral English skills and a hearty sense of humor. A long-time friend of Barriga's, Juana translated for English-speaking visitors who came to visit the program sites throughout the country. The other translators, tied to their desks, saw this as a huge perk. Juana was the ringleader in the occasional mutinies against Elena and in feuds with people from other departments. Elena was reluctant to complain about Juana to Barriga, given their friendship. Perhaps she feared Juana would make her life even more miserable.

Juana's two buddies (*compañeras*) in the department also had many years with the agency. They'd gotten into the habit of helping each other on the infrequent occasions when they had excessive amounts of work. When they were idle or simply wanted to relieve the boredom of their jobs, they socialized and gossiped. Juana in particular was noted for lethal sarcasm and pointed jokes about people she didn't like. This clique was not very welcoming to the newer members of the department. Magdalena simply smiled at them but kept her distance, and the two younger translators kept a low profile to avoid incurring their disfavor. As one of them remarked, "It doesn't pay to get on Juana's bad side."

Like many small offices in Latin America, the agency was located in a spacious former private home. The Donor Services Department was housed in the 40 × 30-foot living room area. The women's desks were set up in two rows, with Elena's desk in the back corner. Since the offices of both Wilson and Barriga were in former back bedrooms, everyone who visited them walked through the department, greeting and stopping to chat with the long-time employees (Elena, Juana, and her two friends). Elena's numerous visitors also spent a good deal of time working their way through the department to reach her desk, further contributing to the amount of socializing going on in the department.

Elena was the only department member who had "official" visitors since she was the liaison person who dealt with program representatives and kept track of enrollments. The translators each were assigned one work process. For example, Marisol prepared case histories on new children and their families for prospective donors while Juana processed gifts. One of the newer translators prepared files for newly enrolled children and did all the filing for the entire department (a daunting task). Most of the jobs were primarily clerical and required little or no English. The letter translations were outsourced to external translators on a piece-work basis and supervised by Magdalena. Hers was the only job that involved extensive translation; for the most part, however, she translated simple messages (such as greeting cards) that were far below her level of language proficiency. The trickier translations, such as queries from donors in other countries, were still handled by Wilson's executive secretary.

Several translators complained that, "We don't have enough opportunity to use our English skills on the job. Not only are we not getting any better in English, we are probably losing fluency because most of our jobs are just clerical work. We do the same simple, boring tasks over and over, day in and day out. Why did they hire bilingual secretaries for these jobs anyway?"

Another obvious problem was the uneven distribution of work in the office. The desks of Magdalena and the new translators were literally overflowing with several months' backlog of work while Juana and her two friends had time to kill. Nobody, including Elena, made any efforts to even out the work assignments or help out those who were buried. The subject had never been broached.

The agency was growing at a rapid pace, and there were piles of paperwork sitting around waiting to be processed. Joanna spent three weeks having each department member explain her job (in mind-numbing detail), drawing up flow charts of how each type of paperwork was handled, and poking around in their files. She found many unnecessary steps that resulted in slow turnaround times for various processes. There were daily output reports submitted to Barriga, but no statistics kept on the length of time it took to respond to requests for information or process paperwork. No data were shared with the translators, so they had no idea how the department was faring and little sense of urgency about their work. The only goal was to meet the monthly quota of case histories, which only affected Marisol. Trying to keep up with what came across their desks summed up the entire focus of the employees.

Joanna found many instances of errors and poor quality, not so much from carelessness as lack of training and supervision. Both Barriga and Wilson revised the case histories, but Joanna was amazed to discover that no one ever looked at any other work done by the department. Joanna found that the employees were very accommodating when asked to explain their jobs and very conscientious about their work (if not the hours devoted to it). She also found, however, the employees were seldom able to explain why things were done in a certain way, because they had received little training for their jobs and only understood their small part of the department. Morale was obviously low, and all the employees seemed frustrated with the situation in the department. With the exception of Magdalena who had experience in other offices, they had few ideas for Joanna about how the department could be improved.

Part Two
Organizational Strategy and Structure

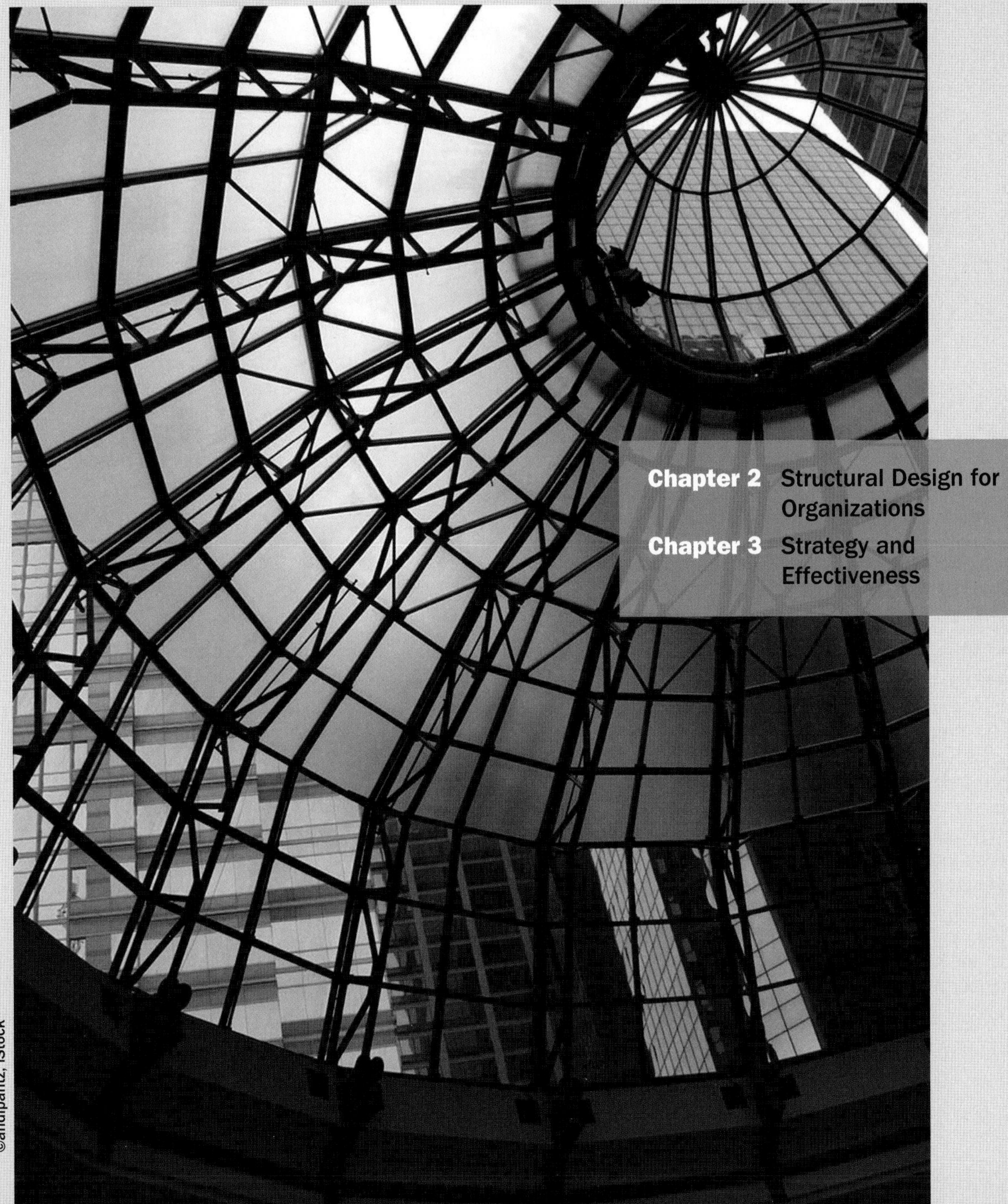

©andipantz, iStock

Chapter 2

Structural Design for Organizations

©andipantz, iStock

Learning Objectives

After reading this chapter you should be able to:

1. Define the three key components of organization structure.
2. Explain the vertical and horizontal information-sharing concepts of structure.
3. Understand the role of task forces and teams in organization structure.
4. Identify departmental grouping options, such as functional, divisional, and matrix.
5. Understand the strengths and weaknesses of various structural forms.
6. Explain new horizontal and virtual network structural forms.
7. Describe the symptoms of structural deficiency within an organization.

Before reading this chapter, please check whether you agree or disagree with each of the following statements:

1 **A popular form of organizing is to have employees work on what they want in whatever department they choose so that motivation and enthusiasm stay high.**

I AGREE _____ I DISAGREE _____

2 **Committees and task forces whose members are from different departments are often worthless for getting things done.**

I AGREE _____ I DISAGREE _____

3 **Top managers are smart to maintain organizational control over the activities of key work units rather than contracting out some work unit tasks to other firms.**

I AGREE _____ I DISAGREE _____

Wyeth Pharmaceuticals makes and sells some very powerful drugs, including Effexor for depression, Zosyn to treat infectious diseases, and Telazol, a combined anesthetic/tranquilizer for animals. But Wyeth no longer manages clinical testing of new drugs or vaccines. Outrageous? Shocking? No, just a new reality. Several years ago, Wyeth formed a joint venture with Accenture called the Alliance for Clinical Data Excellence. The partnership was designed to "bring together the best of both Wyeth and Accenture" for managing Wyeth's entire clinical testing operation—from protocol design to patient recruitment to site monitoring.[1] It's all part of Wyeth's drive to improve quality, efficiency, speed, and innovation by outsourcing some of its operations to firms that can handle them better and faster.

Now, you might wonder how Accenture operates. Let us just say that even CEO Bill Green doesn't have a permanent desk. Accenture doesn't have a formal headquarters, no official branches, no permanent offices. The company's chief technologist is located in Germany, its head of human resources is in Chicago, the chief financial officer is in Silicon Valley, and most of its consultants are constantly on the move.[2]

No doubt about it, many organizations are more complex and amorphous than they used to be. Wyeth and Accenture reflect the structural trend among today's organizations toward outsourcing, alliances, and virtual networking. Today's companies also use other structural innovations, such as teams and matrix designs, to achieve the flexibility they need. Teams, for example, are part of the strategy used by the Federal Bureau of Investigation (FBI) to combat terrorism. Like other organizations, the FBI must find ways to accomplish more with limited resources. One innovation was the creation of Flying Squads, which are teams of volunteer agents and support staff from various offices who are ready to spring into action when minimally staffed FBI offices around the world request assistance.[3] Still other firms continue to be successful with traditional

functional structures that are coordinated and controlled through the vertical hierarchy. Organizations use a wide variety of structural alternatives to help them achieve their purpose and goals, and nearly every firm needs to undergo reorganization at some point to help meet new challenges. Structural changes are needed to reflect new strategies or respond to changes in other contingency factors introduced in Chapter 1: environment, technology, size and life cycle, and culture.

Purpose of This Chapter

This chapter introduces basic concepts of organization structure and shows how to design structure as it appears on the organization chart. First we define structure and provide an overview of structural design. Next, an information-sharing perspective explains how to design vertical and horizontal linkages to provide needed information flow and coordination. The chapter then presents basic design options, followed by strategies for grouping organizational activities into functional, divisional, matrix, horizontal, virtual network, or hybrid structures. The final section examines how the application of basic structures depends on the organization's situation (various contingencies) and outlines the symptoms of structural misalignment.

Organization Structure

As an organization manager, keep these guidelines in mind:

Develop organization charts that describe task responsibilities, reporting relationships, and the grouping of individuals into departments. Provide sufficient documentation so that all people within the organization know to whom they report and how they fit into the total organization picture.

The following three key components define **organization structure**:

1. Organization structure designates formal reporting relationships, including the number of levels in the hierarchy and the span of control of managers and supervisors.
2. Organization structure identifies the grouping together of individuals into departments and of departments into the total organization.
3. Organization structure includes the design of systems to ensure effective communication, coordination, and integration of efforts across departments.[4]

These three elements of structure pertain to both vertical and horizontal aspects of organizing. For example, the first two elements are the structural *framework*, which is the vertical hierarchy.[5] The third element pertains to the pattern of *interactions* among organizational employees. An ideal structure encourages employees to provide horizontal information and coordination where and when it is needed.

Organization structure is reflected in the organization chart. It isn't possible to see the internal structure of an organization the way we might see its manufacturing tools, offices, website, or products. Although we might see employees going about their duties, performing different tasks, and working in different locations, the only way to actually see the structure underlying all this activity is through the organization chart. The organization chart is the visual representation of a whole set of underlying activities and processes in an organization. Exhibit 2.1 shows a simple organization chart for a traditional organization. An organization chart can be quite useful in understanding how a company works. It shows the various parts

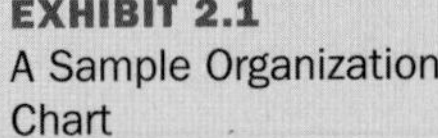

EXHIBIT 2.1
A Sample Organization Chart

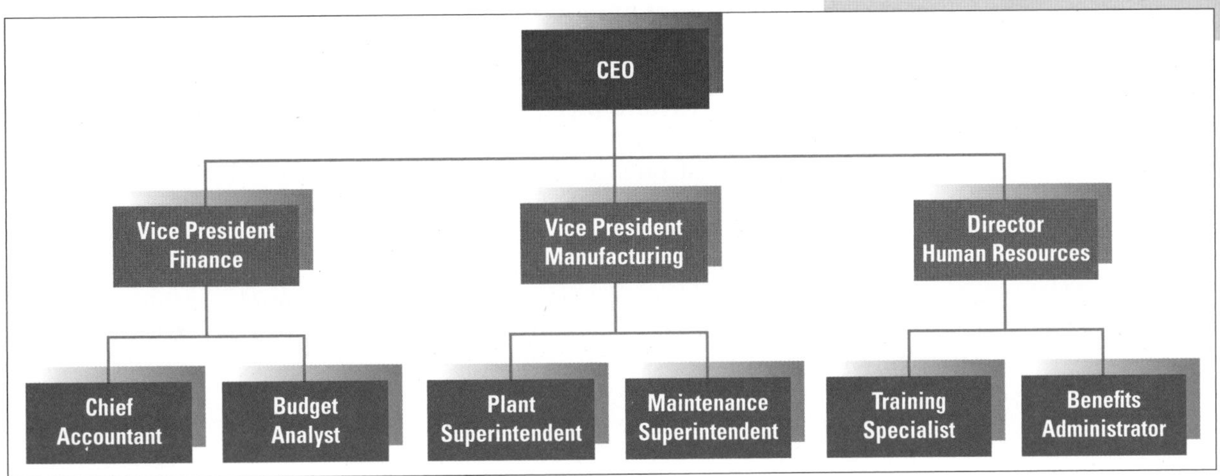

of an organization, how they are interrelated, and how each position and department fits into the whole.

The concept of an organization chart, showing what positions exist, how they are grouped, and who reports to whom, has been around for centuries.[6] For example, diagrams outlining church hierarchy can be found in medieval churches in Spain. However, the use of the organization chart for business stems largely from the Industrial Revolution. As we discussed in Chapter 1, as work grew more complex and was performed by greater numbers of workers, there was a pressing need to develop ways of managing and controlling organizations. The growth of the railroads provides an example. After the collision of two passenger trains in Massachusetts in 1841, the public demanded better control of the operation. As a result, the board of directors of the Western Railroad took steps to outline "definite responsibilities for each phase of the company's business, drawing solid lines of authority and command for the railroad's administration, maintenance, and operation."[7]

EXHIBIT 2.2
Organization Chart for the Erie Railroad, 1855

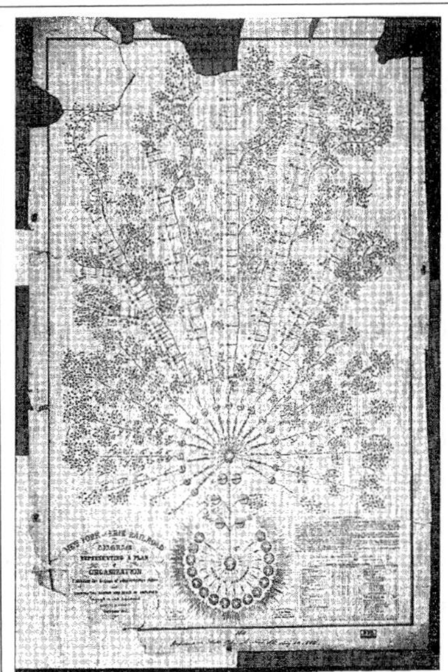

Source: Erie Railroad Organization Chart of 1855. Library of Congress, Haer, N.Y.

Exhibit 2.2 is an interesting example of an early organization chart created by Daniel McCallum for the Erie Railroad in 1855. Faced with financial strain and slumping productivity, McCallum created charts to explain the railroad's operations to investors and to show the division of responsibilities for superintendents along hundreds of miles of rail lines. McCallum divided the railroad up into geographic divisions of manageable size with each division headed by a superintendent.[8]

The type of organization structure that gradually grew out of these efforts in the late nineteenth and early twentieth centuries was one in which the CEO was placed at the top, and there was a clear hierarchy of authority extending to everyone else arranged in layers down below, as illustrated in Exhibit 2.1. The thinking and decision making are done by those at the top, and the physical work is performed by employees who are organized into distinct, functional departments. This structure was quite effective and became entrenched in business, nonprofit, and military organizations for most of the twentieth century. However, this type of vertical structure is not always effective, particularly in rapidly changing environments. Over the years organizations have developed other structural designs, many of them aimed at increasing horizontal coordination and communication and encouraging adaptation to external changes. This chapter's Book Mark suggests that new approaches to organizing and managing people are crucial for companies to attain durable competitive advantages in the twenty-first century.

ASSESS YOUR ANSWER

1 A popular form of organizing is to have employees work on what they want in whatever department they choose so that motivation and enthusiasm stay high.

ANSWER: *Disagree.* A small number of firms have tried this approach with some success, but a typical organization needs to structure its work activities, positions, and departments in a way that ensures work is accomplished and coordinated to meet organizational goals. Many managers try to give some consideration to employee choices as a way to keep enthusiasm high.

Information-Sharing Perspective on Structure

The organization should be designed to provide both vertical and horizontal information flow as necessary to accomplish the organization's overall goals. If the structure doesn't fit the information requirements of the organization, people either will have too little information or will spend time processing information that is not vital to their tasks, thus reducing effectiveness.[9] However, there is an inherent tension between vertical and horizontal mechanisms in an organization. Whereas vertical linkages are designed primarily for control, horizontal linkages are designed for coordination and collaboration, which usually means reducing control.

Organizations can choose whether to orient toward a traditional organization designed for efficiency, which emphasizes vertical communication and control (a mechanistic design, as described in Chapter 1) or toward a contemporary flexible learning organization, which emphasizes horizontal communication and coordination (an organic design). Exhibit 2.3 compares organizations designed for efficiency with those designed for learning and adaptation. An emphasis on efficiency and control is associated with specialized tasks, a hierarchy of authority, rules and regulations, formal reporting systems, few teams or task forces, and **centralized** decision making, which means problems and decisions are funneled to top levels of the

BOOKMARK

2.0 HAVE YOU READ THIS BOOK?

The Future of Management

By Gary Hamel with Bill Breen

Management breakthroughs such as the principles of scientific management, divisionalized organization structure, and using brand managers for horizontal coordination have created more sustained competitive advantage than any hot new product or service innovation, says Gary Hamel in *The Future of Management*, written with Bill Breen. Wait a minute—haven't those ideas been around since—well, *forever*? Exactly the point, says Hamel. In fact, he points out that many of today's managers are running twenty-first century organizations using ideas, practices, and structural mechanisms invented a century or more ago. At that time, the principles of vertical hierarchy, specialization, bureaucratic control, and strong centralization were radical new approaches developed to solve the problem of inefficiency. They are too static, regimented, and binding today when the pace of change continues to accelerate. Today's organizations, Hamel argues, have to become "as strategically adaptable as they are operationally efficient."

SOME STRUCTURAL INNOVATORS

Hamel suggests that the practice of management must undergo a transformation akin to that which occurred with the Industrial Revolution and the advent of scientific management. Here, from *The Future of Management*, are a few examples that offer glimpses of what is possible when managers build structure around principles of community, creativity, and information sharing rather than strict hierarchy:

- *Whole Foods Market.* Teams are the basic organizational unit at Whole Foods, and they have a degree of autonomy nearly unprecedented in the retail industry. Each store is made up of eight or so self-directed teams that oversee departments such as fresh produce, prepared foods, dairy, or checkout. Teams are responsible for all key operating decisions, including pricing, ordering, hiring, and in-store promotions.
- *W. L. Gore.* W. L. Gore's innovation was to organize work so that good things happen whether managers are "in control" or not. Gore, best known for Gore-Tex fabric, lets employees decide what they want to do. There are no management layers, few titles, and no organization charts. As at Whole Foods, the core operating units are small teams, but at Gore people can choose which teams to work on and say no to requests from anyone. Gore also builds in strong accountability—people are reviewed by at least 20 of their peers every year.
- *Visa.* Everybody's heard of Visa, but few people know anything about the organization behind the brand. Visa is the world's first almost-entirely virtual company. In the early 1970s, a group of banks formed a consortium that today has grown into a global network of 21,000 financial institutions and more than 1.3 billion cardholders. The organization is largely self-organizing, continually evolving as conditions change.

HOW TO BE A MANAGEMENT INNOVATOR

Most companies have a system for product innovation, but Hamel notes that few have a well-honed process for management innovation. *The Future of Management* provides detailed steps managers can take to increase the chances of a breakthrough in management thinking. Hamel considers the rise of modern management and organization design the most important innovation of the twentieth century. It is time now, though, for twenty-first century ideas.

The Future of Management, by Gary Hamel with Bill Breen, is published by Harvard Business School Press.

hierarchy for resolution. Emphasis on learning and adaptation is associated with shared tasks; a relaxed hierarchy; few rules; face-to-face communication; many teams and task forces; and informal, **decentralized** decision making. Decentralized decision making means decision-making authority is pushed down to lower organizational levels.

Organizations may have to experiment to find the correct degree of centralization or decentralization to meet their needs. For example, a study by William Ouchi found that three large school districts that shifted to a more flexible, decentralized

EXHIBIT 2.3
The Relationship of Organization Design to Efficiency versus Learning Outcomes

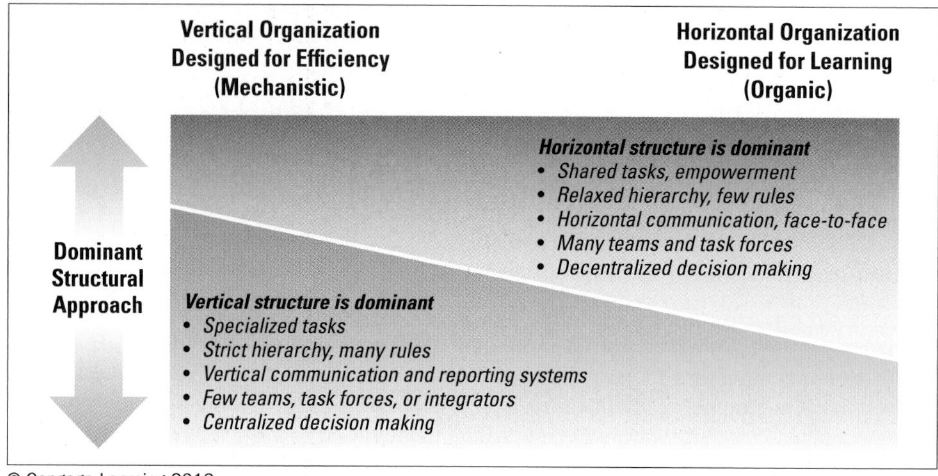

structure, giving school principals more autonomy, responsibility, and control over resources, performed better and more efficiently than large districts that were highly centralized.[10] In Los Angeles, Mayor Antonio Villaraigosa initiated a program to try to turn the struggling public school system around by pushing authority down to principals rather than having all major decisions made at the district level. The Partnership for L.A. Schools initiative currently affects only 10 schools where parents and teachers voted to participate, but leaders hope to expand it quickly once positive results are evident. The initiative is still struggling to gain widespread support, but the schools involved, some of the lowest-performing in the district, are already seeing improvements in test scores. One teacher said that before the change, "every year there would be a new top-down reform fed to us from the district. It was as if the system were set up to be unresponsive."[11]

On the other hand, large decentralized companies sometimes need to build in more centralized communication and control systems to keep these huge, global corporations functioning efficiently. Consider the structural decisions that helped CEO Lewis Campbell revive Textron Inc., a $12 billion industrial conglomerate with headquarters in Providence, Rhode Island.

Textron Inc.

Textron CEO Lewis Campbell was a confirmed believer in decentralization, but in 2001, he took a look at the company's situation and knew something had to change. "We were adrift," says Campbell. "We were doing all the things we used to do but were not getting results." An economic downturn, combined with a steep decline in the industrial and aviation markets from which Textron derived most of its profits, had left Textron in a free fall. Over a two-year period, profits declined 75 percent.

To get the company operating at peak efficiency required some dramatic changes. At the time, Textron's many business units operated autonomously, with each unit handling its own administrative functions and managers making decisions focused on meeting their own division's goals. Many division managers didn't even know what other units of the company did. At the annual management summit, Campbell decreed that the various units would now be required to cooperate and share resources. The new focus would be on how the company as a whole was doing, and bonuses were linked to companywide rather than division performance. To improve efficiency, more than 1,500 payroll systems were cut down to just three, numerous health care plans across the disparate divisions were reduced to just one, and more than 100 data centers were consolidated into a handful. Managers who had been accustomed to making all their own decisions lost some of their autonomy as companywide decisions, such as a Six Sigma quality improvement program, were centralized to headquarters level and implemented top down.

Taking Textron away from its roots as a decentralized organization to one with a single vision and more centralized decision making didn't lead to overnight success, but the efficiencies soon began to accumulate. Within a few years, Textron's economic health had significantly improved, and Campbell was being hailed as a turnaround artist.[12]

It couldn't have been easy, bringing centralization to a company that had thrived on decentralization for its entire existence, but Campbell believed it was necessary for the current situation the company faced. Managers are always searching for the best combination of vertical control and horizontal collaboration, centralization and decentralization, for their own situations.[13]

Vertical Information Sharing

Organization design should facilitate the communication among employees and departments that is necessary to accomplish the organization's overall task. Managers create *information linkages* to facilitate communication and coordination among organizational elements. **Vertical linkages** are used to coordinate activities between the top and bottom of an organization and are designed primarily for control of the organization. Employees at lower levels should carry out activities consistent with top-level goals, and top executives must be informed of activities and accomplishments at the lower levels. Organizations may use any of a variety of structural devices to achieve vertical linkage, including hierarchical referral, rules, plans, and formal management information systems.[14]

Hierarchical Referral. The first vertical device is the hierarchy, or chain of command, which is illustrated by the vertical lines in Exhibit 2.1. If a problem arises that employees don't know how to solve, it can be referred up to the next level in the hierarchy. When the problem is solved, the answer is passed back down to lower levels. The lines of the organization chart act as communication channels.

Rules and Plans. The next linkage device is the use of rules and plans. To the extent that problems and decisions are repetitious, a rule or procedure can be established so employees know how to respond without communicating directly with their manager. Rules and procedures provide a standard information source enabling employees to be coordinated without actually communicating about every task. At PepsiCo's Gemesa cookie business in Mexico, for example, managers carefully brief production workers on goals, processes, and procedures so that employees themselves do most of the work of keeping the production process running smoothly, enabling the plants to operate with fewer managers.[15] Plans also provide standing information for employees. The most widely used plan is the budget. With carefully designed and communicated budget plans, employees

BRIEFCASE

As an organization manager, keep these guidelines in mind:

Provide vertical and horizontal information linkages to integrate diverse departments into a coherent whole. Achieve vertical linkage through hierarchy referral, rules and plans, and vertical information systems. Achieve horizontal linkage through cross-functional information systems, liaison roles, task forces, full-time integrators, and teams.

at lower levels can be left on their own to perform activities within their resource allotment.

Vertical Information Systems. A **vertical information system** is another strategy for increasing vertical information capacity. Vertical information systems include the periodic reports, written information, and computer-based communications distributed to managers. Information systems make communication up and down the hierarchy more efficient.

In today's world of corporate financial scandals and ethical concerns, many top managers are considering strengthening their organization's linkages for vertical information and control. The other major issue in organizing is to provide adequate horizontal linkages for coordination and collaboration.

Horizontal Information Sharing and Coordination

Horizontal communication overcomes barriers between departments and provides opportunities for coordination among employees to achieve unity of effort and organizational objectives. **Horizontal linkage** refers to communication and coordination horizontally across organizational departments. Its importance is articulated by comments made by Lee Iacocca when he took over Chrysler Corporation in the 1980s:

> *What I found at Chrysler were thirty-five vice presidents, each with his own turf . . . . I couldn't believe, for example, that the guy running engineering departments wasn't in constant touch with his counterpart in manufacturing. But that's how it was. Everybody worked independently. I took one look at that system and I almost threw up. That's when I knew I was in really deep trouble . . . .Nobody at Chrysler seemed to understand that interaction among the different functions in a company is absolutely critical. People in engineering and manufacturing almost have to be sleeping together. These guys weren't even flirting!*[16]

During his tenure at Chrysler, Iacocca pushed horizontal coordination to a high level. Everyone working on a specific vehicle project—designers, engineers, and manufacturers, as well as representatives from marketing, finance, purchasing, and even outside suppliers—worked together on a single floor so they could easily communicate.

Horizontal linkage mechanisms often are not drawn on the organization chart, but nevertheless are a vital part of organization structure. Small organizations usually have a high level of interaction among all employees, but in a large organization, providing mechanisms to ensure horizontal information sharing is critical to effective coordination, knowledge-sharing, and decision making.[17] For example, poor coordination and lack of information sharing has been blamed for delaying Toyota's decisions and response time to quality and safety issues related to sticky gas petals, faulty brakes, and other problems.[18] The following devices are structural alternatives that can improve horizontal coordination and information flow.[19] Each device enables people to exchange information.

Information Systems. A significant method of providing horizontal linkage in today's organizations is the use of cross-functional information systems. Computerized information systems enable managers or frontline workers throughout the organization to routinely exchange information about problems, opportunities, activities, or decisions. For example, at Veterans Administration (VA) hospitals around the country, a sophisticated system called Vista enables people all across the organization to access complete patient information and provide better care. By enabling close coordination and collaboration, technology has transformed the VA, once considered subpar, into one of the highest-quality, most cost-effective medical providers in the United States.[20]

Some organizations also encourage employees to use the company's information systems to build relationships all across the organization, aiming to support and enhance ongoing horizontal coordination across projects and geographical boundaries. CARE International, one of the world's largest private international relief organizations, enhanced its personnel database to make it easy for people to find others with congruent interests, concerns, or needs. Each person in the database has listed past and current responsibilities, experience, language abilities, knowledge of foreign countries, emergency experiences, skills and competencies, and outside interests. The database makes it easy for people working across borders to seek each other out, share ideas and information, and build enduring horizontal connections.[21]

Liaison Roles. A higher level of horizontal linkage is direct contact between managers or employees affected by a problem. One way to promote direct contact is to create a special **liaison role**. A liaison person is located in one department but has the responsibility for communicating and achieving coordination with another department. Liaison roles often exist between engineering and manufacturing departments because engineering has to develop and test products to fit the limitations of manufacturing facilities. An engineer's office might be located in the manufacturing area so the engineer is readily available for discussions with manufacturing supervisors about engineering problems with the manufactured products. A research and development person might sit in on sales meetings to coordinate new product development with what sales people think customers are wanting.[22]

Task Forces. Liaison roles usually link only two departments. When linkage involves several departments, a more complex device such as a task force is required. A **task force** is a temporary committee composed of representatives from each organizational unit affected by a problem.[23] Each member represents the interest of a department or division and can carry information from the meeting back to that department.

Task forces are an effective horizontal linkage device for temporary issues. They solve problems by direct horizontal coordination and reduce the information load on the vertical hierarchy. Typically, they are disbanded after their tasks are accomplished. Organizations have used task forces for everything from organizing the annual company picnic to solving expensive and complex manufacturing problems. One example comes from Georgetown Preparatory School in North Bethesda, Maryland, which used a task force made up of teachers, administrators, coaches, support staff, and outside consultants to develop a flu preparedness plan. When the N1 flu threat hit several years ago, Georgetown was much better equipped than most educational institutions to deal with the crisis because they had a plan in place.[24]

ASSESS YOUR ANSWER

2 Committees and task forces whose members are from different departments are often worthless for getting things done.

ANSWER: *Disagree.* The point of cross-functional committees and task forces is to share information to coordinate their departmental activities. Meeting, talking, and disagreeing is the work of the committee. These groups should not try to "get things done" in the sense of being efficient.

Full-time Integrator. A stronger horizontal linkage device is to create a full-time position or department solely for the purpose of coordination. A full-time **integrator** frequently has a title, such as product manager, project manager, program manager, or brand manager. Unlike the liaison person described earlier, the integrator does not report to one of the functional departments being coordinated. He or she is located outside the departments and has the responsibility for coordinating several departments. The brand manager for Planters Peanuts, for example, coordinates the sales, distribution, and advertising for that product.

The integrator can also be responsible for an innovation or change project, such as coordinating the design, financing, and marketing of a new product. An organization chart that illustrates the location of project managers for new product development is shown in Exhibit 2.4. The project managers are drawn to the side to indicate their separation from other departments. The arrows indicate project members assigned to the new product development. New Product A, for example, has a financial accountant assigned to keep track of costs and budgets. The engineering member provides design advice, and purchasing and manufacturing members represent their areas. The project manager is responsible for the entire project. He or she sees that the new product is completed on time, is introduced to the market, and achieves other project goals. The horizontal lines in Exhibit 2.4 indicate that project managers do not have formal authority over team members with respect to giving pay raises, hiring, or firing. Formal authority rests with the managers of the functional departments, who have formal authority over subordinates.

Integrators need excellent people skills. Integrators in most companies have a lot of responsibility but little authority. The integrator has to use expertise and persuasion to achieve coordination. He or she spans the boundary between departments and must be able to get people together, maintain their trust, confront problems, and resolve conflicts and disputes in the interest of the organization.[25]

Teams. Project teams tend to be the strongest horizontal linkage mechanism. **Teams** are permanent task forces and are often used in conjunction with a full-time integrator. When activities among departments require strong coordination over a long period of time, a cross-functional team is often the solution. Special project teams may be used when organizations have a large-scale project, a major innovation, or a new product line. JetBlue Airways put together a special project team made up of crew schedulers, systems operators, dispatchers, reservations agents, and other employees to revise how the airline handles and recovers from "irregular operations," such as severe weather. How effectively airlines manage and recover from these events dramatically affects performance and customer satisfaction, but effectiveness requires close coordination. At the first team meeting, leaders presented a simulated emergency and asked the team to map out how they

EXHIBIT 2.4
Project Manager Location in the Structure

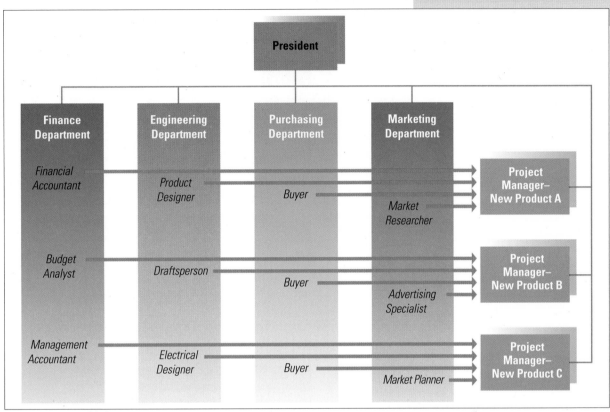

President

Finance Department
Engineering Department
Purchasing Department
Marketing Department

Financial Accountant
Product Designer
Buyer
Market Researcher
Project Manager–New Product A

Budget Analyst
Draftsperson
Buyer
Advertising Specialist
Project Manager–New Product B

Management Accountant
Electrical Designer
Buyer
Market Planner
Project Manager–New Product C

would respond. As team members went through the process, they began to spot problems. The goal of the team is to work out solutions to help JetBlue improve both regular on-time performance and its recovery time from major events.[26]

Many of today's company's use virtual cross-functional teams. A **virtual team** is one that is made up of organizationally or geographically dispersed members who are linked primarily through advanced information and communications technologies. Members frequently use the Internet and collaboration software to work together rather than meet face to face.[27] IBM's virtual teams, for instance, collaborate primarily via internal websites using wiki technology.[28] At Nokia, virtual team members working in several different countries across time zones and cultures have a virtual work space that members can access 24 hours a day. In addition, Nokia provides an online resource where virtual workers are encouraged to post photos and share personal information.[29]

An illustration of how teams provide strong horizontal coordination is shown in Exhibit 2.5. Wizard Software Company develops and markets software for various Web, desktop, and mobile applications, from games and social media products to financial services. Wizard uses teams to coordinate each product line across the research, programming, and marketing departments, as illustrated by the dashed lines and shaded areas in the exhibit. Members from each team meet at the beginning of each day as needed to resolve problems concerning customer needs,

EXHIBIT 2.5
Teams Used for Horizontal Coordination at Wizard Software Company

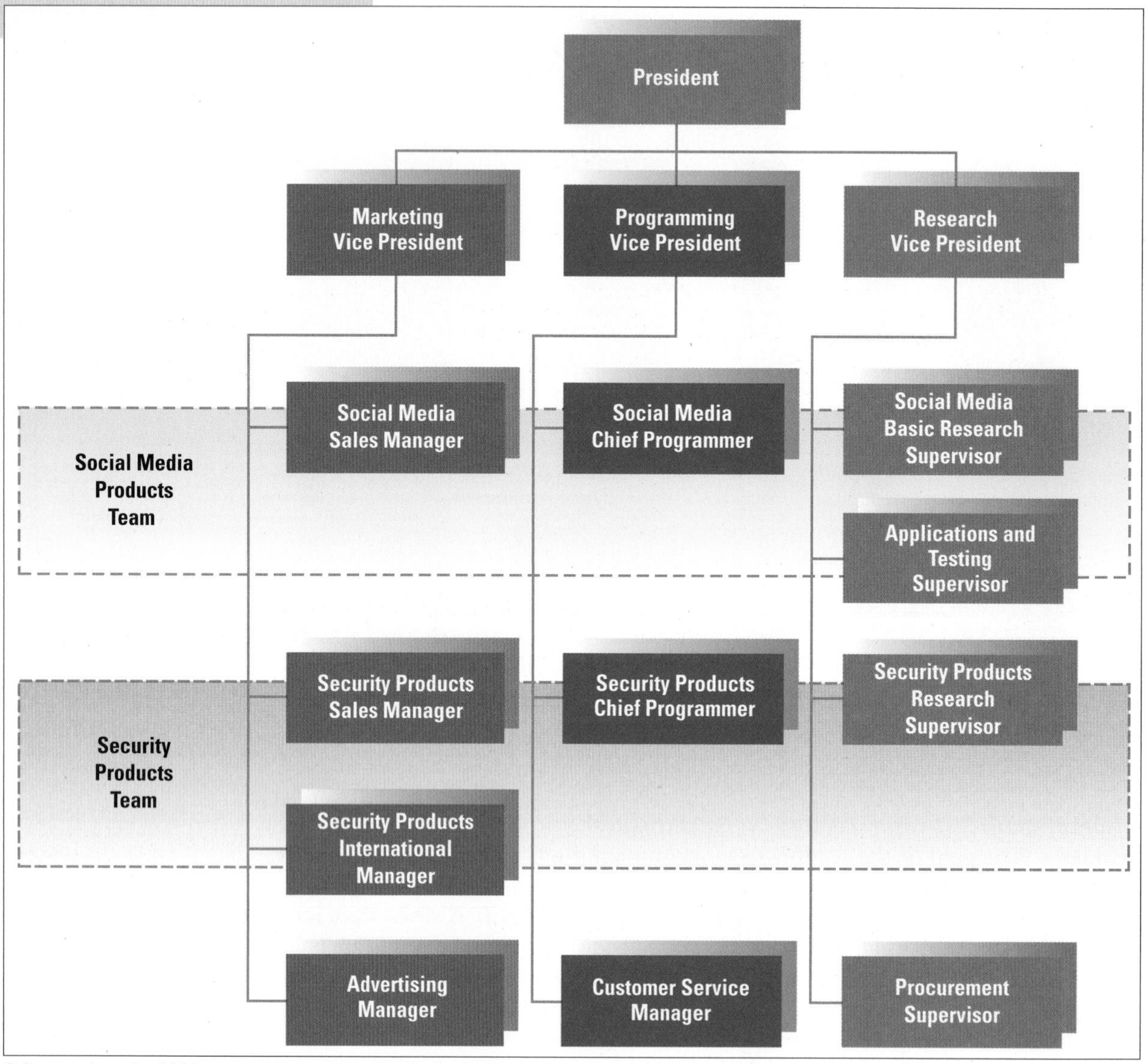

President

Marketing Vice President
Programming Vice President
Research Vice President

Social Media Products Team
Social Media Sales Manager
Social Media Chief Programmer
Social Media Basic Research Supervisor
Applications and Testing Supervisor

Security Products Team
Security Products Sales Manager
Security Products Chief Programmer
Security Products Research Supervisor
Security Products International Manager

Advertising Manager
Customer Service Manager
Procurement Supervisor

backlogs, programming changes, scheduling conflicts, and any other problem with the product line. Are you cut out for horizontal team work? Complete the questionnaire in the "How Do You Fit the Design?" box to assess your feelings about working on a team.

Exhibit 2.6 summarizes the mechanisms for achieving horizontal linkages. These devices represent alternatives that managers can select to increase horizontal coordination in any organization. The higher-level devices provide more horizontal information capacity, although the cost to the organization in terms of time and human resources is greater. If horizontal communication is insufficient, departments

How Do You Fit the Design?

THE PLEASURE/PAIN OF WORKING ON A TEAM

Your approach to your job or schoolwork may indicate whether you thrive on a team. Answer the following questions about your work preferences. Please answer whether each item is Mostly True or Mostly False for you.

	Mostly True	Mostly False
1. I prefer to work on a team rather than do individual tasks.	___	___
2. Given a choice, I try to work by myself rather than face the hassles of group work.	___	___
3. I enjoy the personal interaction when working with others.	___	___
4. I prefer to do my own work and let others do theirs.	___	___
5. I get more satisfaction from a group victory than an individual victory.	___	___
6. Teamwork is not worthwhile when people do not do their share.	___	___
7. I feel good when I work with others, even when we disagree.	___	___
8. I prefer to rely on myself rather than others to do a job or assignment.	___	___

Scoring: Give yourself one point for each odd-numbered item you marked as Mostly True and one point for each even-numbered item you marked Mostly False. Your score indicates your preference for teamwork versus individual work. If you scored 2 or fewer points, you definitely prefer individual work. A score of 7 or above suggests that you prefer working in teams. A score of 3–6 indicates comfort working alone and in a team.

Interpretation. Teamwork can be either frustrating or motivating depending on your preference. On a team you will lose some autonomy and have to rely on others who may be less committed than you. On a team you have to work through other people and you lose some control over work procedures and outcomes. On the other hand, teams can accomplish tasks far beyond what an individual can do, and working with others can be a major source of satisfaction. If you definitely prefer individual work, then you would likely fit better in a functional structure within a vertical hierarchy or in the role of individual contributor. If you prefer teamwork, then you are suited to work in the role of a horizontal linkage, such as on a task force or as an integrator, and would do well in a horizontal or matrix organization structure.

Source: Based on Jason D. Shaw, Michelle K. Duffy, and Eric M. Stark, "Interdependence and Preference for Group Work: Main and Congruence Effects on the Satisfaction and Performance of Group Members," *Journal of Management* 26, no. 2 (2000), 259–279.

will find themselves out of synchronization and will not contribute to the overall goals of the organization. When the amount of horizontal coordination needed is high, managers should select higher-level mechanisms.

Relational Coordination

The highest level of horizontal coordination illustrated in Exhibit 2.6 is relational coordination. **Relational coordination** refers to "frequent, timely, problem-solving communication carried out through relationships of shared goals, shared knowledge, and mutual respect."[30] Relational coordination isn't a device or mechanism like the other elements listed in Exhibit 2.6, but rather is part of the very fabric and

EXHIBIT 2.6
Ladder of Mechanisms for Horizontal Linkage and Coordination

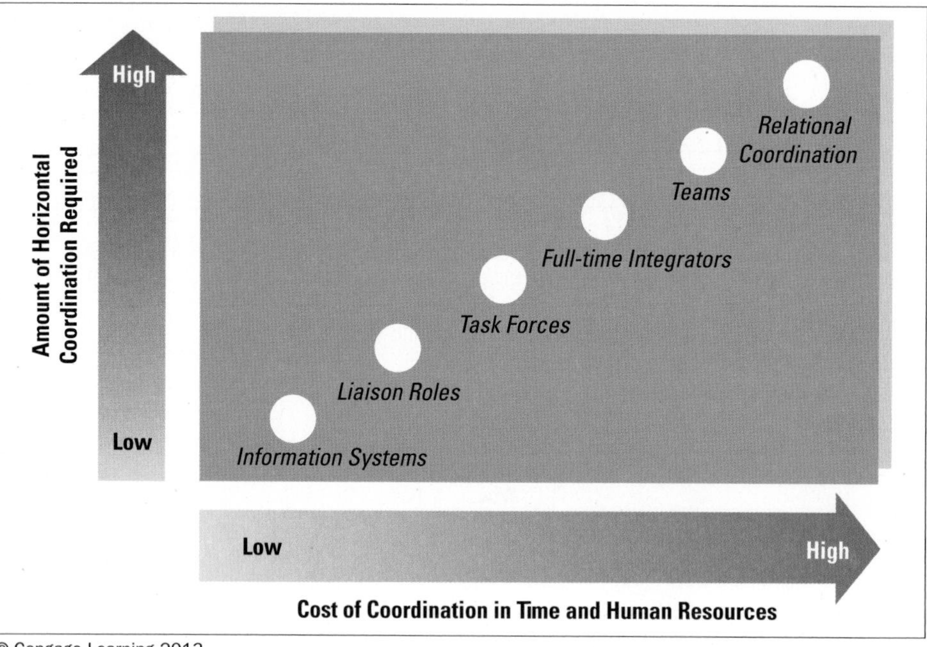

BRIEFCASE

As an organization manager, keep these guidelines in mind:

Recognize that the strongest horizontal linkage mechanisms are more costly in terms of time and human resources but are necessary when the organization needs a high degree of horizontal coordination to achieve its goals. When very high levels of coordination and knowledge sharing are needed, build relational coordination into the culture of the organization.

culture of the organization. In an organization with a high level of relational coordination, people share information freely across departmental boundaries, and people interact on a continuous basis to share knowledge and solve problems. Coordination is carried out through a web of ongoing positive relationships rather than because of formal coordination roles or mechanisms.[31] Employees coordinate directly with each other across units.

Building relational coordination into the fabric of the organization requires the active role of managers. Managers invest in training people in the skills needed to interact with one another and resolve cross-functional conflicts, build trust and credibility by showing they care about employees, and intentionally foster relationships based on shared goals rather than emphasizing goals of the separate departments. People are given freedom from strict work rules so they have the flexibility to interact and contribute wherever they are needed, and rewards are based on team efforts and accomplishments. Front-line supervisors have small spans of control so they can develop close working relationships with subordinates and coach and mentor employees. Managers also create specific cross-functional roles that promote coordination across boundaries. At Southwest Airlines, for example, operations agents span the boundaries across various departments to coordinate the numerous functions involved with flight departures.[32] When relational coordination is high, people share information and coordinate their activities without having to have bosses or formal mechanisms telling them to do so.

U.S. Lieutenant General David M. Rodriguez, the first commander of the International Security Assistance Force Joint Command (IJC) and deputy commander of U.S. forces in Afghanistan, fostered relational coordination among U.S. and Afghan military leaders as well as low-ranking commanders, civilian leaders, and others. His operations center had the feel of a newsroom, in which people eagerly talked to one another and shared their knowledge. Guidelines from high-ranking officers would get bottom-up refinement from captains and sergeants. Rodriguez understood that people have to "work together and figure out how to maximize the effectiveness of the team." He worked hard to build relationships based on mutual trust, respect, and shared goals and commitments. "We ask them to hold us accountable and we attempt to hold them accountable in a type of shared responsibility," Rodriguez said in an interview.[33] Whether in the military or in business, trust grows and knowledge and collaboration result when leaders build solid relationships.

Organization Design Alternatives

The overall design of organization structure indicates three things: required work activities, reporting relationships, and departmental groupings.

Required Work Activities

Departments are created to perform tasks considered strategically important to the company. In a typical manufacturing company, for example, work activities fall into a range of functions that help the organization accomplish its goals, such as a human resource department to recruit and train employees, a purchasing department to obtain supplies and raw materials, a production department to build products, a sales department to sell products, and so forth. As organizations grow larger and more complex, managers find that more functions need to be performed. Organizations typically define new positions, departments, or divisions as a way to accomplish new tasks deemed valuable by the organization. For example, British oil giant BP has added a new safety division in the wake of the Deepwater Horizon oil spill.

IN PRACTICE **BP**

For several years, BP's growth strategy was based on being a leader in pushing the frontiers of the oil industry, such as drilling the world's deepest wells, scouting for oil in the Arctic, and other aggressive efforts. Taking shortcuts and pushing risk to the limit was ingrained in the corporate culture. Previous CEO John Browne had built the company by taking over other oil firms and then ruthlessly cutting costs, many times firing some of the most experienced engineers. His successor, Tony Hayward, continued the hard-driving style. The approach was successful—to a point. BP steadily increased production and overtook Royal Dutch Shell PLC in market capitalization in January 2010. A few months later, though, disaster struck at BP's Deepwater Horizon rig, presenting a crisis that will be tough for BP to weather and requiring a new approach for the oil giant.

New CEO Robert Dudley, who took over in September 2010, is making a number of major changes aimed at shifting how the company operates and rebuilding trust. His earliest moves, which he called "the first and most urgent steps," were structural. Before he even officially became CEO, Dudley announced that he would split the company's exploration and production division into three parts to provide more oversight. In addition, he created a new global safety division with broad power to challenge management decisions if it considers them too risky. The division will also review how the company manages agreements with third-party contractors. The creation of a new division focused on safety and operational risk reflects how the company now must operate, said Dudley, "with safety and risk management our most urgent priority."[34]

Reporting Relationships

Once required work activities and departments are defined, the next question is how these activities and departments should fit together in the organizational hierarchy. Reporting relationships, often called the *chain of command*, are represented by vertical lines on an organization chart. The chain of command should be an unbroken line of authority that links all persons in an organization and shows who reports to whom. In a large organization such as General Electric, BP, L'Oreal, or Microsoft, 100 or more charts might be needed to identify reporting relationships among thousands of employees. The definition of departments and the drawing of reporting relationships define how employees are to be grouped into departments.

Departmental Grouping Options

Options for departmental grouping, including functional grouping, divisional grouping, multi-focused grouping, horizontal grouping, and virtual network grouping, are illustrated in Exhibit 2.7. **Departmental grouping** affects employees because they share a common supervisor and common resources, are jointly responsible for performance, and tend to identify and collaborate with one another.[35]

Functional grouping places together employees who perform similar functions or work processes or who bring similar knowledge and skills to bear. For example, all marketing people work together under the same supervisor, as do all manufacturing employees, all human resources people, and all engineers. For an Internet company, all the people associated with maintaining the website might be grouped together in one department. In a scientific research firm, all chemists may be grouped in a department different from biologists because they represent different disciplines.

Divisional grouping means people are organized according to what the organization produces. All the people required to produce toothpaste—including personnel in marketing, manufacturing, and sales—are grouped together under one executive. In huge corporations, such as Time Warner Corporation, some product or service lines may represent independent businesses, such as Warner Brothers Entertainment (movies and videos), Time Inc. (publisher of magazines such as *Sports Illustrated*, *Time*, and *People*), and Turner Broadcasting (cable television networks).

Multi-focused grouping means an organization embraces two or more structural grouping alternatives simultaneously. These structural forms are often called *matrix* or *hybrid*. They will be discussed in more detail later in this chapter. An organization may need to group by function and product division simultaneously or might need to combine characteristics of several structural options.

Horizontal grouping means employees are organized around core work processes, the end-to-end work, information, and material flows that provide value directly to customers. All the people who work on a core process are brought together in a group rather than being separated into functional departments. At field offices of the U.S. Occupational Safety and Health Administration, for example, teams of workers representing various functions respond to complaints from American workers regarding health and safety issues, rather than having the work divided up among specialized employees.[36]

Virtual network grouping is the most recent approach to departmental grouping. With this grouping, the organization is a loosely connected cluster of separate components. In essence, departments are separate organizations that are electronically

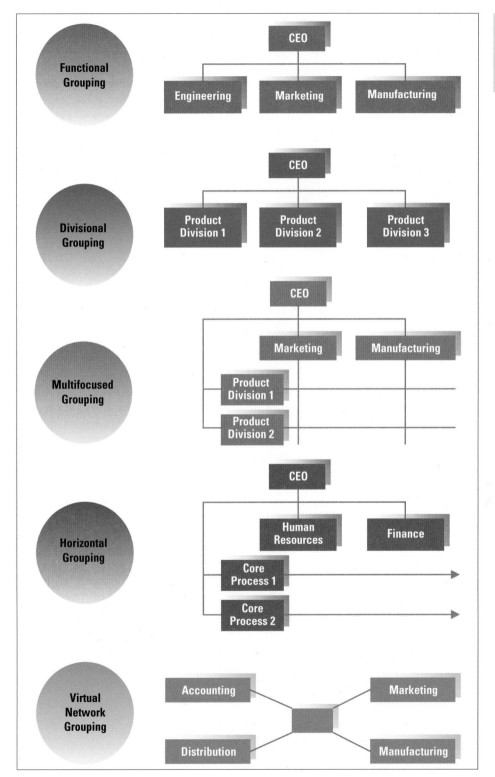

EXHIBIT 2.7
Structural Design Options for Grouping Employees into Departments

Functional Grouping

CEO

Engineering
Marketing
Manufacturing

Divisional Grouping

CEO

Product Division 1
Product Division 2
Product Division 3

Multifocused Grouping

CEO

Marketing
Manufacturing
Product Division 1
Product Division 2

Horizontal Grouping

CEO

Human Resources
Finance
Core Process 1
Core Process 2

Virtual Network Grouping

Accounting
Marketing
Distribution
Manufacturing

Source: Adapted from David Nadler and Michael Tushman, *Strategic Organization Design* (Glenview, IL: Scott Foresman, 1988), 68.

connected for the sharing of information and completion of tasks. Departments can be spread all over the world rather than located together in one geographic location.

The organizational forms described in Exhibit 2.7 provide the overall options within which the organization chart is drawn and the detailed structure is designed. Each structural design alternative has significant strengths and weaknesses, to which we now turn.

Functional, Divisional, and Geographic Designs

Functional grouping and divisional grouping are the two most common approaches to structural design.

Functional Structure

In a **functional structure**, also called a U-form (unitary), activities are grouped together by common function from the bottom to the top of the organization.[37] All engineers are located in the engineering department, and the vice president of engineering is responsible for all engineering activities. The same is true in marketing, R&D, and manufacturing. An example of the functional organization structure was shown in Exhibit 2.1 earlier in this chapter.

With a functional structure, all human knowledge and skills with respect to specific activities are consolidated, providing a valuable depth of knowledge for the organization. This structure is most effective when in-depth expertise is critical to meeting organizational goals, when the organization needs to be controlled and coordinated through the vertical hierarchy, and when efficiency is important. The structure can be quite effective if there is little need for horizontal coordination. Exhibit 2.8 summarizes the strengths and weaknesses of the functional structure.

EXHIBIT 2.8
Strengths and Weaknesses of Functional Organization Structure

Strengths	Weaknesses
1. Allows economies of scale within functional departments	1. Slow response time to environmental changes
2. Enables in-depth knowledge and skill development	2. May cause decisions to pile on top; hierarchy overload
3. Enables organization to accomplish functional goals	3. Leads to poor horizontal coordination among departments
4. Is best with only one or a few products	4. Results in less innovation
	5. Involves restricted view of organizational goals

Source: Based on Robert Duncan, "What Is the Right Organization Structure?" *Organizational Dynamics* (Winter 1979), 59–80.

One strength of the functional structure is that it promotes economy of scale within functions. Economy of scale results when all employees are located in the same place and can share facilities. Producing all products in a single plant, for example, enables the plant to acquire the latest machinery. Constructing only one facility instead of separate facilities for each product line reduces duplication and waste. The functional structure also promotes in-depth skill development of employees. Employees are exposed to a range of functional activities within their own department.[38]

The main weakness of the functional structure is a slow response to environmental changes that require coordination across departments. The vertical hierarchy becomes overloaded. Decisions pile up, and top managers do not respond fast enough. Other disadvantages of the functional structure are that innovation is slow because of poor coordination, and each employee has a restricted view of overall goals.

Some organizations perform very effectively with a functional structure. Consider the case of Blue Bell Creameries, Inc.

IN PRACTICE

Blue Bell Creameries, Inc.

It is the third best-selling brand of ice cream in the United States, but many Americans have never heard of it because Blue Bell Creameries, with headquarters in Brenham, Texas, sells its ice cream in only 20 states, mostly southern. It recently moved into Colorado to serve markets only within a 100-mile radius of Denver. Keeping distribution limited "allows us to focus on making and selling ice cream," says CEO and President Paul Kruse, the fourth generation of Kruses to run Blue Bell. Or, as another family slogan puts it, "It's a cinch by the inch but it's hard by the yard."

The "little creamery in Brenham," as the company markets itself, is obsessed with quality control and doesn't allow anyone outside the company to touch its product from the plant to the freezer case. "We make it all, we deliver it all in our own trucks, and we maintain all the stock in retailers' freezers," says chairman Ed Kruse. At any one time, the company has only about 30 to 40 flavors available. Blue Bell commands a huge percentage of the ice cream market in Texas, Louisiana, and Alabama. People outside the region often pay $89 to have four half-gallons packed in dry ice and shipped to them. Despite the demand, management refuses to compromise quality by expanding into regions that cannot be satisfactorily serviced or by growing so fast that the company can't adequately train employees in the art of making ice cream.

Blue Bell's major departments are sales, quality control, production, maintenance, and distribution. There is also an accounting department and a small R&D group. Most employees have been with the company for years and have a wealth of experience in making quality ice cream. The environment is stable. The customer base is well established. The only change has been the increase in demand for Blue Bell Ice Cream.[39]

The functional structure is just right for Blue Bell Creameries. The organization has chosen to stay medium-sized and focus on making a single product—quality ice cream. As Blue Bell expands, however, it may have problems coordinating across departments, requiring stronger linkage mechanisms.

Functional Structure with Horizontal Linkages

Organizing by functions is still the prevalent approach to organization design.[40] However, in today's fast-moving world, very few companies can be successful with a strictly functional structure. For example, Microsoft's Vista operating system took five years to bring to market, and even then many of the software features weren't ready by the time the product first shipped. The biggest problem was that the group developing Vista was working in functional silos, each dealing with only specific features and details, and there was little communication among the numerous people working on the project. Microsoft managers recognized the need for greater horizontal coordination and collaboration when developing Windows 7.[41]

Organizations compensate for the vertical functional hierarchy by installing horizontal linkages, as described earlier in this chapter. Managers improve horizontal coordination by using information systems, liaison roles, full-time integrators or project managers (illustrated in Exhibit 2.4), task forces, or teams (illustrated in Exhibit 2.5), and by creating the conditions that encourage relational coordination. One interesting use of horizontal linkages occurred at Karolinska Hospital in Stockholm, Sweden, which had 47 functional departments. Even after top executives cut that down to 11, coordination was still inadequate. The top executive team set about reorganizing workflow at the hospital around patient care. Instead of bouncing a patient from department to department, Karolinska now envisions the illness to recovery period as a process with "pit stops" in admissions, X-ray, surgery, and so forth. The most interesting aspect of the approach is the new position of nurse coordinator. Nurse coordinators serve as full-time integrators, troubleshooting transitions within or between departments. The improved horizontal coordination dramatically improved productivity and patient care at Karolinska.[42] The hospital is effectively using horizontal linkages to overcome some of the disadvantages of the functional structure.

BRIEFCASE

As an organization manager, keep these guidelines in mind:

When designing overall organization structure, choose a functional structure when efficiency is important, when in-depth knowledge and expertise are critical to meeting organizational goals, and when the organization needs to be controlled and coordinated through the vertical hierarchy. Use a divisional structure in a large organization with multiple product lines and when you wish to give priority to product goals and coordination across functions.

Divisional Structure

With a **divisional structure**, also called an M-form (multi-divisional) or a decentralized form, separate divisions can be organized with responsibility for individual products, services, product groups, major projects or programs, divisions, businesses, or profit centers.[43] This structure is sometimes also called a product structure or strategic business unit structure. The distinctive feature of a divisional structure is that grouping is based on *organizational outputs*. For example, United Technologies Corporation (UTC), which is among the 50 largest U.S. industrial firms, has numerous divisions, including Carrier (air conditioners and heating), Otis (elevators and escalators), Pratt & Whitney (aircraft engines), and Sikorsky (helicopters).[44] The Chinese online-commerce company Taobao is divided into three divisions that provide three different types of services: linking individual buyers and sellers; a marketplace for retailers to sell to consumers; and a service for people to search across Chinese shopping websites.[45]

The difference between a divisional structure and a functional structure is illustrated in Exhibit 2.9. The functional structure can be redesigned into separate product groups, and each group contains the functional departments of R&D, manufacturing, accounting, and marketing. Coordination is maximized across functional departments within each product group. The divisional structure promotes flexibility and change because each unit is smaller and can adapt to the needs of its environment. Moreover, the divisional structure *decentralizes* decision making

EXHIBIT 2.9
Reorganization from Functional Structure to Divisional Structure at Info-Tech

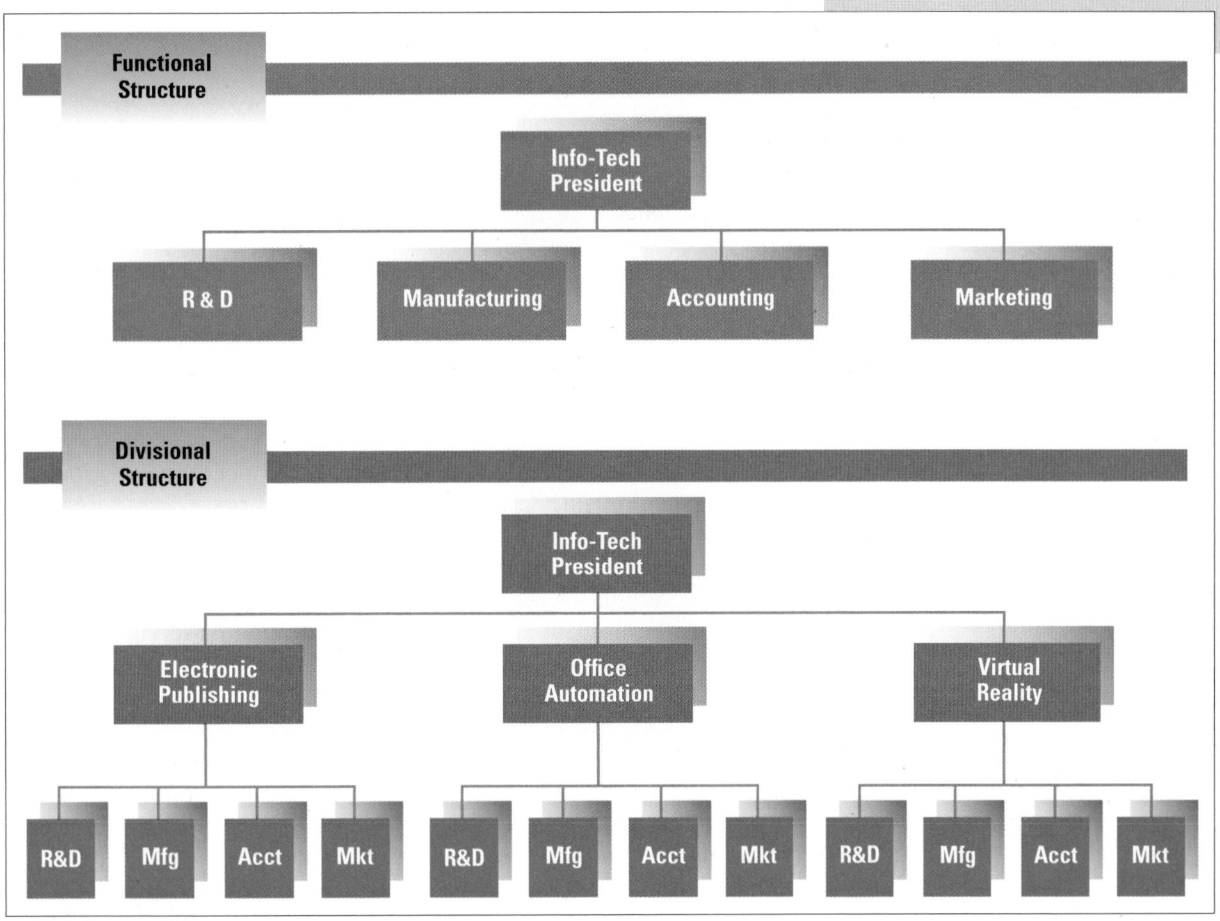

Functional Structure

- Info-Tech President
  - R & D
  - Manufacturing
  - Accounting
  - Marketing

Divisional Structure

- Info-Tech President
  - Electronic Publishing
    - R&D
    - Mfg
    - Acct
    - Mkt
  - Office Automation
    - R&D
    - Mfg
    - Acct
    - Mkt
  - Virtual Reality
    - R&D
    - Mfg
    - Acct
    - Mkt

because the lines of authority converge at a lower level in the hierarchy. The functional structure, by contrast, is *centralized* because it forces decisions all the way to the top before a problem affecting several functions can be resolved.

Strengths and weaknesses of the divisional structure are summarized in Exhibit 2.10. The divisional organization structure is excellent for achieving coordination across functional departments. It works well when organizations can no longer be adequately controlled through the traditional vertical hierarchy and when goals are oriented toward adaptation and change. Giant, complex organizations such as General Electric, Sony, and Johnson & Johnson are subdivided into a series of smaller, self-contained organizations for better control and coordination. In these large companies, the units are sometimes called divisions, businesses, or strategic business units. Johnson & Johnson is organized into three major divisions: Consumer Products, Medical Devices and Diagnostics, and Pharmaceuticals, yet within those three major divisions are 250 separate operating units in 57 countries.[46] Some U.S. government organizations also use a divisional structure to better serve the public. One example is the Internal Revenue Service, which wanted to

EXHIBIT 2.10
Strengths and Weaknesses of Divisional Organization Structure

Strengths	Weaknesses
1. Suited to fast change in unstable environment 2. Leads to customer satisfaction because product responsibility and contact points are clear 3. Involves high coordination across functions 4. Allows units to adapt to differences in products, regions, customers 5. Best in large organizations with several products 6. Decentralizes decision making	1. Eliminates economies of scale in functional departments 2. Leads to poor coordination across product lines 3. Eliminates in-depth competence and technical specialization 4. Makes integration and standardization across product lines difficult

Source: Based on Robert Duncan, "What Is the Right Organization Structure?" *Organizational Dynamics* (Winter 1979).

be more customer oriented. The agency shifted its focus to informing, educating, and serving the public through four separate divisions serving distinct taxpayer groups—individual taxpayers, small businesses, large businesses, and tax-exempt organizations. Each division has its own budget, personnel, policies, and planning staffs that are focused on what is best for each particular taxpayer segment.[47]

The divisional structure has several strengths.[48] This structure is suited to fast change in an unstable environment and provides high product or service visibility. Since each product line has its own separate division, customers are able to contact the correct division and achieve satisfaction. Coordination across functions is excellent. Each product can adapt to requirements of individual customers or regions. The divisional structure typically works best in organizations that have multiple products or services and enough personnel to staff separate functional units. Decision making is pushed down to the divisions. Each division is small enough to be quick on its feet, responding rapidly to changes in the market.

One disadvantage of using divisional structuring is that the organization loses economies of scale. Instead of 50 research engineers sharing a common facility in a functional structure, 10 engineers may be assigned to each of five product divisions. The critical mass required for in-depth research is lost, and physical facilities have to be duplicated for each product line. Another problem is that product lines become separate from each other, and coordination across product lines can be difficult. As a Johnson & Johnson executive once said, "We have to keep reminding ourselves that we work for the same corporation."[49]

Some companies that have a large number of divisions have had real problems with cross-unit coordination. Sony lost the digital music player business to Apple partly because of poor coordination. With the introduction of the iPod, Apple quickly captured 60 percent of the U.S. market versus 10 percent for Sony. The digital music business depends on seamless coordination. Sony's Walkman didn't even recognize some of the music sets that could be made with the company's SonicStage software and thus didn't mesh well with the division selling music downloads.[50] Unless effective horizontal mechanisms are in place, a divisional structure can hurt overall performance. One division may produce products or programs that are incompatible with products sold by another division, as at Sony. Customers can become frustrated when a sales representative from one division is unaware of developments in other divisions. Task forces and other horizontal linkage devices are needed to coordinate across divisions. A lack of technical specialization is also a problem in a divisional structure. Employees identify with the product line rather than with a functional specialty. R&D personnel, for example, tend to do applied research to benefit the product line rather than basic research to benefit the entire organization.

Geographic Structure

Another basis for structural grouping is the organization's users or customers. The most common structure in this category is geography. Each region of the country may have distinct tastes and needs. Each geographic unit includes all functions required to produce and market products or services in that region. Large nonprofit organizations such as the Girl Scouts of the USA, Habitat for Humanity, Make-A-Wish Foundation, and the United Way of America frequently use a type of geographic structure, with a central headquarters and semi-autonomous local units. The national organization provides brand recognition, coordinates fund-raising services, and handles some shared administrative functions, while day-to-day control and decision making is decentralized to local or regional units.[51]

For multi-national corporations, self-contained units are created for different countries and parts of the world. Exhibit 2.11 shows an example of a geographic structure for a cosmetics company. This structure focuses managers and employees on specific geographic regions and sales targets. Walmart Stores are organized by geographic regions, such as Walmart Japan, Walmart India, Walmart Brazil, Walmart China, Walmart Asia, and so forth. Until recently, U.S. operations were organized largely by function, but managers restructured U.S. operations into three geographic divisions, West, South, and North, making the U.S. organization more like how Walmart operates internationally. Using a geographic structure helps the company expand into new markets and use resources more efficiently.[52]

The strengths and weaknesses of a geographic divisional structure are similar to the divisional organization characteristics listed in

EXHIBIT 2.11
Geographic Structure for Cosmetics Company

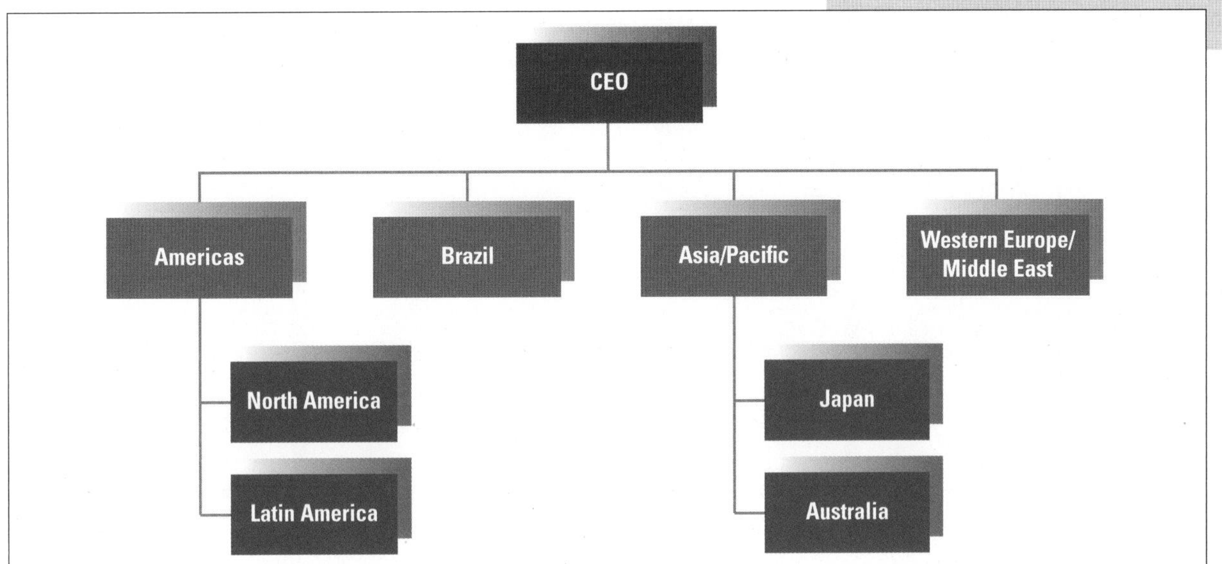

Exhibit 2.10. The organization can adapt to the specific needs of its own region, and employees identify with regional goals rather than with national goals. Horizontal coordination within a region is emphasized rather than linkages across regions or to the national office.

Matrix Structure

Sometimes, an organization's structure needs to be multi-focused in that both product and function or product and geography are emphasized at the same time. One way to achieve this is through the **matrix structure**.[53] The matrix can be used when both technical expertise and product innovation and change are important for meeting organizational goals. The matrix structure often is the answer when organizations find that the functional, divisional, and geographic structures combined with horizontal linkage mechanisms will not work.

The matrix is a strong form of horizontal linkage. The unique characteristic of the matrix organization is that both product divisions and functional structures (horizontal and vertical) are implemented simultaneously, as shown in Exhibit 2.12. The product managers and functional

EXHIBIT 2.12
Dual-Authority Structure in a Matrix Organization

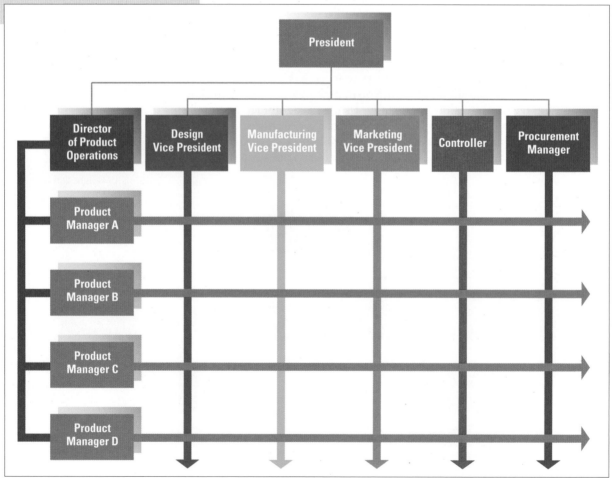

President

Director of Product Operations

Design Vice President

Manufacturing Vice President

Marketing Vice President

Controller

Procurement Manager

Product Manager A

Product Manager B

Product Manager C

Product Manager D

managers have equal authority within the organization, and employees report to both of them. The matrix structure is similar to the use of full-time integrators or product managers described earlier in this chapter (Exhibit 2.4), except that in the matrix structure the product managers (horizontal) are given formal authority equal to that of the functional managers (vertical).

BRIEFCASE

As an organization manager, keep these guidelines in mind:

Consider a matrix structure when the organization needs to give equal priority to both products and functions because of dual pressures from customers in the environment. Use either a functional matrix or a product matrix if the balanced matrix with dual lines of authority is not appropriate for your organization.

Conditions for the Matrix

A dual hierarchy may seem an unusual way to design an organization, but the matrix is the correct structure when the following conditions are present:[54]

- *Condition 1.* Pressure exists to share scarce resources across product lines. The organization is typically medium-sized and has a moderate number of product lines. It feels pressure for the shared and flexible use of people and equipment across those products. For example, the organization is not large enough to assign engineers full-time to each product line, so engineers are assigned part-time to several products or projects.
- *Condition 2.* Environmental pressure exists for two or more critical outputs, such as for in-depth technical knowledge (functional structure) and frequent new products (divisional structure). This dual pressure means a balance of power is needed between the functional and product sides of the organization, and a dual-authority structure is needed to maintain that balance.
- *Condition 3.* The environmental domain of the organization is both complex and uncertain. Frequent external changes and high interdependence between departments require a large amount of coordination and information processing in both vertical and horizontal directions.

Under these three conditions, the vertical and horizontal lines of authority must be given equal recognition. A dual-authority structure is thereby created so the balance of power between them is equal.

Referring again to Exhibit 2.12, assume the matrix structure is for a clothing manufacturer. Product A is footwear, product B is outerwear, product C is sleepwear, and so on. Each product line serves a different market and customers. As a medium-sized organization, the company must effectively use people from manufacturing, design, and marketing to work on each product line. There are not enough designers to warrant a separate design department for each product line, so the designers are shared across product lines. Moreover, by keeping the manufacturing, design, and marketing functions intact, employees can develop the in-depth expertise to serve all product lines efficiently.

The matrix formalizes horizontal teams along with the traditional vertical hierarchy and tries to give equal balance to both. However, the matrix may shift one way or the other. Many companies have found a balanced matrix hard to implement and maintain because one side of the authority structure often dominates. As a consequence, two variations of matrix structure have evolved—the **functional matrix** and the **product matrix**. In a functional matrix, the functional bosses have primary authority and the project or product managers simply coordinate product activities. In a product matrix, by contrast, the project or product managers have primary authority and functional managers simply assign technical personnel to projects and provide advisory expertise as needed. For many organizations, one of these approaches works better than the balanced matrix with dual lines of authority.[55]

All kinds of organizations have experimented with the matrix, including hospitals, consulting firms, banks, insurance companies, government agencies, and many types of industrial firms.[56] This structure has been used successfully by global organizations such as Procter & Gamble, IBM, Unilever, and Dow Chemical, which fine-tuned the matrix to suit their own particular goals and culture.

Strengths and Weaknesses

The matrix structure is best when environmental change is high and when goals reflect a dual requirement, such as for both product and functional goals. The dual-authority structure facilitates communication and coordination to cope with rapid environmental change and enables an equal balance between product and functional bosses. The matrix facilitates discussion and adaptation to unexpected problems. It tends to work best in organizations of moderate size with a few product lines. The matrix is not needed for only a single product line, and too many product lines make it difficult to coordinate both directions at once. Exhibit 2.13 summarizes the strengths and weaknesses of the matrix structure based on what we know of organizations that use it.[57]

One strength of the matrix is that it enables an organization to meet dual demands from customers in the environment. Resources (people, equipment) can be flexibly allocated across different products, and the organization can adapt to changing external requirements.[58] This structure also provides an opportunity for employees to acquire either functional or general management skills, depending on their interests.

One disadvantage of the matrix is that some employees experience dual authority, reporting to two bosses and sometimes juggling conflicting demands. This can be frustrating and confusing, especially if roles and responsibilities are not clearly defined by top managers.[59] Employees working in a matrix need excellent interpersonal and conflict-resolution skills, which may require special training in human relations. The matrix also forces managers to spend a great deal of time in meetings.[60]

EXHIBIT 2.13
Strengths and Weaknesses of Matrix Organization Structure

Strengths	Weaknesses
1. Achieves coordination necessary to meet dual demands from customers 2. Flexible sharing of human resources across products 3. Suited to complex decisions and frequent changes in unstable environment 4. Provides opportunity for both functional and product skill development 5. Best in medium-sized organizations with multiple products	1. Causes participants to experience dual authority, which can be frustrating and confusing 2. Means participants need good interpersonal skills and extensive training 3. Is time consuming; involves frequent meetings and conflict resolution sessions 4. Will not work unless participants understand it and adopt collegial rather than vertical type relationships 5. Requires great effort to maintain power balance

Source: Based on Robert Duncan, "What Is the Right Organization Structure? Decision Tree Analysis Provides the Answer," *Organizational Dynamics* (Winter 1979), 429.

If managers do not adapt to the information and power sharing required by the matrix, the system will not work. Managers must collaborate with one another rather than rely on vertical authority in decision making. The successful implementation of one matrix structure occurred at a steel company in Great Britain.

IN PRACTICE

Englander Steel

As far back as anyone could remember, the steel industry in England was stable and certain. Then in the 1980s and 1990s, excess European steel capacity, an economic downturn, the emergence of the mini mill electric arc furnace, and competition from steelmakers in Germany and Japan forever changed the steel industry. By the turn of the century, traditional steel mills in the United States, such as Bethlehem Steel and LTV Corporation, were facing bankruptcy. Mittal Steel in Asia and Europe's leading steelmaker, Arcelor, started acquiring steel companies to become world steel titans (the two merged in 2006 to become ArcelorMittal). The survival hope of small traditional steel manufacturers was to sell specialized products. A small company could market specialty products aggressively and quickly adapt to customer needs. Complex process settings and operating conditions had to be rapidly changed for each customer's order—a difficult feat for the titans.

Englander Steel employed 2,900 people, made 400,000 tons of steel a year (about 1 percent of Arcelor's output), and was 180 years old. For 160 of those years, a functional structure worked fine. As the environment became more turbulent and competitive, however, Englander Steel managers realized they were not keeping up. Fifty percent of Englander's orders were behind schedule. Profits were eroded by labor, material, and energy cost increases. Market share declined.

In consultation with outside experts, the president of Englander Steel saw that the company had to walk a tightrope. It had to specialize in a few high-value-added products tailored for separate markets, while maintaining economies of scale and sophisticated technology within functional departments. The dual pressure led to an unusual solution for a steel company: a matrix structure.

Englander Steel had four product lines: open-die forgings, ring-mill products, wheels and axles, and sheet steel. A business manager was given responsibility for and authority over each line, which included preparing a business plan and developing targets for production costs, product inventory, shipping dates, and gross profit. The managers were given authority to meet those targets and to make their lines profitable. Functional vice presidents were responsible for technical decisions. Functional managers were expected to stay abreast of the latest techniques in their areas and to keep personnel trained in new technologies that could apply to product lines. With 20,000 recipes for specialty steels and several hundred new recipes ordered each month, functional personnel had to stay current. Two functional departments—field sales and industrial relations—were not included in the matrix because they worked independently. The final design was a hybrid matrix structure with both matrix and functional relationships, as illustrated in Exhibit 2.14.

Implementation of the matrix was slow. Middle managers were confused. Meetings to coordinate orders across functional departments seemed to be held every day. After about a year of training by external consultants, Englander Steel was on track. Ninety percent of the orders were now delivered on time and market share recovered. Both productivity and profitability increased steadily. The managers thrived on matrix involvement. Meetings to coordinate product and functional decisions provided a growth experience. Middle managers began including younger managers in the matrix discussions as training for future management responsibility.[61]

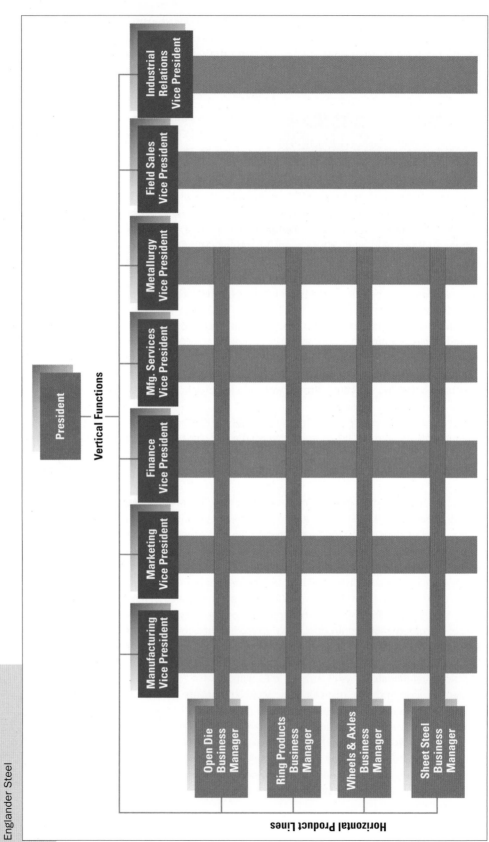

EXHIBIT 2.14
Matrix Structure for Englander Steel

President

Vertical Functions

Manufacturing Vice President

Marketing Vice President

Finance Vice President

Mfg. Services Vice President

Metallurgy Vice President

Field Sales Vice President

Industrial Relations Vice President

Horizontal Product Lines

Open Die Business Manager

Ring Products Business Manager

Wheels & Axles Business Manager

Sheet Steel Business Manager

This example illustrates the correct use of a matrix structure. The dual pressure to maintain economies of scale and to market four product lines gave equal emphasis to the functional and product hierarchies. Through continuous meetings for coordination, Englander Steel achieved both economies of scale and flexibility.

Horizontal Structure

A recent approach to organizing is the **horizontal structure**, which organizes employees around core processes. Organizations typically shift toward a horizontal structure during a procedure called reengineering. **Reengineering**, or *business process reengineering*, basically means the redesign of a vertical organization along its horizontal workflows and processes. A **process** refers to an organized group of related tasks and activities that work together to transform inputs into outputs that create value for customers.[62] Examples of processes include order fulfillment, new product development, and customer service. Reengineering changes the way managers think about how work is done. Rather than focusing on narrow jobs structured into distinct functional departments, they emphasize core processes that cut horizontally across the organization and involve teams of employees working together to serve customers.

A good illustration of process is provided by claims handling at Progressive Casualty Insurance Company. In the past, a customer would report an accident to an agent, who would pass the information to a customer service representative, who, in turn, would pass it to a claims manager. The claims manager would batch the claim with others from the same territory and assign it to an adjuster, who would schedule a time to inspect the vehicle damage. Today, adjusters are organized into teams that handle the entire claims process from beginning to end. One member handles claimant calls to the office while others are stationed in the field. When an adjuster takes a call, he or she does whatever is possible over the phone. If an inspection is needed, the adjuster contacts a team member in the field and schedules an appointment immediately. Progressive now measures the time from call to inspection in hours rather than the 7 to 10 days it once took.[63]

When a company is reengineered to a horizontal structure, all employees throughout the organization who work on a particular process (such as claims handling or order fulfillment) have easy access to one another so they can communicate and coordinate their efforts. The horizontal structure virtually eliminates both the vertical hierarchy and old departmental boundaries. This structural approach is largely a response to the profound changes that have occurred in the workplace and the business environment over the past 15 to 20 years. Technological progress emphasizes computer- and Internet-based integration and coordination. Customers expect faster and better service, and employees want opportunities to use their minds, learn new skills, and assume greater responsibility. Organizations mired in a vertical mindset have a hard time meeting these challenges. Thus, numerous organizations have experimented with horizontal mechanisms such as cross-functional teams to achieve coordination across departments or task forces to accomplish temporary projects. Increasingly, organizations are shifting away from hierarchical, function-based structures to structures based on horizontal processes.

BRIEFCASE

As an organization manager, keep these guidelines in mind:

Consider a horizontal structure when customer needs and demands change rapidly and when learning and innovation are critical to organizational success. Carefully determine core processes and train managers and employees to work within the horizontal structure.

Characteristics

An illustration of a company reengineered into a horizontal structure appears in Exhibit 2.15. Such an organization has the following characteristics:[64]

- Structure is created around cross-functional core processes rather than tasks, functions, or geography. Thus, boundaries between departments are obliterated. Ford Motor Company's Customer Service Division, for example, has core process groups for business development, parts supply and logistics, vehicle service and programs, and technical support.
- Self-directed teams, not individuals, are the basis of organizational design and performance. Schwa, a restaurant in Chicago that serves elaborate multi-course meals, is run by a team. Members rotate jobs so that everyone is sometimes a chef, sometimes a dishwasher, sometimes a waiter, or sometimes the person who answers the phone, takes reservations, or greets customers at the door.[65]
- Process owners have responsibility for each core process in its entirety. For Ford's parts supply and logistics process, for example, a number of teams may work on jobs such as parts analysis, purchasing, material flow, and distribution, but a process owner is responsible for coordinating the entire process.
- People on the team are given the skills, tools, motivation, and authority to make decisions central to the team's performance. Team members are cross-trained to perform one another's jobs, and the combined skills are sufficient to complete a major organizational task.

EXHIBIT 2.15
A Horizontal Structure

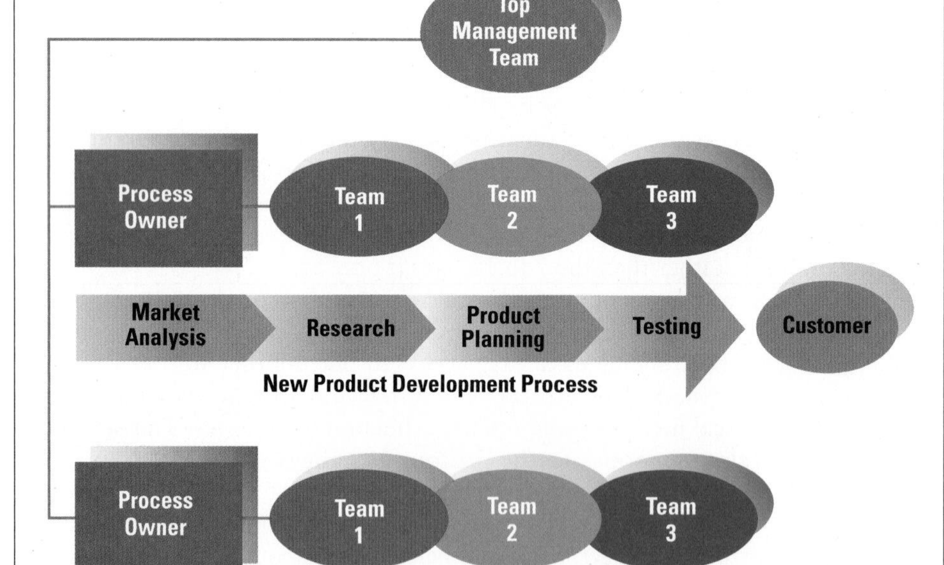

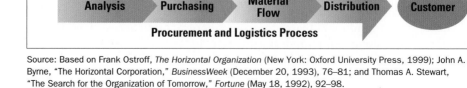

Source: Based on Frank Ostroff, *The Horizontal Organization* (New York: Oxford University Press, 1999); John A. Byrne, "The Horizontal Corporation," *BusinessWeek* (December 20, 1993), 76–81; and Thomas A. Stewart, "The Search for the Organization of Tomorrow," *Fortune* (May 18, 1992), 92–98.

- Teams have the freedom to think creatively and respond flexibly to new challenges that arise.
- Customers drive the horizontal corporation. Effectiveness is measured by end-of-process performance objectives (based on the goal of bringing value to the customer), as well as customer satisfaction, employee satisfaction, and financial contribution.
- The culture is one of openness, trust, and collaboration, focused on continuous improvement. The culture values employee empowerment, responsibility, and well-being.

General Electric's Salisbury, North Carolina, plant shifted to a horizontal structure to improve flexibility and customer service.

IN PRACTICE

GE Salisbury

General Electric's plant in Salisbury, North Carolina, which manufactures electrical lighting panel boards for industrial and commercial purposes, used to be organized functionally and vertically. Because no two GE customers have identical needs, each panel board has to be configured and built to order, which frequently created bottlenecks in the standard production process. In the mid-1980s, faced with high product-line costs, inconsistent customer service, and a declining market share, managers began exploring new ways of organizing that would emphasize teamwork, responsibility, continuous improvement, empowerment, and commitment to the customer.

By the early 1990s, GE Salisbury had made the transition to a horizontal structure that links sets of multi-skilled teams who are responsible for the entire build-to-order process. The new structure is based on the goal of producing lighting panel boards "of the highest possible quality, in the shortest possible cycle time, at a competitive price, with the best possible service." The process consists of four linked teams, each made up of 10 to 15 members representing a range of skills and functions. A production-control team serves as process owner (as illustrated earlier in Exhibit 2.15) and is responsible for order receipt, planning, coordination of production, purchasing, working with suppliers and customers, tracking inventory, and keeping all the teams focused on meeting objectives. The fabrication team cuts, builds, welds, and paints the various parts that make up the steel box that will house the electrical components panel, which is assembled and tested by the electrical components team. The electrical components team also handles shipping. A maintenance team takes care of heavy equipment maintenance that cannot be performed as part of the regular production process. Managers have become *associate advisors* who serve as guides and coaches and bring their expertise to the teams as needed.

The key to success of the horizontal structure is that all the operating teams work in concert with each other and have access to the information they need to meet team and process goals. Teams are given information about sales, backlogs, inventory, staffing needs, productivity, costs, quality, and other data, and each team regularly shares information about its part of the build-to-order process with the other teams. Joint production meetings, job rotation, and cross-training of employees are some of the mechanisms that help ensure smooth integration. The linked teams assume responsibility for setting their own production targets, determining production schedules, assigning duties, and identifying and solving problems.

Productivity and performance have dramatically improved with the horizontal structure. Bottlenecks in the workflow, which once wreaked havoc with production schedules, have been virtually eliminated. A six-week lead time has been cut to two-and-a-half days. More subtle but just as important are the increases in employee and customer satisfaction that GE Salisbury has realized since implementing its new structure.[66]

Strengths and Weaknesses

As with all structures, the horizontal structure has both strengths and weaknesses, as listed in Exhibit 2.16.

The most significant strength of the horizontal structure is enhanced coordination, which can dramatically increase the company's flexibility and response to changes in customer needs. The structure directs everyone's attention toward the customer, which leads to greater customer satisfaction as well as improvements in productivity, speed, and efficiency. In addition, because there are no boundaries between functional departments, employees take a broader view of organizational goals rather than being focused on the goals of a single department. The horizontal structure promotes an emphasis on teamwork and cooperation so that team members share a commitment to meeting common objectives. Finally, the horizontal structure can improve the quality of life for employees by giving them opportunities to share responsibility, make decisions, and contribute significantly to the organization.

A weakness of the horizontal structure is that it can harm rather than help organizational performance unless managers carefully determine which core processes are critical for bringing value to customers. Simply defining the processes around which to organize can be difficult. In addition, shifting to a horizontal structure is complicated and time consuming because it requires significant changes in culture, job design, management philosophy, and information and reward systems. Traditional managers may balk when they have to give up power and authority to serve instead as coaches and facilitators of teams. Employees have to be trained to work effectively in a team environment. Finally, because of the cross-functional nature of work, a horizontal structure can limit in-depth knowledge and skill development unless measures

EXHIBIT 2.16
Strengths and Weaknesses of Horizontal Structure

Strengths	Weaknesses
1. Promotes flexibility and rapid response to changes in customer needs	1. Determining core processes is difficult and time consuming
2. Directs the attention of everyone toward the production and delivery of value to the customer	2. Requires changes in culture, job design, management philosophy, and information and reward systems
3. Each employee has a broader view of organizational goals	3. Traditional managers may balk when they have to give up power and authority
4. Promotes a focus on teamwork and collaboration	4. Requires significant training of employees to work effectively in a horizontal team environment
5. Improves quality of life for employees by offering them the opportunity to share responsibility, make decisions, and be accountable for outcomes	5. Can limit in-depth skill development

Sources: Based on Frank Ostroff, *The Horizontal Organization: What the Organization of the Future Looks Like and How It Delivers Value to Customers* (New York: Oxford University Press, 1999); and Richard L. Daft, *Organization Theory and Design*, 6th ed. (Cincinnati, Ohio: South-Western, 1998), 253.

are taken to give employees opportunities to maintain and build technical expertise.

Virtual Networks and Outsourcing

Recent developments in organization design extend the concept of horizontal coordination and collaboration beyond the boundaries of the traditional organization. The most widespread design trend in recent years has been the outsourcing of various parts of the organization to outside partners.[67] **Outsourcing** means to contract out certain tasks or functions, such as manufacturing, human resources, or credit processing, to other companies.

All sorts of organizations are jumping on the outsourcing bandwagon. The City of Manwood, California, decided to outsource everything from parking enforcement to street maintenance to policing and public safety. The budget for the police department used to be nearly $8 million. Now the city pays about half that to the Los Angeles County Sheriff's Department, and residents say service has improved.[68] The U.S. military is also increasingly using private military company contractors to handle just about everything except the core activity of fighting battles and securing defensive positions. Kellogg Brown & Root, a subsidiary of the Halliburton Corporation, for instance, builds and maintains military bases and provides catering and cleaning services. In the business world, Hitachi once made all its own televisions with Hitachi-made components, but the company now outsources manufacturing and gets key components from outside suppliers. Wachovia Corporation transferred administration of its human resources programs to Hewitt Associates, and British food retailer J. Sainsbury's lets Accenture handle its entire information technology department. About 20 percent of drug manufacturer Eli Lilly & Company's chemistry work is done in China by start-up labs such as Chem-Explorer; and companies such as India's Wipro, France's S.R. Teleperformance, and the U.S.-based Convergys manage call center and technical support operations for big computer and cell phone companies around the world.[69] The pharmaceuticals company Pfizer is using an innovative approach that lets some employees pass off certain parts of their jobs to an outsourcing firm in India with a click of a button. Rather than shifting entire functions to contractors, this "personal outsourcing" approach allows people to shift only certain tedious and time-consuming tasks to be handled by the outsourcing partner while they focus on higher-value work.[70]

BRIEFCASE

As an organization manager, keep these guidelines in mind:

Use a virtual network structure for extreme flexibility and rapid response to changing market conditions. Focus on key activities that give the organization its competitive advantage and outsource other activities to carefully selected partners.

Once, a company's units of operation "were either within the organization and 'densely connected' or they were outside the organization and not connected at all," as one observer phrased it.[71] Today, the lines are so blurred that it can be difficult to tell what is part of the organization and what is not. IBM handles back-office operations for many large companies, but it also outsources some of its own activities to other firms, which in turn may farm out some of their functions to still other organizations.[72]

A few organizations carry outsourcing to the extreme to create a virtual network structure. With a **virtual network structure**, sometimes called a *modular structure*, the firm subcontracts most of its major functions or processes to separate companies and coordinates their activities from a small headquarters organization.[73]

How the Structure Works

The virtual network organization may be viewed as a central hub surrounded by a network of outside specialists. For example, Philip Rosedale runs LoveMachine from his home and coffee shops around San Francisco. LoveMachine makes software that lets employees send Twitter-like messages to say "Thank you," or "Great job!" When the message is sent, everyone in the company gets a copy, which builds morale, and the basic software is free to companies that want to use it. LoveMachine has no full time development staff, but instead works with a network of freelancers who bid on jobs such as creating new features, fixing glitches, and so forth. Rosedale also contracts out payroll and other administrative tasks.[74]

With a network structure, rather than being housed under one roof or located within one organization, services such as accounting, design, manufacturing, marketing, and distribution are outsourced to separate companies or individuals that are connected electronically to a central office. Organizational partners located in different parts of the world may use networked computers or the Internet to exchange data and information so rapidly and smoothly that a loosely connected network of suppliers, manufacturers, and distributors can look and act like one seamless company. The virtual network form incorporates a free-market style to replace the traditional vertical hierarchy. Subcontractors may flow into and out of the system as needed to meet changing needs.

With a network structure, the hub maintains control over processes in which it has world-class or difficult-to-imitate capabilities and then transfers other activities—along with the decision making and control over them—to other organizations. These partner organizations organize and accomplish their work using their own ideas, assets, and tools.[75] The idea is that a firm can concentrate on what it does best and contract out everything else to companies with distinctive competence in those specific areas, enabling the organization to do more with less.[76] The "heart-healthy" food company Smart Balance was able to innovate and expand rapidly by using a virtual network approach.

Smart Balance

IN PRACTICE

Smart Balance has about 67 employees, but nearly 400 people work for the company. Smart Balance started by making a buttery spread and now has a line of spreads, all-natural peanut butter, nutrient-enhanced milk, cheese, sour cream, popcorn, and other products. Managers credit the virtual network approach for helping the company innovate and expand rapidly.

Smart Balance keeps product development and marketing in-house but uses contractors to do just about everything else, including manufacturing, distribution, sales, information technology services, and research and testing. The way the company got into the milk business shows how the network structure increases speed and flexibility. Peter Dray, vice president of product development, was able to get the help he needed to perfect the product from contractors. Outside scientists and research and development consultants worked on the formula. The company contracted with a dairy processor to do tests and trial production runs. An outside laboratory assessed nutritional claims and another company managed consumer taste tests.

Each morning, full-time employees and virtual workers exchange a flurry of e-mail messages and phone calls to update each other on what took place the day before and what needs to happen today. Executives spend much of their time managing relationships. Twice a year they hold all-company meetings that include permanent staff and contractors. Information is shared widely, and managers make a point of recognizing the contributions of contractors to the company's success, which helps create a sense of unity and commitment.[77]

With a network structure such as that used at Smart Balance, it is difficult to answer the question "Where is the organization?" in traditional terms. The different organizational parts are drawn together contractually and coordinated electronically, creating a new form of organization. Much like building blocks, parts of the network can be added or taken away to meet changing needs.[78] Exhibit 2.17 illustrates a simplified network structure for Smart Balance, showing some of the functions that are outsourced to other companies.

Strengths and Weaknesses

Exhibit 2.18 summarizes the strengths and weaknesses of the virtual network structure.[79] One of the major strengths is that the organization, no matter how small, can be truly global, drawing on resources worldwide to achieve the best quality and price and then selling products or services worldwide just as easily through subcontractors. The network structure also enables a new or small company to develop products or services and get them to market rapidly without huge investments in factories, equipment, warehouses, or distribution facilities. The ability to arrange and rearrange resources to meet changing needs and best serve customers gives the network structure extreme flexibility and rapid response. New technologies can be developed quickly by tapping into a worldwide network of experts. The organization can continually redefine itself to meet changing product or market opportunities. A final strength is reduced administrative overhead. Large teams of staff specialists and administrators are not needed. Managerial and technical talent can be focused on key activities that provide competitive advantage while other activities are outsourced.

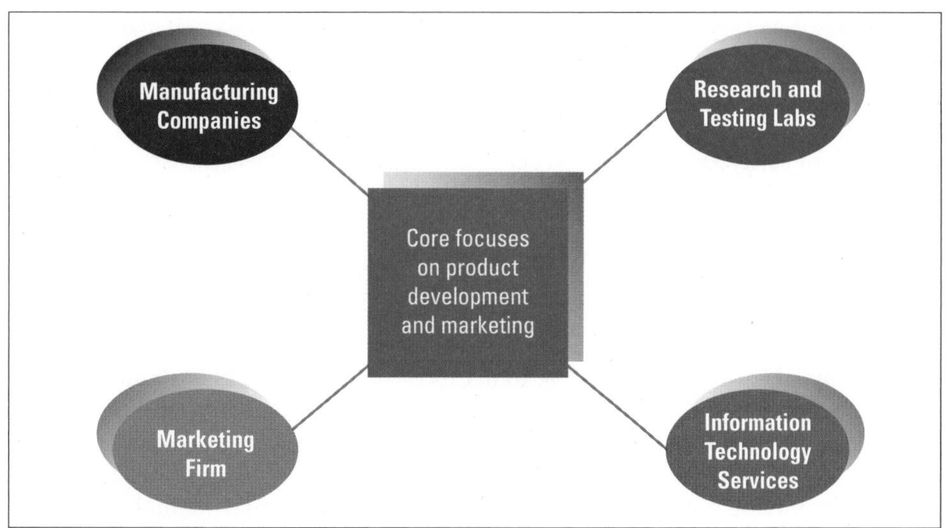

EXHIBIT 2.17
Example of a Virtual Network Structure

EXHIBIT 2.18
Strengths and Weaknesses of Virtual Network Structure

Strengths	Weaknesses
1. Enables even small organizations to obtain talent and resources worldwide	1. Managers do not have hands-on control over many activities and employees
2. Gives a company immediate scale and reach without huge investments in factories, equipment, or distribution facilities	2. Requires a great deal of time to manage relationships and potential conflicts with contract partners
3. Enables the organization to be highly flexible and responsive to changing needs	3. There is a risk of organizational failure if a partner fails to deliver or goes out of business
4. Reduces administrative overhead costs	4. Employee loyalty and corporate culture might be weak because employees feel they can be replaced by contract services

Sources: Based on R.E. Miles and C.C. Snow, "The New Network Firm: A Spherical Structure Built on a Human Investment Philosophy," *Organizational Dynamics* (Spring 1995), 5–18; Gregory G. Dess, Abdul M. A. Rasheed, Kevin J. McLaughlin, and Richard L. Priem, "The New Corporate Architecture," *Academy of Management Executive* 9, no. 3 (1995), 7–20; N. Anand and R.L. Daft, "What Is the Right Organization Design?" *Organizational Dynamics* 36, no. 4 (2007), 329–344; and H.W. Chesbrough and D.J. Teece, "Organizing for Innovation: When Is Virtual Virtuous?" *Harvard Business Review* (August 2002), 127–134.

The virtual network structure also has a number of weaknesses. The primary weakness is a lack of control. The network structure takes decentralization to the extreme. Managers do not have all operations under their jurisdiction and must rely on contracts, coordination, and negotiation to hold things together. This also means increased time spent managing relationships with partners and resolving conflicts.

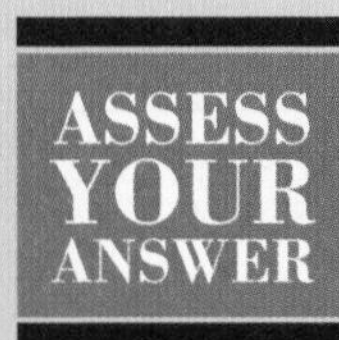

3 Top managers are smart to maintain organizational control over the activities of key work units rather than contracting out some work unit tasks to other firms.

ANSWER: *Disagree.* Virtual networks and outsourcing forms of organization design have become popular because they offer increased flexibility and more rapid response in a fast-changing environment. Outsourced departments can be added or dropped as conditions change. Keeping control over all activities in-house might be more comfortable for some managers, but it discourages flexibility.

A problem of equal importance is the risk of failure if one organizational partner fails to deliver, has a plant burn down, or goes out of business. Managers in the headquarters organization have to act quickly to spot problems and find new arrangements. Finally, from a human resource perspective, employee loyalty can be weak in a network organization because of concerns over job security. Employees may feel that they can be replaced by contract services. In addition, it is more difficult to develop a cohesive corporate culture. Turnover may be higher because emotional commitment between the organization and employees is low. With changing products, markets, and partners, the organization may need to reshuffle employees at any time to get the correct mix of skills and capabilities.

Hybrid Structure

As a practical matter, many structures in the real world do not exist in the pure forms we have outlined in this chapter. Most large organizations, in particular, often use a **hybrid structure** that combines characteristics of various approaches tailored to specific strategic needs. Most companies combine characteristics of functional, divisional, geographic, horizontal, or network structures to take advantage of the strengths of various structures and avoid some of the weaknesses. Hybrid structures tend to be used in rapidly changing environments because they offer the organization greater flexibility.

One type of hybrid that is often used is to combine characteristics of the functional and divisional structures. When a corporation grows large and has several products or markets, it typically is organized into self-contained divisions of some type. Functions that are important to each product or market are decentralized to the self-contained units. However, some functions that are relatively stable and require economies of scale and in-depth specialization are also centralized at headquarters. For example, Starbucks has a number of geographic divisions, but functions such as marketing, legal, and supply chain operations are centralized.[80] Sun Petroleum Products Corporation (SPPC) reorganized to a hybrid structure to be more responsive to changing markets. The hybrid organization structure adopted by SPPC is illustrated in part 1 of Exhibit 2.19. Three major product divisions—fuels, lubricants, and chemicals—were created, each serving a different market and requiring a different strategy and management style. Each product-line vice president is now in charge of all functions for that product, such as marketing, planning, supply and distribution, and manufacturing. However, activities such as human resources, legal, technology, and finance were centralized as functional departments at headquarters in order to achieve economies of scale. Each of these departments provides services for the entire organization.[81]

A second hybrid approach that is increasingly used today is to combine characteristics of functional, divisional, and horizontal structures. Ford Motor Company's Customer Service Division, a global operation made up of 12,000 employees serving nearly 15,000 dealers, provides an example of this type of hybrid. Beginning in 1995, when Ford launched its "Ford 2000" initiative aimed at becoming the world's leading automotive firm in the twenty-first century, top executives grew increasingly concerned about complaints regarding customer service. They decided that the horizontal model offered the best chance to gain a faster, more efficient, integrated approach to customer service. Part 2 of Exhibit 2.19 illustrates a portion of the Customer Service Division's hybrid structure. Several horizontally aligned groups, made up of multi-skilled teams, focus on core processes such as parts supply and logistics (acquiring parts and getting them to dealers quickly and efficiently), vehicle service and programs (collecting and disseminating information about repair problems), and technical support (ensuring that every service department receives

BRIEFCASE

As an organization manager, keep these guidelines in mind:

Implement hybrid structures, when needed, to combine characteristics of functional, divisional, and horizontal structures. Use a hybrid structure in complex environments to take advantage of the strengths of various structural characteristics and avoid some of the weaknesses.

EXHIBIT 2.19
Two Hybrid Structures

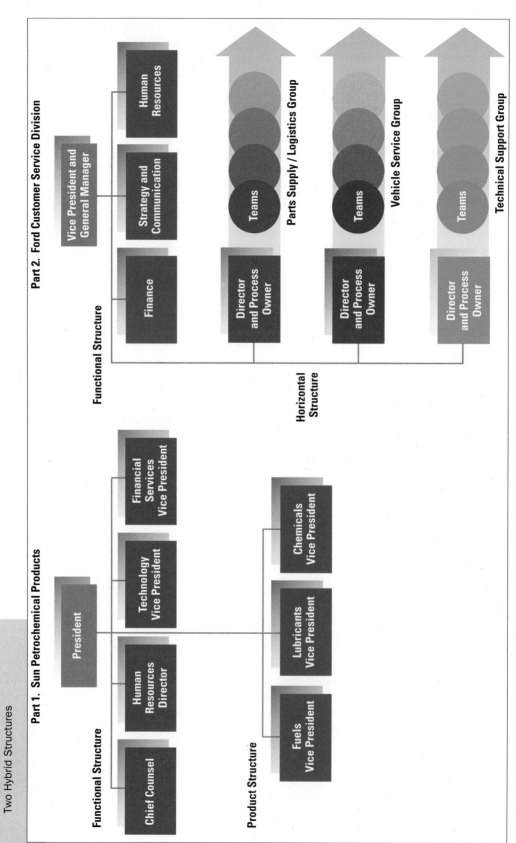

Part 1. Sun Petrochemical Products

President

Functional Structure

Chief Counsel
Human Resources Director
Technology Vice President
Financial Services Vice President

Product Structure

Fuels Vice President
Lubricants Vice President
Chemicals Vice President

Part 2. Ford Customer Service Division

Vice President and General Manager

Functional Structure

Finance
Strategy and Communication
Human Resources

Horizontal Structure

Director and Process Owner
Teams
Parts Supply / Logistics Group

Director and Process Owner
Teams
Vehicle Service Group

Director and Process Owner
Teams
Technical Support Group

Source: Based on Linda S. Ackerman, "Transition Management: An In-Depth Look at Managing Complex Change," *Organizational Dynamics* (Summer 1982), 46–66; and Frank Ostroff, *The Horizontal Organization* (New York: Oxford University Press, 1999), Figure 2.1, p.34.

updated technical information). Each group has a process owner who is responsible for seeing that the teams meet overall objectives. Ford's Customer Service Division retained a functional structure for its finance, strategy and communications, and human resources departments. Each of these departments provides services for the entire division.[82]

In a huge organization such as Ford, managers may use a variety of structural characteristics to meet the needs of the total organization. Like many large organizations, for example, Ford also outsources some of its activities to other firms. A hybrid structure is often preferred over the pure functional, divisional, horizontal, or virtual network structure because it can provide some of the advantages of each and overcome some of the disadvantages.

Applications of Structural Design

Each type of structure is applied in different situations and meets different needs. In describing the various structures, we touched briefly on conditions such as environmental stability or change and organizational size that are related to structure. Each form of structure—functional, divisional, matrix, horizontal, network, hybrid—represents a tool that can help managers make an organization more effective, depending on the demands of its situation.

Structural Alignment

Ultimately, the most important decision that managers make about structural design is to find the right balance between vertical control and horizontal coordination, depending on the needs of the organization. Vertical control is associated with goals of efficiency and stability, while horizontal coordination is associated with learning, innovation, and flexibility. Exhibit 2.20 shows a simplified continuum that illustrates how structural approaches are associated with vertical control versus horizontal coordination. The functional structure is appropriate when the organization needs to be coordinated through the vertical hierarchy and when efficiency is important for meeting organizational goals. The functional structure uses task specialization and a strict chain of command to gain efficient use of scarce resources, but it does not enable the organization to be flexible or innovative. At the opposite end of the scale, the horizontal structure is appropriate when the organization has a high need for coordination among functions to achieve innovation and promote learning. The horizontal structure enables organizations to differentiate themselves and respond quickly to changes, but at the expense of efficient resource use. The virtual network structure offers even greater flexibility and potential for rapid response by allowing the organization to add or subtract pieces as needed to adapt and meet changing needs from the environment and marketplace. Exhibit 2.20 also shows how other types of structure defined in this chapter—functional with horizontal linkages, divisional, and matrix—represent intermediate steps on the organization's path to efficiency or innovation and learning. The exhibit does not include all possible structures, but it illustrates how organizations attempt to balance the needs for efficiency and vertical control with innovation and horizontal coordination. In addition, as described in the chapter, many organizations use a hybrid structure to combine characteristics of various structural types.

BRIEFCASE

As an organization manager, keep these guidelines in mind:

Find the correct balance between vertical control and horizontal coordination to meet the needs of the organization. Consider a structural reorganization when symptoms of structural deficiency are observed.

EXHIBIT 2.20
Relationship of Structure to Organization's Need for Efficiency versus Learning

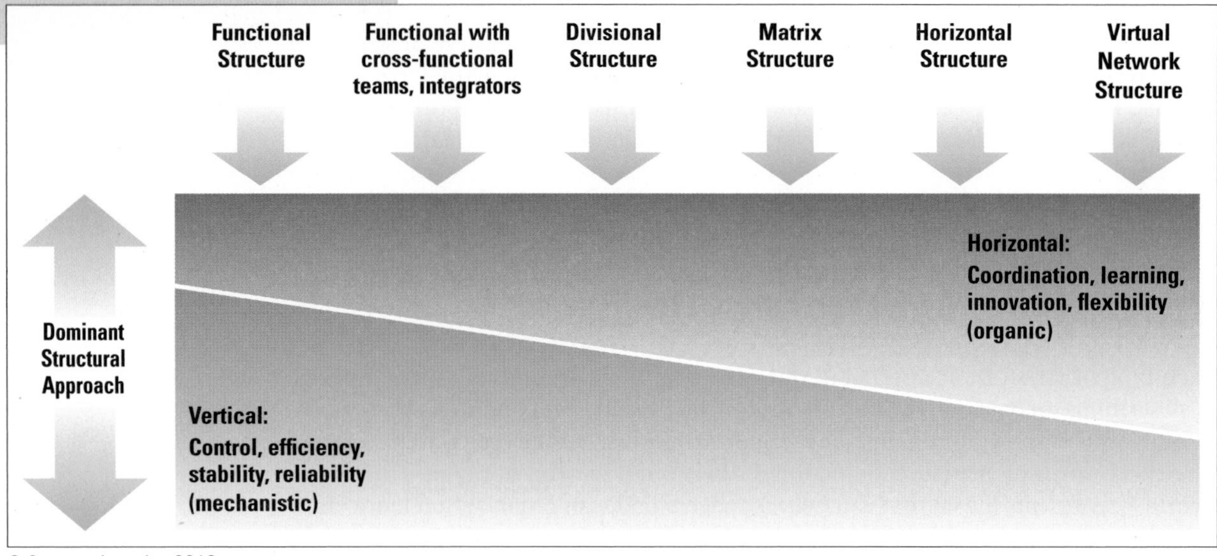

Symptoms of Structural Deficiency

Top executives periodically evaluate organization structure to determine whether it is appropriate to changing needs. Managers try to achieve the best fit between internal reporting relationships and the needs of the external environment. As a general rule, when organization structure is out of alignment with organization needs, one or more of the following **symptoms of structural deficiency** appear.[83]

- *Decision making is delayed or lacking in quality.* Decision makers may be overloaded because the hierarchy funnels too many problems and decisions to them. Delegation to lower levels may be insufficient. Another cause of poor-quality decisions is that information may not reach the correct people. Information linkages in either the vertical or horizontal direction may be inadequate to ensure decision quality.
- *The organization does not respond innovatively to a changing environment.* One reason for lack of innovation is that departments are not coordinated horizontally. The identification of customer needs by the marketing department and the identification of technological developments in the research department must be coordinated. Organization structure also has to specify departmental responsibilities that include environmental scanning and innovation.
- *Employee performance declines and goals are not being met.* Employee performance may decline because the structure doesn't provide clear goals, responsibilities, and mechanisms for coordination. The structure should reflect the complexity of the market environment yet be straightforward enough for employees to effectively work within.

- *Too much conflict is evident.* Organization structure should allow conflicting departmental goals to combine into a single set of goals for the entire organization. When departments act at cross-purposes or are under pressure to achieve departmental goals at the expense of organizational goals, the structure is often at fault. Horizontal linkage mechanisms are not adequate.

Design Essentials

- Organization structure must accomplish two things for the organization. It must provide a framework of responsibilities, reporting relationships, and groupings, and it must provide mechanisms for linking and coordinating organizational elements into a coherent whole. The structure is reflected on the organization chart. Linking the organization into a coherent whole requires the use of information systems and linkage devices in addition to the organization chart.
- Organization structure can be designed to provide vertical and horizontal information linkages based on the information processing required to meet the organization's overall goal. Managers can choose whether to orient toward a traditional organization designed for efficiency, which emphasizes vertical linkages such as hierarchy, rules and plans, and formal information systems (a mechanistic design), or toward a contemporary organization designed for learning and adaptation, which emphasizes horizontal communication and coordination (an organic design). Vertical linkages are not sufficient for most organizations today. Organizations provide horizontal linkages through cross-functional information systems, liaison roles, temporary task forces, full-time integrators, and teams, and by creating the conditions to enable relational coordination.
- Alternatives for grouping employees and departments into overall structural design include functional grouping, divisional grouping, multi-focused grouping, horizontal grouping, and virtual network grouping. The choice among functional, divisional, and horizontal structures determines where coordination and integration will be greatest. With functional and divisional structures, managers also use horizontal linkage mechanisms to complement the vertical dimension and achieve integration of departments and levels into an organizational whole. With a horizontal structure, activities are organized horizontally around core work processes.
- A virtual network structure extends the concept of horizontal coordination and collaboration beyond the boundaries of the organization. Core activities are performed by a central hub while other functions and activities are outsourced to contract partners.
- The matrix structure attempts to achieve an equal balance between the vertical and horizontal dimensions of structure. Most organizations do not exist in these pure forms, using instead hybrid structures that incorporate characteristics of two or more types of structure.
- Ultimately, managers attempt to find the correct balance between vertical control and horizontal coordination. Signs of structural misalignment include delayed decision making, lack of innovation, poor employee performance, and excessive conflict.

- Finally, an organization chart is only so many lines and boxes on a piece of paper. The purpose of the organization chart is to encourage and direct employees into activities and communications that enable the organization to achieve its goals. The organization chart provides the structure, but employees provide the behavior. The chart is a guideline to encourage people to work together, but management must implement the structure and carry it out.

Key Concepts

centralized
decentralized
departmental grouping
divisional grouping
divisional structure
functional grouping
functional matrix
functional structure
horizontal grouping
horizontal linkage
horizontal structure
hybrid structure
integrator
liaison role
matrix structure
multi-focused grouping
organization structure
outsourcing
process
product matrix
reengineering
relational coordination
symptoms of structural deficiency
task force
teams
vertical information system
vertical linkages
virtual network grouping
virtual network structure
virtual team

Discussion Questions

1. What is the definition of *organization structure?* Does organization structure appear on the organization chart? Explain.
2. When is a functional structure preferable to a divisional structure?
3. Large corporations tend to use hybrid structures. Why?
4. What are the primary differences in structure between a traditional, mechanistic organization designed for efficiency and a more contemporary, organic organization designed for learning?
5. What is the difference between a task force and a team? Between liaison role and integrating role? Which of these provides the greatest amount of horizontal coordination?
6. As a manager, how would you create an organization with a high degree of relational coordination?
7. What conditions usually have to be present before an organization should adopt a matrix structure?
8. The manager of a consumer products firm said, "We use the brand manager position to train future executives." Why do you think the brand manager position is considered a good training ground? Discuss.
9. Why do companies using a horizontal structure have cultures that emphasize openness, employee empowerment, and responsibility? What do you think a manager's job would be like in a horizontally organized company?
10. Describe the virtual network structure. What are the advantages and disadvantages of using this structure compared to performing all activities in-house within an organization?

Chapter 2 Workbook You and Organization Structure[84]

To better understand the importance of organization structure in your life, do the following assignment.

Select one of the following situations to organize:

- A copy and print shop
- A travel agency
- A sports rental (such as Jet Skis or snowmobiles) in a resort area
- A bakery

Background

Organization is a way of gaining some power against an unreliable environment. The environment provides the organization with inputs, which include raw materials, human resources, and financial resources. There is a service or product to produce that involves technology. The output goes to clients, a group that must be nurtured. The complexities of the environment and the technology determine the complexity of the organization.

Planning Your Organization

1. Write down the mission or purpose of the organization in a few sentences.
2. What are the specific tasks to be completed to accomplish the mission?
3. Based on the specifics in question 2, develop an organization chart. Each position in the chart will perform a specific task or is responsible for a certain outcome.
4. You are into your third year of operation, and your business has been very successful. You want to add a second location a few miles away. What issues will you face running the business at two locations? Draw an organization chart that includes the two business locations.
5. Five more years go by and the business has grown to five locations in two cities. How do you keep in touch with it all? What issues of control and coordination have arisen? Draw an up-to-date organization chart and explain your rationale for it.
6. Twenty years later you have 75 business locations in five states. What are the issues and problems that have to be dealt with through organizational structure? Draw an organization chart for this organization, indicating such factors as who is responsible for customer satisfaction, how you will know if customer needs are met, and how information will flow within the organization.

CASE FOR ANALYSIS C & C Grocery Stores, Inc.[85]

The first C & C Grocery store was started in 1947 by Doug Cummins and his brother Bob. Both were veterans who wanted to run their own business, so they used their savings to start the small grocery store in Charlotte, North Carolina. The store was immediately successful. The location was good, and Doug Cummins had a winning personality. Store employees adopted Doug's informal style and "serve the customer" attitude. C & C's increasing circle of customers enjoyed an abundance of good meats and produce.

By 1997, C & C had over 200 stores. A standard physical layout was used for new stores. Company headquarters moved from Charlotte to Atlanta in 1985. The organization chart for C & C is shown in Exhibit 2.21. The central offices in Atlanta handled personnel, merchandising, financial, purchasing, real estate, and legal affairs for the entire chain. For management of individual stores, the organization was divided by regions. The southern, southeastern, and northeastern regions each had about seventy stores. Each region was divided into five districts of ten to fifteen stores each. A district director was responsible for supervision and coordination of activities for the 10 to 15 district stores.

Each district was divided into four lines of authority based on functional specialty. Three of these lines reached into the stores. The produce department manager within each store reported directly to the produce specialist for the division, and the same was true for the meat department manager, who reported directly to the district meat specialist. The meat and produce managers were responsible for all activities associated with the acquisition and sale of perishable products. The store manager's responsibility included the grocery line, front-end departments, and store operations. The store manager was responsible for appearance of personnel, cleanliness, adequate checkout service, and price accuracy. A grocery manager reported to the store manager, maintained inventories, and restocked shelves for grocery items. The district merchandising office was responsible for promotional campaigns, advertising circulars, district advertising, and attracting customers into the stores. The grocery merchandisers were expected to coordinate their activities with each store in the district.

Business for the C & C chain has dropped off in all regions in recent years—partly because of a declining economy, but mostly because of increased competition from large discount retailers such as Walmart, Target, and Costco Wholesale. When these large discounters entered the grocery business, they brought a level of competition unlike any C & C had seen before. C & C had managed to hold its own against larger supermarket chains, but now even the big chains were threatened by Walmart, which became number 1 in grocery sales in 2001. C & C managers knew they couldn't compete on price, but they were considering ways they could use advanced information technology to improve service and customer satisfaction and distinguish the store from the large discounters.

However, the most pressing problem was how to improve business with the resources and stores they now had. A consulting team from a major university was hired to investigate store structure and operations. The consultants visited several stores in each region, talking to about 50 managers and employees. The consultants wrote a report that pinpointed four problem areas to be addressed by store executives.

1. *The chain was slow to adapt to change.* Store layout and structure were the same as had been designed fifteen years ago. Each store did things the same way,

EXHIBIT 2.21
Organization Structure for C & C Grocery Stores, Inc.

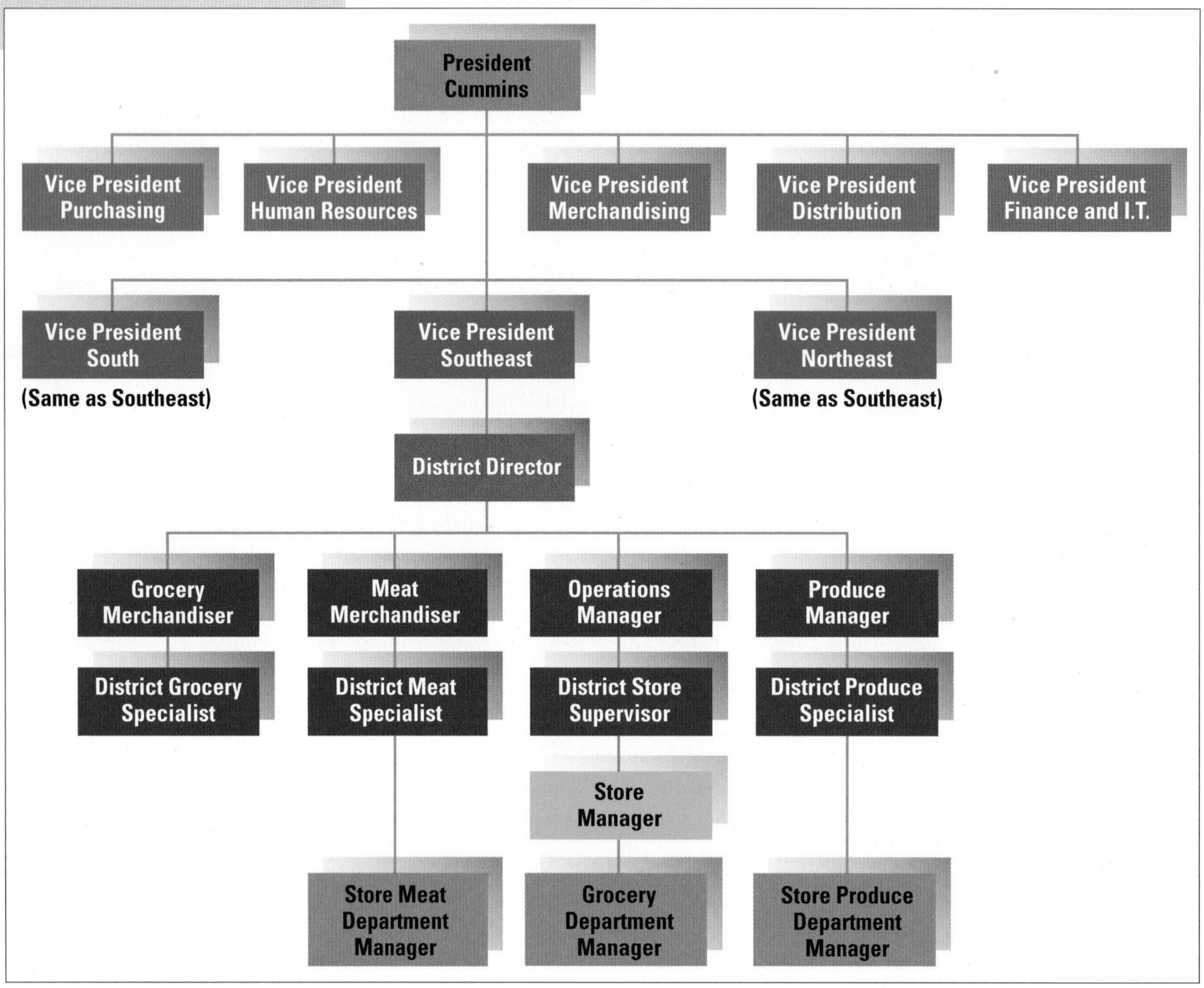

- President Cummins
  - Vice President Purchasing
  - Vice President Human Resources
  - Vice President Merchandising
  - Vice President Distribution
  - Vice President Finance and I.T.
  - Vice President South (Same as Southeast)
  - Vice President Southeast
    - District Director
      - Grocery Merchandiser
        - District Grocery Specialist
      - Meat Merchandiser
        - District Meat Specialist
          - Store Meat Department Manager
      - Operations Manager
        - District Store Supervisor
          - Store Manager
            - Grocery Department Manager
      - Produce Manager
        - District Produce Specialist
          - Store Produce Department Manager
  - Vice President Northeast (Same as Southeast)

even though some stores were in low-income areas and other stores in suburban areas. A new computerized supply chain management system for ordering and stocking had been developed, but after two years it was only partially implemented in the stores. Other proposed information technology (IT) initiatives were still "on the back burner," not yet even in the development stage.

2. *Roles of the district store supervisor and the store manager were causing dissatisfaction.* The store managers wanted to learn general management skills for potential promotion into district or regional management positions. However, their jobs restricted them to operational activities and they learned little about merchandising, meat, and produce. Moreover, district store supervisors used store visits to inspect for cleanliness and adherence to operating standards rather than to train the store manager and help coordinate operations with perishable departments. Close supervision on the operational details had become the focus of operations management rather than development, training, and coordination.
3. *Cooperation within stores was low and morale was poor. The informal, friendly atmosphere originally created by Doug Cummins was gone.* One example of this problem occurred when the grocery merchandiser and store manager in a Louisiana store decided to promote Coke and Diet Coke as a loss leader. Thousands of cartons of Coke were brought in for the sale,

but the stockroom was not prepared and did not have room. The store manager wanted to use floor area in the meat and produce sections to display Coke cartons, but those managers refused. The produce department manager said that Diet Coke did not help his sales and it was okay with him if there was no promotion at all.

4. *Long-term growth and development of the store chain would probably require reevaluation of long-term strategy.* The percent of market share going to traditional grocery stores was declining nationwide due to competition from large superstores and discount retailers. In the near future, C & C might need to introduce nonfood items into the stores for one-stop shopping, add specialty or gourmet sections within stores, and investigate how new technology could help distinguish the company, such as through targeted marketing and promotion, providing superior service and convenience, and offering their customers the best product assortment and availability.

To solve the first three problems, the consultants recommended reorganizing the district and the store structure as illustrated in Exhibit 2.22. Under this reorganization, the meat, grocery, and produce department managers would all report to the store manager. The store manager would have complete store control and would be responsible for coordination of all store activities. The district supervisor's role would be changed from supervision to training and development. The district supervisor would head a team that included himself and several meat, produce, and merchandise specialists who would visit area stores as a team to provide advice and help for the store managers and other employees. The team would act in a liaison capacity between district specialists and the stores.

EXHIBIT 2.22
Proposed Reorganization of C & C Grocery Stores, Inc.

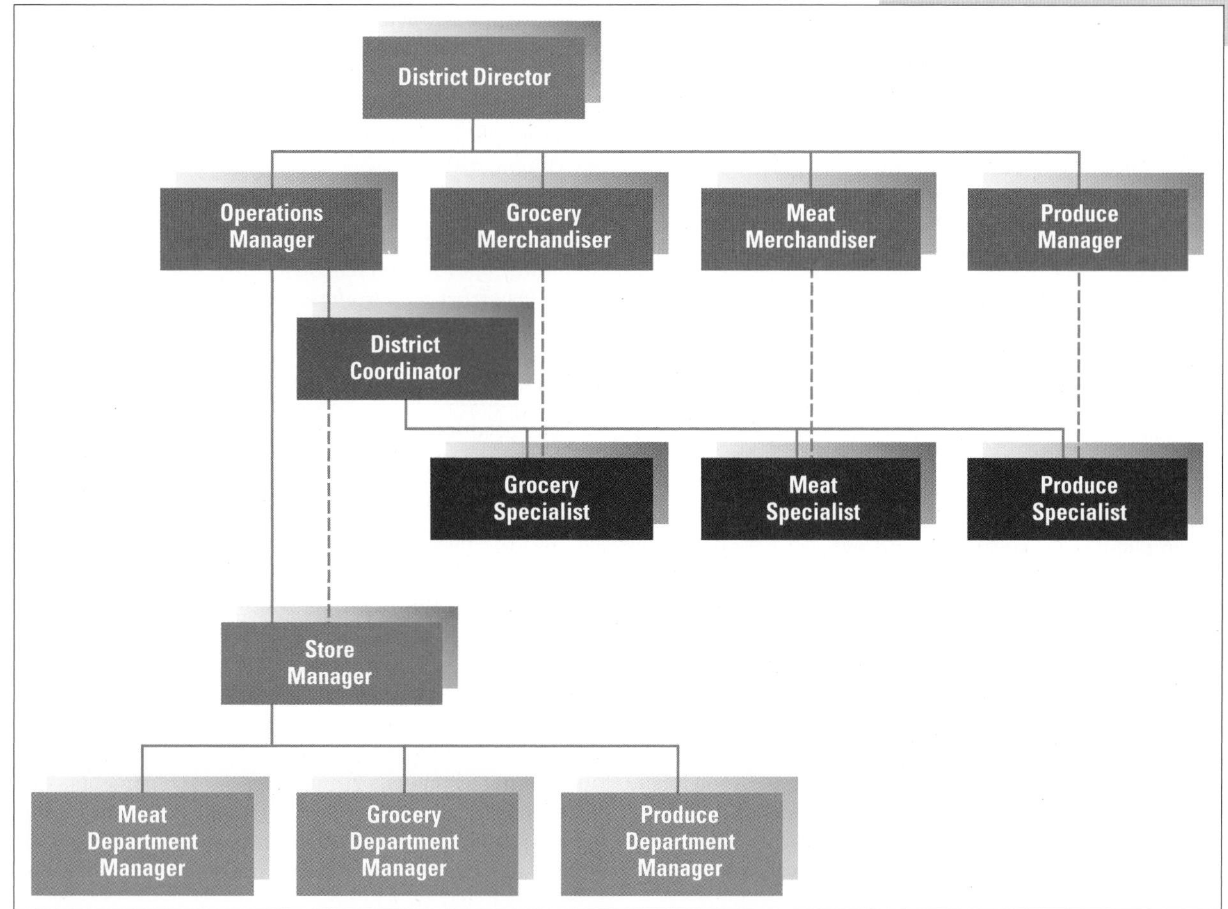

The consultants were enthusiastic about the proposed structure. With the removal of one level of district operational supervision, store managers would have more freedom and responsibility. The district liaison team would establish a cooperative team approach to management that could be adopted within stores. Focusing store responsibility on a single manager would encourage coordination within stores and adaptation to local conditions. It would also provide a focus of responsibility for storewide administrative changes.

The consultants also believed that the proposed structure could be expanded to accommodate non-grocery lines and gourmet units if these were included in C & C's future plans. Within each store, a new department manager could be added for pharmacy, gourmet/specialty items, or other major departments. The district team could be expanded to include specialists in these lines, as well as an information technology coordinator to act as liaison for stores in the district.

CASE FOR ANALYSIS Aquarius Advertising Agency[86]

The Aquarius Advertising Agency is a medium-sized firm that offered two basic services to its clients: customized plans for the content of an advertising campaign (for example, slogans and layouts) and complete plans for media (such as radio, TV, newspapers, billboards, and Internet). Additional services included aid in marketing and distribution of products and marketing research to test advertising effectiveness.

Its activities were organized in a traditional manner. The organization chart is shown in Exhibit 2.23. Each department included similar functions.

Each client account was coordinated by an account executive who acted as a liaison between the client and the various specialists on the professional staff of the operations and marketing divisions. The number of direct communications and contacts between clients and Aquarius specialists, clients and account executives, and Aquarius specialists and account executives is indicated in Exhibit 2.24. These sociometric data were gathered by a consultant who conducted a study of the patterns of formal and informal communication. Each intersecting cell of Aquarius personnel and the clients contains an index of the direct contacts between them.

Although an account executive was designated to be the liaison between the client and specialists within the agency, communications frequently occurred directly between clients and specialists and bypassed the account executive. These direct contacts involved a wide range of interactions, such as meetings, telephone calls, e-mail messages, and so on. A large number of direct communications occurred between agency specialists and their counterparts in the client organization. For example, an art specialist working as one member of a team on a particular client account would often be contacted directly by the client's in-house art specialist, and agency research personnel had direct communication with research personnel of the client firm. Also, some of the unstructured contacts often led to more formal meetings with clients in which agency personnel made presentations, interpreted and defended agency policy, and committed the agency to certain courses of action.

Both hierarchical and professional systems operated within the departments of the operations and marketing divisions. Each department was organized hierarchically with a director, an assistant director, and several levels of authority. Professional communications were widespread and mainly concerned with sharing knowledge and techniques, technical evaluation of work, and development of professional interests. Control in each department was exercised mainly through control of promotions and supervision of work done by subordinates. Many account executives, however, felt the need for more influence, and one commented:

Creativity and art. That's all I hear around here. It is hard as hell to effectively manage six or seven hotshots who claim they have to do their own thing. Each of them tries to sell his or her idea to the client, and most of the time I don't know what has happened until a week later. If I were a despot, I would make all of them check with me first to get approval. Things would sure change around here.

The need for reorganization was made more acute by changes in the environment. Within a short period of time, there was a rapid turnover in the major accounts handled by the agency. It was typical for advertising agencies to gain or lose clients quickly, often with no advance warning as consumer behavior and lifestyle changes emerged and product innovations occurred.

An agency reorganization was one solution proposed by top management to increase flexibility in this unpredictable environment. The reorganization would be aimed at reducing the agency's response time to environmental changes and at increasing cooperation and communication among specialists from different departments. The top managers are not sure what type of reorganization is appropriate. They would like your help analyzing their context and current structure and welcome your advice on proposing a new structure.

EXHIBIT 2.23
Aquarius Advertising Agency Organization Chart

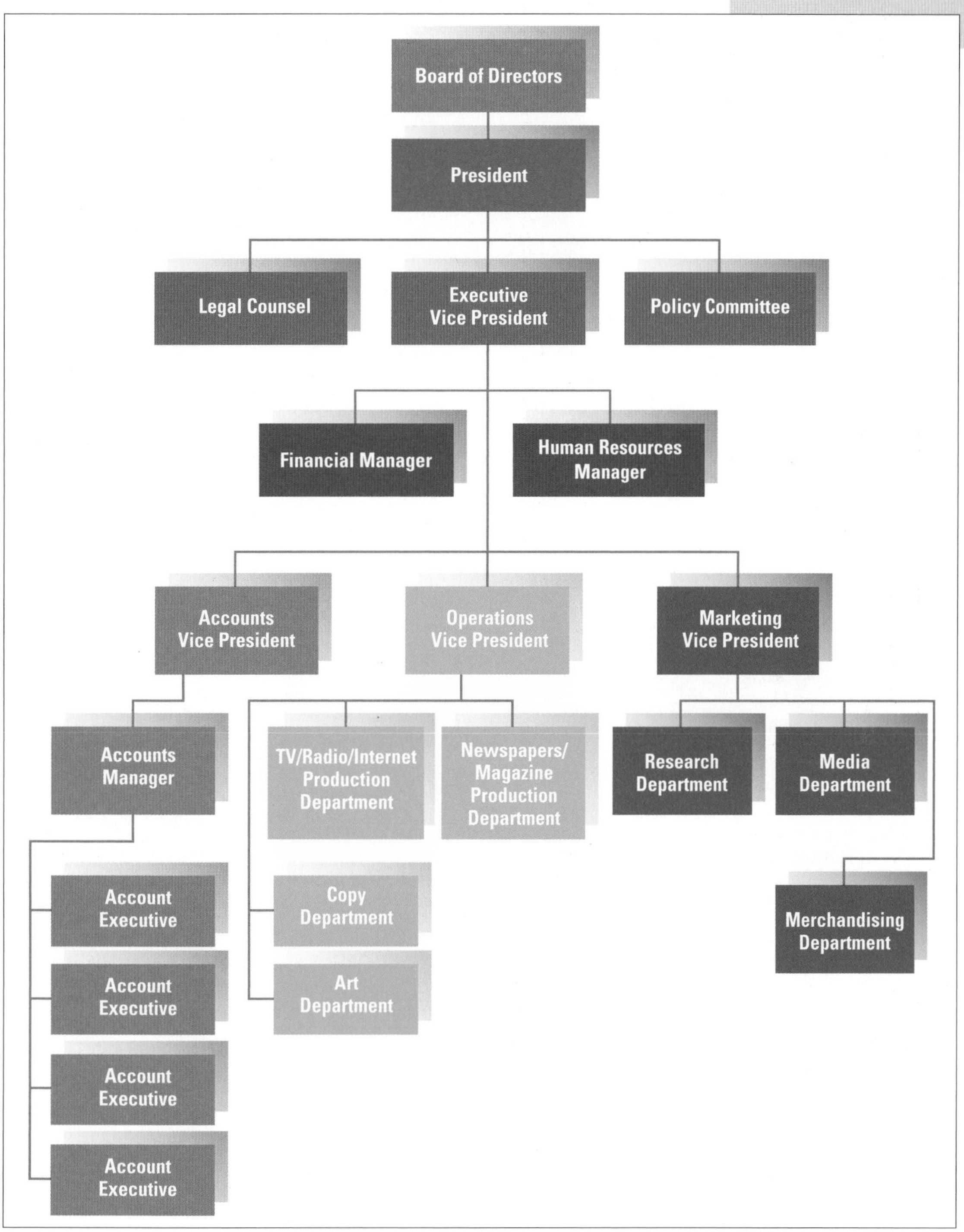

EXHIBIT 2.24
Sociometric Index of Aquarius Personnel and Clients
F = Frequent—daily
O = Occasional—once or twice per project
N = None

	Clients	Account Manager	Account Executives	TV/Radio Specialists	Newspaper/Magazine Specialists	Copy Specialists	Art Specialists	Merchandising Specialists	Media Specialists	Research Specialists
Clients	X	F	F	N	N	O	O	O	O	O
Account Manager		X	F	N	N	N	N	N	N	N
Account Executives			X	F	F	F	F	F	F	F
TV/Radio Specialists				X	N	O	O	N	N	O
Newspaper/Magazine Specialists					X	O	O	N	O	O
Copy Specialists						X	N	O	O	O
Art Specialists							X	O	O	O
Merchandising Specialists								X	F	F
Media Specialists									X	F
Research Specialists										X

Notes

1. Pete Engardio with Michael Arndt and Dean Foust, "The Future of Outsourcing," *BusinessWeek* (January 30, 2006), 50–58; "Working with Wyeth to Establish a High-Performance Drug Discovery Capability," Accenture website, http://www.accenture.com/SiteCollectionDocuments/PDF/wyeth (accessed July 18, 2011); and Ira Spector, "Industry Partnerships: Changing the Way R&D Is Conducted," *Applied Clinical Trials Online* (March 1, 2006), http://appliedclinicaltrialsonline.findpharma.com/appliedclinicaltrials/article/articleDetail.jsp?id=310807 (accessed July 18, 2011).
2. Carol Hymowitz, "Have Advice, Will Travel; Lacking Permanent Offices, Accenture's Executives Run 'Virtual' Company on the Fly," *The Wall Street Journal* (June 5, 2006), B1.
3. Dan Carrison, "Borrowing Expertise from the FBI," *Industrial Management* (May–June 2009), 23–26.
4. John Child, *Organization* (New York: Harper & Row, 1984).
5. Stuart Ranson, Bob Hinings, and Royston Greenwood, "The Structuring of Organizational Structures," *Administrative Science Quarterly* 25 (1980), 1–17; and Hugh Willmott, "The Structuring of Organizational Structures: A Note," *Administrative Science Quarterly* 26 (1981), 470–474.
6. This section is based on Frank Ostroff, *The Horizontal Organization: What the Organization of the Future Looks Like and How It Delivers Value to Customers* (New York: Oxford University Press, 1999).
7. Stephen Salsbury, *The State, the Investor, and the Railroad: The Boston & Albany, 1825–1867* (Cambridge: Harvard University Press, 1967), 186–187.
8. "The Cases of Daniel McCallum and Gustavus Swift," Willamette University, http://www.willamette.edu/~fthompso/MgmtCon/McCallum.htm (accessed July 29, 2011); "The Rise of the Professional Manager in America," *Management-Guru.com*, http://www.mgmtguru.com/mgt301/301_Lecture1Page7.htm (accessed July 29, 2011); and Alfred D. Chandler, *Strategy and Structure: Chapters in the History of the American Industrial Enterprise* (Cambridge, MA: Massachusetts Institute of Technology Press, 1962).
9. David Nadler and Michael Tushman, *Strategic Organization Design* (Glenview, IL.: Scott Foresman, 1988).
10. William C. Ouchi, "Power to the Principals: Decentralization in Three Large School Districts," *Organization Science* 17, no. 2 (March–April 2006), 298–307.
11. Gabriel Kahn, "Los Angeles Sets School-Rescue Program," *The Wall Street Journal* (September 2, 2008), A3; and "L.A. Mayor Antonio Villaraigosa Receives Award, Discusses Education at 18th Annual Charter Schools Conference," California Charter Schools Association (March 9, 2011), http://www.calcharters.org/blog/2011/03/la-mayor-antonio-villaraigosa-receives-award-discusses-education-at-18th-annual-charter-schools-conf.html (accessed July 20, 2011).
12. Brian Hindo, "Making the Elephant Dance," *BusinessWeek* (May 1, 2006), 88–90.
13. "Country Managers: From Baron to Hotelier," *The Economist* (May 11, 2002), 55–56.
14. Based on Jay R. Galbraith, *Designing Complex Organizations* (Reading, MA: Addison-Wesley, 1973), and *Organization Design* (Reading, MA: Addison-Wesley, 1977), 81–127.
15. George Anders, "Overseeing More Employees—With Fewer Managers," *The Wall Street Journal* (March 24, 2008), B6.
16. Lee Iacocca with William Novak, *Iacocca: An Autobiography* (New York: Phantom Books, 1984), 152–153.
17. Kirsten Foss and Waymond Rodgers, "Enhancing Information Usefulness by Line Managers' Involvement in Cross-Unit Activities," *Organization Studies* 32, no. 5 (2011), 683–703; M. Casson, *Information and Organization*, (Oxford: Oxford University Press, 1997); Justin J. P. Jansen, Michiel P. Tempelaar, Frans A. J. van den Bosch, and Henk W. Volberda, "Structural Differentiation and Ambidexterity: The Mediating Role of Integration Mechanisms," *Organization Science* 20, no. 4 (July–August 2009), 797–811; and Galbraith, *Designing Complex Organizations.*
18. "Panel Says Toyota Failed to Listen to Outsiders," *USA Today* (May 23, 2011), http://content.usatoday.com/communities/driveon/post/2011/05/toyota-panel-calls-for-single-us-chief-paying-heed-to-criticism/1 (accessed July 20, 2011).
19. These are based in part on Galbraith, *Designing Complex Organizations.*
20. David Stires, "How the VA Healed Itself," *Fortune* (May 15, 2006), 130–136.
21. Jay Galbraith, Diane Downey, and Amy Kates, "How Networks Undergird the Lateral Capability of an Organization—Where the Work Gets Done," *Journal of Organizational Excellence* (Spring 2002), 67–78.
22. Amy Barrett, "Staying on Top," *BusinessWeek* (May 5, 2003), 60–68.
23. Walter Kiechel III, "The Art of the Corporate Task Force," *Fortune* (January 28, 1991), 104–105; and William J. Altier, "Task Forces: An Effective Management Tool," *Management Review* (February 1987), 52–57.
24. Margaret Frazier, "Flu Prep," *The Wall Street Journal* (March 25–26, 2006), A8.
25. Paul R. Lawrence and Jay W. Lorsch, "New Managerial Job: The Integrator," *Harvard Business Review* (November–December 1967), 142–151.
26. Dan Heath and Chip Heath, "Blowing the Baton Pass," *Fast Company* (July–August 2010), 46–48.
27. Anthony M. Townsend, Samuel M. DeMarie, and Anthony R. Hendrickson, "Virtual Teams: Technology and the Workplace of the Future," *Academy of Management Executive* 12, no. 3 (August 1998); 17–29.
28. Erin White, "How a Company Made Everyone a Team Player," *The Wall Street Journal* (August 13, 2007), B1.
29. Pete Engardio, "A Guide for Multinationals: One of the Greatest Challenges for a Multinational Is Learning How to Build a Productive Global Team," *BusinessWeek* (August 20, 2007), 48–51; and Lynda Gratton, "Working Together. . . . When Apart," *The Wall Street Journal*, June 18, 2007.
30. Jody Hoffer Gittell, *The Southwest Airlines Way: Using the Power of Relationships to Achieve High Performance* (New York: McGraw-Hill, 2003).
31. This discussion is based on Jody Hoffer Gittell, "Coordinating Mechanisms in Care Provider Groups: Relational Coordination as a Mediator and Input Uncertainty as a

Moderator of Performance Effects," *Management Science* 48, no. 11 (November 2002), 1408–1426; J. H. Gittell, "The Power of Relationships," *Sloan Management Review* (Winter 2004),16–17; and J. H. Gittell, *The Southwest Airlines Way*.
32. Gittell, *The Southwest Airlines Way*.
33. "Transcript of Stripes Interview with Lt. Gen. David M. Rodriguez," *Stars and Stripes* (December 31, 2009), http://www.stripes.com/news/transcript-of-stripes-interview-with-lt-gen-david-m-rodriguez-1.97669# (accessed July 21, 2011); and Robert D. Kaplan, "Man Versus Afghanistan," *The Atlantic* (April 2010), 60–71. Note: Rodriguez was scheduled to leave Afghanistan in late July 2011.
34. Guy Chazan, "BP's Worsening Spill Crisis Undermines CEO's Reforms," *The Wall Street Journal*, May 3, 2010, A1; Guy Chazan, "BP's New Chief Puts Stress on Safety," *The Wall Street Journal*, September 30, 2010, B1; and Joe Nocera, "BP Ignored the Omens of Disaster," *The New York Times*, June 18, 2010, B1.
35. Henry Mintzberg, *The Structuring of Organizations* (Englewood Cliffs, N.J.: Prentice-Hall, 1979).
36. Frank Ostroff, "Stovepipe Stomper," *Government Executive* (April 1999), 70.
37. Raymond E. Miles, Charles C. Snow, Øystein D. Fjeldstad, Grant Miles, and Christopher Lettl, "Designing Organizations to Meet 21st-Century Opportunities and Challenges," *Organizational Dynamics* 39, no. 2 (2010), 93–103.
38. Based on Robert Duncan, "What Is the Right Organization Structure?" *Organizational Dynamics* (Winter 1979), 59–80; and W. Alan Randolph and Gregory G. Dess, "The Congruence Perspective of Organization Design: A Conceptual Model and Multivariate Research Approach," *Academy of Management Review* 9 (1984), 114–127.
39. R. W. Apple, Jr., "Making Texas Cows Proud," *The New York Times* (May 31, 2006), F1; Lynn Cook, "How Sweet It Is," *Forbes* (March 1, 2004), 90ff; David Kaplan, "Cool Commander; Brenham's Little Creamery Gets New Leader in Low-Key Switch," *Houston Chronicle* (May 1, 2004), 1; Toni Mack, "The Ice Cream Man Cometh," *Forbes* (January 22, 1990), 52–56; David Abdalla, J. Doehring, and Ann Windhager, "Blue Bell Creameries, Inc.: Case and Analysis" (unpublished manuscript, Texas A&M University, 1981); Jorjanna Price, "Creamery Churns Its Ice Cream into Cool Millions," *Parade* (February 21, 1982), 18–22; Art Chapman, "Lone Star Scoop—Blue Bell Ice Cream Is a Part of State's Culture," http://www.bluebell.com/press/FtWorthStar-july2002.htm; Javier A. Flores, "Bringing Smiles to Faces," *San Antonio Express-News*, July 22, 2010, CX1; and Bill Radford, "The Taste of Blue Bell Is Coming to Colorado Springs," *The Gazette*, February 11, 2011.
40. Survey reported in Timothy Galpin, Rod Hilpirt, and Bruce Evans, "The Connected Enterprise: Beyond Division of Labor," *Journal of Business Strategy* 28, no. 2 (2007), 38–47.
41. Nick Wingfield, "To Rebuild Windows, Microsoft Razed Some Walls," *The Wall Street Journal Asia*, October 21, 2009, 16.
42. Rahul Jacob, "The Struggle to Create an Organization for the 21st Century," *Fortune* (April 3, 1995), 90–99.
43. R. E. Miles et al., "Designing Organizations to Meet 21st Century Opportunities and Challenges."
44. N. Anand and Richard L. Daft, "What Is the Right Organization Design?" *Organizational Dynamics* 36, no. 4 (2007), 329–344.
45. Loretta Chao, "Alibaba Breaks Up E-Commerce Unit," *The Wall Street Journal*, June 17, 2011, B2.
46. Geoff Colvin and Jessica Shambora, "J&J: Secrets of Success," *Fortune* (May 4, 2009), 117–121.
47. Eliza Newlin Carney, "Calm in the Storm," *Government Executive* (October 2003), 57–63; and Brian Friel, "Hierarchies and Networks," *Government Executive* (April 2002), 31–39.
48. Based on Duncan, "What Is the Right Organization Structure?"
49. Joseph Weber, "A Big Company That Works," *BusinessWeek* (May 4, 1992), 124.
50. Phred Dvorak and Merissa Marr, "Stung by iPod, Sony Addresses a Digital Lag," *The Wall Street Journal* (December 30, 2004), B1.
51. Maisie O'Flanagan and Lynn K. Taliento, "Nonprofits: Ensuring That Bigger Is Better," *McKinsey Quarterly*, Issue 2 (2004), 112ff.
52. Mae Anderson, "Wal-Mart Reorganizes U.S. Operations to Help Spur Growth," *USA Today* (January 28, 2010), http://www.usatoday.com/money/industries/retail/2010-01-28-walmart-reorganization_N.htm (accessed July 21, 2011); and "Organizational Chart of Wal-Mart Stores," The Official Board.com, http://www.theofficialboard.com/org-chart/wal-mart-stores (accessed July 21, 2011).
53. Jay R. Galbraith, "The Multi-Dimensional and Reconfigurable Organization," *Organizational Dynamics* 39, no. 2 (2010), 115–125; and Stanley M. Davis and Paul R. Lawrence, *Matrix* (Reading, MA: Addison-Wesley, 1977), 11–24.
54. Davis and Lawrence, *Matrix*.
55. Steven H. Appelbaum, David Nadeau, and Michael Cyr, "Performance Evaluation in a Matrix Organization: A Case Study (Part One)," *Industrial and Commercial Training* 40, no. 5 (2008), 236–241; Erik W. Larson and David H. Gobeli, "Matrix Management: Contradictions and Insight," *California Management Review* 29 (Summer 1987), 126–138; and T. Sy and L. S. D'Annunzio, "Challenges and Strategies of Matrix Organizations: Top-Level and Mid-Level Managers' Perspectives, HR," *Human Resources Planning* 28, no. 1 (2005), 39–48.
56. Davis and Lawrence, *Matrix*, 155–180.
57. Robert C. Ford and W. Alan Randolph, "Cross-Functional Structures: A Review and Integration of Matrix Organizations and Project Management," *Journal of Management* 18 (June 1992), 267–294; and Duncan, "What Is the Right Organization Structure?"
58. Lawton R. Burns, "Matrix Management in Hospitals: Testing Theories of Matrix Structure and Development," *Administrative Science Quarterly* 34 (1989), 349–368; and Sy and D'Annunzio, "Challenges and Strategies of Matrix Organizations."
59. Carol Hymowitz, "Managers Suddenly Have to Answer to a Crowd of Bosses" (In the Lead column), *The Wall Street Journal* (August 12, 2003), B1; and Michael Goold and Andrew Campbell, "Making Matrix Structures Work: Creating Clarity on Unit Roles and Responsibilities," *European Management Journal* 21, no. 3 (June 2003), 351–363.

60. Christopher A. Bartlett and Sumantra Ghoshal, "Matrix Management: Not a Structure, a Frame of Mind," *Harvard Business Review* (July–August 1990), 138–145.
61. This case was inspired by John E. Fogerty, "Integrative Management at Standard Steel" (unpublished manuscript, Latrobe, Pennsylvania, 1980); Stanley Reed with Adam Aston, "Steel: The Mergers Aren't Over Yet," *BusinessWeek* (February 21, 2005), 6; Michael Arndt, "Melting Away Steel's Costs," *BusinessWeek* (November 8, 2004), 48; and "Steeling for a Fight," *The Economist* (June 4, 1994), 63.
62. Michael Hammer, "Process Management and the Future of Six Sigma," *Sloan Management Review* (Winter 2002), 26–32; and Michael Hammer and Steve Stanton, "How Process Enterprises *Really* Work," *Harvard Business Review* 77 (November–December 1999), 108–118.
63. Hammer, "Process Management and the Future of Six Sigma."
64. Based on Ostroff, *The Horizontal Organization*; and Anand and Daft, "What Is the Right Organization Design?"
65. Julia Moskin, "Your Waiter Tonight. . . . Will Be the Chef," *The New York Times* (March 12, 2008), F1.
66. Frank Ostroff, *The Horizontal Organization*, 102–114.
67. See Anand and Daft, "What Is the Right Organization Design?"; Pete Engardio, "The Future of Outsourcing," *BusinessWeek* (January 30, 2006), 50–58; Jane C. Linder, "Transformational Outsourcing," *MIT Sloan Management Review* (Winter 2004), 52–58; and Denis Chamberland, "Is It Core or Strategic? Outsourcing as a Strategic Management Tool," *Ivey Business Journal* (July–August 2003), 1–5.
68. David Streitfeld, "A City Outsources Everything. California's Sky Doesn't Fall," *The New York Times*, July 20, 2010, A1.
69. Anand and Daft, "What Is the Right Organization Design?"; Yuzo Yamaguchi and Daisuke Wakabayashi, "Hitachi to Outsource TV Manufacture," *The Wall Street Journal Online* (July 10, 2009), http://online.wsj.com/article/SB124714255400717925.html (accessed July 17, 2009); Engardio, "The Future of Outsourcing"; Chamberland, "Is It Core or Strategic?"; and Keith H. Hammonds, "Smart, Determined, Ambitious, Cheap: The New Face of Global Competition," *Fast Company* (February 2003), 91–97.
70. Jena McGregor, "The Chore Goes Offshore," *BusinessWeek* (March 23 & 30, 2009), 50–51.
71. David Nadler, quoted in "Partners in Wealth: The Ins and Outs of Collaboration," *The Economist* (January 21–27, 2006), 16–17.
72. Ranjay Gulati, "Silo Busting: How to Execute on the Promise of Customer Focus," *Harvard Business Review* (May 2007), 98–108.
73. The discussion of virtual networks is based on Anand and Daft, "What Is the Right Organization Design?"; Melissa A. Schilling and H. Kevin Steensma, "The Use of Modular Organizational Forms: An Industry-Level Analysis," *Academy of Management Journal* 44, no. 6 (2001), 1149–1168; Raymond E. Miles and Charles C. Snow, "The New Network Firm: A Spherical Structure Built on a Human Investment Philosophy," *Organizational Dynamics* (Spring 1995), 5–18; and R. E. Miles, C. C. Snow, J. A. Matthews, G. Miles, and H. J. Coleman Jr., "Organizing in the Knowledge Age: Anticipating the Cellular Form," *Academy of Management Executive* 11, no. 4 (1997), 7–24.
74. Darren Dahl, "Want a Job? Let the Bidding Begin; A Radical Take on the Virtual Company," *Inc.* (March 2011), 93–96.
75. Paul Engle, "You *Can* Outsource Strategic Processes," *Industrial Management* (January–February 2002), 13–18.
76. Don Tapscott, "Rethinking Strategy in a Networked World," *Strategy & Business* 24 (Third Quarter, 2001), 34–41.
77. Joann S. Lublin, "Smart Balance Keeps Tight Focus on Creativity" (Theory & Practice column), *The Wall Street Journal*, June 8, 2009; and Rebecca Reisner, "A Smart Balance of Staff and Contractors," *BusinessWeek Online* (June 16, 2009), http://www.businessweek.com/managing/content/jun2009/ca20090616_217232.htm (accessed April 30, 2010).
78. Gregory G. Dess, Abdul M. A. Rasheed, Kevin J. McLaughlin, and Richard L. Priem, "The New Corporate Architecture," *Academy of Management Executive* 9, no. 3 (1995), 7–20.
79. This discussion of strengths and weaknesses is based on Miles and Snow, "The New Network Firm"; Dess, et al., "The New Corporate Architecture"; Anand and Daft, "What Is the Right Organization Design?"; Henry W. Chesbrough and David J. Teece, "Organizing for Innovation: When Is Virtual Virtuous?" *Harvard Business Review* (August 2002), 127–134; Cecily A. Raiborn, Janet B. Butler, and Marc F. Massoud, "Outsourcing Support Functions: Identifying and Managing the Good, the Bad, and the Ugly," *Business Horizons* 52 (2009), 347–356; and M. Lynne Markus, Brook Manville, and Carole E. Agres, "What Makes a Virtual Organization Work?" *Sloan Management Review* (Fall 2000), 13–26.
80. "Organization Chart for Starbucks," The Official Board.com, http://www.theofficialboard.com/org-chart/starbucks (accessed July 21, 2011).
81. Linda S. Ackerman, "Transition Management: An In-depth Look at Managing Complex Change," *Organizational Dynamics* (Summer 1982), 46–66.
82. Based on Ostroff, *The Horizontal Organization*, 29–44.
83. Based on Child, *Organization*, Ch. 1; and Jonathan D. Day, Emily Lawson, and Keith Leslie, "When Reorganization Works," *The McKinsey Quarterly*, 2003 Special Edition: The Value in Organization, 21–29.
84. Adapted by Dorothy Marcic from "Organizing," in Donald D. White and H. William Vroman, *Action in Organizations*, 2nd ed. (Boston: Allyn & Bacon, 1982), 154, and Cheryl Harvey and Kim Morouney, "Organization Structure and Design: The Club Ed Exercise," *Journal of Management Education* (June 1985), 425–429.
85. Prepared by Richard L. Daft, from Richard L. Daft and Richard Steers, *Organizations: A Micro/Macro Approach* (Glenview, IL: Scott Foresman, 1986). Reprinted with permission.
86. Adapted from John F. Veiga and John N. Yanouzas, "Aquarius Advertising Agency," *The Dynamics of Organization Theory* (St. Paul, Minn.: West, 1984), 212–217, with permission.

Chapter 3

Strategy and Effectiveness

©andipantz, iStock

Learning Objectives

After reading this chapter you should be able to:

1. Describe the importance of strategy and the strategy process.
2. Understand strategic purpose and operating goals.
3. Know Porter's strategy model and Miles and Snow's strategy typology.
4. Explain how strategy affects organization design.
5. Discuss the goal, resource, internal process, and strategic constituents approaches to measuring effectiveness.
6. Explain the competing values model and how it relates to effectiveness.

Before reading this chapter, please check whether you agree or disagree with each of the following statements:

1 **A company's strategic intent or direction reflects managers' systematic analysis of organizational and environmental factors.**

I AGREE _____ I DISAGREE _____

2 **The best business strategy is to make products and services as distinctive as possible to gain an edge in the marketplace.**

I AGREE _____ I DISAGREE _____

3 **The best measures of business performance are financial.**

I AGREE _____ I DISAGREE _____

One of the primary responsibilities of managers is to position their organizations for success by establishing goals and strategies that can keep the organization competitive. Consider the situation at eBay. A decade ago, eBay was considered unstoppable. At a time when almost every dot-com company was handing out pink slips, scaling back, or going out of business, eBay was thriving. But consumers grew tired of online auctions, the core of eBay's business. Many people began to prefer the simplicity of buying products directly from online retail marketplaces such as Amazon.com. EBay was losing favor with customers.

John Donahoe, the current CEO of eBay, has spent the past few years trying to shift the company's strategic direction by offering a broader array of goods and developing services that make eBay a more attractive place for large merchants to offer new products. To put the strategy into action, he recently completed a $2.4-billion acquisition of GSI Commerce, a company that provides marketing, order-management, packing, and shipping services for scores of retailers. "EBay is clearly going on the offensive," said David Spitz, president of ChannelAdvisor Corporation, a partner firm that helps merchants sell on eBay. The company continues to pull away from its roots as a site for individuals and small vendors to offer odd items and used goods through auctions, but Donahoe knows the company can stay competitive only by shifting strategic direction as e-commerce continues to evolve.[1]

Purpose of This Chapter

Top managers give direction to organizations. They set goals and develop the plans for their organization to attain them. The purpose of this chapter is to help you understand the types of goals that organizations pursue and some of the competitive strategies managers use to reach those goals. We provide an overview of strategic management, examine two significant frameworks for determining strategic action, and look at how strategies affect organization design. The chapter also describes the

most popular approaches to measuring the effectiveness of organizational efforts. To manage organizations well, managers need a clear way to measure how effective the organization is in attaining its goals.

The Role of Strategic Direction in Organization Design

The choice of goals and strategy influences how an organization should be designed. An **organizational goal** is a desired state of affairs that the organization attempts to reach.[2] A goal represents a result or end point toward which organizational efforts are directed.

Top executives decide the end purpose the organization will strive for and determine the direction it will take to accomplish it. It is this purpose and direction that shapes how the organization is designed and managed. Indeed, *the primary responsibility of top management is to determine an organization's goals, strategy, and design, thereby adapting the organization to a changing environment.*[3] Middle managers do much the same thing for major departments within the guidelines provided by top management. Exhibit 3.1 illustrates the relationships through which top managers provide direction and then design.

EXHIBIT 3.1
Top Management Role in Organization Direction, Design, and Effectiveness

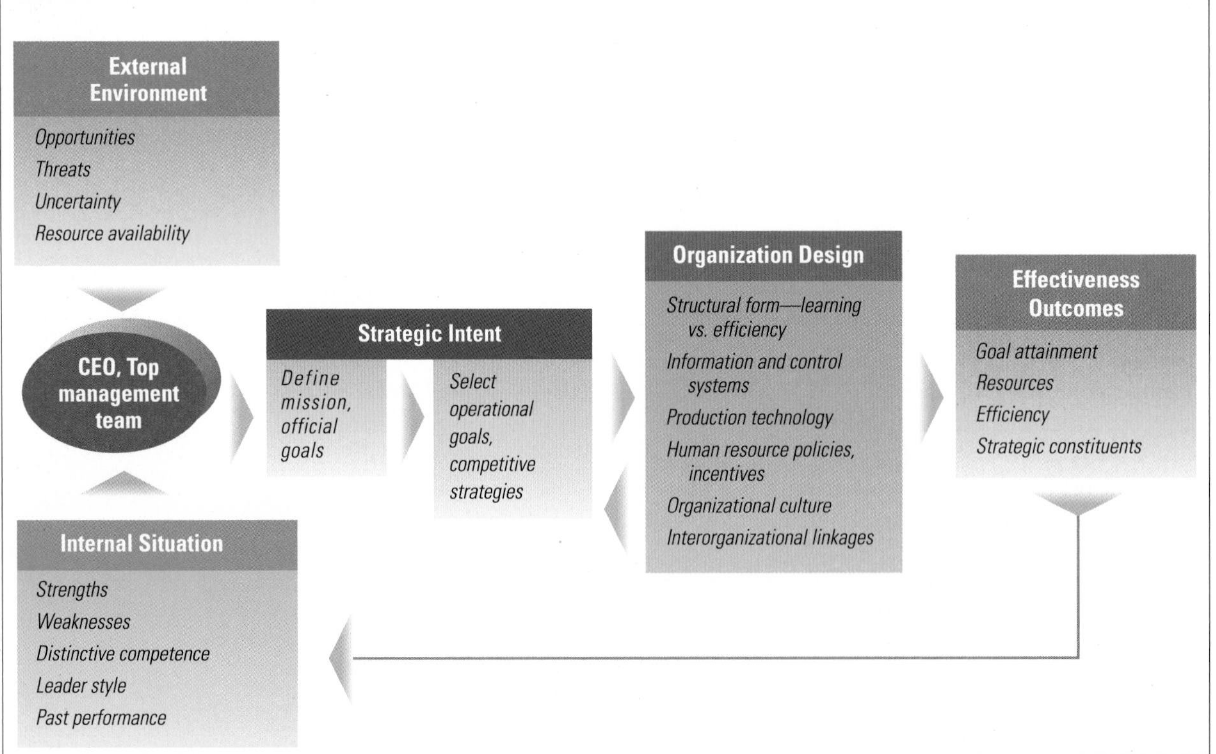

Source: Adapted from Arie Y. Lewin and Carroll U. Stephens, "Individual Properties of the CEO as Determinants of Organization Design," unpublished manuscript, Duke University, 1990; and Arie Y. Lewin and Carroll U. Stephens, "CEO Attributes as Determinants of Organization Design: An Integrated Model," *Organization Studies* 15, no. 2 (1994), 183–212.

The direction-setting process typically begins with an assessment of the opportunities and threats in the external environment, including the amount of change, uncertainty, and resource availability, which we discuss in more detail in Chapter 6. Top managers also assess internal strengths and weaknesses to define the company's distinctive competence compared with other firms in the industry. This competitive analysis of the internal and external environments is one of the central concepts in strategic management.[4]

1 A company's strategic intent or direction reflects managers' systematic analysis of organizational and environmental factors.

ANSWER: *Agree.* The best strategies come from systematic analysis of organizational strengths and weaknesses combined with analysis of opportunities and threats in the environment. Careful study combined with experience enable top managers to decide on specific goals and strategies.

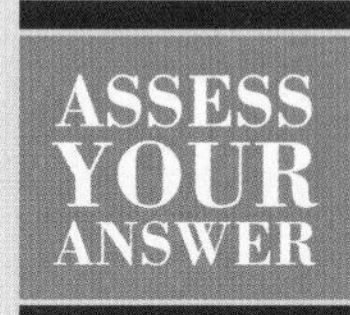

The next step is to define and articulate the organization's *strategic intent,* which includes defining an overall mission and official goals based on the correct fit between external opportunities and internal strengths. Leaders then formulate specific operational goals and strategies that define how the organization is to accomplish its overall mission. In Exhibit 3.1, organization design reflects the way goals and strategies are implemented so that the organization's attention and resources are consistently focused toward achieving the mission and goals.

Organization design is the administration and execution of the strategic plan. Managers make decisions about structural form, including whether the organization will be designed primarily for learning and innovation (an organic approach) or to achieve efficiency (a mechanistic approach), as discussed in Chapter 1. Other choices are made about information and control systems, the type of production technology, human resource policies, culture, and linkages to other organizations. Changes in structure, technology, human resource policies, culture, and interorganizational linkages will be discussed in subsequent chapters. Also note the arrow in Exhibit 3.1 running from organization design back to strategic intent. This means that strategies are often made within the current structure of the organization so that current design constrains, or puts limits on, goals and strategy. More often than not, however, the new goals and strategy are selected based on environmental needs, such as at eBay, described in the opening example, and then top managers attempt to redesign the organization to achieve those ends.

Finally, Exhibit 3.1 illustrates how managers evaluate the effectiveness of organizational efforts—that is, the extent to which the organization realizes its goals. This chart reflects the most popular ways of measuring performance, each of which is discussed later in this chapter. It is important to note here that performance measurements feed back into the internal environment so that past performance of the organization is assessed by top managers in setting new goals and strategic direction for the future.

The role of top management is important because managers can interpret the environment differently and develop different goals. Think about how top managers at Kodak failed to recognize digital photography as a threat to their photographic

film business, while managers at Japanese rival Fuji took early steps to redefine their organization as a digital technology company.[5] The choices top managers make about goals, strategies, and organization design have a tremendous impact on organizational effectiveness. Remember that goals and strategy are not fixed or taken for granted. Top managers and middle managers must select goals for their respective units, and the ability to make good choices largely determines a firm's success. Organization design is used to implement goals and strategy and also determines organization success.

Organizational Purpose

As an organization manager, keep these guidelines in mind:

Establish and communicate organizational mission and goals. Communicate official goals to provide a statement of the organization's mission to external constituents. Communicate operating goals to provide internal direction, guidelines, and standards of performance for employees.

All organizations, including Fuji, eBay, Philips Electronics, Google, Harvard University, the Catholic Church, the U.S. Department of Agriculture, the local laundry, and the neighborhood deli, exist for a purpose. This purpose may be referred to as the overall goal, or mission. Different parts of the organization establish their own goals and objectives to help meet the overall goal, mission, or purpose of the organization.

Strategic Intent

Many types of goals exist in organizations, and each type performs a different function. To achieve success, however, organizational goals and strategies are focused with strategic intent. **Strategic intent** means that all the organization's energies and resources are directed toward a focused, unifying, and compelling overall goal.[6] Examples of ambitious goals that demonstrate strategic intent are Microsoft's early goal to "Put a computer on every desk in every home," Komatsu's motto, "Encircle Caterpillar," and Coca-Cola's goal "To put a Coke within 'arm's reach' of every consumer in the world."[7] Strategic intent provides a focus for management action. Three aspects related to strategic intent are the mission, core competence, and competitive advantage.

Mission. The overall goal for an organization is often called the **mission**—the organization's reason for existence. The mission describes the organization's shared values and beliefs and its reason for being. The mission is sometimes called the **official goals**, which refers to the formally stated definition of business scope and outcomes the organization is trying to achieve. Official goal statements typically define business operations and may focus on values, markets, and customers that distinguish the organization. Whether called a mission statement or official goals, the organization's general statement of its purpose and philosophy is often written down in a policy manual or the annual report. Exhibit 3.2 shows the mission statement for Machias Savings Bank. Note how the overall mission, values, and vision are all defined.

One of the primary purposes of a mission statement is to serve as a communication tool.[8] The *mission statement* communicates to current and prospective employees, customers, investors, suppliers, and competitors what the organization stands for and what it is trying to achieve. A mission statement communicates legitimacy to internal and external stakeholders, who may join and be committed to the organization

EXHIBIT 3.2
Mission Statement for Machias Savings Bank

Mission

To be exceptional in every relationship, in every product developed, in every service rendered and every promise made.

Vision

To provide the most exceptional banking experience in the state of Maine.

Principles

Driven to Be the Best
To be the best, we must look through the lens of the customer to deliver the best products and services in a cost-effective way.

Build a Winning Performance Culture
To create a Winning Performance Culture we need to first operate with the highest standards of integrity.

Execute as One
Together, we will focus on a consistent strong financial performance during good times and bad.

Source: "Banking Today," Vol. 6, Issue 1, Machias Savings Bank.

because they identify with its stated purpose and vision. Most top leaders want employees, customers, competitors, suppliers, investors, and the local community to look on the organization in a favorable light, and the concept of legitimacy plays a critical role. Consider the damage that was done to the legitimate reputation of News Corporation when rivals revealed that reporters for the company's British division had hacked into the phone lines of various celebrities, politicians, and families of murder victims. Rupert Murdoch and other top managers are still struggling to restore the company's legitimacy in the eyes of the public. In today's corporate world of weakened trust, increasing regulation, and concern for the natural environment, many organizations face the need to redefine their mission to emphasize the firm's purpose in more than financial terms.[9] Companies where managers are sincerely guided by mission statements that focus on a larger social purpose, such as Medtronic's "To restore people to full life and health" or Liberty Mutual's "Helping people live safer, more secure lives," typically attract better employees, have better relationships with external parties, and perform better in the marketplace over the long term.[10]

Competitive Advantage. The overall aim of strategic intent is to help the organization achieve a sustainable competitive advantage. **Competitive advantage** refers to what sets the organization apart from others and provides it with a distinctive edge for meeting customer or client needs in the marketplace. Strategy necessarily changes over time to fit environmental conditions, and good managers pay close attention to trends that might require changes in how the company operates. Managers analyze competitors and the internal and external environments to find potential *competitive openings* and learn what new capabilities the organization needs to gain the upper hand against other companies in the industry.[11] The following example illustrates how printing company Mimeo found a competitive opening in a mature industry.

Mimeo

IN PRACTICE

How do you gain a competitive edge in the routine business of printing brochures, manuals, and marketing materials? John Delbridge, David Uyttendaele, and Jeff Stewart knew most office workers would rather place orders for such materials online and let someone else do the work rather than spend hours at Kinko's or toiling in the office copy room. They also knew that most businesses do much of their printing at the last minute in today's fast-paced, high-pressure world.

To compete with local copy shops, Mimeo started a night shift and began accepting orders late into the evening and offering customers nationwide the option of overnight delivery. Mimeo guarantees to get the job delivered wherever it needs to be the next morning, and it has sometimes gone to extreme measures to make good on the promise. When a last-minute international order missed the FedEx cutoff, Mimeo sent two employees on a round-trip flight to London with 14 boxes of human resources manuals. Another time, workers at the Memphis office were scrambling after a customer called late in the day asking if Mimeo could get materials printed and delivered to Houston for a financial analysts' conference by 8:00 AM the next day. The problem was that the content for the materials wouldn't be ready until around 11:00 PM that evening. Unable to complete the complex job in time for FedEx's overnight delivery, Mimeo hired a private plane and delivered the presentations on time.

The ability to smoothly handle rush jobs has given Mimeo a definite edge over other printing companies, and there has been no shortage of businesses needing the "emergency service." Mimeo goes the extra mile for every order, big or small, even though it means occasionally taking a loss. The company once spent $600 to get a $300 order to the customer on time, for example. Managers believe it is worth it to keep customers happy and keep them coming back.[12]

Mimeo makes rush jobs look easy because the company has the right skills, strengths, and tools to get the job done. For example, it locates facilities as close as possible to Fed Ex hubs so employees have more time to complete last-minute orders. Proprietary software prioritizes orders based on deadline, order size, current capacity, and other factors. The company has also developed close relationships with other copy shops so it can outsource work when Mimeo's own resources are overwhelmed.

Core Competence. A company's **core competence** is something the organization does especially well in comparison to its competitors. A core competence may be in the area of superior research and development, expert technological know-how, process efficiency, or exceptional customer service.[13] Mimeo, for example, excels with core competencies of superb customer service and the application of technology to ensure internal process efficiency. At Apple, strategy focuses on superior design and marketing skills. Robinson Helicopter succeeds through technological know-how for building small, two-seater helicopters that are used for everything from police patrols in Los Angeles to herding cattle in Australia.[14] In each case, managers identified what their company does especially well and built the strategy around it.

Operating Goals

The organization's mission and overall goals provide a basis for developing more specific operating goals. **Operating goals** designate the ends sought through the actual operating procedures of the organization and explain what the organization is actually trying to do.[15] Operating goals describe specific measurable outcomes and are often concerned with the short run. Operating goals typically pertain to the primary tasks an organization must perform.[16] Specific goals for each primary task provide direction for the day-to-day decisions and activities within departments. Typical operating goals that define what an organization is trying to accomplish include performance goals, resource goals, market goals, employee development goals, productivity goals, and goals for innovation and change, as illustrated in Exhibit 3.3.

Overall Performance. Profitability reflects the overall performance of for-profit organizations. Profitability may be expressed in terms of net income, earnings per share, or return on investment. Other overall performance goals are growth and output volume. Growth pertains to increases in sales or profits over time. Volume pertains to total sales or the amount of products or services delivered. For example, Toyota Motor Corporation has set performance goals of selling 10 million vehicles and achieving $12 billion in operating profit by the middle of the decade. The company had tried to reach a goal of selling 10 million vehicles in 2009, but it fell short due to the global recession and massive recalls that damaged the company's reputation.[17]

Government and nonprofit organizations such as social service agencies or labor unions do not have goals of profitability, but they do have goals that attempt to specify the delivery of services to clients or members within specified expense levels. The Internal Revenue Service has a goal of providing accurate responses to 85 percent of taxpayer questions about new tax laws. Growth and volume goals also may be indicators of overall performance in nonprofit organizations. Expanding their services to new clients is a primary goal for many social service agencies, for example.

Resources. Resource goals pertain to the acquisition of needed material and financial resources from the environment. They may involve obtaining financing for the construction of new plants, finding less expensive sources for raw materials, or hiring top-quality technology graduates. Starbucks recently formed an alliance

EXHIBIT 3.3
Typical Operating Goals for an Organization

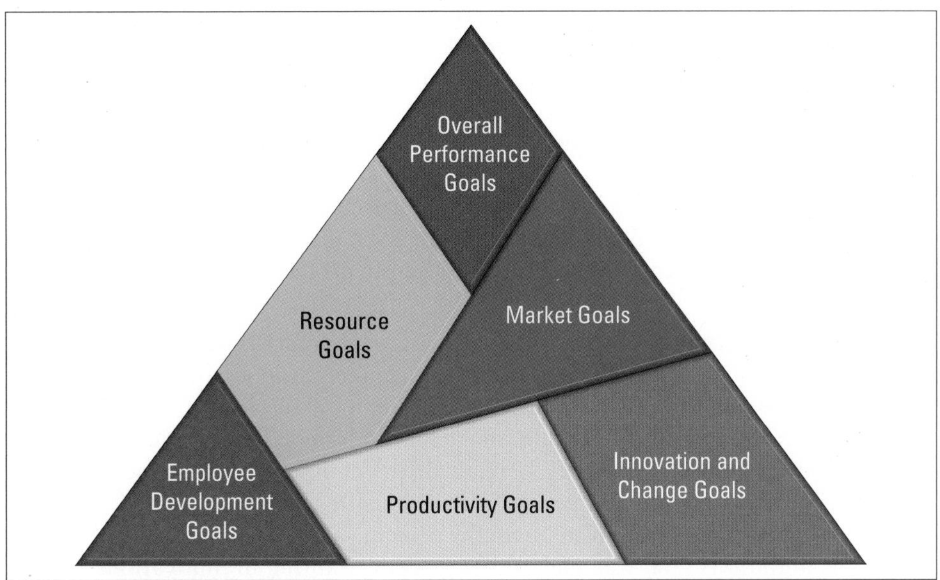

with India's Tata Group to obtain Indian premium Arabica coffee beans for use in Starbucks stores. Eventually, the alliance will also enable Starbucks to find prime locations for outlets in India, which can also be considered valuable resources.[18] Resource goals for the New England Patriots include drafting top-notch players and attracting quality coaches. For nonprofit organizations, resource goals might include recruiting dedicated volunteers and expanding the organization's funding base.

Market. Market goals relate to the market share or market standing desired by the organization. Market goals are largely the responsibility of marketing, sales, and advertising departments. L'Oreal SA, the world's largest cosmetics company, has a goal of doubling its current clientele, adding one billion consumers by 2020. As one step to achieve the goal, managers are making changes in marketing and selling approaches designed to win over more customers in Brazil. Women there are some of the biggest spenders on beauty products, but L'Oreal has had trouble adapting to the Brazilian market.[19] Market goals can also apply to nonprofit organizations. Cincinnati Children's Hospital Medical Center, not content with a limited regional role in health care, has gained a growing share of the national market by developing expertise in the niche of treating rare and complex conditions and relentlessly focusing on quality.[20]

Employee Development. Employee development pertains to the training, promotion, safety, and growth of employees. It includes both managers and workers. Strong employee development goals are one of the characteristics common to organizations that regularly show up on *Fortune* magazine's list of "100 Best Companies to Work For." For example, family-owned Wegmans Food Markets, which has appeared on the list every year since its inception and ranked Number 3 in 2011, has strong employee development goals. The company invests more than 40 hours per year in training for employees and offers employee scholarships and other growth opportunities. One of the requirements of managers is to mentor employees and help people develop to their full potential.[21]

Productivity. Productivity goals concern the amount of output achieved from available resources. They typically describe the amount of resource inputs required to reach desired outputs and are thus stated in terms of "cost for a unit of production," "units produced per employee," or "resource cost per employee." Illumination Entertainment, the production company behind the hit movie "Hop," has productivity goals that help the company make animated films at about half the cost of those made by larger studios. CEO Christopher Meledandri believes strict cost controls and successful animated films are not mutually exclusive, but it means Illumination's 30 or so employees have to be highly productive.[22]

Innovation and Change. Innovation goals pertain to internal flexibility and readiness to adapt to unexpected changes in the environment. Innovation goals are often defined with respect to the development of specific new services, products, or production processes. Procter & Gamble started a program called Connect + Develop in 2001, with a goal of getting 50 percent of the company's innovation through collaboration with people and organizations outside the company by 2010. The goal represented an increase from about 35 percent in 2004 and only 10 percent in 2000. The ambitious goal was met and exceeded, resulting in innovations such as Swiffer Dusters, Olay Regenerist, and Mr. Clean Magic Eraser.[23]

Successful organizations use a carefully balanced set of operating goals. Although profitability goals are important, some of today's best companies recognize that a single-minded focus on bottom-line profits may not be the best way to achieve high performance. Innovation and change goals are increasingly important, even though they may initially cause a *decrease* in profits. Employee development goals are critical for helping to maintain a motivated, committed workforce.

The Importance of Goals

Both official goals and operating goals are important for the organization, but they serve very different purposes. Official goals and mission statements describe a value system for the organization and set an overall purpose and vision; operating goals represent the primary tasks of the organization. Official goals legitimize the organization; operating goals are more explicit and well defined.

Operating goals serve several specific purposes, as outlined in Exhibit 3.4. For one thing, goals provide employees with a sense of direction so that they know what they are working toward. This can help to motivate employees toward specific targets and important outcomes. Numerous studies have shown that specific high goals can significantly increase employee performance.[24] People like having a focus for their activities and efforts. Consider Guitar Center, the largest musical instrument retailer in the United States. Managers establish clear, specific goals for sales teams at every Guitar Center store each morning, and employees do whatever they need to, short of losing the company money, to meet the targets. Guitar Center's unwritten mantra of "Take the deal" means that salespeople are trained to take any profitable deal, even at razor-thin margins, to meet daily sales goals.[25]

Another important purpose of goals is to act as guidelines for employee behavior and decision making. Appropriate goals can act as a set of constraints on individual behavior and actions so that employees behave within boundaries that are acceptable to the organization and larger society.[26] They help to define the appropriate decisions concerning organization structure, innovation, employee welfare, or growth. Finally, goals provide a standard for assessment. The level of organizational performance, whether in terms of profits, units produced, degree of employee satisfaction, level of innovation, or number of customer complaints, needs a basis for evaluation. Operating goals provide this standard for measurement.

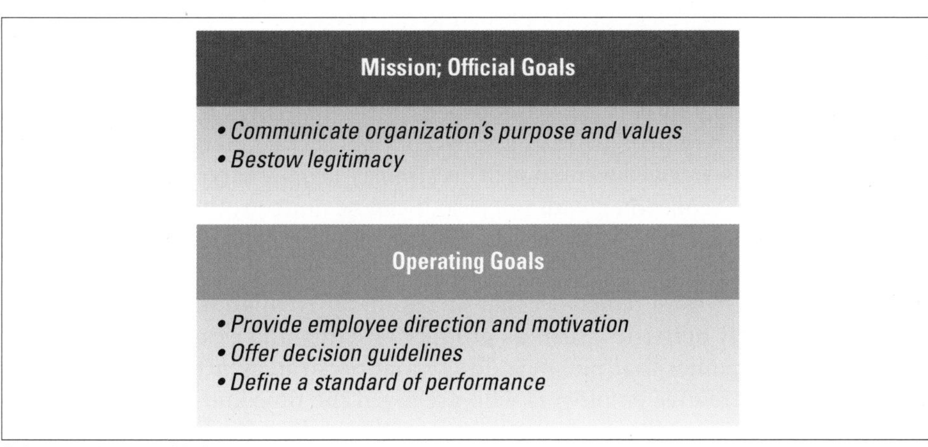

EXHIBIT 3.4
Goal Types and Purposes

A Framework for Selecting Strategy and Design

To support and accomplish the organization's strategic intent and keep people focused in the direction determined by organizational mission, vision, and operating goals, managers have to select specific strategy and design options that can help the organization achieve its purpose and goals within its competitive environment. In this section, we examine a couple of practical approaches to selecting strategy and design. The questionnaire in this chapter's "How Do You Fit the Design?" box will give you some insight into your own strategic management competencies.

A **strategy** is a plan for interacting with the competitive environment to achieve organizational goals. Some managers think of goals and strategies as interchangeable, but for our purposes *goals* define where the organization wants to go and *strategies* define how it will get there. For example, a goal might be to achieve 15 percent annual sales growth; strategies to reach that goal might include aggressive advertising to attract new customers, motivating salespeople to increase the average size of customer purchases, and acquiring other businesses that produce similar products. Strategies can include any number of techniques to achieve the goal. The essence of formulating strategies is choosing whether the organization will perform different activities than its competitors or will execute similar activities more efficiently than its competitors do.[27]

Two models for formulating strategies are the Porter model of competitive strategies and the Miles and Snow strategy typology. Each provides a framework for competitive action. After describing the two models, we discuss how the choice of strategies affects organization design.

Porter's Competitive Strategies

Michael E. Porter studied a number of business organizations and proposed that managers can make the organization more profitable and less vulnerable by adopting either a differentiation strategy or a low-cost leadership strategy.[28] Using a low-cost leadership strategy means managers choose to compete through lower costs, whereas with a differentiation strategy the organization competes through the ability to offer unique or distinctive products and services that can command a premium price. These two basic strategies are illustrated in Exhibit 3.5. Moreover, each strategy can vary in scope from broad to narrow.

BRIEFCASE

As an organization manager, keep these guidelines in mind:

After goals have been defined, select strategies for achieving those goals. Define specific strategies based on Porter's competitive strategies or Miles and Snow's strategy typology.

Differentiation. With a **differentiation strategy** the organization attempts to distinguish its products or services from others in the industry. Managers may use advertising, distinctive product features, exceptional service, or new technology to achieve a product perceived as unique. This strategy usually targets customers who are not particularly concerned with price, so it can be quite profitable.

A differentiation strategy can reduce rivalry with competitors and fight off the threat of substitute products because customers are loyal to the company's brand. However, managers must remember that successful differentiation strategies require a number of costly activities, such as product research and design and extensive advertising. Companies that pursue a differentiation strategy need strong marketing abilities and creative employees who are given the time and resources to seek innovations. One good illustration of a company that benefits from a differentiation strategy is Apple. Apple has never tried to compete on price and likes being perceived as an "elite" brand. Its personal computers, for example, can command significantly higher prices than other PCs because of their distinctiveness. The company has built a loyal customer base by providing innovative, stylish products and creating a prestigious image.

Service firms can use a differentiation strategy as well. Umpqua Bank, based in Portland, Oregon, for instance, wants to become a "lifestyle brand," rather

How Do You Fit the Design?

YOUR STRATEGY/PERFORMANCE STRENGTH

As a potential manager, what are your strengths concerning strategy formulation and implementation? To find out, think about *how you handle challenges and issues* in your school work or job. Then circle *a* or *b* for each of the following items depending on which is more descriptive of your behavior. There are no right or wrong answers. Respond to each item as it best describes how you respond to work situations.

1. When keeping records, I tend to
- **a.** be very careful about documentation.
- **b.** be more haphazard about documentation.

2. If I run a group or a project, I
- **a.** have the general idea and let others figure out how to do the tasks.
- **b.** try to figure out specific goals, time lines, and expected outcomes.

3. My thinking style could be more accurately described as
- **a.** linear thinker, going from A to B to C.
- **b.** thinking like a grasshopper, hopping from one idea to another.

4. In my office or home things are
- **a.** here and there in various piles.
- **b.** laid out neatly or at least in reasonable order.

5. I take pride in developing
- **a.** ways to overcome a barrier to a solution.
- **b.** new hypotheses about the underlying cause of a problem.

6. I can best help strategy by making sure there is
- **a.** openness to a wide range of assumptions and ideas.
- **b.** thoroughness when implementing new ideas.

7. One of my strengths is
- **a.** commitment to making things work.
- **b.** commitment to a dream for the future.

8. I am most effective when I emphasize
- **a.** inventing original solutions.
- **b.** making practical improvements.

Scoring: For *Strategic Formulator* strength, score one point for each "*a*" answer circled for questions 2, 4, 6, and 8, and for each "*b*" answer circled for questions 1, 3, 5, and 7. For *Strategic Implementer* strength, score one point for each "*b*" answer circled for questions 2, 4, 6, and 8, and for each "*a*" answer circled for questions 1, 3, 5, and 7. Which of your two scores is higher and by how much? The higher score indicates your *Strategy Strength*.

Interpretation: Formulator and Implementer are two important ways managers bring value to strategic management and effectiveness. Managers with implementer strengths tend to work on operating goals and performance to make things more efficient and reliable. Managers with the formulator strength push toward out-of-the-box strategies and like to think about mission, vision, and dramatic breakthroughs. Both styles are essential to strategic management and organizational effectiveness. Strategic formulators often use their skills to create whole new strategies and approaches, and strategic implementers often work with strategic improvements, implementation, and measurement.

If the difference between your two scores is 2 or less, you have a balanced formulator/implementer style and work well in both arenas. If the difference is 4–5, you have a moderately strong style and probably work best in the area of your strength. And if the difference is 7–8, you have a distinctive strength and almost certainly would want to contribute in the area of your strength rather than in the opposite domain.

Source: Adapted from Dorothy Marcic and Joe Seltzer, *Organizational Behavior: Experiences and Cases* (South-Western, 1998), 284–287, and William Miller, *Innovation Styles* (Global Creativity Corporation, 1997).

EXHIBIT 3.5
Porter's Competitive Strategies

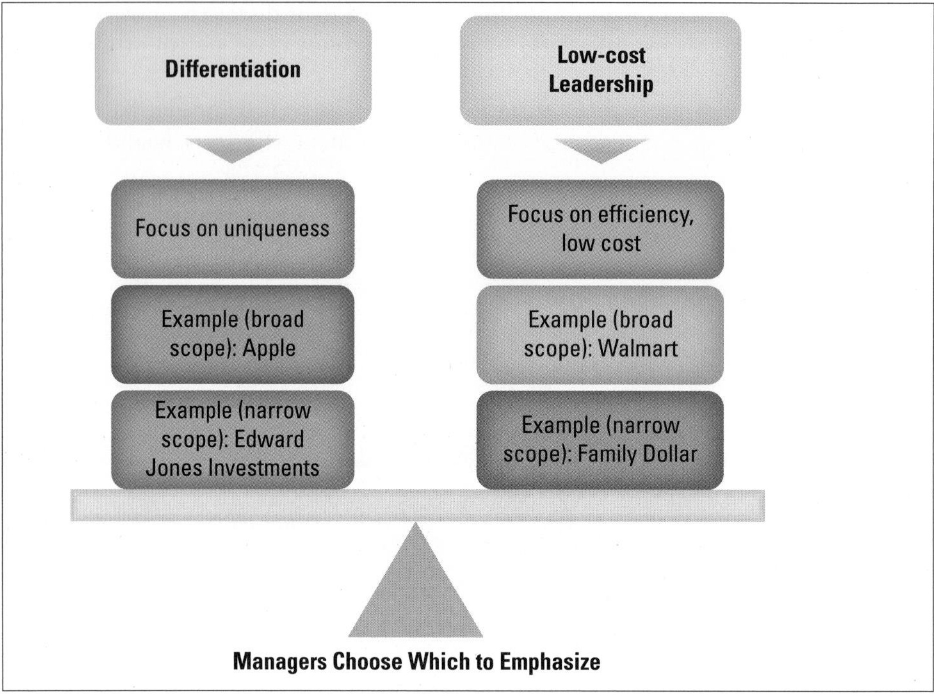

Source: Based on Michael E. Porter, *Competitive Advantage: Creating and Sustaining Superior Performance* (New York: The Free Press, 1988).

than just a financial institution. Many branches have free wi-fi access, spacious seating areas with big-screen televisions, and Umpqua branded coffee. The company recently released its first CD—not a "certificate of deposit," but the kind with music on it. The bank worked with music marketing firm Rumblefish to put together a collection of songs by new or undiscovered artists in the markets where Umpqua operates. Over the past dozen or so years, Umpqua's differentiation strategy has helped it grow from about $150 million in deposits to more than $7 billion.[29]

Low-Cost Leadership. The **low-cost leadership strategy** tries to increase market share by keeping costs low compared to competitors. With a low-cost leadership strategy, the organization aggressively seeks efficient facilities, pursues cost reductions, and uses tight controls to produce products or services more efficiently than its competitors. Low-cost doesn't necessarily mean low price, but in many cases low-cost leaders provide goods and services to customers at cheaper prices. For example, the CEO of Irish airline Ryanair said of the company's strategy: "It's the oldest, simplest formula: Pile 'em high and sell 'em cheap... We want to be the Walmart of the airline business. Nobody will beat us on price. EVER." Ryanair can offer low fares because it keeps costs at rock bottom, lower than anyone else in Europe. The company's watchword is cheap tickets, not customer care or unique services.[30]

The low-cost leadership strategy is concerned primarily with stability rather than taking risks or seeking new opportunities for innovation and growth. A low-cost position means a company can achieve higher profits than competitors because of its efficiency and lower operating costs. Low-cost leaders such as Ryanair can undercut competitors' prices and still earn a reasonable profit. In addition, if substitute products or potential new competitors enter the picture, the low-cost producer is in a better position to prevent loss of market share. Consider how Acer Inc. became the world's second-largest computer maker with a low-cost leadership strategy.

IN PRACTICE

Acer Inc.

In 2004, Acer owned less than 5 percent of the global personal computer market, compared to Hewlett-Packard's 15 percent and Dell's nearly 20 percent. Six years later, the Taiwan-based company had surpassed Dell and was closing in on HP. How did it happen? Managers, led by former CEO Gianfranco Lanci, used a strategy based on exploiting the company's core competencies of extremely lean operations combined with a speedy response to shifting consumer trends.

Acer has a bare-bones cost structure. Unlike rival companies, it sells only through retailers, and the company outsources all manufacturing and assembly to a network of partners. That has helped keep overhead expenses for Acer at about 8 percent of sales, compared to around 14 to 15 percent for rival companies. Cost savings are passed on to consumers, with a high-quality ultrathin laptop selling for around $650, compared to $1,800 for a similar HP model and $2,000 for Dell's ultrathin. Moreover, Acer managers saw the trend toward smaller devices and were able to move quickly to introduce a wide selection of inexpensive netbooks.

Acer introduced its first smartphone in 2009 and has since added numerous other models. It's one of the fastest-growing sectors in the industry. With Acer's low cost structure, it can give consumers quality smartphones at lower cost and still see profit margins in the range of 15 percent to 20 percent.[31]

Porter found that companies that did not consciously adopt a low-cost or differentiation strategy achieved below-average profits compared to those that used one of the strategies. Many Internet companies have failed because managers did not develop competitive strategies that would distinguish them in the marketplace.[32] On the other hand, Google became highly successful with a coherent differentiation strategy that distinguished it from other search engines.

2 The best business strategy is to make products and services as distinctive as possible to gain an edge in the marketplace.

ANSWER: *Disagree.* Differentiation, making the company's products or services distinctive from others in the market, is one effective strategic approach. A low-cost leadership approach can be equally or even more effective depending on the organization's strengths and the nature of competition in the industry.

Competitive Scope Can Be Broad or Narrow. With either strategy, the scope of competitive action can be either broad or narrow. That is, an organization can choose to compete in many market and customer segments or to focus on a specific market or buyer group. For example, both Walmart and Family Dollar use a low-cost leadership strategy, but Walmart competes in a broad market whereas Family Dollar concentrates on a narrow market. Family Dollar stores offer prices on major brands such as Tide or Colgate that are 20 percent to 40 percent lower than those found in major supermarkets. The company locates its stores on inexpensive, unglamorous real estate and markets to people making less than $35,000 a year rather than trying to court a wider customer base.[33] An example of a narrowly focused differentiation strategy is Edward Jones Investments, a St. Louis-based brokerage house. The company concentrates on building its business in rural and small-town America and providing clients with conservative, long-term investment advice. Management scholar and consultant Peter Drucker once said the distinctive safety-first orientation means Edward Jones delivers a product "that no Wall Street house has ever sold before: peace of mind."[34]

Miles and Snow's Strategy Typology

Another strategy typology was developed from the study of business strategies by Raymond Miles and Charles Snow.[35] The Miles and Snow typology is based on the idea that managers seek to formulate strategies that will be congruent with the external environment. Organizations strive for a fit among internal organization characteristics, strategy, and the external environment. The four strategies that can be developed are the prospector, the defender, the analyzer, and the reactor.

Prospector. The **prospector** strategy is to innovate, take risks, seek out new opportunities, and grow. This strategy is suited to a dynamic, growing environment, where creativity is more important than efficiency. Nike, which innovates in both products and internal processes, exemplifies the prospector strategy. For example, the company has introduced a new line of shoes based on designs that can be produced using recycled materials and limited amounts of toxic chemical-based glues.[36] China's Zhejiang Geely Holding Group is setting a prospector strategy for Volvo Car Corporation after acquiring the global automaker from Ford Motor Company in 2010.

Volvo Car Corporation

IN PRACTICE

For several years Volvo has focused on stability, seeking to hang on to customers who appreciate the brand's reputation for safe, reliable family vehicles. But Li Shufu, the company's new hard-charging Chinese owner, is setting a new course for the company, aiming to expand aggressively into the luxury car market and compete head-on with the likes of BMW and Mercedes. Li's company, Zhejiang Geely Holding Group, acquired Volvo from Ford in a landmark deal in 2010.

Li has clashed with Volvo's European CEO, Stefan Jacoby, who wants to move more slowly away from the company's tradition of modest style, but the two eventually agreed on an ambitious turnaround plan that involves $10 billion in investment over a five-year period and a goal of doubling worldwide sales to 800,000 vehicles by 2020. The plan to build three new manufacturing plants in China has been scaled back to one, scheduled to start production in 2013, but Li still wants to build more as soon as possible.

In April 2011, Volvo introduced the Concept Universe, an upscale vehicle that reflects the goal of moving into snazzier luxury models. The car's underpinning, called SPA for "scalable platform architecture," was designed to be able to accommodate a larger car in the future. China's emerging class of rich consumers "behave outrageously," Li says, and he wants Volvo to offer innovative, electrifying designs that turn heads and win new customers. China sales are a growing part of the auto business, and Li says Volvo has no future unless it caters to the flashier tastes of emerging rich consumers in that country.[37]

Li and Jacoby are continuing to work out their differing visions and management styles, but the prospector strategy to upgrade the product lineup and expand aggressively is on course. Online companies such as Facebook, Google, and Zynga, whose motto is "Connecting the World through Games," also reflect a prospector strategy.

Defender. The **defender** strategy is almost the opposite of the prospector. Rather than taking risks and seeking out new opportunities, the defender strategy is concerned with stability or even retrenchment. This strategy seeks to hold on to current customers, but it neither innovates nor seeks to grow. The defender is concerned primarily with internal efficiency and control to produce reliable, high-quality products for steady customers. This strategy can be successful when the organization exists in a declining industry or a stable environment. Paramount Pictures has been using a defender strategy for several years.[38] Paramount turns out a steady stream of reliable hits but few blockbusters. Managers shun risk and sometimes turn down potentially high-profile films to keep a lid on costs. This has enabled the company to remain highly profitable while other studios have low returns or actually lose money.

Analyzer. The **analyzer** tries to maintain a stable business while innovating on the periphery. It seems to lie midway between the prospector and the defender. Some products will be targeted at stable environments in which an efficiency strategy designed to keep current customers is used. Others will be targeted at new, more dynamic environments, where growth is possible. The analyzer attempts to balance efficient production for current product or service lines with the creative development of new product lines. Amazon.com provides an example. The company's current strategy is to defend its core business of selling books and other physical goods over the Internet, but also to build a business in digital media, including initiatives such as a digital book service, an online movie rental business, and a digital music store to compete with Apple's iTunes.[39]

Reactor. The **reactor** strategy is not really a strategy at all. Rather, reactors respond to environmental threats and opportunities in an ad hoc fashion. With a reactor strategy, top management has not defined a long-range plan or given the organization an explicit mission or goal, so the organization takes whatever actions seem to meet immediate needs. Although the reactor strategy can sometimes be successful, it can also lead to failed companies. Some large, once highly successful companies are struggling because managers failed to adopt a strategy consistent with consumer trends. In recent years managers at Dell, long one of the most successful and profitable makers of personal computers in the world, have been floundering to find the appropriate strategy. Dell had a string of disappointing quarterly profits as the company reached the limits of its "make PCs cheap and build them to order" strategy. Competitors caught up, and Dell had failed to identify new strategic directions that could provide a new edge.[40]

BRIEFCASE

As an organization manager, keep these guidelines in mind:

Design the organization to support the firm's competitive strategy. With a low-cost leadership or defender strategy, select design characteristics associated with an efficiency orientation. For a differentiation or prospector strategy, on the other hand, choose characteristics that encourage learning, innovation, and adaptation. Use a balanced mixture of characteristics for an analyzer strategy.

The Miles and Snow typology has been widely used, and researchers have tested its validity in a variety of organizations, including hospitals, colleges, banking institutions, industrial products companies, and life insurance firms. In general, researchers have found strong support for the effectiveness of this typology for organization managers in real-world situations.[41]

The ability of managers to devise and maintain a clear competitive strategy is considered one of the defining factors in an organization's success, but many managers struggle with this crucial responsibility. This chapter's BookMark describes how managers can learn to craft valuable strategies by understanding what distinguishes a good strategy from a bad one.

How Strategies Affect Organization Design

Choice of strategy affects internal organization characteristics. Organization design characteristics need to support the firm's competitive approach. For example, a company wanting to grow and invent new products looks and "feels" different from a company that is focused on maintaining market share for long-established products in a stable industry. Exhibit 3.6 summarizes organization design characteristics associated with the Porter and Miles and Snow strategies.

With a low-cost leadership strategy, managers take a primarily mechanistic, efficiency approach to organization design, whereas a differentiation strategy calls for a more organic, learning approach. Recall from Chapter 1 that mechanistic organizations designed for efficiency have different characteristics from organic organizations designed for learning. A low-cost leadership strategy (efficiency) is associated with strong, centralized authority and tight control, standard operating procedures, and emphasis on efficient procurement and distribution systems. Employees generally perform routine tasks under close supervision and control and are not empowered to make decisions or take action on their own. A differentiation strategy, on the other hand, requires that employees be constantly experimenting and learning. Structure is fluid and flexible, with strong horizontal coordination. Empowered employees work directly with customers and are rewarded for creativity and risk taking. The organization values research, creativity, and innovativeness over efficiency and standard procedures.

The prospector strategy requires characteristics similar to a differentiation strategy, and the defender strategy takes an efficiency approach similar to low-cost leadership. Because the analyzer strategy attempts to balance efficiency for stable product lines with flexibility and learning for new products, it is associated with a mix of characteristics, as listed in Exhibit 3.6. With a reactor strategy, managers have left the organization with no direction and no clear approach to design.

Other Contingency Factors Affecting Organization Design

Strategy is one important factor that affects organization design. Ultimately, however, organization design is a result of numerous contingencies, which will be discussed throughout this book. The emphasis given to efficiency and control (mechanistic) versus learning and flexibility (organic) is determined by the contingencies of strategy, environment, size and life cycle, technology, and organizational

BOOKMARK

3.0 HAVE YOU READ THIS BOOK?

Good Strategy Bad Strategy: The Difference and Why It Matters

By Richard Rumelt

Richard Rumelt, the Harry and Elsa Kunin Chair in Business and Society at UCLA's Anderson School of Management, points out that "winging it is not a strategy." Corporate leaders are always talking about strategy, but Rumelt says many of them are just winging it. "Too many organizational leaders say they have a strategy when they do not," writes Rumelt in *Good Strategy Bad Strategy: The Difference and Why It Matters*. Instead, he explains, they have fallen prey to "the creeping spread of bad strategy."

HOW TO TELL A BAD STRATEGY FROM A GOOD ONE

Some carefully devised strategies founder or fail because of managers' miscalculations or flawed decisions, but what Rumelt calls bad strategy is something else entirely and can be identified by several characteristics. First, many executives mistake goals for strategy. Have you ever heard a CEO proclaim that his company's strategy is "to grow by 20 percent a year" or "to increase profits by 15 percent?" These desired outcomes, emphasizes Rumelt, are not strategy. Goals define where you want the organization to go, whereas "strategy is how you are going to get there." Following are three other ways to tell a bad strategy from a good one.

- *It Fails to Define the Problem.* "A good strategy does more than urge us forward toward a goal or vision; it honestly acknowledges the challenges we face and provides an approach to overcoming them," Rumelt writes. Managers can't craft a good strategy unless they clearly define the challenge or problem. If managers have failed to identify and analyze the obstacles they're aiming to overcome, then they have a bad strategy.
- *It Is Based on Weak or Fuzzy Objectives.* A good strategy is focused. Managers have to carefully choose a few clearly defined goals to pursue, which means other goals have to be set aside. Bad strategy results when managers pursue what Rumelt calls "a dog's dinner of goals"—a long list of desires, objectives, and things to do. Another problem many managers fall prey to is the "blue sky goal." This kind of lofty objective inspires a wish-driven strategy that "skips over the annoying fact that no one has a clue how to get there."
- *It Is Mostly Fluff.* Fluff refers to a "superficial restatement of the obvious combined with a generous sprinkling of buzzwords." Good strategy is clearly stated, based on a careful analysis of problems, opportunities, and sources of strength and weakness, and focuses on actionable objectives. It builds a bridge between the current state of affairs and the desired outcome with specific strategic actions. A "flurry of fluff designed to mask the absence of thought" is a clear sign of a bad strategy.

THREE ELEMENTS OF GOOD STRATEGY

Following is a summary of the elements of good strategy:

- *Diagnosis.* A careful analysis of the challenges and problems facing the organization comes first. To conduct this analysis, managers define specific critical issues in the environment in order to simplify the complexity of the situation.
- *A Guiding Policy.* This is an overall approach that managers choose for how the organization will cope with or overcome the challenges. The guiding policy is designed to give the organization a distinctive *advantage* over competitors.
- *Coherent Action Steps.* Good strategy always specifies *how* the organization will achieve the strategic goals. Execution is often the hardest part and includes action steps that are coordinated to facilitate the accomplishment of the guiding policy.

Good Strategy Bad Strategy is not only thought-provoking but also an enjoyable read. Using examples ranging from Hannibal's defeat of a larger Roman army at Cannae in 216 BC to Steve Jobs' rescue of Apple in the late twentieth and early twenty-first centuries, Rumelt shows us what a good strategy is—and how it can make the difference between success and failure.

Good Strategy Bad Strategy: The Difference and Why It Matters, by Richard Rumelt, is published by Crown Business.

EXHIBIT 3.6
Organization Design Outcomes of Strategy

Porter's Competitive Strategies	Miles and Snow's Strategy Typology
Strategy: Differentiation **Organization Design:** • Learning orientation; acts in a flexible, loosely knit way, with strong horizontal coordination • Strong capability in research • Values and builds in mechanisms for customer intimacy • Rewards employee creativity, risk taking, and innovation **Strategy:** Low-Cost Leadership **Organization Design:** • Efficiency orientation; strong central authority; tight cost control, with frequent, detailed control reports • Standard operating procedures • Highly efficient procurement and distribution systems • Close supervision; routine tasks; limited employee empowerment	**Strategy:** Prospector **Organization Design:** • Learning orientation; flexible, fluid, decentralized structure • Strong capability in research **Strategy:** Defender **Organization Design:** • Efficiency orientation; centralized authority; tight cost control • Emphasis on production efficiency; low overhead • Close supervision; little employee empowerment **Strategy:** Analyzer **Organization Design:** • Balances efficiency and learning; tight cost control with flexibility and adaptability • Efficient production for stable product lines; emphasis on creativity, research, risk-taking for innovation **Strategy:** Reactor **Organization Design:** • No clear organizational approach; design characteristics may shift abruptly, depending on current needs

Source: Based on Michael E. Porter, *Competitive Strategy: Techniques for Analyzing Industries and Competitors* (New York: The Free Press, 1980); Michael Treacy and Fred Wiersema, "How Market Leaders Keep Their Edge," *Fortune* (February 6, 1995), 88–98; Michael Hitt, R. Duane Ireland, and Robert E. Hoskisson, *Strategic Management* (St. Paul, Minn.: West, 1995), 100–113; and Raymond E. Miles, Charles C. Snow, Alan D. Meyer, and Henry J. Coleman, Jr., "Organizational Strategy, Structure, and Process," *Academy of Management Review* 3 (1978), 546–562.

culture. The organization is designed to "fit" the contingency factors, as illustrated in Exhibit 3.7.

In a stable environment, for example, the organization can have a traditional mechanistic structure that emphasizes vertical control, efficiency, specialization, standard procedures, and centralized decision making. However, a rapidly changing environment may call for a more flexible, organic structure, with strong horizontal coordination and collaboration through teams or other mechanisms. Environment will be discussed in detail in Chapters 4 and 6. In terms of size and life cycle, young, small organizations are generally informal and have little division of labor, few rules and regulations, and ad hoc budgeting and performance systems. Large organizations such as Coca-Cola, Sony, or General Electric, on the other hand, have an extensive division of labor, numerous rules and regulations, and standard procedures and systems for budgeting, control, rewards, and innovation. Size and stages of the life cycle will be discussed in Chapter 12.

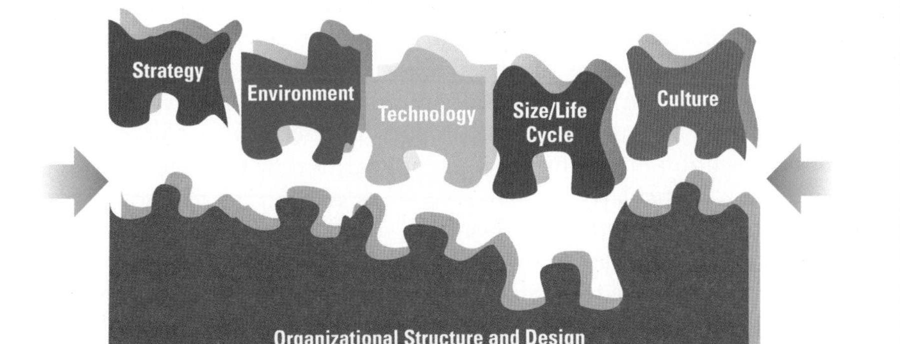

The Right Mix of Design Characteristics Fits the Contingency Factors

EXHIBIT 3.7
Contingency Factors Affecting Organization Design

Design must also fit the workflow technology of the organization. For example, with mass production technology, such as a traditional automobile assembly line, the organization functions best by emphasizing efficiency, formalization, specialization, centralized decision making, and tight control. An e-business, on the other hand, would need to be more informal and flexible. Technology's impact on design will be discussed in detail in Chapters 11 and 13. A final contingency that affects organization design is corporate culture. An organizational culture that values teamwork, collaboration, creativity, and open communication, for example, would not function well with a tight, vertical structure and strict rules and regulations. The role of culture is discussed in Chapter 9.

One responsibility of managers is to design organizations that fit the contingency factors of strategy, environment, size and life cycle, technology, and culture. Finding the right fit leads to organizational effectiveness, whereas a poor fit can lead to decline or even the demise of the organization.

Assessing Organizational Effectiveness

Understanding organizational goals and strategies, as well as the concept of fitting design to various contingencies, is a first step toward understanding organizational effectiveness. Organizational goals represent the reason for an organization's existence and the outcomes it seeks to achieve. The rest of this chapter explores the topic of effectiveness and how effectiveness is measured in organizations.

Definition

Recall from Chapter 1 that organizational effectiveness is the degree to which an organization realizes its goals. *Effectiveness* is a broad concept. It implicitly takes into consideration a range of variables at both the organizational and departmental levels. Effectiveness evaluates the extent to which multiple goals—whether official or operating—are attained. *Efficiency* is a more limited concept that pertains to the internal workings of the organization. Organizational efficiency is the amount of resources used to produce a unit of output.[42] It can be measured as the ratio of inputs to outputs. If one organization can achieve a given production level with fewer resources than another organization, it would be described as more efficient.[43]

Sometimes efficiency leads to effectiveness, but in other organizations efficiency and effectiveness are not related. An organization may be highly efficient but fail to achieve its goals because it makes a product for which there is no demand. Likewise, an organization may achieve its profit goals but be inefficient. Efforts to increase efficiency, particularly through severe cost cutting, can also sometimes make the organization less effective. For example, one regional fast food chain wanting to increase efficiency decided to reduce food waste by not cooking any food until it was ordered. The move reduced the chain's costs, but it also led to delayed service, irritated customers, and lower sales.[44]

Overall effectiveness is difficult to measure in organizations. Organizations are large, diverse, and fragmented. They perform many activities simultaneously, pursue multiple goals, and generate many outcomes, some intended and some unintended.[45] Managers determine what indicators to measure in order to gauge the effectiveness of their organizations. Four possible approaches to measuring effectiveness are:

- The Goal Approach
- The Resource-Based Approach
- The Internal Process Approach
- The Strategic Constituents Approach

Who Decides?

Key people in charge of the organization, such as top managers or board members, have to make a conscious decision about how they will determine the organization's effectiveness. Organizational effectiveness is a **social construct**, meaning that it is created and defined by an individual or group rather than existing independently in the external world.[46] An analogy from baseball that clarifies the concept is the story of three umpires explaining how they call balls and strikes. The first says, "I call 'em as they are." The second says, "I call 'em as I see 'em." The third takes a social construct approach and says, "They ain't nothin' 'til I call 'em."[47] Similarly, organizational effectiveness is nothing until managers or stakeholders "call it."

An employee might consider the organization is effective if it issues accurate paychecks on time and provides promised benefits. A customer might consider it effective if it provides a good product at a low price. A CEO might consider the organization effective if it is profitable. Effectiveness is always multidimensional, and thus assessments of effectiveness are typically multidimensional as well. Managers in businesses typically use profits and stock performance as indicators of effectiveness, but they also give credence to other measures, such as employee satisfaction or customer loyalty.

Managers often use indicators from more than one of the four approaches (goal, resource, internal process, strategic constituents) when measuring effectiveness. Exhibit 3.8 lists a sample of 15 indicators that managers of large, multinational organizations reported using to assess effectiveness. As you read the descriptions of the four approaches to measuring effectiveness in the following sections, try to decide which approach each of these 15 indicators falls under.[48]

As the items in Exhibit 3.8 reveal, indicators of effectiveness are both quantitative and qualitative, tangible and intangible. An indicator such as achieving sales

EXHIBIT 3.8
Some Indicators of Organizational Effectiveness Reported by Multinational Organizations

1. Meeting deadlines; on-time delivery
2. Timely material and equipment acquisition
3. Quality of product or service
4. Customer satisfaction/complaints
5. Market share compared to competitors
6. Employee training and development (number of hours)
7. Staying within budget
8. Shareholder satisfaction
9. Reduction in costs
10. Supply chain delays or improvements
11. Productivity; dollars spent for each unit of output
12. Employee engagement
13. Achieving sales targets
14. Product development cycle time (reduction in cycle time)
15. Number of hours/days/etc. to complete tasks

Source: Based on "Table 1; Initial Items Derived from Interviews," in Cristina B. Gibson, Mary E. Zellmer-Bruhn, and Donald P. Schwab, "Team Effectiveness in Multinational Organizations: Evaluation Across Contexts," *Group & Organizational Management* 28, no. 4 (December 2003), 444–474.

targets or percentage of market share is easy to measure, but indicators such as employee engagement, quality, or customer satisfaction are less clear-cut and often have to be measured qualitatively.[49] Relying solely on quantitative measurements can give managers a limited or distorted view of effectiveness. Albert Einstein is reported to have kept a sign in his office that read, "Not everything that counts can be counted, and not everything that can be counted counts."[50]

Four Effectiveness Approaches

As open systems, organizations bring in resources from the environment, and those resources are transformed into outputs delivered back into the environment, as shown in Exhibit 3.9. In addition, recall from Chapter 1 that organizations interact with a number of stakeholder groups inside and outside the organization. Four key approaches to measuring effectiveness look at different parts of the organization and measure indicators connected with outputs, inputs, internal activities, or key stakeholders, also called strategic constituents.[51]

Goal Approach

The **goal approach** to effectiveness consists of identifying an organization's output goals and assessing how well the organization has attained those goals.[52] This is a logical approach because organizations do try to attain certain levels of output, profit, or client satisfaction. The goal approach measures progress toward the attainment of those goals.

Indicators. The important goals to consider are operating goals, because official goals (mission) tend to be abstract and difficult to measure. Operating goals reflect activities the organization is actually performing.[53]

EXHIBIT 3.9
Four Approaches to Measuring Organizational Effectiveness

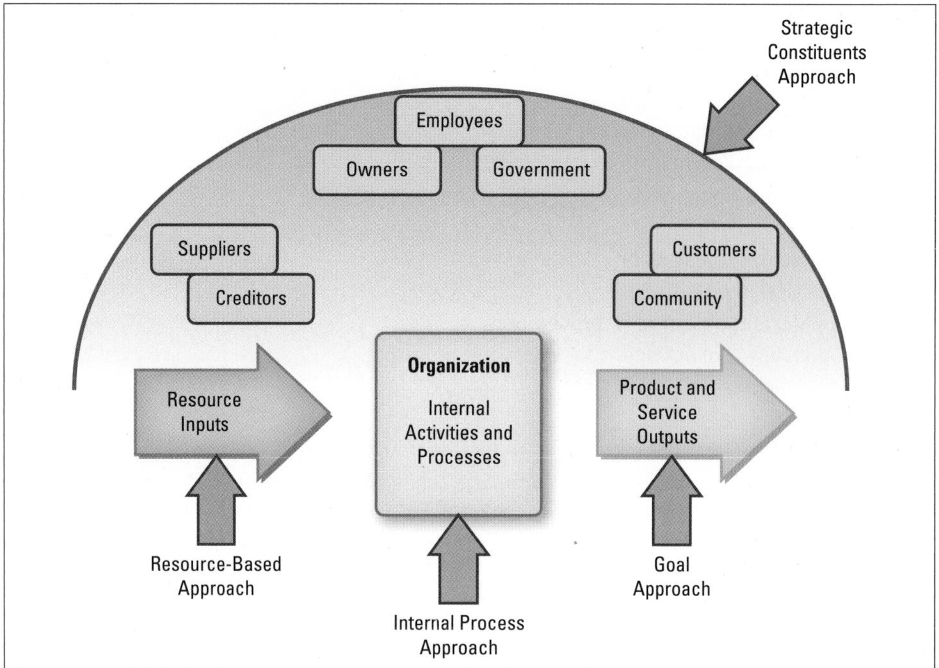

Indicators tracked with the goal approach include:

- Profitability—the positive gain from business operations or investments after expenses are subtracted
- Market share—the proportion of the market the firm is able to capture relative to competitors
- Growth—the ability of the organization to increase its sales, profits, or client base over time
- Social responsibility—how well the organization serves the interests of society as well as itself
- Product quality—the ability of the organization to achieve high quality in its products or services

Usefulness. The goal approach is used in business organizations because output goals can be readily measured. As illustrated by the following example, however, some nonprofit organizations that aim to solve social problems also find the goal approach useful.

Every Child Succeeds

IN PRACTICE

Using a rigorous model of performance measurement based on some of the management practices at Procter & Gamble, Every Child Succeeds is a public-private partnership funded primarily by United Way that aims to reduce infant mortality and improve maternal health in the area surrounding Cincinnati, Ohio. In the seven Ohio and Kentucky counties around the city, 8.3 out of every 1,000 newborns die before they reach their first birthday, on par with countries such as Lithuania and Brunei. Yet among the mothers enrolled in Every Child Succeeds, that statistic is only 2.8 percent, lower than in virtually every industrialized country.

Social workers and nurses from 15 participating organizations, including two Cincinnati hospitals and several social service agencies, visit at-risk mothers in their homes and help them stop smoking, learn to eat better, control their diabetes or high blood pressure, and improve their health in other ways. Unlike many social improvement programs, Every Child Succeeds sets and measures a few narrow and specific goals organized under seven focus areas. The program limits its reach to first time mothers and works with the client from pregnancy until the child's third birthday.

Managers collect reams of data that enable them to measure what is working and fix what is not. A chart hangs in the agency offices that lists 17 indicators, such as immunization rates, rate of breast feeding, and client satisfaction, and shows how well each of the participating agencies is doing on meeting targets. When the Cincinnati Home for Children failed to meet the immunization target of 80 percent, managers created an action plan that quickly improved performance on that indicator.[54]

Usefulness. In businesses as well as in nonprofit organizations such as Every Child Succeeds, identifying operating goals and measuring effectiveness are not always easy. Two problems that must be resolved are the issues of multiple goals and subjective indicators of goal attainment. Since organizations have multiple and sometimes conflicting goals, effectiveness cannot be assessed by a single indicator. High achievement on one goal might mean low achievement on another. Moreover, there are department goals as well as overall organizational goals. The full assessment of effectiveness should take into consideration several goals simultaneously.

The other issue to resolve with the goal approach is how to identify operating goals for an organization and how to measure goal attainment. For business organizations, there are often objective indicators for certain goals, such as profit or growth. Every Child Succeeds can also use objective indicators for some goals, such as tracking how many infants are immunized or how many clients stop smoking during pregnancy. However, subjective assessment is needed for other goals, such as employee welfare, social responsibility, or client satisfaction. Top managers and other key people on the management team have to clearly identify which goals the organization will measure. Subjective perceptions of goal attainment must be used when quantitative indicators are not available. Managers rely on information from customers, competitors, suppliers, and employees, as well as their own intuition, when considering these goals.

Resource-Based Approach

The **resource-based approach** looks at the input side of the transformation process shown in Exhibit 3.9. It assumes organizations must be successful in obtaining and managing valued resources in order to be effective because strategically valuable resources give an organization a competitive edge.[55] From a resource-based perspective, organizational effectiveness is defined as the ability of the organization, in either absolute or relative terms, to obtain scarce and valued resources and successfully integrate and manage them.[56]

Indicators. Obtaining and successfully managing resources is the criterion by which organizational effectiveness is assessed. In a broad sense, resource indicators of effectiveness encompass the following dimensions:[57]

- Bargaining position—the ability of the organization to obtain from its environment scarce and valued resources, including tangible resources such as a prime location, financing, raw materials, and quality employees, and intangible assets such as a strong brand or superior knowledge

- The abilities of the organization's decision makers to perceive and correctly interpret the real properties of the external environment and supply forces
- The abilities of managers to use tangible (e.g., supplies, people) and intangible (e.g., knowledge, corporate culture) resources and capabilities in day-to-day organizational activities to achieve superior performance
- The ability of the organization to respond to changes in resource sectors of the environment

Usefulness. The resource-based approach is valuable when other indicators of performance are difficult to obtain. In many nonprofit and social welfare organizations, for example, it is hard to measure output goals or internal efficiency. The Shriners Hospitals for Children (SHC) system provides an example. The 22 Shriners Hospitals provide free treatment to thousands of children with orthopedic conditions, burns, spinal cord injuries, and cleft lip and palette conditions. For most of its history, the SHC was highly successful in obtaining donations, the main source of funding for the hospitals' operations. However, when the federal government launched a no-cost health insurance program for children of low-income families, Shriners began losing patients to traditional healthcare providers. With a decline in patient registrations, donations began to decline as well. Managers had to search for new ways to respond to the increased competition and obtain needed resources.[58] Many for-profit organizations also use a resource-based approach because resources are critical to competitive success. For example, the British retail firm Marks & Spencer evaluates its effectiveness partly by looking at the company's ability to obtain, manage, and maintain valued resources such as prime locations for stores, a strong brand, quality employees, and effective supplier relationships.[59]

Although the resource-based approach is valuable when other measures of effectiveness are not available, it does have shortcomings. For one thing, the approach only vaguely considers the organization's link to the needs of customers. A superior ability to acquire and use resources is important only if resources and capabilities are used to achieve something that meets a need in the environment. Critics have challenged that the approach assumes stability in the marketplace and fails to adequately consider the changing value of various resources as the competitive environment and customer needs change.[60]

BRIEFCASE

As an organization manager, keep these guidelines in mind:

Use the goal approach, internal process approach, and resource-based approach to obtain specific interpretations of organizational effectiveness in the areas of outputs, internal processes, and inputs. Assess the satisfaction of strategic constituents or use the competing values model to obtain a broader picture of effectiveness.

Internal Process Approach

In the **internal process approach**, effectiveness is measured as internal organizational health and efficiency. An effective organization has a smooth, well-oiled internal process. Employees are happy and satisfied. Department activities mesh with one another to ensure high productivity. This approach does not consider the external environment. The important element in effectiveness is what the organization does with the resources it has, as reflected in internal health and efficiency.

Indicators. One indicator of internal process effectiveness is economic efficiency. However, the best-known proponents of an internal process model are from the human relations approach to organizations. Such writers as Chris Argyris, Warren G. Bennis, Rensis Likert, and Richard Beckhard have all worked extensively with human resources in organizations and emphasize the connection between human resources and effectiveness.[61] Results from a study of nearly 200 secondary schools showed that both human resources and employee-oriented processes were important in explaining and promoting effectiveness in those organizations.[62]

Internal process indicators include:[63]

- A strong, adaptive corporate culture and positive work climate
- Confidence and trust between employees and management
- Operational efficiency, such as using minimal resources to achieve outcomes
- Undistorted horizontal and vertical communication
- Growth and development of employees
- Coordination among the organization's parts, with conflicts resolved in the interest of the larger organization

Usefulness. The internal process approach is important because the efficient use of resources and harmonious internal functioning are good ways to assess organizational effectiveness. In the wake of the economic recession, companies such as DuPont, Campbell Soup, and UPS are looking for ways to be more efficient, such as using existing technology to accomplish more with less. At Campbell's Maxton, North Carolina-based factory, hundreds of small changes and improvements, many suggested by employees, have increased operating efficiency to 85 percent of what managers believe is the maximum possible. UPS trucks carry devices that track how many left-turns against traffic its drivers have to make. By helping drivers optimize their routes with fewer left turns, the system will save UPS 1.4 million gallons of fuel per year.[64]

Today, most managers believe that committed, actively involved employees and a positive corporate culture are also important internal measures of effectiveness. A good example of an internal process approach focused on employees is the Ritz-Carlton hotel chain. Managers carefully track performance data related to employee engagement, customer engagement, and "maintaining the Ritz-Carlton Mystique." If employees aren't engaged, customers can't be satisfied and engaged, the mystique of the brand suffers, and thus financial performance will decline. Employee training is ongoing, and employees have access to data that let them see how well they are doing on meeting performance targets. The culture encourages employees to do whatever it takes to make customers happy. Every employee takes part in a daily pre-shift meeting to discuss actions, events, issues, and the Ritz-Carlton philosophy. The learning environment at Ritz-Carlton, said John Timmerman, vice president of operations, "is how we stay agile in an ever-changing world."[65]

The internal process approach also has shortcomings. Total output and the organization's relationship with the external environment are not evaluated. Another problem is that evaluations of internal health and functioning are often subjective because many aspects of inputs and internal processes are not quantifiable. Managers should be aware that this approach alone represents a limited view of organizational effectiveness.

Strategic Constituents Approach

The strategic constituents approach is related to the stakeholder approach described in Chapter 1. Recall from Exhibit 1.5 that organizations have a variety of internal and external stakeholders that may have competing claims on what they want from the organization. Several important stakeholder groups are also shown at the top of Exhibit 3.9.

In reality, it is unreasonable to assume that all stakeholders can be equally satisfied. The **strategic constituents approach** measures effectiveness by focusing on the satisfaction of key stakeholders, those who are critical to the organization's ability

to survive and thrive. The satisfaction of these strategic constituents can be assessed as an indicator of the organization's performance.[66]

Indicators. The initial work on evaluating effectiveness on the basis of strategic constituents looked at 97 small businesses and seven groups relevant to those organizations. Members of each group were surveyed to determine the perception of effectiveness from each viewpoint.[67] Each constituent group had a different criterion of effectiveness:

Strategic Constituent Group	Effectiveness Criteria
Owners	Financial return
Employees	Pay, good supervision, worker satisfaction
Customers	Quality of goods and services
Creditors	Creditworthiness
Community	Contribution to community affairs
Suppliers	Satisfactory transactions
Government	Obedience to laws and regulations

If an organization fails to meet the needs of several constituent groups, it is probably not meeting its effectiveness goals. Although these seven groups reflect constituents that nearly every organization has to satisfy to some degree, each organization might have a different set of strategic constituents. For example, independent software developers are key to the success of *Facebook* even though they are not necessarily customers, suppliers, or owners. CEO Mark Zuckerberg works hard to win over developers. At a developer's conference, he unveiled a new technology that lets websites install a Facebook "Like" button for free. Users can click on it to signal their interest in a piece of content. The user's approval then shows up on his or her Facebook page with a link back to the site. The technology will drive traffic from Facebook to other websites, and in turn drive traffic back to Facebook.[68]

Usefulness. Research has shown that the assessment of multiple constituents is an accurate reflection of organizational effectiveness, especially with respect to organizational adaptability.[69] Moreover, both profit and nonprofit organizations care about their reputations and attempt to shape perceptions of their performance.[70] The strategic constituents approach takes a broader view of effectiveness and examines factors in the environment as well as within the organization. It looks at several criteria simultaneously—inputs, internal processes, and outputs—and acknowledges that there is no single measure of effectiveness.

The strategic constituents approach is popular because it is based on the understanding that effectiveness is a complex, multidimensional concept and has no single measure.[71] In the following section, we look at another popular approach that takes a multidimensional, integrated approach to measuring effectiveness.

An Integrated Effectiveness Model

The **competing values model** tries to balance a concern with various parts of the organization rather than focusing on one part. This approach to effectiveness acknowledges that organizations do many things and have many outcomes.[72] It combines several indicators of effectiveness into a single framework.

The model is based on the assumption that there are disagreements and competing viewpoints about what constitutes effectiveness. Managers sometimes disagree over which are the most important goals to pursue and measure. One tragic example of conflicting viewpoints and competing interests comes from NASA. After seven astronauts died in the explosion of the space shuttle Columbia in February 2003, an investigative committee found deep organizational flaws at NASA, including ineffective mechanisms for incorporating dissenting opinions between scheduling managers and safety managers. External pressures to launch on time overrode safety concerns with the Columbia launch.[73] Similarly, Congressional investigations of the 2010 Deepwater Horizon oil rig explosion and oil spill in the Gulf of Mexico found that BP engineers and managers made a number of decisions that were counter to the advice of key contractors, putting goals of cost control and timeliness ahead of concerns over well safety.[74] BP and NASA represent how complex organizations can be, operating not only with different viewpoints internally but also from contractors, government regulators, Congress, and the expectations of the American public.

The competing values model takes into account these complexities. The model was originally developed by Robert Quinn and John Rohrbaugh to combine the diverse indicators of performance used by managers and researchers.[75] Using a comprehensive list of performance indicators, a panel of experts in organizational effectiveness rated the indicators for similarity. Their analysis found underlying dimensions of effectiveness criteria that represented competing management values in organizations.

Indicators. The first value dimension pertains to organizational **focus**, which is whether dominant values concern issues that are *internal* or *external* to the firm. Internal focus reflects a management concern for the well-being and efficiency of employees, and external focus represents an emphasis on the well-being of the organization itself with respect to the environment. The second value dimension pertains to organization **structure** and whether *stability* or *flexibility* is the dominant structural consideration. Stability reflects a management value for efficiency and top-down control, whereas flexibility represents a value for learning and change.

The value dimensions of structure and focus are illustrated in Exhibit 3.10. The combination of dimensions provides four approaches to organizational effectiveness, which, though seemingly different, are closely related. In real organizations, these competing values can and often do exist together. Each approach reflects a different management emphasis with respect to structure and focus.[76]

A combination of external focus and flexible structure leads to an **open systems emphasis**. Management's primary goals are growth and resource acquisition. The organization accomplishes these goals through the subgoals of flexibility, readiness, and a positive external evaluation. The dominant value is establishing a good relationship with the environment to acquire resources and grow. This emphasis is similar in some ways to the resource-based approach described earlier.

The **rational goal emphasis** represents management values of structural control and external focus. The primary goals are productivity, efficiency, and profit. The organization wants to achieve output goals in a controlled way. Subgoals that facilitate these outcomes are internal planning and goal setting, which are rational management tools. The rational goal emphasis is similar to the goal approach described earlier.

The **internal process emphasis** is in the lower-left section of Exhibit 3.10; it reflects the values of internal focus and structural control. The primary outcome is a stable organizational setting that maintains itself in an orderly way. Organizations that are well established in the environment and simply want to maintain their current position would reflect this emphasis. Subgoals include mechanisms for efficient communication, information management, and decision making. Although this part

EXHIBIT 3.10
Four Approaches to Effectiveness Values

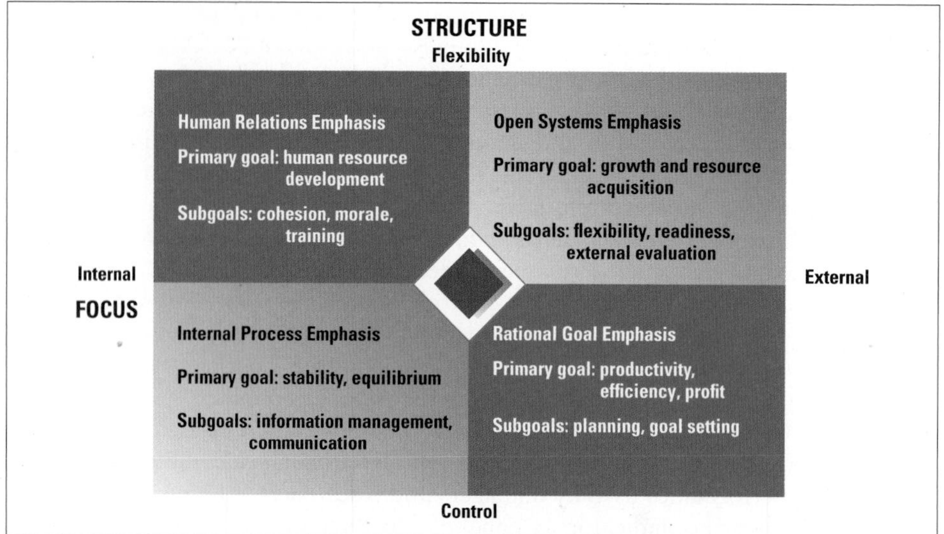

Source: Adapted from Robert E. Quinn and John Rohrbaugh, "A Spatial Model of Effectiveness Criteria: Toward a Competing Values Approach to Organizational Analysis," *Management Science* 29 (1983), 363–377; and Robert E. Quinn and Kim Cameron, "Organizational Life Cycles and Shifting Criteria of Effectiveness: Some Preliminary Evidence," *Management Science* 29 (1983), 33–51.

of the competing values model is similar in some ways to the internal process approach described earlier, it is less concerned with human resources than with other internal processes that lead to efficiency.

The **human relations emphasis** incorporates the values of an internal focus and a flexible structure. Here, management concern is for the development of human resources. Employees are given opportunities for autonomy and development. Management works toward the subgoals of cohesion, morale, and training opportunities. Organizations adopting this emphasis are more concerned with employees than with the environment.

The four cells in Exhibit 3.10 represent opposing organizational values. Managers decide which values will take priority in the organization. The way two organizations are mapped onto the four approaches is shown in Exhibit 3.11.[77] Organization A is a young organization concerned with finding a niche and becoming established in the external environment. Primary emphasis is given to flexibility, innovation, the acquisition of resources from the environment, and the satisfaction of external strategic constituents. This organization gives moderate emphasis to human relations and even less emphasis to current productivity and profits. Satisfying and adapting to the environment are more important. The attention given to open systems values means that the internal process emphasis is practically nonexistent. Stability and equilibrium are of little concern.

Organization B, in contrast, is an established business in which the dominant value is productivity and profits. This organization is characterized by planning and goal setting. Organization B is a large company that is well established in the environment and is primarily concerned with successful production and profits. Flexibility and human resources are not major concerns. This organization prefers stability and equilibrium to learning and innovation because it wants to maximize the value of its established customers.

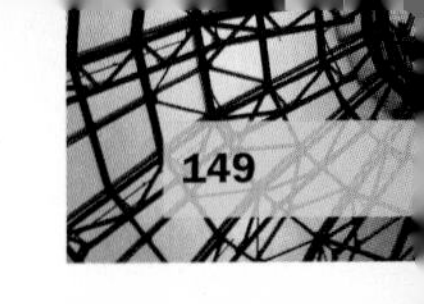

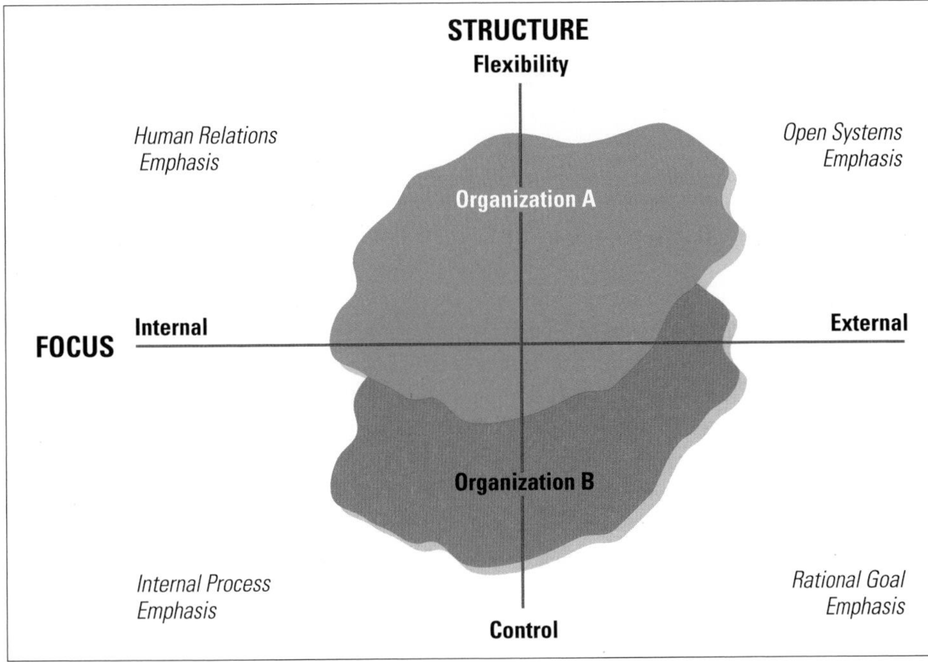

EXHIBIT 3.11
Effectiveness Values for Two Organizations

3 The best measures of business performance are financial.

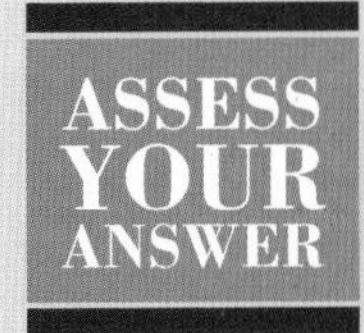

ANSWER: *Disagree.* If you can have only one type of measure of business performance, it might have to be financial. But diverse views of performance, such as using the competing values model, have proven to be more effective than financials alone because managers can understand and control the actions that cause business effectiveness. Financial numbers alone provide narrow and limited information.

Usefulness. The competing values model makes two contributions. First, it integrates diverse concepts of effectiveness into a single perspective. It incorporates the ideas of output goals, resource acquisition, and human resource development as goals the organization tries to accomplish. Second, the model calls attention to how effectiveness criteria are socially constructed from management values and shows how opposing values exist at the same time. Managers must decide which values they wish to pursue and which values will receive less emphasis. The four competing values exist simultaneously, but not all will receive equal priority. For example, a new, small organization that concentrates on establishing itself within a competitive environment will give less emphasis to developing employees than to the external environment.

The dominant values in an organization often change over time as organizations experience new environmental demands, new top leadership, or other changes. For example, the Walt Disney Company's acquisition of Pixar Animation Studios has been relatively smooth, and Disney/Pixar has had a string of critical and commercial hits like "Ratatouille" and "Toy Story 3." However, managers at Disney and those at Pixar are currently struggling with the question of which values they want to pursue—risky creativity and openness or guaranteed financial success and stability.

Disney/ Pixar

IN PRACTICE

When Bob Iger, CEO of the Walt Disney Company, reached a deal to buy Pixar in 2006, some people worried that bringing the successful animation company into Disney's bureaucracy could mean the end of Pixar's flexible, innovative approach—and maybe the end of its string of box-office hits. After all, one of the founders of Pixar, John Lasseter, had earlier been fired from Disney. But Iger took a different approach to the merger. Instead of trying to integrate Pixar into Disney, he gave Pixar's top managers (Lasseter and co-founder Ed Catmull) full control of Walt Disney Animation Studios.

The approach has been successful, and Disney/Pixar films have been both creative and financial successes. However, Pixar's managers and Disney's finance managers are having a difference of opinion over the best way to maintain and measure the organization's effectiveness. For Lasseter, it is all about creativity, risk-taking, and openness. Jay Rasulo, Disney's chief financial officer, on the other hand, has a mindset like most other big studio finance managers—he wants to do the safe thing, the thing that is guaranteed to bring a financial return. For example, most critics felt that the 2011 release "Cars 2" looked like the kind of predictable, risk-free sequel that was created solely to drive merchandise sales for Disney. Rather than "the story being king," as Lasseter once said about Pixar, it seemed that the dollar was becoming king.

The ultimate decisions about which values Pixar/Disney will pursue and which ones will receive less emphasis will be hashed out by managers on both sides. So far, Disney's CEO Bob Iger has seemed willing to give Pixar managers a lot of freedom to run things as they see fit, believing that creative openness and financial stability can coexist.[78]

The effectiveness values that have guided Pixar Animation Studios, which was a relatively young, small, entrepreneurial organization when it was acquired by Disney, reflect a primarily open systems emphasis. Managers value flexibility, the ability to find highly creative employees and give them the freedom to make decisions about story ideas and the direction of projects, being innovative, and giving customers something fresh and unexpected. Pixar was started in the mid-1980s and took an organic approach to organization design. On the other hand, the Walt Disney Company began as a small cartoon studio in the 1920s, but by the time it acquired Pixar it was a large, well-established global company with standard procedures and a hierarchical, mechanistic structure. The values at Disney reflect a strong rational goal approach. The primary goals are productivity and profits, and values of stability outweigh openness and flexibility. Bringing these two organizations together has naturally led to some goal and value conflicts. Remember, all organizations are a mix of competing ideas, goals, and values. Goal emphasis and values change over time.

Design Essentials

- Organizations exist for a purpose. Top managers decide the organization's strategic intent, including a specific mission to be accomplished. The mission statement, or official goals, makes explicit the purpose and direction of an organization. Operating goals designate specific ends sought through actual operating procedures. Official and operating goals are a key element in organizations because they meet these needs—establishing legitimacy with external groups, providing employees with a sense of direction and motivation, and setting standards of performance.

- Two other aspects related to strategic intent are competitive advantage and core competence. Competitive advantage refers to what sets the organization apart from others and provides it with a distinctive edge. A core competence is something the organization does extremely well compared to competitors. Managers look for competitive openings and develop strategies based on their core competencies.
- Strategies may include any number of techniques to achieve the stated goals. Two models for formulating strategies are Porter's competitive strategies and the Miles and Snow strategy typology. Organization design needs to fit the firm's competitive approach to contribute to organizational effectiveness.
- Assessing organizational effectiveness reflects the complexity of organizations as a topic of study. Effectiveness is a social construct, meaning that effectiveness criteria are created and decided upon by people. Different people will have different criteria for what makes the organization "effective." Managers have to decide how they will define and measure organizational effectiveness.
- No easy, simple, guaranteed measure will provide an unequivocal assessment of performance. Organizations must perform diverse activities well—from obtaining resource inputs to delivering outputs—to be successful. Four approaches to measuring effectiveness are the goal approach, resource-based approach, internal process approach, and strategic constituents approach. Effectiveness is multidimensional, so managers typically use indicators from more than one approach and they use qualitative as well as quantitative measures.
- No approach is suitable for every organization, but each offers some advantages that the others may lack. In addition, the competing values model balances a concern with various parts of the organization rather than focusing on one part. This approach acknowledges different areas of focus (internal, external) and structure (flexibility, stability) and allows managers to choose the values to emphasize.

Key Concepts

analyzer
competing values model
competitive advantage
core competence
defender
differentiation strategy
focus
goal approach
human relations emphasis
internal process approach
internal process emphasis
low-cost leadership strategy
mission
official goals
open systems emphasis
operating goals
organizational goal
prospector
rational goal emphasis
reactor
resource-based approach
social construct
strategic constituents approach
strategic intent
strategy
structure

Discussion Questions

1. Discuss the role of top management in setting organizational direction.
2. How might a company's goals for employee development be related to its goals for innovation and change? To goals for productivity? Can you discuss ways these types of goals might conflict in an organization?
3. What is a goal for the class for which you are reading this text? Who established this goal? Discuss how the goal affects your direction and motivation.
4. What is the difference between a goal and a strategy as defined in the text? Identify both a goal and a strategy for a campus or community organization with which you are involved.
5. Discuss the similarities and differences in the strategies described in Porter's competitive strategies and Miles and Snow's typology.
6. Do you believe mission statements and official goal statements provide an organization with genuine legitimacy in the external environment? Discuss.
7. Suppose you have been asked to evaluate the effectiveness of the police department in a medium-sized community. Where would you begin, and how would you proceed? What effectiveness approach would you prefer?
8. What are the advantages and disadvantages of the resource-based approach versus the goal approach for measuring organizational effectiveness?
9. What are the similarities and differences between assessing effectiveness on the basis of competing values versus the strategic constituents approach? Explain.
10. A noted organization theorist once said, "Organizational effectiveness can be whatever top management defines it to be." Discuss.

Chapter 3 Workbook Identifying Company Strategies and Effectiveness Criteria[79]

Choose three organizations in three different industries, including one non-profit organization if possible. Search the Internet for information on the organizations, including annual reports. In each organization look particularly at descriptions of goals and performance criteria. Refer back to the four effectiveness criteria in Exhibit 3.9 and also to Porter's competitive strategies in Exhibit 3.5.

	Effectiveness Criteria from Exhibit 3.9 Articulated	Strategies from Porter Used (Exhibit 3.5)
Company #1		
Company #2		
Company #3		

Questions

1. Which effectiveness criteria seem most important?
2. Look for differences in the goals and strategies of the three companies and develop an explanation for those differences.
3. Which of the goals or strategies might be changed? Why?
4. *Optional:* Compare your table with those of other students and look for common themes. Which companies seem to articulate and communicate their goals and strategies best?

CASE FOR ANALYSIS The University Art Museum[80]

Visitors to the campus were always shown the University Art Museum, of which the large and distinguished university was very proud. A photograph of the handsome neoclassical building that housed the museum had long been used by the university for the cover of its brochures and catalogs.

The building, together with a substantial endowment, was given to the university around 1929 by an alumnus, the son of the university's first president, who had become very wealthy as an investment banker. He also gave the university his own small, but high-quality, collections—one of Etruscan figurines, and one, unique in America, of English pre-Raphaelite paintings. He then served as the museum's unpaid director until his death. During his tenure he brought a few additional collections to the museum, largely from other alumni of the university. Only rarely did the museum purchase anything. As a result, the museum housed several small collections of uneven quality. As long as the founder ran the museum, none of the collections was ever shown to anybody except a few members of the university's art history faculty, who were admitted as the founder's private guests.

After the founder's death, in the mid-1940s, the university intended to bring in a professional museum director. Indeed, this had been part of the agreement under which the founder had given the museum. A search committee was to be appointed, but in the meantime a graduate student in art history, who had shown interest in the museum and who had spent a good many hours in it, took over temporarily. At first, Miss Kirkoff did not even have a title, let alone a salary. She stayed on acting as the museum's director, and over the next 30 years was promoted in stages to that title. But from the first day, whatever her title, she was in charge. She immediately set about changing the museum altogether. She cataloged the collections. She pursued new gifts, again primarily small collections from alumni and other friends of the university. She organized fund raising for the museum, but above all she began to integrate the museum into the work of the university.

When a space problem arose due to increased enrollments and the addition of new professors, Miss Kirkoff offered the third floor of the museum to the art history faculty, which moved its offices there. She remodeled the building to include classrooms and a modern and well-appointed auditorium. She raised funds to build one of the best research and reference libraries in art history in the country. She also began to organize a series of special exhibitions built around one of the museum's own collections, complemented by loans from outside collections. For each of these exhibitions, she had a distinguished member of the university's art faculty write a catalog. These catalogs speedily became the leading scholarly texts in the fields.

Miss Kirkoff ran the University Art Museum for almost half a century. At the age of 68, after suffering a severe stroke, she had to retire. In her letter of resignation she proudly pointed to the museum's growth and accomplishment under her stewardship. "Our endowment," she wrote, "now compares favorably with museums several times our size. We never have had to ask the university for any money other than our share of the university's insurance policies. Our collections in the areas of our strength, while small, are of first-rate quality and importance. Above all, we are being used by more people than any museum of our size. Our lecture series, in which members of the university's art history faculty present a major subject to a university audience of students and faculty, attracts regularly 300 to 500 people; and if we had the seating capacity, we could easily have a larger audience. Our exhibitions are seen and studied by more visitors, most of them members of the university community, than all but the most highly publicized exhibitions in the very big museums ever draw. Above all, the courses and seminars offered in the museum have become one of the most popular and most rapidly growing educational features of the university. No other museum in this country or anywhere else," concluded Miss Kirkoff, "has so successfully integrated art into the life of a major university and a major university into the work of a museum."

Miss Kirkoff strongly recommended that the university bring in a professional museum director as her successor. "The museum is much too big and much too important to be entrusted to another amateur such as I was 45 years ago," she wrote. "And it needs careful thinking regarding its direction, its basis of support, and its future relationship with the university."

The university took Miss Kirkoff's advice. A search committee was duly appointed and, after one year's work, it produced a candidate whom everybody approved. The candidate was himself a graduate of the university who had then obtained his Ph.D. in art history and in museum work from the university. Both his teaching and his administrative record were sound, leading to his current museum directorship in a medium-sized city. There he converted an old, well-known, but rather sleepy museum into a lively, community-oriented museum whose exhibitions were well publicized and attracted large crowds.

The new museum director took over with great fanfare in September 1998. Less than three years later he left—with less fanfare, but still with considerable noise. Whether he resigned or was fired was not quite clear. But that there was bitterness on both sides was only too obvious.

The new director, upon his arrival, had announced that he looked upon the museum as a "major community resource" and intended to "make the tremendous artistic

and scholarly resources of the museum fully available to the academic community as well as to the public." When he said these things in an interview with the college newspaper, everybody nodded in approval. It soon became clear that what he meant by "community resource" and what the faculty and students understood by these words were not the same. The museum had always been "open to the public" but, in practice, it was members of the college community who used the museum and attended its lectures, its exhibitions, and its frequent seminars.

The first thing the new director did, however, was to promote visits from the public schools in the area. He soon began to change the exhibition policy. Instead of organizing small shows, focused on a major collection of the museum and built around a scholarly catalog, he began to organize "popular exhibitions" around "topics of general interest" such as "Women Artists through the Ages." He promoted these exhibitions vigorously in the newspapers, in radio and television interviews, and, above all, in the local schools. As a result, what had been a busy but quiet place was soon knee-deep with schoolchildren, taken to the museum in special buses that cluttered the access roads around the museum and throughout the campus. The faculty, which was not particularly happy with the resulting noise and confusion, became thoroughly upset when the scholarly old chairman of the art history department was mobbed by fourth graders who sprayed him with their water pistols as he tried to push his way through the main hall to his office.

Increasingly, the new director did not design his own shows, but brought in traveling exhibitions from major museums, importing their catalog as well rather than have his own faculty produce one.

The students, too, were apparently unenthusiastic after the first six or eight months, during which the new director had been somewhat of a campus hero. Attendance at the classes and seminars held at the art museum fell off sharply, as did attendance at the evening lectures. When the editor of the campus newspaper interviewed students for a story on the museum, he was told again and again that the museum had become too noisy and too "sensational" for students to enjoy the classes and to have a chance to learn.

What brought all this to a head was an Islamic art exhibit in late 2000. Since the museum had little Islamic art, nobody criticized the showing of a traveling exhibit, offered on very advantageous terms with generous financial assistance from some of the Arab governments. But then, instead of inviting one of the university's own faculty members to deliver the customary talk at the opening of the exhibit, the director brought in a cultural attaché of one of the Arab embassies in Washington. A week later, the university senate decided to appoint an advisory committee, drawn mostly from members of the art history faculty, which, in the future, would have to approve all plans for exhibits and lectures. The director thereupon, in an interview with the campus newspaper, sharply attacked the faculty as "elitist" and "snobbish" and as believing that "art belongs to the rich." Six months later, in June 2001, his resignation was announced.

Under the bylaws of the university, the academic senate appoints a search committee. Normally, this is pure formality. The chairperson of the appropriate department submits the department's nominees for the committee who are approved and appointed, usually without debate. But when the academic senate early the following semester was asked to appoint the search committee, things were far from "normal." The dean who presided, sensing the tempers in the room, tried to smooth over things by saying, "Clearly, we picked the wrong person the last time. We will have to try very hard to find the right one this time."

He was immediately interrupted by an economist, known for his populism, who broke in and said, "I admit that the late director was probably not the right personality. But I strongly believe that his personality was not at the root of the problem. He tried to do what needs doing, and this got him in trouble with the faculty. He tried to make our museum a community resource, to bring in the community and to make art accessible to broad masses of people, to African Americans and Hispanics, to the kids from the ghetto schools and to a lay public. And this is what we really resented. Maybe his methods were not the most tactful ones—I admit I could have done without those interviews he gave. But what he tried to do was right. We had better commit ourselves to the policy he wanted to put into effect, or else we will have deserved his attacks on us as 'elitist' and 'snobbish.'"

"This is nonsense," cut in the usually silent and polite senate member from the art history faculty. "It makes absolutely no sense for our museum to become the kind of community resource our late director and my distinguished colleague want it to be. First, there is no need. The city has one of the world's finest and biggest museums, and it does exactly that and does it very well. Secondly, we have neither the artistic resources nor the financial resources to serve the community at large. We can do something different but equally important and indeed unique. Ours is the only museum in the country, and perhaps in the world, that is fully integrated with an academic community and truly a teaching institution. We are using it, or at least we used to until the last few unfortunate years, as a major educational resource for all our students. No other museum in the country, and as far as I know in the world, is bringing undergraduates into art the way we do. All of us, in addition to our scholarly and graduate work, teach undergraduate courses for people who are not going to be art majors or art historians. We work with the engineering students and show them what we do in our conservation and restoration work. We work with architecture students and show them the development of architecture through the ages. Above all, we work with liberal arts students, who often have had no exposure to art before they came here and who enjoy our courses all the more because they are scholarly and not just 'art appreciation.' This is unique and this is what our museum can do and should do."

"I doubt that this is really what we should be doing," commented the chairman of the mathematics department. "The museum, as far as I know, is part of the graduate faculty. It should concentrate on training art historians in its Ph.D. program, on its scholarly work, and on its research. I would strongly urge that the museum be considered an adjunct to graduate and especially to Ph.D. education, confine itself to this work, and stay out of all attempts to be 'popular,' both on campus and outside of it. The glory of the museum is the scholarly catalogs produced by our faculty, and our Ph.D. graduates who are sought after by art history faculties throughout the country. This is the museum's mission, which can only be impaired by the attempts to be 'popular,' whether with students or with the public."

"These are very interesting and important comments," said the dean, still trying to pacify. "But I think this can wait until we know who the new director is going to be. Then we should raise these questions with him."

"I beg to differ, Mr. Dean," said one of the elder statesmen of the faculty. "During the summer months, I discussed this question with an old friend and neighbor of mine in the country, the director of one of the nation's great museums. He said to me: 'You do not have a personality problem; you have a management problem. You have not, as a university, taken responsibility for the mission, the direction, and the objectives of your museum. Until you do this, no director can succeed. And this is your decision. In fact, you cannot hope to get a good director until you can tell that person what your basic objectives are. If your late director is to blame—I know him and I know that he is abrasive—it is for being willing to take on a job when you, the university, had not faced up to the basic management decisions. There is no point talking about who should manage until it is clear what it is that has to be managed and for what.'"

At this point the dean realized that he had to adjourn the discussion unless he wanted the meeting to degenerate into a brawl. But he also realized that he had to identify the issues and possible decisions before the next senate meeting a month later.

CASE FOR ANALYSIS Covington Corrugated Parts & Services[81]

Larisa Harrison grimaced as she tossed her company's latest quarterly earnings onto the desk. When sales at Virginia-based Covington Corrugated Parts & Services surged past the $10 million mark some time back, Larisa was certain the company was well positioned for steady growth. Today Covington, which provides precision machine parts and service to the domestic corrugated box and paperboard industry, still enjoys a dominant market share, but sales and profits are showing clear signs of stagnation.

More than two decades ago, Larisa's grandfather loaned her the money to start the business and then handed over the barn on what had been the family's Shenandoah Valley farm to serve as her first factory. He had been a progressive thinker compared to many of his contemporaries who scoffed at the idea of a woman running a machine parts plant, and he saw no reason why a smart, ambitious 27-year-old woman couldn't run anything she wanted to. His old-fashioned friends no longer scoffed when Larisa became one of the major employers in the local area. Today, Covington operates from a 50,000 square-foot factory located near I-81 just a few miles from that old family barn. The business allowed Larisa to realize what had once seemed an almost impossible goal: She was making a good living without having to leave her close-knit extended family and rural roots. She also felt a sense of satisfaction at employing about 150 people, many of them neighbors. They were among the most hard-working, loyal workers you'd find anywhere. However, many of her original employees were now nearing retirement. Replacing those skilled workers was going to be difficult, she realized from experience. The area's brightest and best young people were much more likely to move away in search of employment than their parents had been. Those who remained behind just didn't seem to have the work ethic Larisa had come to expect in her employees.

Other problems were looming as well. Covington's market share, once at a formidable 70 percent, was slipping fast, brought about not only by the emergence of new direct competitors but also by changes in the industry. The box and paperboard industry had never been particularly recession resistant, with demand fluctuating with manufacturing output. The rocky economy had hurt the whole industry, including Covington's largest customers. Added to that, alternative shipping products, such as flexible plastic films and reusable plastic containers, were becoming more prevalent. It remained to be seen how much of a dent they'd make in the demand for boxes and paperboard. Even more worrying, consolidation in the industry had wiped out hundreds of the smaller U.S. plants that Covington once served, with many of the survivors either opening overseas facilities or entering into joint ventures abroad. The surviving manufacturers were investing in higher quality machines from Germany that broke down less frequently, thus requiring fewer of Covington's parts.

Covington was clearly at a crossroads, and its managers were arguing about which direction the company should take. If Covington wanted to grow, business as usual wasn't going to work. But no one could seem to agree on the best way to achieve growth. The marketing manager was pushing for moving into new products and services, perhaps even serving other industries, while the director of finance believed the plant needed to become more efficient, even lay off employees, and offer customers the lowest cost. Larisa cringed as she heard that statement because her focus was always on what was best for her employees. The finance director added that efficiency and profitability should be the key criteria by which Covington measured its performance, whereas the marketing manager vehemently argued that the company would be effective only if it focused on customer satisfaction in the changing industry environment, which would mean taking some financial risks. "I know 'corrugated' is in our name," he said, "but we've already moved beyond that to servicing other types of paperboard-making equipment. Why not become the all-around provider, serving any manufacturer that makes containers and packing materials, whether it's paper, plastic, or whatever?" It was truly an ambitious idea, but he was so fired up about it that he had investigated possible acquisitions and partnership opportunities. The finance director was livid. "If anyone is looking into mergers and acquisitions, it should be me, not the marketing manager," she had shouted at the most recent managers' meeting. Meanwhile, the vice president of manufacturing presented a plan for expanding market share by exporting parts globally, which set both the marketing manager and the finance director off. "Why haven't we even heard about this before now?" the marketing manager asked. "I'm not saying I disagree with it, but communication in this place is atrocious. I never even got a copy of the last finance report." The director of finance quickly shot back with a charge that the marketing manager didn't seem to care about profit and loss anyway so why should he need a copy of the report.

As Larisa considered the chaos into which the most recent meeting had degenerated, she thought back to her days in graduate school and realized that organization design was part of the problem. Covington had succeeded for two decades with a loose, even haphazard structure, because everyone seemed focused on building the business. People simply did what needed to be done. However, the company had never been under threat before. "Perhaps we just aren't as well organized as we need to be to handle the challenges Covington is facing," she thought. As she watched the last shift workers walk to their cars, Larissa scribbled a few notes on a pad:

How should we decide what strategy to pursue?
Who should have authority and responsibility for what?
How do we improve communications?
What criteria should we use to measure performance and ensure accountability?

Larisa knew that as soon as she or her team could determine some answers, she would sleep at least a little better.

Chapter 3 Workshop Competing Values and Organizational Effectiveness[82]

1. Divide into groups of four to six members.
2. Select an organization to study for this exercise. It should be an organization for which one of you has worked, or it could be part of the university.
3. Using Exhibit 3.10, "Four Approaches to Effectiveness Values," your group should list eight potential measures that show a balanced view of performance across the four value categories. Use the following table.
4. How will achieving these goals/values help the organization to become more effective? Which goals/values do you think should be given more weight than others? Why?
5. Present your chart to the rest of the class. Each group should explain why it chose those particular measures and which they think are more important. Be prepared to defend your position to the other groups, which are encouraged to question your choices.

Effectiveness Category	Goal or Subgoal	Performance Gauge	How to Measure	Source of Data	What Do You Consider Effective?
(Example)	Equilibrium	Turnover rates	Compare percentages of workers who left	HRM files	25% reduction in first year
Open system	1.				
	2.				
Human Relations	3.				
	4.				

Effectiveness Category	Goal or Subgoal	Performance Gauge	How to Measure	Source of Data	What Do You Consider Effective?
Internal Process	5.				
	6.				
Rational Goal	7.				
	8.				

Notes

1. Miguel Helft, "What Makes eBay Unstoppable?" *The Industry Standard* (August 6–13, 2001), 32–37; and Scott Morrison and Geoffrey A. Fowler, "eBay Pushes Into Amazon Turf," *The Wall Street Journal*, March 29, 2011.
2. Amitai Etzioni, *Modern Organizations* (Englewood Cliffs, NJ: Prentice-Hall, 1964), 6.
3. John P. Kotter, "What Effective General Managers Really Do," *Harvard Business Review* (November–December 1982), 156–167; Henry Mintzberg, *The Nature of Managerial Work* (New York: Harper & Row, 1973); and Henry Mintzberg, *Managing* (San Francisco: Berrett-Kohler Publishers, 2009).
4. Charles C. Snow and Lawrence G. Hrebiniak, "Strategy, Distinctive Competence, and Organizational Performance," *Administrative Science Quarterly* 25 (1980), 317–335; and Robert J. Allio, "Strategic Thinking: The Ten Big Ideas," *Strategy & Leadership* 34, no. 4 (2006), 4–13.
5. Dan Sabbagh, "Digital Revolt Leaves Film-Makers Exposed," *The Times*, October 9, 2004.
6. Gary Hamel and C. K. Prahalad, "Strategic Intent," *Harvard Business Review* (July–August 2005), 148–161.
7. Ibid.
8. Barbara Bartkus, Myron Glassman, and R. Bruce McAfee, "Mission Statements: Are They Smoke and Mirrors?" *Business Horizons* (November–December 2000), 23–28; and Mark Suchman, "Managing Legitimacy: Strategic and Institutional Approaches," *Academy of Management Review* 20, no. 3 (1995), 571–610.
9. Ian Wilson, "The Agenda for Redefining Corporate Purpose: Five Key Executive Actions," *Strategy & Leadership* 32, no. 1 (2004), 21–26.
10. Bill George, "The Company's Mission is the Message," *Strategy + Business*, Issue 33 (Winter 2003), 13–14; and Jim Collins and Jerry Porras, *Built to Last: Successful Habits of Visionary Companies* (New York: Harper Business, 1994).
11. Hamel and Prahalad, *Strategic Intent*.
12. Issie Lapowsky, "Logistics; No Time to Spare; Tackling Last-Minute Jobs," *Inc.* (July–August 2011), 106, 108.
13. Arthur A. Thompson, Jr. and A. J. Srickland III, *Strategic Management: Concepts and Cases*, 6th ed. (Homewood, IL: Irwin, 1992); and Briance Mascarenhas, Alok Baveja, and Mamnoon Jamil, "Dynamics of Core Competencies in Leading Multinational Companies," *California Management Review* 40, no. 4 (Summer 1998), 117–132.
14. Chris Woodyard, "Big Dreams for Small Choppers Paid Off," *USA Today*, September 11, 2005.
15. Charles Perrow, "The Analysis of Goals in Complex Organizations," *American Sociological Review* 26 (1961), 854–866.
16. Johannes U. Stoelwinde and Martin P. Charns, "The Task Field Model of Organization Analysis and Design," *Human Relations* 34 (1981), 743–762; and Anthony Raia, *Managing by Objectives* (Glenview, IL: Scott Foresman, 1974).
17. Chester Dawson and Yoshio Takahashi, "Toyota Hones Focus, Top Ranks; Japanese Car Maker's New Strategy Will Devote More Attention to Hybrids and Emerging Markets," *The Wall Street Journal Online* (March 10, 2011), http://online.wsj.com/article/SB100014240527487041322045761898 24246558988.html (accessed March 10, 2011).
18. Paul Beckett, Vibhuti Agarwal, and Julie Jargon, "Starbucks Brews Plan to Enter India," *The Wall Street Journal Online* (January 14, 2011), http://online.wsj.com/article/SB10001424052748703583404576079593558838756.html (accessed July 16, 2011).
19. Christina Passariello, "To L'Oreal, Brazil's Women Need Fresh Style of Shopping," *The Wall Street Journal*, January 21, 2011, B1.
20. Reed Abelson, "Managing Outcomes Helps a Children's Hospital Climb in Renown," *The New York Times*, September 15, 2007, C1.
21. "Customer Bliss' Jeanne Bliss: Wegmans Food Markets Excels by Throwing Away the Rule Book," The 1to1 Blog, http://www.1to1media.com/weblog/2011/07/customer_bliss_jeanne_bliss_we.html (accessed July 16, 2011); Milton Moskowitz, Robert Levering, and Christopher Tkaczyk, "100 Best Companies to Work For," *Fortune* (February 7, 2011), 91–98; and Wegmans website, http://www.wegmans.com/webapp/wcs/stores/servlet/ProductDisplay?storeId=10052&partNumber=UNIVERSAL_4373 (accessed July 16, 2011).
22. Brooks Barnes, "Animation Meets Economic Reality," *The New York Times*, April 4, 2011, B1.
23. A. G. Lafley and Ram Charan, *The Game Changer: How You Can Drive Revenue and Profit Growth with Innovation* (New York: Crown Business, 2008); Larry Huston and Nabil Sakkab, "Connect and Develop; Inside Procter & Gamble's New Model for Innovation," *Harvard Business Review* (March 2006), 58–66; G. Gil Cloyd, "P&G's Secret: Innovating Innovation," *Industry Week* (December 2004), 26–34; and "P&G Sets Two New Goals for Open Innovation Partnerships," Press Release (October 28, 2010), Procter & Gamble website,

http://www.pginvestor.com/phoenix.zhtml?c=104574&p=irol-newsArticle&ID=1488508 (accessed July 15, 2011).

24. See studies reported in Gary P. Latham and Edwin A. Locke, "Enhancing the Benefits and Overcoming the Pitfalls of Goal Setting," *Organizational Dynamics* 35, no. 4 (2006), 332–340.
25. Paul Sloan, "The Sales Force That Rocks," *Business 2.0* (July 2005), 102–107.
26. James D. Thompson, *Organizations in Action* (New York: McGraw Hill, 1967), 83–98.
27. Michael E. Porter, "What Is Strategy?" *Harvard Business Review* (November–December 1996), 61–78.
28. This discussion is based on Michael E. Porter, *Competitive Strategy: Techniques for Analyzing Industries and Competitors* (New York: Free Press, 1980).
29. Rob Walker, "Branching Out," *New York Times Magazine* (September 24, 2006), 21.
30. Alan Ruddock, "Keeping Up with O'Leary," *Management Today* (September 2003), 48–55; and Jane Engle, "Flying High for Pocket Change; Regional Carriers Offer Inexpensive Travel Alternative," *South Florida Sun Sentinel* (February 13, 2005), 5.
31. Bruce Einhorn, "Acer's Game-Changing PC Offensive," *BusinessWeek* (April 20, 2009), 65; Charmian Kok and Ting-I Tsai, "Acer Makes China Push from Taiwan; PC Maker's Chief Expects Best Gains in New Markets, Including Brazil, As Aims to Surpass H-P," *The Wall Street Journal,* April 1, 2010; and "Experience Will Propel Acer to Top of Smartphone Market by 2013," *Gulf News,* January 22, 2010.
32. Michael E. Porter, "Strategy and the Internet," *Harvard Business Review* (March 2001), 63–78; and John Magretta, "Why Business Models Matter," *Harvard Business Review* (May 2002), 86.
33. Suzanne Kapner, "The Mighty Dollar," *Fortune* (April 27, 2009), 65–66.
34. Richard Teitelbaum, "The Wal-Mart of Wall Street," *Fortune* (October 13, 1997), 128–130.
35. Raymond E. Miles and Charles C. Snow, *Organizational Strategy, Structure, and Process* (New York: McGraw-Hill, 1978).
36. Nicholas Casey, "New Nike Sneaker Targets Jocks, Greens, Wall Street," *The Wall Street Journal* (February 15, 2008), B1.
37. Norihiko Shirouzu, "Chinese Begin Volvo Overhaul," *The Wall Street Journal,* June 7, 2011, B1.
38. Geraldine Fabrikant, "The Paramount Team Puts Profit Over Splash," *The New York Times,* June 30, 2002, Section 3, 1, 15.
39. Mylene Mangalindan, "Slow Slog for Amazon's Digital Media—Earnings Today May Provide Data on What Works," *The Wall Street Journal,* April 23, 2008, B1.
40. Nanette Byrnes and Peter Burrows, "Where Dell Went Wrong," *BusinessWeek* (February 19, 2007), 62–63; and Cliff Edwards, "Dell's Do-Over," *BusinessWeek* (October 26, 2009), 36–40.
41. "On the Staying Power of Defenders, Analyzers, and Prospectors: Academic Commentary by Donald C. Hambrick," *Academy of Management Executive* 17, no. 4 (2003), 115–118.
42. Etzioni, Modern Organizations, 8; and Gary D. Sandefur, "Efficiency in Social Service Organizations," *Administration and Society* 14 (1983), 449–468.
43. Richard M. Steers, *Organizational Effectiveness: A Behavioral View* (Santa Monica, CA: Goodyear, 1977), 51.
44. Michael Hammer, "The 7 Deadly Sins of Performance Measurement (and How to Avoid Them)," *MIT Sloan Management Review* 48, no. 3 (Spring 2007), 19–28.
45. Karl E. Weick and Richard L. Daft, "The Effectiveness of Interpretation Systems," in Kim S. Cameron and David A. Whetten, eds., *Organizational Effectiveness: A Comparison of Multiple Models* (New York: Academic Press, 1982).
46. This discussion is based on Robert D. Herman and David O. Renz, "Advancing Nonprofit Organizational Effectiveness Research and Theory," *Nonprofit Management and Leadership* 18, no. 4 (Summer 2008), 399–415; Eric J. Walton and Sarah Dawson, "Managers' Perceptions of Criteria of Organizational Effectiveness," *Journal of Management Studies* 38, no. 2 (March 2001), 173–199; and K. S. Cameron and D. A. Whetton, "Organizational Effectiveness: One Model or Several?" in *Organizational Effectiveness: A Comparison of Multiple Models*, K. S. Cameron and D. A. Whetton, eds., (New York: Academic Press, 1983), 1–24.
47. Story told in Herman and Renz, "Advancing Nonprofit Organizational Effectiveness Research and Theory."
48. Most of these indicators are from Cristina B. Gibson, Mary E. Zellmer-Bruhn, and Donald P. Schwab, "Team Effectiveness in Multinational Organizations: Evaluation Across Contexts," *Group & Organizational Management* 28, no. 4 (December 2003), 444–474.
49. Herman and Renz, "Advancing Nonprofit Organizational Effectiveness Research and Theory;" Y. Baruch and N. Ramalho, "Communalities and Distinctions in the Measurement of Organizational Performance and Effectiveness Across For-Profit and Nonprofit Sectors," *Nonprofit and Voluntary Sector Quarterly* 35, no. 1 (2006), 39–65; A. M. Parhizgari and G. Ronald Gilbert, "Measures of Organizational Effectiveness: Private and Public Sector Performance," *Omega; The International Journal of Management Science* 32 (2004), 221–229; David L. Blenkhorn and Brian Gaber, "The Use of 'Warm Fuzzies' to Assess Organizational Effectiveness," *Journal of General Management,* 21, no. 2 (Winter 1995), 40–51; and Scott Leibs, "Measuring Up," *CFO* (June 2007), 63–66.
50. Reported in David H. Freedman, "What's Next: The Dashboard Dilemma," *Inc.* (November 1, 2006), http://www.inc.com/magazine/20061101/column-freedman.html (accessed July 14, 2011).
51. Kim S. Cameron, "A Study of Organizational Effectiveness and Its Predictors," *Management Science* 32 (1986), 87–112; and Joseph R. Matthews, "Assessing Organizational Effectiveness: The Role of Performance Measures," *The Library Quarterly* 81, no. 1 (2011), 83–110.
52. James L. Price, "The Study of Organizational Effectiveness," *Sociological Quarterly* 13 (1972), 3–15; and Steven Strasser, J. D. Eveland, Gaylord Cummins, O. Lynn Deniston, and John H. Romani, "Conceptualizing the Goal and Systems Models of Organizational Effectiveness—Implications for Comparative Evaluation Research," *Journal of Management Studies* 18 (1981), 321–340.
53. Richard H. Hall and John P. Clark, "An Ineffective Effectiveness Study and Some Suggestions for Future Research," *Sociological Quarterly* 21 (1980), 119–134; Price, "The Study of Organizational Effectiveness;" and Perrow, "The Analysis of Goals in Complex Organizations."

54. Gautam Naik, "Poverty: The New Search for Solutions; Baby Steps: Cincinnati Applies a Corporate Model to Saving Infants," (Third in a Series), *The Wall Street Journal*, June 20, 2006, A1.
55. David J. Collis and Cynthia A. Montgomery, "Competing on Resources," *Harvard Business Review* (July–August 2008), 140–150.
56. The discussion of the resource-based approach is based in part on Michael V. Russo and Paul A. Fouts, "A Resource-Based Perspective on Corporate Environmental Performance and Profitability," *Academy of Management Journal* 40, no. 3 (June 1997), 534–559; and Jay B. Barney, J. L. "Larry" Stempert, Loren T. Gustafson, and Yolanda Sarason, "Organizational Identity within the Strategic Management Conversation: Contributions and Assumptions," in David A. Whetten and Paul C. Godfrey, eds., *Identity in Organizations: Building Theory through Conversations* (Thousand Oaks, CA: Sage Publications, 1998), 83–98.
57. These are based on David J. Collis and Cynthia A. Montgomery, "Competing on Resources," *Harvard Business Review* (July–August 2008), 140–150; J. Barton Cunningham, "A Systems-Resource Approach for Evaluating Organizational Effectiveness," *Human Relations* 31 (1978), 631–656; and Ephraim Yuchtman and Stanley E. Seashore, "A System Resource Approach to Organizational Effectiveness," *Administrative Science Quarterly* 12 (1967), 377–395.
58. Roger Noble, "How Shriners Hospitals for Children Found the Formula for Performance Excellence," *Global Business and Organizational Excellence* (July–August 2009), 7–15.
59. Based on Collis and Montgomery, "Competing on Resources."
60. Richard I. Priem, " " Is the Resource-Based 'View' a Useful Perspective for Strategic Management Research?" *Academy of Management Review* 26, no. 1 (2001), 22–40.
61. Chris Argyris, *Integrating the Individual and the Organization* (New York: Wiley, 1964); Warren G. Bennis, *Changing Organizations* (New York: McGraw-Hill, 1966); Rensis Likert, *The Human Organization* (New York: McGraw-Hill, 1967); and Richard Beckhard, *Organization Development Strategies and Models* (Reading, MA: Addison-Wesley, 1969).
62. Cheri Ostroff and Neal Schmitt, "Configurations of Organizational Effectiveness and Efficiency," *Academy of Management Journal* 36 (1993), 1345–1361.
63. J. Barton Cunningham, "Approaches to the Evaluation of Organizational Effectiveness," *Academy of Management Review* 2 (1977), 463–474; and Beckhard, *Organization Development.*
64. Craig Torres and Anthony Feld, "Campbell's Quest for Productivity," *BusinessWeek* (November 24, 2010), 15–16.
65. Jennifer Robison, "How the Ritz-Carlton Manages the Mystique: The Luxury Brand Uses Hard Data on Employee and Customer Engagement to Create Its Image and Ambience," *Gallup Management Journal* (December 11, 2008).
66. Anne S. Tusi, "A Multiple Constituency Model of Effectiveness: An Empirical Examination at the Human Resource Subunit Level," *Administrative Science Quarterly* 35 (1990), 458–483; Charles Fombrun and Mark Shanley, "What's In a Name? Reputation Building and Corporate Strategy," *Academy of Management Journal* 33(1990), 233–258; and Terry Connolly, Edward J. Conlon, and Stuart Jay Deutsch, "Organizational Effectiveness: A Multiple Constituency Approach," *Academy of Management Review* 5 (1980), 211–217.
67. Frank Friedlander and Hal Pickle, "Components of Effectiveness in Small Organizations," *Administrative Science Quarterly* 13 (1968), 289–304.
68. Jessica E. Vascellaro, "Facebook Taps Consumer Card—Social Networking Site Wants to Know More Than Just Who Your Friends Are," *The Wall Street Journal*, April 22, 2010, B2.
69. Tusi, "A Multiple Constituency Model of Effectiveness."
70. Fombrun and Shanley, "What's In a Name?"
71. Kim S. Cameron, "The Effectiveness of Ineffectiveness," in Barry M. Staw and L. L. Cummings, eds., *Research in Organizational Behavior* (Greenwich, CT: JAI Press, 1984), 235–286; and Rosabeth Moss Kanter and Derick Brinkerhoff, "Organizational Performance: Recent Developments in Measurement," *Annual Review of Sociology* 7 (1981), 321–349.
72. Eric J. Walton and Sarah Dawson, "Managers' Perceptions of Criteria of Organizational Effectiveness," *Journal of Management Studies* 38, no. 2 (2001), 173–199.
73. Beth Dickey, "NASA's Next Step," *Government Executive* (April 15, 2004), http://www.govexec.com/features/0404-15/0404-15s1.htm 34 (accessed July 19, 2011).
74. Neil King Jr. and Russell Gold, "BP Crew Focused on Costs: Congress," *The Wall Street Journal Online* (June 15, 2010), http://online.wsj.com/article/SB10001424052748704324304575306800201158346.html (accessed July 19, 2011).
75. Robert E. Quinn and John Rohrbaugh, "A Spatial Model of Effectiveness Criteria: Towards a Competing Values Approach to Organizational Analysis," *Management Science* 29, no. 3 (1983), 363–377; and Walton and Dawson, "Managers' Perceptions of Criteria of Organizational Effectiveness."
76. Regina M. O'Neill and Robert E. Quinn, "Editor's Note: Applications of the Competing Values Framework," *Human Resource Management* 32 (Spring 1993), 1–7.
77. Robert E. Quinn and Kim Cameron, "Organizational Life Cycles and Shifting Criteria of Effectiveness: Some Preliminary Evidence," *Management Science* 29 (1983), 33–51.
78. James B. Stewart, "A Collision of Creativity and Cash," *The New York Times*, July 2, 2011, B1.
79. Copyright 1996 by Dorothy Marcic. All rights reserved.
80. Drucker, *Management Cases*, 1st ed., © 1977. Reprinted and Electronically reproduced by permission of Pearson Education, Inc., Upper Saddle River, New Jersey.
81. Based on Ron Stodghill, "Boxed Out," *FSB* (April 2005), 69–72; "SIC 2653 Corrugated and Solid Fiber Boxes," *Reference for Business, Encyclopedia of Business*, 2nd ed., http://www.referenceforbusiness.com/industries/Paper-Allied/Corrugated-Solid-Fiber-Boxes.html (accessed November 11, 2011); "Paper and Allied Products," *U.S. Trade and Industry Outlook 2000*, 10–12 to 10–15; "Smurfit-Stone Container: Market Summary," *BusinessWeek Online* (May 4, 2006); and Bernard A. Deitzer and Karl A. Shilliff, "Incident 15," *Contemporary Management Incidents* (Columbus, Ohio: Grid, Inc., 1977), 43–46.
82. Adapted by Dorothy Marcic from general ideas in Jennifer Howard and Larry Miller, *Team Management*, The Miller Consulting Group, 1994, 92.

INTEGRATIVE CASE 3.0

It Isn't So Simple: Infrastructure Change at Royce Consulting*

The lights of the city glittered outside Ken Vincent's twelfth-floor office. After nine years of late nights and missed holidays, Ken was in the executive suite with the words "Associate Partner" on the door. Things should be easier now, but the proposed changes at Royce Consulting had been more challenging than he had expected. "I don't understand," he thought. "At Royce Consulting our clients, our people, and our reputation are what count, so why do I feel so much tension from the managers about the changes that are going to be made in the office? We've analyzed why we have to make the changes. Heck, we even got an outside person to help us. The administrative support staff are pleased. So why aren't the managers enthusiastic? We all know what the decision at tomorrow's meeting will be—Go! Then it will all be over. Or will it?" Ken thought as he turned out the lights.

Background

Royce Consulting is an international consulting firm whose clients are large corporations, usually with long-term contracts. Royce employees spend weeks, months, and even years working under contract at the client's site. Royce consultants are employed by a wide range of industries, from manufacturing facilities to utilities to service businesses. The firm has over 160 consulting offices located in 65 countries. At this location Royce employees included 85 staff members, 22 site managers, 9 partners and associate partners, 6 administrative support staff, 1 human resource professional, and 1 financial support person.

For the most part, Royce Consulting hired entry-level staff straight out of college and promoted from within. New hires worked on staff for five or six years; if they did well, they were promoted to manager. Managers were responsible for maintaining client contracts and assisting partners in creating proposals for future engagements. Those who were not promoted after six or seven years generally left the company for other jobs.

Newly promoted managers were assigned an office, a major perquisite of their new status. During the previous year, some new managers had been forced to share an office because of space limitations. To minimize the friction of sharing an office, one of the managers was usually assigned to a long-term project out of town. Thus, practically speaking, each manager had a private office.

Infrastructure and Proposed Changes

Royce was thinking about instituting a hoteling office system—also referred to as a "nonterritorial" or "free-address" office. A hoteling office system made offices available to managers on a reservation or drop-in basis. Managers are not assigned a permanent office; instead, whatever materials and equipment the manager needs are moved into the temporary office. These are some of the features and advantages of a hoteling office system:

- No permanent office assigned
- Offices are scheduled by reservations
- Long-term scheduling of an office is feasible
- Storage space would be located in a separate file room
- Standard manuals and supplies would be maintained in each office
- Hoteling coordinator is responsible for maintaining offices
- A change in "possession of space"
- Eliminates two or more managers assigned to the same office
- Allows managers to keep the same office if desired
- Managers would have to bring in whatever files they needed for their stay
- Information available would be standardized regardless of office
- Managers do not have to worry about "housekeeping issues"

The other innovation under consideration was an upgrade to state-of-the-art electronic office technology. All managers would receive a new notebook computer with updated communications capability to use Royce's integrated and proprietary software. Also, as part of the electronic office technology, an electronic filing system was considered. The electronic filing system meant information

*Presented to and accepted by the Society for Case Research.

This case was prepared by Sally Dresdow of the University of Wisconsin at Green Bay and Joy Benson of the University of Illinois at Springfield and is intended to be used as a basis for class discussion. The views represented here are those of the case authors and do not necessarily reflect the views of the Society for Case Research. The authors' views are based on their own professional judgments. The names of the organization, individuals, and location have been disguised to preserve the organization's request for anonymity.

regarding proposals, client records, and promotional materials would be electronically available on the Royce Consulting network.

The administrative support staff had limited experience with many of the application packages used by the managers. While they used word processing extensively, they had little experience with spreadsheets, communications, or graphics packages. The firm had a graphics department and the managers did most of their own work, so the administrative staff did not have to work with those application software packages.

Work Patterns

Royce Consulting was located in a large city in the Midwest. The office was located in the downtown area, but it was easy to get to. Managers assigned to in-town projects often stopped by for a few hours at various times of the day. Managers who were not currently assigned to client projects were expected to be in the office to assist on current projects or work with a partner to develop proposals for new business.

In a consulting firm, managers spend a significant portion of their time at client sites. As a result, the office occupancy rate at Royce Consulting was about 40 to 60 percent. This meant that the firm paid lease costs for offices that were empty approximately half of the time. With the planned growth over the next ten years, assigning permanent offices to every manager, even in doubled-up arrangements, was judged to be economically unnecessary given the amount of time offices were empty.

The proposed changes would require managers and administrative support staff to adjust their work patterns. Additionally, if a hoteling office system was adopted, managers would need to keep their files in a centralized file room.

Organizational Culture

Royce Consulting had a strong organizational culture, and management personnel were highly effective at communicating it to all employees.

Stability of Culture

The culture at Royce Consulting was stable. The leadership of the corporation had a clear picture of who they were and what type of organization they were. Royce Consulting had positioned itself to be a leader in all areas of large business consulting. Royce Consulting's CEO articulated the firm's commitment to being client-centered. Everything that was done at Royce Consulting was because of the client.

Training

New hires at Royce Consulting received extensive training in the culture of the organization and the methodology employed in consulting projects. They began with a structured program of classroom instruction and computer-aided courses covering technologies used in the various industries in which the firm was involved. Royce Consulting recruited top young people who were aggressive and who were willing to do whatever was necessary to get the job done and build a common bond. Among new hires, camaraderie was encouraged along with a level of competition. This kind of behavior continued to be cultivated throughout the training and promotion process.

Work Relationships

Royce Consulting employees had a remarkably similar outlook on the organization. Accepting the culture and norms of the organization was important for each employee. The norms of Royce Consulting revolved around high performance expectations and strong job involvement.

By the time people made manager, they were aware of what types of behaviors were acceptable. Managers were formally assigned the role of coach to younger staff people, and they modeled acceptable behavior. Behavioral norms included when they came into the office, how late they stayed at the office, and the type of comments they made about others. Managers spent time checking on staff people and talking with them about how they were doing.

The standard for relationships was that of professionalism. Managers knew they had to do what the partners asked and they were to be available at all times. A norms survey and conversations made it clear that people at Royce Consulting were expected to help each other with on-the-job problems, but personal problems were outside the realm of sanctioned relationships. Personal problems were not to interfere with performance on a job. To illustrate, vacations were put on hold and other kinds of commitments were set aside if something was needed at Royce Consulting.

Organizational Values

Three things were of major importance to the organization: its clients, its people, and its reputation. There was a strong client-centered philosophy communicated and practiced. Organization members sought to meet and exceed customer expectations. Putting clients first was stressed. The management of Royce Consulting listened to its clients and made adjustments to satisfy the client.

The reputation of Royce Consulting was important to those leading the organization. They protected and enhanced it by focusing on quality services delivered by quality people. The emphasis on clients, Royce Consulting personnel, and the firm's reputation was cultivated by developing a highly motivated, cohesive, and committed group of employees.

Management Style and Hierarchical Structure

The company organization was characterized by a directive style of management. The partners had the final word on all issues of importance. It was common to hear statements like "Managers are expected to solve problems, and do whatever it takes to finish the job" and "Whatever the partners want, we do." Partners accepted and asked for managers' feedback on projects, but in the final analysis, the partners made the decisions.

Current Situation

Royce Consulting had an aggressive five-year plan that was predicated on a continued increase in business. Increases in the total number of partners, associate partners, managers, and staff were forecast. Additional office space would be required to accommodate the growth in staff; this would increase rental costs at a time when Royce's fixed and variable costs were going up.

The partners, led by managing partner Donald Gray and associate partner Ken Vincent, believed that something had to be done to improve space utilization and the productivity of the managers and administrative personnel. The partners approved a feasibility study of the innovations and their impact on the company.

The ultimate decision makers were the partner group who had the power to approve the concepts and commit the required financial investment. A planning committee consisted of Ken Vincent; the human resources person; the financial officer; and an outside consultant, Mary Schrean.

The Feasibility Study

Within two working days of the initial meeting, all the partners and managers received a memo announcing the hoteling office feasibility study. The memo included a brief description of the concept and stated that it would include an interview with the staff. By this time, partners and managers had already heard about the possible changes and knew that Gray was leaning toward hoteling offices.

Interviews with the Partners

All the partners were interviewed. One similarity in the comments was that they thought the move to hoteling offices was necessary but they were glad it would not affect them. Three partners expressed concern about managers' acceptance of the change to a hoteling system. The conclusion of each partner was that if Royce Consulting moved to hoteling offices, with or without electronic office technology, the managers would accept the change. The reason given by the partners for such acceptance was that the managers would do what the partners wanted done.

The partners all agreed that productivity could be improved at all levels of the organization: in their own work as well as among the secretaries and the managers. Partners acknowledged that current levels of information technology at Royce Consulting would not support the move to hoteling offices and that advances in electronic office technology needed to be considered.

Partners viewed all filing issues as secondary to both the office layout change and the proposed technology improvement. What eventually emerged, however, was that ownership and control of files was a major concern, and most partners and managers did not want anything centralized.

Interviews with the Managers

Personal interviews were conducted with all ten managers who were in the office. During the interviews, four of the managers asked Schrean whether the change to hoteling offices was her idea. The managers passed the question off as a joke; however, they expected a response from her. She stated that she was there as an adviser, that she had not generated the idea, and that she would not make the final decision regarding the changes.

The length of time that these managers had been in their current positions ranged from six months to five years. None of them expressed positive feelings about the hoteling system, and all of them referred to how hard they had worked to make manager and gain an office of their own. Eight managers spoke of the status that the office gave them and the convenience of having a permanent place to keep their information and files. Two of the managers said they did not care so much about the status but were concerned about the convenience. One manager said he would come in less frequently if he did not have his own office. The managers believed that a change to hoteling offices would decrease their productivity. Two managers stated that they did not care how much money Royce Consulting would save on lease costs; they wanted to keep their offices.

However, for all the negative comments, all the managers said that they would go along with whatever the partners decided to do. One manager stated that if Royce Consulting stays busy with client projects, having a permanently assigned office was not a big issue.

During the interviews, every manager was enthusiastic and supportive of new productivity tools, particularly the improved electronic office technology. They believed that new computers and integrated software and productivity tools would definitely improve their productivity. Half the managers stated that updated technology would make the change to hoteling offices "a little less terrible," and they wanted their secretaries to have the same software as they did.

The managers' responses to the filing issue varied. The volume of files managers had was in direct proportion to their tenure in that position: The longer a person was a manager, the more files he or she had. In all cases, managers took care of their own files, storing them in their offices and in whatever filing drawers were free.

As part of the process of speaking with managers, their administrative assistants were asked about the proposed changes. Each of the six thought that the electronic office upgrade would benefit the managers, although they were somewhat concerned about what would be expected of them. Regarding the move to hoteling offices, each said that the managers would hate the change, but that they would agree to it if the partners wanted to move in that direction.

Results of the Survey

A survey developed from the interviews was sent to all partners, associate partners, and managers two weeks after the interviews were conducted. The completed survey was returned by 6 of the 9 partners and associate partners and 16 of the 22 managers. This is what the survey showed.

Work Patterns. It was "common knowledge" that managers were out of the office a significant portion of their time, but there were no figures to substantiate this belief, so the respondents were asked to provide data on where they spent their time. The survey results indicated that partners spent 38 percent of their time in the office; 54 percent at client sites; 5 percent at home; and 3 percent in other places, such as airports. Managers reported spending 32 percent of their time in the office, 63 percent at client sites, 4 percent at home, and 1 percent in other places.

For 15 workdays, the planning team also visually checked each of the 15 managers' offices four times each day: at 9 A.M., 11 A.M., 2 P.M., and 4 P.M. These times were selected because initial observations indicated that these were the peak occupancy times. An average of six offices (40 percent of all manager offices) were empty at any given time; in other words, there was a 60 percent occupancy rate.

Alternative Office Layouts. One of the alternatives outlined by the planning committee was a continuation of and expansion of shared offices. Eleven of the managers responding to the survey preferred shared offices to hoteling offices. Occasions when more than one manager was in the shared office at the same time were infrequent. Eight managers reported 0 to 5 office conflicts per month; three managers reported 6 to 10 office conflicts per month. The type of problems encountered with shared offices included not having enough filing space, problems in directing telephone calls, and lack of privacy.

Managers agreed that having a permanently assigned office was an important perquisite. The survey confirmed the information gathered in the interviews about managers' attitudes: All but two managers preferred shared offices over hoteling, and managers believed their productivity would be negatively impacted. The challenges facing Royce Consulting if they move to hoteling offices centered around tradition and managers' expectations, file accessibility and organization, security and privacy issues, unpredictable work schedules, and high-traffic periods.

Control of Personal Files. Because of the comments made during the face-to-face interviews, survey respondents were asked to rank the importance of having personal control of their files. A 5-point scale was used, with 5 being "strongly agree" and 1 being "strongly disagree." Here are the responses.

Respondents	Sample	Rank
Partners	6	4.3
Managers:		
0–1 year	5	4.6
2–3 years	5	3.6
4 years	6	4.3

Electronic Technology. Royce Consulting had a basic network system in the office that could not accommodate the current partners and managers working at a remote site. The administrative support staff had a separate network, and the managers and staff could not communicate electronically. Of managers responding to the survey, 95 percent wanted to use the network but only 50 percent could actually do so.

Option Analysis

A financial analysis showed that there were significant cost differences between the options under consideration:

Option 1: Continue private offices with some office sharing

- Lease an additional floor in existing building; annual cost, $360,000
- Build out the additional floor (i.e., construct, furnish, and equip offices and work areas): one-time cost, $600,000

Option 2: Move to hoteling offices with upgraded office technology

- Upgrade office electronic technology: one-time cost, $190,000

Option 1 was expensive because under the terms of the existing lease, Royce had to commit to an entire floor if it wanted additional space. Hoteling offices showed an overall financial advantage of $360,000 per year and a one-time savings of $410,000 over shared or individual offices.

The Challenge

Vincent met with Mary Schrean to discuss the upcoming meeting of partners and managers, where they would

present the results of the study and a proposal for action. Included in the report were proposed layouts for both shared and hoteling offices. Vincent and Gray were planning to recommend a hoteling office system, which would include storage areas, state-of-the-art electronic office technology for managers and administrative support staff, and centralized files. The rationale for their decision emphasized the amount of time that managers were out of the office and the high cost of maintaining the status quo and was built around the following points:

1. Royce's business is different: offices are empty from 40 to 60 percent of the time.
2. Real estate costs continue to escalate.
3. Projections indicate there will be increased need for offices and cost-control strategies as the business develops.
4. Royce Consulting plays a leading role in helping organizations implement innovation.

"It's still a go," thought Vincent as he and the others returned from a break. "The cost figures support it and the growth figures support it. It's simple—or is it? The decision is the easy part. What is it about Royce Consulting that will help or hinder its acceptance? In the long run, I hope we strengthen our internal processes and don't hinder our effectiveness by going ahead with these simple changes."

INTEGRATIVE CASE 4.0

The Plaza Inn*

David Bart, General Manager of the Plaza Inn, had just finished reading a letter from Jean Dumas, President of the prestigious Relais & Chateaux, a French hotel association of which the Plaza Inn was a member. In the formal and polite tone of the French language, the president stated that the last inspection had determined that the service levels of the Plaza Inn did not measure up to the Relais & Chateaux standards. Moreover, the letter noted that the Front Desk and Reservations, two critical guest contact departments, received the worst ratings among all of the Relais & Chateaux member properties. The letter concluded that unless the management of the Plaza Inn could submit a plan for guest service improvement and pass the next inspection scheduled in six months, the Relais & Chateaux would "regrettably be forced to withhold the Plaza Inn's membership."

Background

Located within walking distance of the Country Club Plaza and the Crown Center districts of Kansas City, the Plaza Inn is a 50-room hotel modeled after the boutique hotels of Europe. The Inn's intimate atmosphere and unobtrusive service attract business and leisure travelers alike.

Built in the 1920s in the classic Victorian style and meticulously renovated in 1985, the Inn occupies a place on the National Register of Historic Places. Guest rooms are decorated in the best country manner with antique furnishings and oriental rugs discreetly coupled with the most modern leisure and business amenities. Luxurious terry cloth robes and marbled baths, for example, await the weary guest. The Plaza Inn also boasts two gourmet restaurants: the romantic, nationally acclaimed St. Jacques with an award winning wine list, and the more casual Andre's bar and bistro. In addition to its overnight guests, the restaurants have an established local clientele.

Nostalgia prompted Andre Bertrand and Tim Boyle, two successful Kansas City entrepreneurs and real estate developers, to purchase the Plaza Inn in 1983. They entered into a partnership with Antoine Fluri, a Swiss hotelier who soon assumed the position of the Inn's general manager. In addition to the three general partners the Inn is owned by approximately 20 limited partners.

"One of the Ten Best New Inns"

Under the charismatic direction of Antoine Fluri, the Inn quickly established a national reputation. In 1987, *Travel* magazine voted the Plaza Inn among the "ten best new inns." A loyal clientele included such famous people as former French President Valery Giscard D'Estaing, Senator Danforth, and Susan Sontag, to name a few. Antoine Fluri also negotiated the Inn's membership in the prestigious, world-renowned Relais & Chateaux association. The existing hotels in the immediate area: a Marriott, a Holiday Inn, and a Hilton gave the Plaza Inn virtually no competition for the upscale traveler.

Despite the success of the Inn, in early 1989 Antoine Fluri sold his share to the remaining two partners and left the Inn citing, "irreconcilable differences" as the reason. A year later, he opened his own restaurant in the Country Club Plaza District.

To continue to promote the European image of the Inn, the owners hired a French couple from Normandy, Marc and Nicole Duval, to replace Antoine Fluri. However, the Duvals soon proved to lack knowledge about European hospitality practices as well as management expertise. They abused their position and power, and within a short time succeeded in alienating many of the Inn's clientele and most of its staff. Under their management, the Inn rapidly incurred heavy financial losses. Alarmed by the practices of the Duvals, the owners looked for new management for the Inn. In December 1989, David Bart was hired as the new general manager. A native of Missouri, he had a solid hotel management background in the middle west, most recently including several years as controller at the headquarters of a large chain hotel.

As David Bart assumed the direction of the Inn in early 1990, he faced several challenges, including steadily declining hotel occupancy and revenues. Many of the regular clientele complained that the Inn had not been the same since Antoine Fluri left. Moreover, contrary to optimistic expectations, the Inn was also losing business to a 300-room, upscale Ritz-Carlton hotel which had just opened a few blocks down the street and was offering introductory room rates as low as $75. Finally, toward the end of 1990 demand also declined as a national recession began to set in.

Given the poor performance of the hotel, David Bart immediately proceeded to cut costs, which included the elimination of several staff positions. In the Food and Beverage Department (F&B), two of the three restaurant managers were eliminated. St. Jacques and Andre's were to be run by the F&B director with the assistance of only

*Written for class discussion by Craig Lundberg, Cornell University, based on field research by Monika Dubaj. This case does not purport to illustrate either effective or ineffective managerial practices. Reprinted with permission.

one restaurant manager. In the Rooms Department, Bart eliminated the position of Private Branch Exchange (PBX) operator, and transferred the responsibility of answering the phone directly to the front desk. Finally, the front office manager position was eliminated, and the front desk staff came under the supervision of the sales manager. Thus, the Inn began to operate with a lean management and staff group. All operating departments, with the exception of F&B, were headed by one person and with no administrative support. Even Bart himself did not retain a secretary.

The Front Desk

The end of David Bart's first year at the Plaza Inn was marked by the outbreak of the Gulf War. During the first quarter of 1990, occupancy hit an all-time low of just 40%. However, business finally began to pick up in April. This increase in demand was especially hard for the front desk. The reception area, consisting of an elegant antique concierge-type desk, was too small to be staffed by more than one person at a time. Consequently, only one front desk receptionist was scheduled per shift. With no PBX operator and no secretarial staff, this meant that the front desk receptionist was responsible for not only providing guest service, but also for answering the telephone, taking messages for the management staff, and booking room and restaurant reservations. Moreover, the sales office was not connected to the computerized Property Management System (PMS), and consequently the sales and catering managers relied on the front desk to check availability and block and update group reservations. Similarly, the housekeeping department was not computerized, and the front desk was charged with the preparation of housekeeping room assignments each morning and evening as well as with the tracking and updating of room status in the PMS. Bart believed that the front desk should perform a central function in the operation of the Inn. Rather than computerize the housekeeping, sales and catering departments, and train the managers to utilize the PMS, Bart preferred the front desk to oversee those activities. This, he believed, allowed for greater consistency and control.

With only one person scheduled per shift, the front desk receptionist had to juggle the telephone, coordinate department activities, and take care of guest needs in the personalized manner that was the trademark of the Inn. On busy days, guests checking in or out were rudely interrupted by the ringing telephone, or alternatively, callers were put on hold for lengthy periods of time while the front desk receptionist helped a guest.

The inability to efficiently expedite phone calls and respond to guest needs became worrisome not only from a guest service perspective, but also from a potential revenue loss standpoint. Room reservation calls usually hung up if they remained on hold for more than two minutes. Moreover, under the pressure to answer the phone and help a guest at the same time, the front desk receptionists frequently underquoted rates, mixed up arrival dates, and booked rooms on sold out nights. Cancellation requests were not handled correctly with the consequence that some guests were billed for reservations that they had canceled. One of the front desk receptionists commented: "It's extremely difficult to make a room sale when I constantly have to ask the customer to hold because I'm trying to pick up the other five lines that are ringing. What is more important: making a $130 room reservation for two nights or taking a message for one of the managers?"

Reinstatement of the Front Office Manager

Lost revenues and customer complaints about front office service finally convinced David Bart of the need to reinstate the position of the front office manager. A manager was needed to monitor the rooms inventory and ensure that no revenues were lost due to un-canceled reservations and unreleased room blocks, to coordinate activities between the departments, and to train the front office staff consisting of front desk receptionists and valets/bellhops. However, to minimize costs, Bart decided that the front office manager would also work three shifts per week at the front desk as a receptionist.

In February 1991, Bart offered the position of front office manager to Ms. Claire Ruiz, who had been working as a front desk receptionist since 1989. The promotion worked out well. Claire knew the job thoroughly and was genuinely interested in hotel management. She was able to effectively combine her managerial duties with the three shifts at the front desk.

Cooperation between the departments soon increased significantly. Claire believed that the Inn would never be able to afford the specialized and extensive front office staff of a larger hotel, and thus its ability to deliver high-quality customer service depended on mutual cooperation between all employees. Consequently, when things got busy, she had the front desk ask other departments for support. For example, if the switchboard was busy, reservation calls were transferred from the front desk to accounting or sales. Even the general manager himself got called on to help the valets park cars or assist guests with luggage, although he clearly preferred being in his office going over reports and records.

The New PBX Position

While other managers were willing to help out, they also had their own duties to tend to and were not always available. Since occupancy remained strong, Claire convinced the general manager to reinstate the PBX position. However, Claire's idea was to have the PBX operator function as an extension of the front desk. A PBX station was set up in an unoccupied reception area in the lobby, and with the exception of checking guests in and out, the PBX operator performed the same duties and was compensated at the same rate of pay as the front desk receptionist. This additional support allowed the front desk to provide more efficient and gracious service to the Inn's guests and improve their room-selling ability. Despite the continuing recession and competition from the Ritz-Carlton, 1991 proved to be a year of record high occupancy and revenues for the Plaza Inn.

In August 1992, Claire left the Plaza Inn to pursue a graduate degree in hotel management at an eastern university. David Bart believed that the situation at the front desk was under control, and did not plan to fill the vacant position of front office manager. The front desk staff once again would be indirectly supervised by the sales manager.

It wasn't long, however, before the same problems Claire had worked so hard to resolve cropped up again. With the start of the school year, the front desk staff were no longer as flexible in terms of scheduling, and the PBX operator was called on to fill vacant shifts at the front desk. More often than not, there was only one person scheduled to work in the front office, and guest service began to suffer again. One day, for example, David Bart discovered that a recently hired front desk receptionist frequently told clients that the hotel was sold out because she was too busy to take a reservation.

Bart believed that there was no one at the front desk capable of being promoted to the position of front office manager. However, he also thought that it would be difficult to hire an outsider who would be willing to work the three shifts at the front desk for the modest salary he was willing to offer (most managers at the Plaza Inn were paid $5,000 to $7,000 less than other Kansas City hotels). Thus, Bart was relieved to learn that Laura Dunbar, who had previously worked at the Plaza Inn as a front desk receptionist, was interested in the position.

A New Front Office Manager

In addition to her experience at the Plaza Inn, Laura had worked as a concierge at one of the convention hotels in downtown Kansas City for several years. She had left the Plaza Inn for a secretarial position that offered more pay than the front desk position at the Inn. However, she missed the excitement and pace of the hospitality industry, and accepted the front office manager position in December 1992 with enthusiasm.

Despite her extensive connections with other Kansas City hotels, as well as the Kansas City Concierge Association, Laura soon found that one of her biggest challenges was the hiring and retaining of the front desk staff. The difficulty of hiring qualified employees forced Laura to work more than three shifts at the front desk. This left her with little time for planning and managing the front office operation. Short-staffed, she sometimes found herself working as much as 30 days in a row without a day off. In addition, the PBX position had not been filled on a regular basis for several months. Laura noticed that the front desk receptionists were not very attentive to the guests and were unable to meet guest expectations of a personalized, concierge-type service. Guest comment cards frequently included negative observations regarding front desk service; in fact, one guest commented that it seemed to him that the front desk receptionists "were responsible for doing everything with the exception of bartending and bussing the tables in the restaurants."

Laura believed that David Bart was reluctant to hire a full-time PBX operator due to financial constraints. She also felt pressured to meet the front office payroll budget, which had been prepared by Bart and which she felt had been grossly underestimated. In a bi-monthly management staff meeting, Laura suggested to the F&B director that perhaps the restaurant should assume responsibility for managing their own reservations and inquiries, so as to free up the front desk staff to improve guest service and sell more rooms. However, the F&B director was quick to point out that the evening restaurant manager was called on to assist with rooms-related issues on a daily basis, and replaced the evening front desk receptionist so that she could take a break. The restaurants, he asserted, could not afford to create a position just to take reservations and answer inquiries.

Laura felt especially pressured with managing the front desk operation on the weekends. During the week she felt she could call on the other managers for help, whether it was to park a car or take a reservation. On the weekends, however, the only manager on duty was the restaurant manager, and he was often too busy with the restaurant to help with rooms issues. The Manager on Duty (MOD) program (in which all department managers rotated in being at the Inn on call and in charge Friday and Saturday nights) that had been established the prior spring at the initiation of Bart, had been a tremendous help; however, it had been canceled when the Inn had hit the slow summer period. David Bart was not in on the weekends, and Laura felt he somehow forgot that the hotel existed on weekends, not to mention that it usually ran at full occupancy.

By mid-fall, Bart agreed with Laura that there was a definite need to reinstate the MOD program, as well as the PBX position. However, Bart thought that Laura herself had reduced her role of front office manager to that of a front desk receptionist. She seemed to him to surround herself with employees who were either not flexible or not qualified enough, and thus was left to fill a lot of shifts at the front desk herself. This didn't leave her with any time to oversee the operation of the front desk, and to ensure everything was in order. She still hadn't even finished writing up job descriptions for the Inn which he had told her to do two months ago. Bart wondered if the problems at the Front Desk stemmed from Laura's rather shy personality,

EXHIBIT 1
Organizational Chart, The Plaza Inn—1993

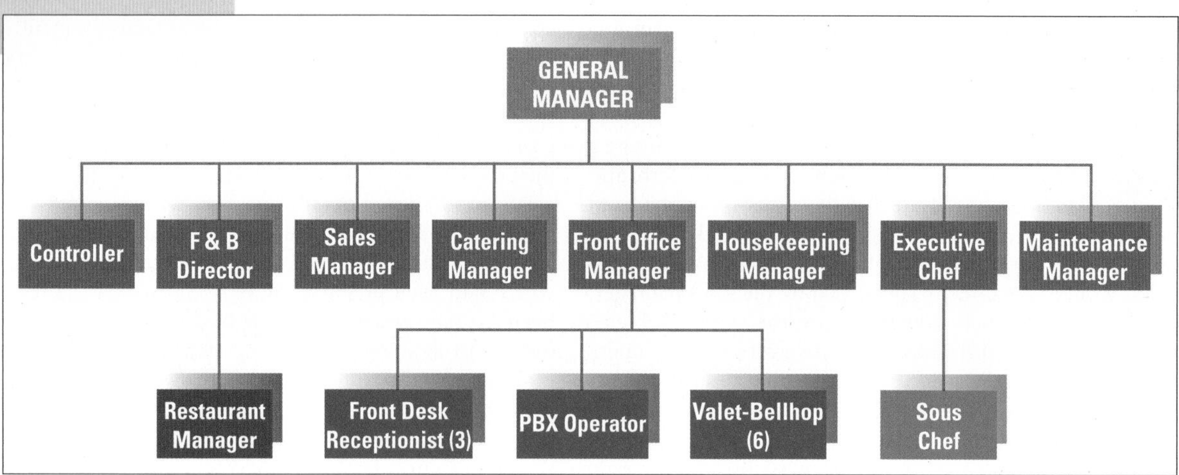

or perhaps from her lack of management expertise. It appeared that she was unable to articulate her needs to him and other managers. Perhaps he needed to give her more direction; however, this was contradictory to his belief that each manager should assume the responsibility of defining his or her own role consistent with the objectives of the Inn. The weakness he saw in the front office manager was of growing concern to David Bart. Clearly, it was a key position in the operation of the Inn and required a highly competent, proactive individual.

As he thought back to the ultimatum he had received from the president of Relais & Chateaux, the general manager wondered what he should do. Perhaps he should look for an experienced manager to head the front office, even if it meant paying a much higher salary. Perhaps he just needed to shake Laura up. Perhaps the situation would just straighten itself out. David Bart reached for a copy of the Inn's organization chart (Exhibit 1); perhaps a major structural change was needed. Perhaps. . . .

Part Three
External Factors and Design

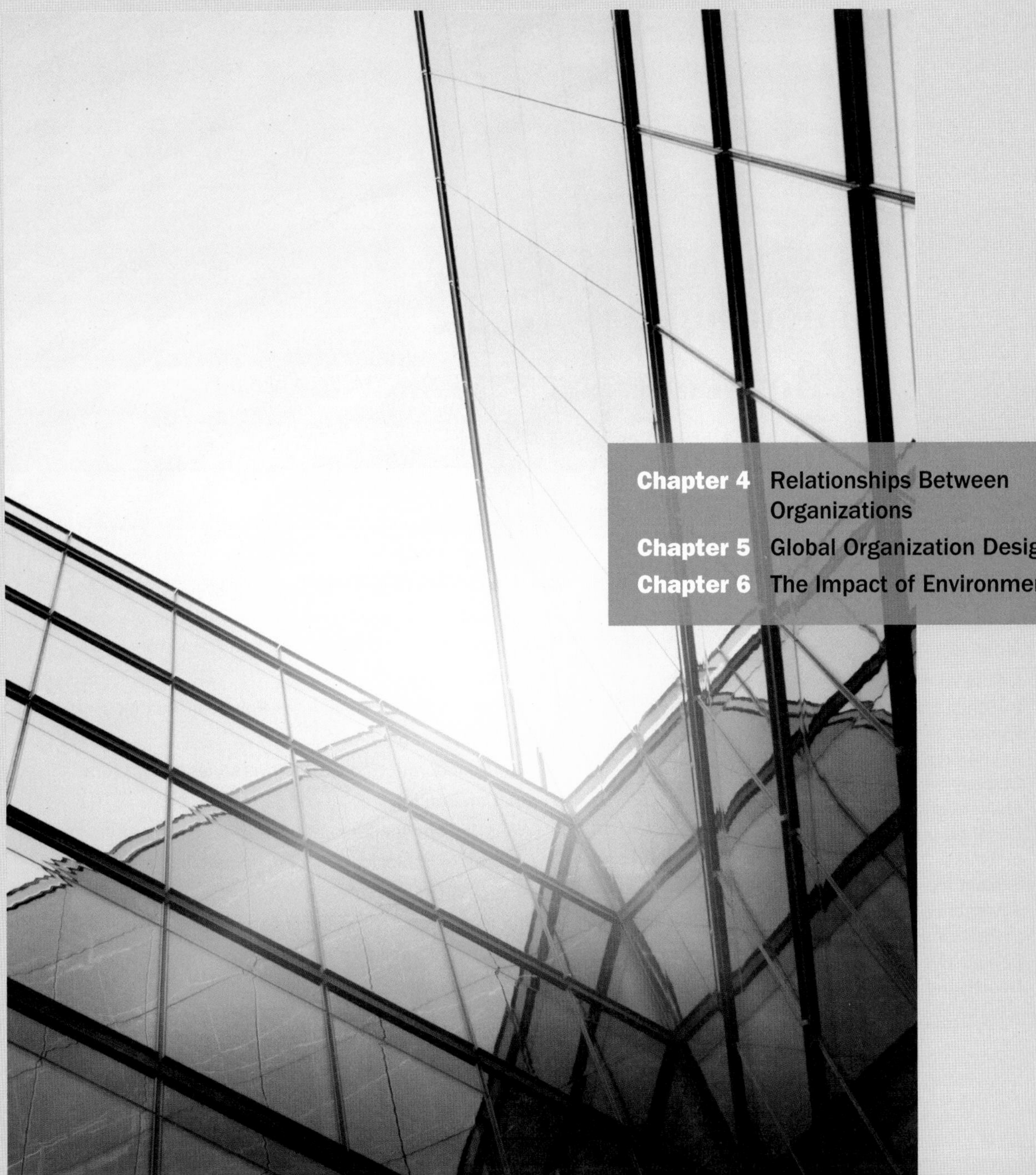

Chapter 4

©Ulrike Neumann, iStock

Relationships Between Organizations

Learning Objectives

After reading this chapter you should be able to:

1. Define an organizational ecosystem and the changing role of competition.
2. Explain the changing role of management in interorganizational relationships.
3. Discuss the power implications of supply-chain relationships.
4. Describe the role of collaborative networks.
5. Explain the interorganizational shift from adversaries to partners.
6. Understand the population-ecology perspective and its key concepts.
7. Specify the key aspects of institutionalism.

Before reading this chapter, please check whether you agree or disagree with each of the following statements:

1 **Organizations should strive to be as independent and self-sufficient as possible so that their managers aren't put in the position of "dancing to someone else's tune."**

I AGREE _____ I DISAGREE _____

2 **The success or failure of a start-up is largely determined by the smarts and management ability of the entrepreneur.**

I AGREE _____ I DISAGREE _____

3 **Managers should quickly copy or borrow techniques being used by other successful companies to make their own organization more effective and to keep pace with changing times.**

I AGREE _____ I DISAGREE _____

Cybercrime is one of the biggest threats to today's organizations, particularly financial firms and other companies that are entrusted with people's money. Poste Italiane S.p.A., which serves as Italy's postal service as well as a bank, a credit card firm, and a mobile phone company, created one of the most sophisticated cyber security operations in the world. Around the clock, employees monitor everything from mail delivery to ATM transactions in real time, tracking the source of possible risks, collecting data, passing information to local authorities, and acting with speed and precision to shut down threats. The problem was that no matter how good the company's cyber security, it was never good enough. "I am impressed by the way they change their behavior from their side," said CEO Massimo Sarmi of the cybercriminals, "how they react immediately."

Sarmi realized that collaboration with other organizations was the only way Poste Italiane could hope to achieve true security for its customers. He began reaching out around the globe. Poste Italiane has signed a memorandum of understanding with the U.S. Secret Service, for example, and is joining the electronic crime task force in New York City. The company has partnered with companies such as software firm Microsoft, energy company Enel, and Visa/MasterCard, and academic organizations such as George Mason University and the University of London, to open a global Cyber Security Program of Excellence. The center is promoting international cooperation regarding cyber security and studying ways to make the Internet more dynamically secure through active defense. "[T]he problem is global," Sarmi says. It's not national or local."[1]

When dealing with a massive, complex problem like cybercrime, even the most sophisticated and capable organization will soon reach the limit of its effectiveness. Today's organizations face numerous complex problems because of the complexity and uncertainty of the environment. Thus, a widespread organizational trend is to reduce boundaries and increase collaboration between companies, sometimes even between competitors. Several dozen U.S. retailers, for instance, have joined a cooperative program called ShopRunner, offering free two-day shipping and free returns, to compete with the growing power of Amazon.com. "It's amazing what people will do when they recognize there is a bigger threat . . . than just competing with each other," said Fiona Dias, executive vice president of strategy and marketing for GSI Commerce.[2]

In many industries, the business environment is so complicated that no single company can develop all the expertise and resources needed to stay competitive. Why? Globalization and rapid advances in technology, communications, and transportation have created amazing new opportunities, but they have also raised the cost of doing business and made it increasingly difficult for any company to take advantage of those opportunities on its own. In this new economy, webs of organizations are emerging. Collaboration and partnership is the new way of doing business. Organizations think of themselves as teams that create value jointly rather than as autonomous companies that are in competition with all others.

Purpose of This Chapter

This chapter explores the most recent trend in organizing, which is the increasingly dense web of relationships among organizations. Companies have always been dependent on other organizations for supplies, materials, and information. The question involves the way these relationships are managed. At one time it was a matter of a large, powerful company tightening the screws on small suppliers. Today a company can choose to develop positive, trusting relationships. The notion of horizontal relationships described in Chapter 2 and the understanding of environmental uncertainty that will be covered in Chapter 6 are leading to the next stage of organizational evolution, which is a web of horizontal relationships *across* organizations. Organizations can choose to build relationships in many ways, such as appointing preferred suppliers, establishing agreements, business partnering, joint ventures, or even mergers and acquisitions.

Interorganizational research has yielded perspectives such as resource dependence, collaborative networks, population ecology, and institutionalism. The sum total of these ideas can be daunting because it means managers no longer can rest in the safety of managing a single organization. They have to figure out how to manage a whole set of interorganizational relationships, which is a great deal more challenging and complex.

Organizational Ecosystems

Interorganizational relationships are the relatively enduring resource transactions, flows, and linkages that occur among two or more organizations.[3] Traditionally, these transactions and relationships have been seen as a necessary evil to obtain what an organization needs. The presumption has been that the world is composed of distinct businesses that thrive on autonomy and compete for supremacy. A company may be forced into interorganizational relationships depending on its needs and the instability and complexity of the environment.

A new view described by James Moore argues that organizations are now evolving into business ecosystems. An **organizational ecosystem** is a system formed by the interaction of a community of organizations and their environment. An ecosystem cuts across traditional industry lines.[4] A similar concept is the *megacommunity approach*, in which businesses, governments, and nonprofit organizations join together across sectors and industries to tackle huge, compelling problems of mutual interest, such as energy development, world hunger, or cybercrime.[5]

BRIEFCASE

As an organization manager, keep these guidelines in mind:

Look for and develop relationships with other organizations. Don't limit your thinking to a single industry or business type. Build an ecosystem of which your organization is a part.

Is Competition Dead?

No company can go it alone under a constant onslaught of international competitors, changing technology, and new regulations. Organizations around the world are embedded in complex networks of confusing relationships—collaborating in some markets, competing fiercely in others. The number of corporate alliances has been increasing at a rate of 25 percent annually, and many of those have been between competitors.[6] Think of the auto industry. Ford and GM compete fiercely, but the two joined together to develop a six-speed transmission. Hyundai, Chrysler, and Mitsubishi jointly run the Global Engine Manufacturing Alliance to build four-cylinder engines. Volvo is now owned by Zhejiang Geely Holding Group of China, but it maintains an alliance with previous owner Ford Motor Company to supply engines and certain other components.[7]

Traditional competition, which assumes a distinct company competing for survival and supremacy with other standalone businesses, no longer exists because each organization both supports and depends on the others for success, and perhaps for survival. However, most managers recognize that the competitive stakes are higher than ever in a world where market share can crumble overnight, and no industry is immune from almost instant obsolescence.[8] In today's world, a new form of competition is in fact intensifying.[9]

For one thing, companies now need to co-evolve with others in the ecosystem so that everyone gets stronger. Consider the wolf and the caribou. Wolves cull weaker caribou, which strengthens the herd. A strong herd means that wolves must become stronger themselves. With co-evolution, the whole system becomes stronger. In the same way, companies co-evolve through discussion with each other, shared visions, alliances, and managing complex relationships.

Exhibit 4.1 illustrates the complexity of an ecosystem by showing the myriad overlapping relationships among high-tech companies. Since the time this chart was created, many of these companies have merged, been acquired, or gone out of business. Ecosystems constantly change and evolve, with some relationships growing stronger while others weaken or are terminated. The changing pattern of relationships and interactions in an ecosystem contributes to the health and vitality of the system as an integrated whole.[10]

In an organizational ecosystem, conflict and cooperation exist at the same time. For example, Google, one of the most successful Internet companies in recent years, has competed most effectively by cooperating.

EXHIBIT 4.1
An Organizational Ecosystem

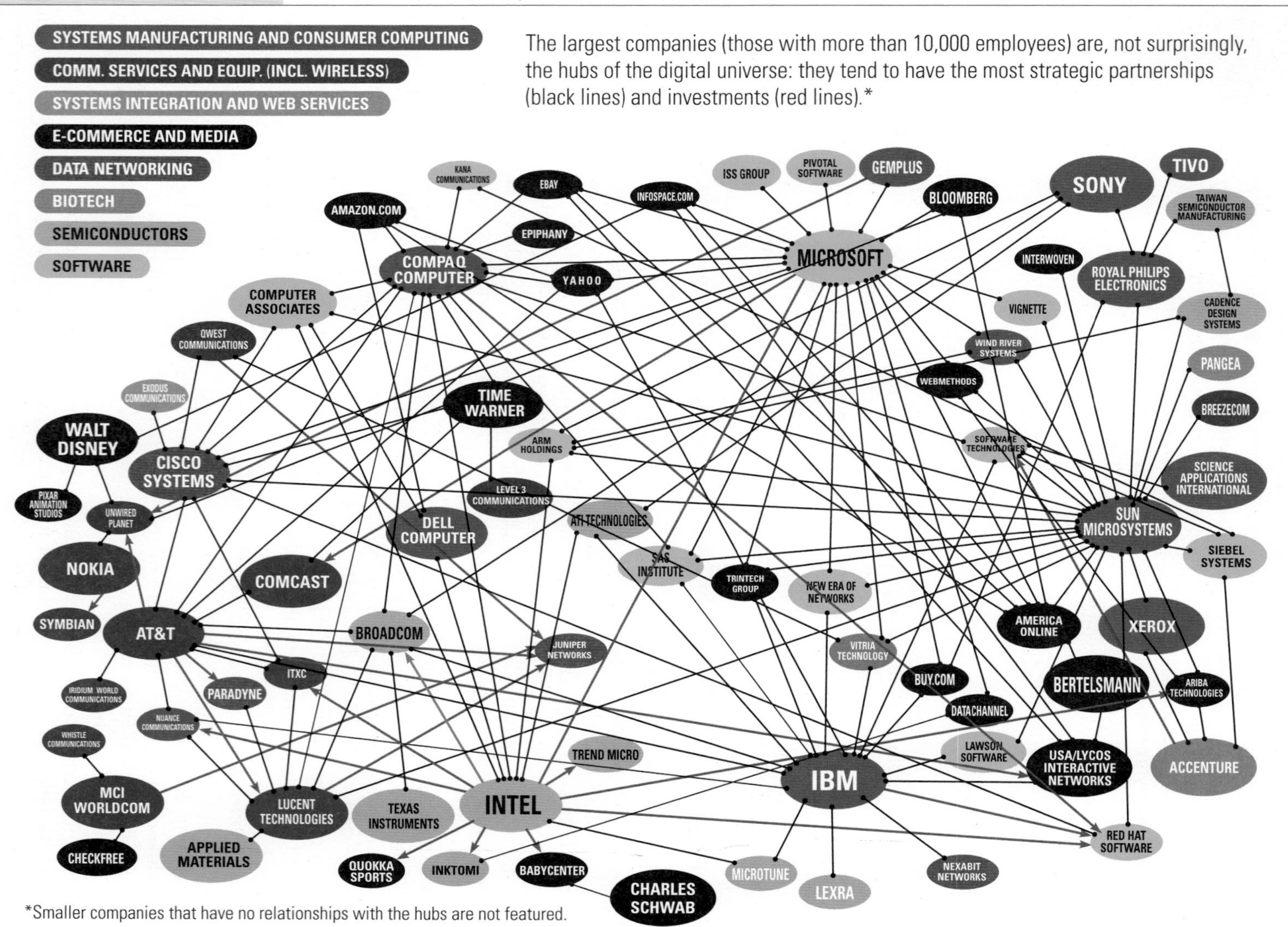

IN PRACTICE

Google

At Google, there's a whole team dedicated to giving business to the competition. If people don't like Google products, such as Gmail or Google Maps, the Google team makes it easy for them to move their data free of charge to any competitor's website. Google has never tried to lock users into its products, believing that when people spend more time online—wherever they spend it—everyone benefits. Helping your competitors get more business might seem like a strange way to run a business, but Google managers don't think so. Take the Google Chrome browser. It's small potatoes compared to Microsoft's Internet Explorer, but Chrome has slowly eaten away at Microsoft's market share. Yet Google Chrome is free and open source, which means any other browser that wants to incorporate pieces of the software can freely do so. What if Microsoft copied entire chunks of Chrome's programming code and built a better Explorer? That's great, says Google. Similarly, Google makes its smartphone operating platform Android free to any handset manufacturer that wants to use it. It created the first real competition to the iPhone, and the open-source approach means there are now many more people using Android-based phones than iPhones. Google believes giving away its technology leads to further Internet advances, which not only fits with Google's mission of improving the way people connect with information but also means Google gets more business—and gets stronger.

Collaboration, Google managers say, is essential to innovation. Consider the recently released Google Body Browser, an interactive 3-D simulation of the human body that allows users to peel back layers of the body and zoom in to study specific organs, bones, muscles, and more. At this time, Body Browser is still a work in progress, but it could be a hit with medical schools as well as other users (and advertisers). So far, few browsers outside of Google's most recent version of Chrome can support such a sophisticated tool. Others will catch up, of course, and that's fine with Google because that will spur even further advances.[11]

Google's emphasis on cooperation might be tested in coming years as it moves more steadily into markets now dominated by Apple. In addition to smartphones, Google is also moving into other businesses, such as digital music services, that put it in direct competition with a tough rival. "Open systems don't always win," warned the recently deceased Steve Jobs, Apple's co-founder and former CEO, who always kept tight control and close watch over his company's products.[12]

However, in general cooperation has become the rule in many industries and especially in high-tech firms. The business press is full of articles that talk about *frenemies*, reflecting the trend toward companies being both friends and enemies, collaborators and competitors. Many companies that long prided themselves on independence have shifted to an ecosystem approach. Mutual dependencies and partnerships have become a fact of life. Is competition dead? Companies today may use their strength to achieve victory over competitors, but ultimately cooperation carries the day.

The Changing Role of Management

Within business ecosystems managers learn to move beyond traditional responsibilities of corporate strategy and designing hierarchical structures and control systems. If a top manager looks down to enforce order and uniformity, the company is missing opportunities for new and evolving external relationships.[13] In this new world, managers think about horizontal processes rather than vertical structures. Important initiatives are not just top down; they cut across the boundaries separating organizational units. Moreover, horizontal relationships now include linkages with suppliers and customers, who become part of the team. Business leaders can learn to lead economic co-evolution. Managers learn to see and appreciate the rich environment of opportunities that grow from cooperative relationships with other contributors to the ecosystem. Rather than trying to force suppliers into low prices or customers into high prices, managers strive to strengthen the larger system evolving around them, finding ways to understand this big picture and how to contribute.

This is a broader leadership role than ever before. Managers in charge of coordinating with other companies must learn new executive skills. For example, Federal investigations have found that the inability of managers to collaborate and communicate effectively across organizational boundaries played a significant role in the BP-Transocean Deepwater Horizon oil spill, as we described in Chapter 1. One question raised by investigators concerned an argument between a BP manager and a Transocean manager that occurred on the rig the day of the explosion. BP and Federal agency managers also had trouble collaborating effectively in clean-up efforts.[14]

A study of executive roles by the Hay Group distinguished between *operations roles* and *collaborative roles*. Most traditional managers are skilled in handling operations roles, which have traditional vertical authority and are accountable for business results primarily through direct control over people and resources. Collaborative roles, on the other hand, don't have direct authority over horizontal colleagues or partners, but are nonetheless accountable for specific business results. Managers in collaborative roles have to be highly flexible and proactive. They achieve results through personal communication and assertively seeking out needed information and resources.[15]

The old way of managing relied almost exclusively on operations roles, defending the organization's boundaries and maintaining direct control over resources. Today, though, collaborative roles are becoming more important for success. When partnerships fail, it is usually because of an inability of the partners to develop trusting, collaborative relationships rather than due to the lack of a solid business plan or strategy. In successful alliances, people work together almost as if they were members of the same organization.[16] Consider the U.S. war against terrorism. As we discussed in the opening section of this chapter, interorganizational collaboration is essential for tackling large, complex problems. To fight terrorism, the U.S. government not only collaborates with governments of other countries but also with numerous private security companies. At the Pentagon's National Military Command Center, employees of private contracting firms work side-by-side with military personnel monitoring potential crises worldwide and providing information to top leaders. "We could not perform our mission without them," said Ronald Sanders, former chief of human capital at the Office of the Director of National Intelligence. "They serve as our reserves, providing flexibility and expertise we can't acquire. Once they are on board, we treat them as if they're part of the total force."[17]

Interorganizational Framework

Appreciating the larger organizational ecosystem is one of the most exciting areas of organization theory. The models and perspectives for understanding interorganizational relationships ultimately help managers change their role from top-down management to horizontal coordination across organizations. Exhibit 4.2 shows a framework for analyzing the different views of interorganizational relationships. Relationships among organizations can be characterized by whether the organizations are dissimilar or similar and whether

EXHIBIT 4.2
A Framework of Interorganizational Relationships*

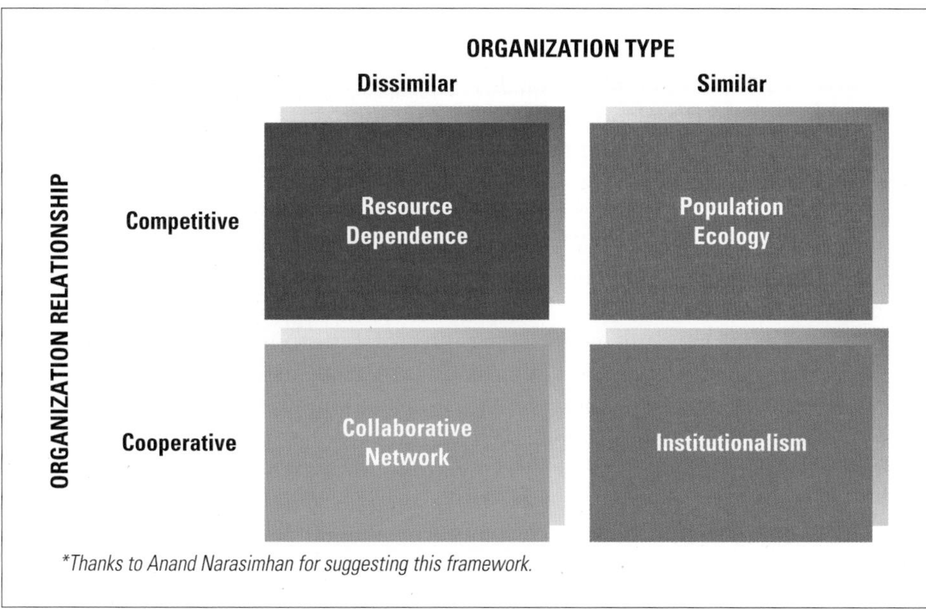

*Thanks to Anand Narasimhan for suggesting this framework.

relationships are competitive or cooperative. By understanding these perspectives, managers can assess their environment and adopt strategies to suit their needs. The first perspective is called resource-dependence theory. It describes rational ways organizations deal with each other to reduce their dependence on the environment. The second perspective is about collaborative networks, wherein organizations allow themselves to become dependent on other organizations to increase value and productivity for all. The third perspective is population ecology, which examines how new organizations fill niches left open by established organizations and how a rich variety of new organizational forms benefits society. The final approach is called institutionalism, which explains why and how organizations legitimate themselves in the larger environment and design structures by borrowing ideas from each other. These four approaches to the study of interorganizational relationships are described in the remainder of this chapter.

Resource Dependence

Resource dependence represents the traditional view of relationships among organizations. **Resource-dependence theory** argues that organizations try to minimize their dependence on other organizations for the supply of important resources and try to influence the environment to make resources available.[18] Organizations succeed by striving for independence and autonomy. When threatened by greater dependence, organizations will assert control over external resources to minimize that dependence.

When organizations feel resource or supply constraints, the resource dependence perspective says they maneuver to maintain their autonomy through a variety of strategies. One strategy is to adapt to or alter the interdependent relationships. This could mean purchasing ownership in suppliers, developing long-term contracts or joint ventures to lock in necessary resources, or building relationships in other ways. For example, the giant Swiss food company Nestlé SA, which is also the world's largest seller of packaged coffee, plans to offer free training and advice to coffee farmers all around the world over the next 10 years and provide them with plants that produce a greater quantity and higher quality of coffee beans. Nestlé does't plan to lock farmers who receive the plants and training into long-term contracts, but managers believe the attention and commitment the company is showing will lead many farmers to sell to Nestlé. The company says it will double the amount of coffee it buys directly from farmers, and more than half of the farmers in one Veracruz coffee cooperative said they would sell to Nestlé. "We're doing it for better quality and securing our raw materials," said Nestlé CEO Paul Bulcke. "We want to build a relationship where the farmer wants to sell to us."[19]

Other techniques include interlocking directorships to include members of supplier companies on the board of directors, joining trade associations to coordinate needs, using lobbying and political activities, or merging with another firm to guarantee resources and material supplies. Organizations operating under the resource-dependence philosophy will do whatever is needed to avoid excessive dependence on the environment and maintain control of resources, thereby reducing uncertainty. Locking in resources through long-term supplier relationships is one of the most common strategies.

Supply Chain Relationships

BRIEFCASE

As an organization manager, keep these guidelines in mind:

Reach out and influence external people and organizations that threaten needed resources. Adopt strategies to control resources, especially when your organization is dependent and has little power. Assert your company's influence when you have power and control over resources.

To operate efficiently and produce high-quality items that meet customers' needs, an organization must have reliable deliveries of high-quality, reasonably priced supplies and materials. Many organizations develop close relationships with key suppliers to gain control over necessary resources. As one example, SCA (Svenska Cellulosa Aktiebolaget) uses fiber from recycled paper to make napkins, toilet paper, and paper towels for restaurants, offices, schools, and other institutions. But the supply of recycled paper has gone down in recent years due to reduced paper waste along with competition for the fiber from Chinese paper companies. To make sure SCA has the supplies it needs, managers developed partnerships with numerous recycling centers, providing them with financial backing to upgrade equipment in exchange for the centers selling recovered fiber exclusively to SCA. The centers can still sell lower grades of fiber to other manufacturers.[20]

Supply chain management refers to managing the sequence of suppliers and purchasers, covering all stages of processing from obtaining raw materials to distributing finished goods to consumers.[21] Exhibit 4.3 illustrates a basic supply chain model. A supply chain is a network of multiple businesses and individuals that are connected through the flow of products or services. Research indicates that formalizing collaborative supply chain relationships can help organizations obtain and use resources more efficiently and improve their performance.[22]

Many organizations manage supply chain relationships using the Internet and other sophisticated technologies, establishing electronic linkages between the organization and these external partners for the sharing and exchange of data.[23] Companies such as Apple, Walmart, Dell, Tesco, and Samsung, for instance, are electronically connected with their partners so that everyone along the supply chain has almost completely transparent information about sales, orders, shipments, and other data. That means suppliers have data about orders, production levels, and needed materials, ensuring that resources are available when needed. In 2011, Gartner Research (previously AMR Research) ranked Apple as the best-performing supply chain in the world for the fourth year in a row. Procter & Gamble ranked No. 3, Samsung Electronics No. 10, and Nestlé No. 18. Amazon.com made the list

EXHIBIT 4.3
A Basic Supply Chain Model

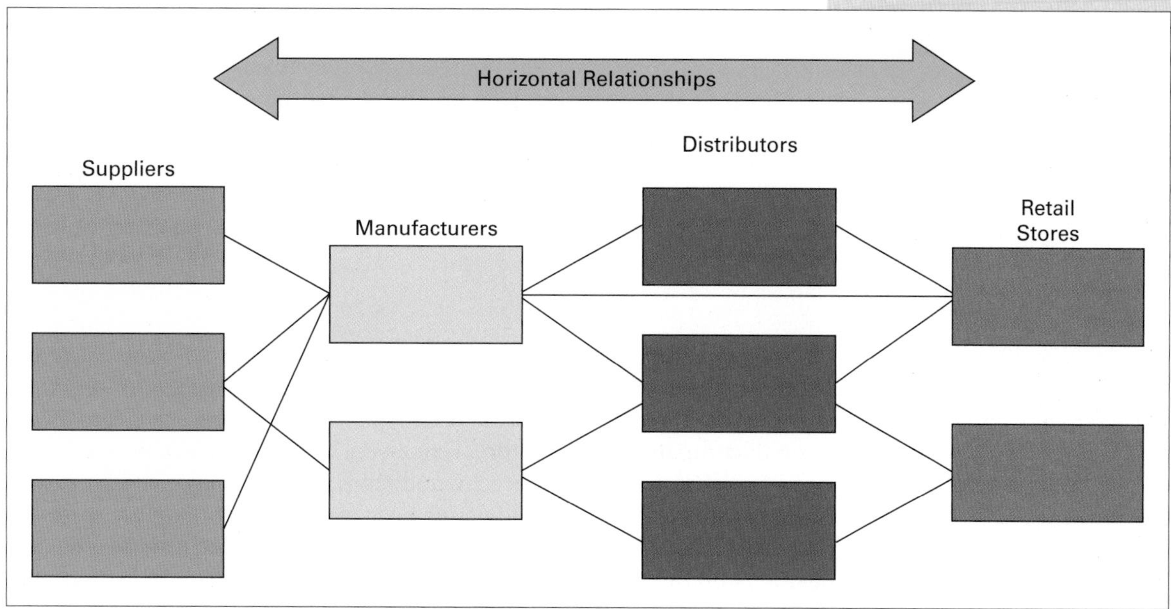

Source: Global Supply Chain Games Project, Delft University and the University of Maryland, R. H. Smith School of Business, *http://www.gscg.org:8080/opencms/export/sites/default/gscg/images/supplychain_simple.gif* (accessed February 6, 2008).

for only the second time in its history, moving from No. 10 in 2010 to No. 5 in 2011. On the other hand, the struggling Finnish cell phone manufacturer Nokia, which ranked at or near the top for several years, fell off the list entirely in 2011.[24]

Power Implications

In resource-dependence theory, large, independent companies have power over small suppliers. When one company has power over another, it can ask suppliers to absorb more costs, ship more efficiently, and provide more services than ever before, often without a price increase. Often the suppliers have no choice but to go along, and those who fail to do so may go out of business. Small suppliers are currently resisting the power tactics of Anheuser-Busch InBev, but so far the large company still has the upper hand.

Anheuser-Busch InBev NV

When Belgian brewing company InBev bought Anheuser-Busch, it created a heavyweight that is wielding new power over suppliers. AB InBev managers said they would aim to save $110 million a year from "procurement scale," or the costs they can save on procuring supplies because of the company's large size.

AB InBev managers used a hard-charging style as they renegotiated contracts with long-term suppliers, including many that once had friendly relationships with U.S.-based Anheuser Busch. In January 2009, for example, the company announced a new worldwide policy that would give InBev up to 120 days to pay once it gets an invoice from a supplier. (Previous terms called for payment in as little as 30 days.) Extending average payment time frees up working capital for InBev, but it hurts the suppliers. Some suppliers banded together and spurred the Belgian government to investigate whether InBev was using its dominant position to impose unfair contract terms. Unfortunately for the suppliers, the competition authority in Belgium said it found no infringements on the part of the large brewer.

Some suppliers say the company has refused to take contracted deliveries of malt or other supplies because of reduced demand for beer during the economic downturn. AB InBev insists that it hasn't broken any contract terms but has "renegotiated to align the supply and demand reality we are facing." By putting the squeeze on suppliers, AB InBev squeezed more profits for itself even as beer sales slumped. Managers said the company would deliver about $1 billion in cost cuts, mostly due to downsizing and negotiating better terms with suppliers.[25]

AB InBev's aggressive tactics show how a large company has power over smaller suppliers. The company's managers are doing whatever they need to do to get the supplies AB InBev needs at the best cost and most favorable terms. Beechwood Corporation, a small company in Millington, Tennessee, went out of business after the company dropped it as a supplier of beechwood chips. The company had been providing beechwood chips for aging Budweiser beer for 62 years. "They were difficult to deal with, but fair," said Beechwood's owner of the former Anheuser-Busch. "With InBev, it's all gone. You're not family. You're the guy who got outbid by a nickel or two."[26]

Resource dependence can work in the opposite direction too. Auto companies such as Toyota and General Motors are working to develop a new type of electric motor that doesn't require the use of neodymium, a rare earth mineral that is almost entirely mined and refined in China. Chinese suppliers have power over the auto companies as they strive to create more hybrid and electric vehicles, and the price of the mineral has soared.[27] Power relationships in various industries are always shifting.

Collaborative Networks

The **collaborative-network perspective** is an emerging alternative to resource-dependence theory. Companies join together to become more competitive and to share scarce resources. Large aerospace firms partner with one another and with smaller companies and suppliers to design next-generation jets. Large pharmaceutical companies join with small biotechnology firms to share resources and knowledge and spur innovation. Consulting firms, investment companies, and accounting firms may join in an alliance to meet customer demands for expanded services.[28] Five leading medical groups spanning several states and millions of patients joined in a consortium to share electronic data, including patient health records. Geisinger Health System, Kaiser Permanente, Mayo Clinic, Intermountain Healthcare, and Group Health Cooperative believe using and sharing digitized patient records can help healthcare providers make smarter decisions and provide better care, such as referring a patient to a specialist in another system.[29] Corporate alliances require managers who are good at building personal networks across boundaries. How effective are you at networking? Complete the questionnaire in the "How Do You Fit the Design?" box to find out.

How Do You Fit the Design?

PERSONAL NETWORKING

Are you a natural at reaching out to others for personal networking? Having multiple sources of information is a building block for partnering with people in other organizations. To learn something about your networking, answer the following questions. Please answer whether each item is Mostly True or Mostly False for you in school or at work.

	Mostly True	Mostly False
1. I learn early on about changes going on in the organization and how they might affect me or my job.	____	____
2. I network as much to help other people solve problems as to help myself.	____	____
3. I join professional groups and associations to expand my contacts and knowledge.	____	____
4. I know and talk with peers in other organizations.	____	____
5. I act as a bridge from my work group to other work groups.	____	____
6. I frequently use lunches to meet and network with new people.	____	____
7. I regularly participate in charitable causes.	____	____
8. I maintain a list of friends and colleagues to whom I send holiday cards.	____	____
9. I maintain contact with people from previous organizations and school groups.	____	____
10. I actively give information to subordinates, peers, and my boss.	____	____

Scoring: Give yourself one point for each item marked as Mostly True. A score of 7 or higher suggests very active networking. If you scored three or less, reaching out to others may not be natural for you and will require extra effort.

Interpretation: In a world of adversarial relationships between organizations, networking across organizational boundaries was not important. In a world of interorganizational partnerships, however, many good things flow from active networking, which will build a web of organizational relationships to get things done. If you are going to manage relationships with other organizations, networking is an essential part of your job. Networking builds social, work, and career relationships that facilitate mutual benefit. People with large, active networks tend to enjoy and contribute to partnerships and have broader impact on interorganizational relationships.

Why Collaboration?

Why all this interest in interorganizational collaboration? Some key reasons include sharing risks when entering new markets, mounting expensive new programs and reducing costs, and enhancing the organizational profile in selected industries or technologies. Cooperation is a prerequisite for greater innovation, problem solving, and performance.[30] Partnerships are also a major avenue for entering global markets, with both large and small firms developing partnerships overseas and in North America. Joint ventures with organizations in other countries, for example, make up a substantial portion of U.S. firms' foreign investment and entry strategies.[31]

North American companies traditionally have worked alone, competing with each other and believing in the tradition of individualism and self-reliance, but they have learned from their international experience just how effective interorganizational relationships can be. Both Japan and Korea have long traditions of corporate clans or industrial groups that collaborate and assist each other. North Americans typically have considered interdependence a bad thing, believing it would reduce competition. However, the experience of collaboration in other countries has shown that competition among companies can be fierce in some areas even as they collaborate in others. It is as if the brothers and sisters of a single family went into separate businesses and want to outdo one another, but they will help each other out when push comes to shove.

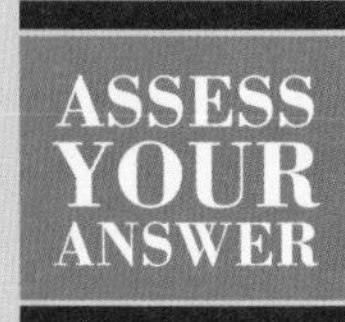

1 Organizations should strive to be as independent and self-sufficient as possible so that their managers aren't put in the position of "dancing to someone else's tune."

ANSWER: *Disagree.* Trying to be separate and independent is the old way of thinking. This view says organizations should minimize their dependence on other firms so that they don't become vulnerable. Today, though, successful companies see collaboration as a better approach to maintaining a balance of power and getting things done.

Interorganizational linkages provide a kind of safety net that encourages long-term investment, information sharing, and risk taking. Organizations can achieve higher levels of innovation and performance as they learn to shift from an adversarial to a partnership mindset.[32] Consider the following examples:

- Sikorsky Aircraft and Lockheed Martin have previously been head-to-head competitors in the fight to build presidential helicopters, but the two teamed up to bid on a new contract for a fleet of Marine One helicopters. The partnership will have Sikorsky building the helicopter and Lockheed Martin providing the vast array of specialized systems each one uses. The two joined together to be more competitive against rivals such as Boeing, Bell Helicopters, and Finmeccanica SpA's Agusta Westland.[33]
- Microsoft struck a deal with the biggest Chinese search engine, Baidu.com, to offer web search services in English. Microsoft's search engine Bing was scheduled to appear on Baidu's website by the end of 2011. Baidu will benefit by being able to improve its English-language search services. English language searches account for as many as 10 million a day on Baidu. For Microsoft, it is a way to get access to the world's largest Internet population of more than 470 million users. Search results will likely be censored by the Chinese government, a fact that led Google to pull its search engine out of mainland China a couple of years ago. A Microsoft spokesperson said of the partnership with Baidu: "We operate in China in a manner that both respects local authority and culture and makes clear that we have differences of opinion with official content management policies."[34]
- German auto maker Daimler forged a five-year partnership with the existing alliance of France's Renault and Japan's Nissan. Renault and Nissan have been partners since 1999. Under the new partnership, Daimler and Renault-Nissan will share small-car technology and engines and collaborate on research and development into fuel-efficient technologies. Soon after the Daimler-Renault-Nissan alliance was announced, Daimler rival BMW AG struck a deal with PSA Peugeot Citroen to develop a full range of hybrid car components and software for hybrid vehicles. Peugeot Citroen has a separate electric vehicle partnership

with Mitsubishi Motors. The demand for meeting tighter fuel efficiency standards has automakers rushing to develop new hybrid and electric vehicles, and teaming up is the only way they can do it cost effectively.[35]

As an organization manager, keep these guidelines in mind:

Seek collaborative partnerships that enable mutual dependence and enhance value and gain for both sides. Get deeply involved in your partner's business, and vice versa, to benefit both.

From Adversaries to Partners

Fresh flowers are blooming on the battle-scarred landscape where once-bitter rivalries once took place. In North America, collaboration among organizations initially occurred in nonprofit social service and mental health organizations, where public interest was involved. Community organizations collaborated to achieve greater effectiveness and better use of scarce resources.[36] With the push from international competitors and international examples, hard-nosed American business managers soon began shifting to a new partnership paradigm on which to base their relationships.

Exhibit 4.4 provides a summary of this change in mindset. Rather than organizations maintaining independence, the new model is based on interdependence and trust. Performance measures for the partnership are loosely defined, and problems are resolved through discussion and dialogue. Managing strategic relationships with other firms has become a critical management skill, as discussed in this chapter's Book Mark. In the new orientation, people try to add value to both sides and believe in high commitment rather than suspicion and competition. Companies work toward equitable profits for both sides rather than just for their own benefit. The new model is characterized by lots of shared information, including electronic linkages and face-to-face discussions to provide feedback and solve problems. Sometimes people from other companies are on site to enable very close coordination. Partners develop equitable solutions to conflicts rather than relying on legal contracts and lawsuits. Contracts

EXHIBIT 4.4
Changing Characteristics of Interorganizational Relationships

Traditional Orientation: Adversarial	New Orientation: Partnership
Low dependence	**High dependence**
Suspicion, competition, arm's length	Trust, addition of value to both sides, high commitment
Detailed performance measures, closely monitored	Loose performance measures; problems discussed
Price, efficacy, own profits	Equity, fair dealing, both profit
Limited information and feedback	Electronic linkages to share key information, problem feedback, and discussion
Legal resolution of conflict	Mechanisms for close coordination; people on site
Minimal involvement and up-front investment, separate resources	Involvement in partner's product design and production, shared resources
Short-term contracts	Long-term contracts
Contract limiting the relationship	Business assistance beyond the contract

Sources: Based on Mick Marchington and Steven Vincent, "Analysing the Influence of Institutional, Organizational, and Interpersonal Forces in Shaping Inter-Organizational Relations," *Journal of Management Studies* 41, no. 6 (September 2004), 1029–1056; Jeffrey H. Dyer, "How Chrysler Created an American *Keiretsu*," *Harvard Business Review* (July–August 1996), 42–56; Myron Magnet, "The New Golden Rule of Business," *Fortune* (February 21, 1994), 60–64; and Peter Grittner, "Four Elements of Successful Sourcing Strategies," *Management Review* (October 1995), 41–45.

BOOKMARK

4.0 HAVE YOU READ THIS BOOK?

Managing Strategic Relationships: The Key to Business Success

By Leonard Greenhalgh

What determines organizational success in the twenty-first century? According to Leonard Greenhalgh, author of *Managing Strategic Relationships: The Key to Business Success*, it's how successfully managers support, foster, and protect collaborative relationships both inside and outside the firm. In separate chapters, the book offers strategies for managing relationships between people and groups within the company and with other organizations. Effectively managing relationships generates a sense of commonwealth and consensus, which ultimately results in competitive advantage.

MANAGING RELATIONSHIPS IN A NEW ERA

Greenhalgh says managers need a new way of thinking to fit the realities of the new era. He offers the following guidelines:

- *Recognize that detailed legal contracts can undermine trust and goodwill.* Greenhalgh stresses the need to build relationships that are based on honesty, trust, understanding, and common goals instead of on narrowly defined legal contracts that concentrate on what one business can give to the other.
- *Treat partners like members of your own organization.* Members of partner organizations need to be active participants in the learning experience by becoming involved in training, team meetings, and other activities. Giving a partner organization's employees a chance to make genuine contributions promotes deeper bonds and a sense of unity.
- *Top managers must be champions for the alliance.* Managers from both organizations have to act in ways that signal to everyone inside and outside the organization a new emphasis on partnership and collaboration. Using ceremony and symbols can help instill a commitment to partnership in the company culture.

A PARTNERSHIP PARADIGM

To succeed in today's environment, old-paradigm management practices based on power, hierarchy, and adversarial relationships must be traded for new-era commonwealth practices that emphasize collaboration and communal forms of organization. The companies that will thrive, Greenhalgh believes, "are those that really have their act together—those that can successfully integrate strategy, processes, business arrangements, resources, systems, and empowered workforces." That can be accomplished, he argues, only by effectively creating, shaping, and sustaining strategic relationships.

Managing Strategic Relationships: The Key to Business Success, by Leonard Greenhalgh, is published by The Free Press.

may be loosely specified, and it is not unusual for business partners to help each other outside whatever is specified in the contract.[37]

In this new view of partnerships, dependence on another company is seen to reduce rather than increase risks. Greater value can be achieved by both parties. By being entwined in a system of interorganizational relationships, everyone does better because they help one another. This is a far cry from the belief that organizations do best by being autonomous. The partnership mindset can be seen in a number of industries. For example, British Airways, American Airlines, and Spain's Iberia Líneas Aéreas de España SA formed an alliance that will enable the carriers to cooperate more closely on trans-Atlantic flights and be more competitive against bigger rivals.[38] Auto companies have formed numerous partnerships to share development costs for new electric vehicles. Canada's Bombardier and its suppliers were linked together almost like one organization to build the Continental business jet.[39]

By breaking down boundaries and becoming involved in partnerships with an attitude of fair dealing and adding value to both sides, today's companies are changing the concept of what makes an organization.

Population Ecology

This section introduces a different perspective on relationships among organizations. The **population-ecology perspective** differs from the other perspectives because it focuses on organizational diversity and adaptation within a population of organizations.[40] A **population** is a set of organizations engaged in similar activities with similar patterns of resource utilization and outcomes. Organizations within a population compete for similar resources or similar customers, such as financial institutions in the Seattle area or car dealerships in Houston, Texas.

Within a population, the question asked by ecology researchers is about the large number and variation of organizations in society. Why are new organizational forms that create such diversity constantly appearing? The answer is that individual organizational adaptation is severely limited compared to the changes demanded by the environment. Innovation and change in a population of organizations take place through the birth of new types of organizations more so than by the reform and change of existing organizations. Indeed, organizational forms are considered relatively stable, and the good of a whole society is served by the development of new forms of organization through entrepreneurial initiatives. New organizations meet the new needs of society more than established organizations that are slow to change.[41]

What does this theory mean in practical terms? It means that large, established organizations often become dinosaurs. Consider that among the companies that appeared on the first *Fortune* 500 list in 1955, only 71 stayed on the list for 50 years. Some were bought out or merged with other companies. Others simply declined and disappeared. Large, established firms often have tremendous difficulty adapting to a rapidly changing environment. Hence, new organizational forms that fit the current environment emerge, fill a new niche, and over time take away business from established companies.[42] According to the population-ecology view, when looking at an organizational population as a whole, the changing environment determines which organizations survive or fail. The assumption is that individual organizations suffer from structural inertia and find it difficult to adapt to environmental changes. Thus, when rapid change occurs, old organizations are likely to decline or fail, and new organizations emerge that are better suited to the needs of the environment.

What Hinders Adaptation?

Why do established organizations have such a hard time adapting? Michael Hannan and John Freeman, originators of the population-ecology model of organization, argue that there are many limitations on the ability of organizations to change. The limitations come from heavy investment in plants, equipment, and specialized personnel; limited information; the established viewpoints of decision makers; the organization's own successful history that justifies current procedures; and the difficulty of changing corporate culture. True transformation is a rare and unlikely event in the face of all these barriers.[43] Consider how Netflix beat giant Blockbuster in the business of video rentals.

Netflix

IN PRACTICE

There was a time when going to the video store was a part of everyday life for many people. Blockbuster, the king of traditional video rental, had faux movie lights, popcorn and candy at the checkouts, and film posters on the walls. Shelves full of VHS (and later DVD) boxes beckoned, and it was a thrill to snap up the last copy of a hot new release. Now, you'd be hard pressed to even *find* a video store. Netflix, which offers movies by mail or via online streaming, didn't even exist when Blockbuster was raking in tons of money in the 1980s and most of the 1990s. When Reed Hastings founded Netflix in 1997, Blockbuster managers failed to take the company and its new business model seriously. Even though sales at video stores began to decline, Blockbuster didn't start offering new options for renting movies until 2003.

Blockbuster had a large customer base, a sophisticated inventory management system, and strong brand recognition. But the company couldn't adapt to a new way of doing business. Blockbuster was run by people at every level who had been there for years, when bricks-and-mortar stores were tremendously profitable. They simply couldn't believe those days were gone forever. The company's huge investment in its traditional stores made managers slow to recognize the importance of the Internet and reluctant to move into uncharted territory. Rather than dramatically shrinking the size and number of retail stores, Blockbuster managers kept investing more money in them. By the time they did get into the online game, Netflix had a big head start. Starting from scratch, Netflix could focus on making its distribution system better and more efficient. Blockbuster, on the other hand, had to invest a tremendous amount of time and money in developing and integrating new technology into its existing systems. Blockbuster finally admitted defeat and filed for bankruptcy in 2010. Meanwhile, Netflix expanded its customer base to more than 13 million and saw its stock price top $118 a share that same year.[44]

Netflix has run into problems of its own in recent years. Changes in pricing and other faulty management decisions angered customers, who began dropping the service. The stock price suffered as a result, plunging nearly 60 percent over a 3-month period. Netflix managers are still struggling to recover from the damage done to the company's reputation and performance. Meanwhile, Blockbuster has been acquired by Dish Network and is back in the game.[45] Despite these developments, the story of how Netflix as a new company defeated giant Blockbuster illustrates that it is extremely difficult for large established companies to shift to a new way of doing things. Another example comes from Kodak, which actually invented some of the earliest digital photographic technology but couldn't accept that customers would give up on the company's traditional film. Kodak had been successful for so long and was so large and entrenched in its way of doing business that it couldn't change substantively even when managers wanted to.[46]

The population-ecology model is developed from theories of natural selection in biology, and the terms *evolution* and *selection* are used to refer to the underlying behavioral processes. Theories of biological evolution try to explain why certain life forms appear and survive whereas others perish. Some theories suggest the forms that survive are typically best fitted to the immediate environment. The environment of the 1940s and 1950s was suitable to Woolworth, but new organizational forms like Walmart and other superstores became dominant in the 1980s. Now, the environment is shifting again, indicating that the "big box" era is coming to a close. With more people shopping online, smaller stores once again have an advantage in bricks-and-mortar retail. Walmart is planning to open dozens of small-scale

Walmart Express stores in urban areas. Best Buy is also opting for smaller storefronts called Best Buy Mobile and searching for ways to fill unused floor space in its large outlets.[47] No company is immune to the processes of social change. In recent years, technology has brought tremendous environmental change, leading to the decline of many outdated organizations and a proliferation of new companies such as Amazon, Facebook, and Twitter.

Organizational Form and Niche

The population-ecology model is concerned with organizational forms. **Organizational form** is an organization's specific technology, structure, products, goals, and personnel, which can be selected or rejected by the environment. Each new organization tries to find a **niche** (i.e., a domain of unique environmental resources and needs) sufficient to support it. The niche is usually small in the early stages of an organization but may increase in size over time if the organization is successful. If the organization doesn't find an appropriate niche, it will decline and may perish.

From the viewpoint of a single firm, luck, chance, and randomness play important parts in survival. New products and ideas are continually being proposed by both entrepreneurs and large organizations. Whether these ideas and organizational forms survive or fail is often a matter of chance—whether external circumstances happen to support them. A woman starting a small electrical contracting business in a rapidly growing area such as Cape Coral, Florida, or St. George, Utah (the two fastest growing cities in 2011), would have an excellent chance of success. If the same woman were to start the same business in a declining community elsewhere in the United States, her chance of success would be far less. Success or failure of a single firm thus is predicted by the characteristics of the environment as much as by the skills or strategies used by the organization's managers.

BRIEFCASE

As an organization manager, keep these guidelines in mind:

Adapt your organization to new variations being selected and retained in the external environment. If you are starting a new organization, find a niche that contains a strong environmental need for your product or service, and be prepared for a competitive struggle over scarce resources.

2 The success or failure of a start-up is largely determined by the smarts and management ability of the entrepreneur.

ANSWER: *Disagree.* Luck is often as important as smarts because larger forces in the environment, typically unseen by managers, allow some firms to succeed and others to fail. If a start-up happens to be in the right place at the right time, chances for success are much higher, regardless of management ability.

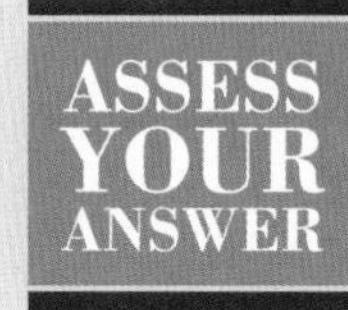

Process of Ecological Change

The population-ecology model assumes that new organizations are always appearing in the population. Thus, organizational populations are continually undergoing change. The process of change in the population occurs in three stages: variation, selection, and retention, as summarized in Exhibit 4.5.

- *Variation.* **Variation** means the appearance of new, diverse forms in a population of organizations. These new organizational forms are initiated by entrepreneurs, established with venture capital by large corporations, or set up by governments seeking to provide new services. Some forms may be conceived to cope with a perceived need in the external environment. In recent years, a large number of new firms have been initiated to develop computer software, to provide consulting

EXHIBIT 4.5
Elements in the Population Ecology Model of Organizations

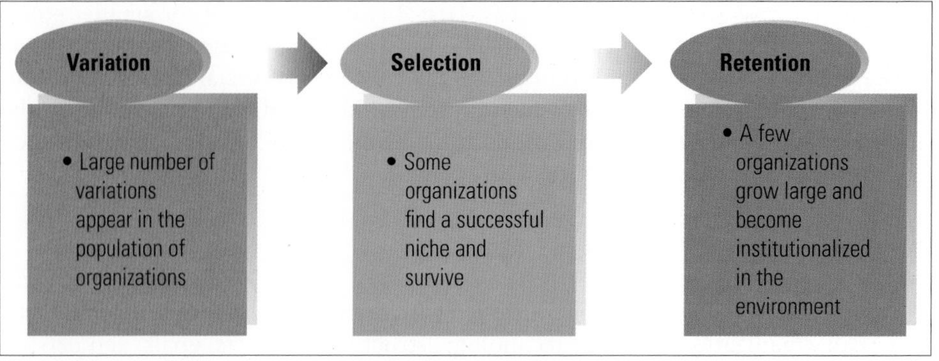

and other services to large corporations, and to develop products and technologies for Internet commerce. Other new organizations produce a traditional product or service, but do it using new technology, new business models, or new management techniques that make the new companies far more able to survive. Organizational variations are analogous to mutations in biology, and they add to the scope and complexity of organizational forms in the environment.

- *Selection.* **Selection** refers to whether a new organizational form is suited to the environment and can survive. Only a few variations are "selected in" by the environment and survive over the long term. Some variations will suit the external environment better than others. Some prove beneficial and thus are able to find a niche and acquire the resources from the environment necessary to survive. Other variations fail to meet the needs of the environment and perish. When there is insufficient demand for a firm's product or service and when insufficient resources are available to the organization, that organization will be "selected out."
- *Retention.* **Retention** is the preservation and institutionalization of selected organizational forms. Certain technologies, products, and services are highly valued by the environment. The retained organizational form may become a dominant part of the environment. Many forms of organization have been institutionalized, such as government, schools, churches, and automobile manufacturers. McDonald's, which owns 43 percent of the fast-food market and provides the first job for many teenagers, has become institutionalized in American life.

Institutionalized organizations like McDonald's seem to be relatively permanent features in the population of organizations, but they are not permanent in the long run. The environment is always shifting, and if the dominant organizational forms don't adapt to external change, they will gradually diminish and be replaced by other organizations.

From the population-ecology perspective, the environment is the important determinant of organizational success or failure. The organization must meet an environmental need or else it will be selected out. The principles of variation, selection, and retention lead to the establishment of new organizational forms in a population of organizations.

Strategies for Survival

Another principle that underlies the population-ecology model is the **struggle for existence**, or competition. Organizations and populations of organizations are engaged in a competitive struggle over resources, and each organizational form is fighting to survive. The struggle is most intense among new organizations, and both the birth and survival frequencies of new organizations are related to factors in the larger environment. Historically, for example, factors such as size of urban area, percentage of immigrants, political turbulence, industry growth rate, and environmental variability have influenced the launching and survival of newspapers, telecommunication firms, railroads, government agencies, labor unions, and even voluntary organizations.[48]

In the population-ecology perspective, **generalist** and **specialist** strategies distinguish organizational forms in the struggle for survival. Organizations with a wide niche or domain—that is, those that offer a broad range of products or services or that serve a broad market—are generalists. Organizations that provide a narrower range of goods or services or that serve a narrower market are specialists.

In the natural environment, a specialist form of flora and fauna would evolve in protective isolation in a place like Hawaii, where the nearest body of land is 2,000 miles away. The flora and fauna are heavily protected. In contrast, a place like Costa Rica, which experienced wave after wave of external influences, developed a generalist set of flora and fauna that has better resilience and flexibility for adapting to a broad range of environments. In the business world, Amazon.com started with a specialist strategy, selling books over the Internet, but evolved to a generalist strategy with the addition of music, DVDs, electronics, and a wide range of other goods; creation of the Kindle digital reader; and most recently the addition of a streaming video service offering thousands of movies and TV shows. A company such as Olmec Corporation, which sells African-American and Hispanic dolls, would be considered a specialist, whereas Mattel is a generalist, marketing a broad range of toys for boys and girls of all ages.[49]

Specialists are generally more competitive than generalists in the narrow area in which their domains overlap. However, the breadth of the generalist's domain serves to protect it somewhat from environmental changes. Though demand may decrease for some of the generalist's products or services, it usually increases for others at the same time. In addition, because of the diversity of products, services, and customers, generalists are able to reallocate resources internally to adapt to a changing environment, whereas specialists are not. However, because specialists are often smaller companies, they can sometimes move faster and be more flexible in adapting to changes.[50] Managerial impact on company success often comes from selecting a strategy that steers a company into an open niche.

Institutionalism

The institutional perspective provides yet another view of interorganizational relationships.[51] The **institutional perspective** describes how organizations survive and succeed through congruence between an organization and the expectations from its environment. The **institutional environment** is composed of norms and values from stakeholders (e.g., customers, investors, associations, boards, other organizations, government, the community, and so on). Thus, the institutional view believes that organizations adopt structures and processes to please outsiders, and these activities come to take on rule-like status in organizations. The institutional environment reflects what the greater society views as correct ways of organizing and behaving.[52]

Legitimacy is defined as the general perception that an organization's actions are desirable, proper, and appropriate within the environment's system of norms, values, and beliefs.[53] Institutional theory thus is concerned with the set of intangible norms and values that shape behavior, as opposed to the tangible elements of technology and structure. Organizations and industries must fit within the cognitive and emotional expectations of their audience. For example, people will not deposit money in a bank unless it sends signals of compliance with norms of wise financial management. Consider also your local government and whether it could raise property taxes for increased school funding if community residents did not approve of the school district's policies and activities.

Most organizations are concerned with legitimacy, as reflected in the annual *Fortune* magazine survey that ranks corporations based on their reputations and the annual Global Rep Trak 100 conducted by the Reputation Institute. In 2011, Apple and Google shared the top spot on the Global Rep Trak and ranked No. 1 and No. 2 on *Fortune*'s list of most admired.[54] Success and a good reputation go hand in hand. The fact that there is a payoff for having a good reputation is verified by a study of organizations in the airline industry. Having a good reputation was significantly related to higher levels of performance based on measures such as return on assets and net profit margin.[55]

Many corporations actively shape and manage their reputations to increase their competitive advantage. In the wake of the mortgage meltdown and the failure of giants Bear Stearns and Lehman Brothers, for example, many companies in the finance industry began searching for new ways to bolster legitimacy. Citigroup, Merrill Lynch, and Wachovia all ousted their chief executives over mortgage-related issues, partly as a way to signal a commitment to better business practices. The board of oil giant BP asked Tony Hayward to resign as CEO due to his mishandling of the Deepwater Horizon oil spill crisis and brought in a new CEO they believed could take the steps needed to restore the company's reputation.[56]

The notion of legitimacy answers an important question for institutional theorists: Why is there so much homogeneity in the forms and practices of established organizations? For example, visit banks, high schools, hospitals, government departments, or business firms in a similar industry, in any part of the country, and they will look strikingly similar. When an organizational field is just getting started, such as in Internet-related businesses, diversity is the norm. New organizations fill emerging niches. Once an industry becomes established, however, there is an invisible push toward similarity. *Isomorphism* is the term used to describe this move toward similarity.

The Institutional View and Organization Design

The institutional view also sees organizations as having two essential dimensions—technical and institutional. The technical dimension is the day-to-day work, technology, and operating requirements. The institutional structure is that part of the organization most visible to the outside public. Moreover, the technical dimension is governed by norms of rationality and efficiency, but the institutional dimension is governed by expectations from people and organizations in the external environment. As a result of pressure to conduct business in a proper and correct way, the formal structures of many organizations reflect the expectations and values of the environment rather than the demand of work activities. This means that an organization may incorporate positions or activities (e.g., e-commerce division, chief compliance officer, social media director) perceived as important by the larger society to increase its legitimacy and survival prospects, even though these elements may decrease efficiency. For example, many small companies set up websites, even though the benefits gained from the site are sometimes outweighed by the costs of maintaining it. Having a website is perceived as essential by the larger society today. The formal structure and design of an organization may not be rational with respect to workflow and products or services, but it will ensure survival in the larger environment.

Organizations adapt to the environment by signaling their congruence with the demands and expectations stemming from cultural norms, standards set by professional bodies, funding agencies, and customers. Structure is something of a facade disconnected from technical work through which the organization obtains approval, legitimacy, and continuing support. The adoption of structures thus might not be linked to actual production needs and might occur regardless of whether specific internal problems are solved. Formal structure is separated from technical action in this view.[57]

BRIEFCASE

As an organization manager, keep these guidelines in mind:

Pursue legitimacy with your organization's major stakeholders in the external environment. Adopt strategies, structures, and management techniques that meet the expectations of significant parties, thereby ensuring their cooperation and access to resources.

Institutional Similarity

Many aspects of structure and behavior may be targeted toward environmental acceptance rather than toward internal technical efficiency. Interorganizational relationships thus are characterized by forces that cause organizations in a similar population to look like one another. **Institutional similarity**, called *institutional isomorphism* in the academic literature, is the emergence of a common structure and approach among organizations in the same field. Isomorphism is the process that causes one unit in a population to resemble other units that face the same set of environmental conditions.[58]

Exactly how does increasing similarity occur? How are these forces realized? Exhibit 4.6 provides a summary of three mechanisms for institutional adaptation. These three core mechanisms are *mimetic forces,* which result from responses to uncertainty; *coercive forces,* which stem from political influence; and *normative forces,* which result from common training and professionalism.[59]

Mimetic Forces. Most organizations, especially business organizations, face great uncertainty. It is not clear to senior executives exactly what products, services, technologies, or management practices will achieve desired goals, and sometimes the goals themselves are not clear. In the face of this uncertainty, **mimetic forces,**

EXHIBIT 4.6
Three Mechanisms for Institutional Adaptation

	Mimetic	Coercive	Normative
Reason to become similar:	Uncertainty	Dependence	Duty, obligation
Events:	Innovation visibility	Political law, rules, sanctions	Professionalism—certification, accreditation
Social basis:	Culturally supported	Legal	Moral
Example:	Reengineering, benchmarking	Pollution controls, school regulations	Accounting standards, consultant training

Source: Adapted from W. Richard Scott, *Institutions and Organizations* (Thousand Oaks, CA: Sage, 1995).

the pressures to copy or model other organizations, occur. Executives observe an innovation in a firm generally regarded as successful, so the practice is quickly copied. McDonald's revised stagnant sales by adding healthier menu items and new types of beverages, so other fast food chains began doing the same. "You need to learn from your competition," said David Novak, CEO of Yum Brands, the parent company of KFC, Taco Bell, and Pizza Hut. SanDisk, Microsoft, Samsung, and other companies came out with their own digital music players to try to capture some of the success Apple enjoyed with its iPod.[60] Many large companies enter specific foreign markets when managers see their firm's biggest rivals doing so, even if entering the market is highly risky. Managers don't want to take a chance on losing out.[61]

Many times, this modeling of other organizations is done without any clear proof that performance will be improved. Mimetic processes explain why fads and fashions occur in the business world. Once a new idea starts, many organizations grab onto it, only to learn that the application is difficult and may cause more problems than it solves. This was the case with the recent merger wave that swept many industries. The past few decades have seen the largest merger and acquisition wave in history, but evidence shows that many of these mergers did not produce the expected financial gains and other benefits. The sheer momentum of the trend was so powerful that many companies chose to merge not because of potential increases in efficiency or profitability but simply because it seemed like the right thing to do.[62]

Techniques such as outsourcing, teams, Six Sigma quality programs, brainstorming, and the balanced scorecard have all been adopted without clear evidence that they will improve efficiency or effectiveness. The one certain benefit is that management's feelings of uncertainty will be reduced, and the company's image will be enhanced because the firm is seen as using the latest management techniques. A study of 100 organizations confirmed that those companies associated with using popular management techniques were more admired and rated higher in quality of management, even though these organizations often did not reflect higher economic performance.[63] Perhaps the clearest example of official copying is the technique of benchmarking that occurs as part of the total quality movement. *Benchmarking* means identifying who is best at something in an industry and then duplicating the technique for creating excellence, perhaps even improving it in the process. Many organizations, however, simply copy what a competitor is doing without understanding why it is successful or how it might mesh—or clash—with their own organization's way of doing business.[64]

The mimetic process occurs because managers face high uncertainty, they are aware of innovations occurring in the environment, and the innovations are culturally supported, thereby giving legitimacy to adopters. This is a strong mechanism by which a group of banks, or high schools, or manufacturing firms begin to look and act like one another.

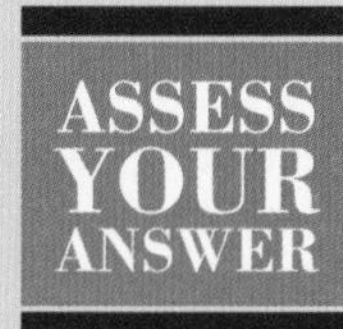

3 Managers should quickly copy or borrow techniques being used by other successful companies to make their own organization more effective and to keep pace with changing times.

ANSWER: *Agree.* Managers frequently copy techniques used by other, successful organizations as a way to appear legitimate and up to date. Copying other firms is one reason organizations may begin to look and act similar in their structures, processes, and management systems.

Coercive Forces. All organizations are subject to pressure, both formal and informal, from government, regulatory agencies, and other important organizations in the environment, especially those on which a company is dependent. **Coercive forces** are the external pressures exerted on an organization to adopt structures, techniques, or behaviors similar to other organizations. For example, large corporations have recently been putting pressure on service providers, such as accounting or law firms, to step up their diversity efforts. Managers in these corporations have felt pressure to increase diversity within their own organizations and they want the firms with which they do business to reflect a commitment to hiring and promoting more women and minorities as well.[65]

Some pressures may have the force of law, such as government mandates to adopt new pollution control equipment or new safety standards. New regulations and government oversight boards have been set up for the mortgage and finance industries following the Wall Street meltdown. As one example, the Credit Card Accountability, Responsibility, and Disclosure (CARD) Act requires credit card companies to add specific warnings regarding late payments and the total amount of interest customers will pay if they make only the minimum payment.

Coercive pressures may also occur between organizations where there is a power difference, as described in the resource-dependence section earlier in this chapter. Large retailers and manufacturers often insist that certain policies, procedures, and techniques be used by their suppliers. As part of its new sustainability push, for instance, Walmart is requiring its 100,000 or so suppliers to calculate the "full environmental costs" of making their products (such as water use, carbon-dioxide emissions, and waste) and provide this information for the company to distill into a rating system that shoppers will see alongside the price of the item.[66]

As with other changes, those brought about because of coercive forces may not make the organization more effective, but it will look more effective and will be accepted as legitimate in the environment. Organizational changes that result from coercive forces occur when an organization is dependent on another, when there are political factors such as rules, laws, and sanctions involved, or when some other contractual or legal basis defines the relationship. Organizations operating under those constraints will adopt changes and relate to one another in a way that increases homogeneity and limits diversity.

BRIEFCASE

As an organization manager, keep this guideline in mind:

Enhance legitimacy by borrowing good ideas from other firms, complying with laws and regulations, and following procedures considered best for your company.

Normative Forces. The third reason organizations change according to the institutional view is normative forces. **Normative forces** are pressures to achieve standards of professionalism and to adopt techniques that are considered by the professional community to be up to date and effective. Changes may be in any area, such as information technology, accounting requirements, marketing techniques, or collaborative relationships with other organizations.

Professionals share a body of formal education based on university degrees and professional networks through which ideas are exchanged by consultants and professional leaders. Universities, consulting firms, trade associations, and professional training institutions develop norms among professional managers. People are exposed to similar training and standards and adopt shared values, which are implemented in organizations with which they work. Business schools teach finance, marketing, and human resource majors that certain techniques are better than others, so using those techniques becomes a standard in the field. In one study, for example, a radio station changed from a functional to a multidivisional structure because a consultant recommended it as a "higher standard" of doing business.

There was no proof that this structure was better, but the radio station wanted legitimacy and to be perceived as fully professional and up to date in its management techniques.

Companies accept normative pressures to become like one another through a sense of obligation or duty to high standards of performance based on professional norms shared by managers and specialists in their respective organizations. These norms are conveyed through professional education and certification and have almost a moral or ethical requirement based on the highest standards accepted by the profession at that time. In some cases, though, normative forces that maintain legitimacy break down, as they did recently in the mortgage and finance industries, and coercive forces are needed to shift organizations back toward acceptable standards.

An organization may use any or all of the mechanisms of mimetic, coercive, or normative forces to change itself for greater legitimacy in the institutional environment. Firms tend to use these mechanisms when they are acting under conditions of dependence, uncertainty, ambiguous goals, and reliance on professional credentials. The outcome of these processes is that organizations become far more homogeneous than would be expected from the natural diversity among managers and environments.

Design Essentials

- This chapter has been about the important evolution in interorganizational relationships. At one time organizations considered themselves autonomous and separate, trying to outdo other companies. Today more organizations see themselves as part of an ecosystem. The organization may span several industries and will be anchored in a dense web of relationships with other companies. In this ecosystem, collaboration is as important as competition. Indeed, organizations may compete and collaborate at the same time, depending on the location and issue. In business ecosystems, the role of management is changing to include the development of horizontal relationships with other organizations.

- Four perspectives have been developed to explain relationships among organizations. The resource-dependence perspective is the most traditional, arguing that organizations try to avoid excessive dependence on other organizations. In this view, organizations devote considerable effort to controlling the environment to ensure ample resources while maintaining independence. One key approach is to develop close relationships with suppliers through supply chain management.

- The collaborative-network perspective is an emerging alternative to resource dependence. Organizations welcome collaboration and interdependence with other organizations to enhance value for both. Many executives are changing mindsets away from autonomy toward collaboration, often with former corporate enemies. The new partnership mindset emphasizes trust, fair dealing, and achieving profits for all parties in a relationship.

- The population-ecology perspective explains why organizational diversity continuously increases with the appearance of new organizations filling niches left open by established companies. This perspective asserts that large companies usually cannot adapt to meet a changing environment; hence, new companies emerge with the appropriate form and skills to serve new needs. Through the process of variation, selection, and retention, some organizations will survive and grow while others perish. Companies may adopt a generalist or specialist strategy to survive in the population of organizations.

- The institutional perspective argues that interorganizational relationships are shaped as much by a company's need for legitimacy as by the need to provide products and services. The need for legitimacy means that the organization will adopt structures and activities that are perceived as valid, proper, and up to date by external stakeholders. In this way, established organizations copy techniques from one another and begin to look very similar. The emergence of common structures and approaches in the same field is called institutional similarity or institutional isomorphism. Three core mechanisms explain increasing organizational homogeneity: mimetic forces, which result from responses to uncertainty; coercive forces, which stem from power differences and political influences; and normative forces, which result from common training and professionalism.
- Each of the four perspectives is valid. They represent different lenses through which the world of interorganizational relationships can be viewed: organizations experience a competitive struggle for autonomy; they can thrive through collaborative relationships with others; the slowness to adapt provides openings for new organizations to flourish; and organizations seek legitimacy as well as profits from the external environment. The important thing is for managers to be aware of interorganizational relationships and to consciously manage them.

Key Concepts

coercive forces
collaborative-network perspective
generalist
institutional environment
institutional perspective
institutional similarity
interorganizational relationships
legitimacy
mimetic forces
niche
normative forces
organizational ecosystem
organizational form
population
population-ecology perspective
resource-dependence theory
retention
selection
specialist
struggle for existence
supply chain management
variation

Discussion Questions

1. The concept of business ecosystems implies that organizations are more interdependent than ever before. From personal experience, do you agree? Explain.
2. How do you feel about the prospect of becoming a manager and having to manage a set of relationships with other companies rather than just managing your own company? Discuss.
3. Assume you are the manager of a small firm that is dependent on a large manufacturing customer that uses the resource-dependence perspective. Put yourself in the position of the small firm, and describe what actions you would take to survive and succeed. What actions would you take from the perspective of the large firm?
4. Many managers today were trained under assumptions of adversarial relationships with other companies. Do you think operating as adversaries is easier or more difficult than operating as partners with other companies? Discuss.
5. Discuss how the adversarial versus partnership orientations work among students in class. Is there a sense of competition for grades? Is it possible to develop true partnerships in which your work depends on others?

6. The population-ecology perspective argues that it is healthy for society to have new organizations emerging and old organizations dying as the environment changes. Do you agree? Why would European countries pass laws to sustain traditional organizations and inhibit the emergence of new ones?
7. Explain how the process of variation, selection, and retention might explain innovations that take place within an organization.
8. Do you believe that legitimacy really motivates a large, powerful organization such as Walmart? Is acceptance by other people a motivation for individuals as well? Explain.
9. How does the desire for legitimacy result in organizations becoming more similar over time?
10. How do mimetic forces differ from normative forces? Give an example of each.

Chapter 4 Workbook Management Fads[67]

Look up one or two articles on current trends or fads in management. Then, find one or two articles on a management fad from several years ago. Finally, use an Internet search engine to locate information on both the current and previous fads.

Questions

1. How were these fads used in organizations? Use real examples from your readings.
2. Why do you think the fads were adopted? To what extent were the fads adopted to truly improve productivity and morale versus the company's desire to appear current in its management techniques compared to the competition?
3. Give an example in which a fad did not work as expected. Explain the reason it did not work.

CASE FOR ANALYSIS **Why Is Cooperation So Hard?**

Armando Bronaldo immigrated to the United States six years ago after working as design leader for an Italian company specializing in home sound systems. Armed with a vision and 15 years of experience, he founded his own company, Technologia, as the supplier of sound translation components including the base radiator, dome tweeter (for high frequency), composite cone (for mid-range sound), the binding post (for sound translator delivery), and ohms impedance (for conducting sound through the speakers). As it builds its reputation for quality and supply chain service and delivery, Technologia relies heavily on continuing a solid relationship with AUD, a manufacturer of home sound systems, under the management of CEO Audie Richards. AUD was the company's first contractual partner, currently accounting for 50 percent of the small supplier's business. The initial agreement with AUD has grown and the current business relationship brings a steady stream of orders that has enabled Bronaldo, even in a tough economy, to add workers over the last three years. Bronaldo loves the reliability of selling to AUD, but he sometimes questions whether the business relationship is overbalanced in favor of the powerful manufacturer.

"I think in the beginning Audie played his hand well, knowing that we were a start-up and trying to secure a solid customer base. In my eagerness to get the contract and in trying to please the head of a big company, I found myself saying 'Yes' and carrying out his wishes and demands," Bronaldo admits. "Because we were a young company and because he is, by far, our biggest customer, I think he got into the habit of assuming the focus would remain on *his* needs and *his* profits throughout the business relationship. But now, with our feet under us as a company, I think it is time to look again at the relationship between the two companies."

Richards is satisfied with the present arrangement he has with Technologia and sees himself as both partner and mentor, as he recently explained to a colleague. "Bronaldo came to this country and started his company and I was willing to give him a chance, set up our logistics, and make it possible for him to grow his company. I think it's worked out very well for AUD. And now he talks about wanting to change the way we do things. I'm suspicious about what he has in mind. But he needs us more than we need him. Look, I've got a good supplier; he gets lots of business from us; I see no reason to change it."

Although the relationship and dialogue at the top management level is strained, mid-level managers at both companies *do* talk and are eager to explore and implement a new vendor managed inventory (VMI) system that builds a partnership of strong interdependence and equity. Instead of sending purchase orders, VMI involves sharing daily electronic information about AUD's sales, so inventory is replaced automatically by Technologia. Mid-level managers Larry Stansell (AUD) and Victoria Santos (Technologia) regularly correspond and meet to find potential areas for close cooperation, information sharing, and problem feedback.

"I know that Richards is suspicious, but it really is time for these two guys to take a new look at this business relationship and how they can address issues that could be beneficial to both," Santos says. "The playing field has changed. Technologia is stronger."

"But the relationship has not changed and I don't think it will until Bronaldo finds a way to reduce his dependence on AUD. In the meantime, flexibility, information-sharing, and reconsidering a range of cost-efficient options is important," Stansell admits, "But we have to start with the discussion of whether AUD calls all the shots between our two organizations."

"Yes, and that discussion must include logistical issues," Santos says.

"Delivery, the disagreements about the pallets . . ."

"Richards set up all of that initially—what would work best for delivery to AUD," Santos says. "But Bronaldo insists that PM rather than AM pick-ups would be better and that a change in pallet companies, from Bradley Packaging to Eastmont Packaging, would cut costs per trip by reducing mileage. Plus Eastmont has a new custom-made pallet that provides greater load stabilization necessary for high tech components. The savings for Technologia would be shared with AUD."

"But Bradley has a long-time business relationship of its own with AUD," Stansell points out.

"So, what we're saying here is that it is not *just* a discussion about these two organizations, but a consideration of the whole supply chain. The cost of lost flexibility, the lack of shared information. It's costing both of them. And the sudden spikes in production requests by AUD, in response to its retail customers, creates unnecessary problems in production planning at Technologia and unnecessary stress for the management and workers at both companies."

"VMI could be a powerful tool that empowers and brings value to both sides," Stansell says. "Through this system, Technologia will be able to create orders for us based on direct access to our orders and demand information—both short and long-range needs. . . ."

"And then, we can work together, determining the most cost-efficient way to manage and deliver the inventory," Santos continues. "We'll look at the entire supply chain to see where changes and even minor tweaks can be made to bring down costs and make the partnership strong, but there would have to be equal give and take."

"Flexibility on both sides is necessary to make this work," Stansell points out. "This is not a competition. Nobody has to be *right.*"

"But getting top management on-board to make this work is our real challenge," Santos says. "And we have to start looking ahead. VMI could be a stepping-stone to Jointly Managed Inventory (JMI), an even deeper collaboration, allowing the increased tactical planning and the real integration of Techologia and AUD's point of sale systems. That will offer optimal cost sharing and real time sales data, allowing us to stay ahead of the curve in production planning as well as logistics to meet AUD's needs in real time."

"So, what's our next step?" Stansell asks. "How can we make this happen?"

CASE FOR ANALYSIS Oxford Plastics Company[68]

Oxford Plastics manufactures high-quality plastics and resins for use in a variety of products, from lawn ornaments and patio furniture to automobiles. The Oxford plant located near Beatty, a town of about 45,000 in a southeastern state, employs about 3,000 workers. It plays an important role in the local economy and, indeed, that of the entire state, which offers few well-paying factory jobs.

In early 2004, Sam Henderson, plant manager of the Beatty facility, notified Governor Tom Winchell that Oxford was ready to announce plans for a major addition to the factory—a state-of-the-art color lab and paint shop that would enable better and faster matching of colors to customer requirements. The new shop would keep Oxford competitive in the fast-paced global market for plastics, as well as bring the Beatty plant into full compliance with updated U.S. Environmental Protection Agency (EPA) regulations.

Plans for the new facility were largely complete. The biggest remaining task was identifying the specific location. The new color lab and paint shop would cover approximately 25 acres, requiring Oxford to purchase some additional land adjacent to its 75-acre factory campus. Henderson was somewhat concerned with top management's preferred site because it fell outside the current industrial zoning boundary, and, moreover, would necessitate destruction of several 400- to 500-year-old beech trees. The owner of the property, a nonprofit agency, was ready to sell, whereas property located on the other side of the campus might be more difficult to obtain in a timely manner. Oxford was on a tight schedule to get the project completed. If the new facility wasn't up and running in a timely manner, there was a chance the EPA could force Oxford to stop using its old process—in effect, shutting down the factory.

The governor was thrilled with Oxford's decision to build the new shop in Beatty and he urged Henderson to immediately begin working closely with local and state officials to circumvent any potential problems. It was essential, he stressed, that the project not be bogged down or thwarted by conflict among different interest groups, as it was too important to the economic development of the region. Governor Winchell assigned Beth Friedlander, director of the Governor's Office of Economic Development, to work closely with Henderson on the project. However, Winchell was not willing to offer his commitment to help push through the rezoning, as he had been an enthusiastic public supporter of environmental causes.

Following his conversation with Governor Winchell, Henderson sat down to identify the various people and organizations that would have an interest in the new color lab project and that would need to collaborate in order for it to proceed in a smooth and timely manner. They are as follows:

Oxford Plastics

- Mark Thomas, vice president of North American Operations. Thomas would be flying in from Oxford's Michigan headquarters to oversee land purchase and negotiations regarding the expansion.
- Sam Henderson, Beatty plant manager, who has spent his entire career at the Beatty facility, beginning on the factory floor fresh out of high school.
- Wayne Talbert, local union president. The union is strongly in favor of the new shop being located in Beatty because of the potential for more and higher-wage jobs.

State Government

- Governor Tom Winchell, who can exert pressure on local officials to support the project.
- Beth Friedlander, director of the Governor's Office of Economic Development.
- Manu Gottlieb, director of the State Department of Environmental Quality.

City Government

- Mayor Barbara Ott, a political newcomer who has been in office for less than a year and who campaigned on environmental issues.
- Major J. Washington, the Chamber of Commerce chair of local economic development.

Public

- May Pinelas, chairman of Historic Beatty who argues vociferously that the future of the region lies in historic and natural preservation and tourism.
- Tommy Tompkins, president of the Save Our Future Foundation, a coalition of private individuals and representatives from the local university who have long been involved in public environmental issues and have successfully thwarted at least one previous expansion project.

Henderson is feeling torn about how to proceed. He thinks to himself, "To move forward, how will I build a coalition among these diverse organizations and groups?" He understands the need for Oxford to move quickly, but he wants Oxford to have a good relationship with the people and organizations that will surely oppose destruction of more of Beatty's natural beauty. Henderson has always liked finding a win-win compromise, but there are so many groups with an interest in this project that he's not sure where to start. Maybe he should begin by working closely with Beth Friedlander from the governor's office—there's no doubt this is an extremely important project for the state's economic development. On the other hand, it's the local people who are going to be most affected and most involved in the final decisions. Oxford's vice president has suggested a press conference to announce the new shop at the end of the week, but Henderson is worried about putting the news out cold. Perhaps he should call a meeting of interested parties now and let everyone get their feelings out into the open? He knows it could get emotional, but he wonders if things won't get much uglier later on if he doesn't.

Chapter 4 Workshop The Shamatosi[69]

Instructions

1. Divide into groups of three. Half the groups, on one side of the room, are "1s" and the other half are "2s."
2. The 1s are Pharmacology; the 2s are Radiology. Read *only* your own role, not the other one.
3. Any students not in a negotiating group can be assigned to observe a specific negotiation meeting.
4. Both groups want to purchase Shamatosi plants owned by DBR.
5. Each group has 10 minutes to prepare a negotiation strategy for meeting with the other side.
6. One Pharmacology group meets with one Radiology group so that all groups meet with one counterpart.
7. You have 15 minutes to try and negotiate a possible agreement to purchase Shamatosi plants from DBR.
8. You should decide whether you can form an agreement to move ahead jointly or whether you will go into competition with each other. An agreement would consider the price offered for the plants, how the cost is shared, to where plants will be delivered (which company), and how plants are best utilized.
9. Groups report to the whole class on results of negotiation. Observers can comment on their observations, such as level of trust and/or disclosure and ease/difficulties of reaching an agreement between companies.
10. Instructor leads a discussion on interorganizational agreements, decision-making, and joint ventures.

Role of Team from Pharmacology, Inc.:

Dr. Bernice Hobbs, a biological researcher for Pharmacology, Inc., a major pharmaceutical company, has monitored with mounting concern the reports from Brazil's Amazon rainforest. Everything from world weather patterns to providing an estimated one in four ingredients in medicine are tied to securing the world's rainforests. But over the past decade, scientists and pharmaceutical companies, along with environmental groups and others, have observed with alarm the destruction of the rainforests, and with them the destruction of entire species of plant, animal, and insect life.

As Hobbs monitors the situation, she is particularly concerned about conditions with regard to a particular plant found in limited quantities near the Rio Negro. Rainforest trees have shallow roots because the major nutrients for growth are located near the surface level. Biologists discovered a rare tiny plant growth called Shamatosi embedded among the trees near the Rio Negro. For a number of years, researchers have explored potential medical uses for these tiny plants.

Dr. Hobbs has been working with the leaves of the tiny Shamatosi plant and has discovered the plant's potential as a cancer-suppressing drug after breast cancer surgery. For a number of years the leading drug in this category has been Tamoxifen, a synthetic drug described as "remarkable" and credited with saving more lives than any other oncological drug by the lead investigator for a major breast cancer research group. However, research has also shown that Tamoxifen raises the risk of cancer in the lining of the uterus and can lead to blood clots in the lungs. There is also a growing level of concern as Tamoxifen resistance has developed. The medicine developed by Hobbs may avoid these problems and bring a new treatment into the list of options for doctors and their patients. But more research is needed. Hobbs needs to have access to as many leaves as possible from the Shamatosi plant.

DBR, the Brazilian timber company, has possession of several thousand Shamatosi plants from this year's season that have been replanted in portable crates. Your company, Pharmacology, Inc., has authorized $1.5 million for your team to bid to obtain the plants. You cannot go over this budget. Your team will meet with a team from Radiology, Inc., who also wants to purchase the Shamatosi plants from DBR, about a possible agreement for purchasing and using the plants for research.

Role of Team from Radiology, Inc.:

Dr. Alberto Dominguez, a biochemist for Radiology, Inc. who has expertise in treating radiation exposure, monitors with mounting concern the reports from Brazil's Amazon rainforest. Everything from world weather patterns to providing an estimated one in four ingredients in medicine are tied to securing the world's rainforests. But over the past decade, scientists and pharmaceutical companies, along with environmental groups and others, have observed with alarm the destruction of the rainforests, and with them the destruction of entire species of plant, animal, and insect life.

As Dominguez monitors the situation, he is particularly concerned about conditions concerning a particular plant found in limited quantities near the Rio Negro. Rainforest trees have shallow roots because the major nutrients for growth are located near the surface level. Biologists discovered a rare tiny plant growth called Shamatosi embedded among the trees near the Rio Negro. For a number of years, researchers have explored potential medical uses for these tiny plants.

Dr. Dominquez has been working with the roots of the Shamatosi plant in response to incidents involving radiation exposure. The worldwide expansion of nuclear facilities, the lessons from the 1986 Chernobyl disaster, and the resulting cases of thyroid cancer among thousands of children and adolescents, led to intensive

research by Dominguez and his colleagues to provide the swiftest response with the most powerful medicine. For years, Potassium iodide (KI) was issued in kits provided by organizations such as the Centers for Disease Control. However, KI was found deficient in protecting many body parts, such as the liver and intestines. Dominguez discovered the tiny Shamatosi plant, and his research indicated the potential for medicines from the root of this plant to provide additional protection, even for incidents of large-scale or prolonged exposure. The March 2011 Tohoku earthquake and tsunami, and the resultant radiation exposure caused by the meltdown at the Fukushima Daiichi nuclear power plant, intensified concerns among scientists to find and develop a new medicine. Dominguez needs as many plants as possible.

DBR, the Brazilian timber company, has possession of several thousand Shamatosi plants from this year's season that have been replanted in portable crates. Your company, Radiology, Inc., has authorized your team to bid $1.5 million to obtain the plants. You cannot go over this budget. Your team will meet with a team from Pharmacology, Inc., who also wants to purchase the Shamatosi plants from DBR, about a possible agreement for purchasing and using the plants for research.

Notes

1. Fernando Napolitano, "The Megacommunity Approach to Tackling the World's Toughest Problems," *Strategy + Business* (August 24, 2010), http://www.strategy-business.com/article/10305?gko=73c6d (accessed August 1, 2011).
2. Geoffrey A. Fowler, "Retailers Team Up Against Amazon," *The Wall Street Journal Online* (October 6, 2010), http://online.wsj.com/article/SB10001424052748703843804575534062509989530.html (accessed August 1, 2011).
3. Christine Oliver, "Determinants of Interorganizational Relationships: Integration and Future Directions," *Academy of Management Review* 15 (1990), 241–265.
4. James Moore, *The Death of Competition: Leadership and Strategy in the Age of Business Ecosystems* (New York: HarperCollins, 1996).
5. Mark Gerencser, Reginald Van Lee, Fernando Napolitano, and Christopher Kelly, *Megacommunities: How Leaders of Government, Business, and Non-profits Can Tackle Today's Global Challenges Together* (New York: Palgrave Macmillan, 2008).
6. Jonathan Hughes and Jeff Weiss, "Simple Rules for Making Alliances Work," *Harvard Business Review* (November 2007), 122–131; Howard Muson, "Friend? Foe? Both? The Confusing World of Corporate Alliances," *Across the Board* (March–April 2002), 19–25; and Devi R. Gnyawali and Ravindranath Madhavan, "Cooperative Networks and Competitive Dynamics: A Structural Embeddedness Perspective," *Academy of Management Review* 26, no. 3 (2001), 431–445.
7. Katie Merx, "Automakers Interconnected Around World," *Edmonton Journal*, April 6, 2007, H14; and Keith Bradsher, "Ford Agrees to Sell Volvo to a Fast-Rising Chinese Company," *The New York Times Online*" (March 28, 2010), http://www.nytimes.com/2010/03/29/business/global/29auto.html (accessed August 1, 2011).
8. Thomas Petzinger, Jr., *The New Pioneers: The Men and Women Who Are Transforming the Workplace and Marketplace* (New York: Simon & Schuster, 1999), 53–54.
9. James Moore, "The Death of Competition," *Fortune* (April 15, 1996), 142–144.
10. Brian Goodwin, *How the Leopard Changed Its Spots: The Evolution of Complexity* (New York: Touchstone, 1994), 181, quoted in Petzinger, *The New Pioneers,* 53.
11. Greg Ferenstein, "In a Cutthroat World, Some Web Giants Thrive by Cooperating," *The Washington Post* (February 19, 2011), http://www.washingtonpost.com/business/in-a-cutthroat-world-some-web-giants-thrive-by-cooperating/2011/02/19/ABmYSYQ_story.html (accessed February 19, 2011); Sam Grobart, "Gadgetwise: Body Browser is a Google Earth for the Anatomy," *The New York Times*, December 23, 2010, B7; Andrew Dowell, "The Rise of Apps, iPad, and Android," *The Wall Street Journal Online* (December 28, 2010), http://online.wsj.com/article/SB10001424052748704774604576035611315663944.html (accessed August 1, 2011); and Beth Kowitt, "100 Million Android Fans Can't Be Wrong," *Fortune* (June 16, 2011), http://tech.fortune.cnn.com/2011/06/16/100-million-android-fans-cant-be-wrong/ (accessed August 2, 2011).
12. Ferenstein, "In a Cutthroat World, Some Web Giants Thrive by Cooperating;" and Jessica E. Vascellaro and Yukari Iwatani Kane, "Apple, Google Rivalry Heats Up," *The Wall Street Journal*, December 11, 2009, B1.
13. Sumantra Ghoshal and Christopher A. Bartlett, "Changing the Role of Top Management: Beyond Structure and Process," *Harvard Business Review* (January–February 1995), 86–96.
14. Ian Urbina, "In Gulf, It Was Unclear Who Was in Charge of Oil Rig," *The New York Times* (June 5, 2010), http://www.nytimes.com/2010/06/06/us/06rig.html (accessed August 5, 2011).
15. "Toward a More Perfect Match: Building Successful Leaders by Effectively Aligning People and Roles," Hay Group Working Paper (2004); and "Making Sure the Suit Fits," *Hay Group Research Brief* (2004). Available from Hay Group, The McClelland Center, 116 Huntington Avenue, Boston, MA 02116, or at *http://www.haygroup.com.*
16. Hughes and Weiss, "Simple Rules for Making Alliances Work."
17. Dana Priest and William M. Arkin, "Top Secret America, A *Washington Post* Investigation; Part II: National Security Inc." (July 20, 2010), http://projects.washingtonpost.com/top-secret-america/articles/national-security-inc/1/ (accessed November 28, 2011).
18. J. Pfeffer and G. R. Salancik, *The External Control of Organizations: A Resource Dependence Perspective* (New York: Harper & Row, 1978); and Amy J. Hillman, Michael

C. Withers, and Brian J. Collins, "Resource Dependence Theory: A Review," *Journal of Management* 35, no. 6 (2009), 1404–1427.

19. Christina Passariello and Laurence Iliff, "Nestlé Plans Ground Attack Over Coffee Beans," *The Wall Street Journal*, August 27, 2010, B1.
20. Ellen Byron, "Theory & Practice: Tight Supplies, Tight Partners," *The Wall Street Journal*, January 10, 2011, B5.
21. Definition based on Steven A. Melnyk and David R. Denzler, *Operations Management: A Value Driven Approach* (Burr Ridge, IL: Irwin, 1996), 613.
22. Patricia J. Daugherty, R. Glenn Richey, Anthony S. Roath, Soonhong Min, Haozhe Chen, Aaron D. Arndt, and Stefan E. Gencehv, "Is Collaboration Paying Off for Firms?" *Business Horizons* 49, no. 2 (January–February 2006), 61–70.
23. Jim Turcotte, Bob Silveri, and Tom Jobson, "Are You Ready for the E-Supply Chain?" *APICS–The Performance Advantage* (August 1998), 56–59.
24. "The Gartner Supply Chain Top 25 for 2011," Gartner.com (June 2, 2010), http://www.gartner.com/technology/supply-chain/top25.jsp (accessed August 1, 2011).
25. Matthew Dalton, "Corporate News: AB InBev Suppliers Feel Squeeze—Smaller Companies Complain of Brewing Behemoth's Newfound Muscle," *The Wall Street Journal*, April 17, 2009, B2; "Business Brief: Anheuser-Busch InBev SA," *The Wall Street Journal Europe*, May 12, 2009, 7; and Jeremiah McWilliams, "Cost Savings Provide a Big Boost to A-B InBev; Profits Blow by Forecasts Despite Drop in Beer Sales," *St. Louis Post-Dispatch*, August 14, 2009, B1.
26. Jeremiah McWilliams, "Suggestion Backfires on A-B Supplier; InBev Took Idea of Single Firm For Beechwood, But Chose Competitor," *St. Louis Post-Dispatch*, April 23, 2009, A8.
27. Mike Ramsey, "Toyota Tries to Break Reliance on China," *The Wall Street Journal*, January 14, 2011, B1.
28. Mitchell P. Koza and Arie Y. Lewin, "The Co-Evolution of Network Alliances: A Longitudinal Analysis of an International Professional Service Network," Center for Research on New Organizational Forms, Working Paper 98–09–02; and Kathy Rebello with Richard Brandt, Peter Coy, and Mark Lewyn, "Your Digital Future," *BusinessWeek* (September 7, 1992), 56–64.
29. Steve Lohr, "Big Medical Groups Begin Patient Data-Sharing Project," *The New York Times* (April 6, 2011), http://bits.blogs.nytimes.com/2011/04/06/big-medical-groups-begin-patient-data-sharing-project/ (accessed April 6, 2011).
30. Christine Oliver, "Determinants of Interorganizational Relationships: Integration and Future Directions," *Academy of Management Review*, 15 (1990), 241–265; and Ken G. Smith, Stephen J. Carroll, and Susan Ashford, "Intra- and Interorganizational Cooperation: Toward a Research Agenda," *Academy of Management Journal* 38 (1995), 7–23.
31. Paul W. Beamish and Nathaniel C. Lupton, "Managing Joint Ventures," *Academy of Management Perspectives* (May 2009), 75–94.
32. Timothy M. Stearns, Alan N. Hoffman, and Jan B. Heide, "Performance of Commercial Television Stations as an Outcome of Interorganizational Linkages and Environmental Conditions," *Academy of Management Journal* 30 (1987), 71–90; David A. Whetten and Thomas K. Kueng, "The Instrumental Value of Interorganizational Relations: Antecedents and Consequences of Linkage Formation," *Academy of Management Journal* 22 (1979), 325–344; G. Ahuja, "Collaboration Networks, Structural Holes, and Innovation: A Longitudinal Study," *Administrative Science Quarterly* 45 (2000), 425–455; and Corey C. Phelps, "A Longitudinal Study of the Influence of Alliance Network Structure and Composition on Firm Exploratory Innovation," *Academy of Management Journal* 53, no. 4 (2010), 890–913.
33. Peter Sanders, "Sikorsky's Business Heads Up," *The Wall Street Journal Online* (April 19, 2010), http://online.wsj.com/article/SB10001424052702304180804575188821353177134.html (accessed April 19, 2010).
34. David Barboza, "Microsoft to Provide Bing to a Chinese Search Engine," *The New York Times*, July 5, 2011, B2.
35. David Jolly, "Daimler, Nissan and Renault Unveil Partnership," *The New York Times* (April 7, 2010), http://www.nytimes.com/2010/04/08/business/global/08autos.html (accessed April 7, 2010); and Vanessa Fuhrmans, "Corporate News: BMW Sets Hybrid Pact with Peugeot," *The Wall Street Journal*, February 3, 2011, B3.
36. Keith G. Provan and H. Brinton Milward, "A Preliminary Theory of Interorganizational Network Effectiveness: A Comparative of Four Community Mental Health Systems," *Administrative Science Quarterly* 40 (1995), 1–33.
37. Peter Smith Ring and Andrew H. Van de Ven, "Developmental Processes of Corporate Interorganizational Relationships," *Academy of Management Review* 19 (1994), 90–118; Jeffrey H. Dyer, "How Chrysler Created an American *Keiretsu*," *Harvard Business Review* (July–August 1996), 42–56; Peter Grittner, "Four Elements of Successful Sourcing Strategies" *Management Review* (October 1995), 41–45; Myron Magnet, "The New Golden Rule of Business," *Fortune* (February 21, 1994), 60–64; and Mick Marchington and Steven Vincent, "Analysing the Influence of Institutional, Organizational and Interpersonal Forces in Shaping Inter-Organizational Relationships," *Journal of Management Studies* 41, no. 6 (September 2004), 1029–1056.
38. Daniel Michaels and Peppi Kiviniemi, "Corporate News: Looming Alliance to Boost BA," *The Wall Street Journal*, July 13, 2010, B3.
39. Philip Siekman, "The Snap-Together Business Jet," *Fortune* (January 21, 2002), 104[A]–104[H].
40. This section draws from Joel A. C. Baum, "Organizational Ecology," in Stewart R. Clegg, Cynthia Hardy, and Walter R. Nord, eds., *Handbook of Organization Studies* (Thousand Oaks, CA: Sage, 1996); Jitendra V. Singh, *Organizational Evolution: New Directions* (Newbury Park, CA: Sage, 1990); Howard Aldrich, Bill McKelvey, and Dave Ulrich, "Design Strategy from the Population Perspective," *Journal of Management* 10 (1984), 67–86; Howard E. Aldrich, *Organizations and Environments* (Englewood Cliffs, NJ: Prentice Hall, 1979); Michael Hannan and John Freeman, "The Population Ecology of Organizations," *American Journal of Sociology* 82 (1977), 929–964; Dave Ulrich, "The Population Perspective: Review, Critique, and Relevance," *Human Relations* 40 (1987), 137–152; Jitendra V. Singh and Charles J. Lumsden, "Theory and Research in Organizational Ecology," *Annual Review of Sociology* 16 (1990), 161–195; Howard E. Aldrich, "Understanding, Not Integration: Vital Signs from Three Perspectives on Organizations," in Michael Reed and

Michael D. Hughes, eds., *Rethinking Organizations: New Directions in Organizational Theory and Analysis* (London: Sage, 1992); Jitendra V. Singh, David J. Tucker, and Robert J. House, "Organizational Legitimacy and the Liability of Newness," *Administrative Science Quarterly* 31 (1986), 171–193; and Douglas R. Wholey and Jack W. Brittain, "Organizational Ecology: Findings and Implications," *Academy of Management Review* 11 (1986), 513–533.

41. Derek S. Pugh and David J. Hickson, *Writers on Organizations* (Thousand Oaks, CA: Sage, 1996); and Lex Donaldson, *American Anti-Management Theories of Organization* (New York: Cambridge University Press, 1995).
42. Jim Collins, "The Secret of Enduring Greatness," *Fortune* (May 5, 2008), 72–76; Julie Schlosser and Ellen Florian, "In the Beginning; Fifty years of Amazing Facts," *Fortune* (April 5, 2004), 152–159; and "The Fortune 500; 500 Largest U. S. Corporations," *Fortune* (May 23, 2011), F1–F26.
43. Hannan and Freeman, "The Population Ecology of Organizations."
44. James Surowiecki, "The Financial Page: The Next Level," *The New Yorker* (October 18, 2010), 28; "Video Store Going the Way of the Milkman," (Rock Hill) *Herald*, March 8, 2010; Anthony Clark and Andrea Rumbaugh, "Did Netflix Kill the Video Store?" *Gainesville Sun*, June 3, 2010; and Damon Darlin, "Always Pushing Beyond the Envelope," *The New York Times*, August 8, 2010, BU5.
45. John D. Sutter, "Netflix Whiplash Stirs Angry Mobs—Again; Stock Has Fallen About 60 Percent Since Mid-July," *WGAL.com* (October 11, 2011), http://www.wgal.com/r/29444179/detail.html (accessed October 11, 2011); and "Netflix's New Competitor: Unlimited Streaming, $10 a Month," *The MainStreet Newsletter* (September 23, 2011), http://www.mainstreet.com/article/smart-spending/technology/netflix-s-new-competitor-unlimited-streaming-10-month (accessed October 11, 2011).
46. Darlin, "Always Pushing Beyond the Envelope."
47. Miguel Bustillo, "As Big Boxes Shrink, They Also Rethink," *The Wall Street Journal*, March 3, 2011, B1.
48. David J. Tucker, Jitendra V. Singh, and Agnes G. Meinhard, "Organizational Form, Population Dynamics, and Institutional Change: The Founding Patterns of Voluntary Organizations," *Academy of Management Journal* 33 (1990), 151–178; Glenn R. Carroll and Michael T. Hannan, "Density Delay in the Evolution of Organizational Populations: A Model and Five Empirical Tests," *Administrative Science Quarterly* 34 (1989), 411–430; Jacques Delacroix and Glenn R. Carroll, "Organizational Foundings: An Ecological Study of the Newspaper Industries of Argentina and Ireland," *Administrative Science Quarterly* 28 (1983), 274–291; Johannes M. Pennings, "Organizational Birth Frequencies: An Empirical Investigation," *Administrative Science Quarterly* 27 (1982), 120–144; David Marple, "Technological Innovation and Organizational Survival: A Population Ecology Study of Nineteenth-Century American Railroads," *Sociological Quarterly* 23 (1982), 107–116; and Thomas G. Rundall and John O. McClain, "Environmental Selection and Physician Supply," *American Journal of Sociology* 87 (1982), 1090–1112.
49. "Amazon.com Inc.; Amazon Announces Digital Video License Agreement with NBCUniversal Domestic TV Distribution," *Computers, Networks & Communication* (August 11, 2011), 93; and Maria Mallory with Stephanie Anderson Forest, "Waking Up to a Major Market," *BusinessWeek* (March 23, 1992), 70–73.
50. Arthur G. Bedeian and Raymond F. Zammuto, *Organizations: Theory and Design* (Orlando, FL: Dryden Press, 1991); and Richard L. Hall, *Organizations: Structure, Process and Outcomes* (Englewood Cliffs, NJ: Prentice-Hall, 1991).
51. M. Tina Dacin, Jerry Goodstein, and W. Richard Scott, "Institutional Theory and Institutional Change: Introduction to the Special Research Forum," *Academy of Management Journal* 45, no. 1 (2002), 45–47. Thanks to Tina Dacin for her material and suggestions for this section of the chapter.
52. J. Meyer and B. Rowan, "Institutionalized Organizations: Formal Structure as Myth and Ceremony," *American Journal of Sociology* 83 (1990), 340–363; and Royston Greenwood and Danny Miller, "Tackling Design Anew: Getting Back to the Heart of Organizational Theory," *Academy of Management Perspectives* (November 2010), 78–88.
53. Mark C. Suchman, "Managing Legitimacy: Strategic and Institutional Approaches," *Academy of Management Review* 20 (1995), 571–610.
54. "World's Most Admired Companies 2011; And the Winners Are . . .," *Fortune*, http://money.cnn.com/magazines/fortune/mostadmired/2011/index.html (accessed August 4, 2011); and "Google, Apple, Disney, BMW and LEGO are the World's Most Reputable Companies According to Consumers Across 15 Countries," *PR Newswire* (June 8, 2011), http://www.prnewswire.com/news-releases/google-apple-disney-bmw-and-lego-are-the-worlds-most-reputable-companies-according-to-consumers-across-15-countries-123454134.html (accessed August 4, 2011).
55. Richard J. Martinez and Patricia M. Norman, "Whither Reputation? The Effects of Different Stakeholders," *Business Horizons* 47, no. 5 (September–October 2004), 25–32.
56. Guy Chazan and Monica Langley, "Dudley Faces Daunting To-Do List," *The Wall Street Journal Europe*, July 27, 2010, 17.
57. Pamela S. Tolbert and Lynne G. Zucker, "The Institutionalization of Institutional Theory," in Stewart R. Clegg, Cynthia Hardy, and Walter R. Nord, eds., *Handbook of Organization Studies* (Thousand Oaks, CA: Sage, 1996).
58. Pugh and Hickson, *Writers on Organizations;* and Paul J. DiMaggio and Walter W. Powell, "The Iron Cage Revisited: Institutional Isomorphism and Collective Rationality in Organizational Fields," *American Sociological Review* 48 (1983), 147–160.
59. This section is based largely on DiMaggio and Powell, "The Iron Cage Revisited;" Pugh and Hickson, *Writers on Organizations;* and W. Richard Scott, *Institutions and Organizations* (Thousand Oaks, CA: Sage, 1995).
60. Janet Adamy, "Yum Uses McDonald's as Guide in Bid to Heat Up Sales," *The Wall Street Journal*, December 13, 2007, A21; Nick Wingfield and Robert A. Guth, "IPod, TheyPod: Rivals Imitate Apple's Success," *The Wall Street Journal*, September 18, 2006, B1.
61. Kai-Yu Hsieh and Freek Vermeulen, "Me Too or Not Me? The Influence of the Structure of Competition on Mimetic

Market Entry," *Academy of Management Annual Meeting Proceedings* (2008), 1–6.

62. Ellen R. Auster and Mark L. Sirower, "The Dynamics of Merger and Acquisition Waves," *The Journal of Applied Behavioral Science* 38, no. 2 (June 2002), 216–244; and Monica Yang and Mary Anne Hyland, "Who Do Firms Imitate? A Multilevel Approach to Examining Sources of Imitation in Choice of Mergers and Acquisitions," *Journal of Management* 32, no. 3 (June 2006), 381–399.
63. Barry M. Staw and Lisa D. Epstein, "What Bandwagons Bring: Effects of Popular Management Techniques on Corporate Performance, Reputation, and CEO Pay," *Administrative Science Quarterly* 45, no. 3 (September 2000), 523–560.
64. Jeffrey Pfeffer and Robert I. Sutton, "The Trouble with Benchmarking," *Across the Board* 43, no. 4 (July–August 2006), 7–9.
65. Karen Donovan, "Pushed by Clients, Law Firms Step Up Diversity Efforts," *The New York Times*, July 21, 2006, C6.
66. Miguel Bustillo, "Wal-Mart to Assign New 'Green' Ratings," *The Wall Street Journal*, July 16, 2009, B1.
67. Copyright 1996 by Dorothy Marcic. All rights reserved.
68. Based in part on "Mammoth Motors' New Paint Shop," a role play originally prepared by Arnold Howitt, executive director of the A. Alfred Taubman Center for State and Local Government at the Kennedy School of Government, Harvard University, and subsequently edited by Gerald Cormick, a principal in the CSE Group and senior lecturer for the Graduate School of Public Affairs at the University of Washington.
69. Based on Donald D. Bowen, Roy J. Lewicki, Francine S. Hall, and Douglas T. Hall, "The Ugli Orange Case," *Experiences in Management and Organizational Behavior*, 4th ed. (Chicago, IL: Wiley, 1997), 134–136; "Amazon Rainforest," BluePlanetBiomes.org, http://www.blueplanetbiomes.org/amazon.htm (accessed August 24, 2011); and "Rainforest Plants,"BluePlanetBiomes.org, http://www.blueplanetbiomes.org/rnfrst_plant_page.htm (accessed August 24, 2011).

©Ulrike Neumann, iStock

Chapter 5 Global Organization Design

Learning Objectives

After reading this chapter you should be able to:

1. Discuss organizational motivations for entering the global arena.
2. Explain the stages of international development.
3. Understand globalization versus multidomestic strategies.
4. Describe structural design options for international operations.
5. Recognize the three major design challenges of global organizations.
6. Identify key mechanisms for global coordination.
7. Describe national approaches to coordination and control.
8. Understand the transnational model of organizing.

Before reading this chapter, please check whether you agree or disagree with each of the following statements:

1 **The only way an organization can reasonably expect to be successful in different countries is to customize its products and services to suit the local interests, preferences, and values in each country.**

I AGREE _____ I DISAGREE _____

2 **It is an especially difficult challenge to work on a global team to coordinate one's own activities and share new ideas and insights with colleagues in different divisions around the world.**

I AGREE _____ I DISAGREE _____

3 **If management practices and coordination techniques work well for a company in its home country, they probably will be successful in the company's international divisions as well.**

I AGREE _____ I DISAGREE _____

Japanese brokerage firm Nomura Holdings Inc. has been trying for decades to expand internationally, and managers cheered when the company acquired Lehman Brothers' international operations after Lehman filed for bankruptcy. But cultural differences plagued the venture from the start. At one training session, for example, managers separated male and female employees and taught the women how to wear their hair, serve tea, and choose appropriate attire. Lehman employees, who included recent Harvard University graduates, were appalled, and some quit their jobs with ill will toward Nomura.[1]

That's the reality of international business. When an organization decides to do business in another country, managers face a whole new set of challenges and roadblocks. They sometimes find that transferring their domestic success internationally requires a totally different approach. For example, British supermarket giant Tesco has become a global powerhouse and is rapidly expanding into emerging countries, but it has struggled to gain a foothold in the coveted U.S. market. Deere & Company, the world's largest maker of farm equipment, is trying hard to penetrate Russia's farm equipment market, but the Russian government passed a law excluding farm machinery built outside the country from financing, so farmers had no way to buy from Deere. The company has now opened a plant near Moscow but still faces tremendous risks and uncertainties in Russia. Giant retailer Walmart entered South Korea with high hopes in 1996, but 10 years later sold all its South Korean stores to a local retailer and withdrew from that country. Similarly, the company abandoned the German market after spending eight years trying to break into the competitive discount retailing environment in that country.[2] It is not the only successful organization to have pulled out of one or another foreign market battered and bruised, its managers scratching their heads over what went wrong.

Succeeding on a global scale isn't easy. Managers have to make tough decisions about strategic approach, how best to get involved in international markets, and how to design the organization to reap the benefits of international expansion. Despite the challenges, managers in most organizations think the potential rewards outweigh the risks. U.S.-based firms set up foreign operations to provide goods and services needed by consumers in other countries, as well as to obtain lower costs or technical know-how for producing products and services to sell domestically. In return, companies from Japan, Germany, the United Kingdom, and other countries compete with U.S. organizations on their own turf as well as abroad. Understanding and addressing the challenges of international business is more important today than ever before.

Purpose of This Chapter

This chapter explores how managers design an organization for the international environment. We begin by looking at some of the primary motivations for organizations to expand internationally, the typical stages of international development, and the use of strategic alliances as a means for international expansion. Then, the chapter examines global strategic approaches and the application of various structural designs for global advantage. Next, we discuss some of the specific challenges global organizations face, mechanisms for addressing them, and cultural differences that influence the organization's approach to designing and managing a global firm. Finally, the chapter takes a look at the *transnational model*, a type of global organization that achieves high levels of the varied capabilities needed to succeed in a complex and volatile international environment.

Entering the Global Arena

Only a few decades ago, many companies could afford to ignore the international environment. Not today. The world is rapidly developing into a unified global field, and every company and manager needs to think globally. Brazil, Russia, India, and China (often referred to as BRIC) as well as other emerging economies are growing rapidly as providers of both products and services to the United States, Canada, Europe, and other developed nations. At the same time, these regions are becoming major markets for the products and services of North American firms.[3] China has emerged as the world's largest auto market, for example. GM sold more cars in China than it did in the United States during the first half of 2010. China also has around 687 million mobile phone subscribers, compared to around 270 million in the United States. That's why Apple has been willing to jump through hoops to sell the iPhone there.[4] Over the next few decades, the BRIC countries will have tremendous spending power as around a billion people become part of a new middle class.[5] For today's companies, the whole world is a source of business threats and opportunities. The Book Mark discusses some of the factors contributing to our increasingly interconnected world and how this interconnection affects organizations.

Motivations for Global Expansion

Economic, technological, and competitive forces have combined to push many companies from a domestic to a global focus. Extraordinary advances in communications, technology, and transportation have created a new, highly competitive landscape.[6]

BOOKMARK

5.0 HAVE YOU READ THIS BOOK?

The World Is Flat: A Brief History of the Twenty-First Century

By Thomas L. Friedman

The global competitive playing field is being leveled. How fast is globalization happening? Three-time Pulitzer-Prize winning *New York Times* columnist Thomas L. Friedman started working on the second edition of his best-selling book, *The World Is Flat*, before the first edition was barely off the press. However, Friedman asserts that the forces causing this accelerated phase of globalization actually began to unfold in the final years of the twentieth century.

WHAT MAKES THE WORLD GO FLAT?

Friedman outlines 10 forces that flattened the world, which he calls Flatteners. Many of these forces are directly or indirectly related to advanced technology, including:

- *Work Flow Software*. A dizzying array of software programs enable computers to easily communicate with one another. That's what makes it possible for a company like animation studio Wild Brain to make films with a team of production employees spread all over the world, or for Boeing airplane factories to automatically resupply global customers with parts. It means companies can create global virtual offices as well as outsource pieces of their operations to whoever can do the job best and most efficiently, no matter in which country they are located.
- *Supply-Chaining*. Work flow software also enhances supply-chaining, the horizontal collaboration among suppliers, retailers, and customers that became a phenomenon in the 1990s. In turn, the more supply chains grow and proliferate, the flatter the world becomes. Supply chaining forces the adoption of common standards and technologies among companies so that every link can interact seamlessly.
- *The Steroids*. Friedman refers to a variety of new technologies as steroids "because they are amplifying and turbocharging all the other flatteners." Perhaps the most significant element is the wireless revolution, which enables you to "take everything that had been digitized, made virtual and personal, and do it from anywhere." As Alan Cohen, senior vice president at Airespace says, "Your desk goes with you everywhere you are now. And the more people have the ability to push and pull information from anywhere to anywhere faster, the more barriers to competition and communication disappear."

HOW TO BENEFIT FROM A FLATTER WORLD

A flatter, interconnected world means employees and organizations can collaborate and compete more successfully than ever, whatever their size and wherever they are located. But the benefits of a flatter world are not automatic. Friedman offers strategies for how companies can align themselves with the new reality of globalization. He warns U.S. companies (and employees) that they should embrace the idea that there will no longer be such a thing as an American firm or an American job. In a flat world, the best companies are the best global collaborators.

The World Is Flat, by Thomas L. Friedman, is published by Farrar, Straus & Giroux.

The importance of the global environment for today's organizations is reflected in the shifting global economy. As one indication, *Fortune* magazine's list of the Global 500, the world's 500 largest companies by revenue, indicates that economic clout is being diffused across a broad global scale. Exhibit 5.1 lists the number of companies on the Global 500 for a variety of countries in 2006, 2008, and 2011. Note the general decline in North America and Western Europe, and the increase in countries such as China, Brazil, Taiwan, and Russia. China, in particular, is coming on strong. China's GDP surpassed Japan's in the second half of 2010, making that country the second-largest economy in the world (after the United States).[7] Consider that in 1993, China had only three

EXHIBIT 5.1
The Shifting Global Economy as Reflected in the *Fortune* Global 500.

	Number of Companies on the Global 500 List		
	2006	2008	2011
United States	170	153	133
Japan	70	64	68
China	20	29	61
France	38	39	35
Germany	35	37	34
Britain	38	34	30
Switzerland	12	14	15
South Korea	12	15	14
Netherlands	14	13	12
Canada	14	14	11
Italy	10	10	10
Spain	9	11	9
India	6	7	8
Taiwan	3	6	8
Australia	8	8	8
Brazil	4	5	7
Russia	5	5	7
Mexico	5	5	3
Sweden	6	6	3
Singapore	1	1	2

Source: Based on data from "Global 500," *Fortune* magazine's annual ranking of the world's largest corporations for 2006, 2008, and 2011, http://money.cnn.com/magazines/fortune/global500/ (accessed December 7, 2011).

companies on the *Fortune* Global 500 list and now has 61. Japan, on the other hand, has declined in importance, dropping from 149 companies in 1993 down to 68 by 2011.[8]

As power continues to shift, organizations are viewing participation in global business as a necessity. Indeed, in some industries a company can be successful only by succeeding on a global scale. In general, three primary factors motivate companies to expand internationally: economies of scale, economies of scope, and low-cost production factors.[9]

Economies of Scale. Building a global presence expands an organization's scale of operations, enabling it to realize **economies of scale**. The trend toward large organizations was initially sparked by the Industrial Revolution, which created pressure in many industries for larger factories that could seize the benefits of economies of scale offered by new technologies and production methods. Through large-volume production, these industrial giants were able to achieve the lowest possible cost per unit of production. However, for many companies, domestic markets no longer provide the high level of sales needed to maintain enough volume to achieve scale economies. In an industry such as automobile manufacturing, for example, a company would need a tremendous share of the domestic market to achieve scale economies. Thus, an organization such as Ford Motor Company is forced to become international in order to survive. The Hollywood movie industry has also recently expanded its international outlook as sales of movie tickets and DVDs have declined in the U.S. and risen in other countries. The studios are using more international stars and retooling scripts to appeal to an international audience. One film industry veteran said, "no studio head is going to make a big expensive movie . . . unless it has worldwide appeal. You can't pay back that production cost on the domestic model alone."[10]

Domestic markets have become saturated for many U.S. companies and the only potential for growth lies overseas. For example, with sales in its U.S. stores falling, Walmart is making an aggressive international push. The company recently bought South Africa's Massmart to try to get a first-mover advantage in that country and is looking for opportunities to enter Russia and the Middle East. Starbucks, after closing hundreds of underperforming stores in the United States, has targeted Asia for rapid international growth, planning to open thousands of stores in China, India, and Vietnam.[11] Economies of scale also enable companies to obtain volume discounts from suppliers, lowering the organization's cost of production.

BRIEFCASE

As an organization manager, keep this guideline in mind:

Consider building an international presence to realize economies of scale, exploit economies of scope, or obtain scarce or low-cost production factors such as labor and raw materials.

Economies of Scope. A second factor is the enhanced potential for exploiting **economies of scope**. *Scope* refers to the number and variety of products and services a company offers as well as the number and variety of regions, countries, and markets it serves. Hollywood's DreamWorks SKG sold a 50 percent stake to India's Reliance Big Entertainment because the company has a presence in every entertainment platform. It can sell DreamWorks movies through its theaters, its satellite networks, its movie rental service, its radio stations, and its mobile phones. Big Entertainment, in turn, gets support for its movie studio, the largest in India, and a better opportunity to sell its films to audiences outside of India.[12]

Companies that have a presence in multiple countries gain marketing power and synergy compared to the same size firm that has a presence in fewer countries. For example, an advertising agency with a presence in several global markets gains a competitive edge serving large companies that span the globe. Or consider the case of McDonald's, which has to obtain nearly identical ketchup and sauce packets for its restaurants around the world. A supplier that has a presence in every country McDonald's serves has an advantage because it provides cost, consistency, and convenience benefits to McDonald's, which does not have to deal with a number of local suppliers in each country. Economies of scope can also increase a company's market power as compared to competitors, because the company develops broad knowledge of the cultural, social, economic, and other factors that affect its customers in varied locations and can provide specialized products and services to meet those needs.

Low-Cost Production Factors. The third major force motivating global expansion relates to **factors of production**. One of the earliest, and still one of the most powerful, motivations for U.S. companies to invest abroad is the opportunity to obtain raw materials, labor, and other resources at the lowest possible cost. Organizations have long turned overseas to secure raw materials that were scarce or unavailable in their home country. In the early twentieth century, for example, tire companies went abroad to develop rubber plantations to supply tires for America's growing automobile industry.

Today, U.S. paper manufacturers such as Weyerhaeuser and U.S. Paper Co., forced by environmental concerns to look overseas for new timberlands, are managing millions of acres of tree farms in New Zealand and other areas.[13]

Many companies also turn to other countries as a source of cheap labor. Apple's iPhones and iPads are made by the world's largest contract manufacturer in Shenzhen, China, for example, where assembly line workers are paid around US$150 a month.[14] Textile manufacturing in the United States is now practically nonexistent as companies have shifted most production to Asia, Mexico, Latin America, and the Caribbean, where the costs of labor and supplies are much lower. Manufacturing of non-upholstered furniture has rapidly followed the same pattern, with companies closing plants in the United States and importing high-quality wooden furniture from China, where as many as 30 workers can be hired for the cost of one cabinetmaker in the United States.[15] But the trend isn't limited to manufacturing. A growing number of service firms in India write software, perform consulting work, and handle technical support, accounting, and data processing for some of the biggest corporations in the United States. One index lists more than 900 business services companies in India that employ around 575,000 people.[16]

Other organizations have gone international in search of lower costs of capital, sources of cheap energy, reduced government restrictions, or other factors that lower the company's total production costs. Aerospace-related companies have built factories in Mexico, for example, not just for the cheaper labor but also because of favorable government regulations.[17] Companies can locate facilities wherever it makes the most economic sense in terms of needed employee education and skill levels, labor and raw materials costs, and other production factors. Companies such as IBM and Google, for instance, can't find the technological brainpower they need in the United States, so they are building research and development facilities in India to take advantage of highly skilled workers.[18] Automobile manufacturers such as Toyota, BMW, General Motors, and Ford have built plants in South Africa, Brazil, and Thailand, where they typically get dramatically lower costs for factors such as land, water, and electricity.[19] Foreign companies also come to the United States to obtain favorable circumstances. Kalexsyn, a small chemical research firm in Kalamazoo, Michigan, does about 25 percent of its business with Western European biotechnology firms that need high quality instead of low prices.[20] Japan's Honda and Toyota, South Korea's Samsung Electronics, and the Swiss drug company Novartis have all built plants or research centers in the United States to take advantage of tax breaks, find skilled workers, or be closer to major customers and suppliers.[21]

Stages of International Development

No company can become a global giant overnight. Managers have to consciously adopt a strategy for global development and growth. Organizations enter foreign markets in a variety of ways and follow diverse paths. However, the shift from domestic to global typically occurs through stages of development, as illustrated in Exhibit 5.2.[22] In stage one, the **domestic stage**, the company is domestically oriented, but managers are aware of the global environment and may want to consider initial foreign involvement to expand production volume and realize economies of scale. Market potential is limited and is primarily in the home country. The structure of the company is domestic, typically functional or divisional, and initial foreign sales are handled through an export department. The details of freight forwarding, customs problems, and foreign exchange are handled by outsiders.

EXHIBIT 5.2
Four Stages of International Evolution

	I. Domestic	II. International	III. Multinational	IV. Global
Strategic Orientation	Domestically oriented	Export-oriented, multidomestic	Multinational	Global
Stage of Development	Initial foreign involvement	Competitive positioning	Explosion	Global
Structure	Domestic structure plus export department	Domestic structure plus international division	Worldwide geographic product structure	Matrix, transnational structure
Market Potential	Moderate, mostly domestic	Large, multidomestic	Very large, multinational	Whole world

Source: Based on Nancy J. Adler, *International Dimensions of Organizational Behavior*, 4th ed. (Cincinnati, Ohio: South-Western, 2002), 8–9; and Theodore T. Herbert, "Strategy and Multinational Organization Structure: An Interorganizational Relationships Perspective," *Academy of Management Review* 9 (1984), 259–271.

In stage two, the **international stage**, the company takes exports seriously and begins to think multidomestically. **Multidomestic** means competitive issues in each country are independent of other countries; the company deals with each country individually. The concern is with international competitive positioning compared with other firms in the industry. At this point, an international division has replaced the export department, and specialists are hired to handle sales, service, and warehousing abroad. Multiple countries are identified as a potential market. Purafil, with headquarters in Doraville, Georgia, manufactures air filters that remove pollution and cleanse the air in 60 different countries.[23] The company first began exporting in the early 1990s and now earns 60 percent of its revenues from overseas. A service example is AlertDriving, a firm that provides online training courses to companies with vehicle fleets. The company must tailor its products and marketing to the expectations, driving habits, and geographical nuances in the 20 or so countries where it exports.[24]

In stage three, the **multinational stage**, the company has extensive experience in a number of international markets and has established marketing, manufacturing, or research and development (R&D) facilities in several foreign countries. The organization obtains a large percentage of revenues from sales outside the home country. Explosive growth occurs as international operations take off, and the company has business units scattered around the world along with suppliers, manufacturers, and distributors. Companies in the multinational stage include Siemens of Germany, Sony of Japan, and Coca-Cola of the United States. Aditya Birla Group is an example of a multinational based in India. The company began in 1850 as the Birla family's trading company. Starting in the 1970s in Southeast Asia, the Birla Group has expanded around the world, producing and selling such products as fiber, chemicals, cement, metals, yarns and textiles, apparel, fertilizer, and carbon black. In 2010, around 60 percent of the company's revenues came from outside India.[25]

The fourth and ultimate stage is the **global stage**, which means the company transcends any single country. The business is not merely a collection of domestic

industries; rather, subsidiaries are interlinked to the point where competitive position in one country significantly influences activities in other countries.[26] Truly **global companies** no longer think of themselves as having a single home country and, indeed, have been called *stateless corporations*.[27] This represents a new and dramatic evolution from the multinational company of the 1960s and 1970s. At this stage, ownership, control, and top management tend to be dispersed among several nationalities.[28] Nestlé SA provides a good example. The company gets most of its sales from outside the "home" country of Switzerland, and its 280,000 employees are spread all over the world. CEO Paul Bulcke is Belgian, chairman Peter Brabeck-Letmathe was born in Austria, and more than half of the company's managers are non-Swiss. Nestlé has hundreds of brands and has production facilities or other operations in almost every country in the world.[29]

Global companies operate in truly global fashion, and the entire world is their marketplace. Global companies such as Nestlé, Royal Dutch/Shell, Unilever, and Matsushita Electric may operate in more than a hundred countries. The structural problem of holding together this huge complex of subsidiaries scattered thousands of miles apart is immense. Organization structure for global companies can be extremely complex and often evolves into an international matrix or transnational model, which will be discussed later in this chapter.

Global Expansion through International Strategic Alliances

One of the most popular ways companies get involved in international operations is through international strategic alliances. Companies in rapidly changing industries such as media and entertainment, pharmaceuticals, biotechnology, and software might have hundreds of these relationships.[30]

BRIEFCASE

As an organization manager, keep this guideline in mind:

Develop international strategic alliances, such as licensing, joint ventures, partnerships, and consortia, as fast and inexpensive ways to become involved in international sales and operations.

Typical alliances include licensing, joint ventures, and consortia.[31] For example, when entering new markets, particularly in developing areas of the world, retailers such as Saks Fifth Avenue and Barneys New York limit their risks by licensing their names to foreign partners. Saks has licensed stores in Riyadh and Dubai, Saudi Arabia, and in Mexico, for instance, and Barneys has a licensed store in Japan. Both firms, as well as other U.S.-based department stores, are currently making a strong international push in light of weak sales and stiff competition in the United States.[32] A **joint venture** is a separate entity created with two or more active firms as sponsors. This is a popular approach to sharing development and production costs and penetrating new markets.[33] Joint ventures may be with either customers or competitors. Competing firms Sprint, Deutsche Telecom, and Telecom France cooperate with each other and with several smaller firms in a joint venture that serves the telecommunication needs of global corporations in 65 countries.[34] Navistar International Corporation, based in Warrenville, Illinois, formed a joint venture with rival Mahindra & Mahindra Ltd., a fast-growing equipment maker in India, to build trucks and buses for export.[35] And Walmart got a foothold in India's fast-growing but difficult retail market through a joint venture with Bharti Enterprises to establish Bharti Walmart Private Limited.[36]

Companies often seek joint ventures to achieve production cost savings through economies of scale, to share complementary technological strengths, to distribute new products and services through another country's distribution channels, or to take advantage of a partner's knowledge of local markets. Consider the case of Spain's largest hotel chain.

IN PRACTICE

Meliá Hotels International (Sol Meliá)

Founded in 1956, Meliá Hotels International (known for decades as Sol Meliá) is the largest hotel chain in Spain and one of the top 20 hotel companies worldwide. Meliá has more than 350 hotels in 35 countries, including China, Bulgaria, the United States, Indonesia, Greece, Croatia, Brazil, Egypt, and the United Kingdom. Its 35,000 employees come from 100 different countries and speak 25 or more different languages.

How did the company successfully adapt its services, technology, and management to so many countries that differ so widely in terms of consumer preferences, political and legal structures, and competitive conditions? One primary approach has been to use joint ventures and other forms of partnership. Meliá has numerous partnerships with companies in the 35 countries where it operates. One recent example is a joint venture with Jin Jiang International Hotel Company, China's leading hotel firm, to cooperate on a joint growth strategy in China and Europe.

Meliá managers know it would be extremely costly—and likely impossible—to acquire the know-how the company would need to operate in so many different markets on its own. Thus, they have established close partnerships with local organizations that already have knowledge and experience in the regions where Meliá wants to grow.[37]

The recent name change from Sol Meliá to Meliá Hotels International, and the corporate slogan, "Where everything is possible," reflect the company's vision of even broader international expansion. During the first half of 2011, Meliá was adding one hotel every three weeks. Joint ventures, leases, and franchises accounted for more than 85 percent of those additions.[38]

Another growing approach is for companies to become involved in **consortia**, groups of independent companies—including suppliers, customers, and even competitors—that join together to share skills, resources, costs, and access to one another's markets.[39] Consortia are often used in other parts of the world, such as the *keiretsu* family of corporations in Japan. In Korea, these interlocking company arrangements are called *chaebol*.

Designing Structure to Fit Global Strategy

As we discussed in Chapter 2, an organization's structure must fit its situation by providing sufficient information processing for coordination and control while focusing employees on specific functions, products, or geographic regions. Organization design for international firms follows a similar logic, with special interest in global versus local strategic opportunities.

Strategies for Global Versus Local Opportunities

When organizations venture into the international domain, managers strive to formulate a coherent global strategy that will provide synergy among worldwide operations for the purpose of achieving common organizational goals. One dilemma they face is choosing whether to emphasize global **standardization** versus local responsiveness. Managers must decide whether they want each global affiliate to act autonomously or whether activities should be standardized across countries. These decisions are reflected in the choice between a *globalization* versus a *multidomestic* global strategy.

The **globalization strategy** means that product design, manufacturing, and marketing strategy are standardized throughout the world.[40] For example, Black & Decker became much more competitive internationally when it standardized its line of power hand tools. Some products, such as Coca-Cola, are naturals for globalization because only advertising and marketing need to be tailored for different regions. In general, services are less suitable for globalization because different customs and habits often require a different approach to providing service. That is one reason Meliá Hotels International, described earlier, partners with local companies, for instance. This was part of Walmart's trouble in the South Korean market. The retailer continued to use Western-style displays and marketing strategies, whereas successful South Korean retailers build bright, eye-catching displays and hire clerks to promote their goods using megaphones and hand-clapping. Walmart similarly flubbed in Indonesia, where it closed its stores after only a year. Customers didn't like the brightly lit, highly organized stores, and because no haggling was permitted, they perceived the goods as being overpriced.[41]

Other companies have also begun shifting away from a strict globalization strategy. Economic and social changes, including a backlash against huge global corporations, have prompted consumers to be less interested in global brands and more in favor of products that have a local feel.[42] However, a globalization strategy can help a manufacturing organization reap economy-of-scale efficiencies by standardizing product design and manufacturing, using common suppliers, introducing products around the world faster, coordinating prices, and eliminating overlapping facilities.[43] Ford Motor Company has introduced a new strategy to build one small car, under the Ford Focus name, for markets around the world rather than different ones tailored to national or regional tastes. By sharing technology, design, suppliers, and manufacturing standards worldwide in a coordinated global automotive operation, Ford can potentially save billions of dollars. The company will also save on advertising by launching a global advertising campaign rather than having ads tailored to local markets. Similarly, Gillette Company, which makes grooming products such as the Mach3 shaving system for men and the Venus razor for women, has large production facilities that use common suppliers and processes to manufacture products whose technical specifications are standardized around the world.[44]

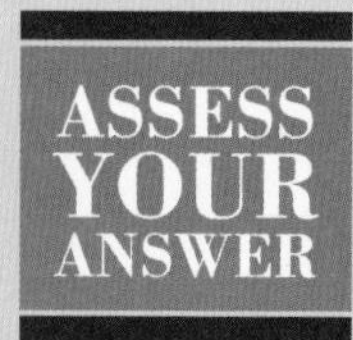

1 The only way an organization can reasonably expect to be successful in different countries is to customize its products and services to suit the local interests, preferences, and values in each country.

ANSWER: *Disagree.* It is the case that people around the world often want products and services that are tailored to their local needs and interests, and many organizations are quite successful by responding to local market demands. However, other international organizations attain competitive advantages by using the same product design and marketing strategies in many countries throughout the world.

A **multidomestic strategy** means that competition in each country is handled independently of competition in other countries. Thus, a multidomestic strategy would encourage product design, assembly, and marketing tailored to the specific needs of each country. Some companies have found that their products do not thrive in a single global market. For instance, people in different countries have very different expectations for personal-care products such as deodorant or toothpaste. Many people in parts of Mexico use laundry detergent for washing dishes. Even American fast food chains, once considered ultimate examples of standardization for a world market, have felt the need to be more responsive to local and national differences. Consider one of the most successful fast-food companies in China, KFC, which is owned by Louisville, Kentucky-based Yum Brands.

KFC (Yum Brands)

IN PRACTICE

In the United States, KFC is like a poor cousin, struggling to keep up with McDonald's. In China, though, Colonel Sanders (the long-dead, white bearded Kentucky colonel who adorns the KFC logo) is King. "We love him," laughs a 21-year-old student at Beijing's Capital University of Economics and Business.

In China, customers can buy a bucket of fried chicken, but they can also get fried dough for breakfast, a bowl of congee for lunch, or a Dragon Twister for supper. Yum Brands, which owns KFC as well as Pizza Hut and Taco Bell, expected to get about 36 percent of its operating profit in 2010 from its 3,700 restaurants in China. In a country where other Western companies have struggled, Yum has thrived. It has a 40 percent market share, compared to 16 percent for McDonald's. The company also recently opened a new chain that serves only Chinese fast food and acquired a 27 percent stake in a company specializing in Mongolian hot-pot dishes.

The key to KFC and Yum's success in China has been getting in early and successfully adapting both their product and their operations. Over the 24 years Yum has been in China, it has formed partnerships with local companies and hired Chinese managers who can build the connections that are essential to doing business in China. Having local managers, for example, opened supply lines that gave Yum access to locations that rival companies run by overseas managers couldn't reach.[45]

KFC is succeeding internationally now, particularly in China, but that wasn't always the case. When the company first expanded into Asia in 1973, it couldn't win over local consumers because it tried to use a globalization strategy. The 11 restaurants it opened closed within two years. Yum Brands managers learned the lesson and began tailoring their business and menu to different countries and regions where they operated. The company gives local managers real decision-making power and allows them to offer regional dishes that appeal to tastes in specific areas of the country. In addition to localizing the menu, KFCs in different regions may host parties associated with certain religious or cultural rituals.

Different global organization designs are better suited to the need for either global standardization or local responsiveness. Research on more than 100 international firms based in Spain provided support for the connection between international structure and strategic focus.[46] The model in Exhibit 5.3 illustrates how organization design and international strategy fit the needs of the environment.[47]

Companies can be characterized by whether their product and service lines have potential for globalization, which means advantages through worldwide standardization. Companies that sell similar products or services across many countries have a globalization strategy. On the other hand, some companies have products

EXHIBIT 5.3
Model to Fit Organization Structure to International Advantages

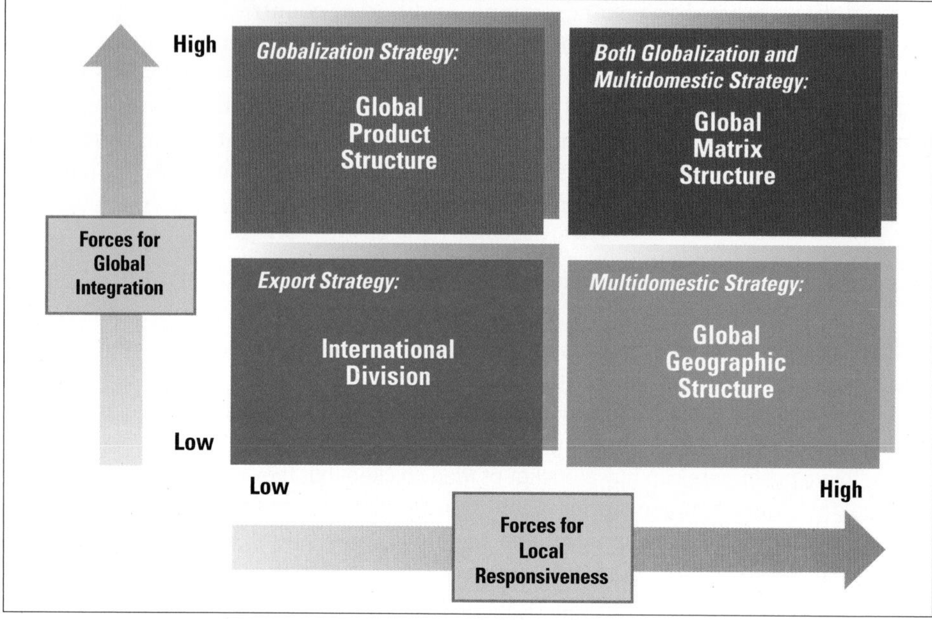

Source: Based on Christopher A. Bartlett and Sumantra Ghoshal, *Text, Cases, and Readings in Cross-Border Management*, 3rd ed. (New York: Irwin McGraw-Hill, 2000), 395; Roderick E. White and Thomas A. Poynter, "Organizing for Worldwide Advantage," *Business Quarterly* (Summer 1989), 84–89. Gunnar Hedlund, "The Hypermodern MNC–A Heterarchy?" *Human Resource Management* 25, no. 1 (Spring 1986), 9–36; and J. M. Stopford and L. T. Wells, Jr., *Managing the Multinational Enterprise* (New York: Basic Books, 1972).

and services appropriate for a multidomestic strategy, which means local-country advantages through differentiation and customization to meet local needs.

As indicated in Exhibit 5.3, when forces for both global standardization and local responsiveness in many countries are low, simply using an international division with the domestic structure is an appropriate way to handle international business. For some industries, however, technological, social, or economic forces may create a situation in which selling standardized products worldwide provides a basis for competitive advantage. In these cases, a global product structure is appropriate. This structure provides product managers with authority to handle their product lines on a global basis and enables the company to take advantage of a unified global marketplace. In other cases, companies can gain competitive advantages through local responsiveness—by responding to unique needs in the various countries in which they do business. For these companies, a worldwide geographic structure is appropriate. Each country or region will have subsidiaries that modify products and services to fit that locale. A good illustration is the advertising firm of Ogilvy & Mather, which divides its operations into four primary geographic regions because advertising approaches need to be modified to fit the tastes, preferences, cultural values, and government regulations in different parts of the world.[48] Children are frequently used to advertise products in the United States, but this approach in France is against the law. The competitive claims of rival products regularly seen on U.S. television would violate government regulations in Germany.[49]

In many instances, companies need to respond to both global and local opportunities simultaneously, in which case the global matrix structure can be used. Part of the product line may need to be standardized globally and other parts tailored to the needs of local countries. Let's discuss each of the structures in Exhibit 5.3 in more detail.

International Division

As companies begin to explore international opportunities, they typically start with an export department that grows into an **international division**. The international division has a status equal to the other major departments or divisions within the company and is illustrated in Exhibit 5.4. Whereas the domestic divisions are typically organized along functional or product lines, the international division is organized according to geographic interests, as illustrated in the exhibit. The international division has its own hierarchy to handle business (licensing, joint ventures) in various countries, selling the products and services created by the domestic divisions, opening subsidiary plants, and in general moving the organization into more sophisticated international operations.

Although functional structures are often used domestically, they are less frequently used to manage a worldwide business.[50] Lines of functional hierarchy running around the world would extend too long, so some form of product or geographic structure is used to subdivide the organization into smaller units. Firms typically start with an international department and, depending on their strategy, later use product or geographic division structures or a matrix. One study found that 48 percent of organizations identified as global leaders use divisional structures, while 28 percent reported using matrix structures.[51]

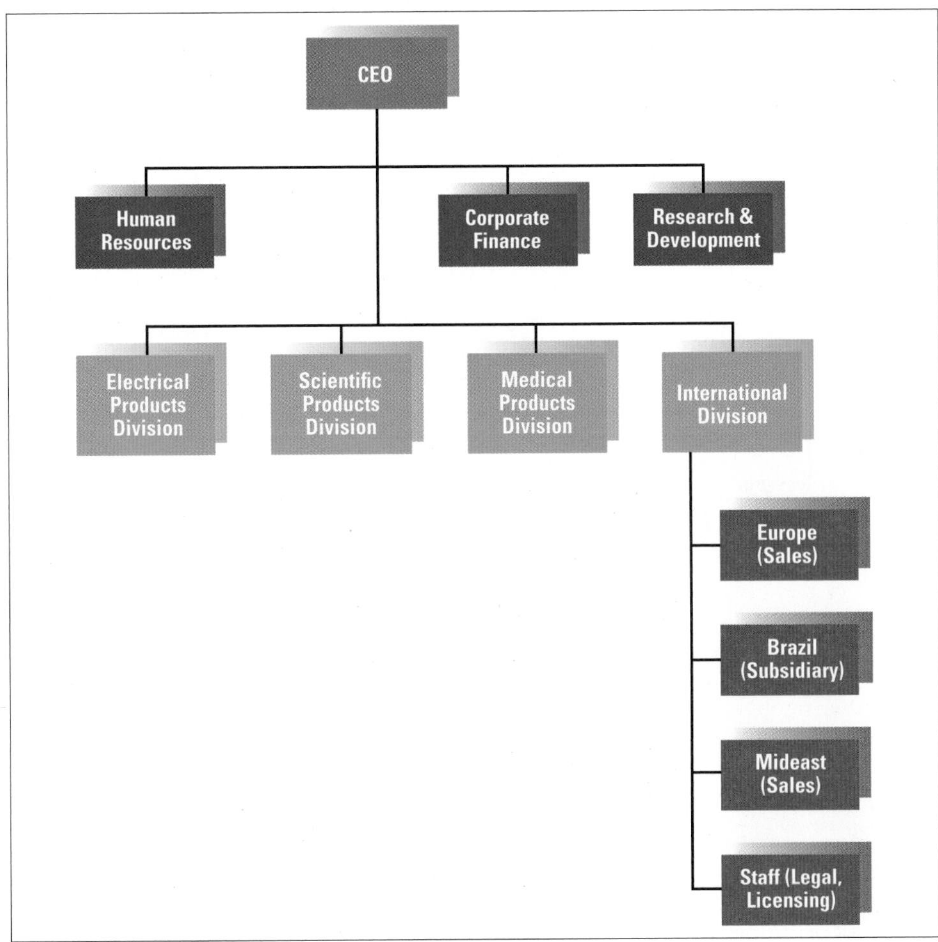

EXHIBIT 5.4
Domestic Hybrid Structure with International Division

Global Product Division Structure

In a **global product structure**, the product divisions take responsibility for global operations in their specific product area. This is one of the most commonly used structures through which managers attempt to achieve global goals because it provides a fairly straightforward way to effectively manage a variety of businesses and products around the world. Managers in each product division can focus on organizing for international operations as they see fit and directing employees' energy toward their own division's unique set of global problems or opportunities.[52] In addition, the structure provides top managers at headquarters with a broad perspective on competition, enabling the entire corporation to respond more rapidly to a changing global environment.[53] Service companies can also use a divisional structure. For example, Italian bank UniCredit, with headquarters in Milan and more than 9,600 branches in 22 countries, has three product divisions: Family and SME (household and small and mid-sized business banking), Corporate and Investment Banking, and Private Banking and Asset Management. The company also has one geographic-based division to focus on operations and growth in Central and Eastern European countries.[54]

With a global product structure, each division's manager is responsible for planning, organizing, and controlling all functions for the production and distribution of its products or services for any market around the world. As we saw in Exhibit 5.3, the global product structure works best when the company has opportunities for worldwide production and sale of standard products for all markets, thus providing economies of scale and standardization of production, marketing, and advertising.

Eaton Corporation has used a form of worldwide product structure, as illustrated in Exhibit 5.5. In this structure, the automotive components group, industrial group, and so on are responsible for the manufacture and sale of products worldwide. The vice president of the international division is responsible for coordinators in each region, including a coordinator for Japan, Australia, South America, and

EXHIBIT 5.5
Partial Global Product Structure Used by Eaton Corporation

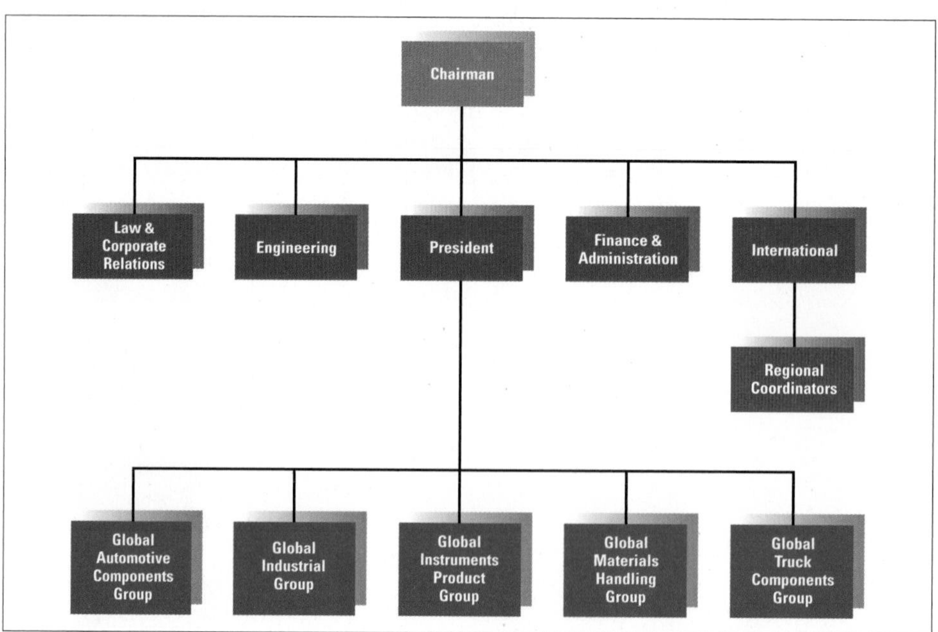

Source: Based on *New Directions in Multinational Corporate Organization* (New York: Business International Corp., 1981).

northern Europe. The coordinators find ways to share facilities and improve production and delivery across all product lines sold in their regions. These coordinators fulfill the same function as integrators described in Chapter 2.

The product structure is great for standardizing production and sales around the globe, but it also has problems. Often the product divisions do not work well together, competing instead of cooperating in some countries; and some countries may be ignored by product managers. The solution adopted by Eaton Corporation of using country coordinators who have a clearly defined role is a superb way to overcome these problems.

BRIEFCASE

As an organization manager, keep these guidelines in mind:

Choose a global product structure when the organization can gain competitive advantages through a globalization strategy (global integration). Choose a global geographic structure when the company has advantages with a multidomestic strategy (local responsiveness). Use an international division when the company is primarily domestic and has only a few international operations.

Global Geographic Division Structure

A regionally based organization is well suited to companies that want to emphasize adaptation to regional or local market needs through a multidomestic strategy, as illustrated earlier in Exhibit 5.3. The **global geographic structure** divides the world into geographic regions, with each geographic division reporting to the CEO. Each division has full control of functional activities within its geographic area. For example, Nestlé, with headquarters in Switzerland, puts great emphasis on the autonomy of regional managers who know the local culture. The largest branded food company in the world, Nestlé rejects the idea of a single global market and has used a partial geographic structure to focus on the local needs and competition in each country. Local managers have the authority to tinker with a product's flavoring, packaging, portion size, or other elements as they see fit. Many of the company's 8,000 brands are registered in only one country.[55]

Companies that use this type of structure have typically been those with mature product lines and stable technologies. They can find low-cost manufacturing within countries as well as meet different needs across countries for marketing and sales. However, several business and organizational trends have led to a broadening of the kinds of companies that use the global geographic structure.[56] The growth of service organizations has outpaced manufacturing for several years, and services by their nature must occur on a local level. In addition, to meet new competitive threats, many manufacturing firms are emphasizing the ability to customize their products to meet specific needs, which requires a greater emphasis on local and regional responsiveness. All organizations are compelled by current environmental and competitive challenges to develop closer relationships with customers, which may lead companies to shift from product-based to geographic-based structures. India's Bupharm, a young and growing pharmaceuticals company, created geographic divisions for its sales operation, such as Asia Pacific, Latin America, and Europe, to help the company better serve customers in the 40 countries where it does business.[57]

The problems encountered by senior management using a global geographic structure result from the autonomy of each regional division. For example, it is difficult to do planning on a global scale—such as new-product R&D—because each division acts to meet only the needs of its region. New domestic technologies and products can be difficult to transfer to international markets because each division thinks it will develop what it needs. Likewise, it is difficult to rapidly introduce products developed offshore into domestic markets, and there is often duplication of line and staff managers across regions. Because regional divisions act to meet specific needs in their own areas, tracking and maintaining control of costs can be a real problem. The following example illustrates how executives at Colgate-Palmolive overcame some of the problems associated with the geographic structure.

Colgate-Palmolive Company

IN PRACTICE

For several years, Colgate-Palmolive Company, which manufactures and markets personal-care, household, and specialty products, used a global geographic structure of the form illustrated in Exhibit 5.6. Colgate has a long, rich history of international involvement and has relied on regional divisions in North America, Europe, Latin America, the Far East, and the South Pacific to stay on the competitive edge. Well over half of the company's total sales are generated outside of the United States.

The regional approach supports Colgate's cultural values, which emphasize individual autonomy, an entrepreneurial spirit, and the ability to act locally. Each regional president reports directly to the chief operating officer, and each division has its own staff functions such as human resources (HR), finance, manufacturing, and marketing. Colgate handled the problem of coordination across geographic divisions by creating an *international business development group* that is responsible for long-term company planning and worldwide product coordination and communication. It used several product team leaders, many of whom had been former country managers with extensive experience and knowledge. The product leaders are essentially coordinators and advisors to the geographic divisions; they have no power to direct, but they have the ability and the organizational support needed to

EXHIBIT 5.6
Global Geographic Structure of Colgate-Palmolive Company

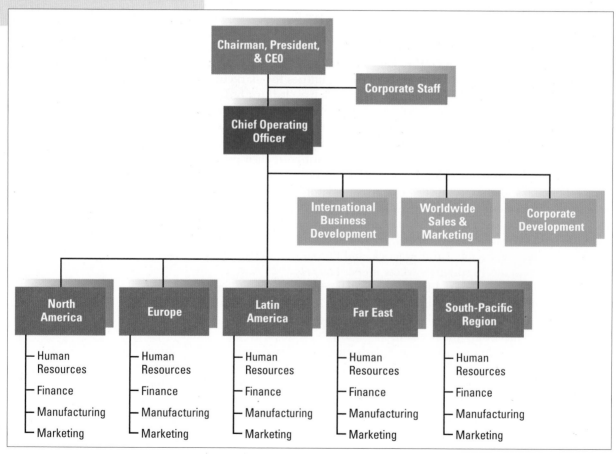

Source: Based on Robert J. Kramer, *Organizing for Global Competitiveness: The Geographic Design* (New York: The Conference Board, 1993), 30.

exert substantial influence. The addition of this business development group quickly reaped positive results in terms of more rapid introduction of new products across all countries and better, lower-cost marketing.

The success of the international business development group prompted Colgate's top management to add two additional coordinating positions—a *vice president of corporate development* to focus on acquisitions, and a *worldwide sales and marketing group* that coordinates sales and marketing initiatives across all geographic locations. With these worldwide positions added to the structure, Colgate maintains its focus on each region and achieves global coordination for overall planning, faster product introductions, and enhanced sales and marketing efficiency.[58]

Global Matrix Structure

We've discussed how Eaton used a global product division structure and found ways to coordinate across worldwide divisions. Colgate-Palmolive used a global geographic division structure and found ways to coordinate across geographic regions. Each of these companies emphasized a single dimension. Recall from Chapter 2 that a matrix structure provides a way to achieve vertical and horizontal coordination simultaneously along two dimensions. A **global matrix structure** is similar to the matrix described in Chapter 2, except that for multinational corporations the geographic distances for communication are greater and coordination is more complex.

The matrix works best when pressure for decision making balances the interests of both product standardization and geographic localization and when coordination to share resources is important. For many years, ABB (Asea Brown Boveri), a global leader in power and automation technologies, with headquarters in Zurich, has used a global matrix structure that works extremely well to coordinate a 130,000-employee company operating in more than 100 countries.

IN PRACTICE

ABB Group

ABB has given new meaning to the notion of "being local worldwide." ABB has used a complex global matrix structure similar to Exhibit 5.7 to achieve worldwide economies of scale combined with local flexibility and responsiveness.

At the top are the chief executive officer and an executive committee of 10 top managers, who hold frequent meetings around the world. Along one side of the matrix are product division managers for Power Products, Power Systems, Discrete Automation and Motion, Low Voltage Products, and Process Automation. Each division manager is responsible for handling business on a global scale, allocating export markets, establishing cost and quality standards, and creating mixed-nationality teams to solve problems. Each division is subdivided into smaller units over which the division manager also has responsibility.

Along the other side of the matrix is a regional structure; ABB has eight regional managers for Northern Europe, Central Europe, Mediterranean, North America, South America, India, Middle East and Africa, North Asia, and South Asia. Under the regional managers are country managers who run local companies that cross business areas and are responsible for local balance sheets, income statements, and career ladders.

The matrix structure converges at the level of the local companies. The presidents of local companies report to two bosses—the product division leader, who coordinates on a global scale, and the country president, who runs the company of which the local organization is a subsidiary.

EXHIBIT 5.7
Global Matrix Structure

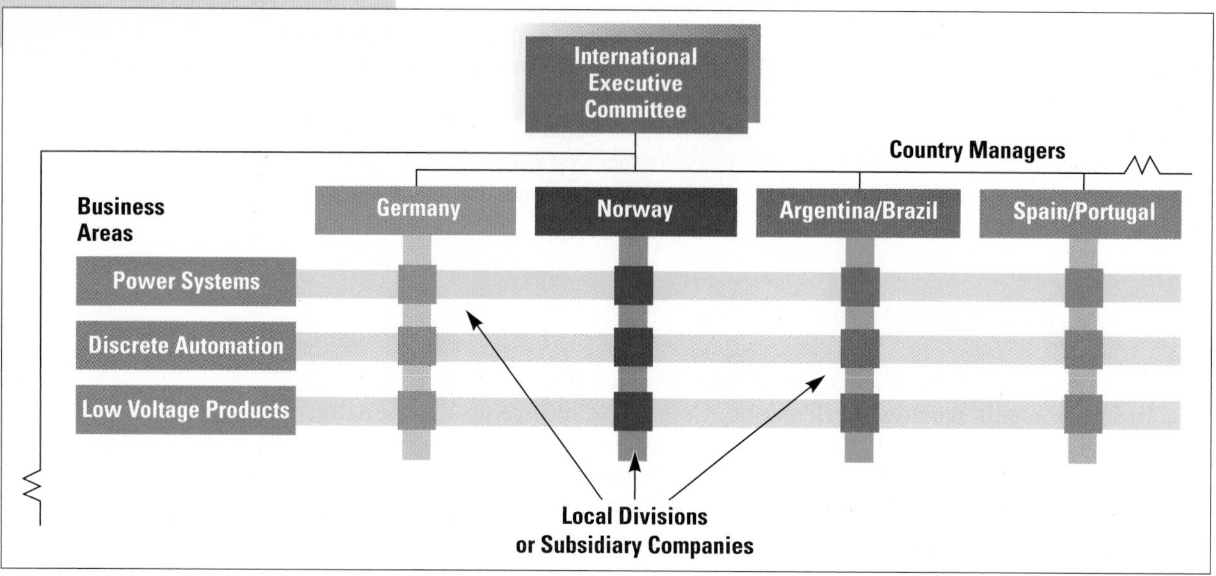

ABB's philosophy is to decentralize things to the lowest levels. Global managers are generous, patient, and multilingual. They must work with teams made up of different nationalities and be culturally sensitive. They craft strategy and evaluate performance for people and subsidiaries around the world. Country managers, by contrast, are line managers responsible for several country subsidiaries. They must cooperate with product division managers to achieve worldwide efficiencies and the introduction of new products. Finally, the presidents of local companies have both a global boss—the product division manager—and a country boss, and they learn to coordinate the needs of both.[59]

ABB is a large, successful company that achieved the benefits of both product and geographic organizations through this matrix structure. However, over the past several years, as ABB has faced increasingly complex competitive issues, leaders have transformed the company toward a complex structure called the *transnational model*, which will be discussed later in this chapter.

In the real world, as with the domestic hybrid structure, many international firms such as ABB, Colgate, UniCredit, Nestlé, or Eaton Corporation apply a *global hybrid* or *mixed structure*, in which two or more different structures or elements of different structures are used. Hybrid structures are typical in highly volatile environments. UniCredit, for example, combines elements of functional, geographic, and product divisions to respond to dynamic market conditions in the multiple countries where it operates.[60]

Organizations that operate on a global scale frequently have to make adjustments to their structures to overcome the challenges of doing business in a global environment. In the following sections, we will look at some specific challenges organizations face in the global arena and mechanisms for successfully addressing them.

Building Global Capabilities

There are many instances of well-known companies that have trouble transferring successful ideas, products, and services from their home country to the international domain. We talked earlier about the struggles Walmart has faced internationally, but Walmart is not alone. PepsiCo set a five-year goal to triple its international soft-drink revenues and boldly expanded its presence in international markets. Yet five years later, the company had withdrawn from some of those markets and had to take a nearly $1 billion loss from international beverage operations.[61] Hundreds of American companies that saw Vietnam as a tremendous international opportunity in the mid-1990s had called it quits by the turn of the century. Political and cultural differences sidetracked most of the ventures, leading to heavy losses. Only a few companies, such as Caterpillar's heavy-equipment business, have found success in that country, although other organizations, such as Starbucks mentioned earlier, are once again looking to Vietnam for growth opportunities.[62] Managers taking their companies international face a tremendous challenge in how to capitalize on the incredible opportunities that global expansion presents.

The Global Organizational Design Challenge

Exhibit 5.8 illustrates the three primary segments of the global organizational challenge: greater complexity and differentiation, the need for integration, and the problem of transferring knowledge and innovation across a global firm. Organizations have to accept an extremely high level of environmental complexity in the international domain and address the many differences that occur among countries. For instance, each country has its own history, culture,

EXHIBIT 5.8
The Global Organizational Challenge

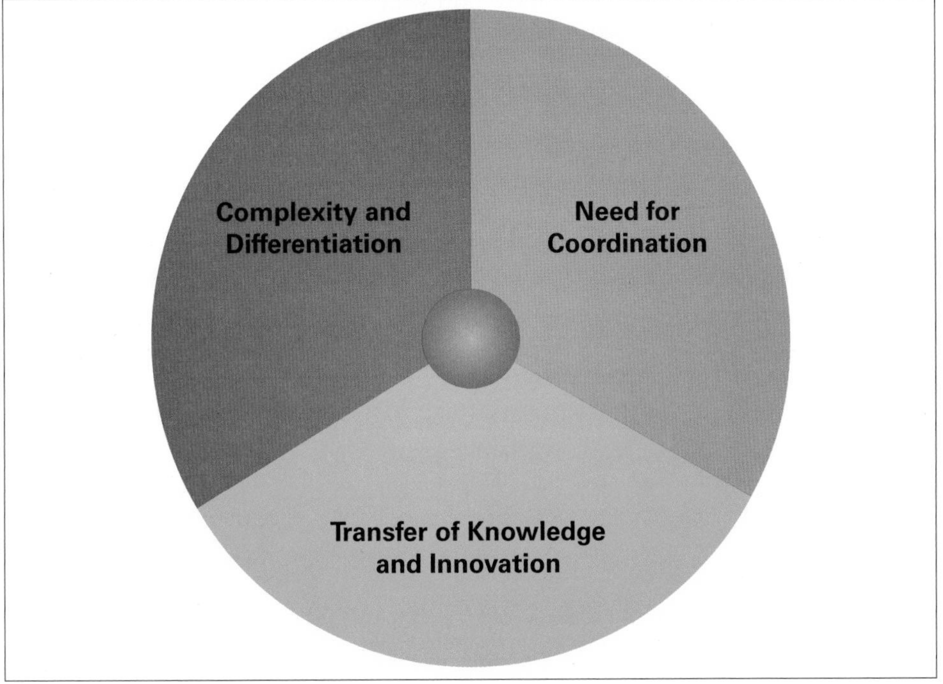

laws, and regulatory system. People eat different foods, observe different religions, have different attitudes, and subscribe to different social customs.[63] This environmental complexity and country variations require greater organizational differentiation.

At the same time, organizations must find ways to effectively achieve coordination and collaboration among far-flung units and facilitate the development and transfer of organizational knowledge and innovation for global learning.[64] Although many small companies are involved in international business, most international companies grow very large, creating a huge coordination problem. Exhibit 5.9 provides some understanding of the size and impact of international firms by comparing the revenues of several large multinational companies with the gross domestic product (GDP) of selected countries.

Increased Complexity and Differentiation. When organizations enter the international arena, they encounter a greater level of internal and external complexity than anything experienced on the domestic front. Companies have to create a structure to operate in numerous countries that differ in economic development, language, political systems and government regulations, cultural norms and values, and infrastructure such as transportation and communication facilities. For example, computer maker Lenovo, incorporated in Hong Kong, has nine operational hubs, and its top managers and corporate functions are spread around the world. The CEO is in Singapore, the chairman in Raleigh, North Carolina, and the chief financial officer in Hong Kong. Worldwide marketing is coordinated in India.[65]

All the complexity in the international environment is mirrored in a greater internal organizational complexity. As environments become more complex and uncertain, organizations grow more highly differentiated, with many specialized positions and departments to cope with specific sectors in the environment. Top management might need to set up specialized departments to deal with the diverse government, legal, and accounting regulations in various countries, for example. Google has a team of lawyers

EXHIBIT 5.9
Comparison of Leading Multinational Companies and Selected Countries, 2008 (in U.S. dollars)

Company	Revenue*	Country	Annual GDP†
Exxon Mobil	404.6 billion	Egypt	403.9 billion
Walmart	378.8 billion	Greece	370.2 billion
Royal Dutch Shell	355.8 billion	Malaysia	355.2 billion
BP	291.4 billion	Nigeria	292.6 billion
Toyota	262.3 billion	Algeria	269.2 billion
ING Group	212.0 billion	Peru	218.8 billion
General Motors	181.1 billion	Finland	182.0 billion
General Electric	172.7 billion	Kazakhstan	167.6 billion

*This size comparison is assuming revenues were valued at the equivalent of GDP.
†Gross domestic product.

Source: "Count: *Really* Big Business," *Fast Company* (December 2008–January 2009), 46.

and other experts in its New Delhi office to monitor complaints from Internet users and local police about questionable content on its social networking site, Orkut, and decide how to respond. India is a democracy and in principle supports freedom of speech on the Internet as well as in print. Yet with its volatile mix of religions and ethnic politics, the Indian government reserves the right to impose "reasonable restrictions" on free speech to maintain public order. Internet companies such as Google, Yahoo, and Facebook are expected to help enforce certain standards and take down content considered incendiary, but the rules can be difficult to interpret. Google, for its part, wants to follow local laws and sentiments, but it also wants to exercise discretion regarding what it believes should be allowable.[66]

In addition to departments to deal with diverse laws and regulations, companies operating internationally need more boundary-spanning departments to sense and respond to the external environment. Some companies disperse operations such as engineering, design, manufacturing, marketing, and sales around the world. In particular, many organizations have set up global product development systems to achieve greater access to international expertise and design products that are better suited to global markets. A Deloitte Research study found that 48 percent of North American and Western European manufacturers surveyed had set up engineering operations in other countries.[67] International organizations also might implement a variety of strategies, a broader array of activities, and a much larger number of products and services on an international level.

Need for Coordination. As organizations become more differentiated, with multiple products, divisions, departments, and positions scattered across numerous countries, managers face a tremendous coordination challenge. *Coordination* refers to the quality of collaboration across organizational units. The question is how to achieve the integration and collaboration that is necessary for a global organization to reap the benefits of economies of scale, economies of scope, and labor and production cost efficiencies that international expansion offers. High differentiation among departments requires that more time and resources be devoted to achieving coordination because employees' attitudes, goals, and work orientations differ widely. Imagine what it must be like for an international organization, whose operating units are divided not only by goals and work attitudes but by geographic distance, time differences, cultural values, and perhaps even language as well. Recall how Colgate-Palmolive created several specific units to achieve coordination and integration among regional divisions. Other companies, too, must find ways to share information, ideas, new products, and technologies across the organization.

All organizations working globally face the challenge of getting all the pieces working together in the right way at the right time and in the right place. Another issue is how to share knowledge and innovations across global divisions.

Transfer of Knowledge and Innovation. The third piece of the international challenge is for organizations to learn from their international experiences by sharing knowledge and innovations across the enterprise. The diversity of the international environment offers extraordinary opportunities for learning, development of diverse capabilities, and startling innovations in products and services. Some experts believe a great percentage of radical innovations will come from companies in emerging markets such as China and India in the coming years.[68] Innovations in products and services used to come primarily from developed countries and gravitate to less developed areas of the world, but a new approach referred to as *trickle-up innovation* or

EXHIBIT 5.10
Examples of Trickle-Up Innovation

Company	Innovation and Application
Groupe Danone:	Built tiny plants in Bangladesh that produce one-hundreth of the yogurt a typical Danone factory produces, and then discovered they can operate almost as efficiently as the firm's large factories, spurring Danone to adapt the concept to other markets
Nestlé:	Took the Maggi brand dried noodles created as a low-cost meal for rural Pakistan and India and repositioned it as a budget-friendly health food in Australia and New Zealand
General Electric	Created an inexpensive portable electrocardiogram machine for sale in India, where medical practitioners face power fluctuations, lack of funding and space for big machines, high levels of dust, and difficulty replacing parts in expensive equipment, and now sells it in the United States as well as other countries around the world
Hewlett-Packard	Has a team in India looking for ways to migrate Web-interface applications created for mobile phones in Asia and Africa to developed markets in the United States and Europe
John Deere	John Deere India developed a high-quality low-cost tractor for farmers in India that is now increasingly in demand in the United States among farmers reeling from the recession and that will play a big role in Deere's expansion in Russia

Sources: These examples are from Michael Fitzgerald, "As the World Turns," *Fast Company* (March 2009), 33–34; Reena Jana, "Inspirations from Emerging Economies," *BusinessWeek* (March 23 & 30, 2009), 38–41; Jeffrey R. Immelt, Vijay Govindarajan, and Chris Trimble, "How GE Is Disrupting Itself," *Harvard Business Review* (October 2009), 3–11; and Navi Radjou, "Polycentric Innovation: A New Mandate for Multinationals," *The Wall Street Journal Online* (November 9, 2009), http://online.wsj.com/article/SB125774328035737917.html (accessed November 13, 2009).

reverse innovation has companies paying attention more than ever to the need for mechanisms that encourage sharing across the international enterprise. Consider the healthcare profession. GE Healthcare had a solid presence in China, but its high-end ultrasound machines and other products didn't meet the needs of healthcare practitioners working in poorly funded, low-tech hospitals or clinics in rural villages. Price, portability, and ease of use were the important criteria. GE Healthcare's team in China created a portable ultrasound machine that sold for less than 15 percent of the cost of the company's high-end ultrasound machines. GE now sells the product around the world, and it grew to a $278 million global product line within six years.[69] Exhibit 5.10 lists some additional examples of trickle-up innovation.

Organizational units in each location acquire the skills and knowledge to meet environmental challenges that arise in that particular locale. As the trend toward trickle-up innovation shows, much of that knowledge, which may be related to product improvements, operational efficiencies, technological advancements, or myriad other competencies, is relevant across multiple countries, so organizations need systems that promote the transfer of knowledge and innovation across the global enterprise. A classic example comes from Procter & Gamble. Liquid Tide was one of P&G's most successful U.S. product launches in the 1980s, but the product came about from the sharing of innovations developed in diverse parts of the firm. Liquid Tide incorporated a technology for helping to suspend dirt in wash water from P&G headquarters in the United States, the formula for its cleaning agents from P&G technicians in Japan, and special ingredients for fighting mineral salts present in hard water from company scientists in Brussels.[70]

Getting employees to transfer ideas and knowledge across national boundaries can be exceedingly challenging. Many organizations tap only a fraction of the potential that is available from the cross-border transfer of knowledge and innovation. People scattered at different locations around the world sometimes have trouble building trusting relationships. Other reasons include:[71]

- Language barriers, cultural dissimilarities, and geographic distances can prevent managers from spotting the knowledge and opportunities that exist across disparate country units.
- Sometimes managers don't appreciate the value of organizational integration and want to protect the interests of their own division rather than cooperate with other divisions.
- Divisions sometimes view knowledge and innovation as power and want to hold onto it as a way to gain an influential position within the global firm.
- The "not-invented-here" syndrome makes some managers reluctant to tap into the know-how and expertise of other units.
- Much of an organization's knowledge is in the minds of employees and cannot easily be written down and shared with other units.

Organizations have to encourage both the development and the sharing of knowledge, implement systems for tapping into knowledge wherever it exists, and share innovations to meet global challenges.

Global Coordination Mechanisms

Managers meet the global challenge of coordination and transferring knowledge and innovation across highly differentiated units in a variety of ways. Some of the most common are the use of global teams, stronger headquarters planning and control, and specific coordination roles.

Global Teams. The popularity and success of teams on the domestic front allowed managers to see firsthand how this mechanism can achieve strong horizontal coordination, as described in Chapter 2, and thus recognize the promise teams held for coordination across a global firm as well. **Global teams**, also called *transnational teams*, are cross-border work groups made up of multiskilled, multinational members whose activities span multiple countries.[72] Typically, teams are of two types: intercultural teams, whose members come from different countries and meet face to face, and virtual global teams, whose members remain in separate locations around the world and conduct their work electronically.[73] Heineken formed the European Production Task Force, a 13-member team made up of multinational members, to meet regularly and come up with ideas for optimizing the company's production facilities across Europe.[74] German steelmaker ThyssenKrupp uses global virtual teams, applying sophisticated computer networks and software to link and coordinate team members working across three continents to run a virtually integrated steel operation.[75]

However, building effective global teams is not easy. Cultural and language differences can create misunderstandings, and resentments and mistrust can quickly derail the team's efforts. Consider what happened in one virtual team made up of members from India, Israel, Canada, the United States, Singapore, Spain, Brussels, Great Britain, and Australia:

> *"Early on . . . team members were reluctant to seek advice from teammates who were still strangers, fearing that a request for help might be interpreted as a sign of incompetence. Moreover, when teammates did ask for help, assistance was not always forthcoming. One team member confessed to carefully calculating how much information she was willing to share. Going the extra mile on behalf of a virtual teammate, in her view, came at a high price of time and energy, with no guarantee of reciprocation."*[76]

As this quote shows, it is easy for an "us against them" mentality to develop, which is just the opposite of what organizations want from global teams.[77] No wonder when the executive council of *CIO* magazine asked global chief information officers to rank their greatest challenges, managing virtual global teams ranked as the most pressing issue.[78] "You need to be intensely international" to help global teams succeed, said Greg Caltabiano, CEO of chip-designer Teknovus Inc. (now part of Broadcom Corporation).[79] Organizations that use global teams effectively invest the time and resources to adequately educate employees and find ways to encourage cross-cultural understanding and trust. At Teknovus, Caltabiano sent U.S. employees on short visits to the company's Asian offices and required that all new overseas hires spend time in the United States.[80]

2 It is an especially difficult challenge to work on a global team to coordinate one's own activities and share new ideas and insights with colleagues in different divisions around the world.

ANSWER: *Agree.* The problems of different languages, locations, cultural values, and business practices make membership on an international team especially difficult. Global teams can be effective only if members have the patience and skills to surmount the barriers and openly share information and ideas. Global teams perform better when they are made up of people who are culturally astute and genuinely want to coordinate and communicate with their counterparts in other countries.

Headquarters Planning. A second approach to achieving stronger global coordination is for headquarters to take an active role in planning, scheduling, and control to keep the widely distributed pieces of the global organization working together and moving in the same direction. In one survey, 70 percent of global companies reported that the most important function of corporate headquarters was to "provide enterprise leadership."[81] Without strong leadership, highly autonomous divisions can begin to act like independent companies rather than coordinated parts of a global whole. To counteract this, top management may delegate responsibility and decision-making authority in some areas, such as adapting products or services to meet local needs, while maintaining strong control through centralized systems in other areas to provide the coordination and integration needed.[82] Plans, schedules, and formal rules and procedures can help ensure greater communication among divisions and with headquarters as well as foster cooperation and synergy among far-flung units to achieve the organization's goals in a cost-efficient way. Top managers can provide clear strategic direction, guide far-flung operations, and resolve competing demands from various units.

Expanded Coordination Roles. Organizations may also implement structural solutions to achieve stronger coordination and collaboration.[83] Creating specific organizational roles or positions for coordination is a way to integrate all the pieces of the enterprise to achieve a strong competitive position. In successful international firms, the role of top *functional managers*, for example, is expanded to include responsibility for coordinating across countries, identifying and linking the organization's expertise and resources worldwide. In an international organization, the manufacturing manager has to be aware of and coordinate with manufacturing operations of the company in various parts of the world so that the company achieves manufacturing efficiency and shares technology and ideas across units. A new manufacturing technology developed to improve efficiency in a company's Brazilian operations may be valuable for European and North American plants as well. Manufacturing managers are responsible for being aware of new developments wherever they occur and for using their knowledge to improve the organization. Similarly, marketing managers, HR managers, and other functional managers at an international company are involved not only in activities for their particular location but in coordinating with their sister units in other countries as well.

Whereas functional managers coordinate across countries, *country managers* coordinate across functions. A country manager for an international firm has to coordinate all the various functional activities located within the country to meet the problems, opportunities, needs, and trends in the local market, enabling the organization to achieve multinational flexibility and rapid response. The country manager in Venezuela for a global consumer products firm such as Colgate-Palmolive would coordinate everything that goes on in that country, from manufacturing to HR to marketing, to ensure that activities meet the language, cultural, government, and legal requirements of Venezuela. The country manager in Ireland or Canada would do the same for those countries. Country managers also help with the transfer of ideas, trends, products, and technologies that arise in one country and might have significance on a broader scale. Some organizations also use *business integrators* to provide coordination on a regional basis that might include several countries. These managers reach out to various parts of the organization to resolve problems and coordinate activities across groups, divisions, or countries.

Another coordination role is that of formal *network coordinator* to coordinate information and activities related to key customer accounts. These coordinators would enable a manufacturing organization, for example, to provide knowledge and integrated solutions across multiple businesses, divisions, and countries for a large retail customer such as Tesco, Walmart, or Carrefour. Top managers in successful global firms also encourage and support informal networks and relationships to keep information flowing in all directions. Much of an organization's information exchange occurs not through formal systems or structures but through informal channels and relationships. By supporting these informal networks, giving people across boundaries opportunities to get together and develop relationships, and then ways to keep in close touch, executives enhance organizational coordination.[84]

BRIEFCASE

As an organization manager, keep these guidelines in mind:

Use mechanisms such as global teams, headquarters planning and specific coordination roles to provide needed coordination and integration among far-flung international units. Emphasize information and knowledge sharing to help the organization learn and improve on a global scale.

Benefits of Coordination. International companies have a hard time staying competitive without strong inter-unit coordination and collaboration. Those firms that stimulate and support collaboration are typically better able to leverage dispersed resources and capabilities to reap operational and economic benefits.[85] Benefits that result from inter-unit collaboration include the following:

- *Cost savings.* Collaboration can produce real, measurable results in the way of cost savings from the sharing of best practices across global divisions. For example, at BP, a business unit head in the United States improved inventory turns and cut the working capital needed to run U.S. service stations by learning the best practices from BP operations in the United Kingdom and the Netherlands.
- *Better decision making.* By sharing information and advice across divisions, managers can make better business decisions that support their own unit as well as the organization as a whole.
- *Greater revenues.* By sharing expertise and products among various divisions, organizations can reap increased revenues. BP again provides an example. More than 75 people from various units around the world flew to China to assist the team developing an acetic acid plant there. As a result, BP finished the project and began realizing revenues sooner than project planners had expected.
- *Increased innovation.* The sharing of ideas and technological innovations across units stimulates creativity and the development of new products and services. McDonald's is taking an approach called "freedom within a framework" that allows regional and national managers to develop practices and products suited to the local area. The company then makes sure international managers have plenty of both formal and informal ways to communicate and share ideas. The Big Tasty, a whopping 5.5 oz. beef patty slathered in barbeque sauce and topped with three slices of cheese, was created in a test kitchen in Germany and launched in Sweden, but as word spread, the sandwich was adopted by restaurants in places like Brazil, Italy, and Portugal, where it became a huge hit.[86]

BRIEFCASE

As an organization manager, keep these guidelines in mind:

Appreciate cultural value differences and strive to use coordination mechanisms that are in tune with local values. When broader coordination mechanisms are needed, focus on education and corporate culture as ways to gain understanding and acceptance.

Cultural Differences in Coordination and Control

Just as social and cultural values differ from country to country, the management values and organizational norms of international companies tend to vary depending on the organization's home country. Organizational norms and values are influenced by the values in the larger national culture, and these in turn influence the organization's structural approach and the ways managers coordinate and control an international firm.

National Value Systems

Studies have attempted to determine how national value systems influence management and organizations. One of the most influential was conducted by Geert Hofstede, who identified several dimensions of national value systems that vary widely across countries.[87] More recent research by Project GLOBE (Global Leadership and Organizational Behavior Effectiveness) has supported and extended

Hofstede's assessment. Project GLOBE used data collected from 18,000 managers in 62 countries to identify nine dimensions that explain cultural differences, including those identified by Hofstede.[88] These studies provide managers with an understanding of key cultural differences that can enhance their and their organizations' effectiveness on a global scale.[89] Complete the questionnaire in the "How Do You Fit the Design?" box to see how prepared you are to work internationally.

How Do You Fit the Design?

ARE YOU READY TO FILL AN INTERNATIONAL ROLE?

Are you ready to negotiate a sales contract with someone from another country? Coordinate a new product for use overseas? Companies large and small deal on a global basis. To what extent do you display the behaviors below? Please answer each item as Mostly True or Mostly False for you.

Are You Typically:	**Mostly True**	**Mostly False**
1. Impatient? Do you have a short attention span? Do you want to keep moving to the next topic?	____	____
2. A poor listener? Are you uncomfortable with silence? Does your mind think about what you want to say next?	____	____
3. Argumentative? Do you enjoy arguing for its own sake?	____	____
4. Not familiar with cultural specifics in other countries? Do you have limited experience in other countries?	____	____
5. Placing more emphasis on the short-term than on the long-term in your thinking and planning?	____	____
6. Thinking that it is a waste of time getting to know someone personally before discussing business?	____	____
7. Legalistic to win your point? Holding others to an agreement regardless of changing circumstances?	____	____
8. Thinking "win/lose" when negotiating? Trying to win a negotiation at the other's expense?	____	____

Scoring: Give yourself one point for each Mostly True answer. A score of 3 or lower suggests that you may have international style and awareness. A score of 6 or higher suggests low presence or awareness with respect to other cultures.

Interpretation: A low score on this exercise is a good thing. American managers often display cross-cultural ignorance during business negotiations compared to counterparts from other countries. American habits can be disturbing, such as emphasizing areas of disagreement over agreement, spending little time understanding the views and interests of the other side, and adopting an adversarial attitude. Americans often like to leave a negotiation thinking they won, which can be embarrassing to the other side. For this quiz, a low score shows better international presence. If you answered "Mostly True" to three or fewer questions, then consider yourself ready to assist with an international negotiation. If you scored six or higher "Mostly True" responses, it is time to learn more about how businesspeople behave in other national cultures before participating in international business deals. Try to develop greater focus on other people's needs and an appreciation for different viewpoints. Be open to compromise and develop empathy for people who are different from you.

Source: Adapted from Cynthia Barnum and Natasha Wolniansky, "Why Americans Fail at Overseas Negotiations," *Management Review* (October 1989), 54–57.

Two value dimensions that seem to have a strong impact within organizations are *power distance* and *uncertainty avoidance*. High **power distance** means that people accept inequality in power among institutions, organizations, and people. Low power distance means that people expect equality in power. High **uncertainty avoidance** means that members of a society feel uncomfortable with uncertainty and ambiguity and thus support beliefs that promise certainty and conformity. Low uncertainty avoidance means that people have a high tolerance for the unstructured, the unclear, and the unpredictable.

The value dimensions of *power distance* and *uncertainty avoidance* are reflected within organizations in beliefs regarding the need for hierarchy, centralized decision making and control, formal rules and procedures, and specialized jobs.[90] In countries that value high power distance, for example, organizations tend to be more hierarchical and centralized, with greater control and coordination from the top levels of the organization. On the other hand, organizations in countries that value low power distance are more likely to be decentralized. A low tolerance for uncertainty tends to be reflected in a preference for coordination through rules and procedures. Organizations in countries where people have a high tolerance for uncertainty typically have fewer rules and formal systems, relying more on informal networks and personal communication for coordination.

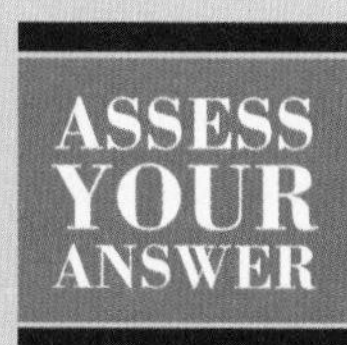

3 If management practices and coordination techniques work well for a company in its home country, they probably will be successful in the company's international divisions as well.

ANSWER: *Disagree.* National culture has a tremendous impact on how people in different countries feel about issues of power and control, rules and procedures, and every other aspect of organizational life. Management practices and coordination and control techniques that work well in a country such as the United States might be ineffective or even offensive in a country such as Japan or China. Managers have to stretch out of their familiar comfort zone to succeed internationally.

Although organizations do not always reflect the dominant cultural values, studies have found rather clear patterns of different management structures when comparing countries in Europe, the United States, and Asia.

Four National Approaches to Coordination and Control

Let's look at four approaches to coordination and control as represented by Japanese, Chinese, American, and European companies. It should be noted that companies in each country use tools and techniques from each of the coordination methods. However, there are broad, general patterns that illustrate cultural differences.

Centralized Coordination in Japanese Companies. When expanding internationally, Japanese companies have typically developed coordination mechanisms that rely on centralization.[91] Top managers at headquarters actively direct and control overseas operations, whose primary focus is to implement strategies handed down from headquarters. A study of R&D activities in high-tech firms in Japan and Germany supported the idea that Japanese organizations tend to be more centralized. Whereas the German firms leaned toward dispersing R&D groups out into different regions, Japanese companies tended to keep these activities centralized in the home country.[92] This centralized approach enables Japanese companies to leverage the knowledge and resources located at the corporate center, attain global efficiencies, and coordinate across units to obtain synergies and avoid turf battles. Top managers use strong structural linkages to ensure that managers at headquarters remain up to date and fully involved in all strategic decisions. However, centralization has its limits. As the organization expands and divisions grow larger, headquarters can become overloaded and decision making slows. The quality of decisions may also suffer as greater diversity and complexity make it difficult for headquarters to understand and respond to local needs in each region.

Strong centralization has been cited as one factor that caused Toyota's poor decision making and delayed response related to safety issues such as sticking gas pedals. After safety scandals tarnished Toyota's quality reputation, company executives formed a panel headed by former U.S. Transportation secretary Rodney Slater to investigate what went wrong. The panel's report said Toyota "has erred too much on the side of global centralization and needs to shift the balance somewhat toward greater local authority and control." Almost every major decision at Toyota is made at headquarters. Toyota's North American division doesn't even have a single executive in charge; instead, major department heads report directly to headquarters in Japan. Decisions regarding vehicle design and development, marketing, communications, public relations, and recalls have always been tightly controlled by headquarters, which slowed the company's response to quality and safety issues.[93]

Tradition in Chinese Companies. China is a rapidly growing part of the international business environment, and research is increasingly being conducted into management structures and coordination mechanisms of Chinese firms.[94] Many Chinese companies are still relatively small and run in a traditional family-like manner. Often, key employees are family members of the founder or CEO. Even large firms are often networks of smaller family-based business alliances that act as one unit. However, similar to Japan, organizations typically reflect a distinct hierarchy of authority and relatively strong centralization. Chinese entrepreneurs, for instance, tend to employ a strong authoritarian style of management, centralizing power in themselves and perhaps key family members. Hierarchy plays an important role in Chinese culture and management, so employees feel obligated to follow orders directed from above, and they are typically loyal not just to the boss but also to company rules and policies. Culture, history, and tradition play a significant role in organizations in China. Guarding one's special skills and knowledge is a central aspect of traditional culture, and many Chinese business managers hold information closely rather than share it across the business. This tendency can also make managers reluctant to partner with other firms. For the Chinese, it takes a long time to develop trusting relationships, or *Guanxi*, both within the organization and with outsiders. An informal, powerful network, called *Quanzi*, consisting of people who share this deep trusting type of relationship, determines power relationships and the pattern of information sharing, cooperation, and collaboration.

Stan Shih, who founded Acer (originally called Multitech) and helped it grow from a tiny startup to a billion-dollar global brand and the second-largest computer maker in the world, embraced many of the traditions of Chinese family-like businesses, such as a focus on the long term and an emphasis on collectivism, harmony, and maintaining a good family reputation. However, he also avoided some traditions that he felt held Chinese companies back, such as the tendency toward mistrust and the tendency toward strong authoritarianism and centralization. Shih encouraged a decentralized approach, delegation, and empowerment.[95] As Chinese organizations grow larger and become a major element of the global business landscape, more insight will be gained into how these firms handle the balance of coordination and control.

European Firms' Decentralized Approach. A different approach has typically been taken by European companies.[96] Rather than relying on strong, centrally directed coordination and control as in the Japanese firms, international units tend to have a high level of independence and decision-making autonomy. Companies rely on a strong mission, shared values, and informal personal relationships for coordination. Thus, great emphasis is placed on careful selection, training, and development of key managers throughout the international organization. Formal management and control systems are used primarily for financial rather than technical or operational control. Many European managers don't appreciate headquarters taking control over operational issues. When SAP AG tried to assert a more centralized control system to speed up development of new software and fend off growing competition, German engineers rebelled at the loss of autonomy. "They said, 'You don't tell us what to do—we tell you what to build,'" one former executive recalls.[97]

With a decentralized approach, each international unit focuses on its local markets, enabling the company to excel in meeting diverse needs. One disadvantage is the cost of ensuring, through training and development programs, that managers throughout a huge, global firm share goals, values, and priorities. Decision making can also be slow and complex, and disagreements and conflicts among divisions are more difficult to resolve.

The United States: Coordination and Control through Formalization. U.S.-based companies that have expanded into the international arena have taken still another direction.[98] Typically, these organizations have delegated responsibility to international divisions, yet retained overall control of the enterprise through the use of sophisticated management control systems and the development of specialist headquarters staff. Formal systems, policies, standards of performance, and a regular flow of information from divisions to headquarters are the primary means of coordination and control. Decision making is based on objective data, policies, and procedures, which provides for many operating efficiencies and reduces conflict among divisions and between divisions and headquarters. However, the cost of setting up complex systems, policies, and rules for an international organization may be quite high. This approach also requires a larger headquarters staff for reviewing, interpreting, and sharing information, thus increasing overhead costs. Finally, standard routines and procedures don't always fit the needs of new problems and situations. Flexibility is limited if managers pay so much attention to the standard systems that they fail to recognize opportunities and threats in the environment.

Clearly, each of these approaches has advantages. But as international organizations grow larger and more complex, the disadvantages of each tend to become more pronounced. Because traditional approaches have been inadequate to meet the demands of a rapidly changing, complex global environment, many large international companies are moving toward a *transnational model* of organization, which is highly differentiated to address the increased complexity of the global environment, yet offers very high levels of coordination, learning, and transfer of organizational knowledge and innovations.

The Transnational Model of Organization

The **transnational model** represents the most advanced kind of international organization. It reflects the ultimate in both organizational complexity, with many diverse units, and organizational coordination, with mechanisms for integrating the varied parts. The transnational model is useful for large, multinational companies with subsidiaries in many countries that try to exploit both global and local advantages as well as technological advancements, rapid innovation, and global learning and knowledge sharing. Rather than building capabilities primarily in one area, such as global efficiency, local responsiveness, or global learning, the transnational model seeks to achieve all three simultaneously. Dealing with multiple, interrelated, complex issues requires a complex form of organization and structure.

The transnational model represents the most current thinking about the kind of structure needed by highly complex global organizations such as Philips NV, illustrated in Exhibit 5.11. Incorporated in the Netherlands, Philips has hundreds of operating units all over the world and is typical of global companies such as Unilever, Matsushita, or Procter & Gamble.[99] Large professional service firms such as KPMG and Pricewaterhouse Coopers also use the transnational structure. PricewaterhouseCoopers (PwC), for example, has more than 160,000 people in 757 offices in 151 countries. The company provides a highly diversified range of knowledge-based services that have to be customized to specific clients in specific locales, so local offices need discretion and autonomy. At the same time, PwC needs consistent operating standards and control systems worldwide.[100]

BRIEFCASE

As an organization manager, keep this guideline in mind:

Strive toward a transnational model of organization when the company has to respond to multiple global forces simultaneously and needs to promote worldwide integration, learning, and knowledge sharing.

The units of a transnational organization network, as illustrated in Exhibit 5.11, are far-flung. Achieving coordination, a sense of participation and involvement by subsidiaries, and a sharing of information, knowledge, new technology, and customers is a tremendous challenge. For example, a global corporation like Philips, Unilever, or PricewaterhouseCoopers is so large that size alone is a huge problem in coordinating global operations. In addition, some subsidiaries become so large that they no longer fit a narrow strategic role defined by headquarters. While being part of a larger organization, individual units need some autonomy for themselves and the ability to have an impact on other parts of the organization.

The transnational model addresses these challenges by creating an integrated network of individual operations that are linked together to achieve the multidimensional goals of the overall organization.[101] The management philosophy is based on *interdependence* rather than either full divisional independence or total dependence of these units on headquarters for decision making and control. The transnational model is more than just an organization chart. It is a managerial state of mind, a set of values, a shared desire to make a worldwide learning system work, and an idealized structure for effectively managing such a system. The following characteristics distinguish the transnational organization from other global organization forms such as the matrix, described earlier.

EXHIBIT 5.11
International Organizational Units and Interlinkages within Philips NV

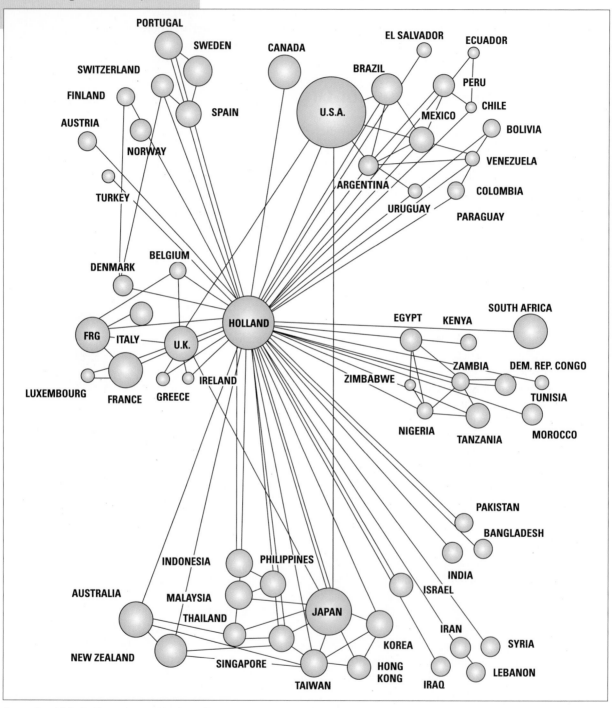

Source: Republished with permission of Academy of Management (NY), from Sumantra Ghoshal and Christopher Bartlett, "The Multinational Corporation as an Interorganizational Network," *The Academy of Management Review*, 15 (1990), 603–625; permission conveyed through Copyright Clearance Center, Inc.

1. *Assets and resources are dispersed worldwide into highly specialized operations that are linked together through interdependent relationships.* Resources and capabilities are widely distributed to help the organization sense and respond to diverse stimuli such as market needs, technological developments, or consumer trends that emerge in different parts of the world. To manage this increased complexity and differentiation, managers forge interdependent relationships among the various product, functional, or geographic units. Mechanisms such as cross-subsidiary teams, for example, compel units to work together for the good of their own unit as well as the overall organization. Rather than being completely self-sufficient, each group has to cooperate to achieve its own goals. At PricewaterhouseCoopers, for example, the client management system connects teams of people drawn from various units, service lines, and areas of expertise around the world. Such interdependencies encourage the collaborative sharing of information and resources, cross-unit problem solving, and collective implementation demanded by today's competitive international environment. Materials, people, products, ideas, resources, and information are continually flowing among the dispersed parts of the integrated network. In addition, managers actively shape, manage, and reinforce informal information networks that cross functions, products, divisions, and countries.
2. *Structures are flexible and ever-changing.* The transnational operates on a principle of *flexible centralization.* It may centralize some functions in one country, some in another, yet decentralize still other functions among its many geographically dispersed operations. An R&D center may be centralized in Holland and a purchasing center may be located in Sweden, while financial accounting responsibilities are decentralized to operations in many countries. A unit in Hong Kong may be responsible for coordinating activities across Asia, while activities for all other countries are coordinated by a large division headquarters in London. The transnational model requires that managers be flexible in determining structural needs based on the benefits to be gained. Some functions, products, and geographic regions by their nature may need more central control and coordination than others. In addition, coordination and control mechanisms will change over time to meet new needs or competitive threats. Some companies have begun setting up multiple headquarters in different countries as the organization gets too large and too complex to manage from one place. Irdeto Holdings BV, for example, has headquarters in both Amsterdam and Beijing. U.S.-based Halliburton Company is planning to open a second corporate headquarters in Dubai.[102]
3. *Subsidiary managers initiate strategy and innovations that become strategy for the corporation as a whole.* In traditional structures, managers have a strategic role only for their division. In a transnational structure, various centers and subsidiaries can shape the company from the bottom up by developing creative responses and initiating programs in response to local needs, then dispersing those innovations worldwide. Transnational companies recognize each of the worldwide units as a source of capabilities and knowledge that can be used to benefit the entire organization. In addition, environmental demands and opportunities vary from country to country, and exposing the whole organization to this broader range of environmental stimuli triggers greater learning and innovation.
4. *Unification and coordination are achieved primarily through corporate culture, shared vision and values, and management style, rather than through formal structures and systems.* A study by Hay Group found that one of the

defining characteristics of companies that succeed on a global scale is that they successfully coordinate worldwide units and subsidiaries around a common strategic vision and values rather than relying on formal coordination systems alone.[103] Achieving unity and coordination in an organization in which employees come from a variety of different national backgrounds, are separated by time and geographic distance, and have different cultural norms is more easily accomplished through shared understanding than through formal systems. Top leaders build a context of shared vision, values, and perspectives among managers who in turn cascade these elements through all parts of the organization. Selection and training of managers emphasizes flexibility and open-mindedness. In addition, people are often rotated through different jobs, divisions, and countries to gain broad experience and become socialized into the corporate culture. Achieving coordination in a transnational organization is a much more complex process than simple centralization or decentralization of decision making. It requires shaping and adapting beliefs, culture, and values so that everyone participates in information sharing and learning.

Taken together, these characteristics facilitate strong coordination, organizational learning, and knowledge sharing on a broad global scale. The transnational model is truly a complex and messy way to conceptualize organization structure, but it is becoming increasingly relevant for large, global firms that treat the whole world as their playing field and do not have a single country base. The autonomy of organizational parts gives strength to smaller units and allows the firm to be flexible in responding to rapid change and competitive opportunities on a local level, while the emphasis on interdependency enables global efficiencies and organizational learning. Each part of the transnational company is aware of and closely integrated with the organization as a whole so that local actions complement and enhance other company parts.

Design Essentials

- This chapter examined how managers design organizations for a complex international environment. Almost every company today is affected by significant global forces, and many are developing overseas operations to take advantage of global markets. Three primary motivations for global expansion are to realize economies of scale, exploit economies of scope, and achieve scarce or low-cost factors of production such as labor, raw materials, or land. One popular way to become involved in international operations is through strategic alliances with international firms. Alliances include licensing, joint ventures, and consortia.

- Organizations typically evolve through four stages, beginning with a domestic orientation, shifting to an international orientation, then changing to a multinational orientation, and finally moving to a global orientation that sees the whole world as a potential market. Organizations typically use an export department, then use an international department, and eventually develop into a worldwide geographic or product structure.

- Geographic structures are most effective for organizations that can benefit from a multidomestic strategy, meaning that products and services will do best if tailored to local needs and cultures. A product structure supports a globalization strategy, which means that products and services can be standardized and sold worldwide. Huge global firms might use a matrix structure to respond to both local and global forces simultaneously. Many firms use hybrid structures by combining elements of two or more different structures to meet the dynamic conditions of the global environment.

- Succeeding on a global scale is not easy. Three aspects of the global organizational design challenge are addressing environmental complexity through greater organizational complexity and differentiation, achieving integration and coordination among the highly differentiated units, and implementing mechanisms for the transfer of knowledge and innovations. Common ways to address the problem of integration and knowledge transfer are through global teams, stronger headquarters planning and control, and specific coordination roles.
- Managers also recognize that diverse national and cultural values influence the organization's approach to coordination and control. Four varied national approaches are the centralized coordination and control typically found in many Japanese-based firms, an emphasis on tradition in China, a decentralized approach common among European firms, and the formalization approach often used by U.S.-based international firms. Most companies, however, no matter their home country, use a combination of elements from each of these approaches.
- Companies operating globally need broad coordination methods, and some are moving toward the transnational model of organization. The transnational model is based on a philosophy of interdependence. It is highly differentiated yet offers very high levels of coordination, learning, and transfer of knowledge across far-flung divisions. The transnational model represents the ultimate global design in terms of both organizational complexity and organizational integration. Each part of the transnational organization is aware of and closely integrated with the organization as a whole so that local actions complement and enhance other company parts.

Key Concepts

consortia
domestic stage
economies of scale
economies of scope
factors of production
global companies
global geographic structure
global matrix structure
global product structure
global stage
global teams
globalization strategy
international division
international stage
joint venture
multidomestic
multidomestic strategy
multinational stage
power distance
standardization
transnational model
uncertainty avoidance

Discussion Questions

1. Under what conditions should a company consider adopting a global geographic structure as opposed to a global product structure?
2. Name some companies that you think could succeed today with a globalization strategy and explain why you selected those companies. How does the globalization strategy differ from a multidomestic strategy?
3. Why would a company want to join a strategic alliance rather than go it alone in international operations? What do you see as the potential advantages and disadvantages of international alliances?

4. Do you think it makes sense for a transnational organization to have more than one headquarters? What might be some advantages associated with two headquarters, each responsible for different things? Can you think of any drawbacks?
5. What are some of the primary reasons a company decides to expand internationally? Identify a company in the news that has recently built a new overseas facility. Which of the three motivations for global expansion described in the chapter do you think best explains the company's decision? Discuss.
6. When would an organization consider using a matrix structure? How does the global matrix differ from the domestic matrix structure described in Chapter 2?
7. Name some of the elements that contribute to greater complexity for international organizations. How do organizations address this complexity? Do you think these elements apply to a company such as Spotify that wants to expand its music streaming service internationally? Discuss.
8. Traditional values in Mexico support high power distance and a low tolerance for uncertainty. What would you predict about a company that opens a division in Mexico and tries to implement global teams characterized by shared power and authority and the lack of formal guidelines, rules, and structure?
9. Do you believe it is possible for a global company to simultaneously achieve the goals of global efficiency and integration, national responsiveness and flexibility, and the worldwide transfer of knowledge and innovation? Discuss.
10. Compare the description of the transnational model in this chapter to the elements of organic vs. mechanistic organization designs described in Chapter 1. Do you think the transnational model seems workable for a huge global firm? Discuss.

Chapter 5 Workbook Made in the U.S.A.?

In March of 2011, ABC World News ran a special series called "Made in America." In the opening program, correspondents David Muir and Sharyn Alfonsi removed all foreign made products from a family's Dallas, Texas, home and found that there was virtually nothing left when they finished. How many items in your home were "made in America"? For this exercise, pick three different consumer products from your home (e.g., a shirt, a toy or game, a phone, a shoe, a sheet or pillowcase, a coffeemaker). Try to find the following information for each product, as shown in the table. To find this information, use websites, articles on the company from various business newspapers and magazines, and the labels on the items or user manuals. You could also try calling the company and talking with someone there.

Product	What country do materials come from?	Where is it manufactured or assembled?	Which country does the marketing and advertising?	In what different countries is the product sold?
1.				
2.				
3.				

What can you conclude about international products and organizations based on your analysis?

CASE FOR ANALYSIS TopDog Software[104]

At the age of 39, after working for nearly 15 years at a leading software company on the West Coast, Ari Weiner and his soon-to-be-wife, Mary Carpenter, had cashed in their stock options, withdrawn all their savings, maxed out their credit cards, and started their own business, naming it TopDog Software after their beloved Alaskan malamute. The two had developed a new software package for root cause analysis (RCA) applications that they were certain was far superior to anything on the market at that time. TopDog's software was particularly effective for use in design engineering organizations because it provided a highly efficient way to eliminate problems in new digital manufacturing processes, including product development, software engineering, hardware design, manufacturing, and installation. The software, which could be used as a standalone product or easily integrated with other software packages, dramatically expedited problem identification and corrective actions in the work of design engineering firms. The use of TopDog's RCA software would find an average of 30-to-50 root cause problems and provide 20-to-30 corrective actions that lowered defect rates by 50 percent, saving tens and sometimes hundreds of thousands of dollars with each application.

The timing proved to be right on target. RCA was just getting hot, and TopDog was poised to take advantage of the trend as a niche player in a growing market. Weiner and Carpenter brought in two former colleagues as partners and were soon able to catch the attention of a venture capitalist firm to gain additional funding. Within a couple of years, TopDog had 28 employees and sales had reached nearly $4 million.

Now, though, the partners are facing the company's first major problem. TopDog's head of sales, Samantha Jenkins, has learned of a new company based in Norway that is beta testing a new RCA package that promises to outpace TopDog's—and the Norway-based company, FastData, has been talking up its global aspirations in the press. "If we stay focused on the United States and they start out as a global player, they'll kill us within months!" Sam moaned. "We've got to come up with an international strategy to deal with this kind of competition."

In a series of group meetings, off-site retreats, and one-on-one conversations, Weiner and Carpenter have gathered opinions and ideas from their partners, employees, advisors, and friends. Now they have to make a decision—should TopDog go global? And if so, what approach would be most effective? There's a growing market for RCA software overseas, and new companies such as FastData will soon be cutting into TopDog's U.S. market share as well. Samantha Jenkins isn't alone in her belief that TopDog has no choice but to enter new international markets or get eaten alive. Others, however, are concerned that TopDog isn't ready for that step. The company's resources are already stretched to the limit, and some advisors have warned that rapid global expansion could spell disaster. TopDog isn't even well established in the United States, they argue, and expanding internationally could strain the company's capabilities and resources. Others have pointed out that none of the managers has any international experience, and the company would have to hire someone with significant global exposure to even think about entering new markets.

Although Mary tends to agree that TopDog for the time being should stay focused on building its business in the United States, Ari has come to believe that global expansion of some type is a necessity. But if TopDog does eventually decide on global expansion, he wonders how on earth they should proceed in a huge, complex world environment. Sam, the sales manager, is arguing that the company should set up its own small foreign offices from scratch and staff them primarily with local people. Building a U.K. office and an Asian office, she asserts, would give TopDog an ideal base for penetrating markets around the world. However, it would be quite expensive, not to mention the complexities of dealing with language and cultural differences, legal and government regulations, and other matters. Another option would be to establish alliances or joint ventures with small European and Asian companies that could benefit from adding RCA applications to their suite of products. The companies could share expenses in setting up foreign production facilities and a global sales and distribution network. This would be a much less costly operation and would give TopDog the benefit of the expertise of the foreign partners. However, it might also require lengthy negotiations and would certainly mean giving up some control to the partner companies.

One of TopDog's partners is urging still a third, even lower-cost approach, that of licensing TopDog's software to foreign distributors as a route to international expansion. By giving foreign software companies rights to produce, market, and distribute its RCA software, TopDog could build brand identity and customer awareness while keeping a tight rein on expenses. Ari likes the low-cost approach, but he wonders if licensing would give TopDog enough participation and control to successfully develop its international presence. As another day winds down, Weiner and Carpenter are no closer to a decision about global expansion than they were when the sun came up.

CASE FOR ANALYSIS **Rhodes Industries**

David Javier was reviewing the consulting firm's proposed changes in organization structure for Rhodes Industries (RI). As Javier read the report, he wondered whether the changes recommended by the consultants would do more harm than good for RI. Javier had been president of RI for 18 months, and he was keenly aware of the organizational and coordination problems that needed to be corrected in order for RI to improve profits and growth in its international businesses.

Company Background

Rhodes Industries was started in the 1950s in Southern Ontario, Canada, by Robert Rhodes, an engineer who was an entrepreneur at heart. He started the business by first making pipe and then glass for industrial uses. As soon as the initial business was established, however, he quickly branched into new areas such as industrial sealants, coatings, and cleaners, and even into manufacturing mufflers and parts for the trucking industry. Much of this expansion occurred by acquiring small firms in Canada and the United States during the 1960s. RI had a conglomerate-type structure with rather diverse subsidiaries scattered around North America, all reporting directly to the Ontario headquarters. Each subsidiary was a complete local business and was allowed to operate independently so long as it contributed profits to RI.

During the 1970s and 1980s, the president at the time, Clifford Michaels, brought a strong international focus to RI. His strategy was to acquire small companies worldwide with the belief that they could be formed into a cohesive unit that would bring RI synergies and profits through low cost of manufacturing and by serving businesses in international markets. Some of RI's businesses were acquired simply because they were available at a good price, and RI found itself in new lines of business such as consumer products (paper and envelopes) and electrical equipment (switchboards, light bulbs, and security systems), in addition to its previous lines of business. Most of these products had local brand names or were manufactured for major international companies such as General Electric or Corning Glass.

During the 1990s, a new president of RI, Sean Rhodes, the grandson of the founder, took over the business and adopted the strategy of focusing RI on three lines of business—Industrial Products, Consumer Products, and Electronics. He led the acquisition of more international businesses that fit these three categories and divested a few businesses that didn't fit. Each of the three divisions had manufacturing plants as well as marketing and distribution systems in North America, Asia, and Europe. The Industrial Products division included pipe, glass, industrial sealants and coatings, cleaning equipment, and truck parts. The Electronics division included specialty light bulbs, switchboards, computer chips, and resistors and capacitors for original equipment manufacturers. Consumer Products included dishes and glassware, paper and envelopes, and pencils and pens.

Structure

In 2004 David Javier replaced Sean Rhodes as president. He was very concerned about whether a new organization structure was needed for RI. The current structure was based on three major geographic areas—North America, Asia, and Europe—as illustrated in Exhibit 5.12. The various autonomous units within those regions reported to the office of the regional vice president. When several units existed in a single country, one of the subsidiary presidents was also responsible for coordinating the various businesses in that country, but most coordination was done through the regional vice president. Businesses were largely independent, which provided flexibility and motivation for the subsidiary managers.

The headquarters functional departments in Ontario were rather small. The three central departments—Corporate Relations and Public Affairs, Finance and Acquisitions, and Legal and Administrative—served the corporate business worldwide. Other functions such as HR management, new product development, marketing, and manufacturing all existed within individual subsidiaries and there was little coordination of these functions across geographic regions. Each business devised its own way to develop, manufacture, and market its products in its own country and region.

Organizational Problems

The problems Javier faced at RI, which were confirmed in the report on his desk, fell into three areas. First, each subsidiary acted as an independent business, using its own

EXHIBIT 5.12
Rhodes Industries Organization Chart

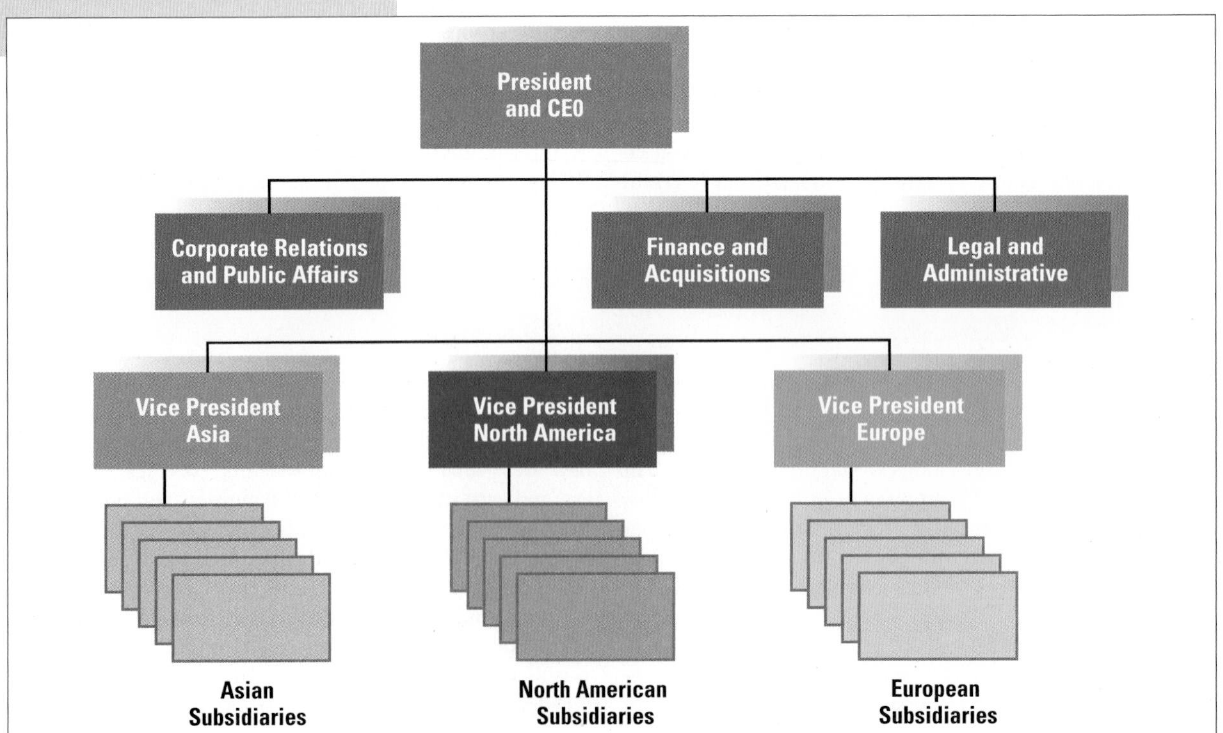

reporting systems and acting to maximize its own profits. This autonomy made it increasingly difficult to consolidate financial reports worldwide and to gain the efficiencies of uniform information and reporting systems.

Second, major strategic decisions were made to benefit individual businesses or for a country's or region's local interests. Local projects and profits received more time and resources than did projects that benefited RI worldwide. For example, an electronics manufacturer in Singapore refused to increase production of chips and capacitors for sale in the United Kingdom because it would hurt the bottom line of the Singapore operation. However, the economies of scale in Singapore would more than offset shipping costs to the United Kingdom and would enable RI to close expensive manufacturing facilities in Europe, increasing RI's efficiency and profits.

Third, there had been no transfer of technology, new product ideas, or other innovations within RI. For example, a cost-saving technology for manufacturing light bulbs in Canada had been ignored in Asia and Europe. A technical innovation that provided homeowners with cell phone access to home security systems developed in Europe had been ignored in North America. The report on Javier's desk stressed that RI was failing to disperse important innovations throughout the organization. These ignored innovations could provide significant improvements in both manufacturing and marketing worldwide. The report said, "No one at RI understands all the products and locations in a way that allows RI to capitalize on manufacturing improvements and new product opportunities." The report also said that better worldwide coordination would reduce RI's costs by 7 percent each year and increase market potential by 10 percent. These numbers were too big to ignore.

Recommended Structure

The report from the consultant recommended that RI try one of two options for improving its structure. The first alternative was to create a new international department at headquarters with the responsibility to coordinate technology transfer and product manufacturing and marketing worldwide (Exhibit 5.13). This department would have a product director for each major product line—Industrial, Consumer, and Electronics—who would have authority to coordinate activities and innovations worldwide. Each product director would have a team that would travel to each region and carry information on innovations and improvements to subsidiaries in other parts of the world.

The second recommendation was to reorganize into a worldwide product structure, as shown in Exhibit 5.14. All subsidiaries worldwide associated with a product line

EXHIBIT 5.13
Proposed Product Director Structure

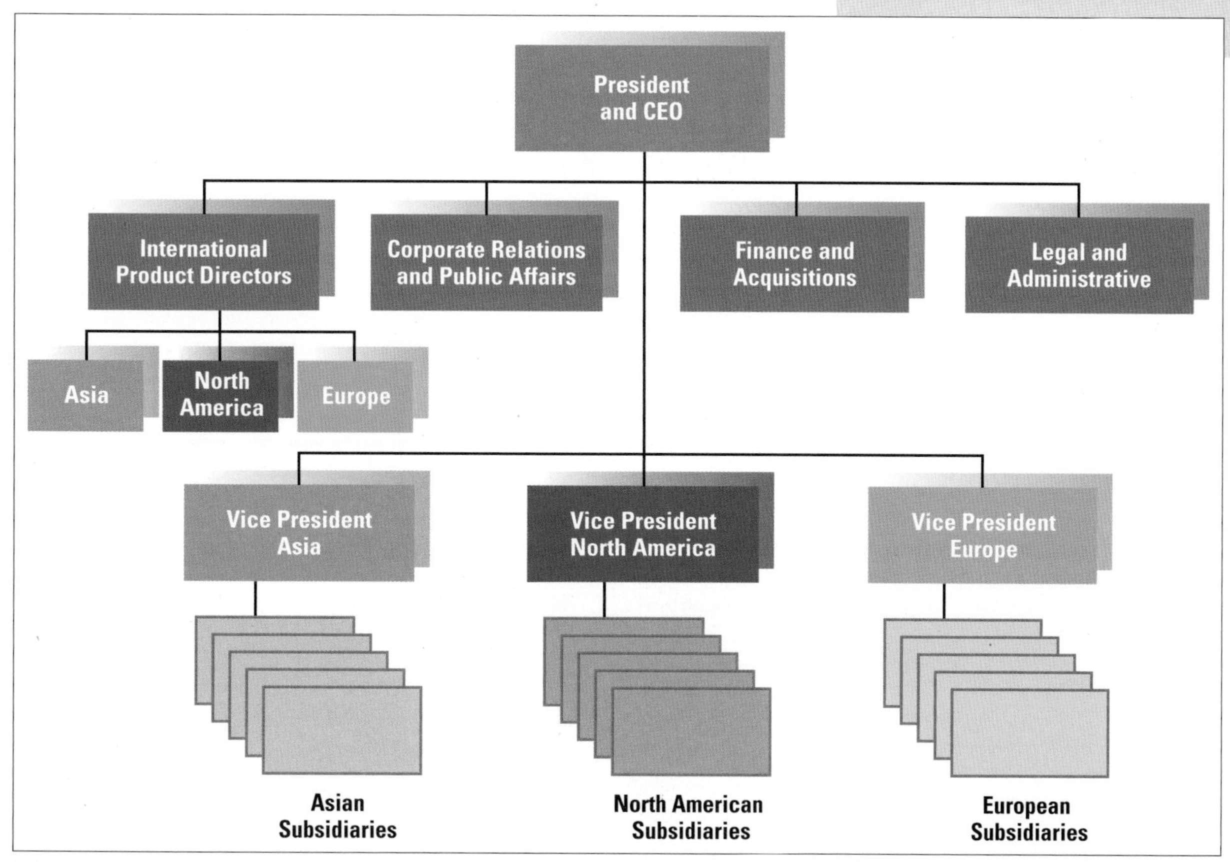

EXHIBIT 5.14
Proposed Worldwide Business Manager Structure

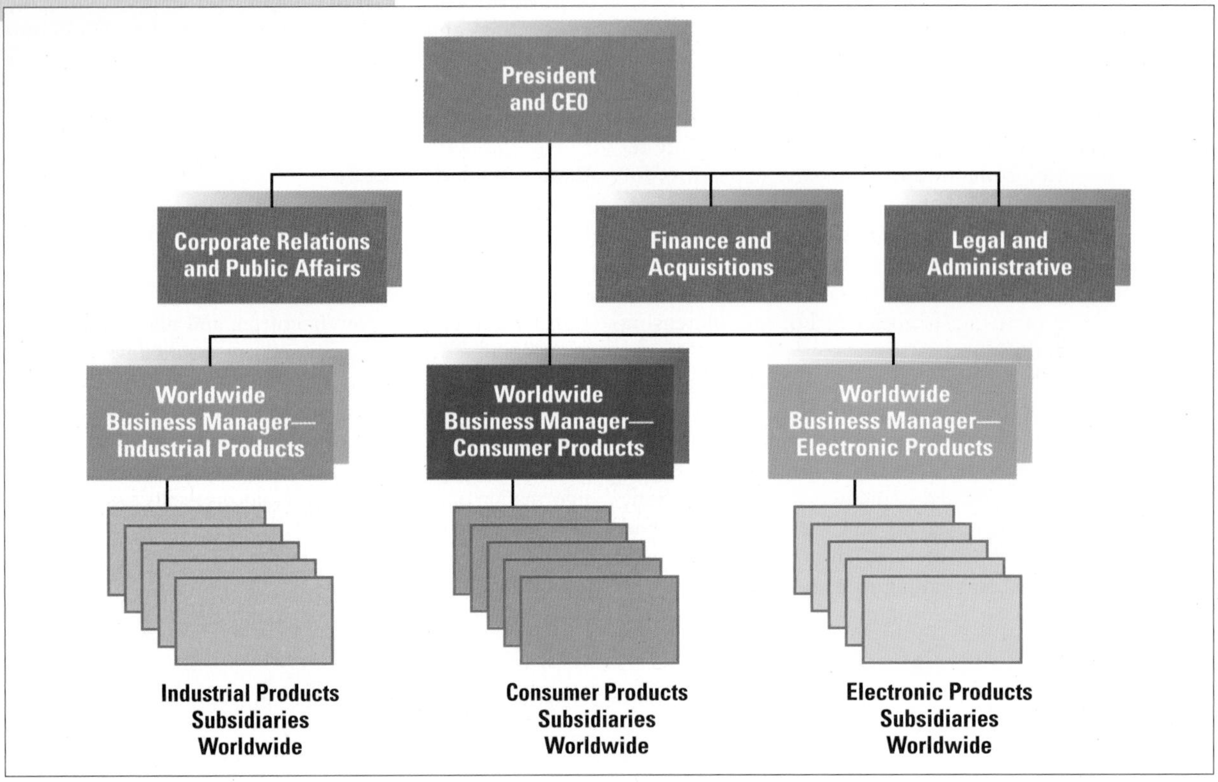

would report to the product line business manager. The business manager and staff would be responsible for developing business strategies and for coordinating all manufacturing efficiencies and product developments worldwide for its product line.

This worldwide product structure would be a huge change for RI. Many questions came to Javier's mind. Would the subsidiaries still be competitive and adaptive in local markets if forced to coordinate with other subsidiaries around the world? Would business managers be able to change the habits of subsidiary managers toward more global behavior? Would it be a better idea to appoint product director coordinators as a first step or jump to the business manager product structure right away? Javier had a hunch that the move to worldwide product coordination made sense, but he wanted to think through all the potential problems and how RI would implement the changes.

Chapter 5 Workshop Comparing Cultures[105]

As a group, rent a foreign movie (or, alternately, go to the cinema when a foreign movie is shown). Take notes as you watch the movie, looking for any differences in cultural norms compared to your own. For example, identify any differences in the following compared to your own cultural norms:

a. The way people interact with one another
b. The formality or informality of relationships
c. The attitudes toward work
d. The amount of time people spend on work versus family
e. The connection to family
f. How people have fun

Questions

1. What were the key differences you observed in the movie's culture versus your own?
2. What are the advantages and disadvantages of using movies to understand another culture?

Notes

1. Alison Tudor, "Nomura Stumbles in New Global Push," *The Wall Street Journal*, July 29, 2009, A1.
2. Paul Sonne, "Tesco's CEO-to-Be Unfolds Map for Global Expansion," *The Wall Street Journal*, June 9, 2010, B1; Bob Tita, "Deere Enhances Focus on Russia," *The Wall Street Journal* (March 24, 2011), http://online.wsj.com/article/SB10001424052748704604704576220684003808072.html (accessed August 9, 2011); Choe Sang-Hun, "Wal-Mart Selling Stores and Leaving South Korea," *The New York Times*, May 23, 2006, C5; and Miguel Bustillo, Robb Stewart, and Paul Sonne, "Wal-Mart Bids $4.6 Billion for South Africa's Massmart," *The Wall Street Journal* (September 28, 2010), http://online.wsj.com/article/SB10001424052748704654004575517300108186976.html (accessed September 28, 2010).
3. Michael A. Hitt and Xiaoming He, "Firm Strategies in a Changing Global Competitive Landscape," *Business Horizons* 51 (2008), 363–369.
4. Norihiko Shirouzu, "Chinese Inspire Car Makers' Designs," *The Wall Street Journal*, October 28, 2009; David Barboza and Nick Bunkley, "G.M., Eclipsed at Home, Soars to Top in China," *The New York Times*, July 22, 2010, A1; and Loretta Chao, Juliet Ye, and Yukari Iwatani Kane, "Apple, Facing Competition, Readies iPhone for Launch in Giant China Market," *The Wall Street Journal*, August 28, 2009, A6.
5. Qamar Rizvi, "Going International: A Practical, Comprehensive Template for Establishing a Footprint in Foreign Markets," *Ivey Business Journal* (May–June 2010), http://www.iveybusinessjournal.com/topics/global-business/going-international-a-practical-comprehensive-template-for-establishing-a-footprint-in-foreign-markets (accessed August 9, 2011).
6. Michael A. Hitt and Xiaoming He, "Firm Strategies in a Changing Global Competitive Landscape," *Business Horizons* 51 (2008), 363–369.
7. D. Barboza, "China Passes Japan as Second-Largest Economy," *The New York Times* (August 14, 2010), http://www.nytimes.com/2010/08/16/business/global/16yuan.html (accessed August 12, 2011).
8. Jenny Mero, "Power Shift," *Fortune*, July 21, 2008, 161; and "The Fortune Global 500," *Fortune*, http://money.cnn.com/magazines/fortune/global500/2011/ (accessed August 8, 2011).
9. This discussion is based heavily on Christopher A. Bartlett and Sumantra Ghoshal, *Transnational Management: Text, Cases, and Readings in Cross-Border Management*, 3rd ed. (Boston: Irwin McGraw-Hill, 2000), 94–96; and Anil K. Gupta and Vijay Govindarajan, "Converting Global Presence into Global Competitive Advantage," *Academy of Management Executive* 15, no. 2 (2001), 45–56.
10. Lauren A. E. Schuker, "Plot Change: Foreign Forces Transform Hollywood Films," *The Wall Street Journal*, July 31, 2010, A1.
11. Bustillo et al., "Wal-Mart Bids $4.6 Billion for South Africa's Massmart;" Mariko Sanchanta, "Starbucks Plans Major China Expansion," *The Wall Street Journal* (April 13, 2010), http://online.wsj.com/article/SB10001424052702304604204575181490891231672.html (accessed April 16, 2010); and Paul Beckett, Vibhuti Agarwal, and Julie Jargon, "Starbucks Brews Plan to Enter India," *The Wall Street Journal* (January 14, 2011), http://online.wsj.com/article/SB10001424052748703583404576079593558838756.html (accessed July 16, 2011).
12. Eric Bellman, "Indian Firm Takes a Hollywood Cue, Using DreamWorks to Expand Empire," *The Wall Street Journal*, September 22, 2009, B1.
13. Jim Carlton, "Branching Out; New Zealanders Now Shear Trees Instead of Sheep," *The Wall Street Journal*, May 29, 2003, A1, A10.
14. Stephanie Wong, John Liu, and Tim Culpan, "Life and Death at the iPad Factory," *BusinessWeek*, June 7–June 13, 2010, 35–36.
15. Dan Morse, "Cabinet Decisions; In North Carolina, Furniture Makers Try to Stay Alive," *The Wall Street Journal*, February 20, 2004, A1.
16. Keith H. Hammonds, "Smart, Determined, Ambitious, Cheap: The New Face of Global Competition," *Fast Company*, February 2003, 91–97; and W. Michael Cox and Richard Alm, "China and India: Two Paths to Economic Power," *Economic Letter*, Federal Reserve Bank of Dallas (August 2008), http://www.dallasfed.org/research/eclett/2008/el0808.html (accessed July 14, 2010).
17. Chris Hawley, "Aircraft Makers Flock to Mexico," *USA Today* (April 6, 2008), http://www.usatoday.com/money/industries/manufacturing/2008-04-06-aerospace_N.htm?loc=interstitialskip (accessed April 7, 2008).
18. James Flanigan, "Now, High-Tech Work Is Going Abroad," *The New York Times*, November 17, 2005, C6; and Sheridan Prasso, "Google Goes to India," *Fortune*, October 29, 2007, 160–166.
19. Todd Zaun, Gregory L. White, Norihiko Shirouzu, and Scott Miller, "More Mileage: Auto Makers Look for Another Edge Farther from Home," *The Wall Street Journal*, July 31, 2002, A1, A8.
20. Alison Stein Wellner, "Turning the Tables," *Inc.*, May 2006, 55–57.
21. Ken Belson, "Outsourcing, Turned Inside Out," *The New York Times*, April 11, 2004, Section 3, 1.
22. Based on Nancy J. Adler, *International Dimensions of Organizational Behavior*, 4th ed. (Cincinnati, OH: South-Western, 2002); Theodore T. Herbert, "Strategy and Multinational Organizational Structure: An Interorganizational Relationships Perspective," *Academy of Management Review* 9 (1984), 259–271; and Laura K. Rickey, "International Expansion—U.S. Corporations: Strategy, Stages of Development, and Structure" (unpublished manuscript, Vanderbilt University, 1991).
23. Julia Boorstin, "Exporting Cleaner Air," segment of "Small and Global," *Fortune Small Business*, June 2004, 36–48; and Purafil website, http://www.purafil.com/company/facts.aspx (accessed August 8, 2011).
24. Emily Maltby, "Expanding Abroad? Avoid Cultural Gaffes," *The Wall Street Journal*, January 19, 2010.
25. Vikas Sehgal, Ganesh Panneer, and Ann Graham, "A Family-Owned Business Goes Global," *Strategy + Business*

(September 13, 2010), http://www.strategy-business.com/article/00045?gko=aba49 (accessed August 9, 2011).

26. Michael E. Porter, "Changing Patterns of International Competition," *California Management Review* 28 (Winter 1986), 9–40.
27. William J. Holstein, "The Stateless Corporation," *BusinessWeek*, May 14, 1990, 98–115.
28. Nancy J. Adler, *International Dimensions of Organizational Behavior,* 4th ed. (Cincinnati, OH: South-Western, 2002), 8–9; and William Holstein, Stanley Reed, Jonathan Kapstein, Todd Vogel, and Joseph Weber, "The Stateless Corporation," *BusinessWeek*, May 14, 1990, 98–105.
29. Deborah Ball, "Boss Talk: Nestlé Focuses on Long Term," *The Wall Street Journal*, November 2, 2009; Transnationale website, http://www.transnationale.org/companies/nestle.php (accessed March 17, 2010); Company-Analytics website, http://www.company-analytics.org/company/nestle.php (accessed March 17, 2010); and Nestle website, http://www.nestle.com (accessed March 17, 2010).
30. Debra Sparks, "Partners," *BusinessWeek,* Special Report: Corporate Finance, October 25, 1999, 106–112.
31. David Lei and John W. Slocum, Jr., "Global Strategic Alliances: Payoffs and Pitfalls," *Organizational Dynamics* (Winter 1991), 17–29.
32. Vanessa O'Connell, "Department Stores: Tough Sell Abroad," *The Wall Street Journal,* May 22, 2008, B1.
33. Paul W. Beamish and Nathaniel C. Lupton, "Managing Joint Ventures," *Academy of Management Perspectives* (May 2009), 75–94; Stratford Sherman, "Are Strategic Alliances Working?" *Fortune,* September 21, 1992, 77–78; and David Lei, "Strategies for Global Competition," *Long-Range Planning* 22 (1989), 102–109.
34. Cyrus F. Freidheim, Jr., *The Trillion-Dollar Enterprise: How the Alliance Revolution Will Transform Global Business* (New York: Perseus Books, 1998).
35. Pete Engardio, "Emerging Giants," *BusinessWeek*, July 31, 2006, 40–49.
36. Eric Bellman and Kris Hudson, "Wal-Mart to Enter India in Venture," *The Wall Street Journal*, November 28, 2006, A3.
37. Paloma Almodóvar Martínez and José Emilio Navas López, "Making Foreign Market Entry Decisions," *Global Business and Organizational Excellence* (January–February 2009), 52–59; "About Meliá Hotels International," SolMelia.com website, http://www.solmelia.com/corporate/about-sol-melia.htm (accessed August 8, 2011); and "Sol Meliá and Jin Jiang Form Partnership," *Hotel News Now* (February, 18, 2011), http://www.hotelnewsnow.com/articles.aspx/4993/Sol-Meli%C3%A1-and-Jin-Jiang-form-partnership (accessed August 8, 2011).
38. "About Meliá Hotels International;" and "MELA HOTE: Meliá Hotels International Confirms the Positive Performance of the Business with an 8% Increase in Ebitda Up to June," 4-Traders.com (July 29, 2011), http://www.4-traders.com/MELA-HOTE-75117/news/MELA-HOTE-Meli%E1-Hotels-International-confirms-the-positive-performance-of-the-business-with-an-8-i-13730991/ (accessed August 8, 2011).
39. Sparks, "Partners."
40. Kenichi Ohmae, "Managing in a Borderless World," *Harvard Business Review* (May–June 1989), 152–161.
41. Choe Sang-Hun, "Wal-Mart Selling Stores and Leaving South Korea;" Constance L. Hays, "From Bentonville to Beijing and Beyond," *The New York Times*, December 6, 2004, C6.
42. Conrad de Aenlle, "Famous Brands Can Bring Benefit, or a Backlash," *The New York Times*, October 19, 2003, Section 3, 7.
43. Cesare R. Mainardi, Martin Salva, and Muir Sanderson, "Label of Origin: Made on Earth," *Strategy + Business* 15 (Second Quarter 1999), 42–53; and Joann S. Lublin, "Place vs. Product: It's Tough to Choose a Management Model," *The Wall Street Journal*, June 27, 2001, A1, A4.
44. David Kiley, "One Ford for the Whole Wide World," *BusinessWeek*, June 15, 2009, 58–59; Stuart Elliott, "Ford Tries a Global Campaign for Its Global Car," *The New York Times* (February 24, 2011), http://www.nytimes.com/2011/02/25/business/media/25adco.html (accessed August 9, 2011); and Mainardi, Salva, and Sanderson, "Label of Origin."
45. Richard Gibson, "U.S. Restaurants Push Abroad" *The Wall Street Journal*, June 18, 2008; and William Mellor, "Local Menu, Managers are KFC's Secret in China," *The Washington Post* (February 12, 2011), http://www.washingtonpost.com/wp-dyn/content/article/2011/02/12/AR2011021202412.html (accessed February 13, 2011).
46. José Pla-Barber, "From Stopford and Wells's Model to Bartlett and Ghoshal's Typology: New Empirical Evidence," *Management International Review* 42, no. 2 (2002), 141–156.
47. Sumantra Ghoshal and Nitin Nohria, "Horses for Courses: Organizational Forms for Multinational Corporations," *Sloan Management Review* (Winter 1993), 23–35; and Roderick E. White and Thomas A. Poynter, "Organizing for Worldwide Advantage," *Business Quarterly* (Summer 1989), 84–89.
48. Robert J. Kramer, *Organizing for Global Competitiveness: The Country Subsidiary Design* (New York: The Conference Board, 1997), 12.
49. Laura B. Pincus and James A. Belohlav, "Legal Issues in Multinational Business: To Play the Game, You Have to Know the Rules," *Academy of Management Executive* 10, no. 3 (1996), 52–61.
50. John D. Daniels, Robert A. Pitts, and Marietta J. Tretter, "Strategy and Structure of U.S. Multinationals: An Exploratory Study," *Academy of Management Journal* 27 (1984), 292–307.
51. Hay Group Study, reported in Mark A. Royal and Melvyn J. Stark, "Why Some Companies Excel at Conducting Business Globally," *Journal of Organizational Excellence* (Autumn 2006), 3–10.
52. Robert J. Kramer, *Organizing for Global Competitiveness: The Product Design* (New York: The Conference Board, 1994).
53. Robert J. Kramer, *Organizing for Global Competitiveness: The Business Unit Design* (New York: The Conference Board, 1995), 18–19.
54. Tina C. Ambos, Bodo B. Schlegelmilch, Björn Ambos, and Barbara Brenner, "Evolution of Organisational Structure and Capabilities in Internationalising Banks," *Long Range Planning* 42 (2009), 633–653; "Divisions," UniCredit website, http://www.unicreditgroup.eu/en/Business/Strategic_Business_Areas.htm (accessed August 10, 2011); and "Organizational Model,"

UniCredit website, http://www.unicreditgroup.eu/en/Business/Organizational_structure.htm (accessed August 10, 2011).

55. Carol Matlack, "Nestlé Is Starting to Slim Down at Last; But Can the World's No. 1 Food Colossus Fatten Up Its Profits As It Slashes Costs?" *BusinessWeek*, October 27, 2003, 56.
56. Robert J. Kramer, *Organizing for Global Competitiveness: The Geographic Design* (New York: The Conference Board, 1993).
57. Rakesh Sharma and Jyotsna Bhatnagar, "Talent Management—Competency Development: Key to Global Leadership," *Industrial and Commercial Training* 41, no 3 (2009), 118–132.
58. Kramer, *Organizing for Global Competitiveness: The Geographic Design,* 29–31.
59. "Group Structure," ABB website, http://www.abb.com/cawp/abbzh252/9c53e7b73aa42f7ec1256ae700541c35.aspx (accessed August 9, 2011); William Taylor, "The Logic of Global Business: An Interview with ABB's Percy Barnevik," *Harvard Business Review* (March–April 1991), 91–105; Carla Rappaport, "A Tough Swede Invades the U.S.," *Fortune,* January 29, 1992, 76–79; Raymond E. Miles and Charles C. Snow, "The New Network Firm: A Spherical Structure Built on a Human Investment Philosophy," *Organizational Dynamics* (Spring 1995), 5–18; and Manfred F. R. Kets de Vries, "Making a Giant Dance," *Across the Board* (October 1994), 27–32.
60. Ambos et al., "Evolution of Organisational Structure and Capabilities in Internationalising Banks;" and "Organizational Structure Map," UniCredit website, http://www.nicreditgroup.eu/ucg-static/downloads/Organizational_structure_map.pdf (accessed August 10, 2011).
61. Gupta and Govindarajan, "Converting Global Presence into Global Competitive Advantage."
62. Robert Frank, "Withdrawal Pains: In Paddies of Vietnam, Americans Once Again Land in a Quagmire," *The Wall Street Journal*, April 21, 2000, A1, A6.
63. C. K. Prahalad and Hrishi Bhattacharyya, "Twenty Hubs and No HQ," *Strategy + Business* (February 26, 2008), http://www.strategy-business.com/article/08102?gko=8c379 (accessed July 25, 2009).
64. The discussion of these challenges is based on Bartlett and Ghoshal, *Transnational Management.*
65. Phred Dvorak, "Why Multiple Headquarters Multiply," *The Wall Street Journal,* November 19, 2007, B1.
66. Amol Sharma and Jessica E. Vascellaro, "Google and India Test the Limits of Liberty," *The Wall Street Journal*, January 4, 2010, A16.
67. Peter Koudal and Gary C. Coleman, "Coordinating Operations to Enhance Innovation in the Global Corporation," *Strategy & Leadership* 33, no. 4 (2005), 20–32; and Steven D. Eppinger and Anil R. Chitkara, "The New Practice of Global Product Development," *MIT Sloan Management Review* (Summer 2006), 22–30.
68. David W. Norton, and B. Joseph Pine II, "Unique Experiences: Disruptive Innovations Offer Customers More 'Time Well Spent,'" *Strategy & Leadership* 37, no. 6 (2009), 4; and "The Power to Disrupt," *The Economist,* April 17, 2010, 16.
69. Jeffrey R. Immelt, Vijay Govindarajan, and Chris Trimble, "How GE is Disrupting Itself," *Harvard Business Review* (October 2009), 3–11; Daniel McGinn, "Cheap, Cheap, Cheap," *Newsweek.com* (January 21, 2010), http://www.newsweek.com/2010/01/20/cheap-cheap-cheap.html (accessed September 3, 2010); and Reena Jana, "Inspiration from Emerging Economies," *BusinessWeek,* March 23 & 30, 2009, 38–41.
70. P. Ingrassia, "Industry Is Shopping Abroad for Good Ideas to Apply to Products," *The Wall Street Journal,* April 29, 1985, A1.
71. Based on Gupta and Govindarajan, "Converting Global Presence into Global Competitive Advantage;" Giancarlo Ghislanzoni, Risto Penttinen, and David Turnbull, "The Multilocal Challenge: Managing Cross-Border Functions," *The McKinsey Quarterly* (March 2008), http://www.mckinseyquarterly.com/The_multilocal_challenge_Managing_cross-border_functions_2116 (accessed August 11, 2011); and Bert Spector, Henry W. Lane, and Dennis Shaughnessy, "Developing Innovation Transfer Capacity in a Cross-National Firm," *The Journal of Applied Behavioral Science* 45, no. 2 (June 2009), 261–279.
72. Vijay Govindarajan and Anil K. Gupta, "Building an Effective Global Business Team," *MIT Sloan Management Review* 42, no. 4 (Summer 2001), 63–71.
73. Charlene Marmer Solomon, "Building Teams Across Borders," *Global Workforce* (November 1998), 12–17.
74. Charles C. Snow, Scott A. Snell, Sue Canney Davison, and Donald C. Hambrick, "Use Transnational Teams to Globalize Your Company," *Organizational Dynamics* 24, no. 4 (Spring 1996), 50–67.
75. Robert Guy Matthews, "Business Technology: Thyssen's High-Tech Relay—Steelmaker Uses Computer Networks to Coordinate Operations on Three Continents," *The Wall Street Journal,* December 14, 2010, B9.
76. Benson Rosen, Stacie Furst, and Richard Blackburn, "Overcoming Barriers to Knowledge Sharing in Virtual Teams," *Organizational Dynamics* 36, no. 3 (2007), 259–273.
77. Gupta and Govindarajan, "Converting Global Presence into Global Competitive Advantage;" and Nadine Heintz, "In Spanish, It's *Un Equipo*; In English, It's a Team; Either Way, It's Tough to Build," *Inc.,* April 2008, 41–42.
78. Richard Pastore, "Global Team Management: It's a Small World After All," *CIO* (January 23, 2008), http://www.cio.com/article/174750/Global_Team_Management_It_s_a_Small_World_After_All (accessed May 20, 2008).
79. Quoted in Phred Dvorak, "Frequent Contact Helps Bridge International Divide" (Theory & Practice column), *The Wall Street Journal*, June 1, 2009, B4.
80. Tanya Mohn, "Going Global, Stateside," *The New York Times*, March 9, 2010, B8; and Dvorak, "Frequent Contact Helps Bridge International Divide."
81. Robert J. Kramer, *Organizing for Global Competitiveness: The Corporate Headquarters Design* (New York: The Conference Board, 1999).
82. Ghislanzoni et al., "The Multilocal Challenge."
83. Based on Christopher A. Bartlett and Sumantra Ghoshal, *Managing Across Borders: The Transnational Solution*, 2nd ed. (Boston: Harvard Business School Press, 1998), Chapter 11, 231–249.
84. See Jay Galbraith, "Building Organizations around the Global Customer," *Ivey Business Journal* (September–October 2001), 17–24, for a discussion of both formal and informal lateral networks in multinational companies.

85. This section and the BP examples are based on Morten T. Hansen and Nitin Nohria, "How to Build Collaborative Advantage," *MIT Sloan Management Review* (Fall 2004), 22ff.
86. Peter Gumbel, "Big Mac's Local Flavor," *Fortune,* May 5, 2008, 114–121.
87. Geert Hofstede, "The Interaction between National and Organizational Value Systems," *Journal of Management Studies* 22 (1985), 347–357; and Geert Hofstede, *Cultures and Organizations: Software of the Mind* (London: McGraw-Hill, 1991).
88. See Mansour Javidan and Robert J. House, "Cultural Acumen for the Global Manager: Lessons from Project GLOBE," *Organizational Dynamics* 29, no. 4 (2001), 289–305; and R. J. House, M. Javidan, Paul Hanges, and Peter Dorfman, "Understanding Cultures and Implicit Leadership Theories across the Globe: An Introduction to Project GLOBE," *Journal of World Business* 37 (2002), 3–10.
89. Mansour Javidan, Peter W. Dorfman, Mary Sully de Luque, and Robert J. House, "In the Eye of the Beholder: Cross Cultural Lessons in Leadership from Project GLOBE," *Academy of Management Perspectives* (February 2006), 67–90.
90. This discussion is based on "Culture and Organization," Reading 2-2 in Christopher A. Bartlett and Sumantra Ghoshal, *Transnational Management*, 3rd ed. (Boston: Irwin McGraw-Hill, 2000), 191–216, excerpted from Susan Schneider and Jean-Louis Barsoux, *Managing Across Cultures* (London: Prentice-Hall, 1997).
91. This discussion is based on Bartlett and Ghoshal, *Managing across Borders*, 181–201.
92. Martin Hemmert, "International Organization of R&D and Technology Acquisition Performance of High-Tech Business Units," *Management International Review* 43, no. 4 (2003), 361–382.
93. "Panel Says Toyota Failed to Listen to Outsiders," *USA Today* (May 23, 2011), http://content.usatoday.com/communities/driveon/post/2011/05/toyota-panel-calls-for-single-us-chief-paying-heed-to-criticism/1 (accessed August 12, 2011).
94. This section is based on Ming-Jer Chen and Danny Miller, "West Meets East: Toward an Ambicultural Approach to Management," *Academy of Management Perspectives* (November 2010), 17–24; Eddie Liu and Timothy Porter, "Culture and KM in China," *Vine* 40, no. 3–4 (2010), 326–333; Vincent A. Conte and Daniel Novello, "Assessing Leadership in a Chinese Company: A Case Study," *The Journal of Management Development* 27, no. 10 (2008), 1002–1016; Jean Lee, "Culture and Management—A Study of a Small Chinese Family Business in Singapore," *Journal of Small Business Management* 34, no. 3 (July 1996), 63ff; Olivier Blanchard and Andrei Shleifer, "Federalism with and without Political Centralization: China versus Russia," *IMF Staff Papers* 48 (2001), 171ff; and Nailin Bu, Timothy J. Craig, and T. K. Peng, "Reactions to Authority," *Thunderbird International Business Review* 43, no. 6 (November–December 2001), 773–795.
95. Ming-Jer Chen and Danny Miller, "West Meets East: Toward an Ambicultural Approach to Management," *Academy of Management Perspectives* (November 2010), 17–24.
96. Based on Bartlett and Ghoshal, *Managing across Borders*, 181–201.
97. Phred Dvorak and Leila Abboud, "Difficult Upgrade: SAP's Plan to Globalize Hits Cultural Barriers; Software Giant's Shift Irks German Engineers," *The Wall Street Journal*, May 11, 2007, A1.
98. Based on Bartlett and Ghoshal, *Managing across Borders*, 181–201.
99. Sumantra Ghoshal and Christopher Bartlett, "The Multinational Corporation as an Interorganizational Network," *Academy of Management Review* 15 (1990), 603–625.
100. Royston Greenwood, Samantha Fairclough, Tim Morris, and Mehdi Boussebaa, "The Organizational Design of Transnational Professional Service Firms," *Organizational Dynamics* 39, no. 2 (2010), 173–183.
101. The description of the transnational organization is based on Bartlett and Ghoshal, *Transnational Management* and *Managing Across Borders.*
102. Phred Dvorak, "How Irdeto Split Headquarters—Move to Run Dutch Firm From Beijing Means Meeting Challenges," *The Wall Street Journal*, January 7, 2008, B3; and Dvorak, "Why Multiple Headquarters Multiply."
103. Royal and Stark, "Why Some Companies Excel at Conducting Business Globally."
104. Based on Timo O. A. Lehtinen, Mika V. Mäntylä, and Jari Vanhanen, "Development and Evaluation of a Lightweight Root Cause Analysis Method (ARCA Method): Field Studies at Four Software Companies," *Information and Software Technology* 53 (2011), 1045–1061; and Walter Kuemmerle, "Go Global—Or No?" *Harvard Business Review* (June 2001), 37–49.
105. Copyright © 2003 by Dorothy Marcic. All rights reserved.

Chapter 6

The Impact of Environment

Learning Objectives

After reading this chapter you should be able to:

1. Define the task environment and its key sectors.
2. Define the general environment and its key sectors.
3. Explain the simple-complex and stable-unstable dimensions of the external environment.
4. Describe the environmental uncertainty model.
5. Explain how organizations adapt to a changing environment.
6. Understand how the environment affects organizational differentiation and integration.
7. Describe how the environment affects organic versus mechanistic management processes.
8. Specify how organizations depend on external resources.
9. Recognize how organizations influence key environment sectors.

Before reading this chapter, please check whether you agree or disagree with each of the following statements:

1 **The best way for an organization to cope with a complex environment is to develop a complex structure (rather than keep it simple and uncomplicated).**

I AGREE _____ I DISAGREE _____

2 **In a volatile, fast-changing environment, serious planning activities are a waste of time and resources.**

I AGREE _____ I DISAGREE _____

3 **Managers of business organizations should not get involved in political activities.**

I AGREE _____ I DISAGREE _____

Whatever happened to MySpace? Well, it is still around, but maybe not for long. At one time, MySpace ruled social networking. Then Facebook came along. After several attempts to revitalize the once-dominant company, including management layoffs and a shift in strategic direction, MySpace is no longer even considered a competitor. In January 2011, the company laid off about half of its 1,000 or so employees. Users had declined to less than 55 million, whereas Facebook was reporting more than 600 million. Yet Facebook has provided opportunities for other companies too. Zoosk, a fast-growing online dating service, owes its existence to Facebook. The company originally launched as an application on Facebook and experienced rapid user growth.

Changes in the environment, such as the appearance of a new company like Facebook, can create both threats and opportunities for organizations. "Facebook is both a great competitor and a benefactor here in Silicon Valley," said one venture capitalist. "Anyone who's trying to get the attention of the young Internet user now has to compete with [Facebook's] dominant position. . . . On the other hand, they have opened up a lot of opportunities." With its wide reach, powerful influence, and growing ambitions, Facebook is considered both a friend and a foe to most technology companies, including Yahoo, eBay, Google, and Microsoft. But the environment is always changing. As one executive put it when talking about MySpace's decline: "There's a lot of people who wonder if the same thing will happen to Facebook."[1]

All organizations—not just Internet companies such as Facebook, Zoosk, and Google, but traditional firms like Toyota, Goldman Sachs, General Electric, and J.C. Penney—face tremendous uncertainty in dealing with events in the external environment and often have to adapt quickly to new competition, economic turmoil, changes in consumer interests, or innovative technologies.

Purpose of This Chapter

The purpose of this chapter is to develop a framework for assessing environments and how organizations can respond to them. First we identify the organizational domain and the sectors that influence the organization. Then we explore two major environmental forces on the organization—the need for information and the need for resources. Organizations respond to these forces through structural design, planning systems, and attempts to adapt to and influence various people, events, and organizations in the external environment.

The Organization's Environment

In a broad sense the environment is infinite and includes everything outside the organization. However, the analysis presented here considers only those aspects of the environment to which the organization is sensitive and must respond to survive. Thus, **organizational environment** is defined as everything that exists outside the boundary of the organization and has the potential to affect all or part of the organization.

The environment of an organization can be understood by analyzing its domain within external sectors. An organization's **domain** is the chosen environmental field of action. It is the territory an organization stakes out for itself with respect to products, services, and markets served. Domain defines the organization's niche and defines those external sectors with which the organization will interact to accomplish its goals.

As an organization manager, keep these guidelines in mind:

Organize elements in the external environment into ten sectors for analysis: industry, raw materials, human resources, financial resources, market, technology, economic conditions, government, sociocultural, and international. Focus on sectors that may experience significant change at any time.

The environment comprises several **sectors** or subdivisions that contain similar elements. Ten sectors can be analyzed for each organization: industry, raw materials, human resources, financial resources, market, technology, economic conditions, government, sociocultural, and international. The sectors and a hypothetical organizational domain are illustrated in Exhibit 6.1. For most companies, the sectors in Exhibit 6.1 can be further categorized as either the task environment or the general environment.

Task Environment

The **task environment** includes sectors with which the organization interacts directly and that have a direct impact on the organization's ability to achieve its goals. The task environment typically includes the industry, raw materials, and market sectors, and perhaps the human resources and international sectors.

The following examples illustrate how each of these sectors can affect organizations:

- In the *industry sector*, Netflix has been a disruptive force in the home entertainment industry since it began in 1997. First, it virtually wiped out the retail video rental business. The biggest player in video rentals, Blockbuster, went bankrupt in the fall of 2010. Now Netflix is becoming a major competitive threat to television and movie providers, offering unlimited movies and television shows streamed to viewers' computers or other devices for a low monthly fee. Cable television long controlled home entertainment, but subscriptions fell for the first time in the cable companies' history in late 2010.[2]

EXHIBIT 6.1
An Organization's Environment

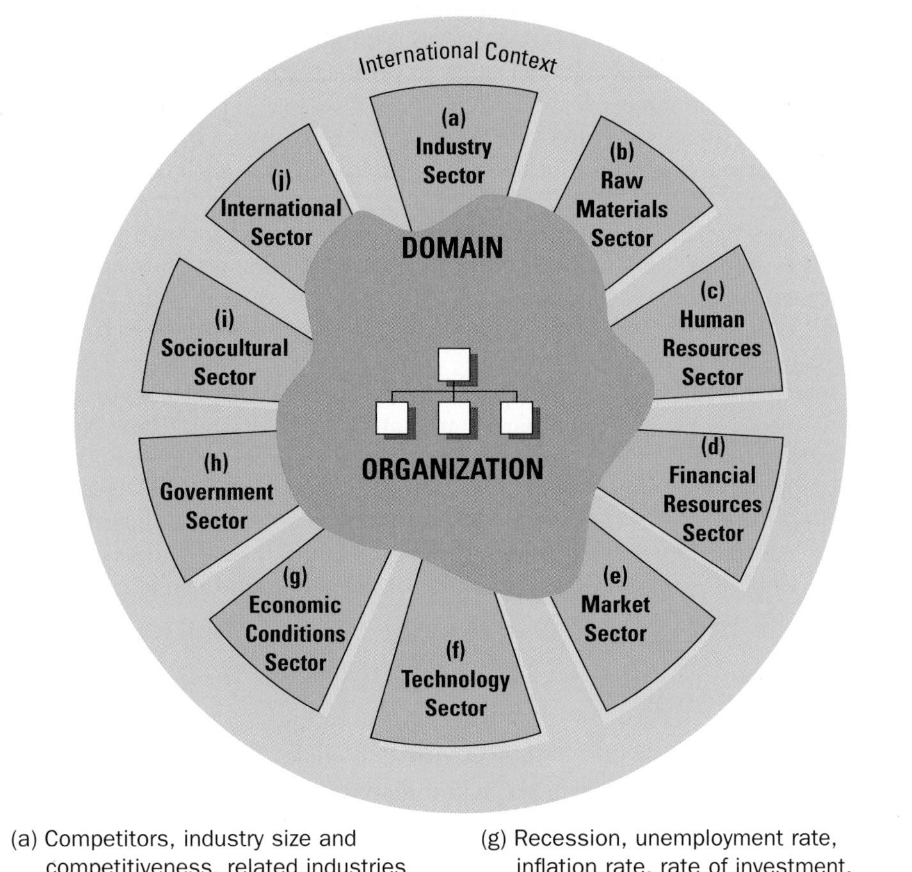

(a) Competitors, industry size and competitiveness, related industries

(b) Suppliers, manufacturers, real estate, services

(c) Labor market, employment agencies, universities, training schools, employees in other companies, unionization

(d) Stock markets, banks, savings and loans, private investors

(e) Customers, clients, potential users of products and services

(f) Techniques of production, science, computers, information technology, e-commerce

(g) Recession, unemployment rate, inflation rate, rate of investment, economics, growth

(h) City, state, federal laws and regulations, taxes, services, court system, political processes

(i) Age, values, beliefs, education, religion, work ethic, consumer and green movements

(j) Competition from and acquisition by foreign firms, entry into overseas markets, foreign customs, regulations, exchange rate

- An interesting historical example in the *raw materials sector* concerns the beverage can industry. Steelmakers owned the beverage can market until the mid-1960s, when Reynolds Aluminum Company launched a huge aluminum recycling program to gain a cheaper source of raw materials and make aluminum cans price-competitive with steel.[3]
- In the *market sector*, smart companies are paying close attention to the "Generation C" consumer. Generation C refers to people born after 1990, who will make up about 40 percent of the population in the U.S., Europe, Brazil, Russia, India, and China by 2020, and about 10 percent of the rest of the world.

For this generation, the world has always been defined by the Internet, mobile devices, social networking, and continuous connectivity. This huge cohort of consumers wants a different approach to products and services than do their parents and grandparents.[4]

- The *human resources sector* is of significant concern to every business. In China, a new labor movement is challenging business leaders, with emerging labor activist groups as well as legal aid and support networks at universities promoting workers rights. Young migrant workers are using the Internet and mobile phones to organize and spread information about poor working conditions. "Every worker is a labor lawyer by himself. They know their rights better than my HR officer," said the German owner of a factory that produces cable connectors in China.[5]
- For most companies today, the *international sector* is also a part of the task environment because of globalization and intense competition. China is already the world's largest producer of raw materials for pharmaceuticals, and several years ago a Chinese company won permission from the Food and Drug Administration to export finished medicines to the United States. India-based companies have been exporting generics to the United States for a decade, but experts believe China's growing firms, blessed with low costs and brilliant scientists, will quickly overtake them.[6]

General Environment

The **general environment** includes those sectors that might not have a direct impact on the daily operations of a firm but will indirectly influence it. The general environment often includes the government, sociocultural, economic conditions, technology, and financial resources sectors. These sectors affect all organizations eventually. Consider the following examples:

- In the *government sector*, regulations influence every phase of organizational life. Two of the most prominent and far-reaching changes in the United States in recent years were the 2010 Patient Protection and Affordable Care Act (the health care overhaul bill) and the Dodd-Frank Act (financial regulatory reform).[7] Overall, federal agencies issued 43 major new rules expanding government financial oversight. Small companies in particular are struggling with the time and expense required to meet provisions of new health care and financial reform laws.
- One significant element in the *sociocultural sector* is the "green movement." People are concerned about the natural environment and want organizations to do more to protect it. Nike began making shoes with recycled materials and eco-friendly glues. The big oil company Valero is using windmills to run its refineries more efficiently and produce petroleum-based fuels more cleanly. Walmart introduced a solar power initiative in California, began shifting to a hybrid truck fleet, and is now requiring suppliers to reduce packaging [8]
- General *economic conditions* often affect the way a company must do business. The global recession has affected companies in all industries. Briggs Inc., a small New York City company that plans customized events for corporations wanting to woo top clients or reward staff or client loyalty, had to make some changes when it began losing customers. Even huge,

elite corporations were hesitant to spend extravagantly in the weakening economy, so Briggs began looking for ways to save clients money, such as moving events to smaller venues, scaling down décor, and adding extras that didn't add to the cost. Companies can hold stylish and unique events in boutique hotels instead of Fifth Avenue locations, for instance. The strategy has been a financial burden for Briggs, but it has helped the company hold onto clients for the long term.[9]

- The *technology sector* is an area in which massive changes have occurred in recent years, from streaming video and advances in mobile technology to cloning and stem-cell research. The green movement mentioned above is also spurring major technological advances. Dozens of new companies and hundreds of academics are using genetic engineering and other biological techniques in an effort to create a "super-algae" that can be converted into diesel or jet fuel.[10]
- All businesses have to be concerned with *financial resources*, and this sector is often first and foremost in the minds of entrepreneurs. Many small business owners turned to online person-to-person (P-to-P) lending networks for small loans as banks tightened their lending standards. Jeff Walsh, for example, borrowed around $22,000 through Prosper.com for his coin laundry business. Alex Kalempa needed $15,000 to expand his business of developing racing shift systems for motorcycles, but banks offered him credit lines of only $500 to $1,000. Kalempa went to LendingClub.com, where he got the $15,000 loan at an interest rate several points lower than the banks were offering.[11]

International Environment

The international sector can directly affect many organizations, and it has become extremely important in the last few years. The auto industry, for example, has experienced profound shifts as China recently emerged as the world's largest auto market. In response, car makers are moving international headquarters into China and designing features that appeal to the Chinese market, including bigger, limousine-like back seats, advanced entertainment systems, and light-colored interiors. These trends, inspired by the Chinese market, are reflected in models sold around the world.[12]

In addition, international events can influence all the domestic sectors of the environment as well. For example, adverse weather and a workers' strike in Western Africa, which supplies about two-thirds of the world's cocoa beans, sharply increased raw materials costs for Choco-Logo, a small maker of gourmet chocolates in Buffalo, New York.[13] Farmers, fertilizer companies, food manufacturers, and grocers in the United States faced new competitive issues because of an unexpected grain shortage and rising costs related to international changes. Strong economic growth in developing countries enabled millions of people to afford richer diets, including grain-fed meat, which directly contributed to the grain shortage in the United States.[14] Countries and organizations around the world are connected as never before, and economic, political, and sociocultural changes in one part of the world eventually affect other areas

Every organization faces uncertainty domestically as well as globally. Consider the challenges facing managers at television network Univision.

Univision

IN PRACTICE

The Latino population in the United States is growing by leaps and bounds, and Univision, the giant of Spanish-language television in the U.S. now challenges the major networks CBS, NBC, ABC, and Fox, especially in large cities. Univision won the loyalty of Latino audiences by keeping English out of its programs and commercials. Its prime-time lineup is based on telenovelas from Mexico, sexy soap-opera stories that attract a vast audience. Nielsen ratings indicate that Univision has 90 of the 100 most-watched Spanish-language shows in the United States.

But there's a shift taking place that Univision managers have so far failed to respond to: the interests and tastes of viewers are changing much more rapidly than Univision's shows. Births, not immigration, are now the main source of Latino growth, and American-born Latinos aren't interested in the same type of programs their parents and grandparents were. "I think of [Univision] as a horse-and-buggy company," said David R. Morse, president and CEO of New American Dimensions, which conducted a study of younger Latino viewers. Younger Latinos are more likely to speak English as their primary language, are better educated than their parents, and are more prone to marry outside their ethnic group. They want a broader variety of programs, and many, particularly teenagers, prefer English-language television or bilingual programming. "I can't even carry a complete conversation [in Spanish] with my grandma," said 18-year-old Esmeralda Hernandez.

Second- and third-generation bilingual or English-speaking Latinos are largely underserved by both Spanish and English language networks. Although they are ethnically proud, they don't feel they have to prove themselves. They just want quality programming that addresses their interests. Jeff Valdez, founder of SiTV, currently the only English language television network for the growing Latino population, says young Latinos "want to see themselves on screen. They want to hear their stories."[15]

Univision has recently boosted its in-house production of programs to be more competitive with English-language rivals and the growing number of Spanish-language networks.[16] Can Univision transform its programming to satisfy younger Latino viewers, or is it destined to gradually decline as more competitors come on the scene with hip programs that attract the coveted audience of 18-to-34-year-olds? Univision is still a powerhouse, and it can succeed for years using its current formula. If the network doesn't keep pace with changing demands from the environment, however, it could indeed go the way of the horse and buggy.

Television networks are not the only organizations that have to adapt to both subtle and massive shifts in the environment. In the following sections, we will discuss in greater detail how companies can cope with and respond to environmental uncertainty and instability.

The Changing Environment

How does the environment influence an organization? The patterns and events occurring in the environment can be described along several dimensions, such as whether the environment is stable or unstable, homogeneous or heterogeneous, simple or complex; the *munificence,* or amount of resources available to support the organization's growth; whether those resources are concentrated or dispersed; and the degree of consensus in the environment regarding the organization's intended domain.[17] These dimensions boil down to two essential ways the environment influences organizations: the need for information about the environment and the need for resources from the environment. The environmental conditions of complexity and change create a greater need to gather information and to respond based on that information. The organization also is concerned with scarce material and financial resources and with the need to ensure availability of resources.

Environmental uncertainty pertains primarily to those sectors illustrated in Exhibit 6.1 that an organization deals with on a regular, day-to-day basis. Although sectors of the general environment—such as economic conditions, social trends, or technological changes—can create uncertainty for organizations, determining an organization's environmental uncertainty generally means focusing on sectors of the *task environment*, such as how many elements (e.g., people, other organizations, events) the organization deals with regularly, how rapidly these various elements change, and so forth. To assess uncertainty, each sector of the organization's task environment can be analyzed along dimensions such as stability or instability and degree of complexity.[18] The total amount of uncertainty felt by an organization is the uncertainty accumulated across relevant task environment sectors.

Organizations must cope with and manage uncertainty to be effective. **Uncertainty** means that decision makers do not have sufficient information about environmental factors, and they have a difficult time predicting external changes. Uncertainty increases the risk of failure for organizational responses and makes it difficult to compute costs and probabilities associated with decision alternatives.[19] The remainder of this section will focus on the information perspective, which is concerned with uncertainty created by the extent to which the environment is simple or complex and the extent to which events are stable or unstable. Later in the chapter, we discuss how organizations influence the environment to acquire needed resources.

Simple–Complex Dimension

The **simple–complex dimension** concerns environmental complexity, which refers to heterogeneity, or the number and dissimilarity of external elements (e.g., competitors, suppliers, industry changes, government regulations) that affect an organization's operations. The more external elements that regularly influence the organization, and the greater number of other companies in an organization's domain, the greater the complexity. A complex environment is one in which the organization interacts with and is influenced by numerous diverse external elements. In a simple environment, the organization interacts with and is influenced by only a few similar external elements.

For example, a family-owned hardware store in a suburban community is in a simple environment. The store does not have to deal with complex technologies or extensive government regulations, and cultural and social changes have little impact. Human resources are not a problem because the store is run by family members and part-time help. The only external elements of real importance are a few competitors, suppliers, and customers. On the other hand, oil companies like BP, Exxon Mobil, and Royal Dutch Shell operate in a highly complex environment. They use multiple, complex technologies, cope with numerous ever-changing government regulations, are significantly affected by international events, compete for scarce financial resources and highly trained engineers, interact with numerous suppliers, customers, contractors, and partners, respond to changing social values, and deal with complex legal and financial systems in multiple countries. This large number of external elements in an oil company's domain creates a complex environment.

Stable–Unstable Dimension

The **stable–unstable dimension** refers to whether the environment in which the organization operates is dynamic. An environmental domain is stable if it remains essentially the same over a period of months or years. Under unstable conditions, environmental elements shift rapidly. Consider what is happening in the environment for video game console manufacturers.

Sony Corporation, Nintendo, Microsoft

IN PRACTICE

Gaming sales are booming, but that isn't helping the PlayStation. Sony Corporation's PlayStation and Sega's Saturn, with their CD drives and 3D graphics, once defined the cutting edge of coolness when it came to videogames. Nintendo got an edge with its DS handheld videogame player and had a decided hit with the Wii. But videogame consoles such as these and others are increasingly insignificant. Does anybody even remember Atari, one of the early giants of the industry? Sega, once the world's Number 3 console seller behind Sony and Nintendo, exited the console business entirely and is finding success developing software and games for PCs and wireless devices as well as for platforms from Sony, Nintendo, and Microsoft.

Today, more people are playing games on their smartphones and computers or on social networking sites like Facebook. Gaming on social networks is expected to grow 46 percent, and on smartphones it will grow 19 percent annually over the next couple of years, while spending on console game discs is projected to drop 6 percent a year. There are around 85,000 game titles available for Apple's iPhone and iPad alone. Why pay $40 for a game disc when you can download one to your smartphone for less than five bucks? The power of consoles for playing interactive games doesn't matter so much in the new digital world. "The traditional videogame guys have lost market share, eyeball share, and coolness share," said market analyst J.T. Taylor. A startup company called OnLive is testing a service to allow people to stream games through a broadband connection the same way Netflix streams movies.

Despite changes in the industry, Sony is developing a new PlayStation 4 and Microsoft is said to be developing a new Xbox. Both companies are aiming to make the new versions all-in-one entertainment devices rather than just game boxes. Slowing sales of Nintendo's Wii and DS handheld caused the company to post lower profits for the first time in six years. Both Sony and Microsoft introduced upgraded products that cut into Nintendo's sales. As competition grows and the industry becomes more fragmented, Sony, Microsoft, and Nintendo, the three big players in consoles, are battling it out for a shrinking part of the gaming dollar. [20]

As this example shows, instability often occurs when consumer interests shift, new technologies are introduced, or competitors react with aggressive moves and countermoves regarding advertising and new products or services. Sometimes specific, unpredictable events—such as reports of lead-tainted paint in

Mattel toys made in China, the Pakistani government's attempt to block access to certain videos on YouTube, or the discovery of heart problems related to pain drugs such as Vioxx and Celebrex—create unstable conditions for organizations. Today, freewheeling bloggers, Twitterers, and YouTubers are a tremendous source of instability for scores of companies. For example, when United Airlines refused to compensate a musician for breaking his $3,500 guitar, he wrote a song and posted a derogatory music video about his lengthy negotiations with the company on YouTube. Word spread quickly across the Internet, and United just as quickly responded with a settlement offer.[21] Similarly, Domino's Pizza managers had to act quickly after two pranksters posted a video showing employees fouling a pizza on the way to delivery. Domino's responded with a video of its own. The company president apologized and thanked the online community for bringing the issue to his attention. He promised that the wrongdoers would be prosecuted and outlined steps Domino's was taking to ensure the episode would never happen again. By engaging in an online conversation about the crisis, Domino's demonstrated concern for its customers and squelched further rumors and fears.[22]

Environmental domains are increasingly unstable for most organizations.[23] This chapter's Book Mark on page 260 examines the volatile nature of today's business world and gives some tips for managing in a fast-shifting environment. Although environments are more unstable for most organizations today, an example of a traditionally stable environment is a public utility.[24] In the rural Midwest, demand and supply factors for a public utility are stable. A gradual increase in demand may occur, which is easily predicted over time. Toy companies, by contrast, have an unstable environment. Hot new toys are difficult to predict, a problem compounded by the fact that children are losing interest in toys at a younger age, their interest captured by video and computer games, electronics, and the Internet. Adding to the instability for toymakers is the shrinking retail market, with big toy retailers going out of business trying to compete with discounters such as Walmart. Toymakers are trying to attract more customers in developing markets such as China, Poland, Brazil, and India to make up for the declining U.S. market, but hitting the target in those countries has proven to be a challenge. Companies such as Fisher-Price, owned by Mattel, can find their biggest products languishing on shelves as shoppers turn to less expensive locally made toys in countries where brand consciousness doesn't come into play. As one toy analyst said, "Chinese kids have been growing for 5,000 years without the benefits of Fisher-Price."[25]

Framework

The simple–complex and stable–unstable dimensions are combined into a framework for assessing environmental uncertainty in Exhibit 6.2. In the *simple, stable* environment, uncertainty is low. There are only a few external elements in a limited number of environmental sectors (e.g. suppliers, customers) to contend with, and they tend to remain stable. The *complex, stable* environment represents somewhat greater uncertainty. A large number of elements (e.g. suppliers, customers, government regulations, industry changes, unions, economic conditions) have to be scanned, analyzed, and acted upon for the organization to perform well. External elements do not change rapidly or unexpectedly in this environment.

BOOKMARK

6.0 HAVE YOU READ THIS BOOK?

Confronting Reality: Doing What Matters to Get Things Right

By Lawrence A. Bossidy and Ram Charan

The business world is changing at an increasingly rapid pace. That is the reality that spurred Larry Bossidy, retired chairman and CEO of Honeywell International, and Ram Charan, a noted author, speaker, and business consultant, to write *Confronting Reality: Doing What Matters to Get Things Right.* Too many managers, they believe, are tempted to hide their heads in the sand of financial issues rather than face the confusion and complexity of the organization's environment.

LESSONS FOR FACING REALITY

For many companies, today's environment is characterized by global hyper-competition, declining prices, and the growing power of consumers. Bossidy and Charan offer some lessons to leaders for navigating in a fast-changing world.

- *Understand the environment as it is now and is likely to be in the future, rather than as it was in the past.* Relying on the past and conventional wisdom can lead to disaster. Kmart, for example, stuck to its old formula as Walmart gobbled its customers and carved out a new business model. Few could have predicted in 1990, for example, that Walmart would now be America's biggest seller of groceries.
- *Seek out and welcome diverse and unorthodox ideas.* Managers need to be proactive and open-minded toward conversing with employees, suppliers, customers, colleagues, and anyone else they come in contact with. What are people thinking about? What changes and opportunities do they see? What worries them about the future?
- *Avoid the common causes of manager failure to confront reality: filtered information, selective hearing, wishful thinking, fear, emotional overinvestment in a failing course of action, and unrealistic expectations.* For example, when sales and profits fell off a cliff at data-storage giant EMC, managers displayed a bias toward hearing good news and believed the company was only experiencing a blip in the growth curve. When Joe Tucci was named CEO, however, he was determined to find out if the slump was temporary. By talking directly with top leaders at his customers' organizations, Tucci was able to face the reality that EMC's existing business model based on high-cost technology was dead. Tucci implemented a new business model to fit that reality.
- *Ruthlessly assess your organization.* Understanding the internal environment is just as important. Managers need to evaluate whether their company has the talent, commitment, and attitude needed to drive the important changes. At EMC, Tucci realized his sales force needed an attitude shift to sell software, services, and business solutions rather than just expensive hardware. The arrogant, hard-driving sales tactics of the past had to be replaced with a softer, more customer-oriented approach.

STAYING ALIVE

Staying alive in today's business environment requires that managers stay alert. Managers should always be looking at their competitors, broad industry trends, technological changes, shifting government policies, changing market forces, and economic developments. At the same time, they work hard to stay in touch with what their customers really think and really want. By doing so, leaders can confront reality and be poised for change.

Confronting Reality: Doing What Matters to Get Things Right, by Lawrence A. Bossidy and Ram Charan, is published by Crown Business Publishing.

Even greater uncertainty is felt in the *simple, unstable* environment.[26] Rapid change creates uncertainty for managers. Even though the organization has few external elements, those elements are hard to predict (such as shifting social trends or changing customer interests), and they react unexpectedly to organizational initiatives. The greatest uncertainty for an organization occurs in the *complex, unstable* environment. A large number of elements in numerous environmental sectors impinge upon the organization, and they shift frequently or react strongly to organizational initiatives. When several sectors change simultaneously, the environment becomes turbulent.[27]

EXHIBIT 6.2
Framework for Assessing Environmental Uncertainty

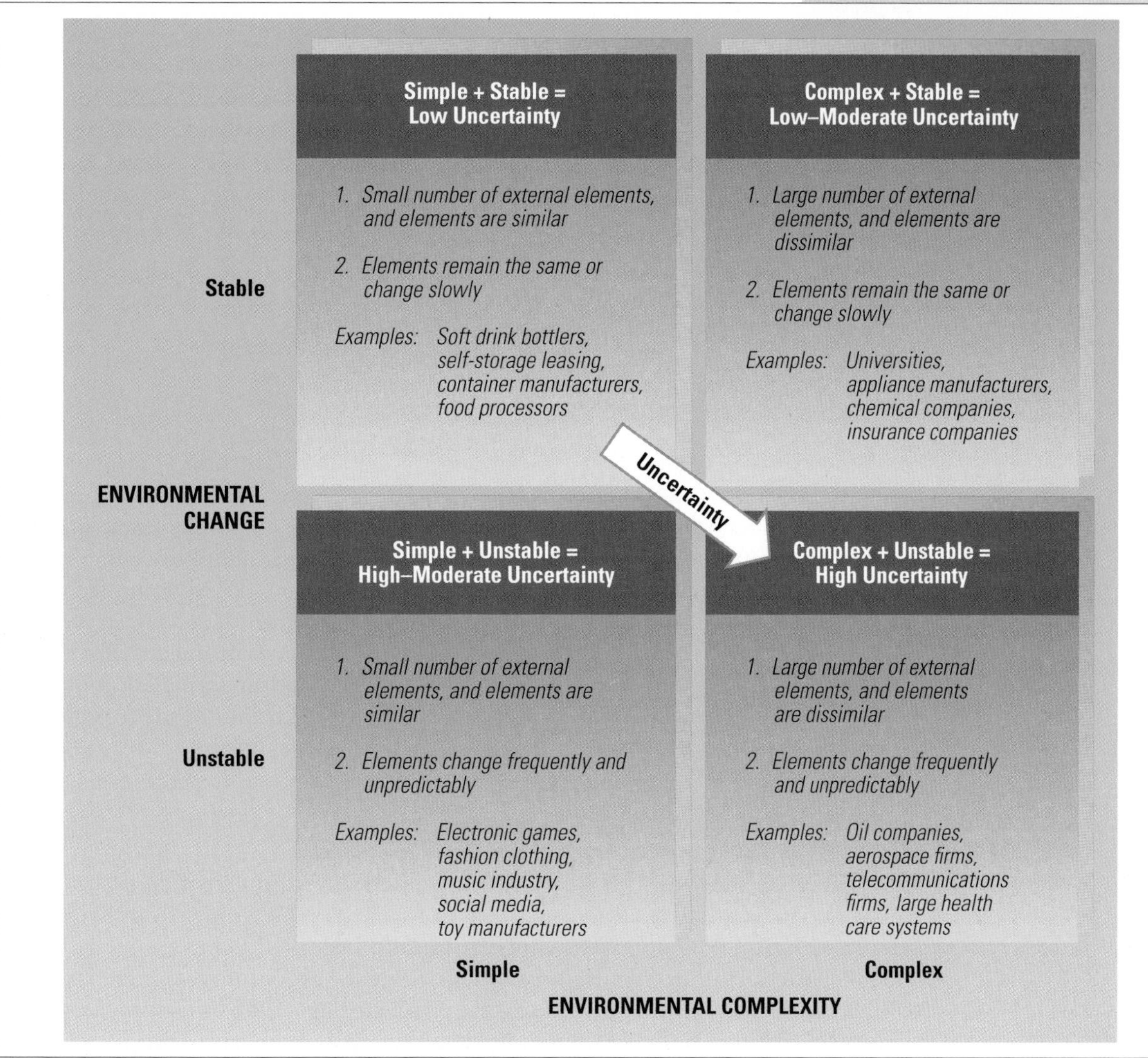

Simple + Stable =
Low Uncertainty
1. Small number of external elements, and elements are similar
2. Elements remain the same or change slowly
Examples: Soft drink bottlers, self-storage leasing, container manufacturers, food processors
Complex + Stable =
Low–Moderate Uncertainty
1. Large number of external elements, and elements are dissimilar
2. Elements remain the same or change slowly
Examples: Universities, appliance manufacturers, chemical companies, insurance companies
Stable
ENVIRONMENTAL CHANGE
Uncertainty
Simple + Unstable =
High–Moderate Uncertainty
1. Small number of external elements, and elements are similar
2. Elements change frequently and unpredictably
Examples: Electronic games, fashion clothing, music industry, social media, toy manufacturers
Complex + Unstable =
High Uncertainty
1. Large number of external elements, and elements are dissimilar
2. Elements change frequently and unpredictably
Examples: Oil companies, aerospace firms, telecommunications firms, large health care systems
Unstable
Simple
Complex
ENVIRONMENTAL COMPLEXITY

Source: *Administrative Science Quarterly*, Characteristics of Organizational Environments and Perceived Environments Uncertainty by Robert Duncan vol. 17, pp. 313–327, September 1972. Reprinted by permission of SAGE Publications.

A soft drink distributor functions in a simple, stable environment. Demand changes only gradually. The distributor has an established delivery route, and supplies of soft drinks arrive on schedule. State universities, appliance manufacturers, and insurance companies are in somewhat stable, complex environments. A large number of external elements are present, but although they change, changes are gradual and predictable.

Toy manufacturers are in simple, unstable environments. Organizations that design, make, and sell toys, as well as those that make electronic games or are involved in the clothing or music industry, face shifting supply and demand.

Fashion apparel company Zara launches around 11,000 new products annually to try to meet changing customer tastes, for example.[28] Although there may be few elements to contend with—e.g., suppliers, customers, competitors—they are difficult to predict and change abruptly and unexpectedly.

The telecommunications industry and the oil industry face complex, unstable environments. Many external sectors are changing simultaneously. In the case of airlines, in just a few years the major carriers were confronted with an air-traffic controller shortage, aging fleets of planes, labor unrest, soaring fuel prices, the entry of new low-cost competitors, a series of major air-traffic disasters, and a drastic decline in customer demand. Between 2001 and 2008, four large airlines and many smaller ones went through bankruptcy, and the airlines collectively laid off 170,000 employees.[29]

Adapting to a Changing Environment

Once you see how environments differ with respect to change and complexity, the next question is, "How do organizations adapt to each level of environmental uncertainty?" Environmental uncertainty represents an important contingency for organization structure and internal behaviors. Recall from Chapter 2 that organizations facing uncertainty often use structural mechanisms that encourage horizontal communication and collaboration to help the company adapt to changes in the environment. In this section we discuss in more detail how the environment affects organizations. An organization in a certain environment will be managed and controlled differently from an organization in an uncertain environment with respect to positions and departments, organizational differentiation and integration, control processes, and future planning and forecasting. Organizations need to have the right fit between internal structure and the external environment.

Adding Positions and Departments

As complexity and uncertainty in the external environment increase, so does the number of positions and departments within the organization, leading to increased internal complexity. This relationship is part of being an open system. Each sector in the external environment requires an employee or department to deal with it. The human resource department deals with unemployed people who want to work for the company. The marketing department finds customers. Procurement employees obtain raw materials from hundreds of suppliers. The finance group deals with bankers. The legal department works with the courts and government agencies. E-business departments handle electronic commerce, and information technology departments deal with the increasing complexity of computerized information and knowledge management systems. For example, President Barack Obama added a Chief Technology Officer position and a Chief Information Officer position to the U.S. government. Many organizations added Chief Compliance Officer or Chief Governance Officer positions to deal with the complexities associated with the 2002 Sarbannes-Oxley Act, often referred to as SOX. SOX required several types of corporate governance reforms, including better internal monitoring to reduce the risk of fraud, certification of financial results by top executives, improved measures for internal auditing, and enhancing public financial disclosure. Adding new positions and departments is a common way for organizations to adapt to growing environmental complexity and uncertainty.

Building Relationships

The traditional approach to coping with environmental uncertainty was to establish buffer departments. The purpose of **buffering roles** is to absorb uncertainty from the environment.[30] The technical core performs the primary production activity of an organization. Buffer departments surround the technical core and exchange materials, resources, and money between the environment and the organization. They help the technical core function efficiently. The purchasing department buffers the technical core by stockpiling supplies and raw materials. The human resource department buffers the technical core by handling the uncertainty associated with finding, hiring, and training production employees.

A more recent approach many organizations use is to drop the buffers and expose the technical core to the uncertain environment. These organizations no longer create buffers because they believe being well connected to customers and suppliers is more important than internal efficiency. Highly uncertain environments require rapid transfer of information and knowledge so the organization can adapt quickly. Teams, as described in Chapter 2, often work directly with customers and other parties outside the organization.[31] At Total Attorneys, a Chicago-based company that provides software and services to small law firms, cross-functional teams work with customers who test and provide feedback on products as they are developed.[32] Opening up the organization to the environment by building closer relationships with external parties makes it more fluid and adaptable.

Boundary-spanning roles link and coordinate an organization with key elements in the external environment. Boundary spanning is primarily concerned with the exchange of information to detect and bring into the organization information about changes in the environment and to send information into the environment that presents the organization in a favorable light.[33]

Organizations have to keep in touch with what is going on in the environment so that managers can respond to market changes and other developments. A study of high-tech firms found that 97 percent of competitive failures resulted from lack of attention to market changes or the failure to act on vital information.[34] To detect and bring important information into the organization, boundary personnel scan the environment. For example, a market-research department scans and monitors trends in consumer tastes. Boundary spanners in engineering and research and development departments scan new technological developments, innovations, and raw materials. Boundary spanners prevent the organization from stagnating by keeping top managers informed about environmental changes. The greater the uncertainty in the environment, the greater the importance of boundary spanners.[35]

One approach to boundary spanning is **business intelligence**, which refers to the high-tech analysis of large amounts of internal and external data to spot patterns and relationships that might be significant. For example, Verizon uses business intelligence to actively monitor customer interactions so that it can catch problems and fix them almost immediately.[36] Tools to automate the process are a hot area of software, with companies spending billions on business-intelligence software in recent years.[37]

Business intelligence is related to another important area of boundary spanning, known as *competitive intelligence* (CI). Competitive intelligence gives top executives a systematic way to collect and analyze public information about rivals and use it to make better decisions.[38] Using techniques that range from Internet

BRIEFCASE

As an organization manager, keep these guidelines in mind:

Scan the external environment for threats, changes, and opportunities. Use boundary-spanning roles, such as market research and intelligence teams, to bring into the organization information about changes in the environment. Enhance boundary-spanning capabilities when the environment is uncertain.

surfing to digging through trash cans, intelligence professionals dig up information on competitors' new products, manufacturing costs, or training methods and share it with top leaders. Intelligence teams are the newest wave of CI activities. An **intelligence team** is a cross-functional group of managers and employees, usually led by a competitive intelligence professional, who work together to gain a deep understanding of a specific business issue, with the aim of presenting insights, possibilities, and recommendations to top leaders.[39] Intelligence teams can provide insights that enable managers to make more informed decisions about goals, as well as devise contingency plans and scenarios related to major competitive issues.

The boundary task of sending information into the environment to represent the organization is used to influence other people's perception of the organization. In the marketing department, advertising and sales people represent the organization to customers. Purchasers may call on suppliers and describe purchasing needs. The legal department informs lobbyists and elected officials about the organization's needs or views on political matters. Many companies set up special Web pages and blogs to present the organization in a favorable light.

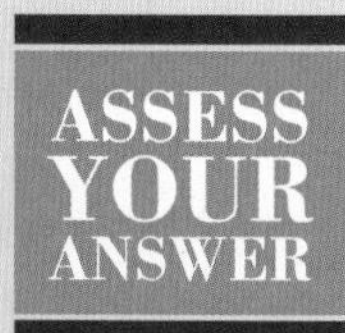

1 The best way for an organization to cope with a complex environment is to develop a complex structure (rather than keep it simple and uncomplicated).

ANSWER: *Agree.* As an organization's environment becomes more complex, the organization has to add jobs, departments, and boundary spanning roles to cope with all the elements in the environment. When environmental sectors are complex, there is no way for an organization to stay simple and uncomplicated and continue to be effective.

Differentiation and Integration

Another response to environmental uncertainty is the amount of differentiation and integration among departments. Organizational **differentiation** refers to "the differences in cognitive and emotional orientations among managers in different functional departments, and the difference in formal structure among these departments."[40] When the external environment is complex and rapidly changing, organizational departments become highly specialized to handle the uncertainty in that part of the external environment each department works with. Success in each environmental sector (human resources, technology, government, and so forth) requires special expertise and behavior. Employees in an R&D department thus have unique attitudes, values, goals, and education that distinguish them from employees in manufacturing or sales departments.

A study by Paul Lawrence and Jay Lorsch examined three organizational departments—manufacturing, research, and sales—in 10 corporations.[41] This study found that each department evolved toward a different orientation and structure to deal with specialized parts of the external environment. Exhibit 6.3 illustrates the market, scientific, and manufacturing subenvironments identified by Lawrence and Lorsch. As shown in the exhibit, each department interacted

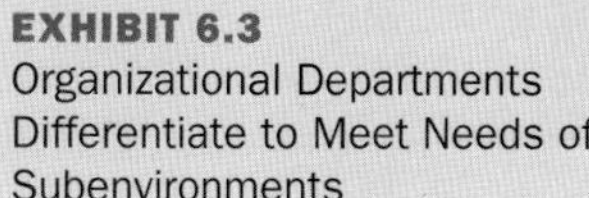

EXHIBIT 6.3
Organizational Departments Differentiate to Meet Needs of Subenvironments

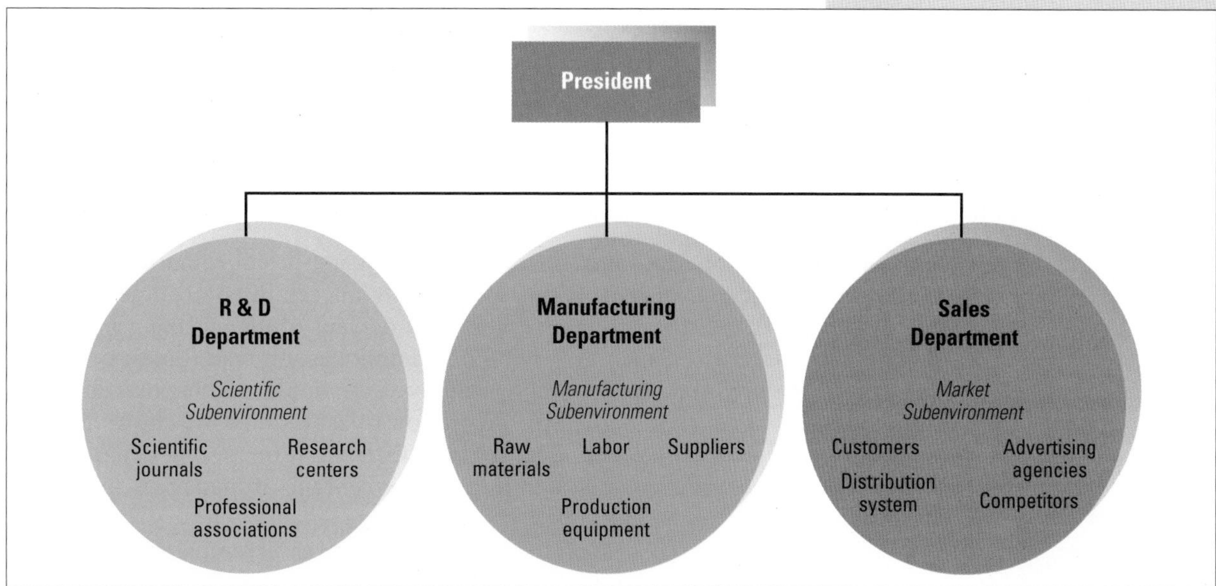

with different external groups. The differences that evolved among departments within the organizations are shown in Exhibit 6.4. To work effectively with the scientific subenvironment, R&D had a goal of quality work, a long time horizon (up to five years), an informal structure, and task-oriented employees. Sales was at the opposite extreme. It had a goal of customer satisfaction, was oriented toward the short term (two weeks or so), had a very formal structure, and was socially oriented.

One outcome of high differentiation is that coordination among departments becomes difficult. More time and resources must be devoted to achieving coordination when attitudes, goals, and work orientation differ so widely. **Integration** is the quality of collaboration among departments.[42] Formal integrators are often required to coordinate departments. When the environment is highly uncertain, frequent changes require more information processing to achieve horizontal coordination, so integrators become a necessary addition to the organization structure. Sometimes integrators are called

EXHIBIT 6.4
Differences in Goals and Orientations among Organizational Departments

Characteristic	R&D Department	Manufacturing Department	Sales Department
Goals	New developments, quality	Efficient production	Customer satisfaction
Time horizon	Long	Short	Short
Interpersonal orientation	Mostly task	Task	Social
Formality of structure	Low	High	High

Source: Based on Paul R. Lawrence and Jay W. Lorsch, *Organization and Environment* (Homewood, IL: Irwin, 1969), 23–29.

EXHIBIT 6.5
Environmental Uncertainty and Organizational Integrators

Industry	Plastics	Foods	Container
Environmental uncertainty	High	Moderate	Low
Departmental differentiation	High	Moderate	Low
Percent management in integrating roles	22%	17%	0%

Source: Based on Jay W. Lorsch and Paul R. Lawrence, "Environmental Factors and Organizational Integration," *Organizational Planning: Cases and Concepts* (Homewood, IL.: Irwin and Dorsey, 1972), 45.

liaison personnel, project managers, brand managers, or coordinators. As illustrated in Exhibit 6.5, organizations with highly uncertain environments and a highly differentiated structure assign about 22 percent of management personnel to integration activities, such as serving on committees, on task forces, or in liaison roles.[43] In organizations characterized by very simple, stable environments, almost no managers are assigned to integration roles. Exhibit 6.5 shows that, as environmental uncertainty increases, so does differentiation among departments; hence, the organization must assign a larger percentage of managers to coordinating roles.

Lawrence and Lorsch's research concluded that organizations perform better when the levels of differentiation and integration match the level of uncertainty in the environment. Organizations that performed well in uncertain environments had high levels of both differentiation and integration, while those performing well in less uncertain environments had lower levels of differentiation and integration.

As an organization manager, keep these guidelines in mind:

Match internal organization structure to the external environment. If the external environment is complex, make the organization structure complex. Associate a stable environment with a mechanistic structure and an unstable environment with an organic structure. If the external environment is both complex and changing, make the organization highly differentiated and organic, and use mechanisms to achieve coordination across departments.

Organic Versus Mechanistic Management Processes

Recall our discussion of organic and mechanistic designs from Chapter 1. The degree of uncertainty in the external environment is one primary contingency that shapes whether an organization will function best with an organic or a mechanistic design. Tom Burns and G.M. Stalker observed 20 industrial firms in England and discovered that internal management processes were related to the external environment.[44] When the external environment was stable, the internal organization was characterized by standard rules, procedures, a clear hierarchy of authority, formalization, and centralization. Burns and Stalker called this a **mechanistic** organization system, as described in Chapter 1 and illustrated in Exhibit 1.7.

In rapidly changing environments, the internal organization was much looser, free-flowing, and adaptive, with a loose hierarchy and decentralized decision making. Burns and Stalker used the term **organic** to characterize this type of organization. Complete the questionnaire in the "How Do You Fit the Design?" box for some insight into whether you are more suited to working in an organic organization or a mechanistic one.

As environmental uncertainty increases, organizations tend to become more organic, which means decentralizing authority and responsibility to lower levels, encouraging employees to take care of problems by working directly with

How Do You Fit the Design?

MIND AND ENVIRONMENT

Does your mind best fit an organization in a certain or an uncertain environment? Think back to how you thought or behaved as a student, employee, or in a formal or informal leader position. Please answer whether each following item was Mostly True or Mostly False for you.

	Mostly True	Mostly False
1. I always offered comments on my interpretation of data or issues.	___	___
2. I welcomed unusual viewpoints of others even if we were working under pressure.	___	___
3. I made it a point to attend industry trade shows and company (school) events.	___	___
4. I explicitly encouraged others to express opposing ideas and arguments.	___	___
5. I asked "dumb" questions.	___	___
6. I enjoyed hearing about new ideas even when working toward a deadline.	___	___
7. I expressed a controversial opinion to bosses and peers.	___	___
8. I suggested ways of improving my and others' ways of doing things.	___	___

Scoring: Give yourself one point for each item you marked as Mostly True. If you scored less than 5, your mindfulness level may be suited to an organization in a stable rather than unstable environment. A score of 5 or above suggests a higher level of mindfulness and a better fit for an organization in an uncertain environment.

Interpretation: In an organization in a highly uncertain environment everything seems to be changing. In that case, an important quality for a professional employee or manager is "mindfulness," which includes the qualities of being open minded and an independent thinker. In a stable environment, an organization will be more "mechanistic," and a manager without mindfulness may perform okay because much work can be done in the traditional way. In an uncertain environment, everyone needs to facilitate new thinking, new ideas, and new ways of working. A high score on this exercise suggests higher mindfulness and a better fit with an "organic" organization in an uncertain environment.

Source: These questions are based on ideas from R.L. Daft and R.M. Lengel, *Fusion Leadership,* Chapter 4 (San Francisco, CA: Berrett Koehler, 2000); B. Bass and B. Avolio, *Multifactor Leadership Questionnaire,* 2nd ed. (Menlo Park, CA: Mind Garden, Inc); and Karl E. Weick and Kathleen M. Sutcliffe, *Managing the Unexpected: Assuring High Performance in an Age of Complexity* (San Francisco, CA: Jossey-Bass, 2001).

one another, encouraging teamwork, and taking an informal approach to assigning tasks and responsibility. Thus, the organization is more fluid and is able to adapt continually to changes in the external environment.[45] Guiltless Gourmet, which sells low-fat tortilla chips and other high-quality snack foods, provides an example. When large companies like Frito Lay entered the low-fat snack-food market, Guiltless Gourmet shifted to a flexible network structure to remain competitive. The company redesigned itself to become basically a full-time marketing organization, while production and other activities were outsourced. An 18,000-square-foot plant in Austin was closed and the workforce cut from 125 to about 10 core people who handle marketing and sales promotions. The flexible structure allowed Guiltless Gourmet to adapt quickly to changing market conditions.[46]

Planning, Forecasting, and Responsiveness

The whole point of increasing internal integration and shifting to a more organic design is to enhance the organization's ability to quickly respond to sudden changes in an uncertain environment. It might seem that in an environment where everything is changing all the time, planning is useless. However, in uncertain environments, planning and environmental forecasting actually become *more* important as a way to keep the organization geared for a coordinated, speedy response. When the environment is stable, the organization can concentrate on current operational problems and day-to-day efficiency. Long-range planning and forecasting are not needed because environmental demands in the future will be much the same as they are today.

With increasing environmental uncertainty, planning and forecasting become necessary.[47] Indeed, surveys of multinational corporations have found that as environments become more turbulent, managers increase their planning activities, particularly in terms of planning exercises that encourage learning, continual adaptation, and innovation.[48] For example, following the September 11, 2001, terrorist attacks in the United States, there was a surge in the use of scenario and contingency planning as a way to manage uncertainty. Although their popularity waned for several years, these approaches made a comeback due to increasing environmental turbulence and the recent global financial crisis. A *McKinsey Quarterly* survey found that 50 percent of respondents said scenario planning was playing a bigger role in planning or was newly added to the planning process in 2009 as compared to the previous year, reflecting managers' greater concern with managing uncertainty.[49]

With scenario planning, managers mentally rehearse different scenarios based on anticipating various changes that could affect the organization. Scenarios are like stories that offer alternative, vivid pictures of what the future will look like and how managers will respond. Royal Dutch/Shell Oil has long used scenario building and has been a leader in speedy response to massive changes that other organizations failed to perceive until it was too late.[50] Planning can soften the adverse impact of external shifts. Organizations that have unstable environments often establish a separate planning department. In an unpredictable environment, planners scan environmental elements and analyze potential moves and countermoves by other organizations.

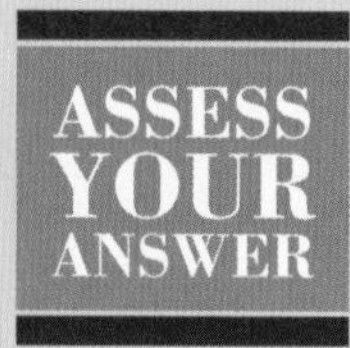

2 In a volatile, fast-changing environment, serious planning activities are a waste of time and resources.

ANSWER: *Disagree.* General Colin Powell once said, "No battle plan survives contact with the enemy."[51] Yet no wise general would go into battle without one. Serious planning becomes more important in a turbulent environment, even though a plan will not last long. Planning and environmental forecasting help managers anticipate and be prepared to respond to changes. Lack of planning makes more sense in a stable, easily predictable environment.

Planning, however, cannot substitute for other actions, such as effective boundary spanning and adequate internal integration and coordination. The organizations that are most successful in uncertain environments are those that keep everyone in close touch with the environment so they can spot threats and opportunities, enabling the organization to respond immediately.

Framework for Responses to Environmental Change

Exhibit 6.6 summarizes the ways in which environmental uncertainty influences organizational characteristics. The change and complexity dimensions are combined and illustrate four levels of uncertainty. The low uncertainty environment is simple and stable. Organizations in this environment can have few departments and a mechanistic design. In a low–moderate uncertainty environment, more departments are needed, along with more integrating roles to coordinate the departments. Some planning may occur. Environments that are high–moderate uncertainty are unstable but simple. Organization design is organic and decentralized. Planning is emphasized and managers are quick to make internal changes as needed. The high uncertainty environment is both complex

EXHIBIT 6.6
Contingency Framework for Environmental Uncertainty and Organizational Responses

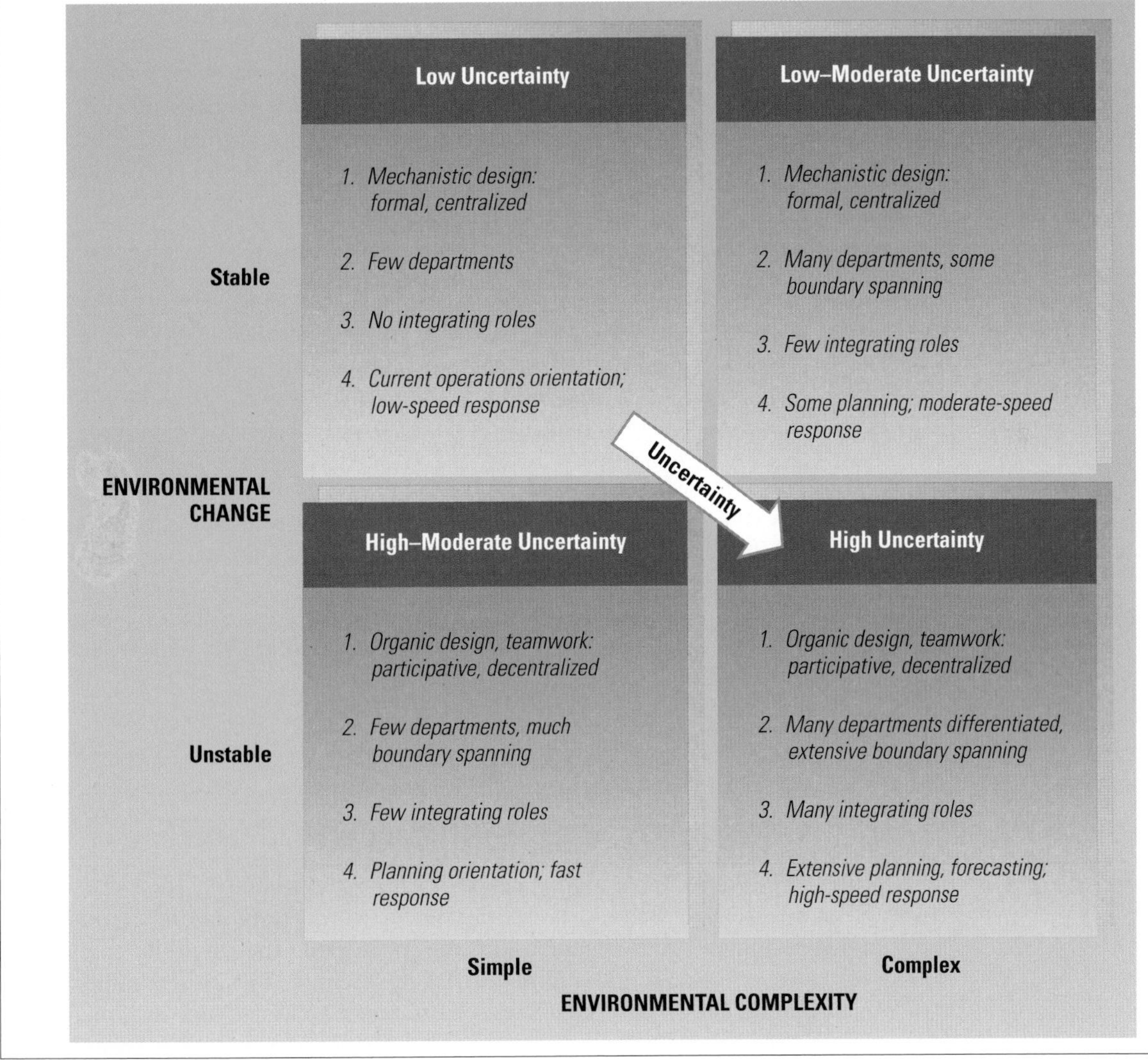

and unstable and is the most difficult environment from a management perspective. Organizations are large and have many departments, but they are also organic. A large number of management personnel are assigned to coordination and integration, and the organization uses boundary spanning, planning, and forecasting to enable a high-speed response to environmental changes.

Dependence on External Resources

Thus far, this chapter has described several ways in which organizations adapt to the lack of information and to the uncertainty caused by environmental change and complexity. We turn now to the third characteristic of the organization–environment relationship that affects organizations, which is the need for material and financial resources. The environment is the source of scarce and valued resources essential to organizational survival. Research in this area is called the *resource-dependence perspective*. **Resource dependence** means that organizations depend on the environment but strive to acquire control over resources to minimize their dependence.[52] Organizations are vulnerable if vital resources are controlled by other organizations, so they try to be as independent as possible. Organizations do not want to become too vulnerable to other organizations because of negative effects on performance.

Although companies like to minimize their dependence, when costs and risks are high they also team up to share scarce resources and be more competitive on a global basis. Formal relationships with other organizations present a dilemma to managers. Organizations seek to reduce vulnerability with respect to resources by developing links with other organizations, but they also like to maximize their own autonomy and independence. Organizational linkages require coordination,[53] and they reduce the freedom of each organization to make decisions without concern for the needs and goals of other organizations. Inter-organizational relationships thus represent a tradeoff between resources and autonomy. To maintain autonomy, organizations that already have abundant resources will tend not to establish new linkages. Organizations that need resources will give up independence to acquire those resources. For example, DHL, the express delivery unit of Germany's Deutsche Post AG, lost billions of dollars trying to take over the U.S. package delivery market. By 2008, the company had entered into a partnership with UPS to have that company handle DHL parcels in the United States. The two organizations continue to compete in overseas markets. In the face of $3 billion in losses, difficulty building a local management team in the United States, and maintenance problems at U.S. package handling facilities, Deutsche Post's CEO Frank Appel called the partnership "a pragmatic and realistic strategy" for his company's U.S. operations.[54] Resource dependence was discussed in more detail in Chapter 4.

Influencing External Resources

In response to the need for resources, organizations try to maintain a balance between depending on other organizations and preserving their own independence. Organizations maintain this balance through attempts to modify, manipulate, or control elements of the external environment (such as other organizations, government regulators) to meet their needs.[55] To survive, the focal organization often tries to reach out and change or control its environment. Two strategies

Establishing Formal Relationships	Influencing Key Sectors
1. Acquire an ownership stake	1. Change where you do business (your domain)
2. Form joint ventures and partnerships	2. Use political activity, regulation
3. Lock in key players	3. Join in trade associations
4. Recruit executives	4. Avoid illegitimate activities
5. Use advertising and public relations	

EXHIBIT 6.7
Organizing Strategies for Controlling the External Environment

can be adopted to influence resources in the external environment: establish favorable relationships with other organizations and shape the organization's environment.[56] Techniques to accomplish each of these strategies are summarized in Exhibit 6.7. As a general rule, when organizations sense that valued resources are scarce, they will use the strategies in Exhibit 6.7 rather than go it alone. Notice how dissimilar these strategies are from the responses to environmental change and complexity described in Exhibit 6.6. The dissimilarity reflects the difference between responding to the need for resources and responding to the need for information.

Establishing Formal Relationships

Building formal relationships includes techniques such as acquiring ownership, establishing joint ventures and partnerships, developing connections with important people in the environment, recruiting key people, and using advertising and public relations.

Acquire an Ownership Stake. Companies use various forms of ownership to reduce uncertainty in an area important to the acquiring company. For example, a firm might buy a part of or a controlling interest in another company, giving it access to technology, products, or other resources it doesn't currently have.

A greater degree of ownership and control is obtained through acquisition or merger. An *acquisition* involves the purchase of one organization by another so that the buyer assumes control, such as when Google bought YouTube, eBay bought PayPal, and Walmart purchased Britain's ASDA Group. A *merger* is the unification of two or more organizations into a single unit.[57] Sirius Satellite Radio and XM Satellite Radio Holdings merged to become Sirius XM Radio. The merger enabled the companies to combine resources and share risks to be more competitive against digital music providers and other emerging types of music distribution. In the past few years, there has been a huge wave of acquisition and merger activity in the telecommunications industry, reflecting how these companies cope with the tremendous uncertainty they face. Health care is another industry where companies use ownership to deal with an uncertain environment.

IN PRACTICE

Johns Hopkins Medicine

Johns Hopkins Hospital in Bethesda, Maryland, is owned by Johns Hopkins Medicine. So is the Howard County General Hospital in Columbia, Maryland, Suburban Hospital in Bethesda, Maryland, and Sibley Hospital, located in one of the wealthiest neighborhoods in the District of Columbia.

A wave of consolidations is hitting the U.S. health care industry, partly because of the uncertainty associated with the new health care reform law. Part of the legislation calls for "accountable care organizations" that will be paid by Medicare to serve all enrollees in a given service area and share in the savings if they meet quality and cost targets. In addition, payments from both government and private insurers will likely be more restrictive under the law. Many people in the health care industry believe that merging with other organizations to create large, integrated systems will be needed to meet the challenge of this shifting environment. "It's fair to say that [independent] hospitals are talking with everyone, feeling like they don't want to be the last one standing," said Steven Thompson, senior vice-president for Johns Hopkins Medicine.

Large systems have a better chance of getting financial capital for new services or equipment, negotiating better deals with suppliers and realizing other efficiencies, and hiring the best doctors targeting critical illnesses. Because of changes in the industry, more doctors prefer working for hospitals rather than running their own private practices, for example, but most standalone hospitals find it a daunting idea to consider hiring groups of doctors.[58]

Form Joint Ventures and Partnerships. When there is a high level of complementarity between the business lines, geographical positions, or skills of two companies, the firms often go the route of a strategic alliance rather than ownership through merger or acquisition.[59] Such alliances are formed through contracts and joint ventures.

Contracts and joint ventures reduce uncertainty through a legal and binding relationship with another firm. Contracts come in the form of *license agreements* that involve the purchase of the right to use an asset (such as a new technology) for a specific time and *supplier arrangements* that contract for the sale of one firm's output to another. Contracts can provide long-term security by tying customers and suppliers to specific amounts and prices. For example, the Italian fashion house Versace forged a deal to license its primary asset—its name—for a line of designer eyeglasses.[60]

Joint ventures result in the creation of a new organization that is formally independent of the parents, although the parents will have some control.[61] Madrid-based tech startup FON formed a joint venture with British phone carrier BT to install FON wi-fi technology in the modems of nearly 2 million BT customers. Office Depot and Reliance Retail Limited, a division of India's largest private-sector employer, entered into a joint venture to provide office products and services to business customers in India. Food and agricultural corporation Cargill Inc. has numerous joint ventures around the world, such as the one with Spanish cooperative Hojiblance to source, trade, and supply customers worldwide with private label and bulk olive oils. As evidenced by these short examples, many joint ventures are undertaken to share risks when companies are doing business in other countries or on a global scale.

Lock in Key Players. **Cooptation** occurs when leaders from important sectors in the environment are made part of an organization. It takes place, for example, when influential customers or suppliers are appointed to the board of directors, such as when the senior executive of a bank sits on the board of a manufacturing company. As a board member, the banker may become psychologically coopted into the interests of the manufacturing firm.

An **interlocking directorate** is a formal linkage that occurs when a member of the board of directors of one company sits on the board of directors of another company. The individual is a communications link between companies and can influence policies and decisions. When one individual is the link between two companies, this is typically referred to as a **direct interlock**. An **indirect interlock** occurs when a director of company A and a director of company B are both directors of company C. They have access to one another but do not have direct influence over their respective companies.[62] Research shows that, as a firm's financial fortunes decline, direct interlocks with financial institutions increase. Financial uncertainty facing an industry also has been associated with greater indirect interlocks between competing companies.[63] However, during the economic turmoil of recent years, some companies, including Apple and Google, have run up against a long-standing U.S. federal law that bars direct interlocks between competing companies. Arthur Levinson, chairman of Roche Holding AG's Genentech, for example, resigned from the Google board after the Federal Trade Commission began investigating his participation on both the Google and Apple boards. Similarly, Eric Schmidt, Executive Chairman and former CEO of Google, resigned from the Apple board for the same reason, as the two companies compete in a growing number of businesses.[64]

Important business or community leaders also can be appointed to other organizational committees or task forces. By serving on committees or advisory panels, these influential people learn about the needs of the company and are more likely to include the company's interests in their decision making. Today, many companies face uncertainty from environmental pressure groups, so organizations are trying to bring in leaders from this sector, such as when DuPont appointed environmentalists to its biotechnology advisory panel.[65]

Recruit Executives. Transferring or exchanging executives also offers a method of establishing favorable linkages with external organizations. For example, the high-frequency trading firm Getco LLC hired a former associate director in the Securities and Exchange Commission's Division of Trading and Markets to be part of its regulatory and compliance team.[66] The aerospace industry often hires retired generals and executives from the Department of Defense. These generals have personal friends in the department, so the aerospace companies obtain better information about technical specifications, prices, and dates for new weapons systems. They can learn the needs of the defense department and are able to present their case for defense contracts in a more effective way. Companies without personal contacts find it nearly impossible to get a defense contract. Having channels of influence and communication between organizations reduces financial uncertainty and dependence for an organization.

Get Your Side of the Story Out. A traditional way of establishing favorable relationships is through advertising. Organizations spend large amounts of money to influence the tastes and opinions of consumers. Advertising is especially important in highly competitive industries and in industries that experience variable demand. For example, since the U.S. Food and Drug Administration loosened regulations to permit advertising of prescription drugs in the United States, the major pharmaceutical companies have spent nearly $5 billion annually on advertisements such as a cute cartoon bee pushing Nasonex spray for allergies or heart attack survivors promoting the benefits of cholesterol-fighting Lipitor.[67]

Public relations is similar to advertising, except that stories often are free and aimed at public opinion. Public relations people cast an organization in a favorable light in speeches, on websites, in press reports, and on television. Public relations attempts to shape the company's image in the minds of customers, suppliers, government officials, and the broader public. Blogging, tweeting, and social networking have become important components of public relations activities for many companies today.[68] General Motors launched an online public-relations campaign to rebuild trust with dealers and customers after emerging from bankruptcy

BRIEFCASE

As an organization manager, keep these guidelines in mind:

Reach out and control external sectors that threaten needed resources. Influence the domain by engaging in political activity, joining trade associations, and establishing favorable relationships. Establish relationships through ownership, joint ventures and strategic partnerships, cooptation, interlocking directorates, and executive recruitment. Reduce the amount of change or threat from the external environment so the organization will not have to change internally.

protection. Part of the campaign includes GM's "Fastlane" blog, designed to give a more transparent glimpse into the workings of the beleaguered automaker.[69]

Influencing Key Sectors

In addition to establishing favorable linkages, organizations often try to change the environment. There are four techniques for influencing or changing a firm's environment.

Change Where You Do Business. Early in this chapter, we talked about the organization's *domain* and the ten sectors of the environment. An organization's domain is not fixed. Managers make decisions about which business to be in, the markets to enter, and the suppliers, banks, employees, and location to use, and this domain can be changed if necessary to keep the organization competitive.[70] Walmart, which has long focused on building big stores in suburban areas, is now planning to open dozens of tiny stores in U.S. cities. Expanding its domain into cities is one way Walmart is coping with the increased competition from dollar chains and other low-cost competitors that are grabbing some of the giant retailer's customers.[71]

An organization can seek new environmental relationships and drop old ones. Managers may try to find a domain where there is little competition, no government regulation, abundant suppliers, affluent customers, and barriers to keep competitors out. Acquisition and divestment are two techniques for altering the domain. For example, Google has acquired a number of companies to expand its domain beyond Internet search, including Android (mobile phone platform), Applied Semantics (search advertising solutions), Slide (social gaming), DoubleClick (display ad technology), and On2 (video compression).[72] Divestment occurred when JC Penney sold off its chain of Eckerd drug stores to focus resources on the department store and when Deutsche Telekom sold T-Mobile USA to AT&T to get out of the U.S. wireless market. Barnes & Noble is altering its domain as more readers switch from print to e-books.

Barnes & Noble

IN PRACTICE

Barnes & Noble, which has dominated the bookstore retail industry for four decades, has a new superstore on Manhattan's Upper East Side. But depending on which direction you look in the store, you might have trouble finding a book. There's a lot of shelf space devoted to Art Deco flight clocks, baby blankets, adult games, and assorted other merchandise.

The digital revolution is changing all the rules of the book industry. E-books are still in their infancy, but they are coming on strong and forcing retailers (as well as others in the industry) to change. Leonard Riggio, Barnes & Noble's chairman, and other managers are trying to shift the company into a more diverse retailer, selling a variety of merchandise as well as showcasing the company's Nook e-reader and digital book products. Some analysts doubt that any traditional book retailers can survive. Borders Group, once the nation's second largest book chain, filed for bankruptcy in mid-2011 and began selling off all its assets and closing its remaining 399 stores. Once-thriving mall bookstores have virtually disappeared, and the number of small independent book retailers continues to decline.

Barnes & Noble stumbled badly several years ago when it pulled the plug on its fledgling digital reading business. The company was one of the first to invest in digital books, investing in a handled device called the Rocket eBook reader in 1998. But managers didn't hang in there through the turmoil and uncertainty of the new business and pulled out in

2003. By the time Barnes & Noble introduced the Nook in 2009, the market was practically owned by Amazon's Kindle, which has about 80 percent of the digital book business. However, Barnes & Noble is making a big investment in software and technology to sell more digital downloads. The company has fired most of its book buyers and is hiring about 20 software and technology engineers to replace them.[73]

Altering its domain is the only way Barnes & Noble can hope to survive. Billionaire investor Ron Burkle recently increased his stake in the company, saying he believes the brand name has staying power. Time will tell. "I would say that there's nothing we wouldn't put under consideration," said chairman Leonard Riggio.[74]

Get Political. Political activity includes techniques to influence government legislation and regulation. Political strategy can be used to erect regulatory barriers against new competitors or to squash unfavorable legislation. Corporations also try to influence the appointment to agencies of people who are sympathetic to their needs.

Health insurance companies are heavily lobbying federal and state officials to try to ward off strict regulation of insurance premiums and company profits under the new health care law. Large retailers such as Walmart and Target are lobbying to change laws so that Amazon.com will be required to collect sales taxes. And Facebook has a Washington office with a staff of eight people lobbying legislators primarily regarding tighter privacy restrictions on online companies.[75]

Many CEOs believe they should participate directly in lobbying. CEOs have easier access than lobbyists and can be especially effective when they do the politicking. Political activity is so important that "informal lobbyist" is an unwritten part of almost any CEO's job description.[76] Top executives at Amerilink Telecom Corporation did some serious politicking as they tried to open the U.S. market to telecommunications equipment manufactured by China's Huawei Technologies Company.

Huawei Technologies

IN PRACTICE

Huawei Technologies has tried for years to break into the U.S. market, but security concerns have thwarted its ambitions. Alleged ties to the Chinese government and military have U.S. officials worried that allowing equipment from the company could disrupt or intercept critical U.S. communications.

For its most recent effort in the United States, a bid for a multibillion-dollar network upgrade at Sprint Nextel, Huawei partnered with U.S. consulting firm Amerilink, a company founded by William Owens, former vice chairman of the Joint Chiefs of Staff under President Bill Clinton. Owens and other top executives immediately launched an extensive lobbying campaign, meeting with numerous officials from Congress and the Obama administration. In addition, the company recruited several former government officials to aid in lobbying, including former Congressional leader Richard Gebhardt, Gordon England, who served as deputy secretary of defense and homeland security under President George W. Bush, and former World Bank President James Wolfensohn.

Despite the heavy lobbying efforts, Huawei's joint bid with Amerilink was rejected by Sprint after government officials allegedly expressed serious concerns to Sprint managers about security risks. In addition, U.S. lawmakers recently approved a provision to the Senate's National Defense Authorization Act that gives military agencies the power to force technology vendors like Sprint to exclude suppliers and subcontractors that the U.S. government considers risky.[77]

Despite the failure of lobbying efforts by Amerilink, this example shows how companies use political activity to try to influence government opinion and legislation that affects the organization's success. Huawei executives staunchly deny that they have any ties to the Chinese military and will continue their campaign to enter the U.S. market. Some analysts believe they will eventually succeed. Huawei is already a mainstream provider of telecommunications equipment in Europe and Asia and was recently selected by India's Bharti Airtel Ltd. as one of the suppliers for its third-generation wireless network.[78]

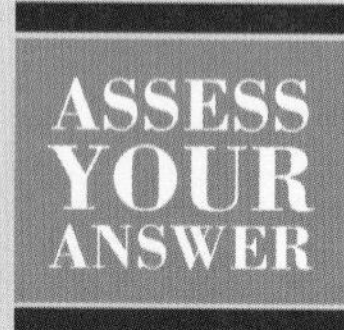

3 Managers of business organizations should not get involved in political activities.

ANSWER: *Disagree.* Smart business managers get involved in lobbying and other political activities to try to make sure the consequences of new laws and regulations are mostly positive for their own firms. Companies pay huge fees to associations and lobbyists to make sure government actions work out in their favor.

Unite with Others. Much of the work to influence the external environment is accomplished jointly with other organizations that have similar interests. For example, most large pharmaceutical companies belong to Pharmaceutical Research and Manufacturers of America. Manufacturing companies are part of the National Association of Manufacturers, and retailers join the Retail Industry Leaders Association. The American Petroleum Institute is the leading trade group for oil and gas companies. By pooling resources, these organizations can pay people to carry out activities such as lobbying legislators, influencing new regulations, developing public relations campaigns, and making campaign contributions. Primerica is using the resources and influence of the American Council of Life Insurers to push for changes in state licensing exams, which the company believes put minorities at a disadvantage. Primerica, unlike most large insurance companies, focuses on selling basic term life insurance and depends almost exclusively on middle-income consumers rather than selling pricier policies. Company managers say the way the test questions are phrased limits their ability to expand their corps of minority agents that could better serve minority communities.[79]

Don't Fall into Illegitimate Activities. Illegitimate activities represent the final technique companies sometimes use to control their environmental domain, but this technique typically backfires. Conditions such as low profits, pressure from senior managers, or scarce environmental resources may lead managers to adopt behaviors not considered legitimate.[80] One study found that companies in industries with low demand, shortages, and strikes were more likely to be convicted for illegal activities, suggesting that illegal acts are an attempt to cope with resource scarcity. Some nonprofit organizations have been found to use illegitimate or illegal actions to bolster their visibility and reputation as they compete with other organizations for scarce grants and donations, for example.[81]

Types of illegitimate activities include payoffs to foreign governments, illegal political contributions, promotional gifts, and wiretapping. Bribery is one of the most frequent types of illegitimate activity, particularly in companies operating globally. Energy companies face tremendous uncertainty, for example, and need foreign governments to approve giant investments and authorize risky projects. Under pressure to win contracts in Nigeria, Albert "Jack" Stanley, a former executive at KBR (then a division of Halliburton Company), admits he orchestrated a total of about $182 million in bribes to get Nigerian officials to approve the construction of a liquefied natural gas plant in that country. Stanley faces up to seven years in prison and a hefty fine after pleading guilty.[82] In Germany, executives at both Siemens and Volkswagen have been charged with bribing labor representatives on their companies' supervisory boards. German law requires that firms give as many as half of their supervisory board seats to labor representatives. Executives need the board's support to carry out their plans and strategies for the company, and some resort to bribery to get the cooperation they need.[83]

Organization–Environment Integrative Framework

The relationships illustrated in Exhibit 6.8 summarize the two major themes about organization–environment relationships discussed in this

EXHIBIT 6.8
Relationship between Environmental Characteristics and Organizational Actions

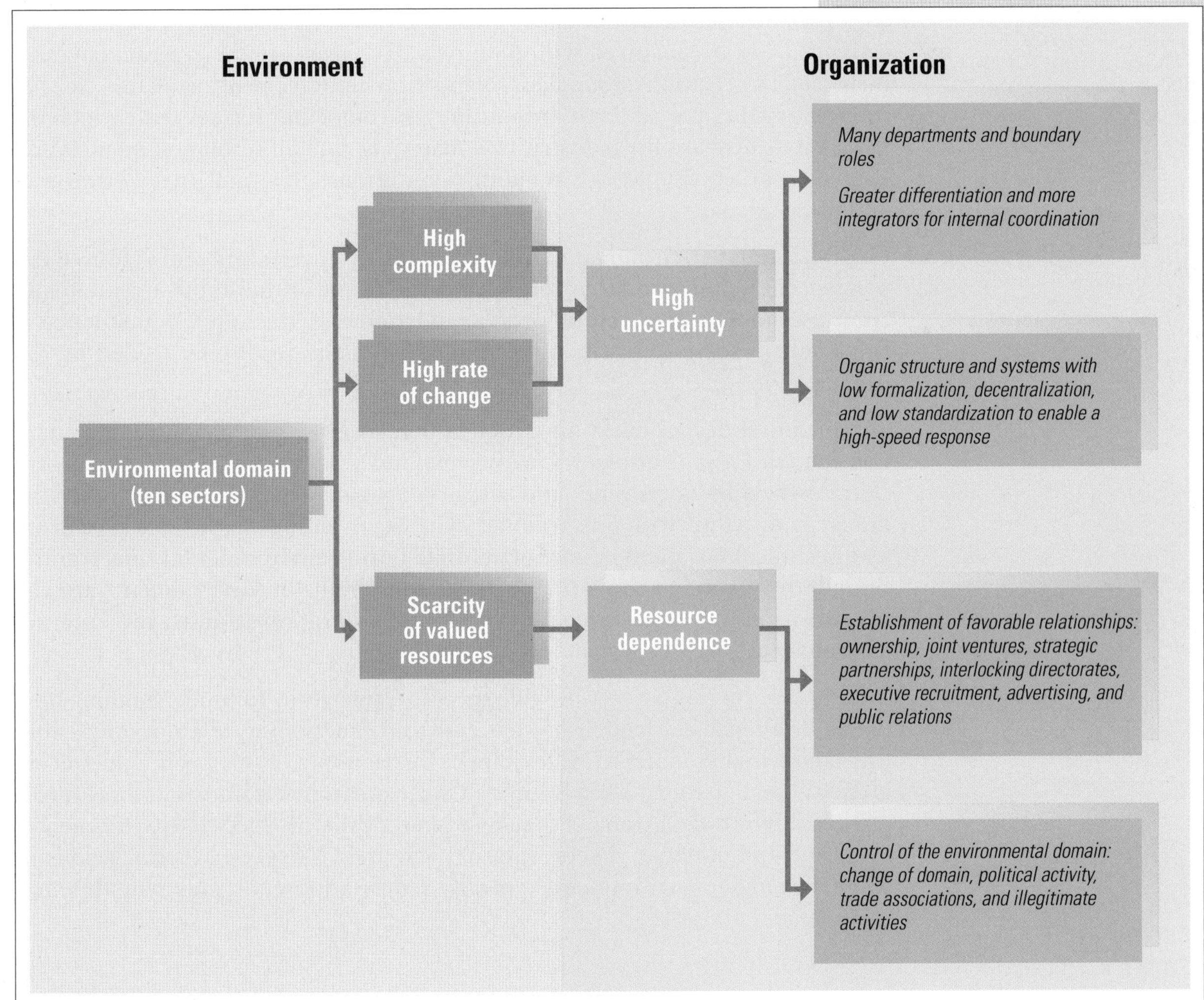

chapter. One theme is that the amount of complexity and change in an organization's domain influences the need for information and hence the uncertainty felt within an organization. Greater information uncertainty is resolved through greater structural flexibility (an organic design) and the assignment of additional departments and boundary roles. When uncertainty is low, management structures can be more mechanistic, and the number of departments and boundary roles can be fewer. The second theme pertains to the scarcity of material and financial resources. The more dependent an organization is on other organizations for those resources, the more important it is to either establish favorable linkages with those organizations or control entry into the domain. If dependence on external resources is low, the organization can maintain autonomy and does not need to establish linkages or control the external domain.

Design Essentials

- Change and complexity in the external environment have major implications for organization design and management action. Organizations are open social systems. Most are involved with hundreds of elements in the external environment, such as customers, suppliers, competitors, government regulators, special interest groups, and so forth. Important environmental sectors with which organizations deal are the industry, raw materials, human resources, financial resources, market, technology, economic conditions, government, sociocultural, and international.
- Organizational environments differ in terms of uncertainty and resource dependence. Organizational uncertainty is the result of the stable–unstable and simple–complex dimensions of the environment. Resource dependence is the result of scarcity of the material and financial resources needed by the organization.
- Organization design takes on a logical perspective when the environment is considered. Organizations try to survive and achieve efficiencies in a world characterized by uncertainty and scarcity. Specific departments and functions are created to deal with uncertainties. The organization can be conceptualized as a technical core and departments that buffer environmental uncertainty. Boundary-spanning roles bring information about the environment into the organization and send information about the organization to the external environment.
- The concepts in this chapter provide specific frameworks for understanding how the environment influences the structure and functioning of an organization. Environmental complexity and change, for example, have specific impact on internal complexity and adaptability. Under great uncertainty, more resources are allocated to departments that will plan, deal with specific environmental elements, and integrate diverse internal activities. Moreover, organizations in rapidly changing environments typically reflect a loose, organic structure and management processes.

- When risk is great or resources are scarce, the organization can establish linkages through acquisitions, strategic alliances, interlocking directorates, executive recruitment, or advertising and public relations that will minimize risk and maintain a supply of scarce resources. Other techniques for influencing the environment include a change of the domain in which the organization operates, political activity, participation in trade associations, and perhaps illegitimate activities.
- Two important themes in this chapter are that organizations can learn and adapt to the environment and that organizations can change and control the environment. These strategies are especially true for large organizations that command many resources. Such organizations can adapt when necessary but can also neutralize or change problematic areas in the environment.

Key Concepts

boundary-spanning roles
buffering roles
business intelligence
cooptation
differentiation
direct interlock
domain
general environment
indirect interlock
integration
intelligence team
interlocking directorate
mechanistic
organic
organizational environment
resource dependence
sectors
simple–complex dimension
stable–unstable dimension
task environment
uncertainty

Discussion Questions

1. Define *organizational environment*. Would the task environment of a new Internet-based company be the same as that of a large government agency? Discuss.
2. What are some forces that influence environmental uncertainty? Which typically has the greatest impact on uncertainty—environmental complexity or environmental change? Why?
3. Name some factors causing environmental complexity for an organization of your choice. How might this environmental complexity lead to organizational complexity? Explain.
4. Discuss the importance of the international sector for today's organizations, compared to domestic sectors. What are some ways in which the international sector affects organizations in your city or community?
5. Describe differentiation and integration. In what type of environmental uncertainty will differentiation and integration be greatest? Least?
6. How do you think planning in today's organizations compares to planning twenty-five years ago? Do you think planning becomes more important or less important in a world where everything is changing fast and crises are a regular part of organizational life? Why?
7. What is an organic organization? A mechanistic organization? How does the environment influence organic and mechanistic designs?
8. Why do organizations become involved in interorganizational relationships? Do these relationships affect an organization's dependency? Performance?
9. Assume you have been asked to calculate the ratio of staff employees to production employees in two organizations—one in a simple, stable environment and one in a complex, shifting environment. How would you expect these ratios to differ? Why?
10. Is changing the organization's domain a feasible strategy for coping with a threatening environment? Explain. Can you think of an organization in the recent news that has changed its domain?

Chapter 6 Workbook Organizations You Rely On[84]

Below, list eight organizations you somehow rely on in your daily life. Examples might be a restaurant, a clothing store, a university, your family, the post office, the telephone company, an airline, a pizzeria that delivers, your place of work, and so on. In the first column, list those eight organizations. Then, in column 2, choose another organization you could use in case the ones in column 1 were not available. In column 3, evaluate your level of dependence on the organizations listed in column 1 as Strong, Medium, or Weak. Finally, in column 4, rate the certainty of that organization being able to meet your needs as High (certainty), Medium, or Low.

Organization	Backup Organization	Level of Dependence	Level of Certainty
1.			
2.			
3.			
4.			
5.			
6.			
7.			
8.			

Questions

1. Do you have adequate backup organizations for those of high dependence? How might you create even more backups?
2. What would you do if an organization you rated high for dependence and high for certainty suddenly became high-dependence and low-certainty? How would your behavior relate to the concept of resource dependence?
3. Have you ever used any behaviors similar to those in Exhibit 6.7 to manage your relationships with the organizations listed in column 1?

CASE FOR ANALYSIS The Paradoxical Twins: Acme and Omega Electronics[85]

Part I

In 1986, Technological Products of Erie, Pennsylvania, was bought out by a Cleveland manufacturer. The Cleveland firm had no interest in the electronics division of Technological Products and subsequently sold to different investors two plants that manufactured computer chips and printed circuit boards. Integrated circuits, or chips, were the first step into microminiaturization in the electronics industry, and both plants had developed some expertise in the technology, along with their superior capabilities in manufacturing printed circuit boards. One of the plants, located in nearby Waterford, was renamed Acme Electronics; the other plant, within the city limits of Erie, was renamed Omega Electronics, Inc.

Acme retained its original management and upgraded its general manager to president. Omega hired a new president who had been a director of a large electronic research laboratory and upgraded several of the existing personnel within the plant. Acme and Omega often competed for the same contracts. As subcontractors, both firms benefited from the electronics boom and both looked forward to future growth and expansion. The world was going digital, and both companies began producing digital microprocessors along with the production of circuit boards. Acme had annual sales of $100 million and employed 550 people. Omega had annual sales of $80 million and employed 480 people. Acme regularly achieved greater net profits, much to the chagrin of Omega's management.

Inside Acme

The president of Acme, John Tyler, was confident that, had the demand not been so great, Acme's competitor would not have survived. "In fact," he said, "we have been able to beat Omega regularly for the most profitable contracts, thereby increasing our profit." Tyler credited his firm's greater effectiveness to his managers' abilities to run a "tight ship." He explained that he had retained the basic structure developed by Technological Products because it was most efficient for high-volume manufacturing. Acme had detailed organization charts and job descriptions. Tyler believed everyone should have clear responsibilities and narrowly defined jobs, which would lead to efficient performance and high company profits. People were generally satisfied with their work at Acme; however, some of the managers voiced the desire to have a little more latitude in their jobs.

Inside Omega

Omega's president, Jim Rawls, did not believe in organization charts. He felt his organization had departments similar to Acme's, but he thought Omega's plant was small enough that things such as organization charts just put artificial barriers between specialists who should be working together. Written memos were not allowed since, as Rawls expressed it, "the plant is small enough that if people want to communicate, they can just drop by and talk things over."

The head of the mechanical engineering department said, "Jim spends too much of his time and mine making sure everyone understands what we're doing and listening to suggestions." Rawls was concerned with employee satisfaction and wanted everyone to feel part of the organization. The top management team reflected Rawls's attitudes. They also believed that employees should be familiar with activities throughout the organization so that cooperation between departments would be increased. A newer member of the industrial engineering department said, "When I first got here, I wasn't sure what I was supposed to do. One day I worked with some mechanical engineers and the next day I helped the shipping department design some packing cartons. The first months on the job were hectic, but at least I got a real feel for what makes Omega tick."

Part II

In the 1990s, mixed analog and digital devices began threatening the demand for the complex circuit boards manufactured by Acme and Omega. This "system-on-a-chip" technology combined analog functions, such as sound, graphics, and power management, together with digital circuitry, such as logic and memory, making it highly useful for new products such as cellular phones and wireless computers. Both Acme and Omega realized the threat to their futures and began aggressively to seek new customers.

In July 1992, a major photocopier manufacturer was looking for a subcontractor to assemble the digital memory units of its new experimental copier. The projected contract for the job was estimated to be $7 million to $9 million in annual sales.

Both Acme and Omega were geographically close to this manufacturer, and both submitted highly competitive bids for the production of 100 prototypes. Acme's bid was slightly lower than Omega's; however, both firms were asked to produce 100 units. The photocopier manufacturer told both firms that speed was critical because its president had boasted to other manufacturers that the firm would have a finished copier available by Christmas. This boast, much to the designer's dismay, required pressure on all subcontractors to begin prototype production before the final design of the copier was complete. This meant Acme and Omega would have at most two weeks to produce the prototypes or would delay the final copier production.

Part III

Inside Acme

As soon as John Tyler was given the blueprints (Monday, July 13, 1992), he sent a memo to the purchasing

department asking to move forward on the purchase of all necessary materials. At the same time, he sent the blueprints to the drafting department and asked that it prepare manufacturing prints. The industrial engineering department was told to begin methods design work for use by the production department supervisors. Tyler also sent a memo to all department heads and executives indicating the critical time constraints of this job and how he expected that all employees would perform as efficiently as they had in the past.

The departments had little contact with one another for several days, and each seemed to work at its own speed. Each department also encountered problems. Purchasing could not acquire all the parts on time. Industrial engineering had difficulty arranging an efficient assembly sequence. Mechanical engineering did not take the deadline seriously and parceled its work to vendors so the engineers could work on other jobs scheduled previously. Tyler made it a point to stay in touch with the photocopier manufacturer to let it know things were progressing and to learn of any new developments. He traditionally worked to keep important clients happy. Tyler telephoned someone at the photocopier company at least twice a week and got to know the head designer quite well.

On July 17, Tyler learned that mechanical engineering was far behind in its development work, and he "hit the roof." To make matters worse, purchasing had not obtained all the parts, so the industrial engineers decided to assemble the product without one part, which would be inserted at the last minute. On Thursday, July 23, the final units were being assembled, although the process was delayed several times. On Friday, July 24, the last units were finished while Tyler paced around the plant. Late that afternoon, Tyler received a phone call from the head designer of the photocopier manufacturer, who told Tyler that he had received a call on Wednesday from Jim Rawls of Omega. He explained that Rawls's workers had found an error in the design of the connector cable and taken corrective action on their prototypes. He told Tyler that he had checked out the design error and that Omega was right. Tyler, a bit overwhelmed by this information, told the designer that he had all the memory units ready for shipment and that, as soon as they received the missing component on Monday or Tuesday, they would be able to deliver the final units. The designer explained that the design error would be rectified in a new blueprint he was sending over by messenger and that he would hold Acme to the Tuesday delivery date.

When the blueprint arrived, Tyler called in the production supervisor to assess the damage. The alterations in the design would call for total disassembly and the unsoldering of several connections. Tyler told the supervisor to put extra people on the alterations first thing Monday morning and to try to finish the job by Tuesday. Late Tuesday afternoon, the alterations were finished and the missing components were delivered. Wednesday morning, the production supervisor discovered that the units would have to be torn apart again to install the missing component. When John Tyler was told this, he again "hit the roof." He called industrial engineering and asked if it could help out. The production supervisor and the methods engineer couldn't agree on how to install the component. John Tyler settled the argument by ordering that all units be taken apart again and the missing component installed. He told shipping to prepare cartons for delivery on Friday afternoon.

On Friday, July 31, 50 prototypes were shipped from Acme without final inspection. John Tyler was concerned about his firm's reputation, so he waived the final inspection after he personally tested one unit and found it operational. On Tuesday, August 4, Acme shipped the last 50 units.

Inside Omega

On Friday, July 10, Jim Rawls called a meeting that included department heads to tell them about the potential contract they were to receive. He told them that as soon as he received the blueprints, work could begin. On Monday, July 13, the prints arrived and again the department heads met to discuss the project. At the end of the meeting, drafting had agreed to prepare manufacturing prints, while industrial engineering and production would begin methods design.

Two problems arose within Omega that were similar to those at Acme. Certain ordered parts could not be delivered on time, and the assembly sequence was difficult to engineer. The departments proposed ideas to help one another, however, and department heads and key employees had daily meetings to discuss progress. The head of electrical engineering knew of a Japanese source for the components that could not be purchased from normal suppliers. Most problems were solved by Saturday, July 18.

On Monday, July 20, a methods engineer and the production supervisor formulated the assembly plans, and production was set to begin on Tuesday morning. On Monday afternoon, people from mechanical engineering, electrical engineering, production, and industrial engineering got together to produce a prototype just to ensure that there would be no snags in production. While they were building the unit, they discovered an error in the connector cable design. All the engineers agreed, after checking and rechecking the blueprints, that the cable was erroneously designed. People from mechanical engineering and electrical engineering spent Monday night redesigning the cable, and on Tuesday morning, the drafting department finalized the changes in the manufacturing prints. On Tuesday morning, Rawls was a bit apprehensive about the design changes and decided to get formal approval. Rawls received word on Wednesday from the head designer at the photocopier firm that they could proceed with the design changes as discussed on the phone. On Friday, July 24, the final units were inspected by quality control and were then shipped.

Part IV

Ten of Acme's final memory units were defective, whereas all of Omega's units passed the photocopier firm's tests. The photocopier firm was disappointed with

Acme's delivery delay and incurred further delays in repairing the defective Acme units. However, rather than give the entire contract to one firm, the final contract was split between Acme and Omega with two directives added: maintain zero defects and reduce final cost. In 1993, through extensive cost-cutting efforts, Acme reduced its unit cost by 20 percent and was ultimately awarded the total contract.

Notes

1. Tim Arango, "A Hot Social Networking Site Cools as Facebook Flourishes," *The New York Times*, January 12, 2011, A1; and Geoffrey A. Fowler, "Facebook's Web of Frenemies," *The Wall Street Journal*, February 15, 2011, B1.
2. Tim Arango and David Carr, "Netflix's Move Onto the Web Stirs Rivalries," *The New York Times*, November 25, 2010, A1; and Cecilia Kang, "Netflix Could Upend Telecom Industry," *Pittsburg Post-Gazette*, March 6, 2011, A4.
3. Dana Milbank, "Aluminum Producers, Aggressive and Agile, Outfight Steelmakers," *The Wall Street Journal*, July 1, 1992, A1.
4. Roman Friedrich, Michael Peterson, and Alex Koster, "The Rise of Generation C," *Strategy + Business*, Issue 62 (Spring 2011), http://www.strategy-business.com/article/11110 (accessed July 25, 2011).
5. Dexter Roberts, "A New Labor Movement is Born in China," *BusinessWeek* (June 14–June 20, 2010), 7–8.
6. Nicholas Zamiska, "U.S. Opens the Door to Chinese Pills," *The Wall Street Journal*, October 9, 2007, B1.
7. "What's In Health Care Bill? Take a Dose," *CBS News.com* (March 19, 2010), http://www.cbsnews.com/stories/2010/03/19/politics/main6314410.shtml (accessed June 1, 2010); "Another View: Full Speed Ahead on Banking Reforms," *San Gabriel Valley Tribune*, February 25, 2010; and "Government and Regulatory Reform," National Federation of Independent Business, http://www.nfib.com/issues-elections/government-and-regulatory-reform?gclid=CIf_5oWLpKoCFcjAKgodhh2GYA& (accessed July 28, 2011).
8. Reena Jana, "Nike Goes Green. Very Quietly," *BusinessWeek* (June 22, 2009), 56; Ana Campoy, "Valero Harnesses Wind Energy to Fuel Its Oil-Refining Process," *The Wall Street Journal*, June 29, 2009, B1; Ann Zimmerman, "Retailer's Image Moves from Demon to Darling," *The Wall Street Journal* (July 16, 2009), http://online.wsj.com/article/SB124770244854748495.html?KEYWORDS=%22Retailer%E2%80%99s+Image+Moves+from+Demon+to+Darling%22 (accessed July 24, 2009).
9. Simona Covel, "Briggs Retains Clients by Helping Them Cut Costs," *The Wall Street Journal Online* (May 2, 2008), http://online.wsj.com/article/SB120943805522951855.html (accessed May 2, 2008).
10. Andrew Pollack, "Not Just Pond Scum," *The New York Times*, July 26, 2010, B1.
11. Jane J. Kim, "Where Either a Borrower or a Lender Can Be," *The Wall Street Journal,* March 12, 2008, D1, D3.
12. Norihiko Shirouzu, "Chinese Inspire Car Makers' Designs," *The Wall Street Journal*, October 28, 2009.
13. Alex Salkever, "Anatomy of a Business Decision; Case Study: A Chocolate Maker Is Buffeted by Global Forces Beyond His Control," *Inc.* (April 2008), 59–63.
14. Scott Kilman, "Consumers Feel Impact of Rising Grain Costs," *The Wall Street Journal*, August 8, 2008, A1, A11.
15. Mireya Navarro, "Changing U.S. Audience Poses Test for a Giant of Spanish TV," *The New York Times*, March 10, 2006, A1; Sam Schechner, "Univision to Add Two New Channels," *The Wall Street Journal*, April 13, 2011, B8; and Yvonne Villarreal, "Television; Embracing English Subtitles; Spanish-Language Stations Hope to Hook Younger Generations by Taking the Fluency Requirement Off Telenovelas and Other Shows," *The Los Angeles Times*, October 3, 2010, D1.
16. Sam Schechner, "Univision to Make More Shows Itself," *The Wall Street Journal*, May 19, 2011, B7.
17. Randall D. Harris, "Organizational Task Environments: An Evaluation of Convergent and Discriminant Validity," *Journal of Management Studies* 41, no. 5 (July 2004), 857–882; Allen C. Bluedorn, "Pilgrim's Progress: Trends and Convergence in Research on Organizational Size and Environment," *Journal of Management* 19 (1993), 163–191; Howard E. Aldrich, *Organizations and Environments* (Englewood Cliffs, N.J.: Prentice-Hall, 1979); and Fred E. Emery and Eric L. Trist, "The Casual Texture of Organizational Environments," *Human Relations* 18 (1965), 21–32.
18. Gregory G. Dess and Donald W. Beard, "Dimensions of Organizational Task Environments," *Administrative Science Quarterly* 29 (1984), 52–73; Ray Jurkovich, "A Core Typology of Organizational Environments," *Administrative Science Quarterly* 19 (1974), 380–394; and Robert B. Duncan, "Characteristics of Organizational Environments and Perceived Environmental Uncertainty," *Administrative Science Quarterly* 17 (1972), 313–327.
19. Christine S. Koberg and Gerardo R. Ungson, "The Effects of Environmental Uncertainty and Dependence on Organizational Structure and Performance: A Comparative Study," *Journal of Management* 13 (1987), 725–737; and Frances J. Milliken, "Three Types of Perceived Uncertainty about the Environment: State, Effect, and Response Uncertainty," *Academy of Management Review* 12 (1987), 133–143.
20. Alex Pham and Ben Fritz, "Game Over? Consoles Lose Ground in Video Gaming as Players Turn to Tablets, Smartphones," *The Los Angeles Times*, June 5, 2011, B1; Alex Pham and Ben Fritz, "Nintendo Unveils New Wii Model: The Company Hopes the Upgraded Game Console Reverses Its Slumping Sales," *The Los Angeles Times*, June 8, 2011, B2; "Sega Corporation," *Hoovers Company Information*, http://www.hoovers.com/company/SEGA_Corporation/ctfrif-1.html (accessed July 28, 2011); and Daisuke Wakabayashi, "Nintendo's Profit Drops As Rivals Move In," *The Wall Street Journal*, May 7, 2010, B5.
21. Reported in Pekka Aula, "Social Media, Reputation Risk and Ambient Publicity Management," *Strategy & Leadership* 38, no. 6 (2010), 43–49.
22. Jay Stuller, "The Need for Speed," *The Conference Board Review* (Fall 2009), 34–41; and Richard S. Levick, "Domino's Discovers Social Media," *BusinessWeek* (April 21, 2009), http://www.businessweek.com/print/managing/content/apr2009/ca20090421_555468.htm (accessed April 21, 2009).

23. See Ian P. McCarthy, Thomas B. Lawrence, Brian Wixted, and Brian R. Gordon, "A Multidimensional Conceptualization of Environmental Velocity," *Academy of Management Review* 35, no. 4 (2010), 604–626, for an overview of the numerous factors that are creating environmental instability for organizations.
24. J. A. Litterer, *The Analysis of Organizations,* 2nd ed. (New York: Wiley, 1973), 335.
25. Constance L. Hays, "More Gloom on the Island of Lost Toy Makers," *The New York Times,* February 23, 2005, C1; and Nicholas Casey, "Fisher-Price Game Plan: Pursue Toy Sales in Developing Markets," *The Wall Street Journal,* May 29, 2008, B1, B2.
26. Rosalie L. Tung, "Dimensions of Organizational Environments: An Exploratory Study of Their Impact on Organizational Structure," *Academy of Management Journal* 22 (1979), 672–693.
27. Joseph E. McCann and John Selsky, "Hyper-turbulence and the Emergence of Type 5 Environments," *Academy of Management Review* 9 (1984), 460–470.
28. McCarthy et al., "A Multidimensional Conceptualization of Environmental Velocity."
29. Susan Carey and Melanie Trottman, "Airlines Face New Reckoning as Fuel Costs Take Big Bite," *The Wall Street Journal,* March 20, 2008, A1, A15.
30. James D. Thompson, *Organizations in Action* (New York: McGraw-Hill, 1967), 20–21.
31. Jennifer A. Marrone, "Team Boundary Spanning: A Multilevel Review of Past Research and Proposals for the Future," *Journal of Management* 36, no. 4 (July 2010), 911–940.
32. Darren Dahl, "Strategy: Managing Fast, Flexible, and Full of Team Spirit," *Inc.* (May 2009), 95–97.
33. David B. Jemison, "The Importance of Boundary Spanning Roles in Strategic Decision-Making," *Journal of Management Studies* 21 (1984), 131–152; and Mohamed Ibrahim Ahmad at-Twaijri and John R. Montanari, "The Impact of Context and Choice on the Boundary-Spanning Process: An Empirical Extension," *Human Relations* 40 (1987), 783–798.
34. Reported in Michelle Cook, "The Intelligentsia," *Business 2.0* (July 1999), 135–136.
35. Robert C. Schwab, Gerardo R. Ungson, and Warren B. Brown, "Redefining the Boundary-Spanning Environment Relationship," *Journal of Management* 11 (1985), 75–86.
36. Tom Duffy, "Spying the Holy Grail," *Microsoft Executive Circle* (Winter 2004), 38–39.
37. Reported in Julie Schlosser, "Looking for Intelligence in Ice Cream," *Fortune* (March 17, 2003), 114–120.
38. Ken Western, "Ethical Spying," *Business Ethics* (September/October 1995), 22–23; Stan Crock, Geoffrey Smith, Joseph Weber, Richard A. Melcher, and Linda Himelstein, "They Snoop to Conquer," *BusinessWeek* (October 28, 1996), 172–176; and Kenneth A. Sawka, "Demystifying Business Intelligence," *Management Review* (October 1996), 47–51.
39. Liam Fahey and Jan Herring, "Intelligence Teams," *Strategy & Leadership* 35, no. 1 (2007), 13–20.
40. Jay W. Lorsch, "Introduction to the Structural Design of Organizations," in Gene W. Dalton, Paul R. Lawrence, and Jay W. Lorsch, eds., *Organizational Structure and Design* (Homewood, IL: Irwin and Dorsey, 1970), 5.
41. Paul R. Lawrence and Jay W. Lorsch, *Organization and Environment* (Homewood, IL: Irwin, 1969).
42. Lorsch, "Introduction to the Structural Design of Organizations," 7.
43. Jay W. Lorsch and Paul R. Lawrence, "Environmental Factors and Organizational Integration," in J. W. Lorsch and Paul R. Lawrence, eds., *Organizational Planning: Cases and Concepts* (Homewood, IL: Irwin and Dorsey, 1972), 45.
44. Tom Burns and G. M. Stalker, *The Management of Innovation* (London: Tavistock, 1961).
45. John A. Courtright, Gail T. Fairhurst, and L. Edna Rogers, "Interaction Patterns in Organic and Mechanistic Systems," *Academy of Management Journal* 32 (1989), 773–802.
46. Dennis K. Berman, "Crunch Time," *BusinessWeek Frontier* (April 24, 2000), F28–F38.
47. Thomas C. Powell, "Organizational Alignment as Competitive Advantage," *Strategic Management Journal* 13 (1992), 119–134; Mansour Javidan, "The Impact of Environmental Uncertainty on Long-Range Planning Practices of the U.S. Savings and Loan Industry," *Strategic Management Journal* 5 (1984), 381–392; Tung, "Dimensions of Organizational Environments," and Thompson, *Organizations in Action.*
48. Peter Brews and Devavrat Purohit, "Strategic Planning in Unstable Environments," *Long Range Planning* 40 (2007), 64–83; and Darrell Rigby and Barbara Bilodeau, "A Growing Focus on Preparedness," *Harvard Business Review* (July–August 2007), 21–22.
49. Bain & Company Management Tools and Trends Survey, reported in Darrell Rigby and Barbara Bilodeau, "A Growing Focus on Preparedness," *Harvard Business Review* (July–August 2007), 21–22; William J. Worthington, Jamie D. Collins, and Michael A. Hitt, "Beyond Risk Mitigation: Enhancing Corporate Innovation with Scenario Planning," *Business Horizons* 52 (2009), 441–450; Cari Tuna, "Pendulum Is Swinging Back on 'Scenario Planning,'" *The Wall Street Journal,* July 6, 2009, B6; and "Strategic Planning in a Crisis: A *McKinsey Quarterly* Survey," *The McKinsey Quarterly: The Online Journal of McKinsey & Co.* (April 2009), http://www.mckinseyquarterly.com (accessed April 20, 2009).
50. Ian Wylie, "There Is No Alternative To . . . .," *Fast Company* (July 2002), 106–110.
51. General Colin Powell, quoted in Oren Harari, "Good/Bad News About Strategy," *Management Review* (July 1995), 29–31.
52. Jeffrey Pfeffer and Gerald Salancik, *The External Control of Organizations: A Resource Dependent Perspective* (New York: Harper & Row, 1978); David Ulrich and Jay B. Barney, "Perspectives in Organizations: Resource Dependence, Efficiency, and Population," *Academy of Management Review* 9 (1984), 471–481; and Amy J. Hillman, Michael C. Withers, and Brian J. Collins, "Resource Dependence Theory: A Review," *Journal of Management* 35, no. 6 (2009), 1404–1427.
53. Andrew H. Van de Ven and Gordon Walker, "The Dynamics of Interorganizational Coordination," *Administrative Science Quarterly* (1984), 598–621; and Huseyin Leblebici and Gerald R. Salancik, "Stability in Interorganizational Exchanges: Rulemaking Processes of the Chicago Board of Trade," *Administrative Science Quarterly* 27 (1982), 227–242.
54. Mike Esterl and Corey Dade, "DHL Sends an SOS to UPS in $1 Billion Parcel Deal," *The Wall Street Journal,* May 29, 2008, B1.
55. Judith A. Babcock, *Organizational Responses to Resource Scarcity and Munificence: Adaptation and Modification in Colleges within a University* (Ph.D. diss., Pennsylvania State University, 1981).
56. Peter Smith Ring and Andrew H. Van de Ven, "Developmental Processes of Corporative Interorganizational Relationships," *Academy of Management Review* 19 (1994), 90–118; Jeffrey

Pfeffer, "Beyond Management and the Worker: The Institutional Function of Management," *Academy of Management Review* 1 (April 1976), 36–46; and John P. Kotter, "Managing External Dependence," *Academy of Management Review* 4 (1979), 87–92.

57. Bryan Borys and David B. Jemison, "Hybrid Arrangements as Strategic Alliances: Theoretical Issues in Organizational Combinations," *Academy of Management Review* 14 (1989), 234–249.
58. Julie Appleby "As More Hospital Systems Consolidate, Experts Say Health Care Prices Will Jump," *The Washington Post* (September 25, 2010), http://www.washingtonpost.com/wp-dyn/content/article/2010/09/25/AR2010092503006.html (accessed July 28, 2011); and Steven Pearlstein, "Connect These Dots to Form a Hospital Chain," *The Washington Post*, July 9, 2010, A13.
59. Julie Cohen Mason, "Strategic Alliances: Partnering for Success," *Management Review* (May 1993), 10–15.
60. Teri Agins and Alessandra Galloni, "After Gianni; Facing a Squeeze, Versace Struggles to Trim the Fat," *The Wall Street Journal*, September 30, 2003, A1, A10.
61. Borys and Jemison, "Hybrid Arrangements as Strategic Alliances."
62. Donald Palmer, "Broken Ties: Interlocking Directorates and Intercorporate Coordination," *Administrative Science Quarterly* 28 (1983), 40–55; F. David Shoorman, Max H. Bazerman, and Robert S. Atkin, "Interlocking Directorates: A Strategy for Reducing Environmental Uncertainty," *Academy of Management Review* 6 (1981), 243–251; and Ronald S. Burt, *Toward a Structural Theory of Action* (New York: Academic Press, 1982).
63. James R. Lang and Daniel E. Lockhart, "Increased Environmental Uncertainty and Changes in Board Linkage Patterns," *Academy of Management Journal* 33 (1990), 106–128; and Mark S. Mizruchi and Linda Brewster Stearns, "A Longitudinal Study of the Formation of Interlocking Directorates," *Administrative Science Quarterly* 33 (1988), 194–210.
64. Miguel Bustillo and Joann S. Lublin, "Board Ties Begin to Trip Up Companies," *The Wall Street Journal*, April 8, 2010, B1.
65. Claudia H. Deutsch, "Companies and Critics Try Collaboration," *The New York Times*, May 17, 2006, G1.
66. Tom McGinty, "SEC 'Revolving Door' Under Review; Staffers Who Join Companies They Once Regulated Draw Lawmakers' Ire," *The Wall Street Journal*, June 16, 2010, C1.
67. Keith J. Winstein and Suzanne Vranica, "Drug Ads' Impact Questioned," *The Wall Street Journal*, September 3, 2008, B7; and Jon Kamp, "Pfizer Drops Celebrity Pitch in New Lipitor Spots," *The Wall Street Journal*, September 2, 2008, B8.
68. Aula, "Social Media, Reputation Risk and Ambient Publicity Management."
69. John D. Stoll, "Repair Job: GM Urges, 'Tell Fritz,' " *The Wall Street Journal Online* (July 20, 2009), http://online.wsj.com/article/SB124804822336763843.html?mod=djem_jiewr_LD (accessed July 27, 2010).
70. Kotter, "Managing External Dependence."
71. Miguel Bustillo, "Wal-Mart Sees Small Stores in Big Cities," *The Wall Street Journal Online* (October 13, 2010), http://online.wsj.com/article/SB10001424052748703673604575550243762557882.html (accessed October 14, 2010).
72. Matt Rosoff, "Google's 15 Biggest Acquisitions and What Happened to Them," *Business Insider* (March 14, 2011), http://www.businessinsider.com/googles-15-biggest-acquisitions-and-what-happened-to-them-2011-3 (accessed July 28, 2011).
73. Jeffrey A. Trachtenberg, "E-Books Rewrite Bookselling," *The Wall Street Journal*, May 21, 2010, A1; and Jeffrey A. Trachtenberg, "Firing Bookworms, Hiring Tech Jocks, Barnes & Noble Strives to Survive," *The Wall Street Journal*, July 20, 2011, B1.
74. Trachtenberg, "E-Books Rewrite Bookselling."
75. Robert Pear, "Health Insurance Companies Try to Shape Rules," *The New York Times* (May 15, 2010), http://www.nytimes.com/2010/05/16/health/policy/16health.html (accessed May 15, 2010); Miguel Bustillo and Stu Woo, "Retailers Push Amazon on Taxes; Wal-Mart, Target and Others Look to Close Loophole for Online Sellers," *The Wall Street Journal*, March 17, 2011, B1; and Sara Forden, "Facebook Seeks Friends in Washington Amid Privacy Talk," *BusinessWeek* (December 2, 2010), http://www.businessweek.com/news/2010-12-02/facebook-seeks-friends-in-washington-amid-privacy-talk.html (accessed July 28, 2011).
76. David B. Yoffie, "How an Industry Builds Political Advantage," *Harvard Business Review* (May–June 1988), 82–89; and Jeffrey H. Birnbaum, "Chief Executives Head to Washington to Ply the Lobbyist's Trade," *The Wall Street Journal*, March 19, 1990, A1, A16.
77. Spencer E. Ante and Shayndi Raice, "Dignitaries Come on Board to Ease Huawei into U.S.," *The Wall Street Journal Online* (September 21, 2010), http://online.wsj.com/article/SB1000142405274870441690457550189244026699 2.html (accessed September 23, 2010); P. Goldstein, "Former Defense Official Joins Amerilink in Huawei Lobbying Bid," *FierceWireless.com* (October 22, 2010), http://www.fiercewireless.com/story/former-defense-official-joins-amerilink-huawei-lobbing-bid/2010-10-22 (accessed July 26, 2011); Joann S. Lublin and Shayndi Raice, "U.S. Security Fears Kill Huawei, ZTE Bids," *The Asian Wall Street Journal*, November 8, 2010, 17; and Shayndi Raice, "Huawei and U.S. Partner Scale Back Business Tie-Up," *The Wall Street Journal*, February 10, 2011, B5.
78. Ante and Raice, "Dignitaries Come on Board to East Huawei into U.S."
79. Leslie Scism, "Insurer Pushes to Weaken License Test," *The Wall Street Journal*, April 25, 2011, A1.
80. Anthony J. Daboub, Abdul M. A. Rasheed, Richard L. Priem, and David A. Gray, "Top Management Team Characteristics and Corporate Illegal Activity," *Academy of Management Review* 20, no. 1 (1995), 138–170.
81. Barry M. Staw and Eugene Szwajkowski, "The Scarcity-Munificence Component of Organizational Environments and the Commission of Illegal Acts," *Administrative Science Quarterly* 20 (1975), 345–354; and Kimberly D. Elsbach and Robert I. Sutton, "Acquiring Organizational Legitimacy through Illegitimate Actions: A Marriage of Institutional and Impression Management Theories," *Academy of Management Journal* 35 (1992), 699–738.
82. Russell Gold, "Halliburton Ex-Official Pleads Guilty in Bribe Case," *The Wall Street Journal*, September 4, 2005, A1, A15.
83. G. Thomas Sims, "German Industry Would Alter Law Requiring Labor Seats on Boards," *The New York Times*, April 6, 2007, C3.
84. Adapted by Dorothy Marcic from "Organizational Dependencies," in Ricky W. Griffin and Thomas C. Head, *Practicing Management*, 2nd ed. (Dallas: Houghton Mifflin), 2–3.
85. Adapted from John F. Veiga, "The Paradoxical Twins: Acme and Omega Electronics," in John F. Veiga and John N. Yanouzas, *The Dynamics of Organizational Theory* (St. Paul, MN: West, 1984), 132–138.

5.0

INTEGRATIVE CASE 5.0
IKEA: Scandinavian Style

"Behind the mountain there are people too." Old Swedish Proverb

As one of the world's most successful businessmen, Ingvar Kamprad never forgot the dreams, aspirations, and hard work of rural people, or their ability to find solutions to difficult problems. Growing up on the farmland of southern Sweden, Kamprad embodied many of the traits of the hearty men and women who surrounded him and, as an ambitious working boy, revealed the business traits that would contribute to his later success and reputation. As a child, Kamprad learned the concept of serving the needs of ordinary people by purchasing matches in bulk, which he then sold to rural customers at a profit. While still in his teens, he expanded his retail operation to sell everything from pencils to Christmas cards and upgraded the efficiency of his distribution by using the regional milk delivery system.

Beginnings

In 1943, at age 17, Kamprad formed IKEA with initials representing his first and last names, along with that of the family farm (Elmtaryd) and the nearby village (Agunnaryd). Anticipating the rising consumerism amid the rebuilding boom that would follow the war, IKEA moved quickly to provide families with low-cost furniture designs through the convenience of catalogue sales. With the opening of the company's first showroom in 1953, Kamprad created a model of vertical integration, uniting a variety of suppliers under the IKEA umbrella, coordinating long run production schedules, and controlling distribution. That model expanded in 1964 with the introduction of the first warehouse store, eliminating an entire step in product distribution by allowing warehouse container pick-up by customers.

The business lessons Kamprad mastered as a boy entrepreneur were evidenced at the corporate level in many ways. For example, the bulk purchasing of matches in his youth was a forerunner to the bulk purchase of fabric that expanded upholstery choices for consumers and made the luxury of fabric options, formerly limited to the wealthy, available to all customers. Likewise, IKEA used imaginative distribution and delivery options, such as when an IKEA employee cleverly discovered the company's "flat box" approach in 1955. While attempting to load a table into a customer's automobile, an employee simply removed the table legs, enabling a new vision of selling furniture unassembled. Practical solutions wedded to a low-cost promise created a new IKEA formula of "knock-down" furniture, flat-box storage and shipping, and assembly by consumers armed with IKEA-developed assembly tools and visual instructions. This formula revolutionized the home furnishings industry.

A major strength of IKEA lies in its pioneering distribution created through unique corporate-supplier relationships. In the earliest days of the company, Swedish fine furniture manufacturers attempted to boycott IKEA and drive it out of business for selling furniture at such low cost. Kamprad outmaneuvered them by forging new partnerships with other Scandinavian manufacturers, providing assurances of long production runs. Moreover, top managers learned that affordable furniture can be provided without the necessity of owning the factories. IKEA is something of a "hollow" or virtual corporation because nearly all of its manufacturing is outsourced. IKEA uses normal short-term purchasing contracts with suppliers, which means it can quickly adjust orders to changes in demand and not be saddled with huge unsold inventory. Suppliers also are in competition with one another to keep costs low. IKEA has indirect control over suppliers because it often purchases 90 to 100 percent of a supplier's production. Aware of the importance of supplier relationships, IKEA maintains a constant vigilance in working with suppliers to find ways to cut costs while keeping quality standards high, occasionally even agreeing to underwrite supplier technical assistance. That can-do attitude with suppliers has served IKEA well over time.

Supplier Relationships

Today, with 1,300 suppliers in 53 countries, IKEA's integrated design, production, and distribution faces new problems. The sheer numbers can weaken long production runs and disperse supply lines. Global reach also means that domestic requirements vary from one region to another or that certain areas, such as Eastern Europe, have few suppliers capable of high-quality, low-cost production. In addition, furniture competitors have not been idly sitting by, but have garnered lessons from the furniture giant. In the face of these challenges, IKEA continues to believe in the power of its ingenuity. Design teams work with suppliers in imaginative ways. For example, the need for expertise in bent-wood design for a popular armchair resulted in a partnership with ski-makers. Likewise, the need throughout Scandinavia for affordable housing resulted in IKEA's expansion into manufactured homes, built on supplier factory floors and delivered to construction sites, ready

to be filled with IKEA furnishings, conveniently assisted through $500 in IKEA gift certificates to the homeowner.

From the outset, IKEA represented more than catch phrases such as low price and convenience. Looking out for the families of modest incomes leads to IKEA's constant adherence to frugality, which is reflected in a cultural abhorrence for corporate office perks such as special parking or dining facilities. IKEA executives are expected to fly "coach." In his effort to bring "a little bit of Sweden to the world," Kamprad created a lifestyle model that would mold consumer habits and attitudes. True to the rural values of his homeland, Kamprad nurtured the ideal of the *IKEA family*, referring to employees as *co-workers*, and bestowing the name *Tillsammans* (Swedish for "Together") on the corporate center.

Mission and Culture

The higher cultural purpose of IKEA was reaffirmed in 1976 with the publication of Kamprad's *Testament of a Furniture Dealer*, which states explicitly that IKEA is about "creating a better everyday life for the majority of people." He went on, "In our line of business, for instance, too many new and beautifully designed products can be afforded by only a small group of better-off people. IKEA's aim is to change this situation." The purpose of providing fine-looking furniture to the masses was to be met via an internal culture that Kamprad described with words such as the following: "informal, cost conscious, humbleness, down to earth, simplicity, will-power, making do, honesty, common sense, facing reality, and enthusiasm." Achieving this purpose meant employees had to have direct personal experience with the needs of the customer majority.

Visualizing the constantly changing needs of a customer base comprised of farmers and college students, young professionals, and on-the-go families, Kamprad defined IKEA's business mission as *"to offer a wide variety of home furnishing items of good design and function at prices so low that the majority of people can afford to buy them."* This is "place-holder" furniture, filling the constantly changing needs in the lives of individuals and families. But the company would go further than merely providing the solution to a consumer's immediate needs. From furniture design to catalogue layout or the arrangement of warehouse showrooms, Kamprad and his co-workers gently imprinted Swedish style and cultural values of home, frugality, and practicality. As CEO Anders Dahlvig explained in a 2005 interview for *Business Week*, "IKEA isn't just about furniture. It's a lifestyle."

That lifestyle is reflected in the consumer shopping experience. The convenience of helpful touches—providing tape measures and pencils, a playroom that frees parents for leisurely shopping, a restaurant midway through the building to provide a shopping break—is a key part of the IKEA experience. Also familiar is the gray pathway, guiding the shopper along wide aisles through the 300,000-square-foot store. A veritable labyrinth, the route provides the charm of surprise as shoppers venture past the showrooms or leads to total confusion for those who venture off the intended path. Everything is carefully orchestrated; price tags are draped always to the left of the object, large bins lure with the promise of practical and inexpensive "must-haves," and room arrangements include special touches that spark vision and stimulate add-on purchases.

IKEA's attention to detail is honed through a variety of strategies that link management and co-workers at all levels to their customers. *Anti-bureaucracy week* places executives on stock-room and selling floors, tending registers, answering customer queries, or unloading merchandise from trucks. IKEAs *Loyalty Program* and *Home Visits* program allow company researchers entrance to consumer homes in order to better determine individual and community needs for furniture designs. The results of such efforts can be practical, such as specially designed storage units for urban apartment dwellers, or deeper drawers to meet the wardrobe needs of Americans. They can also help in detecting or anticipating cultural shifts. IKEA was the first retailer to acknowledge through its advertising the broadening definition of family to include multi-racial, multi-generational, and single-sex family arrangements and to promote its openness to "all families."

Challenges

Over the decades, efforts at strengthening IKEA and consumer family ties and encouraging repeat business as customers moved from one phase of life into another produced a unique global brand famous for innovation. The company's devotion to lifestyle solutions led to rapid movement on two fronts, the expansion of product lines (now over 9,500 products) and the expansion of global markets. By 2010 there were 332 IKEA stores in 41 countries. Global economic woes of recent years—including slumps in world stock markets, rising unemployment, and personal financial insecurity—increased sales and profits for IKEA. As consumers searched for ways to trim overall expenses and cut home furnishing costs, the company continued experiencing steady growth with a sales increase of 7.7 percent to 23.1 billion Euros.

However, the company's rapid global expansion and the rise of imitators in providing low-cost, quality home furnishings led some critics to believe IKEA had abandoned its maverick methods and relinquished its innovative edge. They detected a loosening of the company's strict core values, established more than half a century ago and reinforced in the training of co-workers in the *IKEA Way*.

Other critics take the opposite view and claim that IKEA is provincial. The problems from this viewpoint are the result of those strict core values, monitored on a regular basis through *Commercial Reviews*, measuring how closely the various stores adhere to the IKEA Way.

IKEA repeatedly surveys customers, visitors, suppliers, and co-workers about their satisfaction with the IKEA relationship. Repeating the surveys provides clear feedback and even measures important trends, especially if the results venture from the expected 5's toward the dreaded 1's. The critics would argue that the constant pressure for Kamprad's "little bit of Sweden" creates a culture that scorns strategic planning, is slow to react to cultural nuance in new locations, and offers limited opportunity for professional growth or advancement for non-Swedes. They could point out that the notion of *people behind the mountain* should work both ways.

Globalization

Global expansion into non-European markets, including the United States, Japan, and China, magnified the problems and the need for flexibility. Examples abound. The focus on standardization rather than adaptation poses problems for an industry giant such as IKEA, particularly as it enters Asian markets that are culturally different. IKEA's dependence on standardization for everything from store layout to the Swedish names of all products presented translation problems when informing Asian consumers about shopping and shipping procedures. Addressing cultural differences (women are the prime decision-makers and purchasers for the home), store and product specifications (for example, lowering store shelves and adjusting the length of beds), or consumer purchasing power (a worker may need up to a year and a half to purchase a product) was critical to company success in China. Furthermore, IKEA managers realized the need to shift focus from selling furniture to providing home decorating advice when they discovered that many skilled consumers could use the convenient tape measures and pencils to sketch pieces which they could then build for themselves at home.

In the U.S. market, IKEA was slow to make allowances, such as a shift from measuring in meters to feet and inches. While consumers embraced low pricing and the convenience of break-down furniture, the company's delay in bed size designation to the familiar king, queen, and twin drove U. S. customers bonkers because "160 centimeters" meant nothing to them. Co-worker issues also arose. Angry American workers in locations such as Danville, Virginia moved to unionize amid complaints of discrepancies in pay ($8.00 per hour compared to the $19.00 per hour for workers in Sweden), vacation (12 days annually for U.S. workers compared to five weeks for their counterparts in Sweden), and the constant demands by strict managers in requiring, for example, mandatory overtime.

Officials with IKEA admit they "almost blew it" in America and that they are committed to being both global and local. They insist they are responsive to issues and people. The company points to a history of standing against corruption and to its own quick response when a subcontractor's bribery efforts brought the hint of scandal to IKEAs door. CEO Mikael Ohlsson proudly points to the company's recent record in looking out for the needs of ordinary people through charitable projects such as IKEA Social Initiatives, benefiting over 100 million children. Service to people "behind the mountain" also requires acknowledgement of the mountain. IKEA places a priority on sustainability, working to improve company energy efficiency as reflective of its commitment to thrift, the wise use of natural resources, and a family level regard for stewardship of the earth. From the elimination of wood pallets and the ban on use of plastic bags to the installation of solar panels and the phasing out of sales on incandescent light bulbs, IKEA leads consumers and competitors by example and demonstration of its core values.

Behind the Curtain

Despite the concerns of critics, those values established by Kamprad remain intact through the combination of co-worker training in the IKEA Way and a carefully crafted organization structure that leaves little room for cultural or corporate change. Although retired (since 1986), Kamprad remains senior advisor on a board dominated by fellow Swedes. Organization structure resembles the IKEA flat box, with only four layers separating the CEO and the cashier on the sales floor. And the culture is in good hands with current CEO Mikael Ohlsson, who says bluntly, "we hate waste," as he points with pride at a sofa that his engineers found a way to ship in one-half the container space, thus shaving €100 from the price—and sharply reducing carbon-dioxide emissions while transporting it.

Historically, financial details about IKEA have been kept tight and neat and, until recently, secretive. The full public disclosure of information such as sales, profits, assets, and liabilities appeared for the first time in 2010 on the heels of a Swedish documentary. The ability to maintain such an opaque organization dates back 30 years. Nineteen eighty-two marked the transfer of IKEA ownership to Ingka Holding, held by Stichting INGKA Foundation (a Dutch non-profit). Kamprad chairs the foundation's five-member executive committee. The IKEA trademark is owned by IKEA Systems, another private Dutch company whose parent, IKEA Holding, is registered in Luxembourg and owned by Interogo, a Liechtenstein foundation controlled by the Kamprad family. This complex organizational setup enables IKEA to minimize taxes, avoid disclosure, and through strict guidelines protect Kamprad's vision while minimizing the potential for takeover.

The Future

The vision remains, but with global expansion IKEA's corporate culture ventured into ways to use technology to bond loyal IKEA customers while tapping into their ideas and valuable feedback. The company expanded its

e-commerce sales and initiated the *IKEA Family Club* in order to strengthen ties with existing customers and build long-term relationships. Family club members assist in sharing values and ideas and providing co-creating value for everything from product development to improvements in stores and service. Members are encouraged to increase their visits to stores, on-site "experience rooms," and the website to familiarize themselves with products and to build ties of shared-development in finding real-life solutions to the home furnishings challenges they encounter at various stages of their lives. This latest development in the long history of IKEA reinforces the decades-old goal of the founder to continue to look behind the mountain to meet the needs of the ordinary people.

Sources

Laura Collins, "House Perfect: Is the IKEA Ethos Comfy or Creepy?" *The New Yorker* (October 3, 2011), 54–66.

Colleen Lief, "IKEA: Past, Present & Future," *IMD International* (June 18, 2008), http://www.denisonconsulting.com/Libraries/Resources/IMD-IKEA.sflb.ashx (accessed January 4, 2012).

Kerry Capell, "IKEA: How the Swedish Retailer Became a Global Cult Brand," *BusinessWeek* (November 14, 2005), 96–106.

Bo Edvardsson and Bo Enquist, "'The IKEA Saga': How Service Culture Drives Service Strategy," *The Services Industry Journal* 22, no. 4 (October 2002), 153–186.

Katarina Kling and Ingela Goteman, "IKEA CEO Anders Dahlvig on International Growth and IKEA's Unique Corporate Culture and Brand Identity," *Academy of Management Executive* 17, no. 1(2003), 31–37.

Anonymous, "The Secret of IKEA's Success: Lean Operations, Shrewd Tax Planning, and Tight Control," *The Economist* (February 26, 2011), 57–58.

"IKEA: Creativity Key to Growth," *Marketing Week* (July 19, 2007), 30.

Gareth Jones, "IKEA Takes Online Gamble," *Marketing* (May 25, 2007), 14.

Bob Trebilcock, "IKEA Thinks Global, Acts Local," *Modern Material Handling* 63 no. 2 (February 2008), 22.

Anonymous, "IKEA Focuses on Sustainability," *Professional Services Close-Up* (September 26, 2011).

D. Howell, "IKEA 'LEEDS' the Way," *Chain Store Age* special issue (2006), 97–98.

Ulf Johansson and Asa Thelander, "A Standardized Approach to the World," *International Journal of Quality & Service Sciences* 1, no. 2 (2009), 199–219.

Anonymous, "IKEA Aims to Have 15 Stores in China by 2015," *Asia Pulse* (June 24, 2011).

Mei Fong, "IKEA Hits Home in China: The Swedish Design Giant, Unlike Other Retailers, Slashes Prices For the Chinese," *The Wall Street Journal* (March 3, 2006), B.1.

Ali Yakhlef, "The Trinity of International Strategy: Adaptation, Standardization, and Transformation," *Asian Business & Management* 19, no. 1(November 2009), 47–65.

M. Roger, P. Grol and C. Schoch, "IKEA: Culture as Competitive Advantage," *ECCH Collection* (1998), available for purchase at http://www.ecch.com/educators/products/view?id=22574 (Case reference # 398-173-1).

INTEGRATIVE CASE 6.0

6.0

Perdue Farms*

Background and Company History

"I have a theory that you can tell the difference between those who have inherited a fortune and those who have made a fortune. Those who have made their own fortune forget not where they came from and are less likely to lose touch with the common man." (Bill Sterling, Just Browsin' *column in* Eastern Shore News, *March 2, 1988)*

The history of Perdue Farms is dominated by seven themes: quality, growth, geographic expansion, vertical integration, innovation, branding, and service. Arthur W. Perdue, a Railway Express agent and descendent of a French Huguenot family named Perdeaux, founded the company in 1920 when he left his job with Railway Express and entered the egg business full-time near the small town of Salisbury, Maryland. Salisbury is located in a region immortalized in James Michener's *Chesapeake* that is alternately known as "the Eastern Shore" or "the DelMarVa Peninsula." It includes parts of *Delaware, Maryland* and *Virginia*. Arthur Perdue's only child, Franklin Parsons Perdue, was born in 1920.

A quick look at Perdue Farms' mission statement (Exhibit 1) reveals the emphasis the company has always put on quality. In the 1920s, "Mr. Arthur," as he was called, bought leghorn breeding stock from Texas to improve the quality of his flock. He soon expanded his egg market and began shipments to New York. Practicing small economies such as mixing his own chicken feed and using leather from his old shoes to make hinges for his chicken coops, he stayed out of debt and prospered. He tried to add a new chicken coop every year.

By 1940, Perdue Farms was already known for quality products and fair dealing in a tough, highly competitive market. The company began offering chickens for sale when Mr. Arthur realized that the future lay in selling chickens, not eggs. In 1944, Mr. Arthur made his son Frank a full partner in A.W. Perdue & Son Inc.

In 1950, Frank took over leadership of the company, which employed forty people. By 1952, revenues were $6 million from the sale of 2,600,000 broilers. During this period, the company began to vertically integrate, operating its own hatchery, starting to mix its own feed formulations, and operating its own feed mill. Also, in the 1950s, Perdue Farms began to contract with others to grow chickens for them. By furnishing the growers with peeps (baby chickens) and feed, the company was better able to control quality.

In the 1960s, Perdue Farms continued to vertically integrate by building its first grain receiving and storage facilities and Maryland's first soybean processing plant. By 1967, annual sales had increased to about $35 million. But, it became clear to Frank that profits lay in processing chickens. Frank recalled in an interview for *BusinessWeek* (September 15, 1972) "processors were paying us 10¢ a live pound for what cost us 14¢ to produce. Suddenly, processors were making as much as 7¢ a pound."

A cautious, conservative planner, Arthur Perdue had not been eager for expansion, and Frank Perdue was reluctant to enter poultry processing. But, economics forced his hand and, in 1968, the company bought its first processing plant, a Swift & Company operation in Salisbury.

From the first batch of chickens that it processed, Perdue's standards were higher than those of the federal government. The state grader on the first batch has often told the story of how he was worried that he had rejected too many chickens as not Grade A. As he finished his inspections for that first day, he saw Frank Perdue headed his way and he could tell that Frank was not happy. Frank started inspecting the birds and never argued over one that was rejected. Next, he saw Frank start to go through the ones that the state grader had passed and began to toss some of them over with the rejected birds. Finally, realizing that few met his standards, Frank put all of the birds in the reject pile. Soon, however, the facility was able to process 14,000 Grade A broilers per hour.

From the beginning, Frank Perdue refused to permit his broilers to be frozen for shipping, arguing that it resulted in unappetizing black bones and loss of flavor and moistness when cooked. Instead, Perdue chickens were (and some still are) shipped to market packed in ice, justifying the company's advertisements at that time that it sold only "fresh, young broilers." However, this policy also limited the company's market to those locations that could be serviced overnight from the Eastern Shore of Maryland. Thus, Perdue chose for its primary markets the densely populated towns and cities of the East Coast, particularly New York City, which consumes more Perdue chicken than all other brands combined.

Frank Perdue's drive for quality became legendary both inside and outside the poultry industry. In 1985, Frank and Perdue Farms were featured in the book, *A Passion for Excellence*, by Tom Peters and Nancy Austin.

*Adapted from George C. Rubenson and Frank M. Shipper, Department of Management and Marketing, Franklin P. Perdue School of Business, Salisbury University.

EXHIBIT 1
Perdue Mission 2000

Stand on Tradition

Perdue was built upon a foundation of quality,
a tradition described in our Quality Policy...

Our Quality Policy

"We shall produce products and provide services at all times which meet or exceed the expectations of our customers."

"We shall not be content to be of equal quality to our competitors."

"Our commitment is to be increasingly superior."

"Contribution to quality is a responsibility shared by everyone in the Perdue organization."

Focus on Today

Our mission reminds us of the purpose we serve...

Our Mission

"Enhance the quality of life with great food and agricultural products."

While striving to fulfill our mission, we use our values to guide our decisions...

Our Values

- **Quality:** We value the needs of our customers. Our high standards require us to work safely, make safe food and uphold the Perdue name.
- **Integrity:** We do the right thing and live up to our commitments. We do not cut corners or make false promises.
- **Trust:** We trust each other and treat each other with mutual respect. Each individual's skill and talent are appreciated.
- **Teamwork:** We value a strong work ethic and ability to make each other successful. We care what others think and encourage their involvement, creating a sense of pride, loyalty, ownership and family.

Look to the Future

Our vision describes what we will become and the qualities
that will enable us to succeed...

Our Vision

"To be the leading quality food company with $20 billion in sales in 2020."

Perdue in the Year 2020

- **To our customers:** We will provide food solutions and indispensable services to meet anticipated customer needs.
- **To our consumers:** A portfolio of trusted food and agricultural products will be supported by multiple brands throughout the world.
- **To our associates:** Worldwide, our people and our workplace will reflect our quality reputation, placing Perdue among the best places to work.
- **To our communities:** We will be known in the community as a strong corporate citizen, trusted business partner and favorite employer.
- **To our shareholders:** Driven by innovation, our market leadership and our creative spirit will yield industry-leading profits.

In 1970, Perdue established its primary breeding and genetic research programs. Through selective breeding, Perdue developed a chicken with more white breast meat than the typical chicken. Selective breeding has been so successful that Perdue Farms chickens are desired by other processors. Rumors have even suggested that Perdue chickens have been stolen on occasion in an attempt to improve competitor flocks.

In 1971, Perdue Farms began an extensive marketing campaign featuring Frank Perdue. In his early advertisements, he became famous for saying things like "If you want to eat as good as my chickens, you'll just have to eat my chickens." He is often credited with being the first to brand what had been a commodity product. During the 1970s, Perdue Farms also expanded geographically to areas north of New York City such as Massachusetts, Rhode Island, and Connecticut.

In 1977, "Mr. Arthur" died at the age of 91, leaving behind a company with annual sales of nearly $200 million, an average annual growth rate of 17 percent compared to an industry average of 1 percent a year, the potential for processing 78 thousand broilers per hour, and annual production of nearly 350 million pounds of poultry per year. Frank Perdue said of his father simply "I learned everything from him."

In 1981, Frank Perdue was in Boston for his induction into the Babson College Academy of Distinguished Entrepreneurs, an award established in 1978 to recognize the spirit of free enterprise and business leadership. Babson College President Ralph Z. Sorenson inducted Perdue into the academy, which, at that time, numbered eighteen men and women from four continents. Perdue had the following to say to the college students:

"There are none, nor will there ever be, easy steps for the entrepreneur. Nothing, absolutely nothing, replaces the willingness to work earnestly, intelligently towards a goal. You have to be willing to pay the price. You have to have an insatiable appetite for detail, have to be willing to accept constructive criticism, to ask questions, to be fiscally responsible, to surround yourself with good people and, most of all, to listen." (Frank Perdue, speech at Babson College, April 28, 1981)

The early 1980s saw Perdue Farms expand southward into Virginia, North Carolina, and Georgia. It also began to buy out other producers such as Carroll's Foods, Purvis Farms, Shenandoah Valley Poultry Company, and Shenandoah Farms. The latter two acquisitions diversified the company's markets to include turkey. New products included value-added items such as "Perdue Done It!," a line of fully cooked fresh chicken products.

James A. (Jim) Perdue, Frank's only son, joined the company as a management trainee in 1983 and became a plant manager. The late 1980s tested the mettle of the firm. Following a period of considerable expansion and product diversification, a consulting firm recommended that the company form several strategic business units, responsible for their own operations. In other words, the firm should decentralize. Soon after, the chicken market leveled off and then declined for a period. In 1988, the firm experienced its first year in the red. Unfortunately, the decentralization had created duplication and enormous administrative costs. The firm's rapid plunge into turkeys and other food processing, where it had little experience, contributed to the losses. Characteristically, the company refocused, concentrating on efficiency of operations, improving communications throughout the company, and paying close attention to detail.

On June 2, 1989, Frank celebrated fifty years with Perdue Farms. At a morning reception in downtown Salisbury, the governor of Maryland proclaimed it "Frank Perdue Day." The governors of Delaware and Virginia did the same. In 1991, Frank was named chairman of the Executive Committee and Jim Perdue became chairman of the board. Quieter, gentler, and more formally educated, Jim Perdue focused on operations, infusing the company with an even stronger devotion to quality control and a bigger commitment to strategic planning. Frank Perdue continued to do advertising and public relations. As Jim Perdue matured as the company leader, he took over the role of company spokesperson and began to appear in advertisements.

Under Jim Perdue's leadership, the 1990s were dominated by market expansion south into Florida and west to Michigan and Missouri. In 1992, the international business segment was formalized, serving customers in Puerto Rico, South America, Europe, Japan, and China. By fiscal year 1998, international sales were $180 million per year. International markets are beneficial for the firm because U.S. customers prefer white meat, whereas customers in most other countries prefer dark meat.

Food-service sales to commercial customers has also become a major market. New retail product lines focus on value-added items, individually quick-frozen items, home-meal replacement items, and products for the delicatessen. The "Fit & Easy" label continues as part of a nutrition campaign, using skinless, boneless chicken and turkey products.

The 1990s also saw the increased use of technology and the building of distribution centers to better serve the customer. For example, all over-the-road trucks were equipped with satellite two-way communications and geographic positioning, allowing real-time tracking, rerouting if needed, and accurately informing customers when to expect product arrival.

Currently, nearly 20,000 associates have increased revenues to more than $2.5 billion.

Management and Organization

"From 1950 until 1991, Frank Perdue was the primary force behind Perdue Farms growth and success. During Frank's years as the company leader, the industry entered its high growth period. Industry executives had typically developed professionally during the industry's infancy. Many had little formal education and started their careers in the barnyard, building chicken coops and cleaning them out. They often spent their entire careers with one company, progressing from supervisor of grow-out facilities to management of processing plants to corporate executive positions. Perdue Farms was not unusual in that respect. An entrepreneur through and through, Frank lived up to his marketing image of "it takes a tough man to make a tender chicken." He mostly used a centralized management style that kept decision-making authority in his own hands or those of a few trusted, senior executives whom he had known for a lifetime. Workers were expected to do their jobs.

In later years, Frank increasingly emphasized employee (or "associates" as they are currently called) involvement in quality issues and operational decisions. This emphasis on employee participation undoubtedly eased the transfer of power in 1991 to his son, Jim, which appears to have been unusually smooth. Although Jim grew up in the family business, he spent almost fifteen years earning an undergraduate degree in biology from Wake Forest University, a master's degree in marine biology from the University of Massachusetts at Dartmouth, and a doctorate in fisheries from the University of Washington in Seattle. Returning to Perdue Farms in 1983, he earned an EMBA from Salisbury State University and was assigned positions as plant manager, divisional quality control manager, and vice president of Quality Improvement Process (QIP) prior to becoming chairman.

Jim has a people-first management style. Company goals center on the three Ps: People, Products, and Profitability. He believes that business success rests on satisfying customer needs with quality products. It is important to put associates first, he says, because "If [associates] come first, they will strive to assure superior product quality—and satisfied customers." This view has had a profound impact on the company culture, which is based on Tom Peters's view that "Nobody knows a person's 20 square feet better than the person who works there." The idea is to gather ideas and information from everyone in the organization and maximize productivity by transmitting these ideas throughout the organization.

Key to accomplishing this "employees first" policy is workforce stability, a difficult task in an industry that employs a growing number of associates working in physically demanding and sometimes stressful conditions. A significant number of associates are Hispanic immigrants who may have a poor command of the English language, are sometimes undereducated, and often lack basic health care. In order to increase these associates' opportunity for advancement, Perdue Farms focuses on helping them overcome these disadvantages.

For example, the firm provides English-language classes to help non-English-speaking associates assimilate. Ultimately associates can earn the equivalent of a high-school diploma. To deal with physical stress, the company has an ergonomics committee in each plant that studies job requirements and seeks ways to redesign those jobs that put workers at the greatest risk. The company also has an impressive wellness program that currently includes clinics at ten plants. The clinics are staffed by professional medical people working for medical practice groups under contract to Perdue Farms. Associates have universal access to all Perdue-operated clinics and can visit a doctor for anything from a muscle strain to prenatal care to screening tests for a variety of diseases. Dependent care is available. While benefits to the employees are obvious, the company also benefits through a reduction in lost time for medical office visits, lower turnover, and a happier, healthier, more productive and stable work force.

Marketing

In the early days, chicken was sold to butcher shops and neighborhood groceries as a commodity; that is, producers sold it in bulk and butchers cut and wrapped it. The customer had no idea which firm grew or processed the chicken. Frank Perdue was convinced that higher profits could be made if the firm's products could be sold at a premium price. But, the only reason a product can command a premium price is if customers ask for it by name—and that means the product must be differentiated and "branded." Hence, the emphasis over the years on superior quality, broader-breasted chickens, and a healthy golden color (actually the result of adding marigold petals in the feed to enhance the natural yellow color that corn provided).

Today, branded chicken is ubiquitous. The new task for Perdue Farms is to create a unified theme to market a wide variety of products (e.g., both fresh meat and fully prepared and frozen products) to a wide variety of customers (e.g., retail, food service, and international). Industry experts believe that the market for fresh poultry has peaked while sales of value-added and frozen products continue to grow at a healthy rate. Although domestic retail sales accounted for about 60 percent of Perdue Farms' revenues in the 2000 fiscal year, food service sales now account for 20 percent, international sales account for 5 percent, and grain and oilseed contribute the remaining 15 percent. The company expects food service, international, and grain and oilseed sales to continue to grow as a percentage of total revenues.

Domestic Retail

Today's retail grocery customer is increasingly looking for ease and speed of preparation; that is, value-added products. The move toward value-added products has significantly changed the meat department in the modern grocery store. There are now five distinct meat outlets for poultry:

1. The fresh meat counter—traditional, fresh meat—includes whole chicken and parts
2. The delicatessen—processed turkey, rotisserie chicken

3. The frozen counter—individually quick-frozen items such as frozen whole chickens, turkeys, and Cornish hens
4. Home meal replacement—fully prepared entrees such as Perdue brand "Short Cuts" and Deluca brand entrees (the Deluca brand was acquired and is sold under its own name) that are sold along with salads and desserts so that you can assemble your own dinner
5. Shelf stable—canned products

Because Perdue Farms has always used the phrase "fresh young chicken" as the centerpiece of its marketing, value-added products and the retail frozen counter create a possible conflict with past marketing themes. Are these products compatible with the company's marketing image, and, if so, how does the company express the notion of quality in this broader product environment? To answer that question, Perdue Farms has been studying what the term "fresh young chicken" means to customers who consistently demand quicker and easier preparation and who admit that they freeze most of their fresh meat purchases once they get home. One view is that the importance of the term "fresh young chicken" comes from the customer's perception that "quality" and "freshness" are closely associated. Thus, the real issue may be trust; that is, the customer must believe that the product, whether fresh or frozen, is the freshest, highest quality possible, and future marketing themes must develop that concept.

Operations

Two words sum up the Perdue approach to operations—quality and efficiency—with emphasis on the first over the latter. Perdue, more than most companies, represents the Total Quality Management (TQM) slogan, "Quality, a journey without end." Some of the key events in Perdue's quality improvement process are listed in Exhibit 2.

Both quality and efficiency are improved through the management of details. Exhibit 3 depicts the structure and product flow of a generic, vertically integrated broiler company. A broiler company can choose which steps in the process it wants to accomplish in-house and which it wants suppliers to provide. For example, the broiler company could purchase all grain, oilseed, meal, and other feed products. Or it could contract with hatcheries to supply primary breeders and hatchery supply flocks.

Perdue Farms chose maximum vertical integration to control every detail. It breeds and hatches its own eggs (19 hatcheries), selects its contract growers, builds Perdue-engineered chicken houses, formulates and manufactures its own feed (12 poultry feedmills, 1 specialty feedmill,

EXHIBIT 2
Milestones in the Quality Improvement Process at Perdue Farms

1924 — Arthur Perdue bought leghorn roosters for $25
1950 — Adopted the company logo of a chick under a magnifying glass
1984 — Frank Perdue attended Philip Crosby's Quality College
1985 — Perdue recognized for its pursuit of quality in *A Passion for Excellence*
— 200 Perdue managers attended Quality College
— Adopted the Quality Improvement Process (QIP)
1986 — Established Corrective Action Teams (CAT's)
1987 — Established Quality Training for all associates
— Implemented Error Cause Removal Process (ECR)
1988 — Steering Committee formed
1989 — First Annual Quality Conference held
— Implemented Team Management
1990 — Second Annual Quality Conference held
— Codified Values and Corporate Mission
1991 — Third Annual Quality Conference held
— Customer Satisfaction defined
1992 — Fourth Annual Quality Conference held
— How to implement Customer Satisfaction explained to team leaders and Quality Improvement Teams (QIT)
— Created Quality Index
— Created Customer Satisfaction Index (CSI)
— Created "Farm to Fork" quality program
1999 — Launched Raw Material Quality Index
2000 — Initiated High Performance Team Process

2 ingredient-blending operations), oversees the care and feeding of the chicks, operates its own processing plants (21 processing and further processing plants), distributes via its own trucking fleet, and markets the products (see Exhibit 3). Total process control formed the basis for Frank Perdue's early claims that Perdue Farms poultry is, indeed, higher quality than other poultry. When he stated in his early ads that "A chicken is what it eats... I store my own grain and mix my own feed... and give my Perdue chickens nothing but well water to drink...," he knew that his claim was honest and he could back it up.

Total process control also enables Perdue Farms to ensure that nothing goes to waste. Eight measurable items—hatchability, turnover, feed conversion, livability, yield, birds per man-hour, utilization, and grade—are tracked routinely.

Perdue Farms continues to ensure that nothing artificial is fed to or injected into the birds. No shortcuts are taken. A chemical-free and steroid-free diet is fed to the chickens. Young chickens are vaccinated against disease. Selective breeding is used to improve the quality of the chicken stock. Chickens are bred to yield more white breast meat because that is what the consumer wants.

To ensure that Perdue Farms poultry continues to lead the industry in quality, the company buys and analyzes competitors' products regularly. Inspection associates grade these products and share the information with the highest levels of management. In addition, the company's Quality Policy is displayed at all locations and taught to all associates in quality training (Exhibit 4).

Research and Development

Perdue is an acknowledged industry leader in the use of research and technology to provide quality products and service to its customers. The company spends more on research as a percent of revenues than any other poultry processor. This practice goes back to Frank Perdue's focus on finding ways to differentiate his products based on quality and value. It was research into selective breeding that resulted in the broader breast, an attribute of Perdue Farms chicken that was the basis of his early advertising. Although other processors have also improved their stock, Perdue Farms believes that it still leads the industry. A list of some of Perdue Farms technological accomplishments is given in Exhibit 5.

As with every other aspect of the business, Perdue Farms tries to leave nothing to chance in R&D. The company employs specialists in avian science, microbiology, genetics, nutrition, and veterinary science. Because of its R&D capabilities, Perdue Farms is often involved in United States Food and Drug Administration (FDA) field tests with pharmaceutical suppliers. Knowledge and experience gained from these tests can lead to a competitive advantage. For example, Perdue has the most extensive and expensive vaccination program in the industry. Currently, the company is working with and studying the practices of several European producers who use completely different methods.

The company has used research to significantly increase productivity. For example, in the 1950s, it took fourteen weeks to grow a 3 pound chicken. Today, it takes only seven weeks to grow a 5 pound chicken. This gain in efficiency is due principally to improvements in the conversion rate of feed to chicken. Feed represents about 65 percent of the cost of growing a chicken. Thus, if additional research can further improve the conversion rate of feed to chicken by just 1 percent, it would represent estimated additional income of $2.5–3 million per week or $130–156 million per year.

Environment

Environmental issues present a constant challenge to all poultry processors. Growing, slaughtering, and processing poultry is a difficult and tedious process that demands absolute efficiency to keep operating costs at an acceptable level. Inevitably, detractors argue that the process is dangerous to workers, inhumane to the poultry, hard on the environment, and results in food that may not be safe. Thus, media headlines such as "Human Cost of Poultry Business Bared," "Animal Rights Advocates Protest Chicken Coop Conditions," "Processing Plants Leave Toxic Trail," or "EPA Mandates Poultry Regulations" are routine.

Perdue Farms tries to be proactive in managing environmental issues. In April 1993, the company created an Environmental Steering Committee. Its mission is ". . . to provide all Perdue Farms work sites with vision, direction, and leadership so that they can be good corporate citizens from an environmental perspective today and in the future." The committee is responsible for overseeing how the company is doing in such environmentally sensitive areas as waste water, storm water, hazardous waste, solid waste, recycling, bio-solids, and human health and safety.

For example, disposing of dead birds has long been an industry problem. Perdue Farms developed small composters for use on each farm. Using this approach, carcasses are reduced to an end-product that resembles soil in a matter of a few days. The disposal of hatchery waste is another environmental challenge. Historically, manure and unhatched eggs were shipped to a landfill. However, Perdue Farms developed a way to reduce the waste by 50 percent by selling the liquid fraction to a pet-food processor that cooks it for protein. The other 50 percent is recycled through a rendering process. In 1990, Perdue Farms spent $4.2 million to upgrade its existing treatment facility with a state-of-the-art system at its Accomac, Virginia, and Showell, Maryland, plants. These facilities use forced hot air heated to 120 degrees to cause the microbes to digest all traces of ammonia, even during the cold winter months.

More than ten years ago, North Carolina's Occupational Safety and Health Administration cited Perdue Farms for an unacceptable level of repetitive stress injuries at its Lewiston and Robersonville, North Carolina, processing plants. This sparked a major research program in which Perdue Farms worked with Health and Hygiene Inc. of Greensboro, North Carolina, to learn more about ergonomics, the repetitive

EXHIBIT 3
Perdue Farms Integrated Operations

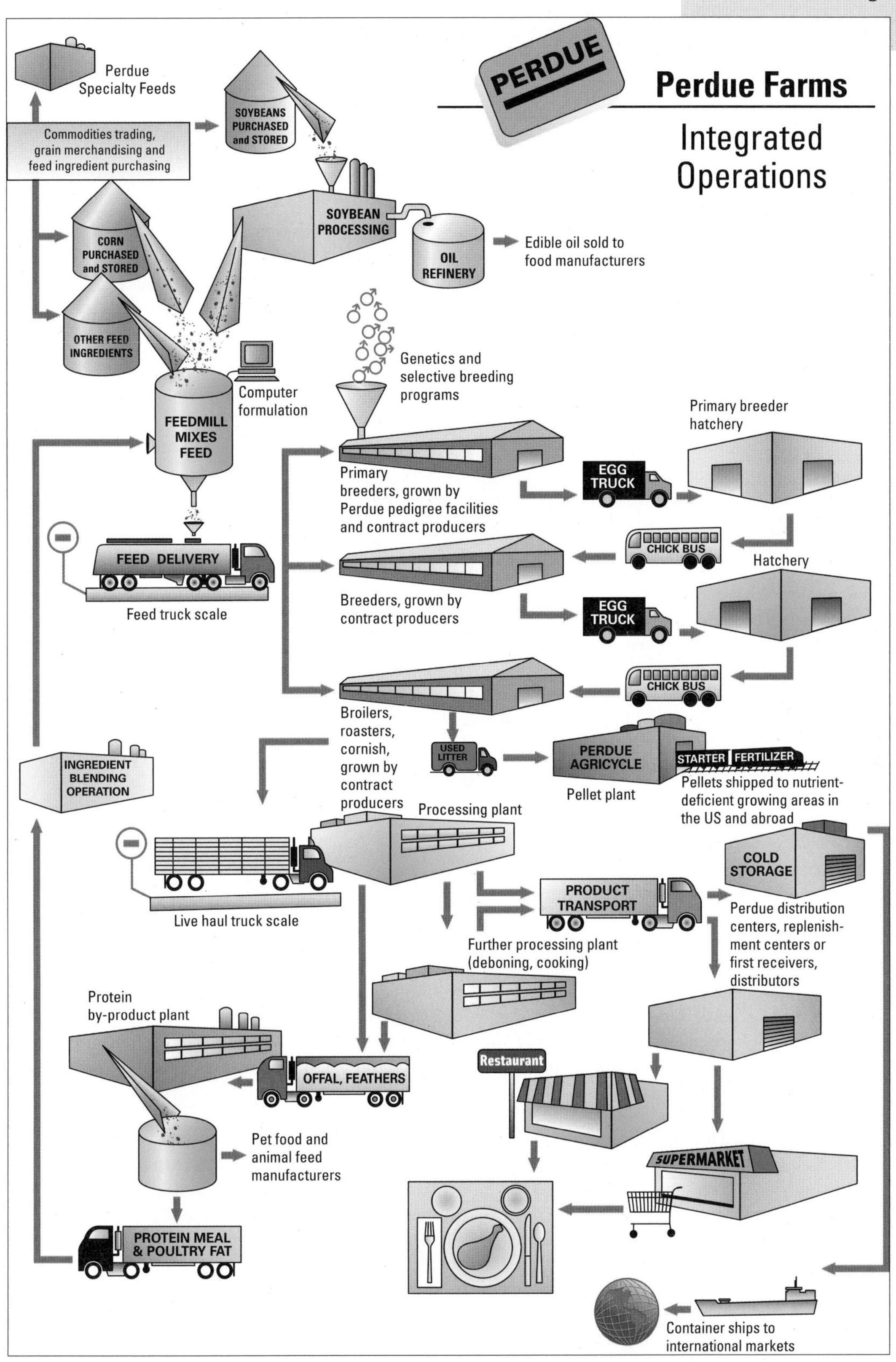
PERDUE
Perdue Farms
Integrated Operations
Perdue Specialty Feeds
Commodities trading, grain merchandising and feed ingredient purchasing
SOYBEANS PURCHASED and STORED
CORN PURCHASED and STORED
OTHER FEED INGREDIENTS
SOYBEAN PROCESSING
OIL REFINERY
Edible oil sold to food manufacturers
FEEDMILL MIXES FEED
Computer formulation
FEED DELIVERY
Feed truck scale
Genetics and selective breeding programs
Primary breeders, grown by Perdue pedigree facilities and contract producers
EGG TRUCK
Primary breeder hatchery
CHICK BUS
Hatchery
Breeders, grown by contract producers
EGG TRUCK
CHICK BUS
Broilers, roasters, cornish, grown by contract producers
USED LITTER
PERDUE AGRICYCLE
Pellet plant
STARTER FERTILIZER
Pellets shipped to nutrient-deficient growing areas in the US and abroad
INGREDIENT BLENDING OPERATION
Processing plant
Live haul truck scale
PRODUCT TRANSPORT
COLD STORAGE
Perdue distribution centers, replenishment centers or first receivers, distributors
Further processing plant (deboning, cooking)
Protein by-product plant
OFFAL, FEATHERS
Restaurant
Pet food and animal feed manufacturers
SUPERMARKET
PROTEIN MEAL & POULTRY FAT
Container ships to international markets

EXHIBIT 4
Quality Policy

- WE SHALL not be content to be of equal quality to our competitors.
- OUR COMMITMENT is to be increasingly superior.
- CONTRIBUTION TO QUALITY is a responsibility shared by everyone in the Perdue organization.

EXHIBIT 5
Perdue Farms Technological Accomplishments

- Conducts more research than all competitors combined
- Breeds chickens with consistently more breast meat than any other bird in the industry
- First to use digital scales to guarantee weights to customers
- First to package fully-cooked chicken products in microwaveable trays
- First to have a box lab to define quality of boxes from different suppliers
- First to test both its chickens and competitors' chickens on 52 quality factors every week
- Improved on-time deliveries 20% between 1987 and 1993
- Built state of the art analytical and microbiological laboratories for feed and end product analysis
- First to develop best management practices for food safety across all areas of the company
- First to develop commercially viable pelletized poultry litter

movements required to accomplish specific jobs. Results have been dramatic. Launched in 1991 after two years of development, the program videotapes employees at all of Perdue Farms' plants as they work in order to describe and place stress values on various tasks. Although the cost to Perdue Farms has been significant, results have been dramatic with workers' compensation claims down 44 percent, lost-time recordables just 7.7 percent of the industry average, an 80 percent decrease in serious repetitive stress cases, and a 50 percent reduction in lost time for surgery for back injuries (Shelley Reese, "Helping Employees get a Grip," *Business and Health,* August 1998).

Despite these advances, serious problems continue to develop. Some experts have called for conservation measures that might limit the density of chicken houses in a given area or even require a percentage of existing chicken houses to be taken out of production periodically. Obviously this would be very hard on the farm families who own existing chicken houses and could result in fewer acres devoted to agriculture. Working with AgriRecycle Inc. of Springfield, Missouri, Perdue Farms has developed a possible solution. The plan envisions the poultry companies processing excess manure into pellets for use as fertilizer. This would permit sales outside the poultry growing region, better balancing the input of grain. Spokesmen estimate that as much as 120,000 tons, nearly one-third of the surplus nutrients from manure produced each year on the DelMarVa Peninsula, could be sold to corn growers in other parts of the country. Prices would be market driven but could be $25 to $30 per ton, suggesting a potential, small profit. Still, almost any attempt to control the problem potentially raises the cost of growing chickens, forcing poultry processors to look elsewhere for locations where the chicken population is less dense.

In general, solving industry environmental problems presents at least five major challenges to the poultry processor:

- How to maintain the trust of the poultry consumer
- How to ensure that the poultry remain healthy
- How to protect the safety of the employees and the process
- How to satisfy legislators who need to show their constituents that they are taking firm action when environmental problems occur
- How to keep costs at an acceptable level

Jim Perdue sums up Perdue Farms' position as follows: ". . . we must not only comply with environmental laws as they exist today, but look to the future to make sure we don't have any surprises. We must make sure our environmental policy statement [see Exhibit 6] is real, that there's something behind it and that we do what we say we're going to do."

Logistics and Information Systems

The explosion of poultry products and increasing number of customers during recent years placed a severe strain on the existing logistics system, which was developed at a time when there were far fewer products, fewer delivery points, and lower volume. Hence, the company had limited

EXHIBIT 6
Perdue Farms Environmental Policy Statement

Perdue Farms is committed to environmental stewardship and shares that commitment with its farm family partners. We're proud of the leadership we're providing our industry in addressing the full range of environmental challenges related to animal agriculture and food processing. We've invested—and continue to invest—millions of dollars in research, new technology, equipment upgrades, and awareness and education as part of our ongoing commitment to protecting the environment.

- Perdue Farms was among the first poultry companies with a dedicated Environmental Services department. Our team of environmental managers is responsible for ensuring that every Perdue facility operates within *100 percent compliance of all applicable environmental regulations and permits*.
- Through our joint venture, Perdue AgriRecycle, Perdue Farms is investing $12 million to build in Delaware a first-of-its-kind pellet plant that will convert surplus poultry litter into a starter fertilizer that will be marketed internationally to nutrient deficient regions. The facility, which will serve the entire DelMarVa region, is scheduled to begin operation in April, 2001.
- We continue to explore new technologies that will reduce water usage in our processing plants without compromising food safety or quality.
- We invested thousands of man-hours in producer education to assist our family farm partners in managing their independent poultry operations in the most environmentally responsible manner possible. In addition, all our poultry producers are required to have nutrient management plans and dead-bird composters.
- Perdue Farms was one of four poultry companies operating in Delaware to sign an agreement with Delaware officials outlining our companies' voluntary commitment to help independent poultry producers dispose of surplus chicken litter.
- Our Technical Services department is conducting ongoing research into feed technology as a means of reducing the nutrients in poultry manure. We've already achieved phosphorous reductions that far exceed the industry average.
- We recognize that the environmental impact of animal agriculture is more pronounced in areas where development is decreasing the amount of farmland available to produce grain for feed and to accept nutrients. That is why we view independent grain *and* poultry producers as vital business partners and strive to preserve the economic viability of the family farm.

At Perdue Farms, we believe that it is possible to preserve the family farm; provide a safe, abundant and affordable food supply; and protect the environment. However, we believe that can best happen when there is cooperation and trust between the poultry industry, agriculture, environmental groups and state officials. We hope Delaware's effort will become a model for other states to follow.

ability to improve service levels, could not support further growth, and could not introduce innovative services that might provide a competitive advantage.

In the poultry industry, companies are faced with two significant problems—time and forecasting. Fresh poultry has a limited shelf life—measured in days. Thus forecasts must be extremely accurate and deliveries must be timely. On one hand, estimating requirements too conservatively results in product shortages. Mega-customers such as Wal-Mart will not tolerate product shortages that lead to empty shelves and lost sales. On the other hand, if estimates are overstated, the result is outdated products that cannot be sold and losses for Perdue Farms. A common expression in the poultry industry is "you either sell it or smell it."

Forecasting has always been extremely difficult in the poultry industry because the processor needs to know approximately eighteen months in advance how many broilers will be needed in order to size hatchery supply flocks and contract with growers to provide live broilers. Most customers (e.g., grocers and food-service buyers) have a much shorter planning window. Additionally, there is no way for Perdue Farms to know when rival poultry processors will put a particular product on special, reducing Perdue Farms sales, or when bad weather and other uncontrollable problems may reduce demand.

In the short run, information technology (IT) has helped by shortening the distance between the customer and Perdue Farms. As far back as 1987, personal computers (PCs) were placed directly on each customer-service associate's desk, allowing the associate to enter customer orders directly. Next, a system was developed to put dispatchers in direct contact with every truck in the system so that they would have accurate information about product inventory and truck location at all times. Now, IT is moving to further shorten the distance between the customer and the Perdue Farms service representative by putting a PC on the customer's desk. All of these steps improve communication and shorten the time from order to delivery.

To control the entire supply chain management process, Perdue Farms purchased a multi-million-dollar information technology system that represents the biggest nontangible asset expense in the company's history. This integrated, state-of-the-art information system required total process re-engineering, a project that took eighteen months and required training 1,200 associates. Major goals of the system were to (1) make it easier and more desirable for the customer to do business with Perdue Farms, (2) make it easier for Perdue Farms associates to get the job done, and (3) take as much cost out of the process as possible.

Industry Trends

The poultry industry is affected by consumer, industry, and governmental regulatory trends. Currently, chicken is the number one meat consumed in the United States, with a 40 percent market share. The typical American consumes about 81 pounds of chicken, 69 pounds of beef, and 52 pounds of pork annually (USDA data). Additionally, chicken is becoming the most popular meat in the world. In 1997, poultry set an export record of $2.5 billion. Although exports fell 6 percent in 1998, the decrease was attributed to Russia's and Asia's financial crisis, and food-industry experts expected this to be only a temporary setback. Hence, the world market is clearly a growth opportunity for the future.

Government agencies whose regulations impact the industry include the Occupational Safety and Health Administration (OSHA) for employee safety and the Immigration and Naturalization Service (INS) for undocumented workers. OSHA enforces its regulations via periodic inspections, and levies fines when noncompliance is found. For example, a Hudson Foods poultry plant was fined more than a million dollars for alleged willful violations causing ergonomic injury to workers. The INS also uses periodic inspections to find undocumented workers. It estimates that undocumented aliens working in the industry vary from 3 to 78 percent of the workforce at individual plants. Plants that are found to use undocumented workers, especially those that are repeat offenders, can be heavily fined.

The Future

The marketplace for poultry in the twenty-first century will be very different from that of the past. Understanding the wants and needs of generation Xers and echo-boomers will be key to responding successfully to these differences.

Quality will continue to be essential. In the 1970s, quality was the cornerstone of Frank Perdue's successful marketing program to "brand" his poultry. However, in the twenty-first century, quality will not be enough. Today's customers expect—even demand—all products to be high quality. Thus, Perdue Farms plans to use customer service to further differentiate the company. The focus will be on learning how to become indispensable to the customer by taking cost out of the product and delivering it exactly the way the customer wants it, where and when the customer wants it. In short, as Jim Perdue says, "Perdue Farms wants to become so easy to do business with that the customer will have no reason to do business with anyone else."

Acknowledgements: The authors are indebted to Frank Perdue, Jim Perdue, and the numerous associates at Perdue Farms, who generously shared their time and information about the company. In addition, the authors would like to thank the anonymous librarians at Blackwell Library, Salisbury State University, who routinely review area newspapers and file articles about the poultry industry—the most important industry on the DelMarVa Peninsula. Without their assistance, this case would not be possible.

Part Four
Managing Organizational Processes

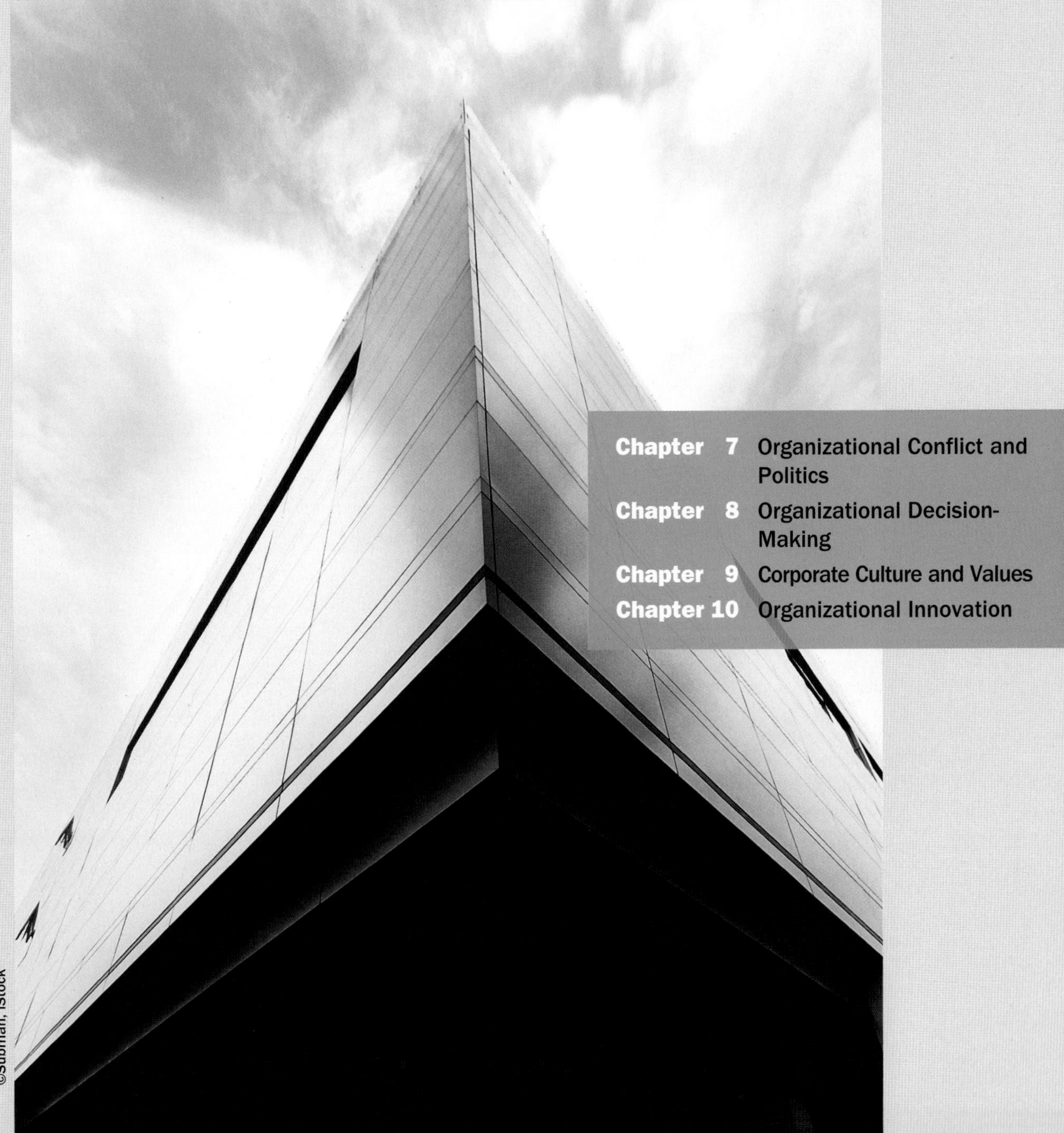

Chapter 7

Organizational Conflict and Politics

©Subman, iStock

Learning Objectives

After reading this chapter you should be able to:

1. Describe the sources of intergroup conflict in organizations.
2. Explain the rational versus political models of conflict.
3. Describe power versus authority and their sources in organizations.
4. Explain the concept of empowerment.
5. Understand the sources of horizontal power in organizations.
6. Define politics and understand when political activity is necessary.
7. Identify tactics for increasing and for using power.

Before reading this chapter, please check whether you agree or disagree with each of the following statements:

1 **A certain amount of conflict is good for an organization.**

I AGREE _____ I DISAGREE _____

2 **A factory worker on the assembly line is in a low power position and should accept that he or she will have little influence over what happens.**

I AGREE _____ I DISAGREE _____

3 **When managers use politics, it usually leads to conflict and disharmony and will likely disrupt the smooth functioning of the organization.**

I AGREE _____ I DISAGREE _____

There's a battle going on inside the executive offices of Research in Motion Ltd. (RIM). Should the company be making products designed and marketed primarily for professionals or should it target a mass consumer market? RIM makes the BlackBerry, which has long been the smartphone favored by corporations, government and military agencies, and many businesspeople. In early 2011 the company introduced its first tablet computer, the PlayBook. But executives couldn't seem to agree on who the product was designed for. Some managers saw the PlayBook as an extension of the BlackBerry, describing it as a "professional tablet" aimed at corporate customers. Others, however, wanted the PlayBook to aggressively focus on ordinary consumers interested in playing games and accessing music and movies. The conflict came to a head around the question of how to market the product. The name itself suggests a focus on ordinary consumers, and an early ad campaign planned to use humor and celebrities such as New England Patriots quarterback Tom Brady to appeal to a broad market. However, the campaign included the tagline "Go Pro" to satisfy those who wanted to target business professionals. The campaign was scrapped, but the battle continued. "There's an internal war going on around the marketing message," said one executive. "Even the guys at the top don't agree." By the time the PlayBook went on sale, RIM had fired two different advertising agencies and the company's marketing director and two of his deputies had resigned. The company's head of global sales and marketing says the PlayBook is aimed at both ordinary consumers and business users who want to enhance the abilities of a BlackBerry. So far, it isn't hitting either target.[1]

All organizations, like Research in Motion, are a complex mix of individuals and groups pursuing various goals and interests. The battle over the PlayBook reflects a conflict among managers over the future direction of the company. Sales of the BlackBerry have been steadily declining due to the popularity of the iPhone and Android-based smartphones, and some executives believe RIM can remain successful only by catering to the desires of ordinary retail consumers. Other executives, however, are resisting the consumer trend and believe the company should retain its corporate and professional focus.

Conflict such as that at RIM is a natural outcome of the close interaction of people who may have diverse opinions and values, pursue different objectives, and have differential access to information and resources within the organization. Individuals and groups use power and political activity to handle their differences and manage the inevitable conflicts that arise.[2] Too much conflict can be harmful to an organization. However, conflict can also be a positive force because it challenges the status quo, encourages new ideas and approaches, and leads to needed change.[3] Some degree of conflict occurs in all human relationships—between friends, romantic partners, and teammates, as well as between parents and children, teachers and students, and bosses and employees. Conflict is not necessarily a negative force; it results from the normal interaction of varying human interests. Within organizations, individuals and groups frequently have different interests and goals they wish to achieve through the organization. Managers can effectively use power and politics to manage conflict, get the most out of employees, enhance job satisfaction and team identification, achieve important goals, and realize high organizational performance.

Purpose of This Chapter

In this chapter we discuss the nature of conflict and the use of power and political tactics to manage and reduce conflict among individuals and groups. The notions of conflict, power, and politics appear in several chapters. In Chapter 2 we talked about horizontal linkages such as task forces and teams that encourage collaboration among functional departments. Chapter 6 introduced the concept of differentiation, which means that different departments pursue different goals and may have different attitudes and values. Chapter 4 touched on conflict and power relationships among organizations. Chapter 9 will discuss the emergence of subcultures, and Chapter 8 will propose that coalition building is one way to resolve disagreements among managers and departments.

The first sections of this chapter explore the nature of intergroup conflict, characteristics of organizations that contribute to conflict, the use of a political versus a rational model of organization to manage conflicting interests, and some tactics for reducing conflict and enhancing collaboration. Subsequent sections examine individual and organizational power, the vertical and horizontal sources of power for managers and other employees, and how power is used to attain organizational goals. We also look at the trend toward empowerment, sharing power with lower-level employees. The latter part of the chapter turns to politics, which is the application of power and influence to achieve desired outcomes. We discuss ways managers increase their power and various political tactics for using power to influence others and accomplish desired goals.

Interdepartmental Conflict in Organizations

Conflict among departments and groups in organizations, called *intergroup conflict*, requires three ingredients: group identification, observable group differences, and frustration. First, employees have to perceive themselves as part of an identifiable group or department.[4] Second, there has to be an observable group difference of some form. Groups may be located on different floors of the building, members may have different social or educational backgrounds, or members may work in different departments. The ability to identify oneself as a part of one group and to observe differences in comparison with other groups is necessary for conflict.[5]

The third ingredient is frustration. Frustration means that if one group achieves its goal, the other will not; it will be blocked. Frustration need not be severe and only needs to be anticipated to set off intergroup conflict. Intergroup conflict will appear when one group tries to advance its position in relation to other groups. **Intergroup conflict** can be defined as the behavior that occurs among organizational groups when participants identify with one group and perceive that other groups may block their group's goal achievement or expectations.[6] Conflict means that groups clash directly, that they are in fundamental opposition. Conflict is similar to competition but more severe. **Competition** is rivalry among groups in the pursuit of a common prize, whereas conflict presumes direct interference with goal achievement.

Intergroup conflict within organizations can occur horizontally across departments or vertically between different levels of the organization.[7] The production department of a manufacturing company may have a dispute with quality control because new quality procedures reduce production efficiency. R&D managers often conflict with finance managers because the finance managers' pressure to control costs reduces the amount of funding for new R&D projects. Teammates may argue about the best way to accomplish tasks and achieve goals. When Matthew Barrett became CEO of Barclays PLC, he found that members of the executive team were frequently in conflict because each member wanted to defend the interests of his or her part of the organization. Barrett took the team to dinner and told them he planned to disband the executive team unless members put the whole of the company first.[8]

Vertical conflict may occur when employees clash with bosses about new work methods, reward systems, or job assignments. Another typical area of conflict is between groups such as unions and management or franchise owners and headquarters. For example, franchise owners for McDonald's, Taco Bell, Burger King, and KFC have clashed with headquarters because of the increase of company-owned stores in neighborhoods that compete directly with franchisees.[9]

Conflict can also occur between different divisions or business units within an organization, such as between the auditing and consulting units of big firms like PricewaterhouseCoopers.[10] In global organizations, conflicts between regional managers and business division managers, among different divisions, or between divisions and headquarters are common because of the complexities of international business, as described in Chapter 5. Similar problems occur between distinct organizations. As we briefly discussed in Chapter 4, with so many companies involved in interorganizational collaboration, conflicts and shifting power relationships are inevitable.

Sources of Conflict

Some specific organizational characteristics can generate conflict. These **sources of intergroup conflict** are goal incompatibility, differentiation, task interdependence, and limited resources. These characteristics of organizational relationships are determined by the organizational structure and the contingency factors of environment, size, technology, and strategy and goals. These characteristics, in turn, help shape the extent to which a rational model of behavior versus a political model of behavior is used to accomplish objectives.

Goal Incompatibility. The goals of each department reflect the specific objectives members are trying to achieve. The achievement of one department's goals often interferes with another department's goals, leading to conflict. University police, for example, have a goal of providing a safe and secure campus. They can achieve their goal by locking all buildings on evenings and weekends and not distributing keys. Without easy access to buildings, however, progress toward the science department's research goals will proceed slowly. On the other hand, if scientists come and go at all hours and security is ignored, police goals for security will not be met. Goal incompatibility throws the departments into conflict with each other.

1 A certain amount of conflict is good for an organization.

ANSWER: *Agree.* Conflict is inevitable in all human relationships, including those in organizations, and is often a good thing. Some conflict can be healthy because it contributes to diverse thinking and leads to change. If there is no conflict whatsoever, there is likely no growth and development either.

In business organizations, the potential for conflict is perhaps greater between marketing and manufacturing than between other departments because the goals of these two departments are frequently at odds. Exhibit 7.1 shows examples of goal conflict between typical marketing and manufacturing departments. Marketing strives to increase the breadth of the product line to meet customer tastes for variety. A broad product line means short production runs, so manufacturing has to bear higher costs.[11] Typical areas of goal conflict are quality, cost control, and new products or services. At newspapers and other media organizations,

EXHIBIT 7.1
Marketing-Manufacturing Areas of Potential Goal Conflict

	MARKETING versus	MANUFACTURING
Goal Conflict	**Operative Goal Is Customer Satisfaction**	**Operative Goal Is Production Efficiency**
Conflict Area	**Typical Comment**	**Typical Comment**
1. Breadth of product line	"Our customers demand variety."	"The product line is too broad—all we get are short, uneconomical runs."
2. New product introduction	"New products are our lifeblood."	"Unnecessary design changes are prohibitively expensive."
3. Product scheduling	"We need faster response. Our customer lead times are too long."	"We need realistic commitments that don't change like wind direction."
4. Physical distribution	"Why don't we ever have the right merchandise in inventory?"	"We can't afford to keep huge inventories."
5. Quality	"Why can't we have reasonable quality at lower cost?"	"Why must we always offer options that are too expensive and offer little customer utility?"

Sources: Based on Benson S. Shapiro, "Can Marketing and Manufacturing Coexist?" *Harvard Business Review* 55 (September–October 1977), 104–114; and Victoria L. Crittenden, Lorraine R. Gardiner, and Antonie Stam, "Reducing Conflict between Marketing and Manufacturing," *Industrial Marketing Management* 22 (1993), 299–309.

there is frequently severe conflict between the business side (controlling costs, luring advertisers) and the journalism side (bias-free, high-quality news reporting). Goal incompatibility is probably the greatest cause of intergroup conflict in organizations.[12]

Differentiation. *Differentiation* was defined in Chapter 6 as "the differences in cognitive and emotional orientations among managers in different functional departments." Functional specialization requires people with specific education, skills, attitudes, and time horizons. For example, people may join a sales department because they have ability and aptitude consistent with sales work. After becoming members of the sales department, they are influenced by departmental norms and values.

Departments or divisions within an organization often differ in values, attitudes, and standards of behavior, and these subcultural differences lead to conflicts.[13] Consider an encounter between a sales manager and a research and development (R&D) scientist about a new product:

> *The sales manager may be outgoing and concerned with maintaining a warm, friendly relationship with the scientist. He may be put off because the scientist seems withdrawn and disinclined to talk about anything other than the problems in which he is interested. He may also be annoyed that the scientist seems to have such freedom in choosing what he will work on. Furthermore, the scientist is probably often late for appointments, which, from the salesman's point of view, is no way to run a business. Our scientist, for his part, may feel uncomfortable because the salesman seems to be pressing for immediate answers to technical questions that will take a long time to investigate. All the discomforts are concrete manifestations of the relatively wide differences between these two men in respect to their working and thinking styles.*[14]

BRIEFCASE

As an organization manager, keep these guidelines in mind:

Recognize that some interdepartmental conflict is natural and can benefit the organization. Associate the organizational design characteristics of goal incompatibility, differentiation, task interdependence, and resource scarcity with greater conflict among groups. Expect to devote more time and energy to resolving conflict in these situations.

Task Interdependence. Task interdependence refers to the dependence of one unit on another for materials, resources, or information. As will be described in Chapter 13, *pooled interdependence* means there is little interaction; *sequential interdependence* means the output of one department goes to the next department; and *reciprocal interdependence* means that departments mutually exchange materials and information.[15]

Generally, as interdependence increases, the potential for conflict increases.[16] In the case of pooled interdependence, units have little need to interact. Conflict is at a minimum. Sequential and reciprocal interdependence require employees to spend time coordinating and sharing information. Employees must communicate frequently, and differences in goals or attitudes will surface. Conflict is especially likely to occur when agreement is not reached about the coordination of services to each other. Greater interdependence means departments often exert pressure for a fast response because departmental work has to wait on other departments.[17]

Limited Resources. Another major source of conflict involves competition between groups for what members perceive as limited resources.[18] Organizations have limited money, physical facilities, staff resources, and human resources to share among departments. In their desire to achieve goals, groups want to increase their resources. This throws them into conflict. Managers may develop strategies, such as inflating budget requirements or working behind the scenes, to obtain a desired level of resources.

Resources also symbolize power and influence within an organization. The ability to obtain resources enhances prestige. Departments typically believe they have a legitimate claim on additional resources. However, exercising that claim results in conflict. Conflict over limited resources also occurs frequently among nonprofit and membership organizations. Consider the nation's labor unions, which are fighting each other these days as much or more than they are fighting corporate management.

Service Employees International Union

IN PRACTICE

On its website, the Service Employees International Union (SEIU) says it is the fastest growing union in North America. Leaders of other unions might say that's because the SEIU has been pulling some dirty tricks. The Service Employees International Union represents some 2.1 million members in about 100 different occupations. The organization recently spent millions of dollars on a campaign in California, but it wasn't aimed at winning favorable legislation or changes in management practices. The goals were to discourage some workers from joining a rival union and to urge other workers to quit their union and join the SEIU instead.

The SEIU isn't the only union engaged in a different kind of fight these days. Labor unions have been on the decline for years and the groups are competing for members and money. The conflict has taken many forms, including fighting within unions, fighting between unions, and even several unions joining forces against another. This is not the first period of internal strife within the labor movement, of course, but this time the conflict is less about philosophical differences and more about jockeying for power and growth in an era of declining resources.

Many union leaders embraced Mary Kay Henry, the SEIU's new president, as a consensus builder who can help to ease the conflicts. Henry quickly negotiated a settlement with rival union Unite Here that had reached the level of litigation. Nevertheless, conflict within and among the unions has continued, with leaders of various groups accusing one another of lying, bullying, and fraud as they vie for new members. Business leaders, meanwhile, are smiling. They know the time, energy, and money the unions spend fighting one another leaves less time and money to fight against corporate America and political candidates who are unfavorable to the labor unions' goals. "The other side doesn't have to take any shots at us," said Amy B. Dean, a longtime labor leader. "We're killing ourselves."[19]

Rational versus Political Model

The sources of intergroup conflict are listed in Exhibit 7.2. The degree of goal incompatibility, differentiation, interdependence, and competition for limited resources determines whether a rational or political model of behavior is used within the organization to accomplish goals.

When goals are in alignment, there is little differentiation, departments are characterized by pooled interdependence, and resources seem abundant, managers can use a **rational model** of organization, as outlined in Exhibit 7.2. As with the rational approach to decision making which will be described in Chapter 8, the rational model of organization is an ideal that is not fully achievable in the real world, though managers strive to use rational processes whenever possible. In the rational organization,

EXHIBIT 7.2
Sources of Conflict and Use of Rational versus Political Model

Sources of Potential Intergroup Conflict	When Conflict Is Low, Rational Model Describes Organization		When Conflict Is High, Political Model Describes Organization
• *Goal incompatibility* • *Differentiation* • *Task interdependence* • *Limited resources*	*Consistent across participants*	*Goals*	*Inconsistent, pluralistic within the organization*
	Centralized	*Power and control*	*Decentralized, shifting coalitions and interest groups*
	Orderly, logical, rational	*Decision process*	*Disorderly, result of bargaining and interplay among interests*
	Norm of efficiency	*Rules and norms*	*Free play of market forces; conflict is legitimate and expected*
	Extensive, systematic, accurate	*Information*	*Ambiguous; information used and withheld strategically*

behavior is not random or accidental. Goals are clear and choices are made in a logical way. When a decision is needed, the goal is defined, alternatives are identified, and the choice with the highest probability of success is selected. The rational model is also characterized by centralized power and control, extensive information systems, and an efficiency orientation.[20]

The opposite view of organizational processes is the **political model**, also described in Exhibit 7.2. When differences are great, organization groups have separate interests, goals, and values. Disagreement and conflict are normal, so power and influence are needed to reach decisions. Groups will engage in the push and pull of debate to decide goals and reach decisions. Information is ambiguous and incomplete. The political model describes the way organizations operate much of the time. Although managers strive to use a rational approach, the political model prevails because each department has different interests it wants met and different goals it wants to achieve. Purely rational procedures do not work for many circumstances.

Typically, both rational and political processes are used in organizations. Neither the rational model nor the political model characterizes things fully, but each will be used some of the time. Managers may strive to adopt rational procedures but will find that politics is needed to accomplish objectives. When managers fail to effectively apply the political model, conflict can escalate and prohibit the organization from achieving important outcomes.

Consider what happened at Premio Foods, where CEO Marc Cinque and Charlean Gmunder, the vice president of operations, tried to use a rational

EXHIBIT 7.3
Top 10 Problems from Too Much Conflict

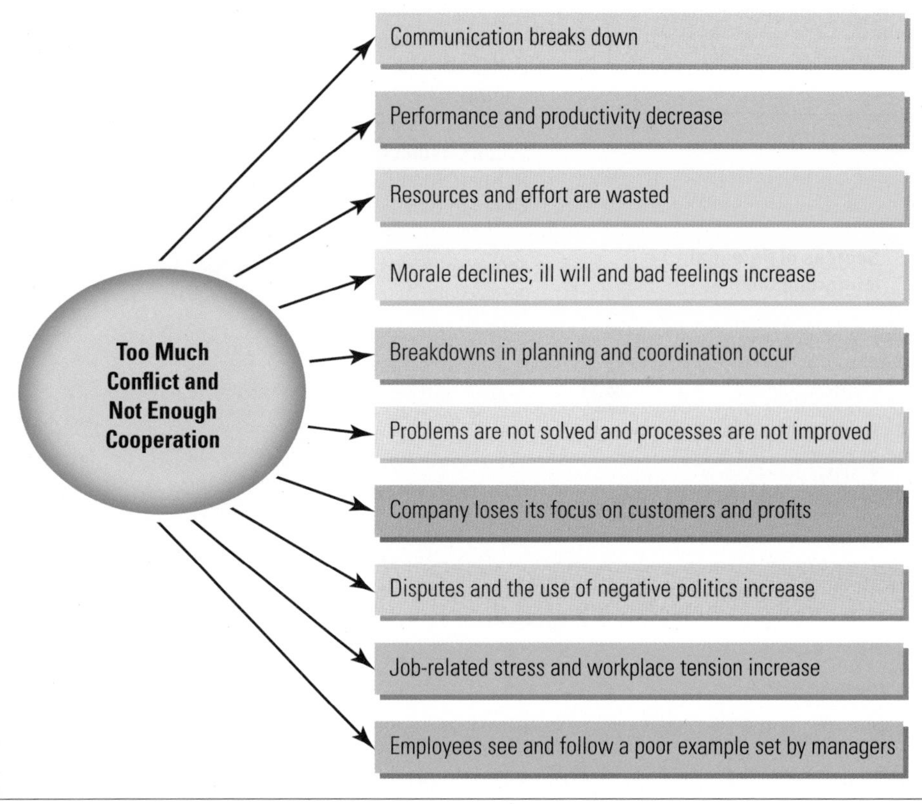
Too Much Conflict and Not Enough Cooperation
Communication breaks down
Performance and productivity decrease
Resources and effort are wasted
Morale declines; ill will and bad feelings increase
Breakdowns in planning and coordination occur
Problems are not solved and processes are not improved
Company loses its focus on customers and profits
Disputes and the use of negative politics increase
Job-related stress and workplace tension increase
Employees see and follow a poor example set by managers

Source: Based on survey results reported in Clinton O. Longenecker and Mitchell Neubert, "Barriers and Gateways to Management Cooperation and Teamwork," *Business Horizons* (November–December 2000), 37–44.

BRIEFCASE

As an organization manager, keep these guidelines in mind:

Use a political model of organization when differences among groups are great, goals are ill-defined, or there is competition for limited resources. Use the rational model when alternatives are clear, goals are defined, and managers can estimate the outcomes accurately. In these circumstances, coalition building, cooptation, or other political tactics are not needed and will not lead to better decisions.

model but discovered that a political model was needed. Gmunder suggested implementing a new computerized system that would overhaul the company's outdated method of forecasting and ordering and require changes in every department. She presented facts and statistics to Cinque showing that the system would increase annual cash flow by $500,000 and save up to $150,000 a year by cutting wasted material. But even though "the numbers made it clear," Cinque hesitated primarily because many of his senior managers expressed strong objections. After Cinque finally decided to go with the system, the conflict intensified. Gmunder couldn't get the information she needed from some managers, and some would show up late to meetings or skip them altogether. Gmunder had failed to build a coalition to support the new system. To salvage the project, Cinque formed a team that included senior managers from various departments to discuss their concerns and involve them in determining how the new system should work.[21]

Most organizations have at least moderate conflict among departments or other organizational groups. When conflict becomes too strong and managers do not work together, it creates many problems for organizations. Exhibit 7.3 lists the top 10 problems caused by a lack of cooperation that were identified by one survey of managers.[22]

Tactics for Enhancing Collaboration

Good managers strive to minimize conflict and prevent it from hurting organizational performance and goal attainment. Effective conflict management can have a direct, positive effect on team and organization performance.[23] Thus, managers consciously apply a variety of techniques to overcome conflict by stimulating cooperation and collaboration among departments to support the attainment of organizational goals. **Tactics for enhancing collaboration** include the following:

1. *Create integration devices.* As described in Chapter 2, teams, task forces, and project managers who span the boundaries between departments can be used as integration devices. Bringing together representatives from conflicting departments in joint problem-solving teams is an effective way to enhance collaboration because representatives learn to understand each other's point of view.[24] Sometimes a full-time integrator is assigned to achieve cooperation and collaboration by meeting with members of the respective departments and exchanging information. The integrator has to understand each group's problems and must be able to move both groups toward a solution that is mutually acceptable.[25]

   Teams and task forces reduce conflict and enhance cooperation because they integrate people from different departments. Integration devices can also be used to enhance cooperation between labor and management. **Labor-management teams**, which are designed to increase worker participation and provide a cooperative model for solving union-management problems, are increasingly being used at companies such as Goodyear, Ford Motor Company, and Alcoa. At the International Specialty Products Corporation plant in Calvert City, Kentucky, a union-management partnership enabled the company to improve quality, reduce costs, and enhance profitability. The plant leadership team is made up of two managers and two union members, and each of the plant's seven operating areas is jointly led by a management representative and a union representative.[26] Although unions continue to battle over traditional issues such as wages, these integration devices are creating a level of cooperation that many managers would not have believed possible just a few years ago. Bob King, president of the United Auto Workers, said the UAW learned the hard way that cooperation was important for helping keep the auto makers profitable. The "old 'Us vs. Them' mentality" is a relic of the past, King says.[27]
2. *Use confrontation and negotiation.* **Confrontation** occurs when parties in conflict directly engage one another and try to work out their differences. **Negotiation** is the bargaining process that often occurs during confrontation and that enables the parties to systematically reach a solution. These techniques bring appointed representatives from the departments together to work out a serious dispute. Confrontation and negotiation involve some risk. There is no guarantee that discussions will focus on a conflict or that emotions will not get out of hand. However, if members are able to resolve the conflict on the basis of face-to-face discussions, they will find new respect for each other, and future collaboration becomes easier. The beginnings of relatively permanent attitude change are possible through direct negotiation.

   Confrontation and negotiation are successful when managers engage in a *win-win strategy.* Win-win means both sides adopt a positive attitude and strive to resolve the conflict in a way that will benefit each other.[28] If the negotiations deteriorate into a strictly win-lose strategy (each group wants to defeat the other), the confrontation will

EXHIBIT 7.4
Negotiating Strategies

Win-Lose Strategy	Win-Win Strategy
1. Define the problem as a win-lose situation.	1. Define the conflict as a mutual problem.
2. Pursue own group's outcomes.	2. Pursue joint outcomes.
3. Force the other group into submission.	3. Find creative agreements that satisfy both groups.
4. Be deceitful, inaccurate, and misleading in communicating the group's needs, goals, and proposals.	4. Be open, honest, and accurate in communicating the group's needs, goals, and proposals.
5. Use threats (to force submission).	5. Avoid threats (to reduce the other's defensiveness).
6. Communicate strong commitment (rigidity) regarding one's position.	6. Communicate flexibility of position.

Source: Adapted from David W. Johnson and Frank P. Johnson, *Joining Together: Group Theory and Group Skills* (Englewood Cliffs, NJ: Prentice-Hall, 1975), 182–183.

be ineffective. The differences between win-win and win-lose strategies of negotiation are shown in Exhibit 7.4. With a win-win strategy—which includes defining the problem as mutual, communicating openly, and avoiding threats—understanding can be changed while the dispute is resolved.

One type of negotiation, used to resolve a disagreement between workers and management, is referred to as **collective bargaining**. The bargaining process is usually accomplished through a union and results in an agreement that specifies each party's responsibilities for the next two to three years.

3. *Schedule intergroup consultation.* When conflict is intense and enduring, and department members are suspicious and uncooperative, top managers may intervene as third parties to help resolve the conflict or bring in third-party consultants from outside the organization.[29] This process, sometimes called *workplace mediation,* is a strong intervention to reduce conflict because it involves bringing the disputing parties together and allowing each side to present its version of the situation. The technique has been developed by such psychologists as Robert Blake, Jane Mouton, and Richard Walton.[30]

   Department members attend a workshop, which may last for several days, away from day-to-day work problems. This approach is similar to the organization development (OD) approach which will be described in Chapter 10. The conflicting groups are separated, and each group is invited to discuss and make a list of its perceptions of itself and the other group. Group representatives publicly share these perceptions, and together the groups discuss the results. Intergroup consultation can be quite demanding for everyone involved, but if handled correctly these sessions can help department employees understand each other much better and lead to improved attitudes and better working relationships for years to come.

4. *Practice member rotation.* Rotation means that individuals from one department can be asked to work in another department on a temporary or permanent basis. The advantage is that individuals become submerged in the values, attitudes, problems, and goals of the other department. In addition, individuals can explain the problems and goals of their original departments to their new colleagues. This enables a frank, accurate exchange of views and information. Rotation works slowly to reduce conflict but is very effective for changing the underlying attitudes and perceptions that promote conflict.[31]

5. *Create shared mission and superordinate goals.* Another strategy is for top management to create a shared mission and establish superordinate goals that require cooperation among departments.[32] As will be discussed in Chapter 9, organizations with strong, constructive cultures, where employees share a larger vision for their company, are more likely to have a united, cooperative workforce. Studies have shown that when employees from different departments see that their goals are linked, they will openly share resources and information.[33] To be effective, superordinate goals must be substantial, and employees must be granted the time and incentives to work cooperatively in pursuit of the superordinate goals rather than departmental subgoals.

BRIEFCASE

As an organization manager, keep these guidelines in mind:

If conflict becomes too strong, use tactics for enhancing collaboration, including integration devices, confrontation, intergroup consultation, member rotation, and superordinate goals. Select the technique that fits the organization and the conflict.

Power and Organizations

Power is an intangible force in organizations. It cannot be seen, but its effect can be felt. *Power* is often defined as the potential ability of one person (or department) to influence other people (or departments) to carry out orders[34] or to do something they would not otherwise have done.[35] Other definitions stress that power is the ability to achieve goals or outcomes that power holders desire.[36] The achievement of desired outcomes is the basis of the definition used here: **Power** is the ability of one person or department in an organization to influence other people to bring about desired outcomes. It is the potential to influence others within the organization with the goal of attaining desired outcomes for power holders. Powerful managers, for instance, are often able to get bigger budgets for their departments, more favorable production schedules, and more control over the organization's agenda.[37]

Power exists only in a relationship between two or more people, and it can be exercised in either vertical or horizontal directions. The source of power often derives from an exchange relationship in which one position, department, or organization provides scarce or valued resources to other people, departments, or organizations. When one is dependent on another, a power relationship emerges in which the side with the resources has greater power.[38] Power holders can achieve compliance with their requests.

As an illustration of dependence increasing one's power, consider AMC's hit show "Mad Men." The show's creator, Matthew Weiner, has had tremendous power in the relationship with AMC and could virtually dictate the terms of his contract. Until recently, AMC had little original programming and was dependent on "Mad Men" for the advertising revenues and prestige it brought to the cable network. In recent negotiations, Weiner walked away with a three-year deal worth $30 million, one of the biggest of its kind in cable television, and the network also dropped some of its demands regarding cast budget cuts and advertising slots. Weiner is considered the heart and soul of "Mad Men," so AMC was dependent upon him to keep the hit show going.[39]

Individual versus Organizational Power

In popular literature, power is often described as a personal characteristic, and a frequent topic is how one person can influence or dominate another person.[40] You probably recall from an earlier management or organizational behavior course that managers have five sources of personal power.[41] *Legitimate power* is the authority granted by the organization to the formal management position a manager holds. *Reward power* stems from the ability to bestow rewards—a promotion, raise, or pat on the back—to other people. The authority to punish or recommend punishment is called *coercive power. Expert power* derives from a person's greater skill or knowledge about the tasks being performed. The last, *referent power,* is derived from personal characteristics: people admire the manager and want to be like or identify with the manager out of respect and admiration. Each of these sources may be used by individuals within organizations.

Power in organizations, however, is often the result of structural characteristics.[42] Organizations are large, complex systems that may contain hundreds, even thousands, of people. These systems have a formal hierarchy in which some tasks are more important regardless of who performs them. In addition, some positions have access to more information and greater resources, or their contribution to the organization is more critical. Thus, the important power processes in organizations reflect larger organizational relationships, both horizontal and vertical.

Power versus Authority

Anyone in an organization can exercise power to achieve desired outcomes. For example, when the Discovery Channel wanted to extend its brand beyond cable television, Tom Hicks began pushing for a focus on the Internet. Even though Discovery's CEO favored exploring interactive television instead, Hicks organized a grassroots campaign that eventually persuaded the CEO to focus on Internet publishing, indicating that Hicks had power within the organization. Eventually, Hicks was put in charge of running Discovery Channel Online.[43]

The concept of formal authority is related to power but is narrower in scope. **Authority** is also a force for achieving desired outcomes, but only as prescribed by the formal hierarchy and reporting relationships. Three properties identify authority:

1. *Authority is vested in organizational positions.* People have authority because of the positions they hold, not because of personal characteristics or resources.
2. *Authority is accepted by subordinates.* Subordinates comply because they believe position holders have a legitimate right to exercise authority.[44] In most North American organizations, employees accept that supervisors can legitimately tell them what time to arrive at work, the tasks to perform while they're there, and what time they can go home.
3. *Authority flows down the vertical hierarchy.*[45] Authority exists along the formal chain of command, and positions at the top of the hierarchy are vested with more formal authority than are positions at the bottom.

Formal authority is exercised downward along the hierarchy. Organizational power, on the other hand, can be exercised upward, downward, and horizontally in organizations. In addition, managers can have formal authority but little real power. Consider what happened when Bill Gates turned the CEO job at Microsoft over to Steven Ballmer. Although Ballmer got the title and the formal authority, Gates retained the power. He continued to hold sway over many day-to-day business decisions, and sometimes his personal power would undermine Ballmer in front of other executives. Though Gates has now fully stepped aside from management of the company and publicly supports Ballmer's decisions, insiders say the power struggle left the company in a weakened position, without a clear strategic direction.[46] In the following sections we examine how employees throughout the organization can tap into both vertical and horizontal sources of power.

Vertical Sources of Power

All employees along the vertical hierarchy have access to some sources of power. Although a large amount of power is typically allocated to top managers by the organization structure, people throughout the organization often obtain power disproportionate to their formal positions and can exert influence in an upward direction, as Tom Hicks did at the Discovery Channel. There are four major sources of vertical power: formal position, resources, control of information, and network centrality.[47]

BRIEFCASE

As an organization manager, keep this guideline in mind:

Understand and use the vertical sources of power in organizations, including formal position, resources, control of information, and network centrality.

Formal Position. Certain rights, responsibilities, and prerogatives accrue to top positions. People throughout the organization accept the legitimate right of top managers to set goals, make decisions, and direct activities. This is *legitimate power,* as defined earlier. Senior managers often use symbols and language to perpetuate their legitimate power. For example, the new administrator at a large hospital in the San Francisco area symbolized his legitimate position power by issuing a newsletter with his photo on the cover and airing a 24-hour-a-day video to personally welcome patients.[48]

The amount of power provided to middle managers and lower-level participants can be built into the organization's structural design. The allocation of power to middle managers and staff is important because power enables employees to be productive. When job tasks are nonroutine, and when employees participate in self-directed teams and problem-solving task forces, this encourages them to be flexible and creative and to use their own discretion. Allowing people to make their own decisions increases their power.

Power is also increased when a position encourages contact with high-level people. Access to powerful people and the development of a relationship with them provide a strong base of influence.[49] For example, in some organizations an administrative assistant to the president might have more power than a department head because the assistant has access to the senior executive on a daily basis.

The logic of designing positions for more power assumes that an organization does not have a limited amount of power to be allocated among high-level and low-level employees. The total amount of power in an organization can be increased by designing tasks and interactions along the hierarchy so everyone can exert more influence. If the distribution of power is skewed too heavily toward the top, research suggests that the organization will be less effective.[50]

Resources. Organizations allocate huge amounts of resources. Buildings are constructed, salaries are paid, and equipment and supplies are purchased. Each year, new resources are allocated in the form of budgets. These resources are allocated downward from top managers. Top managers often own stock, which gives them property rights over resource allocation. In many of today's organizations, however, employees throughout the organization also share in ownership, which increases their power.

In most cases, top managers control the resources and, hence, can determine their distribution. Resources can be used as rewards and punishments, which are additional sources of power. Resource allocation creates a dependency relationship. Lower-level participants depend on top managers for the financial and physical resources needed to perform their tasks. Top management can exchange resources in the form of salaries and bonuses, personnel, promotions, and physical facilities for compliance with the outcomes they desire.

Control of Information. The control of information can be a significant source of power. Managers recognize that information is a primary business resource and that by controlling what information is collected, how it is interpreted, and how it is shared, they can influence how decisions are made.[51] In many of today's companies, information is openly and broadly shared, which increases the power of people throughout the organization.

However, top managers generally have access to more information than do other employees. This information can be released as needed to shape the decisions of other people. In one organization, Clark Ltd., the senior information technology manager controlled information given to the board of directors and thereby influenced the board's decision to purchase a sophisticated computer system.[52] The board of directors had formal authority to decide from which company the system would be purchased. The management services group was asked to recommend which of six computer manufacturers should receive the order. Jim Kenny was in charge of the management services group, and Kenny disagreed with other managers about which system to purchase. As shown in Exhibit 7.5, other managers had to go through Kenny to have their viewpoints heard by the board. Kenny shaped the board's thinking toward selecting the system he preferred by controlling information given to them.

Middle managers and lower-level employees may also have access to information that can increase their power. An assistant to a senior executive can often

EXHIBIT 7.5
Information Flow for Computer Decision at Clark Ltd.

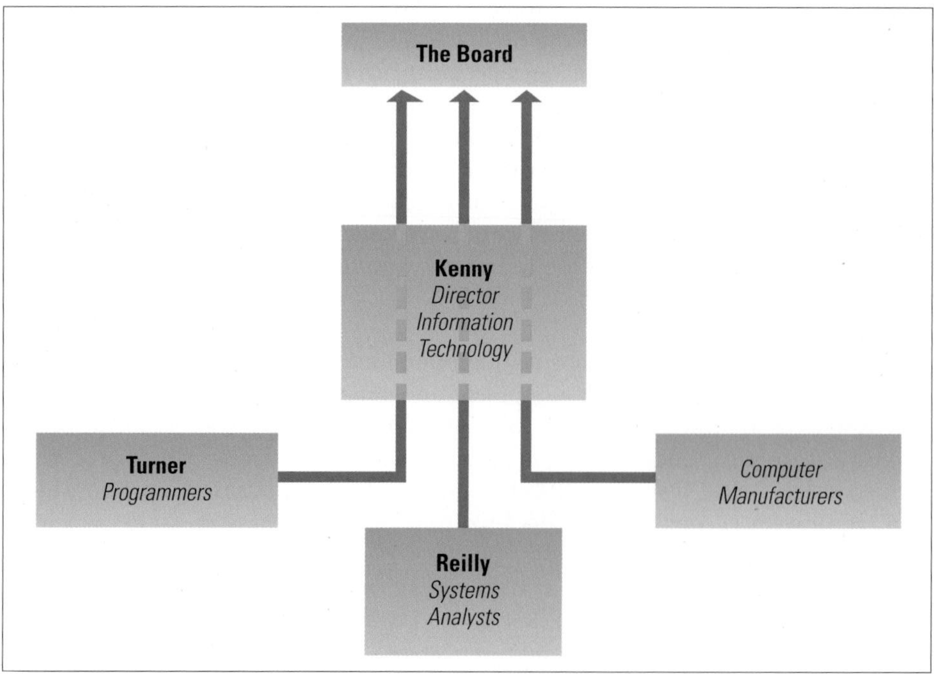

Source: Andrew M. Pettigrew, *The Politics of Organizational Decision-Making* (London: Tavistock, 1973), 235. Reprinted by permission of the author.

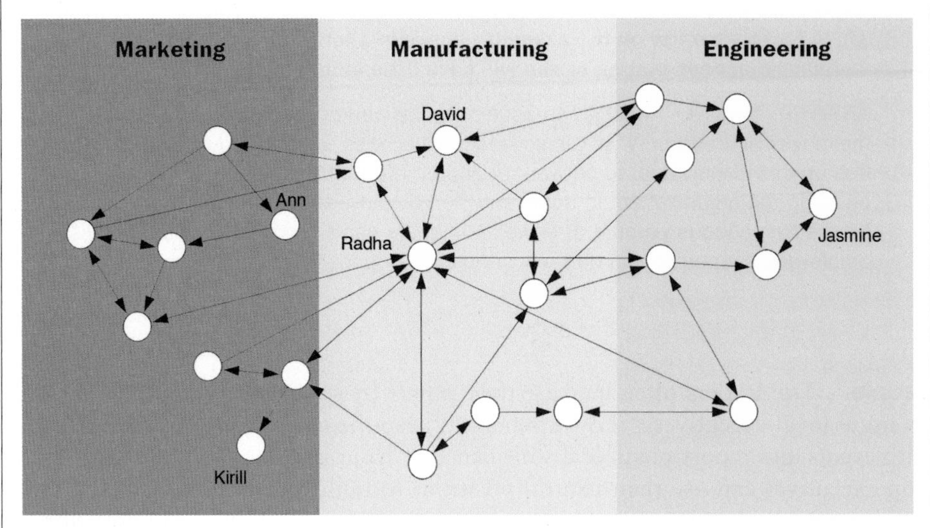

EXHIBIT 7.6
An Illustration of Network Centrality

control information that other people want and will thus be able to influence those people. Top executives depend on people throughout the organization for information about problems or opportunities. Middle managers or lower-level employees may manipulate the information they provide to top managers in order to influence decision outcomes.

Network Centrality. **Network centrality** means being centrally located in the organization and having access to information and people that are critical to the company's success. Managers as well as lower-level employees are more effective and more influential when they put themselves at the center of a communication network, building connections with people throughout the company. For example, in Exhibit 7.6, Radha has a well-developed communication network, sharing information and assistance with many people across the marketing, manufacturing, and engineering departments. Contrast Radha's contacts with those of Jasmine or Kirill. Who do you think is likely to have greater access to resources and more influence in the organization?

People at all levels of the hierarchy can use the idea of network centrality to accomplish goals and be more successful. A real-life example comes from Xerox Corporation. Several years ago, Cindy Casselman, who had little formal power and authority, began selling her idea for an intranet site to managers all over the company. Casselman had a well-developed network, and she worked behind the scenes, gradually gaining the power she needed to make her vision a reality—and win a promotion in the process.[53]

People can increase their network centrality by becoming knowledgeable and expert about certain activities or by taking on difficult tasks and acquiring specialized knowledge that makes them indispensable to managers above them. People who show initiative, work beyond what is expected, take on undesirable but important projects, and show interest in learning about the company and industry often find themselves with influence. Physical location also helps because some locations are in the center of things. Central location lets a person be visible to key people and become part of important interaction networks.

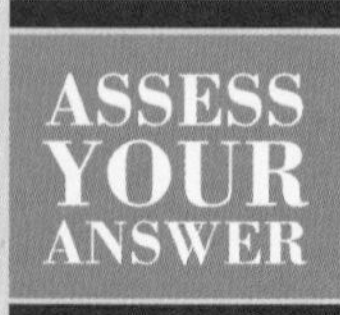

2 A factory worker on the assembly line is in a low power position and should accept that he or she will have little influence over what happens.

ANSWER: *Disagree.* Although an assembly line worker typically has little formal power and authority, all employees have access to some sources of power. It is up to the individual to network or gather information to expand his or her power in the organization. In addition, when employees band together, they can have a tremendous amount of power. Managers can't accomplish goals unless employees cooperate and do the work they're supposed to do.

People. Top leaders often increase their power by surrounding themselves with a group of loyal executives.[54] Loyal managers keep the leader informed and in touch with events and report possible disobedience or troublemaking in the organization. Top executives can use their central positions to build alliances and exercise substantial power when they have a management team that is fully in support of their decisions and actions.

Many top executives strive to build a cadre of loyal and supportive executives to help them achieve their goals for the organization. Smart managers also actively work to build bridges and win over potential opponents. Gary Loveman, who left a position as associate professor at Harvard Business School to be the chief operating officer of casino company Harrah's, provides a good example. Some Harrah's executives, including the CFO, resented Loveman's appointment and could have derailed his plans for the company. Because he knew the CFO's information, knowledge, and support would be critical for accomplishing his plans, Loveman made building a positive relationship with the CFO a priority. He stopped by his office frequently to talk, kept him informed about what he was doing and why, and took care to involve him in important meetings and decisions. Building positive relationships enabled Loveman to accomplish goals that eventually led to him being named CEO of Harrah's.[55]

This idea works for lower-level employees and managers too. Lower-level people have greater power when they have positive relationships and connections with higher-ups. By being loyal and supportive of their bosses, employees sometimes gain favorable status and exert greater influence.

BRIEFCASE

As an organization manager, keep these guidelines in mind:

Do not leave lower organization levels powerless. If vertical power is too heavy in favor of top management, empower lower levels by giving people the tools they need to perform better: information, knowledge and skills, and the power to make substantive decisions.

The Power of Empowerment

In forward-thinking organizations, top managers want lower-level employees to have greater power so they can do their jobs more effectively. These managers intentionally push power down the hierarchy and share it with employees to enable them to achieve goals. **Empowerment** is power sharing, the delegation of power or authority to subordinates in an organization.[56] Increasing employee power heightens motivation for task accomplishment because people improve their own effectiveness, choosing how to do a task and using their creativity.[57]

Empowering employees involves giving them three elements that enable them to act more freely to accomplish their jobs: information, knowledge, and power.[58]

1. *Employees receive information about company performance.* In companies where employees are fully empowered, all employees have access to all financial and operational information.

2. *Employees have knowledge and skills to contribute to company goals.* Companies use training programs and other development tools to help people acquire the knowledge and skills they need to contribute to organizational performance.
3. *Employees have the power to make substantive decisions.* Empowered employees have the authority to directly influence work procedures and organizational performance, such as through quality circles or self-directed work teams.

Many of today's organizations are implementing empowerment programs, but they are empowering employees to varying degrees. At some companies, empowerment means encouraging employees' ideas while managers retain final authority for decisions; at others it means giving people almost complete freedom and power to make decisions and exercise initiative and imagination.[59] The continuum of empowerment can run from a situation in which front-line employees have almost no discretion, such as on a traditional assembly line, to full empowerment, where employees even participate in formulating organizational strategy. One organization that pushes empowerment to the maximum is Semco.

IN PRACTICE

Semco

The Brazil-based company Semco's fundamental operating principle is to harness the wisdom of all its employees. It does so by letting people control their work hours, location, and even pay plans. Employees also participate in all organizational decisions, including what businesses Semco should pursue.

Semco leaders believe economic success requires creating an atmosphere that puts power and control directly in the hands of employees. People can veto any new product idea or business venture. They choose their own leaders and manage themselves to accomplish goals. Information is openly and broadly shared so that everyone knows where they and the company stand. Instead of dictating Semco's identity and strategy, leaders allow it to be shaped by individual interests and efforts. People are encouraged to seek challenge, explore new ideas and business opportunities, and question the ideas of anyone in the company.

This high level of employee empowerment has helped Semco achieve decades of high profitability and growth despite fluctuations in the economy and shifting markets. "At Semco, we don't play by the rules," says Ricardo Semler. Semler, whose father started the company in the 1950s, says it doesn't unnerve him to "step back and see nothing on the company's horizon." He is happy to watch the company and its employees "ramble through their days, running on instinct and opportunity . . . "[60]

Horizontal Sources of Power

Horizontal power pertains to relationships across departments, divisions, or other units. All vice presidents are usually at the same level on the organization chart. Does this mean each department has the same amount of power? No. Horizontal power is not defined by the formal hierarchy or the organization chart. Each department makes a unique contribution to organizational success. Some departments will have greater say and will achieve their desired outcomes, whereas others will not. Researcher and scholar Charles Perrow surveyed managers in several industrial firms.[61] He bluntly asked, "Which department has the most power?" among four major departments: production, sales and marketing, R&D, and finance and accounting. Partial survey results are given in Exhibit 7.7.

EXHIBIT 7.7
Ratings of Power among Departments in Industrial Firms

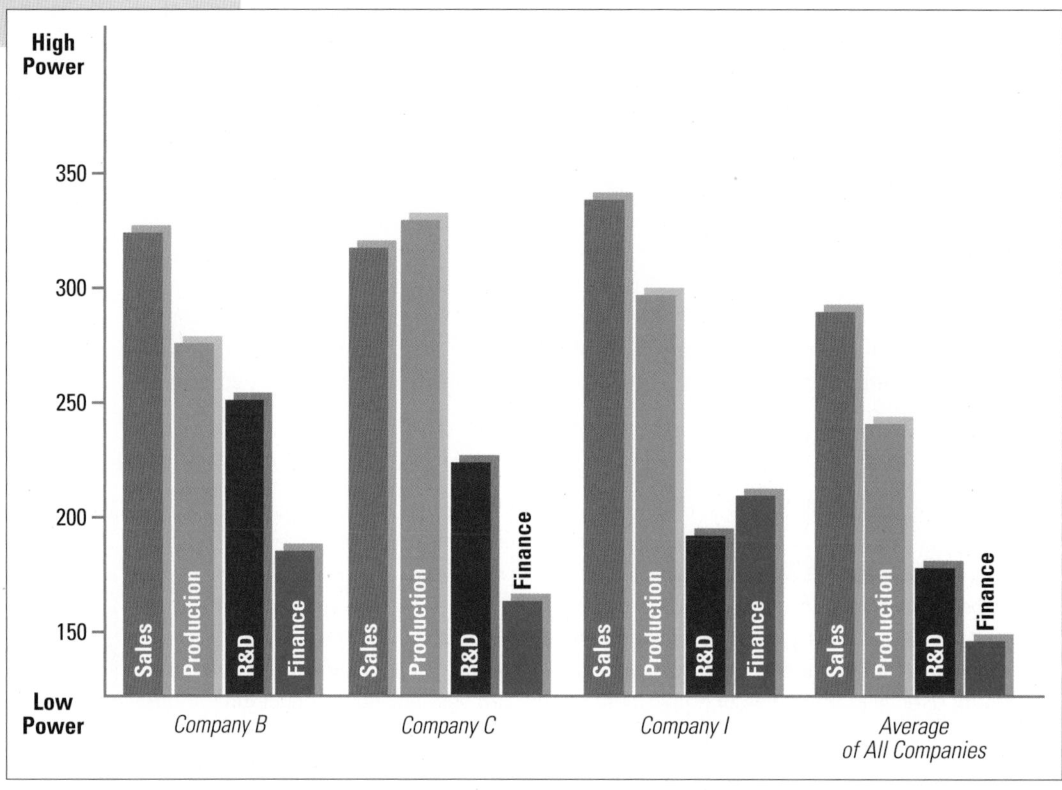

Source: Charles Perrow, "Departmental Power and Perspective in Industrial Firms," in Mayer N. Zald, ed., *Power in Organizations* (Nashville, TN: Vanderbilt University Press, 1970), 64.

In most firms, sales had the greatest power. In a few firms, production was also quite powerful. On average, the sales and production departments were more powerful than R&D and finance, although substantial variation existed. Differences in the amount of horizontal power clearly occurred in those firms. In another recent study of 55 top-level decisions in 14 organizations in the United Kingdom, researchers found that production, finance, and marketing had the greatest influence on strategic decisions compared to R&D, HR, and purchasing.[62] Power shifts among departments depending on circumstances. Today, finance departments have gained power in many companies because of the urgent need to control costs in a tough economy. Ethics and compliance offices may have greater power because they help reduce uncertainty for top leaders regarding ethical scandals and financial malfeasance. In the Federal government, watchdog and regulatory agencies for Wall Street have increased power because of the 2008 financial meltdown. Under the leadership of former chairman Sheila Bair, for example, the Federal Deposit Insurance Corporation (FDIC) gained broad new powers to police large financial institutions, including installing examiners at financial firms to monitor their managers' activities.[63]

Horizontal power is difficult to measure because power differences are not defined on the organization chart. However, some initial explanations for power differences, such as those shown in Exhibit 7.7, have been found. The theoretical concept that explains relative power is called strategic contingencies.[64]

Strategic Contingencies. **Strategic contingencies** are events and activities both inside and outside an organization that are essential for attaining organizational goals. Departments involved with strategic contingencies for the organization tend to have greater power. Departmental activities are important when they provide strategic value by solving problems or crises for the organization. For example, if an organization faces an intense threat from lawsuits and regulations, the legal department will gain power and influence over organizational decisions because it copes with such a threat. If product innovation is the key strategic issue, the power of R&D can be expected to be high.

The strategic contingency approach to power is similar to the resource dependence model described in Chapters 4 and 6. Recall that organizations try to reduce dependence on the external environment. The strategic contingency approach to power suggests that the departments or organizations most responsible for dealing with key resource issues and dependencies in the environment will become most powerful. The National Football League, for instance, bowed to the power of the cable companies and arranged for its television partners, CBS and NBC, to simultaneously broadcast along with the NFL Network the highly-anticipated December 2007 game between the undefeated Patriots and the Giants. The NFL tried for years to get the cable companies to add its network to their basic packages along with ESPN and ESPN2, but the cable companies refused because the price was too high. The NFL has a popular product, but with limited distribution options, it is in a low power position compared to the cable operators.[65]

Power Sources. Jeffrey Pfeffer and Gerald Salancik, among others, have been instrumental in conducting research on the strategic contingencies theory.[66] Their findings indicate that a department rated as powerful may possess one or more of the characteristics illustrated in Exhibit 7.8.[67] In some organizations these five **power sources** overlap, but each provides a useful way to evaluate sources of horizontal power.

1. *Dependency.* Interdepartmental **dependency** is a key element underlying relative power. Power is derived from having something someone else wants. The power of department A over department B is greater when department B depends on department A.[68] Materials, information, and resources may flow between departments in one direction, such as in the case of sequential task interdependence (see Chapter 13). In such cases, the department receiving resources is in a lower power position than the department providing them. The number and strength of dependencies are also important. When seven or eight departments must come for help to the engineering department, for example, engineering is in a strong power position. In contrast, a department that depends on many other departments is in a low power position. Likewise, a department in an otherwise low power position might gain power through dependencies. If a factory cannot produce without the expertise of maintenance workers to keep the machines working, the maintenance department is in a strong power position because it has control over a strategic contingency.
2. *Financial resources.* Control over resources is an important source of power in organizations. Money can be converted into other kinds of resources that

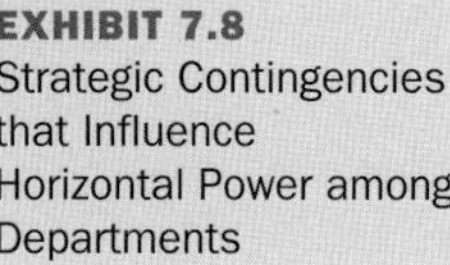

EXHIBIT 7.8
Strategic Contingencies that Influence Horizontal Power among Departments

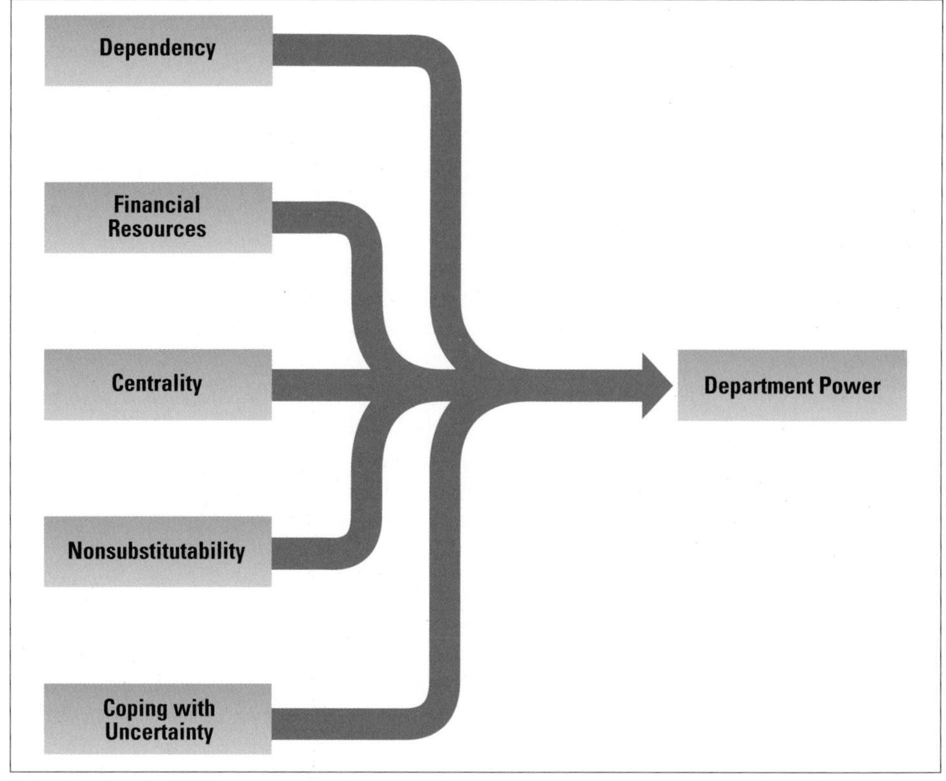

are needed by other departments. Money generates dependency; departments that provide financial resources have something other departments want. Departments that generate income for an organization have greater power. Exhibit 7.7 showed sales as the most powerful unit in most industrial firms. This is because salespeople find customers and bring in money, thereby removing an important problem for the organization. An ability to provide financial resources also explains why certain departments are powerful in other organizations, such as universities.

University of Illinois

IN PRACTICE

You might expect budget allocation in a state university to be a straightforward process. The need for financial resources can be determined by such things as the number of undergraduate students, the number of graduate students, and the number of faculty in each department.

In fact, resource allocation at the University of Illinois is not clear-cut. The University of Illinois has a relatively fixed resource inflow from state government. Beyond that, important resources come from research grants and the quality of students and faculty. University departments that provide the most resources to the university are rated as having the most power. Some departments have more power because of their resource contribution to the university. Departments that generate large research grants are more powerful, for instance, because research grants contain a sizable overhead payment to university administration. This overhead money pays for a large share of the university's personnel and facilities. The size of a department's graduate student body and the national prestige of the department also add to power. Graduate students and national prestige are nonfinancial resources that add to the reputation and effectiveness of the university.

How do university departments use their power? Generally, they use it to obtain even more resources from the rest of the university. Very powerful departments receive university resources, such as graduate-student fellowships, internal research support, and summer faculty salaries, far in excess of their needs based on the number of students and faculty.[69]

As shown in the example of the University of Illinois, power accrues to departments that bring in or provide resources that are highly valued by an organization. Power enables those departments to obtain more of the scarce resources allocated within the organization. "Power derived from acquiring resources is used to obtain more resources, which in turn can be employed to produce more power—the rich get richer."[70]

3. *Centrality.* **Centrality** reflects a department's role in the primary activity of an organization.[71] One measure of centrality is the extent to which the work of the department affects the final output of the organization. For example, the production department is more central and usually has more power than staff groups (assuming no other critical contingencies). Centrality is associated with power because it reflects the contribution made to the organization. The corporate finance department of an investment bank generally has more power than the stock research department. By contrast, in the manufacturing firms described in Exhibit 7.7, finance tends to be low in power. When the finance department has the limited task of recording money and expenditures, it is not responsible for obtaining critical resources or for producing the products of the organization. Today, however, finance departments have greater power in many organizations because of the greater need for controlling costs.
4. *Nonsubstitutability.* Power is also determined by **nonsubstitutability**, which means that a department's function cannot be performed by other readily available resources. If an organization has no alternative sources of skill and information, a department's power will be greater. This can be one reason top managers use outside consultants. Consultants might be used as substitutes for staff people to reduce the power of staff groups.

The impact of substitutability on power was studied for programmers in computer departments.[72] When computers were first introduced, programming was a rare and specialized occupation. Programmers controlled the use of organizational computers because they alone possessed the knowledge to program them. Over a period of about 10 years, computer programming became a more common activity. People could be substituted easily, and the power of programming departments dropped. Substitutability affects the power of organizations as well. Major record labels once had tremendous power over artists in the music industry because they had almost total control over which artists got their music recorded and in front of consumers. Today, though, new and established bands can release albums directly on the Internet without going through a label. In addition, Walmart, the largest music retailer in the United States, has entered the music making and marketing business, buying albums directly from artists like the Eagles and Journey. Intense marketing helped the Eagles' "Long Road Out of Eden" sell 711,000 copies through Walmart in its first week, without a traditional record company ever being involved.[73]

BRIEFCASE

As an organization manager, keep these guidelines in mind:

Be aware of the important horizontal power relationships that come from the ability of a department to deal with strategic contingencies that confront the organization. Increase the horizontal power of a department by increasing involvement in strategic contingencies.

5. *Coping with Uncertainty*. Elements in the environment can change swiftly and can be unpredictable and complex. In the face of uncertainty, little information is available to managers on appropriate courses of action. Departments that reduce this uncertainty for the organization will increase their power.[74] When market research personnel accurately predict changes in demand for new products, they gain power and prestige because they have reduced a critical uncertainty. But forecasting is only one technique. Sometimes uncertainty can be reduced by taking quick and appropriate action after an unpredictable event occurs.

   Departments can cope with critical uncertainties by (1) obtaining prior information, (2) prevention, and (3) absorption.[75] *Obtaining prior information* means a department can reduce an organization's uncertainty by forecasting an event. Departments increase their power through *prevention* by predicting and forestalling negative events. *Absorption* occurs when a department takes action after an event to reduce its negative consequences. Consider the following case from the health care industry.

Carilion Health System

IN PRACTICE

Because hospitals and other health care providers have to deal with so many complex legal and regulatory matters, the legal department is usually in a high power position. That is certainly the case at Carilion Health System, based in Roanoke, Virginia. Some years ago, the legal department successfully fought off a U.S. Department of Justice antitrust lawsuit and played a crucial role in negotiating a merger between Carilion and Roanoke's only other hospital.

Since then, the legal department has been kept busy not only with regulatory issues but also with trying to get payment from patients who say they can't pay their high medical bills. Because Roanoke is now a "one-market town" in terms of health care, critics say Carilion is getting away with charging excessive fees, thereby hurting patients, businesses, insurers, and the entire community. The Roanoke City District Court devotes one morning a week to cases filed by Carilion, which during one recent fiscal year sued nearly 10,000 patients, garnished the wages of more than 5,000 people, and placed liens on nearly 4,000 homes.

The negative press resulting from this, along with a backlash from independent doctors who say Carilion is intentionally stifling competition, means the public relations department has a chance to increase its power as well. The department is actively involved in efforts to bolster Carilion's image as a good corporate citizen, emphasizing that it only sues patients it believes have the ability to pay and pointing out the millions of dollars Carilion dispenses to charity care each year.[76]

At Carilion, the legal department absorbed a critical uncertainty by fighting off the antitrust lawsuit and helping Carilion grow in size and power. It continues to take action after uncertainties appear (such as patients who don't pay).

Horizontal power relationships in organizations change as strategic contingencies change. Whereas the legal department will likely continue in a high power position at Carilion, the need of the hospital to improve its reputation and fend off growing criticism could lead to an increase in the power of the public relations department. The public relations department can gain power by being involved in activities targeted toward both prevention and absorption. Departments that help organizations cope with new strategic issues will increase their power.

Political Processes in Organizations

Politics, like power, is intangible and difficult to measure. It is hidden from view and is hard to observe in a systematic way. Two surveys uncovered the following reactions of managers toward political behavior.[77]

1. Most managers have a negative view toward politics and believe that politics will more often hurt than help an organization in achieving its goals.
2. Managers believe that political behavior is common in practically all organizations.
3. Most managers think that political behavior occurs more often at upper rather than lower levels in organizations.
4. Managers believe political behavior arises in certain decision domains, such as structural change, but is absent from other decisions, such as handling employee grievances.

Based on these surveys, politics seems more likely to occur at the top levels of an organization and around certain issues and decisions. Moreover, managers do not approve of political behavior. The remainder of this chapter explores more fully what political behavior is, when it should be used, the type of issues and decisions most likely to be associated with politics, and some political tactics that may be effective.

Definition

Power has been described as the available force or potential for achieving desired outcomes. *Politics* is the use of power to influence decisions in order to achieve those outcomes. The exercise of power to influence others has led to two ways to define politics: as self-serving behavior or as a natural organizational decision process. The first definition emphasizes that politics is self-serving and involves activities that are not sanctioned by the organization.[78]

In this view, politics involves deception and dishonesty for purposes of individual self-interest and leads to conflict and disharmony within the work environment. This dark view of politics is widely held by laypeople, and political activity certainly can be used in this way. Studies have shown that workers who perceive this kind of political activity within their companies often have related feelings of anxiety and job dissatisfaction. Research also supports the belief that an inappropriate use of politics is related to low employee morale, inferior organizational performance, and poor decision making.[79] This view of politics explains why managers in the aforementioned surveys did not approve of political behavior.

Although politics can be used in a negative, self-serving way, the appropriate use of political behavior can serve organizational goals.[80] The second view sees politics as a natural organizational process for resolving differences among organizational interest groups.[81] Politics is the process of bargaining and negotiation that is used to overcome conflicts and differences of opinion. In this view, politics is similar to the coalition-building decision processes that will be described in Chapter 8.

The organization theory perspective views politics as described in the second definition. Politics is simply the activity through which power is exercised in the resolution of conflicts and uncertainty. Politics is neutral and is not necessarily harmful to the organization. The formal definition of organizational politics is as follows: **organizational politics** involves activities to acquire, develop, and use power and other resources to influence others and obtain the preferred outcome when there is uncertainty or disagreement about choices.[82]

Political behavior can be either a positive or a negative force. Politics is the use of power to get things accomplished—good things as well as bad. Uncertainty and conflict are natural and inevitable, and politics is the mechanism for reaching agreement. Politics includes informal discussions that enable people to arrive at consensus and make decisions that otherwise might be stalemated or unsolvable.

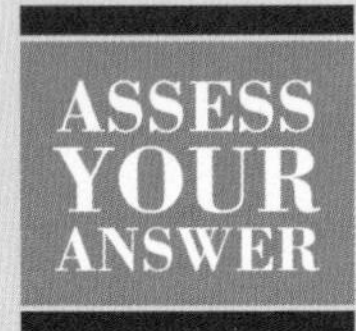

3 When managers use politics, it usually leads to conflict and disharmony and will likely disrupt the smooth functioning of the organization.

ANSWER: *Disagree.* Politics is a natural organizational process for resolving differences and getting things done. Although politics can be used for negative and self-serving purposes, political activity is also the primary way managers are brought together to accomplish good things. Being political is part of the job of a manager, but managers should take care to use politics to serve the interests of the organization rather than themselves.

When Is Political Activity Used?

Politics is a mechanism for arriving at consensus when uncertainty is high and there is disagreement over goals or problem priorities. Recall the rational versus political models described in Exhibit 7.2. The political model is associated with conflict over goals, shifting coalitions and interest groups, ambiguous information, and uncertainty. Thus, political activity tends to be most visible when managers confront nonprogrammed decisions, as will be described in Chapter 8, and is related to the Carnegie model of decision making. Because managers at the top of an organization generally deal with more nonprogrammed decisions than do managers at lower levels, more political activity will appear at higher levels. Moreover, some issues are associated with inherent disagreement. Resources, for example, are critical for the survival and effectiveness of departments, so resource allocation often becomes a political issue. Rational methods of allocation do not satisfy participants. Three **domains of political activity** (areas in which politics plays a role) in most organizations are structural change, management succession, and resource allocation.

Structural reorganizations strike at the heart of power and authority relationships. Reorganizations such as those discussed in Chapter 2 change responsibilities and tasks, which also affects the underlying power base from strategic contingencies. For these reasons, a major reorganization can lead to an explosion of political activity.[83] Managers may actively bargain and negotiate to maintain the responsibilities and power bases they have. Mergers and acquisitions also frequently create tremendous political activity.

Organizational changes such as hiring new executives, promotions, and transfers have great political significance, particularly at top organizational levels where uncertainty is high and networks of trust, cooperation, and communication among executives are important.[84] Hiring decisions can generate uncertainty, discussion, and disagreement. Managers can use hiring and promotion to strengthen network alliances and coalitions by putting their own people in prominent positions.

The third area of political activity is resource allocation. Resource allocation decisions encompass all resources required for organizational performance, including salaries, operating budgets, employees, office facilities, equipment, use of the company airplane, and so forth. Resources are so vital that disagreement about priorities exists, and political processes help resolve the dilemmas.

Using Soft Power and Politics

One theme in this chapter has been that power in organizations is not primarily a phenomenon of the individual. It is related to the resources departments command, the role departments play in an organization, and the environmental contingencies with which departments cope. Position and responsibility, more than personality and style, may determine a manager's ability to influence outcomes in the organization.

However, power is used through individual political behavior. To fully understand the use of power within organizations, it is important to look at both structural components and individual behavior.[85] Although power often comes from larger organizational forms and processes, the political use of power involves individual-level activities and skills. To learn about your political skills, complete the questionnaire in the "How Do You Fit the Design?" box. Managers with political skill are more effective at influencing others and thus getting what they want, for the organization and for their own careers.[86] These managers have

How Do You Fit the Design?

POLITICAL SKILLS

How good are you at influencing people across an organization? To learn something about your political skills, answer the questions that follow. Please answer whether each item is Mostly True or Mostly False for you.

	Mostly True	Mostly False
1. I am able to communicate easily and effectively with others.	___	___
2. I spend a lot of time at work developing connections with people outside my area.	___	___
3. I instinctively know the right thing to say or do to influence others.	___	___
4. I am good at using my connections outside my area to get things done at work.	___	___
5. When communicating with others I am absolutely genuine in what I say and do.	___	___
6. It is easy for me to reach out to new people.	___	___
7. I make strangers feel comfortable and at ease around me.	___	___
8. I am good at sensing the motivations and hidden agendas of others.	___	___

Scoring: Give yourself one point for each item marked as Mostly True.

Interpretation: Having some basic political skill helps a manager gain broad support and influence. Political skills help a manager build personal and organizational relationships that enhance your team's outcomes. A score of 6 or higher suggests active political skills and a good start for your career, especially in an organization in which things get done politically. If you scored three or less, you may want to focus more on building collegial and supportive relationships as you progress in your career. If not, perhaps join an organization in which decisions and actions are undertaken by rational procedures rather than by support of key coalitions.

Source: Adapted from Gerald R. Ferris, Darren C. Treadway, Robert W. Kolodinsky, Wayne A. Hochwarter, Charles J. Kacmer, Ceasar Douglas, and Dwight D. Frink, "Development and Validation of the Political Skill Inventory," *Journal of Management* 31 (February 2005), 126–152.

honed their abilities to observe and understand patterns of interaction and influence in the organization. They are skilled at developing relationships with a broad network of people and can adapt their behavior and approach to diverse people and situations. Politically effective managers understand that influence is about relationships.[87]

Managers can develop political competence, and they can learn to use a wide variety of influence tactics depending on their own position as well as the specific situation. Some tactics rely on the use of "hard power," which is power that stems largely from a person's position of authority. This is the kind of power that enables a supervisor to influence subordinates with the use of rewards and punishments, allows a manager to issue orders and expect them to be obeyed, or lets a domineering CEO force through his or her own decisions without regard for what anyone else thinks. However, effective managers more often use "soft power," which is based on personal characteristics and building relationships.[88] Consider that Jeffrey Immelt, CEO of General Electric, considers himself a failure if he exercises his formal authority more than seven or eight times a year. The rest of the time, Immelt is using softer means to persuade and influence others and to resolve conflicting ideas and opinions.[89]

Even the U.S. military is talking about the importance of building relationships rather than using brute force. Former Defense Secretary Robert Gates, for instance, says that in the battle for hearts and minds abroad, the United States has to be "good at listening to others" rather than just good at kicking down doors, and the Army's new stability operations field manual openly talks about the value of soft power.[90] Wesley Clark, former supreme commander of NATO who led the mission against Serb President Slobodan Milosevic, suggests that, for leaders in businesses as well as nations, building a community of shared interests should be the first choice, rather than using threats, intimidation, and raw power.[91] The effectiveness of soft power is revealed in a study of 49 professional negotiators over a nine-year period of time. Researchers found that the most effective negotiators spent 400 percent more time than their less-effective counterparts looking for areas of mutual benefit and shared interest, rather than just trying to force their own agenda.[92]

The following sections summarize various tactics that managers can use to increase their own or their department's power base, and the political tactics they can use to achieve desired outcomes. Most of these tactics, summarized in Exhibit 7.9, rely on the use of soft rather than hard power.

Tactics for Increasing Power

Four **tactics for increasing power** are as follows:

1. *Enter areas of high uncertainty.* One source of individual or departmental power is to identify key uncertainties and take steps to remove those uncertainties.[93] Uncertainties could arise from stoppages on an assembly line, from the quality demanded of a new product, or from the inability to predict a demand for new services. Once an uncertainty is identified, the department can take action to cope with it. By their very nature, uncertain tasks will not be solved immediately. Trial and error will be needed, which is to the advantage of the department. The trial-and-error process

Tactics for Increasing the Power Base	Political Tactics for Using Power
1. Enter areas of high uncertainty.	1. Build coalitions and expand networks.
2. Create dependencies.	2. Assign loyal people to key positions.
3. Provide scarce resources.	3. Control decision premises.
4. Satisfy strategic contingencies.	4. Enhance legitimacy and expertise.
5. Make a direct appeal.	5. Create superordinate goals.

EXHIBIT 7.9
Power and Political Tactics in Organizations

provides experience and expertise that cannot easily be duplicated by other departments.

2. *Create dependencies.* Dependencies are another source of power.[94] When the organization depends on a department or individual for information, materials, knowledge, or skills, that department or individual will hold power over others. A somewhat amusing example comes from Evan Steingart's consumer products company. A low-level inventory-transfer clerk in the shipping department had to sign off on the shipment of all goods. Salespeople were dependent on the clerk for his signature. Those who wanted their orders shipped quickly learned to cozy up to the clerk. Arrogant ones who treated him badly would find themselves at a disadvantage, as the clerk would have a long list of things to do before he could get to their shipping order, and the salespeople had no recourse but to wait.[95] An equally effective and related strategy is to reduce dependency on other departments by acquiring necessary information or skills when possible, so that your department isn't in a dependent position. For example, the sales manager might seek signing authority to eliminate salespeople's dependence on the inventory clerk and the shipping department.
3. *Provide scarce resources.* Resources are always important to organizational survival. Departments that accumulate resources and provide them to an organization in the form of money, information, or facilities will be powerful. An earlier "In Practice" example described how university departments with the greatest power are those that obtain external research funds for contributions to university overhead. Likewise, sales departments are powerful in industrial firms because they bring in financial resources.
4. *Satisfy strategic contingencies.* The theory of strategic contingencies says that some elements in the external environment and within the organization are especially important for organizational success. A contingency could be a critical event, a task for which there are no substitutes, or a central task that is interdependent with many others in the organization. An analysis of the organization and its changing environment will reveal strategic contingencies. To the extent that contingencies are new or are not being satisfied, there is room for a department to move into those critical areas and increase its importance and power.

In summary, the allocation of power in an organization is not random. Power is the result of organizational processes that can be understood and predicted. The abilities to reduce uncertainty, increase dependency on one's own department, obtain resources, and cope with strategic contingencies all enhance a department's power. Once power is available, the next challenge is to use it to attain desired outcomes.

Political Tactics for Using Power

The use of power in organizations requires both skill and willingness. Many decisions are made through political processes because rational decision processes do not fit. Uncertainty or disagreement is too high. **Political tactics for using power** to influence decision outcomes include the following:

1. *Build coalitions and expand networks.* Effective managers develop positive relationships throughout the organization, and they spend time talking with others to learn about their views and build mutually beneficial alliances and coalitions.[96] Most important decisions are made outside of formal meetings. Managers discuss issues with each other and reach agreement. Effective managers are those who huddle, meeting in groups of twos and threes to resolve key issues.[97] They also make sure their networks cross hierarchical, functional, and even organizational boundaries. One research project found that the ability to build networks has a positive impact on both employees' perception of a manager's effectiveness and the ability of the manager to influence performance.[98] Networks can be expanded by (1) reaching out to establish contact with additional managers and (2) coopting dissenters. Establishing contact with additional managers means building good interpersonal relationships based on liking, trust, and respect. Reliability and the motivation to work with rather than exploit others are part of both networking and coalition building.[99] The second approach to expanding networks, cooptation, is the act of bringing a dissenter into one's network. One example of cooptation involved a university committee whose membership was based on promotion and tenure. Several professors who were critical of the tenure and promotion process were appointed to the committee. Once a part of the administrative process, they could see the administrative point of view. Cooptation effectively brought them into the administrative network.[100]
2. *Assign loyal people to key positions.* Another political tactic is to assign trusted and loyal people to key positions in the organization or department. Top managers as well as department heads often use the hiring, transfer, and promotion processes to place in key positions people who are sympathetic to the outcomes of the department, thus helping to achieve departmental goals.[101] Top leaders frequently use this tactic, as we discussed earlier. When an outside police chief was hired to take over a major metropolitan police department, he brought three assistant chiefs with him because their thinking and management skills were compatible with his goals to transform the department.
3. *Use reciprocity.* There is much research indicating that most people feel a sense of obligation to give something back in return for favors others do for them.[102] This *principle of reciprocity* is one of the key factors affecting influence relationships in organizations. When a manager does a favor for a colleague, the colleague feels obliged to return the favor in the future. Doing additional work that helps out other departments obligates the other departments to respond at a future date. The "unwritten rule of reciprocity" is one reason organizations like Northrup Grumman, Kraft Foods, and Pfizer make donations to the favorite charities of House and Senate members. Leaders attempt to curry favor with lawmakers whose decisions can significantly affect their business.[103] As with other political tactics, managers sometimes use reciprocity for self-serving purposes that can harm the organization and its stakeholders. For instance, investigators have blamed the tight connections and reciprocal favors among nuclear industry managers, regulators, and government officials in Japan for contributing to the disaster at the Fukushima Daiichi power plant.

IN PRACTICE

Fukushima Daiichi (Tokyo Electric Power)

After a major earthquake and tsunami hit Japan in the spring of 2011, the tragedy was made worse when reactors at the Fukushima Daiichi nuclear power plant were damaged, causing the worst disaster of its kind since Chernobyl. As Japan struggled to get the plant under control, many people began questioning whether a "culture of complicity" that involves industry officials, power company managers, politicians, and regulators doing favors for one another had played a role in the accident.

Consider that in 2000, Kei Sugaoka, a Japanese-American nuclear inspector who had done work for General Electric at Daiichi, told Japan's main nuclear regulatory agency about a safety infraction that he believed was being concealed by managers. Instead of investigating, the agency told the plant managers to do their own investigation and allowed the plant to keep operating. Sugaoka's identity was revealed to the plant's operator, Tokyo Electric Power (Tepco), and he was effectively blackballed from the Japanese nuclear industry.

The tight web of connections in Japan's nuclear industry is referred to as the "nuclear power village." Managers, nuclear industry officials, bureaucrats, politicians, and scientists who share similar goals and interests "have prospered by rewarding one another with construction projects, lucrative positions, and political, financial, and regulatory support." For example, politicians and influential regulators who side with the nuclear industry, such as by watering down regulations, can land cushy jobs as executives or consultants at the power companies. In turn, politicians reward their nuclear institutional backers with seats in Parliament. Tokio Kano, a former vice-president of Tepco, was appointed by the Liberal Democratic party to two six-year terms in the upper house of Parliament and later returned to Tepco as an advisor. One critic says Kano worked while in Parliament to rewrite "everything in favor of the power companies."[104]

The pattern of favors revealed by investigations into Japan's nuclear industry reflects the significant role reciprocity plays in influence relationships. Some researchers argue that the concept of exchange—trading something of value for what you want—is the basis of all other influence tactics. For example, rational persuasion works because the other person sees a benefit from going along with the plan, and making people like you is successful because the other person receives liking and attention in return.[105] This chapter's Book Mark further discusses reciprocity and other basic influence principles.

4. *Enhance legitimacy and expertise.* Managers can exert the greatest influence in areas in which they have recognized legitimacy and expertise. This tactic is highly effective with the younger generation of managers and employees. Today's young workers define power based on an individual's knowledge and skills rather than a position of authority over people. They don't appreciate the strong use of politics and expect people to rely on their knowledge to influence others.[106] When managers make a request that is within the task domain of a department and is consistent with the department's vested interest, other departments will tend to comply. Members can also identify external consultants or other experts within the organization to support their cause.[107] For example, a financial vice president in a large retail firm wanted to fire the director of HR management. She hired a consultant to evaluate the HR projects undertaken to date. A negative report from the consultant provided sufficient legitimacy to fire the director, who was replaced with a director loyal to the financial vice president.
5. *Make a direct appeal.* If managers do not ask, they seldom receive. An example of direct appeal comes from Drugstore.com, where Jessica Morrison used direct

BRIEFCASE

As an organization manager, keep these guidelines in mind:

Expect and allow for political behavior in organizations. Politics provides the discussion and clash of interests needed to crystallize points of view and to reach a decision. Build coalitions, expand networks, use reciprocity, enhance legitimacy, and make a direct appeal to attain desired outcomes.

BOOKMARK

7.0 HAVE YOU READ THIS BOOK?

Influence: Science and Practice

By Robert B. Cialdini

Managers use a variety of political tactics to influence others and bring about desired outcomes. In his book *Influence: Science and Practice,* Robert Cialdini examines the social and psychological pressures that cause people to respond favorably to these various tactics. Over years of study, Cialdini, Regents' Professor of Psychology at Arizona State University, has identified some basic *influence principles,* "those that work in a variety of situations, for a variety of practitioners, on a variety of topics, for a variety of prospects."

INFLUENCE PRINCIPLES

Having a working knowledge of the basic set of persuasion tools can help managers predict and influence human behavior, which is valuable for interacting with colleagues, employees, customers, partners, and even friends. Some basic psychological principles that govern successful influence tactics are as follows:

- *Reciprocity.* The principle of reciprocity refers to the sense of obligation people feel to give back in kind what they have received. For example, a manager who does favors for others creates in them a sense of obligation to return the favors in the future. Smart managers find ways to be helpful to others, whether it be helping a colleague finish an unpleasant job or offering compassion and concern for a subordinate's personal problems.
- *Liking.* People say *yes* more often to those they like. Companies such as Tupperware or Pampered Chef have long understood that familiar faces and congenial characteristics sell products. In-home parties allow customers to buy from a friend instead of an unknown salesperson. Salespeople in all kinds of companies often try to capitalize on this principle by finding interests they share with customers as a way to establish rapport. In general, managers who are pleasant, generous with praise, cooperative, and considerate of others' feelings find that they have greater influence.
- *Credible authority.* Legitimate authorities are particularly influential sources. However, research has discovered that the key to successful use of authority is to be knowledgeable, credible, and trustworthy. Managers who become known for their expertise, who are honest and straightforward with others, and who inspire trust can exert greater influence than those who rely on formal position alone.
- *Social validation.* One of the primary ways people decide what to do in any given situation is to consider what others are doing. That is, people examine the actions of others to validate correct choices. For instance, when homeowners were shown a list of neighbors who had donated to a local charity during a fundraiser, the frequency of contributions increased dramatically. By demonstrating, or even implying, that others have already complied with a request, managers gain greater cooperation.

THE PROCESS OF SOCIAL INFLUENCE

Because life as a manager is all about influencing others, learning to be genuinely persuasive is a valuable management skill. Cialdini's book helps managers understand the basic psychological rules of persuasion—how and why people are motivated to change their attitudes and behaviors. When managers use this understanding in an honest and ethical manner, they improve their effectiveness and the success of their organizations.

Influence: Science and Practice (4th edition), by Robert B. Cialdini, is published by Allyn & Bacon.

appeal to get a new title and a salary increase. Morrison researched pay scales on PayScale.com and approached her boss armed with that and other pertinent information. Her direct appeal, backed up with research, won her the promotion.[108] Political activity is effective only when goals and needs are made explicit so the organization can respond. An assertive proposal may be accepted because other managers have no better alternatives. Moreover, an explicit proposal will often receive favorable treatment because other alternatives are ambiguous and less well defined. Effective political behavior requires sufficient forcefulness and risk-taking to at least ask for what you need to achieve desired outcomes.

Managers can use an understanding of these tactics to assert influence and get things done within the organization. When managers ignore soft power and political tactics, they may find themselves failing without understanding why. For example, at the World Bank, Paul Wolfowitz tried to wield hard power without building the necessary relationships he needed to assert influence.

IN PRACTICE

World Bank

After former Deputy Secretary of Defense Paul Wolfowitz lost his bids to become defense secretary or national security advisor in the Bush administration, he jumped at the chance to be the new president of World Bank. But Wolfowitz doomed his career at World Bank from the start by failing to develop relationships and build alliances.

Most World Bank leaders had been in their positions for many years when Wolfowitz arrived, and they were accustomed to "promoting each other's interests and scratching each other's backs," as one board member put it. Wolfowitz came in and tried to assert his own ideas, goals, and formal authority without considering the interests, ideas, and goals of others. He quickly alienated much of the World Bank leadership team and board by adopting a single-minded position on key issues and refusing to consider alternative views. Rather than attempting to persuade others to his way of thinking, Wolfowitz issued directives to senior bank officers, either personally or through his handpicked managers. Several high-level officers resigned following disputes with the new president.

Eventually, the board asked for Wolfowitz's resignation. "What Paul didn't understand is that the World Bank presidency is not inherently a powerful job," said one former colleague. "A bank president is successful only if he can form alliances with the bank's many fiefdoms. Wolfowitz didn't ally with those fiefdoms. He alienated them."[109]

Wolfowitz realized too late that he needed to use a political, soft-power approach rather than trying to force his own agenda. Even when a manager has a great deal of power, the use of power should not be obvious.[110] If a manager formally draws on her power base in a meeting by saying, "My department has more power, so the rest of you have to do it my way," her power will be diminished. Power works best when it is used quietly. To call attention to power is to lose it. People know who has power. Explicit claims to power are not necessary and can even harm the manager's or department's cause.

Also, when using any of the preceding tactics, recall that most people think self-serving behavior hurts rather than helps an organization. If managers are perceived to be throwing their weight around or pursuing goals that are self-serving rather than beneficial to the organization, they will lose respect. On the other hand, managers must recognize the relational and political aspect of their work. It is not sufficient to be rational and technically competent. Developing and using political skill is an important part of being a good manager.

Design Essentials

- The central message of this chapter is that conflict, power, and politics are natural outcomes of organizing. Differences in goals, backgrounds, and tasks are necessary for organizational excellence, but these differences can throw groups into conflict. Managers use power and politics to manage and resolve conflict.

- Two views of organization were presented. The rational model of organization assumes that organizations have specific goals and that problems can be logically solved. The other view, the political model of organization, is the basis for much of the chapter. This view assumes that the goals of an organization are not specific or agreed upon. Departments have different values and interests, so managers come into conflict. Decisions are made on the basis of power and political influence. Bargaining, negotiation, persuasion, and coalition building decide outcomes.

- Although conflict and political behavior are natural and can be used for beneficial purposes, managers also strive to enhance collaboration so that conflict between groups does not become too strong. Tactics for enhancing collaboration include integration devices, confrontation and negotiation, intergroup consultation, member rotation, and shared mission and superordinate goals.

- The chapter also discussed the vertical and horizontal sources of power. Vertical sources of power include formal position, resources, control of information, and network centrality. In general, managers at the top of the organizational hierarchy have more power than people at lower levels. However, positions all along the hierarchy can be designed to increase the power of employees. As organizations face increased competition and environmental uncertainty, top executives are finding that increasing the power of middle managers and lower-level employees can help the organization be more competitive. Empowerment is a popular trend. Empowering employees means giving them three key elements: information and resources, necessary knowledge and skills, and the power to make substantive decisions.

- Research into horizontal power processes has revealed that certain characteristics make some departments more powerful than others. Differences in power can be understood using the concept of strategic contingencies. Departments responsible for dealing with key resource issues and dependencies are more powerful. Such factors as dependency, resources, nonsubstitutability, and dealing with uncertainty determine the influence of departments.

- Managers need political skills to exercise soft power. Many people distrust political behavior, fearing that it will be used for selfish ends that benefit the individual but not the organization. However, politics is often needed to achieve the legitimate goals of a department or organization. Three areas in which political behavior often plays a role are structural change, management succession, and resource allocation because these are areas of high uncertainty. Managers use political tactics, including building coalitions, expanding networks, using reciprocity, enhancing legitimacy, and making a direct appeal, to help their departments achieve desired outcomes.

Key Concepts

authority
centrality
collective bargaining
competition
confrontation
decision premises
dependency
domains of political activity
empowerment
intergroup conflict
labor-management teams
negotiation
network centrality
nonsubstitutability
organizational politics
political model
political tactics for using power
power
power sources
rational model
sources of intergroup conflict
strategic contingencies
tactics for enhancing collaboration
tactics for increasing power

Discussion Questions

1. Give an example from your personal experience of how differences in tasks, personal background, and training lead to conflict among groups. How might task interdependence have influenced that conflict?
2. Consumer products giant Procter & Gamble and Internet leader Google have entered into a marketing partnership. What organizational and environmental factors might determine which organization will have more power in the relationship?
3. In a rapidly changing organization, are decisions more likely to be made using the rational or political model of organization? Discuss.
4. What is the difference between power and authority? Is it possible for a person to have formal authority but no real power? Discuss.
5. Discuss ways in which a department at a health insurance company might help the organization cope with the increased power of large hospital systems such as Carilion by obtaining prior information, prevention, or absorption.
6. In Exhibit 7.7, R&D has greater power in company B than in the other firms. Discuss possible strategic contingencies that might give R&D greater power in this firm.
7. State University X receives 90 percent of its financial resources from the state and is overcrowded with students. It is trying to pass regulations to limit student enrollment. Private University Y receives 90 percent of its income from student tuition and has barely enough students to make ends meet. It is actively recruiting students for next year. In which university will students have greater power? What implications will this have for professors and administrators? Discuss.
8. A financial analyst at Merrill Lynch tried for several months to expose the risks of investments in subprime mortgages, but he couldn't get anyone to pay attention to his claims. How would you evaluate this employee's power? What might he have done to increase his power and call notice to the impending problems at the firm?
9. The engineering college at a major university brings in three times as many government research dollars as does the rest of the university combined. Engineering appears wealthy and has many professors on full-time research status. Yet, when internal research funds are allocated, engineering gets a larger share of the money, even though it already has substantial external research funds. Why would this happen?
10. Some researchers argue that the concept of exchange underlying the principle of reciprocity (trading something of value to another for what you want) is the basis of *all* influence. Do you agree? Discuss. To what extent do you feel obligated to return a favor that is done for you?

Chapter 7 Workbook How Do You Handle Conflict?

Think about how you typically handle a dispute with a team member, friend, or co-worker, and then answer the following statements based on whether they are True or False for you. There are no right or wrong answers, so answer honestly.

	Mostly True	Mostly False
1. I feel that differences are not worth arguing about.	_____	_____
2. I would avoid a person who wants to discuss a disagreement.	_____	_____
3. I would rather keep my views to myself than argue.	_____	_____
4. I typically avoid taking positions that create a dispute.	_____	_____
5. I try hard to win my position	_____	_____
6. I strongly assert my opinion in a disagreement.	_____	_____
7. I raise my voice to get other people to accept my position.	_____	_____
8. I stand firm in expressing my viewpoint.	_____	_____
9. I give in a little if other people do the same.	_____	_____
10. I will split the difference to reach an agreement.	_____	_____
11. I offer trade-offs to reach a solution.	_____	_____
12. I give up some points in exchange for others.	_____	_____
13. I don't want to hurt others' feelings.	_____	_____
14. I am quick to agree when someone I am arguing with makes a good point.	_____	_____
15. I try to smooth over disagreements by minimizing their seriousness.	_____	_____
16. I want to be considerate of other people's emotions.	_____	_____
17. I suggest a solution that includes the other person's point of view.	_____	_____
18. I combine arguments into a new solution from ideas raised in the dispute.	_____	_____
19. I try to include the other person's ideas to create a solution they will accept.	_____	_____
20. I assess the merits of other viewpoints as equal to my own.	_____	_____

Scoring and Interpretation: Five categories of conflict-handling strategies are measured by these 20 questions: avoiding, dominating, bargaining, accommodating, and collaborating. These five strategies reflect different levels of personal desire for *assertiveness* or *cooperation*. The higher your score for a strategy, the more likely that is your preferred conflict-handling approach. A lower score suggests you probably do not use that approach.

Dominating Style (my way) reflects a high degree of assertiveness to get one's own way and fulfill one's self-interest. Sum one point for each Mostly True for items 5–8: _____.

Accommodating Style (your way) reflects a high degree of cooperativeness and a desire to oblige or help others as most important. Sum one point for each Mostly True for items 13–16: _____.

Avoiding Style (no way) reflects neither assertiveness nor cooperativeness, which means that conflict is avoided whenever possible. Sum one point for each Mostly True for items 1–4: _____.

Bargaining Style (half way) reflects a tendency to meet half way by using a moderate amount of both assertiveness and cooperativeness. Sum one point for each Mostly True for items 9–12: _____.

Collaborating Style (our way) reflects a high degree of both assertiveness and cooperativeness to meet the needs of both parties. Sum one point for each Mostly True for items 17–20: _____.

Questions

1. Which strategy do you find easiest to use? Most difficult?
2. How would your answers change if the other party to the conflict was a friend, family member, or co-worker?
3. How do you feel about your approach to handling conflict? What changes would you like to make?

CASE FOR ANALYSIS The Daily Tribune[111]

The *Daily Tribune* is the only daily newspaper serving a six-county region of eastern Tennessee. Even though its staff is small and it serves a region of mostly small towns and rural areas, the *Tribune* has won numerous awards for news coverage and photojournalism from the Tennessee Press Association and other organizations.

Rick Arnold became news editor almost twenty years ago. He has spent his entire career with the *Tribune* and feels a great sense of pride that it has been recognized for its journalistic integrity and balanced coverage of issues and events. The paper has been able to attract bright, talented young writers and photographers thanks largely to Rick's commitment and his support of the news staff. In his early years, the newsroom was a dynamic, exciting place to work—reporters thrived on the fast pace and the chance to occasionally scoop the major daily paper in Knoxville.

But times have changed at the *Daily Tribune*. Over the past five years or so, the advertising department has continued to grow, in terms of both staff and budget, while the news department has begun to shrink. "Advertising pays the bills," publisher John Freeman reminded everyone at this month's managers' meeting. "Today, advertisers can go to direct mail, cable television, even the Internet, if they don't like what we're doing for them."

Rick has regularly clashed with the advertising department regarding news stories that are critical of major advertisers, but the conflicts have increased dramatically over the past few years. Now, Freeman is encouraging greater "horizontal collaboration," as he calls it, asking that managers in the news department and the ad department consult with one another regarding issues or stories that involve the paper's major advertisers. The move was prompted in part by a growing number of complaints from advertisers about stories they deemed unfair. "We print the news," Freeman said, "and I understand that sometimes we've got to print things that some people won't like. But we've got to find ways to be more advertiser-friendly. If we work together, we can develop strategies that both present good news coverage and serve to attract more advertisers."

Rick left the meeting fuming, and he didn't fail to make his contempt for the new "advertiser-friendly" approach known to all, including the advertising manager, Fred Thomas, as he headed down the hallway back to the newsroom. Lisa Lawrence, his managing editor, quietly agreed but pointed out that advertisers were readers too, and the newspaper had to listen to all its constituencies. "If we don't handle this carefully, we'll have Freeman and Thomas in here dictating to us what we can write and what we can't."

Lawrence has worked with Rick since he first came to the paper, and even though the two have had their share of conflicts, the relationship is primarily one of mutual respect and trust. "Let's just be careful," she emphasized. "Read the stories about big advertisers a little more carefully, make sure we can defend whatever we print, and it will all work out. I know this blurring of the line between advertising and editorial rubs you the wrong way, but Thomas is a reasonable man. We just need to keep him in the loop."

Late that afternoon, Rick received a story from one of his corresponding reporters that had been in the works for a couple of days. East Tennessee Healthcorp (ETH), which operated a string of health clinics throughout the region, was closing three of its rural clinics because of mounting financial woes. The reporter, Elisabeth Fraley, lived in one of the communities and had learned about the closings from her neighbor, who worked as an accountant for ETH, before the announcement had been made just this afternoon. Fraley had written a compelling human-interest story about how the closings would leave people in two counties with essentially no access to healthcare, while clinics in larger towns that didn't really need them were being kept open. She had carefully interviewed both former patients of the clinics and ETH employees, including the director of one of the clinics and two high-level managers at the corporate office, and she had carefully documented her sources. After this morning's meeting, Rick knew he should run the story by Lisa Lawrence, since East Tennessee Healthcorp was one of the *Tribune's* biggest advertisers, but Lawrence had left for the day. And he simply couldn't bring himself to consult with the advertising department—that political nonsense was for Lawrence to handle. If he held the story for Lawrence's approval, it wouldn't make the Sunday edition. His only other option was to write a brief story simply reporting the closings and leaving out the human-interest aspect. Rick was sure the major papers from Knoxville and other nearby cities would have the report in their Sunday papers, but none of them would have the time to develop as comprehensive and interesting an account as Fraley had presented. With a few quick keystrokes to make some minor editorial changes, Rick sent the story to production.

When he arrived at work the next day, Rick was called immediately to the publisher's office. He knew it was bad news for Freeman to be in on a Sunday. After some general yelling and screaming, Rick learned that tens of thousands of copies of the Sunday paper had been destroyed and a new edition printed. The advertising manager had called Freeman at home in the wee hours of Sunday morning and informed him of the ETH story, which was appearing the same day the corporation was running a full-page ad touting its service to the small towns and rural communities of East Tennessee.

"The story's accurate, and I assumed you'd want to take advantage of a chance to scoop the big papers," Rick began, but Freeman cut his argument short. "You could have just reported the basic facts without implying that the company doesn't care about the people of this region. The next time something like this happens, you'll find yourself and your reporters standing in the unemployment line!"

Rick had heard it before, but somehow this time he almost believed it. "What happened to the days when the primary purpose of a newspaper was to present the news?" Rick mumbled. "Now, it seems we have to dance to the tune played by the ad department."

CASE FOR ANALYSIS The New Haven Initiative

When Burton Lee took over as plant manager for the New Haven division of a large manufacturing company, he saw the opportunity to transform the lowest performing unit as a pathway to his promotion into top management.

Burton was aware of his reputation within the company as an intellectual, which he credited, in part, to an undergraduate minor in philosophy. Fifteen years after obtaining his MBA, he retained a passion for reading the classics—Homer, Tacitus, Plato, Herodotus, and Cicero—in the original Greek and Latin. Like Thomas Jefferson, he carried a pocket-size Greek grammar with him. Co-workers admiringly and grudgingly accustomed themselves to his familiar phrases, "*When you look at this logically . . .*" or *"it should be obvious that. . . ."*

It was obvious to Burton that changes had to be made at New Haven. The division's reputation as the weak link in the company, with excessive machine downtime, backlogs, and complaints about quality negatively affected employee morale. In a down economy, rumors often circulated that the New Haven plant might be closed.

"My academic background taught me that there is a logical way to approach and solve problems. Manufacturing is often stuck in the past—*the way it has always been done.* Over and over in manufacturing you find that individuals in management have come up through the ranks and are reluctant to change—often even in the face of overwhelming evidence. Because they are stuck in this mindset, they are reluctant to explore ideas, to stay on top of manufacturing trends, or to see the bigger picture. I believe that innovation in thinking, in technology, in streamlining processes and empowering employees is crucial to success at New Haven.

"When I came here to take over New Haven, the plant was a mess, to put it bluntly. We were awash in paper. We were stuck on the traditional assembly line. When I talked to line supervisors, I felt like they were channeling Henry Ford. We needed a new paradigm, a new culture that was not stuck in the past. We had to end the backlogs, move product faster, and improve the quality. I can't do that. The workers in the plant have to do that. But they need the tools to work with. What was it that Churchill told FDR in World War II? 'Give us the tools and we'll finish the job.' That was the culture I wanted here in New Haven.

"I explored everything, talked to everyone, and investigated what was working in other industries. I knew we'd have to take these individual tasks and build a system to coordinate them into complex, but not complicated, interactions with specific targets that raise overall equipment effectiveness. The question was how could we do that?

"When you look at this logically, when you venture outside of your comfort zone and see what other industries have done, you discover a number of models and you find that there are resources in the form of technology and software out there that can help. I somehow managed to convince top management to invest in a pilot project with software that enabled us to create a virtual plant to look at every aspect of the operation—plant layout, material flow, machinery, everything. Initially, my on-site management team really got into this. With this software, we could simulate various problems and do some 'what-if' analysis. The idea was to create lean manufacturing clusters that could serve as a benchmark for the rest of the company.

"On the line, we moved toward dividing the assembly line into cells of self-managed teams. The idea is to empower and motivate the workers to make real-time decisions. Employees seemed enthusiastic and eager to have more control over the day-to-day operations. Supervisors were the first to balk, worried that they were losing prestige and that seniority was being shoved aside, as one long-time supervisor claimed, so that 'Joe Blow, who's only been on the line for ten months, can start making decisions.' Likewise, there were some line workers who balked. You would think that the opportunity to change from being essentially a cog in the wheel to becoming part of a dynamic, self-managed team would be appealing to everyone. But I guess some are afraid of decision-making and feel a need for constant guidance. For some workers the mention of self-managed teams produced a 'deer in the headlights' reaction.

"It should be obvious that these steps would bring improvement, but in order for this whole process to work, we needed worker cooperation and full management support. We had started making some progress and seeing some improvement in production and quality, when suddenly it was as if top management put on the brakes. We need resources and time to make the changes. Managers at other plants complained of preferential treatment for New Haven and argued that they were expected to produce and deliver while we were sitting around 'playing video games' and 'holding hands' – a reference, I'm certain, to the new software and the self-managed teams. Corporate repeatedly delayed funding for the new equipment and training that could transform this plant into a 21st century manufacturing division.

"I admit that I am shocked and disappointed that so many people in this organization fail to see the rationale here, which is obvious to anyone with eyes and a brain, and that they are failing to support our efforts. I'm showing them data that supports everything we're attempting here at New Haven. We're getting knee-jerk reactions when we need enlightened leadership. Now I'm wondering, what is the next step to go forward? A major success is being taken from me. And I heard informally that I am not a candidate for promotion."

Notes

1. Phred Dvorak, Suzanne Vranica, and Spencer E. Ante, "BlackBerry Maker's Issue: Gadgets for Work or Play?" *The Wall Street Journal Online* (September 30, 2011), http://online.wsj.com/article/SB10001424052970204422404576597061591715344.html (accessed September 30, 2011).
2. Lee G. Bolman and Terrence E. Deal, *Reframing Organizations: Artistry, Choice, and Leadership* (San Francisco: Jossey-Bass, 1991).
3. Paul M. Terry, "Conflict Management," *The Journal of Leadership Studies* 3, no. 2 (1996), 3–21; Kathleen M. Eisenhardt, Jean L. Kahwajy, and L. J. Bourgeois III, "How Management Teams Can Have a Good Fight," *Harvard Business Review* (July–August 1997), 77–85; and Patrick Lencioni, "How to Foster Good Conflict," *The Wall Street Journal Online* (November 13, 2008), http://online.wsj.com/article/SB122661642852326187.html (accessed November 18, 2008).
4. Clayton T. Alderfer and Ken K. Smith, "Studying Intergroup Relations Imbedded in Organizations," *Administrative Science Quarterly* 27 (1982), 35–65.
5. Muzafer Sherif, "Experiments in Group Conflict," *Scientific American* 195 (1956), 54–58; and Edgar H. Schein, *Organizational Psychology*, 3d ed. (Englewood Cliffs, NJ: Prentice-Hall, 1980).
6. M. Afzalur Rahim, "A Strategy for Managing Conflict in Complex Organizations," *Human Relations* 38 (1985), 81–89; Kenneth Thomas, "Conflict and Conflict Management," in M. D. Dunnette, ed., *Handbook of Industrial and Organizational Psychology* (Chicago: Rand McNally, 1976); and Stuart M. Schmidt and Thomas A. Kochan, "Conflict: Toward Conceptual Clarity," *Administrative Science Quarterly* 13 (1972), 359–370.
7. L. David Brown, "Managing Conflict among Groups," in David A. Kolb, Irwin M. Rubin, and James M. McIntyre, eds., *Organizational Psychology: A Book of Readings* (Englewood Cliffs, NJ: Prentice-Hall, 1979), 377–389; and Robert W. Ruekert and Orville C. Walker, Jr., "Interactions between Marketing and R&D Departments in Implementing Different Business Strategies," *Strategic Management Journal* 8 (1987), 233–248.
8. Ken Favaro and Saj-nicole Joni, "Getting Tensions Right," *Strategy + Business*, Issue 60 (Autumn 2010), http://www.strategy-business.com/article/10301?gko=4c378 (accessed October 3, 2011).
9. Amy Barrett, "Indigestion at Taco Bell," *BusinessWeek* (December 14, 1994), 66–67; and Greg Burns, "Fast-Food Fight," *BusinessWeek* (June 2, 1997), 34–36.
10. Nanette Byrnes, with Mike McNamee, Ronald Grover, Joann Muller, and Andrew Park, "Auditing Here, Consulting Over There," *BusinessWeek* (April 8, 2002), 34–36.
11. Victoria L. Crittenden, Lorraine R. Gardiner, and Antonie Stam, "Reducing Conflict between Marketing and Manufacturing," *Industrial Marketing Management* 22 (1993), 299–309; and Benson S. Shapiro, "Can Marketing and Manufacturing Coexist?" *Harvard Business Review* 55 (September–October 1977), 104–114.
12. Thomas A. Kochan, George P. Huber, and L. L. Cummings, "Determinants of Intraorganizational Conflict in Collective Bargaining in the Public Sector," *Administrative Science Quarterly* 20 (1975), 10–23.
13. Eric H. Neilsen, "Understanding and Managing Intergroup Conflict," in Jay W. Lorsch and Paul R. Lawrence, eds., *Managing Group and Intergroup Relations* (Homewood, IL: Irwin and Dorsey, 1972), 329–343; and Richard E. Walton and John M. Dutton, "The Management of Interdepartmental Conflict: A Model and Review," *Administrative Science Quarterly* 14 (1969), 73–84.
14. Jay W. Lorsch, "Introduction to the Structural Design of Organizations," in Gene W. Dalton, Paul R. Lawrence, and Jay W. Lorsch, eds., *Organization Structure and Design* (Homewood, IL: Irwin and Dorsey, 1970), 5.
15. James D. Thompson, *Organizations in Action* (New York: McGraw-Hill, 1967), 54–56.
16. Walton and Dutton, "The Management of Interdepartmental Conflict."
17. Joseph McCann and Jay R. Galbraith, "Interdepartmental Relations," in Paul C. Nystrom and William H. Starbuck, eds., *Handbook of Organizational Design*, vol. 2 (New York: Oxford University Press, 1981), 60–84.
18. Roderick M. Cramer, "Intergroup Relations and Organizational Dilemmas: The Role of Categorization Processes," in L. L. Cummings and Barry M. Staw, eds., *Research in Organizational Behavior*, vol. 13 (New York: JAI Press, 1991), 191–228; Neilsen, "Understanding and Managing Intergroup Conflict"; and Louis R. Pondy, "Organizational Conflict: Concepts and Models," *Administrative Science Quarterly* 12 (1968), 296–320.

19. Steven Greenhouse, "Divided, They Risk It All," *The New York Times* (July 9, 2009), B1; "About SEIU," http://www.seiu.org/our-union/ (accessed October 3, 2011); S. Greenhouse, "New Union Leader Wants Group to Be More of a Political Powerhouse," *The New York Times* (May 9, 2010), A23; S. Greenhouse, "Service Unions Agree to End a Long Dispute," *The New York Times* (July 27, 2010), B7; and S. Greenhouse, "Big Union Wins Vote Against a Rival in California," *The New York Times* (October 9, 2010), B2.
20. Jeffrey Pfeffer, *Power in Organizations* (Marshfield, MA: Pitman, 1981).
21. Amy Barrett, "Marc Cinque Hired a Corporate Pro to Upgrade His Sausage Company. Will the Move Pay Off?" *Inc.* (December 2010 – January 2011), 74–77.
22. Clinton O. Longenecker and Mitchell Neubert, "Barriers and Gateways to Management Cooperation and Teamwork," *Business Horizons* (November-December 2000), 37–44.
23. Amanuel G. Tekleab, Narda R. Quigley, and Paul E. Tesluk, "A Longitudinal Study of Team Conflict, Conflict Management, Cohesion, and Team Effectiveness," *Group and Organization Management* 34, no. 2 (April 2009), 170–205.
24. Robert R. Blake and Jane S. Mouton, "Overcoming Group Warfare," *Harvard Business Review* (November–December 1984), 98–108.
25. Blake and Mouton, "Overcoming Group Warfare"; and Paul R. Lawrence and Jay W. Lorsch, "New Management Job: The Integrator," *Harvard Business Review* 45 (November–December 1967), 142–151.
26. Jill Jusko, "Nature vs. Nurture," *Industry Week* (July 2003), 40–46.
27. Neal E. Boudette and Jeff Bennett, "UAW Boss Makes Nice, Touts End of Us vs. Them," *The Wall Street Journal* (August 4, 2011), B1.
28. Robert R. Blake, Herbert A. Shepard, and Jane S. Mouton, *Managing Intergroup Conflict in Industry* (Houston: Gulf Publishing, 1964); and Doug Stewart, "Expand the Pie before You Divvy It Up," *Smithsonian* (November 1997), 78–90.
29. Patrick S. Nugent, "Managing Conflict: Third-Party Interventions for Managers," *Academy of Management Executive* 16, no. 1 (2002), 139–155.
30. Blake and Mouton, "Overcoming Group Warfare"; Schein, *Organizational Psychology*; Blake, Shepard, and Mouton, "Managing Intergroup Conflict in Industry"; and Richard E. Walton, *Interpersonal Peacemaking: Confrontation and Third-Party Consultations* (Reading, MA: Addison-Wesley, 1969).
31. Neilsen, "Understanding and Managing Intergroup Conflict"; and McCann and Galbraith, "Interdepartmental Relations."
32. Ibid.
33. Dean Tjosvold, Valerie Dann, and Choy Wong, "Managing Conflict between Departments to Serve Customers," *Human Relations* 45 (1992), 1035–1054.
34. Robert A. Dahl, "The Concept of Power," *Behavioral Science* 2 (1957), 201–215.
35. W. Graham Astley and Paramijit S. Sachdeva, "Structural Sources of Intraorganizational Power: A Theoretical Synthesis," *Academy of Management Review* 9 (1984), 104–113; and Abraham Kaplan, "Power in Perspective," in Robert L. Kahn and Elise Boulding, eds., *Power and Conflict in Organizations* (London: Tavistock, 1964), 11–32.
36. Gerald R. Salancik and Jeffrey Pfeffer, "The Bases and Use of Power in Organizational Decision-Making: The Case of the University," *Administrative Science Quarterly* 19 (1974), 453–473.
37. Rosabeth Moss Kanter, "Power Failure in Management Circuits," *Harvard Business Review* (July–August 1979), 65–75.
38. Richard M. Emerson, "Power-Dependence Relations," *American Sociological Review* 27 (1962), 31–41.
39. Brian Stelter, "Creator of 'Mad Men' Agrees to Deliver Multiple Seasons," *The New York Times* (April 1, 2011), B2; Lauren A.E. Schuker, "'Mad Men' Put on Ice; AMC's Hit Drama Postponed to 2012 Amid Contract Talks," *The Wall Street Journal* (March 30, 2011) B8; and "Count on AMC to Make it a 'Mad,' 'Mad,' 'Mad,' 'Mad,' 'Mad' World," *The Washington Post* (March 30, 2011), C1.
40. Examples are Robert Greene and Joost Elffers, *The 48 Laws of Power* (New York: Viking, 1999); and Jeffrey J. Fox, *How to Become CEO* (New York: Hyperion, 1999).
41. John R. P. French, Jr. and Bertram Raven, "The Bases of Social Power," in D. Cartwright and A. F. Zander, eds. *Group Dynamics* (Evanston, IL: Row Peterson, 1960), 607–623.
42. Ran Lachman, "Power from What? A Reexamination of Its Relationships with Structural Conditions," *Administrative Science Quarterly* 34 (1989), 231–251; and Daniel J. Brass, "Being in the Right Place: A Structural Analysis of Individual Influence in an Organization," *Administrative Science Quarterly* 29 (1984), 518–539.
43. Michael Warshaw, "The Good Guy's Guide to Office Politics," *Fast Company* (April–May 1998), 157–178.
44. A. J. Grimes, "Authority, Power, Influence, and Social Control: A Theoretical Synthesis," *Academy of Management Review* 3 (1978), 724–735.
45. Astley and Sachdeva, "Structural Sources of Intraorganizational Power."
46. Robert A. Guth, "Gates-Ballmer Clash Shaped Microsoft's Coming Handover," *The Wall Street Journal* (June 5, 2008), A1.
47. Jeffrey Pfeffer, *Managing with Power: Politics and Influence in Organizations* (Boston: Harvard Business School Press, 1992).
48. Monica Langley, "Columbia Tells Doctors at Hospital to End Their Outside Practice," *The Wall Street Journal* (May 2, 1997), A1, A6.
49. Richard S. Blackburn, "Lower Participant Power: Toward a Conceptual Integration," *Academy of Management Review* 6 (1981), 127–131.
50. Kanter, "Power Failure in Management Circuits," 70.
51. Erik W. Larson and Jonathan B. King, "The Systemic Distortion of Information: An Ongoing Challenge to Management," *Organizational Dynamics* 24, no. 3 (Winter 1996), 49–61; and Thomas H. Davenport, Robert G. Eccles, and Laurence Prusak, "Information Politics," *Sloan Management Review* (Fall 1992), 53–65.
52. Andrew M. Pettigrew, *The Politics of Organizational Decision-Making* (London: Tavistock, 1973).
53. Warshaw, "The Good Guy's Guide to Office Politics."

54. Astley and Sachdeva, "Structural Sources of Intraorganizational Power"; and Noel M. Tichy and Charles Fombrun, "Network Analysis in Organizational Settings," *Human Relations* 32 (1979), 923–965.
55. Jeffrey Pfeffer, "Power Play," *Harvard Business Review* (July–August 2010), 84–92.
56. Edwin P. Hollander and Lynn R. Offermann, "Power and Leadership in Organizations," *American Psychologist* 45 (February 1990), 179–189.
57. Jay A. Conger and Rabindra N. Kanungo, "The Empowerment Process: Integrating Theory and Practice," *Academy of Management Review* 13 (1988), 471–482.
58. David E. Bowen and Edward E. Lawler III, "The Empowerment of Service Workers: What, Why, How, and When," *Sloan Management Review* (Spring 1992), 31–39; and Ray W. Coye and James A. Belohav, "An Exploratory Analysis of Employee Participation," *Group and Organization Management* 20, no. 1, (March 1995), 4–17.
59. Robert C. Ford and Myron D. Fottler, "Empowerment: A Matter of Degree," *Academy of Management Executive* 9, no. 3 (1995), 21–31.
60. Ricardo Semler, "Out of This World: Doing Things the Semco Way," *Global Business and Organizational Excellence* (July–August 2007), 13–21.
61. Charles Perrow, "Departmental Power and Perspective in Industrial Firms," in Mayer N. Zald, ed., *Power in Organizations* (Nashville, TN: Vanderbilt University Press, 1970), 59–89.
62. Susan Miller, David Hickson, and David Wilson, "From Strategy to Action: Involvement and Influence in Top Level Decisions," *Long Range Planning* 41 (2008), 606–628.
63. Deborah Solomon, "Bair's Legacy: An FDIC With Teeth," *The Wall Street Journal* (July 7, 2011), C1.
64. D. J. Hickson, C. R. Hinings, C. A. Lee, R. E. Schneck, and J. M. Pennings, "A Strategic Contingencies Theory of Intraorganizational Power," *Administrative Science Quarterly* 16 (1971), 216–229; and Gerald R. Salancik and Jeffrey Pfeffer, "Who Gets Power—and How They Hold onto It: A Strategic-Contingency Model of Power," *Organizational Dynamics* (Winter 1977), 3–21.
65. William C. Rhoden, "The N.F.L. Backed Down for All the World to See," *The New York Times* (December 30, 2007), Sunday Sports section, 1, 3.
66. Pfeffer, *Managing with Power*; Salancik and Pfeffer, "Who Gets Power"; C. R. Hinings, D. J. Hickson, J. M. Pennings, and R. E. Schneck, "Structural Conditions of Intraorganizational Power," *Administrative Science Quarterly* 19 (1974), 22–44.
67. Also see Carol Stoak Saunders, "The Strategic Contingencies Theory of Power: Multiple Perspectives," *Journal of Management Studies* 27 (1990), 1–18; Warren Boeker, "The Development and Institutionalization of Sub-Unit Power in Organizations," *Administrative Science Quarterly* 34 (1989), 388–510; and Irit Cohen and Ran Lachman, "The Generality of the Strategic Contingencies Approach to Sub-Unit Power," *Organizational Studies* 9 (1988), 371–391.
68. Emerson, "Power-Dependence Relations."
69. Jeffrey Pfeffer and Gerald Salancik, "Organizational Decision-Making as a Political Process: The Case of a University Budget," *Administrative Science Quarterly* (1974), 135–151.
70. Salancik and Pfeffer, "Bases and Use of Power in Organizational Decision-Making," 470.
71. Hickson et al., "A Strategic Contingencies Theory."
72. Pettigrew, *The Politics of Organizational Decision-Making*.
73. Robert Levine, "For Some Music, It Has to Be Wal-Mart and Nowhere Else," *The New York Times* (June 9, 2008), C1.
74. Hickson et al., "A Strategic Contingencies Theory."
75. Ibid.
76. John Carreyrou, "Nonprofit Hospitals Flex Pricing Power—In Roanoke, Va., Carilion's Fees Exceed Those of Competitors," *The Wall Street Journal* (August 28, 2008), A1.
77. Jeffrey Gantz and Victor V. Murray, "Experience of Workplace Politics," *Academy of Management Journal* 23 (1980), 237–251; and Dan L. Madison, Robert W. Allen, Lyman W. Porter, Patricia A. Renwick, and Bronston T. Mayes, "Organizational Politics: An Exploration of Managers' Perceptions," *Human Relations* 33 (1980), 79–100.
78. Gerald R. Ferris and K. Michele Kacmar, "Perceptions of Organizational Politics," *Journal of Management* 18 (1992), 93–116; Parmod Kumar and Rehana Ghadially, "Organizational Politics and Its Effects on Members of Organizations," *Human Relations* 42 (1989), 305–314; Donald J. Vredenburgh and John G. Maurer, "A Process Framework of Organizational Politics," *Human Relations* 37 (1984), 47–66; and Gerald R. Ferris, Dwight D. Frink, Maria Carmen Galang, Jing Zhou, Michele Kacmar, and Jack L. Howard, "Perceptions of Organizational Politics: Prediction, Stress-Related Implications, and Outcomes," *Human Relations* 49, no. 2 (1996), 233–266.
79. Ferris et al., "Perceptions of Organizational Politics: Prediction, Stress-Related Implications, and Outcomes"; John J. Voyer, "Coercive Organizational Politics and Organizational Outcomes: An Interpretive Study," *Organization Science* 5, no. 1 (February 1994), 72–85; and James W. Dean, Jr., and Mark P. Sharfman, "Does Decision Process Matter? A Study of Strategic Decision-Making Effectiveness," *Academy of Management Journal* 39, no. 2 (1996), 368–396.
80. Jeffrey Pfeffer, *Managing with Power: Politics and Influence in Organizations* (Boston: Harvard Business School Press, 1992); and Pfeffer, "Power Play."
81. Amos Drory and Tsilia Romm, "The Definition of Organizational Politics: A Review," *Human Relations* 43 (1990), 1133–1154; Vredenburgh and Maurer, "A Process Framework of Organizational Politics"; and Lafe Low, "It's Politics, As Usual," *CIO* (April 1, 2004), 87–90.
82. Pfeffer, *Power in Organizations*, 70.
83. Madison et al., "Organizational Politics"; and Jay R. Galbraith, *Organizational Design* (Reading, MA: Addison-Wesley, 1977).
84. Gantz and Murray, "Experience of Workplace Politics"; and Pfeffer, *Power in Organizations*.
85. Daniel J. Brass and Marlene E. Burkhardt, "Potential Power and Power Use: An Investigation of Structure and Behavior," *Academy of Management Journal* 38 (1993), 441–470.
86. Pfeffer, "Power Play."
87. Gerald R. Ferris, Darren C. Treadway, Pamela L. Perrewé, Robyn L. Brouer, Ceasar Douglas, and Sean Lux, "Political

Skill in Organizations," *Journal of Management* (June 2007), 290–320; "Questioning Authority; Mario Moussa Wants You to Win Your Next Argument" (Mario Moussa interviewed by Vadim Liberman), *The Conference Board Review* (November–December 2007), 25–26; and Samuel B. Bacharach, "Politically Proactive," *Fast Company* (May 2005), 93.

88. Joseph S. Nye, Jr. *Bound to Lead: The Changing Nature of American Power* (New York: Basic Books, 1990); and Diane Coutu, "Smart Power: A Conversation with Leadership Expert Joseph S. Nye, Jr.," *Harvard Business Review* (November 2008), 55–59.
89. Reported in Liberman, "Questioning Authority; Mario Moussa Wants You to Win Your Next Argument."
90. Anna Mulrine, "Harnessing the Brute Force of Soft Power," *US News & World Report* (December 1–December 8, 2008), 47.
91. Wesley Clark, "The Potency of Persuasion," *Fortune* (November 12, 2007), 48.
92. Study reported in Robert Cialdini, "The Language of Persuasion," *Harvard Management Update* (September 2004), 10–11.
93. Hickson et al., "A Strategic Contingencies Theory."
94. Pfeffer, *Power in Organizations.*
95. Jared Sandberg, "How Office Tyrants in Critical Positions Get Others to Grovel," *The Wall Street Journal* (August 21, 2007), B1.
96. Ferris et al., "Political Skill in Organizations"; and Pfeffer, *Power in Organizations.*
97. V. Dallas Merrell, *Huddling: The Informal Way to Management Success* (New York: AMACON, 1979).
98. Ceasar Douglas and Anthony P. Ammeter, "An Examination of Leader Political Skill and Its Effect on Ratings of Leader Effectiveness," *The Leadership Quarterly* 15 (2004), 537–550.
99. Vredenburgh and Maurer, "A Process Framework of Organizational Politics."
100. Pfeffer, *Power in Organizations.*
101. Ibid.
102. Robert B. Cialdini, *Influence: Science and Practice*, 4th ed. (Boston: Allyn & Bacon, 2001); R. B. Cialdini, "Harnessing the Science of Persuasion," *Harvard Business Review* (October 2001), 72–79; Allan R. Cohen and David L. Bradford, "The Influence Model: Using Reciprocity and Exchange to Get What You Need," *Journal of Organizational Excellence* (Winter 2005), 57–80; and Jared Sandberg, "People Can't Resist Doing a Big Favor—Or Asking for One," (Cubicle Culture column), *The Wall Street Journal* (December 18, 2007), B1.
103. Raymond Hernandez and David W. Chen, "Keeping Lawmakers Happy Through Gifts to Pet Charities," *The New York Times* (October 19, 2008), A1.
104. Norimitsu Onishi and Ken Belson, "Culture of Complicity Tied to Stricken Nuclear Plant," *The New York Times* (April 27, 2011), A1.
105. Cohen and Bradford, "The Influence Model."
106. Marilyn Moats Kennedy, "The Death of Office Politics," *The Conference Board Review* (September–October 2008), 18–23.
107. Pfeffer, *Power in Organizations.*
108. Damon Darlin, "Using the Web to Get the Boss to Pay More," *The New York Times* (March 3, 2007), C1.
109. Steven R. Weisman, "How Battles at Bank Ended 'Second Chance' at a Career," *The New York Times* (May 18, 2007), A14.
110. Kanter, "Power Failure in Management Circuits"; and Pfeffer, *Power in Organizations.*
111. This case was inspired by G. Pascal Zachary, "Many Journalists See a Growing Reluctance to Criticize Advertisers," *The Wall Street Journal* (February 6, 1992), A1, A9; and G. Bruce Knecht, "Retail Chains Emerge as Advance Arbiters of Magazine Content," *The Wall Street Journal* (October 22, 1997), A1, A13.

Chapter 8

©Subman, iStock

Organizational Decision-Making

Learning Objectives

After reading this chapter you should be able to:

1. Define organizational decision making.
2. Explain programmed versus nonprogrammed decisions.
3. Discuss the rational and bounded rationality approaches to decision making.
4. Describe the management science approach to decision making.
5. Understand the Carnegie and incremental decision models.
6. Explain the garbage can model of decision making.
7. Discuss the contingency decision-making framework.
8. Explain the role of high-velocity environments, mistakes, and cognitive biases in decision making.

Before reading this chapter, please check whether you agree or disagree with each of the following statements:

1 **Managers should use the most objective, rational process possible when making a decision.**

I AGREE _____ I DISAGREE _____

2 **When a manager knows the best solution to a serious organizational problem and has the necessary authority, it is best to simply make the decision and implement it rather than involve other managers in the decision process.**

I AGREE _____ I DISAGREE _____

3 **Making a poor decision can help a manager and organization learn and get stronger.**

I AGREE _____ I DISAGREE _____

What is one activity every manager—no matter what level of the hierarchy, what industry, or what size or type of organization—engages in every day? Decision making. Managers are often referred to as *decision makers*, and every organization grows, prospers, or fails as a result of the choices managers make. However, many decisions can be risky and uncertain, without any guarantee of success. The decision of managers at companies such as Bear Stearns, Merrill Lynch, and Lehman Brothers to invest in and securitize subprime mortgages virtually destroyed the companies. Managers at Walt Disney Studios decided to spend $175 million to make and market "Mars Needs Moms," but the movie turned out to be one of the biggest box-office bombs in movie history.[1] Or consider the damage done to Toyota's reputation when investigations into quality and safety problems revealed that managers had delayed decisions that might have saved lives. Top executives at Toyota knew of the "sticky-accelerator" defect at least four months before they publicly acknowledged it and recalled millions of vehicles. In the spring of 2010, the U.S. National Highway Traffic Safety Administration levied a record fine of $16.4 million after documents brought the delay to light.[2] In hindsight, the decision to issue a recall seems like a no-brainer, but the situation wasn't so clear-cut at the time. Decision making is done amid constantly changing factors, unclear information, and conflicting points of view, and even the best managers in the most successful companies sometimes make big blunders.

Yet managers also make many successful decisions every day. Apple, which seemed all but dead in the mid-1990s, topped *Fortune* magazine's list of the world's most admired companies for four straight years (2008–2011) thanks to decisions made by recently deceased CEO Steve Jobs and other top managers. At Amazon.com, the decision to launch the Kindle e-reader despite critics who said it would be crushed by the iPad was a definite home run. CEO Jeff Bezos and his key managers made a number of successful decisions that kept Amazon growing and thriving even during the recession.[3] Managers at General Mills are known for making hundreds of small decisions that add up big. For example, the decision to consolidate the purchases of items such as oils, flour, and sugar in the baking division saves the company $12 billion a year.[4]

Purpose of This Chapter

At any time, an organization may be identifying problems and implementing alternatives for hundreds of decisions. Managers and organizations somehow muddle through these processes.[5] The purpose here is to analyze these processes to learn what decision making is actually like in organizational settings. Decision-making processes can be thought of as the brain and nervous system of an organization. Decision making is the end use of the information and control systems which will be described in Chapter 11.

First, the chapter defines decision making and the different types of decisions managers make. The next section describes an ideal model of decision making and then examines how individual managers actually make decisions. The chapter also explores several models of organizational decision making, each of which is appropriate in a different organizational situation. The next section combines the models into a single framework that describes when and how the various approaches should be used. Finally, the chapter discusses special issues related to decision making, such as high-velocity environments, decision mistakes and learning, and ways to overcome cognitive biases that hinder effective decision making.

Types of Decisions

BRIEFCASE

As an organization manager, keep these guidelines in mind:

Adapt decision processes to fit the organizational situation. Understand how processes differ for programmed and nonprogrammed decisions.

Organizational decision making is formally defined as the process of identifying and solving problems. The process has two major stages. In the **problem identification** stage, information about environmental and organizational conditions is monitored to determine if performance is satisfactory and to diagnose the cause of shortcomings. The **problem solution** stage is when alternative courses of action are considered and one alternative is selected and implemented.

Organizational decisions vary in complexity and can be categorized as programmed or nonprogrammed.[6] **Programmed decisions** are repetitive and well defined, and procedures exist for resolving the problem. They are well structured because criteria of performance are normally clear, good information is available about current performance, alternatives are easily specified, and there is relative certainty that the chosen alternative will be successful. Examples of programmed decisions include decision rules, such as when to replace an office copy machine, when to reimburse managers for travel expenses, or whether an applicant has sufficient qualifications for an assembly-line job. Many companies adopt rules based on experience with programmed decisions. For example, a rule for hotel managers assigning staff for banquets is to allow one server per 30 guests for a sit-down function and one server per 40 guests for a buffet.[7]

Nonprogrammed decisions are novel and poorly defined, and no procedure exists for solving the problem. They are used when an organization has not seen a problem before and may not know how to respond. Clear-cut decision criteria do not exist. Alternatives are fuzzy. There is uncertainty about whether a proposed solution will solve the problem. Typically, few alternatives can be developed for a nonprogrammed decision, so a single solution is custom-tailored to the problem.

Many nonprogrammed decisions involve strategic planning because uncertainty is great and decisions are complex. One example comes from the Finnish company Nokia, where managers are struggling with decisions about how to revive the ailing company.

IN PRACTICE

Nokia

As recently as 2007, Nokia was the undisputed king of cellphones, with well over half the global market share for high-end and low-end mobile phones. Then Apple introduced the iPhone. A few years later, Google's Android operating platform dealt another blow. Nokia's share of the smartphone market plummeted. In addition, low-cost Asian companies were cutting into the giant company's market share for simpler, non-smart phones as well.

Stephen Elop was brought in as CEO in 2010 to try to turn things around. One of the first decisions he faced was how to reverse dwindling market share for smartphones. Nokia had virtually been pushed out of some of its largest and most lucrative markets, including the United States, by the iPhone and phones using Android. Many investors and industry insiders believed Nokia should jump on the Android bandwagon. (Google allows any company to use its Android operating platform.) However, Elop and other top managers made a strategic decision to go it alone with the company's homemade operating system, Symbian, and a new software platform called MeeGo being developed with Intel. Elop believed adopting Android would tie the company's hands in terms of being able to differentiate its products with new innovations. "We'd be just another company distributing Android," he said. "It just didn't feel right."

The decision to go it alone, however, didn't work out. Apple and Android had gained too great an advantage. Nokia's Symbian software had fallen too far behind to ever catch up, and the new MeeGo system wasn't ready to pick up the slack. In early 2011, Elop learned that the company was on track to introduce only three MeeGo-based models before 2014, which was way too slow to keep Nokia competitive in the smartphone business. So, Elop made another strategic decision in mid-2011: Nokia would abandon its homemade software and partner with Microsoft to use its Windows Phone7 operating system instead. Although Windows Phone7 had only a tiny share of the smartphone market, the partnership gave Nokia rights to add just about any kind of innovation it wanted to stuff into its Windows-based phones (something it wouldn't have been allowed to do with Android). Elop thinks that flexibility, combined with Nokia's world-class hardware design and a strong distribution network, can put Nokia back on top.[8]

The decision to produce Windows-based smartphones is only part of Elop's turnaround plan. He also wants to invest heavily in developing and protecting Nokia's low-end phone business in emerging and yet-to-emerge nations in Asia and Africa and to fund a skunkworks, staffed by top technicians who will have the freedom and resources to dream up entirely new devices and technologies. Elop is highly optimistic that his strategic decisions will pay off big for Nokia in the next few years. However, these types of decisions are very complex, and there's no guarantee that a particular choice will succeed. For example, although technology partnerships can be highly successful, they can also sometimes turn into nightmares.

The decision to invest heavily in a skunkworks is risky at a time when Nokia is struggling just to stay alive. Nokia "has entered a period of uncertainty," says Elop. "When you go through a transition like this, there are going to be bumps in the road."[9]

Particularly complex nonprogrammed decisions have been referred to as "wicked" decisions because simply defining the problem can turn into a major task. Wicked problems are associated with manager conflicts over objectives and alternatives, rapidly changing circumstances, and unclear linkages among decision elements. Managers dealing with a wicked decision may hit on a solution that merely proves they failed to correctly define the problem to begin with.[10] Under conditions of such extreme uncertainty, even a good choice can produce a bad outcome.[11] Making the decision about how to turn around a company like Nokia could be considered a wicked decision, as could decisions about matters such as how to resolve the European debt crisis, whether to send more U.S. troops into Afghanistan, or how to salvage the reputation of Rupert Murdoch's News Corporation.

Managers and organizations are dealing with a higher percentage of nonprogrammed decisions because of the rapidly changing business environment. As outlined in Exhibit 8.1, the rapid pace, complexity, and uncertainty of today's environment creates new demands on decision makers. For one thing, decisions have to be made faster than when the environment was more stable. No individual manager has the information needed to make all major decisions, which means good decision making depends on cooperation and information sharing. Decisions rely less on hard data, and there is less certainty about the outcomes. Many decisions evolve through trial and error. For example, Walmart managers eliminated 9 percent of merchandise in an effort to simplify and smarten up cluttered stores and increase sales of higher-value items, but the decision hurt sales. Walmart lost market share for the first time in a decade. Managers recently announced a campaign called "It's Back" to showcase the return of about 8,500 items to store shelves and adopted a new motto—"Low prices. Every day. On everything."[12]

EXHIBIT 8.1
Decision Making in Today's Environment

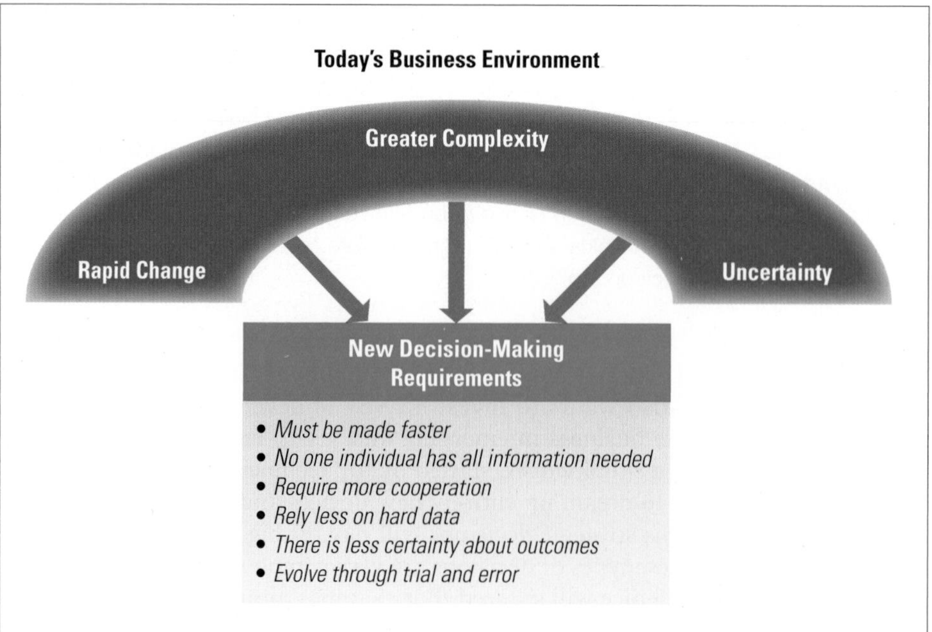

Source: Based on John P. Kotter, *Leading Change* (Boston, MA: Harvard Business School Press, 1996), p. 56.

Individual Decision Making

Individual decision making by managers can be described in two ways. First is the **rational approach**, which suggests an ideal method for how managers should try to make decisions. Second is the **bounded rationality perspective**, which describes how decisions actually have to be made under severe time and resource constraints. The rational approach is an ideal that managers may work toward but rarely reach.

Rational Approach

The rational approach to individual decision making stresses the need for systematic analysis of a problem followed by choice and implementation in a logical, step-by-step sequence. When eighteenth-century politician and diplomat Benjamin Franklin was faced with a difficult problem, for example, he would divide a sheet of paper into two columns labeled "Pro" and "Con" and write down various reasons for or against a particular decision. Over several days Franklin would narrow down the list based on a system of weighting the value of each *pro* or *con* until he reached a determination of the best decision. Franklin believed that by using this rational approach, he was "less liable to make a rash step."[13] For managers, too, the rational approach was developed to guide individual decision making because many managers were observed to be unsystematic and arbitrary in their approach to organizational decisions.

Although the rational model is an ideal not fully achievable in a manager's real world of uncertainty, complexity, and rapid change highlighted in Exhibit 8.1, the model does help managers think about decisions more clearly and rationally. Managers should use systematic procedures to make decisions whenever possible. When managers have a deep understanding of the rational decision-making process, it can help them make better decisions even when there is a lack of clear information. The authors of a popular book on decision making use the example of the U.S. Marines, who have a reputation for handling complex problems quickly and decisively. The Marines are trained to quickly go through a series of mental routines that help them analyze the situation and take action.[14]

According to the rational approach, decision making can be broken down into eight steps, as illustrated in Exhibit 8.2 and demonstrated by department store manager Linda Koslow in the following discussion.[15] Koslow was general manager of the Marshall Field's Oakbrook, Illinois, store before the chain was purchased by Macy's.[16]

1. *Monitor the decision environment.* In the first step, a manager monitors internal and external information that will indicate deviations from planned or acceptable behavior. He or she talks to colleagues and reviews financial statements, performance evaluations, industry indices, competitors' activities, and so forth. For example, during the pressure-packed five-week Christmas season, Linda Koslow checks out competitors around the mall, eyeing whether they are marking down merchandise. She also scans printouts of her store's previous day's sales to learn what is or is not moving.
2. *Define the decision problem.* The manager responds to deviations by identifying essential details of the problem: where, when, who was involved, who was affected, and how current activities are influenced. For Koslow, this means defining whether store profits are low because overall sales are less than expected or because certain lines of merchandise are not moving as expected.

EXHIBIT 8.2
Steps in the Rational Approach to Decision Making

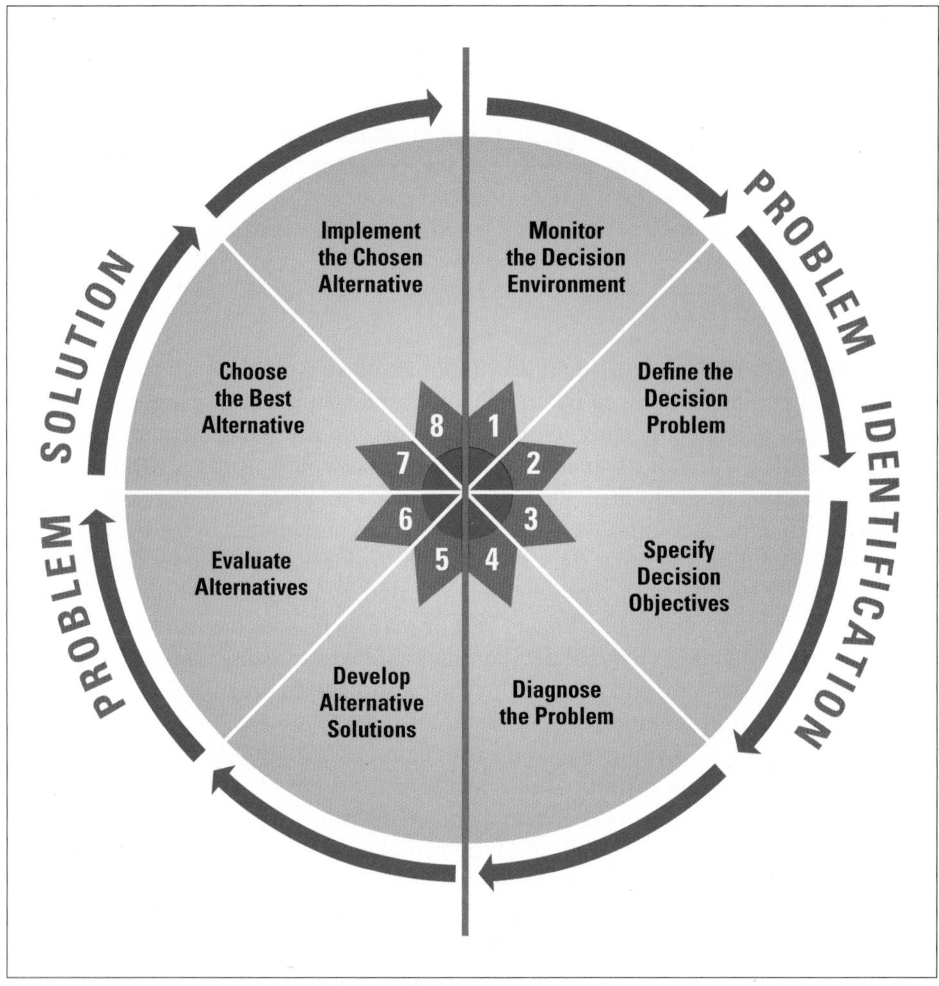

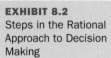

3. *Specify decision objectives.* The manager determines what performance outcomes should be achieved by a decision.
4. *Diagnose the problem.* In this step, the manager digs below the surface to analyze the cause of the problem. He or she might gather additional data to facilitate this diagnosis. Understanding the cause enables appropriate treatment. For Koslow at Marshall Field's, the cause of slow sales might be competitors' marking down of merchandise or Marshall Field's failure to display hot-selling items in a visible location.
5. *Develop alternative solutions.* Before a manager can move ahead with a decisive action plan, he or she must have a clear understanding of the various options available to achieve desired objectives. The manager may seek ideas and suggestions from other people. Koslow's alternatives for increasing profits could include buying fresh merchandise, running a sale, or reducing the number of employees.
6. *Evaluate alternatives.* This step may involve the use of statistical techniques or personal experience to gauge the probability of success. The manager assesses the merits of each alternative, as well as the probability that it will achieve the desired objectives.

7. *Choose the best alternative.* This step is when the manager uses his or her analysis of the problem, objectives, and alternatives to select a single alternative that has the best chance for success. At Marshall Field's, Koslow may choose to reduce the number of staff as a way to meet the profit goals rather than increase advertising or markdowns.
8. *Implement the chosen alternative.* Finally, the manager uses managerial, administrative, and persuasive abilities and gives directions to ensure that the decision is carried out, sometimes called execution of the decision. This might be considered the core of the decision process because any decision that isn't successfully implemented is a failed decision, no matter how good the chosen alternative might be.[17] Managers have to mobilize the people and resources to put the decision into action. Execution may be the hardest step of decision making. The monitoring activity (step 1) begins again as soon as the solution is implemented. For many managers, the decision cycle is a continuous process, with new decisions made daily based on monitoring the environment for problems and opportunities.

The first four steps in this sequence are the problem identification stage, and the next four steps are the problem solution stage of decision making, as indicated in Exhibit 8.2. A manager normally goes through all eight steps in making a decision, although each step may not be a distinct element. Managers may know from experience exactly what to do in a situation, so one or more steps will be minimized. The following example illustrates how the rational approach is used to make a decision about a personnel problem.

IN PRACTICE

Saskatchewan Consulting

1. *Monitor the decision environment.* It is Monday morning, and Joe DeFoe, Saskatchewan Consulting's accounts receivable supervisor, is absent again.
2. *Define the decision problem.* This is the fourth consecutive Monday DeFoe has been absent. Company policy forbids unexcused absenteeism, and DeFoe has been warned about his excessive absenteeism on the last two occasions. A final warning is in order but can be delayed, if warranted.
3. *Specify decision objectives.* DeFoe should attend work regularly and establish the invoice collection levels of which he is capable. The time period for solving the problem is two weeks.
4. *Diagnose the problem.* Discreet discussions with DeFoe's co-workers and information gleaned from DeFoe indicate that DeFoe has a drinking problem. He apparently uses Mondays to dry out from weekend benders. Discussion with other company sources confirms that DeFoe is a problem drinker.
5. *Develop alternative solutions.* (1) Fire DeFoe. (2) Issue a final warning without comment. (3) Issue a warning and accuse DeFoe of being an alcoholic to let him know you are aware of his problem. (4) Talk with DeFoe to see if he will discuss his drinking. If he admits he has a drinking problem, delay the final warning and suggest that he enroll in the company's new employee assistance program for help with personal problems, including alcoholism. (5) Talk with DeFoe to see if he will discuss his drinking. If he does not admit he has a drinking problem, let him know that the next absence will cost him his job.
6. *Evaluate alternatives.* The cost of training a replacement is the same for each alternative. Alternative 1 ignores cost and other criteria. Alternatives 2 and 3 do not adhere to company policy, which advocates counseling where appropriate. Alternative

4 is designed for the benefit of both DeFoe and the company. It might save a good employee if DeFoe is willing to seek assistance. Alternative 5 is primarily for the benefit of the company. A final warning might provide some incentive for DeFoe to admit he has a drinking problem. If so, dismissal might be avoided, but further absences will no longer be tolerated.

7. *Choose the best alternative*. DeFoe does not admit that he has a drinking problem. Choose alternative 5.
8. *Implement the chosen alternative*. Write up the case and issue the final warning.[18]

In the preceding example, issuing the final warning to Joe DeFoe was a programmed decision. The standard of expected behavior was clearly defined, information on the frequency and cause of DeFoe's absence was readily available, and acceptable alternatives and procedures were described. The rational procedure works best in such cases, when the decision maker has sufficient time for an orderly, thoughtful process. Moreover, Saskatchewan Consulting had mechanisms in place to successfully implement the decision once it was made.

When decisions are nonprogrammed, ill-defined, and piling on top of one another, the individual manager should still try to use the steps in the rational approach, but he or she often will have to take shortcuts by relying on intuition and experience. Deviations from the rational approach are explained by the bounded rationality perspective.

Bounded Rationality Perspective

The point of the rational approach is that managers should try to use systematic procedures to arrive at good decisions. When managers are dealing with well-understood issues, they generally use rational procedures to make decisions.[19] Yet research into managerial decision making shows that managers often are unable to follow an ideal procedure. Many decisions must be made very quickly. Time pressure, a large number of internal and external factors affecting a decision, and the ill-defined nature of many problems make systematic analysis virtually impossible. Managers have only so much time and mental capacity and, hence, cannot evaluate every goal, problem, and alternative. The attempt to be rational is bounded (limited) by the enormous complexity of many problems. There is a limit to how rational managers can be.

To understand the bounded rationality approach, think about how most new managers select a job upon graduation from college. Even this seemingly simple decision can quickly become so complex that a bounded rationality approach is used. Graduating students typically will search for a job until they have two or three acceptable job offers, at which point their search activity rapidly diminishes. Hundreds of firms may be available for interviews, and two or three job offers are far short of the maximum number that would be possible if students made the decision based on perfect rationality.

BRIEFCASE

As an organization manager, keep these guidelines in mind:

Use rational decision processes when possible, but recognize that many constraints may impinge on decision makers and prevent a perfectly rational decision. Apply the bounded rationality perspective and use intuition and experience when confronting ill-defined, nonprogrammed decisions.

Constraints and Tradeoffs. Not only are large organizational decisions too complex to fully comprehend, but several constraints impinge on the decision maker, as illustrated in Exhibit 8.3. For many decisions, the organizational circumstances are ambiguous, requiring social support, a shared perspective on what happens, and acceptance and agreement. Other organizational constraints on decision making outlined in Exhibit 8.3 include corporate culture and ethical values and

EXHIBIT 8.3
Constraints and Tradeoffs during Nonprogrammed Decision Making

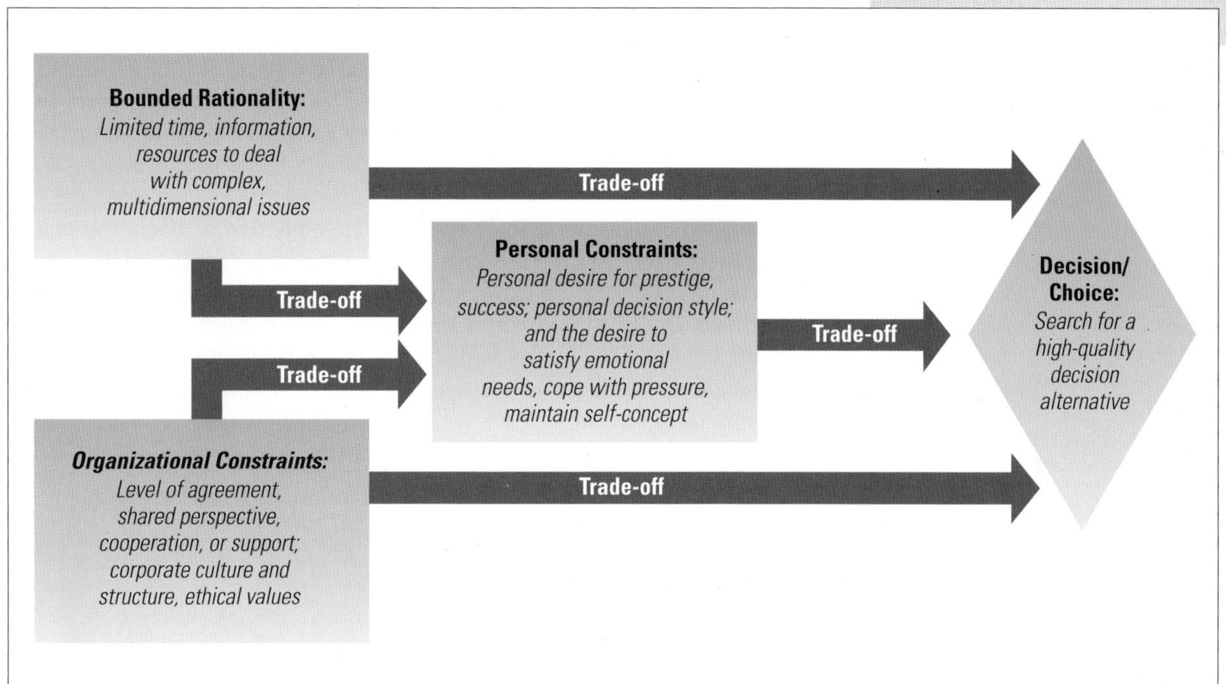

Source: Adapted from Irving L. Janis, *Crucial Decisions* (New York: Free Press, 1989); and A. L. George, *Presidential Decision Making in Foreign Policy: The Effective Use of Information and Advice* (Boulder, CO: Westview Press, 1980).

the organization's structure and design. For example, the corporate culture of BP acted as a constraint on decisions managers made that contributed to the disastrous Deepwater Horizon explosion and oil spill in the Gulf of Mexico. Taking risky shortcuts was deeply ingrained into the culture of the company. BP was drilling one of the deepest oil wells in history, for example, but managers decided to use only one strand of steel casing instead of the recommended two or more. Rather than using the recommended 21 "centralizers," which ensure that the well doesn't veer off-course as it drills deeper, BP managers decided to use only six. They also skipped a crucial test to verify the sturdiness of the cement holding the well at the bottom of the sea, deciding instead to depend solely on the blowout preventer as a safeguard. Other oil companies typically build in additional safeguards so problems can be fixed before the blowout preventer is needed, but BP's aggressive, risk-taking culture constrained managers from taking the more cautious and time-consuming approach.[20]

Constraints also exist at the personal level. Personal constraints—such as decision style, work pressure, desire for prestige, or simple feelings of insecurity—may constrain either the search for alternatives or the acceptability of an alternative. All of these factors constrain a perfectly rational approach that should lead to an obviously ideal choice.[21] Some managers, for example, make many of their decisions within a mindset of trying to please upper managers, people who are perceived to have power within the organization, or others they respect and want to emulate.[22] Other managers are constrained by an unadaptive decision style. Michael Dell reportedly has a cautious decision style that has constrained his acceptance of alternatives for fixing the problems his computer company has been facing. Dell was highly successful for many years, but while other companies such as IBM, Hewlett-Packard, and Apple moved into entirely new businesses, Dell got stuck in the business of making personal computers and providing niche services. Dell failed to appreciate the shifts in the industry away from computer hardware and to search for alternatives for moving his company into new areas. In addition, insiders say he repeatedly blocked former CEO Kevin Rollins's efforts to expand beyond PCs, starting in 2002. His aversion to risk and uncertainty acted as a personal constraint on decision making.[23]

The Role of Intuition. The bounded rationality perspective is often associated with intuitive decision processes. In **intuitive decision making**, experience and judgment rather than sequential logic or explicit reasoning are used to make decisions.[24] Most researchers have found that effective managers use a combination of rational analysis and intuition in making complex decisions under time pressure.[25] Go to the "How Do You Fit the Design?" box for some insight into your use of rationality versus intuition in making decisions.

How Do You Fit the Design?

MAKING IMPORTANT DECISIONS

How do you make important decisions? To find out, think about a time when you made an important career decision or made a major purchase or investment. To what extent does each of the following words describe how you reached the final decision? Please check five words that best describe how you made your final choice.

1. Logic _____
2. Inner knowing _____
3. Data _____
4. Felt sense _____
5. Facts _____
6. Instincts _____
7. Concepts _____
8. Hunch _____
9. Reason _____
10. Feelings _____

Scoring: Give yourself one point for each odd-numbered item you checked, and subtract one point for each even-numbered item you checked. The highest possible score is +5 and the lowest possible score is –5.

Interpretation: The odd-numbered items pertain to a linear decision style and the even-numbered items pertain to a nonlinear decision approach. Linear means using logical *rationality* to make decisions, which would be similar to the decision process in Exhibit 8.2. Nonlinear means using primarily *intuition* to make decisions, as described in the text. If you scored from –3 to –5, then intuition and a satisficing model is your dominant approach to major decisions. If you score +3 to +5, then the rational model of decision making as described in the text is your dominant approach. The rational approach is taught in business schools, but many managers use intuition based on experience, especially at senior management levels when there is little tangible data to evaluate.

Source: Adapted from Charles M. Vance, Kevin S. Groves, Yongsun Paik, and Herb Kindler, "Understanding and Measuring Linear–Nonlinear Thinking Style for Enhanced Management Education and Professional Practice," *Academy of Management Learning & Education* 6, no. 2 (2007), 167–185.

Intuition is not arbitrary or irrational because it is based on years of practice and hands-on experience, often stored in the subconscious. When managers use their intuition based on long experience with organizational issues, they more rapidly perceive and understand problems, and they develop a gut feeling or hunch about which alternative will solve a problem, speeding the decision-making process.[26] The value of intuition for effective decision making is supported by a growing body of research from psychology, organizational science, and other disciplines.[27]

When someone has a depth of experience and knowledge in a particular area, the right decision often comes quickly and effortlessly because the individual recognizes patterns based on information that has been largely forgotten by the conscious mind. This ability can be seen among soldiers in Iraq who have been responsible for stopping many roadside bomb attacks by recognizing patterns. High-tech gear designed to detect improvised explosive devices, or IEDs, is merely a supplement rather than a replacement to the ability of the human brain to sense danger and act on it. Soldiers with experience in Iraq unconsciously know when something doesn't look or feel right. It might be a rock that wasn't there yesterday, a piece of concrete that looks too symmetrical, odd patterns of behavior, or just a different feeling of tension in the air.[28] Similarly, in the business world managers continuously perceive and process information that they may not consciously be aware of, and their base of knowledge and experience helps them make decisions that may be characterized by uncertainty and ambiguity.

Managers use previous experience and judgment to incorporate intangible elements at both the problem identification and problem solution stages.[29] A study of manager problem finding showed that 30 of 33 problems were ambiguous and ill-defined.[30] Bits and scraps of unrelated information from informal sources resulted in a pattern in the manager's mind. The manager could not prove a problem existed but knew intuitively that a certain area needed attention. A too-simple view of a complex problem is often associated with decision failure,[31] so managers learn to listen to their intuition rather than accepting that things are going okay.

Intuitive processes are also used in the problem solution stage. Executives frequently make decisions without explicit reference to the impact on profits or to other measurable outcomes.[32] As we saw in Exhibit 8.3, many intangible factors—such as a person's concern about the support of other executives, fear of failure, and social attitudes—influence selection of the best alternative. These factors cannot be quantified in a systematic way, so intuition guides the choice of a solution. Managers may make a decision based on what they sense to be right rather than on what they can document with hard data.

1 Managers should use the most objective, rational process possible when making a decision.

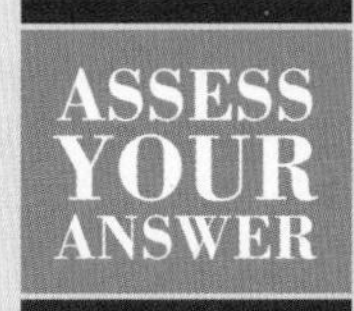

ANSWER: *Disagree.* Striving for perfect rationality in decision making is ideal, but not realistic. Many complex decisions do not lend themselves to a step-by-step analytical process. There are also numerous constraints on decision makers. When making nonprogrammed decisions, managers may try to follow the steps in the rational decision-making process, but they also have to rely on experience and intuition.

This chapter's Book Mark discusses how managers can give their intuition a better chance of leading to successful decisions. Remember that the bounded rationality perspective and the use of intuition apply mostly to nonprogrammed decisions. The novel, unclear, complex aspects of nonprogrammed decisions mean hard data and logical procedures are not available. Studies of executive decision making find that managers simply cannot use the rational approach for nonprogrammed strategic decisions, such as whether to market a controversial new prescription drug, whether to invest in a complex new project, or whether a city has a need for and can reasonably adopt an enterprise resource planning system.[33] For decisions such as these, managers have limited time and resources, and some factors simply cannot be measured and analyzed. Trying to quantify such information could cause

BOOKMARK

8.0 HAVE YOU READ THIS BOOK?

Blink: The Power of Thinking without Thinking

By Malcolm Gladwell

Snap decisions can be just as good as—and sometimes better than—decisions that are made cautiously and deliberately. Yet they can also be seriously flawed or even dangerously wrong. That's the premise of Malcolm Gladwell's *Blink: The Power of Thinking without Thinking*. Gladwell explores how our "adaptive unconscious" arrives at complex, important decisions in an instant—and how we can train it to make those decisions good ones.

SHARPENING YOUR INTUITION

Even when we think our decision making is the result of careful analysis and rational consideration, Gladwell says, most of it actually happens subconsciously in a split second. This process, which he refers to as "rapid cognition," provides room for both amazing insight and grave error. Here are some tips for improving rapid cognition:

- *Remember that more is not better.* Gladwell argues that giving people too much data and information hampers their ability to make good decisions. He cites a study showing that emergency room doctors who are best at diagnosing heart attacks gather less information from their patients than other doctors do. Rather than overloading on information, search out the most meaningful parts.
- *Practice thin-slicing.* The process Gladwell refers to as *thin-slicing* is what harnesses the power of the adaptive unconscious and enables us to make smart decisions with minimal time and information. Thin-slicing means focusing on a thin slice of pertinent data or information and allowing your intuition to do the work for you. Gladwell cites the example of a Pentagon war game, in which an enemy team of commodities traders defeated a U.S. Army that had "an unprecedented amount of information and intelligence" and "did a thoroughly rational and rigorous analysis that covered every conceivable contingency." The commodities traders were used to making thousands of instant decisions an hour based on limited information. Managers can practice spontaneous decision making until it becomes second nature.
- *Know your limits.* Not every decision should be based on intuition. When you have a depth of knowledge and experience in an area, you can put more trust in your gut feelings. Gladwell also cautions to beware of biases that interfere with good decision making. *Blink* suggests that we can teach ourselves to sort through first impressions and figure out which are important and which are based on subconscious biases such as stereotypes or emotional baggage.

PUT IT TO WORK

Blink is filled with lively and interesting anecdotes, such as how experienced firefighters can "slow down a moment" and create an environment where spontaneous decision making can take place. Gladwell asserts that a better understanding of the process of split-second decision making can help people make better decisions in all areas of their lives, as well as help them anticipate and avoid miscalculations.

Blink: The Power of Thinking without Thinking, by Malcolm Gladwell, is published by Little, Brown.

mistakes because it may oversimplify decision criteria. Intuition can balance and supplement rational analysis to help managers make better decisions.

Organizational Decision Making

Organizations are composed of managers who make decisions using both rational and intuitive processes; but organization-level decisions are not usually made by a single manager. Many organizational decisions involve several managers. Problem identification and problem solution involve many departments, multiple viewpoints, and even other organizations, which are beyond the scope of an individual manager.

The processes by which decisions are made in organizations are influenced by a number of factors, particularly the organization's own internal structures and the degree of stability or instability of the external environment.[34] Research into organization-level decision making has identified four primary types of organizational decision-making processes: the management science approach, the Carnegie model, the incremental decision model, and the garbage can model.

Management Science Approach

The **management science approach** to organizational decision making is the analog to the rational approach by individual managers. Management science came into being during World War II.[35] At that time, mathematical and statistical techniques were applied to urgent, large-scale military problems that were beyond the ability of individual decision makers.

Mathematicians, physicists, and operations researchers used systems analysis to develop artillery trajectories, antisubmarine strategies, and bombing strategies such as salvoing (discharging multiple shells simultaneously). Consider the problem of a battleship trying to sink an enemy ship several miles away. The calculation for aiming the battleship's guns should consider distance, wind speed, shell size, speed and direction of both ships, pitch and roll of the firing ship, and curvature of the earth. Methods for performing such calculations using trial and error and intuition are not accurate, take far too long, and may never achieve success.

This is where management science came in. Analysts were able to identify the relevant variables involved in aiming a ship's guns and could model them with the use of mathematical equations. Distance, speed, pitch, roll, shell size, and so on could be calculated and entered into the equations. The answer was immediate, and the guns could begin firing. Factors such as pitch and roll were soon measured mechanically and fed directly into the targeting mechanism. Today, the human element is completely removed from the targeting process. Radar picks up the target, and the entire sequence is computed automatically.

Management science yielded astonishing success for many military problems. This approach to decision making diffused into corporations and business schools, where techniques were studied and elaborated. Operations research departments use mathematical models to quantify relevant variables and develop a quantitative representation of alternative solutions and the probability of each one solving the problem. These departments also use such devices as linear programming, Bayesian statistics, PERT charts, and computer simulations.

BRIEFCASE

As an organization manager, keep this guideline in mind:

Use a rational decision approach—computation, management science—when a problem situation is well understood and can be broken down into variables that can be measured and analyzed.

Management science is an excellent device for organizational decision making when problems are analyzable and when the variables can be identified and measured. Mathematical models can contain a thousand or more variables, each one relevant in some way to the ultimate outcome. Management science techniques have been used to correctly solve problems as diverse as finding the right spot for a church camp, test-marketing the first of a new family of products, drilling for oil, and radically altering the distribution of telecommunications services.[36] Other problems amenable to management science techniques are the scheduling of ambulance technicians, turnpike toll collectors, and airline crew members.[37]

Management science, especially with increasingly sophisticated computer technology and software, can accurately and quickly solve problems that have too many explicit variables for adequate human processing. Imagine being an airline manager during and after the five-day ban on European flights due to a cloud of volcanic ash caused by an eruption under Iceland's Eyjafjallajokull glacier in 2010. The nightmare would have been compounded if airlines didn't have computerized systems to help managers make decisions about where to assign planes and crew members as they struggled to get more than 9 million stranded passengers to their destinations.[38] Alaska Airlines has been using management science techniques to make flight decisions since 1980, when Mount St. Helens erupted near the airline's home base and crippled the company for days. A team of aviation and weather experts developed computer models to predict the trajectory of volcanic ash and often enable flights to work around it.[39]

Management science is covering a broader range of problems than ever before. Consider baseball and the story told in the 2011 movie "Moneyball."[40] Brad Pitt portrays Billy Beane, the legendary general manager for the Oakland As, who in 2002 built one of Major League Baseball's winningest teams with one of its smallest budgets. Rather than rely on the intuition of scouts, who would sometimes reject a player because he "didn't look like a major leaguer," Beane relied heavily on data and statistical analysis. If the analysis said an overweight college catcher that nobody else wanted should be a number-one draft pick, Beane went for it. Since that time, most other teams have adopted management science techniques for analyzing various types of data to make decisions. "There's still a place for [guys with stopwatches or playing hunches], but technology has changed the game forever," said Steve Greenberg, former deputy commissioner of Major League Baseball.[41]

Managers in other types of organizations are also applying technology to make more decisions. Advertising firms optimize online ad campaigns by using software that can easily calculate response rates and return on investment for every advertisement. Many retailers, including Home Depot, Bloomingdale's, and Gap, use software to analyze current and historical sales data and determine when, where, and how much to mark down prices. At Walt Disney World in Orlando, Florida, managers use sophisticated computerized systems to analyze data and make decisions that minimize wait times for visitors, maximize ride capacity, optimize staffing efficiency, and increase souvenir-selling opportunities.[42] Food and beverage companies are using mathematical formulas to precisely study customer data and make decisions about which new products to develop and how to market them. Even doctors' offices are turning to management science to manage their practices more efficiently, such as by predicting demand for appointments based on the number of patients in their practice, the average no-show rate, and other factors.[43]

One problem with the management science approach is that quantitative data are not rich and do not convey tacit knowledge, as will be described in Chapter 11.

Informal cues that indicate the existence of problems have to be sensed on a more personal basis by managers.[44] The most sophisticated mathematical analyses are of no value if the important factors cannot be quantified and included in the model. Such things as competitor reactions, consumer tastes, and product warmth are qualitative dimensions. In these situations, the role of management science is to supplement manager decision making. Quantitative results can be given to managers for discussion and interpretation along with their informal opinions, judgment, and intuition. The final decision can include both qualitative factors and quantitative calculations.

Carnegie Model

The **Carnegie model** of organizational decision making is based on the work of Richard Cyert, James March, and Herbert Simon, who were all associated with Carnegie-Mellon University.[45] Their research helped formulate the bounded rationality approach to individual decision making, as well as provide new insights about organizational decisions.

Until their work, research in economics assumed that business firms made decisions as a single entity, as if all relevant information were funneled to the top decision maker for a choice. Research by the Carnegie group indicated that organization-level decisions involved many managers and that a final choice was based on a coalition among those managers. A **coalition** is an alliance among several managers who agree about organizational goals and problem priorities.[46] It could include managers from line departments, staff specialists, and even external groups, such as powerful customers, bankers, or union representatives.

Management coalitions are needed during decision making for two reasons. First, organizational goals are often ambiguous, and operative goals of departments are often inconsistent. When goals are ambiguous and inconsistent, managers disagree about problem priorities. They must bargain about problems and build a coalition around the question of which problems to address. For example, Randy Komisar, a partner with Kleiner Perkins Caufield & Byers, advises using a technique called "the balance sheet" when a company is facing decisions about which new opportunities to invest in or which problems to solve. Managers from across departments sit around a table, and each person lists on paper the good and bad points about a specific opportunity. This is similar to the "Pro" and "Con" list Benjamin Franklin used for making rational decisions as an individual. In this case, though, managers then share their thoughts and ideas with others and typically find shared interests. The process "mitigates a lot of the friction that typically arises when people marshal the facts that support their case while ignoring those that don't," Komisar says.[47]

The second reason for coalitions is that individual managers intend to be rational but function with human cognitive limitations and other constraints, as described earlier. Managers do not have the time, resources, or mental capacity to identify all dimensions and to process all information relevant to a decision. These limitations lead to coalition-building behavior. Managers talk to each other and exchange points of view to gather information and reduce ambiguity. People who have relevant information or a stake in a decision outcome are consulted. Building a coalition will lead to a decision that is supported by interested parties. Consider how managers at *The New York Times* reached a decision to begin a paid subscription plan for the newspaper's website.

BRIEFCASE

As an organization manager, keep these guidelines in mind:

Use a coalition-building approach when organizational goals and problem priorities are in conflict. When managers disagree about priorities or the true nature of the problem, they should discuss and seek agreement about priorities.

The New York Times

IN PRACTICE

In March 2011, *The New York Times* took a big strategic leap—it asked readers to begin paying for access to its journalism online. The decision wasn't made lightly. In fact, executives and senior editors spent most of 2009 debating the question, analyzing various options, and reaching agreement to implement the new subscription plan.

The economic recession hit the newspaper's revenue hard. Print advertising had already drastically declined, and with the recession online advertising did the same. The company had to borrow money at a high interest rate, and for the first time in its history the paper implemented a round of layoffs in the newsroom. This added urgency to emerging discussions within the organization about an online subscription model. Arthur Sulzberger, Jr., chairman of the company, and several other top executives embraced the idea of a pay model. However, other senior managers and editors vehemently opposed the plan. These managers and editors had spent years working to build *NYTimes.com* into the most visited newspaper site in the world. They argued that a subscription model would jeopardize the paper's online reach and was out of step with the digital age. Some advertising managers were worried that it would also jeopardize digital advertising revenues, which were just starting to recover. Others argued that the paper needed a subscription source of revenue or more layoffs would be needed.

Debate and discussion continued, both formally and informally. Managers studied consumer survey responses to try to gauge how readers would react to a subscription plan. Eventually, a coalition came together around the idea of a tiered subscription service that allows website visitors to read 20 articles a month at no charge before being asked to select one of three subscription models at various price levels. Articles that people access through social networks such as Facebook and Twitter or search engines such as Google won't count toward the monthly limit (there is a limit of five articles a day for those who access the site via Google). The fact that content can still easily be "shared, tweeted, blogged" assuaged some of the concerns from digital managers and helped get them on board to support the decision. As Martin A. Nisenholtz, senior vice president for digital operations, put it, "On the one hand, I think there is [still] some anxiety around it. On the other hand, I think the model we have chosen mitigates 90 percent of it."[48]

The New York Times Company reported in late July 2011 that a quarter of a million people had purchased online subscriptions, but it remains to be seen if the decision to charge for access will pay off for *The Times* in the long run.[49] However, managers successfully built a coalition to support the decision within the organization by engaging in debate and discussion of the concerns of all interested parties.

The process of coalition building has several implications for organizational decision behavior. First, decisions are made to *satisfice* rather than to optimize problem solutions. **Satisficing** means organizations accept a satisfactory rather than a maximum level of performance, enabling them to achieve several goals simultaneously. In decision making, the coalition will accept a solution that is perceived as satisfactory to all coalition members, as at *The New York Times*.

Second, managers are concerned with immediate problems and short-run solutions. They engage in what Cyert and March called *problemistic search*.[50] **Problemistic search** means managers look around in the immediate environment for a solution to quickly resolve a problem. Although managers at *The Times* studied various options that were being used by other companies, they didn't consider every possible approach that could be taken to an online subscription model. Managers don't expect a perfect solution when the situation is ill-defined and conflict-laden. This contrasts with the management science approach, which assumes

EXHIBIT 8.4
Choice Processes in the Carnegie Model

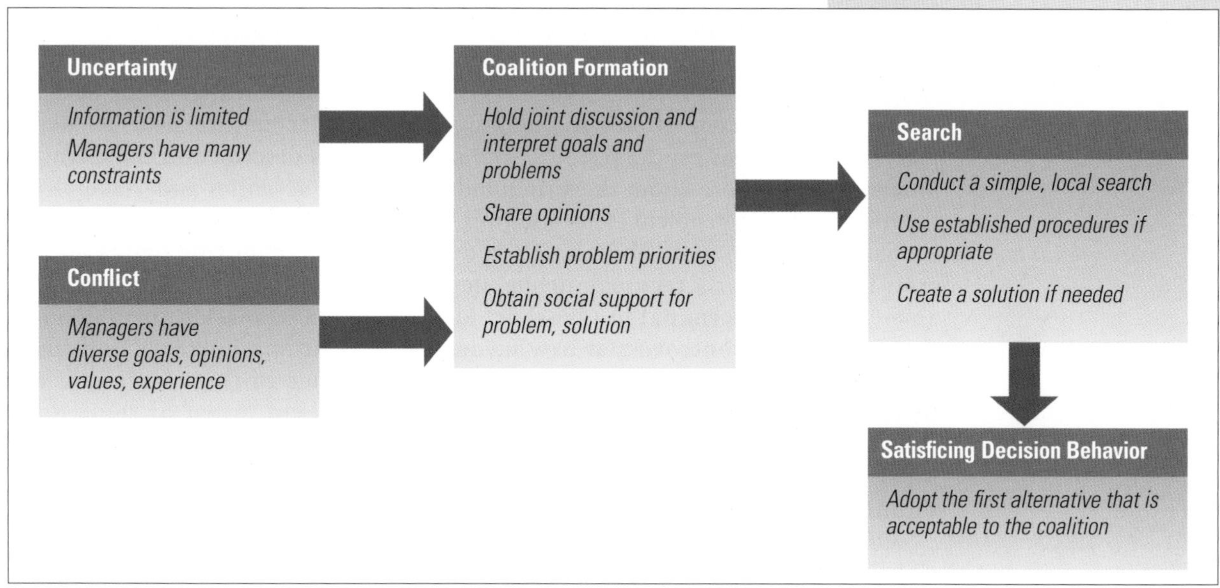

that analysis can uncover every reasonable alternative. The Carnegie model says that search behavior is just sufficient to produce a satisfactory solution and that managers typically adopt the first satisfactory solution that emerges.

Third, discussion and bargaining are especially important in the problem identification stage of decision making. Unless coalition members perceive a problem, action will not be taken. However, a coalition of key managers is also important for smooth implementation of a decision. When top managers perceive a problem or want to make a major decision, they need to reach agreement with other managers to support the decision.[51]

The decision process described in the Carnegie model is summarized in Exhibit 8.4. The Carnegie model points out that building agreement through a managerial coalition is a major part of organizational decision making. This is especially true at upper management levels. Discussion and bargaining are time consuming, so search procedures are usually simple and the selected alternative satisfices rather than optimizes problem solution. When problems are programmed—are clear and have been seen before—the organization will rely on previous procedures and routines. Rules and procedures prevent the need for renewed coalition formation and political bargaining. Nonprogrammed decisions, however, require bargaining and conflict resolution.

2 When a manager knows the best solution to a serious organizational problem and has the necessary authority, it is best to simply make the decision and implement it rather than involve other managers in the decision process.

ANSWER: *Disagree.* Few organizational decisions are made by a single manager. Organizational decision making is a social process that combines multiple perspectives. Managers have to talk to one another about problem priorities and exchange opinions and viewpoints to reach agreement. When managers don't build coalitions, important problems may go unsolved and good decisions may fail because other managers don't buy into the decisions and effectively implement them.

Incremental Decision Model

Henry Mintzberg and his associates at McGill University in Montreal approached organizational decision making from a different perspective. They identified 25 decisions made in organizations and traced the events associated with these decisions from beginning to end.[52] Their research identified each step in the decision sequence. This theory of decision making, called the **incremental decision model**, places less emphasis on the political and social factors described in the Carnegie model, but tells more about the structured sequence of activities undertaken from the discovery of a problem to its solution.[53]

Sample decisions in Mintzberg's research included choosing which jet aircraft to acquire for a regional airline, developing a new supper club, designing a new container terminal in a harbor, identifying a new market for a deodorant, installing a controversial new medical treatment in a hospital, and firing a star radio announcer.[54] The scope and importance of these decisions are revealed in the length of time taken to complete them. Most of these decisions took more than a year, and one-third of them took more than two years. Most of these decisions were nonprogrammed and required custom-designed solutions.

One discovery from this research is that major organizational choices are usually a series of small choices that combine to produce the major decision. Thus, many organizational decisions are a series of nibbles rather than a big bite. Organizations move through several decision points and may hit barriers along the way. Mintzberg called these barriers *decision interrupts*. An interrupt may mean an organization has to cycle back through a previous decision and try something new. Decision loops or cycles are one way the organization learns which alternatives will work. The ultimate solution may be very different from what was initially anticipated.

The pattern of decision stages discovered by Mintzberg and his associates is shown in Exhibit 8.5. Each box indicates a possible step in the decision sequence. The steps take place in three major decision phases: identification, development, and selection.

As an organization manager, keep these guidelines in mind:

Take risks and move the company ahead by increments when a problem is defined but solutions are uncertain. Try solutions step by step to learn whether they work.

Identification Phase. The identification phase begins with *recognition*. Recognition means one or more managers become aware of a problem and the need to make a decision. Recognition is usually stimulated by a problem or an opportunity. A problem exists when elements in the external environment change or when internal performance is perceived to be below standard. In the case of firing a radio announcer, comments about the announcer came from listeners, other announcers, and advertisers. Managers interpreted these cues until a pattern emerged that indicated a problem had to be dealt with.

The second step is *diagnosis*, in which more information is gathered if needed to define the problem situation. Diagnosis may be systematic or informal, depending upon the severity of the problem. Severe problems do not allow time for extensive diagnosis; the response must be immediate. Mild problems are usually diagnosed in a more systematic manner.

Development Phase. In the development phase, a solution is shaped to solve the problem defined in the identification phase. The development of a solution takes one of two directions. First, *search* procedures may be used to seek out alternatives

EXHIBIT 8.5
The Incremental Decision Model

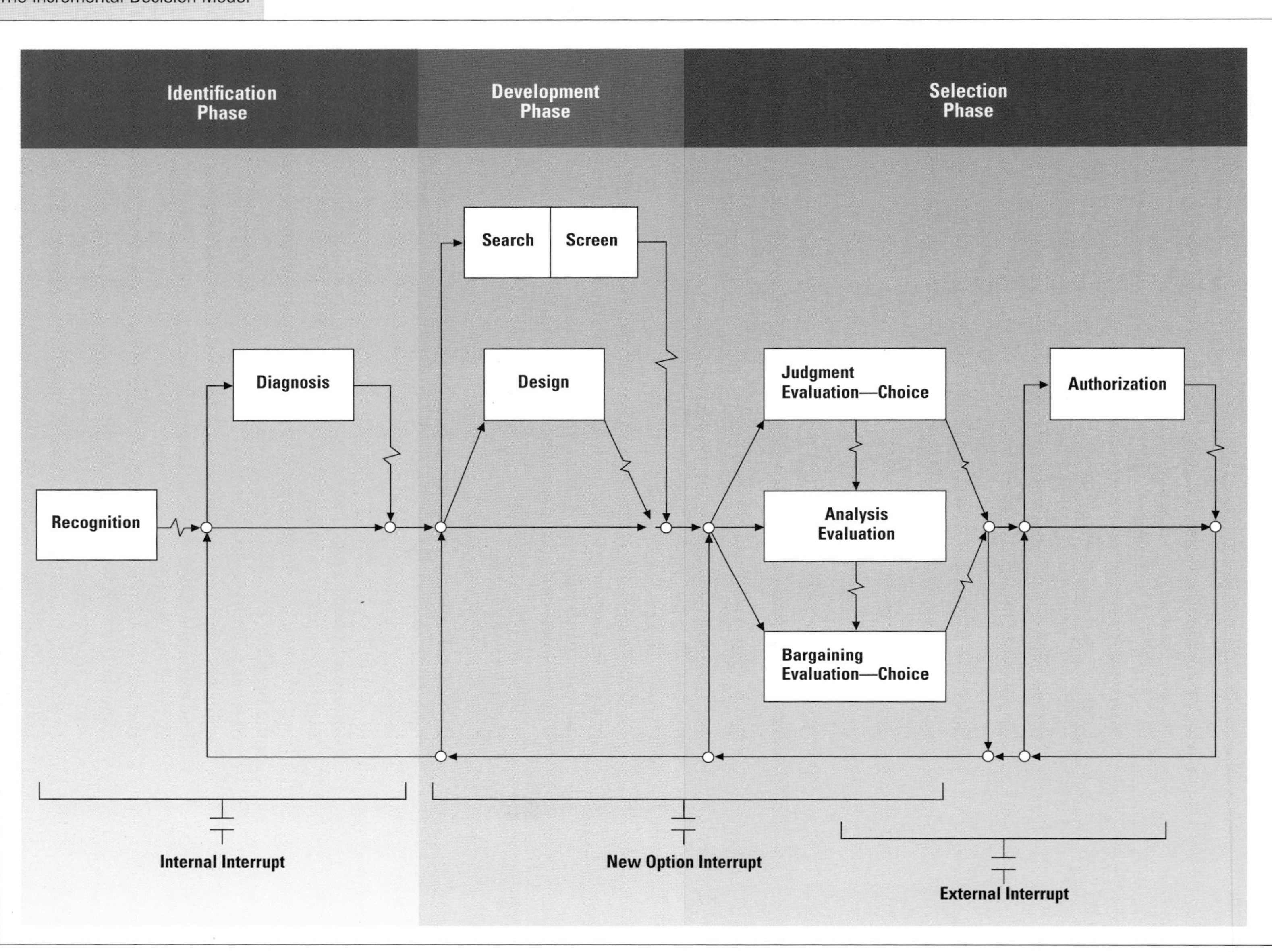

Source: Henry Mintzberg, Duru Raisinghani, and André Théorêt, "Structure of Unstructured Decision Processes," *Administrative Science Quarterly* vol. 21(June 1976), 246–275. Reprinted by permission of SAGE Publications.

within the organization's repertoire of solutions. In the case of firing a star announcer, for example, managers asked what the radio station had done the last time an announcer had to be let go. To conduct the search, organization participants may look into their own memories, talk to other managers, or examine the formal procedures of the organization.

The second direction of development is to *design* a custom solution. This happens when the problem is novel so that previous experience has no value. Mintzberg found that in these cases, key decision makers have only a vague idea of the ideal solution. Gradually, through a trial-and-error process, a custom-designed alternative will emerge. Development of the solution is a groping, incremental procedure, building a solution brick by brick.

Selection Phase. The selection phase is when the solution is chosen. This phase is not always a matter of making a clear choice among alternatives. In the case of custom-made solutions, selection is more an evaluation of the single alternative that seems feasible.

Evaluation and choice may be accomplished in three ways. The *judgment* form of selection is used when a final choice falls upon a single decision maker, and the choice involves judgment based upon experience. In *analysis*, alternatives are evaluated on a more systematic basis, such as with management science techniques. Mintzberg found that most decisions did not involve systematic analysis and evaluation of alternatives. *Bargaining* occurs when selection involves a group of decision makers. Each decision maker may have a different stake in the outcome, so conflict emerges. Discussion and bargaining occur until a coalition is formed, as in the Carnegie model described earlier.

When a decision is formally accepted by the organization, *authorization* takes place. The decision may be passed up the hierarchy to the responsible hierarchical level. Authorization is often routine because the expertise and knowledge rest with the lower-level decision makers who identified the problem and developed the solution. A few decisions may be rejected because of implications not anticipated by lower-level managers.

Dynamic Factors. The lower part of the chart in Exhibit 8.5 shows lines running back toward the beginning of the decision process. These lines represent loops or cycles that take place in the decision process. Organizational decisions do not follow an orderly progression from recognition through authorization. Minor problems arise that force a loop back to an earlier stage. These are decision interrupts. If a custom-designed solution is perceived as unsatisfactory, the organization may have to go back to the very beginning and reconsider whether the problem is truly worth solving. Feedback loops can be caused by problems of timing, politics, disagreement among managers, inability to identify a feasible solution, turnover of managers, or the sudden appearance of a new alternative. For example, when a small Canadian airline made the decision to acquire jet aircraft, the board authorized the decision, but shortly after, a new chief executive was brought in who canceled the contract, recycling the decision back to the identification phase. He accepted the diagnosis of the problem but insisted upon a new search for alternatives. Then a foreign airline went out of business and two used aircraft became available at a bargain price. This presented an unexpected option, and the chief executive used his own judgment to authorize the purchase of the aircraft.[55]

Because most decisions take place over an extended period of time, circumstances change. Decision making is a dynamic process that may require a number of cycles before a problem is solved. An example of the incremental process and cycling that can take place is illustrated in Gillette's decision to create a new razor.

IN PRACTICE

Gillette Company

The Gillette Company, now owned by Procter & Gamble, uses incremental decision making to perfect the design of razors such as the Mach3 Turbo, the vibrating M3Power, or the Fusion shaving system. Consider the development of the original Mach3. While searching for a new idea to increase sales in Gillette's mature shaving market, researchers at the company's British research lab came up with a bright idea to create a razor with three blades to produce a closer, smoother, more comfortable shave (recognition and diagnosis). Ten years later, the Mach3 reached the market, after thousands of shaving tests, numerous design modifications, and a development and tooling cost of $750 million, roughly the amount a pharmaceutical firm invests in developing a blockbuster drug.

The technical demands of building a razor with three blades that would follow a man's face and also be easy to clean had several blind alleys. Engineers first tried to find established techniques (search, screen), but none fit the bill. Eventually a prototype called Manx was built (design), and in shaving tests it "beat the pants off" Gillette's Sensor Excel, the company's best-selling razor at the time. However, Gillette's CEO insisted that the razor had to have a radically new blade edge so the razor could use thinner blades (internal interrupt), so engineers began looking for new technology that could produce a stronger blade (search, screen). Eventually, the new edge, known as DLC for diamond-like carbon coating, would be applied atom by atom with chip-making technology (design).

The next problem was manufacturing (diagnosis), which required an entirely new process to handle the complexity of the triple-bladed razor (design). Although the board gave the go-ahead to develop manufacturing equipment (judgment, authorization), some members became concerned because the new blades, which are three times stronger than stainless steel, would last longer and cause Gillette to sell fewer cartridges (internal interrupt). The board eventually made the decision to continue with the new blades, which have a blue indicator strip that fades to white and signals when it's time for a new cartridge.

The board gave final approval for production of the Mach3, the new razor was introduced a few months later, and it began smoothly sliding off shelves. Gillette recovered its huge investment in record time. Gillette then started the process of searching for the next shaving breakthrough all over again, using new technology that can examine a razor blade at the atomic level and high-speed video that can capture the act of cutting a single whisker. The company moved ahead in increments and rolled out its next major shaving product, the five-bladed Fusion, after only 8 years instead of the decade it took for the Mach3.[56]

At Gillette, the identification phase occurred because executives were aware of the need for a new razor and became alert to the idea of using three blades to produce a closer shave. The development phase was characterized by the trial-and-error custom design leading to the Mach3. During the selection phase, certain approaches were found to be unacceptable, causing Gillette to cycle back and redesign the razor, including using thinner, stronger blades. Advancing once again to the selection phase, the Mach3 passed the judgment of top executives and board members, and manufacturing and marketing budgets were quickly authorized.

Organizational Decisions and Change

At the beginning of this chapter, we discussed how the rapidly changing business environment is creating greater uncertainty for decision makers. Many organizations are marked by a tremendous amount of uncertainty at both the problem identification and problem solution stages. Two approaches to decision making have evolved to help managers cope with this uncertainty and complexity. One approach is to combine the Carnegie and incremental models just described. The second is a unique approach called the garbage can model.

Combining the Incremental and Carnegie Models

BRIEFCASE

As an organization manager, keep these guidelines in mind:

Apply both the Carnegie model and the incremental decision model in a situation with high uncertainty about both problems and solutions. Decision making may also employ garbage can procedures. Move the organization toward better performance by proposing new ideas, spending time working in important areas, and persisting with potential solutions.

The Carnegie description of coalition building is especially relevant for the problem identification stage. When issues are ambiguous, or if managers disagree about problem severity, discussion, negotiation, and coalition building are needed. The incremental model tends to emphasize the steps used to reach a solution. After managers agree on a problem, the step-by-step process is a way of trying various solutions to see what will work. When problem solution is unclear, a trial-and-error solution may be designed.

The application of the Carnegie and incremental models to the stages in the decision process is illustrated in Exhibit 8.6. The two models do not disagree with one another. They describe different approaches for how organizations make decisions when either problem identification or problem solution is uncertain. When both parts of the decision process are simultaneously highly uncertain, the organization is in an extremely difficult position. Decision processes in that situation may be a combination of the Carnegie and incremental models, and this combination may evolve into a situation described in the garbage can model.

Garbage Can Model

The **garbage can model** is one of the most recent and interesting descriptions of organizational decision processes. It is not directly comparable to the earlier models, because the garbage can model deals with the pattern or flow of multiple decisions within organizations, whereas the incremental and Carnegie models focus on how a single decision is made. The garbage can model helps you think of the whole organization and the frequent decisions being made by managers throughout.

Organized Anarchy. The garbage can model was developed to explain the pattern of decision making in organizations that experience extremely high uncertainty. Michael Cohen, James March, and Johan Olsen, the originators of the model, called

EXHIBIT 8.6
Decision Process When Problem Identification and Problem Solution Are Uncertain

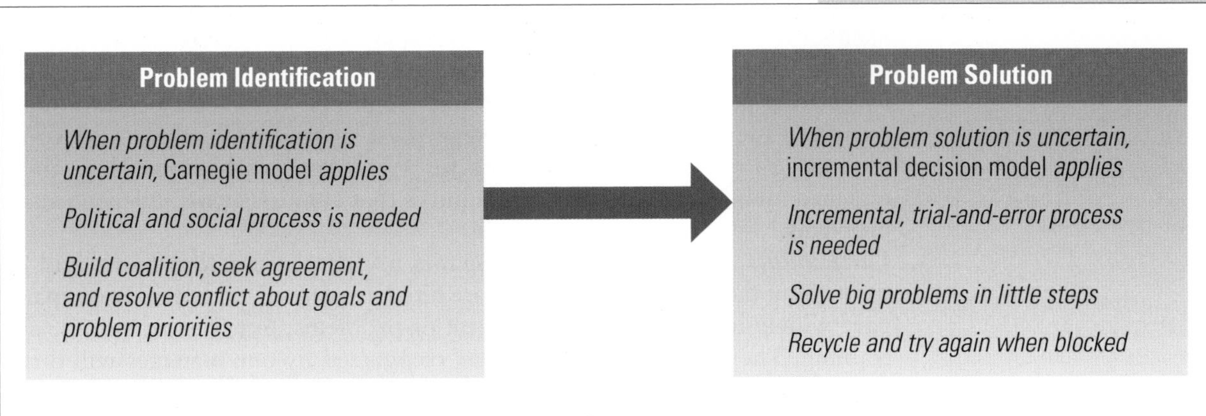

the highly uncertain conditions an **organized anarchy**, which is an extremely organic organization.[57] Organized anarchies do not rely on the normal vertical hierarchy of authority and bureaucratic decision rules. They result from three characteristics:

1. *Problematic preferences.* Goals, problems, alternatives, and solutions are ill-defined. Ambiguity characterizes each step of a decision process.
2. *Unclear, poorly understood technology.* Cause-and-effect relationships within the organization are difficult to identify. An explicit database that applies to decisions is not available.
3. *Turnover.* Organizational positions experience turnover of participants. In addition, employees are busy and have only limited time to allocate to any one problem or decision. Participation in any given decision will be fluid and limited.

An organized anarchy is characterized by rapid change and a collegial, non-bureaucratic environment. No organization fits this extremely organic circumstance all the time, although today's Internet-based companies, as well as organizations in rapidly changing industries, may experience it much of the time. Many organizations will occasionally find themselves in positions of making decisions under unclear, problematic circumstances. The garbage can model is useful for understanding the pattern of these decisions.

Streams of Events. The unique characteristic of the garbage can model is that the decision process is not seen as a sequence of steps that begins with a problem and ends with a solution. Indeed, problem identification and problem solution may not be connected to each other. An idea may be proposed as a solution when no problem is specified. A problem may exist and never generate a solution. Decisions are the outcome of independent streams of events within the organization. The four streams relevant to organizational decision making are as follows:

1. *Problems.* Problems are points of dissatisfaction with current activities and performance. They represent a gap between desired performance and current

activities. Problems are perceived to require attention. However, they are distinct from solutions and choices. A problem may lead to a proposed solution or it may not. Problems may not be solved when solutions are adopted.

2. *Potential solutions.* A solution is an idea somebody proposes for adoption. Such ideas form a flow of alternative solutions through the organization. Ideas may be brought into the organization by new personnel or may be invented by existing personnel. Participants may simply be attracted to certain ideas and push them as logical choices regardless of problems. Attraction to an idea may cause an employee to look for a problem to which the idea can be attached and, hence, justified. The point is that solutions exist independent of problems.
3. *Participants.* Organization participants are employees who come and go throughout the organization. People are hired, reassigned, and fired. Participants vary widely in their ideas, perception of problems, experience, values, and training. The problems and solutions recognized by one manager will differ from those recognized by another manager.
4. *Choice opportunities.* Choice opportunities are occasions when an organization usually makes a decision. They occur when contracts are signed, people are hired, or a new product is authorized. They also occur when the right mix of participants, solutions, and problems exists. Thus, a manager who happened to learn of a good idea may suddenly become aware of a problem to which it applies and, hence, can provide the organization with a choice opportunity. Match-ups of problems and solutions often result in decisions.

With the concept of four streams, the overall pattern of organizational decision making takes on a random quality. Problems, solutions, participants, and choices all flow through the organization. In one sense, the organization is a large garbage can in which these streams are being stirred, as illustrated in Exhibit 8.7. When a problem, solution, and participant happen to connect at one point, a decision may be made and the problem may be solved; but if the solution does not fit the problem, the problem may not be solved.

Thus, when viewing the organization as a whole and considering its high level of uncertainty, one sees problems arise that are not solved and solutions tried that do not work. Organizational decisions are disorderly and not the result of a logical, step-by-step sequence. Events may be so ill-defined and complex that decisions, problems, and solutions act as independent events. When they connect, some problems are solved, but many are not.[58]

Consequences. There are four specific consequences of the garbage can decision process for organizational decision making:

1. *Solutions may be proposed even when problems do not exist.* An employee might be sold on an idea and might try to sell it to the rest of the organization. An example was the adoption of computers by many organizations during the 1970s. The computer was an exciting solution and was pushed by both computer manufacturers and systems analysts within organizations. The computer did not solve any problems in those initial applications. Indeed, some computers caused more problems than they solved.
2. *Choices are made without solving problems.* A choice—for example, creating a new department or revising work procedures—may be made with the intention

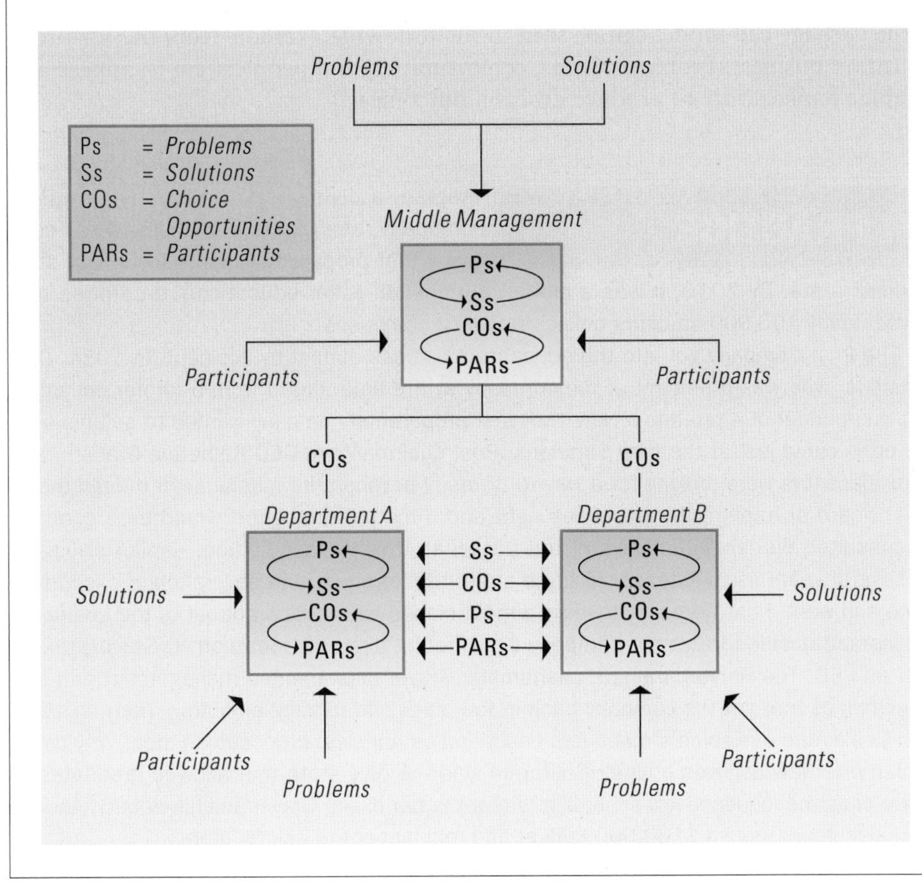

EXHIBIT 8.7
Illustration of Independent Streams of Events in the Garbage Can Model of Decision Making

of solving a problem; but, under conditions of high uncertainty, the choice may be incorrect. Moreover, many choices just seem to happen. People decide to quit, the organization's budget is cut, or a new policy bulletin is issued. These choices may be oriented toward problems but do not necessarily solve them.

3. *Problems may persist without being solved.* Organization participants get used to certain problems and give up trying to solve them; or participants may not know how to solve certain problems because the technology is unclear. A university in Canada was placed on probation by the American Association of University Professors because a professor had been denied tenure without due process. The probation was a nagging annoyance that the administrators wanted to remove. Fifteen years later, the nontenured professor died. The probation continues because the university did not acquiesce to the demands of the heirs to reevaluate the case. The university would like to solve the problem, but administrators are not sure how, and they do not have the resources to allocate to it. The probation problem persists without a solution.
4. *A few problems are solved.* The decision process does work in the aggregate. In computer simulations of the garbage can model, important problems were often resolved. Solutions do connect with appropriate problems and participants so that a good choice is made. Of course, not all problems are resolved when choices are made, but the organization does move in the direction of problem reduction.

The effects of independent streams and the rather chaotic decision processes of the garbage can model can be seen in the following example from the for-profit education business. Problems, ideas, opportunities, and people seem to appear and combine haphazardly to produce decision outcomes.

Kaplan/ The Washington Post Company

IN PRACTICE

Kaplan, a division of The Washington Post Company, used to be a relatively small company that prepared students for taking standardized tests. By 2010, it was a global, multibillion-dollar educational enterprise that served nearly 100,000 students online and at 70 campuses.

The Post Company got into the education business almost by accident. In 1984, Dick Simmons, who was president of the company at the time, heard from a former colleague that the founder of a profitable New York test preparation company wanted to sell his firm. The news came just at the time Simmons, Post chairman and CEO Katherine Graham, and other managers were looking for a way to diversify beyond print media. Even though they'd never heard of Kaplan, the price was right and Simmons thought it would be a good fit. He consulted Warren Buffett, who liked the idea. After the acquisition, Kaplan struggled for several years as rival test-prep firms stole market share and several chief executives came and went. Post Company leaders almost closed Kaplan and got out of the business, but instead decided to let the company's marketing director, Jonathan N. Grayer, take a shot as CEO. The Harvard-trained, charismatic Grayer implemented management and system changes that got the company back in the black and running smoothly. Then, in 1997 Jack Goetz, one of Kaplan's managers based in Los Angeles, proposed an idea: Why didn't Kaplan offer law degrees online? California was the only state that allowed graduates of online or correspondence law schools to sit for the bar exam. Grayer and his deputy, Andrew S. Rosen, gave Goetz a $100,000 budget and told him not to ask for more.

Within two years, Kaplan's Concord Law School, the first online law school in the country, had 600 students. The success of the school spurred mangers to look for other opportunities. In 2000, Kaplan acquired Quest Education, a chain of 30 small, for-profit specialty schools that catered to low-income students. Kaplan was no longer in the business of just preparing students to get into college; it was itself offering degrees. Kaplan's entry into higher education coincided with a U.S. government pilot project in which students could use Federal loans for online courses. Kaplan's success and growth skyrocketed. Other fortuitous political changes also benefitted Kaplan. President George W. Bush appointed a new team at the Education Department that was favorable to for-profit educational firms. The department eased regulations and lifted various restrictions on for-profit schools, which led to increasing enrollments and greater and greater amounts of Federal loan money for Kaplan.

With rapid growth came growing tensions. During this period Grayer left the company and Rosen took over. At the same time, a new team came into the U.S. Education Department under the Obama administration. Unlike previous leaders, the new team was skeptical of for-profit education and began reinstating restrictions. For example, the department proposed 14 new rules to protect students from misleading recruiting practices. The Government Accountability Office sent investigators armed with hidden cameras to pose as applicants at 15 schools, including some Kaplan campuses, and uncovered what they say was a pattern of misleading sales tactics. Kaplan's management quickly went into crisis mode and began its own investigations. Several people were fired or suspended, and the company developed new training programs for recruiters. But new problems continued to arise. Veterans groups began criticizing the company for aggressively recruiting former service members by preying on their fears and uncertainties about the future. Four former employees filed whistle-blower lawsuits accusing the company of breaking the law to recruit more students. The confluence of events demoralized Kaplan staff, damaged the company's reputation, and put executives on the hotseat.

Late in 2010, Kaplan announced the Kaplan Commitment, a plan that allows people to take classes for about a month and then withdraw without owing any money if they decide it is not what they want. Other changes are also underway. Kaplan laid off about 700 workers and is transitioning away from its primary emphasis on serving low-income students. The changes will cut deeply into Kaplan's revenue, which was around $2.9 billion in 2010, mostly from the schools. The original test preparation business has steadily been losing money and closing centers. "The Kaplan story has been one of reinvention over time," said Andrew Rosen.[59]

The shifting fortunes of the Washington Post Company's Kaplan division illustrate the garbage can model of decision making and the flow of people, problems, opportunities, and ideas through an organization. Many events occurred by chance and were intertwined. Post managers bought Kaplan because it became available at the time they were looking to diversify. The company then got into higher education almost by accident when Jack Goetz had the idea of offering law degrees online. Kaplan was able to grow because of favorable legislative actions, but a new administration has brought new problems for the company. Managers are trying various solutions, and some problems will be solved. Others may persist for years. New choices will be made and other opportunities embraced or rejected as people with various ideas come and go and outside forces continue to change.

Contingency Decision-Making Framework

This chapter has covered several approaches to organizational decision making, including management science, the Carnegie model, the incremental decision model, and the garbage can model. It has also discussed rational and intuitive decision processes used by individual managers. Each decision approach is a relatively accurate description of the actual decision process, yet all differ from each other. Management science, for example, reflects a different set of decision assumptions and procedures than does the garbage can model.

One reason for having different approaches is that they appear in different organizational situations. The use of an approach is contingent on the organization setting. Two characteristics of organizations that determine the use of decision approaches are (1) problem consensus and (2) technical knowledge about the means to solve those problems.[60] Analyzing organizations along these two dimensions suggests which approach is most appropriate for making decisions.

Problem Consensus

Problem consensus refers to the agreement among managers about the nature of a problem or opportunity and about which goals and outcomes to pursue. This variable ranges from complete agreement to complete disagreement. When managers agree, there is little uncertainty—the problems and goals of the organization are clear, and so are standards of performance. When managers disagree, organization direction and performance expectations are in dispute, creating a situation of high uncertainty. One example of problem uncertainty occurred at Rockford Health System. Human resource managers wanted to implement a new self-service benefits system, which would allow employees to manage their own benefits and free up HR employees for more strategic activities. Finance managers, on the other hand, argued that the cost of the software licenses was too high and would hurt the company's bottom line. Managers in other departments also disagreed with the new system because they feared adoption of an expensive new HR system meant they might not get their departmental projects approved.[61]

Problem consensus tends to be low when organizations are differentiated, as described in Chapter 6. Recall that uncertain environments cause organizational departments to differentiate from one another in goals and attitudes to specialize in specific environmental sectors. This differentiation leads to disagreement and conflict, so managers must make a special effort to build coalitions during decision making. For example, NASA was severely criticized for failing to identify problems with the *Columbia* space shuttle that might have prevented the February 2003 disaster. Part of the reason was high differentiation and conflicting opinions between safety managers and scheduling managers, in which pressure to launch on time overrode safety concerns. In addition, after the launch, engineers three times requested—and were denied—better photos to assess the damage from a piece of foam debris that struck the shuttle's left wing just seconds after launch. Investigations later indicated that the damage caused by the debris may have been the primary physical cause of the explosion. Mechanisms for hearing dissenting opinions and building coalitions can improve decision making at NASA and other organizations dealing with complex problems.[62]

Problem consensus is especially important for the problem identification stage of decision making. When problems are clear and agreed on, they provide clear standards and expectations for performance. When problems are not agreed on, problem identification is uncertain and management attention must be focused on gaining agreement about goals and priorities.

Technical Knowledge about Solutions

Technical knowledge refers to understanding and agreement about how to solve problems and reach organizational goals. This variable can range from complete agreement and certainty to complete disagreement and uncertainty about cause–effect relationships leading to problem solution. One example of low technical knowledge occurred at Dr. Pepper/Seven-Up Inc. Managers agreed on the problem to be solved—they wanted to increase market share from 6 percent to 7 percent. However, the means for achieving this increase in market share were not known or agreed on. A few managers wanted to use discount pricing in supermarkets. Other managers believed they should increase the number of soda fountain outlets in restaurants and fast-food chains. A few other managers insisted that the best approach was to increase advertising. Managers did not know what would cause an increase in market share. Eventually, the advertising judgment prevailed, but it did not work very well. The failure of its decision reflected managers' low technical knowledge about how to solve the problem.

When means are well understood, the appropriate alternatives can be identified and calculated with some degree of certainty. When means are poorly understood, potential solutions are ill-defined and uncertain. Intuition, judgment, and trial and error become the basis for decisions.

Contingency Framework

Exhibit 8.8 describes the **contingency decision-making framework**, which brings together the two dimensions of problem consensus and technical knowledge about solutions. Each cell represents an organizational situation that is appropriate for the decision-making approaches described in this chapter.

Cell 1. In cell 1 of Exhibit 8.8, rational decision procedures are used because problems are agreed on and cause-effect relationships are well understood, so there is little uncertainty. Decisions can be made in a computational manner. Alternatives can be identified and the best solution adopted through analysis and calculations. The rational models described earlier in this chapter, both for individuals and for the organization, are appropriate when problems and the means for solving them are well defined.

Cell 2. In cell 2, there is high uncertainty about problems and priorities, so bargaining and compromise are used to reach consensus. Tackling one problem might mean the organization must postpone action on other issues. The priorities given to respective problems are decided through discussion, debate, and coalition building.

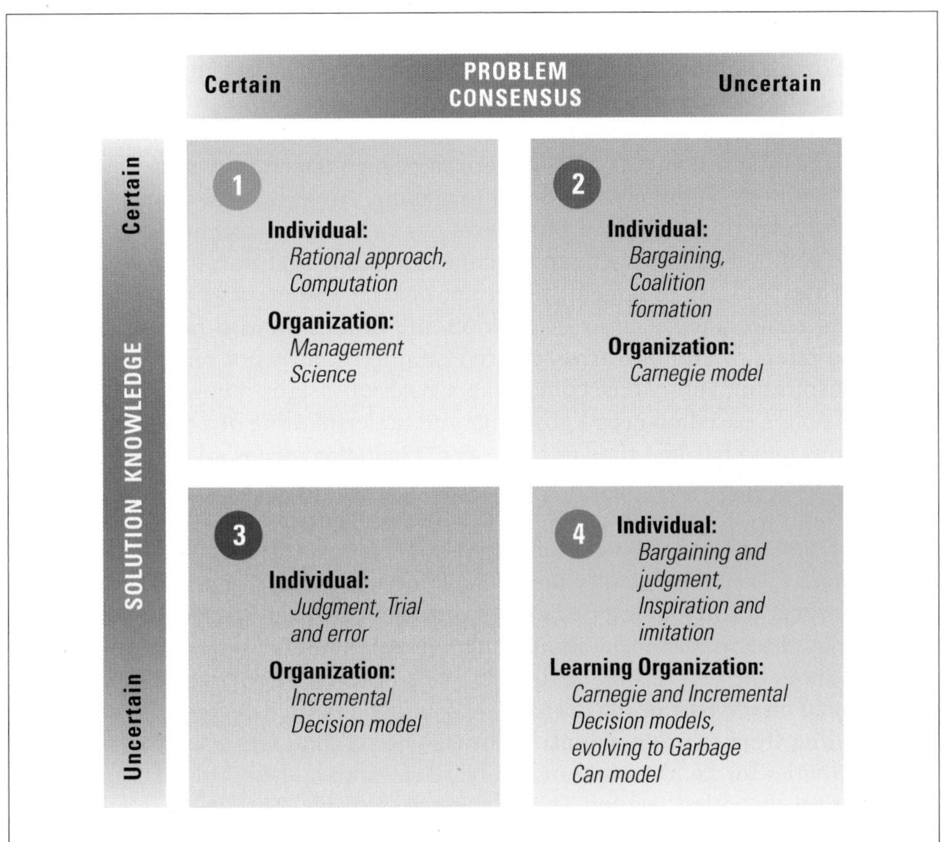

EXHIBIT 8.8
Contingency Framework for Using Decision Models

Managers in this situation should use broad participation to achieve consensus in the decision process. Opinions should be surfaced and discussed until compromise is reached. The organization will not otherwise move forward as an integrated unit. The Carnegie model applies when there is dissension about organizational problems. When groups within the organization disagree, or when the organization is in conflict with constituencies (government regulators, suppliers, unions), bargaining and negotiation are required. The bargaining strategy is especially relevant to the problem identification stage of the decision process. Once bargaining and negotiation are completed, the organization will have support for one direction.

Cell 3. In a cell 3 situation, problems and standards of performance are certain, but alternative technical solutions are vague and uncertain. Techniques to solve a problem are ill defined and poorly understood. When an individual manager faces this situation, intuition will be the decision guideline. The manager will rely on past experience and judgment to make a decision. Rational, analytical approaches are not effective because the alternatives cannot be identified and calculated. Hard facts and accurate information are not available.

The incremental decision model reflects trial and error on the part of the organization. Once a problem is identified, a sequence of small steps enables the organization to learn a solution. As new problems arise, the organization may recycle back to an earlier point and start over. Eventually, over a period of months or years, the organization will acquire sufficient experience to solve the problem in a satisfactory way.

The situation in cell 3, of senior managers agreeing about problems but not knowing how to solve them, occurs frequently in business organizations. If managers use incremental decisions in such situations, they will eventually acquire the technical knowledge to accomplish goals and solve problems.

Cell 4. The situation in cell 4, characterized by high uncertainty about both problems and solutions, is difficult for decision making. An individual manager making a decision under this high level of uncertainty can employ techniques from both cell 2 and cell 3. The manager can attempt to build a coalition to establish goals and priorities and use judgment, intuition, or trial and error to solve problems. Additional techniques, such as inspiration and imitation, also may be required. **Inspiration** refers to an innovative, creative solution that is not reached by logical means. Inspiration sometimes comes like a flash of insight, but—similar to intuition—it is often based on deep knowledge and understanding of a problem that the unconscious mind has had time to mull over.[63] **Imitation** means adopting a decision tried elsewhere in the hope that it will work in this situation.

For example, in one university, accounting department faculty were unhappy with their current circumstances but could not decide on the direction the department should take. Some faculty members wanted a greater research orientation, whereas others wanted greater orientation toward business firms and accounting applications. The disagreement about goals was compounded because neither group was sure about the best technique for achieving its goals. The ultimate solution was inspirational on the part of the dean. An accounting research center was established with funding from major accounting firms. The funding was used to finance research activities for faculty interested in basic research and to provide contact with business firms for other faculty. The solution provided a common goal and unified people within the department to work toward that goal.

When an entire organization is characterized by high uncertainty regarding both problems and solutions, elements of the garbage can model will appear. Managers may first try techniques from both cells 2 and 3, but logical decision sequences starting with problem identification and ending with problem solution will not occur. Potential solutions will precede problems as often as problems precede solutions. In this situation, managers should encourage widespread discussion of problems and idea proposals to facilitate the opportunity to make choices. Eventually, through trial and error, the organization will solve some problems.

Research has found that decisions made following the prescriptions of the contingency decision-making framework tend to be more successful. However, the study noted that nearly six of 10 strategic management decisions failed to follow the framework, leading to a situation in which misleading or missing information decreased the chance of an effective decision choice.[64] Managers can use the contingency framework in Exhibit 8.8 to improve the likelihood of successful organizational decisions.

Special Decision Circumstances

In a highly competitive world beset by global competition and rapid change, decision making seldom fits the traditional rational, analytical model. Today's managers have to make high-stakes decisions more often and more quickly than ever before in an environment that is increasingly less predictable. Interviews with CEOs in high-tech industries, for example, found that they strive to use some type of rational process, but the uncertainty and change in the industry often make that approach unsuccessful. The way these managers actually reach decisions is through a complex interaction with other managers, subordinates, environmental factors, and organizational events.[65] Issues of particular concern for today's decision makers are coping with high-velocity environments, learning from decision mistakes, and understanding and overcoming cognitive biases in decision making.

High-Velocity Environments

In some industries, the rate of competitive and technological change is so extreme that market data are either unavailable or obsolete, strategic windows open and shut quickly, perhaps within a few months, and the cost of poor decisions may be company failure. Research has examined how successful companies make decisions in these **high-velocity environments**, especially to understand whether organizations abandon rational approaches or have time for incremental implementation.[66]

A comparison of successful with unsuccessful decisions in high-velocity environments found the following patterns:

- Successful decision makers tracked information in real time to develop a deep and intuitive grasp of the business. Two to three intense meetings per week with all key players were usual. Decision makers closely tracked operating statistics to constantly feel the pulse of what was happening. Unsuccessful firms were more concerned with future planning and forward-looking information, with only a loose grip on immediate happenings.
- During a major decision, successful companies began immediately to build multiple alternatives. Implementation of alternatives sometimes ran in parallel

BRIEFCASE

As an organization manager, keep this guideline in mind:

Track real-time information, build multiple alternatives simultaneously, and try to involve everyone—but move ahead anyway when making decisions in a high-velocity environment.

before managers settled on a final choice. Companies that made decisions slowly developed just one alternative, moving to another only after the first one failed.

- Fast, successful decision makers sought advice from everyone and depended heavily on one or two savvy, trusted colleagues as counselors. Slow companies were unable to build trust and agreement among the best people.
- Fast companies involved everyone in the decision and tried for consensus; but if consensus did not emerge, the top manager made the choice and moved ahead. Waiting for everyone to be on board created more delays than was warranted. Slow companies delayed decisions to achieve a uniform consensus.
- Fast, successful choices were well integrated with other decisions and the overall strategic direction of the company. Less successful choices considered the decision in isolation from other decisions; the decision was made in the abstract.[67]

When speed matters, a slow decision can be as ineffective as the wrong decision. Managers can learn to make decisions quickly. To improve the chances of a good decision under high-velocity conditions, some organizations stimulate constructive conflict through a technique called **point–counterpoint**, which divides decision makers into two groups and assigns them different, often competing responsibilities.[68] The groups develop and exchange proposals and debate options until they arrive at a common set of understandings and recommendations. Groups can often make better decisions because multiple and diverse opinions are considered. In the face of complexity and uncertainty, the more people who have a say in the decision making, the better.

In group decision making, a consensus may not always be reached, but the exercise gives everyone a chance to consider options and state their opinions, and it gives top managers a broader understanding. Typically, those involved support the final choice. However, if a very speedy decision is required, top managers are willing to make the decision and move forward.

Decision Mistakes and Learning

Organizational decisions result in many errors, especially when made in conditions of great uncertainty. Managers simply cannot determine or predict which alternative will solve a problem. In these cases, the organization must make the decision—and take the risk—often in the spirit of trial and error. If an alternative fails, the organization can learn from it and try another alternative that better fits the situation. Each failure provides new information and insight. The point for managers is to move ahead with the decision process despite the potential for mistakes. "Chaotic action is preferable to orderly inaction."[69]

In some organizations, managers are encouraged to instill a climate of experimentation to facilitate creative decision making. If one idea fails, another idea should be tried. Failure often lays the groundwork for success, such as when technicians at 3M developed Post-it Notes based on a failed product—a not-very-sticky glue. Managers in the most innovative companies believe that if all their new products succeed, they're doing something wrong, not taking the necessary risks to develop new markets. In other words, they recognize that when failure teaches the company something new, it lays the groundwork for success.

Only by making mistakes can managers and organizations go through the process of **decision learning** and acquire sufficient experience and knowledge to perform more effectively in the future. Some companies, such as Intuit, even give awards for failures that lead to learning. One recent winner at Intuit was the team that developed an aggressive marketing campaign to target young tax filers. Through a website called RockYourRefund.com, Intuit offered discounts to Best Buy and other companies and the ability to deposit tax refunds directly into prepaid Visa cards issued by hip-hop star and entrepreneur Russell Simmons. The campaign was a bust, with Intuit doing "very few returns" through the site. A postmortem of the project gave the team lessons they applied to future projects, such as the fact that young people shun websites that feel too much like advertising. "It's only a failure if we fail to get the learning," said Intuit Chairman Scott Cook.[70]

Based on what has been said about decision making in this chapter, one can expect companies to be ultimately successful in their decision making by adopting a learning approach toward solutions. They will make mistakes along the way, but they will resolve uncertainty through the trial-and-error process.

3 Making a poor decision can help a manager and organization learn and get stronger.

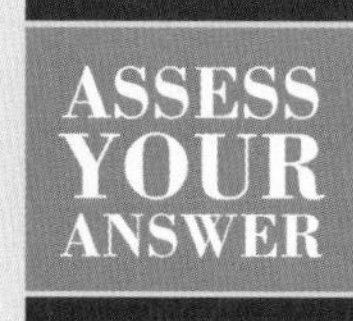

ANSWER: *Agree.* Managers don't want people to intentionally make poor decisions, of course, but smart managers encourage people to take risks and experiment, which can lead to failed decisions. Learning from the failures is the key to growing and improving. In addition, although managers strive to make good decisions, they understand that decisions sometimes must be made quickly based on limited information, and that trial and error is an important way the organization learns and grows stronger.

Cognitive Biases

While encouraging risk-taking and accepting mistakes can lead to learning, one error managers strive to avoid is allowing cognitive biases to cloud their decision making. **Cognitive biases** are severe errors in judgment that all humans are prone to and that typically lead to bad choices.[71] Three common biases are escalating commitment, loss aversion, and groupthink.

Escalating Commitment. One well-known cognitive bias is referred to as **escalating commitment**. Research suggests that organizations often continue to invest time and money in a solution despite strong evidence that it is not working. Several explanations are given for why managers escalate commitment to a failing decision.[72] Many times managers simply keep hoping they can recoup their losses. For example, after the Fukushima Daiichi nuclear power plant was damaged by a 2011 earthquake in Japan, managers at Tokyo Electric Power Company delayed using seawater to cool the damaged nuclear reactors because they wanted to protect their investment and knew that using seawater could render the reactors permanently inoperable. The company reversed its decision and began using seawater only when Japan's prime minister ordered it to do so after an explosion at the facility.[73]

In addition, managers block or distort negative information when they are personally responsible for a bad decision. Another explanation is that consistency and persistence are valued in contemporary society. Consistent managers are considered better leaders than those who switch around from one course of action to another, so managers have a hard time pulling the plug despite evidence that a decision was wrong.

Prospect Theory. Most people are naturally loss averse. The pain one feels from losing a 10-dollar bill is typically much more powerful than the happiness one gets from finding a 20-dollar one. **Prospect theory**, developed by psychologists Daniel Kahneman and Amos Tversky, suggests that the threat of a loss has a greater impact on a decision than the possibility of an equivalent gain.[74] Therefore, most managers have a tendency to analyze problems in terms of what they fear losing rather than what they might gain. When faced with a specific decision, they overweight the value of potential losses and underweight the value of potential gains. In addition, research indicates that the regret associated with a decision that results in a loss is stronger than the regret of a missed opportunity. Thus, managers might avoid potentially wonderful opportunities that also have potentially negative outcomes. This tendency can create a pattern of overly-cautious decisions that leads to chronic underperformance in the organization.[75] Prospect theory also helps to explain the phenomenon of escalating commitment, discussed in the previous section. Managers don't want to lose or be associated with a failing project, so they keep throwing good money after bad.

Groupthink. Many decisions in organizations are made by groups, and the desire to go along with the group can bias decisions. Subtle pressures for conformity exist in almost any group, and particularly when people like one another they tend to avoid anything that might create disharmony. **Groupthink** refers to the tendency of people in groups to suppress contrary opinions.[76] When people slip into groupthink, the desire for harmony outweighs concerns over decision quality. Group members emphasize maintaining unity rather than realistically challenging problems and alternatives. People censor their personal opinions and are reluctant to criticize the opinions of others.

BRIEFCASE

As an organization manager, keep these guidelines in mind:

Don't let cognitive biases cloud your decision making. To avoid the problems of groupthink, escalating commitment, and being influenced by loss aversion, apply evidence-based management and use techniques to encourage diversity and dissent.

Overcoming Personal Biases

How can managers avoid the problems of groupthink, escalating commitment, and being influenced by loss aversion? Several ideas have been proposed that help managers be more realistic and objective when making decisions. Two of the most effective are to use evidence-based management and to encourage dissent and diversity.

Evidence-Based Management. **Evidence-based management** means a commitment to make more informed and intelligent decisions based on the best available facts and evidence.[77] It means being aware of one's biases, seeking and examining evidence with rigor. Managers practice evidence-based decision making by being careful and thoughtful rather than carelessly relying on assumptions, past experience, rules of thumb, or intuition. For example, the Educational Testing Service (ETS), which develops and administers tests such as the SAT and the GRE, created a task force to examine the company's decision-making processes for new products and services. The team found that many product decisions were made without clear information about intellectual property, cycle times, or expected market opportunities. The team then worked with managers to create a more systematic, evidence-based decision-making process, including the use of forms that required specific metrics and information about each proposal and defined standards for what constituted strong evidence that the product or service would fit with ETS strategy and likely market demand.[78]

A global survey by McKinsey & Company found that when managers incorporate thoughtful analysis into decision making, they get better results. Studying the responses of more than 2,000 executives regarding how their companies made a specific decision, McKinsey concluded that techniques such as detailed analysis, risk assessment, financial models, and considering comparable situations typically contribute to better financial and operational outcomes.[79] Evidence-based management can be particularly useful for overcoming fear of loss and the problem of escalating commitment. To practice evidence-based management, managers use data and facts to the extent possible to inform their decisions. Many manager problems are uncertain, and hard facts and data aren't available, but by always seeking evidence, managers can avoid relying on faulty assumptions. Decision makers can also do a postmortem of decisions to evaluate what worked, what didn't, and how to do things better. The best decision makers have a healthy appreciation for what they don't know. They are always questioning and encouraging others to question their knowledge and assumptions. They foster a culture of inquiry, observation, and experimentation.

Encourage Dissent and Diversity. Dissent and diversity can be particularly useful in complex circumstances because they open the decision process to a wide variety of ideas and opinions rather than being constrained by personal biases or groupthink.[80] One way to encourage dissent is to ensure that the group is diverse in terms of age and gender, functional area of expertise, hierarchical level, and experience with the business. Some groups assign a **devil's advocate**, who has the role of challenging the assumptions and assertions made by the group.[81] The devil's advocate may force the group to rethink its approach to the problem and avoid reaching premature decisions. Consider the situation of soldiers involved in volatile military operations in Iraq and Afghanistan, where faulty decisions can be deadly. At Fort Leavenworth's University of Foreign Military and Cultural Studies, the U.S. Army started training a group of soldiers to act as devil's advocates. Members of the "Red Team," as graduates are called, are deployed to various brigades to question prevailing assumptions and make sure decisions are considered from alternate points of view. "This is having someone inside that says, 'Wait a minute, not so fast,'' says Greg Fontenot, the program director. The goal, he says is to avoid "getting sucked into that groupthink."[82]

Another approach, referred to as *ritual dissent*, puts parallel teams to work on the same problem in a large group meeting. Each team appoints a spokesperson who presents the team's finding and ideas to another team, which is required to listen quietly. Then, the spokesperson turns to face away from the team, which rips into the presentation no-holds-barred while the spokesperson is required to listen quietly. Each team's spokesperson does this with every other team in turn, so that by the end of the session all ideas have been well-dissected and discussed.[83] The point–counterpoint method described earlier is also effective for encouraging dissent. Whatever techniques they use, good managers find ways to get a diversity of ideas and opinions on the table when making complex decisions.

Design Essentials

- Most organizational decisions are not made in a logical, rational manner. Most decisions do not begin with the careful analysis of a problem, followed by systematic analysis of alternatives, and finally implementation of a solution. On the contrary, decision processes are characterized by conflict, coalition building, trial and error, speed, and mistakes. Managers operate under many constraints that limit rationality; hence, they use satisficing and intuition as well as rational analysis in their decision making.
- Another important idea is that individuals make decisions, but most organizational decisions are not made by a single individual. Organizational decision-making approaches include the management science approach, the Carnegie model, the incremental decision model, and the garbage can model.
- Only in rare circumstances do managers analyze problems and find solutions by themselves. Many problems are not clear, so widespread discussion and coalition building take place. Once goals and priorities are set, alternatives to achieve those goals can be tried. When a manager does make an individual decision, it is often a small part of a larger decision process. Organizations solve big problems through a series of small steps. A single manager may initiate one step but should be aware of the larger decision process to which it belongs.
- The greatest amount of conflict and coalition building occurs when problems are not agreed on. Priorities must be established to indicate which goals are important and which problems should be solved first. If a manager attacks a problem other people do not agree with, the manager will lose support for the solution to be implemented. Thus, time and activity should be spent building a coalition in the problem identification stage of decision making. Then the organization can move toward solutions. Under conditions of low technical knowledge, the solution unfolds as a series of incremental trials that will gradually lead to an overall solution.
- The most novel description of decision making is the garbage can model. This model describes how decision processes can seem almost random in highly organic organizations. Decisions, problems, ideas, and people flow through organizations and mix together in various combinations. Through this process, the organization gradually learns. Some problems may never be solved, but many are, and the organization will move toward maintaining and improving its level of performance.
- Many organizations operating in high-velocity environments must make decisions with speed, which means staying in immediate touch with operations and the environment. Moreover, in an uncertain world, organizations will make mistakes, and mistakes made through trial and error should be appreciated. Encouraging trial-and-error increments facilitates organizational learning.
- On the other hand, allowing cognitive biases to cloud decision making can have serious negative consequences for an organization. Managers can avoid the biases of escalating commitment, loss aversion, and groupthink by using evidence-based management and by encouraging diversity and dissent in the decision-making process.

Key Concepts

bounded rationality perspective
Carnegie model
coalition
cognitive biases
contingency decision-making framework
decision learning
devil's advocate
escalating commitment
evidence-based management
garbage can model
groupthink
high-velocity environments
imitation
incremental decision model
inspiration
intuitive decision making
management science approach
nonprogrammed decisions
organizational decision making
organized anarchy
point–counterpoint
problem consensus
problem identification
problem solution
problemistic search
programmed decisions
prospect theory
rational approach
satisficing
technical knowledge

Discussion Questions

1. When you are faced with choosing between several valid options, how do you typically make your decision? How do you think managers typically choose between several options? What are the similarities between your decision process and what you think managers do?
2. A professional economist once told his class, "An individual decision maker should process all relevant information and select the economically rational alternative." Do you agree? Why or why not?
3. If managers frequently use experience and intuition to make complex, nonprogrammed decisions, how do they apply evidence-based management, which seems to suggest that managers should rely on facts and data?
4. The Carnegie model emphasizes the need for a political coalition in the decision-making process. When and why are coalitions necessary?
5. What are the three major phases in Mintzberg's incremental decision model? Why might an organization recycle through one or more phases of the model?
6. An organization theorist once told her class, "Organizations never make big decisions. They make small decisions that eventually add up to a big decision." Explain the logic behind this statement.
7. How would you make a decision to select a building site for a new waste-treatment plant in the Philippines? Where would you start with this complex decision, and what steps would you take? Explain which decision model in the chapter best describes your approach.
8. Why would managers in high-velocity environments worry more about the present than the future? Would an individual manager working in this type of environment be more likely to succeed with a rational approach or an intuitive approach? Discuss.
9. Can you think of a decision you have made in your personal, school, or work life that reflects a stronger desire to avoid a loss than to make a gain? How about a time when you stayed with an idea or project for too long, perhaps even escalating your commitment, to avoid a failure? Discuss.
10. Why are decision mistakes usually accepted in organizations but penalized in college courses and exams that are designed to train managers?

Chapter 8 Workbook Decision Styles[84]

Think of some recent decisions you have made, such as buying a car, changing your field of study, joining a volunteer organization, or taking a new job. Now think of two decisions made by other people that influenced your life, such as a new work procedure at your job, a change in a personal relationship, a change at school, or a decision by your family. Fill out the following table, using Exhibit 8.8 to determine decision styles.

Your decisions	Approach used	Advantages and disadvantages	Your recommended decision style
1.			
2.			

Decisions by others

1.			
2.			

Questions

1. How can a decision approach influence the outcome of the decision? What happens when the approach fits the decision? When it doesn't fit?
2. How can you know which approach is best?

CASE FOR ANALYSIS Cracking the Whip[85]

Harmon Davidson stared dejectedly at the departing figure of his management survey team leader. Their meeting had not gone well. Davidson had relayed to Al Pitcher complaints about his handling of the survey. Pitcher had responded with adamant denial and unveiled scorn.

Davidson, director of headquarters management, was prepared to discount some of the criticism as resentment of outsiders meddling with "the way we've always done business," exacerbated by the turbulence of continual reorganization. But Davidson could hardly ignore the sheer volume of complaints or his high regard for some of their sources. "Was I missing danger signals about Pitcher from the start?" Davidson asked himself. "Or was I just giving a guy I didn't know a fair chance with an inherently controversial assignment?"

With his division decimated in the latest round of downsizing at the Department of Technical Services (DTS) earlier that year, Davidson had been asked to return to the headquarters management office after a five-year hiatus. The director, Walton Drummond, had abruptly taken early retirement.

One of the first things Davidson had learned about his new job was that he would be responsible for a comprehensive six-month survey of the headquarters management structure and processes. The DTS secretary had promised the survey to the White House as a prelude to the agency's next phase of management reform. Drummond had already picked the five-person survey team consisting of two experienced management analysts, a promising younger staff member, an intern, and Pitcher, the team leader. Pitcher was fresh from the Treasury Department, where he had participated in a similar survey. But having gone off after retirement for an extended mountain-climbing expedition in Asia, Drummond was unavailable to explain his survey plans or any understandings he had reached with Pitcher.

Davidson had been impressed with Pitcher's energy and motivation. He worked long hours, wrote voluminously if awkwardly, and was brimming with the latest organizational theory. Pitcher had other characteristics, however, that were disquieting. He seemed uninterested in DTS's history and culture and was paternalistic toward top managers, assuming they were unsophisticated and unconcerned about modern management.

A series of presurvey informational briefings for headquarters office heads conducted by Davidson and Pitcher seemed to go swimmingly. Pitcher deferred to his chief on matters of philosophy and confined his remarks to schedule and procedures. He closed his segment on a friendly note, saying, "If we do find opportunities for improvement, we'll try to have recommendations for you."

But the survey was barely a week old when the director of management received his first call from an outraged customer. It was the assistant secretary for public affairs, Erin Dove, and she was not speaking in her usual upbeat tones. "Your folks have managed to upset my whole supervisory staff with their comments about how we'll have to change our organization and methods," she said. "I thought you were going through a fact-finding study. This guy Pitcher sounds like he wants to remake DTS headquarters overnight. Who does he think he is?"

When Davidson asked him about the encounter with public affairs, Pitcher expressed puzzlement that a few summary observations shared with supervisors in the interest of "prompt informal feedback" had been interpreted as such disturbing conclusions. "I told them we'll tell them how to fix it," he reassured his supervisor.

"Listen, Al," Davidson remonstrated gently. "These are very accomplished managers who aren't used to being told they have to fix anything. This agency's been on a roll for years, and the need for reinvention isn't resonating all that well yet. We've got to collect and analyze the information and assemble a convincing case for change, or we'll be spinning our wheels. Let's hold off on the feedback until you and I have reviewed it together."

But two weeks later, Technology Development Director Phil Canseco, an old and treasured colleague, was on Davidson's doorstep looking as unhappy as Erin Dove had sounded on the phone. "Harmon, buddy, I think you have to rein in this survey team a bit," he said. "Several managers who were scheduled for survey interviews were working on a 24-hour turnaround to give a revised project budget to the Appropriations subcommittee that day. My deputy says Pitcher was put out about postponing interviews and grumbled about whether we understood the new priorities. Is he living in the real world?"

Canseco's comments prompted Davidson to call a few of his respected peers who had dealt with the survey team. With varying degrees of reluctance, they all criticized the team leader and, in some cases, team members, as abrasive and uninterested in the rationales offered for existing structure and processes.

And so Davidson marshaled all of his tact for a review with the survey team leader. But Pitcher was in no mood for either introspection or reconsideration. He took the view that he had been brought in to spearhead a White House-inspired management improvement initiative in a glamour agency that had never had to think much about efficiency. He reminded Davidson that even he had conceded that managers were due some hard lessons on this score. Pitcher didn't see any way to meet his deadline except by adhering to a rigorous schedule, since he was working with managers disinclined to cooperate with an outsider pushing an unpopular exercise. He felt Davidson's role was to hold the line against unwarranted criticisms from prima donnas trying to discredit the survey.

Many questions arose in Davidson's mind about the survey plan and his division's capacity to carry it out. Had they taken on too much with too little? Had the right people been picked for the survey team? Had managers and executives, and even the team, been properly prepared for the survey?

But the most immediate question was whether Al Pitcher could help him with these problems.

CASE FOR ANALYSIS The Dilemma of Aliesha State College: Competence Versus Need[86]

Until the 1990s, Aliesha was a well-reputed, somewhat sleepy state teachers college located on the outer fringes of a major metropolitan area. Then with the rapid expansion of college enrollments, the state converted Aliesha to a four-year state college (and the plans called for it to become a state university with graduate work and perhaps even with a medical school in the late 2000s). Within 10 years, Aliesha grew from 1,500 to 9,000 students. Its budget expanded even faster than the enrollment, increasing twentyfold during that period.

The only part of Aliesha that did not grow was the original part, the teachers' college; its enrollment actually went down. Everything else seemed to flourish. In addition to building new four-year schools of liberal arts, business, veterinary medicine, and dentistry, Aliesha developed many community service programs. Among them were a rapidly growing evening program, a mental health clinic, and a speech-therapy center for children with speech defects—the only one in the area. Even within education, one area grew—the demonstration high school attached to the old teachers college. Even though the high school enrolled only 300 students, its teachers were the leading experts in teacher education, and it was considered the best high school in the area.

Then, in 2002 the budget was suddenly cut quite sharply by the state legislature. At the same time the faculty demanded and got a fairly hefty raise in salary. It was clear that something had to give—the budget deficit was much too great to be covered by ordinary cost reductions. When the faculty committee sat down with the president and the board of trustees, two candidates for abandonment emerged after long and heated wrangling: the speech-therapy program and the demonstration high school. Both cost about the same—and both were extremely expensive. The speech-therapy clinic, everyone agreed, addressed itself to a real need and one of high priority. But—and everyone had to agree because the evidence was overwhelming—it did not do the job. Indeed, it did such a poor, sloppy, disorganized job that pediatricians, psychiatrists, and psychologists hesitated to refer their patients to the clinic. The reason was that the clinic was a college program run to teach psychology students rather than to help children with serious speech impediments.

The opposite criticism applied to the high school. No one questioned its excellence and the impact it made on the education students who listened in on its classes and on many young teachers in the area who came in as auditors. But what need did it fill? There were plenty of perfectly adequate high schools in the area.

"How can we justify," asked one of the psychologists connected with the speech clinic, "running an unnecessary high school in which each child costs as much as a graduate student at Harvard?"

"But how can we justify," asked the dean of the school of education, himself one of the outstanding teachers in the demonstration high school, "a speech clinic that has no results even though each of its patients costs the state as much as one of our demonstration high school students, or more?"

Notes

1. Brooks Barnes, "Many Culprits in Fall of a Family Film," *The New York Times* (March 14, 2011).
2. Micheline Maynard, "Toyota Delayed a U.S. Recall, Documents Show," *The New York Times* (April 12, 2010), A1.
3. Betsy Morris, "What Makes Apple Golden?" *Fortune* (March 17, 2008), 68–74; "World's Most Admired Companies 2011," *Fortune*, http://money.cnn.com/magazines/fortune/mostadmired/2011/index.html (accessed September 23, 2011); and "Most Admired Tech Companies 2011: Amazon.com," *Fortune*, http://money.cnn.com/galleries/2011/fortune/1103/gallery.most_admired_tech_companies.fortune/5.html (accessed September 23, 2011).
4. "World's Most Admired Companies: Cereal Cost Cutters" (Top Performers series), *Fortune* (November 10, 2008), 24.
5. Charles Lindblom, "The Science of 'Muddling Through,'" *Public Administration Review* 29 (1954), 79–88.
6. Herbert A. Simon, *The New Science of Management Decision* (Englewood Cliffs, NJ: Prentice-Hall, 1960), 1–8.
7. Paul J. H. Schoemaker and J. Edward Russo, "A Pyramid of Decision Approaches," *California Management Review* (Fall 1993), 9–31.
8. Christopher Lawton, "Nokia's Go-It-Alone Strategy," *The Wall Street Journal* (November 17, 2010), http://online.wsj.com/article/SB10001424052748703628204575618711287993790.html (accessed September 26, 2011); and Peter Burrows, "Elop's Fable," *Bloomberg BusinessWeek* (June 6–June 12 2011), 56–61.
9. Burrows, "Elop's Fable."
10. Michael Pacanowsky, "Team Tools for Wicked Problems," *Organizational Dynamics* 23, no. 3 (Winter 1995), 36–51.
11. The idea of a good choice potentially producing a bad outcome under uncertain conditions is attributed to Robert Rubin, reported in David Leonhardt, "This Fed Chief May Yet Get a Honeymoon," *The New York Times* (August 23, 2006), C1.
12. Ylan Q. Mui, "Wal-Mart to Reinstate Dropped Products, Emphasize Price," *The Washington Post* (April 11, 2011), http://www.washingtonpost.com/business/economy/wal-mart-to-reinstate-products-emphasize-price/2011/04/11/AFrwL-WMD_story.html (accessed September 26, 2011).
13. As described in a letter Franklin wrote in 1772, quoted in J. Edward Russo and Paul J. H. Shoemaker, *Decision Traps: Ten Barriers to Brilliant Decision-Making and How to Overcome Them*, (New York Fireside/Simon & Schuster, 1989).
14. Karen Dillon, "The Perfect Decision" (an interview with John S. Hammond and Ralph L. Keeney), *Inc.* (October 1998), 74–78; and John S. Hammond and Ralph L. Keeney, *Smart Choices: A Practical Guide to Making Better Decisions* (Boston: Harvard Business School Press, 1998).
15. Earnest R. Archer, "How to Make a Business Decision: An Analysis of Theory and Practice," *Management Review* 69 (February 1980), 54–61; Boris Blai, "Eight Steps to Successful Problem Solving," *Supervisory Management* (January 1986), 7–9; and Thomas S. Bateman, "Leading with Competence: Problem-Solving by Leaders and Followers," *Leader to Leader* (Summer 2010), 38–44.
16. Francine Schwadel, "Christmas Sales' Lack of Momentum Tests Store Manager's Mettle," *The Wall Street Journal* (December 16, 1987), 1.
17. Noel M. Tichy and Warren G. Bennis, "Making Judgment Calls: The Ultimate Act of Leadership," *Harvard Business Review* (October 2007), 94–102.
18. Adapted from Archer, "How to Make a Business Decision," 59–61.
19. James W. Dean, Jr., and Mark P. Sharfman, "Procedural Rationality in the Strategic Decision-Making Process," *Journal of Management Studies* 30 (1993), 587–610.
20. Joe Nocera, "BP Ignored the Omens of Disaster," *The New York Times* (June 19, 2010), B1.
21. Irving L. Janis, *Crucial Decisions: Leadership in Policymaking and Crisis Management* (New York: The Free Press,

1989); and Paul C. Nutt, "Flexible Decision Styles and the Choices of Top Executives," *Journal of Management Studies* 30 (1993), 695–721.

22. Art Kleiner, "Core Group Therapy," *Strategy + Business,* Issue 27 (Second Quarter, 2002), 26–31.
23. Katie Benner, "Michael Dell's Dilemma," *Fortune* (June 13, 2011), 41–44.
24. Herbert A. Simon, "Making Management Decisions: The Role of Intuition and Emotion," *Academy of Management Executive* 1 (February 1987), 57–64; and Daniel J. Eisenberg, "How Senior Managers Think," *Harvard Business Review* 62 (November–December 1984), 80–90.
25. Jaana Woiceshyn, "Lessons from 'Good Minds': How CEOs Use Intuition, Analysis, and Guiding Principles to Make Strategic Decisions," *Long Range Planning* 42 (2009), 298–319.
26. Eduardo Salas, Michael A. Rosen, and Deborah DiazGranados, "Expertise-Based Decision Making in Organizations," *Journal of Management* 36, no. 4 (July 2010), 941–973; Kurt Matzler, Franz Bailom, and Todd A. Mooradian, "Intuitive Decision Making," *MIT Sloan Management Review* 49, no. 1 (Fall 2007), 13–15; Stefan Wally and J. Robert Baum, "Personal and Structural Determinants of the Pace of Strategic Decision Making," *Academy of Management Journal* 37, no. 4 (1994), 932–956; and Orlando Behling and Norman L. Eckel, "Making Sense Out of Intuition," *Academy of Management Executive* 5, no. 1 (1991), 46–54.
27. For a recent overview of the research on expertise-based intuition, see Salas et al., "Expertise-Based Decision Making in Organizations." Also see Eric Dane and Michael G. Pratt, "Exploring Intuition and Its Role in Managerial Decision Making," *Academy of Management Review* 32, no. 1 (2007), 33–54; Gary Klein, *Intuition at Work: Why Developing Your Gut Instincts Will Make You Better at What You Do* (New York: Doubleday, 2002); Milorad M. Novicevic, Thomas J. Hench, and Daniel A. Wren, "'Playing By Ear . . . In an Incessant Din of Reasons': Chester Barnard and the History of Intuition in Management Thought," *Management Decision* 40, no. 10 (2002), 992–1002; Alden M. Hayashi, "When to Trust Your Gut," *Harvard Business Review* (February 2001), 59–65; Brian R. Reinwald, "Tactical Intuition," *Military Review* 80, no. 5 (September–October 2000), 78–88; Thomas A. Stewart, "How to Think with Your Gut," *Business 2.0* (November 2002), *http://www.business2.com/articles* (accessed November 7, 2002); Henry Mintzberg and Frances Westley, "Decision Making: It's Not What You Think," *MIT Sloan Management Review* (Spring 2001), 89–93; and Carlin Flora, "Gut Almighty," *Psychology Today* (May–June 2007), 68–75.
28. Benedict Carey, "Hunches Prove To Be Valuable Assets in Battle," *The New York Times* (July 28, 2009), A1.
29. Thomas F. Issack, "Intuition: An Ignored Dimension of Management," *Academy of Management Review* 3 (1978), 917–922.
30. Marjorie A. Lyles, "Defining Strategic Problems: Subjective Criteria of Executives," *Organizational Studies* 8 (1987), 263–280; and Marjorie A. Lyles and Ian I. Mitroff, "Organizational Problem Formulation: An Empirical Study," *Administrative Science Quarterly* 25 (1980), 102–119.
31. Marjorie A. Lyles and Howard Thomas, "Strategic Problem Formulation: Biases and Assumptions Embedded in Alternative Decision-Making Models," *Journal of Management Studies* 25 (1988), 131–145.
32. Ross Stagner, "Corporate Decision-Making: An Empirical Study," *Journal of Applied Psychology* 53 (1969), 1–13.
33. W. A. Agor, "The Logic of Intuition: How Top Executives Make Important Decisions," *Organizational Dynamics* 14, no. 3 (1986), 5–18; and Paul C. Nutt, "Types of Organizational Decision Processes," *Administrative Science Quarterly* 29 (1984), 414–450.
34. Nandini Rajagopalan, Abdul M. A. Rasheed, and Deepak K. Datta, "Strategic Decision Processes: Critical Review and Future Directions," *Journal of Management* 19 (1993), 349–384; Paul J. H. Schoemaker, "Strategic Decisions in Organizations: Rational and Behavioral Views," *Journal of Management Studies* 30 (1993), 107–129; Charles J. McMillan, "Qualitative Models of Organizational Decision Making," *Journal of Management Studies* 5 (1980), 22–39; and Paul C. Nutt, "Models for Decision Making in Organizations and Some Contextual Variables Which Stimulate Optimal Use," *Academy of Management Review* 1 (1976), 84–98.
35. Hugh J. Miser, "Operations Analysis in the Army Air Forces in World War II: Some Reminiscences," *Interfaces 23* (September–October 1993), 47–49; and Harold J. Leavitt, William R. Dill, and Henry B. Eyring, *The Organizational World* (New York: Harcourt Brace Jovanovich, 1973), chap. 6.
36. Stephen J. Huxley, "Finding the Right Spot for a Church Camp in Spain," *Interfaces* 12 (October 1982), 108–114; and James E. Hodder and Henry E. Riggs, "Pitfalls in Evaluating Risky Projects," *Harvard Business Review* (January–February 1985), 128–135.
37. Edward Baker and Michael Fisher, "Computational Results for Very Large Air Crew Scheduling Problems," *Omega* 9 (1981), 613–618; and Jean Aubin, "Scheduling Ambulances," *Interfaces* 22 (March–April, 1992), 1–10.
38. Dan Milmo, Ian Sample, and Sam Jones, "Volcano Chaos: How the Battle for the Skies Ended in Victory for Airlines," *The Guardian* (April 22, 2010), 4; and Daniel Michaels, Sara Schaefer Munox, and Bruce Orwall, "Airlines Rush to Move Millions," *The Wall Street Journal Europe* (April 22, 2010), 1.
39. Scott McCartney, "The Middle Seat: How One Airline Skirts the Ash Cloud," *The Wall Street Journal* (April 22, 2010), D1.
40. The movie is based on the bestselling book by Michael Lewis, *Moneyball: The Art of Winning an Unfair Game* (New York: W. W. Norton & Company, 2003).
41. Matthew Futterman, "Friday Journal—Baseball After Moneyball," *The Wall Street Journal* (September 23, 2011), D1.
42. Stephen Baker, "Math Will Rock Your World," *BusinessWeek* (January 23, 2006), 54–60; Julie Schlosser, "Markdown Lowdown," *Fortune* (January 12, 2004), 40; and Brooks Barnes, "Disney Technology Tackles a Theme Park Headache: Lines," *The New York Times* (December 28, 2010), B1.
43. Baker, "Math Will Rock Your World; and Laura Landro, "The Informed Patient: Cutting Waits at the Doctor's

Office—New Programs Reorganize Practices to Be More Efficient," *The Wall Street Journal* (April 19, 2006), D1.
44. Richard L. Daft and John C. Wiginton, "Language and Organization," *Academy of Management Review* (1979), 179–191.
45. Based on Richard M. Cyert and James G. March, *A Behavioral Theory of the Firm* (Englewood Cliffs, NJ: Prentice-Hall, 1963); and James G. March and Herbert A. Simon, *Organizations* (New York: Wiley, 1958).
46. William B. Stevenson, Joan L. Pearce, and Lyman W. Porter, "The Concept of 'Coalition' in Organization Theory and Research," *Academy of Management Review* 10 (1985), 256–268.
47. Anne Mulcahy, Randy Komisar, and Martin Sorrell, "How We Do It: Three Executives Reflect on Strategic Decision Making," *McKinsey Quarterly* (March, 2010), 46–57.
48. Jeremy W. Peters, "The Times's Online Pay Model Was Years in the Making," *The New York Times* (March 20, 2011), http://www.nytimes.com/2011/03/21/business/media/21times.html?pagewanted=all (accessed September 27, 2011); and J. W. Peters, "New York Times is Set to Begin Charging for Web Access; Chairman Concedes Plan is Risky But Says It's an 'Investment in Our Future,'" *International Herald Tribune* (March 18, 2011), 15.
49. Jeremy W. Peters, "Optimism for Digital Plan; But Times Co. Posts Loss," *The New York Times* (July 22, 2011), B3.
50. Cyert and March, *A Behavioral Theory of the Firm*, 120–222.
51. Lawrence G. Hrebiniak, "Top-Management Agreement and Organizational Performance," *Human Relations* 35 (1982), 1139–1158; and Richard P. Nielsen, "Toward a Method for Building Consensus during Strategic Planning," *Sloan Management Review* (Summer 1981), 29–40.
52. Based on Henry Mintzberg, Duru Raisinghani, and André Théorêt, "The Structure of 'Unstructured' Decision Processes," *Administrative Science Quarterly* 21 (1976), 246–275.
53. Lawrence T. Pinfield, "A Field Evaluation of Perspectives on Organizational Decision Making," *Administrative Science Quarterly* 31 (1986), 365–388.
54. Mintzberg et al., "The Structure of 'Unstructured' Decision Processes."
55. Ibid., 270.
56. William C. Symonds with Carol Matlack, "Gillette's Edge," *BusinessWeek* (January 19, 1998), 70–77; William C. Symonds, "Would You Spend $1.50 for a Razor Blade?" *BusinessWeek* (April 27, 1998), 46; and Peter J. Howe, "Innovative; For the Past Half Century, 'Cutting Edge' Has Meant More at Gillette Co. Than a Sharp Blade," *Boston Globe* (January 30, 2005), D1.
57. Michael D. Cohen, James G. March, and Johan P. Olsen, "A Garbage Can Model of Organizational Choice," *Administrative Science Quarterly* 17 (March 1972), 1–25; and Michael D. Cohen and James G. March, *Leadership and Ambiguity: The American College President* (New York: McGraw-Hill, 1974).
58. Michael Masuch and Perry LaPotin, "Beyond Garbage Cans: An AI Model of Organizational Choice," *Administrative Science Quarterly* 34 (1989), 38–67.
59. Steven Mufson and Jia Lynn Yang, "Hard Lessons: The Trials of Kaplan Higher Ed and the Education of the Washington Post Co.," *The Washington Post* (April 10, 2011), G1.
60. Adapted from James D. Thompson, *Organizations in Action* (New York: McGraw-Hill, 1967), chap. 10; McMillan, "Qualitative Models of Organizational Decision Making," 25; and Clayton M. Christensen, Matt Marx, and Howard H. Stevenson, "The Tools of Cooperation and Change," *Harvard Business Review* (October 2006), 73–80.
61. Ben Worthen, "Cost Cutting Versus Innovation: Reconcilable Difference," *CIO* (October 1, 2004), 89–94.
62. Beth Dickey, "NASA's Next Step," *Government Executive* (April 15, 2004), 34–42; and Jena McGregor, "Gospels of Failure," *Fast Company* (February 2005), 61–67.
63. Mintzberg and Westley, "Decision Making: It's Not What You Think."
64. Paul C. Nutt, "Selecting Decision Rules for Crucial Choices: An Investigation of the Thompson Framework," *The Journal of Applied Behavioral Science* 38, no. 1 (March 2002), 99–131; and Paul C. Nutt, "Making Strategic Choices," *Journal of Management Studies* 39, no. 1 (January 2002), 67–95.
65. George T. Doran and Jack Gunn, "Decision Making in High-Tech Firms: Perspectives of Three Executives," *Business Horizons* (November–December 2002), 7–16.
66. L. J. Bourgeois III and Kathleen M. Eisenhardt, "Strategic Decision Processes in High Velocity Environments: Four Cases in the Microcomputer Industry," *Management Science* 34 (1988), 816–835.
67. Kathleen M. Eisenhardt, "Speed and Strategic Choice: How Managers Accelerate Decision Making," *California Management Review* (Spring 1990), 39–54.
68. David A. Garvin and Michael A. Roberto, "What You Don't Know about Making Decisions," *Harvard Business Review* (September 2001), 108–116.
69. Karl Weick, *The Social Psychology of Organizing*, 2nd ed. (Reading, MA: Addison-Wesley, 1979), 243.
70. Jena McGregor, "How Failure Breeds Success," *BusinessWeek* (July 10, 2006), 42-52.
71. For discussions of various cognitive biases, see Daniel Kahneman, Dan Lovallo, and Olivier Sibony, "Before You Make That Big Decision . . .," *Harvard Business Review* (June 2011), 50–60; John S. Hammond, Ralph L. Keeney, and Howard Raiffa, *Smart Choices: A Practical Guide to Making Better Decisions* (Boston: Harvard Business School Press, 1999); Max H. Bazerman and Dolly Chugh, "Decisions Without Blinders," *Harvard Business Review* (January 2006), 88–97; J. S. Hammond, R. L. Keeney, and H. Raiffa, "The Hidden Traps in Decision Making," *Harvard Business Review* (September–October 1998), 47–58; Oren Harari, "The Thomas Lawson Syndrome," *Management Review* (February 1994), 58–61; and Max H. Bazerman, *Judgment in Managerial Decision Making*, 5th ed. (New York: John Wiley & Sons, 2002).
72. Helga Drummond, "Too Little Too Late: A Case Study of Escalation in Decision Making," *Organization Studies* 15, no. 4 (1994), 591–607; Joel Brockner, "The Escalation of Commitment to a Failing Course of Action: Toward Theoretical Progress," *Academy of Management Review* 17 (1992),

39–61; Barry M. Staw and Jerry Ross, "Knowing When to Pull the Plug," *Harvard Business Review* 65 (March–April 1987), 68–74; and Barry M. Staw, "The Escalation of Commitment to a Course of Action," *Academy of Management Review* 6 (1981), 577–587.

73. Norihiko Shirouzu, Phred Dvorak, Yuka Hayashi, and Andrew Morse, "Bid to 'Protect Assets' Slowed Reactor Fight," *The Wall Street Journal* (March 19, 2011), A1.
74. Daniel Kahneman and Amos Tversky, "Prospect Theory: An Analysis of Decision Under Risk," *Econometrica* 47 (1979), 263–292.
75. Kahneman et al., "Before You Make That Big Decision. . . ."
76. Irving L. Janis, *Groupthink: Psychological Studies of Policy Decisions and Fiascoes*, 2nd ed. (Boston: Houghton Mifflin, 1982).
77. This section is based on Jeffrey Pfeffer and Robert I. Sutton, "Evidence-Based Management," *Harvard Business Review* (January 2006), 62–74; Rosemary Stewart, *Evidence-based Management: A Practical Guide for Health Professionals* (Oxford: Radcliffe Publishing, 2002); and Joshua Klayman, Richard P. Larrick, and Chip Heath, "Organizational Repairs," *Across the Board* (February 2000), 26–31.
78. Thomas H. Davenport, "Make Better Decisions," *Harvard Business Review* (November 2009), 117–123.
79. "How Companies Make Good Decisions: McKinsey Global Survey Results," *The McKinsey Quarterly* (January 2009), http://www.mckinseyquarterly.com/How_companies_make_good_decisions_McKinsey_Global_Survey_Results_2282 (accessed February 3, 2009).
80. Michael A. Roberto, "Making Difficult Decisions in Turbulent Times," *Ivey Business Journal* (May–June 2003), 1–7; Kathleen M. Eisenhardt, "Strategy as Strategic Decision Making," *Sloan Management Review* (Spring 1999), 65–72; and Garvin and Roberto, "What You Don't Know About Making Decisions."
81. David M. Schweiger and William R. Sandberg, "The Utilization of Individual Capabilities in Group Approaches to Strategic Decision Making," *Strategic Management Journal* 10 (1989), 31–43; and "The Devil's Advocate," *Small Business Report* (December 1987), 38–41.
82. Anna Mulrine, "To Battle Groupthink, the Army Trains a Skeptics Corps," *U.S. News & World Report* (May 26–June 2, 2008), 30–32.
83. "Tools for Managing in a Complex Context," sidebar in David J. Snowden and Mary E. Boone, "A Leader's Framework for Decision Making," *Harvard Business Review* (November 2007), 69–76.
84. Adapted by Dorothy Marcic from "Action Assignment" in Jennifer M. Howard and Lawrence M. Miller, *Team Management* (Miller Consulting Group, 1994), 205.
85. This case was prepared by David Hornestay and appeared in *Government Executive*, vol. 30, No. 8 (August 1998), 45–46, as part of a series of case studies examining workplace dilemmas confronting Federal managers. Reprinted by permission of *Government Executive*.
86. Drucker, *Management Cases*, 1st Ed., © 1977, pp. 23–24. Reprinted and Electronically reproduced by permission of Pearson Education, Inc., Upper Saddle River, New Jersey.

Chapter 9

Corporate Culture and Values

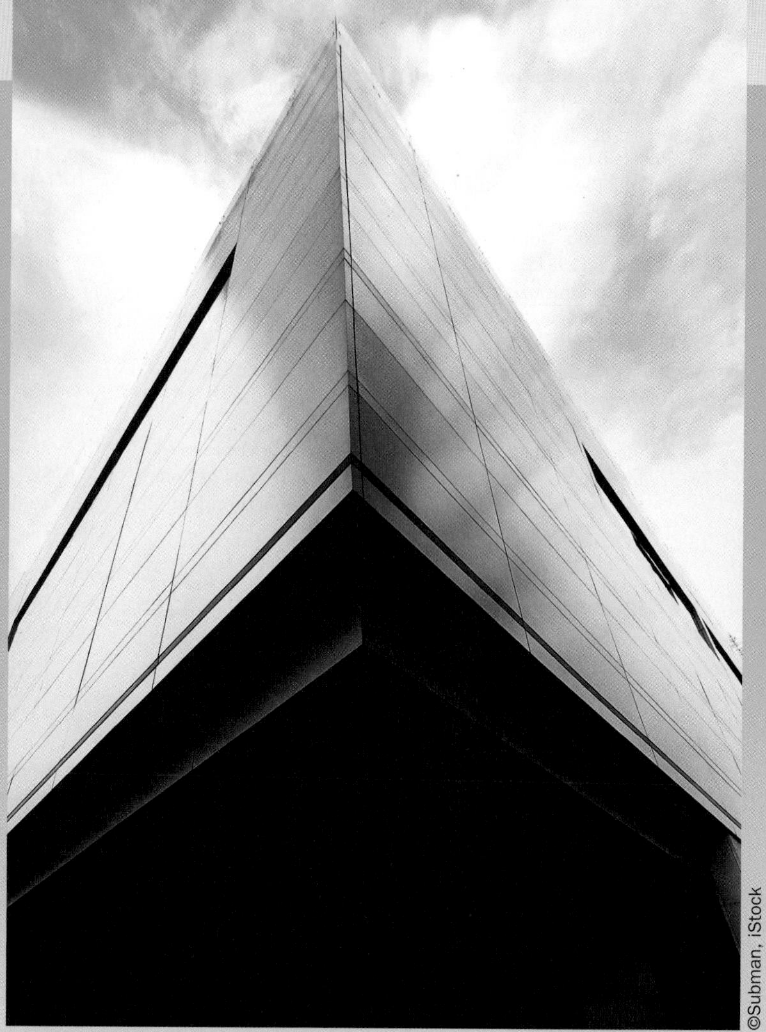

Learning Objectives

After reading this chapter you should be able to:

1. Know the nature of organizational culture and its manifestations.
2. Describe the four types of organizational culture.
3. Explain the relationship between culture and performance.
4. Describe sources of ethical values and principles.
5. Define corporate social responsibility.
6. Explain how managers shape organizational culture and ethical values.

Before reading this chapter, please check whether you agree or disagree with each of the following statements:

1 **Top managers typically should focus their energy more on strategy and structure than on corporate culture.**

I AGREE _____ I DISAGREE _____

2 **Being ethical and socially responsible is not just the right thing for a corporation to do; it is a critical issue for business success.**

I AGREE _____ I DISAGREE _____

3 **The single best way to make sure an organization stays on solid ethical ground is to have a strong code of ethics and make sure all employees are familiar with its guidelines.**

I AGREE _____ I DISAGREE _____

Walk into the headquarters of Patagonia, and you will likely see people wearing flip flops and shorts. Why not? They might be going surfing later. The successful seller of outdoor clothing and equipment is guided by values of creativity, collaboration, simplicity, and caring for the environment. Employees who are eligible can take off two months at full pay to work for environmental groups. The feeling inside headquarters is relaxed, yet vibrant; people work hard, but they also have fun. Compare that to the headquarters at Exxon Mobil, where most employees are in conventional business attire and the atmosphere is tinged with competitiveness and a rigorous, analytical approach to taking care of business. Before the 2010 BP Deepwater Horizon explosion in the Gulf of Mexico, the epitome of a disastrous oil spill was the 1989 grounding of the Exxon Valdez in Prince William Sound off the coast of Alaska. Following that disaster, Exxon managers analyzed their approach to safety and created a system of rules and protocols for company operations that err on the side of caution. That cautious, analytical approach infuses the entire company and has helped Exxon stand out among its peers for its obsessive attention to both safety and high performance. "They're not in the fun business," said one oil industry analyst. "They're in the profit business." No surfing for these guys (or girls). As one investor said with admiration: "They never take a day off."[1]

Patagonia and Exxon represent two very different corporate cultures. Yet both companies are successful, and both have employees who enjoy their jobs and generally like the way things are done at their company. Every organization, like Patagonia and Exxon, has a set of values that characterize how people behave and how the organization carries out everyday business. One of the most important jobs organizational leaders do is instill and support the kind of values needed for the company to thrive.

Strong cultures can have a profound impact on a company, which can be either positive or negative for the organization. At J. M. Smucker & Company, the first manufacturer ever to earn the top spot on *Fortune* magazine's list of "The 100 Best Companies to Work For," strong values of cooperation, caring for employees and customers, and an "all for one, one for all" attitude enable the company to consistently meet productivity, quality, and customer-service goals in the challenging environment of the food industry.[2] Negative cultural norms, however, can damage a company just as powerfully as positive ones can strengthen it. Consider the now-defunct Bear Stearns, which had a strong, highly competitive corporate culture that supported pushing everything to the limits in the pursuit of wealth. As long as an employee was making money for the firm, managers took a hands-off approach, which allowed increasingly risky and sometimes unethical behavior.[3]

A related concept concerning the influence of norms and values on how people work together and how they treat one another and customers is called *social capital.* **Social capital** refers to the quality of interactions among people and whether they share a common perspective. In organizations with a high degree of social capital, for example, relationships are based on trust, mutual understandings, and shared norms and values that enable people to cooperate and coordinate their activities to achieve goals.[4] An organization can have either a high or a low level of social capital. One way to think of social capital is as *goodwill.* When relationships both within the organization and with customers, suppliers, and partners are based on honesty, trust, and respect, a spirit of goodwill exists and people willingly cooperate to achieve mutual benefits. A high level of social capital enables frictionless social interactions and exchanges that help to facilitate smooth organizational functioning. Relationships based on cutthroat competition, self-interest, and subterfuge can be devastating to a company. Social capital relates to both corporate culture and ethics, which is the subject matter of this chapter.

Purpose of This Chapter

This chapter explores ideas about corporate culture and associated ethical values and how these are influenced by organization managers. The first section describes the nature of corporate culture, its origins and purpose, and how to identify and interpret culture by looking at the organization's rites and ceremonies, stories and myths, symbols, organization structures, power relationships, and control systems. We then examine how culture reinforces the strategy and structural design the organization needs to be effective in its environment and discuss the important role of culture in organizational learning and high performance. Next, the chapter turns to ethical values and corporate social responsibility. We consider how managers implement the structures and systems that influence ethical and socially responsible behavior. The chapter also discusses how managers shape culture and ethical values in a direction suitable for strategy and performance outcomes. The chapter closes with a brief overview of the complex cultural and ethical issues that managers face in an international environment.

Organizational Culture

The popularity of the corporate culture topic raises a number of questions. Can we identify cultures? Can culture be aligned with strategy? How can cultures be managed or changed? The best place to start is by defining culture and explaining how it is reflected in organizations.

What Is Culture?

Culture is the set of values, norms, guiding beliefs, and understandings that is shared by members of an organization and taught to new members as the correct way to think, feel, and behave.[5] It is the unwritten, feeling part of the organization. Culture represents the informal organization, whereas topics such as structure, size, and strategy represent the formal organization. Every organization has two sides at work: formal structures and systems and the informal values, norms, and assumptions of the corporate culture.[6] Everyone participates in culture, but culture generally goes unnoticed. It is only when managers try to implement new strategies, structures, or systems that go against basic cultural norms and values that they come face to face with the power of culture.

Organizational culture exists at two levels, as illustrated in Exhibit 9.1. On the surface are visible artifacts and observable behaviors—the ways people dress and act, office layouts, the type of control systems and power structures used by the company, and the symbols, stories, and ceremonies organization members share. The visible elements of culture, however, reflect deeper values in the minds of organization members. These underlying values, assumptions, beliefs, and thought processes operate unconsciously to define the culture.[7] For example, Steelcase built a new pyramid-shaped corporate development center that has scattered, open "thought stations" with white boards and other idea-inspiring features. There is an open atrium from ground floor to top, with a giant ticking pendulum. The new building is a visible symbol; the underlying values are openness, collaboration, teamwork, innovation, and constant change.[8] The attributes of culture display themselves in many ways but typically evolve into a patterned set of activities carried out through social interactions.[9] Those patterns can be used to interpret culture.

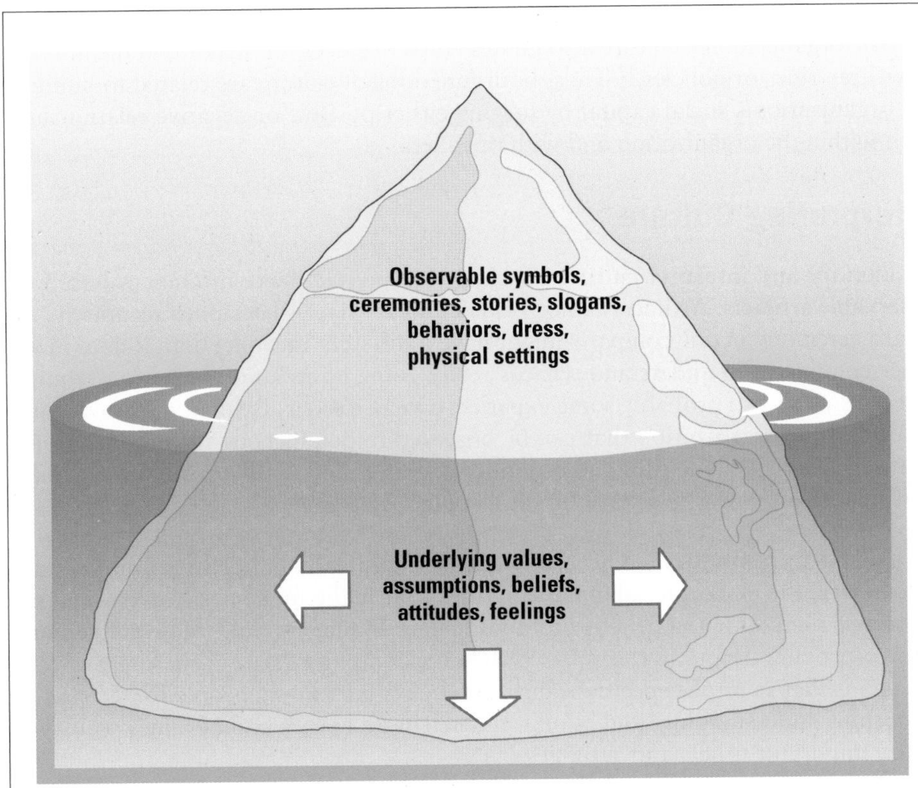

EXHIBIT 9.1
Levels of Corporate Culture

Emergence and Purpose of Culture

Culture provides people with a sense of organizational identity and generates in them a commitment to beliefs and values that are larger than themselves.[10] Though ideas that become part of the culture can come from anywhere within the organization, an organization's culture generally begins with a founder or early leader who articulates and implements particular ideas and values as a vision, philosophy, or business strategy.

When these ideas and values lead to success, they become institutionalized, and an organizational culture emerges that reflects the vision and strategy of the founder or leader. For example, the culture at In-N-Out Burger, a fast-food chain with 232 stores in the western United States, reflects the values and philosophy of founders Harry and Esther Snyder. The Snyders created a corporate culture based on the idea that running a successful business depends on one thing: treating the people on the front lines right. In-N-Out was founded in 1948, but the values of quality, service, and taking care of employees remain at the core of the company's culture, a culture that has inspired intense loyalty among both employees and customers.[11]

Cultures serve two critical functions in organizations: (1) to integrate members so that they know how to relate to one another, and (2) to help the organization adapt to the external environment. **Internal integration** means that members develop a collective identity and know how to work together effectively. It is culture that guides day-to-day working relationships and determines how people communicate within the organization, what behavior is acceptable or not acceptable, and how power and status are allocated. **External adaptation** refers to how the organization meets goals and deals with outsiders. Culture helps guide the daily activities of employees to meet certain goals. It can help the organization respond rapidly to customer needs or the moves of a competitor.

The organization's culture also guides employee decision making in the absence of written rules or policies.[12] Thus, both functions of culture are related to building the organization's social capital by forging either positive or negative relationships both within the organization and with outsiders.

Interpreting Culture

To identify and interpret culture requires that people make inferences based on observable artifacts. Artifacts can be studied but are hard to decipher accurately. An award ceremony in one company might have a different meaning than it does in another company. To understand what is really going on in an organization requires detective work and probably some experience as an insider. Exhibit 9.2 shows some aspects of the organization that can be observed to help decode the organizational culture.[13] These include rites and ceremonies, stories and myths, symbols, organization structures, power relationships, and control systems.[14]

Rites and Ceremonies. Cultural values can typically be identified in **rites and ceremonies**, the elaborate, planned activities that make up a special event and are often conducted for the benefit of an audience. Managers hold rites and ceremonies to provide dramatic examples of what a company values. These are special occasions that reinforce specific values, create a bond among people for sharing an important understanding, and anoint and celebrate heroes and heroines who symbolize important beliefs and activities.[15]

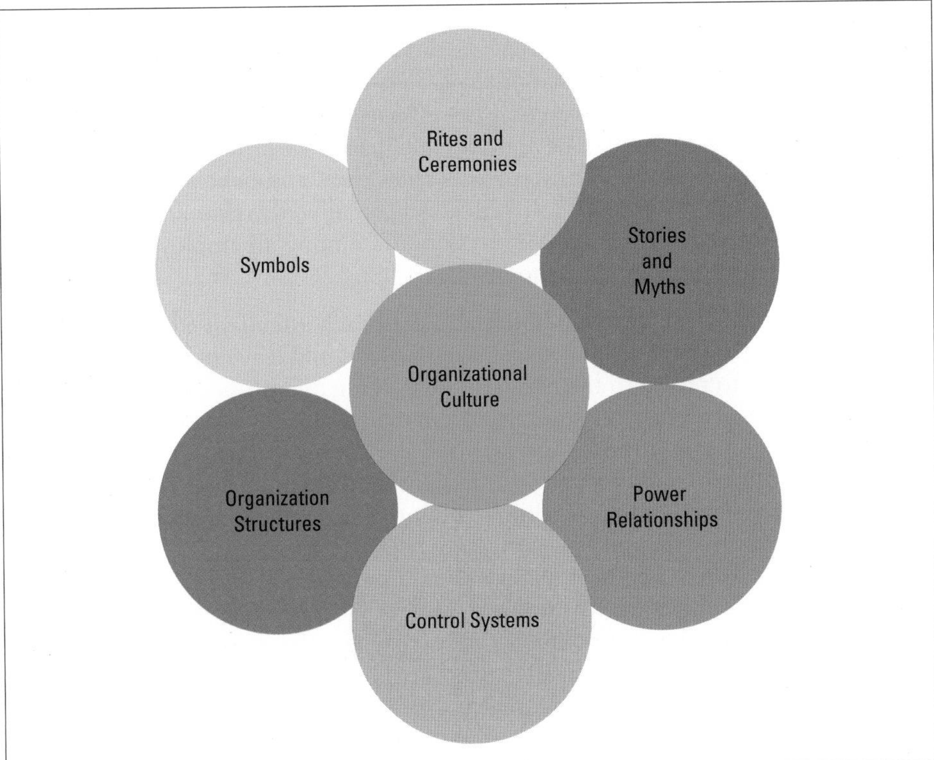

EXHIBIT 9.2
Observable Aspects of Organizational Culture

Source: Reprinted from Gerry Johnson, "Managing Strategic Change—Strategy, Culture, and Action," *Long Range Planning* 25, no. 1 (1992), 28–36, Copyright 1992, with permission from Elsevier.

One type of rite that appears in organizations is a *rite of passage,* which facilitates the transition of employees into new social roles. Organizations as diverse as religious orders, sororities and fraternities, businesses, and the military use rites to initiate new members and communicate important values. Another type often used is a *rite of integration,* which creates common bonds and good feelings among employees and increases commitment to the organization. Consider the following examples:

- A rite of passage at Gentle Giant, a Somerville, Massachusetts moving company that has won nine Best of Boston awards from *Boston* magazine, is the "stadium run." CEO Larry O'Toole decided to have new hires run the tiers of Harvard University stadium as a way to emphasize that people at the company work hard, challenge themselves, and go the distance rather than letting up if things get tough. After the run, O'Toole provides a hearty breakfast and gives an orientation speech. "You're not a Gentle Giant until you've done the run," said employee Kyle Green.[16]
- Whenever a Walmart executive visits one of the stores, he or she leads employees in the Walmart cheer: "Give me a W! Give me an A! Give me an L! Give me a squiggly! (All do a version of the twist.) Give me an M! Give me an A! Give me an R! Give me a T! What's that spell? Walmart! What's that spell? Walmart! Who's No. 1? THE CUSTOMER!" The cheer strengthens bonds among employees and reinforces their commitment to common goals.[17] This is a rite of integration.

Stories and Myths. **Stories** are narratives based on true events that are frequently shared among employees and told to new employees to inform them about an organization. Many stories are about company **heroes** who serve as models or ideals for upholding cultural norms and values. Some stories are considered **legends** because the events are historic and may have been embellished with fictional details. Other stories are **myths**, which are consistent with the values and beliefs of the organization but are not supported by facts.[18] Stories keep alive the primary values of the organization and provide a shared understanding among all employees. Examples of how stories shape culture are as follows:

- A story is told at Ritz-Carlton hotels about a beach attendant who was stacking chairs for the evening when a guest asked if he would leave out two chairs. The guest wanted to return to the beach in the evening and propose to his girlfriend. Although the attendant was going off duty, he not only left out the chairs, he stayed late, put on a tuxedo, and escorted the couple to their chairs, presenting them with flowers and champagne and lighting candles at their table. The story is firmly entrenched in Ritz-Carlton's folklore and symbolizes the value of going above and beyond the call of duty to satisfy guests.[19]
- Employees at IBM often hear a story about the female security guard who challenged IBM's chairman. Although she knew who he was, the guard insisted that the chairman could not enter a particular area because he wasn't carrying the appropriate security clearance. Rather than getting reprimanded or fired, the guard was praised for her diligence and commitment to maintaining the security of IBM's buildings.[20] By telling this story, employees emphasize both the importance of following the rules and the critical contributions of every employee from the bottom to the top of the organization.

BRIEFCASE

As an organization manager, keep these guidelines in mind:

Pay attention to corporate culture. Understand the underlying values, assumptions, and beliefs on which culture is based as well as its observable manifestations. Evaluate corporate culture based on rites and ceremonies, stories and myths, symbols, and the structures, control systems, and power relationships you can observe in the organization.

Symbols. Another tool for interpreting culture is the **symbol**. A symbol is something that represents another thing. In one sense, ceremonies, stories, and rites are all symbols because they symbolize deeper values. Another symbol is a physical artifact of the organization. Physical symbols are powerful because they focus attention on a specific item. Examples of physical symbols are as follows:

- At the headquarters of Mother, a small London-based advertising agency known for its strong culture and offbeat ads, there are no private offices. In fact, except for the restrooms, there are no doors in the whole place. This headquarters design symbolizes and reinforces the cultural values of open communication, collaboration, creativity, and equality.[21]
- When employees at Foot Levelers, a maker of chiropractic products, see the "Rudy in Progress" sign taped to the conference room door, they know there's a group of new employees watching a DVD of *Rudy*, the 1993 inspirational football drama about the ungifted but determined Notre Dame football player Rudy Ruettiger, who finally took the field in the last minutes of a game against Georgia Tech and sacked the quarterback. The film is a symbol of the high value the company puts on determination, passion, commitment, and tenacity. Whenever an employee approaches a manager with a tough problem, the manager will ask "Did you Rudy that?" meaning, did you do all that you possibly can to try to solve the problem.[22]

Organization Structures. How the organization is designed is also a reflection of its culture. Does it have a rigid *mechanistic* structure or a flexible *organic* structure, as described in Chapters 1 and 6? Is there a tall or a flat hierarchy, as discussed in

EXHIBIT 9.3
Organization Chart for Nordstrom Inc.

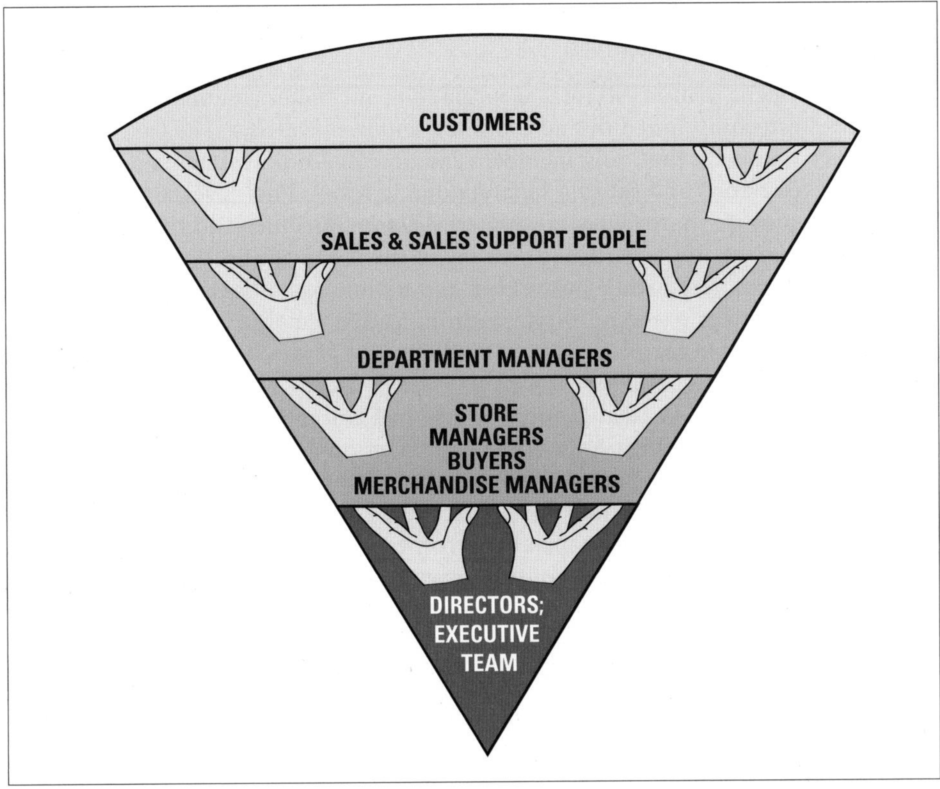

Source: Used with permission of Nordstrom, Inc.

Chapter 2? The way in which people and departments are arranged into a whole, and the degree of flexibility and autonomy people have, tells a lot about which cultural values are emphasized in the organization. Here are a couple of examples:

- Nordstrom's structure reflects the emphasis the department store chain puts on empowering and supporting lower-level employees. Nordstrom is known for its extraordinary customer service. Its organization chart, shown in Exhibit 9.3, symbolizes that managers are to support the employees who give the service rather than exercise tight control over them.[23]
- To get a struggling Chrysler back on its feet quickly after bankruptcy reorganization, CEO Sergio Marchionne cut several layers of management to flatten the structure and get top executives closer to the business of making and selling vehicles. Marchionne also chose a fourth-floor office in the technical center, rather than occupy the top-floor executive suite, to symbolize the importance of top executives being close to the engineers and supervisors making day-to-day decisions.[24]

Power Relationships. Looking at power relationships means deciphering who influences or manipulates or has the ability to do so. Which people and departments are the key power holders in the organization? In some companies, finance people are quite powerful, whereas in others engineers and designers have the most power. Another aspect is considering whether power relationships are formal or informal, such as whether people have power based primarily on their position in the hierarchy or based on other factors, such as their expertise or admirable character. Consider the following examples:

- An investment firm in Atlanta, Georgia, has an "inner sanctum" with special offices, restrooms, and a dining room for senior executives. The entry door has an electronic lock that only members can access. Mid-level managers hold the title of "director" and eat in a separate dining room. First-level supervisors and other employees share a general cafeteria. Dining facilities and titles signal who has more power in the vertical hierarchy of the organization.
- At W. L. Gore, few people have titles, and no one has a boss. Rather than people having power based on their position, leaders emerge based on who has a good idea and can recruit people to work on it.[25]

Control Systems. The final element shown in Exhibit 9.2 relates to control systems, or the inner workings of how the organization controls people and operations. This includes looking at such things as how information is managed, whether managers apply behavior or outcome control related to employee activities, quality control systems, methods of financial control, reward systems, and how decisions are made. Two examples of how control systems reflect culture are:

- At Anheuser-Busch InBev, distribution center managers frequently start the day with a sort of pep rally reviewing the day's sales targets and motivating people to get out and sell more beer. The company's incentive-based compensation system and its focus on increasing sales while relentlessly cutting costs are key elements of a highly competitive corporate culture.[26]
- Netflix lets employees make most of their own choices—even in how to compensate themselves and how much vacation to take. This freedom combined with responsibility reflects what marketing manager Heather McIlhany refers to as a tough, fulfilling, "fully formed adult" culture.[27]

Recall that culture exists at two levels—the underlying values and assumptions and the visible artifacts and observable behaviors. The rites and ceremonies, stories, symbols, organization structures, power relationships, and control systems just described are visible manifestations of underlying company values. These visible artifacts and behaviors can be used to interpret culture, but they are also used by managers to shape company values and to strengthen the desired corporate culture. Thus, the summary of cultural artifacts shown in Exhibit 9.2 can serve as both a mechanism for interpretation and a guideline for action when managers need to change or strengthen cultural values.[28]

Organization Design and Culture

Managers want a corporate culture that reinforces the strategy and structural design that the organization needs to be effective within its environment. For example, if the external environment requires flexibility and responsiveness, such as the environment for Internet-based companies like Twitter, Netflix, Facebook, or Hulu, the culture should encourage adaptability. The correct relationship among cultural values, organizational strategy and structure, and the environment can enhance organizational performance.[29]

Cultures can be assessed along many dimensions, such as the extent of collaboration versus isolation among people and departments, the importance of control

EXHIBIT 9.4
Four Types of Organizational Culture

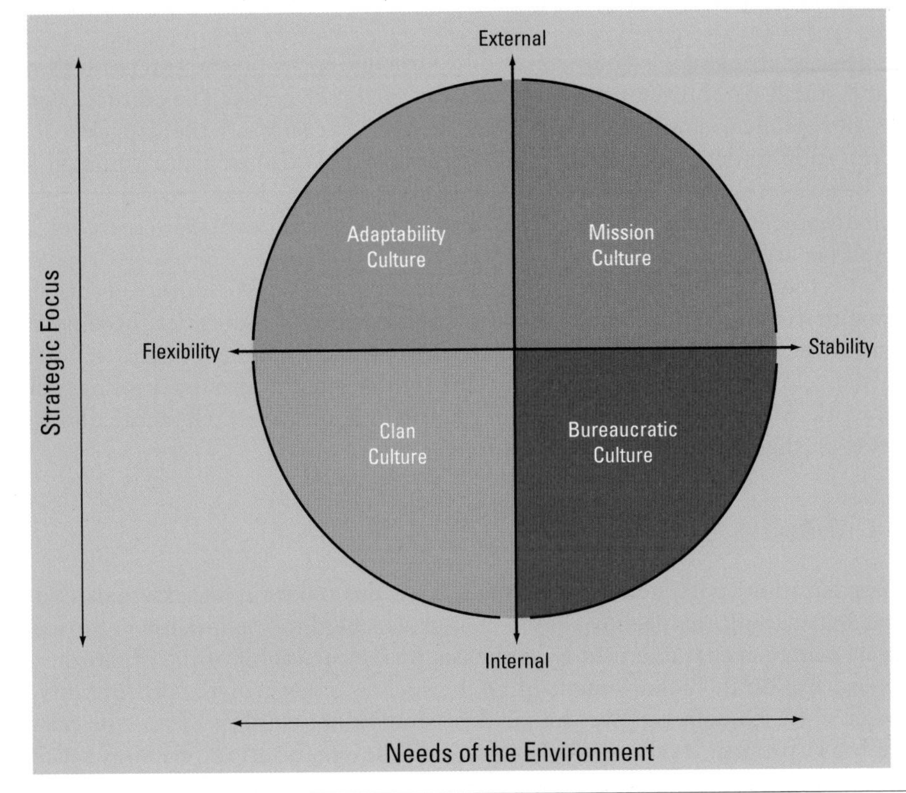

Source: Based on Daniel R. Denison and Aneil K. Mishra, "Toward a Theory of Organizational Culture and Effectiveness," *Organization Science* 6, no. 2 (March–April 1995), 204–223; R. Hooijberg and F. Petrock, "On Cultural Change: Using the Competing Values Framework to Help Leaders Execute a Transformational Strategy," *Human Resource Management* 32 (1993), 29–50; and R. E. Quinn, *Beyond Rational Management: Mastering the Paradoxes and Competing Demands of High Performance* (San Francisco: Jossey-Bass, 1988).

and where control is concentrated, or whether the organization's time orientation is short range or long range.[30] Here we focus on two specific dimensions: (1) the extent to which the competitive environment requires flexibility or stability; and (2) the extent to which the organization's strategic focus and strength are internal or external. Four categories of culture associated with these differences, as illustrated in Exhibit 9.4, are adaptability, mission, clan, and bureaucratic.[31] These four categories relate to the fit among cultural values, strategy, structure, and the environment. Each can be successful, depending on the needs of the external environment and the organization's strategic focus.

1 **Top managers typically should focus their energy more on strategy and structure than on corporate culture.**

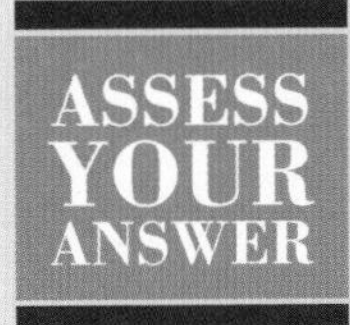

ANSWER: *Disagree.* Smart top managers know that for the organization to be successful, the right culture has to support and reinforce the strategy and structure to be effective in its environment. Someone once said, "Culture eats strategy for lunch." Managers can invest all the time and resources they have in defining a killer strategy, but implementing it will be impossible if the cultural values are out of line.

The Adaptability Culture

The **adaptability culture** is characterized by strategic focus on the external environment through flexibility and change to meet customer needs. The culture encourages entrepreneurial values, norms, and beliefs that support the capacity of the organization to detect, interpret, and translate signals from the environment into new behavior responses. This type of company, however, doesn't just react quickly to environmental changes—it actively creates change. Innovation, creativity, and risk-taking are valued and rewarded.

Most Internet-based companies use the adaptability type of culture, as do many companies in the marketing, electronics, and cosmetics industries, because they must move quickly to satisfy customers. Zappos.com became a hugely successful Internet retailer with an adaptability culture that encourages open-mindedness, teamwork, and a little weirdness. This chapter's Book Mark tells more about the successful, slightly wacky Zappos culture.

The Mission Culture

An organization concerned with serving specific customers in the external environment, but without the need for rapid change, is suited to the mission culture. The **mission culture** is characterized by emphasis on a clear vision of the organization's purpose and on the achievement of goals, such as sales growth, profitability, or market share, to help achieve the purpose. Individual employees may be responsible for a specified level of performance, and the organization promises specified rewards in return. Managers shape behavior by envisioning and communicating a desired future state for the organization. Because the environment is stable, they can translate the vision into measurable goals and evaluate employee performance for meeting them. In some cases, mission cultures reflect a high level of competitiveness and a profit-making orientation.

Anheuser-Busch InBev, mentioned earlier in the chapter, reflects a mission culture. Professionalism, ambition, and aggressiveness are key values. Managers keep employees focused on achieving high sales and profit levels, and those who meet the demanding goals are handsomely rewarded. Bonuses and promotions are based on performance, not seniority, and top executives are unapologetic about giving special treatment to high achievers.[32]

The Clan Culture

The **clan culture** has a primary focus on the involvement and participation of the organization's members and on rapidly changing expectations from the external environment. This culture is similar to the clan form of control. More than any other, this culture focuses on meeting the needs of employees as the route to high performance. Involvement and participation create a sense of responsibility and ownership and, hence, greater commitment to the organization.

In a clan culture, an important value is taking care of employees and making sure they have whatever they need to help them be satisfied as well as productive. Although many companies in the software industry emphasize values associated with an adaptability culture, SAS Institute has been highly successful with a strong clan culture, as described in the following In Practice example.

BOOKMARK

9.0 HAVE YOU READ THIS BOOK?

Delivering Happiness: A Path to Profits, Passion, and Purpose

By Tony Hsieh

How many companies pay employees to quit? Zappos.com does, because CEO Tony Hsieh believes paying someone to leave is $2,000 well spent when it gets rid of a person who doesn't fit in and could damage the company's culture. The successful Internet seller of shoes (and now other products) is renowned for its exceptional customer service, but managers say they don't even talk about customer service at the company. Instead they focus on culture, and exceptional service and high performance happen as a result.

DELIVERING HAPPINESS THE ZAPPOS WAY

Tony Hsieh joined Zappos.com in 2000 and sunk practically all his assets into the business to keep it going during the dot-com bust. By 2009, when Amazon purchased the company for $1.2 billion, Zappos was one of the most successful Internet retailers of all time. Hsieh believes that's because the primary goal of the company was not to sell shoes, but to deliver happiness, both to employees and customers.

Hsieh knew first-hand how important a strong, constructive culture is when it comes to employee and customer happiness. He had experienced the joyless grind of working in a job that had no meaning, where technical skill was all that mattered. Hsieh decided to write *Delivering Happiness* to talk about his journey from "chasing profits to chasing passion," the life lessons he has learned, and how those lessons have been applied at Zappos. Here are some key points for business leaders:

- *Get the right values.* Zappos has a set of 10 core values that include *Create fun and a little weirdness; Deliver WOW through service; Embrace and drive change; Be adventurous, creative, and open-minded; Pursue growth and learning;* and *Be humble.* But Hsieh didn't dictate the values from on high. He sent an e-mail to all employees asking them what values should guide the company. The responses were discussed, condensed, and combined to come up with the final list.
- *Get the right people.* Zappos does two sets of interviews. The first focuses on relevant experience, professional and technical skills, and the ability to work with the team. The second focuses purely on culture fit. There are questions for each of the core values, such as, *How weird are you?* People are carefully selected to fit Zappos' culture, even if it means rejecting people with stronger technical skills.
- *Make culture a top priority.* All employees attend a four-week training session and commit the core values to memory. At the end of training, they're offered $2,000 to resign if they believe they aren't a good fit with the culture. Every year, Zappos puts out a *Culture Book*, in which employees share their own stories about what the Zappos culture means to them. Core values are supported by structures, processes, and systems that give them concrete reality and keep them in the forefront of employees' attention, and performance reviews are based in part on how well people participate in the culture.

PROFITS, PASSION, AND PURPOSE

The book, written in a narrative style, is divided into three sections. In the first, "Profits," Hsieh traces his entrepreneurial ventures from the earthworm farm he had as a child (it failed when all the worms escaped), through college, and on to the founding and sale of LinkExchange in young adulthood. The second section, "Profits and Passion," focuses primarily on his experiences at Zappos, and the final section, "Profits, Passion, and Purpose," outlines broader life lessons and Hsieh's philosophy of spreading happiness. The book is a quick read and offers entertainment, information, and inspiration.

Delivering Happiness: A Path to Profits, Passion, and Purpose, by Tony Hsieh, is published by Business Plus, Hatchette Book Group, Inc.

SAS Institute

IN PRACTICE

In January 2009 alone, America's largest companies laid off 160,000 employees, and more massive layoffs followed. But Jim Goodnight, the co-founder and CEO of SAS Institute, the leader in business analytics software, made a clear and definite promise to his 11,000 employees in early 2009: "There will be no layoffs."

At SAS, people truly are considered the company's most valuable asset, and the cultural values emphasize respect, equality, and caring for employees. Every employee—whether an engineer, an administrative assistant, a food service worker, or a landscaper—is treated the same. The company doesn't outsource any functions, so that people feel secure in their jobs. The role of managers is to support the needs of lower-level employees. One reflection of how much a company cares for its people is the array of benefits it offers, and SAS goes over the top. It pays 90 percent coverage of health insurance premiums, has a free on-site medical clinic, a 66,000-square-foot fitness center, a low-cost on-site child care center, a summer camp for children, and a work-life center with a staff of eight social workers. Employees have flexible work schedules, unlimited sick days, and three weeks of paid vacation (not including the week between Christmas and New Year's). The company also provides other services to "eliminate stress and attract talent," such as an on-site hair and nail salon, a car detailing service, a restaurant and bakery, and break rooms stocked with snacks and beverages.

"The value of SAS walks out of the building at 5 every night," says Goodnight. "My job is to make sure they want to come back." Turnover at SAS is around 2 percent, the lowest in the industry. Even when the economy was booming and there were five jobs for every skilled worker in the software industry, SAS averaged 5 percent turnover, compared to 20 percent industry-wide. SAS has been on the list of *Fortune* magazine's "100 Best Companies to Work For" every year since it was first compiled and ranked Number 1 in both 2010 and 2011.[33]

BRIEFCASE

As an organization manager, keep these guidelines in mind:

Make sure corporate culture is consistent with strategy and the environment. Shape culture to fit the needs of both. Four types of culture are adaptability culture, mission culture, clan culture, and bureaucratic culture.

The clan culture at SAS has helped the company thrive and continue to grow even during the economic downturn. Industry analysts say the exceptionally low turnover enabled SAS to save hundreds of millions of dollars a year that other companies had to spend in recruiting and training new people when the labor market was tight.

The Bureaucratic Culture

The **bureaucratic culture** has an internal focus and a consistency orientation for a stable environment. This type of culture supports a methodical approach to doing business. Symbols, heroes, and ceremonies reinforce the values of cooperation, tradition, and following established policies and practices as ways to achieve goals. Personal involvement is somewhat lower here, but that is outweighed by a high level of consistency, conformity, and collaboration among members. This organization succeeds by being highly integrated and efficient.

Today, most managers are shifting away from bureaucratic cultures because of a need for greater flexibility. However, Pacific Edge Software (now part of Serena Software) successfully implemented elements of a bureaucratic culture to ensure that all its projects stayed on time and on budget. The husband-and-wife co-founders, Lisa Hjorten and Scott Fuller, intentionally established a culture of order, discipline, and control. This emphasis on order and focus meant employees generally went home by 6:00 P.M. rather than working all night to finish an important project.

Although sometimes being careful means being slow, Pacific Edge managed to keep pace with the demands of the external environment.[34]

Some people like the order and predictability of a bureaucratic culture, whereas other people would feel stifled and constrained by too much discipline and would be happier working in some other type of culture. Complete the questionnaire in the "How Do You Fit the Design?" box to get an idea of which type of culture—adaptability, mission, clan, or bureaucratic—you would be most comfortable and successful working in.

Culture Strength and Organizational Subcultures

Culture strength refers to the degree of agreement among members of an organization about the importance of specific values. If widespread consensus exists about the importance of those values, the culture is cohesive and strong; if little agreement exists, the culture is weak.[35]

How Do You Fit the Design?

CORPORATE CULTURE PREFERENCE

The fit between a manager or employee and corporate culture can determine both personal success and satisfaction. To understand your culture preference, rank the following items from 1 to 8 based on the strength of your preference (1 = highest preference; 8 = lowest preference).

1. The organization is very personal, much like an extended family. ___
2. The organization is dynamic and changing, where people take risks. ___
3. The organization is achievement oriented, with the focus on competition and getting jobs done.
4. The organization is stable and structured, with clarity and established procedures.
5. Management style is characterized by teamwork and participation.
6. Management style is characterized by innovation and risk-taking.
7. Management style is characterized by high performance demands and achievement.
8. Management style is characterized by security and predictability.

Scoring: To compute your preference for each type of culture, add together the scores for each set of two questions as follows:

Clan culture—total for questions 1, 5:___
Adaptability culture—total for questions 2, 6:___
Mission culture—total for questions 3, 7:___
Bureaucratic culture—total for questions 4, 8:___

Interpretation: Each of the preceding questions pertains to one of the four types of culture in Exhibit 9.4. A lower score means a stronger preference for that specific culture. You will likely be more comfortable and more effective as a manager in a corporate culture that is compatible with your personal preferences. A higher score means the culture would not fit your expectations, and you would have to change your style to be effective. Review the text discussion of the four culture types. Do your cultural preference scores seem correct to you? Can you think of companies that would fit your culture preference?

Source: Adapted from Kim S. Cameron and Robert E. Quinn, *Diagnosing and Changing Organizational Culture* (Reading, MA: Addison-Wesley, 1999).

A strong culture is typically associated with the frequent use of ceremonies, symbols, and stories, as described earlier, and managers align structures and processes to support the cultural values. These elements increase employee commitment to the values and strategy of a company. However, culture is not always uniform throughout the organization, particularly in large companies. Even in organizations that have strong cultures, there may be several sets of subcultures. **Subcultures** develop to reflect the common problems, goals, and experiences that members of a team, department, or other unit share. An office, branch, or unit of a company that is physically separated from the company's main operations may also take on a distinctive subculture.

For example, although the dominant culture of an organization may be a mission culture, various departments may also reflect characteristics of adaptability, clan, or bureaucratic cultures. The manufacturing department of a large organization may thrive in an environment that emphasizes order, efficiency, and obedience to rules, whereas the research and development (R&D) department may be characterized by employee empowerment, flexibility, and customer focus. This is similar to the concept of differentiation described in Chapter 6, where employees in manufacturing, sales, and research departments studied by Paul Lawrence and Jay Lorsch[36] developed different values with respect to time horizon, interpersonal relationships, and formality in order to perform the job of each particular department most effectively. Consider how the credit division of Pitney Bowes, a huge corporation that manufactures postage meters, copiers, and other office equipment, developed a distinctive subculture to encourage innovation and risk-taking.

Pitney Bowes Credit Corporation

IN PRACTICE

Pitney Bowes, a maker of postage meters and other office equipment, has long thrived in an environment of order and predictability. Its headquarters reflects a typical corporate environment and an orderly culture with its blank walls and bland carpeting. But step onto the third floor of the Pitney Bowes building in Shelton, Connecticut, and you might think you're at a different company. The domain of Pitney Bowes Credit Corporation (PBCC) looks more like an indoor theme park, featuring cobblestone-patterned carpets, faux gas lamps, and an ornate town square-style clock. It also has a French-style café, a 1950s-style diner, and the "Cranial Kitchen," where employees sit in cozy booths to surf the Internet or watch training videos. The friendly hallways encourage impromptu conversations, where people can exchange information and share ideas they wouldn't otherwise share.

PBCC traditionally helped customers finance their business with the parent company. However, Matthew Kisner, PBCC's president and CEO, worked with other managers to redefine the division as a *creator* of services rather than just a provider of services. Rather than just financing sales and leasing of existing products, PBCC now creates new services for customers to buy. For example, Purchase Power is a revolving line of credit that helps companies finance their postage costs. It was profitable within nine months and now has more than 400,000 customers. When PBCC redefined its job, it began redefining its subculture to match by emphasizing values of teamwork, risk-taking, and creativity. "We wanted a fun space that would embody our culture," Kisner says. "No straight lines, no linear thinking. Because we're a financial services company, our biggest advantage is the quality of our ideas." So far, PBCC's new approach is working. In one year, the division, whose 600 employees make up less than 2 percent of Pitney Bowes' total workforce, generated 36 percent of the company's net profits.[37]

Subcultures typically include the basic values of the dominant organizational culture plus additional values unique to members of the subculture. However, subcultural differences can sometimes lead to conflicts between departments, especially in organizations that do not have strong overall corporate cultures. When subcultural values become too strong and outweigh the corporate cultural values, conflicts may emerge and hurt organizational performance. Conflict was discussed in detail in Chapter 7.

BRIEFCASE

As an organization manager, keep this guideline in mind:

Consciously manage culture to shift values toward high performance and goal accomplishment.

Organizational Culture, Learning, and Performance

Culture can play an important role in creating an organizational climate that enables learning and innovative response to challenges, competitive threats, or new opportunities. A strong culture that encourages adaptation and change enhances organizational performance by energizing and motivating employees, unifying people around shared goals and a higher mission, and shaping and guiding behavior so that everyone's actions are aligned with strategic priorities. Thus, creating and influencing a *constructive culture* is one of a manager's most important jobs. The right culture can drive high performance.[38]

A number of studies have found a positive relationship between culture and performance.[39] In *Corporate Culture and Performance,* Kotter and Heskett provided evidence that companies that intentionally managed cultural values outperformed similar companies that did not. Some companies have developed systematic ways to measure and manage the impact of culture on organizational performance. At Caterpillar, top executives used a tool called the Cultural Assessment Process (CAP), which gave them hard data documenting millions of dollars in savings they could attribute directly to cultural factors.[40] Even the U.S. Federal government is recognizing the link between culture and effectiveness. The U.S. Office of Personnel Management created its Organizational Assessment Survey as a way for Federal agencies to measure culture factors and shift values toward high performance.[41]

BRIEFCASE

As an organization manager, keep these guidelines in mind:

To support a learning orientation, emphasize cultural values of openness and collaboration, equality and trust, continuous improvement, and risk-taking. Build a strong internal culture that encourages adaptation to changing environmental conditions.

Strong cultures that don't encourage constructive adaptation, however, can hurt the organization. A danger for many successful organizations is that the culture becomes set and the company fails to adapt as the environment changes. When organizations are successful, the values, ideas, and practices that helped attain success become institutionalized. As the environment changes, these values may become detrimental to future performance. Many organizations become victims of their own success, clinging to outmoded and even destructive values and behaviors. Consider that just a couple of months after the Deepwater Horizon explosion and massive oil spill in the Gulf of Mexico, Tony Hayward, the CEO of BP at the time, went to England to watch his yacht compete in a race around the Isle of Wight. The move sparked outrage, and it was a reflection of a bold, arrogant culture that had become destructive as BP became involved in riskier and riskier ventures. A long series of safety violations, accidents, and costly mistakes were precursors to the Deepwater Horizon disaster. Hayward was soon asked to resign, and a new CEO and other top managers began a close examination of how to fix a once-effective culture gone awry.[42]

Thus, the impact of a strong culture is not always positive. Typically, healthy cultures not only provide for smooth internal integration but also encourage adaptation to the external environment. Non-constructive cultures encourage rigidity and stability. Strong constructive cultures often incorporate the following values:

1. *The whole is more important than the parts, and boundaries between parts are minimized.* People are aware of the whole system, how everything fits together,

and the relationships among various organizational parts. All members consider how their actions affect other parts and the total organization. This emphasis on the whole reduces boundaries both within the organization and with other companies. Although subcultures may form, everyone's primary attitudes and behaviors reflect the organization's dominant culture. The free flow of people, ideas, and information allows coordinated action and continuous learning.

2. *Equality and trust are primary values.* The culture creates a sense of community and caring for one another. The organization is a place for creating a web of relationships that allows people to take risks and develop to their full potential. The emphasis on treating everyone with care and respect creates a climate of safety and trust that allows experimentation, frequent mistakes, and learning. Managers emphasize honest and open communications as a way to build trust.
3. *The culture encourages risk-taking, change, and improvement.* A basic value is to question the status quo. Constant questioning of assumptions opens the gates to creativity and improvement. The culture rewards and celebrates the creators of new ideas, products, and work processes. To symbolize the importance of taking risks, a constructive culture may also reward those who fail in order to learn and grow.

As illustrated in Exhibit 9.5, constructive corporate cultures have different values and behavior patterns than non-constructive cultures.[43] In constructive cultures, managers are concerned with customers and employees, as well as with the internal processes and procedures that bring about useful change. Behavior is flexible, and managers initiate change when needed, even if it involves risk. In non-constructive cultures, managers are more concerned about

EXHIBIT 9.5
Constructive versus Non-Constructive Cultures

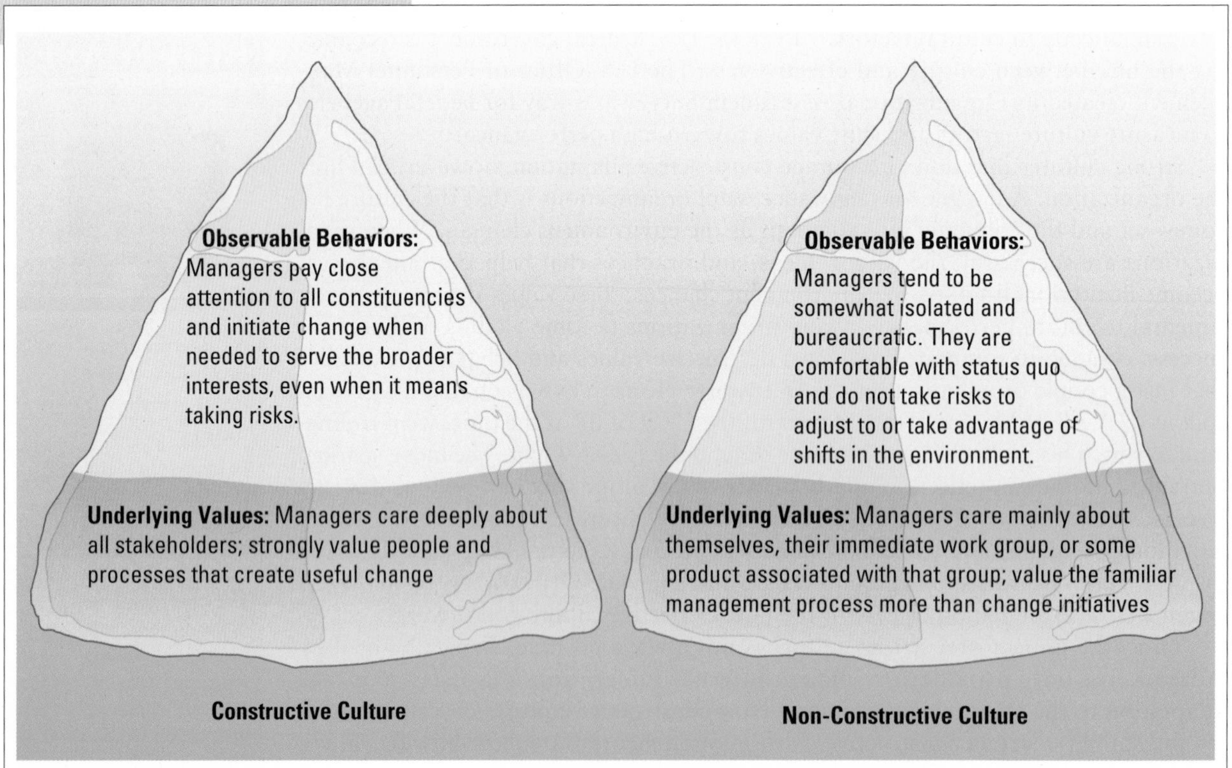

Observable Behaviors: Managers pay close attention to all constituencies and initiate change when needed to serve the broader interests, even when it means taking risks.
Underlying Values: Managers care deeply about all stakeholders; strongly value people and processes that create useful change
Constructive Culture
Observable Behaviors: Managers tend to be somewhat isolated and bureaucratic. They are comfortable with status quo and do not take risks to adjust to or take advantage of shifts in the environment.
Underlying Values: Managers care mainly about themselves, their immediate work group, or some product associated with that group; value the familiar management process more than change initiatives
Non-Constructive Culture

Source: Based on John P. Kotter and James L. Heskett, *Corporate Culture and Performance* (New York: The Free Press, 1992), 51.

themselves or their own special projects, and their values discourage risk-taking and change. Thus, strong, healthy cultures help organizations adapt to the external environment, whereas strong, unhealthy cultures can encourage organizations to march resolutely in the wrong direction. The founders of Menlo Innovations started their company with a goal of creating a strong constructive culture.

Menlo Innovations

IN PRACTICE

Richard Sheridan, James Goebel, Robert Simms, and Thomas Meloche founded Menlo Innovations to create custom software for organizations, but one of their primary goals was to create a unique culture that embraces the values of equality, teamwork, learning, and fun. The founders say they were inspired by the collaborative and creative work environment demonstrated at Thomas Edison's Menlo Park, New Jersey, "Invention Factory" more than 120 years ago.

At many software companies developers work alone, but at Menlo collaboration is valued above anything else. Everyone works in a large, open room with no barriers of any kind to limit communication and information sharing. Employees work in pairs, sharing a single computer and passing the mouse back and forth as they brainstorm ideas and troubleshoot problems. When a pair reports on its work at morning meetings, each partner holds one of the horns of a Viking helmet. The pairs stay together for a week and then all switch around to new partners. Representatives from the client for whom the software is being developed are also brought into the mix and work in pairs with developers. Some complex products might take years to develop, and the variety of partners and tasks helps keep energy high, as well as brings fresh perspectives to ever-evolving projects.

Curiosity, willingness to learn, and the ability to "play well with others" are the qualities Menlo wants in its employees. The goal for each person is not to get the right answer, make the right connection, be the smartest, or know the most, but rather to bring out the best in one's partner. People who apply for jobs are divided into pairs and assigned an exercise, then evaluated on how effective they are at making the other applicant look good. It's tough for some people to handle—trying to make sure a competitor looks good enough to get the job you want. But at Menlo, if you can't do that, you won't fit the culture—and fitting the culture is essential. Menlo doesn't want individual heroes. Anyone who says, "I'm right, so let's do it this way" won't last long. "Constant collaboration means we are constantly transferring knowledge to one another," says Sheridan. "I grow my team an inch every day." Menlo's culture has been a competitive advantage for the company, enabling it to adapt quickly to an ever-shifting environment and meet the changing technology needs of varied clients, including Domino's Pizza, Thomson Reuters, Pfizer, Nationwide Financial, and the University of Michigan.[44]

Ethical Values and Social Responsibility

Of the values that make up an organization's culture, ethical values are now considered among the most important and have gained renewed emphasis in today's era of financial scandals and moral lapses. A study of business news related to the 100 largest U.S. corporations found that a whopping 40 percent of them have recently been involved in activities that can be considered unethical.[45] For example, the giant U.S.-based News Corporation, which owns a string of newspapers, television networks, film studios, and other media outlets around the world, came under widespread attack after the discovery that reporters in London had hacked into the phone lines of murder victims, families of dead soldiers, politicians, and others. The scandal led to a steady stream of revelations about years of sleazy, unethical, and even criminal behavior at the company's newspapers, reflecting a corporate culture that encouraged cutting corners and bending the rules.[46] And the problem isn't limited to U.S. corporations. Business leaders in countries such as Germany and Japan have also been reeling in recent years from one headline-grabbing scandal after another.[47] Top corporate managers are under scrutiny from the public as never before, and even small companies are finding a need to put more emphasis on ethics to restore trust among their customers and the community.

Sources of Individual Ethical Principles

Ethics refers to the code of moral principles and values that governs the behaviors of a person or group with respect to what is right or wrong. Ethical values set standards as to what is good or bad in conduct and decision making.[48] Ethics are personal and unique to each individual, although in any given group, organization, or society there are many areas of consensus about what constitutes ethical behavior. Exhibit 9.6 illustrates the varied sources of individual ethical principles.[49] Each person is a creation of his or her time and place in history. National culture, religious heritage, historical background, and so forth lead to the development of societal morality, or society's view of what is right and wrong. Societal morality is often reflected in norms of behavior and values about what makes sense for an orderly society. Some principles are codified into laws and regulations, such as laws against drunk driving, robbery, or murder.

EXHIBIT 9.6
Sources of Individual Ethical Principles and Actions

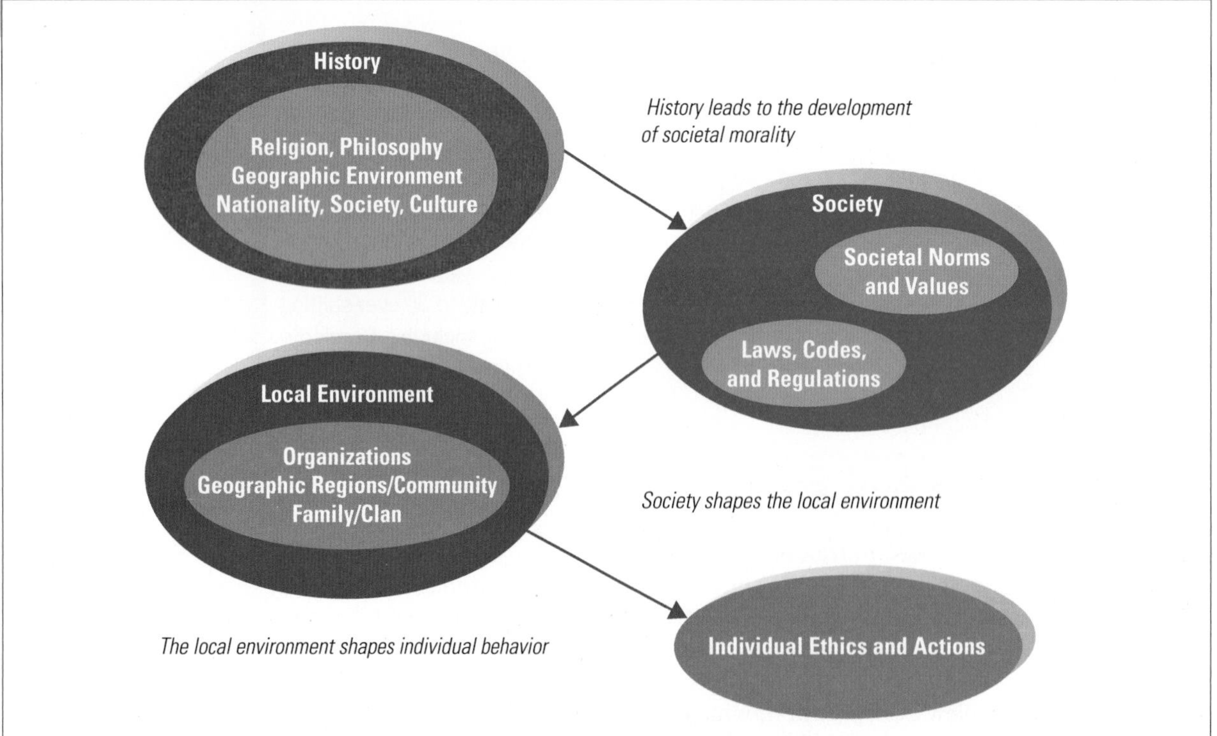

Source: Thanks to Susan H. Taft and Judith White for providing this exhibit, based on their article, "Ethics Education: Using Inductive Reasoning to Develop Individual, Group, Organizational, and Global Perspectives," *Journal of Management Education* 31, no. 5 (October 2007), 614–646.

These laws, as well as unwritten societal norms and values, shape the local environment within which each individual acts, such as a person's community, family, and place of work. Individuals absorb the beliefs and values of their family, community, culture, society, religious community, and geographic environment, typically discarding some and incorporating others into their own personal ethical standards. Each person's ethical stance is thus a blending of his or her historical, cultural, societal, and family backgrounds and influences, as illustrated in Exhibit 9.6.

It is important to look at individual ethics because ethical behavior always involves an individual action, whether it is a decision to act or the failure to take action against wrongdoing by others. In organizations, an individual's ethical stance may be affected by peers, subordinates, and supervisors, as well as by the organizational culture. Organizational culture often has a profound influence on individual choices and can support and encourage ethical actions or promote unethical and socially irresponsible behavior.

Managerial Ethics

Many of the recent scandals in the news have dealt with people and corporations that broke the law. Tyson Foods executives are on the hot seat for allegedly authorizing the payment of bribes in Mexico, for instance, which is a violation of U.S. law.[50] But it is important to remember that ethical decisions go far beyond behaviors governed by law.[51] The **rule of law** arises from a set of codified principles and regulations that describe how people are required to act, that are generally accepted in society, and that are enforceable in the courts.[52]

The relationship between ethical standards and legal requirements is illustrated in Exhibit 9.7. Ethical standards for the most part apply to behavior not covered by the law, and the rule of law applies to behaviors not necessarily covered by ethical standards. Current laws often reflect combined moral judgments, but not all moral judgments are codified into law. The morality of aiding a drowning person, for example, is not specified by law, and driving on the right-hand side of the road has no moral basis; but in acts such as robbery or murder, rules and moral standards

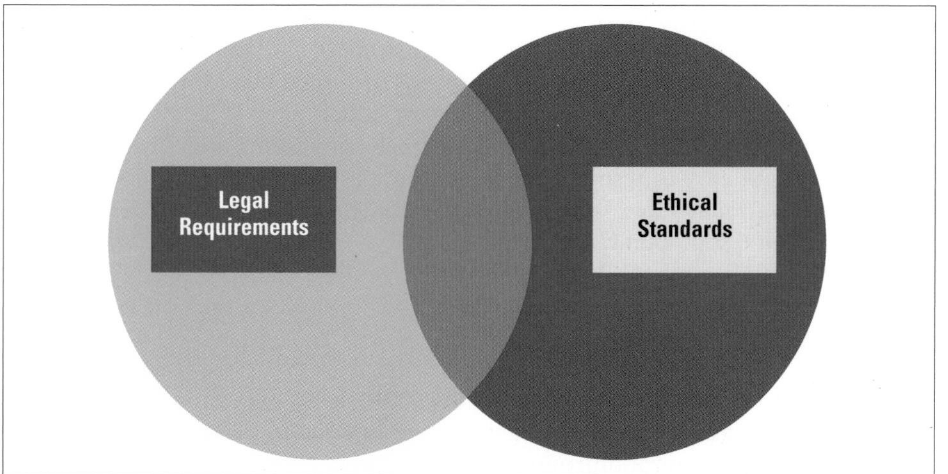

EXHIBIT 9.7
Relationship between the Rule of Law and Ethical Standards

Source: LaRue Tone Hosmer, *The Ethics of Management*, 2nd ed. (Homewood, IL: Irwin, 1991).

overlap. Many people believe that if you are not breaking the law, then you are behaving in an ethical manner, but this is not always true. Many behaviors have not been codified, and managers must be sensitive to emerging norms and values about those issues. For example, prior to the Wall Street meltdown that came about because of millions of bad subprime mortgage loans, there were no laws preventing mortgage companies from providing what some have called "ninja loans" (no income, no job, no assets).[53] However, ethical managers would hold that giving loans to people who most likely cannot afford the payments in order to increase your loan volume is unethical.

Managerial ethics are principles that guide the decisions and behaviors of managers with regard to whether they are right or wrong. The following examples illustrate the need for managerial ethics:[54]

- Top executives are considering promoting a rising sales manager who consistently brings in $70 million a year and has cracked open new markets in places like Brazil and Russia that are important for international growth. However, female employees have been complaining for years that the manager is verbally abusive to them, tells offensive jokes, and throws temper tantrums if female employees don't do exactly as he says.
- The manager of a beauty supply store is told that she and her salespeople can receive large bonuses for selling a specified number of boxes of a new product, a permanent-wave solution that costs nearly twice as much as what most of her salon customers typically use. She orders her salespeople to store the old product in the back and tell customers there's been a delay in delivery.
- A North American manufacturer operating abroad was asked to make cash payments (a bribe) to government officials and was told by local business partners that it was consistent with local customs, despite being illegal in North America.

BRIEFCASE

As an organization manager, keep these guidelines in mind:

Take control of ethical values in the organization and make a commitment to corporate social responsibility. Recognize that ethics is not the same as following the law, and help people learn how to make ethical decisions.

As these examples illustrate, being ethical is about making decisions. Managers make choices every day about whether to be honest or deceitful with customers and suppliers, treat employees with respect or disdain, and be a good or a harmful corporate citizen. Some issues are exceedingly difficult to resolve and often represent ethical dilemmas. An **ethical dilemma** arises in a situation concerning right and wrong in which values are in conflict.[55] Right or wrong cannot be clearly identified in such situations. For a salesperson at the beauty supply store, for example, the value conflict is between being honest with customers and adhering to the boss's expectations. The manufacturing manager may feel torn between respecting and following local customs in a foreign country or adhering to U.S. laws concerning bribes. Sometimes, each alternative choice or behavior seems undesirable. Ethical dilemmas are not easy to resolve, but top executives can aid the process by establishing organizational values that give people guidelines for making the best decision from a moral standpoint.

Corporate Social Responsibility

The notion of **corporate social responsibility (CSR)** is an extension of the idea of managerial ethics and refers to management's obligation to make choices and take action so that the organization contributes to the welfare and interest of all organizational stakeholders, such as employees, customers, shareholders, the community, and the broader society.[56] Ninety percent of companies surveyed by McKinsey & Company said they were doing more than they were five years earlier to incorporate social responsibility issues into their core strategies.[57]

CSR was once seen as the purview of small, offbeat companies like Patagonia or The Body Shop, but it has moved firmly into the mainstream of organizational thinking and behavior. Ernst & Young lends out employees to provide free accounting services to nonprofit organizations or struggling small businesses around the world, paying their salaries and travel expenses. Whirlpool donates a refrigerator and range to every home built by Habitat for Humanity in North America. PepsiCo made a commitment to voluntarily remove high-calorie sweetened drinks from schools in more than 200 countries by 2012. Giant corporations from Walmart to General Electric have announced ambitious environmental responsibility goals. More than 1,000 companies around the world have published reports proclaiming their concern for employees, the environment, and their local communities.[58]

In addition, many companies, including GE, Nestlé, IBM, PepsiCo, and Johnson & Johnson, are pursuing strategies and business opportunities that embrace a *shared value model*. **Shared value** refers to organizational policies and practices that both enhance the economic success of a company and advance the economic and social conditions of the communities in which the company operates.[59] Hindustan Unilever, for example, uses a direct-to-home distribution system for its hygiene products in parts of India, whereby underprivileged women in villages of less than 2,000 people are given micro loans and training to start their own small businesses. The system benefits communities by giving women skills and opportunities that sometimes double their household income, as well as by reducing the spread of disease by bringing hygiene products into isolated areas. It also benefits the company by extending its market and building its brand in hard-to-reach areas. The project now accounts for 5 percent of Hindustan Unilever's revenue in India.[60]

2 Being ethical and socially responsible is not just the right thing for a corporation to do; it is a critical issue for business success.

ANSWER: *Agree.* Following years of scandal, employees and the public are demanding a more ethical and socially responsible approach to business. Businesses as well as nonprofits and governmental organizations are looking for ways to restore trust. A new generation of job seekers takes a company's social responsibility into account when considering job offers, so companies that want to hire the best are paying attention.

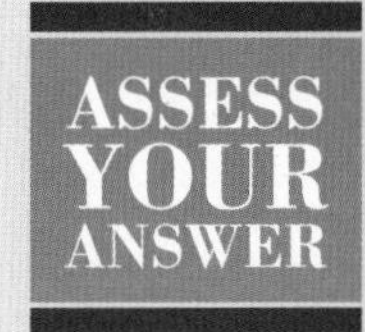

Does It Pay to Be Good?

Why are so many companies embracing CSR? For one thing, employees, customers, investors, and other stakeholders are increasingly demanding that corporations behave in socially responsible ways. People are paying closer attention than ever before to what organizations do, and managers recognize that being a good corporate citizen can enhance their firm's reputation and even its profitability.[61] In the Middle East, 75 percent of leaders surveyed believe CSR helps to attract new investment, increase market share, and gain new markets.[62] A study by researchers at MIT, Michigan State University, and IE Business School in Madrid indicates that having a good reputation for CSR can also help shield companies from the harmful effects of negative publicity. That is, customers are more willing to give a company the benefit of the doubt when it has a solid CSR reputation, rather than automatically accepting that negative reports are true.[63]

The relationship of an organization's ethics and social responsibility to its performance concerns both managers and organization scholars. Studies have provided varying results but generally have found that there is a positive relationship between ethical and socially responsible behavior and financial results.[64] For example, one study of the financial performance of large U.S. corporations that are considered "best corporate citizens" found that they have both superior reputations and superior financial performance.[65] Similarly, Governance Metrics International, an independent corporate governance ratings agency, found that the stocks of companies run on more selfless principles perform better than those run in a self-serving manner. Top-ranked companies also outperformed lower-ranking firms on measures like return on assets, return on investment, and return on capital.[66]

As discussed earlier in the chapter, long-term organizational success relies largely on social capital, which means companies need to build a reputation for honesty, fairness, and doing the right thing. There is evidence that people prefer to work for companies that demonstrate a high level of ethical behavior and corporate social responsibility, so these companies can attract and retain high-quality employees.[67] Sarah Antonette says she joined PNC Financial Services rather than two other companies that offered her a job because of PNC's strong employee volunteer program.[68] One vice president at Timberland says she has turned down lucrative offers from other companies because she prefers to work at a company that puts ethics and social responsibility ahead of just making a profit.[69] And a survey of 13-to-25-year-olds found that 79 percent say they want to work for a company that cares about how it affects or contributes to society.[70]

Customers pay attention to a company's ethics and social responsibility too. A study by Walker Research indicates that, price and quality being equal, two-thirds of people say they would switch brands to do business with a company that makes a high commitment to ethics.[71] Another series of experiments by Remi Trudel and June Cotte of the University of Western Ontario's Ivey School of Business found that consumers were willing to pay slightly more for products they were told had been made using high ethical standards.[72]

Companies that put ethics on the back burner in favor of fast growth and short-term profits ultimately suffer. To gain and keep the trust of employees, customers, investors, and the general public, organizations must put ethics and social responsibility first.

BRIEFCASE

As an organization manager, keep these guidelines in mind:

Act as a leader for the internal culture and ethical values that are important to the organization. Treat people fairly, hold yourself and others to high ethical standards, and communicate a vision for putting ethics before short-term interests. Remember that actions speak louder than words.

How Managers Shape Culture and Ethics

In a study of ethics policy and practice in successful, ethical companies such as Johnson & Johnson and General Mills, no point emerged more clearly than the role of top management in providing commitment, leadership, and examples for ethical behavior.[73] The CEO and other top managers must be committed to specific ethical values and provide constant leadership in tending and renewing the values. Values can be communicated in a number of ways—speeches, company publications, policy statements, and, especially, personal actions. People follow and model what they see managers doing. If managers lie and bend the rules, so will employees. Top leaders are responsible for creating and sustaining a culture that emphasizes the importance of ethical behavior for every employee. When Vic Sarni was CEO of PPG Industries, he often called himself the chief ethics officer. Sarni didn't believe in using special staff departments to investigate ethical complaints; instead, he personally headed the firm's ethics committee. This sent a powerful symbolic message that ethics was important in the organization.[74] However, managers throughout the organizations also need to espouse and model ethical values. Employees are often influenced most by the managers and supervisors they work with closely rather than by distant top leaders. Formal ethics programs are worthless if managers do not live up to high standards of ethical conduct.[75]

The following sections examine how managers signal and implement values through leadership as well as through the formal systems of the organization.

Values-Based Leadership

The underlying value system of an organization cannot be managed in the traditional way. Issuing an authoritative directive, for example, has little or no impact on an organization's value system. Organizational values are developed and strengthened primarily through **values-based leadership**, a relationship between a leader and followers that is based on shared, strongly internalized values that are advocated and acted upon by the leader.[76] Sanjiv Das, president and CEO of CitiMortgage, represents the qualities of a values-based leader.

IN PRACTICE

Sanjiv Das, CitiMortgage

India-born Sanjiv Das, who took over as president and CEO of CitiMortgage in July 2008 in the midst of the housing crisis, had two primary goals when he started the job: (1) to boost the morale of 10,000 employees who were dealing with the agony of the crisis coupled with shrinking public respect for their industry; and (2) to keep people from losing their homes. In his mind, the two goals were related. By keeping people focused on the help they could offer to alleviate the financial pressure of those caught in economic turmoil, Das helped employees find purpose, meaning, and self-respect. For Das, business is not just about money; it's about mutually respectful relationships.

Like many companies, CitiMortgage worked with borrowers who missed several payments to restructure their loans. However, Citi went further than many banks. Das pioneered a first-of-its-kind program to temporarily lower payments and waive interest and penalties for borrowers who had lost their jobs. In addition, he implemented a program to preemptively reach out to approximately 500,000 homeowners who were not late on their payments but might fall behind without help. "These homeowners are often too embarrassed or worried, or simply don't know how to ask . . . for help," Das said. He believes early intervention is one of the best ways to bring down the foreclosure rate, keep people in their homes, help struggling communities, and boost the economy.

Das says his leadership approach is based in the spiritual values he learned growing up in Delhi—such as maintaining purpose and integrity during difficult times and helping others rather than trying to acquire more material goods for oneself. "The No. 1 thing I talk about [to employees] are the customers. Each day, my business is to keep them in their homes, no matter what. That goes back to the values I was brought up with."[77]

Clearly, Sanjiv Das faces a tough leadership situation, and CitiMortgage, like many other companies in the finance and housing industries, is struggling for its very survival. However, Das's values-based leadership has had a significant positive influence on both employee morale and business results. His approach to doing business is helping ease the anxiety and sense of failure that has sapped employee morale.

General Norman Schwarzkopf once said, "Leadership is a combination of strategy and character. If you must be without one, be without the strategy."[78] Good leaders know their every act and statement has an impact on culture and values. Employees learn about values, beliefs, and goals from watching managers, just as students learn which topics are important for an exam, what professors like, and how to get a good grade from watching professors. Actions speak louder than words, so values-based leaders "walk their talk."[79] "Just saying you're ethical isn't very useful," says Charles O. Holliday Jr., former chairman and CEO of DuPont. "You have to earn trust by what you do every day."[80]

Exhibit 9.8 outlines some of the characteristics that define values-based leaders.[81] Values-based leaders treat others with care, are helpful and supportive of others, and put effort into maintaining positive interpersonal relationships. They treat everyone fairly and with respect. Values-based leaders accept others' mistakes and failures and are never condescending. They hold themselves to high ethical standards, continuously strive to be honest, humble, and trustworthy and to be consistently ethical in both their public and private lives. However, they are open about and accept responsibility for their own ethical failings.

Values-based leaders also clearly articulate and communicate an uncompromising vision for high ethical standards in the organization, and they institutionalize

EXHIBIT 9.8
Characteristics of Values-Based Leaders

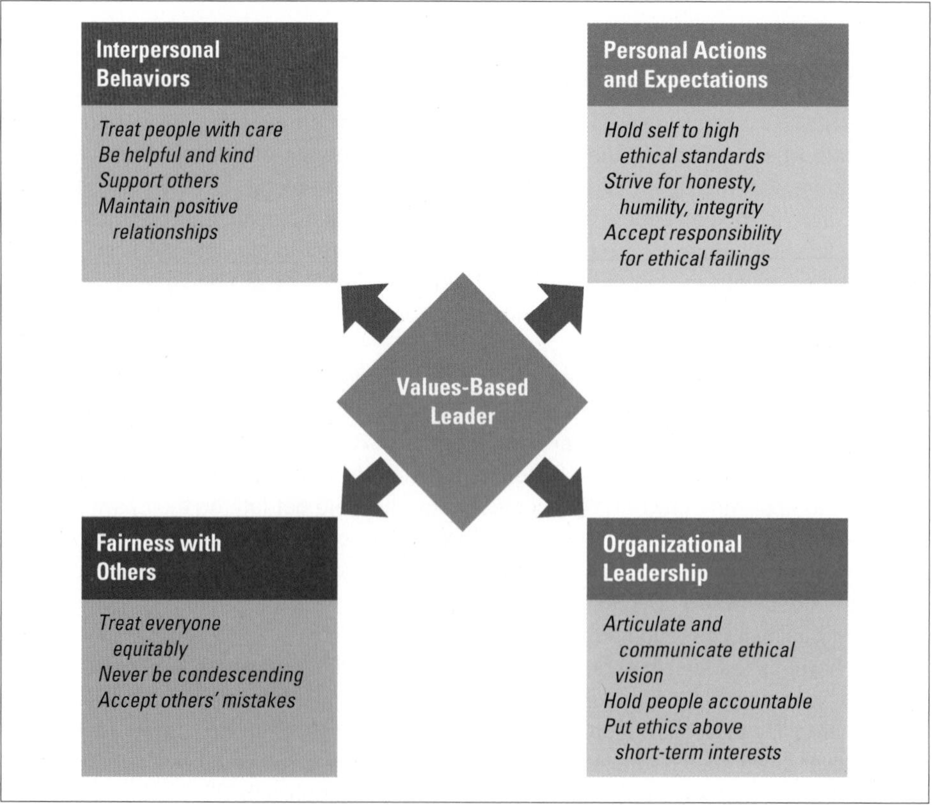

Source: Based on Gary Weaver, Linda Klebe Treviño, and Bradley Agle, "'Somebody I Look Up To': Ethical Role Models in Organizations," *Organizational Dynamics* 34, no. 4 (2005), 313–330.

the vision by holding themselves and others accountable and by putting ethics above short-term personal or company interests. They continuously strengthen ethical values through everyday behaviors, rituals, ceremonies, and symbols, as well as through organizational systems and policies.

BRIEFCASE

As an organization manager, keep this guideline in mind:

Use the formal systems of the organization to implement desired cultural and ethical values. These systems include an ethics committee, a chief ethics officer, disclosure mechanisms, a code of ethics, and ethics training programs.

Formal Structure and Systems

Another set of tools managers can use to shape cultural and ethical values is the formal structure and systems of the organization. These systems can be especially effective for influencing managerial ethics.

Structure. Top executives can assign responsibility for ethical values to a specific position. This not only allocates organization time and energy to the problem but symbolizes to everyone the importance of ethics. One example is an **ethics committee**, which is a cross-functional group of executives who oversee company ethics. The committee provides rulings on questionable ethical issues and assumes responsibility for disciplining wrongdoers. By appointing top-level executives to serve on the committee, the organization signals the importance of ethics.

Today, many organizations are setting up ethics departments that manage and coordinate all corporate ethics activities. These departments are headed by a **chief ethics officer**, a high-level company executive who oversees all aspects of ethics, including establishing and broadly communicating ethical standards, setting up ethics training programs, supervising the investigation of ethical problems, and advising managers on the ethical aspects of corporate decisions.[82] The title of chief ethics officer was almost unheard of a decade ago, but recent ethical and legal problems have created a growing demand for these specialists.

Ethics offices sometimes also work as counseling centers to help employees resolve tricky ethical dilemmas. The focus is as much on helping employees make the right decisions as on disciplining wrongdoers. Most ethics offices have confidential **ethics hotlines** that employees can use to seek guidance as well as report questionable behavior. One organization calls its hotline a "Guide Line" to emphasize its use as a tool for making ethical decisions as well as reporting lapses.[83] According to Gary Edwards, president of the Ethics Resource Center, between 65 and 85 percent of calls to hotlines in the organizations he advises are calls for counsel on ethical issues. Northrup Grumman's "Openline" fields about 1,400 calls a year, of which only one-fourth are reports of misdeeds.[84]

Disclosure Mechanisms. A confidential hotline is also an important mechanism for employees to voice concerns about ethical practices. Holding organizations accountable depends to some degree on individuals who are willing to speak up if they suspect illegal, dangerous, or unethical activities. **Whistle-blowing** involves employee disclosure of illegal, immoral, or illegitimate practices on the part of the organization.[85] As ethical problems in the corporate world increase, many companies are looking for ways to protect whistle-blowers. In addition, calls are increasing for stronger legal protection for those who report illegal or unethical business activities.[86] When there are no protective measures, whistle-blowers suffer, and the company may continue its unethical or illegal practices. For example, Matthew Lee, a former senior vice president in Lehman Brothers' accounting division, lost his job just weeks after he raised concerns about how the firm was hiding risks by temporarily "parking" $50 billion in risky loan assets off its balance sheet. Lawrence McDonald, a former Lehman trader who has written a book about the giant firm's collapse, says Lehman routinely sacked or sidelined whistle-blowers, which allowed the company to continue its risky and unethical behavior.[87]

Many governments, including the United States and Japan, have passed laws aimed at protecting whistle-blowers, but that isn't enough. Enlightened managers strive to create an organizational climate and culture in which people feel free to point out problems and managers take swift action to address concerns about unethical or illegal activities. Organizations can view whistle-blowing as a benefit to the company, helping to prevent the kind of disasters that have hit companies such as Enron, Bear Stearns, Countrywide, News Corporation, and Lehman Brothers.

Code of Ethics. A **code of ethics** is a formal statement of the company's values concerning ethics and social responsibility; it clarifies to employees what the company stands for and its expectations for employee conduct. The code of ethics at Lockheed Martin, for example, states that the organization "aims to set the standard for ethical conduct" through adhering to the values of honesty, integrity, respect, trust, responsibility, and citizenship. The code specifies the types of behaviors expected to honor these values and encourages employees to use available company resources to help make ethical choices and decisions.[88] Codes of ethics may cover a broad range of issues, including statements of the company's guiding values; guidelines related to issues such as workplace safety, the security of proprietary information, or employee privacy; and commitments to environmental responsibility, product safety, and other matters of concern to stakeholders. Swiss bank UBS AG, for example, developed a strong code of ethics addressing issues such as financial crime, competition, and confidentiality, including outlining sanctions against employees who violate the code. The code explicitly bans staff from helping clients cheat on their taxes, in response to a damaging investigation into the use of hidden offshore accounts. In an important step, the new code prohibits retaliation by managers against employees who report misconduct.[89]

Some companies use broader values statements within which ethics is a part. These statements define ethical values as well as corporate culture and contain language about company responsibility, quality of products, and treatment of employees. A formal statement of values can serve as a fundamental organizational document that defines what the organization stands for and clarifies the expected ethical behaviors and choices.[90]

Although written codes of ethics and value statements are important, it is essential that top managers support and reinforce the codes through their actions, including rewards for compliance and discipline for violations. Otherwise, a code of ethics is nothing more than a piece of paper. Indeed, one study found that companies with a written code of ethics are just as likely as those without a code to be found guilty of illegal activities.[91]

3 The single best way to make sure an organization stays on solid ethical ground is to have a strong code of ethics and make sure all employees are familiar with its guidelines.

ANSWER: *Disagree.* Having a strong code of ethics can be an important part of creating an ethical organization, but managers' actions are more powerful in determining whether people live up to high ethical standards. If managers and top leaders are dishonest, unprincipled, or ruthless and create a culture that supports or ignores these behaviors in others, employees will put little stock in the formal ethics code.

Training Programs. To ensure that ethical issues are considered in daily decision making, many companies supplement a written code of ethics with employee training programs.[92] All Texas Instruments (TI) employees go through an eight-hour ethics training course that includes case examples giving people a chance to wrestle with ethical dilemmas. In addition, TI incorporates an ethics component into every training course it offers.[93]

Some training programs also include frameworks for ethical decision making. Learning these frameworks helps employees act autonomously and still think their way through a difficult decision. In a few companies, managers are also taught about the stages of moral development, which helps to bring them to a high level of ethical decision making. This training has been an important catalyst for establishing ethical behavior and integrity as critical components of strategic competitiveness.[94]

These formal systems and structures can be highly effective. However, they alone are not sufficient to build and sustain an ethical company. Managers should integrate ethics into the organizational culture as well as support and renew ethical values through their words and actions. Only when employees are convinced that ethical values play a key role in all management decisions and actions can they become committed to making them a part of their everyday behavior.

Corporate Culture and Ethics in a Global Environment

Organizations operating on a global basis often face particularly tough ethical challenges because of the various cultural and market factors they deal with. The greater complexity of the environment and organizational domain creates a greater potential for ethical problems or misunderstandings.[95] Consider that in Europe, privacy has been defined as a basic human right and there are laws limiting the amount and kind of information companies can collect and governing how they may use it. A new European Union law, for example, requires that websites get user consent before collecting data about Internet users' identities and habits via tracking files commonly referred to as "cookies." In U.S. organizations, collecting data, trading it with partners, using it for marketing, and even selling it are all common practice. Mobile tracking is on the rise as companies attempt to market to consumers on their smartphones.[96]

Employees from different countries may have varied attitudes and beliefs that make it difficult to establish a sense of community and cohesiveness based on the corporate culture. In fact, research has indicated that national culture has a greater impact on employees than does corporate culture, and differences in national culture also create tremendous variance in ethical attitudes.[97] So, how do managers translate the ideas for developing strong, ethical corporate cultures to a complex global environment?

Vijay Govindarajan, a professor of international business and director of the "Global Leadership 2020" management program at Dartmouth College, offers some guidance. His research indicates that, even though organizational cultures may vary widely, there are specific components that characterize a global culture. These include an emphasis on multicultural rather than national values, basing status on merit rather than nationality, being open to new ideas from other cultures, showing excitement rather than trepidation when entering new cultural environments, and being sensitive to cultural differences without being limited by them.[98]

Managers must also think more broadly in terms of ethical issues. Accenture, a management consulting, technology services, and outsourcing company with 140,000 employees in 48 countries, worked with liaisons in each region, called "Geographic Ethics Leads," to make sure the ethics code was written in appropriate language and addressed to the needs of employees in the different regions. These liaisons received input from employees at focus group sessions held in each country. Thus, although there are core ethical values in common, the company's code of ethics is customized for each country where Accenture has offices.[99]

Companies are using a wide variety of mechanisms to support and reinforce their ethics initiatives on a global scale. One of the most useful mechanisms for building global ethics is the **social audit**, which measures and reports the ethical, social, and environmental impact of a company's operations.[100] Concerns about the labor practices and working conditions of many major U.S. corporations' overseas suppliers originally spurred the Council on Economic Priorities Accreditation Agency to propose a set of global social standards to deal with issues such as child labor, low wages, and unsafe working conditions. Today, the Social Accountability 8000, or SA 8000, is the only auditable social standard in the world. The system is designed to work like the ISO 9000 quality-auditing system. Many companies, such as Avon, Eileen Fisher, and Toys "R" Us, are taking steps to ensure that their factories and suppliers meet SA 8000 standards.[101] Yet managers face significant ethical challenges when working internationally. Bribery, in particular, continues to be a tremendous problem. Avon, Ikea, Halliburton, IBM, Tyson Foods, General Electric, and Daimler are just a few of the companies that have been investigated in recent years for allegedly paying bribes to win business or gain favorable circumstances in foreign countries such as Russia, Nigeria, South Korea, China, and Mexico, where some companies still consider bribery a normal part of doing business.[102]

Design Essentials

- This chapter covered a range of material on corporate culture, the importance of cultural and ethical values, and techniques managers can use to influence these values. Cultural and ethical values help determine the organization's social capital, and the right values can contribute to organizational success.
- Culture is the set of key values, beliefs, and norms shared by members of an organization. Organizational cultures serve two critically important functions—to integrate members so that they know how to relate to one another and to help the organization adapt to the external environment. Culture can be interpreted by looking at the organization's rites and ceremonies, stories, symbols, structures, control systems, and power relationships. Managers can also use these elements to influence culture.
- Organizational culture should reinforce the strategy and structure that the organization needs to be successful in its environment. Four types of culture that may exist in organizations are adaptability culture, mission culture, clan culture, and bureaucratic culture. When widespread consensus exists about the

importance of specific values, the organizational culture is strong and cohesive. However, even in organizations with strong cultures, several sets of subcultures may emerge, particularly in large organizations.

- Strong cultures can be either constructive or non-constructive. Constructive cultures have different values and different behavior patterns than non-constructive cultures. Strong but unhealthy cultures can be detrimental to a company's chances for success. On the other hand, strong constructive cultures can play an important role in creating high performance and innovative responses to challenges, competitive threats, or new opportunities.
- An important aspect of organizational values is managerial ethics, which is the set of values governing behavior with respect to what is right or wrong. Corporate social responsibility (CSR) is an extension of managerial ethics and refers to management responsibility to make choices that contribute to the welfare of society as well as the organization. Many companies are embracing the concept of shared value, which means adopting policies and practices that enhance the competitiveness of a company while simultaneously advancing the economic and social conditions of the communities in which it operates.
- The chapter also discussed how managers shape culture and ethics. One important idea is values-based leadership, which means leaders define a vision of proper values, communicate it throughout the organization, and institutionalize it through everyday behavior, rituals, ceremonies, and symbols. We also discussed formal systems that are important for shaping ethical values. Formal systems include an ethics committee, an ethics department, disclosure mechanisms for whistle-blowing, ethics training programs, and a code of ethics or values statement that specifies desired ethical values and behaviors.
- As business increasingly crosses geographical and cultural boundaries, leaders face difficult challenges in establishing strong cultural and ethical values with which all employees can identify and agree. Companies that develop global cultures emphasize multicultural values, base status on merit rather than nationality, are excited about new cultural environments, remain open to ideas from other cultures, and are sensitive to different cultural values without being limited by them. Social audits are important tools for companies trying to maintain high ethical standards on a global basis.

Key Concepts

adaptability culture
bureaucratic culture
chief ethics officer
clan culture
code of ethics
corporate social responsibility (CSR)
culture
culture strength
ethical dilemma
ethics
ethics committee
ethics hotlines
external adaptation
heroes
internal integration
legends
managerial ethics
mission culture
myths
rites and ceremonies
rule of law
shared value
social audit
social capital
stories
subcultures
symbol
values-based leadership
whistle-blowing

Discussion Questions

1. How much do you think it is possible for an outsider to discern about the underlying cultural values of an organization by analyzing symbols, ceremonies, dress, or other observable aspects of culture, compared to an insider with several years of work experience? Specify a percentage (e.g., 10 percent, 70 percent) and discuss your reasoning.
2. Many of the companies on *Fortune* magazine's list of most admired companies are also on its list of most profitable ones. Some people say this proves that high social capital translates into profits. Other people suggest that high profitability is the primary reason the companies have a good culture and are admired in the first place. Discuss your thinking about these two differing interpretations.
3. Can a strong bureaucratic culture also be a constructive culture, as defined in the text and in Exhibit 9.5? Discuss.
4. Why is values-based leadership so important to the influence of culture? Does a symbolic act communicate more about company values than an explicit statement? Discuss.
5. Can you recall a situation in which either you or someone you know was confronted by an ethical dilemma, such as being encouraged to inflate an expense account or trade answers on a test? Do you think the decision was affected more by individual moral values or by the accepted values within the team or company? Explain.
6. In a survey of 20,000 people in 16 European countries plus Russia, Turkey, and the United States, 55 percent of respondents said cheating in business is more common than it was 10 years ago. Do you believe this is truly the case, or have new forms of media simply made cheating more visible? Discuss.
7. What importance would you attribute to leadership statements and actions for influencing ethical values and decision making in an organization?
8. Why has globalization contributed to more complex ethical issues? Do you think it's possible for a company operating in many different countries to have a cohesive corporate culture? To have uniform ethical values?
9. Explain the concept of shared value. Do you think managers in companies that take a shared value approach are more likely to behave in ethical and socially responsible ways? Discuss.
10. Codes of ethics have been criticized for transferring responsibility for ethical behavior from the organization to the individual employee. Do you agree? Do you think a code of ethics is valuable for an organization?

Chapter 9 Workbook Shop 'til You Drop: Corporate Culture in the Retail World[103]

To understand more about corporate culture, visit two retail stores and compare them according to various factors. Go to one discount or low-end store, such as Kmart or Walmart, and to one high-end store, such as Saks Fifth Avenue or Macy's. Do not interview any employees, but instead be an observer or a shopper. After your visits, fill out the following table for each store. Spend at least two hours in each store on a busy day and be very observant.

Culture Item	Discount Store	High-End Department Store
1. Mission of store: What is it, and is it clear to employees?		
2. Individual initiative: Is it encouraged?		
3. Reward system: What are employees rewarded for?		

(continued)

Culture Item	Discount Store	High-End Department Store
4. Teamwork: Do people within one department or across departments work together or talk with each other?		
5. Company loyalty: Is there evidence of loyalty or of enthusiasm to be working there?		
6. Dress: Are there uniforms? Is there a dress code? How strong is it? How do you rate employees' personal appearance in general?		
7. Diversity or commonality of employees: Is there diversity or commonality in age, education, race, personality, and so on?		
8. Service orientation: Is the customer valued or tolerated?		
9. Human resource development: Is there opportunity for growth and advancement?		

Questions

1. How does the culture seem to influence employee behavior in each store?
2. What effect does employees' behavior have on customers?
3. Which store was more pleasant to be in? How does that relate to the mission of the store?

CASE FOR ANALYSIS Implementing Change at National Industrial Products[104]

Curtis Simpson sat staring out the window of his office. What would he say to Tom Lawrence when they met this afternoon? Tom had clearly met the challenge Simpson set for him when he hired him as president of National Industrial Products (National) a little more than a year ago, but the company seemed to be coming apart at the seams. As chairman and CEO of Simpson Industries, which had bought National several years ago, Simpson was faced with the task of understanding the problem and clearly communicating his ideas and beliefs to Lawrence.

National Industrial Products is a medium-sized producer of mechanical seals, pumps, and other flow-control products. When Simpson Industries acquired the company, it was under the leadership of Jim Carpenter, who had been CEO for almost three decades and was very well liked by employees. Carpenter had always treated his employees like family. He knew most of them by name, often visited them in their homes if they were ill, and spent part of each day just chatting with workers on the factory floor. National sponsored an annual holiday party for its workers as well as company picnics and other social events several times a year, and Carpenter was always in attendance. He considered these activities to be just as important as his visits with customers or negotiations with suppliers. Carpenter believed it was important to treat people right so they would have a sense of loyalty to the company. If business was slow, he would find something else for workers to do, even if it was just sweeping the parking lot, rather than lay people off. He figured the company couldn't afford to lose skilled workers who were so difficult to replace. "If you treat people right," he said, "they'll do a good job for you without your having to push them."

Carpenter had never set performance objectives and standards for the various departments, and he trusted his managers to run their departments as they saw fit. He offered training programs in communications and HR for managers and team leaders several times each year. Carpenter's approach had seemed to work quite well for much of National's history. Employees were very loyal to Carpenter and the company, and there were many instances in which workers had gone above and beyond the call of duty. For example, when two National pumps that supplied water to a U.S. Navy ship failed on a Saturday night just before the ship's scheduled departure, two employees worked throughout the night to make new seals and deliver them for installation before the ship left port. Most managers and employees had been with the company for many years, and National boasted the lowest turnover rate in the industry.

However, as the industry began to change in recent years, National's competitiveness began to decline. Four of National's major rivals had recently merged into two large companies that were better able to meet customer needs, which was one factor that led to National being acquired by Simpson Industries. Following the acquisition, National's sales and profits had continued to decline, while costs kept going up. In addition, Simpson Industries' top executives were concerned about low productivity at National. Although they had been happy to have Carpenter stay on through the transition, within a year they had gently pressured him into early retirement. Some of the top managers believed Carpenter tolerated poor performance and low productivity in order to maintain a friendly atmosphere. "In today's world, you just can't do that," one had said. "We've got to bring in someone who can implement change and turn this company around in a hurry, or National's going to go bankrupt." That's when Tom Lawrence was brought on board, with a mandate to cut costs and improve productivity and profits.

Lawrence had a growing reputation as a young, dynamic manager who could get things done fast. He quickly began making changes at National. First, he cut costs by discontinuing the company-sponsored social activities, and he even refused to allow the impromptu birthday celebrations that had once been a regular part of life at National. He cut the training programs in communications and HR, arguing that they were a waste of time and money. "We're not here to make people feel good," he told his managers. "If people don't want to work, get rid of them and find someone else who does." He often referred to workers who complained about the changes at National as "crybabies."

Lawrence established strict performance standards for his vice presidents and department managers and ordered them to do the same for their employees. He held weekly meetings with each manager to review department performance and discuss problems. All employees were now subject to regular performance reviews. Any worker who had substandard performance was to be given one warning and then fired if performance did not improve within two weeks. And, whereas managers and sales representatives had once been paid on a straight salary basis, with seniority being the sole criterion for advancement, Lawrence implemented a revised system that rewarded them for meeting productivity, sales, and profit goals. For those who met the standards, rewards were generous, including large bonuses and perks such as company cars and first-class air travel to industry meetings. Those who fell behind were often chided in front of their colleagues to set an example, and if they didn't shape up soon, Lawrence didn't hesitate to fire them.

By the end of Lawrence's first year as president of National, production costs had been reduced by nearly 20 percent, while output was up 10 percent and sales increased by nearly 10 percent as well. However, three experienced and well-respected National managers had left the company for jobs with competitors, and turnover among production workers had increased alarmingly. In the tight labor market, replacements were not easily found. Most disturbing to Simpson were the results of a survey he had commissioned by an outside consultant. The survey indicated that morale at National was in the pits. Workers viewed their supervisors with antagonism and a touch of fear. They expressed the belief that managers were obsessed with profits and quotas and cared nothing about workers' needs and feelings. They also noted that the collegial, friendly atmosphere that had made National a great place to work had been replaced by an environment of aggressive internal competition and distrust.

Simpson was pleased that Lawrence has brought National's profits and productivity up to the standards Simpson Industries expects. However, he was concerned that the low morale and high turnover would seriously damage the company in the long run. Was Lawrence correct that many of the employees at National are just being "crybabies"? Were they so accustomed to being coddled by Carpenter that they weren't willing to make the changes necessary to keep the company competitive? Finally, Simpson wondered if a spirit of competition can exist in an atmosphere of collegiality and cooperativeness such as that fostered by Carpenter.

CASE FOR ANALYSIS Does This Milkshake Taste Funny?[105]

George Stein, a college student working for Eastern Dairy during the summer, was suddenly faced with an ethical dilemma. George had very little time to think about his choices, less than a minute. On the one hand, he could do what Paul told him to do, and his shift could go home on time. However, he found it tough to shake the gross mental image of all those innocent kids drinking milkshakes contaminated with pulverized maggots. If he chose instead to go against Paul, what would the guys say? He could almost hear their derisive comments already: "wimp . . . college kid. . . ."

Background

George Stein had lived his entire life in various suburbs of a major city on the East Coast. His father's salary as a manager provided the family with a solid middle-class lifestyle. His mother was a homemaker. George's major interests in life were the local teenage gathering place—a drive-in restaurant—hot rod cars, and his girlfriend, Cathy. He had not really wanted to attend college, but relentless pressure by his parents convinced him to try it for a year. He chose mechanical engineering as his major, hoping there might be some similarity between being a mechanical engineer and being a mechanic. After one year of engineering school, however, he has not seen any similarity yet. Once again this summer, his parents had to prod and cajole him to agree to return to school in the fall. They only succeeded by promising to give their blessing to his marriage to Cathy following his sophomore year.

George had worked at menial jobs each of the last four summers to satisfy his immediate need for dating and car money. He did manage to put away a bit to be used for spending money during the school year. He had saved very little for the day that he and Cathy would start their life together, but they planned for Cathy to support them with her earnings as a customer service representative until George either finished or quit school.

The day after George returned home this summer, he heard that Eastern Dairy might hire summer help. He applied at the local plant the next day. Eastern Dairy was unionized, and the wages paid were more than twice the minimum wage George had been paid on previous jobs, so he was quite interested in a position.

Eastern Dairy manufactured milkshake and ice cream mix for a number of customers in the metropolitan area. It sold the ice cream mix in 5- and 10-gallon containers to other firms, which then added the flavoring ingredients (e.g., strawberries or blueberries), packaged and froze the mix, and sold the ice cream under their own brand names. Eastern Dairy sold the milkshake mix in 5-gallon cardboard cartons, which contained a plastic liner. These packages were delivered to many restaurants in the area. The packaging was designed to fit into automatic milkshake machines used in many types of restaurants, including most fast-food restaurants and drive-ins.

George was elated when he received the call asking him to come to the plant on June 8. After a brief visit with the HR director, at which time George filled out the necessary employment forms, he was instructed to report for work at 11:00 P.M. that night. He was assigned to the night shift, working from 11:00 P.M. until 7:00 A.M. six nights per week—Sunday through Friday. With the regular wages paid at Eastern Dairy, supplemented by time-and-a-half pay for 8 hours of guaranteed overtime each week, George thought he could save a tidy sum before he had to return to school at the end of the first week in September.

When George reported to work, he discovered that there were no managers assigned to the night shift. The entire plant was run by a six-person crew of operators. One member of this crew, a young man named Paul Burnham, received each night's production orders from the day shift superintendent as the superintendent left for the day. Although Paul's status was no different from that of his five colleagues, the other crew members looked to him for direction. Paul passed the production orders to the mixer (who was the first stage of the production process) and kept the production records for the shift.

The production process was really quite simple. Mixes moved between various pieces of equipment (including mixing vats, pasteurizers, coolers, homogenizers, and filling machines) through stainless steel pipes suspended from the ceiling. All of the pipes had to be disassembled, thoroughly cleaned, and reinstalled by the conclusion of the night shift. This process took approximately one hour, so all the mix had to be run by 6:00 A.M. in order to complete the cleanup by the 7:00 A.M. quitting time. Paul and one other worker, Fred (the mixer), cleaned the giant mixing vats while the other four on the shift, including George, cleaned and reinstalled the pipes and filters.

George soon learned that Paul felt a sense of responsibility for completing all of the assigned work before the end of the shift. However, as long as that objective was achieved, he did not seem to care about what else went on during the shift. A great deal of story-telling and horseplay was the norm, but the work was always completed by quitting time. George was soon enjoying the easy camaraderie of the work group, the outrageous pranks they pulled on one another, and even the work itself.

George's position required that he station himself beside the conveyor in a large freezer room. He removed containers of mix as they came down the line and stacked them in the appropriate places. Periodically, Paul would decide that they had all worked hard enough and would shut down the line for a while so that they could engage in some non-work activity like joke telling, hiding each other's lunch boxes, or "balloon" fights. The balloons were actually the 5-gallon, flexible liners for the cardboard boxes in which the mix was sold.

While George did not relish being hit by an exploding bag containing 5 gallons of heavy mix, he found it great fun to lob one at one of his co-workers. The loss of 10 to 40 gallons of mix on a shift did not seem to concern anyone, and these fights were never curtailed. George quickly learned that management had only two expectations of the night shift. First, the shift was expected to complete the production orders each night. Second, management expected the equipment, including the pipes, to be spotlessly clean at the conclusion of the shift. Paul told George that inspectors from the county health department would occasionally drop by unannounced at the end of the shift to inspect the vats and pipes after they had been disassembled and scrubbed. Paul also told George that management would be very upset if the inspectors registered any complaints about cleanliness.

George did join the union but saw very little evidence of its involvement in the day-to-day operations of the plant. Labor relations seemed quite amicable, and George thought of the union only when he looked at a pay stub and noticed that union dues had been deducted from his gross pay. The difference George noticed in working for Eastern Dairy compared to his previous employers was not the presence of the union but the absence of management.

The Current Situation

Things seemed to be going quite well for George on the job—until a few minutes ago. The problem first surfaced when the milkshake mix that was being run started spewing out of one of the joints in the overhead pipe network. The pumps were shut down while George disassembled the joint to see what the problem was. George removed the filter screen from the pipe at the leaking joint and saw that it was completely packed with solid matter. Closer inspection revealed that maggots were the culprits. George hurriedly took the filter to Paul to show him the blockage. Paul did not seem too concerned and told George to clean the filter and reassemble the joint. When George asked how this could have happened, Paul said maggots occasionally got into the bags of certain ingredients that were stored in a warehouse at the back of the lot. "But you don't have to worry," said Paul. "The filters will catch any solid matter."

Feeling somewhat reassured, George cleaned the filter and reassembled the pipe. But still, the image of maggots floating in a milkshake was hard to shake. And, unfortunately for George, that was not the end of it.

Shortly after the pumps were restarted, the mix began to flow out of another joint. Once again, a filter plugged with maggots was found to be the cause.

For the second time, George cleaned the filter and reassembled the connection. This time Paul had seemed a bit more concerned as he noted that they barely had enough time to run the last 500 gallons remaining in the vats before they needed to clean up in preparation for the end of the shift.

Moments after the equipment was again restarted, another joint started to spew. When maggots were found to be clogging this filter, too, Paul called George over and told him to remove all five filters from the line so the last 500 gallons could be run without any filters. Paul laughed when he saw the shocked look on George's face.

"George," he said, "don't forget that all of this stuff goes through the homogenizer, so any solid matter will be completely pulverized. And when it's heated in the pasteurization process, any bacteria will be killed. No one will ever know about this, the company can save a lot of mix—that's money—and, most important, we can run this through and go home on time."

George knew that they would never get this lot packaged if they had to shut down every minute to clean filters, and there was no reason to believe it would not be this way for the rest of the run. The product had been thoroughly mixed in the mixing vats at the beginning of the process, which meant that contaminants would be distributed uniformly throughout the 500 gallons. George also knew that the 500 gallons of milkshake was very expensive. He did not think management would just want it dumped down the drain.

Finally, Paul was definitely right about one thing—removing all of the filters, a 10-minute job at most, would ensure that they could get everything cleaned up and be out on time.

As George walked to the first filter joint, he felt a knot forming in his stomach as he thought of kids drinking all of the milkshakes they were about to produce. He had already decided he would not have another milkshake for at least a month, in order to be absolutely sure that this batch was no longer being served at restaurants. After all, he did not know exactly which restaurants would receive this mix. As he picked up his wrench and approached the first pipe joint that contained a filter, he still could not help wondering if he should do or say something more.

Chapter 9 Workshop The Power of Ethics[106]

This exercise will help you to better understand the concept of ethics and what it means to you.

1. Spend about five minutes individually answering the four questions in right hand column.
2. Divide into groups of four to six members.
3. Have each group try to achieve consensus with answers to each of the four questions. For question 3, choose one scenario to highlight. You will have 20 to 40 minutes for this exercise, depending on the instructor.
4. Have groups share their answers with the whole class, after which the instructor will lead a discussion on ethics and its power in business.

Questions

1. In your own words, define the concept of ethics in one or two sentences.
2. If you were a manager, how would you motivate your employees to follow ethical behavior? Use no more than two sentences.
3. Describe a situation in which you were faced with an ethical dilemma. What was your decision and behavior? How did you decide to do that? Can you relate your decision to any concept in the chapter?
4. What do you think is a powerful ethical message for others? Where did you get it from? How will it influence your behavior in the future?

Notes

1. Steve Hamm, "A Passion For the Planet," *BusinessWeek* (August 21–28, 2006), 92–94; "Our Reason for Being," Patagonia website, http://www.patagonia.com/us/patagonia.go?assetid=2047&ln=140 (accessed September 8, 2011); Geoff Colvin, "The Defiant One," *Fortune* (April 30, 2007), 86–92; and Jad Mouawad, "New Culture of Caution at Exxon after Valdez," *The New York Times* (July 12, 2010), http://www.nytimes.com/2010/07/13/business/13bpside.html (accessed September 8, 2011).
2. Julia Boorstin, "Secret Recipe: J. M. Smucker," *Fortune* (January 12, 2004), 58–59.
3. For the story of Bear Stearns and its culture, see William D. Cohan, *House of Cards: A Tale of Hubris and Wretched Excess on Wall Street* (New York: Doubleday 2009); Chuck Leddy, "When Wall Street Bet the House," *Boston Globe,* March 28, 2009, G8; and Robin Sidel and Kate Kelly, "Bear Stearns a Year Later: From Fabled to Forgotten—Bear's Name, and Culture, Fade Away After J.P. Morgan's Fire-Sale Deal," *The Wall Street Journal,* March 14, 2009, B1.
4. Mark C. Bolino, William H. Turnley, and James M. Bloodgood, "Citizenship Behavior and the Creation of Social Capital in Organizations," *Academy of Management Review* 27, no. 4 (2002), 505–522; and Don Cohen and Laurence Prusak, *In Good Company: How Social Capital Makes Organizations Work* (Boston: Harvard Business School Press, 2001), 3–4.
5. W. Jack Duncan, "Organizational Culture: 'Getting a Fix' on an Elusive Concept," *Academy of Management Executive* 3 (1989), 229–236; Linda Smircich, "Concepts of Culture and Organizational Analysis," *Administrative Science Quarterly* 28 (1983), 339–358; and Andrew D. Brown and Ken Starkey, "The Effect of Organizational Culture on Communication and Information," *Journal of Management Studies* 31, no. 6 (November 1994), 807–828.
6. See Jon Katzenbach and Zia Khan, "Leading Outside the Lines," *Strategy + Business* (April 26, 2010), http://www.strategy-business.com/article/10204?gko=788c9 (accessed September 9, 2010) for the idea of the formal versus the informal organization.
7. Edgar H. Schein, "Organizational Culture," *American Psychologist* 45 (February 1990), 109–119.
8. James H. Higgins and Craig McAllaster, "Want Innovation? Then Use Cultural Artifacts That Support It," *Organizational Dynamics* 31, no. 1 (2002), 74–84.
9. Harrison M. Trice and Janice M. Beyer, "Studying Organizational Cultures through Rites and Ceremonials," *Academy of Management Review* 9 (1984), 653–669; Janice M. Beyer and Harrison M. Trice, "How an Organization's Rites Reveal Its Culture," *Organizational Dynamics* 15 (Spring 1987), 5–24; Steven P. Feldman, "Management in Context: An Essay on the Relevance of Culture to the Understanding of Organizational Change," *Journal of Management Studies* 23 (1986), 589–607; and Mary Jo Hatch, "The Dynamics of Organizational Culture," *Academy of Management Review* 18 (1993), 657–693.
10. This discussion is based on Edgar H. Schein, *Organizational Culture and Leadership*, 2nd ed. (Homewood, IL: Richard D. Irwin, 1992); and John P. Kotter and James L. Heskett, *Corporate Culture and Performance* (New York: Free Press, 1992).

11. Stacy Perman, "The Secret Sauce at In-N-Out Burger" (excerpt from *In-N-Out Burger: A Behind-the-Counter Look at the Fast-Food Chain That Breaks All the Rules*, published by HarperBusiness 2009), *BusinessWeek* (April 20, 2009), 68–69.
12. Larry Mallak, "Understanding and Changing Your Organization's Culture," *Industrial Management* (March–April 2001), 18–24.
13. Based on Gerry Johnson, "Managing Strategic Change—Strategy, Culture, and Action," *Long Range Planning* 25, no. 1 (1992), 28–36.
14. For an expanded list of various elements that can be used to assess or interpret corporate culture, see "10 Key Cultural Elements," sidebar in Micah R. Kee, "Corporate Culture Makes a Fiscal Difference," *Industrial Management* (November–December 2003), 16–20.
15. Gazi Islam and Michael J. Zyphur, "Rituals in Organizations: A Review and Expansion of Current Theory," *Group & Organization Management* 34, no. 1 (2009), 114–139; Trice and Beyer, "Studying Organizational Cultures through Rites and Ceremonials"; and Terrence E. Deal and Allan A. Kennedy, "Culture: A New Look through Old Lenses," *Journal of Applied Behavioral Science* 19 (1983), 498–505.
16. Leigh Buchanan, "Managing: Welcome Aboard. Now, Run!" *Inc.* (March 2010), 95–96.
17. Example reported in Don Hellriegel and John W. Slocum, Jr., *Management*, 7th ed. (Cincinnati, OH: South-Western, 1996), 537.
18. Trice and Beyer, "Studying Organizational Cultures through Rites and Ceremonials."
19. Chip Jarnagan and John W. Slocum, Jr., "Creating Corporate Cultures Through Mythopoetic Leadership," *Organizational Dynamics* 36, no. 3 (2007), 288–302
20. Joanne Martin, *Organizational Culture: Mapping the Terrain* (Thousand Oaks, CA: Sage Publications, 2002), 71–72.
21. Joann S. Lublin, "Theory & Practice: Keeping Clients by Keeping Workers; Unique Efforts to Encourage Employee Loyalty Pay Off for U.K. Ad Shop Mother," *The Wall Street Journal,* November 20, 2006, B3.
22. Buchanan, "Managing: Welcome Aboard. Now, Run!"
23. "FYI: Organization Chart of the Month," *Inc.* (April 1991), 14.
24. Neal E. Boudette, "Fiat CEO Sets New Tone at Chrysler," *The Wall Street Journal Online* (June 19, 2009), http://online.wsj.com/article/SB124537403628329989.html?utm_source=feedburner&utm_medium=feed&utm_campaign=Feed%3A+wsj%2Fxml%2Frss%2F3_7011+%28WSJ.com%3A+What%27s+News+US%29#mod=rss_whats_news_us (accessed September 12, 2011).
25. Gary Hamel with Bill Breen, *The Future of Management* (Boston: Harvard Business School Press, 2007).
26. Matt Moffett, "At InBev, a Gung-Ho Culture Rules; American Icon Anheuser, A Potential Target, Faces Prospect of Big Changes," *The Wall Street Journal,* May 28, 2008, B1; and Matt Moffett, "InBev's Chief Built Competitive Culture," *The Wall Street Journal,* June 13, 2008, B6.
27. Michelle Conlin, "Netflix: Flex to the Max," *BusinessWeek* (September 24, 2007), 72–74.
28. Johnson, "Managing Strategic Change—Strategy, Culture, and Action."
29. Jennifer A. Chatman and Sandra Eunyoung Cha, "Leading by Leveraging Culture," *California Management Review* 45, no. 4 (Summer 2003), 20–34; and Abby Ghobadian and Nicholas O'Regan, "The Link between Culture, Strategy, and Performance in Manufacturing SMEs," *Journal of General Management* 28, no. 1 (Autumn 2002), 16–34.
30. James R. Detert, Roger G. Schroeder, and John J. Mauriel, "A Framework for Linking Culture and Improvement Initiatives in Organizations," *Academy of Management Review* 25, no. 4 (2000), 850–863.
31. Based on Daniel R. Denison, *Corporate Culture and Organizational Effectiveness* (New York: Wiley, 1990), 11–15; Daniel R. Denison and Aneil K. Mishra, "Toward a Theory of Organizational Culture and Effectiveness," *Organization Science* 6, no. 2 (March–April 1995), 204–223; R. Hooijberg and F. Petrock, "On Cultural Change: Using the Competing Values Framework to Help Leaders Execute a Transformational Strategy," *Human Resource Management* 32 (1993), 29–50; and R. E. Quinn, *Beyond Rational Management: Mastering the Paradoxes and Competing Demands of High Performance* (San Francisco: Jossey-Bass, 1988).
32. Moffett, "InBev's Chief Built Competitive Culture."
33. Janet Wiscombe, "SAS," *Workforce Management* (October 2010), 36–38; and "100 Best Companies to Work For 2011: SAS," *Fortune*, http://money.cnn.com/magazines/fortune/best-companies/2011/snapshots/1.html (accessed September 12, 2011).
34. Rekha Balu, "Pacific Edge Projects Itself," *Fast Company* (October 2000), 371–381.
35. Bernard Arogyaswamy and Charles M. Byles, "Organizational Culture: Internal and External Fits," *Journal of Management* 13 (1987), 647–659.
36. Paul R. Lawrence and Jay W. Lorsch, *Organization and Environment* (Homewood, IL: Irwin, 1969).
37. Scott Kirsner, "Designed for Innovation," *Fast Company* (November 1998), 54, 56.
38. Chatman and Cha, "Leading by Leveraging Culture"; and Jeff Rosenthal and Mary Ann Masarech, "High-Performance Cultures: How Values Can Drive Business Results," *Journal of Organizational Excellence* (Spring 2003), 3–18.
39. Ghobadian and O'Regan, "The Link between Culture, Strategy and Performance"; G. G. Gordon and N. DiTomaso, "Predicting Corporate Performance from Organizational Culture," *Journal of Management Studies* 29, no. 6 (1992), 783–798; and G. A. Marcoulides and R. H. Heck, "Organizational Culture and Performance: Proposing and Testing a Model," *Organization Science* 4 (1993), 209–225.
40. John P. Kotter and James L. Heskett, *Corporate Culture and Performance* (New York: The Free Press, 1992); and Kee, "Corporate Culture Makes a Fiscal Difference."
41. Tressie Wright Muldrow, Timothy Buckley, and Brigitte W. Schay, "Creating High-Performance Organizations in the Public Sector," *Human Resource Management* 41, no. 3 (Fall 2002), 341–354.
42. Liz Robbins, "Embattled BP Chief Takes In Yacht Race," *The New York Times,* June 20, 2010, A20; Sarah Lyall, "In BP's Record, A History of Boldness and Blunders," *The New*

York Times, July 13, 2010, A1; and Guy Chazan, "BP's Safety Drive Faces Rough Road," *The Wall Street Journal,* February 1, 2011, A1.
43. Kotter and Heskett, *Corporate Culture and Performance.*
44. "Core Value: Teamwork," segment in Leigh Buchanan, "2011 Top Small Company Workplaces: Core Values," *Inc.* (June 2011), 60–74; and "Our Story," Menlo Innovations website, http://www.menloinnovations.com/our-story/history and http://www.menloinnovations.com/our-story/culture (accessed September 12, 2011).
45. Robert W. Clement, "Just How Unethical Is American Business?" *Business Horizons* 49 (2006), 313–327.
46. David Carr, "Troubles That Money Can't Dispel," *The New York Times,* July 18, 2011, B1.
47. Mike Esterl, "Executive Decision: In Germany, Scandals Tarnish Business Elite," *The Wall Street Journal,* March 4, 2008, A1; and Martin Fackler, "The Salaryman Accuses," *The New York Times,* June 7, 2008, C1.
48. Gordon F. Shea, *Practical Ethics* (New York: American Management Association, 1988); Linda K. Treviño, "Ethical Decision Making in Organizations: A Person–Situation Interactionist Model," *Academy of Management Review* 11 (1986), 601–617; and Linda Klebe Treviño and Katherine A. Nelson, *Managing Business Ethics: Straight Talk about How to Do It Right,* 2nd ed. (New York: John Wiley & Sons Inc., 1999).
49. This discussion of the sources of individual ethics is based on Susan H. Taft and Judith White, "Ethics Education: Using Inductive Reasoning to Develop Individual, Group, Organizational, and Global Perspectives," *Journal of Management Education* 31, no. 5 (October 2007), 614–646.
50. James B. Stewart, "Bribery, But Nobody Was Charged," *The New York Times,* June 25, 2011, B1.
51. Dawn-Marie Driscoll, "Don't Confuse Legal and Ethical Standards," *Business Ethics* (July–August 1996), 44.
52. LaRue Tone Hosmer, *The Ethics of Management,* 2nd ed. (Homewood, IL: Irwin, 1991).
53. Brian Griffiths, "Markets Can't Be Improved by Rules, Only by Personal Example," *The Times,* April 9, 2009, 30.
54. Some of these incidents are from Hosmer, *The Ethics of Management.*
55. Linda K. Treviño and Katherine A. Nelson, *Managing Business Ethics: Straight Talk about How to Do It Right* (New York: John Wiley & Sons, Inc., 1995), 4.
56. N. Craig Smith, "Corporate Social Responsibility: Whether or How?" *California Management Review* 45, no. 4 (Summer 2003), 52–76; and Eugene W. Szwajkowski, "The Myths and Realities of Research on Organizational Misconduct," in James E. Post, ed., *Research in Corporate Social Performance and Policy,* vol. 9 (Greenwich, CT: JAI Press, 1986), 103–122.
57. Reported in Beckey Bright, "How More Companies Are Embracing Social Responsibility as Good Business," *The Wall Street Journal,* March 10, 2008, R3.
58. Sarah E. Needleman, "The Latest Office Perk: Getting Paid to Volunteer," *The Wall Street Journal,* April 29, 2008, D1; "Habitat for Humanity," Whirlpool Corporation website, http://www.whirlpoolcorp.com/responsibility/building_communities/habitat_for_humanity.aspx (accessed September 13, 2011); Bruce Horovitz, "Pepsi Is Dropping Out of Schools Worldwide by 2012," *USA Today* (March 16, 2011), http://www.usatoday.com/money/industries/food/2010-03-16-pepsicutsschoolsoda_N.htm (accessed September 13, 2011); Kate O'Sullivan, "Virtue Rewarded," *CFO* (October 2006), 46–52.
59. Michael E. Porter and Mark R. Kramer, "Creating Shared Value: How to Reinvent Capitalism—and Unleash a Wave of Innovation and Growth," *Harvard Business Review* (January–February 2011), 62–77.
60. Ibid.
61. Geoffrey B. Sprinkle and Laureen A. Maines, "The Benefits and Costs of Corporate Social Responsibility," *Business Horizons* 53 (2010), 445–453; O'Sullivan, "Virtue Rewarded"; Bright, "How More Companies Are Embracing Social Responsibility as Good Business"; and Oliver Falck and Stephan Heblich, "Corporate Social Responsibility: Doing Well By Doing Good," *Business Horizons* 50 (2007), 247–254.
62. Survey by the Sustainability Advisory Group on 'What Regional Leaders in the Middle East Think About Corporate Social Responsibility,' reported in "75 Percent of Business Leaders Believe That CSR Grows Business," *Al Bawaba,* May 31, 2010.
63. Study reported in Andreas B. Eisingerich and Gunjan Bhardwaj, "Does Social Responsibility Protect the Company Name?" *National Post,* May 31, 2011, FP7.
64. Philipp Schreck, "Reviewing the Business Case for Corporate Social Responsibility: New Evidence and Analysis," *Journal of Business Ethics* (October 2011), 167–188; Curtis C. Verschoor and Elizabeth A. Murphy, "The Financial Performance of Large U.S. Firms and Those with Global Prominence: How Do the Best Corporate Citizens Rate?" *Business and Society Review* 107, no. 2 (Fall 2002), 371–381; Homer H. Johnson, "Does It Pay to Be Good? Social Responsibility and Financial Performance," *Business Horizons* (November–December 2003), 34–40; Quentin R. Skrabec, "Playing By the Rules: Why Ethics Are Profitable," *Business Horizons* (September–October 2003), 15–18; Marc Gunther, "Tree Huggers, Soy Lovers, and Profits," *Fortune* (June 23, 2003), 98–104; and Dale Kurschner, "5 Ways Ethical Business Creates Fatter Profits," *Business Ethics* (March–April 1996), 20–23. Also see various studies reported in Lori Ioannou, "Corporate America's Social Conscience," *Fortune,* special advertising section (May 26, 2003), S1–S10.
65. Verschoor and Murphy, "The Financial Performance of Large U.S. Firms."
66. Phred Dvorak, "Theory & Practice: Finding the Best Measure of 'Corporate Citizenship,'" *The Wall Street Journal,* July 2, 2007, B3; and Gretchen Morgenson, "Shares of Corporate Nice Guys Can Finish First," *The New York Times,* April 27, 2003, Section 3, 1.
67. Sprinkle and Maines, "The Benefits and Costs of Corporate Social Responsibility"; and Daniel W. Greening and Daniel B. Turban, "Corporate Social Performance as a Competitive Advantage in Attracting a Quality Workforce," *Business and Society* 39, no. 3 (September 2000), 254.
68. Needleman, "The Latest Office Perk."
69. Christopher Marquis, "Doing Well and Doing Good," *The New York Times,* July 13, 2003, Section 3, 2; and Joseph Pereira, "Career Journal: Doing Good and Doing

Well at Timberland," *The Wall Street Journal,* September 9, 2003, B1.
70. Reported in Needleman, "The Latest Office Perk."
71. "The Socially Correct Corporate Business," segment in Leslie Holstrom and Simon Brady, "The Changing Face of Global Business," *Fortune*, special advertising section (July 24, 2000), S1–S38.
72. Remi Trudel and June Cotte, "Does Being Ethical Pay?" *The Wall Street Journal,* May 12, 2008, R4.
73. *Corporate Ethics: A Prime Business Asset* (New York: The Business Round Table, February 1988).
74. Treviño and Nelson, *Managing Business Ethics*, 201.
75. Gary R. Weaver, Linda Klebe Treviño, and Bradley Agle, "'Somebody I Look Up To': Ethical Role Models in Organizations," *Organizational Dynamics* 34, no. 4 (2005), 313–330; Andrew W. Singer, "The Ultimate Ethics Test," *Across the Board* (March 1992), 19–22; Ronald B. Morgan, "Self and Co-Worker Perceptions of Ethics and Their Relationships to Leadership and Salary," *Academy of Management Journal* 36, no. 1 (February 1993), 200–214; and Joseph L. Badaracco Jr., and Allen P. Webb, "Business Ethics: A View from the Trenches," *California Management Review* 37, no. 2 (Winter 1995), 8–28.
76. This definition is based on Robert J. House, Andre Delbecq, and Toon W. Taris, "Value Based Leadership: An Integrated Theory and an Empirical Test" (working paper).
77. Stephanie Armour, "CEO Helps People Keep Their Homes; That's CitiMortgage Chief's Personal Goal," *USA Today,* April 27, 2009, B4; Ruth Simon, "Citi to Allow Jobless to Pay Less on Mortgages for a Time," *The Wall Street Journal Europe,* March 4, 2009, 17; and Sanjiv Das, "Viewpoint: Early Intervention Can Stem Foreclosures," *American Banker* (December 10, 2008), 11.
78. As quoted in Arkadi Kuhlmann, "Culture-Driven Leadership," *Ivey Business Journal* (March-April 2010), http://www.iveybusinessjournal.com/topics/leadership/culture-driven-leadership (accessed September 13, 2011).
79. Thomas J. Peters and Robert H. Waterman, Jr., *In Search of Excellence* (New York: Harper & Row, 1982); and Kuhlmann, "Culture-Driven Leadership."
80. Carol Hymowitz, "CEOs Must Work Hard to Maintain Faith in the Corner Office" (In the Lead column), *The Wall Street Journal,* July 9, 2002, B1.
81. Based on Weaver et al., "'Somebody I Look Up To.'"
82. Alan Yuspeh, "Do the Right Thing," *CIO* (August 1, 2000), 56–58.
83. Treviño and Nelson, *Managing Business Ethics*, 212.
84. Beverly Geber, "The Right and Wrong of Ethics Offices," *Training* (October 1995), 102–118.
85. Janet P. Near and Marcia P. Miceli, "Effective Whistle-Blowing," *Academy of Management Review* 20, no. 3 (1995), 679–708.
86. Jene G. James, "Whistle-Blowing: Its Moral Justification," in Peter Madsen and Jay M. Shafritz, eds., *Essentials of Business Ethics* (New York: Meridian Books, 1990), 160–190; and Janet P. Near, Terry Morehead Dworkin, and Marcia P. Miceli, "Explaining the Whistle-Blowing Process: Suggestions from Power Theory and Justice Theory," *Organization Science* 4 (1993), 393–411.
87. Christine Seib and Alexandra Frean, "Lehman Whistleblower Lost Job Month After Speaking Out," *The Times,* March 17, 2010.
88. "Setting the Standard," Lockheed Martin's website, *http://www.lockheedmartin.com/exeth/html/code/code.html* (accessed August 7, 2001).
89. Katharina Bart, "UBS Lays Out Employee Ethics Code," *The Wall Street Journal* (January 12, 2010), http://online.wsj.com/article/SB10001424052748704586504574653901865050062.html?KEYWORDS=%22Ubs+lays+out+employee+ethics+code%22 (accessed January 15, 2010).
90. Carl Anderson, "Values-Based Management," *Academy of Management Executive* 11, no. 4 (1997), 25–46.
91. Ronald E. Berenbeim, *Corporate Ethics Practices* (New York: The Conference Board, 1992).
92. James Weber, "Institutionalizing Ethics into Business Organizations: A Model and Research Agenda," *Business Ethics Quarterly* 3 (1993), 419–436.
93. Mark Henricks, "Ethics in Action," *Management Review* (January 1995), 53–55; Dorothy Marcic, *Management and the Wisdom of Love* (San Francisco: Jossey-Bass, 1997); and Beverly Geber, "The Right and Wrong of Ethics Offices," *Training* (October 1995), 102–118.
94. Susan J. Harrington, "What Corporate America Is Teaching about Ethics," *Academy of Management Executive* 5 (1991), 21–30.
95. Jerry G. Kreuze, Zahida Luqmani, and Mushtaq Luqmani, "Shades of Gray," *Internal Auditor* (April 2001), 48.
96. David Scheer, "For Your Eyes Only; Europe's New High-Tech Role: Playing Privacy Cop to the World," *The Wall Street Journal* (October 10, 2003), A1, A16; John W. Miller, "Yahoo Cookie Plan in Place," *The Wall Street Journal* (March 19, 2011), http://online.wsj.com/article/SB10001424052748703512404576208700813815570.html (accessed September 13, 2011); and Jennifer Valentino-Devries and Emily Steel, "'Cookies' Cause Bitter Backlash," *The Wall Street Journal,* September 2010, B1.
97. S. C. Schneider, "National vs. Corporate Culture: Implications for Human Resource Management," *Human Resource Management* (Summer 1988), 239; and Terence Jackson, "Cultural Values and Management Ethics: A 10-Nation Study," *Human Relations* 54, no. 10 (2001), 1267–1302.
98. Vijay Govindarajan, reported in Gail Dutton, "Building a Global Brain," *Management Review* (May 1999), 34–38.
99. K. Matthew Gilley, Christopher J. Robertson, and Tim C. Mazur, "The Bottom-Line Benefits of Ethics Code Commitment," *Business Horizons* 53 (2010), 31–37.
100. Homer H. Johnson, "Corporate Social Audits—This Time Around," *Business Horizons* (May–June 2001), 29–36.
101. Cassandra Kegler, "Holding Herself Accountable," *Working Woman* (May 2001), 13; and Louisa Wah, "Treading the Sacred Ground," *Management Review* (July–August 1998), 18–22.
102. David S. Hilzenrath, "Justice Department, SEC Cracking Down on U.S. Companies Engaging in Bribery Abroad," *The Washington Post* (March 21, 2011), http://www.washingtonpost.com/business/economy/justice-department-sec-cracking-down-on-us-companies-engaging-in-bribery-abroad/2011/03/21/ABMlMXLB_story.html (accessed

March 24, 2011); Andrew E. Kramer, "Ikea Fires 2 Officials in Russia Bribe Case," *The New York Times* (February 16, 2010), http://www.nytimes.com/2010/02/16/business/global/16ikea.html (accessed September 13, 2011); and Ellen Byron, "Avon Bribe Investigation Widens," *The Wall Street Journal,* May 5, 2011, B1.

103. Copyright 1996 by Dorothy Marcic. All rights reserved.
104. Based on Gary Yukl, "Consolidated Products," in *Leadership in Organizations*, 4th ed. (Englewood Cliffs, NJ: Prentice-Hall, 1998), 66–67; John M. Champion and John H. James, "Implementing Strategic Change," in *Critical Incidents in Management: Decision and Policy Issues*, 6th ed. (Homewood, IL: Irwin, 1989), 138–140; and William C. Symonds, "Where Paternalism Equals Good Business," *BusinessWeek* (July 20, 1998), 16E4, 16E6.
105. This case was prepared by Roland B. Cousins, LaGrange College, and Linda E. Benitz, InterCel, Inc., as a basis for class discussion and not to illustrate either effective or ineffective handling of an administrative situation. The names of the firm and individuals and the location involved have been disguised to preserve anonymity. The situation reported is factual. The authors thank Anne T. Lawrence for her assistance in the development of this case. Faculty members in nonprofit institutions are encouraged to reproduce this case for distribution to their students without charge or written permission. All other rights are reserved jointly to the author and the North American Case Research Association (NACRA). Reprinted by permission from the *Case Research Journal*. Copyright 1997 by Roland B. Cousins and Linda E. Benitz and the North American Case Research Association. All rights reserved.
106. Adapted by Dorothy Marcic from Allayne Barrilleaux Pizzolatto's "Ethical Management: An Exercise in Understanding Its Power," *Journal of Management Education* 17, no. 1 (February 1993), 107–109.

Chapter 10

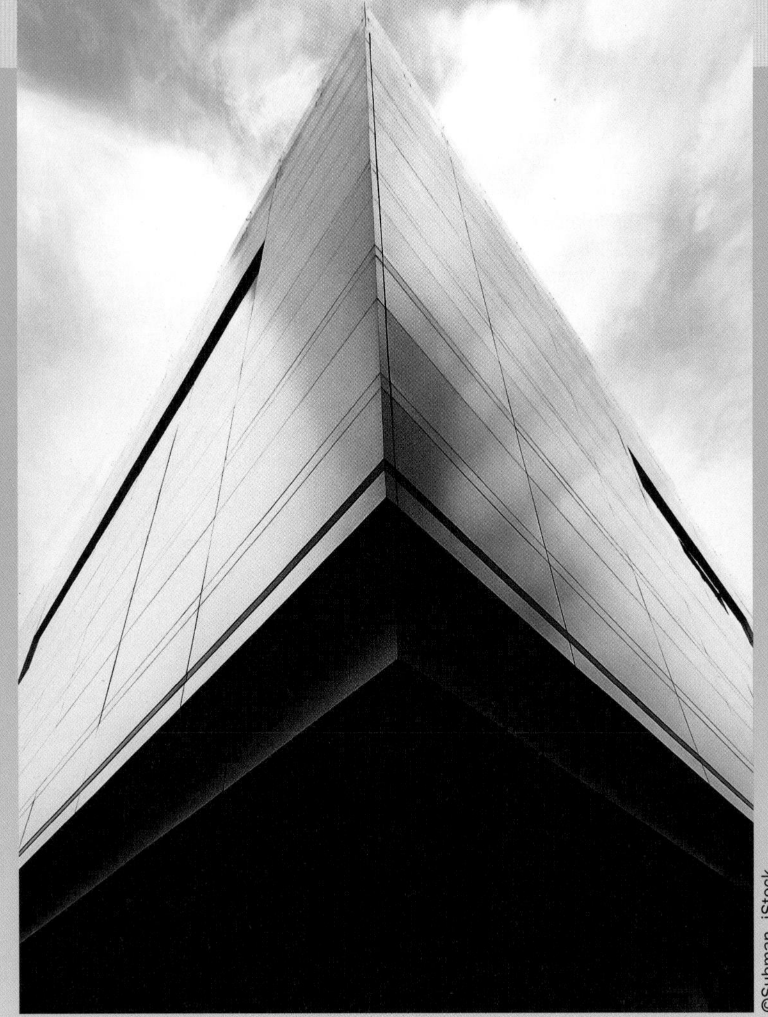

Organizational Innovation

Learning Objectives

After reading this chapter you should be able to:

1. Describe the types of strategic change.
2. Explain the necessary elements for successful organizational change.
3. Understand techniques for encouraging technology change.
4. Discuss the horizontal coordination model for new products.
5. Demonstrate how innovation speed provides competitive advantage.
6. Describe the dual-core approach to organizational change.
7. Explain the techniques for bringing about culture change in organizations.
8. Understand barriers to change and techniques for overcoming resistance.

Before reading this chapter, please check whether you agree or disagree with each of the following statements:

1 **The most important aspect for creating an innovative company is requiring people to come up with new ideas.**

I AGREE _____ I DISAGREE _____

2 **Asking customers what they want is the best way to create new products that will be successful in the marketplace.**

I AGREE _____ I DISAGREE _____

3 **Changing a company's culture is probably one of the hardest jobs a manager can undertake.**

I AGREE _____ I DISAGREE _____

Denise Chudy is a sales team leader at Google, and Aaron Lichtig is a brand manager at Procter & Gamble (P&G), but recently the two have been spending a lot of time together. They are among the two dozen or so Google and P&G employees who are involved in a job-swapping program whereby they sit in on each other's staff training programs and participate in high-level business meetings. What's the point? The job-swapping strategy is all in the name of spurring innovation. P&G, one of the most successful companies in the world at traditional marketing, knows it needs new approaches to reach a new generation of consumers, while Google knows it needs to find better ways of tapping into the advertising dollars of large, traditional companies like P&G.[1]

Every company faces a challenge in keeping up with changes in the external environment. New discoveries, new inventions, and new approaches quickly replace standard ways of doing things. Tremendous leaps in technology have revolutionized the way we live. Many of us now text and tweet and "friend" people online more often than we interact with them face to face. The pace of change is revealed in the fact that the parents of today's college-age students grew up without iPods, social networking, global positioning systems, Kindles, streaming video, and even the Internet. As teenagers, they couldn't have imagined communicating instantly with people around the world, carrying all their favorite music with them wherever they went, or downloading an entire book onto a device as small as a notepad. High-tech industries seem to change every nanosecond, so companies such as Apple, Google, Facebook, Intel, and Twitter are continually innovating to keep up. But companies in all industries face greater pressures for innovation today. Organizations such as Procter & Gamble, Tata Group, Walmart, Sony, and McDonald's are searching for any innovation edge they can find. Bob Jordon, head of technology and strategy at Southwest Airlines, spoke for managers all over the world when he said, "We have to innovate to survive."[2]

Purpose of This Chapter

This chapter explores how organizations change and how managers direct the innovation and change process. First we look at the forces driving a need for change in today's organizations. The next section describes the four types of change—technology, product, structure, people—occurring in organizations, and how to manage change successfully. The chapter then describes the organization structure and management approach for facilitating each type of change. Management techniques for influencing both the creation and implementation of change are also covered. The final section of the chapter looks at barriers to change and implementation techniques managers can use to overcome resistance.

The Strategic Role of Change

If there is one theme or lesson that emerges from previous chapters, it is that organizations must run fast to keep up with changes taking place all around them. Large organizations must find ways to act like small, flexible organizations. Manufacturing firms need to reach out for new digital manufacturing technology and service firms for new information technology (IT). Today's organizations must keep themselves open to continuous innovation, not only to prosper but merely to survive in a world of disruptive change and increasingly stiff competition.

Innovate or Perish

As illustrated in Exhibit 10.1, a number of environmental forces drive this need for major organizational change.[3] Powerful forces associated with advancing technology, international economic integration, shifting economic conditions and sovereign debt, and the growing power of Arab countries and the BRIC nations (Brazil, Russia, India, and China) have brought about an uncertain globalized economy that affects every business, from the largest to the smallest, creating more threats as well as more opportunities.

As illustrated in Exhibit 10.1, the environment creates demands for three types of change.[4] *Episodic change* is what many long-time managers are accustomed to. This type of change occurs occasionally, with periods of relative stability, and managers can respond with technical, product, or structural changes as needed. Most organizations today, however, experience *continuous change* because of a rapidly shifting environment. This type of change occurs frequently, with fewer and shorter periods of stability. Managers embrace change as an ongoing organizational process, using research and development (R&D) to build a flow of new products and services to meet shifting needs. In many industries today, the environment has become so turbulent that managers encounter *disruptive change*. Disruptive change results from sudden shocks and surprises that radically change an industry's rules of the game for producers and consumers. Some disruptive change results from new competition. CDs all but wiped out the phonograph industry, and now Apple's iPod and streaming music from companies such as Europe's Spotify are threatening the same fate for CDs. Netflix's approach to delivering movies through the mail and via streaming was a disruptive change for Blockbuster, which ultimately filed for bankruptcy. Amazon.com's model of selling books over the Internet created

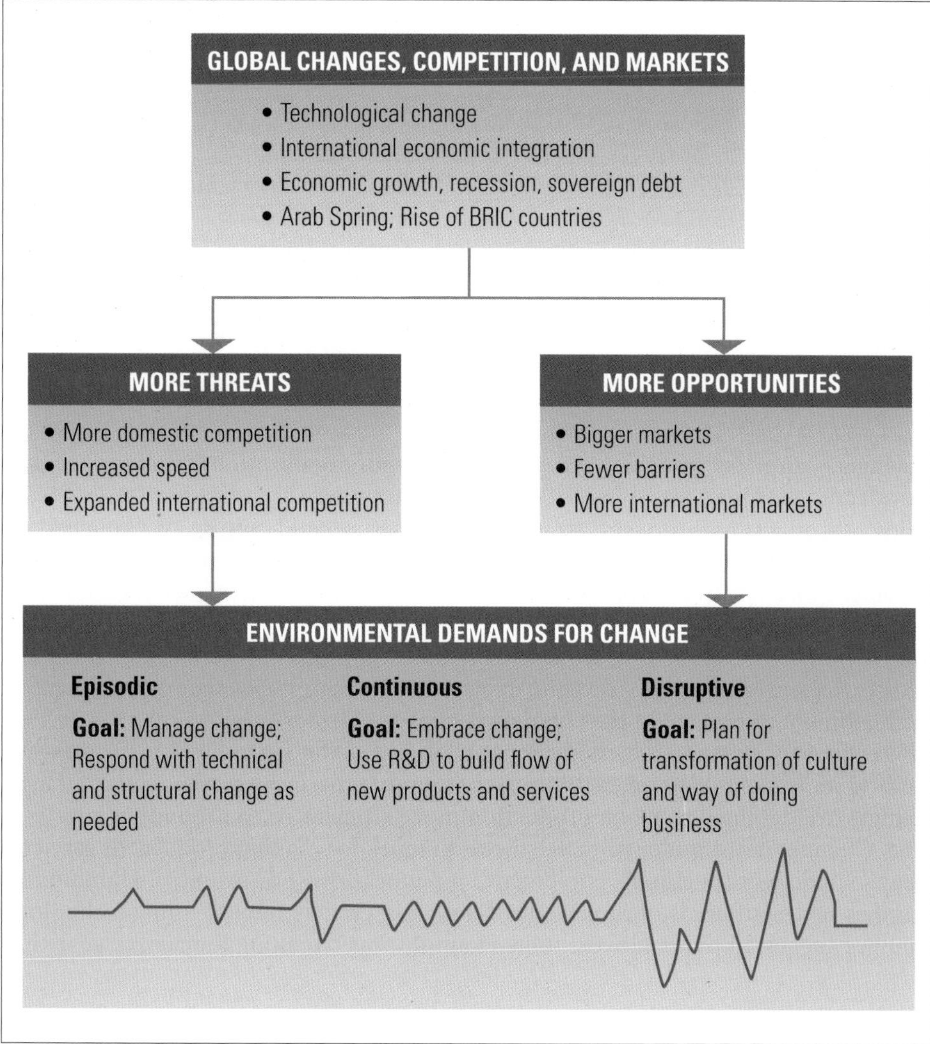

EXHIBIT 10.1
Forces Driving the Need for Major Organizational Change

Source: Based on John P. Kotter, *The New Rules: How to Succeed in Today's Post-Corporate World* (New York: The Free Press, 1995); and Joseph McCann, "Organizational Effectiveness: Changing Concepts for Changing Environments," *Human Resource Planning* 27, no. 1 (2004), 42–50.

disruptive change in the bookselling and publishing industries, and the Kindle and other e-readers are pushing that disruption even further.[5] Disruptive change can also result from natural or man-made disasters, such as the earthquake and tsunami in Japan, the September 11, 2001 terrorist attacks in the United States, or the mortgage crisis and meltdown in the financial services industry. When an organization faces disruptive change, managers often must plan for a total transformation of the company's culture and way of doing business.

For most companies, change, rather than stability, is the norm today. Whereas change once occurred incrementally and infrequently, today it is dramatic and constant. A key ingredient in the success of companies such as Hyundai, Coca-Cola Amazon, Samsung Electronics, and India's fast-growing Tata Group has been their passion for embracing and creating change. Each year, *BusinessWeek* publishes a list of the 50 Most Innovative Companies, and these companies all made the top 25 on the most recent list. The list named the following organizations as the top 10 most innovative companies in the world:[6]

1. Apple
2. Google
3. Microsoft
4. IBM
5. Toyota
6. Amazon
7. LG Electronics
8. BYD (the first Chinese company to make the list)
9. General Electric
10. Sony

Strategic Types of Change

Managers can focus on four types of change within organizations to achieve strategic advantage. These four types of change are summarized in Exhibit 10.2 as technology, products and services, strategy and structure, and culture. We touched on overall leadership and organizational vision in Chapter 3 and in the previous chapter on corporate culture. These factors provide an overall context within which the four types of change serve as a competitive wedge to achieve an advantage in the international environment. Each company has a unique configuration of products and services, strategy and structure, culture, and technologies that can be focused for maximum impact upon the company's chosen markets.[7]

Technology changes are changes in an organization's production process, including its knowledge and skill base, that enable distinctive competence. These changes are designed to make production more efficient or to produce greater volume. Changes in technology involve the techniques for making products or services. They include work methods, equipment, and workflow. For example, Hammond's Candies saves hundreds of thousands of dollars a year by implementing technology changes suggested by employees. One example was tweaking a machine gear that

EXHIBIT 10.2
The Four Types of Change Provide a Strategic Competitive Wedge

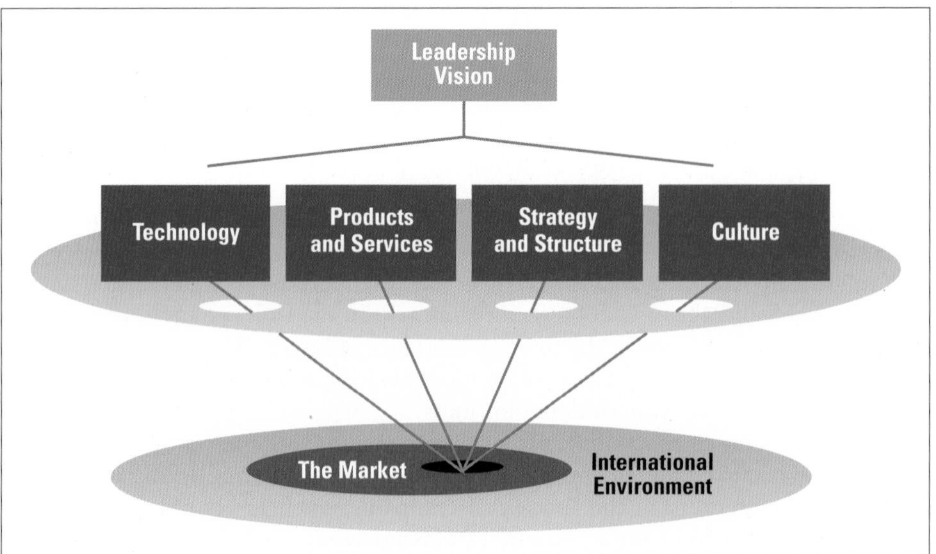

Source: Republished with permission of Academy of Management (NY), from Joseph E. McCann, "Design Principles for an Innovating Company," *Academy of Management Executive* 5, no. 2 (1991), 76–93; permission conveyed through Copyright Clearance Center, Inc.

reduced the number of employees needed on an assembly line from five to four. Another idea was a new way to package candy canes that would protect them from getting broken while en route to stores.[8]

Product and service changes pertain to the product or service outputs of an organization. New products include small adaptations of existing products or entirely new product lines. New products and services are normally designed to increase the market share or to develop new markets, customers, or clients. To expand market share, China's BYD (which stands for Build Your Dreams) introduced a new hybrid car that can be recharged by plugging into a standard home outlet as well as an all-electric car built in partnership with Germany's Daimler. BYD has been selling conventional gas-powered cars mostly in China for 15 years, but it is now selling both electrics and hybrids in the United States and Europe as well.[9] An example of a new service designed to reach new markets and customers comes from India's Tata Consultancy Services. The company's mKrishi service delivers weather information and crop advice to farmers in rural India via cell phone. The service brings together existing technologies, such as remote sensors, voice-enabled text messaging, and camera phones, in a new way to serve a new market.[10]

BRIEFCASE

As an organization manager, keep this guideline in mind:

Recognize that the four types of change are interdependent and that changes in one area often require changes in others.

Strategy and structure changes pertain to the administrative domain in an organization. The administrative domain involves the supervision and management of the organization. These changes include changes in organization structure, strategic management, policies, reward systems, labor relations, coordination devices, management information and control systems, and accounting and budgeting systems. Strategy, structure, and system changes are usually top-down—that is, mandated by top management—whereas product and technology changes often come from the bottom up. At StockPot, a division within the Campbell Soup Company that makes fresh refrigerated soup for the food service industry, former general manager Ed Carolan and his management team changed the strategy to focus more on large grocery retailers. To make the strategy successful, they identified a new set of key performance metrics to track how effectively the company was meeting goals of competitive costs, high quality, and great service. The changes were highly effective for improving the division's financial performance.[11] An example of a top-down structure change comes from ICU Medical Inc., where Dr. George Lopez, founder and CEO, made the decision to implement self-directed teams, even though some managers and employees at first hated the idea. This change also proved to be successful in the long run.[12]

Culture changes refer to changes in the values, attitudes, expectations, beliefs, abilities, and behavior of employees. Culture changes pertain to changes in how employees think; these are changes in mindset rather than technology, structure, or products. The following profile describes how Cathy Lanier is changing the culture of the Washington, D. C. Metropolitan Police Department.

IN PRACTICE

Washington, D.C. Metropolitan Police

"We went from beating people up, wrestling them, handcuffing them, to 'How do we prevent these things from happening?'" said Al Durham, assistant police chief in Washington, D.C. His boss, Cathy Lanier, came into the job of police chief with a goal of changing the culture of crime fighting. She tries hard not to let supervisors and administrators get between her and the beat cops, and she pushes everyone in the department to get close to the people who are involved in and hurt by crime. "Even as a patrol cop, if you work hard, if you focus, you can make major changes in people's lives every single day," Lanier says.

Lanier gives out her business card (and often her private cell phone number) to everyone she meets, and she seeks the advice of people on the front lines of crime fighting. "I hate chain of command," Lanier says about her leadership style. She wants to make sure people inside and outside the department can take their concerns, gripes, or advice directly to her. Lanier has been sharply criticized for some of her decisions, but she doesn't care. The goals she cares about are building trust with local neighborhoods and beat cops, and stopping crime.

Altering ingrained attitudes and habits is difficult, but Lanier has brought significant change to the culture of the Metropolitan Police by believing in and supporting cops from the lowest to the highest level of the force, articulating values that emphasize building trust and preventing crime, and having the courage to do what she thinks is right.[13]

Culture change can be particularly difficult because people don't change their attitudes and beliefs easily. Culture was discussed in detail in the previous chapter, and we will talk about culture change in more detail later in this chapter.

The four types of change in Exhibit 10.2 are interdependent—a change in one often means a change in another. A new product may require changes in the production technology, or a change in structure may require new employee skills. For example, when Shenandoah Life Insurance Company acquired new computer technology to process claims, the technology was not fully used until clerks were restructured into teams of five to seven members that were compatible with the technology. The structural change was an outgrowth of the technology change. Organizations are interdependent systems, and changing one part often has implications for other parts of the organization.

Elements for Successful Change

Regardless of the type or scope of change, there are identifiable stages of innovation, which generally occur as a sequence of events, though innovation stages may overlap.[14] In the research literature on innovation, **organizational change** is considered the adoption of a new idea or behavior by an organization.[15] **Organizational innovation**, in contrast, is the adoption of an idea or behavior that is new to the organization's industry, market, or general environment.[16] The first organization to introduce a new product is considered the innovator, and organizations that copy it are considered to adopt changes. For purposes of managing change, however, the terms *innovation* and *change* will be used interchangeably because the **change process** within organizations tends to be identical whether a change is early or late with respect to other organizations in the environment. Innovations typically are assimilated into an organization through a series of steps or elements. Organization members first become aware of a possible innovation, evaluate its appropriateness, and then evaluate and choose the idea.[17] The required elements of successful change are summarized in Exhibit 10.3. For a change to be successfully implemented, managers must make sure each element occurs in the organization. If one of the elements is missing, the change process will fail.

1. *Ideas.* Change is an outward expression of ideas. No company can remain competitive without new ideas.[18] An idea is a new way of doing things. It may be a new product or service, a new management concept, or a new procedure

EXHIBIT 10.3
Sequence of Elements for Successful Change

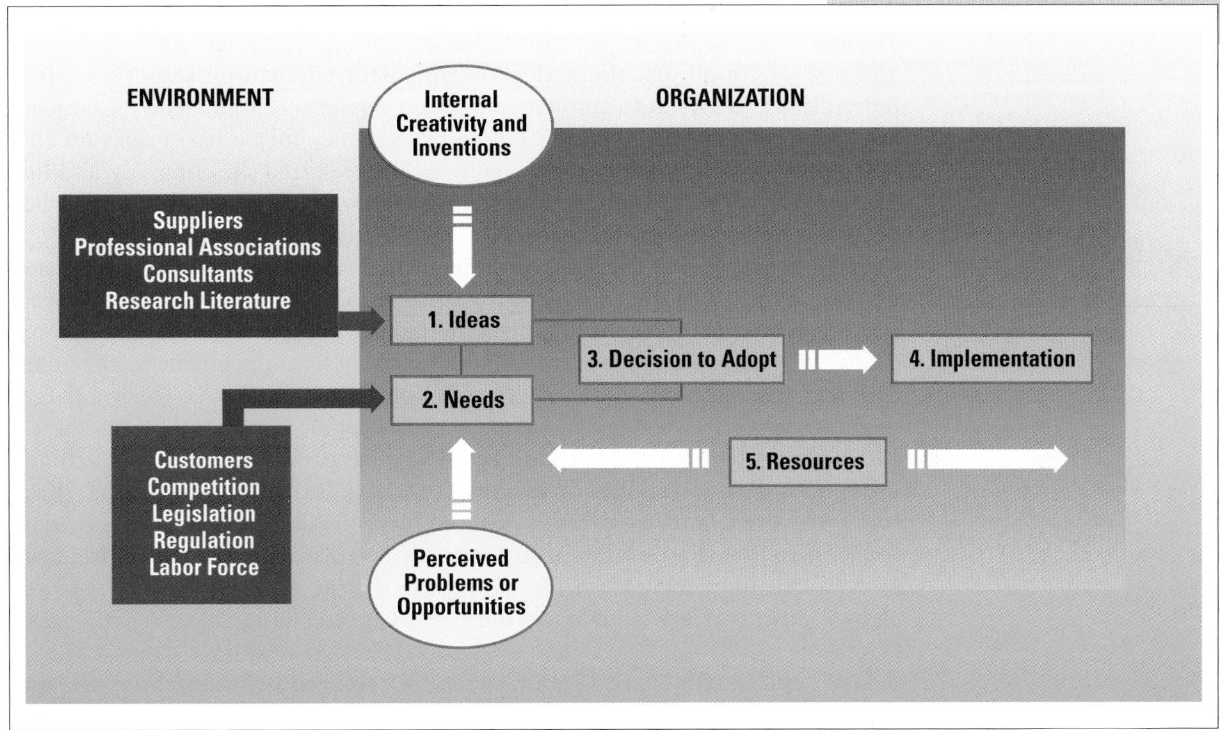

for working together in the organization. Ideas can come from within or from outside the organization. Internal creativity is a dramatic aspect of organizational change. **Creativity** is the generation of novel ideas that may meet perceived needs or respond to opportunities. For example, an employee at Boardroom Inc., a publisher of books and newsletters, came up with the idea of cutting the dimensions of the company's books by a quarter inch. Managers learned that the smaller size would reduce shipping rates, and implementation of the idea led to annual savings of more than $500,000.[19] Some techniques for spurring internal creativity are to increase the diversity within the organization, make sure employees have plenty of opportunities to interact with people different from themselves, give people time and freedom for experimentation, and support risk-taking and learning.[20] Eli Lilly, the Indianapolis-based pharmaceutical company, holds "failure parties" to commemorate brilliant, efficient scientific work that nevertheless resulted in failure. The company's scientists are encouraged to take risks and look for alternative uses for failed drugs. Lilly's osteoporosis drug Evista was a failed contraceptive. Strattera, which treats attention deficit/hyperactivity disorder, had been unsuccessful as an antidepressant. The blockbuster impotence drug Viagra was originally developed to treat severe heart pain.[21]

2. *Need.* Ideas are generally not seriously considered unless there is a perceived need for change. A perceived need for change occurs when managers see a gap between actual performance and desired performance in the organization.

Managers try to establish a sense of urgency so that others will understand the need for change. Sometimes a crisis provides an undoubted sense of urgency. In many cases, however, there is no crisis, so managers have to recognize a need and communicate it to others.[22] A study of innovativeness in industrial firms, for example, suggests that organizations that encourage close attention to customers and market conditions and actively support entrepreneurial activity produce more ideas and are more innovative.[23] Managers at the Walt Disney Company are trying to create those conditions to keep Disney theme parks relevant to a new generation of digitally savvy visitors. They realized the company had lost touch with today's customers, providing ho-hum, passive rides in an era when people expect instant gratification and customized experiences.[24]

3. *Decision to adopt.* The decision to adopt occurs when managers or other decision makers choose to go ahead with a proposed idea. Key managers and employees need to be in agreement to support the change. For a major organizational change, the decision might require the signing of a legal document by the board of directors. For a small change, a middle manager or lower-level manager might be authorized to make the decision to adopt an idea.
4. *Implementation.* Implementation occurs when organization members actually use a new idea, technique, or behavior. Materials and equipment may have to be acquired, and workers may have to be trained to use the new idea. Implementation is a very important step because without it, previous steps are to no avail. Implementation of change is often the most difficult part of the change process. Until people use the new idea, no change has actually taken place.
5. *Resources.* Human energy and activity are required to bring about change. Change does not happen on its own; it requires time and resources, for both creating and implementing a new idea. Employees have to provide energy to see both the need and the idea to meet that need. Someone must develop a proposal and provide the time and effort to implement it. Most innovations go beyond ordinary budget allocations and require special funding. Some companies use task forces, as described in Chapter 2, to focus resources on a change. Others set up seed funds or venture funds that employees with promising ideas can tap into. At Eli Lilly, a "blue sky fund" pays researchers for working on projects that don't appear to make immediate commercial sense.[25]

BRIEFCASE

As an organization manager, keep these guidelines in mind:

Make sure every change undertaken has a definite need, idea, adoption decision, implementation strategy, and resources. Avoid failure by not proceeding until each element is accounted for.

One point about Exhibit 10.3 is especially important. Needs and ideas are listed simultaneously at the beginning of the change sequence. Either may occur first. Many organizations adopted the computer, for example, because it seemed a promising idea for improving efficiency. The search for a vaccine against the HIV virus, on the other hand, was stimulated by a severe need. Whether the need or the idea occurs first, for the change to be accomplished, each of the steps in Exhibit 10.3 must be completed.

Technology Change

In today's business world, any company that isn't continually developing, acquiring, or adapting new technology will likely be out of business in a few years. Managers can create the conditions to encourage technology changes. However, organizations face a contradiction when it comes to technology change because the conditions that promote new ideas are not generally the best for implementing those ideas for routine production. An innovative organization is characterized by flexibility and empowered employees and the absence of rigid work rules.[26] As discussed earlier in this book, an organic, free-flowing organization is typically associated with change and is considered the best organization form for adapting to a chaotic environment. Complete the questionnaire in this chapter's "How Do You Fit the Design?" to see if you have characteristics associated with innovativeness.

The flexibility of an organic organization is attributed to people's freedom to be creative and introduce new ideas. Organic organizations encourage a bottom-up innovation process. Ideas bubble up from middle- and lower-level employees because they have the freedom to propose ideas and to experiment. A mechanistic structure, in contrast, stifles innovation with its emphasis on rules and regulations, but it is often the best structure for efficiently producing routine products. The challenge for

How Do You Fit the Design?

ARE YOU INNOVATIVE?

Think about your current life. Indicate whether each of the following items is Mostly True or Mostly False for you.

	Mostly True	Mostly False
1. I am always seeking new ways to do things.	___	___
2. I consider myself creative and original in my thinking and behavior.	___	___
3. I rarely trust new gadgets until I see whether they work for people around me.	___	___
4. In a group or at work I am often skeptical of new ideas.	___	___
5. I typically buy new foods, gear, and other innovations before other people do.	___	___
6. I like to spend time trying out new things.	___	___
7. My behavior influences others to try new things.	___	___
8. Among my co-workers, I will be among the first to try out a new idea or method.	___	___

Scoring: To compute your score on the Personal Innovativeness scale, add the number of Mostly True answers to items 1, 2, 5, 6, 7, and 8 and the Mostly False answers to items 3 and 4.

Interpretation: *Personal Innovativeness* reflects the awareness of a need to innovate and a readiness to try new things. Innovativeness is also thought of as the degree to which a person adopts innovations earlier than other people in the peer group. Innovativeness is considered a positive quality for people in creative companies, creative departments, venture teams, or corporate entrepreneurship. A score of 6–8 indicates that you are very innovative and likely are one of the first people to adopt changes. A score of 4–5 would suggest that you are average or slightly above average in innovativeness compared to others. A score of 0–3 means that you may prefer the tried and true and hence are not excited about new ideas or innovations. As a manager, a high score suggests you will emphasize innovation and change.

Source: Based on H. Thomas Hurt, Katherine Joseph, and Chester D. Cook, "Scales for the Measurement of Innovativeness," *Human Communication Research* 4, no. 1 (1977), 58–65; and John E. Ettlie and Robert D. O'Keefe, "Innovative Attitudes, Values, and Intentions in Organizations," *Journal of Management Studies* 19, no. 2 (1982), 163–182.

managers is to create both organic and mechanistic conditions within the organization to achieve both innovation and efficiency. To attain both aspects of technological change, many organizations use an ambidextrous approach.

The Ambidextrous Approach

Recent thinking has refined the idea of organic versus mechanistic structures with respect to innovation creation versus innovation utilization. Organic characteristics such as decentralization and employee freedom are excellent for initiating ideas, but these same conditions often make it hard to implement a change because employees are less likely to comply. Employees can ignore the innovation because of decentralization and a generally loose structure.

How does an organization solve this dilemma? One remedy is for the organization to use an **ambidextrous approach**—to incorporate structures and management processes that are appropriate to both the creation and the implementation of innovation.[27] Another way to think of the ambidextrous approach is to look at the organization design elements that are important for *exploring* new ideas versus the design elements that are most suitable for *exploiting* current capabilities.[28] Exploration means encouraging creativity and developing new ideas, whereas exploitation means implementing those ideas to produce routine products. The organization can be designed to behave in an organic way for exploring new ideas and in a mechanistic way to exploit and use the ideas. Exhibit 10.4 illustrates how one department is structured organically to explore and develop new ideas and another department is structured mechanistically for routine implementation of innovations. Research indicates that organizations that use an ambidextrous approach by designing for both exploration and exploitation perform better and are significantly more successful in launching innovative new products or services.[29]

For example, a study of long-established Japanese companies such as Honda and Canon that have succeeded in breakthrough innovations found that these companies use an ambidextrous approach.[30] To develop ideas related to a new technology, the companies assign teams of young staff members who are not entrenched in the "old way of doing things" to work on the project. The teams are headed by an esteemed elder and are charged with doing whatever is needed to develop new ideas and products, even if it means breaking rules that are important in the larger organization for implementing the new ideas.

EXHIBIT 10.4
Division of Labor in the Ambidextrous Organization

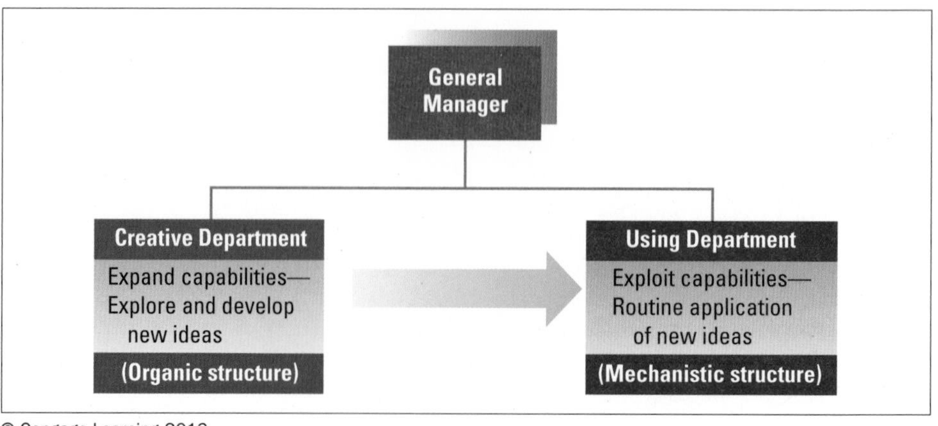

Techniques for Encouraging Technology Change

Some of the techniques used by companies to maintain an ambidextrous approach are switching structures, separate creative departments, venture teams, corporate entrepreneurship, and collaborative teams.

Switching Structures. **Switching structures** means an organization creates an organic structure when such a structure is needed for the initiation of new ideas.[31] Some of the ways organizations have switched structures to achieve the ambidextrous approach are as follows:

- Philips Manufacturing, a building materials producer based in Ohio, each year creates up to 150 transient teams—made up of members from various departments—to develop ideas for improving Philips products and work methods. After five days of organic brainstorming and problem solving, the company reverts to a more mechanistic structure to implement the changes.[32]
- Managers at Gardetto's, a snack-food business acquired by General Mills in 1999, would send small teams of workers to Eureka Ranch for two and a half days of "fun and freedom." Part of each day would be for play, such as Nerf gun battles; then the teams would participate in brainstorming exercises with the idea of generating as many new ideas as possible by the end of the day. After two and a half days, the group returned to the regular organizational structure to put the best of the ideas into action.[33]
- The NUMMI plant, a Toyota–GM joint venture in Fremont, California that operated from 1984 to 2010, created a separate, organically organized, cross-functional subunit, called the Pilot Team, to design production processes for new car and truck models. When the model moved into production, workers returned to their regular jobs on the shop floor.[34]

Each of these organizations found creative ways to be ambidextrous, establishing organic conditions for developing new ideas in the midst of more mechanistic conditions for implementing and using those ideas.

BRIEFCASE

As an organization manager, keep these guidelines in mind:

Facilitate frequent changes in internal technology by adopting an organic organizational structure. Give technical personnel freedom to analyze problems and develop solutions or create a separate, organically structured department or venture group to conceive and propose new ideas. Encourage a bottom-up flow of ideas and make sure they get heard and acted upon by management.

Creative Departments. In many large organizations the initiation of innovation is assigned to separate **creative departments**.[35] Staff departments such as research and development (R&D), engineering, design, and systems analysis create changes for adoption in other departments. Departments that initiate change are organically structured to facilitate the generation of new ideas and techniques. Departments that use those innovations tend to have a mechanistic structure more suitable for efficient production.

One example of a creative department is the research lab at Oksuka Pharmaceutical Company. To get the kind of creative spirit that is willing to try new things and look for the unexpected, Oksuka's president Tatsuo Higuchi says its research labs "put a high value on weird people."[36] However, in the department that manufactures drugs, where routine and precision is important, a pharmaceutical company would prefer to have less-unusual people who are comfortable following rules and standard procedures.

Another type of creative department is the **idea incubator**, an increasingly popular way to facilitate the development of new ideas within the organization. An idea incubator provides a safe harbor where ideas from employees throughout the organization can be developed without interference from company bureaucracy or politics.[37] Companies as diverse as Boeing, Adobe Systems, Yahoo!, Ziff-Davis, and UPS are using incubators to support the development of creative ideas.

Venture Teams. **Venture teams** are a technique used to give free rein to creativity within organizations. Venture teams are often given a separate location and facilities so they are not constrained by organizational procedures. A venture team is like a small company within a large company. Numerous organizations have used the venture team concept to free creative people from the bureaucracy of a large corporation.[38] Mike Lawrie, CEO of London-based software company Misys, for example, created a separate unit for Misys Open Source Solutions, a venture aimed at creating a potentially disruptive technology in the health care industry. Even at the height of the financial crisis, Lawrie protected the autonomy of the Open Source team so creative people would have the time and resources to work on new software that holds the promise of seamless data exchange among hospitals, physicians, insurers, and others involved in the health care system.[39]

One type of venture team is called a *skunkworks*.[40] A **skunkworks** is a separate, small, informal, highly autonomous, and often secretive group that focuses on breakthrough ideas for the business. The original skunkworks was created by Lockheed Martin more than 50 years ago and is still in operation. The essence of a skunkworks is that highly talented people are given the time and freedom to let creativity reign.

A variation of the venture team concept is the **new-venture fund**, which provides financial resources for employees to develop new ideas, products, or businesses. At Pitney Bowes, for example, the New Business Opportunity (NBO) program provides funding for teams to explore potentially lucrative but unproven ideas. The NBO program is intended to generate a pipeline of new businesses for the mail and document management services company. Similarly, Royal Dutch Shell puts 10 percent of its R&D budget into the GameChanger program, which provides seed money for innovation projects that are highly ambitious, radical, or long term and would get lost in the larger product development system.[41]

Corporate Entrepreneurship. Corporate entrepreneurship attempts to develop an internal entrepreneurial spirit, philosophy, and structure that will produce a higher-than-average number of innovations. Corporate entrepreneurship may involve the use of creative departments and new venture teams, but it also attempts to release the creative energy of all employees in the organization. The most successful companies over the long term are ones in which innovation is an everyday way of thinking, an ongoing process rather than a one-time event. ING Direct has built entrepreneurship into the corporate culture. The company's list of guiding principles includes the guideline, "We will never be finished." Managers want people to always be inventing what's next.[42] Google tries hundreds of small experiments at any given time. The company intentionally puts out imperfect or unfinished products to test the response and get ideas for how to perfect them.[43] Many successful innovations start with small experiments rather than with grand ideas. This chapter's Book Mark describes how successful innovation results not from the "epiphanies of geniuses" but instead from a methodical process of experimentation and learning.

An important outcome of corporate entrepreneurship is to facilitate **idea champions**. These go by a variety of names, including *advocate, intrapreneur*, or *change agent*. Idea champions provide the time and energy to make things happen. They fight to overcome natural resistance to change and to convince others of the

BOOKMARK

10.0 HAVE YOU READ THIS BOOK?

Little Bets: How Breakthrough Ideas Emerge from Small Discoveries

By Peter Sims

Why are some companies so good at cranking out hot new products and services while others struggle to find innovative ideas that connect in the marketplace? In *Little Bets*, Peter Sims emphasizes that successful innovation isn't the result of a "Eureka!" moment experienced by a lone, creative employee, but rather the outcome of a disciplined approach to experimentation that depends on making lots of *little bets*. A little bet is a low-risk action taken to discover, test, and develop an idea affordably. Little bets "begin as creative possibilities that get iterated and refined over time, and they are particularly valuable when trying to navigate amid uncertainty, create something new, or attend to open-ended problems."

FROM CHRIS ROCK TO THE U.S. ARMY

Sims conducted extensive research into some great historical achievements and innovations, as well as the psychology of creativity and the field of design thinking. He also interviewed or observed dozens of people about their approach to creativity and innovation, including comedian Chris Rock, architect Frank Gehry, managers at Amazon, Pixar, Procter & Gamble, and Google, and the United States Army's counterinsurgency strategists. Sims describes numerous examples of little bets from these sources, including the following:

- *Get Booed Off the Stage.* When Chris Rock, one of the world's most popular comedians, is planning a new routine for a global tour or a big show, he begins by trying out ideas at small comedy clubs in front of audiences of 40 to 50 people. Rock shows up unannounced, talks with the audience conversationally, and watches for clues to where good ideas might lie. Most of the jokes he tells in the early shows fall flat, and it can be painful to watch as Rock loses his train of thought, tells rambling jokes that don't connect, and endures the sense of disillusionment from the audience. But there are usually a few lines every night that prove to be "ridiculously good." By the time Rock goes on tour, he has tried thousands of preliminary ideas, only a few of which make the final cut and become part of his routine.
- *Use Cheap Prototyping.* People at Procter & Gamble often cobble together product ideas using cardboard and duct tape and show them to potential users. They get better feedback when users have something concrete that they can see and feel. Other companies also put out crude preliminary versions of products or services to see how they work in practice or might be received in the marketplace.
- *Be Willing to Go Down Blind Alleys.* Continually trying new things through little bets is so important at Amazon.com that whether employees do so is a part of their performance reviews. Founder and CEO Jeff Bezos calls it "planting seeds," or "going down blind alleys." If you go down blind alleys, you often hit a dead end, but that's part of the critical learning process. Bezos and Amazon have endured intense criticism over the years for experiments that failed. But, oh, those that succeeded! Amazon is now a hugely successful company—and still making lots of little bets.
- *Keep Your Mind Wide Open.* When doing something new or uncertain, accept that "we rarely know what we don't know." Many of us have been taught to look for solutions to problems, an approach that emphasizes minimizing mistakes and avoiding failure. Innovation, though, depends on a process of discovery about problems we don't understand or don't even know exist. Not knowing what problems they were trying to solve was "the situation the U.S. Army has had to face when confronting Middle Eastern insurgents," Sims writes. General H. R. McMaster and other counterinsurgency strategists used a series of little bets, "doing things to discover what they should do."

DO STUFF AND LEARN FROM IT

Anyone can use little bets to unlock creative potential. The basic idea is to continually experiment and learn by doing. Sims describes six key elements of the little bets approach: fail quickly to learn fast; tap into the power of play; immerse yourself in the world to gain fresh ideas and insights; use insights to define specific problems or needs; be flexible in pursuing solutions; and repeat, refine, and test frequently. Little bets "are at the center of an approach to get to the right idea without getting stymied by perfectionism, risk-aversion, or excessive planning."

Little Bets: How Breakthrough Ideas Emerge from Small Discoveries, by Peter Sims, is published by The Free Press.

merit of a new idea.[44] The importance of the idea champion is illustrated by a fascinating fact discovered by Texas Instruments: When TI reviewed 50 successful and unsuccessful technical projects, it discovered that every failure was characterized by the absence of a volunteer champion. There was no one who passionately believed in the idea, who pushed the idea through every obstacle to make it work. TI took this finding so seriously that now its number-one criterion for approving new technical projects is the presence of a zealous champion.[45] Similarly, at SRI International, a contract research and development firm, managers use the saying "no champion, no product, no exception."[46] Research confirms that successful new ideas are generally those that are backed by someone who believes in the idea wholeheartedly and is determined to convince others of its value. Numerous studies support the importance of idea champions as a factor in the success of new products.[47]

Companies encourage idea champions by providing freedom and slack time to creative people. Companies such as IBM, Texas Instruments, General Electric, and 3M allow employees to develop new technologies without company approval. Sometimes referred to as *bootlegging*, the unauthorized research often pays big dividends. The talking educational toy Speak & Spell was developed "under the table" at TI beginning in the 1970s. The product was a hit, but more importantly, it contained TI's first digital-signal processing-chip, which grew into an enormous, highly profitable business when cell phones and other portable devices came along years later.[48]

Bottom-up Approach. In line with the concept of fostering corporate entrepreneurship, innovative companies recognize that many useful ideas come from the people who are daily doing the work, serving the customers, fighting off the competition, and figuring out how best to get their jobs done. Thus, companies that want to support innovation implement a variety of mechanisms, systems, and processes that encourage a bottom-up flow of ideas and make sure they get heard and acted upon by top executives.[49] Mike Hall, CEO of Borrego Solar Systems, holds internal "innovation challenge" contests on the company intranet to get his shy, introverted engineers to speak up with their ideas for improving the business. Employees vote on their favorites and the winner takes home a cash prize. One idea that was quickly implemented was using software that enables sales and engineering teams to collaborate.[50] At Intuit, managers sponsor Design for Delight (D4D) forums, typically attended by more than 1,000 employees. After the forums, teams are asked to identify the one thing they would do differently at the company. Two employees who had been at Intuit for only a few months came up with the idea of an online social network for the D4D initiative. In the first year, the network generated 32 ideas that made it to market.[51]

Other companies also use this approach, sometimes referred to as "innovation communities." Japanese pharmaceutical firm Eisai Company, for example, has held more than 400 innovation community forums since 2005 to focus on specific healthcare related issues. One idea that is now on the market in Japan is technology for dispensing medications in a jelly-like substance that Alzheimer's patients can easily swallow.[52] Many of today's successful innovators even bring in people from outside the organization. IBM held an online town-hall style meeting, called the Innovation Jam, inviting employees as well as clients, consultants, and employees' family members to an interactive online brainstorming session about new technology ideas.[53]

Just as important as creating ideas is turning them into action. "There's nothing worse for morale than when employees feel like their ideas go nowhere," says Larry Bennett, a professor of entrepreneurship. At Borrego Solar Systems, the CEO assigns each idea he wants to implement to an executive sponsor, and employees can track the progress of implementation on the intranet.[54] At Google, which allows engineers to spend 20 percent of their time on projects of their own choosing, managers realized that many ideas from employees were getting lost because the company didn't have processes for reviewing, prioritizing, and implementing the ideas. Employees with a new idea could lobby their immediate boss for time and resources, but the project could linger or die without getting any attention from top management. In response, executives established "innovation review" meetings, where managers present product ideas bubbling up from their divisions to top executives. It's a way to force management to focus on promising ideas at an early stage and give them the resources needed to turn them into successful products and services.[55]

1 The most important aspect for creating an innovative company is requiring people to come up with new ideas.

ANSWER: *Disagree.* New ideas are essential for innovation, but managers can't simply issue directives ordering people to come up with new ideas. Managers create the conditions that are conducive to both the creation of new ideas and their implementation. Organizing to sustain innovation is as important as organizing to spur creativity.

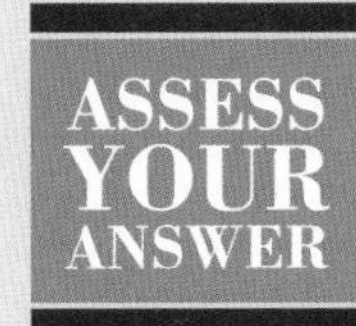

New Products and Services

Although the concepts just discussed are important to product and service as well as technology changes, other factors also need to be considered. In many ways, new products and services are a special case of innovation because they are used by customers outside the organization. Since new products are designed for sale in the environment, uncertainty about the suitability and success of an innovation is very high.

New Product Success Rate

Research has explored the enormous uncertainty associated with the development and sale of new products.[56] To understand what this uncertainty can mean to organizations, consider that Microsoft spent two years and hundreds of millions of dollars creating a new line of smartphones, called Kin One and Kin Two, then pulled them from the market after less than two months because no one was buying. And remember Zune, Microsoft's music player designed to compete with the iPod? If you don't, that's fine; neither does anyone else. Hewlett-Packard was losing so much money trying to compete with Apple's iPad that it pulled the plug on the TouchPad three months after launch. Electronics retailer Best Buy alone returned hundreds of thousands of the products because of low demand.[57] Products from companies in other industries can suffer the same fate. Pfizer invested more than $70 million in the development and testing of an anti-aging drug before it failed in the final testing stages. McDonald's Arch Deluxe hamburger, designed to appeal to "adult tastes," flopped despite millions invested in research and development and a $100 million advertising campaign.[58] Developing and producing products that fail is a part of business in all industries. Toy companies introduce thousands of new

EXHIBIT 10.5
New Product Success Rates

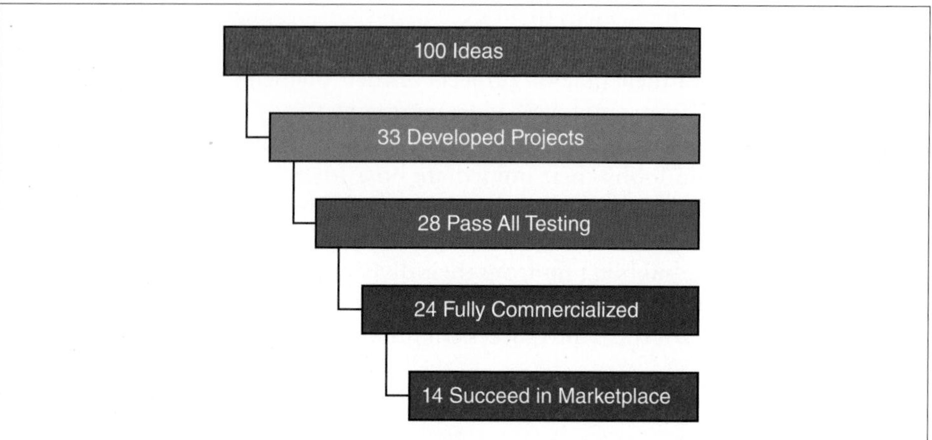

Source: Based on M. Adams and the Product Development and Management Association, "Comparative Performance Assessment Study 2004," available for purchase at http://www.pdma.org (search on CPAS). Results reported in Jeff Cope, "Lessons Learned—Commercialization Success Rates: A Brief Review," *RTI Tech Ventures* newsletter 4, no. 4 (December 2007).

products a year, and many of them fail. U.S. food companies put approximately 5,000 new products in supermarkets each year, but the failure rate of new food products is 70 to 80 percent.[59] Organizations take the risk because product innovation is one of the most important ways companies adapt to changes in markets, technologies, and competition.[60]

Although measuring the success of new products is tricky, a survey by the Product Development and Management Association (PDMA) sheds some light on the commercialization success rates of new products across a variety of industries.[61] PDMA compiled survey results from over 400 PDMA members. The findings about success rates are shown in Exhibit 10.5. On the average, only 28 percent of all projects undertaken in the R&D laboratories passed the testing stage, which means all technical problems were solved and the projects moved on to production. Less than one-fourth of all product ideas (24 percent) were fully marketed and commercialized, and only 14 percent achieved economic success.[62]

Reasons for New Product Success

The next question to be considered is: Why are some products more successful than others? Other studies indicate that innovation success is related to collaboration between technical and marketing departments. Successful new products and services seem to be technologically sound and also carefully tailored to customer needs.[63] A study called Project SAPPHO examined 17 pairs of new product innovations, with one success and one failure in each pair, and concluded the following:

1. Successful innovating companies had a much better understanding of customer needs and paid much more attention to marketing.
2. Successful innovating companies made more effective use of outside technology and outside advice, even though they did more work in-house.
3. Top management support in the successful innovating companies was from people who were more senior and had greater authority.

EXHIBIT 10.6
Horizontal Coordination Model for New Product Innovations

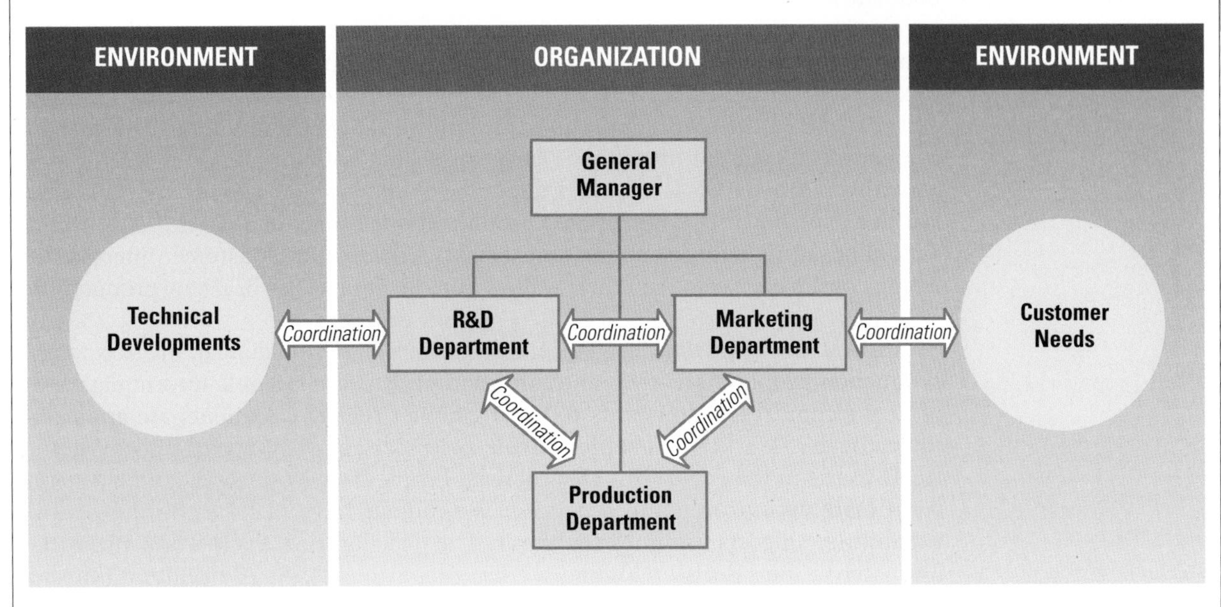

Thus there is a distinct pattern of tailoring innovations to customer needs, making effective use of technology, and having influential top managers support the project. These ideas taken together indicate that the effective design for new product innovation is associated with horizontal coordination across departments.

Horizontal Coordination Model

The organization design for achieving new product innovation involves three components—departmental specialization, boundary spanning, and horizontal coordination. These components are similar to the horizontal coordination mechanisms discussed in Chapter 2, such as teams, task forces, and project managers, and the differentiation and integration ideas discussed in Chapter 6. Exhibit 10.6 illustrates these components in the **horizontal coordination model.**

Specialization. The key departments in new product development are R&D, marketing, and production. The specialization component means that the personnel in all three of these departments are highly competent at their own tasks. The three departments are differentiated from each other and have skills, goals, and attitudes appropriate for their specialized functions.

Boundary Spanning. This component means each department involved with new products has excellent linkage with relevant sectors in the external environment. R&D personnel are linked to professional associations and to colleagues in other R&D departments. They are aware of recent scientific developments. Marketing personnel are closely linked to customer needs. They listen to what customers have to say, and they analyze competitor products and suggestions by distributors. One study compared companies with good product-development track records to those with poor track records and found that the best performers keep in close touch with customers throughout the product development process and carefully research what customers want and need.[64] Kimberly-Clark had amazing success with Huggies Pull-Ups because marketing researchers worked closely with customers in their own homes and recognized the emotional appeal of pull-on diapers for toddlers. By the time competitors caught on, Kimberly-Clark was selling $400 million worth of Huggies annually.[65] Procter & Gamble's product development teams conduct "transaction learning experiments," whereby they produce and sell small quantities of a new product online, at mall kiosks, and at amusement parks to gauge customer interest, thus letting consumers "vote with their wallets" on the desirability of a new product.[66]

Horizontal Coordination. This component means that technical, marketing, and production people share ideas and information. Research people inform marketing of new technical developments to learn whether the developments are applicable to customers. Marketing people provide customer complaints and information to R&D to use in the design of new products. People from both R&D and marketing coordinate with production because new products have to fit within production capabilities so costs are not exorbitant. The decision to launch a new product is ultimately a joint decision among all three departments. At Avocent, an information technology management company, managers redesigned the product development process so that programmers, testers, and customers work on the same team and follow a project from start to finish. After a spate of quality and safety issues and the recall of 8.5 million vehicles, Toyota revamped its process for developing new cars to increase communication across departments.[67] Horizontal coordination, using mechanisms such as cross-functional teams, increases both the amount and the variety of information for new product development, enabling the design of products that meet customer needs and circumventing manufacturing and marketing problems.[68] Corning used a horizontal linkage model to create a new product for the mobile phone industry.

Corning, Inc.

IN PRACTICE

If you have ever had a cell phone with a plastic screen, you probably know that the plastic can scratch and even break easily. A small team in Corning's specialty materials division spotted an opportunity. They began looking for a way that mobile phone screens could be made out of a super-strong but flexible glass that the company had originally attempted (unsuccessfully) to sell for automobile windshields in the 1960s. Just producing an experimental batch to gauge customer interest would cost as much as $300,000, but managers took the risk because the project had a strong idea champion.

Once the test run was completed and potential customers expressed excitement, managers had to move quickly. Corning took the project from concept to commercial success in an amazingly short period of time. One reason is that the company had both the right culture and the right systems. Corning divisions and departments know that top managers expect, support, and reward collaboration on promising new product launches. Innovation at Corning is managed not by lone inventors or small teams in silos, but rather by multidisciplinary groups all across the organization. The company has two units—the Corporate

Technology Council and the Growth and Strategy Council—that are charged with overseeing the innovation process and making sure departments effectively cooperate in new product development efforts that are sanctioned by management. Thus, employees from R&D, manufacturing, and sales quickly agreed to serve on the team developing the new glass product.

By 2010, Corning's cell phone glass, called Gorilla Glass, was used on more than three dozen mobile phones as well as some laptops and other devices. Gorilla Glass is projected to be a $500 million business by 2015.[69]

By using a horizontal linkage model for new product development, Corning has been highly effective in taking products from idea to success in the marketplace. Famous innovation failures—such as New Coke, Microsoft's Zune music player, and the U.S. Mint's Susan B. Anthony dollar, perhaps the most unpopular coin in American history—usually violate the horizontal linkage model. Employees fail to connect with customer needs and market forces or internal departments fail to adequately share needs and coordinate with one another. Research has confirmed a connection between effective boundary spanning that keeps the organization in touch with market forces, smooth coordination among departments, and successful product development.[70]

Open Innovation. Many successful companies include customers, strategic partners, suppliers, and other outsiders directly in the product and service development process. One of the hottest trends is *open innovation.*[71] In the past, most businesses generated their own ideas in-house and then developed, manufactured, marketed, and distributed them, which represents a closed innovation approach. Today, though, forward-looking companies are trying a different method. **Open innovation** means extending the search for and commercialization of new products beyond the boundaries of the organization and even beyond the boundaries of the industry.[72] Collaboration with other firms and with customers and other outsiders provides many benefits, including faster time to market, lower product development costs, improved quality, and better adaptation of products to customer needs. It can also stimulate stronger internal coordination across departments. Because open innovation requires the involvement of people from different areas of the company, it forces managers to set up stronger internal coordination and knowledge-sharing mechanisms.[73]

Booz & Company research shows that firms with robust open innovation capabilities are seven times more effective in terms of generating returns on their overall research and development investment than firms with weak capabilities.[74] Consumer products giant Procter & Gamble is probably the best-known proponent of open innovation. Some of the company's best-selling products, including the Swiffer SweeperVac, Olay Regenerist, and Mr. Clean Magic Eraser, were developed in whole or in part by someone outside the company. P&G get more than 50 percent of its innovation from outside company walls.[75] Even Apple, which has always been famously "closed" in many ways, has found a way to tap into the power of open innovation. The recently deceased CEO, Steve Jobs, maintained close control over the company's product design and development, and the company is tight-lipped about the principles that guided its decade-long journey from virtual irrelevance as a maker of computers to the world's largest technology company, with leading products in the hardware, software, music, video, communication, and e-publishing industries. Managers knew that success in some of these industries requires a more

BRIEFCASE

As an organization manager, keep these guidelines in mind:

Encourage marketing, research, and production departments to develop linkages to each other and to their environments when new products or services are needed. Consider bringing customers, suppliers, and others from outside the boundaries of the organization into the product development process.

open approach. For example, although the company sets guidelines and technological constraints, it allows anyone to create and market mobile applications for the iPhone in exchange for a small share of the revenue generated by the apps. Apple generates around $75 million in revenue a month through its App Store.[76]

Eli Lilly and Company set the standard in the pharmaceuticals industry with its InnoCentive "research without walls" approach. Lilly developed a network of external partners in biotechnology, academia, and other fields. Since 2001, more than 170,000 people from over 175 countries have participated in efforts to solve problems that had stumped Lilly's internal R&D staffs. Over that time period, more than 800 problems have been posted on the InnoCentive website, and almost 400 solutions have been found.[77]

The Internet has made it possible for companies such as Eli Lilly, Procter & Gamble, IBM, and General Electric to tap into ideas from around the world and let hundreds of thousands of people contribute to the innovation process, which is why some approaches to open innovation are referred to as *crowdsourcing*.[78] One company that has taken crowdsourcing to the extreme is online T-shirt retailer Threadless, now owned by skinnyCorp. Threadless sponsors design competitions on an online social network, where people socialize, blog, and discuss ideas. Members submit T-shirt designs by the hundreds each week and then vote on which ones they like best. Managers also built a website that lets Twitter followers suggest their favorite tweets for consideration as T-shirt slogans. In the first five months, the Twitter experiment attracted 100,000 submissions and 3.5 million votes, resulting in new designs that provided hundreds of thousands of dollars in additional revenue.[79]

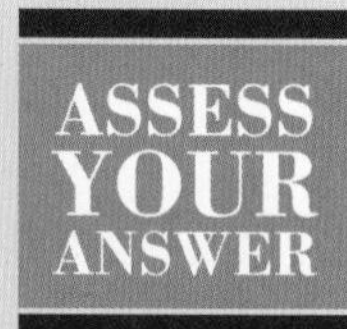

2 Asking customers what they want is the best way to create new products that will be successful in the marketplace.

ANSWER: *Agree or disagree.* It depends on the organization. Bringing customers into the product development process has been highly beneficial for many companies. However, many products developed based on what customers say they want do not succeed. In addition, some highly innovative companies, like Apple, believe relying too much on customer input limits the pie-in-the-sky thinking needed to create truly breakthrough products.

Achieving Competitive Advantage: The Need for Speed

In a survey conducted by IBM and *Industry Week* magazine, 40 percent of respondents identified collaborating with customers and suppliers as having the most significant impact on product development time-to-market.[80] The rapid development of new products and services can be a major strategic weapon in an ever-shifting global marketplace.[81]

Time-based competition means delivering products and services faster than competitors, giving companies a competitive edge. Clothing retailer Zara gets new styles into stores twice a week, for example. Russell Stover got a line of low-carb candies, called Net Carb, on store shelves within three months after perfecting the recipe, rather than the twelve months it usually takes candy companies to get a new product to market.[82] Speed is a cornerstone of Fiat-Chrysler CEO Sergio Marchionne's strategy for reviving Chrysler. Cost cutting by previous managers had led to a dearth of new products, and Marchionne knows Chrysler must catch up fast to stay competitive. The company introduced several new models in both 2011 and 2012 and also revamped older models to keep them fresh and stylish. Urgency and quick decision making are the new watchwords at Chrysler.[83]

Some companies use what are called *fast cycle teams* as a way to support highly important projects and deliver products and services faster than competitors. A fast cycle team is a multifunctional, and sometimes multinational, team that works under stringent timelines and is provided with high levels of company resources and empowerment to accomplish an accelerated product development project.[84]

Another critical issue is designing products that can compete on a global scale and successfully marketing those products internationally. Companies are trying to improve horizontal communication and collaboration across geographical regions, recognizing that they can pick up winning product ideas from customers in other countries. Many new product development teams today are global teams because organizations have to develop products that will meet diverse needs of consumers all over the world.[85]

Strategy and Structure Change

The preceding discussion focused on new production processes and products, which are based in the technology of an organization. The expertise for such innovation lies within the technical core and professional staff groups, such as research and engineering. This section turns to an examination of strategy and structure changes.

All organizations need to make changes in their strategies, structures, management processes, and administrative procedures from time to time. In the past, when the environment was relatively stable, most organizations focused on small, incremental changes to solve immediate problems or take advantage of new opportunities. However, over the past couple of decades, companies throughout the world have faced the need to make radical changes in strategy, structure, and management processes to adapt to new competitive demands.[86] Many organizations are cutting out layers of management and decentralizing decision making. This is one way Sergio Marchionne is speeding things up at Chrysler, for example. Marchionne cut layers of the hierarchy and created a flat organization in which the top 25 Chrysler executives report directly to him. They can reach him by phone or e-mail 24 hours a day seven days a week, and Marchionne makes decisions in minutes that used to take weeks or months traveling through the hierarchy. He also overhauled the management staff, firing some managers who were committed to staying stuck in the old way of doing things and promoting young managers who were hungry for rapid change and willing to put in the long hours to make it happen.[87]

There is a strong shift within organizations toward more horizontal structures, with teams of front-line workers empowered to make decisions and solve problems on their own. Some companies are breaking totally away from traditional organization forms and shifting toward virtual network strategies and structures. Numerous companies are reorganizing and shifting their strategies to incorporate e-business. These types of changes are the responsibility of the organization's top managers, and the overall process of change is typically different from the process for innovation in technology or new products.

The Dual-Core Approach

The **dual-core approach** to organizational change compares management and technical innovation. **Management innovation** refers to the adoption and implementation of a management practice, process, structure, strategy, or technique that is new to the organization and is intended to further organizational goals.[88] This type of change pertains to the design and structure of the organization itself, including restructuring, downsizing, teams, control systems, information systems, and departmental grouping. The implementation of a balanced scorecard, for example, would be a management innovation, as would the establishment of a joint venture for global expansion, as described in Chapter 5, or the shift to a virtual network organization structure, described in Chapter 2. One recent management innovation that many companies are adopting is *jugaad* (pronounced joo-gaardh). Jugaad basically refers to a management mindset used widely by Indian companies such as Tata Group and Infosys Technologies that strives to meet customers' immediate needs quickly and inexpensively. With research and development budgets strained in a difficult economy, it's an approach many U.S. managers are picking up on.[89]

BRIEFCASE

As an organization manager, keep these guidelines in mind:

Facilitate changes in strategy and structure by adopting a top-down approach. Use a mechanistic structure when the organization needs to adopt frequent management changes in a top-down fashion.

Research into management change suggests two things. First, management changes occur less frequently than do technical changes. Second, management changes occur in response to different environmental sectors and follow a different internal process than do technology-based changes.[90] The dual-core approach to organizational change identifies the unique processes associated with management change.[91] Organizations—schools, hospitals, city governments, welfare agencies, government bureaucracies, and many business firms—can be conceptualized as having two cores: a *technical core* and a *management core.* Each core has its own employees, tasks, and environmental domain. Innovation can originate in either core.

The management core is above the technical core in the hierarchy. The responsibility of the management core includes the structure, control, and coordination of the organization itself and concerns the environmental sectors of government, financial resources, economic conditions, human resources, and competitors. The technical core is concerned with the transformation of raw materials into organizational products and services and involves the environmental sectors of customers and technology.[92]

The point of the dual-core approach is that many organizations—especially nonprofit and government organizations—must adopt frequent management changes and need to be structured differently from organizations that rely on frequent technical and product changes for competitive advantage.

Organization Design for Implementing Management Change

The findings from research comparing management and technical change suggest that a mechanistic organization structure is appropriate for frequent management changes, including changes in goals, strategy, structure, control systems, and human resources.[93] Organizations that successfully adopt many management changes often have a larger administrative ratio, are larger in size, and are centralized and formalized compared with organizations that adopt many technical changes.[94] The reason is the top-down implementation of changes in response to changes in the

EXHIBIT 10.7
Dual-Core Approach to Organization Change

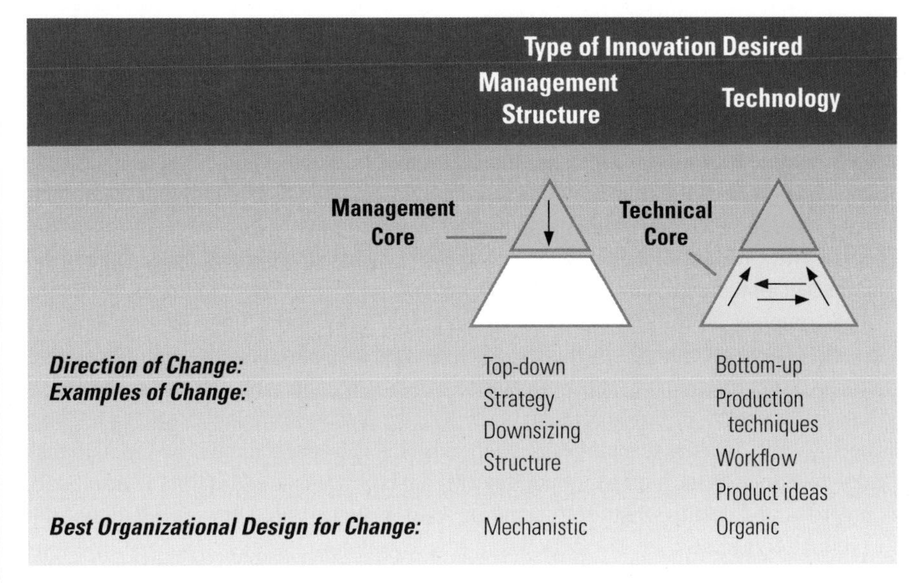

government, financial, or legal sectors of the environment. If an organization has an organic structure, lower-level employees have more freedom and autonomy and, hence, may resist top-down initiatives.

Type of Innovation Desired
Management Structure
Technology
Management Core
Technical Core
Direction of Change:
Examples of Change:
Top-down
Strategy
Downsizing
Structure
Bottom-up
Production techniques
Workflow
Product ideas
Best Organizational Design for Change:
Mechanistic
Organic

The innovation approaches associated with management versus technical change are summarized in Exhibit 10.7. Technical change, such as changes in production techniques and innovative technology for new products, is facilitated by an organic structure, which allows ideas to bubble upward from lower- and middle-level employees. Organizations that must adopt frequent management changes, in contrast, tend to use a top-down process and a mechanistic structure. For example, changes such as implementation of Six Sigma methods, application of the balanced scorecard, decentralization of decision making, or downsizing and restructuring are facilitated by a top-down approach.

Research into civil service reform found that the implementation of management innovation was extremely difficult in organizations that had an organic technical core. The professional employees in a decentralized agency could resist civil service changes. By contrast, organizations that were considered more bureaucratic and mechanistic in the sense of high formalization and centralization adopted management changes readily.[95]

What about business organizations that are normally technologically innovative in bottom-up fashion but suddenly face a crisis and need to reorganize? Or a technically innovative, high-tech firm that must reorganize frequently to accommodate changes in production technology or the environment? Technically innovative firms may suddenly have to restructure, reduce the number of employees, alter pay systems, disband teams, or form a new division.[96] The answer is to use a top-down change process. The authority for strategy and structure change lies with top management, who should initiate and implement the new strategy and structure to meet environmental circumstances. Employee input may be sought, but top managers have the responsibility to direct the change. For example, top managers at GlaxoSmithKline, the large pharmaceutical company with headquarters in the United Kingdom, implemented top-down change to improve drug discovery.

Glaxo-SmithKline

IN PRACTICE

Large pharmaceutical companies such as Pfizer, AstraZeneca, and GlaxoSmithKline have grown even larger over the past decade or so through mergers and acquisitions. Yet, while the increasing size brought power in sales and marketing, the growing bureaucracy hampered research and development (R&D) efforts. The amount of money big companies invested in R&D of new drugs has tripled over the past 15 years, but the number of new drugs has declined, with most new pharmaceuticals being invented by small biotechnology start-ups.

Andrew Witty, CEO of GlaxoSmithKline, decided to try an experimental approach that would get his R&D scientists thinking and acting more like those start-ups. He broke the R&D unit into small groups of 20 to 60 people, called Discovery Performance Units (DPUs). Each group has scientists from all disciplines working together and focusing their combined expertise on finding new drugs for specific types of diseases, such as cancer or auto-immune diseases. Previously, chemist David Wilson says he could go days on end without ever seeing a biologist. Now, he says, the mix of disciplines has led to quick decisions and productive brainstorming.

Witty gave the DPUs three-year budgets with specific goals and set up a review board to track progress and decide whether to continue funding them. The units were told that if they don't produce, they could be disbanded and employees terminated. "If we fail, there must be consequences that may go all the way to termination," said Moncef Slaoui, Glaxo's head of R&D.[97]

Most researchers at Glaxo welcomed the creation of the DPUs. Witty says morale in the research unit was "terrible" when he arrived. Implementing the new R&D approach has spurred an entrepreneurial drive and given people a chance to focus their energies on the most promising areas of research. If the units don't perform as needed to help the company discover cutting-edge drugs, Witty and other top managers may have to implement more difficult top-down changes by terminating employees and outsourcing more R&D work.

Top-down changes related to restructuring and downsizing can be painful for employees, so top managers should move quickly and authoritatively to make them as humane as possible.[98] A study of successful corporate transformations, which frequently involve painful changes, found that managers followed a fast, focused approach. When top managers spread difficult changes such as downsizing over a long time period, employee morale suffers and the change is much less likely to lead to positive outcomes.[99]

Top managers should also remember that top-down change means initiation of the idea occurs at upper levels and is implemented downward. It does not mean that lower-level employees are not educated about the change or allowed to participate in it.

Culture Change

Organizations are made up of people and their relationships with one another. Changes in strategy, structure, technologies, and products do not happen on their own, and changes in any of these areas involve changes in people as well. Employees must learn how to use new technologies, or market new products, or work effectively in interdisciplinary teams, as at GlaxoSmithKline. Sometimes achieving a new way of thinking requires a focused change in the underlying corporate cultural values and norms. Changing corporate culture fundamentally shifts how work is done in an organization and can lead to renewed commitment and empowerment of employees, as well as a stronger bond between the company and its customers.[100]

However, changing culture can be particularly difficult because it challenges people's core values and established ways of thinking and doing things. Mergers and acquisitions often illustrate how tough culture change can be. Consider an example from Japan. Yasuhiro Sato, the new CEO and president of Mizuho Financial Group, which was formed from the merger of Dai-Ichi, Fuji Bank, and Industrial Bank of Japan in 2002, says cultural differences between the units have created the biggest hurdle to integrating operations. Mizuho's structure, culture, and management systems have been under scrutiny since the bank suffered a prolonged computer system breakdown following the March 11, 2011 earthquake that hit Japan. Sato has vowed to create a unified corporate culture and speed the integration to prevent similar problems and improve Mizuho's financial performance, which is lagging that of other large Japanese banks.[101] Although cultural issues can sometimes make or break the success of a merger, many managers fail to consider culture as part of their merger and acquisition plans, says Chuck Moritt, a senior partner in Mercer's M&A consulting business.[102]

Forces for Culture Change

In addition to mergers, a number of other recent trends have contributed to a need for cultural makeovers at many companies. For example, reengineering and the shift to horizontal forms of organizing, which we discussed in Chapter 2, require greater focus on employee empowerment, collaboration, information sharing, and meeting customer needs, which means managers and employees need a new mindset. Mutual trust, risk-taking, and tolerance for mistakes become key cultural values in the horizontal organization.

Another force for culture change is the diversity of today's workforce. Diversity is a fact of life for today's organizations, and many are implementing new recruiting, mentoring, and promotion methods, diversity training programs, tough policies regarding sexual harassment and racial discrimination, and new benefits programs that respond to a more diverse workforce. However, if the underlying culture of an organization does not change, all other efforts to support diversity will fail.

Finally, a growing emphasis on learning and adaptation in organizations calls for new cultural values. Recall from Chapter 1 that flexible, organic organizations that support learning and adaptation typically have more horizontal structures with empowered teams working directly with customers. There are few rules and procedures for performing tasks, and knowledge and control of tasks are located with employees rather than supervisors. Information is broadly shared, and employees, customers, suppliers, and partners all play a role in determining the organization's strategic direction. When managers want to shift to a more organic organization design, they have to instill new values, new attitudes, and new ways of thinking and working together.

3 Changing a company's culture is probably one of the hardest jobs a manager can undertake.

ANSWER: *Agree.* Changing people and culture is typically much more difficult than changing any other aspect of the organization. Managers often underestimate the difficulty of changing culture and fail to appreciate that it takes a determined, consciously planned effort over a long period of time.

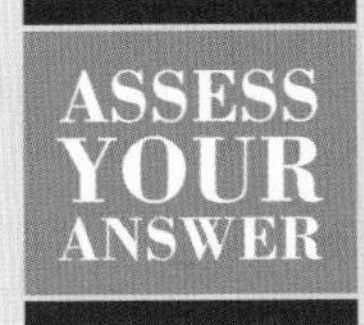

Organization Development Culture Change Interventions

Managers use a variety of approaches and techniques for changing corporate culture, some of which we discussed in Chapter 9. One method of quickly bringing about culture change is known as **organization development** (OD), which focuses on the human and social aspects of the organization as a way to improve the organization's ability to adapt and solve problems. OD emphasizes the values of human development, fairness, openness, freedom from coercion, and individual autonomy that allows workers to perform the job as they see fit, within reasonable organizational constraints.[103] In the 1970s, OD evolved as a separate field that applied the behavioral sciences in a process of planned organization-wide change, with the goal of increasing organizational effectiveness. Today, the concept has been enlarged to examine how people and groups can change to an adaptive culture in a complex and turbulent environment. Organization development is not a step-by-step procedure to solve a specific problem but a process of fundamental change in the human and social systems of the organization, including organizational culture.[104]

BRIEFCASE

As an organization manager, keep this guideline in mind:

Work with organization development consultants for large-scale changes in the attitudes, values, or skills of employees, and when trying to change the overall culture toward a more adaptable one.

OD uses knowledge and techniques from the behavioral sciences to create a learning environment through increased trust, open confrontation of problems, employee empowerment and participation, knowledge and information sharing, the design of meaningful work, cooperation and collaboration between groups, and the full use of human potential.

OD interventions involve training of specific groups or of everyone in the organization. For OD interventions to be successful, senior management in the organization must see the need for OD and provide enthusiastic support for the change. Techniques used by many organizations for improving people skills through OD include the following.

Large Group Intervention. Most early OD activities involved small groups and focused on incremental change. However, in recent years there has been growing interest in the application of OD techniques to large group settings, which are more attuned to bringing about radical or transformational change in organizations operating in complex environments.[105] The **large group intervention** approach, sometimes referred to as "whole system in the room,"[106] brings together participants from all parts of the organization—often including key stakeholders from outside the organization as well—in an off-site setting to discuss problems or opportunities and plan for change. A large group intervention might involve 50 to 500 people and last for several days. For example, the global furniture retailer IKEA used the large-group intervention approach to completely re-conceptualize how the company operates. During 18 hours of meetings held over several days, 52 stakeholders created a new system for product design, manufacturing, and distribution, which involved cutting layers of hierarchy and decentralizing the organization.[107] All of the departments that had information, resources, or an interest in the design outcome worked together to create and implement the new system.

Using an off-site setting limits interference and distractions, enabling participants to focus on new ways of doing things. General Electric's "Work Out" program, an ongoing process of solving problems, learning, and improving, begins with large-scale off-site meetings that get people talking across functional, hierarchical, and organizational boundaries. Hourly and salaried workers come together from many different parts of the organization and join with customers and suppliers to discuss and solve specific problems.[108] The process forces a rapid analysis of ideas, the creation of solutions, and the development of a plan for implementation. Over time, Work Out creates a culture where ideas are rapidly translated into action and positive business results.[109]

Team Building. **Team building** promotes the idea that people who work together can work as a team. A work team can be brought together to discuss conflicts, goals, the decision-making process, communication, creativity, and leadership. The team can then plan to overcome problems and improve results. Team-building activities are also used in many companies to train task forces, committees, and new product development groups. These activities enhance communication and collaboration and strengthen the cohesiveness of organizational groups and teams.

Interdepartmental Activities. Representatives from different departments are brought together in a neutral location to expose problems or conflicts, diagnose the causes, and plan improvements in communication and coordination. This type of intervention has been applied to union–management conflict, headquarters–field office conflict, interdepartmental conflict, and mergers.[110] One archival records-storage company found interdepartmental meetings to be a key means of building a culture based on team spirit and customer focus. People from different departments met for hour-long sessions every two weeks and shared their problems, told stories about their successes, and talked about things they had observed in the company. The meetings helped people understand the problems faced by other departments and see how everyone depended on each other to do their jobs successfully.[111]

Strategies for Implementing Change

Managers and employees can think of inventive ways to improve the organization's technology, creative ideas for new products and services, fresh approaches to strategies and structures, or ideas for fostering adaptive cultural values, but until the ideas are put into action, they are worthless to the organization. Implementation is the most crucial part of the change process, but it is also the most difficult. Change is frequently disruptive and uncomfortable for managers as well as employees. Change is complex, dynamic, and messy, and implementation requires strong and persistent leadership. In this final section, we briefly discuss the role of leadership for change, some reasons for resistance to change, and techniques that managers can use to overcome resistance and successfully implement change.

Leadership for Change

One survey found that among companies that are successful innovators, 80 percent have top leaders who are innovation champions; that is, they frequently reinforce the value and importance of innovation. These leaders think about innovation, demonstrate its importance through their actions, and follow through to make sure people are investing time and resources in innovation issues.[112]

The leadership style of the top executive sets the tone for how effective an organization is at continuous adaptation and innovation. One style of leadership, referred to as *transformational leadership*, is particularly suited for bringing about change. Top leaders who use a transformational leadership style enhance organizational innovation both directly, by creating a compelling vision, and indirectly, by creating an environment that supports exploration, experimentation, risk-taking, and sharing of ideas.[113]

EXHIBIT 10.8
The Change Curve

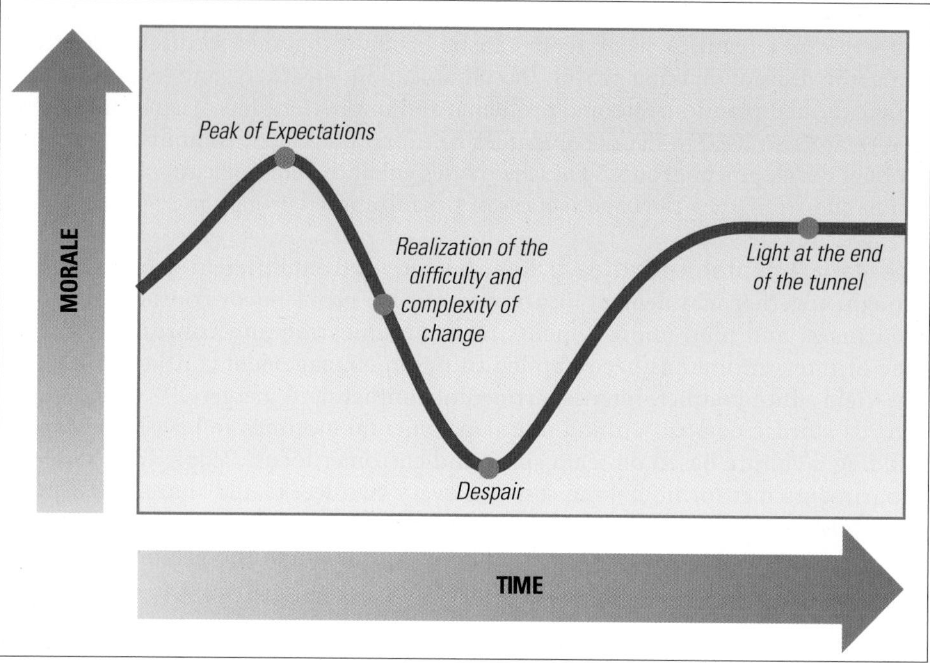

Source: Based on "Gartner Hype Cycle: Interpreting Technology Hype," Gartner Research, http://www.gartner.com/technology/research/methodologies/hype-cycle.jsp (accessed May 20, 2011); "The Change Equation and Curve," 21st Century Leader, http://www.21stcenturyleader.co.uk/change_equation (accessed May 20, 2011); David M. Schneider and Charles Goldwasser, "Be a Model Leader of Change," *Management Review* (March 1998), 41–45; and Daryl R. Conner, *Managing at the Speed of Change* (New York: Villard Books, 1992).

Successful change can happen only when managers and employees are willing to devote the time and energy needed to reach new goals. In addition, people need the coping skills to endure possible stress and hardship. Understanding and appreciating the *curve of change* enables managers to guide people successfully through the difficulties of change. The change curve, illustrated in Exhibit 10.8, is the psychological process people go through during a significant change.

For example, a manager sees a need for a change in work procedures in her department and initiates the change with high expectations for a smooth implementation and a positive outcome. As time progresses, people have difficulty altering their attitudes and behaviors. Employees may question why they need to do things a new way, the supervisor may begin to feel overwhelmed and frustrated, and everyone can potentially reach a point of despair that change is really possible. Performance may decline dramatically as people wrestle with the new procedures and resist the shift to a new way of working. Good change leaders drive through this period of despair rather than allowing it to sabotage the change effort. With effective change leadership, the changes can take hold and lead toward better performance. Managers at Procter & Gamble prepare themselves for a "60-day immune response" from users of a new work process. They expect that it takes 60 days to overcome resistance, work out the bugs in the new process, and reach the light at the end of the tunnel, when everyone begins to see positive results of the change.[114] Having a clearly communicated vision that embodies flexibility and openness to new ideas, methods, and styles sets the stage for a change-oriented organization and helps employees cope with the chaos and tension associated with change.

Barriers to Change

Visionary leadership is crucial for change; however, managers should expect to encounter resistance as they guide the organization along the curve of change. It is natural for people to resist change, and many barriers to change exist at the individual and organizational levels.[115]

1. *Excessive focus on costs.* Management may possess the mindset that costs are all-important and may fail to appreciate the importance of a change that is not focused on costs—for example, a change to increase employee motivation or customer satisfaction.
2. *Failure to perceive benefits.* Any significant change will produce both positive and negative reactions. Education may be needed to help managers and employees perceive more positive than negative aspects of the change. In addition, if the organization's reward system discourages risk-taking, a change process might falter because employees think that the risk of making the change is too high.
3. *Lack of coordination and cooperation.* Organizational fragmentation and conflict often result from the lack of coordination for change implementation. Moreover, in the case of new technology, the old and new systems must be compatible.
4. *Uncertainty avoidance.* At the individual level, many employees fear the uncertainty associated with change. Constant communication is needed so that employees know what is going on and understand how it affects their jobs.
5. *Fear of loss.* Managers and employees may fear the loss of power and status—or even their jobs. In these cases, implementation should be careful and incremental, and all employees should be involved as closely as possible in the change process.

Implementation can typically be designed to overcome many of the organizational and individual barriers to change.

Techniques for Implementation

Top leaders articulate the vision and set the tone, but managers and employees throughout the organization are involved in the process of change. A number of techniques can be used to successfully implement change.[116]

1. *Establish a sense of urgency for change.* Once managers identify a true need for change, they thaw resistance by creating a sense of urgency in others that the change is really needed. Organizational crises can help unfreeze employees and make them willing to invest the time and energy needed to adopt new techniques or procedures. When there is no obvious crisis, managers have to find creative ways to make others aware of the need for change.
2. *Establish a coalition to guide the change.* Effective change managers build a coalition of people throughout the organization who have enough power and influence to steer the change process. For implementation to be successful, there must be a shared commitment to the need and possibilities for change. Top management support is crucial for any major change project, and lack of top management support is one of the most frequent causes of implementation failure.[117] In addition, the coalition should involve lower-level supervisors and

BRIEFCASE

As an organization manager, keep these guidelines in mind:

Understand the curve of change so you can prevent yourself and others from falling prey to frustration and despair when implementing a major change. To achieve successful implementation, use techniques such as obtaining top management support, implementing the change in a series of steps, and assigning change teams or idea champions.

middle managers from across the organization. For smaller changes, the support of influential managers in the affected departments is important.

3. *Create a vision and strategy for change.* Leaders who have taken their companies through major successful transformations often have one thing in common: They focus on formulating and articulating a compelling vision and strategy that will guide the change process. Even for a small change, a vision of how the future can be better and strategies to get there are important motivations for change.
4. *Find an idea that fits the need.* Finding the right idea often involves search procedures—talking with other managers, assigning a task force to investigate the problem, sending out a request to suppliers, or asking creative people within the organization to develop a solution. This is a good opportunity to encourage employee participation because employees need the freedom to think about and explore new options.[118]
5. *Create change teams.* This chapter has emphasized the need for resources and energy to make change happen. Separate creative departments, new-venture groups, and ad hoc teams or task forces are ways to focus energy on both creation and implementation. A separate department has the freedom to create a new technology that fits a genuine need. A task force can be created to see that implementation is completed. The task force can be responsible for communication, involvement of users, training, and other activities needed for change.
6. *Foster idea champions.* One of the most effective weapons in the battle for change is the idea champion. The most effective champion is a volunteer champion who is deeply committed to a new idea. The idea champion sees that all technical activities are correct and complete. An additional champion, such as a manager sponsor, may also be needed to persuade people about implementation, even using coercion if necessary.

Techniques for Overcoming Resistance

Many good ideas are never used because managers failed to anticipate or prepare for resistance to change by consumers, employees, or other managers. No matter how impressive the performance characteristics of an innovation, its implementation will conflict with some interests and jeopardize some alliances in the organization. To increase the chance of successful implementation, managers acknowledge the conflict, threats, and potential losses perceived by employees. Several strategies can be used by managers to overcome resistance:

1. *Alignment with needs and goals of users.* The best strategy for overcoming resistance is to make sure change meets a real need. Employees in R&D often come up with great ideas that solve nonexistent problems. This happens because initiators fail to consult with the intended users. Resistance can be frustrating for managers, but moderate resistance to change is good for an organization. Resistance provides a barrier to frivolous changes and to change for the sake of change. The process of overcoming resistance to change normally requires that the change be good for its users. When David Zugheri wanted to switch to a primarily paperless system at First Houston Mortgage, he emphasized to employees that storing customer records electronically meant they could now work from home when they needed to care for a sick child, or take a vacation

and still keep track of critical accounts. "I could literally see their attitudes change through their body language," Zugheri says.[119]

2. *Communication and training.* Communication means informing users about the need for change and the consequences of a proposed change, preventing rumors, misunderstanding, and resentment. In one study of change efforts, the most commonly cited reason for failure was that employees learned of the change from outsiders. Top managers concentrated on communicating with the public and shareholders but failed to communicate with the people who would be most intimately involved with and most affected by the change—their own employees.[120] Open communication often gives managers an opportunity to explain what steps will be taken to ensure that the change will have no adverse consequences for employees. Training is also needed to help people understand and cope with their role in the change process.
3. *An environment that affords psychological safety.* Psychological safety means that people feel a sense of confidence that they will not be embarrassed or rejected by others in the organization. People need to feel secure and capable of making the changes that are asked of them.[121] Change requires that employees be willing to take risks and do things differently, but many people are fearful of trying something new if they think they might be embarrassed by mistakes or failure. Managers support psychological safety by creating a climate of trust and mutual respect in the organization. "Not being afraid someone is laughing at you helps you take genuine risks," says Andy Law, one of the founders of St. Luke's, an advertising agency based in London.[122]
4. *Participation and involvement.* Early and extensive participation in a change should be part of implementation. Participation gives those involved a sense of control over the change activity. They understand it better, and they become committed to its successful implementation. One study of the implementation and adoption of information technology systems at two companies showed a much smoother implementation process at the company that introduced the new technology using a participatory approach.[123] At Domino's Pizza, some franchise owners resisted the switch to a new point-of-sale system that headquarters managers mandated as part of a drive to improve accuracy, boost efficiency, and increase profits. The franchisees hadn't been involved in the process of designing and configuring the new system, and many of them wanted to stay with the system they were accustomed to. "It was hard for a lot of us to embrace," said Tony Osani, who owns 16 Domino's restaurants in the Huntsville, Alabama, area.[124] The team-building and large group intervention activities described earlier can be effective ways to involve employees in a change process.
5. *Forcing and coercion.* As a last resort, managers may overcome resistance by threatening employees with the loss of jobs or promotions or by firing or transferring them. In other words, management power is used to overwhelm resistance. Recall that Sergio Marchionne fired some executives at Chrysler who refused to go along with his new ideas for the company. According to some insiders, Marchionne "injected an element of fear into [Chrysler's] ranks" to get people to change.[125] In most cases, this approach is not advisable because it leaves people angry at change managers, and the change may be sabotaged. However, this technique may be needed when speed is essential, such as when the organization faces a crisis, as at Chrysler. It may also be required for needed administrative changes that flow from the top down, such as downsizing the workforce.[126]

BRIEFCASE

As an organization manager, keep this guideline in mind:

Overcome resistance to change by actively communicating with workers and encouraging their participation in the change process.

Learning to manage change effectively, including understanding why people resist change and ways to overcome resistance, is crucial, particularly when top-down changes are needed. The failure to recognize and overcome resistance is one of the top reasons managers fail to implement new strategies that can keep their companies competitive.[127] Smart managers approach the change process mindfully and consistently, planning for implementation and preparing for resistance.

Design Essentials

- Organizations face a dilemma. Managers prefer to organize day-to-day activities in a predictable, routine manner. However, change—not stability—is the natural order of things in today's global environment. Thus, organizations need to build in change as well as stability, to facilitate innovation as well as efficiency. Today's environment creates demands for three types of change—episodic change, continuous change, and disruptive change.
- Four types of change—technology, products and services, strategy and structure, and culture—may give an organization a competitive edge, and managers can make certain each of the necessary ingredients for change is present.
- For technology innovation, which is of concern to most organizations, an organic structure that encourages employee autonomy works best because it encourages a flow of ideas throughout the organization. Other approaches are to establish a separate department charged with creating new technical ideas, establish venture teams or idea incubators, apply a variety of mechanisms, systems, and processes that encourage a bottom-up flow of ideas and make sure they get heard and acted upon by top executives, and encourage idea champions. New products and services generally require cooperation among several departments, so horizontal linkage is an essential part of the innovation process. The latest trend is open innovation, which brings customers, suppliers, and other outsiders directly into the search for and development of new products.
- For changes in strategy and structure, a top-down approach is typically best. These innovations are in the domain of top managers who take responsibility for restructuring, for downsizing, and for changes in policies, goals, and control systems.
- Culture changes are also generally the responsibility of top management. Some recent trends that may create a need for broad-scale culture change in the organization are reengineering, the shift to horizontal forms of organizing, greater organizational diversity, and the learning organization. All of these changes require significant shifts in employee and manager attitudes and ways of working together. One method for bringing about this level of culture change is organization development (OD). OD focuses on the human and social aspects of the organization and uses behavioral science knowledge to bring about changes in attitudes and relationships.
- Finally, the implementation of change can be difficult. Strong leadership is needed to guide employees through the turbulence and uncertainty and build organization-wide commitment to change. Understanding the curve of change

can help leaders push through the despair and frustration often associated with major change.

- A number of barriers to change exist, including excessive focus on cost, failure to perceive benefits, lack of organizational coordination, and individual uncertainty avoidance and fear of loss. Managers can increase the likelihood of success by thoughtfully planning how to deal with resistance. Implementation techniques are to establish a sense of urgency that change is needed; create a powerful coalition to guide the change; formulate a vision and strategy to achieve the change; and foster change teams and idea champions. To overcome resistance, managers can align the change with the needs and goals of users, include users in the change process, provide psychological safety, and, in rare cases, force the innovation if necessary.

Key Concepts

ambidextrous approach
change process
creative departments
creativity
culture changes
dual-core approach
horizontal coordination model
idea champions
idea incubator
large group intervention
management innovation
new-venture fund
open innovation
organization development
organizational change
organizational innovation
product and service changes
skunkworks
strategy and structure changes
switching structures
team building
technology changes
time-based competition
venture teams

Discussion Questions

1. Why do you think open innovation has become popular in recent years? What steps might a company take to be more "open" with innovation? What might be some disadvantages of taking an open innovation approach?
2. Describe the dual-core approach. How does the process of management innovation normally differ from technology change? Discuss.
3. What does it mean to say managers should organize for both exploration and exploitation?
4. Do you think factory employees would typically be more resistant to changes in production methods, changes in structure, or changes in culture? Why? What steps could managers take to overcome this resistance?
5. "Change requires more coordination than does the performance of normal organizational tasks. Any time you change something, you discover its connections to other parts of the organization, which have to be changed as well." Discuss whether you agree or disagree with this quote, and why.
6. A noted organization theorist said, "Pressure for change originates in the environment; pressure for stability originates within the organization." Do you agree? Discuss.
7. Of the five elements in Exhibit 10.3 required for successful change, which element do you think managers are most likely to overlook? Discuss.
8. How do the underlying values of organization development compare to the values underlying other types of change? Why do the values underlying OD make it particularly useful in shifting to a constructive culture as described in Chapter 9 (Exhibit 9.5)?
9. The manager of R&D for a drug company said that only 5 percent of the company's new products ever achieve market success. She also said the industry average is 10 percent and wondered how her organization might increase its success rate. If you were acting as a consultant, what advice would you give her about designing organization structure to improve market success?
10. Examine the change curve illustrated in Exhibit 10.8 and the five techniques for overcoming resistance to change discussed at the end of the chapter. Describe at which point along the change curve managers could use each of the five techniques to successfully implement a major change.

Chapter 10 Workbook Innovation Climate[128]

In order to examine differences in the level of innovation encouragement in organizations, you will be asked to rate two organizations. The first should be an organization in which you have worked, or the university. The second should be someone else's workplace—that of a family member, a friend, or an acquaintance. You will have to interview that person to answer the following questions. You should put your own answers in column A, your interviewee's answers in column B, and what you think would be the ideal in column C.

Innovation Measures

Item of Measure	A Your Organization	B Other Organization	C Your Ideal
Score items 1–5 on this scale: 1 = *don't agree at all* to 5 = *agree completely*			
1. Creativity is encouraged here.†			
2. People are allowed to solve the same problems in different ways.†			
3. I get to pursue creative ideas.‡			
4. The organization publicly recognizes and also rewards those who are innovative.‡			
5. Our organization is flexible and always open to change.†			
Score items 6–10 on the opposite scale: 1 = *agree completely* to 5 = *don't agree at all*			
6. The primary job of people here is to follow orders that come from the top.†			
7. The best way to get along here is to think and act like others.†			
8. This place seems to be more concerned with the status quo than with change.†			
9. People are rewarded more if they don't rock the boat.‡			
10. New ideas are great, but we don't have enough people or money to carry them out.‡			

†These items indicate the organization's innovation climate.
‡These items show resource support.

Questions

1. What comparisons in terms of innovation climates can you make between these two organizations?
2. How might productivity differ between a climate that supports innovation and a climate that does not?
3. Where would you rather work? Why?

CASE FOR ANALYSIS Shoe Corporation of Illinois[129]

Shoe Corporation of Illinois (SCI) produces a line of women's shoes that sell in the lower-price market for $27.99 to $29.99 per pair. Profits averaged 30 cents to 50 cents per pair 10 years ago, but according to the president and the controller, labor and materials costs have risen so much in the intervening period that profits today average only 25 cents to 30 cents per pair.

Production at both the company's plants totals 12,500 pairs per day. The two factories are located within a radius of 60 miles of Chicago: one at Centerville, which produces 4,500 pairs per day, and the other at Meadowvale, which produces 8,000 pairs per day. Company headquarters is located in a building adjacent to the Centerville plant.

It is difficult to give an accurate picture of the number of items in the company's product line. Shoes change in style perhaps more rapidly than any other style product, including garments. This is chiefly because it is possible to change production processes quickly and because, historically, each company, in attempting to get ahead of competitors, gradually made style changes more frequently. At present, including both major and minor style changes, SCI offers 100 to 120 different products to customers each year.

A partial organizational chart, showing the departments involved in this case, appears in Exhibit 10.9.

Competitive Structure of the Industry

Very large general shoe houses, such as International and Brown, carry a line of women's shoes and are able to undercut prices charged by SCI, principally because of the policy in the big companies of producing large numbers of "stable" shoes, such as the plain pump and the loafer. They do not attempt to change styles as rapidly as their smaller competitors. Thus, without constant changes in production processes and sales presentations, they are able to keep costs substantially lower.

Charles F. Allison, the president of SCI, feels that the only way for a small independent company to be competitive is to change styles frequently, taking advantage of the flexibility of a small organization to create designs that appeal to customers. Thus, demand can be created and a price set high enough to make a profit. Allison, incidentally, appears to have an artistic talent in styling and a record of successful judgments in approving high-volume styles over the years.

Regarding how SCI differs from its large competitors, Allison has said:

You see, Brown and International Shoe Company both produce hundreds of thousands of the same pair of shoes. They store them in inventory at their factories. Their customers, the large wholesalers and retailers, simply know their line and send in orders. They do not have to change styles nearly as often as we do. Sometimes I wish we could do that, too. It makes for a much more stable and orderly system. There is also less friction between people inside the company. The salespeople always know what they're selling; the production people know what is expected of them. The plant personnel are not shook up so often by someone coming in one morning and tampering with their machine lines or their schedules. The styling people are not shook up so often by the plant saying, "We can't do your new style the way you want it."

To help SCI be more competitive against larger firms, Allison recently created an e-commerce department. Although his main interest was in marketing over the Internet, he also hoped new technology would help reduce some of the internal friction by giving people an easier way to communicate. He invested in a sophisticated new computer system and hired consultants to set up a company intranet and provide a few days' training to upper and middle managers. Katherine Olsen came on board as director of e-commerce, charged primarily with coordinating Internet marketing and sales. When she took the job, she had visions of one day offering consumers the option of customized shoe designs. However, Olsen was somewhat surprised to learn that most employees still refused to use the intranet even for internal communication and coordination. The process for deciding on new styles, for example, had not changed since the 1980s.

Major Style Changes

The decision about whether to put a certain style into production requires information from a number of different people. Here is what typically happens in the company. It may be helpful to follow the organization chart (see Exhibit 10.9) tracing the procedure.

M. T. Lawson, the styling manager, and his designer, John Flynn, originate most of the ideas about shape, size of heel, use of flat sole or heels, and findings (the term used for ornaments attached to, but not part of, the shoes—bows, straps, and so forth). They get their ideas principally from reading style and trade magazines or by copying top-flight designers. Lawson corresponds with publications and friends in large stores in New York, Rome, and Paris to obtain pictures and samples of up-to-the-minute style innovations. Although he uses e-mail occasionally, Lawson prefers telephone contact and receiving drawings or samples by overnight mail. Then, he and Flynn discuss various ideas and come up with design options.

EXHIBIT 10.9
Partial Organization Chart of Shoe Corporation of Illinois

When Lawson decides on a design, he takes a sketch to Allison, who either approves or disapproves it. If Allison approves, he (Allison) then passes the sketch on to L. K. Shipton, the sales manager, to find out what lasts (widths) should be chosen. Shipton, in turn, forwards the design to Martin Freeman, a statistician in the sales department, who maintains summary information on customer demand for colors and lasts.

To compile this information, Freeman visits salespeople twice a year to get their opinions on the colors and lasts that are selling best, and he keeps records of shipments by color and by last. For these needs, he simply totals data that are sent to him by the shipping foreman in each of the two plants.

When Freeman has decided on the lasts and colors, he sends Allison a form that lists the colors and lasts in which the shoe should be produced. Allison, if he approves this list, forwards the information to Lawson, who passes it on to Jenna Richards, an expert pattern maker. Richards makes a paper pattern and then constructs a prototype in leather and paper. She sends this to Lawson, who in turn approves or disapproves it. He forwards any approved prototype to Allison. Allison, if he, too, approves, notifies Lawson, who takes the prototype to Paul Robbins, assistant to the superintendent of the Centerville plant. Only this plant produces small quantities of new or experimental shoe styles. This is referred to as a "pilot run" by executives at the plant.

Robbins then literally carries the prototype through the six production departments of the plant—from cutting to finishing—discussing it with each foreman, who in turn works with employees on the machines in having a sample lot of several thousand pairs made. When the finished lot is delivered by the finishing foreman to the shipping foreman (because of the importance of styling, Allison has directed that each foreman personally deliver styling goods in process to the foreman of the next department), the latter holds the inventory in storage and sends one pair each to Allison and Lawson. If they approve of the finished product, Allison instructs the shipping foreman to mail samples to each of the company's twenty-two salespeople throughout the country. Olsen also receives samples, photos, and drawings to post on the web page and gauge customer interest.

Salespeople have instructions to take the samples immediately (within one week) to at least 10 customers. Orders for already established shoes are normally sent to Ralph Ferguson, a clerk in Shipton's office, who records them and forwards them to the plant superintendents for production. However, salespeople have found by experience that Martin Freeman has a greater interest in the success of new "trials," so they rush these orders to him by overnight mail, and he in turn places the first orders for a new style in the interoffice mail to the plant superintendents. He then sends off a duplicate of the order, mailed in by the salespeople, to Ferguson for entering in his statistical record of all orders received by the company.

Three weeks after the salespeople receive samples, Allison requires Ralph Ferguson to give him a tabulation of orders. At that time, he decides whether the salespeople and the web page should push the item and the superintendents should produce large quantities, or whether he will tell them that although existing orders will be produced, the item will be discontinued in a short time.

According to Allison, the procedures outlined here have worked reasonably well.

The average time from when Lawson decides on a design until we notify the Centerville plant to produce the pilot run is two weeks to a month. Of course, if we could speed that up, it would make the company just that much more secure in staying in the game against the big companies, and in taking sales away from our competitors. There seems to be endless bickering among people around here involved in the styling phase of the business. That's to be expected when you have to move fast—there isn't much time to stop and observe all of the social amenities. I have never thought that a formal organization chart would be good in this company—we've worked out a customary system here that functions well.

M. T. Lawson, manager of styling, said that within his department all work seems to get out in minimum time; he also stated that both Flynn and Richards are good employees and skilled in their work. He mentioned that Flynn had been in to see him twice in the last year

to inquire about his [Flynn's] future in the company. He is 33 years old and has three children. I know that he is eager to make money, and I assured him that over the years we can raise him right along from the $60,000 we are now paying. Actually, he has learned a lot about shoe styles since we hired him from the design department of a fabric company six years ago.

John Flynn revealed:

I was actually becoming dissatisfied with this job. All shoe companies copy styles—it's a generally accepted practice within the industry. But I've picked up a real feel for designs, and several times I've suggested that the company make all its own original styles. We could make SCI a style leader and also increase our volume. When I ask Lawson about this, he says it takes too much time for the designer to create originals—that we have all we can handle to do research in trade magazines and maintain contracts feeding us the results of experts. Beside, he says our styles are standing the test of the marketplace.

Projects X and Y

Flynn also said that he and Martin Freeman had frequently talked about the styling problem. They felt that:

Allison is really a great president, and the company surely would be lost without him. However, we've seen times when he lost a lot of money on bad judgments in styles. Not many times—perhaps six or seven times in the last eighteen months. Also, he is, of course, extremely busy as president of the corporation. He must look after everything from financing from the banks to bargaining with the union. The result is that he is sometimes unavailable to do his styling approvals for several days, or even two weeks. In a business like this, that kind of delay can cost money. It also makes him slightly edgy. It tends, at times when he has many other things to do, to make him look quickly at the styles we submit, or the prototypes Richards makes, or even the finished shoes that are sent for approval by the shipping foreman. Sometimes I worry that he makes two kinds of errors. He simply rubber-stamps what we've done, which makes sending these things to him a waste of time. At other times he makes snap judgments of his own, overruling those of us who have spent so much time and expertise on the shoe. We do think he has good judgment, but he himself has said at times that he wishes he had more time to concentrate on styling and approval of prototypes and final products.

Flynn further explained (and this was corroborated by Freeman) that the two had worked out two plans, which they referred to as "project X" and "project Y." In the first, Flynn created an original design that was not copied from existing styles. Freeman then gave special attention to color and last research for the shoe and recommended a color line that didn't exactly fit past records on consumer purchases—but one he and Flynn thought would have "great consumer appeal." This design and color recommendation was accepted by Lawson and Allison; the shoe went into production and was one of the three top sellers during the calendar year. The latter two men did not know that the shoe was styled in a different way from the usual procedure.

The result of a second, similar project (Y) was put into production the next year, but this time sales were discontinued after three weeks.

Problem between Lawson and Robbins

Frequently, perhaps 10 to 12 times a year, disagreement arises between Mel Lawson, manager of styling, and Paul Robbins, assistant to the superintendent of the Centerville plant. Robbins said:

The styling people don't understand what it means to produce a shoe in the quantities that we do, and to make the changes in production that we have to. They dream up a style quickly, out of thin air. They do not realize that we have a lot of machines that have to be adjusted and that some things they dream up take much longer on certain machines than others, thus creating a bottleneck in the production line. If they put a bow or strap in one position rather than another, it may mean we have to keep people idle on later machines while there is a pileup on the sewing machines on which this complicated little operation is performed. This costs the plant money. Furthermore, there are times when they get the prototype here late, and either the foremen and I work overtime or the trial run won't get through in time to have new production runs on new styles, to take the plant capacity liberated by our stopping production on old styles. Lawson doesn't know much about production and sales and the whole company. I think all he does is to bring shoes down here to the plant, sort of like a messenger boy. Why should he be so hard to get along with? He isn't getting paid any more than I am, and my position in the plant is just as important as his.

Lawson, in turn, said that he has a difficult time getting along with Robbins:

There are many times when Robbins is just unreasonable. I take prototypes to him five or six times a month, and other minor style changes to him six or eight times. I tell him every time that we have problems in getting these ready, but he knows only about the plant, and telling him doesn't seem to do any good. When we first joined the company, we got along all right, but he has gotten harder and harder to get along with.

Other Problems

Ralph Ferguson, the clerk in the sales department who receives orders from salespeople and forwards totals for production schedules to the two plant superintendents, has complained that the salespeople and Freeman are bypassing him in their practice of sending experimental shoe orders to Freeman. He insisted that his job description (one of only two written descriptions in the company) gives him responsibility for receiving all orders throughout the company and for maintaining historical statistics on shipments.

Both the salespeople and Freeman, on the other hand, said that before they started the new practice (that is, when Ferguson still received the experimental shoe orders), there were at least eight or 10 instances a year when these were delayed from one to three days on Ferguson's desk. They reported that Ferguson just wasn't interested in new styles, so the salespeople "just started sending them to Freeman." Ferguson acknowledged that there were times of short delay, but said that there were good reasons for them:

They [the salespeople and Freeman] are so interested in new designs, colors, and lasts that they can't understand the importance of a systematic handling of the whole order procedure, including both old and new shoe styles. There must be accuracy. Sure, I give some priority to experimental orders, but sometimes when rush orders for existing company products are piling up, and when there's a lot of planning I have to do to allocate production between Centerville and Meadowvale, I decide which comes first—processing of these, or processing the experimental shoe orders. Shipton is my boss, not the salespeople or Freeman. I'm going to insist that these orders come to me.

The Push for New Technology

Katherine Olsen believes many of these problems could be solved through better use of technology. She has approached Charles Allison several times about the need to make greater use of the expensive and sophisticated computer information systems he had installed. Although Allison always agrees with her, he has so far done nothing to help solve the problem. Olsen thinks the new technology could dramatically improve coordination at SCI.

Everyone needs to be working from the same data at the same time. As soon as Lawson and Flynn come up with a new design, it should be posted on the intranet so all of us can be informed. And everyone needs access to sales and order information, production schedules, and shipping deadlines. If everyone—from Allison down to the people in the production plants—was kept up to date throughout the entire process, we wouldn't have all this confusion and bickering. But no one around here wants to give up any control—they all have their own little operations and don't want to share information with anyone else. For example, I sometimes don't even know there's a new style in the works until I get finished samples and photos. No one seems to recognize that one of the biggest advantages of the Internet is to help stay ahead of changing styles. I know that Flynn has a good feel for design, and we're not taking advantage of his abilities. But I also have information and ideas that could help this company keep pace with changes and really stand out from the crowd. I don't know how long we expect to remain competitive using this cumbersome, slow-moving process and putting out shoes that are already behind the times.

CASE FOR ANALYSIS Southern Discomfort[130]

Jim Malesckowski remembered the call of two weeks ago as if he had just put down the telephone receiver: "I just read your analysis and I want you to get down to Mexico right away," Jack Ripon, his boss and chief executive officer, had blurted in his ear. "You know we can't make the plant in Oconomo work anymore—the costs are just too high. So go down there, check out what our operational costs would be if we move, and report back to me in a week."

As president of the Wisconsin Specialty Products Division of Lamprey Inc., Jim knew quite well the challenge of dealing with high-cost labor in a third-generation, unionized, U.S. manufacturing plant. And although he had done the analysis that led to his boss's knee-jerk response, the call still stunned him. There were 520 people who made a living at Lamprey's Oconomo facility, and if it closed, most of them wouldn't have a chance of finding another job in the town of 9,900 people.

Instead of the $16-per-hour average wage paid at the Oconomo plant, the wages paid to the Mexican workers—who lived in a town without sanitation and with an unbelievably toxic effluent from industrial pollution—would amount to about $1.60 an hour on average. That would be a savings of nearly $15 million a year for Lamprey, to be offset in part by increased costs for training, transportation, and other matters.

After two days of talking with Mexican government representatives and managers of other companies in the town, Jim had enough information to develop a set of comparative figures of production and shipping costs. On the way home, he started to outline the report, knowing full well that unless some miracle occurred, he would be ushering in a blizzard of pink slips for people he had come to appreciate.

The plant in Oconomo had been in operation since 1921, making special apparel for people suffering from injuries and other medical conditions. Jim had often talked with employees who would recount stories about their fathers or grandfathers working in the same Lamprey company plant—the last of the original manufacturing operations in town.

But friendship aside, competitors had already edged past Lamprey in terms of price and were dangerously close to overtaking it in product quality. Although both Jim and the plant manager had tried to convince the union to accept lower wages, union leaders resisted. In fact, on one occasion when Jim and the plant manager tried to discuss a cell manufacturing approach, which would cross-train employees to perform up to three different jobs, local union leaders could barely restrain their anger. Jim thought he sensed an underlying fear, meaning the union reps were aware of at least some of the problems, but he had been unable to get them to acknowledge this and move on to open discussion.

A week passed and Jim had just submitted his report to his boss. Although he didn't specifically bring up the point, it was apparent that Lamprey could put its investment dollars in a bank and receive a better return than what its Oconomo operation was currently producing.

The next day, he would discuss the report with the CEO. Jim didn't want to be responsible for the plant's dismantling, an act he personally believed would be wrong as long as there was a chance its costs can be lowered. "But Ripon's right," he said to himself. "The costs are too high, the union's unwilling to cooperate, and the company needs to make a better return on its investment if it's to continue at all. It sounds right but feels wrong. What should I do?"

Notes

1. Ellen Byron, "A New Odd Couple: Google, P&G Swap Workers to Spur Innovation," *The Wall Street Journal* (November 19, 2008), A1, A18.
2. Quoted in Anne Fisher, "America's Most Admired Companies," *Fortune* (March 17, 2008), 65–67.
3. Based on John P. Kotter, *Leading Change* (Boston: Harvard Business School Press, 1996), 18–20.
4. This discussion of three types of change is based in part on Joseph McCann, "Organizational Effectiveness: Changing Concepts for Changing Environments," *Human Resource Planning* 27, no. 1 (2004), 42–50.
5. Based in part on David W. Norton, and B. Joseph Pine II, "Unique Experiences: Disruptive Innovations Offer Customers More 'Time Well Spent,'" *Strategy & Leadership* 37, no. 6 (2009), 4–9; and "The Power to Disrupt," *The Economist* (April 17, 2010), 16.
6. Michael Arndt and Bruce Einhorn, "The 50 Most Innovative Companies," *Bloomberg BusinessWeek* (April 25, 2010), 34–40.
7. Joseph E. McCann, "Design Principles for an Innovating Company," *Academy of Management Executive* 5, no. 2 (May 1991), 76–93.
8. Teri Evans, "Entrepreneurs Seek to Elicit Workers' Ideas—Contests with Cash Prizes and Other Rewards Stimulate Innovation in Hard Times," *The Wall Street Journal* (December 22, 2009), B7.
9. Reported in Arndt and Einhorn, "The 50 Most Innovative Companies."
10. Michael Totty, "The Wall Street Journal 2008 Technology Innovation Awards," *The Wall Street Journal* (September 29, 2008), R1, R4, R6.
11. Jon Katzenbach and Zia Khan, "Leading Outside the Lines," *Strategy + Business* (April 26, 2010), http://www.strategy-business.com/article/10204?gko=788c9 (accessed September 9, 2010).
12. Erin White, "How a Company Made Everyone a Team Player," *The Wall Street Journal* (August 13, 2007), B1, B7.
13. Judy Oppenheimer, "A Top Cop Who Gets It," *More* (June 2009), 86–91, 144.
14. Richard A. Wolfe, "Organizational Innovation: Review, Critique and Suggested Research Directions," *Journal of Management Studies* 31, no. 3 (May 1994), 405–431.
15. John L. Pierce and Andre L. Delbecq, "Organization Structure, Individual Attitudes and Innovation," *Academy of Management Review* 2 (1977), 27–37; and Michael Aiken and Jerald Hage, "The Organic Organization and Innovation," *Sociology* 5 (1971), 63–82.
16. Richard L. Daft, "Bureaucratic versus Non-bureaucratic Structure in the Process of Innovation and Change," in Samuel B. Bacharach, ed., *Perspectives in Organizational Sociology: Theory and Research* (Greenwich, CT: JAI Press, 1982), 129–166.
17. Alan D. Meyer and James B. Goes, "Organizational Assimilation of Innovations: A Multilevel Contextual Analysis," *Academy of Management Journal* 31 (1988), 897–923.
18. Richard W. Woodman, John E. Sawyer, and Ricky W. Griffin, "Toward a Theory of Organizational Creativity," *Academy of Management Review* 18 (1993), 293–321.
19. John Grossman, "Strategies: Thinking Small," *Inc.* (August 2004), 34–36.
20. Robert I. Sutton, "Weird Ideas That Spark Innovation," *MIT Sloan Management Review* (Winter 2002), 83–87; Robert Barker, "The Art of Brainstorming," *BusinessWeek* (August 26, 2002), 168–169; Gary A. Steiner, ed., *The Creative Organization* (Chicago: University of Chicago Press, 1965), 16–18; and James Brian Quinn, "Managing Innovation: Controlled Chaos," *Harvard Business Review* (May–June 1985), 73–84.
21. Thomas M. Burton, "Flop Factor: By Learning from Failures, Lilly Keeps Drug Pipeline Full," *The Wall Street Journal* (April 21, 2004), A1, A12.
22. Kotter, *Leading Change*, 20–25; and John P. Kotter, "Leading Change," *Harvard Business Review* (March–April 1995), 59–67.
23. G. Tomas M. Hult, Robert F. Hurley, and Gary A. Knight, "Innovativeness: Its Antecedents and Impact on Business Performance," *Industrial Marketing Management* 33 (2004), 429–438.
24. Brooks Barnes, "Will Disney Keep Us Amused?" *The New York Times* (February 10, 2008), BU1.
25. Burton, "Flop Factor."
26. D. Bruce Merrifield, "Intrapreneurial Corporate Renewal," *Journal of Business Venturing* 8 (September 1993), 383–389; Linsu Kim, "Organizational Innovation and Structure," *Journal of Business Research* 8 (1980), 225–245; and Tom Burns and G. M. Stalker, *The Management of Innovation* (London: Tavistock Publications, 1961).

27. Robert B. Duncan, "The Ambidextrous Organization: Designing Dual Structures for Innovation," in Ralph H. Killman, Louis R. Pondy, and Dennis Slevin, eds., *The Management of Organization*, vol. 1 (New York: North-Holland, 1976), 167–188; Constantine Andriopoulos and Marianne W. Lewis, "Managing Innovation Paradoxes: Ambidexterity Lessons from Leading Product Design Companies," *Long Range Planning* 43 (2010), 104–122; Charles A. O'Reilly III and Michael L. Tushman, "The Ambidextrous Organization," *Harvard Business Review* (April 2004), 74–81; M. L. Tushman and C. A. O'Reilly III, "Building an Ambidextrous Organization: Forming Your Own 'Skunk Works,'" *Health Forum Journal* 42, no. 2 (March–April 1999), 20–23; and J. C. Spender and Eric H. Kessler, "Managing the Uncertainties of Innovation: Extending Thompson (1967)," *Human Relations* 48, no. 1 (1995), 35–56.
28. J. G. March, "Exploration and Exploitation in Organizational Learning," *Organization Science* 2 (1991), 71–87; and R. Duane Ireland and Justin W. Webb, "Crossing the Great Divide of Strategic Entrepreneurship: Transitioning Between Exploration and Exploitation," *Business Horizons* 52 (2009), 469–479. For a review of the research on exploration and exploitation, see A. K. Gupta, K. G. Smith, and C. E. Shalley, "The Interplay Between Exploration and Exploitation," *Academy of Management Journal* 49, no. 4 (2006), 693–706.
29. M. H. Lubatkin, Z. Simsek, Y. Ling, and J. F. Veiga, "Ambidexterity and Performance in Small- to Medium-Sized Firms: The Pivotal Role of Top Management Team Behavioral Integration," *Journal of Management* 32, no. 5 (October 2006), 646–672; and O'Reilly and Tushman, "The Ambidextrous Organization."
30. Tushman and O'Reilly, "Building an Ambidextrous Organization."
31. Edward F. McDonough III and Richard Leifer, "Using Simultaneous Structures to Cope with Uncertainty," *Academy of Management Journal* 26 (1983), 727–735.
32. John McCormick and Bill Powell, "Management for the 1990s," *Newsweek* (April 25, 1988), 47–48.
33. Todd Datz, "Romper Ranch," *CIO Enterprise* Section 2 (May 15, 1999), 39–52.
34. Paul S. Adler, Barbara Goldoftas, and David I. Levine, "Ergonomics, Employee Involvement, and the Toyota Production System: A Case Study of NUMMI's 1993 Model Introduction," *Industrial and Labor Relations Review* 50, no. 3 (April 1997), 416–437.
35. Judith R. Blau and William McKinley, "Ideas, Complexity, and Innovation," *Administrative Science Quarterly* 24 (1979), 200–219.
36. Peter Landers, "Back to Basics; With Dry Pipelines, Big Drug Makers Stock Up in Japan," *The Wall Street Journal* (November 24, 2003), A1, A7.
37. Sherri Eng, "Hatching Schemes," *The Industry Standard* (November 27–December 4, 2000), 174–175.
38. Donald F. Kuratko, Jeffrey G. Covin, and Robert P. Garrett, "Corporate Venturing: Insights from Actual Performance," *Business Horizons* 52 (2009), 459-467.
39. Michael L. Tushman, Wendy K. Smith, and Andy Binns, "The Ambidextrous CEO," *Harvard Business Review* (June 2011), 74–80.
40. Christopher Hoenig, "Skunk Works Secrets," *CIO* (July 1, 2000), 74–76.
41. David Dobson, "Integrated Innovation at Pitney Bowes," *Strategy + Business Online* (October 26, 2009), http://www.strategy-business.com/article/09404b?gko=f9661 (accessed December 30, 2009); and James I. Cash, Jr., Michael J. Earl, and Robert Morison, "Teaming up to Crack Innovation and Enterprise Integration," *Harvard Business Review* (November 2008), 90–100.
42. Arkadi Kuhlmann, "Reinventing Innovation," *Ivey Business Journal* (May–June 2010), 6.
43. Erik Brynjolfsson and Michael Schrage, "The New, Faster Face of Innovation; Thanks to Technology, Change Has Never Been So Easy or So Cheap," *The Wall Street Journal* (August 17, 2009); and Vindu Goel, "Why Google Pulls the Plug," *The New York Times* (February 15, 2009).
44. Jane M. Howell and Christopher A. Higgins, "Champions of Technology Innovation," *Administrative Science Quarterly* 35 (1990), 317–341; and Jane M. Howell and Christopher A. Higgins, "Champions of Change: Identifying, Understanding, and Supporting Champions of Technology Innovations," *Organizational Dynamics* (Summer 1990), 40–55.
45. Thomas J. Peters and Robert H. Waterman, Jr., *In Search of Excellence* (New York: Harper & Row, 1982).
46. Curtis R. Carlson and William W. Wilmot, *Innovation: The Five Disciplines for Creating What Customers Want* (New York: Crown Business, 2006).
47. Robert I. Sutton, "The Weird Rules of Creativity," *Harvard Business Review* (September 2001), 94–103; and Julian Birkinshaw and Michael Mol, "How Management Innovation Happens," *MIT Sloan Management Review* (Summer 2006), 81–88. See Lionel Roure, "Product Champion Characteristics in France and Germany," *Human Relations* 54, no. 5 (2001), 663–682, for a review of the literature related to product champions.
48. Peter Lewis, "Texas Instruments' Lunatic Fringe," *Fortune* (September 4, 2006), 120–128.
49. J. C. Spender and Bruce Strong, "Who Has Innovative Ideas? Employees." *The Wall Street Journal* (August 23, 2010), R5; and Rachel Emma Silverman, "How to Be Like Apple," *The Wall Street Journal* (August 29, 2011), http://online.wsj.com/article/SB10001424053111904009304576532842667854706.html (accessed September 16, 2011).
50. Darren Dahl, "Technology: Pipe Up, People! Rounding Up Staff Ideas," *Inc.* (February 2010), 80–81.
51. Roger L. Martin, "The Innovation Catalysts," *Harvard Business Review* (June 2011), 82–87.
52. Spender and Strong, "Who Has Innovative Ideas?"
53. Jessi Hempel, "Big Blue Brainstorm," *BusinessWeek* (August 7, 2006), 70.
54. Dahl, "Technology: Pipe Up, People!"
55. Jessica E. Vascellaro, "Google Searches for Ways to Keep Big Ideas at Home," *The Wall Street Journal* (June 18, 2009), B1.

56. G. A. Stevens and J. Burley, "3,000 Raw Ideas = 1 Commercial Success!" *Research Technology Management* 40, no. 3 (May–June 1997), 16–27; R. P. Morgan, C. Kruytbosch, and N. Kannankutty, "Patenting and Invention Activity of U.S. Scientists and Engineers in the Academic Sector: Comparisons with Industry," *Journal of Technology Transfer* 26 (2001), 173–183; Edwin Mansfield, J. Rapaport, J. Schnee, S. Wagner, and M. Hamburger, *Research and Innovation in Modern Corporations* (New York: Norton, 1971); Christopher Power with Kathleen Kerwin, Ronald Grover, Keith Alexander, and Robert D. Hof, "Flops," *BusinessWeek* (August 16, 1993), 76–82; and Modesto A. Maidique and Billie Jo Zirger, "A Study of Success and Failure in Product Innovation: The Case of the U.S. Electronics Industry," *IEEE Transactions in Engineering Management* 31 (November 1984), 192–203.
57. Nic Fildes, "Savvy Customers Make the Profit on the Tab that Flopped," *The Times* (September 1, 2011), 43; and Holman W. Jenkins, Jr., "The Microsoft Solution," *The Wall Street Journal Europe* (July 29, 2010), 13.
58. Scott Hensley, "Bleeding Cash: Pfizer 'Youth Pill' Ate Up $71 Million Before It Flopped," *The Wall Street Journal* (May 2, 2002), A1, A8; Andrew Bordeaux, "10 Famous Product Failures and the Advertisements That Did Not Sell Them," *Growthink.com* (December 17, 2007), http://www.growthink.com/content/10-famous-product-failures-and-advertisements-did-not-sell-them (accessed September 16, 2011); and Jane McGrath, "Five Failed McDonald's Menu Items," HowStuffWorks.com, http://money.howstuffworks.com/5-failed-mcdonalds-menu-items3.htm (accessed September 16, 2011).
59. Linton, Matysiak & Wilkes Inc. study results reported in "Market Study Results Released: New Product Introduction Success, Failure Rates Analyzed," *Frozen Food Digest* (July 1, 1997).
60. Deborah Dougherty and Cynthia Hardy, "Sustained Product Innovation in Large, Mature Organizations: Overcoming Innovation-to-Organization Problems," *Academy of Management Journal* 39, no. 5 (1996), 1120–1153.
61. M. Adams and the Product Development and Management Association, "Comparative Performance Assessment Study 2004," available for purchase at http://www.pdma.org. Results reported in Jeff Cope, "Lessons Learned—Commercialization Success Rates: A Brief Review," *RTI Tech Ventures* newsletter 4, no. 4 (December 2007).
62. Ibid.
63. Shona L. Brown and Kathleen M. Eisenhardt, "Product Development: Past Research, Present Findings, and Future Directions," *Academy of Management Review* 20, no. 2 (1995), 343–378; F. Axel Johne and Patricia A. Snelson, "Success Factors in Product Innovation: A Selective Review of the Literature," *Journal of Product Innovation Management* 5 (1988), 114–128; Antonio Bailetti and Paul F. Litva, "Integrating Customer Requirements into Product Designs," *Journal of Product Innovation Management* 12 (1995), 3–15; Jay W. Lorsch and Paul R. Lawrence, "Organizing for Product Innovation," *Harvard Business Review* (January–February 1965), 109-122; and Science Policy Research Unit, University of Sussex, *Success and Failure in Industrial Innovation* (London: Centre for the Study of Industrial Innovation, 1972).
64. Study reported in Mike Gordon, Chris Musso, Eric Rebentisch, and Nisheeth Gupta, "Business Insight (A Special Report): Innovation—The Path to Developing Successful New Products," *The Wall Street Journal* (November 30, 2009), R5.
65. Dorothy Leonard and Jeffrey F. Rayport, "Spark Innovation through Empathic Design," *Harvard Business Review* (November–December 1997), 102–113.
66. Bruce Brown and Scott D. Anthony, "How P&G Tripled Its Innovation Success Rate," *Harvard Business Review* (June 2011), 64–72.
67. Janet Rae-Dupree, "Even the Giants Can Learn to Think Small," *The New York Times* (August 3, 2008), BU4; and Mike Ramsey and Norihiko Shirouzu, "Toyota Is Changing How It Develops Cars," *The Wall Street Journal* (July 5, 2010), http://www.in.com/news/business/fullstory-toyota-is-changing-how-it-develops-cars-14559691-in-1.html (accessed September 16, 2011).
68. Brown and Eisenhardt, "Product Development"; and Dan Dimancescu and Kemp Dwenger, "Smoothing the Product Development Path," *Management Review* (January 1996), 36–41.
69. William J. Holstein, "Five Gates to Innovation," *Strategy + Business* (March 1, 2010), http://www.strategy-business.com/article/00021?gko=0bd39 (accessed September 16, 2011).
70. Kenneth B. Kahn, "Market Orientation, Interdepartmental Integration, and Product Development Performance," *The Journal of Product Innovation Management* 18 (2001), 314–323; and Ali E. Akgün, Gary S. Lynn, and John C. Byrne, "Taking the Guesswork Out of New Product Development: How Successful High-Tech Companies Get That Way," *Journal of Business Strategy* 25, no. 4 (2004), 41–46.
71. The discussion of open innovation is based on Henry Chesbrough, *Open Innovation* (Boston, MA: Harvard Business School Press, 2003); Henry Chesbrough, "The Era of Open Innovation," *MIT Sloan Management Review* (Spring 2003), 35–41; Julian Birkinshaw and Susan A. Hill, "Corporate Venturing Units: Vehicles for Strategic Success in the New Europe," *Organizational Dynamics* 34, no. 3 (2005), 247–257; Amy Muller and Liisa Välikangas, "Extending the Boundary of Corporate Innovation," *Strategy & Leadership* 30, no. 3 (2002), 4–9; and Navi Radjou, "Networked Innovation Drives Profits," *Industrial Management* (January–February 2005), 14–21.
72. Chesbrough, *Open Innovation.*
73. Martin W. Wallin and Georg Von Krogh, "Organizing for Open Innovation: Focus on the Integration of Knowledge," *Organizational Dynamics* 39, no. 2 (2010), 145–154; Bettina von Stamm, "Collaboration with Other Firms and Customers: Innovation's Secret Weapon," *Strategy & Leadership* 32, no. 3 (2004), 16–20; and Bas Hillebrand and Wim G. Biemans, "Links between Internal and External Cooperation in Product Development: An Exploratory Study," *The Journal of Product Innovation Management* 21 (2004), 110–122.

74. Barry Jaruzelski and Richard Holman, "Casting a Wide Net: Building the Capabilities for Open Innovation," *Ivey Business Journal* (March–April 2011), http://www.iveybusinessjournal.com/topics/innovation/casting-a-wide-net-building-the-capabilities-for-open-innovation (accessed September 19, 2011).
75. A. G. Lafley and Ram Charan, *The Game Changer: How You Can Drive Revenue and Profit Growth with Innovation* (New York: Crown Business, 2008); Larry Huston and Nabil Sakkab, "Connect and Develop; Inside Procter & Gamble's New Model for Innovation," *Harvard Business Review* (March 2006),58–66; and G. Gil Cloyd, "P&G's Secret: Innovating Innovation," *Industry Week* (December 2004), 26–34.
76. Farhad Manjoo, "Apple Nation," *Fortune* (July–August 2010), 68–112; and Jorge Rufat-Latre, Amy Muller, and Dave Jones, "Delivering on the Promise of Open Innovation," *Strategy & Leadership* 38, no. 6 (2010), 23–28.
77. John Hagel and John Seely Brown, "The Next Wave of Open Innovation," *BusinessWeek* (April 8, 2009), http://www.businessweek.com/innovate/content/apr2009/id2009048_360417.htm (accessed September 19, 2011); and Lawrence Owne, Charles Goldwasser, Kristi Choate, and Amy Blitz, "Collaborative Innovation throughout the Extended Enterprise," *Strategy & Leadership* 36, no. 1 (2008), 39–45.
78. David Lerman and Liz Smith, "Wanted: Big Ideas from Small Fry," *Bloomberg BusinessWeek* (August 30–September 5, 2010), 49–51; Steve Lohr, "The Crowd Is Wise (When It's Focused)," *The New York Times* (July 19, 2009), BU4; and S. Lohr, "The Corporate Lab As Ringmaster," *The New York Times* (August 16, 2009), BU3.
79. Max Chafkin, "The Customer Is the Company," *Inc.* (June 2008), 88–96; and Max Chafkin, "5 Ways to Actually Make Money on Twitter," *Inc.* (December 2009–January 2010), 96–101.
80. Reported in Jill Jusko, "A Team Effort," *Industry Week* (January 2007), 42, 45.
81. John A. Pearce II, "Speed Merchants," *Organizational Dynamics* 30, no. 3 (2002), 191–205; Kathleen M. Eisenhardt and Behnam N. Tabrizi, "Accelerating Adaptive Processes: Product Innovation in the Global Computer Industry," *Administrative Science Quarterly* 40 (1995), 84–110; Dougherty and Hardy, "Sustained Product Innovation in Large, Mature Organizations"; and Karne Bronikowski, "Speeding New Products to Market," *Journal of Business Strategy* (September–October 1990), 34–37.
82. Cecilie Rohwedder and Keith Johnson, "Pace-Setting Zara Seeks More Speed to Fight Its Rising Cheap-Chic Rivals," *The Wall Street Journal* (February 20, 2008), B1; Janet Adamy, "Leadership (A Special Report); Catch the Wave: Russell Stover Candies Wanted to Get a Piece of the Low-Carb Craze; But to Do So It Had to Be Quick—and Smart," *The Wall Street Journal* (October 25, 2004), R8.
83. Alex Taylor III, "Chrysler's Speed Merchant," *Fortune* (September 6, 2010), 77–82; and "Upcoming Chryslers, Dodges, Rams, and Jeeps," *Allpar.com*, http://www.allpar.com/model/upcoming.html (accessed September 20, 2011).
84. V. K. Narayanan, Frank L. Douglas, Brock Guernsey, and John Charnes, "How Top Management Steers Fast Cycle Teams to Success," *Strategy & Leadership* 30, no. 3 (2002), 19–27.
85. Edward F. McDonough III, Kenneth B. Kahn, and Gloria Barczak, "An Investigation of the Use of Global, Virtual, and Colocated New Product Development Teams," *The Journal of Product Innovation Management* 18 (2001), 110–120.
86. Raymond E. Miles, Henry J. Coleman, Jr., and W. E. Douglas Creed, "Keys to Success in Corporate Redesign," *California Management Review* 37, no. 3 (Spring 1995), 128–145.
87. Alex Taylor III, "Chrysler's Speed Merchant"; and Kate Linebaugh and Jeff Bennett, "Marchionne Upends Chrysler's Ways," *The Wall Street Journal* (January 12, 2010), B1.
88. Julian Birkinshaw, Gary Hamel, and Michael J. Mol, "Management Innovation," *Academy of Management Review* 33, no. 4 (2008), 825–845.
89. Reena Jana, "From India, The Latest Management Fad," *BusinessWeek* (December 14, 2009), 57.
90. Fariborz Damanpour and William M. Evan, "Organizational Innovation and Performance: The Problem of 'Organizational Lag,'" *Administrative Science Quarterly* 29 (1984), 392–409; David J. Teece, "The Diffusion of an Administrative Innovation," *Management Science* 26 (1980), 464–470; John R. Kimberly and Michael J. Evaniski, "Organizational Innovation: The Influence of Individual, Organizational and Contextual Factors on Hospital Adoption of Technological and Administrative Innovation," *Academy of Management Journal* 24 (1981), 689–713; Michael K. Moch and Edward V. Morse, "Size, Centralization, and Organizational Adoption of Innovations," *American Sociological Review* 42 (1977), 716–725; and Mary L. Fennell, "Synergy, Influence, and Information in the Adoption of Administrative Innovation," *Academy of Management Journal* 27 (1984), 113–129.
91. Richard L. Daft, "A Dual-Core Model of Organizational Innovation," *Academy of Management Journal* 21 (1978), 193–210.
92. Daft, "Bureaucratic versus Nonbureaucratic Structure"; and Robert W. Zmud, "Diffusion of Modern Software Practices: Influence of Centralization and Formalization," *Management Science* 28 (1982), 1421–1431.
93. Daft, "A Dual-Core Model of Organizational Innovation"; and Zmud, "Diffusion of Modern Software Practices."
94. Fariborz Damanpour, "The Adoption of Technological, Administrative, and Ancillary Innovations: Impact of Organizational Factors," *Journal of Management* 13 (1987), 675–688.
95. Gregory H. Gaertner, Karen N. Gaertner, and David M. Akinnusi, "Environment, Strategy, and the Implementation of Administrative Change: The Case of Civil Service Reform," *Academy of Management Journal* 27 (1984), 525–543.
96. Claudia Bird Schoonhoven and Mariann Jelinek, "Dynamic Tension in Innovative, High Technology Firms: Managing Rapid Technology Change through Organization Structure," in Mary Ann Von Glinow and Susan Albers Mohrman, eds.,

Managing Complexity in High Technology Organizations (New York: Oxford University Press, 1990), 90–118.
97. Jeanne Whalen, "Glaxo Tries Biotech Model to Spur Drug Innovations," *The Wall Street Journal* (July 1, 2010), A1.
98. David Ulm and James K. Hickel, "What Happens after Restructuring?" *Journal of Business Strategy* (July–August 1990), 37–41; and John L. Sprague, "Restructuring and Corporate Renewal: A Manager's Guide," *Management Review* (March 1989), 34–36.
99. Stan Pace, "Rip the Band-Aid Off Quickly," *Strategy & Leadership* 30, no. 1 (2002), 4–9.
100. Benson L. Porter and Warrington S. Parker, Jr., "Culture Change," *Human Resource Management* 31 (Spring–Summer 1992), 45–67.
101. Atsuko Fukase, "New CEO, New Mizuho Culture," *The Asian Wall Street Journal* (June 23, 2011), 22.
102. Reported in "Mergers Don't Consider Cultures," *ISHN* (September 2011), 14.
103. W. Warner Burke, "The New Agenda for Organization Development," in Wendell L. French, Cecil H. Bell, Jr., and Robert A. Zawacki, *Organization Development and Transformation: Managing Effective Change* (Burr Ridge, IL: Irwin McGraw-Hill, 2000), 523–535.
104. W. Warner Burke, *Organization Development: A Process of Learning and Changing*, 2nd ed. (Reading, MA: Addison-Wesley, 1994); and Wendell L. French and Cecil H. Bell, Jr., "A History of Organization Development," in French, Bell, and Zawacki, *Organization Development and Transformation*, 20–42.
105. French and Bell, "A History of Organization Development."
106. The information on large group intervention is based on Kathleen D. Dannemiller and Robert W. Jacobs, "Changing the Way Organizations Change: A Revolution of Common Sense," *The Journal of Applied Behavioral Science* 28, no. 4 (December 1992), 480–498; Barbara B. Bunker and Billie T. Alban, "Conclusion: What Makes Large Group Interventions Effective?" *The Journal of Applied Behavioral Science* 28, no. 4 (December 1992), 570–591; and Marvin R. Weisbord, "Inventing the Future: Search Strategies for Whole System Improvements," in French, Bell, and Zawacki, *Organization Development and Transformation*, 242–250.
107. Marvin Weisbord and Sandra Janoff, "Faster, Shorter, Cheaper May Be Simple; It's Never Easy," *The Journal of Applied Behavioral Science* 41, no. 1 (March 2005), 70–82.
108. J. Quinn, "What a Workout!" *Performance* (November 1994), 58–63; and Bunker and Alban, "Conclusion: What Makes Large Group Interventions Effective?"
109. Dave Ulrich, Steve Kerr, and Ron Ashkenas, with Debbie Burke and Patrice Murphy, *The GE Work Out: How to Implement GE's Revolutionary Method for Busting Bureaucracy and Attacking Organizational Problems—Fast!* (New York: McGraw-Hill, 2002).
110. Paul F. Buller, "For Successful Strategic Change: Blend OD Practices with Strategic Management," *Organizational Dynamics* (Winter 1988), 42–55.
111. Norm Brodsky, "Everybody Sells," (Street Smarts column), *Inc.* (June 2004), 53–54.
112. Pierre Loewe and Jennifer Dominiquini, "Overcome the Barriers to Effective Innovation," *Strategy & Leadership* 34, no. 1 (2006), 24–31.
113. Bernard M. Bass, "Theory of Transformational Leadership Redux," *Leadership Quarterly* 6, no. 4 (1995), 463–478; and Dong I. Jung, Chee Chow, and Anne Wu, "The Role of Transformational Leadership in Enhancing Organizational Innovation: Hypotheses and Some Preliminary Findings," *The Leadership Quarterly* 14 (2003), 525–544.
114. Todd Datz, "No Small Change," *CIO* (February 15, 2004), 66–72.
115. These are based in part on Carol A. Beatty and John R. M. Gordon, "Barriers to the Implementation of CAD/CAM Systems," *Sloan Management Review* (Summer 1988), 25–33.
116. These techniques are based on John P. Kotter's eight-stage model of planned organizational change, Kotter, *Leading Change*, 20–25.
117. Everett M. Rogers and Floyd Shoemaker, *Communication of Innovations: A Cross Cultural Approach*, 2nd ed. (New York: Free Press, 1971); and Stratford P. Sherman, "Eight Big Masters of Innovation," *Fortune* (October 15, 1984), 66–84.
118. Richard L. Daft and Selwyn W. Becker, *Innovation in Organizations* (New York: Elsevier, 1978); and John P. Kotter and Leonard A. Schlesinger, "Choosing Strategies for Change," *Harvard Business Review* 57 (1979), 106–114.
119. Darren Dahl, "Trust Me: You're Gonna Love This; Getting Employees to Embrace New Technology," *Inc.* (November 2008), 41.
120. Peter Richardson and D. Keith Denton, "Communicating Change," *Human Resource Management* 35, no. 2 (Summer 1996), 203–216.
121. Edgar H. Schein and Warren Bennis, *Personal and Organizational Change via Group Methods* (New York: Wiley, 1965); and Amy Edmondson, "Psychological Safety and Learning Behavior in Work Teams," *Administrative Science Quarterly* 44 (1999), 350–383.
122. Diane L. Coutu, "Creating the Most Frightening Company on Earth; An Interview with Andy Law of St. Luke's," *Harvard Business Review* (September–October 2000), 143–150.
123. Philip H. Mirvis, Amy L. Sales, and Edward J. Hackett, "The Implementation and Adoption of New Technology in Organizations: The Impact on Work, People, and Culture," *Human Resource Management* 30 (Spring 1991), 113–139; Arthur E. Wallach, "System Changes Begin in the Training Department," *Personnel Journal* 58 (1979), 846–848, 872; and Paul R. Lawrence, "How to Deal with Resistance to Change," *Harvard Business Review* 47 (January–February 1969), 4–12, 166–176.
124. Julie Jargon, "Business Technology: Domino's IT Staff Delivers Slick Site, Ordering System," *The Wall Street Journal* (November 24, 2009), B5.
125. Linebaugh, "Marchionne Upends Chrysler's Ways."
126. Dexter C. Dunphy and Doug A. Stace, "Transformational and Coercive Strategies for Planned Organizational Change: Beyond the O.D Model," *Organizational Studies* 9 (1988), 317–334; and Kotter and Schlesinger, "Choosing Strategies for Change."

127. Lawrence G. Hrebiniak, "Obstacles to Effective Strategy Implementation," *Organizational Dynamics* 35, no. 1 (2006), 12–31.
128. Adapted by Dorothy Marcic from Susanne G. Scott and Reginald A. Bruce, "Determinants of Innovative Behavior: A Path Model of Individual Innovation in the Workplace," *Academy of Management Journal* 37, no. 3 (1994), 580–607.
129. Written by Charles E. Summer. Copyright 1978.
130. Doug Wallace, "What Would You Do?" *Business Ethics* (March/April 1996), 52–53. Reprinted with permission from *Business Ethics*, PO Box 8439, Minneapolis, MN 55408; phone: 612-879-0695.

INTEGRATIVE CASE 7.0

7.0

Custom Chip, Inc.*

Introduction

It was 7:50 on Monday morning. Frank Questin, product engineering manager at Custom Chip, Inc., was sitting in his office making a TO DO list for the day. From 8:00 to 9:30 A.M., he would have his weekly meeting with his staff of engineers. After the meeting, Frank thought he would begin developing a proposal for solving what he called "Custom Chip's manufacturing documentation problem"—inadequate technical information regarding the steps to manufacture many of the company's products. Before he could finish his TO DO list, he answered a phone call from Custom Chip's human resource manager, who asked him about the status of two overdue performance appraisals and reminded him that this day marked Bill Lazarus's fifth-year anniversary with the company. Following this call, Frank hurried off to the Monday morning meeting with his staff.

Frank had been product engineering manager at Custom Chip for fourteen months. This was his first management position, and he sometimes questioned his effectiveness as a manager. Often he could not complete the tasks he set out for himself due to interruptions and problems brought to his attention by others. Even though he had not been told exactly what results he was supposed to accomplish, he had a nagging feeling that he should have achieved more after these fourteen months. On the other hand, he thought maybe he was functioning pretty well in some of his areas of responsibility given the complexity of the problems his group handled and the unpredictable changes in the semiconductor industry—changes caused not only by rapid advances in technology, but also by increased foreign competition and a recent downturn in demand.

Company Background

Custom Chip, Inc., was a semiconductor manufacturer specializing in custom chips and components used in radars, satellite transmitters, and other radio frequency devices. The company had been founded in 1977 and had grown rapidly with sales exceeding $25 million in 1986. Most of the company's 300 employees were located in the main plant in Silicon Valley, but overseas manufacturing facilities in Europe and the Far East were growing in size and importance. These overseas facilities assembled the less complex, higher-volume products. New products and the more complex ones were assembled in the main plant. Approximately one-third of the assembly employees were in overseas facilities.

While the specialized products and markets of Custom Chip provided a market niche that had thus far shielded the company from the major downturn in the semiconductor industry, growth had come to a standstill. Because of this, cost reduction had become a high priority.

The Manufacturing Process

Manufacturers of standard chips have long production runs of a few products. Their cost per unit is low and cost control is a primary determinant of success. In contrast, manufacturers of custom chips have extensive product lines and produce small production runs of special applications. Custom Chip, Inc., for example, had manufactured over 2,000 different products in the last five years. In any one quarter the company might schedule 300 production runs for different products, as many as one-third of which might be new or modified products that the company had not made before. Because they must be efficient in designing and manufacturing many product lines, all custom chip manufacturers are highly dependent on their engineers. Customers are often first concerned with whether Custom Chip can design and manufacture the needed product *at all*; second, with whether they can deliver it on time; and only third, with cost.

After a product is designed, there are two phases to the manufacturing process. (See Exhibit 1.) The first is wafer fabrication. This is a complex process in which circuits are etched onto the various layers added to a silicon wafer. The number of steps that the wafer goes through plus inherent problems in controlling various chemical processes make it very difficult to meet the exacting specifications required for the final wafer. The wafers, which are typically "just a few" inches in diameter when the fabrication process is complete, contain hundreds, sometimes thousands, of tiny identical die. Once the wafer has been tested and sliced up to produce these die, each die will be used as a circuit component.

If the completed wafer passes the various quality tests, it moves on to the assembly phase. In assembly, the die from the wafers, very small wires, and other components are attached to a circuit in a series of precise operations. This finished circuit is the final product of Custom Chip, Inc.

Each product goes through many independent and delicate operations, and each step is subject to operator or machine error. Due to the number of steps and tests involved, the wafer fabrication takes eight to twelve weeks

EXHIBIT 1
Manufacturing Process

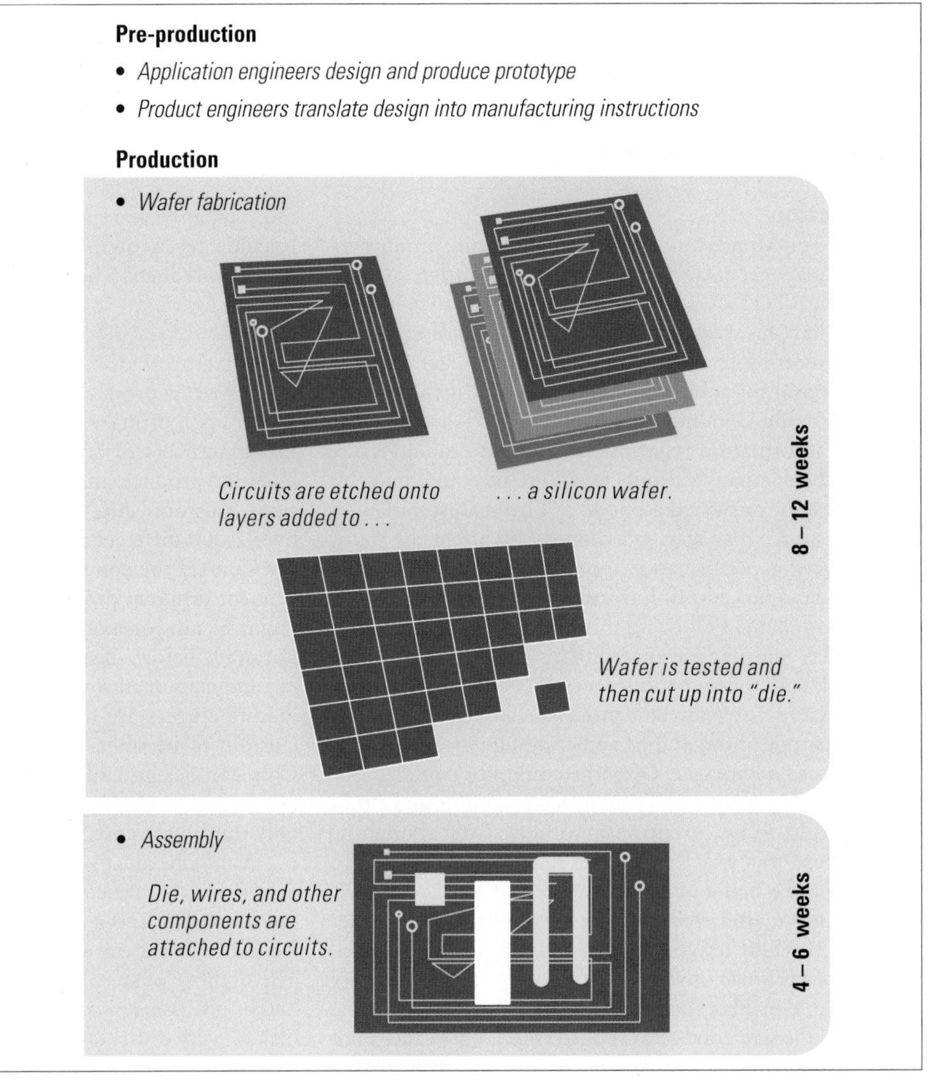

and the assembly process takes four to six weeks. Because of the exacting specifications, products are rejected for the slightest flaw. The likelihood that every product starting the run will make it through all of the processes and still meet specifications is often quite low. For some products, average yield[1] is as low as 40 percent, and actual yields can vary considerably from one run to another. At Custom Chip, the average yield for all products is in the 60 to 70 percent range.

Pre-production
• Application engineers design and produce prototype
• Product engineers translate design into manufacturing instructions
Production
• Wafer fabrication
Circuits are etched onto layers added to . . .
. . . a silicon wafer.
Wafer is tested and then cut up into "die."
8 – 12 weeks
• Assembly
Die, wires, and other components are attached to circuits.
4 – 6 weeks

Because it takes so long to make a custom chip, it is especially important to have some control of these yields. For example, if a customer orders one thousand units of a product and typical yields for that product average 50 percent, Custom Chip will schedule a starting batch of 2,200 units. With this approach, even if the yield falls as low as 45.4 percent (45.4 percent of 2,200 is 1,000) the company can still meet the order. If the actual yield falls below 45.4 percent, the order will not be completed in that run, and a very small, costly run of the item will be needed to complete the order. The only way the company can effectively control these yields and stay on schedule is for the engineering groups and operations to cooperate and coordinate their efforts efficiently.

Role of the Product Engineer

The product engineer's job is defined by its relationship to applications engineering and operations. The applications engineers are responsible for designing and developing prototypes when incoming orders are for new or

[1]Yield refers to the ratio of finished products that meet specifications relative to the number that initially entered the manufacturing process.

modified products. The product engineer's role is to translate the applications engineering group's design into a set of manufacturing instructions and then to work alongside manufacturing to make sure that engineering-related problems get solved. The product engineers' effectiveness is ultimately measured by their ability to control yields on their assigned products. The organization chart in Exhibit 2 shows the engineering and operations departments. Exhibit 3 summarizes the roles and objectives of manufacturing, applications engineering, and product engineering.

The product engineers estimate that 70 to 80 percent of their time is spent in solving day-to-day manufacturing problems. The product engineers have cubicles in a room directly across the hall from the manufacturing facility. If a manufacturing supervisor has a question regarding how to build a product during a run, that supervisor will call the engineer assigned to that product. If the engineer is available, he or she will go to the manufacturing floor to help answer the question. If the engineer is not available, the production run may be stopped and the product put

EXHIBIT 2
Custom Chip, Inc., Partial Organization Chart

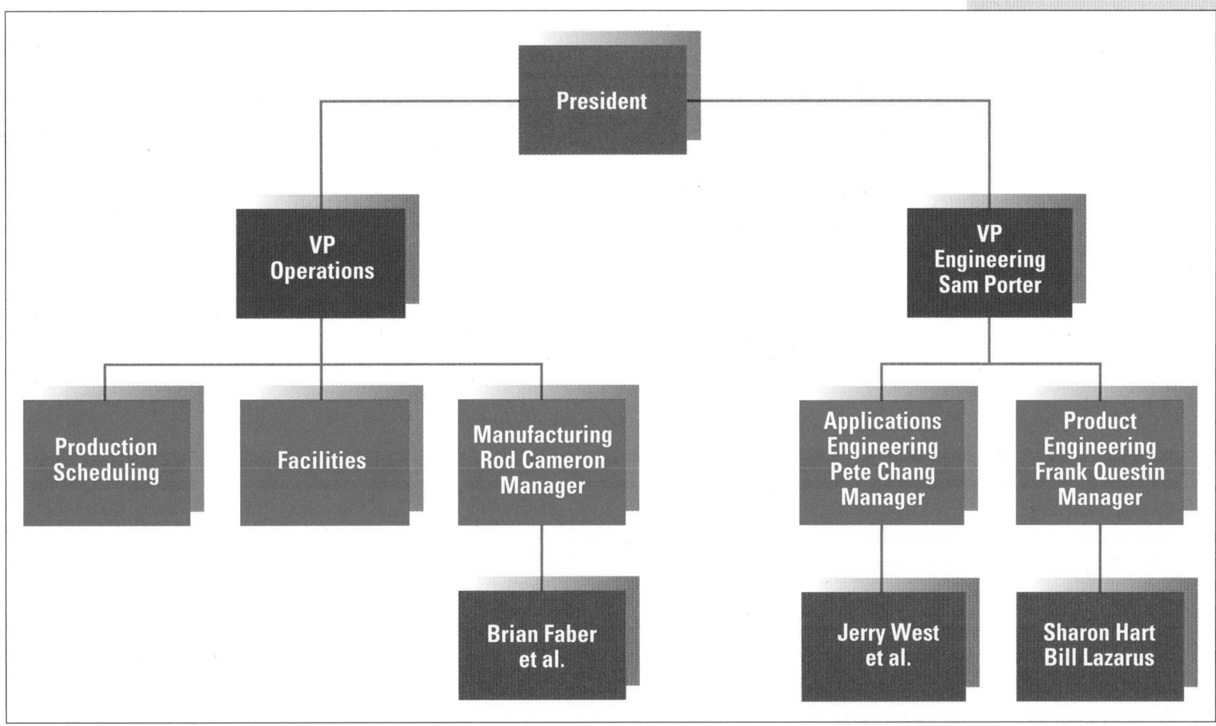

EXHIBIT 3
Departmental Roles and Objectives

Department	Role	Primary Objective
Applications Engineering	Designs and develops prototypes for new or modified products	Satisfy customer needs through innovative designs
Product Engineering	Translates designs into manufacturing instructions and works alongside manufacturing to solve "engineering-related" problems	Maintain and control yields on assigned products
Manufacturing	Executes designs	Meet productivity standards and time schedules

aside so that other orders can be manufactured. This results in delays and added costs. One reason that product engineers are consulted is that documentation—the instructions for manufacturing the product—is unclear or incomplete.

The product engineer will also be called if a product is tested and fails to meet specifications. If a product fails to meet test specifications, production stops, and the engineer must diagnose the problem and attempt to find a solution. Otherwise, the order for that product may be only partially met. Test failures are a very serious problem, which can result in considerable cost increases and schedule delays for customers. Products do not test properly for many reasons, including operator errors, poor materials, a design that is very difficult to manufacture, a design that provides too little margin for error, or a combination of these.

On a typical day, the product engineers may respond to half a dozen questions from the manufacturing floor, and two to four calls to the testing stations. When interviewed, the engineers expressed a frustration with this situation. They thought they spent too much time solving short-term problems, and, consequently, they were neglecting other important parts of their jobs. In particular, they felt they had little time in which to:

- *Coordinate with applications engineers during the design phase.* The product engineers stated that their knowledge of manufacturing could provide valuable input to the applications engineers. Together they could improve the manufacturability and thus, the yields of the new or modified products.
- *Engage in yield improvement projects.* This would involve an in-depth study of the existing process for a specific product in conjunction with an analysis of past product failures.
- *Accurately document the manufacturing steps for their assigned products, especially for those that tend to have large or repeat orders.* They said that the current state of the documentation is very poor. Operators often have to build products using only a drawing showing the final circuit, along with a few notes scribbled in the margins. While experienced operators and supervisors may be able to work with this information, they often make incorrect guesses and assumptions. Inexperienced operators may not be able to proceed with certain products because of this poor documentation.

Weekly Meeting

As manager of the product engineering group, Frank Questin had eight engineers reporting to him, each responsible for a different set of Custom Chip products. According to Frank:

When I took over as manager, the product engineers were not spending much time together as a group. They were required to handle operations problems on short notice. This made it difficult for the entire group to meet due to constant requests for assistance from the manufacturing area.

I thought that my engineers could be of more assistance and support to each other if they all spent more time together as a group, so one of my first actions as a manager was to institute a regularly scheduled weekly meeting. I let the manufacturing people know that my staff would not respond to requests for assistance during the meeting.

The meeting on this particular Monday morning followed the usual pattern. Frank talked about upcoming company plans, projects, and other news that might be of interest to the group. He then provided data about current yields for each product and commended those engineers who had maintained or improved yields on most of their products. This initial phase of the meeting lasted until about 8:30 A.M. The remainder of the meeting was a meandering discussion of a variety of topics. Since there was no agenda, engineers felt comfortable in raising issues of concern to them.

The discussion started with one of the engineers describing a technical problem in the assembly of one of his products. He was asked a number of questions and given some advice. Another engineer raised the topic of a need for new testing equipment and described a test unit he had seen at a recent demonstration. He claimed the savings in labor and improved yields from this machine would allow it to pay for itself in less than nine months. Frank immediately replied that budget limitations made such a purchase unfeasible, and the discussion moved into another area. They briefly discussed the increasing inaccessibility of the applications engineers and then talked about a few other topics.

In general, the engineers valued these meetings. One commented that:

The Monday meetings give me a chance to hear what's on everyone's mind and to find out about and discuss companywide news. It's hard to reach any conclusions because the meeting is a freewheeling discussion. But I really appreciate the friendly atmosphere with my peers.

Coordination with Applications Engineers

Following the meeting that morning, an event occurred that highlighted the issue of the inaccessibility of the applications engineers. An order of 300 units of custom chip 1210A for a major customer was already overdue. Because the projected yield of this product was 70 percent, they had started with a run of 500 units. A sample tested at one of the early assembly points indicated a major performance problem that could drop the yield to below 50 percent. Bill Lazarus, the product engineer assigned to the 1210A, examined the sample and determined that the problem could be solved by redesigning the wiring. Jerry West, the applications engineer assigned to that product category, was responsible for revising the design. Bill tried to contact Jerry, but he was not immediately available, and didn't get back to Bill until later in the day. Jerry explained that he was on a tight schedule trying to finish a design for a customer who was coming into town in two days, and could not get to "Bill's problem" for a while.

Jerry's attitude that the problem belonged to product engineering was typical of the applications engineers. From their point of view there were a number of reasons for making the product engineers' needs for assistance a lower priority. In the first place, applications engineers were rewarded and acknowledged primarily for satisfying customer needs through designing new and modified products. They got little recognition for solving manufacturing problems. Second, applications engineering was perceived to be more glamorous than product engineering because of opportunities to be credited with innovative and groundbreaking designs. Finally, the size of the applications engineering group had declined over the past year, causing the workload on each engineer to increase considerably. Now they had even less time to respond to the product engineers' requests.

When Bill Lazarus told Frank about the situation, Frank acted quickly. He wanted this order to be in process again by tomorrow, and he knew manufacturing was also trying to meet this goal. He walked over to see Pete Chang, head of applications engineering (see the organizational chart in Exhibit 2). Meetings like this with Pete to discuss and resolve interdepartmental issues were common.

Frank found Pete at a workbench talking with one of his engineers. He asked Pete if he could talk to him in private, and they walked to Pete's office.

Frank: *We've got a problem in manufacturing in getting out an order of 1210As. Bill Lazarus is getting little or no assistance from Jerry West. I'm hoping you can get Jerry to pitch in and help Bill. It should take no more than a few hours of his time.*

Pete: *I do have Jerry on a short leash trying to keep him focused on getting out a design for Teletronics. We can't afford to show up empty-handed at our meeting with them in two days.*

Frank: *Well, we are going to end up losing one customer in trying to please another. Can't we satisfy everyone here?*

Pete: *Do you have an idea?*

Frank: *Can't you give Jerry some additional support on the Teletronics design?*

Pete: *Let's get Jerry in here to see what we can do.*

Pete brought Jerry back to the office, and together they discussed the issues and possible solutions. When Pete made it clear to Jerry that he considered the problem with the 1210As a priority, Jerry offered to work on the 1210A problem with Bill. He said, "This will mean I'll have to stay a few hours past 5:00 this evening, but I'll do what's required to get the job done."

Frank was glad he had developed a collaborative relationship with Pete. He had always made it a point to keep Pete informed about activities in the product engineering group that might affect the applications engineers. In addition, he would often chat with Pete informally over coffee or lunch in the company cafeteria. This relationship with Pete made Frank's job easier. He wished he had the same rapport with Rod Cameron, the manufacturing manager.

Coordination with Manufacturing

The product engineers worked closely on a day-to-day basis with the manufacturing supervisors and workers. The problems between these two groups stemmed from an inherent conflict between their objectives (see Exhibit 3). The objective of the product engineers was to maintain and improve yields. They had the authority to stop production of any run that did not test properly. Manufacturing, on the other hand, was trying to meet productivity standards and time schedules. When a product engineer stopped a manufacturing run, he or she was possibly preventing the manufacturing group from reaching its objectives.

Rod Cameron, the current manufacturing manager, had been promoted from his position as a manufacturing supervisor a year ago. His views on the product engineers:

The product engineers are perfectionists. The minute a test result looks a little suspicious they want to shut down the factory. I'm under a lot of pressure to get products out the door. If they pull a few $50,000 orders off the line when they are within a few days of reaching shipping, I'm liable to miss my numbers by $100,000 that month.

Besides that, they are doing a lousy job of documenting the manufacturing steps. I've got a lot of turnover, and my new operators need to be told or shown exactly what to do for each product. The instructions for a lot of our products are a joke.

At first, Frank found Rod very difficult to deal with. Rod found fault with the product engineers for many problems and sometimes seemed rude to Frank when they talked. For example, Rod might tell Frank to "make it quick; I haven't got much time." Frank tried not to take Rod's actions personally, and through persistence was able to develop a more amicable relationship with him. According to Frank:

Sometimes, my people will stop work on a product because it doesn't meet test results at that stage of manufacturing. If we study the situation, we might be able to maintain yields or even save an entire run by adjusting the manufacturing procedures. Rod tries to bully me into changing my engineers' decisions. He yells at me or criticizes the competence of my people, but I don't allow his temper or ravings to influence my best judgment in a situation. My strategy in dealing with Rod is to try not to respond defensively to him. Eventually he cools down, and we can have a reasonable discussion of the situation.

Despite this strategy, Frank could not always resolve his problems with Rod. On these occasions, Frank took the issue to his own boss, Sam Porter, the vice president in charge of engineering. However, Frank was not satisfied with the support he got from Sam. Frank said:

Sam avoids confrontations with the operations VP. He doesn't have the influence or clout with the other VPs or the president to do justice to engineering's needs in the organization.

Early that afternoon, Frank again found himself trying to resolve a conflict between engineering and manufacturing. Sharon Hart, one of his most effective product engineers, was responsible for a series of products used in radars—the 3805A–3808A series. Today she had stopped a large run of 3806As. The manufacturing supervisor, Brian Faber, went to Rod Cameron to complain about the impact of this stoppage on his group's productivity. Brian felt that yields were low on that particular product because the production instructions were confusing to his operators, and that even with clearer instructions, his operators would need additional training to build it satisfactorily. He stressed that the product engineer's responsibility was to adequately document the production instructions and provide training. For these reasons, Brian asserted that product engineering, and not manufacturing, should be accountable for the productivity loss in the case of these 3806As.

Rod called Frank to his office, where he joined the discussion with Sharon, Brian, and Rod. After listening to the issues, Frank conceded that product engineering had responsibility for documenting and training. He also explained, even though everyone was aware of it, that the product engineering group had been operating with reduced staff for over a year now, so training and documentation were lower priorities. Because of this staffing situation, Frank suggested that manufacturing and product engineering work together and pool their limited resources to solve the documentation and training problem. He was especially interested in using a few of the long-term experienced workers to assist in training newer workers. Rod and Brian opposed his suggestion. They did not want to take experienced operators off of the line because it would decrease productivity. The meeting ended when Brian stormed out, saying that Sharon had better get the 3806As up and running again that morning.

Frank was particularly frustrated by this episode with manufacturing. He knew perfectly well that his group had primary responsibility for documenting the manufacturing steps for each product. A year ago he told Sam Porter that the product engineers needed to update and standardize all of the documentation for manufacturing products. At that time, Sam told Frank that he would support his efforts to develop the documentation, but would not increase his staff. In fact, Sam had withheld authorization to fill a recently vacated product engineering slot. Frank was reluctant to push the staffing issue because of Sam's adamance about reducing costs. "Perhaps," Frank thought, "if I develop a proposal clearly showing the benefits of a documentation program in manufacturing and detailing the steps and resources required to implement the program, I might be able to convince Sam to provide us with more resources." But Frank could never find the time to develop that proposal. And so he remained frustrated.

Later in the Day

Frank was reflecting on the complexity of his job when Sharon came to the doorway to see if he had a few moments. Before he could say "Come in," the phone rang. He looked at the clock. It was 4:10 P.M. Pete was on the other end of the line with an idea he wanted to try out on Frank, so Frank said he could call him back shortly. Sharon was upset and told him that she was thinking of quitting because the job was not satisfying for her.

Sharon said that although she very much enjoyed working on yield improvement projects, she could find no time for them. She was tired of the applications engineers acting like "prima donnas," too busy to help her solve what they seemed to think were mundane day-to-day manufacturing problems. She also thought that many of the day-to-day problems she handled wouldn't exist if there was enough time to document manufacturing procedures to begin with.

Frank didn't want to lose Sharon, so he tried to get into a frame of mind where he could be empathetic to her. He listened to her and told her that he could understand her frustration in this situation. He told her the situation would change as industry conditions improved. He told her that he was pleased that she felt comfortable in venting her frustrations with him, and he hoped she would stay with Custom Chip.

After Sharon left, Frank realized that he had told Pete that he would call back. He glanced at the TO DO list he had never completed, and realized that he hadn't spent time on his top priority—developing a proposal relating to solving the documentation problem in manufacturing. Then, he remembered that he had forgotten to acknowledge Bill Lazarus's fifth-year anniversary with the company. He thought to himself that his job felt like a roller coaster ride, and once again he pondered his effectiveness as a manager.

INTEGRATIVE CASE 8.0
Lean Initiatives and Growth at Orlando Metering Company*

It was late August 2002 and Ed Cucinelli, vice president of Orlando Metering Company (OMC), sat in his office on a late Saturday morning. He had come in to prepare for some strategic planning meetings that were scheduled for the upcoming week. As he noticed the uncommon silence in the building, Ed contemplated the current situation in his organization.

The Orlando Metering Company was one of several facilities owned by a leading manufacturer of water meters for the worldwide utility industry. The facility specialized in the assembly, testing, and repair of water meters used to measure the amount of water consumed by private homes, organizations, and large cities. In 1999, OMC started the process of moving from a traditional manufacturing to a lean manufacturing organization with a fully empowered workforce. Due to the tremendous success the organization achieved, the corporate headquarters decided to transfer four new product lines to the Orlando facility in 2001. This transfer resulted in considerable expansion of the business, doubling the number of employees and shifts needed at the plant and quadrupling the revenues of the organization. As Ed looked through some old pictures on his desk, he reflected on how proud he was of everything that his leadership team and employees had been able to accomplish in the short year-and-a-half timeframe that was given to them by the headquarters.

However, the organization was currently experiencing some very tough challenges due to the recent change and expansion. Although OMC successfully brought in the new business, Ed and his management team made some mistakes in the transition. When he walked through the production floor, Ed could feel that the energy and commitment of the employees were at an all time low. He knew that his current 108 employees were stressed and unhappy. Turnover and absenteeism were at an all time high, and productivity and quality were suffering. The organization had lost a lot of the momentum it had gained in its implementation of lean manufacturing. Just last week, Ed had received a call from his supervisor at corporate expressing concerns about the current situation at OMC. The corporate headquarters had given Ed and his leadership team three months to turn things around and show some improvements.

Ed knew that it was time to take some serious action. He knew that the process side of planning the inventory and physically assembling the meters according to the principles of lean manufacturing were working efficiently in his facility. However, the company had lost the team-based, lean manufacturing culture in which the employees took ownership and worked together as a team to solve problems and run their own work cells. He knew that to truly take advantage of the potential of the lean layout and processes operating in his plant, the company needed to have the culture to support it. Ed knew that it was the right decision to keep the lean production process in the operation, inventory planning, and assembling meters. However, he needed to decide whether to refocus the organization on reestablishing the *team-based, lean culture and thinking* that it had lost or return to the traditional top-down management methods of the past.

Background

Fresh out of college, Ed began his career at OMC in 1993 as a mechanical engineer. The company was originally founded in Orlando, Florida in 1974. The PMG group, OMC's parent company based in Europe, was seeking growth opportunities and saw the United States as a great opportunity given the size of the market and the fact that OMC's product offered a new technology compared to those available at that time. There were many styles of water meters for different applications, and OMC's new product at that time provided a solution to issues within the market, mainly suspended solids (i.e., sand) in the water. Traditional meters would slow down and stop due to suspended solids, thus reducing a water utility's revenues. This new meter allowed the suspended solids to pass through and provided better accuracy for measuring water use, thus increasing revenues. Therefore, the meter quickly gained acceptance in many markets and the company had grown since the new meter's introduction.

As sales continued to increase, so did the number of employees and the need for more space. Ed was in charge of designing and overseeing the construction of a new facility. Having no prior experience working within a lean enterprise,

**This case was prepared by Wanda Chaves from Ringling College of Art and Design and Ed Cucinelli from Crummer Business School. The views presented here are those of the case authors and do not necessarily reflect the views of the Society for Case Research. The authors' views are based on their own professional judgments.*

Ed designed the new facility as a larger model of the old. Adding more space and more equipment did not create a more efficient workplace, but with the right people, the company still accomplished the job. As he sat in his office, Ed remembered the long nights working side by side with maintenance, quality, and production personnel, all trying to insure that the new facility move would be successful. The power of teamwork was evident as the employees completed the project in a timely fashion and production efficiencies remained stable. At this time, many of the employees at OMC had been with the company for nearly 10 years. Employees knew each other and each other's families, and they felt a sense of responsibility to one another. Even though OMC did not have the best tools, offered a compensation package that did not exceed the market average, and ran without air-conditioning, the employees felt that they belonged to something special.

The Decision to Go Lean

In 1998, OMC's parent company was purchased by a much larger competitor. Soon after, the board of directors came to Orlando for a board meeting. The board decided to pursue a lean manufacturing culture within the organization. At that time, however, none of the company's facilities operated in a lean manner. As a test and learning experience, the board decided to challenge the Orlando plant, and it gave the facility an aggressive nine-week time frame within which to implement the reconstruction of the production floor and change the manufacturing process to lean.

At this point, Ed accepted the position of Lean Champion, where he became responsible for implementing the lean changes and initiatives. Ed knew that all of the employees at OMC would need to be involved if the organization was to successfully achieve this nine-week goal. Immediately, the leaders of the plant held a plant-wide meeting and outlined the goals. Everyone quickly realized that the small Orlando facility would be closed and relocated to one of the large sister facilities if the change was not successful. Ed organized the employees into teams, conducted lean training, and provided constant management of the project and deadlines. All employees responded, and through long hours, many weekends, and a lot of sweat, all production lines and half of the office processes were converted to utilize the lean concepts. Exhibit 1 details the specific timeline that was developed and accomplished.

Background on Lean Manufacturing

The goals of implementing lean manufacturing at the OMC facility included improving material handling, inventory, quality, scheduling, personnel, and customer satisfaction. In general, the key objectives of the lean facility's layout and flow were to deliver high-quality, low-cost products quickly while maintaining a safe and pleasant working environment (Henderson & Larco, 1999). By implementing just-in-time (JIT) production, one piece flow, self-directed work teams, and cellular manufacturing, the leaders expected the following improvements to occur as part of the new lean environment:

1. a decrease in the cost of space, inventory and capital equipment;
2. a reduction in throughput time, cycle time, or lead time;
3. an increase in capacity utilization;
4. a reduction in lost-time accidents.

Exhibit 2 details the strategic advantages of implementing lean manufacturing.

Lean is not only a production system of tools and processes to continually improve, but it also involves implementing a culture and atmosphere in which the systems and tools can be best utilized. Without the culture and support of all the people, the benefits cannot be maximized. Exhibit 3 illustrates the principal components of lean production, and Exhibit 4 provides details on lean management and the key elements needed to sustain a lean manufacturing culture.

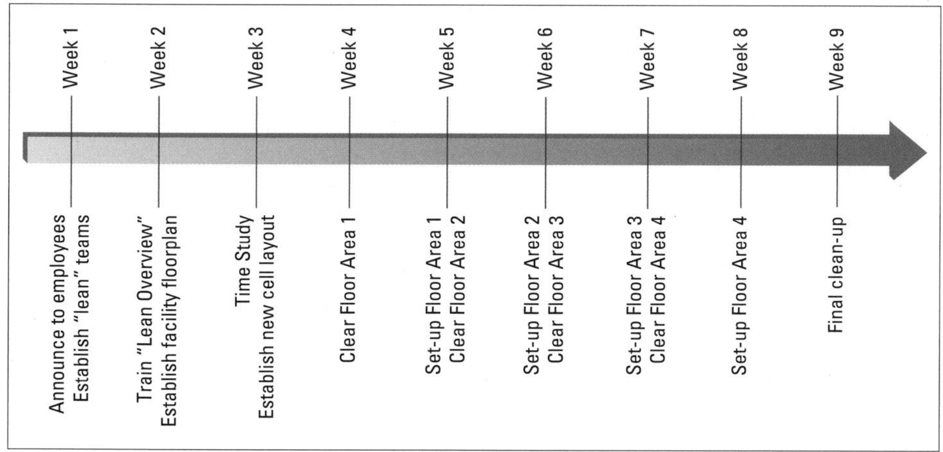

EXHIBIT 1
Nine Week Project Timeline

EXHIBIT 2
Strategic Advantages of Lean Manufacturing

Manufacturing Lead Time	Reduced by one day
Delivered Quality	3 Parts Per Million (PPM)
Delivery Performance	99+ percent
Inventory Turns	Greater than 50
Conversion Cost (materials to finished goods)	25 to 40 percent less than mass producers
Manufacturing Space	35 to 50 percent less than mass producers
New Product Development	Less than six months

Source: B. A. Henderson and J. L. Larco, *Lean Transformation: How to Change Your Business into a Lean Enterprise* (Richmond, VA: The Oaklea Press, 1999), 42.

EXHIBIT 3
Principal Components of Lean Production

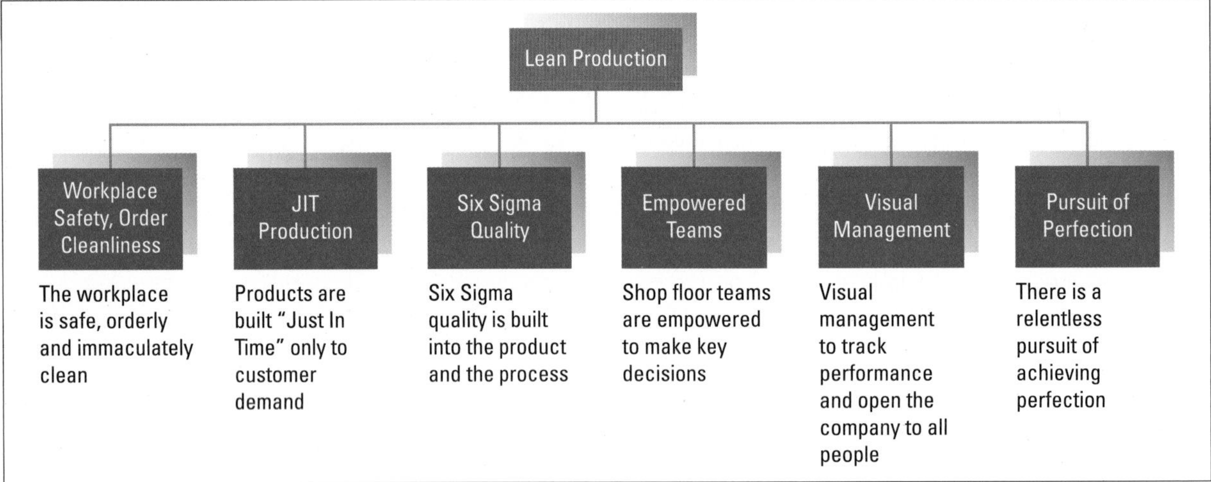

Source: B. A. Henderson and J. L. Larco, *Lean Transformation: How to Change Your Business into a Lean Enterprise*, 46.

EXHIBIT 4
Principal Elements of Lean Management

Element	Key Characteristics
Leader Standard Work	Daily checklists for line production leaders—team leaders, supervisors, and value stream managers—that state explicit expectations for what it means to focus on the process
Visual Controls	Tracking charts and other visual tools that reflect actual performance compared with expected performance of virtually any process in a lean operation, production and non-production alike
Daily Accountability Process	Brief, structured, tiered meetings that are focused on performance with visual action assignments and follow-up to close gaps between actual results versus expected performance
Discipline	Leaders themselves consistently following and following up on others' adherence to the processes that define the first three elements

Source: D. Mann, *Creating a Lean Culture: Tools to Sustain Lean Conversions* (New York: Productivity Press, 2005), vi.

Source: Henderson, B. A. & Larco, J. L. (1999) Lean Transformation: How to change your business into a lean enterprise. *The Oaklea Press.*

Source: Henderson, B. A. & Larco, J. L. (1999) Lean Transformation: How to change your business into a lean enterprise. *The Oaklea Press.*

EXHIBIT 5
Physical Changes to OMC Facility

Becoming the Lean Showcase

Next, the employees and leaders needed to work together to transform the company into a lean showcase. Ed knew that simply making changes to the production processes would not create the lean showcase that the board expected. Although employees were supportive and dedicated, the management team provided most of the direction and led the change. As discussed above, one of the critical elements to the successful implementation of a lean environment is the development and maintenance of a self-directed, empowered workforce (Henderson and Larco, 1999). Ed realized that the time had come to transition to team-based production lines. Over the next few months Ed and the OMC leadership team, with the help of a trainer, began an intensive team-based training program. The employees went through team skills training, including sessions on feedback and communication, problem solving, meeting skills, team dynamics, and an informal session on company financials. The teams began to see the results of the training and hard work. They began to run their own team meetings and suggested and implemented 8 to 10 improvements a week in areas such as quality, safety, and productivity. The employees were motivated and encouraged by all of the progress and success.

At the same time, the leaders at OMC were focused on making a more comfortable and friendly work environment. This was accomplished by adding new lighting that tripled the brightness of the facility; painting the floor, walls, and equipment; and installing air-conditioning. Leaders even placed live plants throughout the facility. These changes helped promote the concept that employees played a key part in the success of OMC. The facility looked clean and beautiful. Exhibit 5 provides before and after pictures of the facility.

After an 18-month implementation cycle (which included the physical changes to the manufacturing floor as well as the implementation of lean manufacturing production and administrative processes), the organization was able to achieve the following benefits:

- The managers and employees were able to reduce inventory by 50 percent and completely eliminate finished goods.
- Quality control changes resulted in the conversion to 100 percent testing of all products without adding any additional employees or equipment.
- The plant was able to cut total production cycle times from days to minutes (typically one to two days to process reduced to 5 to 15 minutes).
- Total floor space was reduced by 41 percent (so much that a basketball court was added within the facility), as displayed in Exhibit 6.

Exhibit 7 details the cost involved during the nine-week transformation of the physical manufacturing floor to lean production.

Working together, the employees and leaders had succeeded in establishing the lean showcase, and the board of directors took full advantage. People from sister companies around the world came to Orlando. They toured the facility to learn about lean manufacturing and the best methods to implement it. Tours were given by the employees. There was no better evidence in the power of lean manufacturing and empowerment than seeing an hourly employee give a presentation to a Vice President of Operations of another facility. Morale was at its highest point ever. There were no obstacles that this Orlando facility could not overcome. At this point, Ed and the leadership team knew that the OMC facility was being underutilized. They needed more business.

Over the next year, the Orlando facility continued to be the "showcase." Performance continued to improve. The rapid success of OMC captured the attention of OMC's customers as well as other corporate officers. In 2001, the board decided to relocate four new product lines from a sister facility to OMC. Although OMC had installed new production lines in the past, this change represented a much larger scale. It would require doubling the workforce, quadrupling sales, and converting the existing production lines to utilize the lean concepts, all within 18 months.

Rapid Growth at OMC

Ed was the project manager responsible for the transition of the new business into the Orlando facility. However, nine months into this project the current VP of Operations

EXHIBIT 6
Reduction of Floor Space at OMC

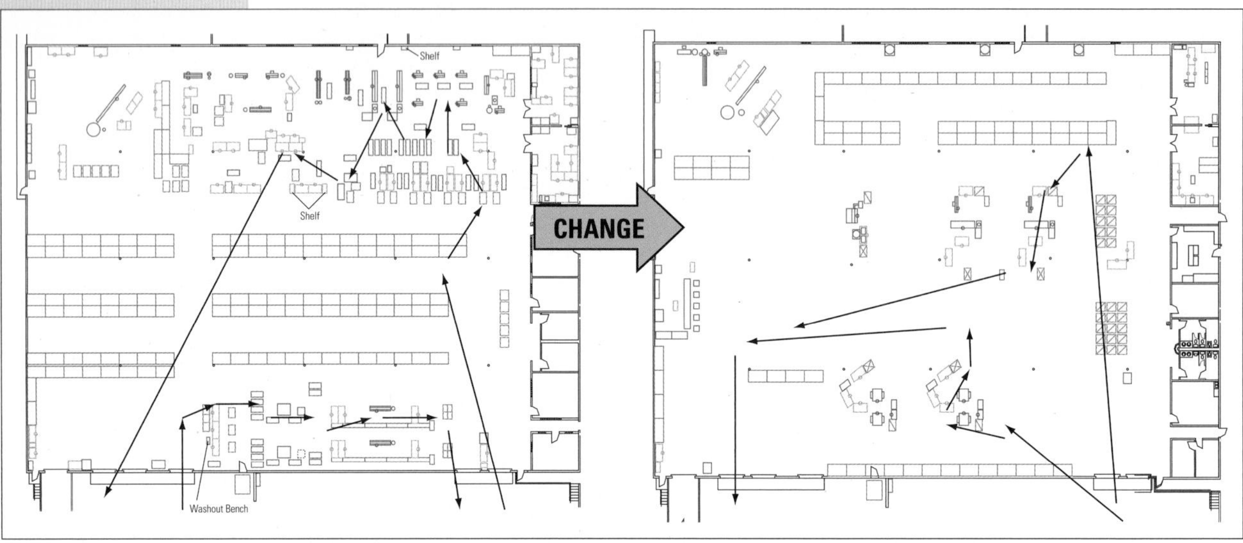

EXHIBIT 7
Project Costs

"Nine-Week" Phase Costs		"Showcase" Phase Costs	
Equipment & Tools	$ 15,000	Air-Conditioning	$ 250,000
Lost Productivity	$ 10,000	Floor Coating	$ 120,000
Lighting	$ 10,000	Equipment & Tools	$ 45,000
Training	$ 6,000	Painting	$ 33,000
Supplies	$ 4,000	Training	$ 12,000
	$ 45,000	Supplies	$ 10,000
			$ 470,000

EXHIBIT 8
Savings Achieved Through Lean at OMC

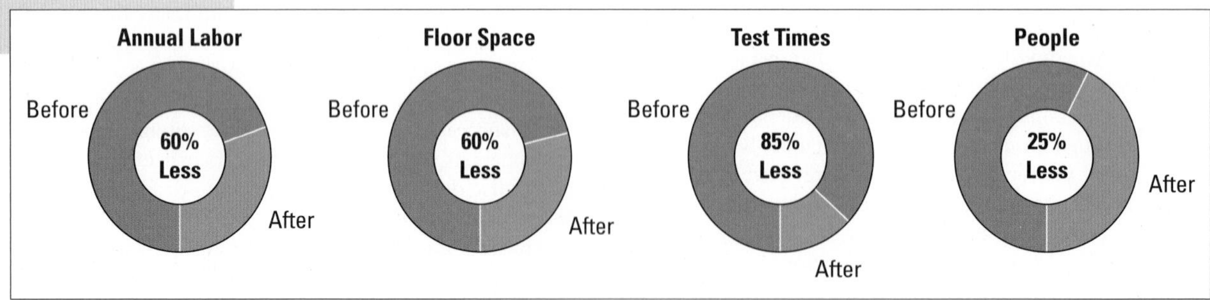

was promoted and Ed became the VP of Operations, in charge of the entire Orlando facility.

Although slightly behind schedule, Ed and his leadership team and employees completed the project in 20 months, and they exceeded the projected savings. Lean manufacturing again provided significant benefits to the OMC operations. Through the change, OMC achieved significant savings in labor costs, floor space, and process times, as exhibited in Exhibit 8.

Ed enthusiastically led the new change, but the technical challenges in the transition of this product proved more difficult than expected. The union facility from which the product was transferred relied solely on the worker's experience in manufacturing the meters, so the facility had kept limited product and process documentation. The engineers at OMC constructed new test equipment to replace the 40-year-old technology previously used. There were also many challenges with the products, as many of them were designed nearly 50 years earlier, and meeting current quality demands proved difficult. The project had placed a large strain on the resources in the Orlando facility, and many sacrifices were made. In order to ensure that the project was completed on time and that the change was seamless for the customer, the leadership team focused heavily on overcoming the technical hurdles with the production of the new meters. In doing so, the team failed to address the impact on the employees and the other critical people issues that arose during the change process. The leadership team quickly learned that the success it had experienced in the recent past would be short-lived, as the lean culture had deteriorated and the team-based structure no longer existed at OMC. Exhibits 9, 10, and 11 detail the longitudinal changes in on-time delivery, turnover, and inventory turns as a function of OMC's sales.

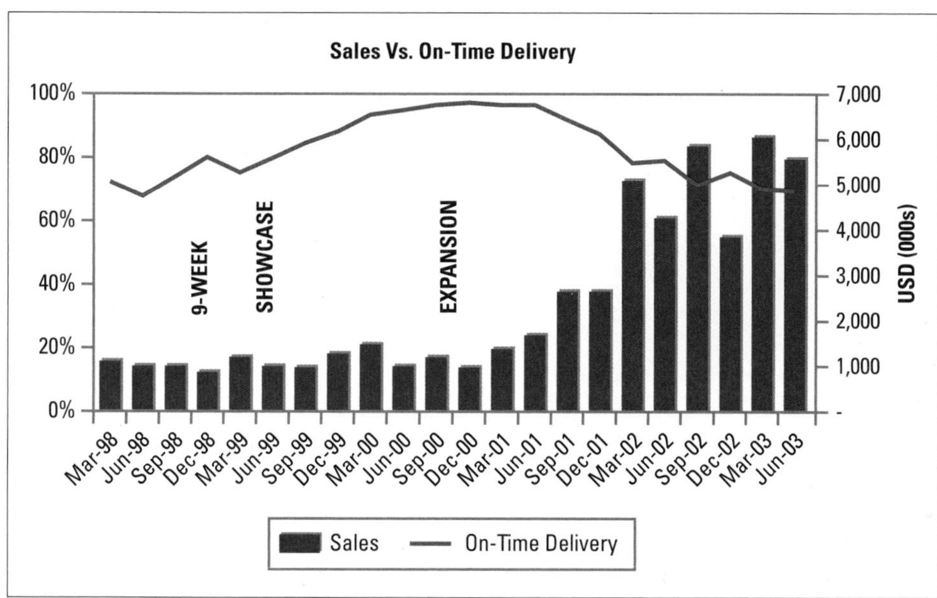

EXHIBIT 9
Changes in On-time Delivery

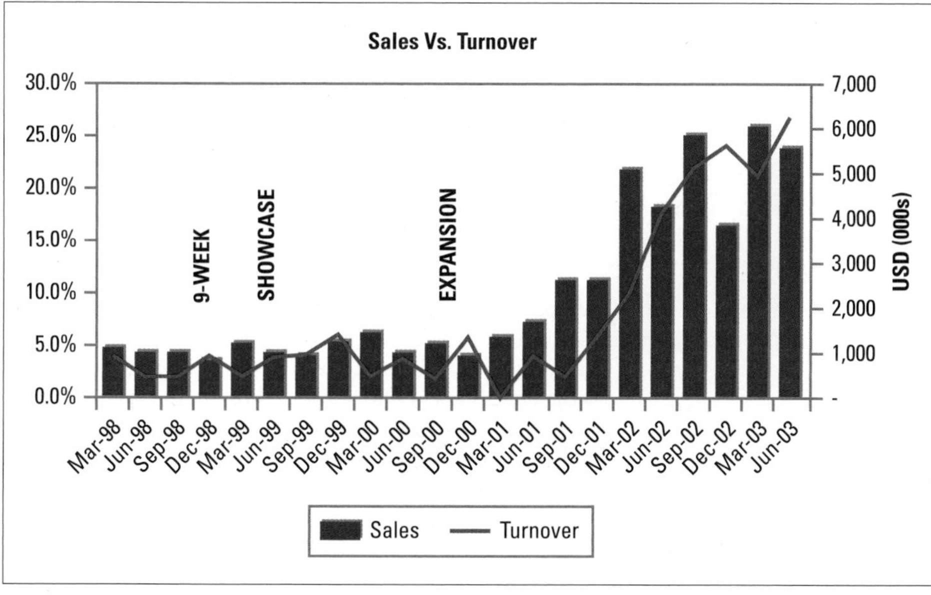

EXHIBIT 10
Changes in Turnover

EXHIBIT 11
Changes in Inventory Turns

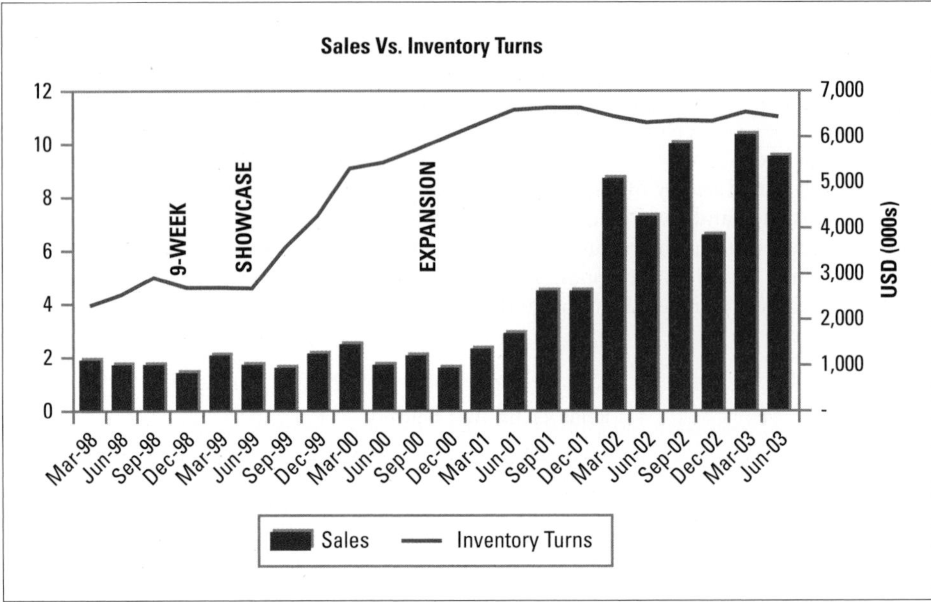

EXHIBIT 12
Overall Timeline for OMC Changes

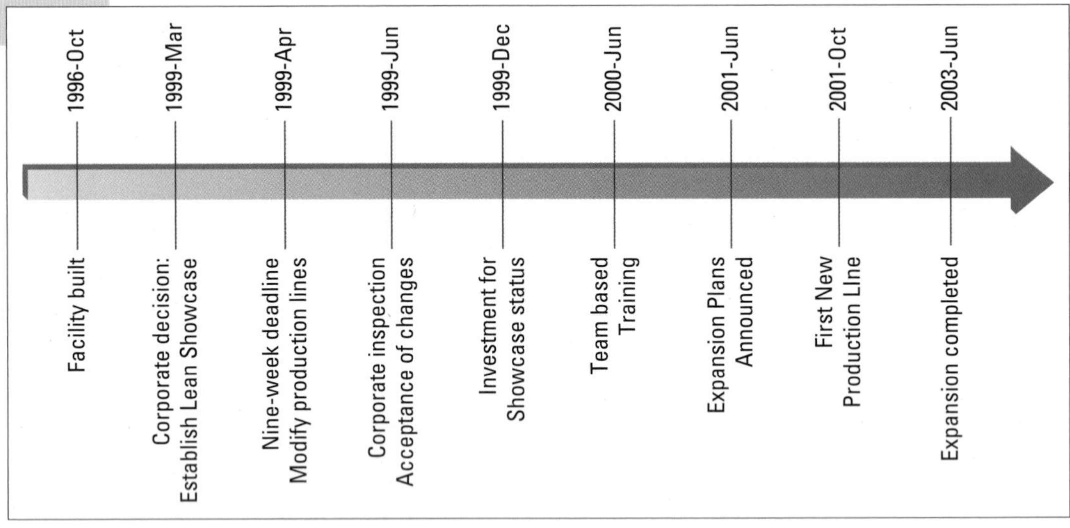

Exhibit 12 summarizes the overall timeline of the changes that have occurred at OMC since the facility was built in 1996.

Current State at OMC

Ed now sat in his office contemplating the current state of the organization. It had taken 20 months to complete the project, and OMC had increased its number of employees from 50 to its current total of 108. Ed and his leadership team had relied heavily on the use of temporary agencies to provide them with new employees. Ed looked at the latest staffing sheets on his desk and calculated that 40 percent of OMC's current employees were temporary workers hired through the staffing agencies. The decision to use temporary employees was not Ed's preference. Without a human resource department to accommodate the rapid growth, Ed lacked enough qualified staff to help with the rapid recruiting, interviewing, and hiring of 58 additional employees. Therefore, he and the leadership team had resorted to the use of temporary agencies. His hope had been that the temporary agency would do the pre-screening for OMC and recruit qualified individuals whom OMC could later hire into full-time positions. However, the lack of appropriate qualifications, low levels of loyalty, and high turnover of the temporary staff, as well as the fees and costs involved in maintaining the temporary employees, had caused a large setback for OMC in its maintenance of the lean team-based culture that had started to develop when the organization was much smaller.

Ed also reevaluated the decision made by him and the leadership team regarding the training and integration of the new employees into the workforce. Ed and his team had decided to disperse the existing employees throughout the various production lines, both new and old.

The intent was to provide a solid base of experienced and self-directed employees within each cell, "lean-thinking" employees in each new production area, as well as to retain some experience in the already existing production lines. However, the leadership team failed to provide the proper training and attention needed by the employees and relied too heavily on the experienced employees to help and informally share their knowledge and experience on lean and the production process with the new employees. The new employees received very little formal training on the technical aspects of their job and on lean culture and teams. Instead, they were placed within the work cells and expected to learn primarily by observing and doing. This had worked well for OMC in the past when it was a much smaller company; however, the changes that had occurred at OMC in the past had not been such large-scale changes that needed to be completed within a very tight timeframe. In hindsight, Ed now realized the importance of formal training and the constant support needed by employees through such a large, accelerated change. The lack of both had now resulted in the dismantling of the lean team-based culture that had previously been established at OMC. The company still had the lean production processes in place, but the fact that it had neglected to sustain the lean culture throughout the growth processes had caused the serious problems that OMC now faced.

The culture of the organization changed drastically due to the tremendous growth that OMC had undergone. The organization moved from a small, one-shift, family-oriented organization to a midsized, two-shift organization in which many of the employees did not know each other's names or each other's jobs. At this time, 60 percent of the workforce had been with OMC for less than one year, including most of the management team. This was an especially difficult change for those employees who had been with the organization for 10 or more years and had seen the organization's culture change so significantly. The constant flux of new employees, the lack of effective training, and limited communications had challenged, frustrated, and stressed the employees on all the teams in the facility on a daily basis. Ed thought back to just a short year and a half ago when OMC was the lean showcase. At that time, the teams were so successful and confident that the teams and the leaders felt that there was nothing the teams could not accomplish. Today, he thought in dismay, every team in the facility was faltering.

Even members of the management team had lost focus on the lean culture as day-to-day activities consumed all their efforts. With more than half of the management team arriving after the lean transformation, the personal commitment and management styles varied. The manufacturing manager had been at OMC for one year. He was experienced in team-based organizations and slowly won the support of the production employees. His preference was a high level of team-based management. The engineering manager had worked at the company for seven years. He was a major contributor to the success in growth and development of new equipment and had excellent technical and design abilities. His preference was for top-down management and tight control of the engineering and maintenance department. OMC's finance manager was in her sixth year with the organization. She was very experienced and understood business in general and saw the financial impact of the lean implementation and culture. Her preference was for a team-based approach to management.

The materials manager had been with OMC for one year and was very experienced in materials and processing. However, he struggled with lack of information from OMC's outdated business systems. He supported team-based management functions within a salaried workforce; however, he did not believe hourly workers would perform at optimal levels without direct supervision. The quality manager was in his sixth month at OMC. His prior experience was within tightly controlled industries where teams existed, but strict controls limited the ability of these teams to make significant changes. Given his experience, he preferred team-based operations with a limited scope on team's abilities. Finally, the human resources manager was in his first month at OMC and had strong prior experience in recruitment and personnel development; however, he had limited experience in lean manufacturing. His focus was to rely heavily on the policies, procedures, and benefits provided by the corporate office. Overall, Ed felt that the team had the technical skills necessary to move the organization to the next level of lean in terms of production. Yet he had struggled in bringing the team together in terms of their understanding and support for the lean, team-based culture that he was trying to maintain within his organization.

Ed once again examined the staffing data on his desk and reviewed the turnover and absenteeism figures he had been tracking. Turnover in the organization had risen to alarming numbers, with an average of one new temporary or full-time employee leaving every day for the first six months after the change. Ed cringed at the thought of the costs that OMC was incurring due to the turnover and the temporary agency fees the company was still paying. Absenteeism rates were also very high, averaging nearly 50 individual absences each month.

The instability in the workforce had also elevated labor costs which, in turn, increased manufacturing costs to a point where corporate had started to show concern and demanded immediate improvements. Productivity dropped 25 percent in comparison to the past performance of the organization. This instability had also impacted the quality of the product and on-time deliveries, and as a result there had been an increase in the number of customer complaints.

Ed had received a phone call last week from corporate. The expectations were that the organization needed to improve results within three months; otherwise, corporate would dictate future changes to the people in Orlando. Ed now stood by the window in his office and reflected on just how quickly success and performance can diminish and disappear. He was confident that OMC would meet the goal set by headquarters, as it had done in the past. This time, however, the situation was different given the current levels of low morale and instability in the workforce. He needed to take immediate action. The question was: should he try to re-implement the lean manufacturing culture and lean thinking in the new organization or should he abandon this goal and instead focus on reestablishing the traditional management methods of the past?

Sources

B. A. Henderson and J. L. Larco, *Lean Transformation: How to Change Your Business into a Lean Enterprise* (Richmond, VA: The Oaklea Press, 1999).

D. Mann, *Creating a Lean Culture: Tools to Sustain Lean Conversions* (New York: Productivity Press, 2005).

INTEGRATIVE CASE 9.0
Cisco Systems: Evolution of Structure

The evolution of Cisco from a university campus networking solution devised by the husband and wife Stanford team of Len Bosack and Sandy Lerner to a global technology leader has been a dynamic process. The speed of technological innovation means that managers are already talking about the "next new thing" during the launch of each new product or service. Parallel with the rapid technological evolution at Cisco are the changes in organization structure necessary to meet the management and decision-making needs of the corporate giant.

Growth

Faced with the challenge of devising a system that would allow Stanford University computer networks to talk to each other, Bosack and Lerner created a multi-protocol router to break through the communication barriers. The perceived need by many organizations for increasingly sophisticated routers and related products led to the founding of the Silicon Valley hi-tech powerhouse Cisco Systems in 1984. As a start-up company, Cisco had a vision, eight employees, and a host of financial challenges. The early days were financed by credit cards, home mortgages, and periods when payrolls were delayed, but in 1986 Cisco shipped its first router. The company turned to a venture capitalist, Sequoia Capital, which moved Cisco toward financial stability, but founders Bosack and Lerner were forced out. Cisco quickly became established as a viable business and, armed with a growing reputation in the industry, went public in 1990.

A leader in the development of routers, Cisco faced new challenges with the emergence of competitors for rapid, less expensive technology. Facing the threat of losing high-profile customers and industry leadership, Cisco management took a bold move in its innovation strategy through the acquisition of small, innovative companies such as Crescendo Communication, a company that had attracted the attention of major customers, including Boeing.

Cisco was selective in its acquisitions, focusing on small start-up companies working on a great product that could be moved from development into production within six to 12 months. The company's goal was to purchase the *future* by acquiring the engineers who were working on the *next generation* of products and services. Therefore, the retention of employees was critical to a successful acquisition. For its part of the deal, Cisco could offer the start-up company the power of Cisco's financial resources, manufacturing, and distribution channels. Cisco's reputation for finding and bringing into the fold the best of the smaller companies reminded admirers and critics alike of *the Borg*, the notorious alien being from Star Trek fame that absorbed species as it expanded across the universe.

As Cisco expanded into wireless devices for home (Linksys) and business, data center switching systems, networking equipment, communications gear, and network security apparatus, visionary John Chambers was brought in as CEO. One of a generation of gurus who championed the power and practical solutions of technology, Chambers expanded the company into advanced technologies, including digital voice and data, web-conferencing, and more diverse security products. By 2000, Cisco had attained a brief designation as the world's most valuable company.

Cisco 1

During the early period that would later become designated as Cisco 1, the organization had created a three-division organization structure. The three self-contained product divisions were each focused on a distinct customer segment: Service Products (such as AT&T), Enterprises (usually multinational corporations), and Small to Mid-Size Commercial Companies. Each of the three divisions was responsible for its own engineering, manufacturing, and marketing activities. Goals were established by each division's managers to develop products and services customized to address the specific and changing needs within that customer group.

With corporate headquarters in San Jose and a dominance of U.S. sales, Cisco found that it could minimize costs with a move toward outsourcing manufacturing from within each of the divisions to contract manufacturers. Cisco had, in effect, a structure wherein managers were rewarded for the performance of their own division. Flexibility and coordination occurred across the functional departments within each division, but there was little collaboration across the three divisions. This decentralized structure seemed to work fine in a prosperous and rapidly growing company.

What a difference a year can make. In 2001, one year after a brief designation as the world's most valuable company, a sharp economic downturn hit Cisco and other companies in the high-tech industry. The techno bubble of the 1990s had burst. Across Silicon Valley, tech stocks tumbled, layoffs proliferated, and companies struggled to adjust and survive. At the same time, increasing product complexity and technical advancement within the field pushed management at Cisco to reconsider whether the existing divisional organization structure was sufficient to carry the company into the future.

Cisco 2

Reviewing the three-division structure, Chambers and his management team detected serious overlap in the work of departments across product groups. One glaring example was the overlap of engineering groups in each of the three divisions who were all working on similar products without knowing it. This meant there was a huge excess of engineering talent focused on relatively straightforward new products. The lack of communication across the three divisions created a lack of awareness and cooperation necessary for finding shared solutions, avoiding repetition, and speeding the process time required to introduce a new product. Likewise, the complete independence and separation of each division resulted in a glut of separate vendors and suppliers for the divisions, in addition to the duplication of employees working on similar projects—all of which added to company costs.

To address the need for efficient use of resources while trying to meet the need for new products and geographic expansion, Cisco moved toward a functional structure. Changes came swiftly in the move to streamline operations and bring costs down. Between 2001 and 2006, the company moved through the reorganization, designated Cisco 2, cutting the workforce by 8,000 employees, reducing the number of vendors (1,500 to 200) and suppliers (600 to 95), and trimming outsourced manufacturing from 13 major plants to four. The company's costs as well as overlap were further cut as the major functions of sales, accounting, and engineering were combined into single centralized groups that reported to headquarters. The three separate and autonomous divisions were gone. The huge engineering staff was broken down into 11 functional groups that reflected the core technologies on which they worked, resulting in added efficiency and reduced overlap.

Cisco 2 provided senior management of each function much vertical control over the work of their engineers, salespeople, and so forth. Top managers could set goals and expect to achieve those goals, along with performance bonuses, because of direct control over their functional departments and the projects on which employees worked. Cisco became much more efficient with fewer people needed within each function, but it was also becoming more hierarchical and less coordinated as each department acted more like a separate silo, with people focused on their own goals and projects with little concern for the needs of other groups.

Cisco 3

By 2006, expanded globalization and product lines and the continued need and movement toward horizontal collaboration brought further structural evolution, called Cisco 3. The new structure added 12 business councils, one for each key customer segment. Each council was composed of approximately 14 executive VPs and senior VPs—roughly one from each major function. The intention of the new structure was to instill a culture of collaboration that would provide better horizontal coordination across functions. The business councils worked at the policy level, involving representatives from each function to select and coordinate new programs and products to meet customer needs in their segment. Beneath the business council level, 47 Boards were created, consisting of vice presidents who would collaborate across functions to implement the new product decisions from the councils. Beneath the VP level, temporary "working groups" were created as needed, composed of about 10 people each, to execute the details of implementation. The new matrix-type structure was viewed as a better way to address a complex environment characterized by uncertainty and rapid change that required internal teamwork, coordination, innovation, and information sharing.

The twenty-first century tech giant's structural evolution brought difficult cultural adjustments. While growth and performance targets remained, emphasis was now placed on collaboration to find solutions for customer needs by involving people from other functions. Executive compensation changed from achieving one's own department goals to cooperation with other departments, and bonuses for some senior executives, as Chambers admits, "went poof." No longer dependent solely on hitting targets within a tightly controlled function, the organization experienced initial executive resistance to giving up control, sharing information and resources, and making joint decisions. The new focus for performance evaluation was on peer review ratings based on successful teamwork. Chambers estimated a loss of approximately 20 percent of top management who "couldn't make the transition" to collaborative work, but the new structure eventually fell into place as its benefits became apparent, and Cisco successfully rode out the loss of key managers.

The structure continued to evolve as Cisco evolved. Five years later, in 2011, the number of business councils had been reduced to three and the number of boards to 15. This was sufficient to make collaborative decisions on key new products for customer segments. Cisco announced a further simplification of this structure around international geographic zones (the Americas, Asia/Pacific, Europe, Africa, and the Middle East) and customer segments within those zones. The previous years had seen the need to reduce the number of business councils from 12 to nine and then to three. Cisco also slashed the number of internal boards and working groups as members of management grumbled about the staggering number of boards and council meetings taking up their time.

Simultaneously, Cisco planned to further strengthen the coordination across functions and departments by tapping into social media. Since 2006, company executives have used TelePresence, a system of lifelike videoconferencing, to connect customers and colleagues around the globe. Today, with the introduction of *Ciscopedia*, the organization is allowing a greater level of information sharing and consultation among employees and among members of the remaining business councils and boards. Employees use social media, blogs, video, and bookmarking to post ideas, coordinate teams, share information, and avoid duplication across departments, product lines, and geographic areas.

Will the evolution of Cisco continue? And if so, what will it look like? Company history indicates that, just as a quick response is needed in the rapid evolution of technology products and services, the company must remain aware of structural changes needed within the organization to maintain its leadership position.

Sources

Dick Clark and Shara Tibkin, "Corporate News: Cisco to Reduce Its Bureaucracy," *The Wall Street Journal* (May 6, 2011), B.4.

Hau Lee and Maria Shao, "Cisco Systems, Inc.: Collaborating on New Product Introduction," *Harvard Business Review*, Product #GS66-PDF-ENG (June 5, 2009), http://hbr.org/product/cisco-systems-inc-collaborating-on-new-product-int/an/GS66-PDF-ENG (accessed January 4, 2012).

Matt Rosoff, "Cisco's Crazy Management Structure Wasn't Working, So Chambers Is Changing It," *Business Insider* (May 5, 2011), http://articles.businessinsider.com/2011-05-05/tech/30062558_1_cisco-ceo-john-chambers-councils-structure (accessed January 4, 2012).

Craig Matsumoto, "Cisco Cuts Down On Councils," *News Analysis, LightReading.com* (May 5, 2011) http://www.lightreading.com/document.asp?doc_id=207537 (accessed January 4, 2012).

Ranjay Gulati, "Cisco Business Councils (2007): Unifying a Functional Enterprise with an Internal Governance System," Harvard Business School, *Case N5-409-062* (June 11, 2010).

Brad Reese, "Cisco's Restructuring Embeds Operating Committee, Councils, Boards, and Working Groups Deeper into Cisco's New Management Structure," (May 5, 2011), http://bradreese.com/blog/5-5-2011.htm (accessed January 4, 2010).

Mina Kimes, "Cisco Systems Layers It On," *Fortune* (December 8, 2008).

Rik Kirkland, "Cisco's Display of Strength," *Fortune* (November 12, 2007).

Jay Galbraith, "How Do You Manage in a Downturn?" *Talent Management Magazine* (August 2009), 44–46.

Nir Breuller and Laurence Capron, "Cisco Systems: New Millennium—New Acquisition Strategy?" *INSEAD Case 03/2010-5669* (March 2010), http://www.insead.edu/facultyresearch/faculty/personal/lcapron/teaching/documents/CiscoIronPort.pdf (accessed January 4, 2012).

Part Five
Internal Factors and Design

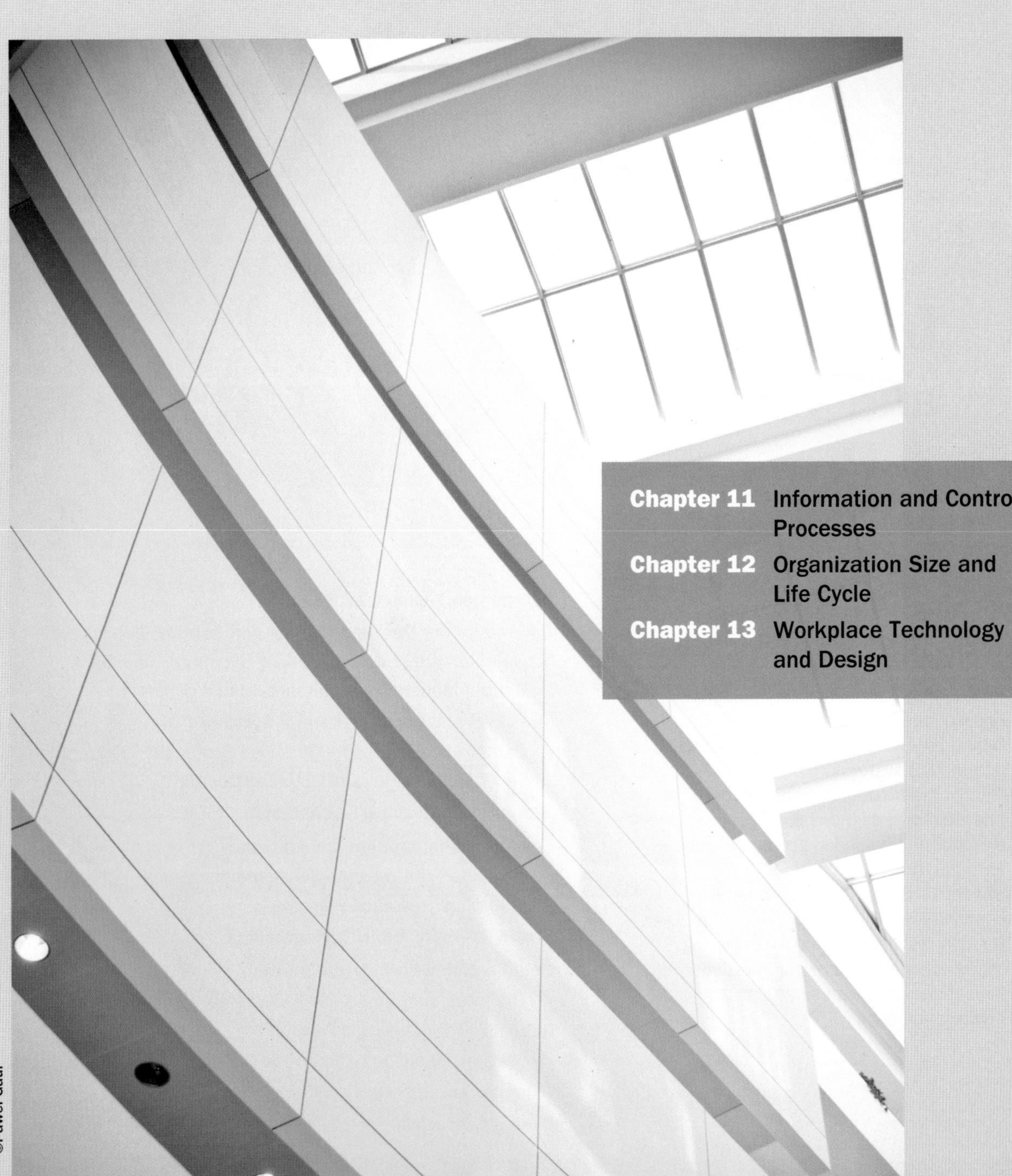

Chapter 11

©Pawel Gaul

Information and Control Processes

Learning Objectives

After reading this chapter you should be able to:

1. Explain how information technology applications have evolved.
2. Define the two levels of management information systems.
3. Explain the feedback control model and executive dashboard.
4. Describe the balanced scorecard's value for organizational control.
5. Specify IT mechanisms for internal coordination.
6. Describe IT mechanisms for achieving coordination with other organizations.
7. Indicate how e-business affects organization design.

Before reading this chapter, please check whether you agree or disagree with each of the following statements:

1 **For a manager, it should not matter much exactly how or when people get their work done, just as long as they produce good results.**

I AGREE _____ I DISAGREE _____

2 **Every manager should have a blog.**

I AGREE _____ I DISAGREE _____

3 **The best way for a large company to set up an Internet division is to create a separate, free-standing unit because the unit will have the autonomy and flexibility to operate at Internet speed rather than being hampered by the larger organization's rules and procedures.**

I AGREE _____ I DISAGREE _____

Wood Flooring International (WFI), based in Delran, New Jersey, uses a sophisticated Internet-based system to manage every link of its supply chain, from vendors all the way through to its customers' customers. The company buys exotic wood overseas, mostly from small, family-owned mills in Latin America, turns the wood into floorboards, and sells the flooring to distributors. Whenever WFI takes an order, the vendor can see an update instantly on the website and adjust its production levels accordingly. The mills can also check real-time reports of their sales histories, check whether their shipments have arrived, and ensure that WFI's accounting squares with their own.[1] Olive Garden, a restaurant chain, uses computerized systems to measure and control everything from bathroom cleanliness to food preparation time. And Memorial Health Services in Long Beach, California, uses medical identification cards (available over the Internet) that can be swiped into a computer to speed registration and give emergency room personnel immediate access to vital patient information, which means better care and fewer errors.[2]

As these examples illustrate, many organizations have been transformed by information technology (IT). Effectively using IT in knowledge-based firms such as consulting firm KPMG, Amerex Energy, a brokerage firm specializing in energy resources, and Business Wire, which provides business and corporate information, has long been fundamental. Today, IT has become a crucial factor helping companies in all industries maintain a competitive edge in the face of growing global competition and rising customer demands for speed, convenience, quality, and value. The primary benefits of IT for organizations include its potential for improving decision making as well as for enhancing control, efficiency, and coordination of the organization internally and with external partners and customers. Some organization theorists believe IT is gradually replacing the traditional hierarchy in coordinating and controlling organizational activities.[3]

Purpose of This Chapter

Managers spend at least 80 percent of their time actively exchanging information. They need this information to hold the organization together. The vertical and horizontal information linkages described in Chapter 2 are designed to provide managers with relevant information for decision making, coordination, evaluation, and control. It isn't just facilities, equipment, or even products and services that define organization success, but rather the information that managers possess and how they use it. Highly successful organizations today are typically those that apply information technology most effectively.

This chapter examines the evolution of IT. The chapter begins by looking at IT systems applied to organizational operations and then examines how IT is used for decision making and control of the organization. The next sections consider how IT can add strategic value through the use of internal coordination applications such as intranets, enterprise resource planning, knowledge management systems, and social networking, as well as applications for external coordination and collaboration, such as extranets, customer-relationship systems, e-business, and the integrated enterprise. The final section of the chapter presents an overview of how IT affects organization design and interorganizational relationships.

Information Technology Evolution

Exhibit 11.1 illustrates the evolution of IT. First-line management is typically concerned with well-defined problems about operational issues and past events. Top management, by contrast, deals mostly with uncertain, ambiguous issues, such as strategy and planning. As computer-based IT systems have grown increasingly sophisticated, applications have grown to support effective management coordination, control, and decision making about complex and uncertain problems.

Initially, IT systems in organizations were applied to operations. These initial applications were based on the notion of machine-room efficiency—that is, current operations could be performed more efficiently with the use of computer technology. The goal was to reduce labor costs by having computers take over some tasks. These systems became known as **transaction processing systems** (TPS), which automate the organization's routine, day-to-day business transactions. A TPS collects data from transactions such as sales, purchases from suppliers, and inventory changes, and stores them in a database. For example, at Enterprise Rent-a-Car, a computerized system keeps track of the 1.4 million transactions the company logs every hour. The system can provide front-line employees with up-to-the-minute information on car availability and other data, enabling them to provide exceptional customer service.[4] Midland Memorial Hospital in Texas recently adopted information technology for electronic medical records. The system helped Midland catch up on a $16.7 million coding and billing backlog for 4,500 patient records in only four weeks, a process that likely would have taken six months or more without the system.[5]

In recent years, the use of data warehousing and business intelligence software has expanded the usefulness of these accumulated data. **Data warehousing** is the use of huge databases that combine all of a company's data and allow users to access the data directly, create reports, and obtain responses to what-if questions. Building a database at a large corporation is a huge undertaking that includes defining hundreds

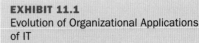

EXHIBIT 11.1
Evolution of Organizational Applications of IT

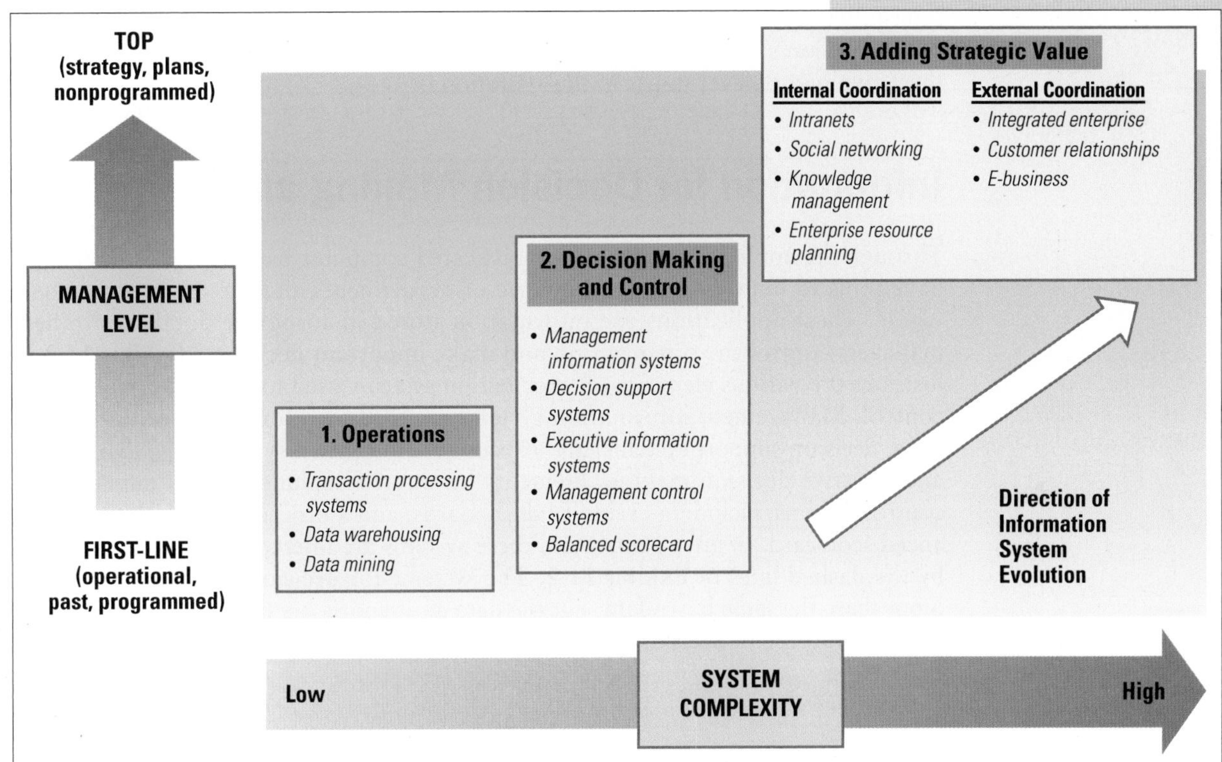

of gigabytes of data from many existing systems, providing a means of continually updating the data, making it all compatible, and linking it to software that makes it possible for users to search and analyze the data and produce helpful reports. Software for business intelligence, also called *analytic software*, helps users make sense of all these data. **Business intelligence** refers to the high-tech analysis of a company's data in order to make better strategic decisions.[6] Sometimes referred to as *data mining*, business intelligence means searching out and analyzing data from multiple sources across the enterprise, and increasingly from outside sources as well, to identify patterns and relationships that might be significant. Retailers are some of the biggest users of business intelligence software. Managers at companies such as Wet Seal, a specialty clothing store selling mainly to teenage girls, and Elie Tahari, a maker of designer clothes, need to spot changing trends fast, so they are continually mining sales data. Wet Seal created a web feature called Outfitter that allows users to put together their own outfits online; mining the 300,000 user-generated outfits gave managers an early lead on the trend toward wearing dressy tops with casual pants and jeans.[7]

By collecting the right data and using business intelligence software to analyze it and spot trends and patterns, managers can make smarter decisions. For example, 1-800-Flowers.com uses data mining to tweak its marketing. Over a six-month period, the company improved its conversion rate (turning browsers into buyers) by 20 percent because of more targeted pages and promotions.[8] Thus, IT has evolved to more complex systems for managerial decision making and control of the organization, the second stage illustrated in Exhibit 11.1. Further advancements have led to the use of IT to add strategic value by providing tight coordination both internally and with external customers, suppliers, and partners, the highest level of application shown in Exhibit 11.1. The remainder of this chapter will focus on these two higher-level stages in the evolution of IT.

Information for Decision Making and Control

Through the application of more sophisticated computer-based systems, managers have tools to improve the performance of departments and the organization as a whole. These applications use information stored in corporate databases to help managers control the organization and make important decisions. Exhibit 11.2 illustrates the various elements of information systems used for decision making and control. Management information systems—including information reporting systems, decision support systems, and executive information systems—facilitate rapid and effective decision making. Elements for control include various management control systems, including executive dashboards, and a procedure known as the balanced scorecard. In an organization, these systems are interconnected, as illustrated by the dashed lines in Exhibit 11.2. The systems for decision making and control often share the same basic data, but the data and reports are designed and used for a primary purpose of decision making versus control.

EXHIBIT 11.2
Information Systems for Managerial Control and Decision Making

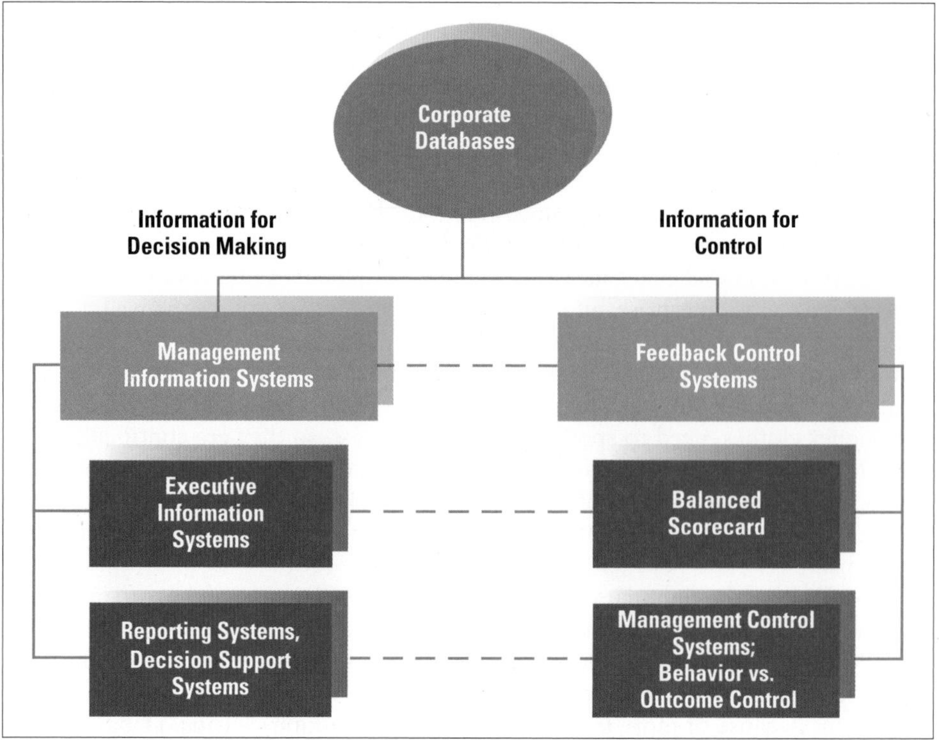

Organizational Decision-Making Systems

A **management information system** (MIS) is a computer-based system that provides information and support for managerial decision making. The MIS is supported by the organization's transaction processing systems and by organizational and external databases. The **information reporting system**, the most common form of MIS, provides mid-level managers with reports that summarize data and support day-to-day decision making. For example, when managers need to make decisions about production scheduling, they can review data on the anticipated number of orders within the next month, inventory levels, and availability of human resources.

At Harrah's casinos, an information reporting system keeps track of detailed information on each player and uses quantitative models to predict each customer's potential long-term value. The information helps managers create customized marketing plans as well as provide customers just the right combination of services and rewards to keep them coming back rather than moving on to another casino. "Almost everything we do in marketing and decision making is influenced by technology," says Harrah's CEO Gary Loveman.[9]

An **executive information system** (EIS) is a higher-level application that facilitates decision making at the highest levels of management. These systems are typically based on software that can convert large amounts of complex data into pertinent information and provide that information to top managers in a timely fashion. For example, Motorola's Semiconductor Products Sector, based in Austin, Texas, had massive amounts of stored data, but managers couldn't find what they needed. The company implemented an EIS using online analytical processing software so that more than a thousand senior executives, as well as managers and project analysts in finance, marketing, sales, and accounting departments around the world, could quickly and easily get information about customer buying trends, manufacturing, and so forth, right from their desktop computers without having to learn complex and arcane search commands.[10]

A **decision support system** (DSS) provides specific benefits to managers at all levels of the organization. These interactive, computer-based systems rely on decision models and integrated databases. Using decision-support software, users can pose a series of what-if questions to test possible alternatives. Based on assumptions used in the software or specified by the user, managers can explore various alternatives and receive information to help them choose the alternative that will likely have the best outcome. The German airline Deutsche Lufthansa AG and Fraport AG, owner of Lufthansa's hub airport, have collaborated on a valuable computerized system that helps make decisions to improve luggage handling.

BRIEFCASE

As an organization manager, keep these guidelines in mind:

Improve the performance of the organization by using IT for better decision making. Implement management information systems, decision support systems, and information reporting systems to provide lower- and middle-level managers with reports and information that support day-to-day decision making. Use executive information systems to facilitate better decision making at the highest levels of the organization.

IN PRACTICE

Deutsche Lufthansa AG and Fraport AG

People have a lot of complaints about air travel these days, but one of the biggest is lost luggage. There's nothing quite as frustrating as arriving at your destination only to discover that your bags didn't arrive with you. Passengers feel like the airlines don't care, but actually they care a great deal—because lost bags means lost money. Airlines spend $100 on average per mishandled bag, for tracking, shipping, and reimbursing passengers.

German carrier Deutsche Lufthansa AG handles some 100,000 bags each day at Frankfurt Airport, and 80 percent of them have to change planes, which is when bags are most likely to go astray. Lufthansa and Fraport AG, owner of the Frankfurt Airport, decided it was time to seriously attack the problem. An important aspect of better baggage handling is using the bar codes on check-in tags, but most airlines and airports have computer systems that don't communicate with one another. Lufthansa and Fraport linked their computers and tied them to a system that helps track bags and decide what to do with them. Employees use scanners to register every bag or container going on or off a plane. The bags are scanned again as they enter the airport's automated sorting system, and they are repeatedly scanned by the system to decide where they should be sent.

The system really pays off for bags making tight flight connections. Two employees, each with six computer screens, continually monitor arrival and departure data of passengers who have little time between connecting flights. Decision support software scans through hundreds of thousands of reservations and real-time air-traffic data to spot potential problems and identify "hot bags," those that are prone to a missed connection. The employees can then flag the bags and notify baggage loaders to quickly get them off the incoming flight and on to the next one.[11]

Lufthansa and the Frankfurt Airport are exceptionally well-coordinated in the use of technology for handling baggage. The constant flow of information enables Lufthansa to locate almost any bag within seconds and make decisions that will get it where it needs to be when it needs to be there.

Feedback Control Model

Another primary use of information in organizations is for control. Effective control systems involve the use of feedback to determine whether organizational performance meets established standards to help the organization attain its goals. Managers set up systems for organizational control that consist of the four key steps in the **feedback control model** illustrated in Exhibit 11.3.

EXHIBIT 11.3
A Simplified Feedback Control Model

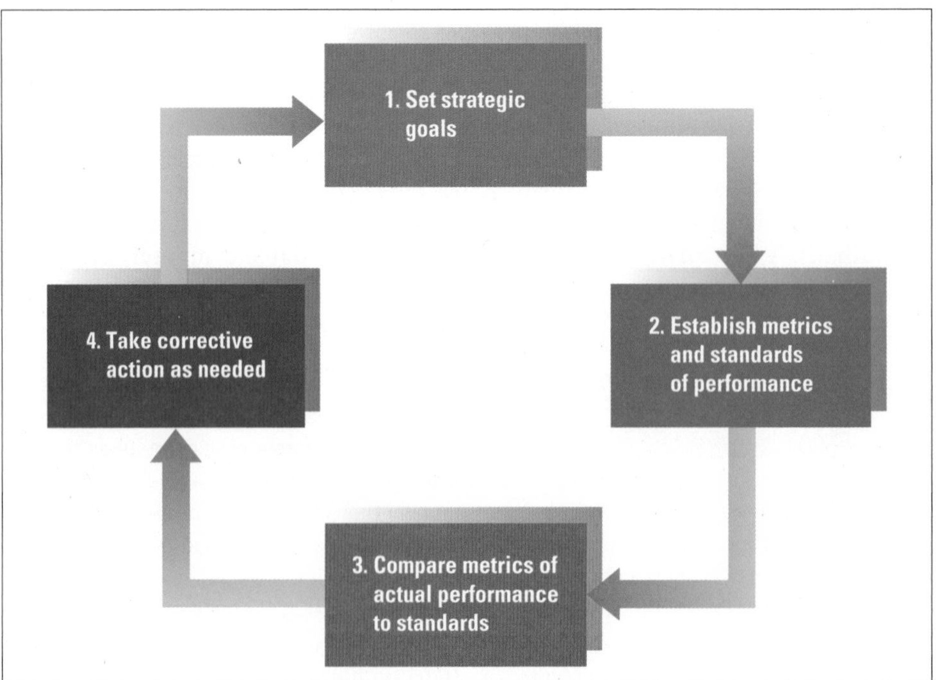

The cycle of control includes setting strategic goals for departments or the organization as a whole, establishing metrics and standards of performance, comparing metrics of actual performance to standards, and correcting or changing activities as needed. An example from Jefferson Pilot Financial, a full-service life insurance and annuities company, illustrates the feedback control model. Executives established goals for one department to reduce the time between receiving an application and issuing a policy by 60 percent and to reduce the number of reissued policies due to errors by 40 percent. When performance was measured, the unit had met its goal of reducing reissues by 40 percent and had surpassed the application-to-policy goal, reducing turnaround time by 70 percent.[12] Feedback control helps managers make needed adjustments in work activities, standards of performance, or goals to help the organization be successful. Complete the questionnaire in the "How Do You Fit the Design?" box to see how effective you are at setting goals.

How Do You Fit the Design?

IS GOAL-SETTING YOUR STYLE?

How do your work habits fit with making plans and setting goals? Answer the following questions as they apply to your work or study behavior. Please answer whether each item is Mostly True or Mostly False for you.

	Mostly True	Mostly False
1. I set clear, specific goals in more than one area of my work and life.	____	____
2. I have a definite outcome in life I want to achieve.	____	____
3. I prefer general to specific goals.	____	____
4. I work better without specific deadlines.	____	____
5. I set aside time each day or week to plan my work.	____	____
6. I am clear about the measures that indicate when I have achieved a goal.	____	____
7. I work better when I set more challenging goals for myself.	____	____
8. I help other people clarify and define their goals.	____	____
9. Trying for specific goals makes life more fun than being without goals.	____	____

Scoring: Give yourself one point for each item you marked as Mostly True, except items 3 and 4. For items 3 and 4 give yourself one point for each one you marked Mostly False. If you scored 4 or less, goal-setting behavior may not be natural for you. A score of 6 or above suggests a positive level of goal-setting behavior and better preparation for a managerial role in an organization.

Interpretation: An important part of organization life is setting goals, measuring results, and reviewing progress for people and departments. Most organizations have goal-setting and review systems. The preceding questions indicate the extent to which you have already adopted the disciplined use of goals in your life and work. Research indicates that setting clear, specific, and challenging goals in key areas will produce better performance. Not everyone thrives under a disciplined goal-setting system, but as an organization manager, setting goals, assessing results, and holding people accountable will enhance your impact. Goal-setting can be learned.

Managers carefully assess what they will measure and how they define it. At Sprint Nextel Corporation, a new CEO discovered that the company was struggling because managers were measuring the wrong things. For example, managers in the customer care department focused on metrics that controlled costs but didn't solve problems. Consequently, Sprint had a terrible customer service reputation, was losing customers, and wasn't meeting its financial targets. When Dan Hesse came on board as CEO, he told managers to stop worrying about how long it took for a care agent to handle a call and start focusing on how effectively the agent solved the customer's problem. Before long, Sprint had moved way up in the consumer satisfaction ratings and was adding new customers.[13] In the auto industry, crash test ratings provide a standard of performance established by the National Highway Traffic Safety Administration. When crash test ratings are below standard, managers rethink design and manufacturing processes to improve crash test results.[14] For pharmaceutical companies such as Wyeth, getting more productivity from research and development is a top priority, so Wyeth sets targets and measures how many compounds move forward at each stage of the drug-development process. Managers at most companies, like Wyeth and Sprint Nextel, use a number of different operational metrics to track performance and control the organization rather than rely on financial measures alone. They track metrics in such areas as customer satisfaction, product quality, employee commitment and turnover, operational performance, innovation, and corporate social responsibility, for example, as well as financial results.

Management Control Systems

Management control systems are broadly defined as the formal routines, reports, and procedures that use information to maintain or alter patterns in organizational activities.[15] These feedback control systems include the formalized information-based activities for planning, budgeting, performance evaluation, resource allocation, and employee rewards. Targets are set in advance, outcomes compared to targets, and variances reported to managers for corrective action. Exhibit 11.4 lists four control system elements that are often considered the core of management control systems: the budget and financial reports; periodic nonfinancial statistical reports; reward systems; and quality-control systems.[16]

EXHIBIT 11.4
Management Control Systems

Subsystem	Content and Frequency
Budget, financial reports	Financial, resource expenditures, profit and loss; monthly
Statistical reports	Nonfinancial outputs; weekly or monthly, often computer-based
Reward systems	Evaluation of managers based on department goals and performance, set rewards; yearly
Quality control systems	Participation, benchmarking guidelines, Six Sigma goals; continuous

Source: Based on Richard L. Daft and Norman B. Macintosh, "The Nature and Use of Formal Control Systems for Management Control and Strategy Implementation," *Journal of Management* 10 (1984), 43–66.

The *budget* is typically used to set targets for the organization's expenditures for the year and then report actual costs on a monthly or quarterly basis. As a means of control, budgets report actual as well as planned expenditures for cash, assets, raw materials, salaries, and other resources so that managers can take action to correct variances. Sometimes, the variance between budgeted and actual amounts for each line item is listed as a part of the budget. Managers also rely on a variety of other financial reports. The *balance sheet* shows a firm's financial position with respect to assets and liabilities at a specific point in time. An *income statement*, sometimes called a *profit and loss statement (P&L)*, summarizes the company's financial performance for a given time interval, such as for the week, month, or year. This statement shows revenues coming into the organization from all sources and subtracts all expenses, such as cost of goods sold, interest, taxes, and depreciation. The *bottom line* indicates the net income—profit or loss—for the given time period.

Managers use periodic statistical reports to evaluate and monitor nonfinancial performance, such as customer satisfaction, employee performance, or rate of staff turnover. For e-commerce organizations, important measurements of nonfinancial performance include metrics such as *stickiness* (how much attention a site gets over time), the *conversion rate*, the ratio of buyers to site visitors, and *site performance data*, such as how long it takes to load a page or how long it takes to place an order.[17] E-commerce managers regularly review reports on conversion rates, customer drop-off, and other metrics to identify problems and improve their business. For all organizations, nonfinancial reports typically are computer based and may be available daily, weekly, or monthly.

Managers often track both nonfinancial and financial data by means of an executive dashboard. An **executive dashboard**, sometimes called a *business performance dashboard*, is a software program that presents key business information in graphical, easy-to-interpret form and alerts managers to any deviations or unusual patterns in the data. Dashboards pull data from a variety of organizational systems and databases; gauge the data against key performance metrics; and pull out the right nuggets of information to deliver to managers' laptops or PCs for analysis and action.[18] For example, at Emergency Medical Associates, a physician-owned medical group that manages emergency rooms for hospitals in New York and New Jersey, dashboards enable managers to quickly see when performance thresholds related to patient wait times or other metrics aren't being met at various hospitals.[19]

Exhibit 11.5 shows an example of an executive dashboard. Managers can see at a glance key control indicators such as sales in relation to targets, fill rates on orders, number of products on back-order, production status, or percentage of customer service calls resolved, and then drill down for additional details.[20] Dashboard systems coordinate, organize, and display the metrics that managers consider most important to monitor on a regular basis, with software automatically updating the figures. Managers at Erickson Retirement Communities use a dashboard to monitor and control costs in areas such as salaries and resident meals. At Verizon Communications, a dashboard system keeps track of more than 300 different measures of business performance in three broad categories: market pulse (including daily sales numbers and market share); customer service (for example, call center wait times and problems resolved on the first call); and cost drivers (such as number of repair trucks in the field). Managers in the various units choose which metrics their dashboard will display based on what relates most to their unit.[21]

BRIEFCASE

As an organization manager, keep these guidelines in mind:

Devise control systems that consist of the four essential steps of the feedback control model: set goals, establish standards of performance, measure actual performance, and correct or change activities as needed. Use executive dashboards so managers can keep tabs on important performance metrics.

EXHIBIT 11.5
An Executive Dashboard

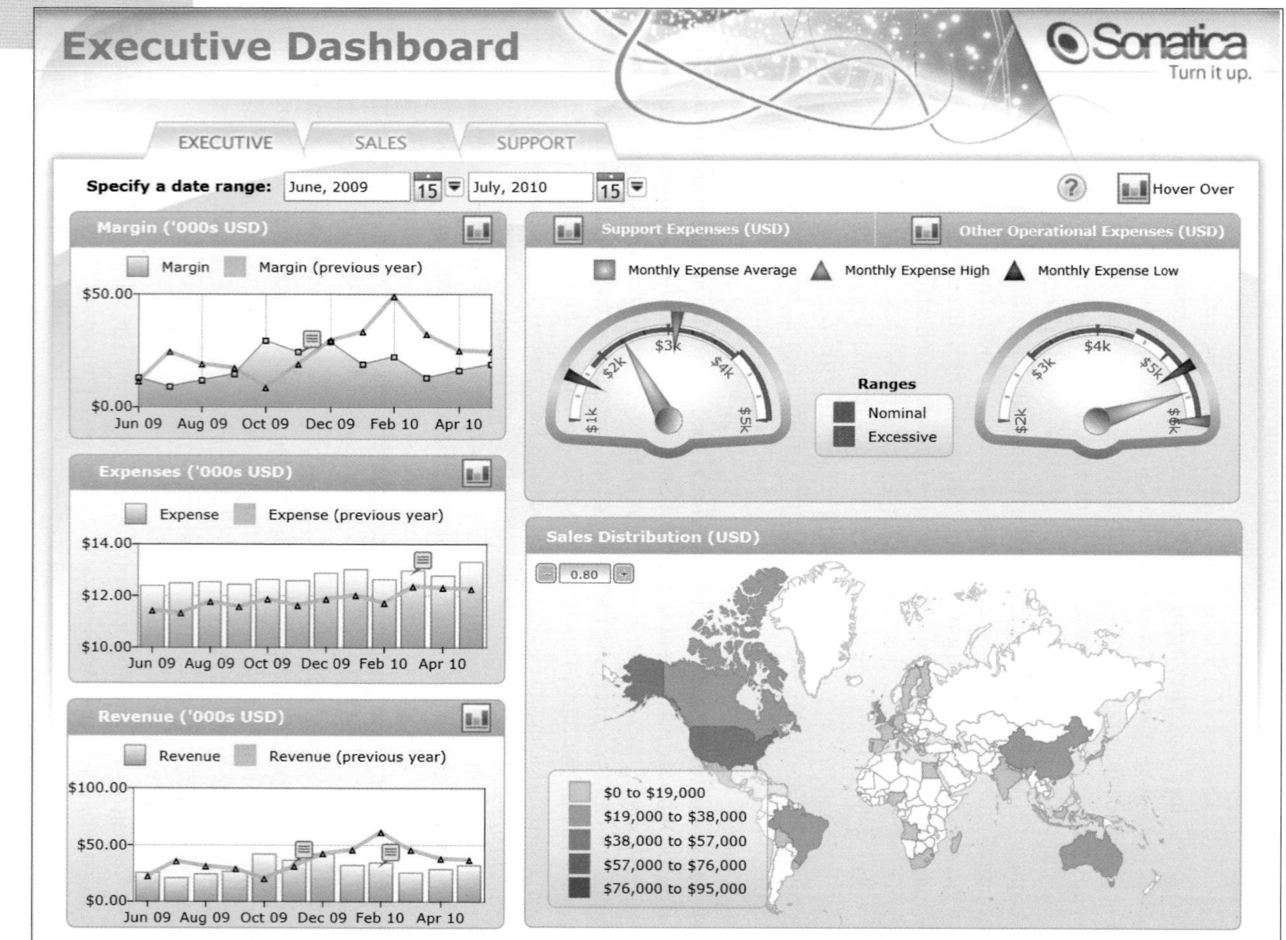

Dundas Data Visualization, Inc.

Other elements of the overall control system listed in Exhibit 11.4 are reward systems and quality control systems. Reward systems offer incentives for managers and employees to improve performance and meet departmental goals. Managers and employees evaluate how well previous goals were met, set new goals, and establish rewards for meeting the new targets. Rewards are often tied to the annual performance appraisal process, during which managers assess employee performance and provide feedback to help people improve performance and obtain rewards.

Quality-control systems involve training employees in quality-control methods, setting targets for employee participation, establishing benchmarking guidelines, and assigning and measuring *Six Sigma* goals. **Benchmarking** means the process of persistently measuring products, services, and practices against tough competitors or other organizations recognized as industry leaders.[22] **Six Sigma** specifically means a highly ambitious quality standard that specifies a goal of no more than 3.4 defects per million parts. However, it has deviated from that precise meaning to refer to a whole set of control procedures that emphasize the relentless pursuit of higher quality and lower costs.[23] The discipline is based on a methodology referred to as DMAIC (Define, Measure, Analyze, Improve, and Control, pronounced de-MAY-ick), which provides a structured way for organizations to approach and solve problems.[24] Companies such as General Electric, ITT Industries, Dow Chemical, ABB Ltd., and 3M have saved millions of dollars by rooting out inefficiencies and waste through Six Sigma processes.[25]

One finding from research into management control systems is that each of the four control system elements listed in Exhibit 11.4 focuses on a different aspect of the production process. These four systems thus form an overall management control system that provides middle managers with control information about resource inputs, process efficiency, and outputs.[26] Moreover, the specific use of control systems depends on the strategic targets set by top management.

The budget is used primarily to allocate resource inputs. Managers use the budget for planning the future and reducing uncertainty about the availability of human and material resources needed to perform department tasks. Computer-based statistical reports are used to control outputs. These reports contain data about output volume and quality and other indicators that provide feedback to middle management about departmental results. The reward system and quality control system are directed at the production process. Quality control systems specify standards for employee participation, teamwork, and problem solving. Reward systems provide incentives to meet goals and can help guide and correct employee behavior. Managers may also use direct supervision to keep departmental work activities within desired limits.

The Level and Focus of Control Systems

Managers consider both control of the overall organization and control of departments, teams, and individuals. Some control strategies apply to the top levels of an organization, where the concern is for the entire organization or major divisions. Control is also an issue at the lower, operational level, where department managers and supervisors focus on the performance of teams and individual employees.

Organization Level: The Balanced Scorecard

As discussed earlier, most companies use a combination of metrics for measuring organizational performance and effectively controlling the organization. A recent control system innovation is to integrate internal financial measurements and statistical reports with a concern for markets and customers, as well as employees. The **balanced scorecard** (BSC) is a comprehensive management control system that balances traditional financial measures with operational measures relating to a company's critical success factors.[27] A balanced scorecard contains four major perspectives, as illustrated in Exhibit 11.6: financial performance, customer service, internal business processes, and the organization's capacity for learning and growth.[28]

EXHIBIT 11.6
Major Perspectives of the Balanced Scorecard

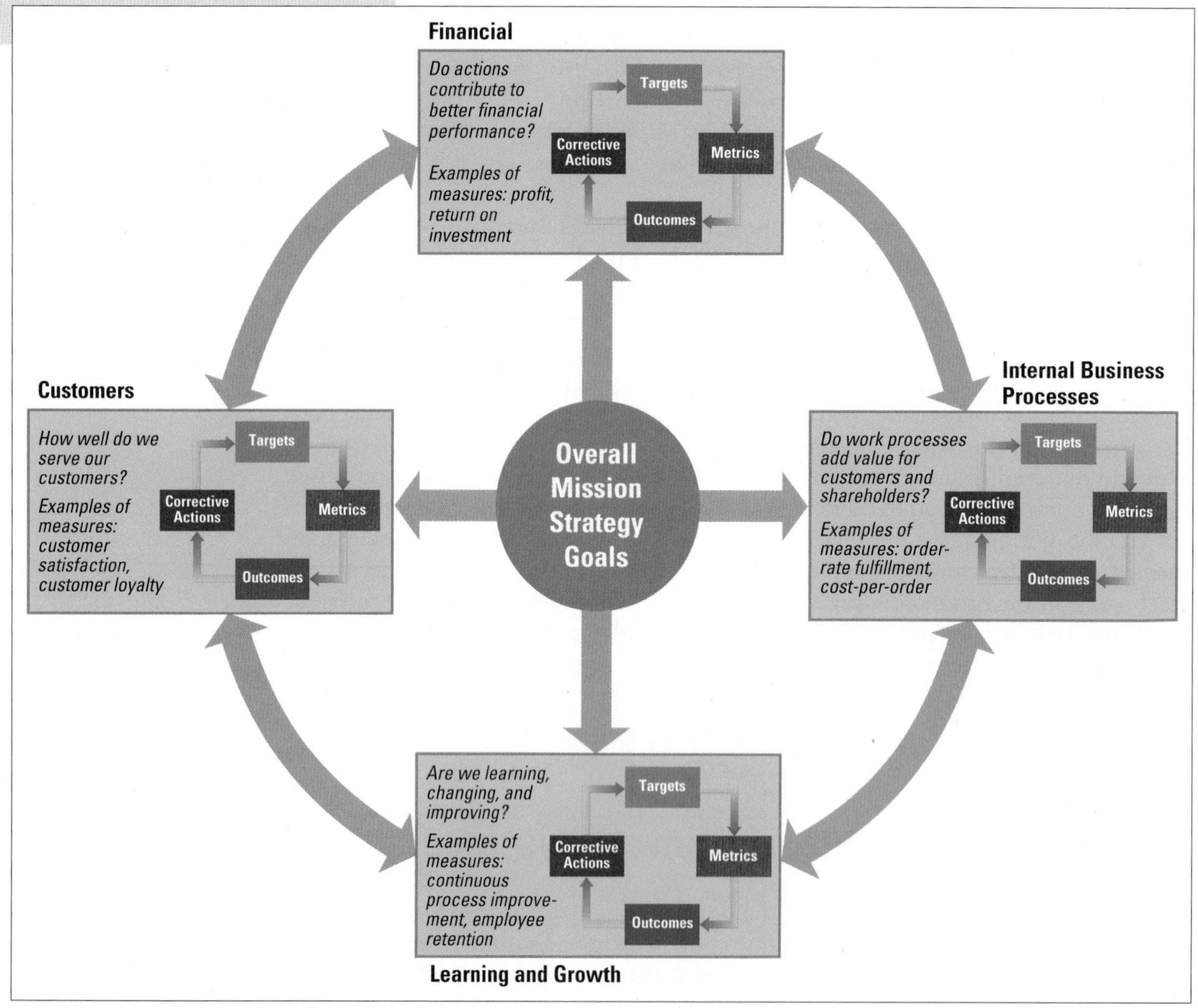

Source: Based on Robert S. Kaplan and David P. Norton, "Using the Balanced Scorecard as a Strategic Management System," *Harvard Business Review* (January–February 1996), 75–85; Chee W. Chow, Kamal M. Haddad, and James E. Williamson, "Applying the Balanced Scorecard to Small Companies," *Management Accounting* 79, no. 2 (August 1997), 21–27; and Cathy Lazere, "All Together Now," CFO (February 1998), 28–36.

Within these four areas, managers identify key performance indicators the organization will track. The *financial perspective* reflects a concern that the organization's activities contribute to improving short- and long-term financial performance. It includes traditional measures such as net income and return on investment. *Customer service indicators* measure such things as how customers view the organization as well as customer retention and satisfaction. *Business process indicators* focus on production and operating statistics, such as order fulfillment or cost per order. The final component looks at the organization's *potential for learning and growth*, focusing on how well resources and human capital are being managed for the company's future. Measurements include such things as employee retention, business process improvements, and the introduction of new products. The components of the scorecard are designed in an integrative manner so that they reinforce one another and link short-term actions with long-term strategic goals, as illustrated in Exhibit 11.6. Managers can use the scorecard to set goals, allocate resources, plan budgets, and determine rewards.

Executive information systems and dashboards facilitate use of the balanced scorecard by enabling top managers to easily track metrics in multiple areas, rapidly analyze the data, and convert huge amounts of data into clear information reports. The scorecard has become the core management control system for many organizations, including Hilton Hotels, Allstate, British Airways, and Cigna Insurance. British Airways clearly ties its use of the balanced scorecard to the feedback control model shown earlier in Exhibit 11.3. Scorecards serve as the agenda for monthly management meetings, where managers evaluate performance, discuss what corrective actions need to be taken, and set new targets for the various BSC categories.[29]

In recent years, the balanced scorecard has evolved into a system that helps managers see how organizational performance results from cause-effect relationships among these four mutually supportive areas. Overall effectiveness is a result of how well these four elements are aligned, so that individuals, teams, and departments are working in concert to attain specific goals that cause high organizational performance.[30]

The cause-effect control technique is the strategy map. A **strategy map** provides a visual representation of the key drivers of an organization's success and shows how specific outcomes in each area are linked.[31] The strategy map is a powerful way for managers to see the cause-and-effect relationships among various performance metrics. The simplified strategy map in Exhibit 11.7 illustrates the four key areas that contribute to a firm's long-term success—learning and growth, internal processes, customer service, and financial performance—and how the various outcomes in one area link directly to performance in another area. The idea is that effective performance in terms of learning and growth serves as a foundation to help achieve excellent internal business processes. Excellent business processes, in turn, enable the organization to achieve high customer service and satisfaction, which enables the organization to reach its financial goals and optimize its value to all stakeholders.

In the strategy map shown in Exhibit 11.7, the organization has learning and growth goals that include employee training and development, continuous learning and knowledge sharing, and building a culture of innovation. Achieving these will help the organization build efficient internal business processes that promote good relationships with suppliers and partners, improve the quality and flexibility of operations, and excel at developing innovative products and services. Accomplishing internal process goals, in turn, enables the organization to maintain strong relationships with customers, be a leader in quality and reliability, and provide innovative solutions to emerging customer needs. At the top of the strategy map, the

BRIEFCASE

As an organization manager, keep these guidelines in mind:

Use a balanced scorecard to integrate various control dimensions and get a more complete picture of organizational performance. Select indicators in the areas of financial performance, customer service, internal processes, and learning and growth, and consider a strategy map to visualize how outcomes are linked.

EXHIBIT 11.7
A Strategy Map for Performance Management

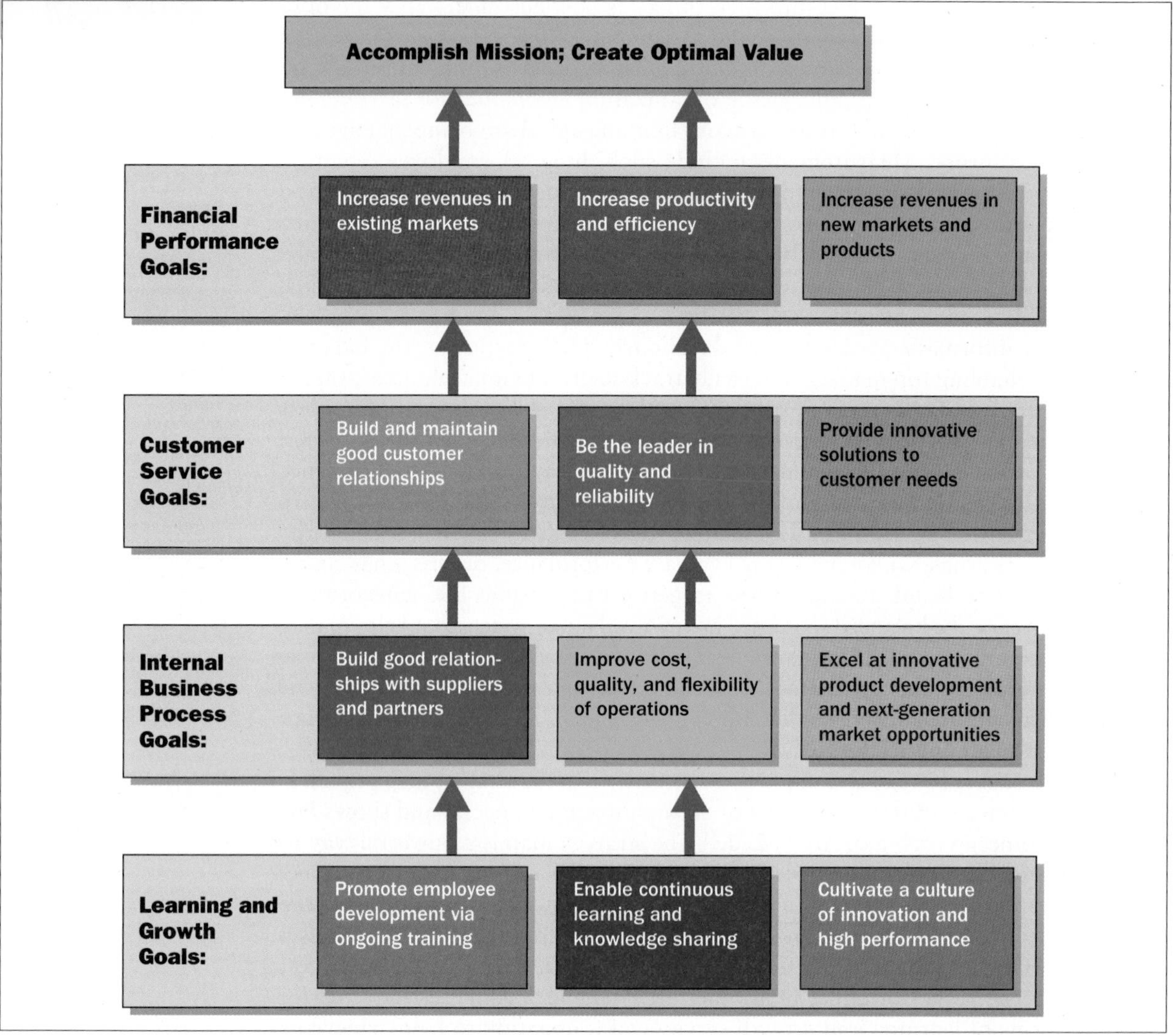

Source: Based on Robert S. Kaplan and David P. Norton, "Mastering the Management System," *Harvard Business Review* (January 2008), 63–77; and R. S. Kaplan and D. P. Norton, "Having Trouble with Your Strategy? Then Map It," *Harvard Business Review* (September–October 2000), 167–176.

accomplishment of these lower-level goals helps the organization increase revenues in existing markets, reduce costs through better productivity and efficiency, and grow by selling new products and services in new market segments.

In a real-life organization, the strategy map would typically be more complex and would state concrete, specific goals, desired outcomes, and metrics relevant to the particular business. However, the generic map in Exhibit 11.7 gives an idea of how managers can use strategy maps to set goals, track metrics, assess performance, and make changes as needed.

Department Level: Behavior Versus Outcome Control

The balanced scorecard and strategy map are techniques used primarily by top and upper-level managers. Lower-level managers focus on the performance of people at the department level, who must meet goals and standards if the organization is to attain its overall goals. Although lower-level managers may use any of the control systems listed earlier in Exhibit 11.4, the reward system is often of paramount concern at the supervisory level.

There are two different approaches to evaluating and controlling team or individual performance and allocating rewards. One approach focuses primarily on *how* people do their jobs, whereas the other focuses primarily on the *outcomes* people produce.[32] **Behavior control** is based on manager observation of employee actions to see whether the individual follows desired procedures and performs tasks as instructed. Do people get to work on time? Do they stay focused on their tasks or spend a lot of time socializing with colleagues? Do they dress appropriately for the job? Do they perform their jobs according to established methods or supervisor instructions? With behavior control, managers provide heavy supervision and monitoring, pay attention to the methods people use to accomplish their jobs, and evaluate and reward people based on specific criteria, which might include areas such as appearance, punctuality, skills, activities, and so forth.

Information technology has increased the potential for managers to use behavior control. For example, GPS tracking devices installed on government-issued vehicles are helping many communities reduce waste and abuse, in part by catching employees shopping, working out at the gym, or otherwise loafing while on the clock. In Denver, 76 vehicles equipped with GPS units were driven 5,000 fewer miles than the unequipped fleet during the same period the year before, indicating the value of this type of quantitative measure.[33] Managers in many companies monitor employees' e-mail and other online activities. Some retailers use cash-register management software that monitors cashiers' activities in real time.[34]

A second approach to control is to pay less attention to what people *do* than to what they *accomplish*. **Outcome control** is based on monitoring and rewarding results, and managers might pay little attention to how those results are obtained. With outcome control, managers don't supervise employees in the traditional sense. People have a great deal of autonomy in terms of how they do their jobs—and sometimes in terms of where and when they do their jobs—as long as they produce desired outcomes. Rather than monitoring how many hours an employee works, for example, managers focus on how much work the employee accomplishes. The Results-Only Work Environment program at Best Buy provides an illustration of outcome control carried to the extreme.

BRIEFCASE

As an organization manager, keep these guidelines in mind:

Don't overdo the use of behavior control. Set some reasonable guidelines for behavior and work activities, but emphasize outcome control by focusing on results and allowing employees some discretion and autonomy about how they accomplish outcomes.

IN PRACTICE

Best Buy

When Best Buy managers noticed an alarming increase in turnover of headquarters employees, they began looking for ways to reverse the trend. They realized that the Best Buy culture that emphasized long hours, mandatory procedures, and managers "acting like hall monitors" was no longer working. So, what was the best approach to keep talented people from reaching burnout?

The answer turned out to be an innovative initiative known as ROWE (Results-Only Work Environment), which lets people work when and where they want as long as they get the job done. The experiment started in one department, where morale had reached a dismal low. Under the ROWE system, claims processors and data entry clerks now focus on how many forms they can process in a week rather than how many hours they put in each day or how many keystrokes it takes to complete a form. The program worked so well that it quickly spread to other departments.

The results? From 2005 to 2007, the turnover rate in departments using ROWE decreased nearly 90 percent, while productivity shot up 41 percent. Managers have now implemented ROWE throughout corporate headquarters. There are no set working hours, no mandatory meetings, and no managers keeping tabs on employees' activities. Senior vice-president John Thompson, who was at first skeptical of ROWE, became a strong believer when he saw the results. "For years I had been focused on the wrong currency," Thompson says. "I was always looking to see if people were here. I should have been looking at what they were getting done."[35]

Switching from behavior control to outcome control had significant positive effects at Best Buy headquarters, and managers are now implementing a form of the ROWE system in the retail stores. With outcome control, IT is used not to monitor and control individual employee behavior but rather to assess performance outcomes. For example, at Best Buy, the manager of the online orders department can use IT to measure how many orders per hour his team processes, even if one team member is working down the hall, one working from home, one taking the afternoon off, and another working from her vacation cabin 400 miles away.[36] Good performance metrics are key to making an outcome control system work effectively.

However, outcome control is not necessarily the best for all situations. In some cases, behavior control is more appropriate and effective, but in general, managers in successful organizations are moving away from closely monitoring and controlling behavior toward allowing employees more discretion and autonomy in how they do their jobs. The BookMark describes a simple tool that managers can use to give employees more autonomy yet at the same time maintain control over critical work activities. In most organizations, managers use both behavior and outcome control.

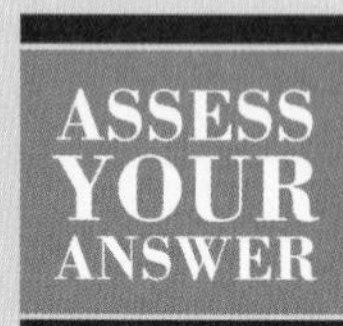

1 For a manager, it should not matter much exactly how or when people get their work done, just as long as they produce good results.

ANSWER: *Agree.* Focusing on results, or outcomes, can be a highly effective approach to department level control in many organizations. Employees resent being micromanaged and don't like being treated like children. Most managers find it necessary to set some reasonable boundaries for correct behavior, but greater control emphasis is placed on outcome control to achieve highest performance.

BOOKMARK

11.0 HAVE YOU READ THIS BOOK?

The Checklist Manifesto: How to Get Things Right

By Atul Gawande

Buildings crumble because design modifications don't take critical engineering specifications into account. Factory fires, oil rig explosions, and mine accidents occur because important safety measures are overlooked. And every year in the United States alone nearly 100,000 people die from hospital-acquired infections because simple sterilization steps are missed. "The volume and complexity of what we know has exceeded our individual ability to deliver its benefits correctly, safely, or reliably," says Atul Gawande, a physician and author of *The Checklist Manifesto: How to Get Things Right*.

A SIMPLE WAY TO CONTROL COMPLEX WORK

Gawande's book describes how using a checklist can reduce and eliminate many errors in complex jobs by making priorities clear, helping people remember specific critical steps that can easily be forgotten in the midst of complexity, and preventing communication breakdowns. Using examples from surgery, foreign intelligence, construction, aviation, rock concerts, software design, and other areas, Gawande shows how the right checklist improves outcomes by catching the "mental flaws inherent in all of us—flaws of memory and attention and thoroughness." Here's how to effectively use a checklist:

- *Keep it simple.* A checklist shouldn't try to detail every step involved in a process such as conducting surgery, setting up for a rock concert, or designing a new piece of software. Rather, it should be simple and precise, spelling out "only the most critical and important steps" that are prone to errors. A good checklist makes priorities clear to everyone using it.
- *Remember that complexity obscures the obvious.* A checklist should make sure people don't make stupid mistakes because they are overwhelmed by a complex situation. A critical care specialist created a five-step checklist designed to reduce IV line infections of patients in the Intensive Care Unit: Wash your hands with soap; Sterilize the patient's skin; Put sterile drapes over the entire patient; Wear a mask, gown, and gloves; Put a sterile dressing over the insertion site. The rate of infections dropped from 11 percent to zero within a year.
- *Make it a communication tool.* A checklist forces communication where it is needed. For instance, in construction, even a minor change in the support structure can affect a range of other planned steps, such as plumbing and electrical. Checklists can be used to make sure people in charge of different aspects of a project are consulted about any decision that potentially affects their part of the project. "Just ticking boxes is not the ultimate goal here," Gawande writes. "Embracing a culture of teamwork and discipline is."

CHECKLISTS HELP DECENTRALIZE POWER

Good checklists enable managers to "push the power of decision making out to the periphery and away from the center," Gawande says. Checklists mean managers can focus less on strict forms of behavior control. "They supply a set of checks to ensure the stupid but critical stuff is not overlooked, and they supply another set of checks to ensure people talk and coordinate and accept responsibility while nonetheless being left the power to manage the nuances and unpredictabilities the best they know how."

The Checklist Manifesto: How to Get Things Right, by Atul Gawande, is published by Metropolitan Books.

Strategic Approach I: Strengthening Employee Coordination and Efficiency

Following the use of information systems for managerial decision making and control, IT has evolved further as a strategic tool for both increasing internal coordination and efficiency and enhancing coordination with customers and external partners. This is the highest level of application, as illustrated in Exhibit 11.1 at the

BRIEFCASE

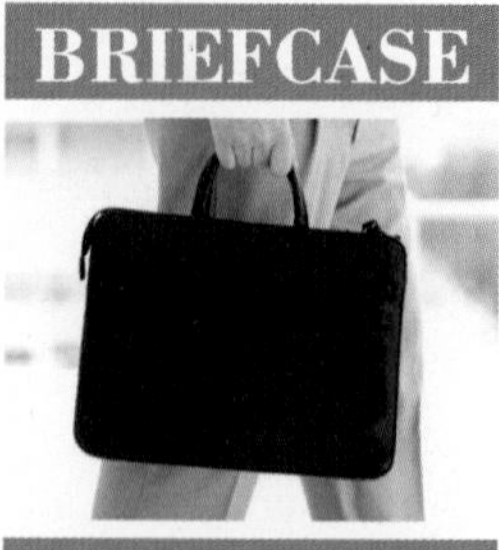

As an organization manager, keep these guidelines in mind:

Improve internal coordination and information sharing with intranets, knowledge management, social networking, and enterprise resource planning systems.

beginning of the chapter. Primary IT applications for increasing internal coordination and efficiency are intranets, knowledge-management, social networking, and enterprise resource planning (ERP). Enhancing coordination with external parties will be discussed in the next section.

Intranets

Networking, which links people and departments within a particular building or across corporate offices, enabling them to share information and cooperate on projects, is an important strategic tool for many companies. For example, a networked electronic medical records system links employees at the hospitals of Partners HealthCare System, the largest hospital network in New England, with the offices of more than 4,000 physicians with admitting privileges. The system ties doctors, nurses, staff specialists, and others into a coordinated team to provide better care, avoid redundant tests, and prevent potentially conflicting prescriptions. Explaining the reasoning behind the system, the head of the Partners' physician group said, "I don't want doctors just to work better. I want them to work better with their colleagues."[37]

One prevalent form of corporate networking is an **intranet**, a private, companywide information system that uses the communications protocols and standards of the Internet but is accessible only to people within the company. To view files and information, users simply navigate the site with a standard web browser, clicking on links. Today, most companies with intranets have moved their management information systems, executive information systems, and so forth over to the intranet so they are accessible to anyone who needs them. In addition, having these systems as part of the intranet means new features and applications can easily be added and accessed through a standard browser. Intranets can improve internal communications and unlock hidden information. They enable employees to keep in touch with what's going on around the organization, quickly and easily find information they need, share ideas, and work on projects collaboratively.

Knowledge Management

Knowledge management refers to the efforts to systematically find, organize, and make available a company's intellectual capital and to foster a culture of continuous learning and knowledge sharing.[38] The company's **intellectual capital** is the sum of its knowledge, experience, understanding, relationships, processes, innovations, and discoveries.

Companies need ways to transfer both codified knowledge and tacit knowledge across the organization.[39] **Codified knowledge** is formal, systematic knowledge that can be articulated, written down, and passed on to others in documents, rules, or general instructions. Tacit knowledge, on the other hand, is often difficult to put into words. **Tacit knowledge** is based on personal experience, rules of thumb, intuition, and judgment. It includes professional know-how and expertise, individual insight and experience, and creative solutions that are difficult to communicate and pass on to others. As much as 80 percent of an organization's valuable knowledge may be tacit knowledge that is not easily captured and transferred.[40] Thus, one

EXHIBIT 11.8
Two Approaches to Knowledge Management

Codified	Knowledge Management Strategy	Tacit
Provide high-quality, reliable, and fast information systems for access of explicit, reusable knowledge		Channel individual expertise to provide creative advice on strategic problems
People-to-documents approach *Develop an electronic document system that codifies, stores, disseminates, and allows reuse of knowledge*	**Knowledge Management Strategy**	**Person-to-person approach** *Develop networks for linking people so that tacit knowledge can be shared*
Invest heavily in information technology, with a goal of connecting people with reusable, codified knowledge	**Information Technology Approach**	*Invest moderately in information technology, with a goal of facilitating conversations and the personal exchange of tacit knowledge*

Source: Based on Morten T. Hansen, Nitin Nohria, and Thomas Tierney, "What's Your Strategy for Managing Knowledge?" *Harvard Business Review* (March–April 1999), 106–116.

hot topic in corporate IT concerns **expert-locator systems** that identify and catalog experts in a searchable database so people can quickly identify who has knowledge they can use.[41]

Two approaches to knowledge management are outlined in Exhibit 11.8.[42] The first approach deals primarily with the collection and sharing of codified knowledge, largely through the use of sophisticated IT systems. Codified knowledge may include intellectual properties such as patents and licenses; work processes such as policies and procedures; specific information on customers, markets, suppliers, or competitors; competitive intelligence reports; benchmark data; and so forth. The second approach focuses on leveraging individual expertise and know-how—tacit knowledge—by connecting people face to face or through interactive media. Tacit knowledge includes professional know-how, individual insights and creativity, and personal experience and intuition. With this approach, managers concentrate on developing personal networks that link people together for the sharing of tacit knowledge. The organization uses IT systems primarily for facilitating conversation and person-to-person sharing of experience, insight, and ideas.

Consider the example of Converteam, a company with headquarters in the United Kingdom that maintains power generation and propulsion systems for hundreds of ships and oil exploration platforms around the world. Employees working in China, India, Brazil, the United States, and Norway need a way to share knowledge and expertise among themselves and with headquarters. An IT system includes contact details for engineers working in various countries along with an expertise inventory. Engineers can contact one another directly regarding new products, challenges, and so forth, rather than having to go through headquarters.[43]

BRIEFCASE

As an organization manager, keep these guidelines in mind:

Establish systems to facilitate both codified and tacit knowledge sharing to help the organization learn and improve.

Social Networking

Encouraging and facilitating the sharing of tacit knowledge isn't easy. Despite the fact that companies have spent billions on software and other technology for knowledge management, there is some indication that knowledge sharing has fallen short of managers' goals. For instance, 60 percent of employees surveyed by a Harris poll said work was often duplicated in their organizations because people were unaware of one another's work. Fifty-four percent said their companies missed opportunities to innovate because of poor collaboration and information sharing, and 51 percent said managers regularly made poor decisions because employee knowledge isn't effectively tapped.[44]

A recent approach that holds promise for more effective sharing of tacit knowledge is the use of *social media*, including corporate social networking and other social technology tools such as blogs and wikis.[45] A **blog** is a running web log that allows an individual to post opinions and ideas about work projects and processes. The simplicity and informality of blogs make them an easy and comfortable medium for people to communicate and share ideas. In addition, the microblogging service Twitter is increasingly being used by companies as a fast way to solve problems. People can send a question and quickly get responses from all over the organization or from outsiders. A **wiki** is similar to a blog and uses software to create a website that allows people to create, share, and edit content through a browser-based interface. Rather than simply sharing opinions and ideas as with a blog, wikis are free-form, allowing people to edit what they find on the site and add content.[46] At Rosen Law, a Raleigh, North Carolina-based law firm, managers moved all contracts, court orders, case files, and other documents to a secure wiki. If people see a better way to organize information, they go ahead and do it. Lawyers and paralegals, for instance, have different needs, so the two groups edited one another's entries until both were happy with certain categorizations.[47] Another benefit besides enhanced coordination is that search engines can mine company blogs and wikis to help people identify who has expertise in a specific area or knowledge that could be useful to a particular project.

Social networking is an extension of blogs and wikis. Social networking sites provide an unprecedented peer-to-peer communication channel where people interact in an online community, sharing personal and professional information and photos, producing and sharing all sorts of ideas and opinions. Because of the popularity of Facebook in people's personal lives, most employees are comfortable with the idea of "following" and communicating with their colleagues online. Using social networks for a business enables people to easily connect with one another across organizational and geographical boundaries based on professional relationships, shared interests, problems, or other criteria. A Symantec salesman in Dubai created a group on the company's social network that exchanges sales tips from employees around the world.[48] People can use the social network to search for tags that will identify others with knowledge and resources that can help them solve a problem or do their jobs better. Moreover, the nature of social networking builds trust so that people are more likely to cooperate and share information.[49]

Many organizations, from small entrepreneurial firms and nonprofit agencies to huge corporations, are experimenting with using social media for business purposes. One organization that has implemented a clearly thought-out social media strategy is Cognizant.

IN PRACTICE

Cognizant

Few companies have applied social media as effectively as Cognizant, based in Teaneck, New Jersey and with employees in development centers around the world. Cognizant provides information technology, consulting, and business process outsourcing services to companies that span five continents and every major industry.

Many of Cognizant's employees are young and they appreciate the opportunity to use social media to build their personal and professional networks both inside and outside the company. All projects and project managers are rated on how well they use social media, and Cognizant regularly analyzes the strength of its employee networks. By looking at who has a large number of followers, managers can tap into these people to help spread new ideas or get feedback from across the organization. CEO Frank D'Souza contributes regularly to blogging forums and uses blogs to communicate new initiatives and get feedback.

Much of the knowledge at Cognizant's is tacit knowledge that can't easily be captured in a structured way. Rather, it has to be located and accessed through social and personal ties among colleagues. One aspect of the social media system is a knowledge management platform, called Knowledge Management Appliance, which includes the ability to "tag" both documents and people so an employee can easily search for those with expertise related to specific technologies or projects. In addition to questions and answers, employees post blogs, comments, and Twitter-like messages that help build connections. KM Appliance is integrated with the Cognizant C2 initiative, which is designed to provide people with access to specific codified knowledge in the context of a particular work process. For any task, a user can see task dependencies, guidance information, templates, similar project artifacts, notes, and checklists.

The final aspect is using social media to connect with external stakeholders, such as clients, industry experts, and academics. An important point is that Cognizant doesn't use this for sales or marketing purposes, but rather for building a trusted online environment where people can connect with one another, share content and opinions, follow one another's activities, and have a dialogue about important business issues.[50]

At Cognizant, social media is used to create a learning and knowledge-sharing environment for both its employees and its partners and clients. As stated on the company's website, the high-level use of social media enables Cognizant to "access the specialized skills of our deep talent pool from anywhere in the world, to solve any problem." Clients and industry experts agree that this approach has given Cognizant a competitive advantage in its industry.

Enterprise Resource Planning

Another approach to information and knowledge management pulls together various types of information to see how decisions and actions in one part of the organization affect other parts of the firm. Many companies are using broad-scale information systems that take a comprehensive view of the organization's activities. These **enterprise resource planning** (ERP) systems collect, process, and provide information about a company's entire enterprise, including order processing, product design, purchasing, inventory, manufacturing, distribution, human resources (HR), receipt of payments, and forecasting of future demand.[51] ERP systems can be expensive and difficult to implement, but when applied successfully, an ERP system

EXHIBIT 11.9
Example of an ERP Network

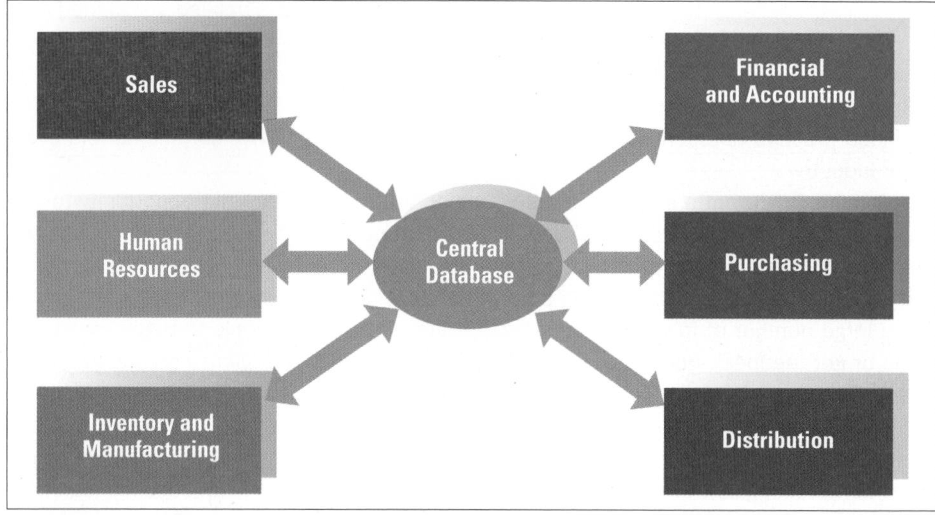

can serve as the backbone for an organization by integrating and optimizing all the various business processes across the entire firm.[52]

Such a system links all of these areas of activity into a network, as illustrated in Exhibit 11.9. When a salesperson takes an order, the ERP system checks to see how the order affects inventory levels, scheduling, HR, purchasing, and distribution. The system replicates organizational processes in software, guides employees through the processes step by step, and automates as many of them as possible. For example, ERP software can automatically cut an accounts payable check as soon as a clerk confirms that goods have been received in inventory, send an online purchase order immediately after a manager has authorized a purchase, or schedule production at the most appropriate plant after an order is received.[53] In addition, because the system integrates data about all aspects of operations, managers and employees at all levels can see how decisions and actions in one part of the organization affect other parts, using this information to make better decisions. ERP can provide the kind of information furnished by transaction processing systems as well as that provided by information reporting systems, decision support systems, or executive information systems. The key is that ERP weaves all of these systems together so people can see the big picture and act quickly, helping the organization be smarter and more effective. More recently, ERP has incorporated tools for supply chain management so that coordination across organizational boundaries is strengthened as well.[54]

BRIEFCASE

As an organization manager, keep this guideline in mind:

Use IT applications such as extranets, supply chain management systems, and e-business systems to strengthen relationships with customers, suppliers, and business partners.

Strategic Approach II: Strengthening Coordination with External Partners

External applications of IT for strengthening coordination with customers, suppliers, and partners include systems for supply chain management and the integrated enterprise, tools for enhancing customer relationships, and e-business organization design. One basic approach is to extend the corporate intranet to include customers and partners. An **extranet** is an external communications system that uses the

Internet and is shared by two or more organizations. Each organization moves certain data outside of its private intranet, but makes the data available only to the other companies sharing the extranet.

The Integrated Enterprise

Extranets play a critical role in today's integrated enterprise. The **integrated enterprise** is an organization that uses advanced IT to enable close coordination within the company as well as with suppliers, customers, and partners. An important aspect of the integrated enterprise is using *supply chain management systems*, which manage the sequence of suppliers and purchasers covering all stages of processing from obtaining raw materials to distributing finished goods to consumers.[55]

Information Linkages. Applying supply chain management systems enables organizations to achieve the right balance of low inventory levels and customer responsiveness. Exhibit 11.10 illustrates horizontal information linkages in the integrated enterprise. By establishing electronic linkages between the organization and key partners for the sharing and exchange of data, the integrated enterprise creates a seamless, integrated line stretching from end consumers to raw materials suppliers.[56] For example, in the exhibit, as consumers purchase products in retail stores, the data are automatically fed into the retail chain's information system. In turn, the chain gives access to this constantly updated data to the manufacturing company through a secure extranet. With knowledge of this demand data, the manufacturer can produce and ship products when needed. As products are made by the manufacturer, data about raw materials used in the production process, updated inventory information, and updated forecasted demand are electronically provided to the manufacturer's suppliers, and the suppliers automatically replenish the manufacturer's raw materials inventory as needed.

Horizontal Relationships. The purpose of integrating the supply chain is for everyone to work closely together, moving in lockstep to meet customers' product and time demands. Honeywell Garrett Engine Boosting Systems, which makes turbochargers for cars, trucks, and light aircraft, uses an extranet to give suppliers access to its inventory and production data so they can respond rapidly to the

BRIEFCASE

As an organization manager, keep these guidelines in mind:

Transform your organization into an integrated enterprise by establishing horizontal information linkages between the organization and key outsiders. Create a seamless, integrated line stretching from end consumers to raw materials suppliers that will meet customers' product and time demands.

EXHIBIT 11.10
The Integrated Enterprise

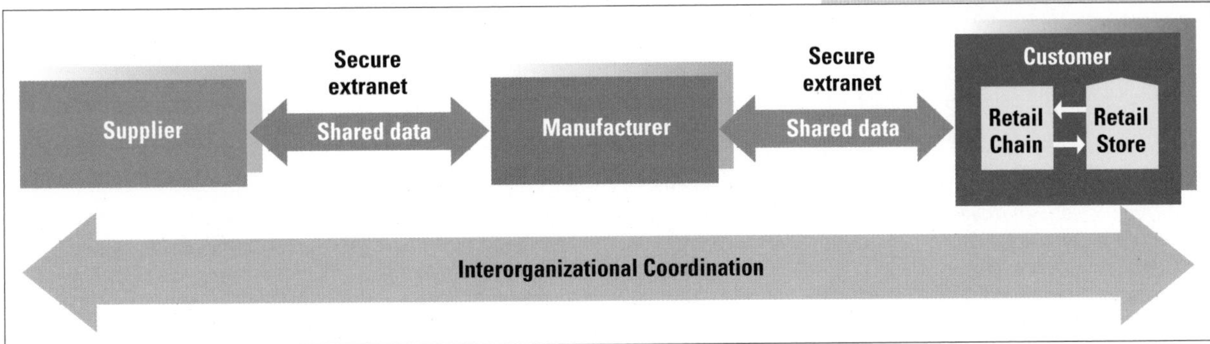

Source: Based on Jim Turcotte, Bob Silveri, and Tom Jobson, "Are You Ready for the E-Supply Chain?" *APICS–The Performance Advantage* (August 1998), 56–59.

manufacturer's need for parts. Honeywell is also working with big customers such as Ford and Volkswagen to integrate their systems so the company will have better information about turbocharger demands from customers as well. "Our goal," says Honeywell's Paul Hopkins, "is seamless value-chain connectivity from customer demand to suppliers."[57] Another organization that has made superb use of technology to forge integrated horizontal relationships is Corrugated Supplies.

Corrugated Supplies

IN PRACTICE

You might not expect a cardboard manufacturer to be on the cutting edge of information technology, but Rick Van Horne transformed Corrugated Supplies into one of the world's first completely web-based production plants. The plant's equipment continually feeds data to the Internet, where the rest of the company, as well as suppliers and customers, can keep track of what's happening on the factory floor in real time. Using a password, customers call up Corrugated's production schedules to see exactly where their orders are in the process and when they will arrive. Suppliers tap into the system to manage inventory.

Exhibit 11.11 illustrates how the system works for a customer placing an order: The customer logs onto the website and types in an order for corrugated paper precisely cut and folded for 20,000 boxes. The order is downloaded into the database and computers at Corrugated's factory determine the best way to blend that order with numerous other orders

EXHIBIT 11.11
Corrugated Supplies System in Action

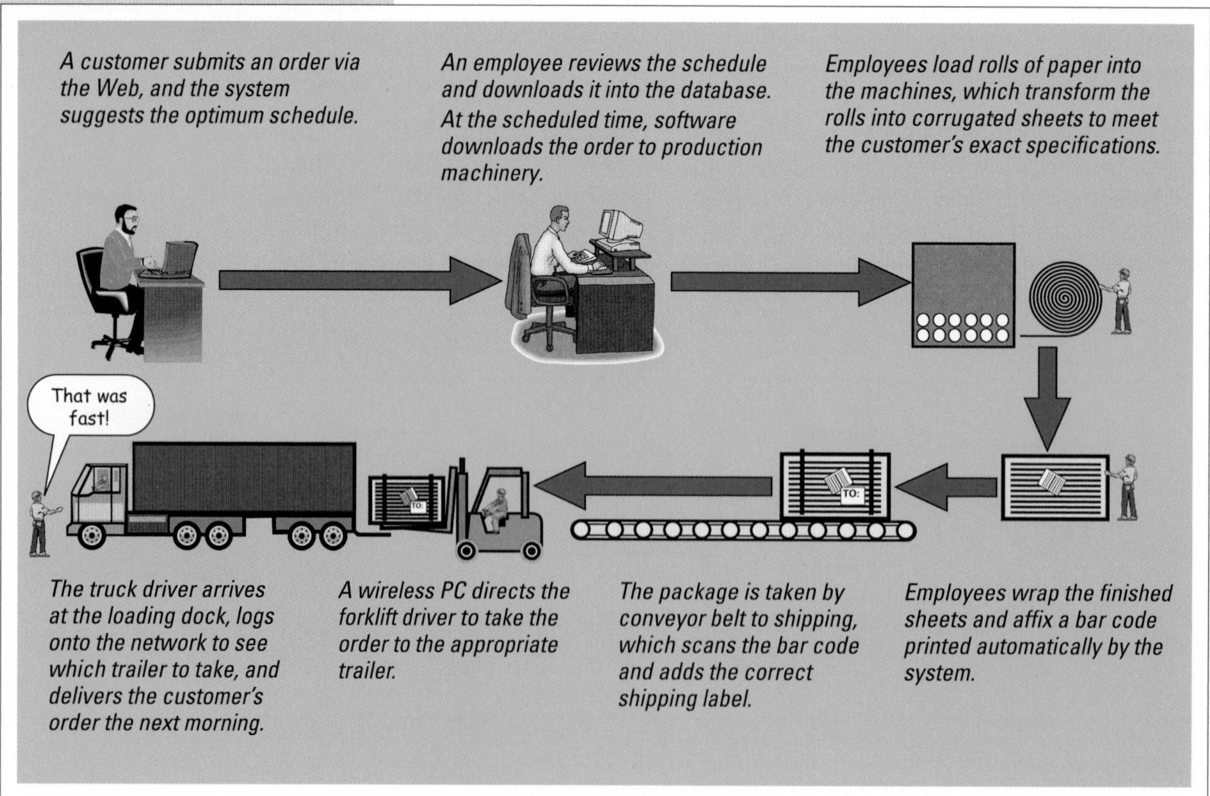

A customer submits an order via the Web, and the system suggests the optimum schedule.
An employee reviews the schedule and downloads it into the database. At the scheduled time, software downloads the order to production machinery.
Employees load rolls of paper into the machines, which transform the rolls into corrugated sheets to meet the customer's exact specifications.
That was fast!
TO:
TO:
The truck driver arrives at the loading dock, logs onto the network to see which trailer to take, and delivers the customer's order the next morning.
A wireless PC directs the forklift driver to take the order to the appropriate trailer.
The package is taken by conveyor belt to shipping, which scans the bar code and adds the correct shipping label.
Employees wrap the finished sheets and affix a bar code printed automatically by the system.

Source: Adapted from Bill Richards, "Superplant," *eCompany* (November 2000), 182–196.

ranging from a few dozen boxes to 50,000. The computer comes up with the optimum schedule—that is, the one that gets the most orders out of a single roll with little leftover paper. A human operator checks the schedule on one of the numerous linked computer screens scattered around the plant and hits the *Send* button. Computer software directs the massive corrugators, trimmers, slitters, and other equipment, which begin spewing out paper orders at 800 feet per minute. Computer-controlled conveyor belts carry the order to the loading dock, where forklifts equipped with wireless PCs take the load to the designated trailer. Truck drivers log on to the website and are told which trailer to haul to maximize their trip's efficiency. The order is usually delivered to the customer the very next day.

About 70 percent of Corrugated's orders are submitted via the Internet and routed electronically to the plant floor. The system saves time and money for Corrugated by automatically scheduling special-order details and cutting out paper waste. For customers, it means faster service and fewer mix-ups. One customer, Gene Mazurek, co-owner of Suburban Corrugated Box Co., says it is "the best thing that's ever happened. . . . It's like Rick put his corrugating machine right inside my plant."[58]

For the integrated enterprise to work, horizontal relationships, such as those between Corrugated and its suppliers and customers, get more emphasis than vertical relationships. Enterprise integration can create a level of cooperation not previously imaginable if managers approach the practice with an attitude of trust and partnership, as in the interorganizational relationships described in Chapter 4.

Customer Relationships

Recall from the previous section the example of Cognizant, which extends its use of social media to clients and partners. It isn't the only company that is applying new technology to build stronger relationships. Many organizations, including Ford Motor Company, Harrah's Entertainment, McDonald's, Petco, and AT&T, have hired *social media directors* that are in charge of a blend of activities such as marketing and promotions, customer service, and support.[59] Social media directors use blogs, Twitter, Facebook, company websites, and other technology primarily to do one thing—strengthen customer relationships. Managers responding to one survey say they use these technologies for improving customer service, developing new markets, getting customer participation in product development, and offering opportunities for customers to interact with one another.[60] For example, Dr. Pepper has built a Facebook fan base of 8.5 million people. Managers put out two messages a day on the company's fan page and then mine the data to see what people are thinking.[61]

Social networks and blogs are particularly popular customer-facing technologies. In 2011, 65 percent of businesses surveyed reported having a company blog to communicate with customers, up from 48 percent in 2009.[62] Blogs give organizations a human voice, enable companies to influence opinion, and provide an easy way to share company news directly with outsiders. For many CEOs, having a blog or a Twitter account is no longer a matter of choice but a requirement of being a good leader. To increase sales for his family's wine business, Wine Library, Gary Vaynerchuk offered free shipping of online orders and promoted it three ways. A direct marketing mailing cost $15,000 and attracted 200 new customers. A billboard ad cost $7,500 and brought in 300 new customers. When Vaynerchuk tweeted the promotion on Twitter, it cost him nothing and attracted 1,800 new customers. Vaynerchuk also posts a daily webcast to connect with consumers that has won a wide following. He calls it "virtual handshaking, working the room."[63]

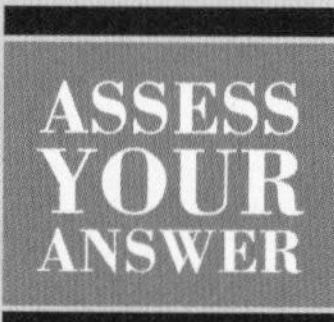

2 **Every manager should have a blog.**

ANSWER: *Disagree.* Blogs are an increasingly popular way for managers to communicate, both with employees and with customers. Blogging has become almost as common for some managers as using e-mail. But blogs are not necessarily appropriate for every manager in every work environment.

BRIEFCASE

As an organization manager, keep these guidelines in mind:

- Use an in-house e-business division to provide tight integration between the Internet operation and the traditional operation and leverage the brand name, customer information, suppliers, and marketing muscle of the parent company.
- Create a separate company if the e-business unit needs greater autonomy and flexibility to adapt to rapidly changing market conditions.
- Consider a blended design that fully integrates the e-business with the traditional business if your company is in an industry that competes heavily with Internet-based firms.

E-Business Organization Design

E-business can be defined as any business that takes place by digital processes over a computer network rather than in physical space. However, e-business most commonly refers to electronic linkages over the Internet with customers, partners, suppliers, employees, or other key constituents. *E-commerce* is a more limited term that refers specifically to business exchanges or transactions that occur electronically. Today, e-commerce is transforming into *m-commerce*, which simply means the ability to conduct business transactions through a mobile device. The world has gone mobile. For many people, their cell phone is always within reach, and they use it for everything from ordering a pizza to accessing their bank account.[64] A study by ABI Research suggests that by 2015 shoppers from around the world will spend about $119 billion on goods and services bought via their mobile phones.[65] Since mobile phones greatly outnumber personal computers in developing markets such as China, India, and Thailand, mobile devices are the primary Internet connection for many consumers.

Many traditional organizations have set up Internet operations, but managers have to make a decision about how best to integrate *bricks and clicks*—that is, how to blend their traditional operations with an Internet initiative. In the early days of e-business, many companies set up dot-com initiatives with little understanding of how those activities could and should be integrated with the overall business. As the reality of e-business has evolved, companies have gained valuable lessons in how to merge online and offline activities.[66]

The range of basic strategies for setting up an Internet operation is illustrated in Exhibit 11.12. One option is to set up an Internet division as a separate business, either by creating a spin-off company or by participating in a joint venture with another organization. Some companies choose to establish an in-house division that is more closely integrated with the traditional business. As the Internet continues to evolve, other companies are moving to a third option, which is to blend traditional and e-business operations in a totally integrated design. Each of these options presents distinct advantages and disadvantages.[67]

Separate Business

To give the Internet operation autonomy and flexibility, some organizations choose to create a separate company, using either a spin-off or a joint venture. A separate business is a free-standing Internet business that competes with other Internet companies. Advantages of a separate business include faster decision making, increased flexibility and responsiveness to changing market conditions, an entrepreneurial culture, and management that is totally focused on the success of the online

EXHIBIT 11.12
Strategies for Integrating Bricks and Clicks

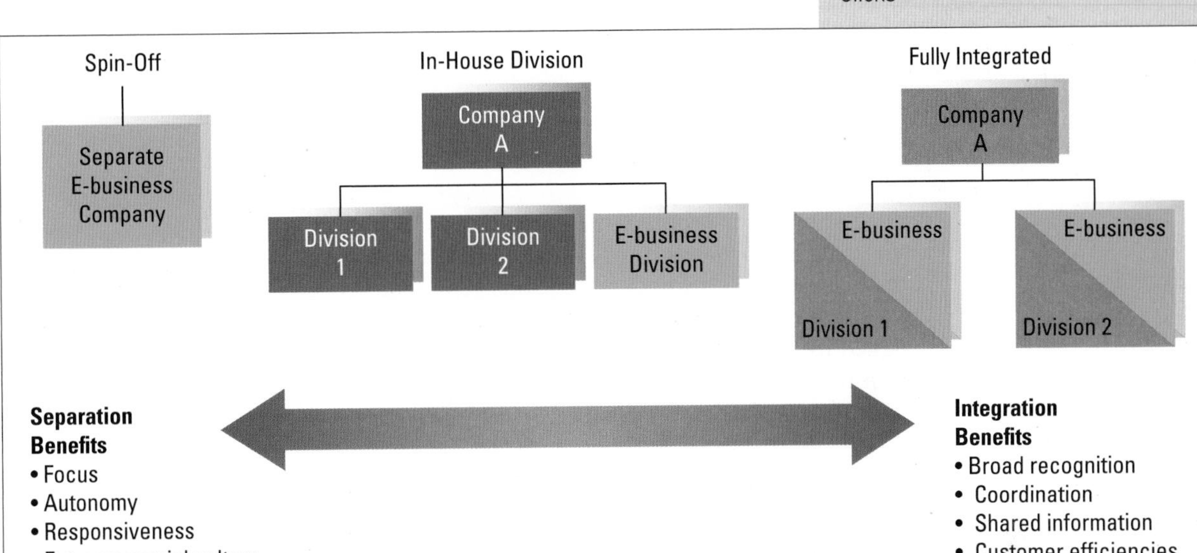

Source: Based on Ranjay Gulati and Jason Garino, "Get the Right Mix of Bricks and Clicks," *Harvard Business Review* (May–June 2000), 107–114.

operation. Potential disadvantages are the loss of brand recognition and marketing opportunities, higher start-up costs, and loss of leverage with suppliers. For example, retailer Kmart originally created a spin-off division called Bluelight.com, and the drugstore CVS originally launched CVS.com as a separate business. In both cases, operating e-business as a separate unit proved to be inefficient for the retailers in the long run. Managers began bringing online operations back under the umbrella of the traditional business so that functions such as marketing, merchandising, and purchasing could be handled more efficiently. The autonomy, flexibility, and focus of the spin-off was an advantage during the start-up phase, but the organizations later gained efficiencies by bringing the web business back in-house for better coordination with other departments.[68] Another approach to creating a separate business is to enter into a joint venture or partnership. Particularly for companies that have little Internet experience, forming a joint venture with an experienced partner can be more successful than going it alone. For example, in 2011, Belle International Holdings Ltd., China's largest retailer of women's shoes, formed a joint venture with Baidu, the largest Internet search provider in China, to launch a business selling shoes online.[69]

In-House Division

An in-house division offers tight integration between the Internet operation and the organization's traditional operation. The organization creates a separate unit within the company that functions within the structure and guidance of the traditional organization. For example, Disney.com is a division under the guidance and control of the Walt Disney Company, and Lowes.com is totally operated and controlled by Lowe's. *The New York Times* embraced the web early on with an in-house division that today provides a growing percentage of the newspaper outfit's business and advertising revenue.[70] The in-house approach gives the new division several advantages by piggybacking on the established company. These include brand recognition, purchasing leverage with suppliers, shared customer information and marketing opportunities, and distribution efficiencies. A potential problem with an in-house division, however, is that the new operation doesn't have the flexibility needed to move quickly in the Internet world.

Integrated Design

A third option is the totally integrated design. With this approach, there is no separation between what is defined as the traditional part of the business and what is defined as the e-business part. E-business is incorporated into every employee's work. That is, what might have started out as an in-house division is broken up and assigned to various departments and business units as part of the everyday way of operating. Virtually every employee is involved in both traditional and e-business activities. The magazine *The Atlantic* provides a good example.

The Atlantic

IN PRACTICE

It was the magazine that first published the "Battle Hymn of the Republic" and ushered the first stories of Mark Twain, Henry James, and Ernest Hemingway into print—153 years old and looking like it wouldn't get much older when Justin Smith arrived in 2007. Smith had to find a way to reinvent *The Atlantic* (originally *The Atlantic Monthly*) for the twenty-first century. Smith and editor James Bennet got managers and editorial people together to brainstorm: "What would we do," they asked, "if the goal was to aggressively cannibalize ourselves?"

The outcome was that *The Atlantic* became one of the first magazines to assertively combine its print and digital sides. Walls between the print and the digital staffs literally and figuratively came crashing down. Advertising salespeople were told it no longer mattered what percentage of their sales were digital or print. Young, web-savvy writers were hired to write blogs and opinion columns, a scary move for a magazine accustomed to producing highly polished, totally fact-checked, error-free articles. To make sure people were reading, managers dismantled the website's subscription paywall so that anyone could freely browse *The Atlantic Online*. Within three years, the company was in the black, and Smith and Bennett were hailed as a marvel in the publishing world because of the decisions they had made to get it there. Fully integrating print and digital (the traditional business side and the e-business side) proved to be the right move for reviving *The Atlantic* for a new generation.[71]

As the Internet matures as a place for doing business, more companies are shifting toward a totally integrated design. Walmart, for example, is restructuring its e-commerce operations as it faces growing pressure to compete with web rivals such as Amazon. Walmart's e-commerce managers in the United States, Japan, the United Kingdom, and Canada will now report to executives in charge of the bricks-and-mortar stores in each country rather than being managed and coordinated by the global e-commerce team. E-commerce in emerging markets is still handled separately because the brand is less well-established in those countries. Walmart executives say the primary reason for the restructuring is that "our customer [in developed markets] is demanding continuity between both channels—a seamless experience as she shops in her store and online."[72]

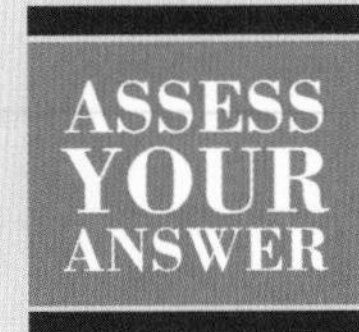

3 The best way for a large company to set up an Internet division is to create a separate, free-standing unit because the unit will have the autonomy and flexibility to operate at Internet speed rather than being hampered by the larger organization's rules and procedures.

ASSESS YOUR ANSWER

ANSWER: *Disagree.* Each approach to creating an e-business operation has advantages and disadvantages. Creating a free-standing business can give the new unit greater autonomy and flexibility, but it can also reduce efficiency and require higher start-up costs. Managers carefully consider whether to use an in-house division, a separate business, or an integrated design, any of which may work out best depending on the organization's circumstances.

IT Impact on Organization Design

Managers and organization theorists have been studying the relationship between technology and organization design and functioning for more than half a century. In recent years, the advances in information technology have had the greatest impact in most organizations.[73] Some specific implications of these advances for organization design are smaller organizations, decentralized structures, improved internal and external coordination, and new network organization structures.

1. *Smaller organizations.* Some Internet-based businesses exist almost entirely in cyberspace; there is no formal organization in terms of a building with offices, desks, and so forth. One or a few people may maintain the site from their homes or a rented work space. Even for traditional businesses, new IT enables the organization to do more work with fewer people. Customers can buy insurance, clothing, tools and equipment, and practically anything else over the Internet without ever speaking to an agent or salesperson. In addition, ERP and other IT systems automatically handle many administrative duties within organizations, reducing the need for clerical staff. The Michigan Department of Transportation (MDOT) used to need an army of workers to verify contractors' work. Large projects often required as many as 20 inspectors on-site every day to keep track of thousands of work items. Today, MDOT rarely sends more than one field technician to a site. The employee enters data into a laptop computer using road construction management software tied to computers at headquarters. The system can automatically generate payment estimates and handle other administrative processes that used to take hours of labor.[74] Thanks to IT, today's companies can also outsource many functions and thus use fewer in-house resources.
2. *Decentralized organization structures.* Although management philosophy and corporate culture have a substantial impact on whether IT is used to decentralize information and authority or to reinforce a centralized authority structure,[75] most organizations today use technology to further decentralization. With IT, information that may have previously been available only to top managers at headquarters can be quickly and easily shared throughout the organization, even across great geographical distances. Managers in varied business divisions or offices have the information they need to make important decisions quickly rather than waiting for decisions from headquarters. Technologies that enable people to meet, coordinate, and collaborate online facilitate communication and decision making among

BRIEFCASE

As an organization manager, keep this guideline in mind:

With greater use of IT, consider smaller organizational units, decentralized structures, improved internal coordination, and greater interorganizational collaboration, including the possibility of outsourcing or a network structure.

distributed, autonomous groups of workers, such as in virtual teams. In addition, technology allows for telecommuting, whereby individual workers can perform work that was once done in the office from their computers at home or other remote locations. Margaret Hooshmand moved to Texas, but she still works as an executive assistant to Cisco Senior Vice President Marthin De Beer in California. Hooshmand reports to work virtually, appearing each morning on a 65-inch high-definition plasma screen that faces De Beer's office. She fields his calls, arranges meetings, and can see and hear what's going on in the Silicon Valley hallways.[76]

3. *Improved horizontal coordination.* Perhaps one of the greatest outcomes of IT is its potential to improve coordination and communication within the firm. IT applications can connect people even when their offices, factories, or stores are scattered around the world. IBM, for example, makes extensive use of virtual teams, whose members use a wide variety of IT tools to easily communicate and collaborate. One team made up of members in the United States, Germany, and the United Kingdom used collaboration software as a virtual meeting room to solve a client's technical problem resulting from Hurricane Katrina within the space of just a few days.[77] Siemens uses a global intranet that connects 450,000 employees around the world to share knowledge and collaborate on projects.[78] MITRE Corporation, an organization that provides consulting and research and development services, primarily to U.S. government clients such as the Department of Defense and the Federal Aviation Administration, uses social networking to overcome traditional barriers such as tenure, location, and functional affiliation that had previously limited information sharing and collaboration at the firm.[79]
4. *Improved interorganizational relationships.* IT can also improve horizontal coordination and collaboration with external parties such as suppliers, customers, and partners. Exhibit 11.13 shows differences between traditional interorganizational relationship characteristics and emerging relationship characteristics. Traditionally, organizations had an arm's-length relationship with suppliers. However, as we discussed in Chapter 4, suppliers are

EXHIBIT 11.13
Key Characteristics of Traditional versus Emerging Interorganizational Relationships

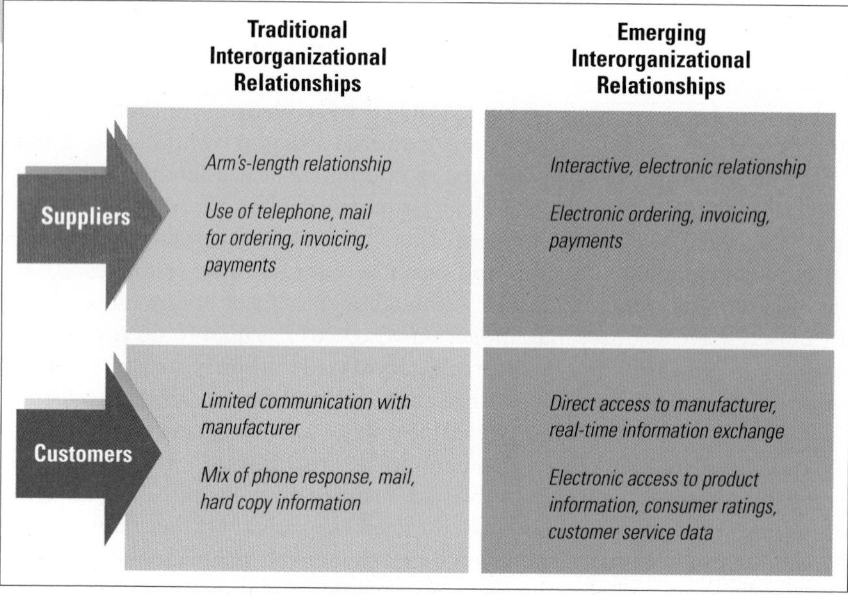

Source: Based on Charles V. Callahan and Bruce A. Pasternack, "Corporate Strategy in the Digital Age," *Strategy + Business*, Issue 15 (Second Quarter 1999), 10–14.

becoming closer partners, tied electronically to the organization for orders, invoices, and payments.

Studies have shown that interorganizational information networks tend to heighten integration, blur organizational boundaries, and create shared strategic contingencies among firms.[80] One good example of interorganizational collaboration is the PulseNet alliance, sponsored by the Centers for Disease Control and Prevention (CDC). The PulseNet information network uses collaborative technology to help U.S. state and federal agencies anticipate, identify, and prevent food-borne disease outbreaks. Through more frequent communication and real-time information sharing, rich relationships among the various agencies have evolved. State health labs and the CDC once had infrequent contact but are now involved in joint strategic planning regarding the PulseNet project.[81]

5. *Enhanced network structures*. The high level of interorganizational collaboration needed in a network organization structure, described in Chapter 2, would not be possible without the use of advanced IT. In the business world, these are also sometimes called *modular structures* or *virtual organizations*. Outsourcing has become a major trend, thanks to computer technology that can tie companies together into a seamless information flow. For example, Hong Kong's Li & Fung is one of the biggest providers of clothing for retailers such as Abercrombie & Fitch, Guess, Ann Taylor, the Limited, and Disney, but the company doesn't own any factories, machines, or fabrics. Li & Fung specializes in managing information, relying on an electronically connected web of 7,500 partners in 37 countries to provide raw materials and assemble the clothes. Using an extranet allows Li & Fung to stay in touch with worldwide partners and move items quickly from factories to retailers. It also lets retailers track orders as they move through production and make last-minute changes and additions.[82] With a network structure, most activities are outsourced so that different companies perform the various functions needed by the organization. The speed and ease of electronic communication makes the network structure a viable option for companies that want to keep costs low but expand activities or market presence.

Design Essentials

- Today's most successful organizations are generally those that most effectively apply information technology. IT systems have evolved to a variety of applications to meet organizations' information needs. Operations applications are applied to well-defined tasks at lower organization levels and help improve efficiency. These include transaction processing systems, data warehousing, and data mining.

- Advanced computer-based systems are also used for better decision making, coordination, and control of the organization. Decision-making systems include management information systems, reporting systems, decision support systems, and executive information systems, which are typically used at middle and upper levels of the organization. Management control systems include budgets and financial reports, periodic nonfinancial statistical reports, reward systems, and quality control systems.

- At the organization level of control, an innovation called the *balanced scorecard* provides managers with a balanced view of the organization by integrating traditional financial measurements and statistical reports with a concern for markets, customers, and employees. Managers also use strategy maps to see the cause-effect relationships among these critical success factors. At the department level, managers use behavior control or outcome control. Behavior control involves close monitoring of employee activities, whereas outcome control measures and rewards results. Most managers use a combination of behavior and outcome control, with a greater emphasis on outcome control because it leads to better performance and higher motivation.
- Today, all the various computer-based systems have begun to merge into an overall IT system that adds strategic value by enabling close coordination internally and with outside parties. Intranets, knowledge management systems, social media, and ERP are used primarily to support greater internal coordination and flexibility. Systems that support and strengthen external relationships include extranets and supply chain management systems, customer relationship systems, and e-business. The integrated enterprise uses advanced IT to enable close coordination among a company and its suppliers, partners, and customers. To establish an e-business, companies can choose to set up a separate business, use an in-house division, or blend the two sides of the business into an integrated whole.
- Advanced IT is having a significant impact on organization design, and some experts suggest that it will eventually replace traditional hierarchy as a primary means of coordination and control. Technology has enabled creation of the network organization structure, in which a company subcontracts most of its major functions to separate companies. In addition, most other organizations are also rapidly evolving toward greater interorganizational collaboration. Other specific implications of advanced IT for organization design include smaller organizations, decentralized organization structures, and improved internal and external coordination.

Key Concepts

balanced scorecard
behavior control
benchmarking
blog
business intelligence
codified knowledge
data warehousing
decision support system
e-business
enterprise resource planning
executive dashboard
executive information system
extranet
feedback control model
information reporting system
integrated enterprise
intellectual capital
intranet
knowledge management
management control systems
management information system
networking
outcome control
Six Sigma
social networking
strategy map
tacit knowledge
transaction processing systems
wiki

Discussion Questions

1. Do you think technology will eventually enable top managers to do their jobs with little face-to-face communication? Discuss.
2. What types of information technology do you as a student use on a regular basis? How might your life be different if this technology were not available to you?
3. How might an enterprise resource planning system be used to improve the management of a manufacturing organization?
4. Discuss some ways a large insurance company such as Allstate, Progressive, or State Farm might use social media tools such as blogs, wikis, or social networking. Do you think these tools are more applicable to a service company than to a manufacturing organization? Discuss.
5. Describe how the four balanced scorecard components discussed in the chapter might be used for feedback control within organizations. Which of these components is more similar to outcome control? Behavior control?
6. Describe your use of codified knowledge when you research and write a term paper. Do you also use tacit knowledge regarding this activity? Discuss.
7. Why is knowledge management particularly important to a company that wants to learn and change continuously rather than operate at a stable state?
8. What is meant by the *integrated enterprise*? Describe how organizations can use extranets to extend and enhance horizontal relationships required for enterprise integration.
9. What are some competitive issues that might lead a company to fully integrate e-business operations with its traditional business? What issues might lead it to keep its e-business as a separate unit or division? Discuss some advantages and disadvantages of each approach.
10. Why does the application of advanced IT typically lead to greater decentralization? Could it also be used for greater centralization in some organizations? Explain.

Chapter 11 Workbook Balanced Scorecard Exercise

Read the measures and objectives listed below for a business firm and a healthcare organization. Make a check for each objective/measure in the correct balanced scorecard column. If you think an objective/measure fits into two balanced scorecard categories, write the numbers 1 and 2 for your first versus second preference.

	Financial	Customers	Business Processes	Learning & Growth
Business Firm				
Return on capital employed (ROCE)	______	______	______	______
Build employee recreation venue by December 2014	______	______	______	______
Develop new products within a time period of eight months	______	______	______	______
Provide team leader training program by July 2012	______	______	______	______
Achieve 98 percent customer satisfaction by December 2014	______	______	______	______
Number of monthly customer complaints	______	______	______	______
Reduce cost per unit sold by 10 percent	______	______	______	______
Increase customer retention by 15 percent	______	______	______	______
Improve employee satisfaction scores by 20 percent	______	______	______	______
Lead market in speed of delivery by 2013	______	______	______	______
Lowest industry cost by 2014	______	______	______	______
Improve profits by 12 percent over the next year	______	______	______	______
Budget forecast accuracy	______	______	______	______
Introduce three new products by December 2013	______	______	______	______
Percent training completed	______	______	______	______
Number of leaders ready for promotion	______	______	______	______
Completed succession plan	______	______	______	______

(continued)

	Financial	Customers	Business Processes	Learning & Growth
Percentage of employees part-time	______	______	______	______
Sales growth to increase 1 percent monthly	______	______	______	______
Number of employee grievances	______	______	______	______
Employee engagement scores	______	______	______	______
Number of employee terminations	______	______	______	______
Policy implementation time lag	______	______	______	______
Vendor on-time delivery rate	______	______	______	______
Total annual revenues	______	______	______	______
Utility consumption costs	______	______	______	______
Workers compensation claims	______	______	______	______
EBITDA	______	______	______	______
Healthcare Organization				
Fundraising targets	______	______	______	______
Patient satisfaction	______	______	______	______
Appointments accommodated on time	______	______	______	______
Percentage of patients restored to full functioning	______	______	______	______
Number of patients wanting service	______	______	______	______
Percentage clinical support staff	______	______	______	______
Nurse satisfaction	______	______	______	______
Length of physician employment	______	______	______	______
Patient satisfaction with scheduling	______	______	______	______
Wait time satisfaction	______	______	______	______
Patient perception of quality	______	______	______	______
Cost of patient care	______	______	______	______
Profitability	______	______	______	______
Staff compliance with privacy regulations	______	______	______	______
Bed utilization rate	______	______	______	______
Falls per 100 patients	______	______	______	______
Percentage of nurse master's degrees	______	______	______	______
Speed of patient admissions & discharge	______	______	______	______
Education for family member care giving	______	______	______	______
Quality of pain control	______	______	______	______
Percentage of medicines filled accurately	______	______	______	______
Nurse turnover rate	______	______	______	______
Nurse shortage rate	______	______	______	______
Completion rate of prescribed services	______	______	______	______
Total labor costs	______	______	______	______
Operating margins	______	______	______	______
Amount of charity care	______	______	______	______
Unpaid cost of public programs	______	______	______	______
Smoking cessation program effectiveness	______	______	______	______
Medicare reimbursement audit results	______	______	______	______
Education completion rate	______	______	______	______

CASE FOR ANALYSIS Century Medical[83]

Sam Nolan clicked the mouse for one more round of solitaire on the computer in his den. He'd been at it for more than an hour, and his wife had long ago given up trying to persuade him to join her for a movie or a rare Saturday night on the town. The mind-numbing game seemed to be all that calmed Sam enough to stop thinking about work and how his job seemed to get worse every day.

Nolan was chief information officer at Century Medical, a large medical products company based in Connecticut. He had joined the company four years ago, and since that time Century had made great progress integrating technology into its systems and processes. Nolan had already led projects to design and build two highly successful systems for Century. One was a benefits-administration system for the company's HR department. The other was a complex web-based purchasing system that streamlined the process of purchasing supplies and capital goods. Although the system had been up and running for only a few months, modest projections were that it would save Century nearly $2 million annually.

Previously, Century's purchasing managers were bogged down with shuffling paper. The purchasing process would begin when an employee filled out a materials request form. Then the form would travel through various offices for approval and signatures before eventually being converted into a purchase order. The new web-based system allowed employees to fill out electronic request forms that were automatically e-mailed to everyone whose approval was needed. The time for processing request forms was cut from weeks to days or even hours. When authorization was complete, the system would automatically launch a purchase order to the appropriate supplier. In addition, because the new system had dramatically cut the time purchasing managers spent shuffling paper, they now had more time to work collaboratively with key stakeholders to identify and select the best suppliers and negotiate better deals.

Nolan thought wearily of all the hours he had put in developing trust with people throughout the company and showing them how technology could not only save time and money but also support team-based work and give people more control over their own jobs. He smiled briefly as he recalled one long-term HR employee, 61-year-old Ethel Moore. She had been terrified when Nolan first began showing her the company's intranet, but she was now one of his biggest supporters. In fact, it had been Ethel who had first approached him with an idea about a web-based job posting system. The two had pulled together a team and developed an idea for linking Century managers, internal recruiters, and job applicants using artificial intelligence software on top of an integrated web-based system. When Nolan had presented the idea to his boss, Executive Vice President Sandra Ivey, she had enthusiastically endorsed it, and within a few weeks the team had authorization to proceed with the project.

But everything began to change when Ivey resigned her position six months later to take a plum job in New York. Ivey's successor, Tom Carr, seemed to have little interest in the project. During their first meeting, Carr had openly referred to the project as a waste of time and money. He immediately disapproved several new features suggested by the company's internal recruiters, even though the project team argued that the features could double internal hiring and save millions in training costs. "Just stick to the original plan and get it done. All this stuff needs to be handled on a personal basis anyway," Carr countered. "You can't learn more from a computer than you can talking to real people—and as for internal recruiting, it shouldn't be so hard to talk to people if they're already working right here in the company." Carr seemed to have no understanding of how and why technology was being used. He became irritated when Ethel Moore referred to the system as "web-based." He boasted that he had never visited Century's intranet site and suggested that "this Internet fad" would eventually blow over anyway. Even Ethel's enthusiasm couldn't get through to him. She tried to show him some of the HR resources available on the intranet and explain how it had benefited the department and the company, but he waved her away. "Technology is for those people in the IT department. My job is people, and yours should be too." Ethel was crushed, and Nolan realized it would be like beating his head against a brick wall to try to persuade Carr to the team's point of view. Near the end of the meeting, Carr even jokingly suggested that the project team should just buy a couple of filing cabinets and save everyone some time and money.

Just when the team thought things couldn't get any worse, Carr dropped the other bomb. They would no longer be allowed to gather input from users of the new system. Nolan feared that without the input of potential users, the system wouldn't meet their needs, or even that users would boycott the system because they hadn't been allowed to participate. No doubt that would put a great big "I told you so" smile right on Carr's face.

Nolan sighed and leaned back in his chair. The project had begun to feel like a joke. The vibrant and innovative HR department his team had imagined now seemed like nothing more than a pipe dream. But despite his frustration, a new thought entered Nolan's mind: "Is Carr just stubborn and narrow-minded or does he have a point that HR is a people business that doesn't need a high-tech job-posting system?"

CASE FOR ANALYSIS **Is Anybody Listening?**

Bart Gaines glanced at the caller ID panel and reluctantly answered the phone.

"Bart, you and Craig and I need to discuss what we plan to do about T-latch."

Again? Bart thought, but he answered back, "Sure, LeRon. You set up something. I'm in."

T-latch was an innovative specialty rear-seat door latch and a highly touted safety feature for a major auto maker's new line of family vehicles. For an industry plagued by several years of mechanical recalls, disastrous investigative media reports, and high-profile lawsuits, top management and marketing enthusiastically embraced the emphasis on family safety. In a tough economy, a new mid-priced, high-mileage family vehicle appealed to consumers, and a series of touching ads reassured potential buyers of the auto company's renewed focus on "safety for those you love."

However, amid the advertising media blitz, the first nervous rumblings about T-latch safety began, strangely from three of the auto makers' plant managers: Bart Gaines, LeRon Cathy, and Craig Langley. The problem they uncovered, almost simultaneously, was that extreme temperatures could cause cracks resulting in product failure during even minor mishaps, putting rear-seat passengers (particularly children) at a small risk of injury or death. In these initial stages of their concern, the three agreed that any discussion of the issue would take place via phone rather than through e-mails until they knew the extent of the problem.

"As more of these vehicles hit the highway, it is a matter of time until the press and public will be screaming for investigations and filing lawsuits," LeRon mentioned during one conference call. "A huge chunk of responsibility falls into our laps, guys."

"But we need to look at several issues here," Craig pointed out. "We can't just hand top management a bombshell like this when sales are skyrocketing and when our own evidence is minimal. This will not be well-received and we can't just give them a '*what if*' scenario. I mean, our guys are saying this can happen, but do we need more tests or what?"

"Let's do this," Bart suggested. "Let's take some time and carefully word a memo to some of the guys in middle management saying that we've detected a potential problem that shows up in extreme conditions and suggesting they determine the next step before contacting top management."

"That sounds good," Craig said. "But let's limit the chatter about this in the memo and not sound like we're panicking over this. We just want them to see what should be done here and we will do what they suggest."

The trio carefully crafted a memo voicing their concerns and sent it up the chain of command to middle managers at corporate headquarters. Within a short time, they received a curt, "We'll check it out." A subsequent report that the team saw no problems with T-latch surprised the plant managers. "Did you check it in extreme temperatures?" the trio countered.

"Everything is fine," was the reply. "Listen, this is the best family vehicle produced in years. Top management is thrilled with sales, the public loves it, and we've seen no evidence of a major safety problem."

When the plant managers teleconferenced days later, Bart told his friends that he felt like the NASA engineers who repeatedly complained about the O-rings before the tragic *Challenger* explosion in 1986. "That was also a problem with temperature and remember, no one listened to them either," he warned. Then Bart added, "Why don't the people above us know about this problem from their own information systems? Are they distracted by big sales or are their information systems not providing detailed data on this kind of problem?"

Of the three, Craig was least convinced of the danger or the need to keep pursuing the issue. "You know, maybe we are over-reacting. Sure, there's some danger that has shown up, but is it any more than the danger that's present any time you get behind the wheel of a vehicle?"

"Tell me, Craig," LeRon said. "Knowing what we know, would you put your kids in the back seat of this vehicle?"

"That's not fair, LeRon. I believe in our company and all I'm saying is that we sent them our concerns and that managers higher up the chain have looked into this and they are satisfied. Let's just give this some time."

"Maybe he's right," Bart said. "It may work itself out or middle management may send something to design. They'll certainly issue a recall for buyers to take the vehicle into the dealership for adjustments if there is a major problem."

The fact that *someone* at corporate knew of their concerns, and that top management would probably be unresponsive to bad news about the vehicle with sales running high, convinced the trio to back off and let middle managers handle the issue.

Over the winter months two tragic accidents (one in Minnesota and the other in Colorado) resulted in the deaths of three children, and while investigations by the National Highway Traffic Safety Administration were still underway, no mention had been made connecting the tragedies to problems with T-latch. Nevertheless, Bart placed a call to LeRon.

"What do you think, LeRon?"

"I'm one step ahead, Bart. I've already placed a call to mid-management, the same guys we spoke to before, and they said it's too early to jump the gun on this thing. But they are willing to release a few summarized versions of memos to the top brass. They will be the kind of bullet-point summaries that management likes. This will make them aware of potential problems without going too negative on their major new line."

"That will mean more delays."

"Production is running high and the company is grabbing every possible award. The guys believe we don't have sufficient evidence of a major problem and that it is still too early to force the company to make announcements or changes in the vehicle. Listen, they're not trying to put anyone at risk. The main focus here is on family safety. But there's no definitive information on this even from NHTSA. The information will be issued as needed. I'm thinking that maybe I agree on this and I'm sure Craig would agree also."

"Ok." Bart hung up the phone, picked up a T-latch sample from his desk and examined it. *Well, we'll just wait and see what happens*, he thought and placed in a desk drawer.

Notes

1. Leigh Buchanan, "Working Wonders on the Web," *Inc. Magazine*, November 2003, 76–84, 104.
2. James Cox, "Changes at Olive Garden Have Chain Living 'La Dolce Vita,'" *USA Today*, December 18, 2000, B1; and Bernard Wysocki Jr., "Hospitals Cut ER Waits," *The Wall Street Journal*, July 3, 2002, D1, D3.
3. Raymond F. Zammuto, Terri L. Griffith, Ann Majchrzak, Deborah J. Dougherty, and Samer Faraj, "Information Technology and the Changing Fabric of Organization," *Organization Science* 18, no. 5 (September–October 2007), 749–762.
4. Erik Berkman, "How to Stay Ahead of the Curve," *CIO*, February 1, 2002, 72–80; and Heather Harreld, "Pick-Up Artists," *CIO* (November 1, 2000), 148–154.
5. Laura Landro, "An Affordable Fix for Modernizing Medical Records," *The Wall Street Journal*, April 30, 2009, A11.
6. "Business Intelligence," special advertising section, *Business 2.0*, February 2003, S1–S4; Alice Dragoon, "Business Intelligence Gets Smart," *CIO*, September 15, 2003, 84–91; and Steve Lohr, "A Data Explosion Remakes Retailing," *The New York Times*, January 3, 2010, BU3.
7. Lohr, "A Data Explosion Remakes Retailing."
8. Ibid.
9. Gary Loveman, "Diamonds in the Data Mine," *Harvard Business Review* (May 2003), 109–113; Joe Ashbrook Nickell, "Welcome to Harrah's," *Business 2.0*, April 2002, 48–54; and Meridith Levinson, "Harrah's Knows What You Did Last Night," *Darwin Magazine*, May 2001, 61–68.
10. Megan Santosus, "Motorola's Semiconductor Products Sector's EIS," Working Smart column, *CIO*, Section 1, November 15, 1998, 84.
11. Daniel Michaels, "Airline Industry Gets Smarter with Bags—Carriers, Airports Use Scanners, Radio Tags, and Software to Improve Tracking of Luggage," *The Wall Street Journal*, September 30, 2009, B5.
12. Cynthia Karen Swank, 'The Lean Service Machine," *Harvard Business Review* (October 2003), 123–129.
13. Shayndi Raice, "Sprint Tackles Subscriber Losses; Carrier Stems Defections as Customer-Service Gains Take Root," *The Wall Street Journal Online* (December 17, 2010), http://online.wsj.com/article/SB10001424052748704073804576023572789952028.html (accessed December 17, 2010).
14. Peter Valdes-Dapena, "Tiny Smart Car Gets Crash Test Kudos," *Fortune* (May 14, 2008), http://money.cnn.com/2008/05/14/autos/smart_fortwo_iihs_crash_test/index.htm (accessed May 14, 2008).
15. Robert Simons, "Strategic Organizations and Top Management Attention to Control Systems," *Strategic Management Journal* 12 (1991), 49–62.
16. Richard L. Daft and Norman B. Macintosh, "The Nature and Use of Formal Control Systems for Management Control and Strategy Implementation," *Journal of Management* 10 (1984), 43–66.
17. Susannah Patton, "Web Metrics That Matter," *CIO*, November 14, 2002, 84–88; and Ramin Jaleshgari, "The End of the Hit Parade," *CIO*, May 14, 2000, 183–190.
18. Spencer E. Ante, "Giving the Boss the Big Picture," *BusinessWeek* (February 13, 2006), 48–51; Doug Bartholomew, "Gauging Success," *CFO-IT* (Summer 2005), 17–19; and Russ Banham, "Seeing the Big Picture: New Data Tools Are Enabling CEOs to Get a Better Handle on Performance Across Their Organizations," *Chief Executive* (November 2003), 46.
19. Bartholomew, "Gauging Success."
20. Kevin Ferguson, "Mission Control," *Inc. Magazine*, November 2003, 27–28; and Banham, "Seeing the Big Picture."
21. Carol Hymowitz, "Dashboard Technology: Is It a Helping Hand or a New Big Brother?" *The Wall Street Journal*, September 26, 2005, B1; and Christopher Koch, "How Verizon Flies by Wire," *CIO*, November 1, 2004, 94–96.
22. Howard Rothman, "You Need Not Be Big to Benchmark," *Nation's Business* (December 1992), 64–65.
23. Tom Rancour and Mike McCracken, "Applying 6 Sigma Methods for Breakthrough Safety Performance," *Professional Safety* 45, no. 10 (October 2000), 29–32; and Lee Clifford, "Why You Can Safely Ignore Six Sigma," *Fortune*, January 22, 2001, 140.
24. Michael Hammer and Jeff Goding, "Putting Six Sigma in Perspective," *Quality* (October 2001), 58–62; and Michael Hammer, "Process Management and the Future of Six Sigma," *Sloan Management Review* (Winter 2002), 26–32.
25. Michael Arndt, "Quality Isn't Just for Widgets," *BusinessWeek*, July 22, 2002, 72–73.
26. Daft and Macintosh, "The Nature and Use of Formal Control Systems for Management Control and Strategy Implementation;" and Scott S. Cowen and J. Kendall Middaugh II,

"Matching an Organization's Planning and Control System to Its Environment," *Journal of General Management* 16 (1990), 69–84.

27. Robert Kaplan and David Norton, "The Balanced Scorecard: Measures That Drive Performance," *Harvard Business Review* (January–February 1992), 71–79; "On Balance," a CFO Interview with Robert Kaplan and David Norton, *CFO* (February 2001), 73–78; Chee W. Chow, Kamal M. Haddad, and James E. Williamson, "Applying the Balanced Scorecard to Small Companies," *Management Accounting* 79, no. 2 (August 1997), 21–27; and Meena Chavan, "The Balanced Scorecard: A New Challenge," *Journal of Management Development* 28, no. 5 (2009), 393–406.
28. Based on Kaplan and Norton, "The Balanced Scorecard;" Chow, Haddad, and Williamson, "Applying the Balanced Scorecard;" and C. A. Latshaw and Y. Choi, "The Balanced Scorecard and the Accountant as a Valued Strategic Partner," *Review of Business* 23, no, 1 (2002), 27–29.
29. Nils–Göran Olve, Carl-Johan Petri, Jan Roy, and Sofie Roy, "Twelve Years Later: Understanding and Realizing the Value of Balanced Scorecards," *Ivey Business Journal* (May–June 2004), 1–7.
30. Geary A. Rummler and Kimberly Morrill, "The Results Chain," *TD* (February 2005), 27–35; Chavan, "The Balanced Scorecard: A New Challenge;" and John C. Crotts, Duncan R. Dickson, and Robert C. Ford, "Aligning Organizational Processes with Mission: The Case of Service Excellence," *Academy of Management Executive* 19, no. 3 (August 2005), 54–68.
31. This discussion is based on Robert S. Kaplan and David P. Norton, "Mastering the Management System," *Harvard Business Review* (January 2008), 63–77; and Robert S. Kaplan and David P. Norton, "Having Trouble with Your Strategy? Then Map It," *Harvard Business Review* (September–October 2000), 167–176.
32. This discussion of behavior versus outcome control is based on Erin Anderson and Vincent Onyemah, "How Right Should the Customer Be?" *Harvard Business Review* (July–August 2006), 59–67.
33. Frank Eltman, "Tracking Systems Help Cities Monitor Employees, Save," *The Tennessean*, November 16, 2007.
34. Pui-Wing Tam, Erin White, Nick Wingfield, and Kris Maher, "Snooping E-Mail by Software Is Now a Workplace Norm," *The Wall Street Journal*, March 9, 2005, B1; and Jennifer S. Lee, "Tracking Sales and the Cashiers," *The New York Times*, July 11, 2001, C1, C6.
35. Bill Ward, "Power to the People: Thanks to a Revolutionary Program Called ROWE, Best Buy Employees Can Lead Lives—Professional and Personal—On Their Own Terms," *Star Tribune*, June 1, 2008, E1; Michelle Conlin, "Smashing the Clock," *BusinessWeek*, December 11, 2006, 60ff; and Jyoti Thottam, "Reworking Work," *Time*, July 25, 2005, 50–55.
36. Conlin, "Smashing the Clock."
37. Catherine Arnst, "Upsetting the Caste System," *BusinessWeek*, May 4, 2009, 36.
38. Based on Andrew Mayo, "Memory Bankers," *People Management* (January 22, 1998), 34–38; William Miller, "Building the Ultimate Resource," *Management Review* (January 1999), 42–45; and Todd Datz, "How to Speak Geek," *CIO Enterprise*, Section 2 (April 15, 1999), 46–52.
39. The discussion of codified and tacit knowledge is based on Gustavo Guzman and Luiz F. Trivelato, "Transferring Codified Knowledge: Socio-technical Versus Top-Down Approaches," *The Learning Organization* 15, no. 3 (2008), 251–276; Ikujiro Nonaka and Hirotaka Takeuchi, *The Knowledge-Creating Company: How Japanese Companies Create the Dynamics of Innovation* (New York: Oxford University Press, 1995), 8–9; Robert M. Grant, "Toward a Knowledge-Based Theory of the Firm," *Strategic Management Journal* 17 (Winter 1996), 109–122; and Martin Schulz, "The Uncertain Relevance of Newness: Organizational Learning and Knowledge Flows," *Academy of Management Journal* 44, no. 4 (2001), 661–681.
40. C. Jackson Grayson, Jr., and Carla S. O'Dell, "Mining Your Hidden Resources," *Across the Board* (April 1998), 23–28.
41. Dorit Nevo, Izak Benbasat, and Yair Wand, "Knowledge Management; Who Knows What?" *The Wall Street Journal*, October 26, 2009.
42. Based on Morten T. Hansen, Nitin Nohria, and Thomas Tierney, "What's Your Strategy for Managing Knowledge?" *Harvard Business Review* (March–April 1999), 106–116.
43. Mark Easterby-Smith and Irina Mikhailava, "Knowledge Management: In Perspective," *People Management* (June 2011), 34–37.
44. David Gilmore, "How to Fix Knowledge Management," *Harvard Business Review* (October 2003), 16–17.
45. This discussion is based on Verne G. Kopytoff, "Companies Stay in the Loop by Using In-House Social Networks," *The New York Times*, June 27, 2011, B3; Daniel Burrus, "Social Networks in the Workplace: The Risk and Opportunity of Business 2.0," *Strategy & Leadership* 38, no. 4 (2010), 50–53; Evelyn Nussenbaum, "Tech to Boost Teamwork," *Fortune Small Business* (February 2008), 51–54; Nevo et al., "Who Knows What?"; and "Building the Web 2.0 Enterprise: McKinsey Global Survey Results," *The McKinsey Quarterly* (July 2008), http://www.mckinseyquarterly.com/Building_the_Web_20_Enterprise_McKinsey_Global_Survey_2174 (accessed October 18, 2011).
46. Cindy Waxer, "Workers of the World—Collaborate," *Fortune Small Business* (April 2005), 57–58.
47. Nussenbaum, "Tech to Boost Teamwork."
48. Kopytoff, "Companies Stay in the Loop."
49. Nevo et al., "Who Knows What?
50. Bala Iyer, Salvatore Parise, Sukumar Rajagopal, and Thomas H. Davenport, "Putting Social Media to Work at Cognizant," *Ivey Business Journal* (July–August 2011), http://www.iveybusinessjournal.com/topics/strategy/putting-social-media-to-work-at-cognizant (accessed August 15, 2011); and "About Us," Cognizant Website, http://www.cognizant.com/aboutus/about-us (accessed August 25, 2011).
51. Derek Slater, "What Is ERP?" *CIO Enterprise*, Section 2 (May 15, 1999), 86; and Jeffrey Zygmont, "The Ties That Bind," *Inc. Tech* no. 3 (1998), 70–84.
52. Vincent A. Mabert, Ashok Soni, and M. A. Venkataramanan, "Enterprise Resource Planning: Common Myths Versus Evolving Reality," *Business Horizons* (May–June 2001), 69–76.
53. Slater, "What Is ERP?"
54. Zammuto et al., "Information Technology and the Changing Fabric of Organization."

55. Steven A. Melnyk and David R. Denzler, *Operations Management: A Value-Driven Approach* (Burr Ridge, IL: Richard D. Irwin, 1996), 613.
56. Jim Turcotte, Bob Silveri, and Tom Jobson, "Are You Ready for the E-Supply Chain?" *APICS–The Performance Advantage* (August 1998), 56–59.
57. Sandra Swanson, "Get Together," *Information Week* (July 1, 2002), 47–48.
58. Bill Richards, "Superplant," *eCompany* (November 2000), 182–196.
59. Felix Gillette, "Twitter, Twitter, Little Stars," *Bloomberg Businessweek* (July 19–July 25, 2010), 64–67.
60. "Building the Web 2.0 Enterprise: McKinsey Global Survey Results."
61. Geoffrey A. Fowler, "Leadership: Information Technology (A Special Report)—Are You Talking to Me?" *The Wall Street Journal* (April 25, 2011), R5.
62. Andreas M. Kaplan and Michael Haenlein," Users of the World, Unite! The Challenges and Opportunities of Social Media," *Business Horizons* 53 (2010), 59–68; and Hubspot marketing software company data, reported in Andrew Shafer, "*Inc.* Data Bank: Crunching the Numbers," *Inc.* (July–August 2011), 30.
63. Jan M. Rosen, "Be It Twittering or Blogging, It's All About Marketing," *The New York Times* (March 12, 2009), http://www.nytimes.com/2009/03/12/business/smallbusiness/12social.ready.html (accessed March 12, 2009).
64. Stephanie Marcus, "Top 5 Mobile Commerce Trends for 2010," Mobile Trends Series, Mashable.com (July 22, 2010), http://mashable.com/2010/07/22/2010-mobile-commerce-trends/ (accessed August 25, 2011); and Julie Jargon, "Business Technology: Domino's IT Staff Delivers Slick Site, Ordering System," *The Wall Street Journal*, November 24, 2009, B5.
65. ABI Research study reported in Stephanie Marcus, "Top 5 Mobile Commerce Trends for 2010."
66. Christopher Barnatt, "Embracing E-Business," *Journal of General Management* 30, no. 1 (Autumn 2004), 79–96.
67. This discussion is based in part on Ranjay Gulati and Jason Garino, "Get the Right Mix of Bricks and Clicks," *Harvard Business Review* (May–June 2000), 107–114.
68. George Westerman, F. Warren McFarlan, and Marco Iansiti, "Organization Design and Effectiveness Over the Innovation Life Cycle," *Organization Science* 17, no. 2 (March–April 2006), 230–238; and Miguel Bustillo and Geoffrey Fowler, "Struggling Sears Scrambles Online," *The Wall Street Journal*, January 15, 2010, A1.
69. "Belle, Baidu Launch Online Shoe Market," *China Business News* (July 11, 2011).
70. Merissa Marr, "Updated Disney.com Offers Networking for Kids; Web Site's Strategic Revamp Encourages More Interaction—But Parents Will Be in Charge," *The Wall Street Journal*, January 2, 2007, B1; John Heilemann, "All the News That's Fit for Bits," *Business 2.0* (September 2006), 40–43.
71. Jeremy W. Peters, "Web Focus Helps Revitalize *The Atlantic*," *The New York Times*, December 13, 2010, B1; and "A History of *The Atlantic Monthly*," from a presentation given in 1994 by Cullen Murphy, *The Atlantic Online*, http://www.theatlantic.com/past/docs/about/atlhistf.htm (accessed February 25, 2011).
72. Miguel Bustillo, "Wal-Mart Shakes Up Its Online Business," *The Wall Street Journal*, August 13–14, 2011, B1.
73. Zammuto et al., "Information Technology and the Changing Fabric of Organization."
74. Stephanie Overby, "Paving over Paperwork," *CIO* (February 1, 2002), 82–86.
75. Siobhan O'Mahony and Stephen R. Barley, "Do Digital Telecommunications Affect Work and Organization? The State of Our Knowledge," *Research in Organizational Behavior* 21 (1999), 125–161.
76. Robert D. Hof, "The End of Work As You Know It," (The Future of Work: Technology on the March section), *BusinessWeek* (August 20, 2007), 80–83.
77. "Big and No Longer Blue," *The Economist* (January 21–27, 2006), http://www.economist.com/node/5380442 (accessed October 18, 2011).
78. "Mandate 2003: Be Agile and Efficient," *Microsoft Executive Circle* (Spring 2003), 46–48.
79. Salvatore Parise, Bala Iyer, Donna Cuomo, and Bill Donaldson, "MITRE Corporation: Using Social Technologies to Get Connected," *Ivey Business Journal* (January–February 2011), http://www.iveybusinessjournal.com/topics/strategy/mitre-corporation-using-social-technologies-to-get-connected (accessed August 25, 2011).
80. O'Mahony and Barley, "Do Digital Telecommunications Affect Work and Organization?"
81. Michael A. Fontaine, Salvatore Parise, and David Miller, "Collaborative Environments: An Effective Tool for Transforming Business Processes," *Ivey Business Journal* (May–June 2004), http://wwwold.iveybusinessjournal.com/view_article.asp?intArticle_ID=489 (accessed October 18, 2011).
82. Joanne Lee-Young and Megan Barnett, "Furiously Fast Fashions," *The Industry Standard* (June 11, 2001), 72–79.
83. Based on Carol Hildebrand, "New Boss Blues," *CIO Enterprise,* Section 2 (November 15, 1998), 53–58; and Megan Santosus, "Advanced Micro Devices' Web-Based Purchasing System," *CIO*, Section 1 (May 15, 1998), 84.

Chapter 12

Organization Size and Life Cycle

Learning Objectives

After reading this chapter you should be able to:

1. Explain the advantages and disadvantages of large organization size.
2. Define organizational life cycle and explain the four stages.
3. Define the characteristics of bureaucracy.
4. Explain how bureaucracy is used for control.
5. Discuss approaches to reducing bureaucracy in large organizations.
6. Contrast market and clan control with bureaucratic control.
7. Describe the model of decline stages and methods of downsizing.

Before reading this chapter, please check whether you agree or disagree with each of the following statements.

1 **It is wise for the entrepreneur who starts a new company to maintain hands-on management control as the company grows.**

I AGREE _____ I DISAGREE _____

2 **A manager should emphasize shared values, trust, and commitment to the organization's mission as the primary means of controlling employee behavior.**

I AGREE _____ I DISAGREE _____

3 **After a necessary downsizing, managers should not spend much time helping laid off workers but focus instead on making sure the remaining employees are taken care of to do what is needed to revive the company.**

I AGREE _____ I DISAGREE _____

If you asked someone at the close of the twentieth century "Do you Google?" you would likely have gotten one of two responses: A big smile and an enthusiastic *Isn't it wonderful?!* Or a puzzled look and a frustrated *What are you talking about?* In 1999, Google had eight employees and averaged around 500,000 Internet searches a day. It didn't take too many years, however, for almost everyone to know what Google was—and many considered the innovative search engine the best thing since sliced bread. The company gained an almost cult-like following. By 2011, Google had nearly 27,000 employees worldwide and more than 3.6 billion searches a day. But for founders Larry Page and Sergey Brin, something unnerving happened: Google lost its coolness factor—it became a big corporation rather than a young, hip startup. Page and Brin understand that the shift is part of "growing up" as a company, but they also know that with growth comes problems as well as opportunities. As organizations like Google grow large and complex, they need more complex systems and procedures for guiding and controlling the organization. Moreover, the addition of more complex systems and procedures can cause problems of inefficiency, rigidity, and slow response time, meaning that the company has a hard time innovating or adapting quickly to client or customer needs. Page recently returned as CEO to try to take Google back to its entrepreneurial roots and reignite the culture of zaniness, passion, and creativity that initially made the company a household name.[1]

Every organization—from locally owned restaurants and auto body shops to large international firms, nonprofit organizations, and law-enforcement agencies—wrestles with questions about organizational size, bureaucracy, and control. During the twentieth century, large organizations became widespread, and bureaucracy has become a major topic of study in organization theory.[2] Most large organizations have bureaucratic characteristics, which can be very effective.

These organizations provide us with abundant goods and services and accomplish astonishing feats—explorations of Mars, overnight delivery of packages to any location in the world, the scheduling and coordination of thousands of airline flights a day—that are testimony to their effectiveness. On the other hand, bureaucracy is also accused of many sins, including inefficiency, rigidity, and demeaning routinized work that alienates both employees and the customers an organization tries to serve.

Purpose of This Chapter

In this chapter, we explore the question of large versus small organizations and how size relates to structure and control. Organization size is a major contingency that influences organization design and functioning, just as do the contingencies—technology, environment, goals—discussed in previous chapters. In the first section, we look at the advantages of large versus small size. Then, we explore what is called an organization's life cycle and the structural characteristics at each stage. Next, we examine the historical need for bureaucracy as a means to control large organizations and compare bureaucratic control to various other control strategies. Finally, the chapter looks at the causes of organizational decline and discusses some methods for dealing with downsizing. By the end of this chapter you should be able to recognize when bureaucratic control can make an organization effective and when other types of control are more appropriate.

Organization Size: Is Bigger Better?

The question of big versus small begins with the notion of growth and the reasons so many organizations feel the need to grow large.

Pressures for Growth

Do you ever dream of starting a small company? Many people do, and entrepreneurial start-ups are the lifeblood of the U.S. economy. Yet the hope of practically every entrepreneur is to have his or her company grow fast and grow large, maybe even to eventually make the *Fortune* 500 list.[3] Sometimes this goal is more urgent than to make the best products or show the greatest profits. However, there are some thriving companies where managers have resisted the pressure for endless growth to focus instead on different goals, as discussed in this chapter's Book Mark.

Recent economic woes and layoffs at many large firms have spurred budding entrepreneurs to take a chance on starting their own company or going it alone in a sole proprietorship. Yet despite the proliferation of new, small organizations, giants such as Toyota, General Electric, Samsung, and Walmart have continued to grow. For example, the employee base of Walmart in 2010 was slightly larger than the population of Houston, Texas. Apple, with 50,000 employees and annual revenues approaching $100 billion, continues to grow 60 percent a year. Despite its problems and having just emerged from bankruptcy in November 2010, General Motors' revenues increased nearly 30 percent to place it at number 8 on *Fortune* magazine's 2011 list of the largest U.S. corporations.[4]

BOOKMARK

12.0 HAVE YOU READ THIS BOOK?

Small Giants: Companies that Choose to Be Great Instead of Big

By Bo Burlingham

The conventional business mind-set is to equate growth with success, but Bo Burlingham, an editor-at-large at *Inc.* magazine, reminds us that there is a different class of great companies that focus not on getting bigger, but on getting better. He calls them *Small Giants*. In his book of the same name, Burlingham looks at 14 small companies that are admired in their industries and recognized for their accomplishments—and in which managers have made a conscious decision not to significantly expand, go public, or become part of a larger firm.

WHAT GIVES SMALL GIANTS THEIR *MOJO*?

The companies Burlingham profiles come from a wide range of industries and vary a great deal in terms of number of employees, corporate structure, management approach, and stage of the life cycle. What makes them similar? Burlingham describes seven shared characteristics that give these companies an almost magical quality. Here are three of them:

- *The founders and leaders made a mindful choice to build the kind of business they wanted to "live in" rather than accommodate a business shaped by outside forces.* Danny Meyer, owner of the Union Square Café, says he "earned more money by choosing the right things to say no to than by choosing things to say yes to." Fritz Maytag of Anchor Brewery, content to limit his distribution to northern California, even helped rival brewers develop their skills to accommodate growing demand for his kind of beer.
- *Each of the small giants is intimately connected with the community in which it does business.* CitiStorage, the premier independent records-storage company in the United States, built its warehouse in a depressed inner-city neighborhood to save money. But it quickly bonded with the community by hiring local residents, opening the facility for community events, and making generous donations to the local school.
- *Their leaders have a passion for the business.* Whether it's making music, creating special effects, designing and manufacturing constant torque hinges, brewing beer, or planning commercial construction projects, the leaders of these companies show a true passion for the subject matter as well as a deep emotional commitment to the business and its employees, customers, and suppliers.

DO YOU WANT TO BUILD A SMALL GIANT?

One beneficial outcome of Burlingham's book has been to prove to new or aspiring entrepreneurs that better doesn't have to mean bigger. For some, this strategy eases the urge to seize every opportunity to expand. But Burlingham warns that resisting the pressures for growth takes strength of character. This fun-to-read book provides great insight into some entrepreneurs and managers who summoned the fortitude to make the choices that were right for them.

Small Giants: Companies That Choose to Be Great Instead of Big, by Bo Burlingham, is published by Portfolio, a division of the Penguin Group.

Companies in all industries, from retail, to aerospace, to media, strive for growth to acquire the size and resources needed to compete on a global scale, to invest in new technology, and to control distribution channels and guarantee access to markets.[5] There are a number of other pressures for organizations to grow. Many executives have found that firms must grow to stay economically healthy. To stop growing is to stagnate. To be stable means that customers may not have their demands fully met or that competitors will increase market share at the expense of your company. As Mark Hurd, former CEO of Hewlett-Packard put it, "if you don't have scale and you don't have leverage, you won't be able to give the customer what the customer wants."[6] At Walmart, managers have vowed to continue an emphasis on growth even if it means a decreasing return on investment (ROI). They are ingrained with the idea that to stop growing is to stagnate and die. Walmart's chief financial officer Tom Schoewe said that even if the ROI could "come down a bit and we could grow faster, that would be just fine by me."[7]

Large size enables companies to take risks that could ruin smaller firms, and scale is crucial to economic health in some industries. There is currently a wave of mergers in the U.S. healthcare industry, for example, as hospitals, medical groups, and insurers strive to control healthcare costs and meet challenges brought about by the Federal healthcare reform law.[8] For marketing-intensive companies such as Coca-Cola and Procter & Gamble, greater size provides power in the marketplace and thus increased revenues.[9] Through a series of mergers and acquisitions, the Belgium brewing company Interbrew (now Anheuser-Busch InBev) became the world's largest brewer and distributor of beer, giving the company tremendous power in the industry. In addition, growing organizations are vibrant, exciting places to work, which enables these companies to attract and keep quality employees. When the number of employees is expanding, the company can offer many challenges and opportunities for advancement.

Dilemmas of Large Size

Organizations feel compelled to grow, but how much and how large? What size organization is better poised to compete in a fast-changing global environment? The arguments are summarized in Exhibit 12.1.

EXHIBIT 12.1
Differences between Large and Small Organizations

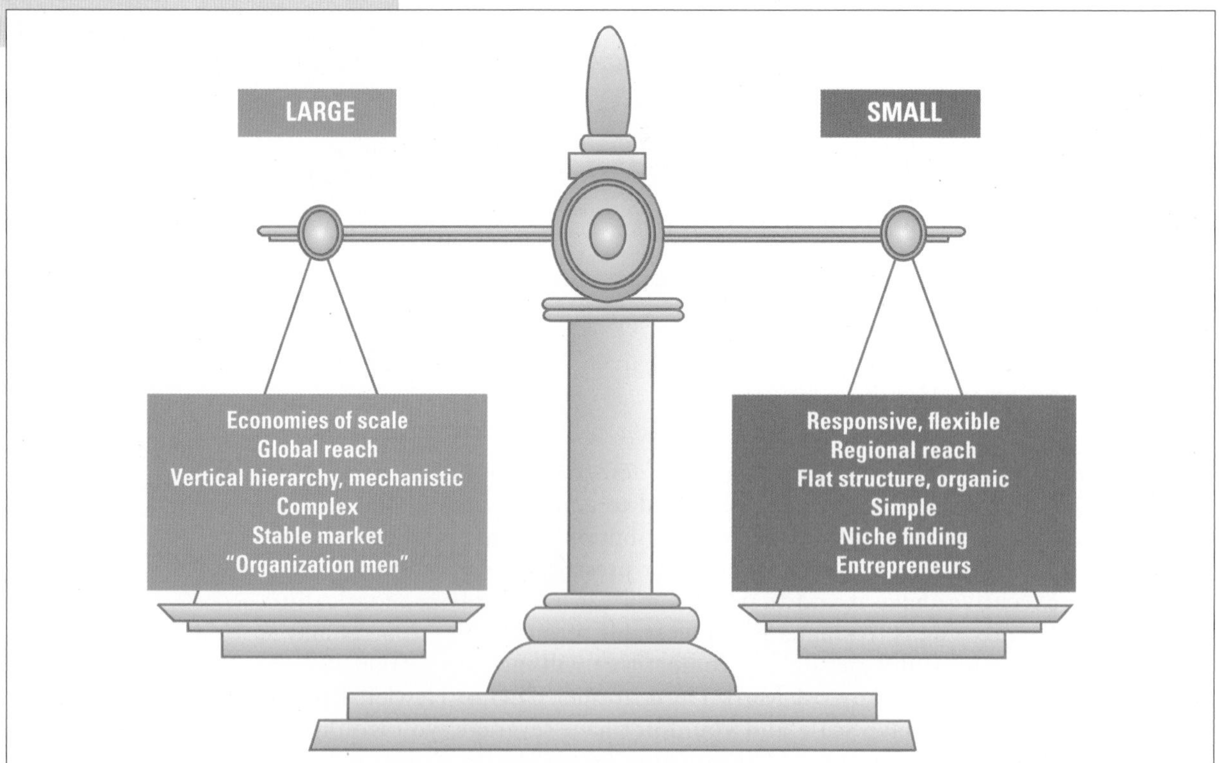

Source: Based on John A. Byrne, "Is your Company Too Big?" *BusinessWeek* (March 27, 1989), 84–94.

Large. Huge resources and economies of scale are needed for many organizations to compete globally. Only large organizations can build a massive pipeline in Alaska. Only a large corporation like General Electric can afford to build ultra-efficient $2 million wind turbines that contain 8,000 different parts.[10] Only a large Johnson & Johnson can invest hundreds of millions of dollars in new products such as bifocal contact lenses and a patch that delivers contraceptives through the skin. In addition, large organizations have the resources to be a supportive economic and social force in difficult times. After the 2011 earthquake, tsunami, and nuclear disaster in Japan, the insurance company Aflac, which derives most of its revenue from that country, gave customers a six-month grace period to pay their insurance premiums. In addition, Aflac donated millions of dollars to relief efforts.[11] Large organizations also are able to get back to business more quickly following a disaster, giving employees and communities a sense of security during an uncertain time. Following Hurricane Irene in the United States, Allstate was able to quickly set up mobile claims centers equipped with generators, satellite technology, and high-speed Internet connections in the hardest-hit areas, enabling people to get their lives back in order more quickly.[12]

Large companies are standardized, often mechanistically run, and complex. The complexity offers hundreds of functional specialties within the organization to perform multifaceted tasks and to produce varied and complicated products. Moreover, large organizations, once established, can be a presence that stabilizes a market for years. Managers can join the company and expect a career reminiscent of the "organization men" of the 1950s and 1960s. The organization can provide longevity, raises, and promotions.

BRIEFCASE

As an organization manager, keep these guidelines in mind:

Decide whether your organization should act like a large or small company. To the extent that economies of scale, global reach, and complexity are important, introduce greater bureaucratization as the organization increases in size. As it becomes necessary, add rules and regulations, written documentation, job specialization, technical competence in hiring and promotion, and decentralization.

Small. The competing argument says small is beautiful because the crucial requirements for success in a global economy are responsiveness and flexibility in fast-changing markets. Small scale can provide significant advantages in terms of quick reaction to changing customer needs or shifting environmental and market conditions.[13] In addition, small organizations often enjoy greater employee commitment because it is easier for people to feel like part of a community. Employees typically work on a variety of tasks rather than narrow, specialized jobs. For many people, working in a small company is more exciting and fulfilling than working in a huge organization. Where would you be happier as a manager? Complete the questionnaire in this chapter's "How Do You Fit the Design?" box on page 542 for some insight.

Many large companies have grown even larger through merger or acquisition in recent years, yet research indicates that few mergers live up to their expected performance levels. Studies by consulting firms such as McKinsey & Company, the Hay Group, and others suggest that performance declines in almost 20 percent of acquired companies after acquisition. By some estimates, 90 percent of mergers and acquisitions never live up to expectations. Consider Pulte Group, the nation's second largest home-builder, which acquired Centex Corporation in 2009. The challenges of integrating the two companies, combined with a weakening housing market, wreaked havoc on Pulte's profitability. Between the time of the acquisition and mid-2011, Pulte had just one profitable quarter and had lost millions of

How Do You Fit the Design?

WHAT SIZE ORGANIZATION FOR YOU?

How do your work preferences fit organization size? Answer the following questions as they reflect your likes and dislikes. Please answer whether each item is Mostly True or Mostly False for you.

	Mostly True	Mostly False
1. I value stability and predictability in the organization I work for.	_____	_____
2. Rules are meant to be broken.	_____	_____
3. Years of service should be an important determinant of pay and promotion.	_____	_____
4. I generally prefer to work on lots of different things rather than specialize in a few things.	_____	_____
5. Before accepting a job, I would want to make sure the company had good benefits.	_____	_____
6. I would rather work on a team where managerial responsibility is shared than work in a department with a single manager.	_____	_____
7. I would like to work for a large, well-known company.	_____	_____
8. I would rather earn $90,000 a year as a VP in a small company than earn $100,000 a year as a middle manager in a big company.	_____	_____

Scoring: Give yourself one point for each odd-numbered item you marked Mostly True and one point for each even-numbered item you marked Mostly False.

Interpretation: Working in a large organization is a very different experience from working in a small organization. The large organization is well-established, provides good benefits, is stable, and has rules, well-defined jobs, and a clear management hierarchy of authority. A small organization may be struggling to survive, but it offers excitement, multitasking, risk, and the sharing of responsibility. If you scored 6 or more, a large organization may be for you. If you scored 3 or less, you may be happier in a smaller, less structured organization.

dollars.[14] Exhibit 12.2 lists some well-known mergers and acquisitions that went wrong. Although there are numerous factors involved in the problems these organizations experienced, many researchers and analysts agree that, frequently, bigness just doesn't add up to better performance.[15]

Despite the increasing size of many companies, the economic vitality of the United States as well as most of the rest of the developed world is tied to small and midsized businesses. According to the Small Business Administration, small businesses represent around 99 percent of all firms in the United States and employ just over half of all private sector employees. In addition, small businesses have generated 64 percent of new jobs annually over the past 15 years.[16] A large percentage of exporters are small businesses. The growth of the Internet and other information

EXHIBIT 12.2
Five Famous Mergers and Acquisitions Gone Wrong

Acquisition	Year of Deal	Results
Bank of America/ Countrywide ($4.1 billion)	2008	In the fourth quarter of 2011, Bank of America reported a nearly $5 billion loss in its mortgage unit, primarily from loans it absorbed from Countrywide
Time Warner/AOL ($111 billion)	2001	Time Warner stock dropped 80 percent, destroying $148 billion of shareholder value. The "marriage" was dissolved in 2009
Yahoo/Broadcast.com ($5.7 billion)	1999	Yahoo's stock price has fallen from above $100 to less than $17
Daimler/Chrysler ($37 billion)	1998	After a decade of heavy losses Daimler sold Chrysler for around $7 billion.
Quaker/Snapple ($1.7 billion)	1994	The Snapple brand couldn't hold its own in large grocery stores. After 27 months, Quaker sold it for a mere $300 million.

Sources: Based on Mary DiMaggio, "The Top 10 Best (and Worst) Corporate Mergers of All Time . . . Or, the Good, the Bad, and the Ugly," Rasmussen.edu (September 15, 2009), http://www.rasmussen.edu/degrees/business/blog/best-and-worst-corporate-mergers/ (accessed August 31, 2011); and Chris Roush, "10 Worst Deals of All Time," LifeGoesStrong.com (January 24, 2011), http://work.lifegoesstrong.com/news-corp-buys-dow-jones-co (accessed August 31, 2011).

technologies has made it easier for small companies to compete with larger firms. The growing service sector also contributes to a decrease in average organization size, as many service companies remain small to better serve customers.

Small organizations have a flat structure and an organic, free-flowing management style that encourages entrepreneurship and innovation. Today's leading biotechnology drugs, for example, were all discovered by small firms such as Gilead Sciences, which developed anti-retroviral drugs to treat HIV, rather than by huge pharmaceutical companies such as Pfizer.[17] Moreover, the personal involvement of employees in small firms encourages motivation and commitment because employees personally identify with the company's mission. Based on studies of primitive societies, religious sects, military organizations, and some businesses, anthropologist Robin Dunbar proposed that 150 is the optimum size for any group trying to achieve a goal. Dunbar says that beyond that size, the group's effectiveness wanes because too many rules, procedures, and red tape slow things down and sap group morale, enthusiasm, and commitment.[18]

BRIEFCASE

As an organization manager, keep these guidelines in mind:

If responsiveness, flexibility, simplicity, and niche finding are important, subdivide the organization into simple, autonomous divisions that have freedom and a small-company approach.

Big-Company/Small-Company Hybrid. The paradox is that the advantages of small companies sometimes enable them to succeed and, hence, grow large. Small companies can become victims of their own success as they grow, shifting to a mechanistic design emphasizing vertical hierarchy and spawning "organization men" rather than entrepreneurs. Giant companies are "built for optimization, not innovation."[19] Big companies become committed to their existing products and technologies and have a hard time supporting innovation for the future.

The solution is what Jack Welch, retired chairman and CEO of General Electric, called the "big-company/small-company hybrid" that combines a large corporation's resources and reach with a small company's simplicity and flexibility. The divisional structure, described in Chapter 2, is one way some large organizations attain a big-company/small-company hybrid. By reorganizing into groups of small companies, huge corporations such as Johnson & Johnson capture the mindset and advantages of smallness. Johnson & Johnson is actually a group of 250 separate companies operating in 60 countries.[20]

The development of new organizational forms, with an emphasis on decentralizing authority and cutting out layers of the hierarchy, combined with the increasing use of information technology described in Chapter 11, is making it easier than ever for companies to be simultaneously large and small, thus capturing the advantages of each. The shift can even be seen in the U.S. military. Unlike World War II, for example, which was fought with large masses of soldiers guided by decisions made at top levels, today's "war on terrorism" depends on decentralized decision making and smaller forces of highly skilled soldiers who have access to up-to-the-minute information.[21] Big companies also find a variety of ways to act both large and small. Consider how W. L. Gore & Associates keeps a small-company mindset.

W. L. Gore & Associates

IN PRACTICE

Bill and Vieve Gore founded W. L. Gore & Associates in the basement of their home in 1958. Today, it is one of the 200 largest privately held companies in the United States. The company, perhaps best known for Gore-Tex fabrics and Elixir guitar strings, has 9,000 employees in 30 countries around the world and $2.5 billion in annual revenues. The company isn't huge, but it's definitely big enough to lose some of the creativity and flexibility that it had in the early years. But Gore's managers, starting with the philosophy of the founder, made sure that didn't happen.

Gore has an extremely loose, flexible, organic design. Overall, the company is divided into four divisions that serve different industries: electronics, fabrics, industrial, and medical. Gore establishes clusters of small manufacturing plants in an area rather than using one large factory so that people can know one another and establish close relationships. Work is done by small teams; some are continuous, but others emerge based on need. Formal authority isn't vested in specific leaders. Instead, leaders emerge because they gain credibility with other associates based on their knowledge, expertise, or special abilities. The loose structure works well when quick response time is needed. A leader with expertise emerges and assembles a knowledge-based team to examine and resolve a problem quickly.

Current CEO Terry Kelly and three other leaders serve on an Enterprise Leadership Team that is responsible for the overall health and growth of the company, but otherwise there are few titles, organization charts, or other structural arrangements that are typically used by big companies. People are expected to interact with everyone else in the work system rather than having to go through a chain of command. Gore has a strong orientation and training program, which emphasizes building relationships. New associates are expected to spend the first three to six months simply building a network of relationships all over the company.[22]

Other companies also find ways to be both big and small. Retail giant Lowe's, for example, uses the advantage of size in areas such as advertising, purchasing, and raising capital, but it also gives each individual store manager the autonomy needed to serve customers as if it were a small, hometown shop. To avoid the problem of isolated top managers, mutual fund manager Vanguard requires everyone—even the CEO—to spend some time each month manning the phones and talking directly to customers.[23] Small companies that are growing can use these ideas to help their organizations retain the flexibility and customer focus that fueled their growth.

Organizational Life Cycle

A useful way to think about organizational growth and change is the concept of an organizational **life cycle**,[24] which suggests that organizations are born, grow older, and eventually die. Organization structure, leadership style, and administrative systems follow a fairly predictable pattern through stages in the life cycle. Stages are sequential and follow a natural progression.

Stages of Life Cycle Development

Research on organizational life cycle suggests that four major stages characterize organizational development.[25] Exhibit 12.3 illustrates these four stages and the problems associated with transition to each stage.

Definitions. Growth is not easy. Each time an organization enters a new stage in the life cycle, it enters a whole new ball game with a new set of rules for how the organization functions internally and how it relates to the external environment.[26]

1. *Entrepreneurial stage.* When an organization is born, the emphasis is on creating a product or service and surviving in the marketplace. The founders are entrepreneurs, and they devote their full energies to the technical activities of production and marketing. The organization is informal and non-bureaucratic. The hours of work are long. Control is based on the owners' personal supervision. Growth is from a creative new product or service. For example, Dennis Crowley and Naveen Selvadurai created the first version of Foursquare—a mobile networking service that lets users share their locations with friends, bookmark information about venues they want to visit, and share tips and experiences—at Crowley's kitchen table in New York City's East Village. They launched the service in 2009 in Austin, Texas, and by April 2011 it had 10 million users worldwide. Crowley acts as CEO and continues to personally provide oversight of the company, which has grown to 75 employees.[27]

   The founding of Foursquare is reminiscent of Apple (originally Apple Computer), which was in the **entrepreneurial stage** when it was created by Steve Jobs and Stephen Wozniak in Wozniak's parents' garage in 1976.

   Crisis: Need for leadership. As the organization starts to grow, the larger number of employees causes problems. The creative and technically oriented owners are confronted with management issues, but they may prefer to focus their energies on making and selling the product or inventing new products and services. At this time of crisis, entrepreneurs must either adjust the structure of the organization to accommodate continued growth or else bring in strong managers who can do so. When Apple began a period of rapid growth, for example, A. C. Markkula was brought in as a leader because neither Jobs nor Wozniak was qualified or cared to manage the expanding company.
2. *Collectivity stage.* If the leadership crisis is resolved, strong leadership is obtained and the organization begins to develop clear goals and direction. Departments are established along with a hierarchy of authority, job assignments, and a beginning division of labor. In the **collectivity stage**, employees identify with the mission of the organization and spend long

BRIEFCASE

As an organization manager, keep these guidelines in mind:

Grow when possible. With growth, you can provide opportunities for employee advancement and greater profitability and effectiveness. Apply new management systems and structural configurations at each stage of an organization's development. Interpret the needs of the growing organization and respond with the management and internal systems that will carry the organization through to the next stage of development.

EXHIBIT 12.3
Organizational Life Cycle

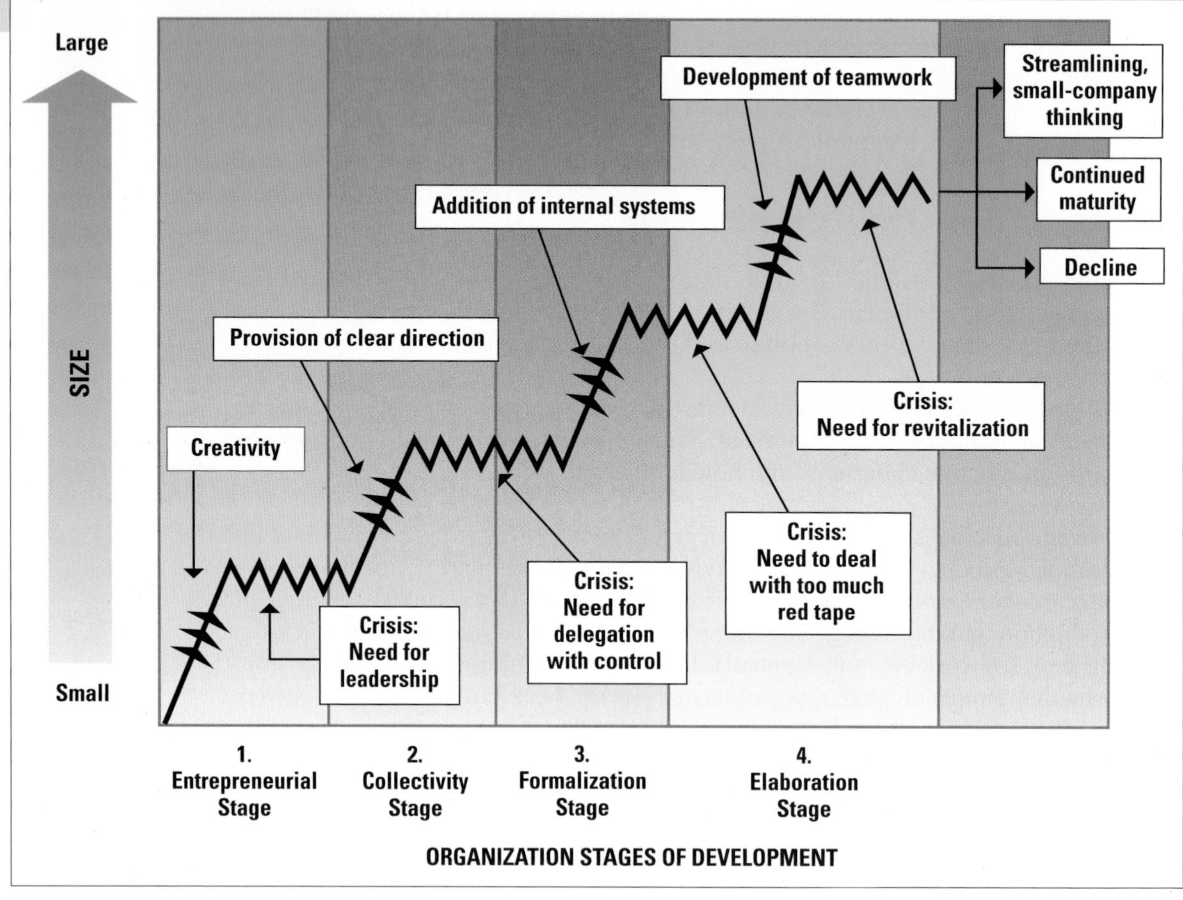

Source: Adapted from Robert E. Quinn and Kim Cameron, "Organizational Life Cycles and Shifting Criteria of Effectiveness: Some Preliminary Evidence," *Management Science* 29 (1983), 33–51; and Larry E. Greiner, "Evolution and Revolution as Organizations Grow," *Harvard Business Review* 50 (July–August 1972), 37–46.

hours helping the organization succeed. Members feel part of a collective. Communication and control are mostly informal, although a few formal systems begin to appear. Apple was in the collectivity stage during its rapid growth years from 1978 to 1981. Jobs remained as CEO and visionary leader, although Markkula and other executives handled most of the management responsibilities. Employees threw themselves into the business as the major product line was established and more than 2,000 dealers signed on.

Crisis: Need for delegation. If the new management has been successful, lower-level employees gradually find themselves restricted by the strong top-down leadership. Lower-level managers begin to acquire confidence in their own functional areas and want more discretion. An autonomy crisis occurs when top managers, who were successful because of their strong leadership and vision, do not want to give up responsibility. Top managers want to make sure that all parts of the organization are coordinated and pulling together. The organization needs to find mechanisms to control and coordinate departments without direct supervision from the top. For example, when Diamond Wipes International reached a point where costly mistakes were being made because of poor communication among departments, Taiwanese entrepreneur Eve Yen hired a general manager and charged him with coordinating the work of all departments.[28]

1 It is wise for the entrepreneur who starts a new company to maintain hands-on management control as the company grows.

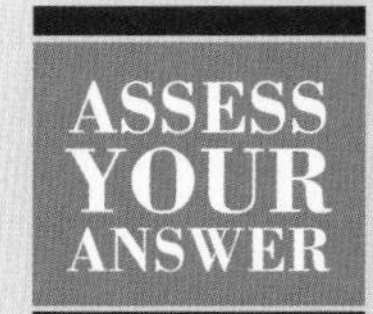

ANSWER: *Disagree.* Entrepreneurs typically enjoy using their creativity to make and sell a new product or service. Many stay hands-on too long because they have a hard time shifting to the role of managing other people and setting up procedures and systems the company needs as it grows. In most cases, successful entrepreneurs bring in skilled managers to run the business and take the organization to the next level.

3. *Formalization stage.* The **formalization stage** involves the installation and use of rules, procedures, and control systems. In the formalization stage, communication is less frequent and more formal, and more likely to follow the hierarchy of authority. Engineers, human resource specialists, and other staff may be added. Top management becomes concerned with issues such as strategy and planning and leaves the operations of the firm to middle management. Product groups or other decentralized units may be formed to improve coordination. Incentive systems based on profits may be implemented to ensure that managers work toward what is best for the overall company. When effective, the new coordination and control systems enable the organization to continue growing by establishing linkage mechanisms between top management and field units. Internet companies such as eBay and Amazon.com are currently in the formalization stage of the life cycle, with managers devising new systems to manage the growing complexity of operations. Apple was in the formalization stage in the 1980s and early 1990s.

   Crisis: Too much red tape. At this point in the organization's development, the proliferation of systems and programs may begin to strangle middle-level executives. The organization seems bureaucratized. Middle management may resent the intrusion of staff. Innovation may be restricted. The organization seems too large and complex to be managed through formal programs. Google, described at the opening of this chapter, is currently at this crisis point, with co-founder Larry Page returning to try to cut the bureaucracy and bring back an entrepreneurial spirit. It was during this crisis stage at Apple that Steve Jobs resigned in 1985 and a new CEO took control to face his own management challenges.
4. *Elaboration stage.* The solution to the red tape crisis is a new sense of collaboration and teamwork. Throughout the organization, managers develop skills for confronting problems and working together. Bureaucracy may have reached its limit. Social control and self-discipline reduce the need for additional

formal controls. Managers learn to work within the bureaucracy without adding to it. Formal systems may be simplified and replaced by manager teams and task forces. To achieve collaboration, teams are often formed across functions or divisions of the company. The organization may also be split into multiple divisions to maintain a small-company philosophy. Apple is currently in the **elaboration stage** of the life cycle, as are such large companies as Toyota, General Electric, and Caterpillar.

Crisis: Need for revitalization. After the organization reaches maturity, it may enter periods of temporary decline.[29] A need for renewal may occur every 10 to 20 years. The organization shifts out of alignment with the environment or perhaps becomes slow moving and over-bureaucratized, so it must go through a stage of streamlining and innovation. Top managers are often replaced during this period. At Apple, the top spot changed hands a number of times as the company struggled to revitalize. CEOs John Sculley, Michael Spindler, and Gilbert Amelio were each ousted by the board as Apple's problems deepened. Steve Jobs returned in mid-1997 to run the company he had founded nearly 25 years earlier. Jobs quickly reorganized the company, weeded out inefficiencies, and refocused Apple on innovative products for the consumer market. Jobs moved the company into a whole new direction with the iPod music system and the iPhone. Sales and profits zoomed and Apple entered a long period of success.[30] In the years since he had left Apple, Jobs had gained management skills and experience, but he was also smart enough to bring in other skilled managers. For instance, Timothy D. Cook, hired by Jobs in 1998, has been referred to as "the story behind the story" and has long handled day-to-day operations while Jobs provided visionary leadership. Cook took over as CEO in mid-2011 following Jobs's resignation and subsequent death.[31] Apple is hot right now, but it will continue to face the problems all mature organizations deal with. All mature organizations must go through periods of revitalization or they will decline, as shown in the last stage of Exhibit 12.3.

Summary. Eighty-four percent of businesses that make it past the first year still fail within five years because they can't make the transition from the entrepreneurial stage.[32] The transitions become even more difficult as organizations progress through future stages of the life cycle. Organizations that do not successfully resolve the problems associated with these transitions are restricted in their growth and may even fail. From within an organization, the life cycle crises are very real. Consider the challenges Facebook managers are confronting as the company grows.

Facebook

IN PRACTICE

For technology companies, life cycles are getting shorter. To stay competitive, companies like Facebook, Netflix, and Google have to successfully progress through stages of the cycle faster. Social networking company Facebook, for example, launched in 2004 and originally restricted to Harvard University students, now has around 750 million users around the world. With rapid growth and the fast-changing nature of the Internet, Facebook moved quickly from the entrepreneurial through the collectivity and into the formalization stage. Founder and CEO Mark Zuckerberg realized his company would have to "grow up at Internet speed," so in early 2008 he began recruiting experienced managers to help develop the procedures and structures needed to effectively manage the growing company.

In the early years, technology smarts, enthusiasm, commitment, and personal oversight by the founders were enough, but Facebook needed more traditional management skills for continued success. Zuckerberg began consulting with investors and mentors about how to design the company and build a management team. He recruited a top Google executive, Sheryl Sandberg, to be second-in-command as chief operating officer and also began hiring other skilled executives to manage various functions such as marketing, finance, legal, and communications and public policy. Human resources managers helped institute new guidelines for performance reviews, recruiting processes, and training programs.

Although they know formal procedures are needed at this stage of growth, Zuckerberg and other executives are trying to find ways to maintain an entrepreneurial spirit at the company. For instance, a real estate advisor recently helped negotiate a deal for the company to move its offices from Palo Alto into the former Sun Microsystems offices in Menlo Park. That site, plus an additional "West Campus" site Facebook plans to build, will house more than 9,000 employees, about twice as many as currently at the company. Zuckerberg has said he plans to install garage doors throughout the complex to echo a Silicon Valley hallmark—the start-up garage. It will serve as "a symbol of the creative, collaborative, and scrappy culture" Facebook wants to retain.[33]

Organizational Characteristics during the Life Cycle

As organizations evolve through the four stages of the life cycle, changes take place in structure, control systems, innovation, and goals. The organizational characteristics associated with each stage are summarized in Exhibit 12.4.

Entrepreneurial. Initially, the organization is small, non-bureaucratic, and a one-person show. The top manager provides the structure and control system. Organizational energy is devoted to survival and the production of a single product or service.

Collectivity. This is the organization's youth. Growth is rapid, and employees are excited and committed to the organization's mission. The structure is still mostly informal, although some procedures are emerging. Strong charismatic leaders provide direction and goals for the organization. Continued growth is a major goal.

Formalization. At this point, the organization is entering midlife. Bureaucratic characteristics emerge. The organization adds staff support groups, formalizes procedures, and establishes a clear hierarchy and division of labor. At the formalization stage, organizations may also develop complementary products to offer a complete product line. Innovation may be achieved by establishing a separate research and development (R&D) department. Major goals are internal stability and market expansion. Top management delegates, but it also implements formal control systems.

Elaboration. The mature organization is large and bureaucratic, with extensive control systems, rules, and procedures. Organization managers attempt to develop a team orientation within the bureaucracy to prevent further bureaucratization. Top managers are concerned with establishing a complete organization. Organizational

EXHIBIT 12.4
Organization Characteristics during Four Stages of Life Cycle

Characteristic	1. Entrepreneurial Nonbureaucratic	2. Collectivity Prebureaucratic	3. Formalization Bureaucratic	4. Elaboration Very Bureaucratic
Structure	Informal, one-person show	Mostly informal, some procedures	Formal procedures, division of labor, new specialties added	Teamwork within bureaucracy, small-company thinking
Products or services	Single product or service	Major product or service, with variations	Line of products or services	Multiple product or service lines
Reward and control systems	Personal, paternalistic	Personal, contribution to success	Impersonal, formalized systems	Extensive, tailored to product and department
Innovation	By owner-manager	By employees and managers	By separate innovation group	By institutionalized R&D department
Goal	Survival	Growth	Internal stability, market expansion	Reputation, complete organization
Top management style	Individualistic, entrepreneurial	Charismatic, direction-giving	Delegation with control	Team approach, attack bureaucracy

Source: Adapted from Larry E. Greiner, "Evolution and Revolution as Organizations Grow," *Harvard Business Review* 50 (July–August 1972), 37–46; G. L. Lippitt and W. H. Schmidt, "Crises in a Developing Organization," *Harvard Business Review* 45 (November–December 1967), 102–112; B. R. Scott, "The Industrial State: Old Myths and New Realities," *Harvard Business Review* 51 (March–April 1973), 133–148; and Robert E. Quinn and Kim Cameron, "Organizational Life Cycles and Shifting Criteria of Effectiveness," *Management Science* 29 (1983), 33–51.

stature and reputation are important. Innovation is institutionalized through an R&D department. Management may attack the bureaucracy and streamline it.

Summary. Growing organizations move through stages of a life cycle, and each stage is associated with specific characteristics of structure, control systems, goals, and innovation. The life cycle phenomenon is a powerful concept used for understanding problems facing organizations and how managers can respond in a positive way to move an organization to the next stage.

Organizational Size, Bureaucracy, and Control

As organizations progress through the life cycle, they usually take on bureaucratic characteristics as they grow larger and more complex. The systematic study of bureaucracy was launched by Max Weber, a sociologist who studied government organizations in Europe and developed a framework of administrative characteristics that would make large organizations rational and efficient.[34] Weber wanted to understand how organizations could be designed to play a positive role in the larger society.

What Is Bureaucracy?

Although Weber perceived **bureaucracy** as a threat to basic personal liberties, he also recognized it as the most efficient possible system of organizing. He predicted the triumph of bureaucracy because of its ability to ensure more efficient functioning of organizations in both business and government settings. Weber identified a set of organizational characteristics, shown in Exhibit 12.5, that could be found in successful bureaucratic organizations.

Rules and standard procedures enabled organizational activities to be performed in a predictable, routine manner. Specialized duties meant that each employee had a clear task to perform. Hierarchy of authority provided a sensible mechanism for supervision and control. Technical competence was the basis by which people were hired rather than friendship, family ties, and favoritism. The separation of the position from the position holder meant that individuals did not own or have an inherent right to the job, which promoted efficiency. Written records provided an organizational memory and continuity over time.

Although bureaucratic characteristics carried to an extreme are widely criticized today, the rational control introduced by Weber was a significant idea and a new form of organization. Bureaucracy provided many advantages over organization forms based on favoritism, social status, family connections, or graft. Consider the

EXHIBIT 12.5
Weber's Dimensions of Bureaucracy

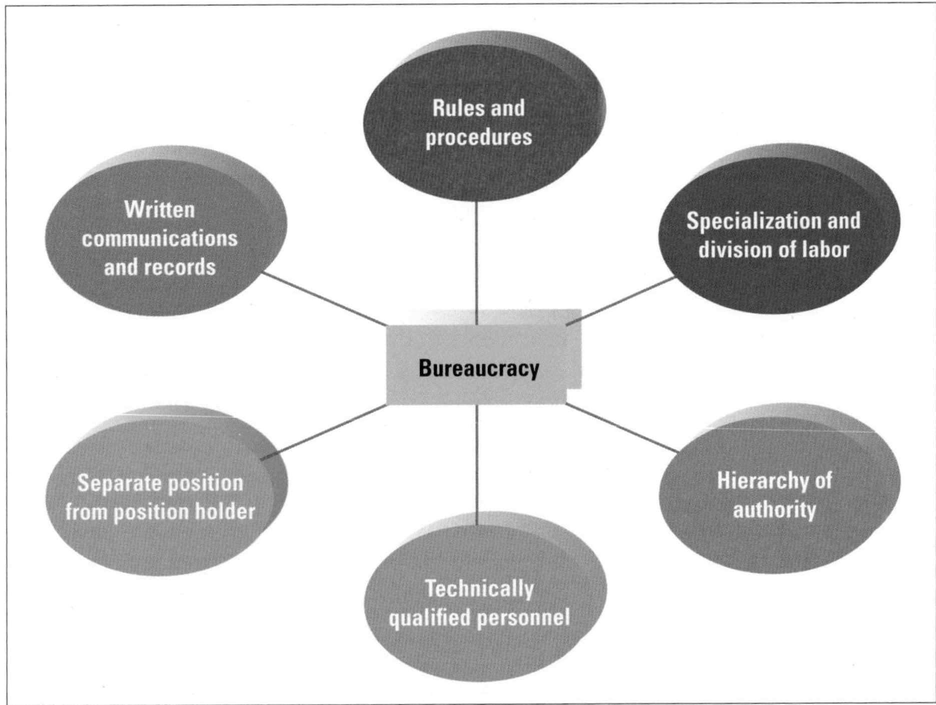

situation in many Latin American countries, where graft, corruption, and nepotism are rampant throughout government and business institutions. In Brazil, for example, government officials have been accused of paying bribes to legislators for their support, favoring contractors who made clandestine campaign contributions, and using their influence to gain jobs or favorable circumstances for family members.[35] In China, the tradition of giving government posts to relatives is still widespread, but China's emerging class of educated people doesn't like seeing the best jobs going to children and other relatives of officials.[36] The United States, as well, sees its share of corruption, as evidenced by the case of Illinois Governor Rod Blagojevich, who was accused of a wide-ranging corruption that included trying to sell the Senate seat vacated by President Barack Obama.[37] By comparison with these examples, the logical and rational form of organization described by Weber allows work to be conducted fairly, efficiently, and according to established rules.

A study of empirical organization research over four decades confirms the validity and persistence of Weber's model of bureaucracy, showing positive relationships among elements such as specialization, formalization, and standardization, as shown in Exhibit 12.5.[38] Bureaucratic characteristics can have a positive effect for many large organizations, such as United Parcel Service (UPS), one of today's most efficient large corporations.

United Parcel Service (UPS)

IN PRACTICE

UPS, sometimes called *Big Brown* for the color of delivery trucks and employee uniforms, is the largest package-distribution company in the world, delivering over 15 million packages a day, and a global leader in supply chain, logistics, and information services. The company operates in more than 200 countries and territories around the world.

How did UPS become so successful? Many efficiencies were realized through adoption of the bureaucratic model of organization. UPS operates according to a mountain of rules and regulations. It teaches drivers an astounding 340 precise steps to correctly deliver a package. For example, it tells them how to load their trucks, how to fasten their seat belts, how to step off the truck, how to walk, and how to carry their keys. Strict dress codes are enforced—clean uniforms (called *browns*) every day, black or brown polished shoes with nonslip soles, no shirt unbuttoned below the first button, no hair below the shirt collar, no beards, no tattoos visible during deliveries, and so on. Before each shift, drivers conduct a "Z-scan," a Z-shaped inspection of the sides and front of their vehicles. There are safety rules for drivers, loaders, clerks, and managers. Employees are asked to clean off their desks at the end of each day so they can start fresh the next morning. Managers are given copies of policy books with the expectation that they will use them regularly, and memos on various policies and rules circulate by the hundreds every day.

Despite the strict rules and numerous policies, employees are satisfied and UPS has a high employee retention rate. Employees are treated well and paid well, and the company has maintained a sense of equality and fairness. Everyone is on a first-name basis. The policy book states, "A leader does not have to remind others of his authority by use of a title. Knowledge, performance, and capacity should be adequate evidence of position and leadership." Technical qualification, not favoritism, is the criterion for hiring and promotion. Top executives started at the bottom—former CEO James Kelly began his career as a temporary holiday-rush driver, for example. The emphasis on equality, fairness, and a promote-from-within mentality inspires loyalty and commitment throughout the ranks.[39]

UPS illustrates how bureaucratic characteristics increase with large size. UPS is so productive and dependable that it dominates the small package delivery market. As it expands and transitions into a global, knowledge-based logistics business, UPS managers may need to find effective ways to reduce the bureaucracy. New technology and new services place more demands on workers, who may need more flexibility and autonomy to perform well. Now, let's look at some specific ways size affects organization structure and control.

Size and Structural Control

In the field of organization theory, organization size has been described as an important contingency that influences structural design and methods of control. Should an organization become more bureaucratic as it grows larger? In what size organizations are bureaucratic characteristics most appropriate? More than 100 studies have attempted to answer these questions.[40] Most of these studies indicate that large organizations are different from small organizations along several dimensions of bureaucratic structure, including formalization, centralization, and personnel ratios.

BRIEFCASE

As an organization manager, keep these guidelines in mind:

As the organization grows, provide greater formalization to achieve standardization and control. Guard against excessive overhead by keeping administrative, clerical, and support staff costs low.

Formalization and Centralization. **Formalization**, as described in Chapter 1, refers to rules, procedures, and written documentation, such as policy manuals and job descriptions, that prescribe the rights and duties of employees.[41] The evidence supports the conclusion that large organizations are more formalized, as at UPS. The reason is that large organizations rely on rules, procedures, and paperwork to achieve standardization and control across their large numbers of employees and departments, whereas top managers can use personal observation to control a small organization.[42] For example, a locally owned coffee shop in a small town doesn't need the detailed manuals, policies, and procedures that Starbucks uses to standardize and control its operations around the world.

Centralization refers to the level of hierarchy with authority to make decisions. In centralized organizations, decisions tend to be made at the top. In decentralized organizations, similar decisions would be made at a lower level.

Decentralization represents a paradox because, in the perfect bureaucracy, all decisions would be made by the top administrator, who would have perfect control. However, as an organization grows larger and has more people and departments, decisions cannot be passed to the top because senior managers would be overloaded. Thus, the research on organization size indicates that larger organizations permit greater decentralization.[43] In small start-up organizations, on the other hand, the founder or top executive can effectively be involved in every decision, large and small.

Personnel Ratios. Another characteristic of bureaucracy relates to **personnel ratios** for administrative, clerical, and professional support staff. The most frequently studied ratio is the administrative ratio.[44] Two patterns have emerged. The first is that the ratio of top administration to total employees is actually smaller in large organizations,[45] indicating that organizations experience administrative economies as they grow larger. The second pattern concerns clerical and professional support staff ratios.[46] These groups tend to *increase* in proportion to organization size. The clerical ratio increases because of the greater communication and reporting requirements needed as organizations grow larger. The professional staff ratio increases because of the greater need for specialized skills in larger, complex organizations.

EXHIBIT 12.6
Percentage of Personnel Allocated to Administrative and Support Activities

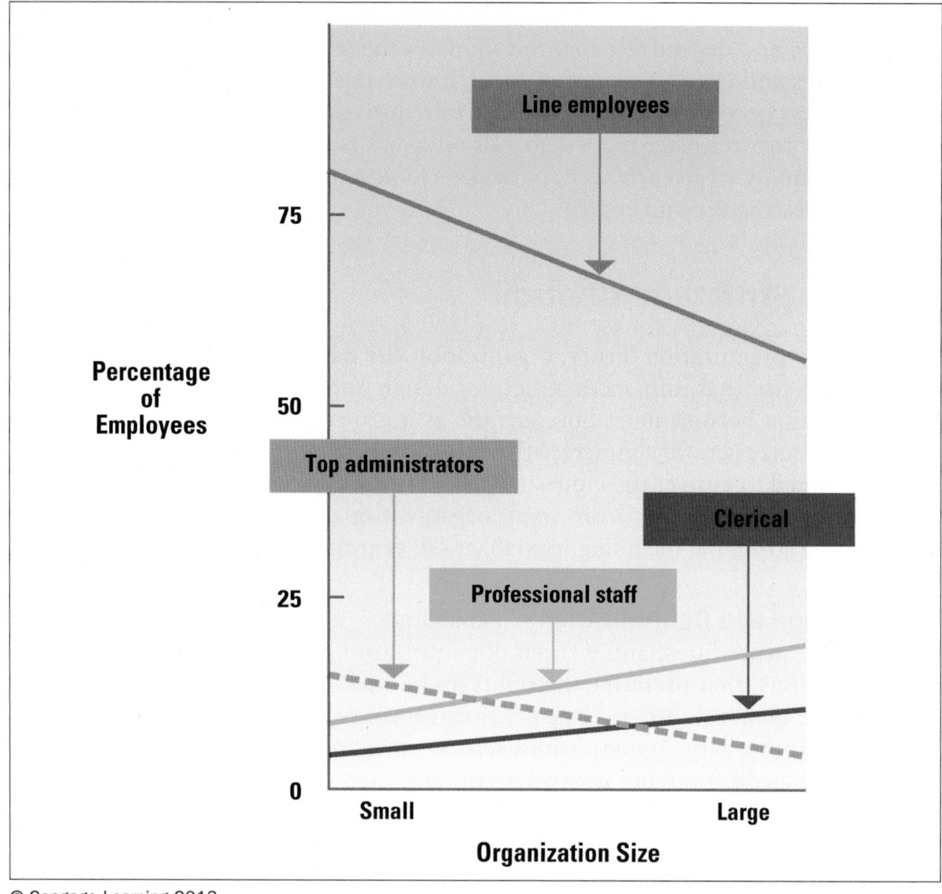

Exhibit 12.6 illustrates administrative and support ratios for small and large organizations. As organizations increase in size, the administrative ratio declines and the ratios for other support groups increase.[47] The net effect for direct workers is that they decline as a percentage of total employees. In summary, whereas top administrators do not make up a disproportionate number of employees in large organizations, the idea that proportionately greater overhead is required in large organizations is supported. With the declining U.S. economy, many companies have been struggling to cut overhead costs. Keeping costs for administrative, clerical, and professional support staff low represents an ongoing challenge for large organizations.

Bureaucracy in a Changing World

Weber's prediction of the triumph of bureaucracy proved accurate. Bureaucratic characteristics have many advantages and have worked extremely well for many of the needs of the industrial age.[48] By establishing a hierarchy of authority and specific rules and procedures, bureaucracy provided an effective way to bring order to large groups of people and minimize abuses of power. Impersonal relationships based on roles rather than people reduced the favoritism and nepotism characteristic of many preindustrial organizations. Bureaucracy also provided for systematic and rational ways to organize and manage tasks too complex to be understood and handled by a few individuals, thus greatly improving the efficiency and effectiveness of large organizations.

Today's world is in constant flux, however, and the machinelike bureaucratic system of the industrial age no longer works so well as organizations face new challenges and need to respond quickly. Consider Microsoft, which some current and former employees complain has become slow and muscle-bound by heavy bureaucracy in recent years. Almost every significant action requires a lawyer's signature, they say, and getting approval for even routine matters can take weeks. One employee left the company because he was tired of being inundated with paperwork. "The smallest issue would balloon into a nightmare of a thousand e-mails," he says.[49] Managers are trying to find ways to cut the bureaucracy so people can do their jobs more effectively and help Microsoft stay competitive. Like Microsoft, many organizations are fighting against increasing formalization and professional staff ratios. ConAgra Foods, for instance, implemented an initiative called RoadMap, which brought together people from all across the company to simplify and streamline processes for reporting, planning, performance management, and so forth. The simplified processes cut overhead costs as well as improved the quality and speed of communication and decision making.[50]

The problems caused by over-bureaucratization are evident in the inefficiencies of some large U.S. government organizations. In response to President Barack Obama's demand that his cabinet secretaries find $100 million in budget cuts, for example, the U.S. Office of Thrift Supervision (a division of the Treasury Department) identified unused phone lines that were costing $320,000 annually.[51] One recent study found an average of 18 Federal management layers between the top and bottom of most agencies, such as between the secretary of agriculture and the forest ranger or the secretary of the interior and the oil rig inspector.[52] Some agencies have so many clerical staff members and confusing job titles that no one is really sure who does what. Richard Cavanagh, once an aide to President Jimmy Carter, reports his favorite Federal title as the "administrative assistant to the assistant administrator for administration of the General Services Administration."[53] Some critics have blamed government bureaucracy for intelligence, communication, and accountability failures related to the 2001 terrorist attacks, the Columbia space shuttle disaster, the abuses at Abu Ghraib prison, and slow responses to the 2010 Gulf oil spill and the 2005 Hurricane Katrina disasters. "Every time you add a layer of bureaucracy, you delay the movement of information up the chain of command. . . . And you dilute the information because at each step some details are taken out," says Richard A. Posner, a Federal appeals court judge who has written a book on intelligence reform.[54] Many business organizations, too, need to reduce formalization and bureaucracy. Narrowly defined job descriptions and excessive rules, for example, tend to limit the creativity, flexibility, and rapid response needed in today's knowledge-based organizations.

Organizing Temporary Systems

How can organizations overcome the problems of bureaucracy in rapidly changing environments? Some are implementing innovative structural solutions. One structural concept is to use temporary systems or structures to respond to an emergency or crisis situation. This approach is often used by organizations such as police and fire departments or other emergency management agencies to maintain the efficiency and control benefits of bureaucracy yet prevent the problem of slow response.[55] The approach is being adapted by other types of organizations to help them respond quickly to new opportunities, unforeseen competitive threats, or organizational crises.

The basic idea is that the organization can glide smoothly between a highly formalized, hierarchical structure that is effective during times of stability and a more flexible, loosely structured one needed to respond well to unexpected and demanding environmental conditions. The hierarchical side with its rules, procedures, and chain of command helps maintain control and ensure adherence to rules that have been developed and tested over many years to cope with well-understood problems and situations. During times of high uncertainty, however, the most effective structure is one that loosens the lines of command and enables people to work across departmental and hierarchical lines to anticipate, avoid, and solve unique problems within the context of a clearly understood mission and guidelines. The approach can be seen in action at the Salvation Army, which has been called "the most effective organization in the world."

Salvation Army

IN PRACTICE

The Salvation Army provides day-to-day assistance to the homeless and economically disadvantaged. In addition, the organization rushes in whenever there is a major disaster—whether it be a tornado, flood, hurricane, airplane crash, or terrorist attack—to network with other agencies to provide disaster relief. The Army's management realizes that emergencies demand high flexibility. At the same time, the organization must have a high level of control and accountability to ensure its continued existence and meet its day-to-day responsibilities. As a former national commander puts it, "We have to have it both ways. We can't choose to be flexible and reckless or to be accountable and responsive. . . . We have to be several different kinds of organization at the same time."

In the early emergency moments of a crisis, the Salvation Army deploys a temporary organization that has its own command structure. People need to have a clear sense of who's in charge to prevent the rapid response demands from degenerating into chaos. For example, if the Army responds to a flood in Mississippi or a tornado in Oklahoma, manuals clearly specify in advance who is responsible for talking to the media, who is in charge of supply inventories, who liaises with other agencies, and so forth. This model for the temporary organization keeps the Salvation Army responsive and consistent. However, in the later recovery and rebuilding phases of a crisis, supervisors frequently give people general guidelines and allow them to improvise the best solutions. There isn't time for supervisors to review and sign off on every decision that needs to be made to get families and communities reestablished.

Thus, the Salvation Army actually has people simultaneously working in all different types of structures, from traditional vertical command structures, to horizontal teams, to a sort of network form that relies on collaboration with other agencies. Operating in such a fluid way enables the organization to accomplish amazing results. In one year, the Army assisted more than 2.3 million people caught in disasters in the United States, in addition to many more served by regular day-to-day programs. It has been recognized as a leader in putting money to maximal use, meaning donors are willing to give because they trust the organization to be responsible and accountable at the same time it is flexible and innovative in meeting human needs.[56]

Other Approaches to Busting Bureaucracy

Organizations are taking a number of other, less dramatic steps to reduce bureaucracy, often *driven by top leaders*. Many are cutting layers of the hierarchy, keeping headquarters staff small, and giving lower-level workers greater freedom to make decisions rather than burdening them with excessive rules and regulations. The commitment of top leadership is essential when an organization needs to reduce bureaucracy and become more flexible and responsive.[57] Consider the following examples:

- As described earlier, Larry Page recently returned as CEO of Google to try to cut through the bureaucracy that has built up as Google became a big corporation. One mechanism Page is using to speed decision making and restore the sense of a start-up is a daily "bullpen" session. Every afternoon, Page and other top executives work together in a public area of Google's headquarters so employees can directly approach them about issues or concerns. "The more people say that you can't have a big company act like a small company, the more determined [Larry Page] is to figure out how to do just that," said Steven Levy, the author of a book about Google.[58]
- Executives at a multinational consumer goods manufacturer created small teams based in each geographic region to focus on customer needs and competitive conditions in each area. They also streamlined procedures for how teams and divisions communicate and work with headquarters. This cut in half the number of rounds of consultations related to an issue, leading to faster decision making and less frustration and wasted time for employees and customers.[59] The point is to reduce red tape that inhibits the flexibility and autonomy of divisions and teams.
- At the London-based pharmaceuticals company GlaxoSmithKline PLC, top executives gave frontline scientists, not managers or a research committee, the authority to set priorities and allocate resources for drugs in development. The shift in who decides which drug research projects to fund has brought an entrepreneurial spirit to the giant firm similar to that of a small biotechnology company.[60]

Another attack on bureaucracy is from the increasing professionalism of employees. *Professionalism* is defined as the length of formal training and experience of employees. More employees need college degrees, MBAs, and other professional degrees to work as attorneys, researchers, engineers, or doctors at Google, Zurich Financial Services, or GlaxoSmithKline. Some Internet-based companies are staffed entirely by well-educated knowledge workers. Studies of professionals show that formalization is not needed because professional training regularizes a high standard of behavior for employees, which acts as a substitute for bureaucracy.[61] Companies enhance this trend when they provide ongoing training for *all* employees, from the front office to the shop floor, in a push for continuous individual and organizational learning. Increased training substitutes for bureaucratic rules and procedures that can constrain the creativity of employees in solving problems and also enhances individual and organizational capability.

BRIEFCASE

As an organization manager, keep these guidelines in mind:

Consider using a temporary systems approach to maintain the efficiency and control benefits of bureaucracy but prevent the problem of slow response to rapid environmental change. Enable the organization to glide smoothly from a formalized system during times of stability to a more flexible, loosely structured one when facing threats, crises, or unexpected environmental changes.

A form of organization called the *professional partnership* has emerged that is made up completely of professionals.[62] These organizations include accounting firms, medical practices, law firms, and consulting firms. The general finding concerning professional partnerships is that branches have substantial autonomy and decentralized authority to make necessary decisions. They work with a consensus orientation rather than the top-down direction typical of traditional business and government organizations. Thus, the trend of increasing professionalism combined with rapidly changing environments is leading to less bureaucracy in corporate North America.

Bureaucracy versus Other Forms of Control

Even though many organizations are trying to reduce bureaucracy and streamline rules and procedures that constrain employees, every organization needs systems for guiding and controlling the organization. Employees may have more freedom in today's companies, but control is still a major responsibility of management.

Managers at the top and middle levels of an organization can choose among three overall control strategies. These strategies come from a framework for organizational control proposed by William Ouchi of the University of California at Los Angeles. Ouchi suggested three control strategies that organizations could adopt—bureaucratic, market, and clan.[63] Each form of control uses different types of information. However, all three types may appear simultaneously in an organization. The requirements for each control strategy are given in Exhibit 12.7.

Bureaucratic Control

Bureaucratic control is the use of rules, policies, hierarchy of authority, written documentation, standardization, and other bureaucratic mechanisms to standardize behavior and assess performance. Bureaucratic control uses the bureaucratic characteristics defined by Weber and illustrated in the UPS case. The primary purpose of bureaucratic rules and procedures is to standardize and control employee behavior.

Recall that as organizations progress through the life cycle and grow larger, they become more formalized and standardized. Within a large organization, thousands of work behaviors and information exchanges take place both vertically

EXHIBIT 12.7
Three Organizational Control Strategies

Type	Requirements
Bureaucratic	Rules, standards, hierarchy, legitimate authority
Market	Prices, competition, exchange relationship
Clan	Tradition, shared values and beliefs, trust

Source: Based on William G. Ouchi, "A Conceptual Framework for the Design of Organizational Control Mechanisms," *Management Science* 25 (1979), 833–848.

EXHIBIT 12.8
Examples of Rules at a Yacht Club

Northeast Harbor Yacht Club Rules for Employees

- ⊕ Employees shall maintain a clean and well-dressed appearance at work.
- ⊕ The summer uniform is green shorts, black or brown belt, white shirt tucked in, and boat shoes. Frayed clothing is not allowed at the club.
- ⊕ Employees should arrive at work at or before the agreed-upon shift time.
- ⊕ Employees shall not smoke or consume alcohol on club property at any time.
- ⊕ Employees are required to be polite and helpful to members at all times.
- ⊕ Employees should remain a respectful distance from members and should not accept social invitations from members.
- ⊕ Employees should not be on club property when they are not working.
- ⊕ Employees are not permitted to use the club phones to make or receive personal calls.
- ⊕ Instructors must provide their own manuals and radio.
- ⊕ Maintenance employees must provide and use their own tools.

and horizontally. Rules and policies evolve through a process of trial and error to regulate these behaviors. Some degree of bureaucratic control is used in virtually every organization. Rules, regulations, and directives contain information about a range of behaviors. For example, note the variety of behaviors managers seek to control through the rules at an exclusive yacht club, listed in Exhibit 12.8.

To make bureaucratic control work, managers must have the authority to maintain control over the organization. Weber argued that legitimate, rational authority granted to managers was preferred over other types of control (e.g., favoritism or payoffs) as the basis for organizational decisions and activities. Within the larger society, however, Weber identified three types of authority that could explain the creation and control of a large organization.[64]

Rational–legal authority is based on employees' belief in the legality of rules and the right of those elevated to positions of authority to issue commands. Rational-legal authority is the basis for both creation and control of most government organizations and is the most common base of control in organizations worldwide. **Traditional authority** is the belief in traditions and in the legitimacy of the status of people exercising authority through those traditions. Traditional authority is the basis for control for monarchies, churches, and some organizations in Latin America and the Persian Gulf. **Charismatic authority** is based on devotion to the exemplary character or to the heroism of an individual person and the order defined by him or her. Revolutionary military organizations are often based on the leader's charisma, as are North American organizations led by charismatic individuals such as Steve Jobs, the recently deceased CEO of Apple, or media entrepreneur Oprah Winfrey, who runs a successful magazine and a television network among other enterprises.

More than one type of authority—such as long tradition and the leader's special charisma—may exist in organizations, but rational–legal authority is the most widely used form to govern internal work activities and decision making, particularly in large organizations. Bureaucratic control can be highly effective, but when carried to an extreme it can also create problems. Consider the following examples from Japan.

Shizugawa Elementary School Evacuation Center and Toyota Motors

IN PRACTICE

One newspaper reporter recently described Japan as "a rule-obsessed nation with a penchant for creating bureaucracy, designating titles and committees for even the most mundane of tasks." When the fishing village of Minamisanriku was ravaged by a tsunami in the spring of 2011, that propensity served a valuable purpose. The creation of rules, procedures, and authority structures helped create a sense of normalcy and comfort at the Shizugawa Elementary School Evacuation Center. The group of evacuees created six divisions to oversee various aspects of daily life, such as cooking, cleaning, inventory control, and medical care, and each function had detailed rules and procedures to follow. The cleaning crews, for instance, followed an instruction sheet describing in minute detail how to separate types of garbage and recyclables, how to replace the garbage bags, and so forth. The exhaustive and meticulous procedures kept the center running smoothly and helped people cope with a devastating situation. "The Japanese people are the type to feel more reassured the more rules are in place," said Shintaro Goto, a 32-year-old actor and electrician who moved back to the village from Tokyo just months before the tsunami.

However, whereas rules, procedures, and detailed lists were highly beneficial at the tsunami evacuation centers, they have been partially blamed for quality and safety problems that have plagued Japan's Toyota Motors in recent years. "The bottom line is that we succumbed to 'Big Company Disease,'" said Shinichi Sasaki, a Toyota board member and executive vice president in charge of quality. "That has led us to question some of our basic assumptions." Toyota's strong top-down bureaucratic system helped obscure problems. For example, the company wanted suppliers, dealers, and other partners, as well as employees, to follow strict guidelines to the letter. The rules and checklists got in the way of executives seeing when things started going wrong, however, and customer complaints started piling up. Toyota has since implemented a number of reforms to its operations, many of them designed to overcome the problems brought about by large size and bureaucracy.[65]

Toyota isn't the only large company to find that too many rules can get in the way of serving customers. Employees at Starbucks, which grew rapidly from six stores in 1987 into a huge corporation with thousands of stores around the world, are being strangled by meticulous rules and policies that no longer work. Consistency is important for any company, and rules and procedures that facilitated predictable outcomes enabled Starbucks to grow and succeed. However, applying rules inflexibly and blindly soon started to cause problems. One software entrepreneur and *Inc.* magazine contributor tells a story about an order taker in a Starbucks store who got into a prolonged shouting match with a customer who wanted to pick up her sandwich at the front counter. "They're not allowed to give it to you up here!" the employee kept shouting at the shocked and frustrated customer.[66]

Market Control

Market control occurs when price competition is used to evaluate the output and productivity of an organization or its major departments and divisions. The idea of market control originated in economics.[67] A dollar price is an efficient form of control because managers can compare prices and profits to evaluate the efficiency of the corporation. Top managers nearly always use the price mechanism to evaluate performance in their corporations. Corporate sales and costs are summarized in a profit-and-loss statement that can be compared against performance in previous years or with that of other corporations.

The use of market control requires that outputs be sufficiently explicit for a price to be assigned and that competition exist. Without competition, the price does not accurately reflect internal efficiency. Even some government and nonprofit organizations are effectively using market control. For example, the U.S. Federal Aviation Administration took bids to operate its payroll computers. The Department of Agriculture beat out IBM and two other private companies to win the bid.[68] The city of Indianapolis requires all its departments to bid against private companies. When the transportation department was underbid by a private company on a contract to fill potholes, the city's union workers made a counterproposal that involved eliminating most of the department's middle managers and reengineering union jobs to save money. Eighteen supervisors were laid off, costs were cut by 25 percent, and the department won the bid.[69]

Market control was once used primarily at the level of the entire organization, but it is increasingly used in product divisions or individual departments. Profit centers are self-contained product divisions, such as those described in Chapter 2. Each division contains resource inputs needed to produce a product. Each division can be evaluated on the basis of profit or loss compared with other divisions. ABB, a global electrical contractor and manufacturer of electrical equipment, includes three different types of profit centers, all operating according to their own bottom line and all interacting through buying and selling with one another and with outside customers.[70] The network organization, also described in Chapter 2, illustrates market control as well. Different companies compete on price to provide the functions and services required by the hub organization. The organization typically contracts with the company that offers the best price and value.

BRIEFCASE

As an organization manager, keep these guidelines in mind:

Implement one of the three basic choices—bureaucratic, clan, market—as the primary means of organizational control. Use bureaucratic control when organizations are large, have a stable environment, and use routine technology. Use clan control in small, uncertain departments. Use market control when outputs can be priced and when competitive bidding is available.

Clan Control

Clan control is the use of social characteristics, such as shared values, commitment, traditions, and beliefs, to control behavior. Organizations that use clan control have strong cultures that emphasize shared values and trust among employees.[71] Clan control is important when ambiguity and uncertainty are high. High uncertainty means the organization cannot put a price on its services, and things change so fast that rules and regulations are not able to specify every correct behavior. Under clan control, people may be hired because they are committed to the organization's purpose, such as in a religious organization or an organization focused on a social mission. New employees are typically subjected to a long period of socialization to gain acceptance by colleagues. There is strong pressure to conform to group norms, which govern a wide range of employee behaviors. Managers act primarily as mentors, role models, and agents for transmitting values.[72]

2 A manager should emphasize shared values, trust, and commitment to the organization's mission as the primary means of controlling employee behavior.

ANSWER: *Agree or disagree.* Clan control, which relies on culture, trust, commitment, and shared values and traditions, can be highly effective and is particularly useful in departments or organizations experiencing high uncertainty or environmental turbulence. However, other forms of control, such as bureaucratic or market control, are also effective and appropriate under the right circumstances.

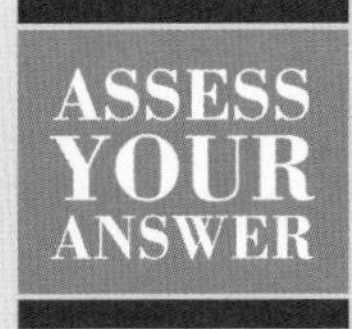

Traditional control mechanisms based on strict rules and close supervision are inadequate for controlling behavior in conditions of high uncertainty and rapid change.[73] In addition, the use of computer networks and the Internet, which often leads to a democratic spread of information throughout the organization, is influencing companies to depend less on bureaucratic control and more on shared values that guide individual actions for the corporate good.[74] Clan control is most often used in small, informal organizations where people are strongly committed to the organization's purpose. Some large companies do use clan control rather than rely on rules and regulations, but large size increases the demands on managers to maintain strong cultural values that support this type of control.

A similar concept is *self-control*. Whereas clan control is a function of being socialized into a group, self-control stems from individual values, goals, and standards. Managers attempt to induce a change such that individual employees' own internal values and work preferences are brought in line with the organization's values and goals.[75] With self-control, employees generally set their own goals and monitor their own performance, yet companies relying on self-control need strong leaders who can clarify boundaries within which people exercise their own knowledge and discretion.

Clan control or self-control may also be used in some departments, such as strategic planning, where uncertainty is high and performance is difficult to measure. Managers of departments that rely on these informal control mechanisms must not assume that the absence of written, bureaucratic control means no control is present. Clan control is invisible yet very powerful. One study found that the actions of employees were controlled even more powerfully and completely with clan control than with a bureaucratic hierarchy.[76] When clan control works, bureaucratic control is not needed.

Organizational Decline and Downsizing

Earlier in the chapter, we discussed the organizational life cycle, which suggests that organizations are born, grow older, and eventually die. Size can become a burden for many organizations. For example, General Motors collapsed under its own weight and had to go through bankruptcy and a forced restructuring. Not only was the company laboring under a financial burden of huge pension and healthcare obligations, but its cumbersome bureaucracy had made it hard for GM to connect with the needs of consumers. Regional managers said their ideas and suggestions for product changes or advertising approaches never reached decision makers or fell on deaf ears.[77] Every organization goes through periods of temporary decline. In addition, a reality in today's environment is that for some companies, continual growth and expansion may not be possible.

All around, we see evidence that some organizations have stopped growing, and many are declining. Huge financial services firms, such as Lehman Brothers and Bear Stearns, disintegrated partly as a result of unfettered growth and ineffective control. Starbucks had to bring its period of rampant expansion to an end when it became clear that it was cannibalizing sales and threatening the chain's success. When Howard Schultz returned as CEO in 2008, he immediately halted new store openings, and Starbucks closed 900 stores over the next three years.[78] With the declining economy, many big organizations have made significant job cuts in recent years. Local governments have been forced to close schools, lay off police officers, and shut down fire stations as tax revenues have declined. Colleges and universities have instituted hiring freezes, halted construction projects, and scaled back on maintenance tasks such as power washing of windows and sidewalks.[79]

In this section, we examine the causes and stages of organizational decline and then discuss how leaders can effectively manage the downsizing that is a reality in today's companies.

Definition and Causes

The term **organizational decline** is used to define a condition in which a substantial, absolute decrease in an organization's resource base occurs over time.[80] Organizational decline is often associated with environmental decline in the sense that an organizational domain experiences either a reduction in size (such as shrinkage in customer demand or erosion of a city's tax base) or a reduction in shape (such as a shift in customer demand). In general, the following three factors are considered responsible for causing organizational decline.

1. *Organizational atrophy.* Atrophy occurs when organizations grow older and become inefficient and overly bureaucratized. The organization's ability to adapt to its environment deteriorates. Often, atrophy follows a long period of success because an organization takes success for granted, becomes attached to practices and structures that worked in the past, and fails to adapt to changes in the environment.[81] Some warning signals for organizational atrophy include excess administrative and support staff, cumbersome administrative procedures, lack of effective communication and coordination, and outdated organizational structure.[82]
2. *Vulnerability.* Vulnerability reflects an organization's strategic inability to prosper in its environment. This often happens to small organizations that are not yet fully established. They are vulnerable to shifts in consumer tastes or in the economic health of the larger community. Small e-commerce companies that had not yet become established were the first to go out of business when the technology sector began to decline. Some organizations are vulnerable because they are unable to define the correct strategy to fit the environment. Vulnerable organizations typically need to redefine their environmental domain to enter new industries or markets.
3. *Environmental decline or competition.* Environmental decline refers to reduced energy and resources available to support an organization. When the environment has less capacity to support organizations, the organization has to either scale down operations or shift to another domain.[83] Managers at the American Red Cross, for example, are struggling with raising enough funds to cover expenses. Donations have been declining for several years, and recent major disasters such as the earthquake in Haiti, the earthquake and tsunami in Japan, and Hurricane Irene in the United States, have strained the organization's resources. Steep drops in the stock market, widespread job losses, rising prices, and general pessimism about the U.S. economy have created a tough fund-raising environment for all nonprofits.[84] New competition can also be a problem, especially for small organizations. Consider what's happening to U.S. toolmakers, the companies that make the dies, molds, jigs, fixtures, and gauges used on factory floors to manufacture everything from car doors to laser-guided bombs. Hundreds of these companies—including one of only two

firms in the United States capable of making tools used to build components of stealth aircraft—have gone out of business in recent years, unable to compete with the super-low prices their counterparts in China are offering. As more and more toolmakers go out of business, the National Tooling and Machining Association has urged Congress to pass legislation that would "level the playing field" and enable these small firms to stay competitive with Chinese companies.[85]

All three of these factors were involved in the decline of Borders Group, once the nation's second-largest bookseller.

Borders Group Inc.

IN PRACTICE

In 1971, Tom and Louis Borders opened an 800-square-foot used bookstore in Ann Arbor, Michigan. By the late 1990s, the little bookstore had grown into Borders Group, the second-largest bookseller in the United States, with an international chain of book superstores and smaller Waldenbooks outlets in shopping malls. The company's innovative inventory management system was considered the envy of the bookselling industry.

In 2006, Borders Group had 36,000 employees and more than 1,000 stores. By mid-2011, the company was dead, with managers liquidating the remaining 399 stores and shutting down the chain for good. What happened? Borders was hit simultaneously by all three factors that cause organizational decline. The primary cause was increased *competition* from discount stores such as Walmart and from online sellers. Amazon.com forever changed the rules of bookselling. Online book sales soared while sales at bookstores began to decline. Borders managers weren't able to adapt to the changes, partly because of *organizational atrophy*. The company had been highly successful for many years, and managers couldn't accept that their way of doing business was no longer effective. They stuck with the strategy of building more big stores, opting to partner with Amazon for online sales rather than establish their own e-commerce unit. By the time Borders decided to halt the expansion of stores and "become a force in online bookselling," it was too late. *Vulnerability* was also a factor in the death of Borders. The increasing popularity of digital books has left all traditional booksellers vulnerable, and Borders managers were unable to find the right strategy and redefine their organizational domain to go beyond the traditional bookstore. Sales of traditional books declined an estimated 11.4 percent in 2011, while sales of digital books increased 111 percent during the same period.[86]

Managers at Borders were unable to overcome the triple-whammy of organizational atrophy, vulnerability, and environmental competition. After the company filed for bankruptcy, there were signs that Borders might survive under new ownership. Ultimately, though, the deal fell through, and there was nothing left to do but shut down the company. In the next section, we examine the stages of organizational decline and some common mistakes managers make that can lead to dissolution, such as at Borders Group.

A Model of Decline Stages

Based on an extensive review of organizational decline research, a model of decline stages has been proposed and is summarized in Exhibit 12.9. This model suggests that decline, if not managed properly, can move through five stages resulting in organizational dissolution.[87]

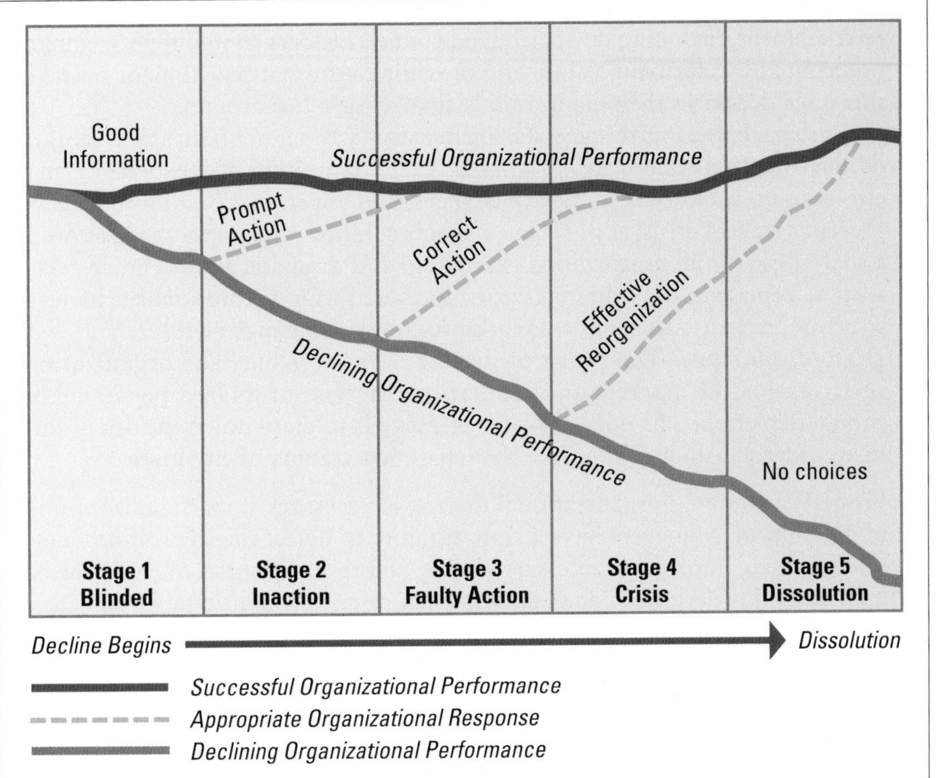

EXHIBIT 12.9
Stages of Decline and the Widening Performance Gap

Source: William Weitzel and Ellen Jonsson, *Administrative Science Quarterly*. "Decline in Organizations: A Literature Integration and Extension," by, vol. 34, pp. 99–109, March 1989. Reprinted by Permission of SAGE Publications.

1. *Blinded stage.* The first stage of decline is the internal and external change that threatens long-term survival and may require the organization to tighten up. The organization may have excess personnel, cumbersome procedures, or lack of harmony with customers. Leaders often miss the signals of decline at this point, and the solution is to develop effective scanning and control systems that indicate when something is wrong. With timely information, alert executives can bring the organization back to top performance.
2. *Inaction stage.* The second stage of decline is called *inaction* in which denial occurs despite signs of deteriorating performance. Leaders may try to persuade employees and other stakeholders that all is well. In 2008, for example, with sales declining and the stock plummeting, Borders's then-CEO told a newspaper reporter who interviewed him about the company's situation: "We're not in trouble; we're not in trouble at all."[88] In some cases, managers use "creative accounting" to make things look fine during this period. The solution is for leaders to acknowledge decline and take prompt action to realign the organization with the environment. Leadership actions may include adopting new problem-solving approaches, increasing decision-making participation, and encouraging employee and customer expression of dissatisfaction to learn what is wrong.
3. *Faulty action stage.* In the third stage, the organization is facing serious problems, and indicators of poor performance cannot be ignored. Failure to adjust to the declining spiral at this point can lead to organizational failure. Leaders are

BRIEFCASE

As an organization manager, keep these guidelines in mind:

Understand the causes and stages of decline. Be vigilant to detect signs of decline in the organization and take action as quickly as possible to reverse course. Quick action in the early stages prevents the organization from deteriorating to a stage-4 crisis, when a turnaround becomes much more difficult.

forced by severe circumstances to consider major changes. Actions may involve retrenchment, including downsizing personnel. Leaders should reduce employee uncertainty by clarifying values and providing information. A major mistake at this stage decreases the organization's chance for a turnaround.

4. *Crisis stage.* In the fourth stage, the organization still has not been able to deal with decline effectively and is facing a panic. The organization may experience chaos, efforts to go back to basics, sharp changes, and anger. It is best for managers to prevent a stage-4 crisis; at this stage, the only solution is major reorganization. The social fabric of the organization is eroding, and dramatic actions are necessary, such as replacing top administrators and instituting revolutionary changes in structure, strategy, and culture. Workforce downsizing may be severe.
5. *Dissolution stage.* This stage of decline is irreversible. The organization is suffering loss of markets and reputation, the loss of its best personnel, and capital depletion. The only available strategy is to close down the organization in an orderly fashion and reduce the separation trauma of employees.

Properly managing organizational decline is necessary if an organization is to avoid dissolution. Managers have a responsibility to detect the signs of decline, acknowledge them, implement necessary action, and reverse course. Some of the most difficult decisions pertain to **downsizing**, which refers to intentionally reducing the size of a company's workforce.

Downsizing Implementation

BRIEFCASE

As an organization manager, keep these guidelines in mind:

When layoffs are necessary, handle them with care. Treat departing employees humanely, communicate with employees and provide as much information as possible, provide assistance to displaced workers, and remember the emotional needs of remaining employees.

The economic downturn has made downsizing a common practice in U.S. corporations. In addition, downsizing has been an integral part of organizational life for the past couple of decades as companies make changes to cope with global competition and a rapidly shifting environment.[89] Reengineering projects, mergers and acquisitions, the implementation of advanced technology, and the trend toward outsourcing have all led to job reductions.[90]

Some researchers have found that massive downsizing has often not achieved the intended benefits, and in some cases has significantly harmed the organization.[91] Honeywell CEO David Cote agrees that widespread layoffs hurt companies in the long run. He says the massive layoff of 31,000 Honeywell employees in the early 2000s "decimated our industrial base." During the recent recession, Honeywell took a more limited and targeted approach to downsizing.[92] There are times when downsizing is a necessary part of managing organizational decline. A number of techniques can help smooth the downsizing process and ease tensions for employees who leave and for those who remain.[93]

1. *Search for alternatives.* Managers can use creative approaches to cut costs and limit the number of people they have to let go during a decline. Honeywell used furloughs and benefit cuts to limit layoffs during the recent recession. Connecticut's state government, Tri-Star Industries, and numerous other organizations are using work-sharing programs, where employees work fewer hours. Other organizations are cutting pay, offering unpaid or partially paid sabbaticals, having mandatory shut-down days, and applying other techniques to avoid across-the-board job cuts.[94]
2. *Communicate more, not less.* Some managers seem to think the less that's said about a pending layoff, the better. Not so. Rumors can be much more damaging

than open communication. At 3Com Corporation (now part of Hewlett-Packard), managers drew up a three-stage plan as they prepared for layoffs. First, they warned employees several months ahead that layoffs were inevitable. Soon thereafter, they held on-site presentations at all locations to explain to employees why the layoffs were needed and to provide as much information as they could about what employees should expect.[95] Managers should remember that it is impossible to "overcommunicate" during turbulent times. Remaining employees need to know what is expected of them, whether future layoffs are a possibility, and what the organization is doing to help co-workers who have lost their jobs.

3. *Provide assistance to displaced workers.* The organization has a responsibility to help displaced workers cope with the loss of their jobs and get reestablished in the job market. The organization can provide training, severance packages, extended benefits, and outplacement assistance. At eBay, managers allowed laid-off employees to stay for up to four weeks to take care of personal needs. The company provided each laid-off employee five months of severance pay, four months of health benefits, and several months of outplacement services. "How you treat the leavers has a strong impact on how the stayers feel about the company," said eBay's senior HR executive.[96] Counseling services for both employees and their families can ease the trauma associated with a job loss. A growing number of companies are giving laid-off workers continued access to employee assistance programs to help them cope with stress, depression, and other problems.[97] Another key step is to allow employees to leave with dignity, giving them an opportunity to say goodbye to colleagues and meet with leaders to express their hurt and anger.
4. *Help the survivors thrive.* There has been much research on the "layoff survivor syndrome."[98] Many people experience guilt, anger, confusion, and sadness after the loss of colleagues, and managers should acknowledge these feelings. Survivors also might be concerned about losing their own jobs, lose confidence in company management, and grow depressed and cynical. People sometimes have difficulty adapting to the changes in job duties, responsibilities, and reporting relationships after a downsizing. It is extremely important that managers don't hide behind closed doors, no matter how depressed they might be feeling themselves. They need to get out and interact with employees, doing everything they can to reduce the uncertainty, stress, and confusion people are feeling. "One of the worst actions management can take during this time is to not acknowledge the situation and the impact it is having on employees," advises management consultant Simma Lieberman.[99]

3 After a necessary downsizing, managers should not spend much time helping laid-off workers but focus instead on making sure the remaining employees are taken care of to do what is needed to revive the company.

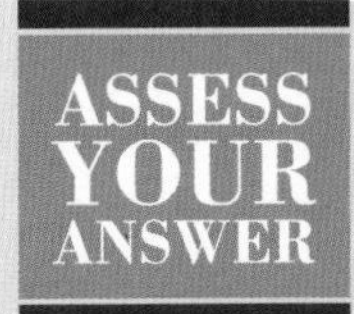

ANSWER: *Disagree.* One way to take care of remaining employees after a downsizing is to take care of the people who were laid off. Helping laid-off employees sends a signal to remaining workers that the organization cares about the departed co-workers and friends, which helps get the company going again. Managing downsizing means providing assistance to both departing and remaining employees.

Even the best-managed organizations may sometimes need to lay off employees in a turbulent environment or to revitalize the organization and reverse decline. Leaders can attain positive results if they handle downsizing in a way that lets departing employees leave with dignity and enables remaining organization members to be motivated, productive, and committed to a better future.

Design Essentials

- Organizations experience many pressures to grow, and large size is crucial to economic health in some industries. Size enables economies of scale, provides a wide variety of opportunities for employees, and allows companies to invest in expensive and risky projects. However, large organizations have a hard time adapting to rapid changes in the environment. Large organizations are typically standardized, mechanistically run, and complex. Small organizations typically have a flatter structure and an organic, free-flowing management. They can respond more quickly to environmental changes and are more suited to encouraging innovation and entrepreneurship. Managers in large or growing firms try to find mechanisms to make their organizations more flexible and responsive.
- Organizations evolve through distinct life-cycle stages as they grow and mature. Organization structure, internal systems, and management issues are different for each stage of development. Growth creates crises and revolutions along the way toward large size. A major task of managers is to guide the organization through the entrepreneurial, collectivity, formalization, and elaboration stages of development.
- As organizations progress through the life cycle and grow larger and more complex, they generally take on bureaucratic characteristics, such as rules, division of labor, written records, hierarchy of authority, and impersonal procedures. Bureaucracy is a logical form of organizing that lets firms use resources efficiently. In many large corporate and government organizations, however, bureaucracy has come under attack with attempts to decentralize authority, flatten organization structure, reduce rules and written procedures, and create a small-company mindset. These companies are willing to trade economies of scale for responsive, adaptive organizations. Many companies are subdividing to gain small-company advantages. Another approach to overcoming the problems of bureaucracy is to use temporary systems, enabling the organization to glide smoothly between a highly formalized, hierarchical style that is effective during times of stability and a more flexible, loosely structured one needed to respond to unexpected or volatile environmental conditions.
- All organizations, large and small, need systems for control. Managers can choose among three overall control strategies: bureaucratic, market, and clan. Bureaucratic control relies on standard rules and the rational–legal authority of managers. Market control is used where product or service outputs can be priced and competition exists. Clan control and self-control are associated with uncertain and rapidly changing organization processes.

They rely on commitment, tradition, and shared values for control. Managers may use a combination of control approaches to meet the organization's needs.

- Many organizations have stopped growing, and some are declining. Organizations go through stages of decline, and it is the responsibility of managers to detect the signs of decline, implement necessary action, and reverse course. One of the most difficult decisions pertains to downsizing the workforce. To smooth the downsizing process, managers can search for creative alternatives to massive layoffs, communicate with employees and provide as much information as possible, provide assistance to displaced workers, and remember to address the emotional needs of those who remain with the organization.

Key Concepts

bureaucracy
bureaucratic control
centralization
charismatic authority
clan control
collectivity stage
downsizing
elaboration stage
entrepreneurial stage
formalization
formalization stage
life cycle
market control
organizational decline
personnel ratios
rational–legal authority
traditional authority

Discussion Questions

1. Why do large organizations tend to have larger ratios of clerical and administrative support staff? Why are they typically more formalized than small organizations?
2. Apply the concept of life cycle to an organization with which you are familiar, such as a local business. What stage is the organization in now? How did the organization handle or pass through its life cycle crises?
3. Why do you think organizations feel pressure to grow? How do you think the companies described in the chapter Book Mark, *Small Giants*, resist that pressure?
4. Describe the three bases of authority identified by Weber. Is it possible for each of these types of authority to function at the same time within an organization? Discuss.
5. Look through several recent issues of a business magazine such as *Fortune*, *BusinessWeek*, or *Fast Company* and find examples of two companies that are using approaches to busting bureaucracy. Discuss the techniques these companies are applying.
6. In writing about types of control, William Ouchi said, "The Market is like the trout and the Clan like the salmon, each a beautiful highly specialized species which requires uncommon conditions for its survival. In comparison, the bureaucratic method of control is the catfish—clumsy, ugly, but able to live in the widest range of environments and ultimately, the dominant species." Discuss what Ouchi meant with that analogy.
7. Government organizations often seem more bureaucratic than for-profit organizations. Could this partly be the result of the type of control used in government organizations? Explain.
8. How does the Salvation Army manage to be "several different kinds of organization at the same time"? Does the Salvation Army's approach seem workable for a large media company like Time Warner or Disney that wants to reduce bureaucracy?
9. Numerous large financial institutions, including Lehman Brothers and Merrill Lynch, experienced significant decline or dissolution in recent years. Which of the three causes of organizational decline described in the chapter seems to apply most clearly to these firms?
10. Do you think a "no growth" philosophy of management should be taught in business schools? Discuss.

Chapter 12 Workbook Control Mechanisms[100]

Think of two situations in your life: your work and your school experiences. How is control exerted? Fill out the tables.

On the Job

Your job responsibilities	How your boss controls	Positives of this control	Negatives of this control	How you would improve control
1.				
2.				
3.				
4.				

At the University

Items	How professor A (small class) controls	How professor B (large class) controls	How these controls influence you	What you think is a better control
1. Exams				
2. Assignments/ papers				
3. Class participation				
4. Attendance				
5. Other				

Questions

1. What are the advantages and disadvantages of the various controls?
2. What happens when there is too much control? Too little?
3. Does the type of control depend on the situation and the number of people involved?
4. *Optional:* How do the control mechanisms in your tables compare to those of other students?

CASE FOR ANALYSIS: Sunflower Incorporated[101]

Sunflower Incorporated is a large distribution company with more than 5,000 employees and gross sales of more than $700 million (2008). The company purchases salty snack foods and liquor and distributes them to independent retail stores throughout the United States and Canada. Salty snack foods include corn chips, potato chips, cheese curls, tortilla chips, pretzels, and peanuts. The United States and Canada are divided into 22 regions, each with its own central warehouse, salespeople, finance department, and purchasing department. The company distributes national and local brands and packages some items under private labels. Competition in this industry is intense. The demand for liquor has been declining, and snack food competitors like Procter & Gamble and Frito-Lay have developed new products and low-carb options to gain market share from smaller companies like Sunflower. The head office encourages each region to be autonomous because of local tastes and practices. In the northeastern United States, for example, people consume a greater percentage of Canadian whiskey and American bourbon, whereas in the West they consume more light liquors, such as vodka, gin, and rum. Snack foods in the Southwest are often seasoned to reflect Mexican tastes, and customers in the Northeast buy a greater percentage of pretzels.

Early in 2003, Sunflower began using a financial reporting system that compared sales, costs, and profits across company regions. Each region was a profit center, and top management was surprised to learn that profits varied widely. By 2006, the differences were so great that management decided some standardization was necessary. Managers believed highly profitable regions were sometimes using lower-quality items, even seconds, to boost profit margins. This practice could hurt Sunflower's image. Most regions were facing cutthroat price competition to hold market share. Triggered by price cuts by Eagle Snacks, national distributors such as Frito-Lay, Borden, Nabisco, Procter & Gamble (Pringles), and Kraft Foods (Planters Peanuts) were pushing to hold or increase market share by cutting prices and launching new products. Independent snack food distributors had a tougher and tougher time competing, and many were going out of business.

As these problems accumulated, Joe Steelman, president of Sunflower, decided to create a new position to monitor pricing and purchasing practices. Loretta Williams was hired from the finance department of a competing organization. Her new title was director of pricing and purchasing, and she reported to the vice president of finance, Peter Langly. Langly gave Williams great latitude in organizing her job and encouraged her to establish whatever rules and procedures were necessary. She was also encouraged to gather information from each region. Each region was notified of her appointment by an official memo sent to the 22 regional directors. A copy of the memo was posted on each warehouse bulletin board. The announcement was also made in the company newspaper.

After three weeks on the job, Williams decided two problems needed her attention. Over the long term, Sunflower should make better use of information technology. Williams believed information technology could provide more information to headquarters for decision making. Top managers in the divisions were connected to headquarters by an intranet, but lower-level employees and salespeople were not connected. Only a few senior managers in about half the divisions used the system regularly.

In the short term, Williams decided fragmented pricing and purchasing decisions were a problem and these decisions should be standardized across regions. This strategy should be undertaken immediately. As a first step, she wanted the financial executive in each region to notify her of any change in local prices of more than 3 percent. She also decided that all new contracts for local purchases of more than $5,000 should be cleared through her office. (Approximately 60 percent of items distributed in the regions were purchased in large quantities and supplied from the home office. The other 40 percent were purchased and distributed within the region.) Williams believed the only way to standardize operations was for each region to notify the home office in advance of any change in prices or purchases. She discussed the proposed policy with Langly. He agreed, so they submitted a formal proposal to the president and board of directors, who approved the plan. The changes represented a complicated shift in policy procedures, and Sunflower was moving into peak holiday season, so Williams wanted to implement the new procedures right away. She decided to send an e-mail message followed by a fax to the financial and purchasing executives in each region notifying them of the new procedures. The change would be inserted in all policy and procedure manuals throughout Sunflower within four months.

Williams showed a draft of the message to Langly and invited his comments. Langly said the message was a good idea but wondered if it was sufficient. The regions handled hundreds of items and were accustomed to decentralized decision making. Langly suggested that Williams ought to visit the regions and discuss purchasing and pricing policies with the executives. Williams refused, saying that such trips would be expensive and time consuming. She had so many things to do at headquarters and said that the trips were impossible to schedule. Langly also suggested waiting to implement the procedures until after the annual company meeting in three months, when Williams could meet the regional directors personally. Williams said this would take too long because the procedures would then not take effect until after the peak sales season. She believed the procedures were needed now. The messages went out the next day.

During the next few days, e-mail replies came in from seven regions. The managers said they were in agreement and were happy to cooperate.

Eight weeks later, Williams had not received notices from any regions about local price or purchase changes. Other executives who had visited regional warehouses indicated to her that the regions were busy as usual. Regional executives seemed to be following usual procedures for that time of year. She telephoned one of the regional managers and discovered that he did not know who she was and had never heard of her position. Besides, he said, "we have enough to worry about reaching profit goals without additional procedures from headquarters." Williams was chagrined that her position and her suggested changes in procedure had no impact. She wondered whether field managers were disobedient or whether she should have used another communication strategy.

Chapter 12 Workshop Windsock Inc.[102]

1. *Introduction.* Class is divided into four groups: Central Office, Product Design, Marketing/Sales, and Production. Central Office is a slightly smaller group. If groups are large enough, assign observers to each one. Central Office is given 500 straws and 750 pins. Each person reads *only* the role description relevant to that group. *Materials needed:* plastic milk straws (500) and a box of straight pins (750).
2. *Perform task.* Depending on length of class, step 2 may take 30 to 60 minutes. Groups perform functions and prepare for a two-minute report for stockholders.
3. *Group reports.* Each group gives a two-minute presentation to stockholders.
4. *Observers' reports (optional).* Observers share insights with subgroups.
5. Class discussion.
   a. What helped or blocked intergroup cooperation and coordination?
   b. To what extent was there open versus closed communication? What impact did that have?
   c. What styles of leadership were exhibited?
   d. What types of team interdependencies emerged?

Roles

Central Office

Your team is the central management and administration of Windsock Inc. You are the pulse of the organization because without your coordination and resource allocation, the organization would go under. Your task is to manage the operations of the organization, which is not an easy responsibility because you have to coordinate the activities of three distinct groups of personnel: the Marketing/Sales group, the Production group, and the Product Design group. In addition, you have to manage resources including materials (pins and straws), time deadlines, communications, and product requirements.

In this exercise, you are to do whatever is necessary to accomplish the mission and to keep the organization operating harmoniously and efficiently.

Windsock Inc. has a total of 30 minutes (more if instructor assigns) to design an advertising campaign and ad copy, to design the windmill, and to produce the first windmill prototypes for delivery. Good luck to you all.

Product Design

Your team is the research and product design group of Windsock Inc. You are the brain and creative aspect of the operation because without an innovative and successfully designed product, the organization would go under. Your duties are to design products that compete favorably in the marketplace, keeping in mind function, aesthetics, cost, ease of production, and available materials.

In this exercise, you are to come up with a workable plan for a product that will be built by your production team. Your windmill must be light, portable, easy to assemble, and aesthetically pleasing. Central Office controls the budget and allocates material for your division.

Windsock Inc. as an organization has a total of 30 minutes (more if instructor assigns) to design an advertising campaign, to design the windmill (your group's task), and to produce the first windmill prototypes for delivery. Good luck to you all.

Marketing/Sales

Your team is the marketing/sales group of Windsock Inc. You are the backbone of the operation because without customers and sales, the organization would go under. Your task is to determine the market, develop an advertising campaign to promote your company's unique product, produce ad copy, and develop a sales force and sales procedures for both potential customers and the public at large.

For the purpose of this exercise, you may assume that a market analysis has been completed. Your team is now in a position to produce an advertising campaign and ad copy for the product. To be effective, you have to become very familiar with the characteristics of the product and how it is different from those products already on the market. The Central Office controls your budget and allocates materials for use by your division.

Windsock Inc. has a total of 30 minutes (more if instructor assigns) to design an advertising campaign and ad (your group's task), to design the windmill, and to produce the first windmill prototypes for delivery. Good luck to you all.

Production

Your team is the production group of Windsock Inc. You are the heart of the operation because without a group to produce the product, the organization would go under. You have the responsibility to coordinate and produce the product for delivery. The product involves an innovative design for a windmill that is cheaper, lighter, more portable, more flexible, and more aesthetically pleasing than other designs currently available in the marketplace. Your task is to build windmills within cost guidelines, according to specifications, and within a prescribed period, using predetermined materials.

For the purpose of this exercise, you are to organize your team, set production schedules, and build the windmills. Central Office controls your budget, materials, and specifications.

Windsock Inc. has a total of 30 minutes (more if instructor assigns) to design an advertising campaign, to design the windmill, and to produce the first windmill prototypes (your group's task) for delivery. Good luck to you all.

Notes

1. Beth Kowitt, "100 Million Android Fans Can't Be Wrong," *Fortune* (June 16, 2011), http://tech.fortune.cnn.com/2011/06/16/100-million-android-fans-cant-be-wrong/ (accessed August 2, 2011); and Douglas Edwards, "Review—Google: The Beginning," *The Wall Street Journal,* July 16, 2011, C1.
2. James Q. Wilson, *Bureaucracy* (New York: Basic Books, 1989); and Charles Perrow, *Complex Organizations: A Critical Essay* (Glenview, IL: Scott, Foresman, 1979), 4.
3. Tom Peters, "Rethinking Scale," *California Management Review* (Fall 1992), 7–29.
4. "1. Wal-Mart Stores," Global 500 Snapshots, *Fortune,* http://money.cnn.com/magazines/fortune/global500/2011/snapshots/2255.html (accessed August 31, 2011); "New 2010 Census Numbers Document Houston's Trickle-In Decade," Houston's Real Estate Landscape, Swamplot.com, (February 17, 2011), http://swamplot.com/new-2010-census-numbers-document-houstons-trickle-in-decade/2011-02-17/ (accessed August 31, 2011); Adam Lashinsky, "Inside Apple," *Fortune* (May 23, 2011), 124–134; and "500 Largest U.S. Corporations," *Fortune,* (May 23, 2011), F1–F26.
5. Donald V. Potter, "Scale Matters," *Across the Board* (July–August 2000), 36–39.
6. Ashlee Vance, "Does H.P. Need a Dose of Anarchy?" *The New York Times,* April 26, 2009, BU1.
7. Kris Hudson, "Wal-Mart Sticks with Fast Pace of Expansion Despite Toll on Sales," *The Wall Street Journal,* April 13, 2006, A1.
8. Christopher Weaver, "Managed Care Enters the Exam Room as Insurers Buy Doctors Groups," *The Washington Post* (July 1, 2011), http://www.washingtonpost.com/insurers-quietly-gaining-control-of-doctors-covered-by-companies-plans/2011/06/29/AG5DNftH_story.html (accessed September 6, 2011).
9. James B. Treece, "Sometimes, You Still Gotta Have Size," *BusinessWeek* (October 22, 1993), 200–201.
10. Nelson D. Schwartz, "Is G.E. Too Big for Its Own Good?" *The New York Times,* July 22, 2007, Section 3, 1.
11. Ken Belson, "After the Disasters in Japan, a Stoic Response from Aflac," *The New York Times,* April 16, 2011, B4.
12. "Allstate Assisting Homeowners After Hurricane Irene; Allstate Brings Mobile Claims Centers to North Carolina, Maryland, Virginia, New York, New Jersey and Connecticut," *U.S. Newswire* (August 30, 2011).
13. Frits K. Pil and Matthias Holweg, "Exploring Scale: The Advantages of Thinking Small," *MIT Sloan Management Review* (Winter 2003), 33–39; and David Sadtler, "The Problem with Size," *Management Today* (November 2007), 52–55.
14. Chip Jarnagan and John W. Slocum, Jr., "Creating Corporate Cultures Through Mythopoetic Leadership," *Organizational Dynamics* 36, no. 3 (2007), 288–302; Robbie Whelan and Dawn Wotapka, "Corporate News: Home Builder Pulte to Lay Off Executives," *The Wall Street Journal,* May 13, 2011, B2.
15. See Keith H. Hammonds, "Size Is Not a Strategy," *Fast Company* (September 2002), 78–86; David Henry, "Mergers: Why Most Big Deals Don't Pay Off," *BusinessWeek* (October 14, 2002), 60–70; and Tom Brown, "How Big Is Too Big?" *Across the Board* (July–August 1999), 15–20, for a discussion.
16. "How Important Are Small Businesses to the U.S. Economy?" U.S. Small Business Administration Office of Advocacy, http://www.sba.gov/advocacy/7495/8420 (accessed August 31, 2011).
17. "The Hot 100," *Fortune* (September 5, 2005), 75–80.
18. Reported in Sadtler, "The Problem with Size."
19. Gary Hamel, quoted in Hammonds, "Size Is Not a Strategy."
20. "Our Company," Johnson & Johnson website, http://www.jnj.com/connect/about-jnj/ (accessed August 31, 2011).
21. Michael Barone, "Not a Victory for Big Government," *The Wall Street Journal,* January 15, 2002, A16.
22. Charles C. Manz, Frank Shipper, and Greg L. Steward, "Everyone a Team Leader: Shared Influence at W. L. Gore & Associates," *Organizational Dynamics* 38, no. 3 (2009), 239–244; and "About Gore," W. L Gore website, http://www.gore.com/en_xx/aboutus/ (accessed August 31, 2011).
23. Reported in Jerry Useem, "The Big...Get Bigger," *Fortune* (April 30, 2007), 81–84.
24. John R. Kimberly, Robert H. Miles, and associates, *The Organizational Life Cycle* (San Francisco: Jossey-Bass, 1980); Ichak Adices, "Organizational Passages—Diagnosing and Treating Lifecycle Problems of Organizations," *Organizational Dynamics* (Summer 1979), 3–25; Danny Miller and Peter H. Friesen, "A Longitudinal Study of the Corporate Life Cycle," *Management Science* 30 (October 1984), 1161–1183; and Neil C. Churchill and Virginia L. Lewis, "The Five Stages of Small Business Growth," *Harvard Business Review* 61 (May–June 1983), 30–50.
25. Larry E. Greiner, "Evolution and Revolution as Organizations Grow," *Harvard Business Review* 50 (July–August 1972), 37–46; and Robert E. Quinn and Kim Cameron, "Organizational Life Cycles and Shifting Criteria of Effectiveness: Some Preliminary Evidence," *Management Science* 29 (1983), 33–51.
26. George Land and Beth Jarman, "Moving beyond Breakpoint," in Michael Ray and Alan Rinzler, eds., *The New Paradigm* (New York: Jeremy P. Tarcher/Perigee Books, 1993), 250–266; and Michael L. Tushman, William H. Newman, and Elaine Romanelli, "Convergence and Upheaval: Managing the Unsteady Pace of Organizational Evolution," *California Management Review* 29 (1987), 1–16.
27. Sam Gustin, "The Next Tech Titan? 10 Hottest Technology Start-Ups of 2010," DailyFinance.com (August 12, 2010), http://www.dailyfinance.com/2010/08/12/the-next-tech-tian-10-hottest-technology-start-ups-of-2010/ (accessed September 1, 2011); and "About Foursquare," https://foursquare.com/about (accessed September 1, 2011).
28. Eve Yen, "Delegate Smart," *Fortune Small Business* (April 2009), 33–34.
29. David A. Whetten, "Sources, Responses, and Effects of Organizational Decline," in Kimberly, Miles, and Associates, *The Organizational Life Cycle*, 342–374.
30. Peter Burrows, "Opening Remarks; The Essence of Apple," *Bloomberg Businessweek* (January 24–January 30, 2011), 6–8; Brent Schlender, "How Big Can Apple Get?" *Fortune* (February 21, 2005), 67–76; and Josh Quittner with Rebecca

Winters, "Apple's New Core—Exclusive: How Steve Jobs Made a Sleek Machine That Could Be the Home-Digital Hub of the Future," *Time* (January 14, 2002), 46.

31. Nick Wingfield, "Apple's No. 2 Has Low Profile, High Impact," *The Wall Street Journal,* October 16, 2006, B1, B9; Garrett Sloane, "Apple Gets Cored; End of an Era as Legend Steve Jobs Resigns," *The New York Post,* August 25, 2011, 27.
32. Land and Jarman, "Moving beyond Breakpoint."
33. Vauhini Vara, "Facebook CEO Seeks Help as Site Grows—Google Veteran to Be Zuckerberg's No. 2," *The Wall Street Journal,* March 5, 2008, A1; Robert A. Guth and Jessica E. Vascellaro, "At Facebook, Departures Seen as Part of Evolution," *The Wall Street Journal,* October 6, 2008, B1; Jon Swartz, "Facebook Says Membership Has Grown to 750 Million," *USA Today* (July 6, 2011), http://www.usatoday.com/tech/news/2011-07-06-facebook-skype-growth_n.htm (accessed September 5, 2011); and Mike Swift, "Facebook Reveals Plans for Second Campus in Menlo Park," MercuryNews.com (August 22, 2011), http://www.mercurynews.com/ci_18734322 (accessed September 5, 2011).
34. Max Weber, *The Theory of Social and Economic Organizations,* translated by A. M. Henderson and T. Parsons (New York: Free Press, 1947).
35. Larry Rohter and Juan Forero, "Unending Graft Is Threatening Latin America," *The New York Times,* July 30, 2005, A1.
36. Barry Kramer, "Chinese Officials Still Give Preference to Kin, Despite Peking Policies," *The Wall Street Journal,* October 29, 1985, 1, 21.
37. John Chase, "Delay Requested for Indictment; 3 More Months Sought in Case against Governor," *The Chicago Tribune,* January 1, 2009, 4.
38. Eric J. Walton, "The Persistence of Bureaucracy: A Meta-Analysis of Weber's Model of Bureaucratic Control," *Organization Studies* 26, no. 4 (2005), 569–600.
39. Nadira A. Hira, "The Making of a UPS Driver," *Fortune* (November 12, 2007), 118–129; "Logistics: Squeezing More Green Out of Brown," *Bloomberg Businessweek* (September 20–September 26, 2010), 43; David J. Lynch, "Thanks to Its CEO, UPS Doesn't Just Deliver," *USA Today,* July 24, 2006, http://www.usatoday.com/money/companies/management/2006-07-23-ups_x.htm?tab1=t2 (accessed July 24, 2006); Kelly Barron, "Logistics in Brown," *Forbes* (January 10, 2000), 78–83; Scott Kirsner, "Venture Vèritè: United Parcel Service," *Wired* (September 1999), 83–96; Kathy Goode, Betty Hahn, and Cindy Seibert, *United Parcel Service: The Brown Giant* (unpublished manuscript, Texas A&M University, 1981); and "About UPS," UPS corporate website, http://www.ups.com/content/ corp/about/index.html?WT.svl=SubNav (accessed October 27, 2008).
40. See Allen C. Bluedorn, "Pilgrim's Progress: Trends and Convergence in Research on Organizational Size and Environment," *Journal of Management Studies* 19 (Summer 1993), 163–191; John R. Kimberly, "Organizational Size and the Structuralist Perspective: A Review, Critique, and Proposal," *Administrative Science Quarterly* (1976), 571–597; and Richard L. Daft and Selwyn W. Becker, "Managerial, Institutional, and Technical Influences on Administration: A Longitudinal Analysis," *Social Forces* 59 (1980), 392–413.
41. James P. Walsh and Robert D. Dewar, "Formalization and the Organizational Life Cycle," *Journal of Management Studies* 24 (May 1987), 215–231.
42. Nancy M. Carter and Thomas L. Keon, "Specialization as a Multidimensional Construct," *Journal of Management Studies* 26 (1989), 11–28; Cheng-Kuang Hsu, Robert M. March, and Hiroshi Mannari, "An Examination of the Determinants of Organizational Structure," *American Journal of Sociology* 88 (1983), 975–996; Guy Geeraerts, "The Effect of Ownership on the Organization Structure in Small Firms," *Administrative Science Quarterly* 29 (1984), 232–237; Bernard Reimann, "On the Dimensions of Bureaucratic Structure: An Empirical Reappraisal," *Administrative Science Quarterly* 18 (1973), 462–476; Richard H. Hall, "The Concept of Bureaucracy: An Empirical Assessment," *American Journal of Sociology* 69 (1963), 32–40; and William A. Rushing, "Organizational Rules and Surveillance: A Proposition in Comparative Organizational Analysis," *Administrative Science Quarterly* 10 (1966), 423–443.
43. Jerald Hage and Michael Aiken, "Relationship of Centralization to Other Structural Properties," *Administrative Science Quarterly* 12 (1967), 72–91.
44. Peter Brimelow, "How Do You Cure Injelitance?" *Forbes* (August 7, 1989), 42–44; Jeffrey D. Ford and John W. Slocum, Jr., "Size, Technology, Environment and the Structure of Organizations," *Academy of Management Review* 2 (1977), 561–575; and John D. Kasarda, "The Structural Implications of Social System Size: A Three-Level Analysis," *American Sociological Review* 39 (1974), 19–28.
45. Graham Astley, "Organizational Size and Bureaucratic Structure," *Organization Studies* 6 (1985), 201–228; Spyros K. Lioukas and Demitris A. Xerokostas, "Size and Administrative Intensity in Organizational Divisions," *Management Science* 28 (1982), 854–868; Peter M. Blau, "Interdependence and Hierarchy in Organizations," *Social Science Research* 1 (1972), 1–24; Peter M. Blau and R. A. Schoenherr, *The Structure of Organizations* (New York: Basic Books, 1971); A. Hawley, W. Boland, and M. Boland, "Population Size and Administration in Institutions of Higher Education," *American Sociological Review* 30 (1965), 252–255; Richard L. Daft, "System Influence on Organization Decision-Making: The Case of Resource Allocation," *Academy of Management Journal* 21 (1978), 6–22; and B. P. Indik, "The Relationship between Organization Size and the Supervisory Ratio," *Administrative Science Quarterly* 9 (1964), 301–312.
46. T. F. James, "The Administrative Component in Complex Organizations," *Sociological Quarterly* 13 (1972), 533–539; Daft, "System Influence on Organization Decision-Making: The Case of Resource Allocation"; E. A. Holdaway and E. A. Blowers, "Administrative Ratios and Organization Size: A Longitudinal Examination," *American Sociological Review* 36 (1971), 278–286; and John Child, "Parkinson's Progress: Accounting for the Number of Specialists in Organizations," *Administrative Science Quarterly* 18 (1973), 328–348.
47. Richard L. Daft and Selwyn Becker, "School District Size and the Development of Personnel Resources," *Alberta Journal of Educational Research* 24 (1978), 173–187.
48. Based on Gifford and Elizabeth Pinchot, *The End of Bureaucracy and the Rise of the Intelligent Organization* (San Francisco: Berrett-Koehler Publishers, 1993), 21–29.
49. Victoria Murphy, "Microsoft's Midlife Crisis," *Forbes* (October 3, 2005), 88.
50. Ron Ashkenas, "Simplicity-Minded Management," *Harvard Business Review* (December 2007), 101–109.

51. Jonathan Weisman, "In a Savings Shocker, the Government Discovers that Paper Has Two Sides," *The Wall Street Journal,* July 29, 2009, A1.
52. Study by Paul C. Light, reported in Paul C. Light, "The Easy Way Washington Could Save $1 Trillion; How an Independent Agency Could Squeeze $1 Trillion in Savings from the Bureaucracy," *The Wall Street Journal* (July 7, 2011), http://online.wsj.com/article/SB10001424052702304760604576428262419935394.html (accessed September 6, 2011).
53. Jack Rosenthal, "Entitled: A Chief for Every Occasion, and Even a Chief Chief," *New York Times Magazine* (August 26, 2001), 16.
54. Scott Shane, "The Beast That Feeds on Boxes: Bureaucracy," *The New York Times,* April 10, 2005, Section 4, 3.
55. Gregory A. Bigley and Karlene H. Roberts, "The Incident Command System: High-Reliability Organizing for Complex and Volatile Task Environments," *Academy of Management Journal* 44, no. 6 (2001), 1281–1299.
56. Robert A. Watson and Ben Brown, *The Most Effective Organization in the U.S.: Leadership Secrets of the Salvation Army* (New York: Crown Business, 2001), 159–181.
57. Julian Birkinshaw and Suzanne Heywood, "Putting Organizational Complexity in Its Place," *McKinsey Quarterly*, Issue 3 (2010), 122–127.
58. Amir Efrati, "At Google, Page Aims to Clear Red Tape," *The Wall Street Journal,* March 26, 2011, B1; and Jessica Guynn, "New CEO Stirs Up Google Ranks; Larry Page Promotes Seven Execs to Run the Company's Most Important Divisions," *Los Angeles Times,* April 9, 2011, B1.
59. Birkinshaw and Heywood, "Putting Organizational Complexity in Its Place."
60. Jeanne Whalen, "Bureaucracy Buster? Glaxo Lets Scientists Choose Its New Drugs," *The Wall Street Journal,* March 27, 2006, B1.
61. Philip M. Padsakoff, Larry J. Williams, and William D. Todor, "Effects of Organizational Formalization on Alienation among Professionals and Nonprofessionals," *Academy of Management Journal* 29 (1986), 820–831.
62. Royston Greenwood, C. R. Hinings, and John Brown, "'P2-Form' Strategic Management: Corporate Practices in Professional Partnerships," *Academy of Management Journal* 33 (1990), 725–755; and Royston Greenwood and C. R. Hinings, "Understanding Strategic Change: The Contribution of Archetypes," *Academy of Management Journal* 36 (1993), 1052–1081.
63. William G. Ouchi, "Markets, Bureaucracies, and Clans," *Administrative Science Quarterly* 25 (1980), 129–141; idem, "A Conceptual Framework for the Design of Organizational Control Mechanisms," *Management Science* 25 (1979), 833–848; and Jay B. Barney, "An Interview with William Ouchi," *Academy of Management Executive* 18, no. 4 (November 2004), 108–116.
64. Weber, *The Theory of Social and Economic Organizations,* 328–340.
65. Daisuke Wakabayashi and Toko Sekiguchi, "Disaster in Japan: Evacuees Set Rules to Create Sense of Normalcy," *The Wall Street Journal,* March 26, 2011, A8; and Chester Dawson and Yoshio Takahashi, "A Year Later, Toyota Quietly Tackles Quality," *The Wall Street Journal,* February 23, 2011, B2.
66. Joel Spolsky, "Good System, Bad System; Starbucks' Meticulous Policy Manual Shows Employees How to Optimize Profits. Too Bad It Undercuts Basic Customer Service," *Inc.* (August 2008), 67.
67. Oliver A. Williamson, *Markets and Hierarchies: Analyses and Antitrust Implications* (New York: Free Press, 1975).
68. David Wessel and John Harwood, "Capitalism Is Giddy with Triumph: Is It Possible to Overdo It?" *The Wall Street Journal,* May 14, 1998, A1, A10.
69. Anita Micossi, "Creating Internal Markets," *Enterprise* (April 1994), 43–44.
70. Raymond E. Miles, Henry J. Coleman, Jr., and W. E. Douglas Creed, "Keys to Success in Corporate Redesign," *California Management Review* 37, no. 3 (Spring 1995), 128–145.
71. Ouchi, "Markets, Bureaucracies, and Clans."
72. Jeffrey Kerr and John W. Slocum, Jr., "Managing Corporate Culture Through Reward Systems," *Academy of Management Executive* 19, no. 4 (2005), 130–138.
73. Richard Leifer and Peter K. Mills, "An Information Processing Approach for Deciding upon Control Strategies and Reducing Control Loss in Emerging Organizations," *Journal of Management* 22, no. 1 (1996), 113–137.
74. Stratford Sherman, "The New Computer Revolution," *Fortune* (June 14, 1993), 56–80.
75. Leifer and Mills, "An Information Processing Approach for Deciding upon Control Strategies"; and Laurie J. Kirsch, "The Management of Complex Tasks in Organizations: Controlling the Systems Development Process," *Organization Science* 7, no. 1 (January–February 1996), 1–21.
76. James R. Barker, "Tightening the Iron Cage: Concertive Control in Self-Managing Teams," *Administrative Science Quarterly* 38 (1993), 408–437.
77. Lee Hawkins Jr., "Lost in Transmission—Behind GM's Slide: Bosses Misjudged New Urban Tastes; Local Dealers, Managers Tried Alerting Staid Bureaucracy," *The Wall Street Journal,* March 8, 2006, A1.
78. Claudia H. Deutsch, "In 2007, Some Giants Went Smaller," *The New York Times,* January 1, 2008, C1; Clair Cain Miller, "A Changed Starbucks. A Changed C.E.O.," *The New York Times,* March 13, 2011, BU1.
79. Deepak K. Datta, James P. Guthrie, Dynah Basuil, and Alankrita Pandey, "Causes and Effects of Employee Downsizing: A Review and Synthesis," *Journal of Management* 36, no. 1 (January 2010), 281–348; Jack Healy, "Big Companies Around Globe Lay Off Tens of Thousands," *The New York Times,* January 27, 2009; Kevin Sack, "A City's Wrenching Budget Choices," *The New York Times,* July 4, 2011; Tamar Lewin, For Colleges, Small Cutbacks Are Adding Up to Big Savings," *The New York Times,* June 19, 2009, A19.
80. Kim S. Cameron, Myung Kim, and David A. Whetten, "Organizational Effects of Decline and Turbulence," *Administrative Science Quarterly* 32 (1987), 222–240.
81. Danny Miller, "What Happens after Success: The Perils of Excellence," *Journal of Management Studies* 31, no. 3 (May 1994), 325–358.
82. Leonard Greenhalgh, "Organizational Decline," in Samuel B. Bacharach, ed., *Research in the Sociology of Organizations* 2 (Greenwich, CT: JAI Press, 1983), 231–276; and Peter Lorange and Robert T. Nelson, "How to Recognize—and Avoid—Organizational Decline," *Sloan Management Review* (Spring 1987), 41–48.
83. Kim S. Cameron and Raymond Zammuto, "Matching Managerial Strategies to Conditions of Decline," *Human Resources Management* 22 (1983), 359–375; and Leonard Greenhalgh, Anne T. Lawrence, and Robert I. Sutton, "Determinants of

Workforce Reduction Strategies in Organizations," *Academy of Management Review* 13 (1988), 241–254.
84. Stephanie Strom, "Short on Fund-Raising, Red Cross Will Cut Jobs," *The New York Times,* January 16, 2008, A15.
85. Timothy Aeppel, "Die Is Cast; Toolmakers Know Precisely What's the Problem: Price," *The Wall Street Journal,* November 21, 2003, A1, A6; "NTMA Urges Congress to Level the Playing Field for U.S. Manufacturers," National Tooling and Machining Association press release (June 21, 2007), https://www.ntma.org/eweb/Dynamicpage.aspx?webcode=PRTemplate&wps_key=17e03068-0ad9-4ef5-ae50-779610c5f025&post_year=2007&post_month_name=Jun (accessed October 29, 2008).
86. Nathan Bomey, "Timeline: From the Founding of Borders in Ann Arbor to Chapter 11 Bankruptcy," *AnnArbor.com* (February 16, 2011), http://www.annarbor.com/business-review/timeline-of-borders-groups-decline/ (accessed September 8, 2011); Mike Spector and Jeffrey A. Trachtenberg, "Borders Succumbs to Digital Era in Books," *The Wall Street Journal* (July 20, 2011), http://online.wsj.com/article/SB10001424052702304567604576456430727129532.html (accessed September 8, 2011); Julie Bosman, "Struggling Borders to Meet with Publishers," *The New York Times,* January 4, 2011, B2; and Jeffrey A. Trachtenberg, "Borders Business Plan Gets a Rewrite; It Will Reopen Web Site, Give Up Most Stores Abroad, Close Many Waldenbooks," *The Wall Street Journal*, March 22, 2007, B1. Book sales data from Albert N. Greco, Institute for Publishing Research, reported in Spector and Trachtenberg, "Borders Succumbs to Digital Era in Books."
87. William Weitzel and Ellen Jonsson, "Reversing the Downward Spiral: Lessons from W. T. Grant and Sears Roebuck," *Academy of Management Executive* 5 (1991), 7–21; and William Weitzel and Ellen Jonsson, "Decline in Organizations: A Literature Integration and Extension," *Administrative Science Quarterly* 34 (1989), 91–109.
88. "Bookseller Borders Group Inc. Explores a Sale," *Capital,* March 23, 2008, B2.
89. Datta et al., "Causes and Effects of Employee Downsizing"; and William McKinley, Carol M. Sanchez, and Allen G. Schick, "Organizational Downsizing: Constraining, Cloning, Learning," *Academy of Management Executive* 9, no. 3 (1995), 32–42.
90. Datta et al., "Causes and Effects of Employee Downsizing"; Gregory B. Northcraft and Margaret A. Neale, *Organizational Behavior: A Management Challenge*, 2nd ed. (Fort Worth, TX: The Dryden Press, 1994), 626; and A. Catherine Higgs, "Executive Commentary" on McKinley, Sanchez, and Schick, "Organizational Downsizing: Constraining, Cloning, Learning," *Academy of Management Executive* 9, no. 3 (1995), 43–44.
91. Wayne Cascio, "Use and Management of Downsizing as a Corporate Strategy," Society for Human Resource Management Foundation (2009), http://www.shrm.org/about/foundation/products/Documents/609%20Exec%20Briefing-%20Downsizing%20FINAL.pdf (accessed September 8, 2011); Wayne Cascio, "Strategies for Responsible Restructuring," *Academy of Management Executive* 16, no. 3 (2002), 80–91; James R. Morris, Wayne F. Cascio, and Clifford E. Young, "Downsizing after All These Years: Questions and Answers about Who Did It, How Many Did It, and Who Benefited from It," *Organizational Dynamics* (Winter 1999), 78–86; Brett C. Luthans and Steven M. Sommer, "The Impact of Downsizing on Workplace Attitudes," *Group and Organization Management* 2, no. 1 (1999), 46–70; and Pat Galagan, "The Biggest Losers: The Perils of Extreme Downsizing," *T+D* (November 2010), 27–29.
92. Scott Thurm, "Recalculating the Cost of Big Layoffs," *The Wall Street Journal,* May 5, 2010, B1.
93. These techniques are based on Cascio, "Use and Management of Downsizing as a Corporate Strategy"; Mitchell Lee Marks and Kenneth P. De Meuse, "Resizing the Organization: Maximizing the Gain While Minimizing the Pain of Layoffs, Divestitures, and Closings," *Organizational Dynamics* 34, no. 2 (2005), 19–35; Bob Nelson, "The Care of the Un-Downsized," *Training and Development* (April 1997), 40–43; Joel Brockner, "Managing the Effects of Layoffs on Survivors," *California Management Review* (Winter 1992), 9–28; Kim S. Cameron, "Strategies for Successful Organizational Downsizing," *Human Resource Management* 33, no. 2 (Summer 1994), 189–211; and Stephen Doerflein and James Atsaides, "Corporate Psychology: Making Downsizing Work," *Electrical World* (September–October 1999), 41–43.
94. Thurm, "Recalculating the Cost of Big Layoffs"; Steven Greenhouse, "To Avoid Layoffs, Some Companies Turn to Work-Sharing," http://www.nytimes.com/2009/06/16/business/economy/16workshare.html?pagewanted=all (accessed September 8, 2011); Kathleen Madigan, "More Firms Cut Pay to Save Jobs," *The Wall Street Journal,* June 9, 2009, A4; and Cascio, "Use and Management of Downsizing as a Corporate Strategy."
95. Matt Murray, "Stress Mounts as More Firms Announce Large Layoffs, But Don't Say Who or When" (Your Career Matters column), *The Wall Street Journal,* March 13, 2001, B1, B12.
96. Ebay example reported in Cascio, "Use and Management of Downsizing as a Corporate Strategy."
97. Joann S. Lublin, "Theory & Practice: Employers See Value in Helping Those Laid Off; Some Firms Continue Access to Programs That Assist Workers," *The Wall Street Journal,* September 24, 2007, B3.
98. Marks and De Meuse, "Resizing the Organization"; Jeanenne LaMarch, "How Companies Reduce the Downside of Downsizing," *Global Business and Organizational Excellence* 29, no. 1 (November–December 2009), 7–16; and Cascio, "Use and Management of Downsizing as a Corporate Strategy."
99. Matt Villano, "Career Couch: Dealing with Low Morale after Others Are Laid Off," *The New York Times,* July 29, 2007, BU17.
100. Copyright 1996 Dorothy Marcic. All Rights reserved.
101. This case was inspired by "Frito-Lay May Find Itself in a Competition Crunch," *BusinessWeek* (July 19, 1982), 186; Jim Bohman, "Mike-Sells Works to Remain on Snack Map," *Dayton Daily News,* February 27, 2005, D1; "Dashman Company" in Paul R. Lawrence and John A. Seiler, *Organizational Behavior and Administration: Cases, Concepts, and Research Findings* (Homewood, IL: Irwin and Dorsey, 1965), 16–17; and Laurie M. Grossman, "Price Wars Bring Flavor to Once Quiet Snack Market," *The Wall Street Journal,* May 23, 1991, B1, B3.
102. Adapted by Dorothy Marcic from Christopher Taylor and Saundra Taylor in "Teaching Organizational Team-Building through Simulations," *Organizational Behavior Teaching Review* XI (3), 86–87.

Chapter 13

©Pawel Gaul

Workplace Technology and Design

Learning Objectives

After reading this chapter you should be able to:

1. Identify and define an organization's core technology.
2. Explain the impact of core technology on organization design.
3. Describe Woodward's model of technical complexity, structure, and performance.
4. Understand lean manufacturing and the digital factory.
5. Describe the nature of service technology and its impact on organization design.
6. Recognize departmental technology and its relationship to department design.
7. Identify three types of interdependence and the respective structural priority.
8. Understand job design and sociotechnical systems.

Before reading this chapter, please check whether you agree or disagree with each of the following statements:

1 **Lean manufacturing is a super-efficient form of manufacturing that produces products of top quality.**

I AGREE _____ I DISAGREE _____

2 **The best way for a company to provide good service is to have abundant and clear rules and procedures and make sure everyone follows them to the letter.**

I AGREE _____ I DISAGREE _____

3 **The design characteristics and management processes that are effective for a television station's sales department probably would not work so well for the news department.**

I AGREE _____ I DISAGREE _____

An auto parts factory sends engineers around the world to learn about new production methods. A team of airline employees studies the pit stop techniques used by NASCAR racing crews. A small clothing manufacturer in New York invests in a computerized German-made knitting machine. What do all these organizations have in common? They are looking for ways to provide goods and services more efficiently and effectively.

For many manufacturers in the United States, it's a do-or-die situation. Manufacturing has been on the decline in the United States and other developed countries for years. The service sector has increased three times as fast as the manufacturing sector in the North American economy. However, some manufacturing companies are applying new technology to gain a new competitive edge. By integrating computerized production equipment and sophisticated information systems, for example, American Axle & Manufacturing (AAM) dramatically improved efficiency and productivity to the point where it began winning contracts to make components in Detroit that a competitor had previously been making in China.[1] Service companies also need to keep pace with changing technology and continually strive for better approaches. Many service firms are fighting for their lives as global competition intensifies, and the cost of ineffective or outdated technology and procedures can be organizational decline and failure.

This chapter explores both service and manufacturing technologies. **Technology** refers to the work processes, techniques, machines, and actions used to transform organizational inputs (materials, information, ideas) into outputs (products and services).[2] Technology is an organization's production process and includes work procedures as well as machinery.

One important theme in this chapter is how core technology influences organization design. Understanding core technology provides insight into how an organization can be designed for efficient performance.[3] An organization's **core technology**

EXHIBIT 13.1
Core Transformation Process for a Manufacturing Company

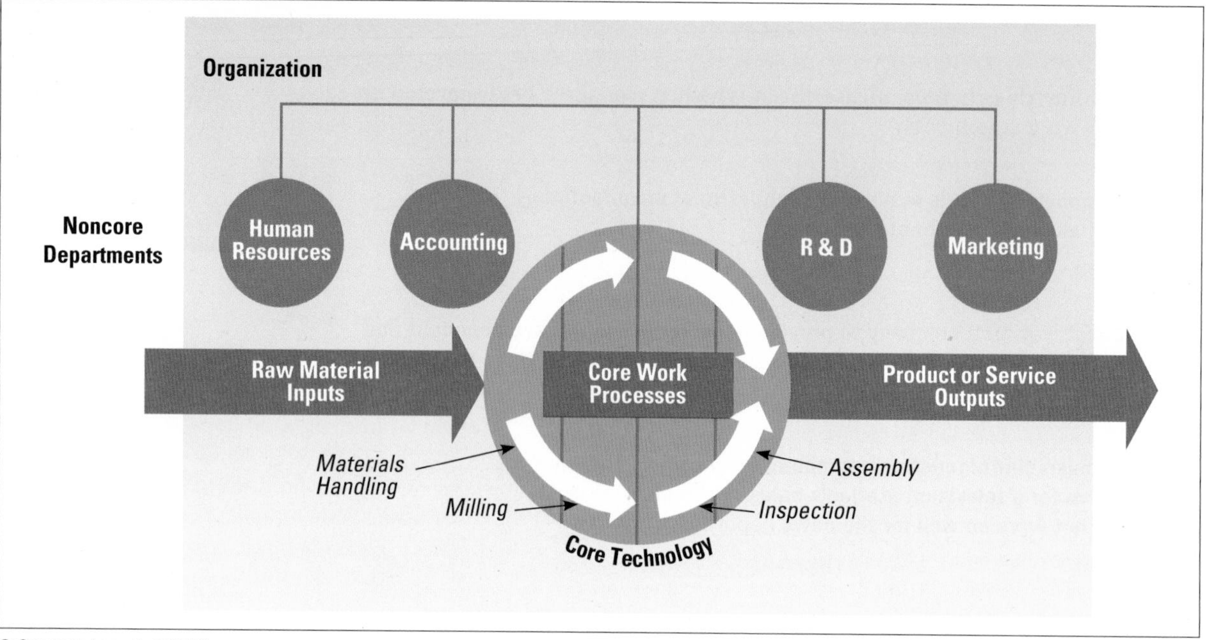

is the work process that is directly related to the organization's mission, such as teaching in a high school, medical services in a health clinic, or manufacturing at AAM. At AAM, the core technology begins with raw materials (e.g., steel, aluminum, and composite metals). Employees take action on the raw material to make a change in it (e.g., they cut and forge metals and assemble parts), thus transforming the raw material into the output of the organization (e.g., axles, drive shafts, crankshafts, and transmission parts). For a service organization like UPS, the core technology includes the production equipment (e.g., sorting machines, package handling equipment, trucks, and airplanes) and procedures for delivering packages and overnight mail. In addition, as at companies like UPS and AAM, computers and information technology have revolutionized work processes in both manufacturing and service organizations. The specific impact of new information technology on organizations was described in Chapter 11.

Exhibit 13.1 features an example of core technology for a manufacturing plant. Note how the core technology consists of raw material inputs, a transformation work process (e.g., milling, inspection, assembly) that changes and adds value to the raw material and produces the ultimate product or service output that is sold to consumers in the environment. In today's large, complex organizations, core work processes vary widely and sometimes can be hard to pinpoint. A core technology can be partly understood by examining the raw materials flowing into the organization,[4] the variability of work activities,[5] the degree to which the production process is mechanized,[6] the extent to which one task depends on another in the workflow,[7] or the number of new product or service outputs.[8]

Organizations are also made up of many departments, each of which may use a different work process (technology) to provide a good or service within the organization.

A **noncore technology** is a department work process that is important to the organization but is not directly related to its primary mission. In Exhibit 13.1, noncore work processes are illustrated by the departments of human resources (HR), accounting, research and development (R&D), and marketing. Thus, R&D transforms ideas into new products, and marketing transforms inventory into sales, each using a somewhat different work process. The output of the HR department is people to work in the organization, and accounting produces accurate statements about the organization's financial condition.

Purpose of This Chapter

In this chapter, we discuss both core and noncore work processes and their relationship to organization design. The nature of the organization's work processes must be considered in designing the organization for maximum efficiency and effectiveness. The optimum organization design is based on a variety of elements. Exhibit 13.2 illustrates that forces affecting organization design come from both outside and inside the organization. External strategic needs, such as environmental conditions, strategic direction, and organizational goals, create top-down pressure for designing the organization in such a way as to fit the environment and accomplish goals. These pressures on design have been discussed in previous chapters. However, decisions about design should also take into consideration pressures from the bottom up—from the work processes that are performed to produce the organization's products or services. The operational work processes will influence the structural design associated with both the core technology and noncore departments. Thus, the subject with which this chapter is concerned is, "How should the organization be designed to accommodate and facilitate its operational work processes?"

The remainder of the chapter will unfold as follows. First, we examine how the technology for the organization as a whole influences organization structure

EXHIBIT 13.2
Pressures Affecting Organization Design

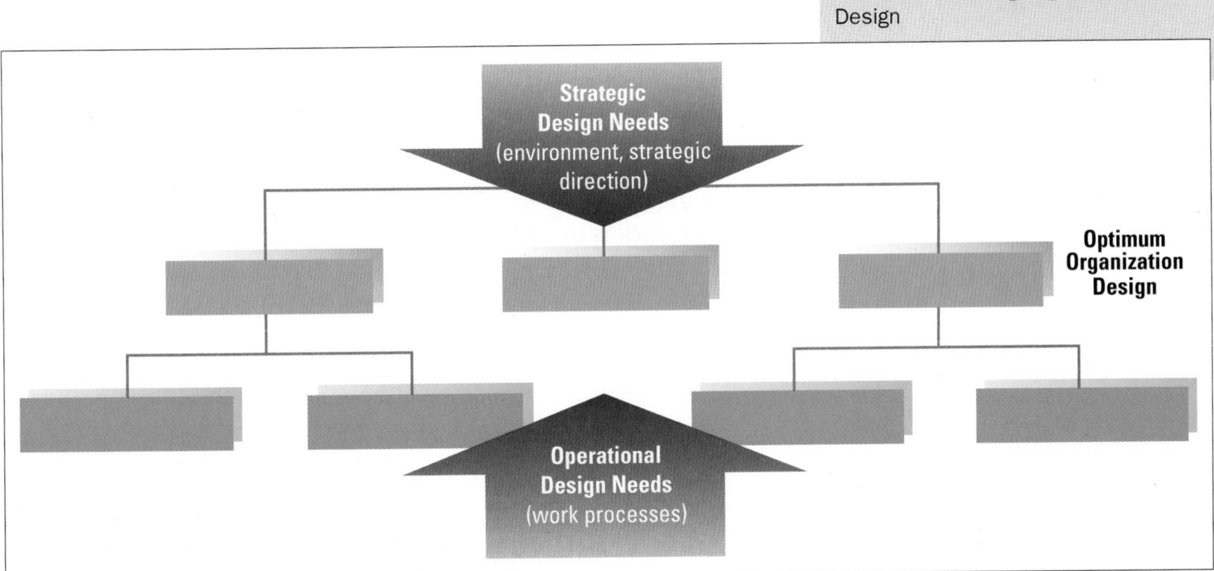

Source: Based on David A. Nadler and Michael L. Tushman, with Mark B. Nadler, *Competing by Design: The Power of Organizational Architecture* (New York: Oxford University Press, 1997), 54.

and design. This discussion includes both manufacturing and service technologies. Next, we examine differences in departmental technologies and how the technologies influence the design and management of organizational subunits. Third, we explore how interdependence—flow of materials and information—among departments affects organization design.

Core Organization Manufacturing Technology

Manufacturing technologies include traditional manufacturing processes and contemporary applications, such as the digital factory and lean manufacturing.

Manufacturing Firms

The first and most influential study of manufacturing technology was conducted by Joan Woodward, a British industrial sociologist. Her research began as a field study of management principles in south Essex. The prevailing management wisdom at the time (1950s) was contained in what were known as universal principles of management. These principles were "one best way" prescriptions that effective organizations were expected to adopt. Woodward surveyed 100 manufacturing firms firsthand to learn how they were organized.[9] She and her research team visited each firm, interviewed managers, examined company records, and observed the manufacturing operations. Her data included a wide range of structural characteristics (e.g., span of control, levels of management), dimensions of management style (e.g., written versus verbal communications, use of rewards), and the type of manufacturing process. She also collected data that reflected the commercial success of the firms.

BRIEFCASE

As an organization manager, keep these guidelines in mind:

Use the categories developed by Woodward to diagnose whether the production technology in a manufacturing firm is small batch, mass production, or continuous process. Use a more organic structure with small-batch or continuous-process technologies and with digital manufacturing systems. Use a mechanistic structure with mass-production technologies.

Woodward developed a scale and organized the firms according to the technical complexity of the manufacturing process. **Technical complexity** represents the extent of mechanization of the manufacturing process. High technical complexity means most of the work is performed by machines. Low technical complexity means workers play a larger role in the production process. Woodward's scale of technical complexity originally had 10 categories, as summarized in Exhibit 13.3. These categories were further consolidated into three basic technology groups, as follows:

- *Group I: Small-batch and unit production.* These firms tend to be job shop operations that manufacture and assemble small orders to meet specific needs of customers. Custom work is the norm. **Small-batch production** relies heavily on the human operator; it is thus not highly mechanized. One example of small-batch production is Hermes International's Kelly handbag, named for the late actress Grace Kelly. Craftsmen stitch the majority of each $7,000 bag by hand and sign it when they finish.[10] Another example comes from Rockwell Collins, which makes electronic equipment for airplanes. Although sophisticated computerized machinery is used for part of the production process, final assembly requires highly skilled human operators to ensure absolute reliability of products used by aerospace companies, defense contractors, and the U.S. military. The company's workforce is divided into manufacturing cells, some of which produce only ten units a day. In one plant, 140 workers build Joint Tactical Information Distribution Systems, for managing battlefield communications from a circling plane, at a rate of 10 a month.[11]

EXHIBIT 13.3
Woodward's Classification of 100 British Firms According to Their Systems of Production

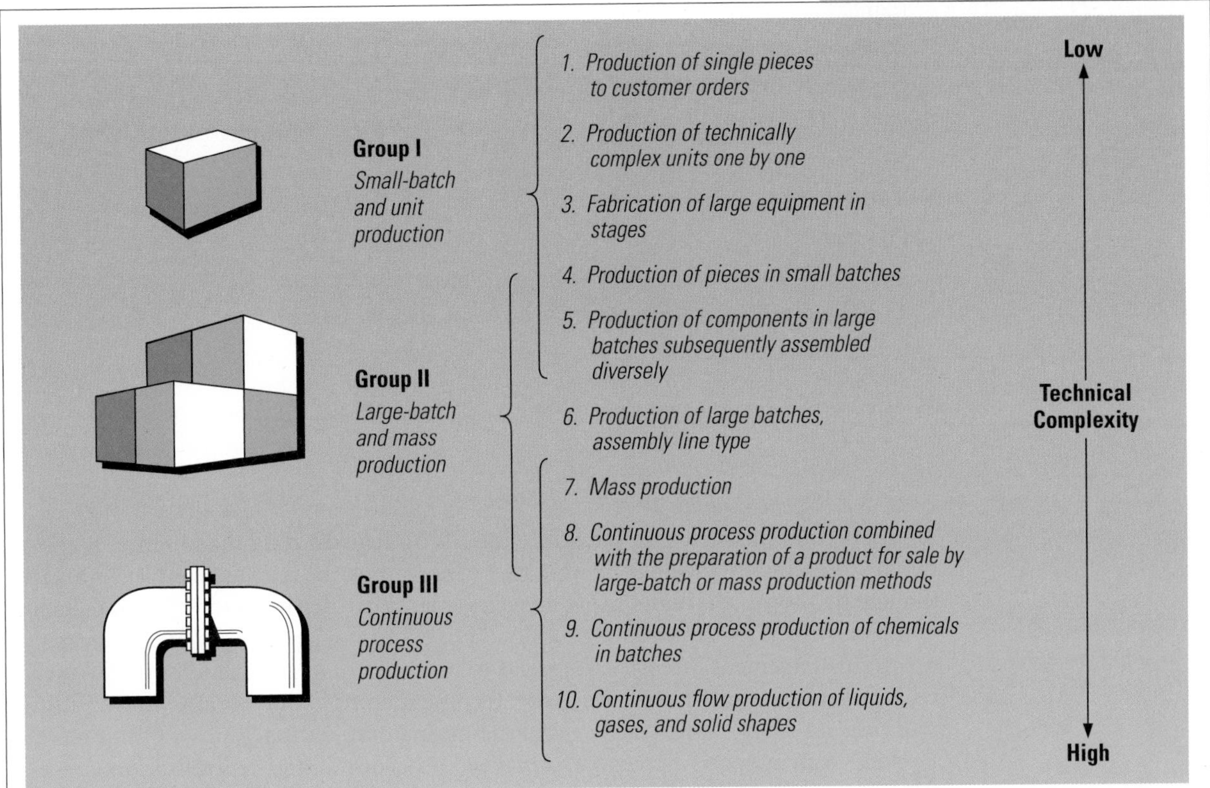

Source: Adapted from Joan Woodward, *Management and Technology* (London: Her Majesty's Stationery Office, 1958). Used with permission of Her Britannic Majesty's Stationery Office.

- *Group II: Large-batch and mass production.* **Large-batch production** is a manufacturing process characterized by long production runs of standardized parts. Output often goes into inventory from which orders are filled because customers do not have special needs. Examples include traditional assembly lines, such as for automobiles.
- *Group III: Continuous-process production.* In **continuous-process production**, the entire process is mechanized. There is no starting and stopping. This represents mechanization and standardization one step beyond those in an assembly line. Automated machines control the continuous process, and outcomes are highly predictable. Examples would include chemical plants, oil refineries, liquor producers, pharmaceuticals, and nuclear power plants. Royal Dutch Shell's new "Pearl GTL" (gas-to-liquid) plant in Qatar, scheduled to begin operation in late 2011, provides an illustration. At the new processing facility, natural gas flows through a maze of pipes, storage tanks, gasification units, distillers, reactors, and other equipment, while highly skilled employees monitor operations from a central control room. GTL uses chemical processes to physically change the composition of gas molecules to produce a colorless, odorless fuel similar to diesel but without diesel's pollutants.[12]

EXHIBIT 13.4
Relationship between Technical Complexity and Structural Characteristics

Structural Characteristic	Technology: Unit Production	Mass Production	Continuous Process
Number of management levels	3	4	6
Supervisor span of control	23	48	15
Direct/indirect labor ratio	9:1	4:1	1:1
Manager/total personnel ratio	Low	Medium	High
Workers' skill level	High	Low	High
Formalized procedures	Low	High	Low
Centralization	Low	High	Low
Amount of verbal communication	High	Low	High
Amount of written communication	Low	High	Low
Overall structure	Organic	Mechanistic	Organic

Based on: Management and Technology by Joan Woodward, (London: Her Majestys Stationery Office, 1958).

Using this classification of technology, Woodward's data made sense. A few of her key findings are given in Exhibit 13.4. The number of management levels and the manager-to-total personnel ratio, for example, show definite increases as technical complexity increases from unit production to continuous process. This indicates that greater management intensity is needed to manage complex technology. The direct-to-indirect labor ratio decreases with technical complexity because more indirect workers are required to support and maintain complex machinery. Other characteristics, such as span of control, formalized procedures, and centralization, are high for mass-production technology because the work is standardized, but low for other technologies. Unit (small batch) production and continuous-process technologies require highly skilled workers to run the machines and verbal communication to adapt to changing conditions. Mass production is standardized and routinized, so few exceptions occur, little verbal communication is needed, and employees are less skilled.

Overall, the structure and management systems in both unit production and continuous-process technology are characterized as organic, as defined in Chapters 1 and 6. They are more free-flowing and adaptive, with fewer formal procedures and less standardization. Mass production, however, is mechanistic, with standardized jobs and formalized procedures. Woodward's discovery about technology thus provided substantial new insight into the causes of organization structure. In Joan Woodward's own words, "Different technologies impose different kinds of demands on individuals and organizations, and those demands had to be met through an appropriate structure."[13]

Strategy, Technology, and Performance

Another portion of Woodward's study examined the success of the firms along dimensions such as profitability, market share, stock price, and reputation. As indicated in Chapter 3, the measurement of effectiveness is not simple or precise, but Woodward was able to rank firms on a scale of commercial success according to whether they displayed above-average, average, or below-average performance on strategic objectives.

Woodward compared the structure-technology relationship against commercial success and discovered that successful firms tended to be those that had complementary structures and technologies. Many of the organizational characteristics of the successful firms were near the average of their technology category, as shown in Exhibit 13.4. Below-average firms tended to depart from the structural characteristics for their technology type. Another conclusion was that structural characteristics could be interpreted as clustering into organic and mechanistic management systems, as defined in Chapters 1 and 6. Successful small-batch and continuous process organizations had organic designs, and successful mass-production organizations had mechanistic designs. Subsequent research has replicated her findings.[14]

What this illustrates for today's companies is that strategy, structure, and technology need to be aligned, especially when competitive conditions change.[15] For example, some years ago when Dell created a business model to build personal computers faster and cheaper, other computer manufacturers had to realign strategy, structure, and technology to stay competitive. Dell made PCs to order for each customer and sold most of them directly to consumers without the expense of distributors or retailers. Manufacturers such as IBM that once tried to differentiate their products and charge a premium price switched to a low-cost strategy, adopted new technology to enable them to customize PCs, revamped supply chains, and began outsourcing manufacturing to other companies that could do the job more efficiently.

Failing to adopt appropriate new technologies to support strategy, or adopting a new technology and failing to realign strategy to match it, can lead to poor performance. Today's increased global competition means more volatile markets, shorter product life cycles, and more sophisticated and knowledgeable consumers; and flexibility to meet these new demands has become a strategic imperative.[16] Manufacturing companies can adopt new technologies to support the strategy of flexibility. However, organization design and management processes must also be realigned, as a highly mechanistic design hampers flexibility and prevents the company from reaping the benefits of the new technology.[17] Managers should always remember that the technological and human systems of an organization are intertwined. This chapter's Book Mark on page 586 provides a different perspective on technology by looking at the dangers of failing to understand the human role in managing highly complex technological advances.

BRIEFCASE

As an organization manager, keep this guideline in mind:

When adopting a new technology, realign strategy, structure, and management processes to achieve top performance.

Contemporary Applications

In the years since Woodward's research, new developments have occurred in manufacturing technology. The factory of today is far different from the industrial firms Woodward studied in the 1950s. In particular, computers and information technology have revolutionized all types of manufacturing—small batch, large batch, and continuous process. At the Marion, North Carolina, plant of Rockwell Automation's Power Systems Division, for example, highly trained employees can quickly handle a build-on-demand unit of one, thanks to computers, wireless technology, and radio-frequency identification (RFID) systems. In one instance, the Marion plant

BOOKMARK

13.0 HAVE YOU READ THIS BOOK?

Inviting Disaster: Lessons from the Edge of Technology

By James R. Chiles

Dateline: Paris, France, July 25, 2000. Less than two minutes after Air France Concorde Flight 4590 departs from Charles DeGaulle Airport, something goes horribly wrong. Trailing fire and billowing black smoke, the huge plane rolls left and crashes into a hotel, killing all 109 people aboard and four more on the ground. It's just one of the technological disasters James R. Chiles describes in his book, *Inviting Disaster: Lessons from the Edge of Technology*.

One of Chiles's main points is that advancing technology makes possible the creation of machines that strain the human ability to understand and safely operate them. For example, managers' overconfidence that they understood blowout preventer technology contributed to the 2010 BP-Transocean oil rig disaster at Deepwater Horizon, and the inability to safely manage complex nuclear technology led to dangerous radiation leaks at Japan's Fukushima Daiichi nuclear power plant following a 2011 earthquake and tsunami. Chiles asserts that the margins of safety are growing thinner as the energies we harness become more powerful and the time between invention and use grows shorter. He believes that today, "for every twenty books on the pursuit of success, we need a book on how things fly into tiny pieces despite enormous effort and the very highest ideals." All complex systems, he reminds us, are destined to fail at some point.

HOW THINGS FLY INTO PIECES: EXAMPLES OF SYSTEM FRACTURES

Chiles uses historical calamities such as the sinking of the *Titanic* and modern disasters such as the explosion of the space shuttle *Challenger* to illustrate the dangers of *system fracture*, a chain of events that involves human error in response to malfunctions in complex machinery. Disaster begins when one weak point links up with others.

- *Sultana* (American steamboat on the Mississippi River near Memphis, Tennessee), April 25, 1865. The boat, designed to carry a maximum of 460 people, was carrying more than 2,000 Union ex-prisoners north—as well as 200 additional crew and passengers—when three of the four boilers exploded, killing 1,800 people. One of the boilers had been temporarily patched to cover a crack, but the patch was too thin. Operators failed to compensate by resetting the safety valve.
- *Piper Alpha* (offshore drilling rig in the North Sea), July 6, 1988. The offshore platform processed large volumes of natural gas from other rigs via pipe. A daytime work crew, which didn't complete the repair of a gas-condensate pump, relayed a verbal message to the next shift, but workers turned the pump on anyway. When the temporary seal on the pump failed, a fire trapped crewmen with no escape route, killing 167 crew and rescue workers.
- *Union Carbide (India) Ltd.* (release of highly toxic chemicals into a community), Bhopal, Madhya Pradesh, India, December 3, 1984. Three competing theories exist for how water got into a storage tank, creating a violent reaction that sent highly toxic methyl isocyanate for herbicides into the environment, causing an estimated 7,000 deaths: (1) poor safety maintenance, (2) sabotage, or (3) worker error.

WHAT CAUSES SYSTEM FRACTURES?

There is a veritable catalog of causes that lead to such disasters, from design errors, insufficient operator training, and poor planning to greed and mismanagement. Chiles wrote his book as a reminder that technology takes us into risky locales, whether it be outer space, up a 2,000-foot tower, or into a chemical processing plant. Chiles also cites examples of potential disasters that were averted by quick thinking and appropriate response. To help prevent system fractures, managers can create organizations in which people throughout the company are expert at picking out the subtle signals of real problems—and where they are empowered to report them and take prompt action.

Inviting Disaster: Lessons from the Edge of Technology, by James R. Chiles, is published by HarperBusiness.

built, packaged, and delivered a replacement bearing for installation in an industrial air conditioning unit in Texas only 15 hours after the customer called for help.[18]

Mass production manufacturing has seen similar transformations. Two significant contemporary applications of manufacturing technology are the digital factory and lean manufacturing.

The Digital Factory

Most of today's factories use a variety of new manufacturing technologies, including robots, numerically controlled machine tools, RFID, wireless technology, and computerized software for product design, engineering analysis, and remote control of machinery. A study found, for example, that manufacturers in the United States use more than six times the amount of information-processing equipment (computers, etc.) as they used 20 years ago.[19] This increase reflects the growing uncertainty and tough challenges manufacturing organizations face, including globalization of operations, increased competition, greater product complexity, and the need to coordinate with a larger number of business partners.[20] The ultimate automated factories are referred to as **digital factories.**[21] Also called *computer-integrated manufacturing, flexible manufacturing systems, smart factories, advanced manufacturing technology*, or *agile manufacturing,* digital factories link manufacturing components that previously stood alone. Thus, robots, machines, product design, and engineering analysis are coordinated by a single computer system.

The digital factory is typically the result of several subcomponents:

- *Computer-aided design (CAD).* Computers are used to assist in the drafting, design, and engineering of new parts. Designers guide their computers to draw specified configurations on the screen, including dimensions and component details. Hundreds of design alternatives can be explored, as can scaled-up or scaled-down versions of the original.[22]
- *Computer-aided manufacturing (CAM).* Computer-controlled machines in materials handling, fabrication, production, and assembly greatly increase the speed at which items can be manufactured. CAM also permits a production line to shift rapidly from producing one product to any variety of other products by changing software codes in the computer. CAM enables the production line to quickly honor customer requests for changes in product design and product mix.[23]
- *Manufacturing processes management (MPM).* New software referred to as manufacturing processes management gives managers the ability to "build" an entire virtual factory with manufacturing layout, robotics, machines, and conveyor lines before beginning physical construction. The virtual plant can test productivity and performance early on when things can still be changed, enabling companies to achieve optimal manufacturing processes.[24]
- *Integrated information network.* A computerized system links all aspects of the firm—including accounting, purchasing, marketing, inventory control, design, production, and so forth. This system, based on a common data and information base, enables managers to make decisions and direct the manufacturing process in a truly integrated fashion.
- *Product life-cycle management (PLM).* PLM software can manage a product from idea through development, manufacturing, testing, and even maintenance in the field. This allows the activities of manufacturers, suppliers, and other

partners to be tightly integrated and coordinated.[25] Using PLM software, managers can evaluate products and production processes in a virtual simulation and link product design to all departments and even outside suppliers involved in new product development. PLM has been used to coordinate people, tools, and facilities around the world for the design, development, and manufacture of products as diverse as roller skates produced by GID of Yorba Linda, California, product packaging for Procter & Gamble consumer products, and Boeing's new 787 Dreamliner passenger jet.[26]

The combination of CAD, CAM, MPM, integrated information systems, and PLM means that a new product can be designed on the computer and a prototype can be produced untouched by human hands. The ideal factory can switch quickly from one product to another, working fast and with precision, without paperwork or record keeping to bog down the system.[27] In addition, new software can coordinate information from multiple departments and organizations involved in a design, and virtual designs can even include an entirely new factory.

Automakers provide good examples of the benefits of the digital factory. Ford's Kansas City, Missouri plant, one of the largest manufacturing facilities in the world, produces around 490,000 F-150s, Ford Escapes, and Mazda Tributes a year. With just a little tweaking, the assembly lines can be programmed to manufacture any kind of car or truck Ford makes. Robots in wire cages do most of the work, while people act as assistants—taking measurements, refilling parts, and altering the system if something goes wrong. Assembly is synchronized by computers, right down to the last rearview mirror. Ford's digital factory is projected to save the company $2 billion over the next 10 years.[28] Honda has achieved an even greater degree of flexibility at its plant in East Liberty, Ohio. Considered the most flexible auto manufacturer in North America, the Honda plant can switch from making Civic compacts to making the longer, taller CRV crossover in as little as five minutes. Most of the company's vehicles are designed to be put together the same way, even if their parts are different. All that's needed to switch assembly from one type of vehicle to another is to put different "hands" on the robots to handle different parts. The ability to quickly adjust inventory levels of different types of vehicles has been a key strategic advantage for Honda in an era of volatile gasoline prices and shifting vehicle popularity.[29]

Lean Manufacturing

The digital factory reaches its ultimate level to improve quality, customer service, and cost cutting when all parts are used interdependently and combined with flexible management processes in a system referred to as lean manufacturing. **Lean manufacturing** uses highly trained employees at every stage of the production process, who take a painstaking approach to details and problem solving to cut waste and improve quality. In a survey by *Industry Week* and the Manufacturing Performance Institute asking 745 manufacturers which improvement programs they used, lean manufacturing was by far the most common answer, with more than 40 percent reporting the use of lean manufacturing techniques.[30]

Lean manufacturing incorporates technological elements, such as CAD/CAM and PLM, but the heart of lean manufacturing is not machines or software, but people. Lean manufacturing requires changes in organizational systems, such as decision-making processes and management processes, as well as an organizational culture that supports active employee participation, a quality perspective, and focus on the customer. Employees are trained to attack waste and strive for continuous improvement in all areas.[31] One lesson of lean manufacturing is that there is always room for improvement. Sealy, the world's top mattress maker, implemented lean manufacturing as a way to cut costs and improve operations.

IN PRACTICE

Sealy

Faced with cost pressures brought about by global competition combined with a recession, manufacturers can't afford to tie up hundreds of millions of dollars in raw materials that sit in factories for months or have partially finished products taking up floor space. Sealy managers have positioned their company for success in tough times by using lean manufacturing techniques.

Sealy operates 25 factories in North America and sells mattresses through thousands of retail outlets. The company conducts a *kaizen* (continuous improvement) event each month at every factory. In the beginning, Sealy focused on cutting unnecessary parts movement, eliminating waste, and eliminating unnecessary handling of materials. Employees are trained to "think lean" and look for any area of potential improvement. Previously, workers produced dozens of unfinished mattresses at a time that sat on the factory floor waiting for the next step. After implementing lean processes, teams of workers produce a complete mattress at a time matched closely to customer orders, which cuts the amount of time handling and moving materials. Today, Sealy has taken lean thinking even further, applying it to product design, for instance, to take waste out of engineering processes and design products that can be manufactured with less time and waste.

Using lean manufacturing helped Sealy reduce its scrap by 69 percent. Raw materials inventory is down 50 percent, to 16 days' worth, and the reduction in piles of partially finished mattresses freed up enough space that managers could combine two shifts, further slashing manufacturing costs. During the recent recession, Sealy maintained its commitment to continuous improvement and employee involvement. "Because of our lean culture we continued to get better . . . despite a downturn in volume," said Mike Hofmann, executive vice president of operations. "We're trying to keep our plants in condition by pushing kaizen and lean initiatives. When the market does return, if we can produce product in 20 percent to 30 percent less time than our competitors, we could seize market share." [32]

Hoffman and other Sealy managers embarked on their lean manufacturing quest some years ago, as did many North American companies that started studying the practices of lean manufacturing pioneer Toyota and other Japanese companies. A lean manufacturing system includes techniques such as just-in-time inventory, product life-cycle management, continuous-flow production, quick changeover of assembly lines, continuous improvement, and preventive maintenance with a management system that encourages employee involvement, creativity, and problem solving. Besides installing the methodology for running an efficient assembly line, managers instill the necessary attitudes, such as concern for quality and a desire to innovate.[33] For example, when Milliken & Company, a manufacturer of textiles and chemicals, first applied lean manufacturing techniques, efficiency and improvement gains were minimal because managers failed to make it part of the organizational culture. They had success when managers made a full commitment to involving and empowering employees.[34]

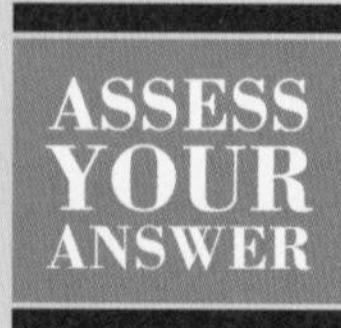

1 **Lean manufacturing is a super-efficient form of manufacturing that produces products of top quality.**

ANSWER: *Agree.* Lean manufacturing techniques have been implemented in hundreds of organizations all over the world and have led to dramatic improvements in quality, productivity, and efficiency. Lean manufacturing continues to be an important tool for manufacturing firms, and smart managers in service firms are also learning to benefit from lean thinking.

Lean manufacturing and the digital factory have paved the way for **mass customization**, which refers to using mass-production technology to quickly and cost-effectively assemble goods that are uniquely designed to fit the demands of individual customers. The goal is to provide customers with exactly what they want when they want it.[35] Mass customization has been applied to products as diverse as farm machinery, water heaters, clothing, computers, and industrial detergents.[36] A customer can order a Sony laptop with one of several hard drive capacities, processing chip speeds, and software packages, or a BMW automobile with the exact combination of features and components desired. About 60 percent of the cars BMW sells in Europe are built to order.[37] Oshkosh Truck Company thrived during an industrywide slump in sales by offering customized fire, cement, garbage, and military trucks. Firefighters often travel to the plant to watch their new vehicle take shape, sometimes bringing paint chips to customize the color of their fleet.[38]

Performance and Structural Implications

The awesome advantage of the digital factory is that products of different sizes, types, and customer requirements freely intermingle on the assembly line, enabling large factories to deliver a wide range of custom-made products at low mass-production costs.[39] Computerized machines can make instantaneous changes—such as putting a larger screw in a different location—without slowing the production line. A manufacturer can turn out an infinite variety of products in unlimited batch sizes, as illustrated in Exhibit 13.5. In traditional manufacturing systems studied by Woodward, choices were limited to the diagonal. Small batch allowed for high product flexibility and custom orders, but because of the "craftsmanship" involved in custom-making products, batch size was necessarily small. Mass production could have large batch size, but offered limited product flexibility. Continuous process could produce a single standard product in unlimited quantities. The digital factory allows plants to break free of this diagonal and to increase both batch size and product flexibility at the same time. When taken to its ultimate level, the digital factory allows for mass customization, with each specific product tailored to customer specification. This high-level use of digital systems has been referred to as *computer-aided craftsmanship*.[40]

Studies suggest that in digital factories, machine utilization is more efficient, labor productivity increases, scrap rates decrease, and product variety and customer satisfaction increase.[41] Many U.S. manufacturing companies are reinventing the factory using digital systems and lean manufacturing techniques to increase productivity.

Research into the relationship between the digital factory and organizational characteristics has discovered the organizational patterns summarized in

EXHIBIT 13.5
Relationship of Flexible Manufacturing Technology to Traditional Technologies

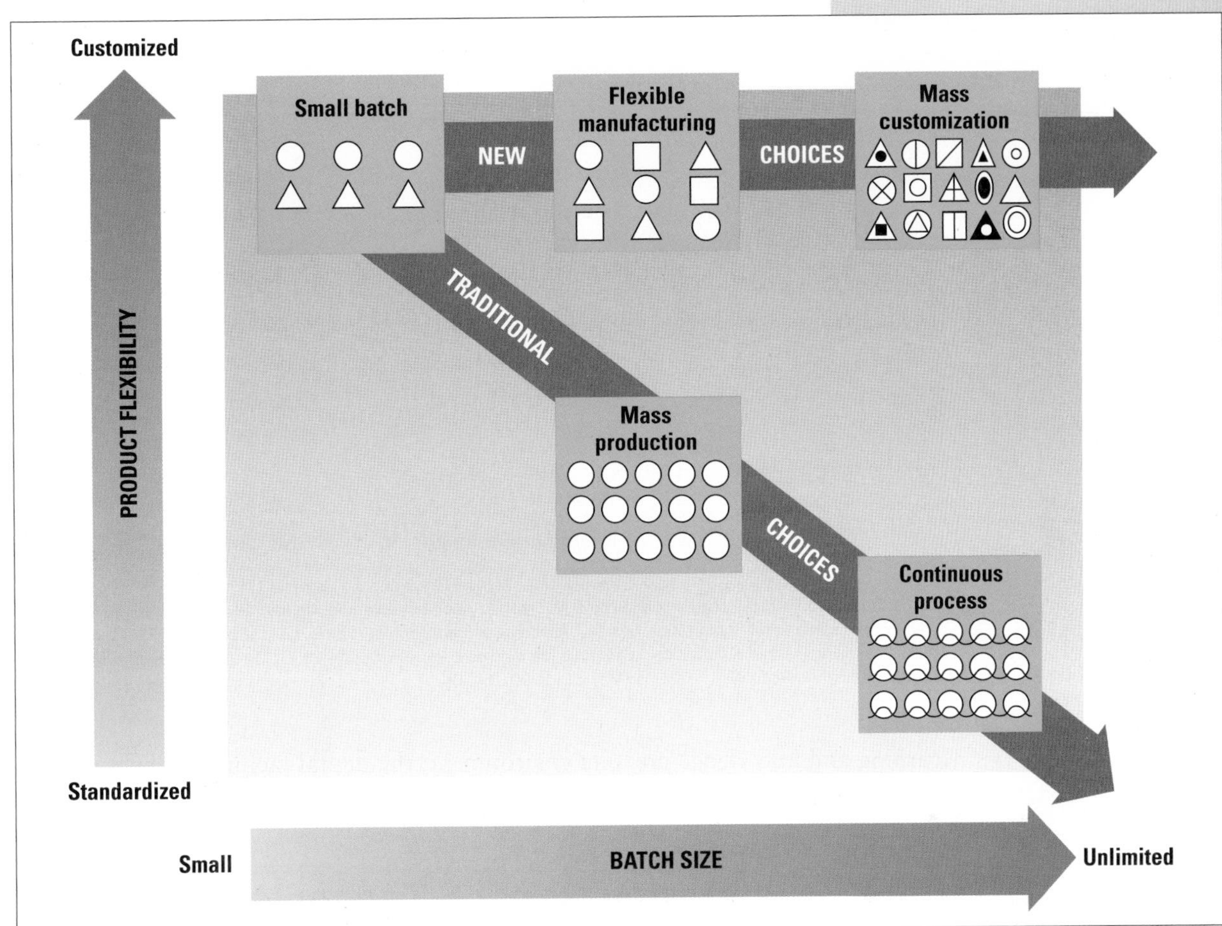

Source: Based on Jack Meredith, "The Strategic Advantages of New Manufacturing Technologies for Small Firms," *Strategic Management Journal* 8 (1987), 249–258; Paul Adler, "Managing Flexible Automation," *California Management Review* (Spring 1988), 34–56; and Otis Port, "Custom-made Direct from the Plant," *BusinessWeek*/21st Century Capitalism (November 18, 1994), 158–159.

Exhibit 13.6. Compared with traditional mass-production technologies, the digital factory has a narrow span of control, few hierarchical levels, adaptive tasks, low specialization, and decentralization, and the overall environment is characterized as organic and self-regulative. Employees need the skills to participate in teams; training is broad (so workers are not overly specialized) and frequent (so workers are up to date). Expertise tends to be cognitive so workers can process abstract ideas and solve problems. Interorganizational relationships in digital factories are characterized by changing demand from customers—which is easily handled with the new technology—and close relationships with a few suppliers that provide top-quality raw materials.[42]

Technology alone cannot give organizations the benefits of flexibility, quality, increased productivity, and greater customer satisfaction. Research suggests that organizational structures and management processes also must be redesigned to take advantage of the new technology.[43] When top managers make a commitment to implement new structures and processes that empower workers and support a

EXHIBIT 13.6
Comparison of Organizational Characteristics Associated with Mass Production and Digital Factories

Characteristic	Mass Production	Digital Factory
Structure		
Span of control	Wide	Narrow
Hierarchical levels	Many	Few
Tasks	Routine, repetitive	Adaptive, craftlike
Specialization	High	Low
Decision making	Centralized	Decentralized
Overall	Bureaucratic, mechanistic	Self-regulating, organic
Human Resources		
Interactions	Standalone	Teamwork
Training	Narrow, one time	Broad, frequent
Expertise	Manual, technical	Cognitive, social; solve problems
Interorganizational		
Customer demand	Stable	Changing
Suppliers	Many, arm's length	Few, close relationships

Source: Based on Patricia L. Nemetz and Louis W. Fry, "Flexible Manufacturing Organizations: Implications for Strategy Formulation and Organization Design," *Academy of Management Review* 13 (1988), 627–638; Paul S. Adler, "Managing Flexible Automation," *California Management Review* (Spring 1988), 34–56; and Jeremy Main, "Manufacturing the Right Way," *Fortune* (May 21, 1990), 54–64.

learning and knowledge-creating environment, the digital factory can help companies be more competitive.[44]

Core Organization Service Technology

Another big change occurring in the technology of organizations is the growing service sector. More than half of all businesses in the United States are service organizations, and according to one estimate nearly 90 percent of the U.S. workforce is employed in services, such as restaurants, hospitals, hotels and resorts, airlines, retail, financial services, and information services.[45]

Service Firms

Service technologies are different from manufacturing technologies and, in turn, require a different organization design.

Definition. Whereas manufacturing organizations achieve their primary purpose through the production of products, service organizations accomplish their primary purpose through the production and provision of services, such as education, healthcare, transportation, banking, and hospitality. Studies of service organizations have focused on the unique dimensions of service technologies. The characteristics of **service technology** are compared to those of manufacturing technology in Exhibit 13.7.

EXHIBIT 13.7
Differences between Manufacturing and Service Technologies

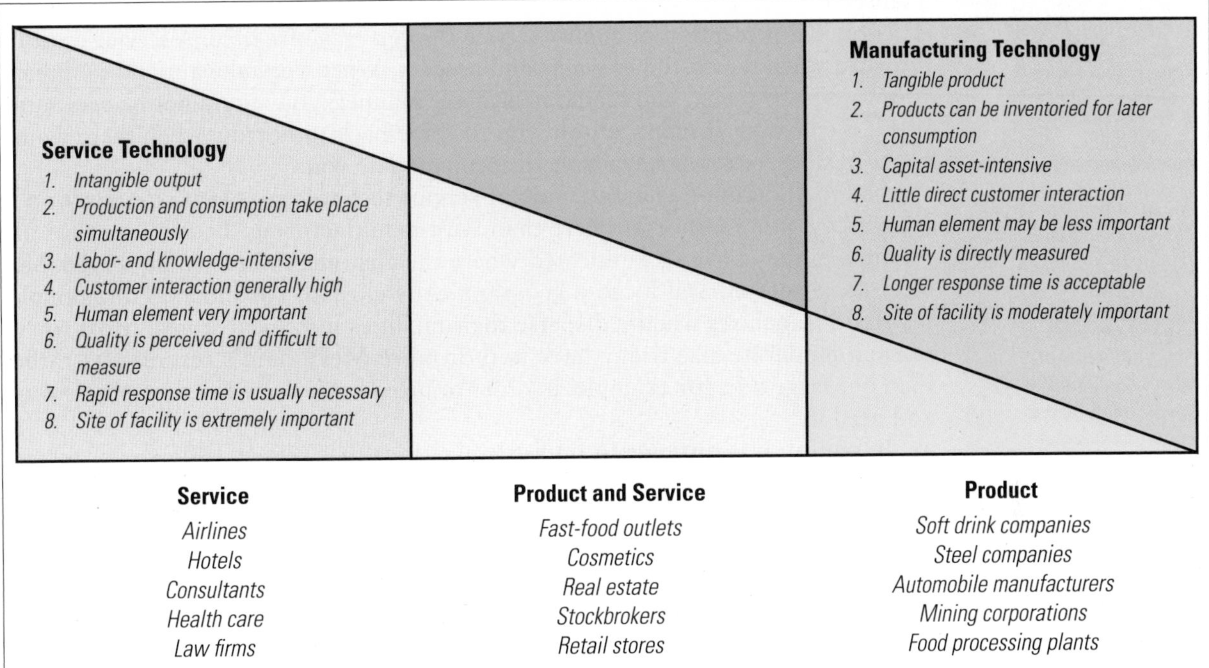

Service Technology
1. Intangible output
2. Production and consumption take place simultaneously
3. Labor- and knowledge-intensive
4. Customer interaction generally high
5. Human element very important
6. Quality is perceived and difficult to measure
7. Rapid response time is usually necessary
8. Site of facility is extremely important
Manufacturing Technology
1. Tangible product
2. Products can be inventoried for later consumption
3. Capital asset-intensive
4. Little direct customer interaction
5. Human element may be less important
6. Quality is directly measured
7. Longer response time is acceptable
8. Site of facility is moderately important
Service
Airlines
Hotels
Consultants
Health care
Law firms
Product and Service
Fast-food outlets
Cosmetics
Real estate
Stockbrokers
Retail stores
Product
Soft drink companies
Steel companies
Automobile manufacturers
Mining corporations
Food processing plants

Source: Based on F. F. Reichheld and W. E. Sasser, Jr., "Zero Defections: Quality Comes to Services," *Harvard Business Review* 68 (September–October 1990), 105–111; and David E. Bowen, Caren Siehl, and Benjamin Schneider, "A Framework for Analyzing Customer Service Orientations in Manufacturing," *Academy of Management Review* 14 (1989), 75–95.

The most obvious difference is that service technology produces an *intangible output* rather than a tangible product, such as a refrigerator produced by a manufacturing firm. A service is abstract and often consists of knowledge and ideas rather than a physical product. Thus, whereas manufacturers' products can be inventoried for later sale, services are characterized by *simultaneous production and consumption*. A client meets with a doctor or attorney, for example, and students and teachers come together in the classroom or over the Internet. A service is an intangible product that does not exist until it is requested by the customer. It cannot be stored, inventoried, or viewed as a finished good. If a service is not consumed immediately upon production, it disappears.[46] This typically means that service firms are *labor and knowledge intensive*, with many employees needed to meet the needs of customers, whereas manufacturing firms tend to be *capital intensive,* relying on mass production, continuous process, and digital manufacturing technologies.[47]

Direct interaction between customer and employee is generally very high with services, while there is little direct interaction between customers and employees in the technical core of a manufacturing firm. This direct interaction means that the *human element* (employees) becomes extremely important in service firms. Whereas most people never meet the workers who manufactured their cars, they interact directly with the salesperson who sells them a new truck or the Enterprise associate who rents them a car while on vacation. The treatment received from the

BRIEFCASE

As an organization manager, keep these guidelines in mind:

Use the concept of service technology to evaluate the production process in nonmanufacturing firms. Service technologies are intangible and must be located close to the customer. Hence, service organizations may have an organization design with fewer boundary roles, greater geographical dispersion, decentralization, highly skilled employees in the technical core, and generally less control than in manufacturing organizations.

salesperson—or from a doctor, lawyer, or hairstylist—affects the perception of the service received and the customer's level of satisfaction. The *quality of a service is perceived* and cannot be directly measured and compared in the same way that the quality of a tangible product can. Another characteristic that affects customer satisfaction and perception of quality service is *rapid response time*. A service must be provided when the customer wants and needs it. When you take a friend to dinner, you want to be seated and served in a timely manner; you would not be very satisfied if the hostess or manager told you to come back tomorrow when there would be more tables or servers available to accommodate you.

The final defining characteristic of service technology is that *site selection is often much more important* here than with manufacturing. Because services are intangible, they have to be located where the customer wants to be served. Services are dispersed and located geographically close to customers. For example, fast-food franchises usually disperse their facilities into local stores. Most towns of even moderate size today have two or more McDonald's restaurants rather than one large one, for example, in order to provide service where customers want and need it.

In reality, it is difficult to find organizations that reflect 100 percent service or 100 percent manufacturing characteristics. Some service firms take on characteristics of manufacturers, and vice versa. Many manufacturing firms are placing a greater emphasis on customer service to differentiate themselves and be more competitive. In addition, manufacturing organizations have departments such as purchasing, human resources, and marketing that are based on service technology. On the other hand, organizations such as gas stations, stockbrokers, retail stores, and restaurants belong to the service sector, but the provision of a product is a significant part of the transaction. The vast majority of organizations involve some combination of products and services. The important point is that all organizations can be classified along a continuum that includes both manufacturing and service characteristics, as illustrated in Exhibit 13.7. This chapter's "How Do You Fit the Design?" questionnaire will give you some insight into whether you are better suited to be a manager in a service organization or a manufacturing firm.

The Trend toward Lean Services. Service firms have always tended toward providing *customized output*—that is, providing exactly the service each customer wants and needs. When you visit a hairstylist, you don't automatically get the same cut the stylist gave the three previous clients. The stylist cuts your hair the way you request it. Pandora.com, whose mission is "to play only music you love," provides its 100 million or so registered users with a custom radio channel that broadcasts a set of music that fits their preferences.[48]

Customer expectations of what constitutes good service are rising. Zappos.com provides free shipping on both orders and returns. Amazon.com not only aims to have the lowest price and the fastest delivery, it also helps outside retailers bring their customer service up to par and covers for their service shortcomings if they don't. Insurance and financial services giant USAA cross-trained its agents and call center representatives so that customers can get answers to their questions about any product or service rather than being switched around from one agent to another.[49]

The expectation for better service has pushed service firms in industries from package delivery to healthcare to take a lesson from manufacturing.[50] Japan Post,

How Do You Fit the Design?

MANUFACTURING VERSUS SERVICE

The questions that follow ask you to describe your behavior. For each question, check the answer that best describes you.

1. I am usually running late for class or other appointments:
   a. Yes
   b. No
2. When taking a test I prefer:
   a. Subjective questions (discussion or essay)
   b. Objective questions (multiple choice)
3. When making decisions, I typically:
   a. Go with my gut—what feels right
   b. Carefully weigh each option
4. When solving a problem, I would more likely:
   a. Take a walk, mull things over, and then discuss
   b. Write down alternatives, prioritize them, and then pick the best
5. I consider time spent daydreaming as:
   a. A viable tool for planning my future
   b. A waste of time
6. To remember directions, I typically:
   a. Visualize the information
   b. Make notes
7. My work style is mostly:
   a. Juggle several things at once
   b. Concentrate on one task at a time until complete
8. My desk, work area, and laundry area are typically:
   a. Cluttered
   b. Neat and organized

Scoring: Count the number of checked "a" items and "b" items. Each "a" represents right-brain processing, and each "b" represents left-brain processing. If you scored 6 or higher on either, you have a distinct processing style. If you checked fewer than 6 for either, you probably have a balanced style.

Interpretation: People have two thinking processes—one visual and intuitive in the right half of the brain, and the other verbal and analytical in the left half of the brain. The thinking process you prefer predisposes you to certain types of knowledge and information—technical reports, analytical information, and quantitative data (left brain) versus talking to people, thematic impressions, and personal intuition (right brain)—as effective input to your thinking and decision making. Manufacturing organizations typically use left-brain processing to handle data based on physical, measurable technology. Service organizations typically use right-brain processing to interpret less tangible situations and serve people in a direct way. Left-brain processing has been summarized as based on logic; right-brain processing has been summarized as based on love.

Source: Adapted from Carolyn Hopper, *Practicing Management Skills* (Houghton Mifflin, 2003); and Jacquelyn Wonder and Priscilla Donovan, "Mind Openers," *Self* (March 1984).

under pressure to cut a $191 million loss on operations, hired Toyota's Toshihiro Takahashi to help apply the principles of the lean Toyota Production System to the collection, sorting, and delivery of mail. In all, Takahashi's team came up with 370 improvements and reduced the post office's person-hours by 20 percent. The waste reduction is expected to cut costs by around $350 million a year.[51] Numerous other service firms, in the United States as well as in other countries, have also applied lean principles in recent years. Starbucks Corporation hired a vice president of lean thinking who has been traveling the world with a *lean team* to work with employees to find ways to cut waste and improve customer service. Rival Dunkin' Donuts uses lean thinking techniques "everywhere from manufacturing to in-store organization and work flow," says Joe Scafido, Dunkin' Brands' chief creative and innovation officer.[52] Another good example comes from Seattle Children's Hospital, which applied lessons from manufacturing to increase efficiency and improve patient care.

Seattle Children's Hospital

IN PRACTICE

Ten years ago, Seattle Children's Hospital set a goal to become the top hospital of its type in the country. But with healthcare costs rising nationwide, administrators needed to find ways not only to improve patient care but also cut costs. They did it by applying lean techniques through a program called "Continuous Performance Improvement" (CPI). The main goals of CPI are to reduce waste and increase value for customers (patients).

CPI examines every aspect of patients' experience, from the time they arrive in the parking lot until they are discharged. Managers involved all hospital staff in studying the flow of medicines, patients, and information in the same way plant managers study the flow of materials in a manufacturing plant, and asked them to find ways to improve processes. Patients often had to wait for a non-emergency MRI for nearly a month. Now, that wait time has been cut to one or two days thanks to more efficient scheduling. Standardizing the instrument cart for specific types of surgeries cut inventory costs and reduced instrument preparation errors. An operating room team saw that a tonsillectomy procedure required filling out 21 separate forms and worked to cut that number down to 11. Overhauling the procedure for sterilizing surgical instruments increased the number of surgeries the hospital could perform. Overall, the CPI program helped cut costs per patient by 3.7 percent in 2009, for a savings of $23 million. The hospital has also been able to serve thousands more patients without expanding or adding beds.

A key aspect of the CPI program was shifting corporate culture by training doctors, nurses, administrators, and others in new methods and ways of thinking. Using CPI, teams can make changes any time they think they can improve a process or cut waste (defined as anything that doesn't add value for the patient). Even small changes that increase efficiency and improve patient care are celebrated by hospital administrators. "Their support fosters the idea that everyone can make positive changes in their departments," said one physician.[53]

With the costs of medical care soaring, other healthcare organizations are also taking a continuous improvement approach to cutting costs without sacrificing quality of care. "In healthcare, you can't do one big thing and reduce the price," says Dr. Devi Shetty, who runs a hospital in India that performs open-heart surgery for about 10 percent of the cost charged by hospitals in the United States. "We have to do 1,000 small things."[54]

Designing the Service Organization

The feature of service technologies with a distinct influence on organizational structure and control systems is the need for technical core employees to be close to the customer.[55] The differences between service and product organizations necessitated by customer contact are summarized in Exhibit 13.8.

EXHIBIT 13.8
Configuration and Structural Characteristics of Service Organizations versus Product Organizations

	Service	Product
Structural Characteristic		
1. Separate boundary roles	Few	Many
2. Geographical dispersion	Much	Little
3. Decision making	Decentralized	Centralized
4. Formalization	Lower	Higher
Human Resources		
1. Employee skill level	Higher	Lower
2. Skill emphasis	Interpersonal	Technical

The impact of customer contact on organization design is reflected in the use of boundary roles and structural disaggregation.[56] Boundary roles are used extensively in manufacturing firms to handle customers and to reduce disruptions for the technical core. They are used less in service firms because a service is intangible and cannot be passed along by boundary spanners, so service customers must interact directly with technical employees, such as doctors or brokers.

A service firm deals in information and intangible outputs and does not need to be large. Its greatest economies are achieved through disaggregation into small units that can be located close to customers. Stockbrokers, doctors' clinics, consulting firms, and banks disperse their facilities into regional and local offices. Manufacturing firms, on the other hand, tend to aggregate operations in a single area that has raw materials and an available workforce. A large manufacturing firm can take advantage of economies derived from expensive machinery and long production runs.

Service technology also influences internal organization characteristics used to direct and control the organization. For one thing, the skills of technical core employees typically need to be higher. These employees need enough knowledge and awareness to handle customer problems rather than just enough to perform mechanical tasks. Employees need social and interpersonal skills as well as technical skills.[57] Because of higher skills and structural dispersion, decision making often tends to be decentralized in service firms, and formalization tends to be low. Although some service organizations, such as many fast-food chains, have set rules and procedures for customer service, employees in service organizations typically have more freedom and discretion on the job. Managers at Home Depot have learned that how employees are managed has a great deal to do with the success of a service organization.

IN PRACTICE

Home Depot Inc.

Home Depot grew to be the world's largest home improvement retailer largely on the strength of its employees. Many people hired to work in the stores were former plumbers, carpenters, or other skilled tradesmen who understood the products and took pride in helping do-it-yourselfers find the right tools and supplies and know how to use them.

To cut costs, however, the company began hiring more part-time employees and instituted a salary cap that made jobs less appealing to experienced workers. As a further way to reduce costs, managers began measuring every aspect of the stores' productivity, such as how long it took to unload shipments of goods or how many extended warranties each employee sold per week. What got overlooked, though, was how well employees were providing service. Customers began complaining that they could never find anyone to assist them—and even when they did, many employees didn't have the knowledge and experience to be of much help. Some customers took their business elsewhere, even if it meant going to small shops where they would pay higher prices but get better service.

Home Depot managers have been working hard to get things back on track. The stores are hiring more full-timers again, instituting new training programs, and looking for other ways to make sure employees are knowledgeable and helpful. The CEO even reached out to the company's founders, Bernie Marcus and Arthur Blank, for advice on how to put the shine back on Home Depot's customer service reputation.[58]

Managers at Home Depot can use an understanding of the nature of service technology to help them align strategy, structure, and management processes and make the retailer more effective. Service technologies require structures and systems that are quite different from those for a traditional manufacturing technology. For example, the concept of separating complex tasks into a series of small jobs and exploiting economies of scale is a cornerstone of traditional manufacturing, but researchers have found that applying it to service organizations often does not work so well.[59] Some service firms have redesigned jobs to separate low- and high-customer-contact activities, with more rules and standardization in the low-contact jobs. High-touch service jobs, like those on the Home Depot sales floor, need more freedom and less control to satisfy customers.

2 The best way for a company to provide good service is to have abundant and clear rules and procedures and make sure everyone follows them to the letter.

ANSWER: *Disagree.* Service employees need good interpersonal skills and a degree of autonomy to be able to satisfy each customer's specific needs. Although many service organizations have some standard procedures for serving customers, service firms are typically low on both centralization and formalization. Abundant rules can take away both personal autonomy and the personal touch.

Now let's turn to another perspective on technology, that of production activities within specific organizational departments. Departments often have characteristics similar to those of service technology, providing services to other departments within the organization.

Noncore Departmental Technology

This section shifts to the department level of analysis for departments not within the technical core. For example, refer back to Exhibit 13.1 on page 580, which illustrates human resources, accounting, research and development, and marketing departments that are outside of the technical core. Each of these (and other noncore) departments in an organization has its own production process that consists of a distinct technology. A company such as Tenneco, a maker of auto parts, might have departments for engineering, research and development, human resources, marketing, quality control, finance, and dozens of other functions. This section analyzes the nature of departmental technology and its relationship with departmental design.

The framework that has had the greatest impact on the understanding of departmental technologies was developed by Charles Perrow.[60] Perrow's model has been useful for a broad range of technologies, which made it ideal for research into departmental activities.

Variety

Perrow specified two dimensions of departmental activities that were relevant to organization structure and processes. The first is the number of exceptions in the work. This refers to task **variety**, which is the frequency of unexpected and novel events that occur in the conversion process. Task variety concerns whether work activities are performed the same way every time or differ from time to time as employees transform the organization's inputs into outputs.[61] When individuals encounter a large number of unexpected situations, with frequent problems, variety is considered high. When there are few problems, and when day-to-day job requirements are repetitious, technology contains little variety. Variety in departments can range from repeating a single act, such as on a traditional assembly line, to working on a series of unrelated problems, such as in a hospital emergency room.

Analyzability

The second dimension of technology concerns the **analyzability** of work activities. When the conversion process is analyzable, the work can be reduced to mechanical steps and participants can follow an objective, computational procedure to solve problems. Problem solution may involve the use of standard procedures, such as instructions and manuals, or technical knowledge, such as that in a textbook or handbook. On the other hand, some work is not analyzable. When problems arise, it is difficult to identify the correct solution. There is no store of techniques or procedures to tell a person exactly what to do. The cause of or solution to a problem is not clear, so employees rely on accumulated experience, intuition, and judgment. The final solution to a problem is often the result of wisdom and experience and not the result of standard procedures. For example, Philippos Poulos, a tone regulator at Steinway & Sons, has an unanalyzable technology. Tone regulators carefully check each piano's hammers to ensure that they produce the proper "Steinway sound."[62] These quality-control tasks require years of experience and practice. Standard procedures will not tell a person how to do such tasks.

Framework

The two dimensions of technology and examples of departmental activities on Perrow's framework are shown in Exhibit 13.9. The dimensions of variety and analyzability form the basis for four major categories of technology: routine, craft, engineering, and nonroutine.

Categories of Technology. **Routine technologies** are characterized by little task variety and the use of objective, computational procedures. The tasks are formalized and standardized. Examples include an automobile assembly line and a bank teller department.

EXHIBIT 13.9
Framework for Department Technologies

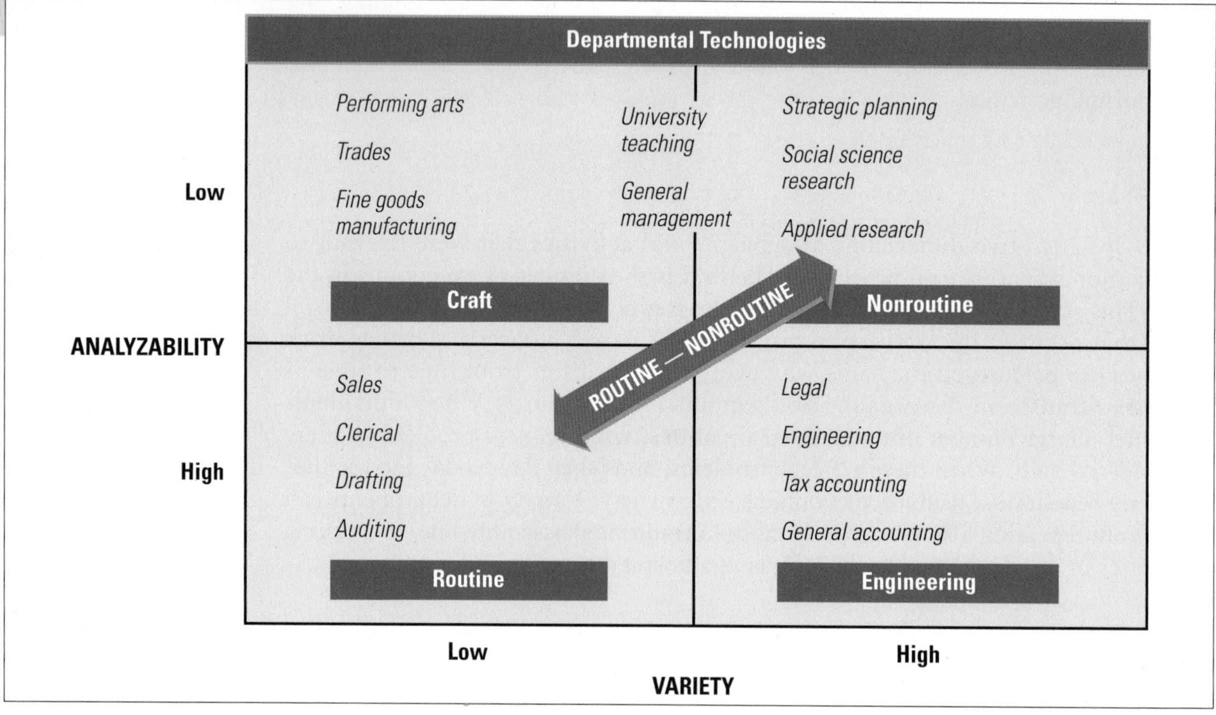

Source: Daft, R. L. and N. Macintosh, "A New Approach to the Design and Use of Management Information," in *California Management Review* 20 (August 1978), pp. 82–92. © 1978 by the Regents of the University of California. Reprinted by permission of the University of California Press.

Craft technologies are characterized by a fairly stable stream of activities, but the conversion process is not analyzable or well understood. Tasks require extensive training and experience because employees respond to intangible factors on the basis of wisdom, intuition, and experience. Although advances in machine technologies seem to have reduced the number of craft technologies in organizations, craft technologies are still important. For example, steel furnace engineers continue to mix steel based on intuition and experience, pattern makers at fashion houses such as Louis Vuitton, Zara, or H&M convert rough designers' sketches into salable garments, and teams of writers for television series such as *Glee* or *The Mentalist* convert ideas into story lines.

Engineering technologies tend to be complex because there is substantial variety in the tasks performed. However, the various activities are usually handled on the basis of established formulas, procedures, and techniques. Employees normally refer to a well-developed body of knowledge to handle problems. Engineering and accounting tasks usually fall in this category.

Nonroutine technologies have high task variety, and the conversion process is not analyzable or well understood. In nonroutine technology, a great deal of effort is devoted to analyzing problems and activities. Several equally acceptable options typically can be found. Experience and technical knowledge are used to solve problems and perform the work. Basic research, strategic planning, and other work that involves new projects and unexpected problems are nonroutine. The blossoming biotechnology industry also represents a nonroutine technology. Breakthroughs in understanding metabolism and physiology at a cellular level depend on highly trained employees who use their experience and intuition, as well as scientific knowledge.[63]

Routine Versus Nonroutine. Exhibit 13.9 also illustrates that variety and analyzability can be combined into a single dimension of technology. This dimension is called *routine versus nonroutine technology*, and it is the diagonal line in Exhibit 13.9. The analyzability and variety dimensions are often correlated in departments, meaning that technologies high in variety tend to be low in analyzability, and technologies low in variety tend to be analyzable. Departments can be evaluated along a single dimension of routine versus nonroutine that combines both analyzability and variety, which is a useful shorthand measure for analyzing departmental technology.

The following questions show how departmental technology can be analyzed for determining its placement on Perrow's technology framework in Exhibit 13.9.[64] Employees normally circle a number from 1 to 7 in response to each question.

Variety:

1. To what extent would you say your work is routine?
2. Does almost everyone in this unit do about the same job in the same way most of the time?
3. Are unit members performing repetitive activities in doing their jobs?

Analyzability:

1. To what extent is there a clearly known way to do the major types of work you normally encounter?
2. To what extent is there an understandable sequence of steps that can be followed in doing your work?
3. To do your work, to what extent can you actually rely on established procedures and practices?

If answers to the preceding questions indicate high scores for analyzability and low scores for variety, the department would have a routine technology. If the opposite occurs, the technology would be nonroutine. Low variety and low analyzability indicate a craft technology, and high variety and high analyzability indicate an engineering technology. As a practical matter, most departments fit somewhere along the diagonal and can be most easily characterized as routine or nonroutine.

Department Design

Once the nature of a department's technology has been identified, the appropriate design can be determined. Department technology tends to be associated with a cluster of departmental characteristics, such as the skill level of employees, formalization, and methods of communication. Definite patterns exist in the relationship between work unit technology and design characteristics, which are associated with departmental performance.[65] Key relationships between technology and other dimensions of departments are described in this section and are summarized in Exhibit 13.10.

The overall design of departments may be characterized as either organic or mechanistic. Routine technologies are associated with a mechanistic design, with formal rules and rigid management processes. Nonroutine technologies are associated with an organic design, and department management is more flexible

EXHIBIT 13.10
Relationship of Department Technology to Structural and Management Characteristics

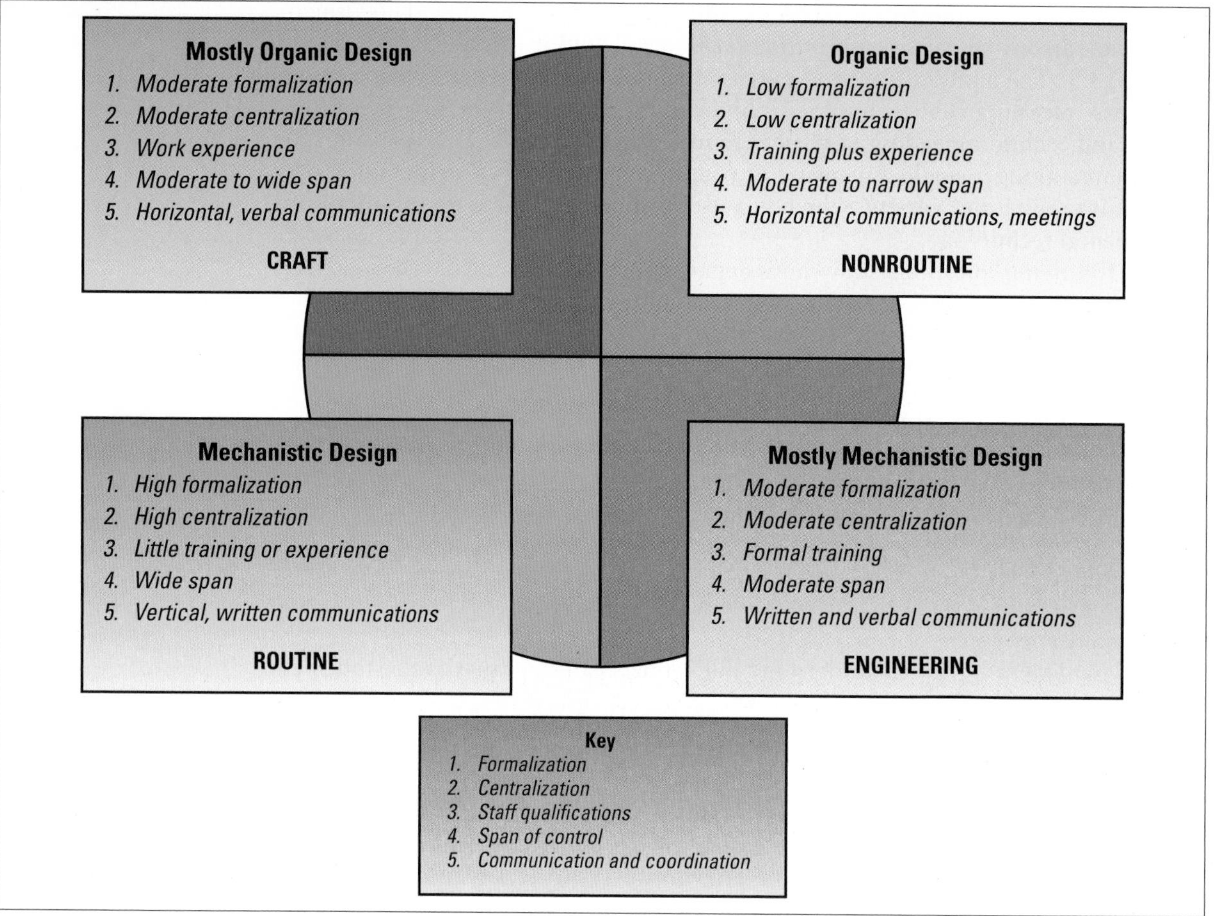

and free-flowing. The specific design characteristics of formalization, centralization, employee skill level, span of control, and communication and coordination vary, depending on work unit technology.

1. *Formalization.* Routine technology is characterized by standardization and division of labor into small tasks that are governed by formal rules and procedures. For nonroutine tasks, the structure is less formal and less standardized. When variety is high, as in a research department, fewer activities are covered by formal procedures.[66]
2. *Decentralization.* In routine technologies, most decision making about task activities is centralized to management.[67] In engineering technologies, employees with technical training tend to acquire moderate decision authority because technical knowledge is important to task accomplishment. Production employees who have years of experience obtain decision authority in craft technologies because they know how to respond to problems. Decentralization to employees is greatest in nonroutine settings, where many decisions are made by employees.

3. *Employee skill level.* Work staff in routine technologies typically require little education or experience, which is congruent with repetitious work activities. In work units with greater variety, staff are more skilled and often have formal training in technical schools or universities. Training for craft activities, which are less analyzable, is more likely to be through job experience. Nonroutine activities require both formal education and job experience.[68]
4. *Span of control.* Span of control is the number of employees who report to a single manager or supervisor. This characteristic is normally influenced by departmental technology. The more complex and nonroutine the task, the more problems arise in which the supervisor becomes involved. Although the span of control may be influenced by other factors, such as skill level of employees, it typically should be smaller for complex tasks because on such tasks the supervisor and subordinate must interact frequently.[69]
5. *Communication and coordination.* Communication activity and frequency increase as task variety increases.[70] Frequent problems require more information sharing to solve problems and ensure proper completion of activities. The direction of communication is typically horizontal in nonroutine work units and vertical in routine work units.[71] The form of communication varies by task analyzability.[72] When tasks are highly analyzable, statistical and written forms of communication (e.g., memos, reports, rules, and procedures) are frequent. When tasks are less analyzable, information typically is conveyed face to face, over the telephone, or in group meetings.

Two important points are reflected in Exhibit 13.10. First, departments differ from one another and can be categorized according to their workflow technology.[73] Second, structural and management processes differ based on departmental technology. Managers should design their departments so that requirements based on technology can be met. Design problems are most visible when the design is clearly inconsistent with technology. Studies have found that when structure and communication characteristics did not reflect technology, departments tended to be less effective.[74] Employees could not communicate with the frequency needed to solve problems.

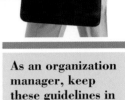

As an organization manager, keep these guidelines in mind:

Use the two dimensions of variety and analyzability to discover whether the work in a department is routine or nonroutine. If the work in a department is routine, use a mechanistic design, with a rigid structure and processes. If the work in a department is nonroutine, use an organic design and flexible management processes.

3 The design characteristics and management processes that are effective for a television station's sales department probably would not work so well for the news department.

ANSWER: *Agree.* The news department has a nonroutine technology compared to the sales department. No one knows what newsworthy events are going to happen during the day, when or where they will happen, or how they will need to be covered. Sales tasks, particularly telephone sales to repeat customers involving standard rates for advertising, can be performed using standard procedures, but gathering and reporting news events can't be standardized. A sales department would be characterized as routine because there is little variety and tasks are well understood.

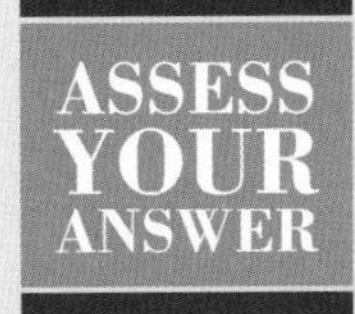

Workflow Interdependence among Departments

The final characteristic of technology that influences organization design is called interdependence. **Interdependence** means the extent to which departments depend on each other for information, resources, or materials to accomplish their tasks. Low interdependence means that departments can do their work independently of each other and have little need for interaction, consultation, or exchange of materials. High interdependence means departments must constantly exchange resources.

Types

James Thompson defined three types of interdependence that influence organization structure.[75] These interdependencies are illustrated in Exhibit 13.11 and are discussed in the following sections.

Pooled. **Pooled interdependence** is the lowest form of interdependence among departments. In this form, work does not flow between units. Each department is part of the organization and contributes to the common good of the organization, but works independently. Subway restaurants or Bank of America branches are examples of pooled interdependence. An outlet in Chicago need not interact with an outlet in Urbana. Pooled interdependence may be associated with the relationships within a *divisional structure*, defined in Chapter 2. Divisions or branches share financial resources from a common pool, and the success of each division contributes to the success of the overall organization.

Thompson proposed that pooled interdependence would exist in firms with what he called a mediating technology. A **mediating technology** provides products or services that mediate or link clients from the external environment and, in so doing, allows each department to work independently. Banks, brokerage firms, and real

EXHIBIT 13.11
Thompson's Classification of Interdependence and Management Implications

Form of Interdependence	Demands on Horizontal Communication, Decision Making	Type of Coordination Required	Priority for Locating Units Close Together
Pooled (bank) Clients	Low communication	Standardization, rules, procedures Divisional structure	Low
Sequential (assembly line) Client	Medium communication	Plans, schedules, feedback Task forces	Medium
Reciprocal (hospital) Client	High communication	Mutual adjustment, relational coordination, teamwork Horizontal structure	High

estate offices all mediate between buyers and sellers, but the offices work independently within the organization.

The management implications associated with pooled interdependence are quite simple. Thompson argued that managers should use rules and procedures to standardize activities across departments. Each department should use the same procedures and financial statements so the outcomes of all departments can be measured and pooled. Very little day-to-day coordination is required among units.

Sequential. When interdependence is of serial form, with parts produced in one department becoming inputs to another department, it is called **sequential interdependence**. The first department must perform correctly for the second department to perform correctly. This is a higher level of interdependence than pooled interdependence because departments exchange resources and depend on others to perform well. Sequential interdependence creates a greater need for horizontal mechanisms such as integrators or task forces.

Sequential interdependence occurs in what Thompson called **long-linked technology**, which "refers to the combination in one organization of successive stages of production; each stage of production uses as its inputs the production of the preceding stage and produces inputs for the following stage."[76] An example of sequential interdependence comes from the shipbuilding industry. Until recently, ship designers made patterns and molds out of paper and plywood, which were passed on to assembly. The cutting department depended on accurate measurements from the designers, and the assembly department depended on accurate parts from the cutting department. This sequential interdependence meant that mistakes in measurements or pattern mix-ups often caused errors in the cutting and assembly process, leading to delays and increased costs. Naval architect Filippo Cali created a complex software program that computerizes the process of making patterns and molds, thus eliminating many of the problems between design and assembly.[77] Another example of sequential interdependence would be an automobile assembly line, which must have all the parts it needs to keep production rolling, such as engines, steering mechanisms, and tires.

The management requirements for sequential interdependence are more demanding than those for pooled interdependence. Coordination among the linked plants or departments is required. Since the interdependence implies a one-way flow of materials, extensive planning and scheduling are generally needed. Department B needs to know what to expect from Department A so both can perform effectively. Some day-to-day communication among plants or departments is also needed to handle unexpected problems and exceptions that arise.

Reciprocal. The highest level of interdependence is **reciprocal interdependence**. This exists when the output of operation A is the input to operation B, and the output of operation B is the input back again to operation A. The outputs of departments influence those departments in reciprocal fashion.

Reciprocal interdependence tends to occur in organizations with what Thompson called **intensive technologies**, which provide a variety of products or services in combination to a client. A firm developing new products provides an example of reciprocal interdependence. Intense coordination is needed between design, engineering, manufacturing, and marketing to combine all their resources to suit the customer's product need. Hospitals, such as Seattle Children's Hospital described earlier, are also excellent examples because they provide coordinated services to patients. At Seattle Children's, the hospital's managers are taking care that the entire

BRIEFCASE

As an organization manager, keep these guidelines in mind:

Evaluate the interdependencies among organizational departments. Use the general rule that, as interdependencies increase, mechanisms for coordination must also increase. Consider a divisional structure for pooled interdependence. For sequential interdependence, use task forces and integrators for greater horizontal coordination. At the highest level of interdependence (reciprocal interdependence), support relational coordination and consider a horizontal structure.

organization is considered in its continuous improvement project because of the high level of interdependence as a patient moves through different departments.

Reciprocal interdependence requires that departments work together intimately and be tightly coordinated. A study of top management teams confirms that the effective performance of teams characterized by high interdependence depends on good communication and close coordination.[78] With reciprocal interdependence, the structure must allow for frequent horizontal communication and adjustment, perhaps using cross-functional teams or a horizontal structure. Extensive planning is required, but plans will not anticipate or solve all problems. Daily interaction and mutual adjustment among departments are required. People from several departments might need to be involved in face-to-face coordination, teamwork, and decision making. For these reasons, managers in organizations characterized by reciprocal interdependence often organize work in such a way to encourage and support *relational coordination*, as described in Chapter 2, so that people share information and coordinate across departments as a normal part of their everyday work lives. Coordination and information sharing is built into the fabric of the organization.[79] Southwest Airlines provides a good example.

Southwest Airlines

IN PRACTICE

Airlines face many challenges, but one that they face hundreds of times a day is getting airplanes loaded and off the ground safely and on time. Flight departure is a highly complex process. It involves numerous employees from various departments, performing multiple tasks within a limited time period, under uncertain and ever-changing conditions.

Exhibit 13.12 illustrates the highly interdependent nature of the flight departure process, which involves ticket agents, pilots, flight attendants, baggage handlers, gate agents, operations agents, mechanics, cabin cleaners, ramp agents, cargo handlers, fuel attendants, and caterers. If all these groups are not tightly coordinated, a successful on-time departure is difficult to achieve.

Southwest Airlines has the shortest turnaround time in the business. How do they do it? Southwest promotes relational coordination among the groups in Exhibit 13.12 to achieve superior on-time performance and a high level of customer satisfaction. In any airline, there can be serious disagreements among employees about who is to blame when a flight is delayed, so Southwest managers created what they call *team delay*. Rather than searching for who is to blame when something goes wrong, the team delay is used to point out problems in coordination between various groups. The emphasis on the team focuses everyone on their shared goals of on-time departure, accurate baggage handling, safety, and customer satisfaction. Because delay becomes a team problem, people are motivated to work closely together and coordinate their activities rather than look out for themselves and try to avoid or shift blame. Supervisors work closely with employees, but their role is less “being the boss” as it is facilitating learning and helping people do their jobs. Southwest uses a small supervisory span of control—about one supervisor for every eight or nine front line employees—so that supervisors have the time to coach and assist employees, who are viewed as internal customers.

Southwest puts a lot of emphasis on hiring people with a collaborative attitude. Rather than focusing on technical skills, Southwest focuses on hiring people who are oriented toward teamwork. Training and development activities and organizational stories reinforce teamwork and mutual respect. One story is told that a pilot came for an interview at Southwest and treated an administrative assistant with disrespect. He didn’t get the job. “We all succeed together—and all fail together,” is the philosophy at Southwest, as one field manager put it.[80]

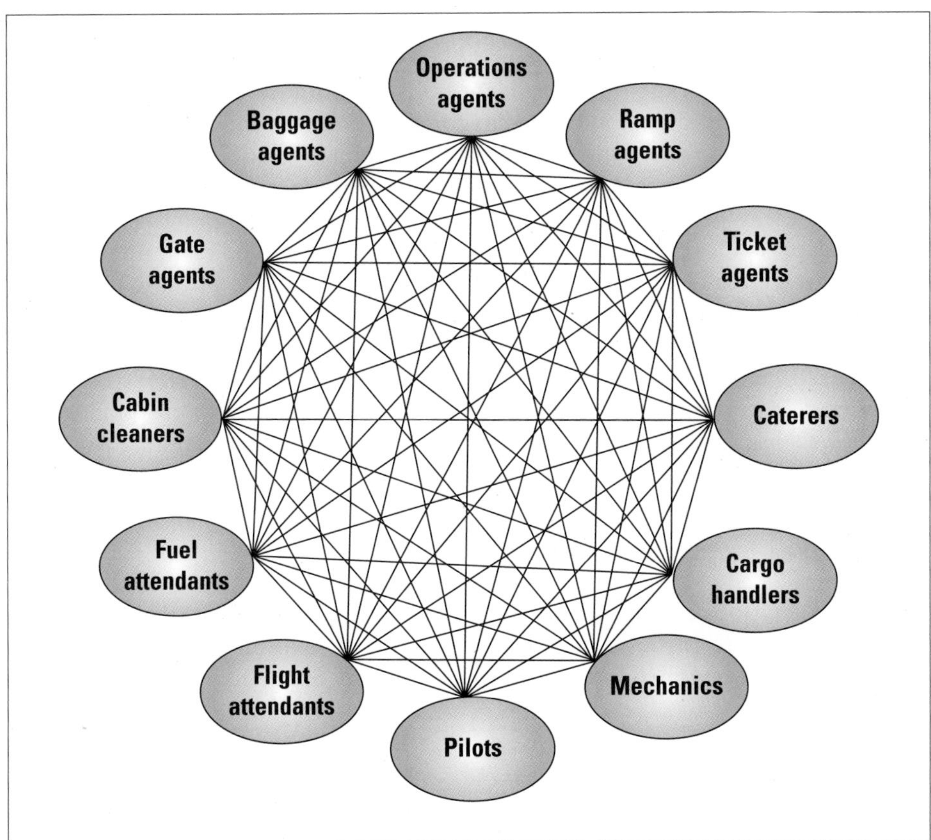

EXHIBIT 13.12
Interdependence of Departments Involved in the Flight Departure Process

Source: Jody Hoffer Gitzell, "Organizing Work to Support Relational Coordination," *International Journal of Human Resource Management* 11, no. 3 (June 2000), 517–539, reprinted by permission of Taylor & Francis Ltd, http://www.tandf.co.uk/journals.

By using practices that support teamwork, shared goals, mutual respect, and shared responsibility and accountability, Southwest facilitates relational coordination so that interdependent departments are tightly coordinated. Reciprocal interdependence is the most complex interdependence for organizations to handle and the most challenging for managers in designing the organization.

Structural Priority

As indicated in Exhibit 13.11, because decision making, communication, and coordination problems are greatest for reciprocal interdependence, reciprocal interdependence should receive first priority in organization structure. New product development is one area of reciprocal interdependence that is of growing concern to managers, as companies face increasing pressure to bring new products to market fast. Many firms are revamping the design-manufacturing relationship by closely integrating CAD and CAM technologies and using PLM software, discussed earlier in this chapter.[81] Activities that are reciprocally interdependent should be grouped close together in the organization so that managers have easy access to one another for mutual adjustment. These units should report to the same person on the organization chart and should be physically close so the time and effort for coordination can be minimized. A horizontal structure, with linked sets of teams working on core processes, can provide the close coordination needed to support reciprocal interdependence. Poor coordination will result in poor performance for the organization. If reciprocally interdependent units are not located close together, the organization should design mechanisms for coordination, such as daily meetings between departments or an intranet to facilitate communication. The next priority is given to sequential interdependencies, and finally to pooled interdependencies.

This strategy of organizing keeps the communication channels short where coordination is most critical to organizational success. For example, customers of Boise Cascade Corporation experienced poor service because customer-service reps located in New York City were not coordinating with production planners in Oregon plants. Customers couldn't get delivery as needed. Boise was reorganized, and the two groups were consolidated under one roof and began reporting to the same supervisor at division headquarters. Now customer needs are met because customer-service reps work with production planning to schedule customer orders.

Structural Implications

Most organizations experience various levels of interdependence, and structure can be designed to fit these needs, as illustrated in Exhibit 13.13.[82] In a manufacturing firm, new product development entails reciprocal interdependence

EXHIBIT 13.13
Primary Means to Achieve Coordination for Different Levels of Task Interdependence in a Manufacturing Firm

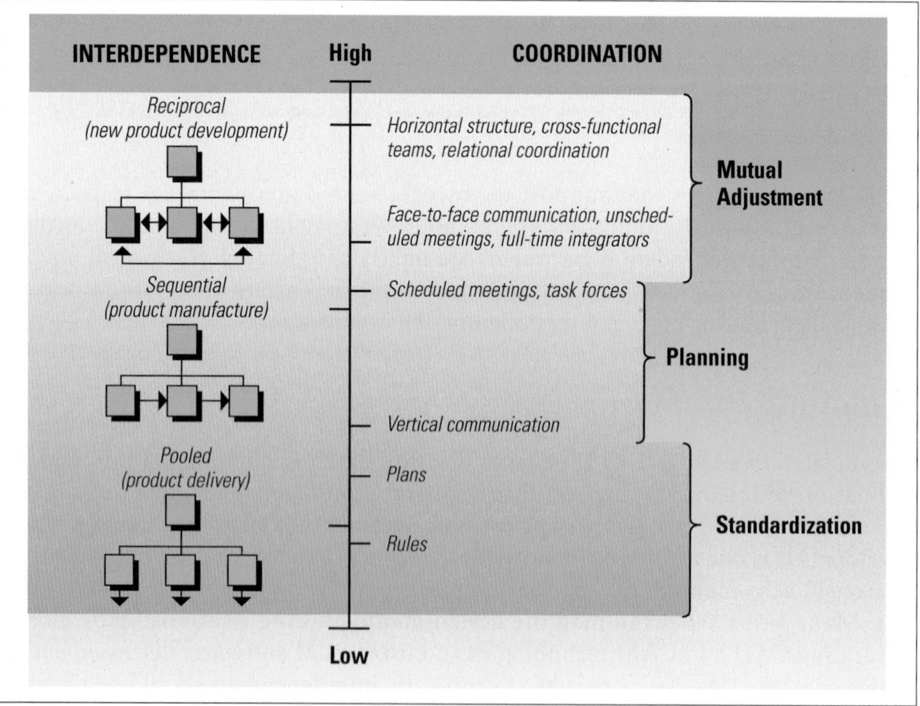

Source: Adapted from Andrew H. Van de Ven, Andre Delbecq, and Richard Koenig, "Determinants of Communication Modes within Organizations," *American Sociological Review* 41 (1976), 330.

among the design, engineering, purchasing, manufacturing, and sales departments. Perhaps a horizontal structure or cross-functional teams could be used to handle the back-and-forth flow of information and resources. Once a product is designed, its actual manufacture would be sequential interdependence, with a flow of goods from one department to another, such as among purchasing, inventory, production control, manufacturing, and assembly. The actual ordering and delivery of products is pooled interdependence, with warehouses working independently. Customers could place an order with the nearest facility, which would not require coordination among warehouses, except in unusual cases such as a stock outage.

The three levels of interdependence are illustrated by a study of athletic teams that examined interdependency among players and how it influences other aspects of baseball, football, and basketball teams.

IN PRACTICE

Athletic Teams

A major difference among baseball, football, and basketball is the interdependence among players. Baseball is low in interdependence, football is medium, and basketball represents the highest player interdependence. The relationships among interdependence and other characteristics of team play are illustrated in Exhibit 13.14.

Pete Rose said, "Baseball is a team game, but nine men who reach their individual goals make a nice team." In baseball, interdependence among team players is low and can be defined as pooled. Each member acts independently, taking a turn at bat and playing his or her own position. When interaction does occur, it is between only two or three players, as in a double play. Players are physically dispersed, and the rules of the game are the primary means of coordinating players. Players practice and develop their skills individually, such as by taking batting practice and undergoing physical conditioning. Management's job is to select good players. If each player is successful as an individual, the team should win.

In football, interdependence among players is higher and tends to be sequential. The line first blocks the opponents to enable the backs to run or pass. Plays are performed

EXHIBIT 13.14
Relationships among Interdependence and Other Characteristics of Team Play

	Baseball	Football	Basketball
Interdependence	Pooled	Sequential	Reciprocal
Physical dispersion of players	High	Medium	Low
Coordination	Rules that govern the sport	Game plan and position roles	Mutual adjustment and shared responsibility
Key management job	Select players and develop their skills	Prepare and execute game	Influence flow of game

Source: Based on William Pasmore, Carol E. Francis, and Jeffrey Haldeman, "Sociotechnical Systems: A North American Reflection on the Empirical Studies of the 70s," *Human Relations* 35 (1982), 1179–1204.

sequentially from first down to fourth down. Physical dispersion is medium, which allows players to operate as a coordinated unit. The primary mechanism for coordinating players is developing a game plan along with rules that govern the behavior of team members. Each player has an assignment that fits with other assignments, and management designs the game plan to achieve victory.

In basketball, interdependence tends to be reciprocal. The game is free-flowing, and the division of labor is less precise than in other sports. Each player is involved in both offense and defense, handles the ball, and attempts to score. The ball flows back and forth among players. Team members interact in a dynamic flow to achieve victory. Management skills involve the ability to influence this dynamic process, either by substituting players or by working the ball into certain areas. Players must learn to adapt to the flow of the game and to one another as events unfold.

Interdependence among players is a primary factor explaining the difference among the three sports. Baseball is organized around an autonomous individual, football around groups that are sequentially interdependent, and basketball around the free flow of reciprocal players.[83]

Impact of Technology on Job Design

So far, this chapter has described models for analyzing how manufacturing, service, and department technologies influence structure and management processes. The relationship between a new technology and the organization seems to follow a pattern, beginning with immediate effects on the content of jobs followed (after a longer period) by impact on the design of the organization. The ultimate impact of technology on employees can be partially understood through the concepts of job design and sociotechnical systems.

Job Design

Job design includes the assignment of goals and tasks to be accomplished by employees. Managers may consciously change job design to improve productivity or worker motivation. However, managers may also unconsciously influence job design through the introduction of new technologies, which can change how jobs are done and the very nature of jobs.[84] Managers should understand how the introduction of a new technology may affect employees' jobs. The common theme of new technologies in the workplace is that they in some way substitute machinery for human labor in transforming inputs into outputs. Automated teller machines (ATMs) have replaced thousands of human bank tellers, for example. Robots used in digital manufacturing systems are replacing laborers on the production line and creating jobs that require people to have higher-level skills for operating complex machinery.

In addition to actually replacing human workers, technology may have several different effects on the human jobs that remain. Research has indicated that mass-production technologies tend to produce **job simplification**, which means that the variety and difficulty of tasks performed by a single person are reduced. The consequence is boring, repetitive jobs that generally provide little satisfaction. Sometimes, managers introduce **job rotation**, which means moving employees from job to job to give them a greater variety of tasks. More advanced technology, on the other hand, tends to cause **job enrichment**, meaning that the job provides greater responsibility, recognition, and opportunities for growth and development. Advanced technologies create a greater need for employee training and education because workers need higher-level skills and greater competence to master their tasks. For example, ATMs took most of the routine tasks (deposits and withdrawals) away from bank tellers and left them with the more complex tasks that require higher-level skills. Studies of digital manufacturing found that it produces three noticeable results for employees: more opportunities for intellectual mastery and enhanced cognitive skills; more employee responsibility for results; and greater interdependence among employees, enabling more social interaction and the development of teamwork and coordination skills.[85] Digital manufacturing and other advanced technology may also contribute to **job enlargement**, which is an expansion of the number of different tasks performed by an employee. Fewer people are needed with the new technology, and each employee has to be able to perform a greater number and variety of tasks.

With advanced technology, workers have to keep learning new skills because technology changes so rapidly. Advances in *information technology* are having a significant effect on jobs in the service industry, including doctors' offices and medical clinics, law firms, financial planners, and libraries. Workers may find that their jobs change almost daily because of new software programs, changes in the use of the Internet, and other advances in information technology.

Advanced technology does not always have a positive effect on employees, but research findings in general are encouraging, suggesting that jobs are enriched rather than simplified, engaging people's higher mental capacities, offering opportunities for learning and growth, and providing greater job satisfaction.

BRIEFCASE

As an organization manager, keep these guidelines in mind:

Be aware that the introduction of a new technology has significant impact on job design. Consider using the sociotechnical systems approach to balance the needs of workers with the requirements of the new technological system.

Sociotechnical Systems

The **sociotechnical systems approach** recognizes the interaction of technical and human needs in effective job design, combining the needs of people with the organization's need for technical efficiency. The *socio* portion of the approach refers to the people and groups that work in organizations and how work is organized and coordinated. The *technical* portion refers to the materials, tools, machines, and processes used to transform organizational inputs into outputs.

Exhibit 13.15 illustrates the three primary components of the sociotechnical systems model.[86] The *social system* includes all human elements—such as individual and team behaviors, organizational culture, management practices, and degree of communication openness—that can influence the performance of work. The *technical system* refers to the type of production technology, the level of interdependence, the complexity of tasks, and so forth. The goal of the sociotechnical systems approach is to design the organization for **joint optimization**, which means that an organization functions best when the social and technical systems are designed to fit the needs of one another. Designing the organization to meet human needs while ignoring the technical systems, or changing technology to improve efficiency while ignoring human needs, may inadvertently cause performance problems. The sociotechnical systems approach attempts to find a balance between what workers want and need and the technical requirements of the organization's production system.[87]

One example comes from a museum that installed a closed-circuit television system. Rather than having several guards patrolling the museum and grounds, the television could easily be monitored by a single guard. Although the technology

EXHIBIT 13.15
Sociotechnical Systems Model

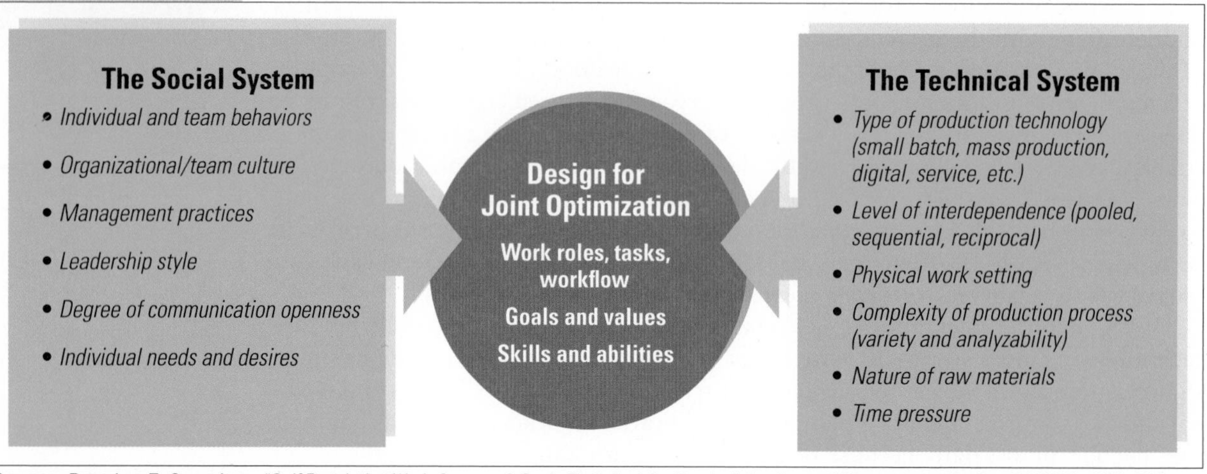

Sources: Based on T. Cummings, "Self-Regulating Work Groups: A Socio-Technical Synthesis," *Academy of Management Review* 3 (1978), 625–634; Don Hellriegel, John W. Slocum, and Richard W. Woodman, *Organizational Behavior*, 8th ed. (Cincinnati, OH: South-Western, 1998), 492; and Gregory B. Northcraft and Margaret A. Neale, *Organizational Behavior: A Management Challenge*, 2nd ed. (Fort Worth, TX: The Dryden Press, 1994), 551.

saved money because only one guard was needed per shift, it led to unexpected performance problems. Guards had previously enjoyed the social interaction provided by patrolling; monitoring a closed-circuit television led to alienation and boredom. When a Federal agency did an 18-month test of the system, only 5 percent of several thousand experimental covert intrusions were detected by the guard.[88] The system was inadequate because human needs were not taken into account.

Sociotechnical principles evolved from the work of the Tavistock Institute, a research organization in England, during the 1950s and 1960s.[89] Examples of organizational change using sociotechnical systems principles have occurred in numerous organizations, including General Motors, Volvo, the Tennessee Valley Authority (TVA), and Procter & Gamble.[90] Although there have been failures, in many of these applications the joint optimization of changes in technology and structure to meet the needs of people as well as efficiency improved performance, safety, quality, absenteeism, and turnover. In some cases, work design was not the most efficient based on technical and scientific principles, but employee involvement and commitment more than made up for the difference. Thus, once again research shows that new technologies need not have a negative impact on people because the technology often requires higher-level mental and social skills and can be organized to encourage the involvement and commitment of employees, thereby benefiting both the employee and the organization.

The sociotechnical systems principle that states that people should be viewed as resources and provided with appropriate skills, meaningful work, and suitable rewards becomes even more important in today's world of growing technological complexity.[91] One study of paper manufacturers found that organizations that put too much faith in machines and technology and pay little attention to the appropriate management of people do not achieve advances in productivity and flexibility. Today's most successful companies strive to find the right mix of machines, digital systems, and people and the most effective way to coordinate them.[92]

Although many principles of sociotechnical systems theory are still valid, current scholars and researchers are also arguing for an expansion of the approach to capture the dynamic nature of today's organizations, the chaotic environment, and the shift from routine to nonroutine jobs brought about by advances in technology.[93]

Design Essentials

- Several important ideas in the technology literature stand out. The first is Woodward's research into manufacturing technology. Woodward went into organizations and collected practical data on technology characteristics, organization structure, and management systems. She found clear relationships between technology and structure in high-performing organizations. Her findings are so clear that managers can analyze their own organizations along the same dimensions of technology and structure. In addition, technology and structure can be co-aligned with organizational strategy to meet changing needs and provide new competitive advantages.
- The second important idea is that service technologies differ in a systematic way from manufacturing technologies. Service technologies are characterized by intangible outcomes and direct client involvement in the production process. Service firms do not have the fixed, machine-based technologies that appear in manufacturing organizations; hence, organization design often differs as well.
- A third significant idea is Perrow's framework applied to department technologies. Understanding the variety and analyzability of a technology tells one about the management style, structure, and process that should characterize that department. Routine technologies are characterized by a mechanistic design and nonroutine technologies by an organic design. Applying the wrong management system to a department will result in dissatisfaction and reduced efficiency.
- The fourth important idea is interdependence among departments. The extent to which departments depend on each other for materials, information, or other resources determines the amount of coordination required between them. As interdependence increases, demands on the organization for coordination increase. Organization design must allow for the correct amount of communication and coordination to handle interdependence across departments.
- The fifth idea is that advanced digital factories and lean manufacturing are being adopted by organizations and having impact on organization design. For the most part, the impact is positive, with shifts toward more organic designs both on the shop floor and in the management hierarchy. These technologies replace routine jobs, give employees more autonomy, produce more challenging jobs, encourage teamwork, and let the organization be more flexible and responsive. The new technologies are enriching jobs to the point where organizations are happier places to work.
- Several principles of sociotechnical systems theory, which attempts to design the technical and human aspects of an organization to fit one another, are increasingly important as advances in technology alter the nature of jobs and social interaction in today's companies.

Key Concepts

analyzability
continuous-process production
core technology
craft technologies
digital factories
engineering technologies
intensive technologies
interdependence
job design
job enlargement
job enrichment
job rotation
job simplification
joint optimization
large-batch production
lean manufacturing
long-linked technology
mass customization
mediating technology
noncore technology
nonroutine technologies
pooled interdependence
reciprocal interdependence
routine technologies
sequential interdependence
service technology
small-batch production
sociotechnical systems approach
technical complexity
technology
variety

Discussion Questions

1. Where would your university or college department be located on Perrow's technology framework? Would a department devoted exclusively to teaching be in a different quadrant from a department devoted exclusively to research?
2. Explain Thompson's levels of interdependence. What is the level of interdependence among departments (finance, marketing) in a business school? What kinds of coordination mechanisms might be used to handle that interdependence?
3. What relationships did Woodward discover between supervisor span of control and technological complexity?
4. How do digital factories and lean manufacturing differ from other manufacturing technologies? Why are these new approaches needed in today's environment?
5. What is a service technology? Are different types of service technologies likely to be associated with different organization designs? Explain.
6. Lean concepts such as continuous improvement and waste reduction have long been used by manufacturing companies. Discuss how service firms can apply the same concepts. Why do you think many service companies are adopting these ideas?
7. Why might administrators at a hospital such as Seattle Children's Hospital, described on page 596, want to foster relational coordination?
8. A top executive claimed that top-level management is a craft technology because the work contains intangibles, such as handling personnel, interpreting the environment, and coping with unusual situations that have to be learned through experience. If this is true, is it appropriate to teach management in a business school? Does teaching management from a textbook assume that the manager's job is analyzable, and hence that formal training rather than experience is most important?
9. To what extent does the development of new technologies simplify and routinize the jobs of employees? Can you give an example? How can new technology lead to job enlargement? Discuss.
10. Describe the sociotechnical systems model. Why might some managers oppose a sociotechnical systems approach?

Chapter 13 Workbook Bistro Technology[94]

You will be analyzing the technology used in three different restaurants—McDonald's, Subway, and a typical family restaurant. Your instructor will tell you whether to do this assignment as individuals or in a group.

You must visit all three restaurants and infer how the work is done, according to the following criteria. You are not allowed to interview any employees, but instead you will be an observer. Take lots of notes when you are there.

	McDonald's	Subway	Family Restaurant
Organization goals: Speed, service, atmosphere, etc.			
Authority structure.			
Type of technology using Woodward's model.			
Organization structure: Mechanistic or organic?			
Team versus individual: Do people work together or alone?			
Interdependence: How do employees depend on each other?			
Tasks: Routine versus nonroutine.			
Specialization of tasks by employees.			
Standardization: How varied are tasks and products?			
Expertise required: Technical versus social.			
Decision making: Centralized versus decentralized.			

Questions

1. Is the technology used the best one for each restaurant, considering its goals and environment?
2. From the preceding data, determine if the structure and other characteristics fit the technology.
3. If you were part of a consulting team assigned to improve the operations of each organization, what recommendations would you make?

CASE FOR ANALYSIS Acetate Department[95]

The acetate department's product consisted of about 20 different kinds of viscous liquid acetate used by another department to manufacture transparent film to be left clear or coated with photographic emulsion or iron oxide.

Before the change: The department was located in an old four-story building, as in Exhibit 13.16. The workflow was as follows:

1. Twenty kinds of powder arrived daily in 50-pound paper bags. In addition, storage tanks of liquid would be filled weekly from tank trucks.
2. Two or three acetate helpers would jointly unload pallets of bags into the storage area using a lift truck.
3. Several times during a shift, the helpers would bring the bagged material up in the elevator to the third floor, where it would be stored temporarily along the walls.
4. Mixing batches was under the direction of the group leader and was rather like baking a cake. Following a prescribed formula, the group leader, mixers, and helpers operated valves to feed in the proper solvent and manually dump in the proper weight and mixture of solid material. The glob would be mixed by giant eggbeaters and heated according to the recipe.
5. When the batch was completed, it was pumped to a finished-product storage tank.
6. After completing each batch, the crew would thoroughly clean the work area of dust and empty bags because cleanliness was extremely important to the finished product.

To accomplish this work, the department was structured as in Exhibit 13.17.

The helpers were usually 18 to 25 years of age; the mixers, 25 to 40; and the group leaders and foremen, 40 to 60. Foremen were on salary; group leaders, mixers, and helpers were on hourly pay.

To produce 20 million pounds of product per year, the department operated 24 hours a day, 7 days a week. Four crews rotated shifts. For example, shift foreman A and his two group leaders and crews would work two weeks on the day shift (8:00 A.M. to 4:00 P.M.), then two weeks on the evening shift (4:00 P.M. to midnight), and then two weeks on the night shift (midnight to 8:00 A.M.). There were two days off between shift changes.

During a typical shift, a group leader and his crew would complete two or three batches. A batch would

EXHIBIT 13.16
Elevation View of Acetate Department before Change

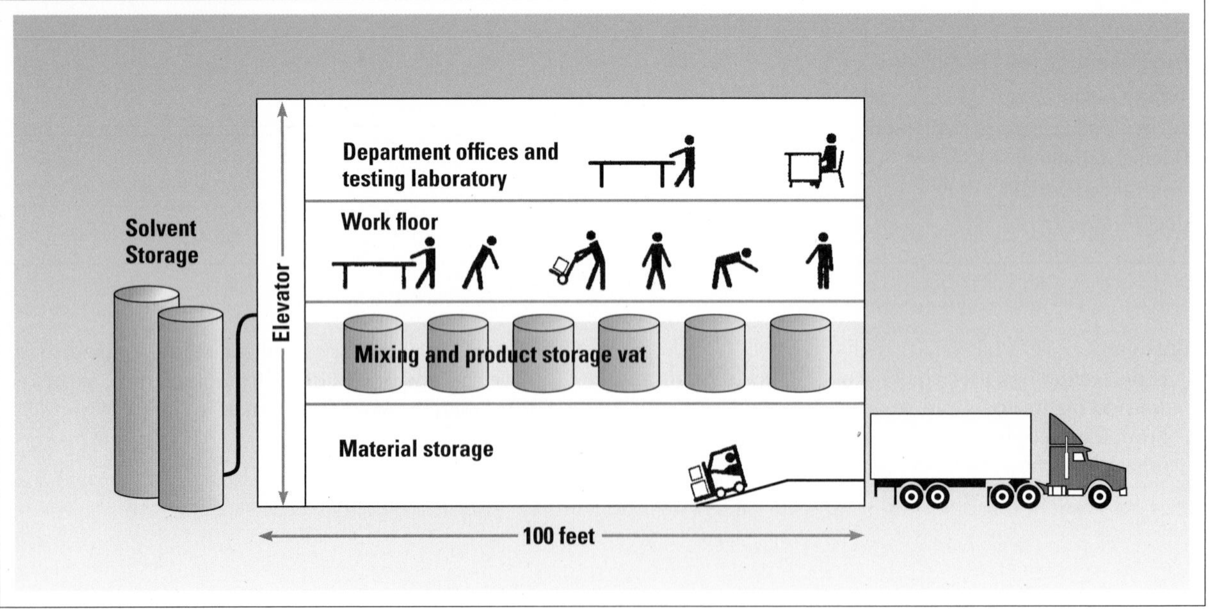

Source: Hampton/Summer/Webber, *Organizational Behavior Practice Management*, 4th ed., © 1982. Reprinted and Electronically reproduced by permission of Pearson Education, Inc., Upper Saddle River, New Jersey.

EXHIBIT 13.17
Organizational Chart of Acetate Department before Change

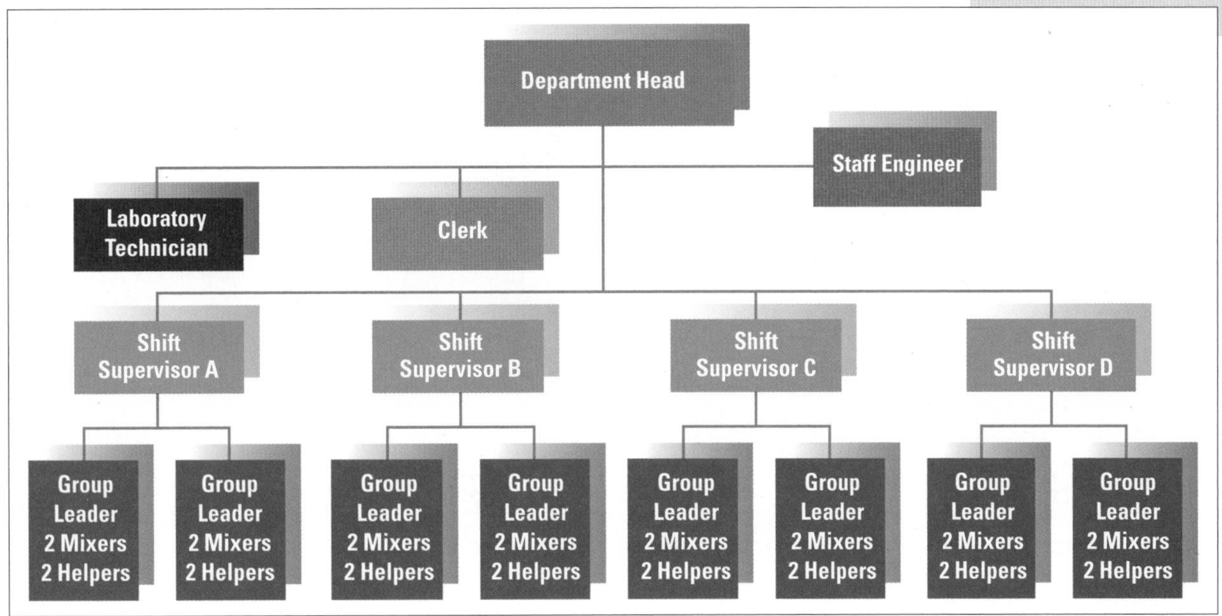

frequently be started on one shift and completed by the next shift crew. There was slightly less work on the evening and night shifts because no deliveries were made, but these crews engaged in a little more cleaning. The shift foreman would give instructions to the two group leaders at the beginning of each shift as to the status of batches in process, batches to be mixed, what deliveries were expected, and what cleaning was to be done. Periodically throughout the shift the foreman would collect samples in small bottles, which he would leave at the laboratory technicians' desk for testing.

The management and office staff (e.g., department head, staff engineer, lab technician, and department clerk) worked only on the day shift, although the foreman might call if an emergency arose on the other shifts.

All in all, the department was a pleasant place in which to work. The work floor was a little warm, but well lit, quiet, and clean. Substantial banter and horseplay occurred when the crew wasn't actually loading batches, particularly on the evening and night shifts. There was a dartboard in the work area, and competition was fierce and loud. Frequently a crew would go bowling right after work, even at 1:00 A.M., because the community's alleys were open 24 hours a day. Department turnover and absenteeism were low. Most employees spent their entire career with the company, many in one department. The corporation was large, paternalistic, and well paying and offered attractive fringe benefits, including large, virtually automatic bonuses for all. Then came the change.

The new system: To improve productivity, the acetate department was completely redesigned; the technology changed from batches to continuous processing. The basic building was retained but substantially modified, as in Exhibit 13.18. The modified workflow is as follows:

1. Most solid raw materials are delivered via trucks in large aluminum bins holding 500 pounds.
2. One handler (formerly helper) is on duty at all times on the first floor to receive raw materials and to dump the bins into the semiautomatic screw feeder.
3. The head operator (former group leader) directs the mixing operations from a control panel on the fourth floor located along one wall across from the department offices. The mixing is virtually an automatic operation once the solid material has been sent up the screw feed; a tape program opens and closes the necessary valves to add solvent, heat, mix, and so on. Sitting at a table before his panel, the head operator monitors the process to see that everything is operating within specified temperatures and pressures.

This technical change allowed the department to greatly reduce its workforce. The new structure is illustrated in Exhibit 13.19. One new position was created, that of a pump operator who is located in a small, separate shack about 300 feet from the main building. This person operates the pumps and valves that move the finished product among various storage tanks.

EXHIBIT 13.18
Elevation View of Acetate Department after Change

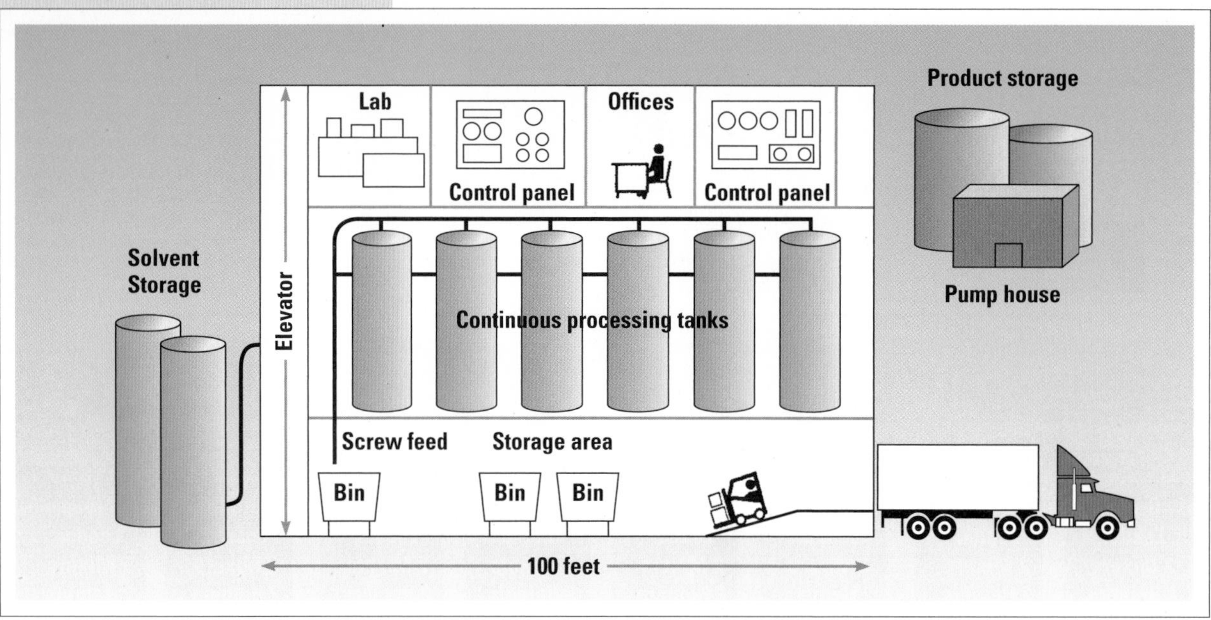

EXHIBIT 13.19
Organizational Chart of Acetate Department after Change

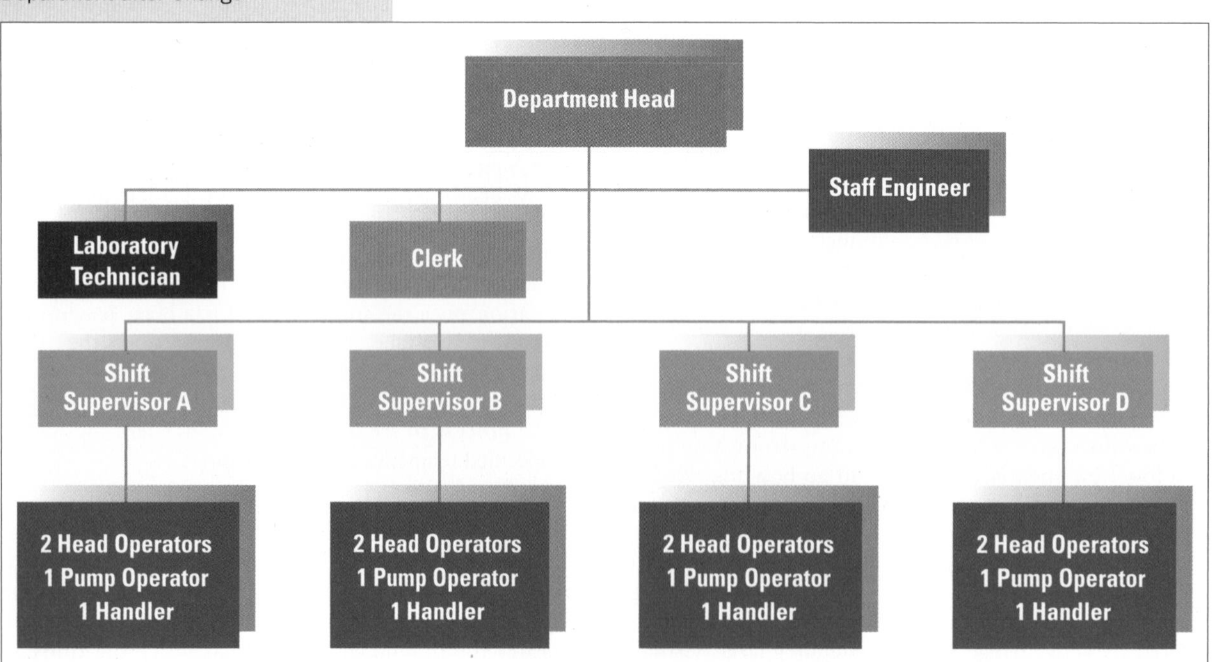

Under the new system, production capacity was increased to 25 million pounds per year. All remaining employees received a 15 percent increase in pay. Former personnel not retained in the acetate department were transferred to other departments in the company. No one was dismissed.

Unfortunately, actual output has lagged well below capacity in the several months since the construction work and technical training were completed. Actual production is virtually identical with that under the old technology. Absenteeism has increased markedly, and several judgmental errors by operators have resulted in substantial losses.

Notes

1. Gene Bylinsky, "Heroes of Manufacturing," *Fortune,* March 8, 2004, 190[B]–190[H].
2. Charles Perrow, "A Framework for the Comparative Analysis of Organizations," *American Sociological Review* 32 (1967), 194–208; and R. J. Schonberger, *World Class Manufacturing: The Next Decade* (New York: The Free Press, 1996).
3. Wanda J. Orlikowski, "The Duality of Technology: Rethinking the Concept of Technology in Organizations," *Organization Science* 3 (1992), 398–427.
4. Linda Argote, "Input Uncertainty and Organizational Coordination in Hospital Emergency Units," *Administrative Science Quarterly* 27 (1982), 420–434; Charles Perrow, *Organizational Analysis: A Sociological Approach* (Belmont, CA: Wadsworth, 1970); and William Rushing, "Hardness of Material as Related to the Division of Labor in Manufacturing Industries," *Administrative Science Quarterly* 13 (1968), 229–245.
5. Lawrence B. Mohr, "Organizational Technology and Organization Structure," *Administrative Science Quarterly* 16 (1971), 444–459; and David Hickson, Derek Pugh, and Diana Pheysey, "Operations Technology and Organization Structure: An Empirical Reappraisal," *Administrative Science Quarterly* 14 (1969), 378–397.
6. Joan Woodward, *Industrial Organization: Theory and Practice* (London: Oxford University Press, 1965); and Joan Woodward, *Management and Technology* (London: Her Majesty's Stationery Office, 1958).
7. Hickson, Pugh, and Pheysey, "Operations Technology and Organization Structure"; and James D. Thompson, *Organizations in Action* (New York: McGraw-Hill, 1967).
8. Edward Harvey, "Technology and the Structure of Organizations," *American Sociological Review* 33 (1968), 241–259.
9. Based on Woodward, *Industrial Organization* and *Management and Technology.*
10. Christina Passariello, "Brand-New Bag: Louis Vuitton Tried Modern Methods on Factory Lines—For Craftsmen, Multitasking Replaces Specialization," *The Wall Street Journal,* October 9, 2006, A1.
11. Philip Siekman, "A Big Maker of Tiny Batches," *Fortune,* May 27, 2002, 152[A]–152[H].
12. Guy Chazan, "Clean-Fuels Refinery Rises in Desert," *The Wall Street Journal,* April 16, 2010, B8; and "Renewed Optimism for the Future of GTL, CTL, and BTL," *Oil and Gas News,* July 11, 2011.
13. Woodward, *Industrial Organization*, vi.
14. William L. Zwerman, *New Perspectives on Organizational Theory* (Westport, CT: Greenwood, 1970); and Harvey, "Technology and the Structure of Organizations."
15. Dean M. Schroeder, Steven W. Congden, and C. Gopinath, "Linking Competitive Strategy and Manufacturing Process Technology," *Journal of Management Studies* 32, no. 2 (March 1995), 163–189.
16. Fernando F. Suarez, Michael A. Cusumano, and Charles H. Fine, "An Empirical Study of Flexibility in Manufacturing," *Sloan Management Review* (Fall 1995), 25–32.
17. Raymond F. Zammuto and Edward J. O'Connor, "Gaining Advanced Manufacturing Technologies' Benefits: The Roles of Organization Design and Culture," *Academy of Management Review* 17, no. 4 (1992), 701–728; and Schroeder, Congden, and Gopinath, "Linking Competitive Strategy and Manufacturing Process Technology."
18. John S. McClenahen, "Bearing Necessities," *Industry Week* (October 2004), 63–65.
19. Heritage Foundation statistic, based on data from the U.S. Department of Labor, Bureau of Labor Statistics, "Multifactor Productivity, 1987–2007," and reported in James Sherk, "Technology Explains Drop in Manufacturing Jobs," *Backgrounder* (October 12, 2010), 1–8.
20. John Teresko, "Winning with Digital Manufacturing," *Industry Week* (July 2008), 45–47.
21. Jim Brown, "Leveraging the Digital Factory," *Industrial Management* (July–August 2009), 26–30; Teresko, "Winning with Digital Manufacturing"; Jack R. Meredith, "The Strategic Advantages of the Factory of the Future," *California Management Review* 29 (Spring 1987), 27–41; and Althea Jones and Terry Webb, "Introducing Computer Integrated Manufacturing," *Journal of General Management* 12 (Summer 1987), 60–74.

22. Paul S. Adler, "Managing Flexible Automation," *California Management Review* (Spring 1988), 34–56.
23. Bela Gold, "Computerization in Domestic and International Manufacturing," *California Management Review* (Winter 1989), 129–143.
24. Brown, "Leveraging the Digital Factory."
25. Teresko, "Winning with Digital Manufacturing."
26. Graham Dudley and John Hassard, "Design Issues in the Development of Computer Integrated Manufacturing (CIM)," *Journal of General Management* 16 (1990), 43–53; and Tom Massung, "Manufacturing Efficiency," *Microsoft Executive Circle* (Winter 2004), 28–29.
27. Dudley and Hassard, "Design Issues in the Development of Computer Integrated Manufacturing."
28. Grainger David, "One Truck a Minute," *Fortune,* April 5, 2004, 252–258; and Scott McMurray, "Ford F-150: Have It Your Way," *Business 2.0,* March 2004, 53–55.
29. Kate Linebaugh, "Honda's Flexible Plants Provide Edge; Company Can Rejigger Vehicle Output to Match Consumer Demand Faster Than Its Rivals," *The Wall Street Journal,* September 23, 2008, B1.
30. 2006 Census of Manufacturers, reported in "Lean Choices," sidebar in Jonathan Katz, "Back to School," *Industry Week* (May 2007), 14.
31. Jeffrey K. Liker and James M. Morgan, "The Toyota Way in Services: The Case of Lean Product Development," *Academy of Management Perspectives* (May 2006), 5–20; and Brian Heymans, "Leading the Lean Enterprise," *Industrial Management* (September–October 2002), 28–33.
32. Jake Stiles, "Lean Initiatives Help Sealy Prepare for Market Rebound," *IndustryWeek.com* (May 6, 2009) http://www.industryweek.com/articles/lean_initiatives_help_sealy_prepare_for_market_rebound_19073.aspx?ShowAll=1 (accessed August 17, 2011); "Stiles Associates, LLC: Lean Companies Gain Even Greater Edge in Recessionary Times," *Science Letter* (March 17, 2009), 4089; Paul Davidson, "Lean Manufacturing Helps Companies Survive Recession," *USA Today,* November 1, 2009; and "About Sealy: Environmental Footprint," Sealy.com, http://www.sealy.com/About-Sealy/Environmental-Footprint.aspx (accessed August 17, 2011).
33. Art Kleiner, "Leaning Toward Utopia," *Strategy + Business,* no. 39 (Second Quarter 2005), 76–87; Fara Warner, "Think Lean," *Fast Company,* February 2002, 40, 42; Norihiko Shirouzu, "Gadget Inspector: Why Toyota Wins Such High Marks on Quality Surveys," *The Wall Street Journal*, March 15, 2001; and James P. Womack and Daniel T. Jones, *The Machine That Changed the World: The Story of Lean Production* (New York: HarperCollins, 1991).
34. Jonathan Katz, "Meeting of the Minds: Where Process and Discrete Manufacturing Converge," *Industry Week* (February 2009), 34-36.
35. B. Joseph Pine II, *Mass Customization: The New Frontier in Business Competition* (Boston: Harvard Business School Press, 1999); and Fabrizio Salvador, Pablo Martin De Holan, and Frank Piller, "Cracking the Code of Mass Customization," *Sloan Management Review* (Spring, 2009), 71–78.
36. Barry Berman, "Should Your Firm Adopt a Mass Customization Strategy?" *Business Horizons* (July–August 2002), 51–60.
37. Erick Schonfeld, "The Customized, Digitized, Have-It-Your-Way Economy," *Fortune,* September 28, 1998, 115–124.
38. Mark Tatge, "Red Bodies, Black Ink," *Forbes,* September 18, 2000, 114–115.
39. Zammuto and O'Connor, "Gaining Advanced Manufacturing Technologies' Benefits."
40. Joel D. Goldhar and David Lei, "Variety Is Free: Manufacturing in the Twenty-First Century," *Academy of Management Executive* 9, no. 4 (1995), 73–86.
41. Meredith, "The Strategic Advantages of the Factory of the Future."
42. Patricia L. Nemetz and Louis W. Fry, "Flexible Manufacturing Organizations: Implementations for Strategy Formulation and Organization Design," *Academy of Management Review* 13 (1988), 627–638; Paul S. Adler, "Managing Flexible Automation," *California Management Review* (Spring 1988), 34–56; Jeremy Main, "Manufacturing the Right Way," *Fortune,* May 21, 1990, 54–64; and Frank M. Hull and Paul D. Collins, "High-Technology Batch Production Systems: Woodward's Missing Type," *Academy of Management Journal* 30 (1987), 786–797.
43. Goldhar and Lei, "Variety Is Free: Manufacturing in the Twenty-First Century"; P. Robert Duimering, Frank Safayeni, and Lyn Purdy, "Integrated Manufacturing: Redesign the Organization before Implementing Flexible Technology," *Sloan Management Review* (Summer 1993), 47–56; and Zammuto and O'Connor, "Gaining Advanced Manufacturing Technologies' Benefits."
44. Goldhar and Lei, "Variety Is Free: Manufacturing in the Twenty-First Century."
45. Estimate reported in "Services Firms Expand at Slowest Pace in 17 Months," *MoneyNews.com* (August 3, 2011), http://www.moneynews.com/Economy/ism-economy-Service-Sector/2011/08/03/id/405915 (accessed August 15, 2011).
46. Byron J. Finch and Richard L. Luebbe, *Operations Management: Competing in a Changing Environment* (Fort Worth, TX: The Dryden Press, 1995), 51.
47. This discussion is based on David E. Bowen, Caren Siehl, and Benjamin Schneider, "A Framework for Analyzing Customer Service Orientations in Manufacturing," *Academy of Management Review* 14 (1989), 79–95; Peter K. Mills and Newton Margulies, "Toward a Core Typology

of Service Organizations," *Academy of Management Review* 5 (1980), 255–265; and Peter K. Mills and Dennis J. Moberg, "Perspectives on the Technology of Service Operations," *Academy of Management Review* 7 (1982), 467–478.

48. "Pandora Announces Listener Milestone," Pandora Press Release (July 12, 2011), http://blog.pandora.com/archives/press/2011/07/pandora_announc_1.html (accessed August 17, 2011).
49. Jena McGregor, "When Service Means Survival," *BusinessWeek,* March 2, 2009, 26–30; and Heather Green, "How Amazon Aims to Keep You Clicking," *BusinessWeek,* March 2, 2009, 37–40.
50. Liker and Morgan, "The Toyota Way in Services."
51. Paul Migliorato, "Toyota Retools Japan," *Business 2.0,* August 2004, 39–41.
52. Julie Jargon, "Latest Starbucks Buzzword: 'Lean' Japanese Techniques," *The Wall Street Journal*, August 4, 2009.
53. Julie Weed, "Factory Efficiency Comes to the Hospital," *The New York Times*, July 9, 2010.
54. Geeta Anand, "The Henry Ford of Heart Surgery," *The Wall Street Journal*, November 25, 2009, A16.
55. Richard B. Chase and David A. Tansik, "The Customer Contact Model for Organization Design," *Management Science* 29 (1983), 1037–1050.
56. Ibid.
57. David E. Bowen and Edward E. Lawler III, "The Empowerment of Service Workers: What, Why, How, and When," *Sloan Management Review* (Spring 1992), 31–39: Gregory B. Northcraft and Richard B. Chase, "Managing Service Demand at the Point of Delivery," *Academy of Management Review* 10 (1985), 66–75; and Roger W. Schmenner, "How Can Service Businesses Survive and Prosper?" *Sloan Management Review* 27 (Spring 1986), 21–32.
58. Ann Zimmerman, "Home Depot Tries to Make Nice to Customers," *The Wall Street Journal,* February 20, 2007, D1.
59. Richard Metters and Vincente Vargas, "Organizing Work in Service Firms," *Business Horizons* (July–August 2000), 23–32.
60. Perrow, "A Framework for the Comparative Analysis of Organizations" and *Organizational Analysis.*
61. Brian T. Pentland, "Sequential Variety in Work Processes," *Organization Science* 14, no. 5 (September–October 2003), 528–540.
62. Jim Morrison, "Grand Tour. Making Music: The Craft of the Steinway Piano," *Spirit,* February 1997, 42–49, 100.
63. Stuart F. Brown, "Biotech Gets Productive," *Fortune*, special section, "Industrial Management and Technology," January 20, 2003, 170[A]–170[H].
64. Michael Withey, Richard L. Daft, and William C. Cooper, "Measures of Perrow's Work Unit Technology: An Empirical Assessment and a New Scale," *Academy of Management Journal* 25 (1983), 45–63.
65. Christopher Gresov, "Exploring Fit and Misfit with Multiple Contingencies," *Administrative Science Quarterly* 34 (1989), 431–453; and Dale L. Goodhue and Ronald L. Thompson, "Task-Technology Fit and Individual Performance," *MIS Quarterly* (June 1995), 213–236.
66. Gresov, "Exploring Fit and Misfit with Multiple Contingencies;" Charles A. Glisson, "Dependence of Technological Routinization on Structural Variables in Human Service Organizations," *Administrative Science Quarterly* 23 (1978), 383–395; and Jerald Hage and Michael Aiken, "Routine Technology, Social Structure and Organizational Goals," *Administrative Science Quarterly* 14 (1969), 368–379.
67. Gresov, "Exploring Fit and Misfit with Multiple Contingencies;" A. J. Grimes and S. M. Kline, "The Technological Imperative: The Relative Impact of Task Unit, Modal Technology, and Hierarchy on Structure," *Academy of Management Journal* 16 (1973), 583–597; Lawrence G. Hrebiniak, "Job Technologies, Supervision and Work Group Structure," *Administrative Science Quarterly* 19 (1974), 395–410; and Jeffrey Pfeffer, *Organizational Design* (Arlington Heights, IL: AHM, 1978), Chapter 1.
68. Patrick E. Connor, *Organizations: Theory and Design* (Chicago: Science Research Associates, 1980); and Richard L. Daft and Norman B. Macintosh, "A Tentative Exploration into Amount and Equivocality of Information Processing in Organizational Work Units," *Administrative Science Quarterly* 26 (1981), 207–224.
69. Paul D. Collins and Frank Hull, "Technology and Span of Control: Woodward Revisited," *Journal of Management Studies* 23 (1986), 143–164; Gerald D. Bell, "The Influence of Technological Components of Work upon Management Control," *Academy of Management Journal* 8 (1965), 127–132; and Peter M. Blau and Richard A. Schoenherr, *The Structure of Organizations* (New York: Basic Books, 1971).
70. W. Alan Randolph, "Matching Technology and the Design of Organization Units," *California Management Review* 22–23 (1980–81), 39–48; Daft and Macintosh, "A Tentative Exploration into Amount and Equivocality of Information Processing"; and Michael L. Tushman, "Work Characteristics and Subunit Communication Structure: A Contingency Analysis," *Administrative Science Quarterly* 24 (1979), 82–98.
71. Andrew H. Van de Ven and Diane L. Ferry, *Measuring and Assessing Organizations* (New York: Wiley, 1980); and Randolph, "Matching Technology and the Design of Organization Units."
72. Richard L. Daft and Robert H. Lengel, "Information Richness: A New Approach to Managerial Behavior

and Organization Design," in Barry Staw and Larry L. Cummings, eds., *Research in Organizational Behavior*, vol. 6 (Greenwich, CT: JAI Press, 1984), 191–233; Richard L. Daft and Norman B. Macintosh, "A New Approach into Design and Use of Management Information," *California Management Review* 21 (1978), 82–92; Daft and Macintosh, "A Tentative Exploration into Amount and Equivocality of Information Processing;" W. Alan Randolph, "Organizational Technology and the Media and Purpose Dimensions of Organizational Communication," *Journal of Business Research* 6 (1978), 237–259; Linda Argote, "Input Uncertainty and Organizational Coordination in Hospital Emergency Units," *Administrative Science Quarterly* 27 (1982), 420–434; and Andrew H. Van de Ven and Andre Delbecq, "A Task Contingent Model of Work Unit Structure," *Administrative Science Quarterly* 19 (1974), 183–197.

73. Peggy Leatt and Rodney Schneck, "Criteria for Grouping Nursing Subunits in Hospitals," *Academy of Management Journal* 27 (1984), 150–165; and Robert T. Keller, "Technology-Information Processing," *Academy of Management Journal* 37, no. 1 (1994), 167–179.
74. Gresov, "Exploring Fit and Misfit with Multiple Contingencies;" Michael L. Tushman, "Technological Communication in R&D Laboratories: The Impact of Project Work Characteristics," *Academy of Management Journal* 21 (1978), 624–645; and Robert T. Keller, "Technology-Information Processing Fit and the Performance of R&D Project Groups: A Test of Contingency Theory," *Academy of Management Journal* 37, no. 1 (1994), 167–179.
75. James Thompson, *Organizations in Action* (New York: McGraw-Hill, 1967).
76. Ibid., 40.
77. Gene Bylinsky, "Shipmaking Gets Modern," *Fortune*, special section, "Industrial Management and Technology," January 20, 2003, 170[K]–170[L].
78. Murray R. Barrick, Bret H. Bradley, Amy L. Kristof-Brown, and Amy E. Colbert, "The Moderating Role of Top Management Team Interdependence: Implications for Real Teams and Working Groups," *Academy of Management Journal* 50, no. 3 (2007), 544–557.
79. Jody Hoffer Gittell, "Organizing Work to Support Relational Coordination," *The International Journal of Human Resource Management* 11, no. 3 (June 2000), 517–539.
80. Jody Hoffer Gittell, "Paradox of Coordination and Control," *California Management Review* 42, no. 3 (Spring 2000), 101–117.
81. Paul S. Adler, "Interdepartmental Interdependence and Coordination: The Case of the Design/Manufacturing Interface," *Organization Science* 6, no. 2 (March–April 1995), 147–167.
82. This discussion is based on Christopher Gresov, "Effects of Dependence and Tasks on Unit Design and Efficiency," *Organization Studies* 11 (1990), 503–529; Andrew H. Van de Ven, Andre Delbecq, and Richard Koenig, "Determinants of Coordination Modes within Organizations," *American Sociological Review* 41 (1976), 322–338; Argote, "Input Uncertainty and Organizational Coordination in Hospital Emergency Units;" Jack K. Ito and Richard B. Peterson, "Effects of Task Difficulty and Interdependence on Information Processing Systems," *Academy of Management Journal* 29 (1986), 139–149; and Joseph L. C. Cheng, "Interdependence and Coordination in Organizations: A Role-System Analysis," *Academy of Management Journal* 26 (1983), 156–162.
83. Robert W. Keidel, "Team Sports Models as a Generic Organizational Framework," *Human Relations* 40 (1987), 591–612; Robert W. Keidel, "Baseball, Football, and Basketball: Models for Business," *Organizational Dynamics* (Winter 1984), 5–18; and Nancy Katz, "Sports Teams as a Model for Workplace Teams: Lessons and Liabilities," *Academy of Management Executive* 15, no. 3 (2001), 56–67.
84. Michele Liu, Héléné Denis, Harvey Kolodny, and Benjt Stymne, "Organization Design for Technological Change," *Human Relations* 43 (January 1990), 7–22.
85. Gerald I. Susman and Richard B. Chase, "A Sociotechnical Analysis of the Integrated Factory," *Journal of Applied Behavioral Science* 22 (1986), 257–270; and Paul Adler, "New Technologies, New Skills," *California Management Review* 29 (Fall 1986), 9–28.
86. Based on Don Hellriegel, John W. Slocum, Jr., and Richard W. Woodman, *Organizational Behavior*, 8th ed. (Cincinnati, OH: SouthWestern, 1998), 491–495; and Gregory B. Northcraft and Margaret A. Neale, *Organizational Behavior: A Management Challenge*, 2nd ed. (Fort Worth, TX: The Dryden Press, 1994), 550–553.
87. F. Emery, "Characteristics of Sociotechnical Systems," Tavistock Institute of Human Relations, document 527 (1959); William Pasmore, Carol Francis, and Jeffrey Haldeman, "Sociotechnical Systems: A North American Reflection on Empirical Studies of the 70s," *Human Relations* 35 (1982), 1179–1204; and William M. Fox, "Sociotechnical System Principles and Guidelines: Past and Present," *Journal of Applied Behavioral Science* 31, no. 1 (March 1995), 91–105.
88. W. S. Cascio, *Managing Human Resources* (New York: McGraw-Hill, 1986), 19.
89. Eric Trist and Hugh Murray, eds., *The Social Engagement of Social Science: A Tavistock Anthology*, vol. II (Philadelphia: University of Pennsylvania Press, 1993); and William A. Pasmore, "Social Science Transformed: The Socio-Technical Perspective," *Human Relations* 48, no. 1 (1995), 1–21.
90. R. E. Walton, "From Control to Commitment in the Workplace," *Harvard Business Review* 63, no. 2 (1985), 76–84; E. E. Lawler, III, *High Involvement Management* (San Francisco: Jossey-Bass, 1986), 84; and Hellriegel, Slocum, and Woodman, *Organizational Behavior*, 491.

91. William A. Pasmore, "Social Science Transformed: The Socio-Technical Perspective," *Human Relations* 48, no. 1 (1995), 1–21.
92. David M. Upton, "What Really Makes Factories Flexible?" *Harvard Business Review* (July–August 1995), 74–84.
93. Pasmore, "Social Science Transformed: The Socio-Technical Perspective;" and H. Scarbrough, "Review Article: *The Social Engagement of Social Science: A Tavistock Anthology*, Vol. II," *Human Relations* 48, no. 1 (1995), 23–33.
94. Adapted loosely by Dorothy Marcic from "Hamburger Technology," in Douglas T. Hall et al., *Experiences in Management and Organizational Behavior*, 2nd ed. (New York: Wiley, 1982), 244–247, as well as "Behavior, Technology, and Work Design" in A. B. Shani and James B. Lau, *Behavior in Organizations* (Chicago: Irwin, 1996), M16–23 to M16–26.
95. Hampton/Summer/Webber, *Organizational Behavior Practice Management*, 4th ed., © 1982. Reprinted and Electronically reproduced by permission of Pearson Education, Inc., Upper Saddle River, New Jersey.

INTEGRATIVE CASE 10.0

First Union: An Office Without Walls[1]

Meg Rabb was a self-made woman. Having started her full-time career at 18, she was at the pinnacle of her career as vice president of training for First Union Federal, a large (fictitious name) savings and loan located in the eastern United States. Meg's division was responsible for both employee training and management development, and the services that her staff provided were very visible in the organization. Her unit was known as a "staff" one in the organization; that is, the training and development division served the needs of other units that were directly tied to serving consumers. These later "line" divisions were closer to final customers and, therefore, enjoyed high status in the organization.

Having recently survived several years of financial crisis and regulatory scrutiny, First Union was embarking on a new customer focus that it took very seriously. Significant amounts of financial resources were directed to employee training. All branch delivery mechanisms and systems were aimed at the achievement of a single service target: meeting consumers' changing financial needs. New approaches to service focused on customers' convenience needs and on the delivery of consistently high-quality personal service. At the same time, attention to cost containment was necessary to avoid further financial crisis and to please the board of directors; the organization spent resources available for internal programs very carefully. In sum, then, the fact that the training and development division was getting a big slice of the available resources gave it some stature in the organization as well as the clout that went with it, even though the division was still a staff function and not involved in direct customer interactions or service delivery.

Meg's achievements were financially rewarding and personally satisfying. She was very good at both the design and implementation phases of the training process, and the 12 trainers and management development specialists under her charge were highly qualified and respectful of her developmental and caring leadership style. Vice president titles at First Union Federal were hard to get, and Meg had only recently been promoted to the position of vice president. Five years ago, when she had been hired at the level of assistant vice president, not a single woman enjoyed the V.P. rank and title, and only a handful of men were V.P.s, out of a total work force of 1,700 employees. After five years of hard work and measurable success in her job, Meg was promoted to the level of vice president. One week after the announcement of her promotion, her boss, Dan Cummings, told her that she would receive a new office and that new furniture would be available to her should she be interested in replacing her existing desk and other fixtures, lamps, and equipment.

The Office As an Incentive

Being a V.P. at First Union brought certain perquisites, or nonfinancial rewards. An office, a travel allowance, a larger share of human and other departmental financial resources, and a parking space in the corporate lot—all of these traditionally accompanied an assistant vice president in the trip up the corporate ladder to vice president.

Meg looked forward to the privacy that her new office would afford. That, above all other nonfinancial perquisites, was to be cherished in her very busy office. The office was characteristically noisy, with lots of people shuffling in and out of the office area all day long to attend training sessions or to schedule programs.

The physical office layout in her department was uncomplicated. Each employee, in a total staff of 12, had his or her own "section," a partitioned area walled off with movable screens. Employees had variable quality office furniture within their areas, depending on their level in the organizational hierarchy. All areas had desks; however, the lowest-level employees received cheaper-quality furniture of the hand-me-down variety, a desk chair, and possibly a guest chair. Lower-level employees typically had just enough room to move around in their space and often had to share space within screened-off areas with other employees. Meg herself had been seated within a screened-off area located in the corner of the work area; this space had two floor-to-ceiling glass walls that overlooked the expansive city, 10 stories below. Her plan was to make this same space her office.

The Walls Came Down

The construction of the office was completed quickly, within three weeks of her promotion. The office was simply decorated, with grey carpet and sparse decorations that included some tasteful (but inexpensive) modern prints, a desk lamp of modern design (selected from an office supply catalog), and utilitarian desk accessories of simple design. Meg planned on using her existing office furniture in order to economize. The old furniture suited the décor of the new office, and she felt good about saving money for First Union. Her own preference was for modern décor—a

[1]This case was written by Susan Stites-Doe and Melissa Waite, SUNY College/at Brockport, and Rajnandini Pillai, California State University at San Marcos. Used with permission. Originally published in the Journal of Private Enterprise.

stark contrast to the other executives' offices, which were decorated in conservative colonial décor. She occupied her new office space comfortably for one day.

Upon arriving at work the following morning, she was summoned into her boss's office. Dan Cummings was the senior vice president of human resources. He was well liked and was very accurately "tuned in" to the political rules of the game; his influence in the organization seemed to blossom after he organized the first annual "Dan Cummings Golf Invitational," now in its fourth year of operation. Golfers from the old guard at First Union, those V.P.s and assistant V.P.s close to the senior management group, always felt honored by their invitations. Invitations denoted status in the organization. Meg had taken golf lessons this past summer in hopes of being included in next year's tournament, despite the fact that no female employees had ever received an invitation to the tournament. Even though her boss knew about her golf lessons, she had not been invited that year, and she'd never voiced her disappointment over not being included to anyone.

Upon entering Dan's office, Meg was perfunctorily informed that the president of First Union had expressed concern over the size of Meg's office. A close friend of the building manager, the president had strolled down to the construction site two days ago to meet the manager for lunch. The bottom line was this: the president had ruled that the office was too large. Meg was told that the existing office would have to be "modified" to conform to new building regulations set in place just that week. The plan was to tear down her office walls and to rebuild them using the proper 10 feet by 10 feet specifications detailed in the new regulations. Her office, unfortunately, had been built using 12 feet by 12 feet specifications deemed by the building manager to be appropriate.

Meg's immediate reaction to this troubling news was one of anger. She masked her true feelings behind a demeanor of cooperative resistance. She was very concerned about what this decision would mean to her employees—how they would take the news and how she could present it to them to mitigate damage to her department's normally healthy morale. She had other concerns, too. She worried that this event would cause her to lose power and esteem among her peers. Meg questioned the building manager later that morning to try to get a handle on how and why such an expensive mistake had been made. He told her that the 12 feet by 12 feet specifications that had been used for her office were set in place by him personally to take advantage of the view and to make the best use of the surrounding building structure. Other contacts told her that the former building regulations that were more lax than the current ones, yet were similar to the existing ones, had been frequently ignored to suit individual employees' tastes. She couldn't help but feel sorry for the building manager. He had used his skills in office design to try to match form with function, and his friendship with the president had apparently not been enough to shield him from personal repercussions. The tone of his voice and his eagerness to end their telephone conversation suggested that he was annoyed about the entire affair. Her empathy for him was joined with confusion. Had he not taken risks in the past by deviating from strict adherence to the regulations? Had he not already considered these risks? And, why was she the first person to fall victim to strict adherence to this regulation?

The Culture and Power Base at First Union

The overall culture of the bank was marked by conservatism. As one might expect when money is involved, cautiousness and conservatism were valued, as was care in retaining tight financial control over depositors' money. Power and influence at First Union were clustered primarily in the line units and at the executive levels of the organization. The mortgage division was particularly powerful. First Union had only recently remodeled the floor on which the mortgage division was located. As the "bread and butter" arm of the organization, the mortgage division enjoyed substantial power because of the revenues it generated and its contribution to the bottom line. Visitors to the newly remodeled offices never failed to remark on the beauty of the mortgage offices and on their distinctiveness from the rest of the bank. Rumor had it that the president of the bank was disturbed about the cost of the renovations but failed to act on the matter due to the high share of profits that the division generated.

In terms of power distribution across genders, First Union had no ranking female executives at or above the level of vice president prior to Meg's promotion. This fact prompted intervention from the Equal Employment Opportunity Commission, which encouraged First Union to seek out qualified female managers for promotion to executive status. The EEOC's scrutiny was public information, and Meg often felt awkward about being the first female to pave the way. Meg did not have a mentor at a higher rank than she was in the organization. Her philosophy had always been that hard work pays off, and she was not particularly sensitive to social and political cues in the environment. Her male counterparts were very active and visible across the political terrain at First Union, as her boss's golf tournament activities attested. Friendships mattered a lot in the organization, and many of her male counterparts in other divisions were socially connected with their superiors outside of work.

Some of the artwork at First Union seemed to be very telling of values held to be near and dear to the organization. One lithograph was particularly indicative of the gender values in the organization. It featured a series of free-floating female breasts arranged in a decorative manner. The print was located in the president's conference room and was visible to board members, outside clients, and to internal staff members who attended regular meetings in the room. One lower-level female manager who visited the room perhaps 15 times had never deciphered the objects in the lithograph. A higher-ranking male colleague proudly pointed out the identity of the shapes to her, laughing as he said, "Hey, did you see what this print is made up of?" She was embarrassed by his remark, but joined in his laughter to get past the moment.

What Should She Do?

Meg sat down and made notes about how she would proceed. One thing was sure: If she was going to survive at First Union, she would have to learn how to play ball. As a V.P. in a staff unit, she had to do what she could to elevate her political status in the organization. Her worst fear was that she might lose her job; her very survival might depend on developing more political savvy. She had no one to turn to in the organization for advice and felt that she couldn't afford to make even a single mistake. Meg resolved to supplement her golf lessons with a crash course in organizational politics.

INTEGRATIVE CASE 11.0

Costco: Join the Club

Following high school, James Sinegal worked for discount warehouse Fed Mart unloading mattresses. Then, in the 1970s as an employee of California-based Price Club, he absorbed every detail of the high-volume, low-cost warehouse club formula pioneered by Sol Price.

Armed with knowledge and ideas, Sinegal partnered with Jeffrey Brotman to establish Costco Wholesale Corporation. The duo opened their first store in Seattle in 1983. Today, nearing 30 years in business, Sinegal's vision and success not only eclipsed those of his mentor but led to the merger of Costco and Price Club.

No Frills

In 2010, Costco's reputation for rock-bottom pricing and razor-thin profit margins helped the company maintain its position as the nation's fourth-largest retailer and the number-one membership warehouse retailer with 572 stores (425 in the United States), 142,000 employees, and 55 million members. Sales reached $76 billion, up 9.1 percent and reflecting, in part, a consumer tendency in a poor economy to focus on value, but more significantly a unique corporate culture that gives not only lip-service to the value of its employees, but maintains a reputation for honoring that value.

The no-frills warehouse-club concept exemplifies the much-maligned "big box" store—merchandise stacked floor to ceiling on wooden pallets, housed in 150,000 square footage of bare concrete, and illuminated by fluorescent lighting. Customers flash member cards and push oversized carts or flatbeds down wide aisles, unadorned by advertising or display. Costco reflects industry standards and consumer expectations for providing limited selection, volume buying, and low pricing.

Valuing People

But the owners believe the secret to Costco's success lies in the many ways the company ventures from the norm by overturning conventional wisdom. Because the owners view people as the organization's "competitive edge," labor and benefits comprise 70 percent of Costco's operating costs. Despite Wall Street criticism, the company maintains its devotion to a well-compensated workforce and scoffs at the notion of sacrificing the well-being of employees for the sake of profits. The 2010 Annual Report declares, "With respect to expenses relating to the compensation of our employees, our philosophy is not to seek to minimize the wages and benefits they earn. Rather, we believe that achieving our longer-term objectives of reducing turnover and enhancing employee satisfaction requires maintaining compensation levels that are better than the industry average." The report admits Costco's willingness to "absorb costs" of higher wages that other retailers routinely squeeze from their workforce. As a result, what the company lacks in margin per item, management believes it makes up in volume, in maintaining "pricing authority" by "consistently providing the most competitive values," and in purchased loyalty memberships which, Sinegal points out, "locks them into shopping with you."

Sinegal is a no-nonsense CEO whose annual salary ($550,000) is a fraction of the traditional pay for large corporate executives and reflects an organizational culture that attempts to minimize disparity between management and workers. Luxury corporate offices are out of the question. Sinegal dresses in casual attire, wears a nametag, answers his own phone, and like all members of management, spends a significant amount of time (upwards of 200 days annually) on the warehouse sales floor.

This unorthodox employer-employee relationship is in sharp contrast to the industry norm, with employees in most companies feeling the added stress of infrequent site visits by suited corporate executives. During an interview for ABC's news magazine "20/20" in 2006, Sinegal provided a simple explanation for the frequency of warehouse visits. "The employees know that I want to say hello to them, because I like them." Indeed, Costco employees marvel at the CEO's ability to remember names and to connect with them as individuals. It is that "in the trenches together" mind-set that defines Costco's corporate culture, contributing to a level of mutual support, teamwork, empowerment, and rapid response that can be activated for confronting any situation. A dramatic example occurred when employees instantly created a Costco emergency brigade, armed with forklifts and fire extinguishers, whose members organized themselves and rushed to offer first aid and rescue trapped passengers following the wreck of a commuter train behind a California warehouse store.

Costco's benevolent and motivational management approach manifests itself most dramatically in wages and benefits. Employees sign a one-page employment contract and then join co-workers as part of the best-compensated workforce in retail. Hourly wages of $17.00 smash those of competitors ($10 to $11.50 per hour). Rewards and bonuses for implementation of time-saving ideas submitted by an individual employee can provide up to 150 shares of company stock. In addition, employees receive a generous benefits package including health care (82 percent of premiums are paid by the company) as well as retirement plans.

Costco's generosity to employees flies in the face of industry and Wall Street conventional wisdom whereby companies attempt to improve profits and shareholder earnings by keeping wages and benefits low. Sinegal insists the investment in human capital is good business. "You get what you pay for," he asserts. As a result, Costco enjoys the reputation of a loyal, highly productive workforce, and store openings attract thousands of quality applicants.

By turning over inventory rather than people, Costco can boast an annual employee turnover of only 6 percent, compared to retail's dismal 50 percent average. Taking into account the cost of worker replacement (1.5 to 2.5 times the individual's annual salary), the higher wages and benefits package pays off in the bigger picture with higher retention levels, a top-quality workforce, low shrinkage from theft (0.2 percent), and greater sales per employee. The combination results in increased operating profit per hour. Whether used for attracting customers or employees, the need for PR or advertising is nonexistent. Sinegal told ABC that the company doesn't spend a dime on advertising, as it already has over 140,000 enthusiastic ambassadors scattered through Costco's warehouses.

Design to Fit

Equal care has been given to organization design. Sinegal's belief in a "flat, fast, and flexible" organization encourages de-facto CEO designation for local warehouse managers who have the freedom and authority to make quick, independent decisions that suit the local needs of customers and employees. The only requirement is that any decision must fit into the organization's five-point code of ethics. Decisions must be lawful, serve the best interests of customers and employees, respect suppliers, and reward shareholders. Likewise, employee training places a high priority on coaching and empowerment over command and control.

All of this fits together in a culture and structure in which the focus on meeting customer needs goes beyond rock-bottom pricing. Costco's new store location efforts seek "fit" between the organization and the community it serves. Typical suburban locations emphasize the bulk shopping needs of families and small businesses, and Costco has extended its own private label, Kirkland Signature. While other companies downsize or sell their private labels, Costco works to develop Kirkland, which now accounts for approximately 400 of Costco's 4,000 in-stock items. The private label provides additional savings of up to 20 percent off of products produced by top manufacturers, such as tires made by Michelin specifically for the Kirkland label. Additional efforts to better meet the needs of customers contributed to Costco's decision to run selected stores as test labs. Over the past decade, selected Costco stores paved the way for launching a variety of ancillary businesses, including pharmacies, optical services, and small business services to better serve the one-stop-shopping needs of the company's suburban customers.

Meanwhile, urban Costco locations acknowledge the customer's desire to purchase in bulk while also serving the upscale shopping desires of condo-dwellers. In these locations, the urgency to "purchase before it's gone" tempts consumers into treasure hunts with special deals on luxury items such as Dom Perignon Champagne, Waterford crystal, or Prada watches.

The rapid growth of Costco from one store in Seattle to America's warehouse club leader and global retailer has come with a share of growing pains as the organization attempts to adapt to its various environments. The merger with Price Club brought an infusion of unionized workers, forcing Sinegal and management officials to push Costco's "superior" wages and benefits as a way to negate the need for unionization.

New Issues

Costco's own reputation for high ethical standards and self-regulation has, in the face of rapid expansion, come up against myriad new problems ranging from complaints about a lack of notification for management job openings to persistent complaints of a glass-ceiling that provides few opportunities for the advancement of women within the organization. In response, the company instituted online job postings, automated recruiting, the use of an outside vendor for hiring, and a recommitment to equity in promotion.

International issues are often more complex and often run up against local needs and perceptions. For example, efforts to expand into Cuernavaca, Mexico, were viewed from the company perspective as a win-win situation, opening a new market and providing jobs and high-quality, low-priced items for area shoppers. When the site of a dilapidated casino became available, Costco moved quickly, but suddenly found itself facing charges of cultural insensitivity in Mexico. Accusations in Cuernavaca that Costco was locating a parking lot over an area with significance in artistic and national heritage led to negotiations under which Costco set aside millions of dollars to preserve landscape, restore murals, and work alongside city planners and representatives of the Mexican Institute of Fine Arts & Literature in the building of a state-of-the-art cultural center and museum.

The story illustrates the emphasis on moral leadership that has come to characterize Costco and its senior management. Business decisions based strictly on financial terms take a back seat to success based on broader criteria: Are we creating greater value for the customer? Are we doing the right thing for employees and other stakeholders? Management believes that the answers to these broader questions help keep the company relevant to the issues and trends shaping the future of business.

Indications are bright for Costco's future, but questions loom on the horizon. Company visionary Sinegal signals no plans to retire, but everyone from Wall Street pundits to customers, shareholders, and employees wonders how the organization might change after he has stepped down. Will future leaders be willing to maintain the modest levels of compensation for top management and maintain the company's above-average wages and benefits for employees? And how will increased globalization alter the strong corporate culture?

Sources

Richard L. Daft, "Costco Wholesale Corporation, Parts One-Six," in *Management*, 8th ed. (Mason, OH: Southwestern, 2008).

"Table of Contents, Item 7—Management's Discussion and Analysis of Financial Conditions," *Costco 2010 Annual Report.*

Wayne F. Cascio, "The High Cost of Low Wages," *Harvard Business Review* 84, no. 2 (December 2006).

Alan B. Goldberg and Bill Ritter, "Costco CEO Finds Pro-Worker Means Profitability," ABC News 20/20, August 2, 2006, http://abcnews.go.com/2020/Business/story?id=1362779 (accessed January 4, 2012).

Doug Desjardins, "Culture of Inclusion: Where Top Executives Lead by Example and Honesty and Frugality Are Valued Virtues," *DSN Retailing Today* (December 2005).

Michelle V. Rafter, "Welcome to the Club," *Workforce Management* 84, no. 4 (April 2005), 40–46.

12.0

INTEGRATIVE CASE 12.0

Hartland Memorial Hospital (A): An Inbox Exercise*

Introduction

Hartland Memorial Hospital, established 85 years ago when wealthy benefactor Sir Reginald Hartland left an estate valued at more than $2 million, is a 285-bed, free-standing community general hospital located in Westfield, a ski resort community of 85,000 people. Ridgeview Hospital is the only other hospital in the area, situated some 18 miles away in the village of Easton. Hartland Memorial is a fully accredited institution that provides a full range of medical and surgical services. It has an excellent reputation for delivering high-quality medical care for the citizens of Westfield and the surrounding area.

You and the Hospital

You are Elizabeth Parsons, BSN, MSN, PhD, vice president for Nursing Services at Hartland Memorial. You accepted this position 17 months ago and have been instrumental in introducing a number of innovations in nursing practice and management. In particular, these innovations have included the establishment of job sharing, self-scheduling, and a compressed work week for all general-duty nurses. In addition, you have also developed a new performance appraisal system and are contemplating using it to create a merit pay system for the nursing staff.

Your administrative assistant is Wilma Smith, who handles your correspondence, as well as scheduling meetings and conferences. Each morning she opens whatever hard-copy mail and memos you have received, and puts them on your desk. She also places hard-copy phone messages on your desk from those people who did not want to be routed to your voicemail. Although she has access to your e-mail, voice mail, and electronic calendar, she does not routinely monitor them. Wilma is only moderately comfortable with the new modes of communicating, generally preferring the ways of the "pre-electronic" era.

Your second in command is Anne Armstrong, who is assistant director for Nursing Services. Anne has worked at Hartland Memorial for seven years, and is very competent. She has only recently returned to work, however, after spending some time in the hospital recovering from the suicide of her husband. A list of the key personnel at Hartland Memorial is presented in Exhibit 1, and selected biographical sketches can be found in Exhibit 2.

EXHIBIT 1
List of Key Personnel at Hartland Hospital

Name	Position
Allan Reid	President and CEO
Scott Little	Assistant to the President
Elizabeth Parsons	Vice President-Nursing Service
Anne Armstrong	Assistant Director-Nursing Service
Cynthia Nichols	Vice President-Human Resources
Clement Westaway, MD	President-Medical Staff
Janet Trist	Nursing Supervisor-3 East
Sylvia Godfrey	Weekend Supervisor
Jane Sawchuck	Clinical Nurse Specialist
Norm Sutter	Vice President-Finance
Marion Simpson	Auditing Clerk
Fran Nixon	Staff Relations Officer
George Cross	Nurses Union Representative
Bernard Stevens	Chairman of the Board
Wilma Smith	Administrative Assistant

The Situation

You have just returned from a greatly needed long weekend off. At your husband's insistence, the two of you left Thursday evening for a mountain resort, and just got back last night. Long hours, high stress, and constantly being accessible by cell phone, voice mail, and e-mail have been taking their toll—you seem to have been "on-call" continuously for months now. Compounding these "curses-of-the-modern-job" have been meeting the needs ("being there") for your school-age kids, and, a recent development, the demands of addressing your parents' needs as they age. In particular, your mom

*This case was written by Kent V. Rondeau, University of Alberta, Edmonton, John E. Paul, University of North Carolina at Chapel Hill, and Jonathon S. Rakich, Indiana University Southeast, New Albany. The case is intended solely as a vehicle for classroom discussion, and is not intended to illustrate either effective or ineffective handling of the situation described.

EXHIBIT 2
Brief Biographical Sketches of Key Players at Hartland

Elizabeth Parsons	A professionally trained and degreed registered nurse (BSN, MSN, PhD). Age 45, with 20 years of progressive management and nursing experience. Married, two children, 10 and 12.
Allan Reid	CEO at Hartland Hospital for 2 years. Age 35, with 6 years experience as an assistant administrator at a 100-bed rural hospital. MHA degree. Married, two children.
Bernard Stevens	Colonel, U.S. Army Infantry (retired). Chairman of the board for Hartland Hospital for the past 12 years. Age 70. Widower, four grown children.
Clement Westaway, MD	Medical degree from the University of Pennsylvania. Internist. Member of the Hartland medical staff for 30 years and president of medical staff for the past 10 years. Age 64. Divorced, two grown children.
Anne Armstrong	Assistant director of Nursing Service at Hartland for the past five years. Has MSN degree. Age 35. Recently widowed, two children.
Janet Trist	Nursing supervisor. Interrupted career at age 26 to raise her children. Resumed working two years ago. RN (diploma program). Age 41. Married.
Wilma Smith	Administrative assistant in her present position for the past 15 years. Has worked at Hartland for 28 years. Age 50. Single, no children.

seems increasingly incapable of taking care of your dad, for whom some other living arrangements may have to be found. Caught between responsibilities with kids and parents (to say nothing about spouse) you are truly in the "sandwich" generation.

The weekend away, however, was wonderful. You were out of cell phone coverage, and the inn did not make its computer generally available to guests. In any case, your husband would have probably left you if you'd logged on or called in. Sunday night after getting home you had planned on logging on and assessing the situation facing you at work, after four blessed days out of touch. The kids, however, needed attention, the dog needed walking, and Mom called and talked for over an hour about what to do about Dad. You never got to your voice mail, either.

It is now 7:45 A.M. on Monday morning, and you have just a little over one hour until your first meeting of the day with Norm Sutter, vice president for Finance. You really have to get through your e-mail, voice mail, and the hard-copy items Wilma left on your desk—letters, phone messages, etc.—and take some action before meeting with Norm. You know the rest of the day will be a blur, and you'll have no further opportunities to get caught up. Moreover, new stuff will be coming in and piling up constantly. The refreshed feeling you had after the weekend out of town is rapidly slipping away. . . A hard copy schedule of your appointments for the day left on Friday by Wilma is shown in Exhibit 3. You know that it will likely be changing.

What Needs to Be Done

This case includes the various e-mails, voice mails, and hard-copy letters and messages that Elizabeth finds awaiting her. Since Wilma doesn't arrive until 8:30 A.M. Elizabeth has the office by herself. Note that the Hartland Hospital IT system does a fairly good job of filtering out spam and junk mail. The occasional item does make it through, which Elizabeth immediately deletes. Additionally, however, there are the e-newsletters from The Kaiser Family Foundation, the Commonwealth Fund, ACHE, etc. to which Elizabeth subscribes, but which she rarely has time to read. She tends to let these pile up in her in-box, sometimes making it hard to find the critical material there. The newsletters that came in over her mini holiday are not included.

For each item, indicate the course of action you think Elizabeth should pursue. You can choose from one of the following action alternatives. Because you may not have all the information needed to make a decision, please make notes that explain your assumptions, thinking and justification for that item. Be prepared to defend your

EXHIBIT 3
Schedule of Appointments, Monday, October 7 (as of 7:45 A.M.; left on your desk by Wilma, Friday afternoon at 5 P.M.)

8:00 A.M.	
8:30	
9:00	Meeting with Norm Sutter
9:30	
10:00	Reg. Monday morning meeting with nursing supervisors
10:30	
11:00	Meeting with Clement Westaway
11:30	
12:00 P.M.	Lunch with Anne Armstrong
12:30"	
1:00	Orientation talk to new nursing recruits
1:30"	
2:00	
2:30	Meeting of infection control committee
3:00"	
3:30	
4:00	Meeting with Allan Reid
4:30"	
5:00	
5:30	

Elizabeth Parson's "Inbox" Monday, October 7

ITEM 1: E-mail

To: Elizabeth Parsons, VP-Nursing Service
From: Scott Little, Assistant to the President
Date: October 4, 8:00 AM
Subject: Wandering patients—IMPORTANT!

On Thursday evening, Mrs. Grace O'Brien, a patient with diabetes and Alzheimer's disease, was missing from her room when her daughter came to visit her. It took the staff more than 3 hours to finally locate her. She was found naked and unconscious in the basement washroom of the Stuart Annex. Her daughter is extremely upset and is threatening to sue the hospital.
We don't need another lawsuit!!!
–Scott

ITEM 2: Letter

> *Eliz - Please note what actions are needed! ~A.*

September 26
President, Hartland Hospital

Dear Sir,

I have been a patient in your hospital on three different occasions over the last 4 years. In the past I have been very satisfied with the nursing care that I have received; however, my last stay there has left much to be desired. For the most part I have found that many of your nurses are very rude and arrogant. On a number of times when I asked these people for assistance, they would either refuse to help me, tell me they were too busy, or ignore me altogether.

I have great respect for Hartland Hospital and I trust that you would want to correct this problem. My late husband, Horace, was once a trustee at your hospital and would never have allowed this to happen.

Sincerely,
Mable Coleman Westfield

ITEM 3: Voice Mail

(Voice message left at 7:30 A.M. on office phone—you forgot to turn on your cell phone driving into work.)

"Elizabeth, this is Mom. I tried to get you before you left home this morning, but just missed you—Dad got up today upset and saying that he was 'a burden.' He's gone back to sleep now. What should I do? Please call when you get a chance!"

ITEM 4: E-Mail

To: Elizabeth Parsons, VP-Nursing Service
From: Allan Reid, President/CEO
Date: October 4
Time: 2:10 PM
Subject: EOM

I have heard that a number of other hospitals have been very successful at motivating their staff by implementing employee recognition programs. These programs can go a long way toward increasing employee commitment and morale. I would like to institute an "Employee-of-the-Month" award here at Hartland. I have a few ideas and would like to discuss them with you. A.

ITEM 5: E-Mail

> To: Elizabeth Parsons, VP-Nursing Service
> From: Sylvia Godfrey, R.N., Weekend Supervisor
> Date: October 6
> Time: 9:07 PM
> Subject: Insufficient staffing
>
> Again this weekend we had a number of nurses call in sick and we were subsequently short staffed. I had to call in nurses from the "availability list" that was provided by the Temp Placement Agency. I don't really think these nurses are any good because they are poorly tr ained and make too many errors. I am sick and tired of having to go through this **hassle every week**!
>
> Sylvia

ITEM 6: E-Mail

> To: Elizabeth Parsons, VP-Nursing Service
> From: Janet Trist, R.N., Supervisor-3 East
> Date: October 4
> Time: 1:23 PM
> Subject: Scheduling problems
>
> I am really having a problem with this new self-scheduling system that we adopted last month. A number of my senior nurses are refusing to go along with it and are threatening to quit unless we go back to the old system. It's affecting the morale on my unit and making my life miserable. We need to discuss this right away.
>
> Janet

ITEM 7: Letter

> **WESTFIELD HIGH SCHOOL**
>
> September 28
> Elizabeth Parsons
> Vice President-Nursing Service
> Hartland Hospital Westfield
>
> Dear Mrs. Parsons;
>
> The Future Careers Club of Westfield High School would like to invite you to be the guest speaker at our November meeting. The meeting will be held on November 14 at 8:00 P.M. in the school auditorium. We would like you to discuss "The Changing Role of the Professional Nurse."
>
> We believe that your presentation will be quite informative for us because several of our students are interested in pursuing a nursing career.
>
> We hope that you will be able to accept this invitation. Please call our sponsor, Mrs. Bonnie Tartabull, to confirm at your earliest convenience. Thank you.
>
> Sincerely,
> Kathy Muller
> President, Westfield High Future Careers Club

ITEM 8: E-Mail

To: Elizabeth Parsons, VP-Nursing Service
From: Marion Simpson, Auditing
Date: October 4
Time: 9:45 AM
Subject: Hours of work for part-time nurses

Once again, many part-time nurses are working between 25 and 30 hours per week. If we permit this to continue, under the terms of the collective agreement, we must give full-time benefits to those involved.
The agreement slates that full-time benefits must be given to those working in excess of 25 hours per week.
The actual number of hours worked per week for part-timers averaged 24.5 hours for the month of September.
Marion Simpson

ITEM 9: Written note from Wilma

To: Elizabeth Parsons
From: Scott Little, Assistant to the President
Time: 10:20
Mr. Little called, but did not leave a message.

ITEM 10: E-mail

To: Elizabeth Parsons, Vice President-Nursing Service
From: Cynthia Nichols, Vice President-Human Resources
Date: October 2
Time: 4:45 PM
Subject: Sexual harassment charges

STRICTLY CONFIDENTIAL
We have just received a notification from a nurse employed here at Hartland alleging sexual harassment by one of our physicians on staff. The charges, if verified, are extremely serious. I would like to appoint you, along with Fran Nixon, from our staff relations department, and George Cross, union representative for the nurses association, to form a committee to investigate these charges. I have been told that the individual claiming harassment has already begun legal action, so we need to proceed with haste.

Cynthia Nichols, Vice President

ITEM 11: Hard Copy

MEMO
To: Elizabeth Parsons, Vice President-Nursing Service
From: Marion Simpson, Auditing
Date: October 3
Subject: Reimbursement for travel

Further to your request for travel reimbursement for your upcoming conference, I regret to inform you that you have already used up this year's travel budget allocation and therefore will not be reimbursed from this account.

Marion Simpson

ITEM 12: Written note from Wilma

Telephone Message
To: Elizabeth Parsons
From: Norm Sutter
Date: October 4
Time: 3:05 P.M.

Mr. Sutter called and asked if the next year's budget projections for nursing have been finished. He needs these figures by Monday. Wilma

ITEM 13: Hard copy

MEMO
To: Elizabeth Parsons, VP-Nursing Service
From: Scott Little, Assistant to the President
Date: October 3
Subject: United Way Campaign

This is a follow-up to our discussion of last week concerning the appointment of someone from your department to serve as a representative for our hospital's annual United Way Campaign. I need to have the name of your representative by Friday, October 4th. —Scott

ITEM 14: Written note from Wilma

To: Betty Parsons
Date: October 4
Time: 2:12 P.M.

Mr. Stevens dropped in and was looking for you. He seemed quite upset and was muttering something about a lawsuit. He wants you to call him as soon as you get back from your trip.
Wilma

ITEM 15: E-Mail

October 4
4:45 PM

Ms Parsons - Can you "please" bring the snacks for the team for Jimmy's tee-ball game Monday night? Several other moms have already said they couldn't! Please confirm if this is OK. Thanks so much!! You're the true "Super-Mom"! Regards, Coach Bailey

ITEM 16: E-mail

To: Elizabeth Parsons, VP-Nursing Service
From: Jane Sawchuck, Clinical Nurse Specialist
Date: October 3
Subject: Nosocomial Infections

It has come to my attention that, again last month, we have recorded high levels of Staphylococcus and Pseudomonas in operating rooms B and C. It is becoming apparent that we need to review our standard procedures in this area before an epidemic breaks out.
Jane

ITEM 17: E-mail

To: Betty Parsons
From: Allan Reid
Date: October 3

My niece, Jennifer, just graduated from nursing school and will be in town just one day-Monday, October 7. She is looking for a job in her field and I have asked her to talk to you. She is a delightful girl. Would you please see her? Allan

ITEM 18: E-mail

To: Elizabeth Parsons, VP-Nursing Service
From: Scott Little, Assistant to the President
Date: October 4
Subject: Nurse working illegally

Carmen Espinoza, the woman I talked to you about, was working illegally for us. She was using a stolen Social Security number. The Immigration and Naturalization Services (INS) contacted me yesterday and a representative will be corning Monday afternoon to inquire about the matter.
Please give me a call right away. Scott

ITEM 19: Telephone Message

(Wilma intercepted the call and took a message; put note in front of you)

To: Elizabeth Parsons, Vice President-Nursing Service
From: Bernard Stevens, Chairman of the Board
Date: October 7
Time: 8:55 A.M.

Mr. Stevens just called and says that he needs to meet with you and Allan Reid this morning at 10:00 A.M.

ITEM 20: E-mail

To: Elizabeth Parsons, Vice President-Nursing Service
From: Dr. Clement Westaway, President-Medical Staff
Date: October 2
Subject: Nurse-physician relations

Further to our discussion last week concerning the pressing need to improve communication between physicians and nurses at Hartland Memorial, I am hoping that the suggestions that I gave you will be successfully implemented by your staff. Remember, we are all trying to provide the best possible medical care for our patients. *C.W., MD*

ITEM 21: E-mail

To: Elizabeth Parsons, Vice President-Nursing Service
From: Cynthia Nichols, VP-Human Resources
Date: October 3
Subject: Firing Ms. Jean White, R.N.

As we discussed yesterday, it is important to conduct the termination interview of nurse Jean White as soon as possible. Her last day of work at Hartland will be October 18 and, according to our collective agreement, she requires 2 weeks' notice. Please call me when the deed is done.

Cynthia Nichols, VP-HR

STOP!!

Do not proceed to the next page until you have responded to all previous items.

ITEM 22: Telephone Call (LIVE**)**

Time: 9:45 A.M., Monday, October 7

Allan Reid just calls, and tells you that Mrs. Grace O'Brien, the patient with diabetes and Alzheimer's disease, is again missing from her room, apparently since late last night. He advises you that he was just informed of this by a local newspaper reporter who had gotten wind of the story. He instructs you to call Mrs. O'Brien's daughter to tell her of this recent development before she hears or reads it in the media. Reid gives you no opportunity to respond, saying, "I have the reporter on the other line and have to go." He then hangs up the telephone.

underlying rationale. If delegating a task, identify who should be responsible for each item. *Work sequentially through each item.*

Action Alternatives
_Call immediately
_Note to call within 2–3 days
_E-mail immediately
_E-mail within a day
_Meet with ASAP
_Forward to: ________
_Note to meet within 2–3 days
_Other (Specify: _______)
_No response needed

Exhibit 4 is a partial diagram of the formal organization structure at Hartland Memorial Hospital.

After completing your action alternatives and justifications for each inbox item, use your knowledge of relationships to construct an informal organization chart, or *sociogram,* for the hospital. Use the organization chart in Exhibit 4 to draw lines between Elizabeth Parsons and other people. Portray positive/neutral/negative relationships with lines of different colors or thickness. Also indicate power relationships, the level of trust, frequency of communication, and criticality of relationships for her successful performance. Include all players about whom you have information. What does your diagram reveal about what is going on that day?

EXHIBIT 4
Hartland Memorial Hospital (Partial Organization Chart)

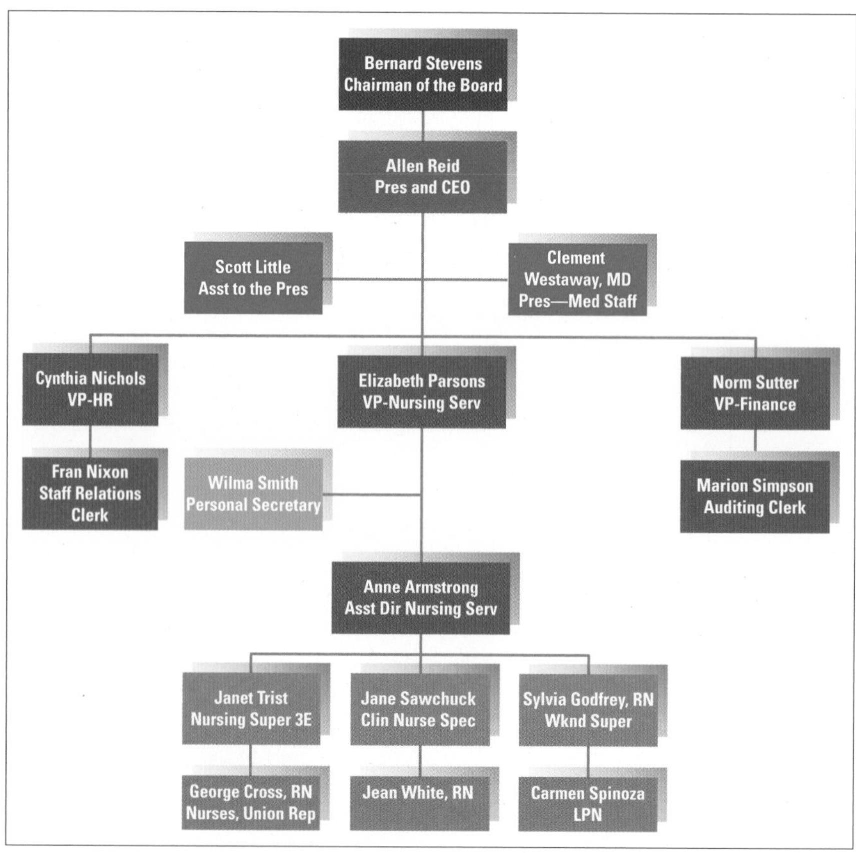

Glossary

A

adaptability culture a culture characterized by strategic focus on the external environment through flexibility and change to meet customer needs.

administrative principles a management perspective that focuses on the design and functioning of the organization as a whole.

ambidextrous approach a design approach that incorporates structures and management processes that are appropriate to both the creation and the implementation of innovation.

analyzability a dimension of technology in which work can be reduced to mechanical steps and participants can follow an objective, computational procedure to solve problems.

analyzer a business strategy based on maintaining a stable business while innovating on the periphery.

authority a force for achieving desired outcomes that is prescribed by the formal hierarchy and reporting relationships.

B

balanced scorecard a comprehensive management control system that balances traditional financial measures with operational measures relating to a company's critical success factors.

behavior control manager observation of employee actions to see whether the individual follows desired procedures and performs tasks as instructed.

benchmarking the process of continually measuring products, services, and practices against tough competitors or other organizations recognized as industry leaders.

blog a running Web log that allows an individual to post opinions and ideas.

boundary-spanning roles activities that link and coordinate an organization with key elements in the external environment.

bounded rationality perspective a perspective that describes how decisions are made when problems are ill-defined, numerous factors affect the decision, and time is limited.

buffering roles activities that absorb uncertainty from the environment.

bureaucracy an organizational framework marked by rules and procedures, specialization and division of labor, hierarchy of authority, emphasis on technically qualified personnel, and written communications and records.

bureaucratic control the use of rules, policies, hierarchy of authority, written documentation, standardization, and other bureaucratic mechanisms to standardize behavior and assess performance.

bureaucratic culture a culture with an internal focus and a consistency orientation for a stable environment.

bureaucratic organizations organizations that emphasize designing and managing on an impersonal, rational basis through such elements as clearly defined authority and responsibility, formal recordkeeping, and uniform application of standard rules.

business intelligence high-tech analysis of large amounts of internal and external data to spot patterns and relationships that might be significant in helping managers make better strategic decisions.

C

Carnegie model organization decision making that involves many managers making a final choice based on a coalition among those managers.

centrality a source of horizontal power for a department that is engaged in the primary activity of an organization.

centralization refers to the level of hierarchy with authority to make decisions.

centralized decision making decision making in which problems and decisions are funneled to top levels of the hierarchy for resolution.

change process the way in which changes occur in an organization.

chaos theory a theory that suggests that relationships in complex, adaptive systems—including organizations—are nonlinear and made up of numerous interconnections and divergent choices that create unintended effects and render the whole unpredictable.

charismatic authority authority based on devotion to the exemplary character or to the heroism of an individual person and the order defined by him or her.

chief ethics officer a high-level company executive who oversees all aspects of ethics.

clan control the use of social characteristics, such as shared cultural values, commitment, traditions, and beliefs, to control behavior.

clan culture a culture with a primary focus on the involvement and participation of the organization's members and on rapidly changing expectations from the external environment.

closed system a system that would not depend on or interact with the environment. It would be autonomous, closed off, and sealed from the outside world.

coalition an alliance among several managers who agree about organizational goals and problem priorities.

code of ethics a formal statement of the organization's values concerning ethics and social responsibility.

codified knowledge formal, systematic knowledge that can be articulated, written down, and passed on to others in documents, rules, or general instructions.

coercive forces the external pressures exerted on an organization to adopt structures, techniques, or behaviors similar to other organizations.

cognitive biases severe errors in judgment that all humans are prone to and that typically lead to bad choices.

collaborative-network perspective a perspective whereby organizations join together to become more competitive and to share scarce resources to increase value and productivity for all.

collective bargaining the negotiation of an agreement between management and workers.

collectivity stage the life cycle phase in which an organization has strong leadership and begins to develop clear goals and direction.

competition rivalry among groups in the pursuit of a common prize.

competing values model a model that tries to balance a concern with various parts of the organization rather than focusing on one part.

competitive advantage what sets the organization apart from others and provides it with a distinctive edge for meeting customer or client needs in the marketplace.

confrontation a situation in which parties in conflict directly engage one another and try to work out their differences.

consortia groups of independent companies (suppliers, customers, and possibly competitors) that join together to share skills, resources, costs, and access to one another's markets.

contingency theory meaning that one thing depends on other things; for organizations to be effective, there must be a "goodness of fit" between their structure and the conditions in their external environment.

contingency decision-making framework a perspective that brings together the two organizational dimensions of problem consensus and technical knowledge about solutions.

contingency factors encompass larger elements that influence structural dimensions, including the organization's size, technology, environment, culture, and goals.

continuous-process production a completely mechanized manufacturing process in which there is no starting or stopping.

cooptation occurs when leaders from important sectors in the environment are made part of an organization and thus are more engaged in that organization's interests.

core competence describes what the organization does especially well in comparison to its competitors.

core technology the work process that is directly related to the organization's mission.

corporate social responsibility (CSR) the concept of management's obligation to make choices and take action so that the organization contributes to the welfare and interest of all organizational stakeholders.

craft technologies technologies characterized by a fairly stable stream of activities, but the conversion process is not analyzable or well understood.

creative departments departments that initiate change, such as research and development, engineering, design, and systems analysis.

creativity the generation of novel ideas that may meet perceived needs or respond to opportunities.

culture the set of values, norms, guiding beliefs, and understandings that is shared by members of an organization and taught to new members as the correct way to think, feel, and behave.

culture changes changes in the values, attitudes, expectations, beliefs, and behavior of employees.

culture strength the degree of agreement among members of an organization about the importance of specific values.

customer relationship management systems that help companies track customers' interactions with the firm and allow employees to call up a customer's past sales and service records, outstanding orders, or unresolved problems.

D

data warehousing the use of huge databases that combine all of a company's data and allow users to access the data directly, create reports, and obtain responses to what-if questions.

decentralization means that decision-making authority is pushed down to lower organizational levels.

decentralized decision making decision making in which authority is pushed down to lower organizational levels.

decision learning a process of recognizing and admitting mistakes that allows managers to acquire sufficient experience and knowledge to perform more effectively in the future.

decision premises constraining frames of reference and guidelines placed by top managers on decisions made at lower levels.

decision support system an interactive, computer-based system that relies on decision models and integrated databases.

defender a business strategy that is concerned with stability or even retrenchment.

departmental grouping a grouping in which employees share a common supervisor and common resources, are jointly responsible for performance, and tend to identify and collaborate with one another.

dependency an aspect of horizontal power, in which one department is dependent on another and the latter is in a position of greater power.

devil's advocate the role of challenging the assumptions and assertions made by the group.

differentiation the cognitive and emotional differences among managers in various functional departments of an organization and formal structure differences among these departments.

differentiation strategy a business strategy that attempts to distinguish an organization's products or services from others in the industry.

digital factories the ultimate automated factories that link manufacturing components that previously stood alone.

direct interlock occurs when one individual is the link between two companies, such as when a member of one company's board also sits on the board of another company.

divisional grouping a grouping in which employees are organized according to what the organization produces.

divisional structure structure in which divisions can be organized according to individual products, services, product groups, major projects or programs, divisions, businesses, or profit centers; sometimes called a *product structure* or *strategic business units.*

domain the chosen environmental field of action; the territory an organization stakes out for itself with respect to products, services, and markets served.

domains of political activity areas in which politics plays a role. Three domains in organizations are structural change, management succession, and resource allocation.

domestic stage the first stage of international development in which a company is domestically oriented while managers are aware of the global environment.

downsizing intentionally reducing the size of a company's workforce by laying off employees.

dual-core approach an organizational change perspective that identifies the unique processes associated with administrative change compared to those associated with technical change.

E

e-business any business that takes place by digital processes over a computer network rather than in physical space.

economies of scale achieving lower costs through large volume production; often made possible by global expansion.

economies of scope achieving economies by having a presence in many product lines, technologies, or geographic areas.

effectiveness the degree to which an organization achieves its goals.

efficiency the amount of resources used to achieve an organization's goals; based on the quantity of raw materials, money, and employees necessary to produce a given level of output.

elaboration stage a mature stage of the life cycle in which a red tape crisis is resolved through the development of a new sense of teamwork and collaboration.

empowerment the delegation of power or authority to subordinates in an organization, also known as *power sharing.*

engineering technologies technologies that tend to be complex because there is substantial variety in the tasks performed, but activities are usually handled on the basis of established formulas, procedures, and techniques.

enterprise resource planning a system that collects, processes, and provides information about a company's entire enterprise.

entrepreneurial stage the life cycle stage in which an organization is born and its emphasis is on creating a product and surviving in the marketplace.

escalating commitment persisting to invest time and money in a solution despite strong evidence that it is not working.

ethical dilemma the result of when each alternative choice or behavior seems undesirable because of a potentially negative ethical consequence.

ethics the code of moral principles and values that governs the behaviors of a person or group with respect to what is right or wrong.

ethics committee a cross-functional group of executives who oversee company ethics.

ethics hotlines telephone numbers employees can call to seek guidance as well as report questionable behavior.

evidence-based management a commitment to make more informed and intelligent decisions based on the best available facts and evidence.

executive dashboard a software program that presents key business information in graphical, easy-to-interpret form and alerts managers to any deviations or unusual patterns in the data; sometimes called a *business performance dashboard.*

executive information system a higher-level application that facilitates decision making at the highest levels of management, these systems are typically based on software that can convert large amounts of complex data into pertinent information and provide that information to top managers in a timely fashion.

external adaptation the manner in which an organization meets goals and deals with outsiders.

extranet an external communications system that uses the Internet and is shared by two or more organizations.

F

factors of production resources necessary for production, such as land, raw materials, and labor.

feedback control model a control cycle that involves setting goals, establishing standards of performance, measuring actual performance and comparing it to standards, and changing activities as needed based on the feedback.

focus the first value dimension that states whether dominant values concern issues that are *internal* or *external* to the firm.

formalization the degree to which an organization has rules, procedures, and written documentation.

formalization stage the life cycle stage that involves the installation and use of rules, procedures, and control systems.

functional grouping a grouping that consists of employees who perform similar functions or work processes or who bring similar knowledge and skills to bear.

functional matrix type of matrix structure in which the functional bosses have primary authority and the project or product managers simply coordinate product activities.

functional structure organization structure in which activities are grouped together by common function from the bottom to the top of the organization.

G

garbage can model decision-making model that describes the pattern or flow of multiple decisions within an organization.

general environment those sectors that might not have a direct impact on the daily operations of a firm but will indirectly influence it.

generalist an organization that offers a broad range of products or services or serves a broad market.

global companies companies that no longer think of themselves as having a single home country; sometimes called *stateless corporations.*

global geographic structure structure that divides the world into geographic regions, with each geographic division reporting to the CEO.

global matrix structure a form of horizontal linkage in an international organization in which both product and geographical structures are implemented simultaneously to achieve a balance between standardization and globalization.

global product structure structure in which the product divisions take responsibility for global operations in their specific product area.

global stage the stage of international development in which the company transcends any one country.

global teams cross-border work groups made up of multiskilled, multinational members whose activities span multiple countries; also called *transnational teams.*

globalization strategy the standardization of product design, manufacturing, and marketing strategy throughout the world.

goal approach an approach to effectiveness that is concerned with an organization's outputs and how well the organization has met its output goals.

groupthink the tendency of people in groups to suppress contrary opinions for the sake of group harmony.

H

Hawthorne Studies a series of experiments on worker productivity begun in 1924 at the Hawthorne plant of Western Electric Company in Illinois; attributed employees' increased output to managers' better treatment of them during the study.

heroes organization members who serve as models or ideals that illustrate and support desired cultural norms and values.

high-velocity environments industries in which competitive and technological change is so extreme that market data is either unavailable or obsolete, strategic windows open and shut quickly, and decisions must be make quickly with limited information.

horizontal coordination model a model of the three components of organizational design needed to achieve new product innovation: departmental specialization, boundary spanning, and horizontal linkages.

horizontal grouping a grouping in which employees are organized around core work processes, the end-to-end work, information, and material flows that provide value directly to customers.

horizontal linkage communication and coordination horizontally across organizational departments.

horizontal structure organization structure that organizes employees around core processes rather than by function, product, or geography.

human relations emphasis incorporates the values of an internal focus and a flexible structure.

hybrid structure structure that combines characteristics of various structural approaches tailored to specific strategic needs.

I

idea champions organization members who provide the time and energy to make change happen; sometimes called *advocates, intrapreneurs,* and *change agents.*

idea incubator a safe harbor in which ideas from employees throughout the organization can be developed without interference from company bureaucracy or politics.

imitation the act of adopting a decision tried elsewhere in the hope that it will work in this situation.

incremental decision model decision-making model that describes the structured sequence of activities undertaken from the discovery of a problem to its solution.

indirect interlock occurs when a director of company A and a director of company B are both directors of company C.

information reporting system the most common form of management information system, this type of system provides mid-level managers with reports that summarize data and support day-to-day decision making.

inspiration an innovative, creative solution that is not reached by logical means.

institutional environment norms, values, and expectations from stakeholders (customers, investors, boards, government, community, etc.).

institutional perspective the view of how organizations survive and succeed through congruence between an organization and the expectations from its institutional environment.

institutional similarity the emergence of a common structure and approach among organizations in the same field; called *institutional isomorphism* in the academic literature.

integrated enterprise an organization that uses advanced IT to enable close coordination within the company as well as with suppliers, customers, and partners.

integration the quality of collaboration among departments or organizations.

integrator a position or department created solely to coordinate several departments.

intellectual capital the sum of an organization's knowledge, experience, understanding, relationships, processes, innovations, and discoveries.

intelligence team cross-functional group of managers and employees, usually led by a competitive intelligence professional, who work together to gain a deep understanding of a specific competitive issue.

intensive technologies technologies that provide a variety of products or services in combination to a client.

interdependence the extent to which departments depend on each other for resources or materials to accomplish their tasks.

intergroup conflict the behavior that occurs among organizational groups when participants identify with one group and perceive that other groups may block their group's goal achievement or expectations.

interlocking directorate formal linkage that occurs when a member of the board of directors of one company sits on the board of directors of another company.

internal integration a state in which members develop a collective identity and know how to work together effectively.

internal process approach an approach that looks at internal activities and assesses effectiveness by indicators of internal health and efficiency.

internal process emphasis reflects the values of internal focus and structural control.

international division a division organized to handle business in other countries.

international stage the second stage of international development, in which the company takes exports seriously and begins to think multidomestically.

interorganizational relationships the relatively enduring resource transactions, flows, and linkages that occur among two or more organizations.

intranet a private, companywide information system that uses the communications protocols and standards of the Internet and the World Wide Web but is accessible only to people within the company.

intuitive decision making decision making based on experience and judgment rather than sequential logic or explicit reasoning.

J

job design the assignment of goals and tasks to be accomplished by employees.

job enlargement an expansion of the number of different tasks performed by an employee in a job.

job enrichment designing a job to provide greater responsibility, recognition, and opportunities for growth and development.

job rotation moving employees from job to job to give them a greater variety of tasks.

job simplification the variety and difficulty of tasks performed by a single person are reduced.

joint optimization the goal of the sociotechnical systems approach, which states that an organization functions best when the social and technical systems are designed to fit the needs of one another.

joint venture a separate entity created with two or more active firms as sponsors.

K

knowledge management the ability to systematically find, organize, and make available a company's intellectual capital and to foster a culture of continuous learning and knowledge sharing so that organizational activities build on what is already known.

L

labor-management teams a cooperative approach designed to increase worker participation and provide a cooperative model for union-management problems.

large group intervention an approach that brings together participants from all parts of the organization, often including key stakeholders from outside the organization as well, in an off-site setting to discuss problems or opportunities and plan for change.

large-batch production a manufacturing process characterized by long production runs of standardized parts.

lean manufacturing a process that uses highly trained employees at every stage of the production process, who take a painstaking approach to details and problem solving to cut waste and improve quality.

legends stories of historic events that may have been embellished with fictional details.

legitimacy the general perception that an organization's actions are desirable, proper, and appropriate within the environment's system of norms, values, and beliefs.

level of analysis in systems theory, the subsystem on which the primary focus is placed; four levels of analysis normally characterize organizations.

liaison role a role in which a person is located in one department but has the responsibility for communicating and achieving coordination with another department.

life cycle the concept that organizations are born, grow older, and eventually die.

long-linked technology the combination within one organization of successive stages of production, with each stage using as its inputs the production of the preceding stage.

low-cost leadership strategy a strategy of increasing market share by keeping costs low compared to competitors.

M

management control systems broadly def ned as the formal routines, reports, and procedures that use information to maintain or alter patterns in organizational activities.

management information system a computer-based system that provides information and support for managerial decision making.

management innovation refers to the adoption and implementation of a management practice, process, structure, strategy, or technique that is new to the organization and is intended to further organizational goals.

management science approach organization decision making that uses quantitative models to analyze numerous variables and arrive at the best solution; the analog to the rational approach by individual managers.

managerial ethics principles that guide the decisions and behaviors of managers with regard to whether they are right or wrong.

market control the use of price competition to evaluate the output and productivity of an organization or its major departments and divisions.

mass customization using mass-production technology to quickly and cost-effectively assemble goods that are uniquely designed to fit the demands of individual customers.

matrix structure organization structure in which both product division and functional structures (horizontal and vertical) are implemented simultaneously.

mechanistic an organization system marked by rules, procedures, a clear hierarchy of authority, and centralized decision making.

mediating technology technology that allows each department to work independently by virtue of providing products or services that mediate or link clients from the external environment.

mimetic forces the pressure to copy or model other organizations that appear to be successful.

mission the organization's reason for existence; describes the organization's shared values and beliefs and its reason for being.

mission culture a culture characterized by emphasis on a clear vision of the organization's purpose and on the achievement of goals, such as sales growth, profitability, or market share, to help achieve the purpose.

multidomestic manager mindset in which competitive issues in each country are viewed independently of other countries; the company deals with each country individually.

multidomestic strategy strategy in which competition in each country is handled independently of competition in other countries.

multifocused grouping a grouping in which the organization embraces two or more structural grouping alternatives simultaneously, often called *matrix* or *hybrid*.

multinational stage the stage of international development in which a company has marketing and production facilities in many countries and more than one-third of its sales outside its home country.

myths stories that are consistent with the values and beliefs of the organization but are not supported by facts.

N

negotiation the bargaining process that often occurs during confrontation and that enables the parties to systematically reach a solution.

network centrality a source of power based on being centrally located in the organization and having access to information and people that are critical to the company's success.

networking electronically linking people and departments within a particular building or across corporate offices, enabling them to share information and cooperate on projects.

new-venture fund a fund that provides financial resources for employees to develop new ideas, products, or businesses.

niche a domain of unique environmental resources and needs.

non-core technology a department work process that is important to the organization but is not directly related to its primary mission.

nonprogrammed decisions novel and poorly defined, these decisions are required when no procedure exists for solving a problem.

nonroutine technologies technologies characterized by high task variety, and the conversion process is not analyz-able or well understood.

nonsubstitutability a source of horizontal power when a department's function cannot be performed by other readily available resources.

normative forces pressures to achieve standards of professionalism and to adopt techniques that are considered by the professional community to be up to date and effective.

O

official goals formally stated definition of business scope and outcomes the organization is trying to achieve.

open innovation an approach that extends the search for and commercialization of new products beyond the boundaries of the organization.

open system a system that must interact with the environment in order to survive. It cannot seal itself off and must continuously adapt to the environment.

open systems emphasis an approach that is led by a combination of external focus and flexible structure

operating goals goals stated in terms of outcomes sought through the actual operating procedures of the organization.

organic an organization system marked by free-flowing, adaptive processes, an unclear hierarchy of authority, and decentralized decision making.

organization development a behavioral science field devoted to improving performance through trust, open confrontation of problems, employee empowerment and participation, the design of meaningful work, cooperation between groups, and the full use of human potential.

organization structure designates formal reporting relationships, including the number of levels in the hierarchy and the span of control of managers and supervisors; identifies the grouping together of individuals into departments and of departments into the total organization; and includes the design of systems to ensure effective communication, coordination, and integration of efforts across departments.

organization theory a macro examination of organizations that analyzes the whole organization as a unit.

organizational behavior a micro approach to organizations that focuses on the individuals within organizations as the relevant units of analysis.

organizational change the adoption of a new idea or behavior by an organization.

organizational decision making the process of identifying and solving problems.

organizational decline a condition in which a substantial, absolute decrease in an organization's resource base occurs over a period of time.

organizational ecosystem a system formed by the interaction of a community of organizations and their environment.

organizational environment all elements that exist outside the boundary of the organization and have the potential to affect all or part of the organization.

organizational form an organization's specific technology, structure, products, goals, and personnel.

organizational goal a desired state of affairs that the organization attempts to reach.

organizational innovation the adoption of an idea or behavior that is new to the organization's industry, market, or general environment.

organizational politics the activities of acquiring, developing, and using power and other resources to influence others and obtain the preferred outcome when there is uncertainty or disagreement about choices.

organizations social entities that are goal-directed, designed as deliberately structured and coordinated activity systems, and are linked to the external environment.

organized anarchy extremely organic organizations characterized by highly uncertain conditions.

outcome control a management focus on monitoring and rewarding results rather than on how those results are obtained.

outsourcing contracting out certain functions or tasks, such as manufacturing or credit processing, to other companies.

P

personnel ratios the proportions of administrative, clerical, and professional support staff.

point–counterpoint a decision-making technique that divides decision makers into two groups and assigns them different, often competing responsibilities.

political model a definition of an organization as being made up of groups that have separate interests, goals, and values in which power and influence are needed to reach decisions.

political tactics for using power these include building coalitions, expanding networks, controlling decision premises, enhancing legitimacy and expertise, and making a direct appeal.

pooled interdependence the lowest form of interdependence, in which work does not f ow between departments.

population a set of organizations engaged in similar activities with similar patterns of resource utilization and outcomes.

population-ecology perspective focuses on organizational diversity and adaptation within a population of organizations.

power the potential ability of one person (or department) to influence other people (or departments) to carry out orders or to do something they would not otherwise have done.

power distance the level of inequality people are willing to accept in an organization.

power sources the five sources of horizontal power in organizations are dependency, financial resources, centrality, nonsubstitutability, and the ability to cope with uncertainty.

problem consensus the level of agreement among managers about the nature of a problem or opportunity and about which goals and outcomes to pursue.

problem identification the decision-making stage during which information about environmental and organizational conditions is monitored to determine if performance is satisfactory and to diagnose the cause of shortcomings.

problem solution the decision-making stage during which alternative courses of action are considered and one alternative is selected and implemented.

problemistic search search that occurs when managers look around in the immediate environment for a solution to quickly resolve a problem.

process an organized group of related tasks and activities that work together to transform inputs into outputs that create value for customers.

product and service changes changes that pertain to the product or service outputs of an organization.

product matrix type of matrix structure in which the project or product managers have primary authority and functional managers simply assign technical personnel to projects and provide advisory expertise as needed.

programmed decisions repetitive and well defined, these decisions are used when procedures exist for resolving the problem.

prospect theory theory that suggests that the threat of a loss has a greater impact on a decision than the possibility of an equivalent gain.

prospector a business strategy of innovating, taking risks, seeking out new opportunities, and growing.

R

rational approach decision-making process based on systematic analysis of a problem followed by choice and implementation in a logical sequence.

rational goal emphasis represents management values of structural control and external focus.

rational model a model of organization characterized by rational decision processes, clear goals and choices, centralized power and control, an efficiency orientation, and little conflict among groups; an ideal not fully achievable in the real world.

rational–legal authority authority based on employees' belief in the legality of rules and the right of those elevated to positions of authority to issue commands.

reactor a response to environmental threats and opportunities in an ad hoc rather than strategic fashion.

reciprocal interdependence the highest level of interdependence, in which the output of one operation is the input of a second, and the output of the second operation is the input of the first (for example, a hospital).

reengineering the redesign of a vertical organization along its horizontal workflows and processes.

relational coordination frequent, timely, problem-solving communication carried out through relationships of shared goals, shared knowledge, and mutual respect.

resource dependence a situation in which organizations depend on the environment but strive to acquire control over resources to minimize their dependence.

resource-based approach an organizational perspective that assesses effectiveness by observing how successfully the organization obtains, integrates, and manages valued resources.

resource-dependence theory theory that organizations try to minimize their dependence on other organizations for the supply of important resources and try to influence the environment to make resources available.

retention the preservation and institutionalization of selected organizational forms.

rites and ceremonies the elaborate, planned activities that make up a special event and are often conducted for the benefit of an audience.

role a part in a dynamic social system that allows an employee to use his or her discretion and ability to achieve an outcome or meet a goal.

routine technologies technologies characterized by little task variety and the use of objective, computational procedures.

rule of law that which arises from a set of codified principles and regulations that describe how people are required to act, that are generally accepted in society, and that are enforceable in the courts.

S

satisficing the acceptance of a satisfactory rather than a maximum level of performance, enabling an organization to achieve several goals simultaneously.

scientific management emphasizes scientifically determined jobs and management practices as the way to improve efficiency and labor productivity.

sectors subdivisions of the external environment that contain similar elements.

selection the process by which a new organizational form is determined to suit the environment and survive, or is "selected out" and fails.

sequential interdependence a serial form of interdependence in which the output of one operation becomes the input to another operation.

service technology technology characterized by simultaneous production and consumption, customized output, customer participation, intangible output, and being labor intensive.

shared value organizational policies and practices that both enhance the economic success of a company and advance the economic and social conditions of the communities in which the company operates.

simple–complex dimension the number and dissimilarity of external elements relevant to an organization's operations.

Six Sigma a highly ambitious quality standard that specifies a goal of no more than 3.4 defects per million parts; also, a set of control procedures that emphasizes the relentless pursuit of quality.

skunkworks a separate, small, informal, highly autonomous, and often secretive group that focuses on breakthrough ideas for the business.

small-batch production a manufacturing process, often custom work, that relies heavily on the human operator and is not highly mechanized.

social audit measures and reports the ethical, social, and environmental impact of an organization's operations.

social capital the quality of interactions among people and the degree to which they share a common perspective.

social construct created and defined by an individual or group rather than existing independently in the external world.

social networking a peer-to-peer communication channel, where people interact in an online community, share personal data and photos, and produce and share a variety of information and opinions.

sociotechnical systems approach an approach that combines the needs of people with the organization's need for technical efficiency.

sources of intergroup conflict factors that generate conflict, including goal incompatibility, differentiation, task interdependence, and limited resources.

specialist an organization that provides a narrower range of goods or services or that serves a narrower market.

stable–unstable dimension refers to whether elements in the environment are dynamic.

stakeholder any group within or outside of an organization that has a stake in the organization's performance.

stakeholder approach integrates and balances diverse organizational activities by looking at various organizational stakeholders and what they want from the organization.

standardization policies that ensure all branches of the company at all locations operate in the same way.

stories narratives based on true events that are frequently shared among organizational employees and told to new employees to inform them about an organization.

strategic constituents approach an approach that measures effectiveness by focusing on the satisfaction of key stakeholders, those who are critical to the organization's ability to survive and thrive.

strategic contingencies events and activities both inside and outside an organization that are essential for attaining organizational goals.

strategic intent a situation in which all the organization's energies and resources are directed toward a focused, unifying, and compelling overall goal.

strategy a plan for interacting with the competitive environment to achieve organizational goals.

strategy and structure change change that pertains to the administrative domain in an organization.

strategy map a visual representation of the key drivers of an organization's success that shows how specific outcomes in each area are linked.

structural dimensions describe the internal characteristics of an organization, and create a basis for measuring and comparing organizations.

structure the formal reporting relationships, groupings, and systems of an organization.

struggle for existence the concept that organizations and populations of organizations are engaged in a competitive struggle over resources, and each organizational form is fighting to survive.

subcultures cultures that develop within an organization that reflect the common problems, goals, and experiences that members of a team, department, or other unit share.

subsystems interrelated parts of a system that function as a whole to achieve a common purpose.

supply chain management managing the sequence of suppliers and purchasers, covering all stages of processing from obtaining raw materials to distributing finished goods to consumers.

sustainability economic development that generates wealth and meets the needs of the current generation while saving the environment so future generations can meet their needs as well.

switching structures an organization creates an organic structure when such a structure is needed for the initiation of new ideas and reverts to a more mechanistic structure to implement the ideas.

symbol something that represents another thing.

symptoms of structural deficiency signs that the organization structure is out of alignment, including delayed or poor-quality decision making, failure to respond innovatively to environmental changes, and too much conflict.

system a set of interrelated parts that function as a whole to achieve a common purpose.

T

tacit knowledge knowledge based on personal experience, rules of thumb, intuition, and judgment; knowledge that is difficult to put into writing.

tactics for enhancing collaboration these include techniques such as integration devices, confrontation and negotiation, intergroup consultation, member rotation, and shared mission and superordinate goals that enable groups to overcome differences and work together.

tactics for increasing power these include entering areas of high uncertainty, creating dependencies, providing resources, and satisfying strategic contingencies.

task a narrowly defined piece of work assigned to a person.

task environment sectors with which the organization interacts directly and that have a direct impact on the organization's ability to achieve its goals.

task force a temporary committee composed of representatives from each organizational unit affected by a problem.

team building activities that promote the idea that people who work together can work as a team.

teams permanent task forces, often used in conjunction with a full-time integrator.

technical complexity the extent of mechanization of the manufacturing process.

technical knowledge the degree of understanding and agreement about how to solve problems and reach organizational goals.

technology the work processes, techniques, machines, and actions used to transform organizational inputs into outputs.

technology changes changes in an organization's production process, including its knowledge and skill base, that enable distinctive competence.

time-based competition competition based on delivering products and services faster than competitors, giving companies a competitive edge.

traditional authority authority based on a belief in traditions and in the legitimacy of the status of people exercising authority through those traditions.

transaction processing systems a system that automates the organization's routine, day-to-day business transactions.

transnational model a form of horizontal organization that has multiple centers, subsidiary managers who initiate strategy and innovations for the company as a whole, and unity and coordination achieved through corporate culture and shared vision and values.

U

uncertainty condition that exists when decision makers do not have sufficient information about environmental factors, and they have a difficult time predicting external changes.

uncertainty avoidance within a cultural group, the degree to which members are uncomfortable with uncertainty and ambiguity and thus support beliefs that promise certainty.

V

values-based leadership a relationship between a leader and followers that is based on shared, strongly internalized values that are advocated and acted upon by the leader.

variation the appearance of new, diverse forms in a population of organizations.

variety in terms of tasks, the frequency of unexpected and novel events that occur in the conversion process.

venture teams a technique used to foster creativity within an organization by setting up a small team as its own company to pursue innovations.

vertical information system a strategy for increasing vertical information capacity.

vertical linkages communication and coordination activities connecting the top and bottom of an organization.

virtual network grouping a loosely connected cluster of separate components.

virtual network structure the firm subcontracts many or most of its major processes to separate companies and coordinates their activities from a small headquarters organization, sometimes called a *modular structure.*

virtual team a team made up of organizationally or geographically dispersed members who are linked primarily through advanced information and communications technologies.

W

whistle-blowing employee disclosure of illegal, immoral, or illegitimate practices on the part of the organization.

wiki a Web page or collection of pages designed to allow people to freely create, share, and edit content using any Web browser.

Name Index

Page numbers followed by the letter n indicate the note in which the entry is located.

C

D

E

F

G

M

N

O

S

T

U

V

Corporate Name Index

Subject Index

Note: Page numbers in *italic* type indicate exhibits.

D

P

R

S

T

U

V

W